WEST ACADEMIC PUBLISHING'S EMERITUS ADVISORY BOARD

WEST ACADEMIC PUBLISHING'S LAW SCHOOL ADVISORY BOARD

DOMESTIC VIOLENCE LAW

Sixth Edition

■ ■ ■

Nancy K. D. Lemon
Retired Herma Hill Kay Lecturer in Domestic Violence Law
Former Director of the Domestic Violence Field Placement
Berkeley Law School
University of California, Berkeley

AMERICAN CASEBOOK SERIES®

860 Blue Gentian Road, Suite 350
Eagan, MN 55121
1-877-888-1330

Published in the United States of America

ISBN: 978-1-63659-458-3

PREFACE AND ACKNOWLEDGMENTS: SIXTH EDITION

As I write this Preface, I am looking back over my 34 years of teaching Domestic Violence Law at Berkeley School of Law, from which I graduated. I was the first person to create such a course and to teach it and a Domestic Violence Clinic/Practicum/Field Placement consistently, year in and year out from 1988 to 2022. While I am now retired from teaching, Berkeley Law continues to offer these two courses, taught by Mallika Kaur, another attorney/lecturer like myself who came out of the domestic violence movement, and who I chose to succeed me. I am most grateful.

I believe the teacher's job, especially in a course like Domestic Violence Law, is to create a safe space for students to not only learn about the history and current practice of this area of law, but to share their sometimes widely divergent points of view in a space which is open to considering the many approaches that students bring. My students told me that they deeply valued having a place where future prosecutors and future criminal defense attorneys as well as prison abolitionists could have respectful discussions about how the legal system should treat the complicated problem of domestic violence.

This is why there are sometimes contradictory pieces in this book, such as two in Chapter 10, the Law Enforcement chapter, one calling for no longer involving the police in domestic violence cases and the other reminding us of the importance of basing policy decisions on what survivors of abuse say they need and want, which may include involving the police. My goal is to encourage students to think critically about these difficult and complex issues and move away from a polarized view of the world where things appear to be black and white, good and bad, open and shut.

As the world and the legal system takes domestic violence more seriously, it is increasingly challenging to sift through the large numbers of domestic violence studies, cases, statutes, books, articles, fact sheets, etc. to choose key materials, and to edit them or turn them into Editor's Notes so they can fit into a one-semester textbook. Since this book is rather long, teachers should feel free to assign only some of the materials and summarize the others in lectures.

For this edition, in addition to the law enforcement pieces mentioned above, I have updated or added materials on COVID and domestic violence, the impact of the Supreme Court's abortion decision in *Dobbs* on survivors of domestic violence, the overlap between human trafficking and domestic violence, abusers as vexatious litigants/litigation abuse, Black women and partner abuse, abused Latinas in the U.S., tribal sovereignty and its relationship to violence against Native women and girls, transgender survivors of intimate partner abuse, mutual restraining orders' impact on LGBTQ+ abuse survivors, suing in tort, coercive control, effectiveness of restraining orders, protective mothers/endangered children, domestic violence custody cases in the U.S. and internationally, strangulation in domestic violence cases, batterers and firearms, U.S. military adjudication of domestic violence, the Internet of Things, coerced debt, workplace injunctions, domestic violence survivors as tenants, battered immigrants' rights, domestic violence survivors seeking asylum, and international human rights law related to domestic violence. As is evident from this long list, domestic violence issues arise in many varied areas of law.

Thanks are due to the agency I co-founded, Family Violence Appellate Project (now in Washington state as well as California), which since 2012 has advanced the law through the appellate process, winning dozens of victories. I have included two of FVAP's recent cases, *F.M. v. M.M.* and *Nicole G. v. Brathwaite*, in the Civil Restraining Order chapter. Other FVAP cases dealing with restraining orders, child custody, immigration, torts, etc. can be found at www.fvaplaw.org.

I also appreciate all the journalists, researchers, law teachers, attorneys, judges, legislators, and others who are working to end domestic violence through conducting key research studies, writing thought provoking articles, educating law students, fighting for abused clients in court, passing impactful laws, and making important judicial decisions. All of us are needed in this effort.

I miss many of my former students at Berkeley Law and meeting new ones. Some of my former students are now my colleagues and friends. I have learned a lot from all of you. I have added excerpts from four of the writing requirements I supervised to this edition, written by Jacquie Andreano, Rishita Apsani, Hailey Guinn, and Madison Lo. Thanks for your scholarship!

Mary Fata, one of my former students recently emailed me an unsolicited message about the effect of my teaching the Domestic Violence Law class on her law school experience and her career, then consented to my quoting her.

> The DV seminar was my first time learning about domestic violence law and policy. Doctrinal courses often do not explore how systemic issues such as poverty, racism, and gender based violence impact our legal systems. Taking this course changed how I viewed the cases we reviewed in doctrinal classes. I began to pay attention to facts suggesting evidence of domestic violence. I began to think critically about laws and how they impact victims of violence and how poverty law intersects with domestic violence

> law. Each time I had a research project, I chose to focus on different areas of domestic violence law. It was important to me because it impacts every area of law, from criminal to civil to administrative. I don't think that one can do public interest lawyering without considering the impact of domestic violence and ensuring that we screen clients. Because I took the class as a first semester 2L, the seminar really set the course for both my work as a student and my work as a legal aid attorney after law school.

Statements like this make me grateful that Berkeley Law asked me to pioneer this course in 1988 and that I was able to continue to do so for so many years.

Thanks are due to Tara Branine, a former student who volunteered to help me comb through dozens of articles and cases, summarizing the ones she thought I might include, and Shepardized all the cases in the last edition to determine if they were still good law. And to my niece Kaelyn Lemon, who is new to legal research but agreed to check all the statutes in the last edition for any changes, thanks for your help. Julia Weber also consulted with me on the materials dealing with firearms, which I appreciated.

I am also grateful to Saskia Ledezma, a recent law school graduate, for our many hours of parallel work sessions on Facetime, checking in every hour and exchanging counseling time when barriers arose for either one of us. This process was invaluable in getting me started on the daunting task of updating this book and keeping me going through reading and editing potential materials, as well as seeking copyright permissions from dozens of publishers and authors, a tedious task. At one point Saskia said that "the revisions to this textbook are dismantling systems of oppression," which I wrote on a Post-It note so I could remember why I am doing this work. Disha Bhatt, another friend, also did countless online work sessions with me while she was studying for the bar exam, which was very helpful.

And finally, as I said in the preface to the last edition, I am grateful to the many thousands of domestic violence survivors in the U.S. and around the world who get up every day and do their best to protect themselves and their loved ones, figure out how to keep a roof over their heads if possible, determine when it is safer to stay or leave or go back, and when it's better to testify or to disappear. You inspire me.

I am also mindful of the many survivors who are currently incarcerated due to committing crimes stemming from being abused by their partners. We need to work harder to get you released and prevent other abuse survivors from becoming incarcerated for such crimes.

I hope this book will contribute to making this world a safer place.

NANCY K. D. LEMON

Berkeley, California
January 2024

PREFACE AND ACKNOWLEDGMENTS: FIFTH EDITION

Plutarch reportedly said, "Education is not the filling of a pail, but the lighting of a fire." The longer I teach law students, the more I agree with this approach. I hope that this edition, like the former ones, prompts teachers and students to ask hard questions and see that there are often not simple answers to how our legal system should approach our societal epidemic of domestic violence. I think the best we can do as teachers is not to pour information into our students, but to light fires in them, tapping in to every human's innate curiosity to learn about the world and everyone's innate desire to solve complex problems.

It is a daunting task to create a book called Domestic Violence Law. There are now so many issues to cover, and so many excellent books, articles, studies, policy papers, and cases that could be included that one could write an encyclopedia rather than a textbook.

In this edition I have worked hard not only to update the materials, but also to shorten pieces and turn many into editor's notes—in the hope that teachers and students will be able to read at least most of the book in one semester. I managed to cut the total page length, compared to the fourth edition, by about 200 pages; I hope I have picked the most salient and useful pieces so the key points in this area of law remain present.

For this edition, I have added non-case materials on an array of topics, including teen dating violence, coercive control, risk factors for men's likelihood of becoming abusive, Family Justice Centers across the country, the Adverse Childhood Experiences (ACE) study, tribal sovereignty over non-Indian batterers, critiques of the battered women's movement and its reliance on the criminal justice system and the government more generally, the connections between domestic violence and animal abuse and litigation abuse, new tools in assessing dangerousness for first responders, law enforcement officers who are also abusers, LGBTQ+ relationships, recommendations for child protective services and domestic violence advocates to work together, parenting issues for abusive fathers, restorative justice, the impact of so-called nuisance and crime-free ordinances on survivors' access to housing, and immigrant survivors—among a plethora of other subjects.

There are also new cases showing the latest issues raised by firearms prohibitions for batterers, evidentiary issues raised in criminal domestic violence cases, mutual restraining orders, children who witness their mothers being abused, children abducted by abusive parents, suits against law enforcement for failing to protect survivors of intimate partner violence, survivors' re-entry to the community from prison, obtaining leave from work and unemployment benefits based on domestic violence, and the first appellate decision in the U.S. holding that domestic violence by itself can be a basis for asylum—among myriad other topics.

Thanks are due to the many people who helped make this book possible. These of course include the authors of the many studies, policy papers, and articles excerpted here. I appreciate your using scholarship resources to help continue the discourse on domestic violence and end the epidemic of abuse of intimate partners.

I am also thankful to the attorneys who have represented domestic violence survivors in trials and appeals, and the judges who have made decisions in the cases I have included. These legal professionals often grappled with difficult situations, involving traumatized clients and children, and often unclear areas of law. Your work shows you have paid witness to abuse, a difficult feat for anyone.

I am thrilled to include in this edition some of the twenty-eight, or so, cases that my own agency, Family Violence Appellate Project—based in Oakland, CA—has won or obtained publication of in the five and a half years of its short existence. These include *Keisha W. v. Marvin M., In re Jonathan B.*, and other cases discussed in Editor's Notes. The staff at FVAP are extremely hard-working, deeply caring, very smart, and lovely human beings, a clearly winning combination. I enjoy learning from all of you. I hope that other law schools can incubate similar appellate projects in other states, as U.C. Berkeley, School of Law did for us.

I am also grateful to my students at Berkeley Law, who often educate and challenge me during our discussions and in their research papers. Every year since I started teaching in 1988, you have taught me as well; I am proud to use excerpts from some of your work. For instance, in this edition, I've added pieces by Brandi Jackson and Dr. Jill Messing.

Eliza Duggan and Emmaline Campbell, two of my former students, have helped with this edition by volunteering to winnow down a long list of potential articles for some of the chapters, and summarizing the best ones for me to review. Thanks to both of you.

Another former student of mine, Cory Hernandez, volunteered to help with producing this edition about a year ago. Cory worked tirelessly for months, reading articles on my list for most of the chapters, summarizing these, and further editing several articles, cases, and other materials for brevity after I had done the first pass. Cory also wrote a short piece I have included on safety planning, and created the Google spreadsheet to track this whole project, including obtaining the dozens of copyright permissions necessary. Furthermore, Cory patiently explained many of the technical aspects of this project to me (who knew there was a difference between "fill-ins" and highlights in a Word document, and how to remove each of those?). Cory, I literally could not have done this without your help, for which I am deeply grateful.

And finally, I am grateful to the many thousands of domestic violence survivors in the U.S. and around the world who get up every day and do their best to protect themselves and their loved ones, figure out how to keep a roof over their heads if possible, determine when it is safer to stay or leave or go back, and when it's better to testify or to disappear. You inspire me.

I hope this book will contribute to making this world a safer place.

NANCY K. D. LEMON

Berkeley, California
January 2018

PREFACE AND ACKNOWLEDGMENTS: FOURTH EDITION

I have been teaching Domestic Violence Law at Boalt Hall School of Law, now Berkeley Law, for over twenty-five years. I continue to grow and learn each year from my amazing students, who are hard-working, eager to learn, committed to social justice, and very bright. I am pleased that several of the new articles excerpted in this book were written by them. Thanks to Yvonne Lindgren, Shane Trawick, Gina Szeto, Erin Liotta, Erica Franklin, and Claire Kelleher-Smith for letting me include your work.

I am also fortunate to be in a field that is constantly evolving, with ever-more sophisticated scholarship and research being conducted, and a huge body of interdisciplinary information to draw on in creating a textbook.

Besides teaching, and serving as the Legal Director of the new Family Violence Appellate Project, I continue to work as a domestic violence expert witness, from which I have learned a great deal about many types of law, some of which are reflected in this book. I thank the many survivors of domestic violence who share very personal and difficult stories with me, and my fellow experts, as we educate and support each other, and think together about how best to educate judges and juries about domestic violence issues. Thanks are also due to my excellent faculty assistant, Leslie Stone, for her many hours of help in obtaining the many permissions necessary for this edition.

I am pleased to report that this is the first edition of this textbook that is shorter than the previous edition. As I updated it and added new pieces, I also edited the materials to streamline the work, so that no chapter is longer than 93 pages, and the average length is 69 pages. Hopefully this will result in professors not having to choose the assigned readings, and in students actually reading what is assigned.

This edition contains many new materials. One piece focuses on the backlash in the U.S. and Canada from groups trying to defund programs for battered women through a skewed interpretation of the concept of equal protection. A national survey describes how domestic violence agencies are forced to serve more clients with less funding, given current cutbacks. Another new article focuses on birth control sabotage as a form of domestic violence, demonstrating the overlap between domestic violence and reproductive justice.

A new study from the field of psychology examines different typologies of men who are violent toward their female partners. A piece from the field of public health notes that culture is a double-edged sword when it comes to intimate partner violence, and that there are positive aspects of many traditional cultures that can be called upon to help stop abuse. Another article notes a way that racism often operates, where the actions of white battered women are seen as based in psychology, while actions of immigrant battered women of the global majority (women of color) are seen as based in their native cultures. There are also new articles about Asian American battered women, and African American battered women, and the racism they face, which limits their access to resources needed to free themselves from abuse.

A new article about domestic violence against women with disabilities includes a discussion of cognitive and psychological disabilities, an emerging field equally as important as physical disabilities. Another piece discusses the Ohio statute that limited domestic violence relief to heterosexual married couples, analyzing the constitutional issues presented by such a law. The transcript of a panel discussion focuses on domestic violence toward transgender people. A case illustrates how a gay man's threats to out his partner, a member of the Marine Corps, comprised another tool that abusers often choose to use.

A new tort case discusses the doctrines of *res judicata* and *collateral estoppel*, and concludes that a victim of spousal abuse could receive an award of spousal support in which abuse was a factor, and then file a tort suit based on the same abuse. Another new tort case holds that intentional infliction of emotional distress in an intimate partner relationship can be the basis for upholding an award of punitive damages, even in the absence of assault. And a case from the bankruptcy court holds that a husband held liable for assaulting his wife in tort cannot discharge the unliquidated damages in bankruptcy.

A new article argues that the statutory definition of domestic violence for restraining orders should be expanded to include all types of power and control typically seen in abusive relationships, while another new piece advocates for legislation that would enable victims of stalking to obtain such orders. New state statutes define domestic violence as including extreme psychological abuse, and interference with personal liberty. Another new article focuses on the need for abused teens to be able to access civil protective orders; we now understand that teens, along with young adults, are at the highest risk for partner abuse. A new case reverses the trial court's award of mutual protective orders where a man injured his girlfriend while there was no evidence that she posed a danger to him. A new piece I wrote analyzes a US Supreme Court decision regarding whether petitioners in restraining order cases are allowed to enforce their orders through contempt actions. A recent resolution by a major law enforcement group opposes the arrest of petitioners for violations of their own protection orders. An editor's note discusses a new case in which text messages from an out of state ex-boyfriend were found to be a sufficient basis for the victim's state to exercise jurisdiction in issuing a protective order. A new guide for prosecutors enforcing protective orders issued in another state outlines best practices.

In the family law arena, a new article expresses concerns that courts are often awarding supervised visitation to abusive parents when it may be in the best interest of the children to suspend or terminate visitation instead. A recent article and case focus on situations in which the battered mother seeks court permission to relocate with the children away from the abuser in order to prevent further abuse. Two new cases regarding international child abduction are included, one stating that the father's abuse of the mother could be the basis for finding a grave risk to the children if they were sent back to the home country, even in the absence of physical abuse of the children, while the other finds no grave risk to the child in spite of extensive abuse of the mother and possible abuse of the child.

A new article about juvenile courts notes that in some jurisdictions they continue to punish battered mothers by removing children due to a concern that the mothers are failing to protect the children from exposure to domestic violence. An article by a long-time consultant and trainer regarding batterers as fathers notes that it is important to focus on the men in children's lives, and not just on the abused mothers, stressing the importance of working with batterers on their parenting, holding them accountable for their actions, and attempting to prevent further abuse.

A new article calls for empirical studies on the effectiveness of mediation in domestic violence cases. Another examines the use of restorative justice modalities in such cases, with practical examples from one jurisdiction.

A new article on marital rape points out the striking disconnect between this area of law and other areas of domestic violence law, noting that antiquated attitudes regarding rape in marriage continue to result in outdated statutes and practices. This is illustrated by several Model Penal Code sections that exempt from criminal liability husbands who rape or sexually assault their wives. Two new cases deal with victim recantation and the applicability of rape shield laws in marital rape cases.

The chapter on law enforcement includes a new article about the federal Secure Communities program and how it works to encourage battered immigrant women to stay silent. Another new article examines mandatory interventions in domestic violence cases and argues that these violate the autonomy of survivors of abuse. Two new articles and a new case examine a series of landmark cases in which survivors of domestic violence or their heirs sued law enforcement for failing to respond properly. In another new case, a man arrested for abusing his girlfriend sued the police for false arrest; the suit was dismissed after the court agreed that he was the dominant aggressor. A recent expert witness declaration I wrote is included, in which the Sheriff of San Francisco was charged with official misconduct based on his pleading guilty to a domestic violence charge.

The chapter on prosecution includes a new case and article discussing the significant US Supreme Court decisions involving statements made by recanting or dead victims in domestic violence and sexual assault cases: *Crawford, Davis/Hammon,* and *Giles*. The materials discuss the issue of when a statement is testimonial, and when the rule of forfeiture applies, allowing admission of the statement of an unavailable victim. Another article questions whether victimless prosecution is really the best approach in domestic violence cases, and argues that if victims are given more resources they could participate in prosecution, which could be empowering for them as well as leading to more convictions. Two new cases discuss the appropriateness and scope of expert testimony in domestic violence prosecutions, one with a recanting victim and one where the victim had been killed. The chapter ends with a new amicus brief filed in a domestic violence homicide case, arguing that the defendant should not be allowed to use a provocation defense where there is a history of domestic violence by the defendant toward the victim.

In the chapter about victims as criminal defendants, a new article explains how when battered women fight back, they may not be perceived as real victims, and how this particularly impacts African American women and lesbians or queer women. An excerpt of a new piece written by me describes the transformative process of working as a domestic violence expert witness in criminal defense cases. Another new article explains how battered women convicted of killing their abusers are double victims, and discusses the difficulties with obtaining their release from prison through parole or habeas petitions.

The federal chapter contains an overview of the history of the Violence Against Women Act and outlines its many iterations, including the 2013 amendments. It also includes many new pieces demonstrating the links between gun possession and domestic violence, and describing promising practices in enforcing the statutes prohibiting possession of guns by abusers. A case and an article discuss the phenomenon of trial court judges ignoring these prohibitions and the constitutional implications of such rogue behavior. Another case deals with instances where the court wrongly ordered such a prohibition and was reversed on appeal.

Three new articles cover domestic violence in the US military, including a description of the scope of the problem, how well the military is complying with federal statutes and policies in the domestic violence arena, and whether veterans who abuse their partners should be dealt with in specialized veterans' courts.

The chapter on confidentiality includes a new article about identity protection for women fleeing domestic violence, a news release about a service member who cyberstalked his girlfriend, a new article explaining the many versions of cyberstalking now being employed by abusers and relevant laws designed to prevent or punish this behavior, and a new case in which a husband used a GPS device to stalk his wife. This chapter also contains a new article arguing against mandatory reporting of suspected domestic violence to the police by medical professionals, and a case in which a hospital was sued by a battered woman's heirs after the woman was released to her abuser, who killed her.

The chapter on financial, employment, and housing issues contains a new article on the inadequacies of the Family Violence Option in the welfare arena, and an article on coerced debt in domestic violence cases, a new understanding of tactics used by abusers. Another new article describes how gender violence affects the victim's work life and calls for reinterpreting existing anti-discrimination statutes to cover this type of situation. A recent case holds that the employer had no liability when an employee shot and killed another employee, his ex-fiancee, at the workplace. A new article describes housing issues that survivors of domestic violence often face and proposes possible legal solutions; a recently enacted state statute serves as a model of how legislatures can protect survivors in such situations. A new case holds that termination of a husband's section 8 voucher violated his due process rights where the termination was based on uncorroborated and vague allegations of domestic violence by his wife and child.

The last chapter starts with a new article using the lens of equal protection analysis to describe the ongoing legal problems faced by immigrant battered women. Two new articles discuss the high frequency of domestic violence toward "mail-order brides," describing the ways US laws fail to protect foreign brides and arguing that these women are being illegally trafficked. A new article challenges the distinction between public and private violence in intimate partner violence-based asylum claims, arguing that batterers often serve as agents of the state. An amicus brief in a recently filed appeal argues that the Board of Immigration Appeals overlooked the gender-based nature of the asylum case, that the would-be boyfriend's actions towards the applicant were abusive and gender-based, and that the home country's failure to prevent and punish domestic violence amounts to acquiescence.

The book ends with a new article focusing on domestic violence as a human rights issue, and describing the decision by the Inter American Commission on Human Rights holding that the U.S. violated the rights of Jessica Gonzales (now Lenahan) and the rights of her three children when it failed to hold police accountable for not enforcing her protective order, resulting in the death of the children. This is followed by a model resolution being passed in various US cities and counties declaring that freedom from domestic violence is a fundamental human right and that local governments have a responsibility to continue securing this right on behalf of their citizens.

I hope this work is useful to many professors, students, advocates, attorneys, researchers, and policy makers, and that some day we will have no need for materials focusing on domestic violence issues, as we will finally have eradicated it.

NANCY K. D. LEMON

Berkeley, California
April, 2013

PREFACE AND ACKNOWLEDGMENTS: THIRD EDITION

Domestic violence law is an exciting field to work in, as it is constantly changing and involves almost every area of law, in addition to non-legal issues.

In the social sciences, new studies are frequently being conducted on the numerous aspects of intimate partner violence. And the body of literature relating to health care response to this problem has mushroomed in the last few years.

The increased use of electronic devices like GPS's, texting, and the internet has caused legislatures and courts applying the precepts of criminal law and civil procedure to chart new territory in domestic violence statutes and opinions. While new technologies offer us access to vast amounts of information and the ability to communicate widely and easily, these same technologies are sometimes very dangerous for those targeted by abusers and stalkers.

The area of the rights of domestic violence survivors who are tenants is also developing rapidly, with courts and legislatures increasingly protecting survivors from eviction and starting to allow them to terminate leases early in order to avoid further abuse.

At least one jurisdiction has now passed a statute allowing survivors of domestic violence, among others, to take paid leave from work when necessary to address the abuse. And increasingly we see public policy arguments being used to prevent survivors from losing their jobs when domestic violence interferes with their employment.

The U.S. Supreme Court has issued several key evidentiary cases in the last few years, all involving domestic violence or sexual assault scenarios. Since these decisions have tended to narrow the admissibility of out of court statements by unavailable victims, prosecutors face new challenges in trying these cases. But many prosecutors have risen to the task, and several state court decisions have been issued which uphold the admission of such statements in certain instances.

We also face ongoing attacks from those who use the courts to try to cut or diminish funding for services for battered women. While these will no doubt continue, attorneys and law professors are publishing exciting new scholarship and submitting amicus briefs elucidating the need for specialized services for women abused by men.

On a brighter note, thanks to the persistence of advocates working on legal issues facing immigrant survivors of domestic violence, remedies available for this very vulnerable population continue to expand. Many undocumented victims of domestic violence are now able to obtain legal residence and are helping to curtail the power of their batterers by working with the criminal justice system.

And in another landmark case, when the U.S. Supreme Court denied enforcement of one survivor's restraining order, holding that the state statute which appeared to mandate arrest was in fact discretionary, the appellant sued the U.S. government in the Inter-American Commission on Human Rights. While the decision is still pending as this edition goes to press, this case reminds us that legal remedies in domestic violence cases are not limited to U.S. laws, that the U.S. is part of the international community, and that governmental failure to respond appropriately to domestic violence may be a violation of human rights.

Thanks to all the people who sent me suggestions for material I used in this new edition, including Susan Bowyer, Jennifer Wyllie-Pletcher, Joan Meier, Sally Goldfarb, Joan Zorza, Anya Lakner, Megan Burke, and Barbara Hart. Thanks also to those of you who suggested other excellent material which I was not able to use due to space and time constraints.

Major kudos are due to my new assistant at Berkeley Law School, Leslie Stone, for her technical help and cheerful competence as I prepared this edition. Thanks also to the administration of the school for assigning her to assist me with it. I really appreciate this support.

I am also indebted to the many colleagues I learn from every day, including other law teachers, domestic violence practitioners, advocates, our state expert witness listserv, our state coalition, and my sister editors at Domestic Violence Report, with whom I worked for many years. It is a pleasure to think with all of you about the challenges before us and to work together to address them.

Though I have taught Domestic Violence Law annually at Berkeley Law School since 1988, I continue to enjoy every class, as I invariably learn a great deal from my students. They are bright and hard-working, and many are moved deeply by our guest speakers and by their own work with survivors of domestic violence in the companion Practicum class. Many have gone on to work in the domestic violence field, and some of their writing is included here. As described on the Practicum's website, one student used what she learned from my course to initiate Taiwan's first domestic violence legislation. Another student, building on her work, is now teaching this course in Taiwan and using this book.

I am also grateful to all the survivors of domestic violence whose stories I have had the honor of listening to as an expert witness. Many of these interviews last five or six hours, and people often share parts of their lives they have never spoken of to anyone else. I usually leave these interactions with a deeper sense of compassion, and admiration for the strength and resourcefulness of survivors. The more I do this work, the more clear it is to me that all of us are more alike than we are different, and that I am simply fortunate not to be struggling with abuse in my own life. It is not that I am somehow better, smarter, or more deserving than my clients, friends, colleagues, and family members who have been abused, but that I have been luckier.

Toward a future where this book will no longer be necessary,

NANCY K. D. LEMON

Berkeley, California
January 2009

PREFACE TO THE SECOND EDITION

In reviewing the points made in the Preface to the first edition of this book, I have a few additional comments regarding to this next edition.

The literature on domestic violence issues continues to grow at an exponential rate, with new articles, studies, cases, statutes, and other materials constantly being generated. These materials also cover a wide range of disciplines, from anthropology and criminology to medicine and law. This makes a task like mine both fascinating, as I review and edit the hundreds of possible pieces to include, and also a bit daunting, as I believe in a somewhat interdisciplinary approach. It is no longer possible to merely find the one piece on a particular topic; instead it is necessary to read many such pieces and choose the one which seems most useful for this textbook. Every chapter now has updated materials, and several chapters were almost entirely replaced by new pieces.

For example, the US Supreme Court's decision in *Crawford v. Washington*, 124 S.Ct. 1354 (2004) has had a huge impact on the prosecution of alleged batterers, given the frequency with which victims recant in these cases. I have included several appellate cases decided after this decision was announced, as well as a law review article which is "hot off the press," analyzing how prosecutors and legislators can best respond.

I have also included a new section in the chapter on victims of domestic violence as defendants, dealing with post-conviction issues, such as parole and habeas corpus. This is an emerging and significant area within the domestic violence field.

Similarly, the chapter on law enforcement response to domestic violence includes a new section on officers who are also batterers, an alarming and serious situation calling for creative responses within the legal system. And an important recent study is included which casts new light on the efficacy of mandatory arrest in reducing recividism.

The chapter on welfare and workplace issues now includes a new section on victims of domestic violence as tenants, as there are now a few cases and articles looking at the many issues raised in this context, such as eviction and early lease termination.

The chapter on safety and confidentiality has been greatly expanded to show both how batterers are increasingly using new technology (e.g., cyberstalking, Global Positioning Systems) to keep their partners or ex-partners under control. This chapter also looks at ways the legal system may inadvertently assist these batterers, e.g., through courts publishing case information on the Internet. But it is not all bad news—there are also many new state statutes designed to help protect victims of domestic violence and their children, and to keep them safe. I have included a representative sample of those statutes.

In response to suggestions by my own students, as well as other law teachers and students around the country, I am including more cases and statutes in this edition in relationship to the number of articles. This should make for more varied reading, and more practice in analyzing both case law and legislation.

Given the huge array of pieces to choose from, I used several criteria. These included materials which show:

- the history or development of a particular area of domestic violence law;
- current trends or typical responses of courts, legislators, commentators;
- unusual, model legislation, cases, or concepts; or
- materials which are controversial, sparking important policy discussions among the readers.

My overall goals are both to give readers a picture of the current thinking and laws regarding domestic violence, and to stimulate new, creative thought and discussion about the cutting edge issues in the field at this time.

NANCY K. D. LEMON

Berkeley, California
November 2005

PREFACE TO THE FIRST EDITION

History of This Book and Course

This book began in 1988, when I was first hired to teach a seminar on Domestic Violence Law at Boalt Hall School of Law, at the University of California at Berkeley, my alma mater. I made many transcontinental phone calls to find a text for the course, only to discover that not only was there no such book in existence, but there had been no courses offered on this subject at that point.

Consequently, I spent many weeks that summer compiling materials to create a photocopied reader. I have continued to teach the course each year. It has grown to three units and up to forty-five students, and has included auditors who are judges, domestic violence activists, scholars from other countries, social welfare students, etc. In 1989, I added an optional companion clinical course for students who wish to gain practical experience in this field. Each year between 1988 and 1995 I updated the substantive materials and tested them in the classroom.

After using photocopied readers for many years, I arranged for publication of the first edition of this book, the first law school textbook on the topic of domestic violence law, in 1996. This coincided with a rapid expansion in the number of law schools offering some type of course or clinical on this topic, from none in 1987 to fifty-seven in 1997 ("When Will They Ever Learn? Educating to End Domestic Violence: A Law School Report," American Bar Association Commission on Domestic Violence, 1997).

Purpose and Uses of These Materials

The changes in the materials I included over the years have reflected a change in my philosophy of teaching. When I started, I saw my role primarily as imparting information to students, and at times, I am afraid, may have lapsed into basically expecting them to learn "the party line." However, I soon came to realize that a more useful approach is to present students with an overview of the policy issues presented in the area of domestic violence law, including the most controversial ones, and to help them think critically about those issues. I now see the class as a "domestic violence think tank," where we are all free to express any opinion or point of view, and there are seldom clear answers. This is why the materials include pieces which are in direct contradiction to each other. As a teacher, I find this approach exciting and dynamic, an opportunity to be instrumental in the development of the academic arm of the domestic violence movement.

As someone who spent most of my professional life from 1981–1993 in the trenches as a practicing attorney working in non-profit agencies, this domestic violence law seminar is a luxurious opportunity to step back a bit and reflect on the larger picture, to think about where we've come from and where we're going. One of my goals as a teacher is thus to bridge the gap between theory and practice. I hope that this bridge contributes both to the law school curriculum and to the larger domestic violence movement. In the law school context, it is my desire that both the first and second editions of this book contribute to the numerical growth and sophistication of law school classes focusing on domestic violence issues, as well as to increased awareness of domestic violence issues in other law school classes (e.g. family law, torts, immigration, criminal law, evidence, constitutional law, etc.).

In other educational settings, these materials can be assigned as the main textbook for a class, or as supplemental readings in any graduate or upperlevel undergraduate course designed to address issues of gender, critical approaches to law and the legal system, or jurisprudence and social policy. Please share it with your colleagues in other disciplines.

Finally, I also hope that this book will be useful to attorneys, advocates, and policymakers in the sometimes daunting task of making the legal system more responsive to the needs of survivors of domestic violence and their children.

Overview of Materials

This book is a collection of articles, book excerpts, cases, and statutes focusing on the role of the legal system in regard to domestic violence. I am defining domestic violence as the various types of abuse occurring in an intimate partner relationship; thus, I am not focusing on other types of family violence, such as elder abuse and child abuse.

My primary goal is not to impart knowledge of what the actual laws are with regard to domestic violence, which would be impossible in one volume, and would need to be updated monthly. Instead, it is to provide an overview of the principal legal issues raised by domestic violence situations, and to enable the reader to think critically about those issues.

The materials are quite interdisciplinary, especially in the introductory chapters. This is because the phenomenon of domestic violence cannot be understood in purely legal terms. In addition, it is important for the reader to be aware of the complexity and variety in terms of who victims of domestic violence are, so that proposed solutions (e.g. mandatory arrest, issuance of restraining orders, physicians reporting abuse to law enforcement, no-drop prosecution policies, etc.) can be evaluated with that awareness in mind.

The four introductory chapters cover some of the history of the legal system's treatment of domestic violence, both in the US and internationally. They also ask what causes domestic violence, what effects the abuse has on the victims, and what approaches are effective in trying to rehabilitate perpetrators; obviously, one's approach to rehabilitation will vary depending on one's analysis of the cause of the problem, and the reader is thus encouraged to think critically about the various treatments which are described.

The third chapter looks at the issue of racism as related to the domestic violence movement and to the legal system's response to domestic violence. The increased emphasis placed on this topic in this edition is partly due to an increased awareness on my part and on the part of the battered women's movement of the issue of racism and its major impact on US society. The women's movement generally and the battered women's movement in particular have struggled with this issue, and need to struggle more, until we all can look squarely at the differences between battered women, as well as at the commonalities. If proposed solutions to the problem of domestic violence do not work for all victims, rather than attempting to implement these solutions and ignoring potential adverse consequences, we need to go back to the drawing board. We as a movement are strong enough to withstand close examination of the hardest issues, racism being one such issue, and to critique how the movement itself has addressed these.

The introductory materials conclude with a chapter focusing on gay and lesbian domestic violence issues. In my opinion, the most interesting aspect of these materials is the way they invite us to question our basic analysis as to what causes domestic violence. Are sex roles actually key in causing this problem? If so, how do we explain such abuse in same-sex couples? This is an example of an area where there is no easy answer.

The second section of the book deals with the response to domestic violence by the civil legal system in the US. These four chapters focus on tort actions between victim and perpetrator, civil restraining orders, children in homes where domestic violence takes place, and alternative dispute resolution. The materials highlight the current issues in each of these areas; two of the most challenging include the response of the legal system to mothers who allegedly have "failed to protect" their children from witnessing the mother's own battering, and the questions which arise when attempting to resolve domestic violence cases outside the courtroom setting, using mediation or peacemaking.

The five chapters in the third section of the book focus primarily on the response of the criminal justice system. Again, policy issues are replete throughout. The chapter on law enforcement response looks at the issue of mandatory arrest in the context of domestic violence, a very controversial issue. The chapter on prosecution questions whether no-drop policies further empower or disempower victims of domestic violence, as well as discussing innovations in the nuts and bolts of prosecuting such cases. The materials on judges invite the reader to examine the development and usefulness of domestic violence courts. The final chapter, on victims of domestic violence as criminal defendants, analyzes the concept and term "Battered Woman Syndrome," and argues for another approach, namely the typical effects of intimate partner abuse upon its victims.

The four chapters in the fourth and last section of the book deal with issues which do not fit neatly into the "civil" or "criminal" categories typically used in the US legal system. They start with current federal responses to domestic violence, including the Violence Against Women Act (VAWA) and restrictions on possession of firearms by batterers. As this book went to press, the US Supreme Court issued its opinion finding unconstitutional the civil rights remedy provided for in VAWA, possibly the most important domestic violence issue the high court has ever addressed. The next chapter looks at confidentiality issues affecting victims of domestic violence, including the controversial question whether medical personnel should be mandated to report domestic violence to law enforcement. Domestic violence victims as welfare recipients and workers is the topic of the following chapter; this is another new area of law, which is just starting to be developed. This book concludes with the issues presented by immigration and international human rights laws as these impact victims of domestic violence; again we see a controversial issue being debated in the appellate courts, namely whether being a victim of domestic violence can be the basis for a request for asylum. The book thus comes full circle, starting and finishing with an international perspective.

A Final Note, An Apology to Some Readers, and An Invitation

Creating this second edition, while sometimes difficult and time-consuming, was also a labor of joy. It is inspiring to see the wealth of legal scholarship bursting forth all over this country, on dozens of domestic-violence related topics. It is exciting to have so much to choose from, and to see the ways practitioners, scholars, and students have been able to build on each other's work to create a body of sophisticated literature.

Some of the users of this book may be dismayed by the deletion of most of the endnotes, tables, references, and internal citations. This decision was made due to space constraints, so that the book could include more substantive pieces. I trust that readers who would like to see the omitted material will be able to access the original articles and cases. If this is very difficult, I would be happy to send a copy of a particular piece.

As a book like this is always a work in progress, I also welcome suggestions from readers or other teachers for what materials to include in the next edition, as well as comments on these materials and how they were useful to you.

NANCY K. D. LEMON

2000
Berkeley, California

COPYRIGHT PERMISSIONS

Virginia H. Murray, A Comparative Survey of the Historic Civil, Common, and American Indian Tribal Law Responses to Domestic Violence, 23 Oklahoma City U. L. Rev. 433 (1998).

Reva Siegel, "The Rule of Love": Wife Beating as Prerogative and Privacy, 105 Yale L. J. 2117 (1996).

Corporate Alliance to End Partner Violence, Financial Costs, http://www.caepv.org/getinfo/facts_stats.php?factsec=2. Reprinted with permission.

Molly Dragiewicz and Yvonne Lindgren, The Gendered Nature of Domestic Violence: Statistical Data for Lawyers Considering Equal Protection Analysis, 17 American U. J. of Gender, Soc. Pol'y & L. 229 (2009).

Break the Cycle, Dating Abuse Statistics (2017), http://www.breakthecycle.org/sites/default/files/Dating%20Statistics%20Fact%20Sheet_National_updated%2012.4.2017.pdf. Reprinted with permission.

Mary Kay Corporation, Mary Kay's 2015 "Truth About Abuse" Survey (press release), MaryKay.com (2015).

Kelly Weisberg, Supreme Court Abortion Decision Harms Domestic Violence Survivors, 28(2) Domestic Violenc Report 1 (Oct/Nov 2022). Domestic Violence Report is a professional report letter devoted to innovative programs, legal developments, and current services and research for those protecting, assisting, counseling, and treating the victims of domestic violence and sexual assault, respectively. For subscription information, write to the Civic Research Institute—4478 U.S. Route 27, P.O. Box 585, Kingston, N.J. 08528—or visit www.civicresearchinstitute.com.

Leigh Goodmark, Law is the Answer? Do We Really Know That for Sure?: Questioning the Efficacy of Legal Interventions for Battered Women, 23 St. Louis U. Pub. L. Rev. 7 (2004). Reprinted with permission of the Saint Louis University Public L. Rev., © 2004 St. Louis University School of Law, St. Louis, Missouri.

Judith Armatta, Getting Beyond the Law's Complicity in Intimate Violence Against Women, 33 Willamette L. Rev. 773 (1997).

Nancy K. D. Lemon, Summary of Deborah M. Weissman, The Personal is Political—And Economic: Rethinking Domestic Violence, 2007 Brigham Young U. L. Rev. 387 (2007), summarized in 13 Domestic Violence Report 69 (June/July 2008).

Domestic Abuse Intervention Programs, Home of the Duluth Model, Power and Control Wheel, https://www.theduluthmodel.org/wheel-gallery/.

Claire Houston, How Feminist Theory Became (Criminal) Law: Tracing the Path to Mandatory Criminal Intervention in Domestic Violence Cases, 21 Michigan J. of Gender & L. 217 (2014). Houston is an assistant professor of law at Western University, Ontario, Canada.

Evan Stark, Current Controversies: Coercive Control, in Sourcebook on Violence Against Women pp. 26–28 (3d ed. 2018, C. Renzetti et al. edits.). Copyright 2018 by Sage Publications. Reprinted by permission of Sage Publications, Inc.

Edward Gondolf & Ellen Fisher, The Survivor Theory, Battered Women as Survivors: An Alternative to Treating Learned Helplessness pp. 11–18, 20–24 (Lexington Books 1988).

Shane M. Trawick, Birth Control Sabotage as Domestic Violence: A Legal Response, 100 California L. Rev. 721 (2012). Reprinted with permission from the California Law Review. © 2012 by the California Law Review, Inc.

The Human Trafficking Legal Center, Human Trafficking and Domestic Violence, info@htlegalcenter.org. (2018).

Michael Paymar, Violent No More: Helping Men End Domestic Abuse pp. 10–16 (2d ed., Hunter House 2000). © 2000 by Michael Paymar. To order, please call (800) 266-5592, fax (510) 865-4295, visit the website www.hunterhouse.com, or write to Hunter House Publishers, P.O. Box 2914 Alameda, CA 94501. Reprinted by permission.

Alyce LaViolette, Assessing Dangerousness in Domestic Violence Cases, California Statewide Dispute Resolution Institute, San Jose, CA (2016). Reprinted with permission of Alyce LaViolette, MFT, and Founder of Alternatives to Violence, Long Beach, CA.

Joan Zorza, The New Domestic Violence Typologies: An Accurate Reconceptualization or Another Trivialization?, 3 Family & Intimate Partner Violence Q. 225 (2011).

Jacquelyn C. Campbell, Sanctions and Sanctuary: Wife-Battering within Cultural Contexts, in To Have and to Hit: Cultural Perspectives on Wife Beating pp. 277–279 (2d ed., Dorothy Ayers Counts et al. edits., 1999). © 1999 by the Board of Trustees of the University of Illinois. Used with permission of the University of Illinois Press and Dr. Campbell.

Paul J. Fleming, Jennifer McCleary-Sill, Matthew Morton, Ruti Levtov, Brian Heilman, Gary Barker, Risk Factors for Men's Lifetime Perpetration of Physical Violence Against Intimate Partners: Results from the International Men and Gender Equality Survey (IMAGES) in

Eight Countries, PLoS ONE 10(3): e0118639, doi:10.1371/journal.pone.0118639 (2015).

David Levinson, Societies Without Family Violence, in Family Violence in Cross-Cultural Perspectives, pp. 102–107 (1987). Copyright 1987 by Sage Publications. (Reprinted by permission of SAGE Publications, Inc.).

William E. Mitchell, Why Wape Men Don't Beat Their Wives: Constraints Toward Domestic Tranquility in a New Guinea Society, in To Have and to Hit: Cultural Perspectives on Wife Beating pp. 100–109 (2d ed., Dorothy Ayers Counts et al. edits., 1999). © 1999 by the Board of Trustees of the University of Illinois. Used with permission of the University of Illinois Press and Dr. Mitchell.

Leti Volpp, On Culture, Difference, and Domestic Violence, 11 Am. U. J. of Gender, Soc. Pol'y & L. 393 (2003).

Angela Davis, The Color of Violence Against Women, 3 ColorLines 4 (Fall 2000). Reprinted with permission.

Gina Szeto, The Asian American Domestic Violence Movement, unpublished Writing Requirement, U.C., Berkeley, School of Law (2012).

Amber Simmons, Why Are We So Mad? The Truth Behind Angry Black Women and Their Legal Invisibility as Victims of Domestic Violence, 36 Harvard BlackLetter L. J. 47 (2020).

Stacey A. Guthartz, Domestic Violence and the Jewish Community, 11 Mich. J. of Gender & L. 27 (2004).

Nooria Faizi, Domestic Violence in the Muslin Community, 10 Texas J. of Women & L. 209 (2001).

Doug Jones, Domestic Violence Against Women with Disabilities: A Feminist Legal Theory Analysis, 2 Fla. A & M U. L. Rev. 207 (2007).

LGBTQ Power and Control Wheel, Produced and distributed by the National Center on Domestic and Sexual Violence, www.ncdsv.org; Developed by Roe & Jagodinsky, Inspired and adapted from Domestic Abuse Intervention Project, Duluth, MN.

Caroline Morin, Re-Traumatized: How Gendered Laws Exacerbate the Harm for Same-Sex Victims of Intimate Partner Violence, 40 New England J. of Crim. & Civ. Confinement 477 (2014). This law journal is now part of the New England Law Review.

Jacquie Andreano, Disproportionate Effect of Mutual Restraining Orders on Same-Sex Domestic Violence Victims, 108 Calif. L. Rev. 1047 (2020).

Kae Greenberg, Still Hidden in the Closet: Trans Women and Domestic Violence, 27 Berkeley J. of Gender, L. & J. 198 (2012).

Rishita Apsani, Are Women's Spaces Trangender Spaces? Single-Sex Domestic Violence Shelters, Transgender Inclusion, and the Equal Protection Clause, 106 Calif. L. Rev. 1689 (2018).

Jessica Dayton, Intersection of Family Law and Torts in Domestic Violence Cases, Calif. Family Law Specialist (summer 2021, no. 3, p.1).

Merle H. Weiner, Domestic Violence and the *Per Se* Standard of Outrage, 54 Maryland L. Rev. 188 (1995).

Jane K. Stoever, Enjoining Abuse: The Case for Indefinite Domestic Violence Protection Orders, 67 Vanderbilt L. Rev. 1015 (2014).

Sally Goldfarb, Reconceiving Civil Protection Orders for Domestic Violence: Can Law Help End the Abuse Without Ending the Relationship?, 29 Cardozo L. Rev. 1487 (2008).

Lisa Vollendorf Martin, What's Love Got to Do with It: Securing Access to Justice for Abused Teens, 61 Cath. U. L. Rev. 457 (2012).

Reinie Cordier, Donna Chung, Sarah Wilkes-Gillan, and Renee Speyer, The Effectiveness of Protection Orders in Reducing Recidivism in Domestic Violence: A Systematic Review and Meta-Analysis, 22(4) Trauma, Violence, & Abuse 804 (2019). Copyright 2019 by Sage Publications. Reprinted by permission of Sage Publications, Inc.

Battered Women's Justice Project, National Center on Protection Orders and Full Faith and Credit, A Prosecutor's Guide to Full Faith and Credit for Protection Orders: Protecting Victims of Domestic Violence (2011). Reprinted with permission.

Jan Jeske and Mary Louise Klas, Adverse Childhood Experiences: Implications for Family Law Practice and the Family Court System, 50 Family L. Q. 123 (2016). Reprinted with permission from the American Bar Association, Ms. Jeske, and Judge Klas.

Zoe Garvin, The Unintended Consequences of Rebuttable Presumptions to Determine Child Custody in Domestic Violence Cases, 50 Family L. Q. 173 (2016). Reprinted with permission from the American Bar Association and Ms. Garvin.

Nancy K. D. Lemon, Statutes Creating Rebuttable Presumptions Against Custody to Batterers: How Effective Are They?, 28 William Mitchell L. Rev. 601 (2001). Reprinted by permission.

Elizabeth Barker Brandt, Concerns At The Margins Of Supervised Access To Children, 9 J. of L. & Family Studies 201 (2007).

Deborah M. Goelman, Shelter from the Storm: Using Jurisdictional Statutes to Protect Victims of Domestic Violence after the Violence Against Women Act of 2000, 13 Columbia J. of Gender & L. 101 (2004).

National Council of Juvenile and Family Court Judges, Relocating After Dissolution in Domestic Violence Cases, 15 Synergy 10 (Winter 2011).

Coffey, D. S., MSW, Ph.D. (2009). Parenting After Violence, A Guide for Practitioners (pp. 1–64, Publication). Philadelphia, PA: Institute for Safe Families. Health Federation of Philadelphia.

Susan Landrum, The Ongoing Debate About Mediation in the Context of Domestic Violence: A Call for Empirical Studies of Mediation Effectiveness, 12 Cardozo J. of Conflict Resolution 425 (2011).

Nancy E. Johnson, Dennis P. Saccuzzo, and Wendy J. Koen, Child Custody Mediation in Cases of Domestic Violence: Empirical Evidence of a Failure to Protect, 11 Violence Against Women 1022 (2005).

Judge Bennett Burkemper and Nina Balsam, Examining the Use of Restorative Justice Practices in Domestic Violence Cases, 27 St. Louis U. Pub. L. Rev. 121 (2007). Reprinted with permission of the Saint Louis University Public Law Review © 2007.

Leigh Goodmark, "Law and Justice Are Not Always the Same": Creating Community-Based Justice Forums for People Subjected to Intimate Partner Abuse, 42 Florida State U. L. Rev. 707 (2015).

Donna Coker, Enhancing Autonomy for Battered Women: Lessons from Navajo Peacemaking, 47 UCLA L. Rev. 1 (1999).

Jessica Klarfeld, A Striking Disconnect: Marital Rape Law's Failure to Keep up with Domestic Violence Law, 48 American Criminal L. Rev. 1819 (2011).

Jenny E. Mitchell & Chitra Raghavan, The Impact of Coercive Control on Use of Specific Sexual Coercion Tactics, 27(2) Violence Against Women 1 (2019). Copyright 2019 by Sage Publications. Reprinted by permission of Sage Publications, Inc.

International Association of Chiefs of Police, Intimate Partner Violence Response Policy and Training Guidelines (2017), http://www.theiacp.org/MPDomesticViolence. Reprinted with permission. Further reproduction without the express permission from IACP is strictly prohibited.

Mallika Kaur, Victims Must Not be Lost in Domestic Violence and Policing Debates, Ms. Magazine online, 10/6/20.

Radna Vishnuvajjala, Insecure Communities: How an Immigration Enforcement Program Encourages Battered Women to Stay Silent, 32 British Columbia. J. of L. & Soc. J. 185 (2012).

Martha McMahon and Ellen Pence, Making Social Change: Reflections on Individual & Institutional Advocacy, 9 Violence Against Women 47 (2003). Reprinted with permission of SAGE Publications.

Lisa Snead, Domestic Violence Litigation in the Wake of *DeShaney* and *Castle Rock,* 18 Texas J. of Women & L. 305 (2009).

Jacqueline M. Mazzola, Honey I'm Home: Addressing the Problem of Officer Domestic Violence, 27 J. of Civil Rights & Economic Development 347 (2014).

International Association of Chiefs of Police, Discussion Paper on IACP's Policy on Domestic Violence by Police Officers, A Product of the IACP Police Response to Violence Against Women Project, http://www.theiacp.org/model-policy/html_policies/domestic-violence-by-police-officers-paper/ (July 2003). © by the IACP, Inc., 515 N. Washington St., Alexandria, VA 22314. Reprinted with permission. Further reproduction without the express permission from IACP is strictly prohibited.

Leigh Goodmark, Autonomy Feminism: An Anti-Essentialist Critique of Mandatory Interventions in Domestic Violence Cases, 37 Florida State U. L. Rev. 1 (2009).

Eleanor Simon, Confrontation and Domestic Violence Post-*Davis*: Is There and Should There Be a Doctrinal Exception?, 17 Michigan J. of Gender & L. 175 (2011).

Victoria Ajayi, Violence Against Women: The Ethics of Incorporating the Cultural Defense in Legal Narrative, 25 Georgetown J. of Legal Ethics 401 (2012).

Melissa Labriola, Sarah Bradley, Chris S. O'Sullivan, Michael Rempel, and Samantha Moore, A National Portrait of Domestic Violence Courts, Center for Court Innovation, http://www.courtinnovation.org/sites/default/files/national_portrait.pdf (2010). Reprinted with permission.

Anat Maytal, Specialized Domestic Violence Courts: Are They Worth the Trouble in Massachusetts?, 18 Boston U. Public Interest L. J. 197 (2008).

Ann E. Freedman, Fact Finding in Civil Domestic Violence Cases: Secondary Traumatic Stress and the Need for Compassionate Witnesses, 11 American U. J. of Gender, Soc. Pol'y & L. 567 (2003). Reprinted with permission.

Andrew R. Klein, Battered Women's Justice Project, Practical Implications of Current Domestic Violence Research for Probation Officers and Administrators, http://www.bwjp.org/assets/documents/pdfs/practical_implications_of_current_domestic_violence_research_for_probation_officers_and_administrators.pdf (2015). Reprinted with permission.

Center for Justice Intervention, Domestic Violence Court Compliance Monitoring, info@innovatingjustice.org (2013).

Shelby A. D. Moore, Understanding the Connection between Domestic Violence, Crime, and Poverty: How Welfare Reform May Keep Battered Women from Leaving Abusive Relationships, 12 Texas J. of Women & L. 451 (2003).

Leigh Goodmark, When Is a Battered Woman Not a Battered Woman? When She Fights Back, 20 Yale J. of L. & Feminism 75 (2008).

Zelda B. Harris, The Predicament of the Immigrant Victim/Defendant: "VAWA Diversion" and Other Considerations in Support of Battered Women, 23 St. Louis U. Public L. Rev. 49 (2004).

Brandi L. Jackson, No Ground on Which to Stand: Review Stand Your Grand Laws so Survivors of Domestic Violence Are No Longer Incarcerated for Defending Their Lives, 30 Berkeley J. of Gender, L. & J. 154 (2015).

Nancy K. D. Lemon, A Transformative Process: Working as a Domestic Violence Expert Witness, 24 Berkeley J. of Gender, L. & J. 208 (2009).

Erin Liotta, Double Victims: Ending the Incarceration of California's Battered Women, 26 Berkeley J. of Gender, L. & J. 253 (2011).

Courtney Cross, Reentering Survivors: Invisible at the Intersection of the Criminal Legal System and the Domestic Violence Movement, 31 Berkeley J. of Gender, L. & J. 60 (2016).

Claire M. DeMatteis, Protecting the Freedom for Women to Be Free from Violence: The Violence Against Women Act Endures, 22 Widener L. Rev. 267 (2016).

Jane Stoever, Firearms and Domestic Violence Fatalities: Preventable Deaths, 53 Fam. L. Q. 183 (2020).

Julia Weber, Texas Court's Radical Firearms Decision Jeoparidizes Domestic Violence Survivors, 28(4) Domestic Violence Report 57 (April/May 2023).

Christine Zellar Church, The Servicemembers Civil Relief Act: Protecting Victims of Domestic Violence in Protection Order Cases Involving the Military, 12 Thomas M. Cooley J. of Practical & Clinical L. 335, http://www.bwjp.org/assets/documents/pdfs/service_members_civil_relief_act_protecting_victims_of_domestic_violence_in_protection_order_cases.pdf (2010). Reprinted with permission.

Hailey Guinn, Military Adjudications of Domestic Violence, (unpublished) (2021), on file with author.

Pamela Kravetz, Way Off Base: An Argument Against Intimate Partner Violence Cases In Veterans Treatment Courts, 4 Veterans Law Rev. 162 (2012).

Kristen M. Driskell, Identity Confidentiality for Women Fleeing Domestic Violence, 20 Hastings Women's L. J. 129 (2009).

National Safe and Strategic Technology Project, National Network to End Domestic Violence, Internet Access to Court Records: Safety & Privacy Risks for Victims of Domestic Violence & All Citizens Using the Justice System, http://www.ncdsv.org/images/TCFV-LegalAdvocatesGuide.pdf (2006). Reprinted with permission.

Madison Lo, Domestic Violence and the Internet of Things, 26(6) Domestic Violence Report 81 (Aug/Sept 2021).

Thomas L. Hafemeister, If All You Have Is a Hammer: Society's Ineffective Response to Intimate Partner Violence, 60 Catholic U. L. Rev. 919 (2011).

Donna Coker, Shifting Power for Battered Women: Law, Material Resources, and Poor Women of Color, 33 UC Davis L. Rev. 1009 (2000). © 2000 by Donna Coker, originally published in the UC Davis Law Review, vol. 33, pp. 1009–1055. © 2000 by the Regents of the University of California. All rights reserved. Reprinted with permission.

Rachel Gallagher, Welfare Reforms' Inadequate Implementation of the Family Violence Option: Exploring the Dual Oppression of Poor Domestic Violence Victims, 19 American U. J. of Gender, Soc. Pol'y & L. 987 (2011). Ms. Gallagher is an associate at Blank Rome LLP.

Megan Adams, Assuring Financial Stability for Survivors: Coerced Debt, 84 Brooklyn L. Rev. 1387 (2019).

Michael D. Moberly, The Workplace Injunction: An Emerging But Imperfect Weapon in the Fight Against Domestic Violence, 26 Am. U. J. Gender Soc. Pol'y & L. 831 (2018).

Monica Batra Kashyap, Heartless Immigration Law: Rubbing Salt into the Wounds of Immigrant Survivors of Domestic Violence, 9 Tulane L. Rev. 51 (2020)

Leslye E. Orloff, Haley Iesha Magwood, Yasmin Campos-Mendez, and Giselle A. Hass, Transforming Lives: How the VAWA Self-Petition and U Visa Change the Lives of Survivors and Their Children After Employment Authorization and Legal Immigration Status, National Immigrant Women's Advocacy Project (NIWAP), American University, Washington College of Law (2021).

National Network to End Domestic Violence (NNEDV), Public Charge and IPV (2022), Regarding *Arizona v. City and County of San Francisco*, California (U.S. Supreme Court, 2022), 142 S.Ct. 1926 (MEM), from NNEDV website.

Olga Grosh, Foreign Wives, Domestic Violence: U.S. Law Stigmatizes and Fails to Protect "Mail-Order Brides," 22 Hastings Women's L. J. 81 (2011).

Harvard Law Review Members, Attorney General Garland Vacates *Matter of A-B-, Matter of A-B-,* 28 I. & N. Dec. 307 (A.G. 2021), 135 Harvard L. Rev. 1174 (2022).

Rhonda Copelon, International Human Rights Dimensions of Intimate Violence: Another Strand in the Dialect of Feminist Lawmaking, 11 American U. J. of Gender Soc. Pol'y & L. 865 (2003). Reprinted with permission.

Max D. Siegel, Surviving *Castle Rock*: The Human Rights of Domestic Violence, 18 Cardozo J. of L. & Gender 727 (2012).

Maggie Woods, Trying to Remove the *Gender* From "Gender-Based Violence": Poland's Policy Framework is War on Women, not Domestic Violence, (2020), unpublished, on file with author.

SUMMARY OF CONTENTS

TABLE OF CONTENTS

TABLE OF CASES

The principal cases are in bold type.

DOMESTIC VIOLENCE LAW

Sixth Edition

CHAPTER 1

HISTORY AND OVERVIEW

■ ■ ■

This chapter introduces the topic of this book, domestic violence law in the United States.

Starting with Roman Law, the materials trace the development of the response of the Roman and Anglo-American legal system to domestic violence, and the influence of Judeo-Christian religion on this response. A nineteenth century U.S. case illustrates the fact that at that time, it was typical for our legal system to not only tolerate domestic violence, but to actually condone it. The materials start to examine the repudiation of this "doctrine of chastisement," but question whether real change took place, asking whether what occurred was merely a change in the rationale for non-interference in cases of domestic violence.

The next section focuses on statistics regarding domestic violence in the U.S.: financial costs, the gendered nature of this form of abuse, dating abuse, and how public awareness is growing. New materials include the impact of the COVID pandemic on domestic violence in the U.S. and how technology enables stalking of intimate partners.

The third part of the chapter focuses on contemporary issues, starting with the impact on domestic violence survivors of the Supreme Court's decision in *Dobbs*, holding that states may severely restrict or ban abortion. The materials also look at the role of the State generally, noting that the legal system and government actors in the U.S. are much more involved in addressing the problem of domestic violence than ever before, but that this also creates additional challenges.

An article brings an international perspective to these questions, and notes that legal changes alone are not sufficient to end domestic violence, though such changes are a key part of the solution. Another piece analyzes the relationship between economics and domestic violence, both on a societal scale and within families. The final piece focuses on the tension between ending violence against women and relying on the U.S. prison industrial complex, a theme that will continue throughout this book.

A. HISTORY

VIRGINIA H. MURRAY, A COMPARATIVE SURVEY OF THE HISTORIC CIVIL, COMMON, AND AMERICAN INDIAN TRIBAL LAW RESPONSES TO DOMESTIC VIOLENCE

23 Okla. City U. L. Rev. 435–443 (1998)
(citations and footnotes omitted)

II. THE HISTORIC RESPONSE OF CIVIL AND COMMON LAW TO DOMESTIC VIOLENCE

"By the old law, a husband might give his wife moderate correction . . . but it is declared in black and white that he may not beat her black and blue, (though the civil law allowed) a man to bestow in moderation his fist upon any woman who had bestowed upon him her hand."

Women in European and American societies have traditionally held a subordinate position to men, a status that dates back to the early Greeks, Romans, and Hebrews. Male dominance in these societies was a result of social and legal structures and religious beliefs. Thus, male dominance and domestic violence in western civilization is not new, nor is it a rarity. Instead, it is an expression of traditional cultural and religious norms. As one author has noted, "it has been with us for more than two thousand years . . . seeded the fields of law from which our notions of justice were harvested. It is rooted in the denial of equality to women."

A. The Influence of Judeo-Christian Religion

Historic Roman, Hebrew, European, and American societies were vertically structured because they were modeled after, and in some cases controlled by, Judeo-Christian religion. Early Judeo-Christian religion, like Muslim and Hindu beliefs, taught that societies should be based on the model of the patriarchal family, with men holding positions of power and authority.

In addition, several prominent religious leaders such as Saint Augustine, Calvin, and Martin Luther believed in the male right to dominate and control women and in the subservient nature of women. The Old and New Testaments instruct the subordination of women, beginning with the creation of Eve from the rib of Adam. Biblical women who were not considered docile, chaste, and passive were subject to death by mutilation or stoning. Women were the property of men, and rape was an encroachment of the father or husband's property interest.

Through the twelfth century, the Christian church's position toward women remained unchanged. Medieval canon law, based in part on Roman law, argued that women were the subjects of men, and as such, should be deprived of all authority.

In the fourteenth century, the Christian church recognized a husband's right of chastisement, adopted in the English common law. Father Cherubino wrote The Rules of Marriage, later officially sanctioned by the Catholic Church, in which he stated that when a wife committed an offense against her husband, he should "scold her sharply, bully and terrify her. And if this still doesn't work . . . take up a stick and beat her soundly. . . ."

Like early Christian teachings, Hebrew religious leaders taught that Hebrew society must be vertically structured, with men holding positions of power and authority at the top. Hebrew women were controlled by men and their value connected to childbearing. Some early Hebrew teachers argued that men could compel their wives to perform household chores, take care of the children, and perform her duties, through wife-beating. A Hebrew husband possessed the power to condemn his wife to death for committing adultery. In the sixteenth century, Solomon Luria stated in Yam Shel Shelomo, a commentary on the Talmud, that a husband is permitted to beat his wife "in any manner when she acts against the laws of the divine Torah. He can beat her until her soul departs, even if she transgresses only a negative commandment."

Some commentators argue that even in the modern era, religious beliefs and the authority of religious institutions perpetuate domestic violence in Europe and America. The basic social and legal structures initially instituted pursuant to the influence of Judeo-Christian religion are still in place, and although women have gained considerable rights in recent decades, men continue to overwhelmingly control the governmental and church hierarchy.

For example, one commentator who studied domestic violence in Ireland noted that traditional cultural and religious influences still encourage Irish women to "take your oil." In addition, most conservative Irish religious dogma continues to "extol[ ] the virtues of preserving the marriage bond, which takes priority over the happiness and security of women's lives."

In modern Jewish society, unequal treatment of men and women continues in at least one form, the issuance of a Get, or bill of divorce. Traditional Hebrew law allowed a man to divorce his wife without cause, and the woman was unable to protest. About A.D. 200, women were also allowed to request a Get in limited circumstances, but a man could not be forced to accept the divorce.

Today, Jewish men can still apply for a Get without cause and a wife can be forced to accept the divorce against her will. However, the traditional restrictions on a woman obtaining a Get continue, including the rule that a husband cannot be forced to accept a Get obtained by his wife.

B. Domestic Violence in Roman Society and Civil Law

European and American societies and legal systems have been greatly influenced by the Romans. Roman society was structured vertically in pyramid form. Slaves constituted the broad base of the pyramid, with men who were Roman citizens in positions of power and authority at the top.

Throughout Roman history, *patria potestas*, or paternal power, was the legal authority of the paterfamilias, the oldest male head of a Roman family. The paterfamilias had control over all members of his family, including *ius vitae necisque*, the power of life and death. The legal concept of *patria potestas* made the wife and mother a legal sister to her own children, and daughter to her husband or master. The Roman wife, like her children, was legally subject to the paterfamilias' power of life and death.

Roman marriages were not regulated by the law, with the exceptions of requiring an individual to have the mental capacity to marry, be of a certain age, and to obtain their father's consent. Subject to these conditions, all that was required for a valid marriage was a manifestation of an intention to be married. Divorce was also without legal regulation. By the time of Justinian in A.D. 527–65, women had increased freedoms and legal rights, and either party could terminate a marriage by simply indicating they no longer wished to be married.

Under early Roman civil law, however, a husband could beat, divorce, or murder his wife for offenses she committed that disparaged his honor or threatened his property rights. In addition, a husband's family could likewise kill his wife for adultery, without participation by the husband. During the Augustan era, the husband or his family members who killed his wife for adultery would be acquitted of murder.

The evolution of the crime of rape in Roman civil law is indicative of the status of women in early Roman society. Rape arose from the early Roman law of *raptus*, a form of violent theft applied to both property and persons. Women, like children, were the property of men in Roman society, and under Roman civil law, injury for rape was based on damages to a father, husband, or brother. In other words, rape was an economic crime against property, and not a crime against the female victim.

With the advent of Christianity as the official religion of the Roman Empire, much of the social and legal progress benefitting women was reversed. For example, in A.D. 542 Justinian changed the Roman divorce laws, forbidding divorce by consent of either party. Although the new law was repealed after five years, it was eventually reinstated in addition to other Canon Law.

C. Domestic Violence and the Common Law

1. England

Historic English common law sanctioned two contradictory roles for husbands: first, husbands were to act as their wives' disciplinarians, and second, husbands were to be their wives' protectors. These roles developed due to women's legal subordination and perceived inferiority.

Unlike Roman civil law, English common law required a man and woman seeking to be married to go through certain legal "formalities." Marriage was a contract, changing the legal status of both parties, and divorce was rarely obtained, and only through legal means. Under the "chattel theory," introduced around the sixth century, a woman was first the property of her father and then, upon marriage, the property of her husband. Two important customs developed from this theory, "bride capture" and "stealing an heiress." In the former a man could conquer a woman through rape; in the latter, a man could literally kidnap a woman for marriage.

Early common law rape laws were similar to those of Roman civil law, and derived from "bride capture" and "stealing an heiress." These laws protected the "property rights" of the male relatives of the female victim. For example, if a man raped a young unmarried woman, he was guilty of stealing her father's property, and not guilty of a crime against the victim herself. To the contrary, if a husband raped his wife, he was merely "using his property."

Under the feudal doctrine of coverture, which prevailed from the eleventh to sixteenth centuries, women lost their legal identity upon marriage. At that time, the husband and wife became one—the husband. This legal fiction was referred to as the "unities theory," and pursuant to it, a wife could not own personal property, make a will, nor be a party to a contract. In fact, it was recognized that a husband did not make contracts with his wife since it was tantamount to making a contract with himself.

The chattel and coverture theories combined to make husbands legally responsible for their wives' misbehavior. This responsibility, along with the desire to maintain family discipline and order, and the influence of Christianity, brought about the doctrine of "chastisement," which allowed a husband to beat his wife. Sir William Blackstone wrote about the doctrine of chastisement in the late eighteenth century, stating: "as he is to answer for her misbehavior, the law thought it reasonable to intrust him with this power of restraining her, by domestic chastisement, in the same moderation that a man is allowed to correct his apprentices or children. . . ." The only limits placed on a husband's right to beat his wife were that he do so in a moderate manner. In accord with the doctrine of chastisement, English jurists in 1782 developed the "rule of thumb," whereby a husband could beat his wife with a rod no thicker than his thumb.

During the late nineteenth century, an era of feminist agitation for reform began in England. Influential women such as Frances Power Cobbe persuaded the English Parliament to pass laws rejecting chastisement, making domestic violence illegal. Although these new laws were a marked departure from the traditional English common law, and a victory for the women's movement in England, the "marital rape exemption" and the rule of primogeniture limiting women's property rights continued well into the twentieth century.

2. The United States

Early American colonies enacted laws proscribing wife abuse, believing it to be a threat to a settlement's orderliness and stability. These laws were not strictly enforced, and domestic assaults were typically excused if a husband could "justify" his behavior. Shortly after settlement, Colonial courts were pressured to follow English jurisprudence.

So long as it did not conflict with the Constitution or state statutes, new states after the Revolutionary War generally incorporated English common law. For example, Blackstone's Commentaries played an important role in shaping American legal thought. Courts in the United States, particularly in the mid-Atlantic region and the South, began adopting the "chastisement" doctrine articulated by Blackstone and accepting the English "rule of thumb." For example, in 1824 the Supreme Court of Mississippi stated that in exercising his right to chastise his wife, a husband should not be subjected to "vexatious prosecutions" by his wife, and that courts should be hesitant to expose such private conduct to public scrutiny. Likewise, courts in North Carolina, Alabama, and Pennsylvania, among others, recognized the doctrine of chastisement.

In the mid-nineteenth century, changes in conceptions of authority and family structure occurred in American society.

For example, many experts argued that corporal punishment of children was an ineffective method of instilling respect for authority and bringing about good behavior. Eventually, the fledgling American women's movement adopted these views regarding the doctrine of chastisement. In 1848, the movement's leaders publicly denounced the common law doctrines of marital status and the hierarchical, vertical structure of American society and marriage in a formal Declaration of Sentiments.

In addition to the women's movement, several nineteenth century American legal scholars issued treatises on American common law recognizing a "softened" right of chastisement. For example, in 1827 James Kent wrote: "As the husband is the guardian of the wife, and bound to protect and maintain her, the law has given him a reasonable superiority and control over her person, and he may even put gentle restraints upon her liberty, if her conduct be such to require it."

Although changes in the law were initially heralded by women's groups as a success, it soon became clear that for the immediate future, true reform was limited. For example, a relatively liberal state such as Massachusetts rejected all remedies for domestic violence that allowed wives to separate from their violent husbands. In many states that did pass laws allowing a wife to petition for divorce to escape abuse, husbands could defeat the petition by claiming their behavior was "provoked," or their wife delayed petitioning and thus "condoned" the abuse.

It was not until the modern women's movement of the 1960s that domestic violence once again became a national issue. As a result, the federal and state governments enacted new laws in the 1970s, 1980s, and 1990s, and existing laws were revised. In some respects, these changes in the American legal system reflected an international legal movement against domestic violence.

CALVIN BRADLEY V. THE STATE

1 Miss. (Walker) 156 (1824)
[Overruled in *Harris v. State,* 71 Miss. 462, 14 South. 266]
(citations omitted)

This cause was tried in the circuit court before the honorable Judge Turner, at the April term of 1824. The defendant was indicted for a common assault and battery, and upon his arraignment, pleaded not guilty, *son assault demesne*, and that Lydia Bradley was his lawful wife & c. Issue was taken upon all the pleas. After the evidence was submitted, and before the jury retired, the counsel for the defendant moved the court to instruct the jury. If they believed the person named in the bill of indictment, and upon whom the assault and battery was committed, was the wife of the defendant, at the time of the assault and battery,—that then and in such case they could not find the defendant guilty. The court refused to give the instructions prayed for by the defendant, and charged the jury, that a husband could commit an assault and battery on the body of his wife, to which opinion of the court, a bill of exceptions was filed, and the case comes up by writ of error upon petition.

The only question submitted for the consideration of the court, is, whether a husband can commit an assault and battery upon the body of his wife. This, as an abstract proposition, will not admit of doubt. But I am fully persuaded, from the examination I have made, an unlimited license of this kind cannot be sanctioned, either upon principles of law or humanity. It is true, according to the old law, the husband might give his wife moderate correction, because he is answerable for her misbehavior; hence it was thought reasonable, to intrust him, with a power, necessary to restrain the indiscretions of one, for whose conduct he was to be made responsible. Sir William Blackstone says, during the reign of Charles the first, this power was much doubted.—Notwithstanding the lower orders of people still claimed and exercised it as an inherent privilege, which could not be abandoned, without entrenching upon their rightful authority, known and acknowledged from the earliest periods of the common law, done in a case before Mr. Justice Raymond, when the same doctrine was recognised, with proper limitations and restrictions, well suited to the condition and feelings of those, who might think proper to use a whip or rattan, no bigger than my thumb. In order to enforce the salutary restraints of domestic discipline, I think his lordship might have narrowed down the rule in such a manner, as to restrain the exercise of the right, within the compass of great moderation, without producing a destruction of the principle itself. If the defendant now before us, could shew from the record in this case, he continued himself within reasonable bounds, when he thought proper to chastise his wife, we would deliberate long before an affirmance of the judgment.

The indictment charges the defendant with having made an assault upon one Lydia Bradley, and then and there did beat, bruise, & c.—and the jury have found the defendant guilty, which never could have taken place, if the evidence supported either the second or third pleas of the accused. It was not necessary for the defendant below to introduce his second and third pleas, as we think he could have made a full and ample defence, upon the same matter, under the plea of the general issue. However abhorrent to the feelings of every member of the bench, must be the exercise of the remnant of federal authority, to inflict pain and suffering, when all the finer feelings of the heart should be warmed into devotion, by our most affectionate regards, yet every principle of public policy and expediency, in reference to the domestic relations, would seem to require, the establishment of the rule we have laid down, in order to prevent the deplorable spectacle of the exhibition of similar cases in our courts of justice.—Family broils and dissensions cannot be investigated before the tribunals of the country, without casting a shade over the character of those who are unfortunately engaged in the controversy. To screen from public reproach those who may be thus unhappily situated, let the husband be permitted to exercise the right of moderate chastisement, in cases of great emergency, and use salutary restraints in every case of misbehavior, without being subjected to vexatious prosecutions, resulting in the mutual discredit and shame of all parties concerned. *Judgment affirmed.*

REVA B. SIEGEL, "THE RULE OF LOVE": WIFE BEATING AS PREROGATIVE AND PRIVACY

105 Yale L. J. 2117, 2118–2120 (1996)
(citations and footnotes omitted)

INTRODUCTION

The Anglo-American common law originally provided that a husband, as master of his household, could subject his wife to corporal punishment or "chastisement" so long as he did not inflict permanent injury upon her.

During the nineteenth century, an era of feminist agitation for reform of marriage law, authorities in England and the United States declared that a husband no longer had the right to chastise his wife. Yet, for a century after courts repudiated the right of chastisement, the American legal system continued to treat wife beating differently from other cases of assault and battery. While authorities denied that a husband had the right to beat his wife, they intervened only intermittently in cases of marital violence: Men who assaulted their wives were often granted formal and informal immunities from prosecution, in order to protect the privacy of the family and to promote "domestic harmony." In the late 1970s, the feminist movement began to challenge the concept of family privacy that shielded wife abuse, and since then, it has secured many reforms designed to protect women from marital violence. Yet violence in the household persists. The U.S. Surgeon General recently found that "battering of women by husbands, ex-husbands or lovers [is] the single largest cause of injury to women in the United States." "[T]hirty-one percent of all women murdered in America are killed by their husbands, ex-husbands, or lovers."

The persistence of domestic violence raises important questions about the nature of the legal reforms that abrogated the chastisement prerogative. By examining how regulation of marital violence evolved after the state denied men the privilege of beating their wives, we can learn much about the ways in which civil rights reform changes a body of status law. In the nineteenth century, and again in the twentieth century, the American feminist movement has attempted to reform the law of marriage to secure for wives equality with their husbands. Its efforts in each century have produced significant changes in the law of marriage. The status of married women has improved, but wives still have not attained equality with their husbands—if we measure equality as the dignitary and material "goods" associated with the wealth wives control, or the kinds of work they perform, or the degree of physical security they enjoy. Despite the efforts of the feminist movement, the legal system continues to play an important role in perpetuating these status differences, although, over time, the role law plays in enforcing status relations has become increasingly less visible.

As this Article will show, efforts to reform a status regime do bring about change—but not always the kind of change advocates seek. When the legitimacy of a status regime is successfully contested, lawmakers and jurists will both cede and defend status privileges—gradually relinquishing the original rules and justificatory rhetoric of the contested regime and finding new rules and reasons to protect such status privileges as they choose to defend. Thus, civil rights reform can breathe new life into a body of status law, by pressuring legal elites to translate it into a more contemporary, and less controversial, social idiom. I call this kind of change in the rules and rhetoric of a status regime "preservation through transformation," and illustrate this modernization dynamic in a case study of domestic assault law as it evolved in rule structure and rationale from a law of marital prerogative to a law of marital privacy.

Parts I–III of this Article illustrate that as the nineteenth-century feminist movement protested a husband's marital prerogatives, the movement helped bring about the repudiation of chastisement doctrine; but, in so doing, the movement also precipitated changes in the regulation of marital violence that "modernized" this body of status law. A survey of criminal and tort law regulating marital violence during the Reconstruction Era reveals that the American legal system did not simply internalize norms of sex equality espoused by feminist critics of the chastisement prerogative; instead, during the Reconstruction Era, chastisement law was supplanted by a new body of marital violence policies that were premised on a variety of gender-, race-, and class-based assumptions. This new body of common law differed from chastisement doctrine, both in rule structure and rhetoric. Judges no longer insisted that a husband had the legal prerogative to beat his wife; instead, they often asserted that the legal system should not interfere in cases of wife beating, in order to protect the privacy of the marriage relationship and to promote domestic harmony. Judges most often invoked considerations of marital privacy when contemplating the prosecution of middle and upper-class men for wife beating. Thus, as I show, the body of formal and informal immunity rules that sprang up in criminal and tort law during the Reconstruction Era was both gender-and class-salient: It functioned to preserve authority relations between husband and wife, and among men of different social classes as well.

These changes in the rule structure of marital status law were justified in a distinctive rhetoric: one that diverged from the traditional idiom of chastisement doctrine. Instead of reasoning about marriage in the older, hierarchy-based norms of the common law, jurists began to justify the regulation of domestic violence in the language of privacy and love associated with companionate marriage in the industrial era. Jurists reasoning in this discourse of "affective privacy" progressively abandoned tropes of hierarchy and began to employ tropes of interiority to describe the marriage relationship, justifying the new regime of common law immunity rules in languages that invoked the feelings and spaces of domesticity. Once translated from an antiquated to a more contemporary gender idiom, the state's justification for treating wife beating differently from other kinds of assault seemed reasonable in ways the law of chastisement did not.

As the history of domestic violence law illustrates, political opposition to a status regime may bring about changes that improve the welfare of subordinated groups. With the demise of chastisement law, the situation of married women improved—certainly, in dignitary terms, and perhaps materially as well. At the same time, the story of chastisement's demise suggests that there is a price for such dignitary and material gains as civil rights reform may bring. If a reform movement is at all successful in advancing its justice claims, it will bring pressure to bear on lawmakers to rationalize status-enforcing state action in new and less socially controversial terms. This process of adaptation can actually revitalize a body of status law, enhancing its capacity to legitimate social inequalities that remain among status-differentiated groups. Examined from this perspective, the reform of chastisement doctrine can teach us much about the dilemmas confronting movements for social justice in America today.

[Editor's Note: However, in Judicial Patriarchy And Domestic Violence: A Challenge To The Conventional Family Privacy Narrative, 21 Wm. & Mary J. of Women & L. 379 (2015), historian Elizabeth Katz argues that at least between 1900–1910, criminal and family courts in the U.S. roundly condemned wife beating, as did the newspapers and general public. Katz disputes Siegel's thesis that U.S. courts condoned wife beating, except they did not believe wives should be allowed to sue their husbands in tort suits, which would give wives too much power and would allow husbands to sue wives in tort, which courts thought was inadvisable. See also excerpt from Katz article in Chapter 5, Torts.]

B. STATISTICS

U.S. CENTERS FOR DISEASE CONTROL, PREVENTING INTIMATE PARTNER VIOLENCE (2022)

1-800-CDC-INFO (232–4636) • www.cdc.gov/violenceprevention
(references omitted)

What is intimate partner violence?

Intimate partner violence (IPV) is abuse or aggression that occurs in a romantic relationship. "Intimate partner" refers to both current and former spouses and dating partners. IPV can vary in how often it happens and how severe it is. It can range from one episode of violence that could have lasting impact to chronic and severe episodes over multiple years.

IPV can include any of the following types of behavior:

- Physical violence is when a person hurts or tries to hurt a partner by hitting, kicking, or using another type of physical force.

- Sexual violence is forcing or attempting to force a partner to take part in a sex act, sexual touching, or a non-physical sexual event (e.g., sexting) when the partner does not or cannot consent.
- Stalking is a pattern of repeated, unwanted attention and contact by a partner that causes fear or concern for one's own safety or the safety of someone close to the victim.
- Psychological aggression is the use of verbal and non-verbal communication with the intent to harm a partner mentally or emotionally and/or to exert control over a partner.
- IPV is connected to other forms of violence and is related to serious health issues and economic consequences. However, IPV and other forms of violence can be prevented.

How big is the problem?

IPV is common. It affects millions of people in the United States each year. Data from CDC's National Intimate Partner and Sexual Violence Survey (NISVS) indicate:

- About 41% of women and 26% of men experienced contact sexual violence, physical violence, and/or stalking by an intimate partner and reported an intimate partner violence-related impact during their lifetime. Injury, posttraumatic stress disorder (PTSD) symptoms, concern for safety, fear, needing help from law enforcement, and missing at least one day of work are common impacts reported.
- Over 61 million women and 53 million men have experienced psychological aggression by an intimate partner in their lifetime. IPV starts early and continues throughout people's lives. When IPV occurs in adolescence, it is called teen dating violence (TDV). TDV affects millions of U.S. teens each year. About 16 million women and 11 million men who reported experiencing contact sexual violence, physical violence, or stalking by an intimate partner in their lifetime said that they first experienced these forms of violence before the age of 18.

While violence impacts all people in the United States, some individuals and communities experience inequities in risk for violence due to the social and structural conditions in which they live, work and play. Youth from groups that have been marginalized, such as sexual and gender minority youth, are at greater risk of experiencing sexual and physical dating violence.

About 1 in 3 women and 1 in 4 men report having experienced severe physical violence from an intimate partner in their lifetime. About 1 in 5 women and 1 in 13 men have experienced contact sexual violence by an intimate partner. 14% of women and 5% of men report having been stalked by an intimate partner.

What are the consequences?

IPV is a significant public health issue that has many individual and societal costs. About 75% of female IPV survivors and 48% of male IPV survivors experience some form of injury related to IPV.

IPV can also result in death. Data from U.S. crime reports suggest that about 1 in 5 homicide victims are killed by an intimate partner. The reports also found that over half of female homicide victims in the United States are killed by a current or former male intimate partner.

Many other negative health outcomes are associated with IPV. These include a range of conditions affecting the heart, muscles and bones, and digestive, reproductive, and nervous systems, many of which are chronic.

Survivors can experience mental health problems such as depression and PTSD symptoms. They are at higher risk for engaging in behaviors such as smoking, binge drinking, and sexual risk activity.

People from groups that have been marginalized, such as people from racial and ethnic minority groups, are at higher risk for worse consequences. Although the personal consequences of IPV are devastating, there are also many costs to society. The lifetime economic cost associated with medical services for IPV-related injuries, lost productivity from paid work, criminal justice, and other costs is $3.6 trillion. The cost of IPV over a victim's lifetime was $103,767 for women and $23,414 for men.

How can we prevent intimate partner violence?

Promoting healthy, respectful, and nonviolent relationships and communities can help reduce the occurrence of IPV. It also can prevent the harmful and long-lasting effects of IPV on individuals, families, and communities. CDC developed a resource, Preventing Intimate Partner Violence Across the Lifespan: A Technical Package of Programs, Policies, and Practices, to help communities use the best available evidence to prevent intimate partner violence. This resource can be used as a tool in efforts to impact individual behaviors as well as family, community, and society factors that influence risk and protective factors for intimate partner violence.

Teach safe and healthy relationship skills

- Social-emotional learning programs for youth
- Healthy relationship programs for couples

Engage Influential adults and peers

- Men and boys as allies in prevention

- Bystander empowerment and education
- Family-based programs

Disrupt the developmental pathways toward partner violence

- Early childhood home visitation
- Preschool enrichment with family engagement
- Parenting skill and family relationship programs
- Treatment for at-risk children, youth, and families

Create protective environments

- Improve school climate and safety
- Improve organizational policies and workplace climate
- Modify the physical and social environments of neighborhoods

Strengthen economic supports for families

- Strengthen household financial security
- Strengthen work-family supports

Support survivors to increase safety and lessen harms

- Victim-centered services
- Housing programs
- First responder and civil legal protections
- Patient-centered approaches
- Treatment and support for survivors of IPV, including teen dating violence

[Editor's Notes: 1. In "Gender Equality and Prevalence of Domestic Violence: What is the 'Nordic Paradox'?," 25(2) DVR Dec/Jan 2020 at 35, Megan Amanda Miller states that women in countries with greater gender equality, such as the Nordic countries, report higher levels of DV than women in countries with lower gender equality, e.g., Spain. This is called The Nordic Paradox. She states that one possible explanation for this is that women in countries with greater gender equality may be more willing to disclose their experiences in a survey. But there may be additional reasons for this seeming paradox.

2. COVID and DV—from the U.S. National DV Hotline:

Calls to the U.S. National DV Hotline decreased 6% at the start of the pandemic in March 2020 compared to March 2019. The Hotline stated that DV survivors likely felt less safe to call because of being in close proximity to their abusive partners.

Calls, digital chats and texts to the Hotline increased 6–33% during Sept 2021–Jan 2022 compared to 2020.

In Feb 2022 they reached the highest number in the 25 year history of the Hotline: 74,000 calls, chats and texts in only 28 days. Once life returned to any kind of normalcy, there were more survivors needing support who had not felt safe to reach out during the height of the pandemic.]

SB 1141 (CA, 2020) CHAPTER 248

THE PEOPLE OF THE STATE OF CALIFORNIA
DO ENACT AS FOLLOWS:

SECTION 1.

The Legislature finds and declares all of the following:

(a) In times of natural disasters and crises, rates of interpersonal violence historically rise, especially among households experiencing significant financial strain.

(b) The COVID-19 pandemic has proven this historical trend to be the reality for survivors of domestic violence as police chiefs nationwide reported increases of 10 percent to 30 percent in domestic violence assaults in the first two weeks after a national emergency was declared in March, also revealing more severe violence as compared with past years.

(c) During the COVID-19 crisis, reports show this is a worst-case scenario for victims experiencing domestic violence, with the data showing the virus is being used as a scare tactic to keep victims isolated from their support systems, or even their children.

(d) Shelter-in-place orders and other restrictions related to COVID-19 have also resulted in victims being isolated from family, friends, and their community.

(e) While some jurisdictions have reported a drop in domestic violence calls, this does not necessarily equate to a reduction in domestic violence. Increased isolation of victims has created an environment where abuse, including coercive control, is more likely to go undetected and therefore unreported.

NATIONAL COMMISSION ON COVID-19 AND CRIMINAL JUSTICE: DV DURING COVID-19

(Feb 2021)

Summary

- The findings presented here are based on a systematic review of multiple [18] domestic [U.S.] and international studies that compared changes in the number of domestic violence incidents before and after jurisdictions began imposing pandemic-related lockdowns in early 2020.

- The review found that domestic violence incidents in the U.S. increased by 8.1% following the imposition of stay-at-home orders.
- The studies included in this review draw on a wide range of data, from logs of police calls for service to domestic violence crime reports, emergency hotline registries, health records, and other administrative documents.
- While evidence to support the findings is strong, it is unclear precisely which factors drove the 2020 spike in domestic violence. The authors believe lockdowns and pandemic-related economic impacts may have exacerbated factors typically associated with domestic violence, such as increased unemployment, stress associated with childcare and homeschooling, and increased financial insecurity.
- The authors also note that by isolating parents and children in their homes, the pandemic separated potential victims from the network of friends, neighbors, teachers, and other individuals capable of reporting signs of abuse and helping those at risk escape a dangerous environment.

STALKING CONCERNS RAISED BY TRACKING TECHNOLOGIES

- National Crime Victimization Survey: Among the estimated 3.4 million US people 16+ who reported experiencing stalking, 80% indicated that technology was involved. Among this group, 14% reported they had their whereabouts tracked with an electronic device. There is a well-established connection between stalking and DV, and some abusers use technology to track their victims. The onus is often on victims to download apps on their phone, etc. to prevent this. Congressional Research Service (2/15/22)—by Emily J. Hanson and Kristin Finklea
- 40% of stalkers are current or former intimate partners, according to the National Intimate Partner and Sexual Violence Survey (2016–2017), CDC: National Center for Injury Prevention and Control.
- This statistic is significant when it comes to tech safety as current/former intimate partners have or had digital access to things an outsider does not, like passwords, devices, apps, accounts, password reset question answers and more. This places these victims at higher risk of tech-facilitated abuse and we should always prioritize digital safety planning with these folks. Adam Dodge, End Technology Facilitated Abuse (End TAB) (2023)

- VAWA 2022: the U.S. Attorney General is developing a national strategy to prevent and address cybercrimes against individuals, including cyberstalking and the non-consensual distribution of intimate images of adults, and will direct the FBI to improve data collection regarding these crimes.

CORPORATE ALLIANCE TO END PARTNER VIOLENCE, FINANCIAL COSTS

http://www.caepv.org/getinfo/facts_stats.php?factsec=2 (accessed 6/8/17)
(references omitted)

The cost of domestic violence to the U.S. economy is more than $8.3 billion. This cost includes medical care, mental health services, and lost productivity (e.g., time away from work).

A study released by the U.S. Centers for Disease Control and Prevention (CDC) in October 2005 found that health care costs associated with each incident of domestic violence were $948 in cases where women were the victims and $387 in cases where men were the victims. The study also found that domestic violence against women results in more emergency room visits and inpatient hospitalizations, including greater use of physician services than domestic violence where men are the victims.

CDC researchers determined healthcare costs by looking at mental health services; the use of medical services such as emergency departments, inpatient hospitals, and physician services; and losses in productivity such as time off from work, childcare or household duties because of injuries. The average medical cost for women victimized by physical domestic violence was $483 compared to $83 for men; mental health services costs for women was $207 compared to $80 for men; while productivity losses were similar at $257 for women and $224 for men.

The annual cost of lost productivity due to domestic violence is estimated as $727.8 million with over 7.9 million paid workdays lost per year.

A study that examined 1997–2002 medical records of several groups of adult female patients of a Health Maintenance Organization (HMO) in Seattle found that women who are victims of physical or sexual domestic violence visit their doctors more often than other women. Annual health-care costs were significantly higher for the women who were victims of domestic violence. Their health-care costs averaged more than $5,000 per year, compared to about $3,400 for those in the second group and $2,400 for those in the third group.

The health-related costs of rape, physical assault, stalking, and homicide by intimate partners exceed $5.8 billion each year [in the U.S.]. Of this total, nearly $4.1 billion are for direct medical and mental health care services, and productivity losses account for nearly $1.8 billion, according to a report by the CDC.

The National Association of Crime Victim Compensation Boards reports that 28 percent of adults receiving crime victim compensation benefits in 2001 were domestic violence victims.

In 2000, 36 percent of rape and sexual assault victims lost more than 10 days of work after their victimization.

The direct cost of medical treatment for battered women annually is estimated at $1.8 billion.

A study conducted at a large health plan in Minneapolis and St. Paul, Minnesota in 1994 found that an annual difference of $1,775 more was spent on abused women who utilized hospital services than on a random sample of general enrollees. The study concluded that early identification and treatment of victims and potential victims are most likely to benefit health care systems in the long run.

The National Institute of Justice found that the aggregate annual cost to victims of domestic violence is about $8.8 billion, or $67 billion when pain, suffering, and lost quality of life is included.

A study conducted at Rush Medical Center in Chicago found that the average charge for medical services provided to abused women, children and older people was $1,633 per person per year. This would amount to a national annual cost of $857.3 million.

Experts indicate that intimate partner violence costs US businesses an estimated $3 to $5 billion annually in lost time and productivity.

[Editor's Note: In addition to the above costs, the legal system expends a great deal of money on domestic violence. This includes attorneys, staff, and judges in family law courts, probate courts, juvenile courts, criminal courts, and courts handling civil suits. Furthermore, a large percentage of matters dealt with by law enforcement, probation and parole staff, jails and prisons, re-entry programs, etc. involve domestic violence, requiring very substantial expenditures.]

MOLLY DRAGIEWICZ AND YVONNE LINDGREN, THE GENDERED NATURE OF DOMESTIC VIOLENCE: STATISTICAL DATA FOR LAWYERS CONSIDERING EQUAL PROTECTION ANALYSIS

17 Am. U. J. Gender Soc. Pol'y & L. 229 (2009)
(citations and footnotes omitted)

In *Woods v. Horton* [167 Cal.App.4th 658 (2008)], California's Third District Court of Appeal ruled that a state Health and Safety Code section funding domestic violence shelter services specifically for battered women and their children violated equal protection. Using the strict scrutiny standard of review, the court held that under the state's Equal Protection Clause, women and men are "similarly situated" with regard to domestic violence and, therefore, the language in the code should be revised to make state funding for domestic violence shelter services under that code gender-neutral. *Woods* is the first successful legal decision for the anti-feminist "fathers' rights" movement in a series of lawsuits filed against battered women's shelters and their funders. The case is important because it highlights the limits of formal equality review of laws that confer benefits upon women. Specifically, in its formal equality review, the court failed to sufficiently consider the gendered nature of domestic violence and the social and political context in which violence against women occurs. Women are battered much more frequently, suffer much greater injuries, and are at much higher risk of being killed by their batterer than their male counterparts, particularly at separation. Further, women who are battered are in greater need of the specific services offered by shelters because of the profoundly gendered nature of battering, wherein women and children bear substantial risk of homicide, assault, rape, and stalking following separation from an abuser, whereas men do not. Women also have fewer economic resources and often are more dependent on their abusers than men due to women's persistently lower income and greater participation in child care. For these reasons, disparate funding for battered women's shelters should survive a strict scrutiny challenge because women and men are not similarly situated with regard to domestic violence. Because the risks faced by women and men following separation are essentially different, shelter services tailored to women and their dependent children are narrowly designed to address a compelling state interest in decreasing separation assault, assisting battered women in safely leaving abusers, and decreasing preventable homicides. By failing to acknowledge the important role that gender plays in domestic violence, the *Woods* decision set a precedent that threatens to erode the already inadequate laws and services specifically created in response to the quantitatively and qualitatively different types of violence faced by women, men, and children. * * *

C. Women's Grossly Disproportionate Risk of Violence from Male Partners

Those who assert that women and men are similarly situated with regard to domestic violence often make facile claims that women "initiate domestic violence as often as men" in intimate relationships. Alternatively, they claim that gender is irrelevant to domestic violence because male victims and female perpetrators exist. The implication in either case is that women's and men's experiences of domestic violence are similar enough to merit identical treatment. Proponents of the ideology of sex symmetry in violence refer to texts they claim show that women are as violent as men, frequently suggesting that this position represents an "uncontroverted" consensus in the research field. However, such texts have been extensively and consistently critiqued for more than thirty years for their failure to contextualize violence in a way that makes their findings intelligible. Symmetry claims fail to account for the majority of quantitative and qualitative studies on domestic violence, which demonstrate significant sex differences and the highly gendered nature of the problem. In addition to this omission, many sources cited in the lawsuits proclaiming sex symmetry simply do not support the claim. Symmetry denotes exact correspondence, equivalence, or balance. Claims of sex symmetry in domestic violence can only be arrived at when researchers fail to consider homicide, rape, separation assault, injury, and other negative outcomes of violence and abuse. A concept of domestic violence that omits these factors can bear only the most cursory resemblance to the pressing social problem that domestic violence shelters and services were created to address. As such, these claims do not demonstrate that women are similarly situated to men.

1. Homicide

We begin our discussion of sex differences in domestic violence with homicide for two reasons. First, homicide statistics are the most objective measure of the most serious form of domestic violence. Unlike sublethal violence and abuse, homicides are almost always reported. Homicide statistics are also much less disputed than other estimates because they avoid definitional and measurement issues endemic to the study of sublethal violence and abuse. Thanks to domestic violence death review practices, many states now have multi-disciplinary death review teams that investigate domestic violence homicides, note patterns and trends in the violence, and make recommendations for prevention. The vast majority of domestic homicide victims are women. Most perpetrators of domestic homicide are men.

In California, there were eighty-six domestic homicides by a spouse or common law partner in 2006. Seventeen of those victims, or 20%, were male, while sixty-nine victims, or 80%, were female. These numbers do not include homicides of ex-partners, which is significant because women are much more likely than men to be killed by former partners. It is important to remember that not all male deaths in domestic homicides indicate female perpetrators. There are occasionally same-sex domestic homicides. Male-perpetrated homicide-suicides also mean that body counts may not be as transparent as they appear at first glance. For example, San Diego's 2006 domestic homicide review report indicated that 80% of victims were female and 20% were male, but 12.5% of perpetrators were female and 87.5% were male. The research showing domestic homicide as predominately male-perpetrated against female victims makes clear the sex differences in domestic homicide, but the research on the nature of domestic homicide brings this picture into even sharper focus. In order to understand homicide rates, it is essential to understand the context in which the homicide occurred.

Domestic homicide comprises a much greater portion of all homicides of women than men. In California between 1997 and 2006, overall homicide rates dropped significantly for both women and men. Homicides of male victims dropped 9% and homicides of female victims dropped 21.4%. Although there are many factors contributing to homicide rates, this was a period of expansion for services targeting abused women and the implementation of aggressive policing of domestic violence. Both of these initiatives benefited from federal funding under the Violence Against Women Act (VAWA) as well as state initiatives to address domestic violence. These practices appear to have helped both women and men.

In 2006, 23.2% of female homicide victims in California were killed by their spouses, while only 1.6% of male homicide victims were killed by their spouses. Where the circumstances leading up to homicide were known, domestic violence related homicide was the single largest category of female victims. More than one-third of homicides of women fit into this category. The largest category of male victims was gang-related homicides (38.9%), followed by all other arguments (32.7%), all other contributing factors (12.9%), robbery/burglary (7.6%), and drug related homicides (6.2%). Unlike female victims for whom domestic homicide was most common, the 1.6% of homicides of men that were domestic violence related comprised the smallest category of homicides of men. Strangulation, which is correlated with domestic violence against women, is the only category of homicide that in absolute numbers had more female than male victims in the state between 1992 and 1999. Any review of homicide records finds that men make up the vast majority of perpetrators and victims, and clearly violence prevention is needed to address men's disproportionate violence. However, because these statistics reveal the very different dynamics of homicide for women and men, we should not assume that the etiology of violence is similar for women and men.

National homicide statistics reflect the same broad trends. According to the Bureau of Justice Statistics (BJS), "[f]emale murder victims are substantially more likely than male murder victims to have been killed by an intimate." BJS notes that in 2005, 33.3% of female homicide victims and 2.5% of male homicide victims were killed by intimate partners. Furthermore, the proportion of female homicide victims killed by an intimate has been increasing in recent years while the proportion of male homicide victims killed by an intimate is decreasing. National trends from 1976 to 2005 show a decline in all domestic homicides with an especially steep decline of 75% for male victims. Nationally, lethal violence by women against male intimates is much less frequent than lethal violence by men against women. Domestic homicides comprise a third of all homicides of women and less than 3% of all homicides of men. Clearly, women and men are dissimilarly situated with regard to domestic homicide. Indeed, the huge drop in domestic homicides of men since the establishment of battered women's shelters and services suggests that current programs are working to address domestic homicides of men. For the entire United States, the decrease has been four times greater for men than for women.

2. Homicide-Suicide

A subset of domestic homicide is homicide-suicide. Although there is no national database for tracking homicide-suicide, analyses of available data indicate that most homicide-suicides are domestic violence related. The vast majority of homicide-suicides are also perpetrated by men. In Dee Wood Harper and Lydia Voigt's study of forty-two homicide-suicides in New Orleans between 1989 and 2001, thirty were domestic violence related, twenty-nine of which were perpetrated by men, and twenty-nine of the victims were women. Most of the studies on domestic homicide-suicide link it to male dominance and controlling behavior. Familicide, where a parent kills a partner and one or more children, is also highly gendered, with studies indicating that over 90% of perpetrators are male. Margo Wilson, Martin Daly, and Antonietta Daniele write, "[f]amilicide is virtually a male monopoly" and "[f]amilicide perpetration is strikingly and highly significantly more male-dominated than nonfamilicidal spouse-killing and filicide." Wilson, Daly, and Daniele have also noted that the small number of women who perpetrate homicide-suicide almost never kill male partners.

3. Sublethal Violence

Despite scholarly debates about the best method of measurement for domestic violence, dramatic sex differences in violence are also clear at the sublethal level. The National Violence Against Women Survey (NVAWS) found that "women were significantly more likely than men to report being victimized by an intimate partner, whether the period was the individual's lifetime or the twelve months preceding the survey and whether the type of violence was rape, physical assault, or stalking." The authors stress that

> differences between women's and men's rates of physical assault by an intimate partner become greater as the seriousness of the assault increases. For example, women were two to three times more likely than men to report that an intimate partner threw something that could hurt or pushed, grabbed, or shoved them. However, they were 7 to 14 times more likely to report that an intimate partner beat them up, choked or tried to drown them, threatened them with a gun, or actually used a gun on them.

Again, these findings indicate not only significant sex differences in the prevalence of domestic violence against women and men, but also different dynamics of the violence. The NVAWS stresses that men are the perpetrators in most violence against adults, and argues that prevention should focus primarily on men's violence.

4. Injury

Prevalence rates for a limited set of violent acts can obscure another major impact of domestic violence: injury. Women are much more likely to be injured than men in domestic violence cases, and injuries due to domestic violence make up a much larger portion of total injuries from violence for women than for men. California created a "cause of injury code" in 1996 to identify hospital cases where domestic violence was the primary cause of injury to patients. Since that time, the code has been applied to 530 women and 42 men, with women receiving 93% of injuries primarily due to domestic violence. When contributing or secondary causes are considered, the code identified 754 women and 72 men injured due to domestic violence, indicating that over 90% of those coded as injured due to domestic violence were women. The injury rates alone cannot indicate the context of the injury, or whether the injury was defensive or offensive. This injury code also does not capture all cases of domestic violence-related injury since information on the identity of the perpetrator is often missing from hospital records.

These numbers are in line with national statistics. The BJS report, Violence-Related Injuries Treated in Hospital Emergency Departments, found that "[a] higher percentage of women than men were treated for injuries inflicted by an intimate—a current or former spouse, boyfriend, or girlfriend. Men were more likely than women to be treated for injuries caused by nonrelatives: acquaintances and strangers." Thirty-seven percent of the women and five percent of men were injured by a current or former partner. As with the prevalence of violence, injuries due to domestic violence comprise a very different social problem for women than men.

5. Sexual Violence

Rape is seriously under-reported in both the National Crime Victimization Survey (NCVS) and NVAWS, but these are the largest scale studies available and they can be viewed as conservative estimates. A scholarly review of the sexual assault literature published in 1993 found that published rates for women's lifetime rape prevalence ranged from 2% to 24%. NVAWS found higher estimates of sexual assault than the NCVS because it asked about all sexual assaults, not just those that respondents identified as crimes. NVAWS found that 17.6% of women and 3% of men had experienced attempted or completed rape at some time in their lives. Of these assaults, 7.7% of women and 0.3% of men in the sample reported having been raped by a current or former partner in their lifetime.

The NCVS found that rates of sexual assaults of adult men were too small to analyze statistically, but 96% of all rape victims identified were women and 4% were men. The NCVS found that sexual assaults by partners were not usually reported to police: "[w]hen the offender was a current or former husband or boyfriend, about three-fourths of all victimizations were not reported to police (77% of completed rapes, 77% of attempted rapes, and 75% of sexual assaults not reported)." Women are not only more likely to have been raped in the past year or in their lifetimes, but the statistics on these sexual assaults indicate that rape is a highly gendered social problem.

6. Stalking

Stalking is another form of abuse that is correlated with domestic violence against women. Stalking is "a course of conduct directed at a specific person that involves repeated visual or physical proximity, nonconsensual communication, or verbal, written or implied threats, or a combination thereof, that would cause a reasonable person fear." National statistics on stalking find that 87% of perpetrators are male and 78% of victims are female. Over a lifetime, women are four times more likely to be stalked than men, 8.1% and 2.2% respectively. The dynamics of stalking are different for women and men. Patricia Tjaden and Nancy Thoennes write:

> Though stalking is a gender-neutral crime, women are the primary victims of stalking and men are the primary perpetrators. Seventy-eight percent of the stalking victims identified by the survey were women, and 22 percent were men. Thus, four out of five stalking victims are women. By comparison, 94 percent of the stalkers identified by female victims and 60 percent of the stalkers identified by male victims were male. Overall, 87 percent of the stalkers identified by victims were male.

The language used by the researchers in this passage illustrates one source of confusion about what the research really says about the nature of domestic violence. Clearly, Tjaden and Thoennes are conceptualizing "gender neutral" very loosely. They describe large, statistically significant differences in the rates of stalking experienced and perpetrated by women and men. In other parts of the article, Tjaden and Thoennes stress that men are more likely to be stalked by strangers and women are more likely to be stalked by intimates. In other words, while women and men are clearly both affected by stalking, they are affected in ways that are substantially quantitatively and qualitatively different. The connection between women's experiences of being stalked and being physically abused makes this issue directly relevant to the provision of shelter services. Fifty-nine percent of female victims of stalking and thirty percent of male victims of stalking identified by the NVAWS were stalked by a current or former intimate partner. Seventy-nine percent of female victims said they were stalked after they broke up with the perpetrator. Eighty-one percent of the women who were stalked by a current or former partner were also physically assaulted by them, and 31% were sexually assaulted by the stalker. Tjaden and Thoennes found that men who stalk female partners are four times more likely to physically assault them and six times more likely to rape them than men who do not stalk. The most frequently reported reason for the end of stalking was the victim moving. These statistics reveal that the nature of stalking indicates emergency shelter may be particularly essential for female victims of domestic violence and stalking.

7. Self Defense

While statistics about the prevalence of violence can provide general information about what kinds of violence constitute a social problem, and for whom, they leave out many relevant factors. The research on women's use of violence that pays attention to the context in which violence is used indicates that a significant portion of women's violence against intimates is defensive. While no one claims that all of women's violence is defensive, research on the motives and context of violence is essential to understanding prevalence numbers.

Research has repeatedly documented that male victim domestic homicides are often victim precipitated. A report on risk factors for intimate partner homicide says, "[i]n 70 to 80 percent of intimate partner homicides, no matter which partner was killed, the man physically abused the woman before the murder. Thus, one of the primary ways to decrease intimate partner homicide is to identify and intervene promptly with abused women at risk." The message is clear: protecting women from men's domestic violence also protects men. Another researcher noted that

> [p]erhaps the most important sex difference to emerge in the St. Louis data on intimate partner homicide, however, concerns the degree and nature of the victim's involvement in the events leading up to his or her death. In more than half of intimate partner homicides with male victims, the victim precipitated the conflict in which the killing occurred. Only 12.5% of the events with female victims were victim precipitated.

Other studies have also found that female perpetrated domestic homicide is often defensive.

8. Separation Assault

Separation assault has often been absent from discussions about sex differences in domestic violence. The studies cited to claim sex symmetry in domestic violence often exclude violence and abuse by former partners, which is a serious limitation. Research has consistently found significant sex differences in the risk of lethal violence by ex-spouses and partners. Between 1976 and 2005, former spouses perpetrated 1.4% of domestic homicides of women and 0.2% of domestic homicides of men in the United States. A larger portion of domestic homicides are likely properly conceived as separation assault in cases occurring during separation but prior to divorce, or at the time a woman announces her intention to separate.

A California study that reviewed domestic homicide cases found that 45% of women were killed when they were recently separated or in the process of separating from their abuser. Separation has been identified as a risk factor for domestic homicide even in relationships where there is no documented history of abuse. Harper and Voigt found that domestic homicide-suicides in their sample were typically in the context of actual or impending separation. San Diego's 2006 domestic homicide report indicated that while 28% of male perpetrators of domestic homicide killed a former or estranged partner, no women in the sample killed estranged or former partners. The San Diego report also states that pending or actual separation was the most common risk factor for domestic homicide: 79.2% of cases shared this risk factor. These differences are extremely pertinent to the provision of shelter services targeting women. In addition, they highlight what is at stake for shelters that admit men who are perpetrators, but who have falsely identified themselves as victims.

The body of literature on domestic violence as a whole clearly indicates that women and men are significantly dissimilarly and asymmetrically situated with regard to domestic violence, especially at separation. Their experiences are both quantitatively and qualitatively different according to both large, random sample studies and small, targeted studies. Women are not only at greater risk from current and previous male partners than men are from female partners, but homicide and injury of women by male partners also makes up a disproportionately large portion of the total amount of violence against women. This means that although there is a small minority of men who are abused or assaulted by women, these incidents neither comprise a significant portion of all violence against men nor constitute a significant social problem for the public the way that violence against women does. The risk to women of domestic violence and abuse after separation is clearly documented. No parallel risk has been demonstrated for men. This difference is directly relevant to the provision of shelter services. * * *

[Editor's Note: The homicide statistics cited in Dragiewizc and Lindgren's article are still valid. Based on 2020 data, The Violence Policy Center noted in 2022 in When Men Murder Women that the rate of men killing women in the U.S. decreased significantly between 1996 and 2014, rose for 3 years and decreased in 2018–2019. It rose dramatically in 2020 during the COVID lockdown. VAWA was first enacted in 1994, and various federal and state gun prohibitions were enacted starting around that time. The VPC concluded that these policies were significant in lowering rates of DV homicides, since firearms are the weapons in most DV murders.

"In 2020, there were 2,059 females murdered by males in single victim/single offender incidents that were submitted to the FBI for its

Supplementary Homicide Report. The key findings of this study... dispel many of the myths regarding the nature of lethal violence against females.

- *For homicides in which the victim to offender relationship could be identified, 89 percent of female victims (1,604 out of 1,801) were murdered by a male they knew.*
- *Eight times as many females were murdered by a male they knew (1,604 victims) than were killed by male strangers (197 victims).*
- *For victims who knew their offenders, 60 percent (967) of female homicide victims were wives or intimate acquaintances of their killers.*
- *There were 298 women shot and killed by either their husband or intimate acquaintance during the course of an argument.*
- *Nationwide, for homicides in which the weapon could be determined (1,735), more female homicides were committed with firearms (61 percent) than with all other weapons combined. Knives and other cutting instruments accounted for 18 percent of all female murders, bodily force nine percent, and murder by blunt object five percent. Of the homicides committed with firearms, 64 percent were committed with handguns.*
- *In 88 percent of all incidents where the circumstances could be determined, homicides were not related to the commission of any other felony, such as rape or robbery."]*

BREAK THE CYCLE, DATING ABUSE STATISTICS

(visited 6/1/2017)
(footnotes omitted)

Dating abuse affects people from all ages, backgrounds and identities, which is why is it important to talk about how abuse can happen in young people's relationships. Just check out these statistics:

Dating Abuse Is a Public Health Crisis

- One in three high school students experience either physical or sexual violence, or both, that is perpetrated by someone they are dating or going out with.
- Young women between the ages of 18–24 experience the highest rate of intimate partner violence, almost double the national average.
- One in ten high school students has been purposefully hit, slapped or physically hurt by a boyfriend or girlfriend.

- Lesbian, gay and bisexual (LGB) youth are more likely to experience physical and psychological dating abuse, sexual coercion, and cyber dating abuse than their heterosexual peers.

The Abuse Starts Early

- More than half of women (69.5%) and men (53.6%) who have been physically or sexually abused, or stalked by a dating partner, first experienced abuse between the ages of 11–24.
- Of the 8.5% of middle and school students who report having bullied a classmate, nearly 1 in 5 have been a victim of dating abuse.
- Nearly half of female and 1 in 4 male high school students who report experiencing sexual or physical abuse by a dating partner, have also been bullied electronically.

The Impact is Severe

- Among male high school students who have experienced sexual and physical abuse by a dating partner, more than 1 in 4 have seriously contemplated suicide, and almost as many have attempted suicide.
- Among female high school students who have experienced sexual and physical abuse by a dating partner, nearly half have seriously contemplated suicide, and more than 1 in 4 have attempted suicide.
- High school girls who have experienced dating abuse are 2.6 times more likely to report an STI diagnosis.
- High school students who have been hit, slapped, or physically hurt on purpose by their partner earned grades of C and D twice as often as earning grades of A or B.
- Women who have experienced sexual assault, physical abuse, or stalking by an intimate partner are three times more likely to report poor mental health.

It's Not Just Teens

- An estimated 20–25 percent of female college students will experience attempted or completed rape before graduation, and those are only the ones who self-disclose.
- Nearly half (43%) of all college women and one third (28%) of college men report having experienced either abuse or controlling behaviors in a dating relationship.

The Time to Talk Is Now

- Education and raising awareness is important! More than half (58%) of college students do not know how to help someone who is experiencing dating abuse, and nearly all (89%) are not confident in their ability to recognize the warning signs.
- More than half of all college students report experiencing either abuse or controlling behaviors in a dating relationship while in college, with 70% reporting they were not aware they were in an abusive relationship at the time.

[Editor's Note: As Professor D. Kelly Weisberg noted in Lindsay's Legacy: The Tragedy that Triggered Law Reform to Prevent Teen Dating Violence, 24 Hastings Women's Law Journal 27 (2013),

"Dating violence has severe physical consequences for teen victims, often resulting in serious injuries. Homicides occur with alarming frequency, even among the youngest victims. Females ages sixteen to nineteen are victims in 22% of all homicides committed by an intimate partner. An even more chilling fact is that younger girls, ages twelve to fifteen, are victims in 10% of all intimate partner homicides. Despite its prevalence and severity, teen dating violence remains stubbornly hidden from adults who might be able to intervene. Teenagers rarely disclose the abuse to authority figures. Most violent incidents involving teen dating relationships are not reported to law enforcement. Fewer than one in three teens talk to a parent about the abuse, and far fewer teens talk to a school counselor or social worker. If teens do disclose the abuse, they are more likely to make such disclosures to peers rather than to adults." (footnotes omitted)]

U.S. NATIONAL INSTITUTES OF JUSTICE, WHAT HAS LONGITUDINAL RESEARCH ON TEEN DATING VIOLENCE TAUGHT US?

(2023)
(footnotes omitted)

For a long time, intimate partner violence in the United States was considered a private matter that was best handled behind closed doors, not one that warranted support and intervention from the criminal justice system.

But the passage of the Violence Against Women Act in 1994 was part of a paradigm shift. The act sought to improve services for victims of domestic violence, dating violence, sexual assault, and stalking, and improve the criminal justice system's response to these crimes. The landmark act has been reauthorized four times since its passage, most recently in 2022.

The National Institutes of Justice (NIJ) has invested more than $150 million in research on violence against women beginning in the 1970s with a study focused on sexual violence. NIJ funded the first project on teen dating violence in 2005 and has continued to support studies in this area, including longitudinal studies that allow for examining risk and protective factors, and patterns and consequences of teen dating violence that extend into adulthood.

Spotlight on Teens: Longitudinal Study Reveals Trends, Characteristics, and Contexts of Teen Dating Abuse

In 2011, researchers received the first of four NIJ awards supporting the examination of the extent and nature of teen dating violence that would span a decade of continuous research. The researchers developed the National Survey on Teen Relationships and Intimate Violence (STRiV), the first comprehensive national household survey focused on teen dating violence using detailed measures of victimization and perpetration.

STRiV was designed to collect data from parents/caregivers and youths, with six waves of data collection being conducted over seven years. At baseline (2013), the researchers collected completed surveys from 2,354 parent-child dyads, which included 1,804 youths ages 12–18. One year later, 1,471 parent-child dyads (62.5% of the original baseline sample) completed follow-up surveys.

Research from these first two waves of data collection produced nationally representative estimates of the prevalence of different types of relationship abuse, documented the characteristics of abusive relationships, assessed risk factors, and placed these estimates in the context of adolescents' key social relationships. Unfortunately, the STRiV data did not have a sufficient sample for detailed examination of sexual or gender minority experiences.

However, a comprehensive portrait of teen dating violence emerged, with research highlighting:

- **Higher rates of dating violence victimization** by a wide margin compared to other national studies. However, local and regional studies using more detailed measures have found rates closer to the STRiV estimates.
- **High overlap between victimization and perpetration**. Over 84% of victims also reported perpetrating abuse, emphasizing that relationships that are characterized by violence typically involve mutual violence.
- **No differences between teen boys and girls regarding victimization rates, but girls reported perpetrating more physical abuse than boys**. Specifically, girls ages 15–18 reported perpetrating moderate threats or physical

violence at more than three times the rate of boys ages 15–18, and serious psychological abuse at more than four times the rate of boys.

[Editor's Note: This finding contrasts with the data described by Dragiewicz and Lindgren in their preceding article, which consistently found that in heterosexual relationships, adult women were significantly more likely to be victimized than were men and to be seriously injured or killed much more frequently than men were. Perhaps this difference is based on the ages of the study participants or to the previously documented tendency of females to overreport their perpetration of intimate partner abuse and males' tendency to underreport theirs. Furthermore, females are more likely to report defensive violence as offensive than males are.]

. . .Over the subsequent five years follow-up studies examined the *development* of relationship abuse from early adolescence to young adulthood, and identified risk and protective factors that could be used to inform intervention efforts that consider gender and developmental and contextual characteristics, including neighborhood-level factors.

STRiV researchers found:

- Youths showed **different patterns of dating and dating violence perpetration** over a period of four years, including a group representing non-daters (37.3%), a group showing steady and significant increases in both non-abusive dating *and* dating with violence perpetration (44.6%), and a group with consistently high levels of dating violence perpetration (18.1%).
- Increasing or consistently high levels of dating violence perpetration were associated with **individual characteristics** (for example, negative mental health) and **family characteristics** (for example, exposure to violence). In particular, **when parents experienced verbal abuse and physical violence by their partners**, their children were more likely to experience abuse and violence in their dating relationships than those whose parents did not perpetrate violence.
- Youths who were characterized as having "**positive parenting**" based on their relationships and interactions with their parents were significantly less likely than those who were not to be tolerant of certain types of violence, particularly violence against boyfriends, as well as less likely to commit dating violence or be a victim one year later.
- **Fights about money issues** in youths' dating relationships were associated with future physical violence perpetration in the context of a dating relationship.

- Teen dating violence victimization and perpetration were found in both low and high crime neighborhoods. However, male youths living in **neighborhoods with higher gender equality** were less likely than those who lived in other neighborhoods to report perpetrating relationship abuse three years later.
- Many youths reported **problematic dating relationships**. Higher levels of **controlling behaviors** (by both the partner and the respondent) were associated with higher rates of dating abuse victimization and perpetration. Relationships characterized by unhealthy and intense relationship dynamics (for example, cheating, controlling behaviors, or lack of closeness) were associated with a higher probability of relationship abuse.
- Problematic relationship dynamics were also associated with **negative mental health** for male youths and **dating victimization** for female youths. In addition, dating victimization was associated with poorer mental health for male youths and reduced intimacy in subsequent relationships for female youths when compared to youths who had not experienced dating victimization.
- **Sexual harassment co-occurred with dating abuse, especially psychological abuse**. Youths who were previously exposed to any violence were three times as likely to experience high levels of relationship abuse and sexual harassment (defined as unwelcome sexual comments, jokes or gestures or physical intimidation in a sexual way), compared to those who were not previously exposed to violence. In addition, male youths who believed in **traditional gender stereotypes** were more likely than those who did not to perpetrate sexual harassment.

Implications for Intervention and Prevention

Findings from the STRiV studies offer insight into potential intervention and prevention strategies to reduce teen dating violence and sexual harassment. Based on the studies, the investigators emphasized the following:

- **Addressing the family environment and youth's previous experiences with violence** may be especially constructive in preventing violence and abuse in the context of dating relationships, as the exposure to interparental or other types of violence is a key risk factor in patterns of increasing or consistently high adolescent dating violence perpetration over time.

- **Minimizing traditional gender stereotypes** and **supporting a community/neighborhood environment characterized by gender equality** may reduce male perpetration of abusive dating behaviors and sexual harassment.
- **Educating adolescents to constructively manage conflicts about money** and other financial matters with their dating partners could help prevent perpetration of physical dating violence.
- **Prevention programs should address both sexual harassment and dating abuse** to improve healthy adolescent interactions and relationships.
- **Addressing patterns of relationship dynamics** (for example, cheating, controlling behaviors, or lack of closeness) is crucial to building healthy relationship skills and preventing violence in youths. In addition, supporting youths' mental health should also be prioritized, given that the mental health of the individuals in the relationship has an impact on dating relationship dynamics and those dynamics also affect mental health over time, especially for male youths.

Consider These Findings Within Their Context and Apply With Care

Appreciating that the STRiV findings have greatly expanded our understanding of teen dating violence, the results should be considered within the context of the recognized study limitations. First, the STRiV data are subject to the usual limitations of self-reported surveys, such as subjects inaccurately recalling events or under-reporting of certain behaviors. Second, the measurement of sexual abuse was limited to four items due to the sensitive nature of these items and the wide age range of youths completing the surveys. Third, the study design did not allow for collecting contextual details regarding specific incidents, such as intensity, motivations, or acts of offense or defense, which is a goal for future research in this area. Fourth, recruitment to participate in STRiV research was limited to youths living in households, so incarcerated youths, homeless youths, or youths in foster care were not included.

MARY KAY.COM, AMERICANS MORE AWARE AND INVESTED IN THE ISSUE OF DOMESTIC VIOLENCE: MARY KAY'S 'TRUTH ABOUT ABUSE' SURVEY REVEALS NEED FOR INCREASED EDUCATION ON HEALTHY RELATIONSHIPS

(accessed 6/1/17)

DALLAS—Oct. 2, 2015—Awareness isn't enough to stop abuse. Today Mary Kay released the results of its sixth annual *Truth About Abuse* survey revealing that Americans' awareness of domestic violence is on the rise. The survey also reveals Americans believe increased education on healthy relationships can make a difference and millennials show confidence that the U.S. can end domestic abuse for the next generation.

"This year's *Truth About Abuse* survey showcases meaningful progress and highlights real opportunities to combat violence against women. Today, 1 in 2 male millennials believe domestic abuse can be eliminated in America. That is a powerful and very hopeful statistic," said Crayton Webb, Vice President of Corporate Communications and Corporate Social Responsibility for Mary Kay Inc. "With increased awareness and earlier education, we can help prevent abuse and ultimately end domestic violence by teaching kids about healthy relationships from an early age."

Highlights from the survey include:

- **It's personal:** 65% of those surveyed have experienced domestic abuse, experiencing it themselves or through someone they know
- **Awareness is on the rise:** 53% of those surveyed say their understanding of domestic violence has improved in the past five years
- **Equipped to help:** 71% feel confident that they would know what to do if someone they know is in an abusive relationship
- **From awareness to action:** 1 in 2 say they would intervene if someone they knew was in a verbally or physically abusive relationship

"It is heartening to see that Americans are becoming more aware and invested in the issue of domestic violence," said Brian Pinero, Chief Programs Officer at The National Domestic Violence Hotline and loveisrespect. "However, many are still struggling to recognize the signs of abuse and more education is needed to ensure that adults and teens are building healthy relationships."

In partnership with loveisrespect, the *2015 Mary Kay Truth About Abuse Survey* aims to explore how Americans' understanding of domestic violence is changing, and gauge attitudes with respect to this evolving issue. One thousand men and women nationwide participated in the online survey Sept. 3–11, 2015, sharing their insights and stories on the issue of domestic violence.

The 2015 survey is part of Mary Kay's "Don't Look Away" campaign which works to educate the public on recognizing the signs of an abusive relationship, how to take action and to raise awareness for support services. To date, Mary Kay Inc. and The Mary Kay Foundation have given $50 million to domestic violence prevention and awareness programs in an effort to end the cycle of abuse. Mary Kay is also the lead sponsor of the nation's first-ever text-based helpline operated by loveisrespect. By simply texting 'loveis' to 22522, teens and young adults are safely and discretely connected to trained peer advocates who provide support, safety tips and referrals for their own relationships or a friend's.

[Editor's Note: The 2016 Mary Kay survey focused on the role of men in the movement to end domestic violence, noting that domestic violence is not just a women's issue. It found that 92% of the 850 domestic violence organizations polled nationwide have made concerted efforts to involve men who engage other men in domestic violence prevention. Men can be role models and mentors to younger men in order to break the cycle of abuse. In some situations, they can also support survivors of abuse. Mary Kay hosted a summit to provide a framework for how to involve men in this work as advocates, volunteers, and ambassadors on a grassroots level.]

C. CURRENT CONTROVERSIES

KELLY WEISBERG, SUPREME COURT ABORTION DECISION HARMS DOMESTIC VIOLENCE SURVIVORS

28(2 Domestic Violence Report 1 (Oct/Nov 2022)
(endnotes and most citations omitted)

In a devastating setback for women's rights, the U.S. Supreme Court recently revoked the constitutional right to abortion. The Court's June 2022 decision in *Dobbs v. Jackson Women's Health Organization*, 142 S.Ct. 2228 (2022), will deprive many women of reproductive choice. Its impact will be especially profound for survivors of intimate partner violence.

By revoking the right to abortion, the Supreme Court abandoned 50 years of precedent beginning with *Roe v. Wade*, 410 U.S. 113 (1973), and including *Planned Parenthood v. Casey*, 505 U.S. 833 (1992). The Supreme Court's *Dobbs* decision was based on the reasoning that unwritten ("unenumerated") rights, to be enforced by courts, must be "deeply rooted" in the country's history at the time of ratification of the Fourteenth Amendment of the Constitution (a view known as "originalism"). The right to abortion, of course, was not in the minds of the framers of the Constitution and therefore was not included in the Constitution—and therefore, according to the majority, should no longer be recognized.

Dobbs marks the first time in history that the Supreme Court has abrogated a previously recognized fundamental right. At the same time, the opinion led to questions about the legitimacy of other unenumerated fundamental rights. Specifically, Justice Thomas, in his concurring opinion, cast doubt on the continued vitality of rights related to contraception, as well as marriage equality, by declaring that these areas were ripe for reversal in a future Supreme Court ruling.

The Court's ruling in *Dobbs* paves the way for widespread passage of state abortion bans. According to a statement by the Center for Reproductive Rights, "The Court's decision will likely lead to half of U.S. states immediately taking action to ban abortion outright, forcing people to travel hundreds and thousands of miles to access abortion care or to carry pregnancies against their will, a grave violation of their human rights." *[Editor's Note: This started to happen soon after the decision in* Dobbs.*]* Moreover, the infringement of rights was magnified by the Court's failure to require any exemptions in cases of rape and incest.

At issue before the Supreme Court was a Mississippi law banning abortion after 15 weeks of pregnancy. A federal district court previously declared the Mississippi law unconstitutional based on the precedents of *Roe v. Wade* and *Planned Parenthood v. Casey,* and therefore prevented enforcement of the Mississippi law by means of preliminary injunctions. The Fifth Circuit Court of Appeals affirmed. Significantly, in petitioning for the Supreme Court to hear the case, the state of Mississippi asked the Court not only to uphold the state abortion ban but also to overrule *Roe v. Wade* (*i.e.*, thereby ruling that there is no constitutional right to abortion).

The Supreme Court's decision in *Dobbs*, and ensuing state actions in implementing it, is devastating for women in general but particularly so for survivors [of domestic violence]. The relationship of intimate partner violence and women's reproductive choice is multi-faceted. First, for some survivors, pregnancy enhances the risk of intimate partner violence, sometimes with fatal consequences.

Approximately 256,000 to 332,000 pregnant women experience intimate partner violence annually. Moreover, many new or expectant mothers die violent deaths at the hands of their intimate partners. Homicide is the most frequent cause of death for pregnant or postpartum women. In fact, homicide of pregnant and postpartum women accounts for 31% of maternal injury deaths annually. This percentage is likely a gross underestimate because few states track homicides and pregnancy status comprehensively.

For many abused women, intimate partner violence is just a routine part of a pregnancy. However, for other women, the pregnancy may trigger or intensify the violence. Violent outbursts occur for many abusers when they feel jealous of the attention that the pregnant woman is receiving. Some men use violence toward their pregnant partners to express their resentment at the pregnancy and the responsibility/stress that the pregnancy adds to their lives.

Second, for those survivors who do not face fatal consequences, intimate partner violence during pregnancy may be harmful to maternal health. Women who are abused during pregnancy often avoid seeing health care providers for fear that the abuse might come to light. For that reason, they are more likely to receive no prenatal care or to delay care until later in the pregnancy than recommended. According to the National Partnership for Women and Families, women experiencing domestic violence during pregnancy are three times more likely to report symptoms of depression in the postnatal period than women who did not experience domestic violence while pregnant. Maternal exposure to domestic violence is associated with significantly increased risk of low birth weight and preterm birth.

Third, a growing body of research has recognized the connection between intimate partner sexual assault and unintended pregnancies. Unwanted pregnancies are a common outcome of sexual assault by an intimate partner. According to one study, from 10%–14% of married woman are raped by their husbands, and approximately 17% of marital rape victims report an unwanted pregnancy.

Moreover, data provided by Planned Parenthood reveal that victims of intimate partner violence are more likely to be in relationships with partners who control their contraceptive methods. These women, therefore, experience frequent unwanted pregnancies. "Practicing contraception is more difficult for women who have experienced IPV because of partner unwillingness to use contraception. Women who are exposed to IPV by the man who got them pregnant are more likely than non-abused women to have a second-trimester abortion. Abusive men are more likely than their non-abusive peers to report being involved in pregnancies ending in abortion. There is a strong association between IPV and involvement in three or more abortions."

Abortion has an important benefit for survivors by facilitating their right to leave abusive relationships. The *Dobbs* decision will result in widescale elimination of that right. It will lead to survivors' being forced to remain in abusive intimate partner relationships because these survivors will be forced to bear perpetrators' children against their wishes.

Survey data reveal that intimate partner violence plays a significant role as a motivator of women's reproductive choices. According to one study, 31% of women seeking to terminate pregnancies cite a "partner-related reason," such as not wanting a child with the man, wanting to end the intimate relationship or believing that the father would not care for the child. Of those women, approximately 8% indicate that abuse by the man was the primary reason for seeking the abortion. Twice that many disclose that their partner had physically abused them within the previous six months.

An economist at the Rand Corporation, Kathryn A. Edwards, compares the access to abortion to access to no-fault divorce in terms of their positive effects for domestic violence survivors who wish to leave their partners. Edwards notes that around the time of *Roe v. Wade* in 1973, exit from abusive marriages was facilitated by nation-wide passage of no-fault divorce laws. Instead of states' requiring spousal agreement to dissolve a marriage or requiring one party to prove fault, states allowed either spouse to act unilaterally to terminate the marriage. Paradoxically, according to Edwards, the most significant result of no-fault divorce laws involved women's mortality: 10% fewer women died at the hands of their spouses and 8% fewer women died by suicide.

Access to abortion similarly facilitates women's departure from abusive relationships. Because of the right to abortion, women may choose not to be bound to an abusive partner through legal parental relationships in terms of custody, visitation, and child support. In the case of both divorce and abortion, Edwards points out that "the issue at hand is bargaining power and the relevant policy is the ability to exit." Whereas unilateral divorce made it easier for women to end an abusive marital relationship, the Supreme Court's abortion ruling makes it more difficult for women to prevent a parental relationship with an abusive partner. This judicial ruling results in redistributing and reducing women's bargaining power in intimate relationships. As a result, Edward concludes, "This [judicial ruling] will have dire consequences for women's physical safety and well-being."

LEIGH GOODMARK, LAW IS THE ANSWER? DO WE REALLY KNOW THAT FOR SURE?: QUESTIONING THE EFFICACY OF LEGAL INTERVENTIONS FOR BATTERED WOMEN

23 St. Louis U. Pub. L. Rev. 7 (2004)
(citations and footnotes omitted)

II. UNINTENDED CONSEQUENCES

A. Penalizing Women Who Choose to Stay

Like many battered women's advocates, I have done a substantial amount of training for judges, lawyers, social workers, and others on the dynamics of domestic violence—a sort of "DV 101" class. One of the major objectives of such training is to help participants understand the barriers battered women face when seeking to leave abusive relationships. I generally ask my audiences to brainstorm a list of reasons why a battered woman remains in an abusive relationship. They usually offer, "Religion. Money. Immigration. Culture. Kids. Low self-esteem." They can articulate a number of factors that keep battered women in their relationships against their will. But when I raise the possibility that the battered woman still loves her abuser despite the violence and wants to make the relationship work, there is often an uncomfortable silence.

The majority of our responses to domestic violence, and certainly the legal responses, are largely premised on the idea that all battered women want—or should want—to separate from their abusers. As Susan Schechter notes,

> Current solutions to domestic violence offer tremendous help and important options to women who have resources and who want to leave their partners or end their relationships. Women can petition the court to evict violent men, can move to a shelter, can ask the police to arrest their partners, and can fight more effectively for custody in some states.

"But," Schechter asks, "what about everyone else?" Advocates have always said that women have the right to be in safe and respectful relationships. The domestic violence movement's historic goal has been to end violence and coercion, not to have women leave their relationships.

Similarly, Professor Esther Jenkins of Chicago State University argues, "Black women don't want men removed from their families. They want their relationships fixed." While their reasons may be emotional, economic, religious, cultural, or child-centered, the reality is that a substantial number of battered women have no intention of leaving their partners. As Donna Coker notes, "Some marriages are worth saving. Sometimes women are successful at getting their partner to stop the violence."

Most people are uncomfortable with the idea that a woman would choose to maintain a relationship with an abusive man. Staying in a violent relationship (and refusing to assist with prosecution) has been cited as proof that a woman is not acting on her own volition. Kate Waits explains, "Ideally, with enough understanding and encouragement, the battered woman will assess her situation realistically, start to unlearn her helplessness, and will agree to help the legal system as a witness against her husband." At best, staying in a violent relationship is seen as evidence that the victim has not been provided with sufficient services, legal and otherwise.

As is clear from the story that began this article, I too believed that all battered women should leave their abusers, and I was happiest when I could help them get divorced. But along with a growing number of voices, I find myself asking the question Schechter asks: what about everyone else? What about those women who are looking for ways to stop the violence from within their relationships? What does the legal system offer them?

The short answer is—not much. Having your husband or boyfriend arrested and jailed may be an unappealing prospect if your goal is to minimize violence from within the relationship. Civil protection orders can offer a blanket provision precluding the partner from assaulting, harassing, or physically abusing the victim while they continue to live together—but those things are already unlawful. Custody and divorce laws do nothing for women who choose to remain with their partners. The significant progress made to improve the legal system for women who are interested in leaving their partners offers very little for those who want to stay.

B. Lawyers Know Best

Embedded in the belief that all battered women want to or should want to leave their abusers is another assumption: that all women should turn to the legal system for assistance in leaving. While battered women's lay advocates routinely argue that legal remedies are not the best choice for all battered women, those who work within the legal system increasingly fall prey to this assumption.* * *

C. The Legal System Is Dangerous

Pushing battered women to use the legal system is particularly problematic because turning to the system can be dangerous for battered women. Most obviously, battered women are frequently warned by their abusers not to contact the police or the courts for help; when they do, the results can be disastrous. Separation related violence is alarmingly common among battered women reaching out for assistance. But there are a number of other ways in which legal recourse can create huge problems for battered women.* * *

D. The Law Demands Physical Violence

The legal system reacts to and punishes crimes—assaults, batteries, harassments, stalking, and destruction of property. These are offenses for which abusers can be arrested, tried, and convicted; for which restraining orders can be issued; and which, in many states, constitute the type of evidence admissible in custody cases where domestic violence is alleged. But, the legal system's definition of domestic violence and the totality of battered women's experiences of domestic violence bear little resemblance to one another. While many abused women are victims of physical violence, the daily reality of their abuse is so much more than physical violence, a reality not reflected in the narrow range of behaviors that the legal system can reach.* * *

E. The Legal System Deprives Battered Women of Agency and Dignity

Victim empowerment is the guiding philosophy behind most domestic violence programs. The empowerment model is based on the belief that the battered woman will best know how to keep herself safe given her "unique ability to predict the abuse, to use techniques to minimize the violence, and to assess when it is safe to leave." Battered women's advocates argue that for women leaving violent, controlling relationships, it is crucial not to replace one form of control with another by having advocates and others tell the battered woman what she should do and how she should do it. The most common legal responses to domestic violence in criminal cases—mandatory arrest and no-drop policies—stand in stark contrast to this empowerment focus.* * *

Despite ongoing efforts to educate police, prosecutors, lawyers, and judges, some still look suspiciously at battered women, doubting their claims, their parenting ability, their judgment, and sometimes, their sanity. The stories of abuse narrated by battered women are discounted; battered women are told that their fears are groundless, overblown, or concocted to deprive their abusers of their liberty or contact with their children. Victims who don't fit the "profile"—physically injured, afraid for their lives, willing to separate—are treated skeptically. Client after client has told me how the police refused to arrest their batterers, refused to listen to their stories, and refused to honor their restraining orders. Legal system professionals also question the capacity of battered women to make judgments about whether to pursue cases. While many judges treat battered women seeking assistance with dignity and respect, "in some cases judges' responses amounted to a secondary victimization." Of particular concern to battered women and their advocates is the perception that judges doubt battered women's honesty and question their motives for seeking protection, particularly when children are involved. Even when the system reaches the right conclusion, it often damages the dignity of battered women along the way.

F. The Legal System Can't Deliver on Its Promises

Battered women who seek the assistance of the legal system do so because the system holds out the promise that it can stop the abuse and keep them and their children safe. Instead, what many women find is that the legal system itself becomes the batterer's forum for terrorizing his victim, and judges and others often give him the tools to perpetuate the abuse.* * *

G. The Legal System, Women of Color, Immigrant Women, and Poor Women

To build support for legislative and policy changes benefiting victims of domestic violence, battered women's advocates stressed that domestic violence occurred among all races, ethnicities, religions, and classes. While this may be true, the experience of domestic violence is profoundly different for women of color, battered immigrant women, and poor women—as is the impact of using the legal system to address violence against them.* * *

H. Fathers and the Legal System

The legal system imprisons fathers, gives them inappropriate custody and visitation, and allows them to use the courts to continue abusing their children's mothers. What it does not do, however, is ask how we can improve batterers' parenting abilities, reducing danger to both children and their mothers and providing a more nurturing environment for the children of battering fathers.* * *

I. The Legal System as the Default

On both the individual and systemic level, the legal system overshadows other, potentially more effective strategies for addressing domestic violence. Attorneys who are unfamiliar with the resources and initiatives focused on domestic violence in the community may fail to connect clients with those resources, focusing instead on the legal solutions they know best. Clients may assume either that their non-legal needs are irrelevant or, not being asked about them, decide not to raise these issues. Believing that an attorney would certainly provide advice as to all available options, the client may take the attorney's failure to address these issues as evidence that no other options exist.

On a systemic level, the focus of the last thirty years on the development of the legal response to domestic violence has certainly diverted money, attention, and energy from other initiatives. Nonetheless, there are a number of promising initiatives for addressing domestic violence that bypass the legal system altogether, focusing on prevention rather than reacting to violence that has already occurred, the legal system's typical posture. * * *

Strategies for ensuring batterer accountability outside of the traditional adversarial legal model are being studied as well. * * * These methods challenge our assumptions about how domestic violence cases "should" be handled, infusing the process with a kind of bargaining that battered women's advocates may feel is inappropriate. Exploring innovative strategies is crucial, however, if we are to expand the options available to battered women outside of the legal system. Lawyers dedicated to serving battered women need to stay abreast of efforts to develop alternatives to the legal system and be ready to counsel their clients on their merits.

III. LAWYERING FOR BATTERED WOMEN: WITHIN AND BEYOND THE LEGAL SYSTEM

* * * The legal system can be a powerful tool in the lives of battered women, and I am not suggesting that we dismantle that system, stop seeking ways to improve it, or return to the days when domestic violence was considered a private matter, justifying the unwillingness of the system to intervene. But those of us who believe law can be a solution for battered

women also need to acknowledge that the legal system can create more problems than it solves and counsel our clients appropriately. * * *

JUDITH ARMATTA, GETTING BEYOND THE LAW'S COMPLICITY IN INTIMATE VIOLENCE AGAINST WOMEN

33 Willamette L. Rev. 773, 842–845 (1997)
(citations and footnotes omitted)

IV. CONCLUSION

From an international perspective, domestic violence is a nearly universal phenomenon. It exists in countries with unduly varying political, economic, and cultural structures. The extensiveness of domestic violence establishes that the problem does not originate with the pathology of an individual person. Rather, domestic violence is embedded in the values, relationships, and social and institutional structures of society. Its roots are found in a hierarchical social structure of male dominance and female subordination. To end domestic violence, societal models based on dominance must be changed.

While change will not occur through legal reform alone, legal structural change is a necessary component of broader social change. At the very least, legal approval of domestic violence must be ended. Moreover, to end the legal system's complicity in domestic violence, the legal system cannot lend itself to use by an abuser seeking to control and harm another. Nor can the law act as an impediment to women seeking safety and well-being. As a survey of women's advocates in ninety-four countries concluded, there is a "need for gender specific, comprehensive and systematically integrated domestic violence legislation."

Ending legal complicity in domestic violence requires abolishing the laws of a gender-neutral stance. Justice must remove her blindfold and see the context that shapes people's lives. The principle of neutrality cannot provide justice between groups with a great disparity in power and resources without taking the disparity into account. Gender-conscious laws are necessary to make the law less of a tool in the hands of abusers.

The issue of family, family privacy, and legally sanctioned violence also must be addressed in any legal reform strategy. Domestic violence takes root in a family structure that gives men power over women and approves of violence as a disciplinary and conflict resolution method, but then declares itself off-limits from state interference. While the state should not unnecessarily interfere in personal relationships, the state must interfere to protect its citizens from harm.

Any legal reform effort must take an integrated approach to the problem of not only domestic violence but all forms of violence against women.

"[M]ost legal systems have not displayed a synthetic approach to the problem [of violence against women]." In other words, the laws of most legal systems address the various manifestations of violence against women separately, with no suggestion that they may have a uniform or even related structural cause. This has meant that, practically speaking, laws concerning different forms of such violence are located in different legal remedies and texts. From a theoretical viewpoint, this failure to adopt a synthetic legal approach has resulted in a general failure to link the various manifestations of violence against women to subordination of and discrimination against women generally. The failure to adopt a synthetic approach in legal remedy has affected other areas, so that service provision and other strategies employed to address the problem have also developed in a fragmented way. It cannot be overemphasized that a fragmented approach practically ensures that root causes will be ignored. Addressing domestic violence in isolation from other forms of violence and discrimination against women has resulted in characterizing domestic violence as a problem of family systems, rather than a problem rooted in a patriarchal social structure. In the same way, this fragmented approach has led to viewing sexual assault as the pathological acts of a few individuals without any understanding of social conditioning, and addressing female poverty as a social service instead of a political issue.

> It is highly likely that the various forms of violence against women are linked and are based on a common cause—the subordination of women. It is likely, therefore, that many of the measures that are now employed to address this violence are merely treating the symptom, rather than the cause of the phenomenon. Work is now required to ensure that all measures interrelate and encompass effective approaches to address the legal, social and economic injustices that women face.

The international human rights community has formulated international standards of behavior. Recently, the international community declared its consensus that violence against women is a human rights violation, and that states have an affirmative duty to protect women from such violence. Further, the international community has recognized that neither family privacy nor religious or cultural traditions should outweigh a woman's right to safety, health, and well-being.

The Beijing Platform for Action, agreed to by all participating countries at the Fourth World Conference on Women in 1995, clarifies the interrelatedness of all forms of violence and discrimination against women. "Developing a holistic and multidisciplinary approach to the challenging task of promoting families, communities and States that are free of violence against women is necessary and achievable. Equality, partnership between woman and men and respect for human dignity must permeate all stages of the socialization process." The Beijing Platform for Action further sets out a comprehensive program for addressing the different manifestations of women's subordination. As such, it provides an important guide for any strategy designed to address domestic violence.

Law reformers at the national and local levels should follow the leadership of the international community and declare that violence against women is a serious and widespread problem that must be addressed for the well-being and progress of the entire world community. And they should make addressing it a priority.

EDITOR'S SUMMARY OF DEBORAH M. WEISSMAN, THE PERSONAL IS POLITICAL—AND ECONOMIC: RETHINKING DOMESTIC VIOLENCE

2007 Brigham Young University Law Rev. 387–450 (2007)
Reprinted with permission from Domestic Violence Report (2008)

Deborah Weissman, a professor at North Carolina School of Law, has written a very thought-provoking article about the relationship between the economic system and domestic violence. While Weissman concedes that the legal approach has some merit, she asks whether this emphasis has precluded alternative explanations for domestic violence, and whether punishment is really the primary means of preventing further abuse. She also notes many structural weaknesses of the criminal justice system.

The author argues that patriarchy alone is not an adequate explanation for domestic violence, and that a paradigm shift is needed in order to consider multi-faceted circumstances contributing to this problem. In particular, community economic hardships and the consequent demise of resources, both caused by globalization, are social conditions also contributing to domestic violence. She says that given the changing circumstances both in the U.S. and around the world, the theory of what causes domestic violence must evolve. Private households are not separate from public workplaces, and patriarchy is not separate from the material conditions of daily life.

In the U.S., globalization has resulted in the loss of many manufacturing jobs which used to sustain households for generations. As a result, many communities in this country now have chronically high unemployment, and workers who still have jobs have been forced into concessions involving lower wages, loss of health care benefits, and loss of pensions. Unions have been weakened. All of this has led to a working environment full of uncertainty, which is very stressful for both the workers and their families. While many workers are unemployed, some workers are forced to work much longer hours than they would choose. Of course, in communities without work, neighborhoods decline, and tax revenues go down, leading to decreased ability of local governments to fund social services. People are forced to move, and the entire community has a lowering of self-worth. This leads to feelings of despair and weakened social controls which then increases crime rates. Studies have shown that domestic violence is higher where there are fewer opportunities for neighbors and coworkers to provide social support, reduced police presence, and general social fragmentation. While the U.S. has been through many economic slumps and of course the Depression, the current situation may be worse in terms of social disorganization because of the heightened expectations when conditions were better. Communities without work can lead to domestic violence even in families not considered previously at risk, as the jobless individuals feel shame, worthlessness, and hopelessness. Dr. Jacquelyn Campbell's study of domestic violence homicides found that the strongest risk factor is the perpetrator's lack of employment—this factor alone resulted in a four-fold increase of risk of homicide.

Of course joblessness by itself does not cause domestic violence. It is the combination of that factor with our social construction of gender which is key: men's role is to support the family financially, which is usually seen as even more important than their being present in the home. Thus economic insecurity is felt as a threat to the male partner's masculinity. Women are very aware of this, feeling more distress over their male partner's job security than over their own. Men with job insecurity or unemployed men may resort to "hypermasculine" behaviors such as violence to try to gain back their lost social status, while women in the same situation tend to seek support from friends and relatives. However, this seeking of support may make the man feel even more of a failure. Furthermore, men experiencing job insecurity may feel they have to compete even more with other men at work to keep their jobs, and may feel that the employer is asserting a patriarchal hierarchy over the workers. This increased stress can lead to workers resorting to violence, both at work and at home, with women disproportionately the targets in both locations. Shockingly, homicide is the leading cause of occupational death for women. And when times are tough economically, women are less likely than men to be hired, and may not qualify for unemployment benefits due to the contingent nature of many women's jobs. Their lack of income then contributes to their powerlessness at home.

Weissman suggests some interesting solutions to this rather depressing picture. She stresses the importance of looking at domestic violence from a group perspective—e.g., the problem is not just that a particular battered woman is economically dependent on her male partner but that women as a group are disproportionately affected by economic instability. Seeing domestic violence as related to market forces also helps us see battered women's survival strategies in the context of these larger social issues, which helps us see the ways they are powerful actors rather than helpless victims. We also need to look more closely at the relationship between poverty and domestic violence, in the context of global economic restructuring.

But what does this all mean for domestic violence advocates and agencies? One of its implications is that rather than seeing themselves as "apolitical service delivery centers" domestic violence agencies need to join the struggle for sustainable social change. The domestic violence movement has done an outstanding job of pointing out that what was formerly seen as private (abuse in the home) is in fact a matter of public concern; this same viewpoint can be very helpful in looking at issues such as plant closures, big-box stores putting local proprietors out of business, or local employers filing for bankruptcy. In such situations, domestic violence advocates can fight for the government to intervene, raising the interests of the larger community, just as they fought for prosecutors to intervene to help stop domestic violence. And the skills that advocates have developed in creating and dealing with the Family Violence Option can be used to improve the administration of Trade Adjustment Assistance programs for laid-off workers: pushing for effective case management, real training, and good jobs. *[Editor's Note: Weissman appears here to be speaking only of helping battered women obtain good jobs, but based on her analysis of the problem, she could also argue that it would be worthwhile for advocates to help potential batterers obtain and keep jobs, as part of a larger prevention strategy.]* And of course, domestic violence advocates could work with workers' rights advocates to accomplish these goals.

Another implication of this changed viewpoint is incorporating economics into the criminal justice system, which should address poverty and joblessness as part of sentencing, batterer's programs, probation, and re-entry after incarceration. Community policing could connect people to housing, treatment, employment training, and education, all of which help prevent crime. Restorative justice models could be utilized more, repairing harm rather than just punishing perpetrators. This focus also would help align the domestic violence movement more with women of color and poor women, help resist the current affiliation with the criminal justice system, and emphasize the movement's potential for being "catalysts of social change."

Concurrently, worker's rights groups, anti-globalization groups, and unions could take on domestic violence issues, helping battered women workers obtain protective orders and new jobs, pushing for improved working conditions and wages for women as part of lowering rates of domestic violence, and pointing out that plant closures tend to increase abuse at home. Unions could join the domestic violence coordinated community response teams currently in place in many areas that tend now to focus on law enforcement and courts.

Weissman ends by noting that there is an "urgent need to shift the course," which can lead to more "creative advocacy," a "transformative project," and a "conceptual revolution." "For those committed to ending domestic violence, working both at the global and local level to address the excesses of global capital . . . may be a meaningful alternative to the narrow strategies of adherence to criminalization policies that paralyze progressive action."

[Editor's Notes: 1. In 2001, two national organizations, INCITE! and Critical Resistance, joined by numerous other organizations and individuals, issued a statement entitled, "Gender Violence and the Prison Industrial Complex," which can be found at http://www.incite-national.org/page/incite-critical-resistance-statement. The central message of the statement was to call on anti-gender-based-violence organizations, such as domestic and sexual assault agencies and also on anti-prison groups, to better support survivors—and especially women survivors of color—without "depend[ing] on a sexist, racist, classist, and homophobic criminal justice system."

In support of this, the statement notes how the anti-violence movement's overreliance on the criminal legal system—including mandatory arrest laws, funneling funding into policing and prisons instead of social service agencies, and the disturbing rise of mass incarceration, especially of people of color—has actually made survivors less safe.

Moreover, the statement shows that the current anti-prison movement's focus has been largely on men and prison abolition, thus ignoring the plight of women and LGBTQI+ communities, and further endangering them by not proposing a viable alternative solution to prisons for offenders like rapists and murderers.

The statement ends with 11 calls to action for social justice movements, including relying more on the community than on the government, moving poor women of color from the margins to the center, "[p]romot[ing] holistic political education," and "[c]halleng[ing] . . . all men . . . to take particular responsibility" in ending violence against women.

2. Reading this book and talking about its contents in class may be upsetting for some people, especially if they have a history of abuse or are close to someone who does. I recommend setting up a buddy system with a friend where the two of you exchange regular and equal time, with one listening and one talking/processing feelings about what is coming up for you, then you switch roles. I have done this since the late 1970's, through Re Evaluation Counseling, www.reevaluationcounseling.org, and have found it an invaluable tool in my life.]

CHAPTER 2

DESCRIPTIONS, CAUSES, AND EFFECTS OF ABUSE

■ ■ ■

This chapter starts by examining the dynamics in abusive relationships, including typical experiences of victims/survivors with the legal system and typical behaviors of abusers. The concepts of power and control, and of coercive control, are introduced. A Ninth Circuit case focuses on the ways the cycle of violence manifests in a long-term abusive relationship. An excerpt focuses on the concept of learned helplessness versus seeing abused women as survivors seeking help, two conflicting theories about the typical responses of survivors. Four pieces focusing on more recently recognized aspects of domestic violence describe birth control sabotage, the overlap between domestic violence and human trafficking, animal abuse as a form of intimate partner abuse, and litigation abuse.

The materials then examine whether there are different types of batterers, what causes them to abuse their partners, and how men who terrorize their partners are similar to or different from those who do not take the abuse to such an extreme level.

Continuing to ask what causes domestic violence, the materials then utilize a cross-cultural perspective, looking at whether domestic violence occurs in all societies, and if not, what is different about those societies where we do not find it.

Many of the materials in this chapter are from disciplines other than law. The issues they raise—conflicting theories as to the causes of domestic violence, differing descriptions of typical responses of those subjected to abuse, information about societies not plagued by violence between partners—have major policy implications for how the U.S. legal system attempts to solve this problem.

A. DYNAMICS OF DOMESTIC VIOLENCE RELATIONSHIPS

DOMESTIC ABUSE INTERVENTION PROJECT, DULUTH, MN, POWER AND CONTROL WHEEL

CLAIRE HOUSTON, HOW FEMINIST THEORY BECAME (CRIMINAL) LAW: TRACING THE PATH TO MANDATORY CRIMINAL INTERVENTION IN DOMESTIC VIOLENCE CASES

21 Mich. J. Gender & L. 217 (2014)
(footnotes omitted)

IV. EARLY FEMINIST THEORIES OF DOMESTIC VIOLENCE

Early feminist theories of domestic violence, like family violence theories, were sociological: they rejected individual factors in favor of social conditions. Feminist theories diverged from family violence theories, however, in their identification of male domination as the primary source of domestic violence. I begin this Part by exploring two early feminist texts on domestic violence: *Battered Wives* by Del Martin, and Rebecca and Russell Dobash's *Violence Against Wives: A Case Against the Patriarchy.* While both texts identified male domination as central to domestic violence, the respective authors differed in their understanding of its function. While Martin envisioned domestic violence as a reaction to gender inequality, the Dobashes saw it as maintenance of male control. It was the Dobashes' perspective, I argue, that informed the feminist position in favor of mandatory criminal interventions.

At the same time, another author was laying the groundwork for the mandatory intervention campaign. Lenore Walker was not concerned with the etiology of domestic violence but rather with why women stayed in abusive relationships. Walker was a psychologist, but rejected traditional psychological theories, including masochism, as anti-feminist. Walker avoided implicating women in domestic violence, arguing instead that women stay with abusive men in part because the abuse renders them psychologically incapable of leaving. This claim ultimately encouraged feminist disregard for the preferences of battered women who refused criminal intervention.

A. Domestic Violence and Sexism: Battered Wives and Violence Against Wives

In *Battered Wives,* Del Martin set out a theory of domestic violence that placed not only sexual inequality but also marriage front and center. Following the radical feminists, Martin described marriage as "the mechanism by which the patriarchy is maintained." Like Millett, she emphasized socialization, and it was here that Martin made the connection to wife beating. According to Martin, wife beating was a consequence of sex roles, which developed out of marriage. Concepts of "masculinity" and "femininity" came from the traditional roles of husband and wife. She argued that gender roles are not natural, but instead a product of the institution of marriage. Men and women struggle to live up to the socially constructed expectations of their gender, and this struggle creates conflict. Each intimate partner expects the other to act according to a socially prescribed role and becomes frustrated when they do not. When violence erupts, the woman—as the physically disadvantaged partner—is more likely to be injured. This explanation sounds blame-neutral, and in fact Martin did not single men out for reproach. In Martin's formulation, men and women were *both* victims of sexism.

In describing sex roles as frustrating, Martin sounded similar to [Richard] Gelles, who suggested that socially defined sex roles create stress that leads to marital violence. Unlike Gelles, however, Martin was not prepared to factor stresses other than sexism into her analysis. She explicitly denied the suggestion that wife beating was more prevalent among the poor, a denial that would continue in future feminist advocacy.

For Martin, marriage not only contributed to wife beating, it also condoned the practice. Traditional beliefs about marriage confined wife beating to the private sphere, which allowed the practice to continue. Speaking of the criminal justice system, Martin explained, "A man's home is his castle, and police, district attorneys, and judges hesitate to interfere with what goes on behind that tightly closed door." Moreover, the perceived intimacy between a husband and wife caused wife-beating cases to be treated as exceptional: "The husband never faces the harsh penalties he would suffer if found guilty . . . for assaulting a stranger." Finally, belief in the sanctity of marriage informed policies that encouraged reconciliation of spouses over separation. Martin offered New York's Family Court Act as an example. "In New York," she reported, "a woman seeking protection or trying to escape from her violent husband is forced to rely on a system intent on 'stabilizing' her family." *[Editor's Note: The author explains earlier that this court, established in 1962, had no criminal jurisdiction, rarely transferred cases to criminal court, and while it could offer protection orders, was also tasked with helping spouses reconcile. In 1977 the FCA was amended to confer concurrent jurisdiction to the criminal court, due to pressure from feminists.]* Social service agencies adopted a similar stance: "the view that reconciliation is the only answer is . . . all too prevalent among representatives of the social system." The problem with promoting reconciliation, in Martin's view, was that it pushed domestic violence back into the private sphere. Once again private, domestic violence was protected, and thereby encouraged.

But what about women who chose not to separate from their husbands after experiencing violence? According to Martin, "Battered wives give many reasons or rationalizations for staying, but fear is the common denominator. Fear immobilizes them, ruling their actions, their decisions, their very lives." She appears to argue that battered women cannot think rationally; if they could, they would leave. This was not the whole story, however. Martin explained that battered women's judgment is also clouded by gender role expectations. Women, she argued, are socialized to believe that wifehood is their greatest calling. Thus, even a woman with the means to leave an abusive relationship might be psychologically blocked from doing so: "a woman with her *own* money! What can she be thinking when she says she *needs* a man who takes her money and her will? . . . *The fact is, she may not be thinking for herself at all.*" This is false consciousness: it is a feminist claiming that another woman cannot see how the oppression under which she lives distorts her worldview. It is distinct from the argument that fear prevents women from leaving abusive relationships, but the result is the same: women's psychology—even if a product of sexism or abuse—leads to the irrational conclusion that staying with an abusive partner is preferable to leaving.

The Dobashes argued that marriage was significant because it granted husbands control over their wives. This control was historically and socially constructed. Male control was historically constructed through the patriarchal family in which husbands exercised power over wives. Socially, it was constructed through institutions and ideology. Echoing Martin (and Millett), the Dobashes explained that gender roles conditioned girls to become submissive wives, and boys to become authoritarian husbands. In situations, like the formal economy that limited women's participation in the workforce, ensured that wives would remain financially dependent on husbands and, thus, under their control.

But social forces alone were not to blame. Violence against wives was also an expression of what the Dobashes called "coercive control" on the part of husbands: "The use of physical force against wives should be seen as an attempt on the part of the husband to bring about a desired state of affairs. *It is primarily purposeful behavior* . . ." From this perspective, violence against wives was not a reaction to gender inequality but a concentrated effort on the part of husbands to perpetuate it. Husbands were not victims of sexism, as Martin had claimed; they were perpetrators.

The Dobashes' conception of wife beating as "coercive control" is analogous to the radical feminist notion of violence against women as patriarchal force. Domestic violence, like rape, is a means of keeping women subordinate to men. While the Dobashes did not make this point explicitly, they seemed to view individual instances of domestic violence as reinforcing not only a husband's domination of his wife, but also male domination of women generally. Other feminists of the time certainly did. The Dobashes believed wife abuse to be an expression of male domination. They also viewed wife abuse as socially condoned, writing that, "men who assault their wives are actually living up to cultural prescriptions that are cherished in Western society—aggressiveness, male domination, and female submission—and they are using physical force as a means to enforce that domination."

The Dobashes were sociologists, like the family violence researchers. However, from the Dobashes' perspective, family violence theory failed to account for the social and historical context in which domestic violence occurred. *[Editor's Note: The author explains earlier that "family violence theory," propounded by Richard Gelles and others, sees the root of domestic violence as an adaptation to structural stress, including sexism and economic factors, and believes that victims of abuse are also to blame, in part, for the abuse.]* By doing so, family violence theory gave short shrift to male domination, which, for the Dobashes, was central to explaining domestic violence. This led family violence theorists to erroneously group wife abuse with other forms of family violence. It also drove spurious hypotheses about "husband abuse." The suggestion that husbands and wives abuse each other at similar rates was, according to the Dobashes, simply not true.

The Dobashes' emphasis on male domination as the foundation of wife abuse informed their view of "victim blaming." They noted two forms: "female provocation" and female masochism. Interpreted through the lens of male domination, both forms could be properly read as acts of resistance by wives. However, without a feminist framework, victim blaming was effectively deployed to maintain the patriarchal status quo, an argument familiar from radical feminist rape discussions. For example, "The idea of provocation is a very powerful tool used in justifying the husband's dominance and control and in removing moral indignation about his resort to force in securing, maintaining, and punishing challenges to his authority." Shifting the locus of blame toward the wife allowed the husband's violence to continue. It also guaranteed his control. The notion of female provocation was based on an assumption that a wife should not challenge her husband's authority, because doing so could lead to violence. To the Dobashes, this view was naive, representing "a failure to see the marital relationship within which the wife must negotiate with her husband in order to conduct her daily life and to see that she must do so from a greatly disadvantaged position." From the Dobashes' perspective, a wife who "provokes" her husband is simply resisting his control.

A similar interpretation was offered for female masochism. Like provocation, masochism shifts blame away from husbands towards innocent wives, "It removes the moral outrage over the wife's victimization and it means outsiders can quietly ignore the problem without feeling guilty." Deploying female masochism to blame wives means the husband's exercise of control goes unchecked.

Because male domination was the problem, combating male domination was the solution. Members of the helping and legal professions had to rethink their responses. To challenge male domination, professionals had to "stop denying the seriousness of the offence, blaming the victim, and/or seeking causes in the man's supposed mental aberrations," or "more insidiously," in the woman's "personal pathologies." The implication was that legal and mental health responses that focused on psychological factors or implicated women in abuse were anti-feminist.

While Martin and the Dobashes' positions were generally in agreement, there were two exceptions. The first, already mentioned, was disagreement over the relative culpability of men. As I demonstrate in the next Part, it was the Dobashes' interpretation that eventually became more popular among feminists advocating for greater criminal justice involvement in domestic violence cases. A second tension lay in the reasons offered for why wives stay with abusive husbands. On this issue, the Dobashes' perspective did not become the popular view. The Dobashes relied on their interpretation of wife abuse as male control to reinterpret the act of staying. Unlike Martin, they did not rely on fear. Women had good reason to *choose* to stay with violent husbands, argued the Dobashes, most often lack of material and personal support. Women who left and then returned to violent husbands were also depicted as rational. The Dobashes described these women as attempting to shift the relationship's balance of power in their favor by demonstrating that they could walk away. These were not women incapable of thinking for themselves, but rational agents challenging their husbands' authority.

B. The Battered Woman

Susan Brownmiller has called the question, "Why doesn't she leave?" the battered women's movement's "bugaboo." It has been a problem from the beginning: Martin and the Dobashes each devoted an entire chapter to the question. It was a question that had to be answered. If, as feminists claimed, domestic violence were a serious crime warranting a traditional criminal response, why were some battered women acting otherwise? Every time a woman stayed or returned to an abusive partner, it undermined the movement's agenda.

One option was to explain a woman's decision to stay with sociological factors, most importantly lack of resources. The Dobashes favored this approach. But as Martin pointed out, this explanation could not account for women of means. The fact that women with resources also returned to violent relationships suggested a deeper problem. This quandary pushed theorists—like Martin—in the direction of psychology. For battered women's advocates, this was a very dangerous course. From the feminist perspective, psychology, and especially its concept of female masochism, was in large part to blame for allowing violence against women to continue. Advocates wanted to steer clear of explanations for why women stayed in abusive relationships that redirected blame toward the victim.

In 1979, Lenore Walker published *The Battered Woman*, a study of "the psychology of battered women as victims." The book introduced "the battered woman syndrome," a set of psychological characteristics common to battered women, including low self-esteem, feelings of guilt, and traditional views about marriage and gender. It also elaborated on two theories: the psychosocial theory of learned helplessness, and the cycle theory of violence.

Walker believed her findings could answer the question, "Why doesn't she leave?" *The Battered Woman* leads with two propositions: one, "that the problem [of battering] is far more pervasive—and terrible—than it was ever thought to be," and two, "that the myths which had previously rationalized" battering were "untrue." Here she addressed and countered the idea of female masochism. "Most people label [battered] women 'masochistic,' for not leaving the relationship," she explained, "unaware or preferring to ignore the battered woman's *inability to help herself.*"

Walker attributed a battered woman's inability to help herself to learned helplessness, a concept from the field of experimental psychology. Applied to battered women, it referred to the belief that a woman has no control over what happens to her, a state of consciousness that develops after multiple "battering cycles":

> The battered woman does not believe anything she does will alter any outcome, not just the specific situation that has occurred. She says, "No matter what I do, I have no influence." She cannot think of alternatives. She says, "I am incapable and too stupid to learn how to change things." Finally, her sense of emotional well-being becomes precarious. She is more prone to depression and anxiety.

It was not that women enjoyed violence. Nor was the violence not serious enough to warrant separation. According to Walker, it was the traumatic nature of the abuse that left women believing they could not leave. Walker offered a psychological explanation, but did not implicate personal pathology. There was nothing in the battered woman's psychological makeup to predispose her to abuse. Her psychological deficiencies came *after* the abuse, according to Walker. A battered woman's psychology was the reason the violent relationship continued, but the continuation was not her fault.

While individual women were not prone to victimization, women as a class were more likely to experience learned helplessness. This was especially true for married women. The culprit, again, was gender inequality, a sociological fact. However, it manifested, according to Walker, in women's psychology. In a patriarchal system, girls are socialized to be more passive than boys. They therefore enter marriage with a "psychological disadvantage." The social and legal institution of marriage, which confers power over wives, compounds this disadvantage. Married women come to believe they have limited control over their lives.

Just as a particular woman's psychology did not make her vulnerable to abuse, neither did her socioeconomic status. Walker's agenda included debunking the "myth" that wife battering was a problem of the poor. What made a woman vulnerable to battering was her gender. "Battered Women," Walker explained, "are found in all age groups, races, ethnic and religious groups, educational levels, and socioeconomic groups. Who are the battered women? If you are a woman, there is a 50 percent chance it could be you!" Indeed, under this high estimate it would be impossible for battering to be concentrated among one socioeconomic group.

Identifying gender as the common denominator supported a feminist theory of domestic violence. It also lent support to feminist reforms. For example, if domestic violence were a socioeconomic problem, the solution would be a reduction in poverty. If domestic violence were a product of sexism, the solution had to be eradication of male domination. Walker's estimate of wife-beating's prevalence made finding a solution all the more pressing. With "as many as 50 percent of all women [becoming] battering victims at some point in their lives," the problem was pervasive.

Bound up with Walker's theory of learned helplessness was her cycle theory of violence. Walker defined a battered woman as one "who is repeatedly subjected to any forceful physical or psychological behavior by a man in order to coerce her to do something he wants her to do without any concern for her rights." Walker's description resembled the Dobashes' account, which defined domestic violence as a conscious effort by men to subordinate women. Battered women are those who have experienced at least two battering cycles. Walker envisioned the battering cycle as comprised of three phases: (1) tension building, (2) the acute battering incident, and (3) loving contrition. In the first phase, friction between the couple builds. The husband acts aggressively toward the wife, and the wife attempts to placate the husband. Eventually the tension becomes so intense that violence erupts, and the couple enters the second stage. Walker noted that sometimes the wife triggers the second stage. Knowing abuse is on the horizon (she has been through this cycle before), but suffering because she cannot predict when it will come, the wife *provokes* the husband in order to get it over with. This is another feminist re-reading of female provocation. Women might provoke violence but it is not their fault. They do it to exercise some control over their violent spouse. In the third stage, the couple returns to a calmer place. The husband expresses remorse for his actions and promises reform. The woman, reminded of happier times, agrees to stay, hoping this time things will be different.

While there is overlap between learned helplessness and the cycle theory of violence (i.e., cycles of violence contribute to learned helplessness), the theories can be understood as offering distinct answers to the question, "Why doesn't she leave?" According to learned helplessness, women exposed to systemic abuse become psychologically incapable of helping themselves. Under the cycle theory of violence, women stay because they believe their husbands will change.

Walker first introduced the cycle theory of violence in 1978. After reviewing the three phases, she offered a morbid prediction: if, in individual cases, the cycle of violence was not broken, the likely outcome was death. "The [battered] woman," according to Walker, "sees death as the *only way out* of her situation, either the batterer's death or her own. The batterer similarly would rather die or kill her than voluntarily leave." This assessment supported Walker's claim that domestic violence was more "terrible" than previously imagined. It also supported her choice of remedy: separation. Because staying in a battering relationship was likely to lead to death, a woman could only save herself by leaving.

Other commentators have suggested that learned helplessness is victim blaming from a feminist perspective. It is a substitute for female masochism, and like female masochism it rests on women's mental pathology. The cycle theory of violence's explanation for why women stay could also be an example of feminist victim blaming. Women's experiences in the phase of loving contrition can be interpreted as false consciousness. *[Editor's Note: The author explains in an earlier section that the term "false consciousness," used by Professor Catharine MacKinnon in the 1980's, refers to women adopting a male point of view about their own experiences.]* Rather than seeing domestic violence for what it is—an act of male domination—the battered woman interprets the actions of her husband as anomalous. She fails to see that violence inflicted upon her is not a demonstration of weakness by an individual man but a concerted effort to control her as a woman.

If victim blaming perpetuates domestic violence, and if, as I argue, a woman's decision to stay in a relationship can sometimes be explained by false consciousness, then leaving is not only self-protective but it is also a remedy to victim blaming. According to Walker, a woman who stays in an abusive relationship with the (erroneous) hope that her partner will change "becomes an accomplice to her own battering." Like society's "*laissez faire* attitude" toward battering, a woman who stays encourages a batterer's violent behavior. Through "passive acceptance" she allows the violence to continue. From a feminist perspective, this has broader implications. If domestic violence is patriarchal force—like rape—then allowing it to continue against an individual woman reinforces male control over women as a class. Thus, separation is required not only for the individual woman's safety, but for the liberation of the group.

Separation, not surprisingly, was also Walker's remedy for learned helplessness. The research Walker relied upon was based on experiments with dogs. Walker believed analogies could still be drawn. Just as dogs "could *only* be taught to overcome their passivity by being dragged repeatedly out of the punishing situation and shown how to avoid the shock," battered women could only be cured of learned helplessness by being forcefully separated from their abusive partners. "This 'dragging' [of battered women]," explained Martin, "may require help from outside, such as the dogs received from the researchers." It did not take long for Walker's prescription to become reality.

V. FEMINIST THEORY BECOMES CRIMINAL LAW

The previous four Parts of this Article demonstrate how early feminist theories of domestic violence were based on a rejection of alternative psychological and family violence theories, and informed by the radical feminist position on rape. I emphasized the development of a strong anti-victim-blaming stance, traceable to radical feminist theories of rape and a rejection of psychological theories of domestic violence. I highlighted the feminist focus on male domination as the primary explanation for domestic violence, based on the notion that domestic violence is a patriarchal tool. This emphasis on male domination was an explicit rejection of family violence theory. In this Part, I will show how this foundation contributed to the feminist "turn" to criminal law as a preferred solution to domestic violence. * * *

CONCLUSION

Over the course of four decades, our popular understanding and legal approach to domestic violence has shifted dramatically. There has been a shift from the "private" response, where domestic violence was considered a product of relationship dysfunction, to a fully "public" campaign in which the state takes the lead in combating domestic violence through arrest and prosecution of abusers. This shift, I have argued, reflects a feminist understanding of domestic violence as patriarchal force. This understanding grew out of a rejection of alternative understandings of domestic violence, namely those offered by psychological and family violence theory, and was informed by earlier radical feminist theorizing on rape.

While my account is descriptive, it carries important normative implications. Since the 1960s, our response to domestic violence has been informed by our interpretation of the problem. My account suggests that our current system of criminalization, marked by mandatory criminal intervention policies, reflects a distinctly feminist interpretation of domestic violence as patriarchal force. Feminists looking to move away from mandatory policies will need a new way of understanding domestic violence. The alternative theories I canvass in the article offer some possibilities. Drawing from the psychological and family violence approaches, feminists may wish to consider the possibility of multiple types of domestic violence, stemming from a variety of factors, including structural stress, psychology, and interrelational dynamics. Being mindful of the legacy and destructive power of victim blaming, feminists may also want to ask about violence initiated by women, and try to understand the role of women in relationship conflict more generally. By developing an alternative to the feminist understanding of domestic violence as patriarchal force, feminists may discover (or come to support) options for managing the problem of domestic violence in ways that do not threaten the autonomy interests of individual women.

EVAN STARK, CURRENT CONTROVERSIES: COERCIVE CONTROL

In C. Renzetti, J. Edleson & R. Bergen (eds.) Sourcebook on Violence Against Women (3rd ed, 2018) (references omitted)

U.S. policy, law, interventions and most research on domestic violence continue to rely on a narrow "violence model" that equates partner abuse with discrete assaults. In the last decade, however, Europe and many other regions of the world have identified "violence against women" in relationships as a form of gender-based discrimination that violates human rights and broadened the definition to encompass "coercive control," defined as a strategic course of conduct that consists of physical and sexual violence, stalking and other forms of intimidation, emotional abuse, isolation, "economic violence," and "control," illustrated by what are termed "arbitrary violations of liberty." Rather than gauging the seriousness of abuse by injury, the new model considers the degree to which coercive control has disabled a woman's capacity to effectively resist or escape abuse, a condition referred to as "entrapment." The wrong here is subordination, depriving women of liberty, autonomy, dignity and equality, and is identified with what men keep women from doing for themselves as well as with the violence they do to women. Coercive control harms children because of their prolonged exposure to subjugation/inequality as well as to violence and because perpetrators subject children to coercive control by isolating, controlling, degrading or hurting them alongside their mother and by using them to control their mother, a pattern termed "child abuse as tangential spouse abuse." Coercive control has become part of common parlance among domestic violence researchers and service providers. But there are as yet no simple measurement tools for coercive control (as there are to measure violence) and federal and state governments in the U.S. have yet to identify coercive control as a specific offense (as it is England, e.g.) or to acknowledge its significance.

The term "coercive control" has evolved from a description of the "psychological abuse" observed among P.O.W.'s who were "brain washed" to an account of how battered women are structurally subordinated when abusive partners compliment their physical/sexual violence and intimidation with tactics that exploit and reinforce women's second-class status, deprive them of basic rights and resources, regulate their everyday lives and degrade them into a condition of dependence that is independent of personality, familial or cultural factors. Shifting the focus from ending violence to ending women's subjugation in personal life allows researchers to explore the full range of tactics used to achieve this end, even when no violence is involved.

Some coercive control tactics are criminal offenses, such as violence and marital rape; some tactics, like stalking or taking money, are considered criminal among strangers; and some tactics only contribute to entrapment when they occur against a background of fear and deprivation, such as when women comply with a partner's "rules" about housework or dress out of fear, the "or else" proviso. The fact remains: coercive control remains "invisible in plain sight" to U.S. law makers regardless of the legal status of the tactics used.

Coercive control has identifiable temporal and spatial dimensions, typical dynamics and predictable consequence. The tactical components of coercive control include those used to hurt, degrade and intimidate victims (coercion) and those designed to isolate and control them (control). Perpetrators adapt these tactics through trial and error based on their relative benefits and costs in a given relationship and the privileged knowledge of their partner afforded by intimacy. Women also assault male partners in large numbers. But, there is no evidence there is a "hidden" population of men suffering the pattern of violence, intimidation, isolation and control evident among 60% to 80% of abused women.

Coercion entails the use of physical and sexual violence, stalking and other intimidation tactics to cause pain, exact punishment, instill fear, compel or dispel a particular response and secure privileges. A high proportion of abusive relationships include episodes of severe injury. However, well over 95% of partner violence is non-injurious and is missed when police, courts or health services wait for injury to get involved. In fact, the significance of the violence used in coercive control derives from the cumulative effects of frequent, but generally low-level physical abuse extending for a period of 5.5 to 7.2 years on average. Thirty-five percent of abused women in the general population report being "beaten" 11 to 50 times (21%) or > 50 times (18%); 42% report being "slapped, pushed or shoved" in similar proportions. Repeated sexual assaults and other forms of sexual coercion accompany frequent physical abuse in between 43% to 55%, of cases with the result that partners account for the majority of all reported rapes. Among women in shelter, 27% reported they had been forced to have sex against their will "often" or "all the time." Sexual assault falls on a continuum of sexual coercion that extends from forced anal sex to forced pregnancies or abortions, sabotage of birth control, sexual inspection, sex trafficking, exposure to pornography and what Stark calls "rape as routine," where women comply with their partner's demands because they are afraid to refuse.

Intimidation tactics are used to instill fear, dependence, compliance, loyalty, and shame in four ways primarily—through threats, deprivation, surveillance, and degradation. Threats run the gamut from threats to kill a partner, friends or family members to threats that are only understood by the victim and may seem caring to outsiders, such as confining a woman to the home to "protect" her from the dangers lurking outside. Stalking is the most prevalent and devastating of surveillance tactics, includes cyber stalking, monitoring and internal stalking (where the abuser tracks a victim's behavior in the home), and is closely linked to physical and sexual violence. Many perpetrators establish their omnipotence through "search and destroy" missions to find and close "safety zones" women carve out to consider their options. Degradation involves targeting a woman's sources of personal esteem or shame, such as her weight, intelligence, parenting, personal hygiene or achievements at work.

Control tactics extend abuse through social space by isolating victims from sources of support, depriving them of basic rights and resources and micro-managing their behavior within and outside the home through implied to explicit "rules" that remain in play even when the perpetrator is absent. Isolation may encompass all the moorings of a victim's identity and extend from literal prohibitions against contacts with significant others, to denying women the means needed to communicate or be with others, to "harassment through the network," where the abusive partner "enters" and "poisons" his partner's social world.

Control tactics include depriving women of basic necessities, taking their money (54%), monitoring their time and movement (85%) and extend to rules about how they enact their default gender roles as wives, mothers and homemakers.

Alongside the empirical rationale for adapting the coercive control model is its practical rationale, the failure of legal, criminal justice and other intervention strategies wedded to the violence definition to improve the long-term prospects of battered women and their children. A conservative estimate is that > 8.7 million women in the U.S. are being subjected to coercive control. Yet, only 2 or 3 of every 100 perpetrators reported to police are sent to jail, an attrition rate of 98%. The 50th offense is treated no more seriously than the first. Identifying coercive control, broadening the definition of domestic violence accordingly, criminalizing coercive control and recognizing the historical and multi-faceted nature of partner abuse in Family and Juvenile Court proceedings would be first steps to closing the gap between the current approach and the oppression women are actually experiencing in their personal lives.

CONN. G.S.A. § 46B–1. FAMILY RELATIONS MATTERS AND DOMESTIC VIOLENCE DEFINED

(effective 10/1/22)

[In family law and guardianship cases,]

(b) As used in this title, "domestic violence" means: (1) A continuous threat of present physical pain or physical injury against a family or household member, as defined in section 46b–38a; (2) stalking, including, but not limited to, stalking as described in section 53a–181d, of such family or household member; (3) a pattern of threatening, including, but not limited to, a pattern of threatening as described in section 53a–62, of such family or household member or a third party that intimidates such family or household member; or (4) coercive control of such family or household member, which is a pattern of behavior that in purpose or effect unreasonably interferes with a person's free will and personal liberty. "Coercive control" includes, but is not limited to, unreasonably engaging in any of the following:

(A) Isolating the family or household member from friends, relatives or other sources of support;

(B) Depriving the family or household member of basic necessities;

(C) Controlling, regulating or monitoring the family or household member's movements, communications, daily behavior, finances, economic resources or access to services;

(D) Compelling the family or household member by force, threat or intimidation, including, but not limited to, threats based on actual or suspected immigration status, to (i) engage in conduct from which such family or household member has a right to abstain, or (ii) abstain from conduct that such family or household member has a right to pursue;

(E) Committing or threatening to commit cruelty to animals that intimidates the family or household member; or

(F) Forced sex acts, or threats of a sexual nature, including, but not limited to, threatened acts of sexual conduct, threats based on a person's sexuality or threats to release sexual images. . .

[Editor's Notes: 1. This Connecticut legislation also includes a provision giving indigent people seeking protective orders the right to representation. It gives litigants in protective order proceedings the option of emailing court papers when requesting service by a marshal and to give testimony remotely. It makes domestic violence the first factor when courts are determining child custody, makes violations of protective orders a family violence crime, and requires courts to consider risks to survivors of DV when determining bond for restraining order violations.

2. Changing the definition of domestic violence to include coercive control in state statutes applying to protective or restraining orders has other impacts. In some states it triggers the presumption against awarding custody to abusers (e.g., Ca. Family Code § 3044) and the rules allowing evidence of prior DV in prosecutions for DV crimes (e.g., Ca. Evid. Code § 1109).

3. Some states and countries have criminalized coercive control, while others (e.g., CT, CA) have made it grounds for a civil domestic violence restraining order. In Coercive Control: To criminalize or not to criminalize?, 18 Criminology & Crim Justice 50 (2018), Julia Tolmie writes:

> *"Criminalizing coercive or controlling behaviour in an intimate relationship, as has been done in England and Wales [and Hawaii and Ireland] and is proposed in Scotland, has the advantage of offering an offence structure to match the operation and wrong of intimate partner violence. This article raises the question as to whether other jurisdictions should follow suit. It argues that the successful implementation of such an offence may require a complexity of analysis that the criminal justice system is not currently equipped to provide and will require significant reforms in practice and thinking. If it is not successful such an offence could conceivably operate to minimize the criminal justice response to intimate partner violence and be used to charge primary victims."*

Courtney K. Cross reaches the same conclusion in "Coercive Control and the Limits of Criminal Law," 56 U.C. Davis L. Rev. 195 (2022), arguing that "criminalizing coercive control will do far more harm than good. Analyzing the domestic violence movement's prior attempt to use criminal law to address coercive behavior—the adoption of mandatory arrest and no-drop prosecution policies—underscores how, yet again, the most vulnerable survivors and their families will bear the brunt of these new criminal laws. As with mandatory policies, coercive control criminal laws will be coopted by abusive partners and used against survivors. . ."

4. In Coercive Control in Intimate Partner Violence: Relationship with Women's Experience of Violence, Use of Violence, and Danger, 8(5) Psychol. Violence 596 (2018), Melissa E. Dichter, Kristie A. Thomas, Paul Crits-Christoph, Shannon N. Ogden, and Karin V. Rhodes report on a study they conducted with 553 women patients at two emergency rooms, almost ¾ of whom were Black, who had experienced recent Intimate Partner Violence (IPV) and unhealthy drinking. A few were in relationships with other women or nonbinary people.

The researchers found that women experiencing coercive control in the last 3 months reported higher frequency of experiencing psychological, physical, and sexual IPV, and higher levels of danger, compared to women IPV survivors who were not experiencing coercive control. There was no statistically significant association between experience of coercive control and women's use of psychological or sexual IPV against their partners. However, women who experienced coercive control were more likely to report using physical IPV (43%) and to be poor than women who were not experiencing coercive control (19%). The authors note that we need to remember that women experiencing coercive control may also use violence, indicating that a woman's use of violence does not necessarily mean that she is not also experiencing severe and dangerous violence as well as coercive control. In fact, experience of coercive control may increase victims' use of physical violence as a survival strategy, especially if they have fewer resources like calling the police, escaping, or becoming independent from their partners.]

LAURA LUIS HERNANDEZ V. JOHN ASHCROFT, ATTORNEY GENERAL

345 F.3d 824 (9th Cir. 2003)
(citations and most footnotes omitted)

While living in Mexico, Laura Luis Hernandez ("Hernandez") experienced life-threatening violence at the hands of her husband, a legal permanent resident of the United States. She fled to the United States, but her husband tracked her down, promised not to hurt her again, and begged her to return to Mexico with him. After Hernandez submitted to his demand and returned to Mexico, the physical abuse began again.

Having escaped her husband permanently, and now living without legal status in the United States, Hernandez applied for suspension of deportation under a provision of the Violence Against Women Act of 1994 ("VAWA") intended to protect immigrants who have suffered domestic violence. With the passage of VAWA, Congress provided a mechanism for women who have been battered or subjected to extreme cruelty to achieve lawful immigration status independent of an abusive spouse. However, the Board of Immigration Appeals ("BIA") affirmed the immigration judge's ("IJ's") denial of Hernandez's application because it determined that Hernandez had not "been battered or subjected to extreme cruelty in the United States," as the statute then required. Hernandez also applied for adjustment of status on the basis of a petition for permanent residency that her husband had filed for her while they were still together. The BIA affirmed the IJ's denial of this application as well, first stating that she failed to adequately show that she had an approved visa petition or that an immigrant visa was immediately available to her, and secondly affirming the IJ's "discretionary determination to deny the respondent's application for adjustment of status for the reason that the marriage is no longer in existence." We reverse the BIA's denial of both the suspension of deportation and adjustment of status. * * *

I. BACKGROUND

Hernandez was thirty years old when she met her future husband, Refugio Acosta Gonzalez ("Refugio"), early in 1990. Refugio frequently ate at a restaurant where Hernandez worked in Mexicali, and after a short while they began dating. Initially, the relationship seemed idyllic. Hernandez believed that Refugio "was a marvelous person, a good person.... he used to give me flowers.... everything was marvelous."

After dating for a few months, the two decided to move in together. Several months later, "we were already in love and he asked me to get married." They were married in October 1990, in a small civil ceremony with a few friends present. After the wedding, they continued living in the same apartment in Mexicali.

Following the marriage, however, Refugio's behavior changed drastically. He began drinking heavily and verbally abusing Hernandez, and ultimately began physically abusing her as well. Although the verbal and physical abuse appear to have been constant throughout the marriage, Hernandez described several specific instances of particularly serious physical assault.

On the first occasion, a few months after their marriage, Refugio and Hernandez had gone to the movies. They became separated, and Hernandez was unable to find Refugio. After searching for him without success, she returned home and went to sleep. She was awakened some time later by the shattering of the bedroom window above her head. Refugio entered the darkened room through the broken window, landing on Hernandez. Seeing her, Refugio lifted her by her hair and threw her forcefully against the wall. Hernandez lay where she fell, stunned. Refugio stumbled drunkenly into the kitchen, seized a chair, and broke it across Hernandez's back. He continued hitting and kicking her while uttering insults and other verbal abuse.

Hernandez's head was wounded by the assault, and it was noted during the hearing that she still bears a visible scar from the injury. However, Refugio refused to allow her to leave the house or seek medical treatment. While testifying about this assault Hernandez became upset and began crying. She stated:

> I merely cleaned my head and for two days he wouldn't let me go out. He didn't let me go to the hospital to get treatment. I was bleeding alone. He was afraid that I will denounce him to the police, that's why he wouldn't let me go out.

Following this incident Refugio became "the same man that I knew. He was very good and he will behave very well."

In December of 1992 another violent assault occurred. Intoxicated, Refugio broke through the mosquito netting of the kitchen window while Hernandez was sleeping, and again attacked her. He smashed a pedestal fan over her head, breaking it on her forehead.

Hernandez was convinced that Refugio intended to kill her. She was afraid to return to her family in Mexico, because Refugio knew where they lived, and she feared he would follow her and kill her. With the help of a neighbor, Hernandez fled to the United States, to the home of her sister who lived in Los Angeles. However, after two weeks Refugio convinced the neighbor to give him the telephone number of Hernandez's sister. Refugio began calling every day. Ultimately, Hernandez agreed to talk to him. Refugio told Hernandez that he needed her. Hernandez testified, "He was crying. He asked me forgiveness and he said that he wouldn't do it again. And he asked why I had come here. . . . [I responded,] if I hadn't gone, fled, he would have killed me."

Refugio came to Los Angeles. He told Hernandez that "if I would go back with him he would look for a marriage counselor so that we could save our marriage, because he didn't want to lose me and I also didn't want to leave him." Hernandez believed him, particularly because he had never previously raised the possibility of seeking professional help. Still loving him, and believing his remorse and his promises to change, she returned to Mexico with him.

Upon their return, Hernandez found a marriage counselor. However, despite his earlier promise, Refugio refused to see the counselor. After a brief period, Refugio's violence returned.

The violence culminated several months later when Refugio came home drunk one evening. He beat Hernandez savagely, broke the windows in the house, and destroyed all of the furniture. After the beating, Hernandez "stayed in the corner sitting there in the corner, because I was very hurt." The next morning, Hernandez arose and began cooking breakfast. Behaving as though nothing had occurred, Refugio got up and began helping her. Then, suddenly, Refugio lunged at her with the knife he was using to chop vegetables. Sensing the attack, Hernandez blocked the knife thrust with her arm as Refugio attempted to stab her in the back. The knife gouged Hernandez's hand, slicing through to the bone.

Despite the severity of the wound, Hernandez was unable to go to the hospital to treat the injury. Instead, Refugio kept her trapped inside the house for two days. During these two days, Refugio stayed home with her, no longer beating her. On the third day Refugio returned to work, but he placed a padlock on the front door in order to keep Hernandez locked in the house while he was gone. However, Hernandez had an extra key to the padlock, and she was able to attract the attention of a passing neighbor. She slid the key under the door, and the neighbor unlocked the padlock and released her.

Hernandez went straight to the hospital to get treatment for her hand, but the delay in treatment had resulted in permanent damage to the nerves. The hand continues to give Hernandez great pain, and her use of it is restricted. At the hearing, Hernandez showed the IJ a scar approximately an inch and a half long on her right hand between her index finger and thumb.

In fear for her life, Hernandez again fled to the United States. She did not return to her sister's house, because Refugio knew its location. She explained, "I didn't go there anymore, because he has the address of my sister. He knew where I lived and I didn't want him to—and I didn't want him to find me again. I was very afraid. In fact, I am very afraid that he will find me again and he will kill me." She stayed with a friend in the town of Huron, California, for a few months, and then moved to Salinas.

A year later, in Salinas, she met Paulino Garcia, now her domestic partner, who "has helped me economically and morally with all the problems that I have suffered from my—from the abuse of my—the constant abuse that I suffer from my husband." In 1995, she and Paulino attempted to go to Alaska to work on a fishing boat, but Hernandez was intercepted by the INS at the airport and deportation proceedings were initiated against her.

Hernandez is still married to Refugio, but she has not had any contact with him and does not want him to find her. She believes that if she were required to return to Mexico, Refugio would find her and kill her. * * *

Procedural Background

* * * Following a hearing, the IJ issued a written opinion, finding Hernandez's testimony to lack credibility due to inconsistencies and the absence of corroborating testimony. The IJ denied her application for suspension of deportation because she had failed to prove she was a victim of domestic violence, and denied her application for adjustment of status because there was no evidence showing that the I-130 application had been approved.

On appeal, the BIA reversed the negative credibility determination, which it determined was unfounded. Nonetheless, the BIA affirmed the IJ's denial of both suspension of deportation and adjustment of status. With regard to the application for suspension of deportation under VAWA, the BIA determined that Hernandez met the three-year continuous physical presence requirement and the good moral character requirement. However, the BIA concluded that because the acts of physical violence occurred in Mexico, Hernandez was unable to show that she was "battered or subjected to extreme cruelty in the United States," as required by the 1994 version of the statute. * * *

The BIA provided two grounds for denying the application for adjustment of status. First, the BIA found that Hernandez had not established that a visa was immediately available to her or that her visa petition had been approved. Secondly, the BIA stated that the deterioration of the marriage provided an independent, discretionary basis for denying the adjustment of status. The BIA did, however, grant Hernandez's request for voluntary departure. * * *

III. SUSPENSION OF DEPORTATION UNDER VAWA

Hernandez applied for suspension of deportation. The former section 244 of the INA provided a method for certain aliens to establish eligibility for a discretionary suspension of deportation and obtain a grant of lawful status. Section 244(a)(3) was added to the INA as part of the passage of the Violence Against Women Act of 1994, in order to assist certain immigrants suffering from domestic violence. This provision provided that the Attorney General had the discretion to suspend deportation proceedings against an individual who:

> 1) has been physically present in the United States for a continuous period of not less than 3 years immediately preceding the date of such application;
>
> 2) has been battered or subjected to extreme cruelty in the United States by a spouse or parent who is a United States citizen or lawful permanent resident;
>
> 3) proves that during all of such time in the United States the alien was and is a person of good moral character;
>
> 4) and is a person whose deportation would, in the opinion of the Attorney General, result in extreme hardship to the alien or the alien's parent or child.

Hernandez bears the burden of establishing each of these four factors in order to qualify for suspension of deportation under section 244(a)(3). The BIA concluded that Hernandez had established both continuous physical presence and good moral character, the first and third prongs. Hernandez asks us to reverse the BIA's determination that she did not "suffer[ ] extreme cruelty in the United States." * * *

B. Extreme Cruelty

There is no dispute that the egregious abuse that Hernandez suffered in Mexico would qualify as battery or extreme cruelty. However, it is also clear that none of the acts of battery that occurred took place in the United States. Although Congress has since removed the requirement that an alien must have suffered from domestic abuse within the United States [in 2000], Hernandez's case is subject to an older version of VAWA, which did include this requirement. Thus, the question presented is whether the actions taken by Refugio in seeking to convince Hernandez to leave her safe haven in the United States in which she had taken refuge can be deemed to constitute extreme cruelty.[10]

---

[10] The INS contends that neither Refugio's actions in incessantly calling Hernandez's sister's home from Mexico nor his representations in the course of his telephone conversation with Hernandez are relevant to the question of whether extreme cruelty occurred in the United States, because Refugio was in Mexico when these actions took place. However, the statutory text demonstrates that it is Hernandez's location, not Refugio's, which is significant: the question is

1) Refugio's Behavior in the Context of Domestic Violence

Hernandez and amici argue that the interaction between Hernandez and Refugio in Los Angeles made up an integral stage in the cycle of domestic violence, and thus the actions taken by Refugio in order to lure Hernandez back to the violent relationship constitute extreme cruelty. Although according to common understanding, Refugio's actions might not be perceived as cruel, in enacting VAWA, Congress recognized that lay understandings of domestic violence are frequently comprised of "myths, misconceptions, and victim blaming attitudes," and that background information regarding domestic violence may be crucial in order to understand its essential characteristics and manifestations. Thus, in order to evaluate Hernandez's argument, we must first consider the nature and effects of violence in intimate relationships.

The field of domestic violence and our own case law reflect the fact that Refugio's actions represent a specific phase that commonly recurs in abusive relationships. Abuse within intimate relationships often follows a pattern known as the cycle of violence, "which consists of a tension building phase, followed by acute battering of the victim, and finally by a contrite phase where the batterer's use of promises and gifts increases the battered woman's hope that violence has occurred for the last time." Indeed, Hernandez's relationship with Refugio reflected just such a cycle: as described in Hernandez's testimony, following each violent episode, Refugio would for a time again become the man she had loved.

The literature also emphasizes that, although a relationship may appear to be predominantly tranquil and punctuated only infrequently by episodes of violence, "abusive behavior does not occur as a series of discrete events," but rather pervades the entire relationship. The effects of psychological abuse, coercive behavior, and the ensuing dynamics of power and control mean that "the pattern of violence and abuse can be viewed as a single and continuing entity." Thus, "the battered woman's fear, vigilance, or perception that she has few options may persist, . . . even when the abusive partner appears to be peaceful and calm." The psychological role of kindness is also significant in understanding the impact of Refugio's actions on Hernandez, since in combination with the batterer's physical dominance, such kindness often creates an intense emotional dependence by the battered woman on the batterer. Significantly, research also shows that women are often at the highest risk of severe abuse or death when they attempt to leave their abusers.

---

whether Hernandez was "*subjected* to extreme cruelty in the United States." INA § 244(a)(3) (emphasis added). Clearly, actions taken by a person in one location may subject a person in another location to extreme cruelty. Thus, we consider actions taken by Refugio in Mexico in determining whether Hernandez experienced extreme cruelty in the United States.

Although the INS implies otherwise, the record before the IJ and BIA contained substantial evidence regarding the cycle of violence and clinical and psychological understandings of domestic violence, evidence that was entirely unrebutted. * * * Information in the record also explained that "[d]omestic violence is not an isolated, individual event, but rather a pattern of perpetrator behaviors used against the victim." * * * The INS presented no evidence contradicting or undermining any of Hernandez's evidence.

Understood in light of the familiar dynamics of violent relationships, Refugio's seemingly reasonable actions take on a sinister cast. Following Refugio's brutal and potentially deadly beating, Hernandez fled her job, home, country, and family. Hernandez believed that if she had not fled, Refugio would have killed her. Unwilling to lose control over Hernandez, Refugio stalked her, convincing the very neighbor who helped Hernandez to escape to give him her phone number and calling her sister repeatedly until Hernandez finally agreed to speak with him. Once Refugio was able to speak with Hernandez, he emanated remorse, crying and telling Hernandez that he needed her. Refugio promised not to hurt Hernandez again, and told her that if she would go back to him he would seek counseling. Wounded both emotionally and physically by someone she trusted and loved, Hernandez was vulnerable to such promises. Moreover, Hernandez was well aware of Refugio's potential for violence. Behind Refugio's show of remorse, there also existed the lurking possibility that if Hernandez adamantly refused, Refugio might resort to the extreme violence or murder that commonly results when a woman attempts to flee her batterer. Refugio successfully manipulated Hernandez into leaving the safety that she had found and returning to a deadly relationship in which her physical and mental well-being were in danger.

2) Statutory Analysis of "Extreme Cruelty"

No court has yet interpreted the meaning of 8 U.S.C. § 1254(a)(3)'s reference to extreme cruelty. * * * The [INS] regulation states in relevant part:

> For the purpose of this chapter, the phrase "was battered by or was the subject of extreme cruelty" includes, but is not limited to, being the victim of any act or threatened act of violence, including any forceful detention, which results or threatens to result in physical or mental injury. Psychological or sexual abuse . . . shall be considered acts of violence. *Other abusive actions may also be acts of violence under certain circumstances, including acts that, in and of themselves, may not initially appear violent but that are a part of an overall pattern of violence.*

(emphasis added). * * * This interpretation is congruent with Congress's goal of protecting battered immigrant women and recognition of past governmental insensitivity regarding domestic violence, and consistent with the clinical understanding of domestic violence. * * *

Congress's intent in allowing a showing of either battery or extreme cruelty was to protect survivors of domestic violence. Under the INS's regulation, any act of physical abuse is deemed to constitute domestic violence without further inquiry, while "extreme cruelty" describes all other manifestations of domestic violence. Non-physical actions rise to the level of domestic violence when "tactics of control are intertwined with the threat of harm in order to maintain the perpetrator's dominance through fear." * * *

Here, there is no question that the relationship between Hernandez and Refugio was a violent one. Hernandez's interaction with Refugio in the United States clearly occurred within this context, an observation reaffirmed by the fact that domestic violence is not a phenomenon that appears only at brief isolated times, but instead pervades an entire relationship. Refugio's success in this "contrite" or "hearts and flowers" phase occurred because of Hernandez's emotional vulnerability, the strong emotional bond to Refugio necessitated by his violence, and the underlying threat that the failure to accede to his demands would bring renewed violence. Against this violent backdrop, Refugio's actions in tracking Hernandez down and luring her from the safety of the United States through false promises and short-lived contrition are precisely the type of acts of extreme cruelty that "may not initially appear violent but that are part of an overall pattern of violence." As a result, we hold that Hernandez has established that she was subjected to extreme cruelty in the United States.

[Editor's Note: This case was superseded by a statutory change as stated in Johnson v. A.G., *602 F3d 508 (3rd Cir. 2010), dealing with whether Federal Courts of Appeal have jurisdiction to review decisions by the Board of Immigration Appeals. The issue of what constitutes "extreme cruelty" in a domestic violence context is now seen as non-reviewable because the BIA's determination is discretionary. But since* Hernandez *is excerpted here to illustrate the model of the Cycle of Violence, it is still relevant.]*

EDWARD GONDOLF & ELLEN FISHER, THE SURVIVOR THEORY, BATTERED WOMEN AS SURVIVORS: AN ALTERNATIVE TO TREATING LEARNED HELPLESSNESS

11–18, 20–24 (Lexington Books, 1988)

Our assertion that battered women are active survivors raises a fundamental theoretical issue. It appears to contradict the prevailing characterization that battered women suffer from learned helplessness. According to learned helplessness, battered women tend to "give up" in the course of being abused; they suffer psychological paralysis and an underlying masochism that needs to be treated by specialized therapy. Our survivor hypothesis, on the other hand, suggests that women respond to abuse with help-seeking efforts that are largely unmet. What the women most need are the resources and social support that would enable them to become more independent and leave the batterer. (See table 2–1.)

In this chapter, we examine in more detail the theoretical basis for these two contrasting characterizations of battered women. First, the assumptions of learned helplessness are discussed. We consider also the experimental research underlying learned helplessness and its application to battered women. Second, we present the basis of a survivor theory with an overview of our survivor hypothesis, a summary of the supportive empirical research, and a redefinition of the symptoms of learned helplessness.

Finally, the implications of the alternative survivor theory are raised. There appears to be learned helplessness among the help sources designed to aid the battered women. The help sources need to be "treated," and the patriarchal assumptions that debilitate the available help sources need to be addressed.

LEARNED HELPLESSNESS

The Prevailing Characterization

The battered woman has been typically characterized as a helpless and passive victim. Lenore Walker's ground-breaking book, *The Battered Woman* (1979), noted that the battered woman becomes "psychologically paralyzed" as a result of learned helplessness. As animal experiments have demonstrated, there is a tendency to become submissive in the face of intermittent punishments or abuse. Similarly, the battered woman is immobilized amidst the uncertainty of when abuse will occur. She begins to feel that she has no control over her experience. No matter what she does, she "gets it." In the process, the victim begins to blame herself for the abuse. This self-blame implies some recourse or control over the otherwise unpredictable abuse. "If only I change myself, then the abuse will stop."

Lenore Walker (1979:49–50) summarizes the victimization this way:

> In applying the learned helplessness concept to battered women, the process of how the battered woman becomes victimized grows clearer. Repeated batterings, like electrical shocks (in animal experiments), diminish the woman's motivation to respond. She becomes passive. Secondly, her cognitive ability to perceive success is changed. She does not believe her response will result in a favorable outcome, whether or not it might. Next, having generalized her helplessness, the battered woman does not believe anything she does will alter any outcome, not just the specific situation that has occurred. she says "no matter what I do, I have

no influence." She cannot think of alternatives. She says, "I am incapable and too stupid to learn how to change things." Finally, her sense of emotional well-being becomes precarious. She is more prone to depression and anxiety.

Battered women, therefore, appear to need specialized counseling to address their debilitated psychological state. A number of clinical studies have, in fact, prescribed treatment for the battered woman's lack of self-esteem and fragmented identity, feelings of loss and inadequacy, or isolation and anxiety that is traced to abuse as a child. Feminist critics, however, have strongly objected to the implication that battered women provoke or prolong abuse and generally require psychological counseling.

Table 2-1

Learned Helplessness	Survivor Hypothesis
Severe abuse fosters a sense of helplessness in the victim. Abuse as a child and the neglect of help sources intensifies this helplessness. The battered woman is consequently severely victimized.	Severe abuse prompts innovative coping strategies from battered women and efforts to seek help. Previous abuse and neglect by help sources lead women to try other help sources and strategies to lessen the abuse. The battered woman, in this light, is a "survivor."
The victim experiences low self-esteem, self-blame, guilt, and depression. The only way to feel some sense of control over what is otherwise an unpredictable environment is to think that "if I change my ways, things will get better." But the abuse continues.	The survivor may experience anxiety or uncertainty over the prospects of leaving the batterer. The lack of options, know-how, and finances raise fears about trying to escape the batterer. The battered woman may therefore attempt to change the batterer instead of attempting to leave.
The victim eventually becomes psychologically paralyzed. She fails to seek help for herself and may even appear passive before the beatings. When she does contact a help source she is very tentative about receiving help and is likely to return to the batterer despite advice or opportunity to leave.	The survivor actively seeks help from a variety of informal and formal help sources. There is most often inadequate or piecemeal helpgiving that leaves the woman little alternative but to return to the batterer. The helpseeking continues, however.
This vulnerability and indecisiveness prolongs the violence and may contribute to its intensification. Some observers argue that this tendency may reflect an underlying masochism in the battered woman. The woman may feel that she deserves to be beaten and accepts it as a fulfillment of her expectations.	The failure of help sources to intervene in a comprehensive and decisive fashion allows abuse to continue and escalate. The inadequacy of help sources may be attributed to a kind of learned helplessness experienced in many community services. Service providers feel too overwhelmed and limited in their resources to be effective and therefore do not try as hard as they might.
Battered women as victims need primarily psychological counseling to treat their low self esteem, depression, and masochism. Cognitive therapy that addresses attributions of blame for the abuse may also be particularly effective in motivating the victim.	Battered women as survivors of abuse need, most of all, access to resources that would enable them to escape the batterer. Community services need to be coordinated to assure the needed allocation of resources and integrated to assure long-term comprehensive intervention.

* * *

Explanations of Battered Women

It is not surprising, then, that the notion of learned helplessness has become a fixture in the domestic violence field as well. Battered women, as the theory goes, typically are conditioned to tolerate the abuse as a result of persistent and intermittent reinforcement from the batterer. The community lack of response to the abuse, and frequent accusation that the woman contributed to the abuse, further the helplessness. The cage door is shut, so to speak, and the women have no apparent way out.

Additionally, studies have suggested that learned helplessness may be rooted in childhood exposure to violence. Exposure to violence as a child may, in fact, predispose a woman to an abusive relationship as an adult. She may grow up thinking that abuse is normal, or feel such shame and rejection that she expects and accepts the worst. The relationship between abuse as a child and as an adult may, however, be spurious or inevitable given the amount of violence in and around our homes. Perhaps a more acceptable position is that the batterers appear to be "violence prone," and not battered women.

Another popular explanation for what appears as learned helplessness is the "brainwashing" that a woman experiences in an abusive relationship as an adult. The batterer's manipulation and control of the woman has, in fact, been likened to the tactics used by brainwashers in prisoner-of-war camps. Eventually the captive is psychologically broken down to the point of relinquishing any sense of autonomy and complying to all the wishes of the captor.

Psychologists Donald Dutton and Susan Painter have similarly applied the theory of "traumatic bonding" to battered women. They point out that the abuse leaves the victim emotionally and physically drained and in desperate need of some human support or care. She is therefore likely to respond to the batterer's apologies and affection after the abuse. In this vulnerable state, she may sympathize and overidentify with the batterer, much as some prisoners of war or concentration camps have become sympathetic toward their guards. In essence, the trauma makes the woman prone to a kind of masochism.

Helplessness as Masochism

Although the initial application of learned helplessness to battered women was not intended to implicate masochism, it has been explicitly extended to do so. * * *

In Dr. Natalie Shainess's conception, however, masochism is learned developmentally and culturally, rather than predestined as the Freudians suggest. This may in part be related to growing up in abusive homes and thinking, as a result, that abuse is normal, or to internalizing the persistent subjugation and degradation of women in society at large. The masochism can be unlearned, therefore, by being more assertive and decisive in interpersonal relations. The popularity of books like *Women Who Love Too Much* appears to speak to this notion that women make themselves vulnerable and dependent and can solve this problem by simply being more assertive.

Reformulations of Helplessness

The learned helplessness theory has admittedly been critiqued and reformulated in recent years. Its earlier versions reflected the assumptions of behaviorist conditioning. Like the animals in Seligman's experiments, humans appeared to be "trained" into submission and learned helplessness. Their situation appeared to determine their behavior. In sum, learned helplessness was a conditioned reaction to the unpredictable punishments one received.

The advent of cognitive psychology has introduced the role of individual expectations and attributions in mediating learned helplessness. In this view, one's perceptions of the environment are what most influence one's reaction to it. If an individual perceives a series of punishments or failures as outside of his or her control, then learned helplessness is more likely.

Similarly, several qualitative studies of battered women have shown that their assumptions about their social environment contribute to their reactions to abuse. However, rather than confirm learned helplessness, these studies actually open the door to alternative explanations. The women, rather than being passive recipients of the violence, appear instead as participants in the definition of the relationship and of themselves. If anything, the battered women learn, as the abuse escalates, that the self-blame associated with learned helplessness is inappropriate.

Interviews with self-identified battered women show that the women are more likely to blame themselves for the abuse after the first incident. Consequently they may attempt to change their behavior to please their batterers and avoid further abuse. As is usually the case, the violence recurs and escalates despite the women's efforts to please their batterers. They begin, therefore, to increasingly blame the batterer (that is, attribute the cause to him) and seek ways to change him. When these fail, the women then seek more decisive intervention and means to establish their own safety.

There is some suggestion, however, that there is a limit to this initiative. After repeated unsuccessful attempts to control the battering, some women may then begin to give up and lessen their helpseeking. This resignation, after an intermediate phase of active helpseeking, differs from the conventional notion of learned helplessness in which there is a progression toward total brainwashing. (See table 2–2 for a summary of this attributional helpseeking progression.)

Another interview study, with a small sample of shelter residents, suggests that the women experience a loss of self; for example, they mention feeling like a zombie, a robot, or simply numb amidst the violence. They begin to lose their "observing self" as well, in that they doubt and question their judgment and interpretation of events. However, the battered women continue to have "insights" about their relationship and their batterers' definition of the situation. They occasionally act on these insights by seeking verification of or response to them. The women also creatively and valiantly develop coping strategies intended to reduce the severity of the abuse. Eventually, with sufficient confirmation of the insights, they begin to define themselves as "survivors,"—as individuals who are aware of their strength in enduring the abuse. They muster self-respect for that endurance and attempt to improve their situation.

This shift in perception begins to occur after any one of a variety of catalysts: a change in the level of violence, a change in resources, a change in the relationship, severe despair, a change in the visibility of violence, and external interventions that redefine the relationship. Any of these prompt a rejection of the previous rationalizations or denials of abuse, according to a qualitative study by Kathleen Ferraro and John Johnson.

Not only are the women's perceptions seen as basic to their reaction, these perceptions also evolve and change. In fact, the tentative findings suggest that battered women are rational in their response. They hold to societal conceptions of their duty in a relationship until that conception is no longer plausible. The catalysts for change are not "treatment" of the symptoms of learned helplessness but rather a change in situational evidence or events that necessitates an adjustment in one's perceptions and attribution. As has been argued about other oppressed or victimized people, the women's "grievance" has to be confirmed and resources made available in order for them to become "mobilized." * * *

TOWARD A SURVIVOR THEORY

The Survivor Hypothesis

The alternative characterization of battered women is that they are active survivors rather than helpless victims. As suggested above, battered women remain in abusive situations not because they have been passive but because they have tried to escape with no avail. We offer, therefore, a survivor hypothesis that contradicts the assumptions of learned helplessness: Battered women increase their helpseeking in the face of increased violence, rather than decrease helpseeking as learned helplessness would suggest. More specifically, we contend that helpseeking is likely to increase as wife abuse, child abuse, and the batterer's antisocial behavior (substance abuse, general violence, and arrests) increase. This helpseeking may be mediated, as current research suggests, by the resources available to the woman, her commitment to the relationship, the number of children she has, and the kinds of abuse she may have experienced as a child.

The fundamental assumption is, however, that woman seek assistance in proportion to the realization that they and their children are more and more in danger. They are attempting, in a very logical fashion, to assure themselves and their children protection and therefore survival. Their effort to survive transcends even fearsome danger, depression or guilt, and economic constraints. It supersedes the "giving up and giving in" which occurs according to learned helplessness. In this effort to survive, battered women are, in fact, heroically assertive and persistent.

Empirical Research

There are at least a few empirical studies that substantiate this hypothesis that battered women are survivors. The studies by Lee Bowker (1983), Mildred Pagelow (1981), and Lenore Walker (1984) indicate quantitatively that the helpseeking efforts of battered women are substantial.

Perhaps the most significant of these empirical works is Walker's *The Battered Women's Syndrome* (1984), designed to verify the author's original learned helplessness and "cycle of violence" theorization. Walker found, however, that the women in her Rocky Mountain sample were not necessarily beaten into submissiveness; rather, helpseeking increased as the positive reinforcements within the relationship decreased and the costs of the relationship in terms of abusiveness and injury increased. * * *

Redefining the Symptoms

This is not to deny the observations of shelter workers that some battered women do experience severe low self-esteem, guilt, self-blame, depression, vulnerability, and futility—all of which are identified with learned helplessness. Some battered women may even appear to act carelessly and provocatively at times, as the proponents of masochism argue. But cast in another light, these "symptoms" take on a different meaning, as well as a different proportion.

The so-called symptoms of learned helplessness may in fact be part of the adjustment to active helpseeking. They may represent traumatic shock from the abuse, a sense of commitment to the batterer, or separation anxiety amidst an unresponsive community. All of these are quite natural and healthy responses but not entirely acceptable ones in a patriarchal (or male-dominated) society that values cool detachment. Not to respond with some doubts, anxiety, or depression would suggest emotional superficiality and denial of the real difficulties faced in helpseeking.* * *

TREATING THE HELPERS

Helplessness Among Helpers

In sum, many battered women make contact with a variety of helping sources in response to their abuse. As the abuse becomes more severe and the batterer more apparently beyond change, the diversity of the woman's contacts actually increases. We argue that this represents a survivor tendency of strength and resiliency. Depression, guilt, and shame may accompany a battered woman, but these should not be used to characterize battered women in general or to label them as victims of learned helplessness.

The prevailing notion of learned helplessness may, in fact, be misleading. Learned helplessness suggests that it is the woman who needs to be diagnosed and treated. Admittedly, some women do need tremendous emotional support and mental health care in the wake of devastating abuse. However, we believe that there is a more important side to consider: the insufficient response of community help sources.

If learned helplessness is a valid conception, it is ironically prevalent in the system of helping sources. It is more likely that agency personnel suffer from insufficient resources, options, or authority to make a difference, and therefore are reluctant to take decisive action. Too often, community services respond singularly to a problem rather than in some coordinated and mutually reinforcing fashion. This too cannot help but cause a sense of diffusion and duplication. There remains, furthermore, a reductionism that would treat abuse as a symptom of some other disorder or accident. In fact, emergency room staff have been accused of "cooling out" the abused woman with tranquilizer medications that actually reduce the woman's ability to respond effectively to her abuse.

It is our community systems of care and intervention that need treatment. Granted, the battered woman's contact with the clergy, human services, police, and legal assistance may at times be tentative. But the women meet an equally tentative response from the helpers. Malpractice suits, no-risk clauses, privatization of services, severe funding cutbacks, and a laissez-faire public attitude have brought reluctance rather than initiative to the helping professions.

Certainly more than new community programs are needed to counteract the impact of this state of affairs. Many of the social problems we face today—pockets of severe unemployment, generations of poverty among minority groups, increased immigration and opposing discrimination—require governmental leadership, if not activism, and perhaps some personal intrusions. * * *

SHANE M. TRAWICK, BIRTH CONTROL SABOTAGE AS DOMESTIC VIOLENCE: A LEGAL RESPONSE

100 Ca. L. Rev. 721 (2012)
(citations and footnotes omitted)

INTRODUCTION

Birth control sabotage is a tactic of domestic violence when an intimate partner ignores the reproductive preferences of his or her partner by tampering with contraception or using coercion to induce pregnancy. Given the disturbing prevalence of birth control sabotage, I hope to use this Comment as a medium to discuss the legal remedies currently and potentially available to victims of birth control sabotage. An investigation of birth control sabotage is not just an exercise in intellectual excess. Birth control sabotage impacts the lives of women in myriad ways—ways that merit exploration and deserve our compassion. While the following narratives may not capture the full range of birth control sabotage experienced in relationships involving domestic violence, they do illustrate some of the emotional and physical distress a woman may suffer as a result of birth control sabotage.

The story of "Janey" involves multiple forms of reproductive coercion by an abusive male partner who hoped to prevent Janey from ever leaving the relationship. Janey was nineteen when she began a relationship with a "romantic" man in his mid-twenties. She acknowledges that there was abuse very early on in the relationship; however, at first the abuse was not physical. Instead, her partner lied about practically everything, including his fidelity. When Janey confronted him about his lies, he forced himself upon her sexually, refused to use a condom, and considered her suggestion of condom usage as a personal attack. In time, Janey became pregnant with his baby—a baby she did not want in the first place—and ultimately decided to carry the baby to term. Unsurprisingly, she was diagnosed on several occasions with sexually transmitted infections (STIs), despite having only one sexual partner.

Eventually, Janey became pregnant a second time by the same abusive partner. He had promised he would "pull out," but on multiple occasions, intentionally did not. Though the sabotage of Janey's reproductive preferences often brought her to tears, her partner merely laughed at her devastation and called her "crazy." Believing another baby would keep her in his life permanently, he refused to pay for an abortion, despite her inability to pay for one herself. Janey eventually obtained a protection order after her abuser broke into her home. Notwithstanding her abuse, Janey now leads a successful life.

"Carollee" is another survivor of domestic abuse who was also subjected to birth control sabotage. At the age of nineteen, Carollee began a sexual relationship with a thirty-two-year-old man. When her birth control pills began to disappear, she confronted him, only to be told that he "knew she wanted to have his child." Carollee also noticed that her partner had been piercing the condoms they were using, but she did not address it. When she became pregnant with his child, he became more controlling—demanding to know where she was at all times and inspecting her clothing when she went out. When she went to Planned Parenthood for an abortion, he quickly found her, dragged her home, and threatened to kill her if she went through with the procedure. Like Janey's abuser, Carollee's aggressor likely did not want her to terminate the one permanent tie he could force upon her. Since then, her partner has been in and out of prison multiple times and is currently serving a sentence for attempting to detonate a bomb in a crowded building.

It is important to note that birth control sabotage is not limited to women of a particular class. Rather, experiences of birth control sabotage impact an array of women along the economic and educational spectrum. The story of "Sandi" provides an apt example. Sandi was a model Ph.D. student on scholarship at a prestigious university. The early part of Sandi's relationship with her partner seemed perfect, but it all changed when they began having sex. Her partner would remove the condom just before ejaculation and insist that the condom had slipped or broken. When Sandi grew concerned about the possibility of an unplanned pregnancy, she obtained emergency contraception. In response, her partner "became absolutely livid." He accused her of being a whore, spat in her face, and attempted to hit her. In fury, he forced Sandi into a car, drove her two hours from her dorm, and dropped her off without any form of return transportation.

These stories exhibit the host of ways in which birth control sabotage can impact the lives of women. Importantly, they also suggest one uniform message: the sabotage of contraception is a form of domestic violence that is detrimental to female autonomy. The consequences of sabotage and violence not only impact the survivor's dignity, but also deteriorate her mental and physical health, financial position, and long-term stability. Even further, they impact the lives of the people close to the survivor, including the children either miscarried, aborted, or born to women who did not want them.

This Comment is a vital step in devising legal remedies for women like Janey, Carolee, and Sandi. Recent scholarship has failed to recognize the important intersection of birth control sabotage and domestic violence even though birth control sabotage occurs at a significantly higher rate in violent intimate partner relationships than in other relationships. The increasingly apparent relationship between birth control sabotage and violence demonstrates the imminent need to reevaluate how sabotage may fit into existing family law and domestic violence civil liability schemes;

this correlation also underscores the importance of criminalizing sabotage as a deterrent to other ongoing violence.

Part I of this Comment is a general discussion of the current contraception usage rates in the United States as well as a brief explanation of current national attitudes about contraceptives. Further, Part I presents a discussion of the birth control sabotage phenomenon—what it is, how it occurs, how often it happens, and why women are subjected to it. Part II discusses the remedies potentially available to survivors of birth control sabotage under current tort and domestic violence law. Specifically, I question whether a woman who experiences an unwanted pregnancy through her partner's sabotage of her contraceptive device or plan of withdrawal may claim damages from his fraudulent misrepresentation of "protected sex." I argue that new studies bringing sabotage under the umbrella of domestic violence should be sufficient to permit a fraudulent misrepresentation claim with punitive damages awarded to a survivor in the form of pregnancy-related costs and increased child support awards.

Part III proposes the criminalization of birth control sabotage. In light of the recent studies showing the relationship between sabotage and violence, criminalizing birth control sabotage is an important step in preventing further violence to a survivor and her family. I examine a 2010 Canadian case holding that fraudulent destruction of a contraceptive device is an offense under modern Canadian sexual assault statutes. I query whether this model could be harmoniously integrated into U.S. law and conclude that a wiser solution would be independent legislation to make birth control sabotage a separate criminal offense.

Part IV considers counterarguments and concerns related to the evidentiary hurdles and potential for fraud raised by allowing civil and criminal liability for birth control sabotage. I reason that pre-existing police procedure in domestic violence and sexual assault cases coupled with recent trends regarding rules of evidence should help allay any concerns about evidentiary difficulty or fraud. * * *

CONCLUSION

The high rate of birth control sabotage, documented by recent studies, has elicited concern in the domestic violence and reproductive rights advocacy communities. Despite identification of the emerging problem, no scholarship has recommended tort or criminal remedies for women subjected to this form of reproductive abuse. This Comment takes that initiative. Adoption of compensatory and punitive tort damages for abusers who intentionally misrepresent contraceptive usage to induce a pregnancy is an important legal tool to put female survivors of violence in control of their reproductive lives. Recognizing birth control sabotage as a form of domestic violence puts the tort claim beyond traditional rationales for rejecting wrongful pregnancy claims. Additionally, criminalization of contraceptive sabotage as an independent crime is another important remedy that legislatures should consider in order to effectively address the growing problem of birth control sabotage and domestic violence. An independent crime of sabotage is essential in curtailing domestic violence. A thoughtful reconsideration of the civil and criminal approach to birth control sabotage can better protect survivors and move our country closer to eradicating domestic violence.

THE HUMAN TRAFFICKING LEGAL CENTER, HUMAN TRAFFICKING AND DOMESTIC VIOLENCE

htlegalcenter.org (2018)
(footnotes omitted)

FACT SHEET

Advocates have long pointed to links between domestic violence and human trafficking. The federal government also has acknowledged the link between these two crimes, recognizing that cases that initially appear to be domestic violence may mask sex or labor trafficking. Understanding the connections between human trafficking and domestic violence is key to identifying appropriate criminal, civil, and immigration remedies. This Fact Sheet provides examples in each context, highlighting cases in which courts and administrative bodies recognized the nexus between human trafficking and domestic violence.

The Department of Justice's Human Trafficking Task Force eGuide expressly lists domestic violence as a crime that may overlap with human trafficking. A recent Government Accountability Office (GAO) publication revealed that 12 of 27 tribal law enforcement agencies reported identifying domestic violence in their human trafficking investigations. Decisions by the Administrative Appeals Office (AAO) of the Department of Homeland Security on T-visas similarly reflect this linkage. In a 2011 AAO decision, an applicant for a T-visa alleged that her husband forced her into prostitution in the United States, threatening to tell her children if she did not engage in forced commercial sex. And a recent AAO decision stated, "[t]he Applicant correctly notes on appeal that a personal relationship involving domestic violence may qualify as human trafficking in some cases, and that forced sex may qualify as a type of involuntary servitude."

It is not uncommon in federal trafficking prosecutions for the trafficker to be the husband, boyfriend, or romantic partner of the victim. The fact that a trafficker is married to—or in an intimate relationship with—his victim does not vitiate the trafficking crime. And while the most widely understood domestic violence-human trafficking scenario involves perpetrators holding their domestic partners in forced prostitution, advocates also should look for forced labor in intimate-partner cases.

Forced non-commercial sex may qualify as involuntary servitude, even in the context of an intimate- partner relationship. And intimate partners also may hold wives and girlfriends in forced labor.

Domestic Violence and Sex Trafficking

In some instances, a marriage or intimate relationship may be a fraud instigated by the trafficker from the start. This fact pattern is particularly common in sex trafficking cases, in which young victims are lured into marriages or romantic relationships only to be exploited by their partners through forced prostitution. . . [gives examples of young women brought from outside the U.S. by U.S. citizens].

Domestically, traffickers use the same tactics on U.S. citizen victims. Boyfriends, husbands, and romantic partners have forced their U.S. citizen victims into commercial sex:. . . [includes child pornography where victim was a minor].

Domestic Violence and Forced Labor

Traffickers also have used the promise of a relationship or marriage to obtain forced labor. . . [gives examples of forced domestic servitude in defendant's home and being forced to work without pay in the defendant's business.].

It is not always the case that the relationship between a trafficking victim and trafficker is a fraud at its inception. Trafficking victims often have complex relationships with their traffickers. A bona fide marriage or relationship may devolve into a situation of human trafficking. . .

[gives example: violation of Trafficking Victims Protection Reauthorization Act supported tort claim by Russian wife brought to US, forced to perform heavy manual labor, her teen daughter was sexually abused by husband and his son.]

Domestic Violence and Human Trafficking
Involving Other Family Members

Human trafficking can occur alongside domestic violence, particularly when other family members direct the forced labor. Traffickers may use the victim's fear of retaliation by her community or extended family as a form of coercion. . .

Family-controlled human trafficking may also include identity theft, tax fraud, and the filing of false tax returns. These fraudulent tax returns can result in IRS enforcement actions against the trafficking victims even years after they escape. Trafficker-perpetrated tax fraud is a risk for all trafficking victims, but the risk is particularly pronounced in situations of domestic violence and family-controlled trafficking.

Conclusion

As these cases illustrate, victims of domestic violence may also be victims of sex trafficking and/ or labor trafficking. Growing recognition of the connection between domestic violence and human trafficking will enable survivors to achieve justice and immigration relief.

[Editor's Note: Tennessee Statute 62–4–110, effective 7/1/22, requires anyone applying for a license to be a cosmetologist, aesthetician, natural hair stylist, manicurist, or teacher of these must first complete an hour of free training by a recognized DV organization on how to recognize the signs of domestic violence, how to respond to these signs, and how to refer a client to resources.

Illinois and Arkansas enacted similar legislation in 2017, and California did so in 2018. Signs of potential domestic violence highlighted in some of the trainings include physical injuries, self-blame, sudden lifestyle changes, and irregular appointments. The Professional Beauty Association adopted a voluntary program called Cut It Out in 2003 designed to teach hair stylists and cosmetologists to recognize signs of domestic violence and give phone numbers for resources.]

STATE V. ABDI-ISSA

504 P3d 223 (WA, 2022)
(footnotes and citations omitted)

(Note: This opinion contains facts which
may be upsetting to the reader.)

Under Washington law, some crimes may be designated crimes of domestic violence. A domestic violence designation makes additional protections available for victims. We are asked whether the trial court correctly concluded that animal cruelty may be such a crime. We are also asked whether the trial court properly instructed the jury that it could find this crime had a destructive and foreseeable impact on persons other than the victim. We affirm the trial court on both issues.

BACKGROUND

Julie Fairbanks began dating Charmarke Abdi-Issa shortly after she moved to Seattle with her dog, Mona. Mona was a small Chihuahua and Dachshund mix. Fairbanks testified she was close to Mona. Abdi-Issa, however, had a history of disliking Mona. Abdi-Issa was abusive toward Fairbanks and Mona, even threatening to kill them both.

One evening, while they were out in Seattle's International District, Abdi-Issa insisted Fairbanks let him take Mona on a walk. Fairbanks objected, but Abdi-Issa ignored her and left with Mona. Fairbanks felt powerless, claiming, "[I]t didn't matter[; if] he wanted to [take her on a walk,] he was going to do it either way."

Not long after he left, Abdi-Issa called Fairbanks, claiming that Mona had gotten out of her harness and that he could not find her. Fairbanks did not believe him, as Mona had never gotten out of her harness before. Abdi-Issa refused to tell her more. Fairbanks began to panic after she heard Mona yelping over the phone.

Around that same time, Melissa Ludin and William Moe heard a sound of great distress. They followed the sound and saw Abdi-Issa beating and making "brutal stabbing" motions toward Mona. They saw Abdi-Issa kick Mona so hard that she went up into the air and "flew into the bushes." Each time Mona was struck she made a "screeching[,] screaming[,] pained[,] awful sound" that was at last followed by silence.

While Ludin called the police, Moe yelled at Abdi-Issa to stop hitting Mona. Abdi-Issa turned toward Moe and yelled, "[D]o you want to get some?" When Moe once again told Abdi-Issa to stop, Abdi-Issa walked away.

Seattle Police Officers Young Lim and Kyle Corcoran responded to Ludin's call. While Lim talked to Abdi-Issa, Corcoran went to find Mona. With Ludin's help, Corcoran found Mona, still alive, underneath a bush. Officers transported Mona to an emergency veterinary clinic.

Ludin testified she was very upset by the incident. When the police arrived Ludin was in distress, "[h]yperventilating and having a panic attack." Ludin cried as she explained to the officers what she saw and where she had last seen Mona. Ludin suffered a severe panic attack that night and continued to experience flashbacks in the following week.

Meanwhile, Fairbanks was frantically searching for Mona. During her search, she ran into Lim and Corcoran, who realized that Fairbanks was Mona's owner. The officers directed Fairbanks to the veterinary clinic.

Mona arrived at the clinic nearly comatose, with severe swelling in her brain, bruising on her chest, and a wound to the top of her head. By the time Fairbanks arrived at the veterinary clinic Mona had died. A necropsy found that Mona had died from multiple instances of blunt force trauma.

The State charged Abdi-Issa with first degree animal cruelty under RCW 16.52.205 and sought a domestic violence designation under RCW 10.99.020 and RCW 9A.36.041(4). The State also charged two sentencing aggravators: (1) that the crime had a destructive and foreseeable impact on persons other than the victim under RCW 9.94A.535(3)(r) and (2) that Abdi-Issa's conduct during the crime of domestic violence manifested deliberate cruelty or intimidation of the victim, RCW 9.94A.635(3)(h)(iii). Abdi-Issa unsuccessfully moved to dismiss the domestic violence designation and aggravators multiple times.

The jury found Abdi-Issa guilty of animal cruelty. The jury also found that Abdi-Issa and Fairbanks were in a domestic relationship prior to the crime, which allowed for a domestic violence designation. The jury returned mixed verdicts on the sentencing aggravators, finding that the crime involved a destructive and foreseeable impact on persons other than the victim, but they did not find that it manifested deliberate cruelty or intimidation of the victim.

The court imposed the maximum 12-month sentence for the crime of animal cruelty, and an additional 6 months for the aggravator, sentencing Abdi-Issa to an 18-month exceptional sentence. Based on the domestic violence designation, the court also imposed a no-contact order prohibiting Abdi-Issa from having contact with Fairbanks.

The Court of Appeals vacated the domestic violence designation, the no-contact order, and the impact on others sentencing aggravator. We granted review.

ANALYSIS

The questions before us are questions of statutory interpretation that we review de novo. When interpreting statutes, our goal is to determine and carry out the intent of the legislature. Statutory interpretation begins with an examination of the statute's plain language. "In discerning the plain meaning of a provision, we consider the entire statute in which the provision is found, as well as related statutes or other provisions in the same act that disclose legislative intent." If the words of a statute are clear, we end our inquiry. If not, we may consult other tools of statutory construction, such as legislative history.

1. Animal Cruelty as a Crime of Domestic Violence

First, we must decide whether animal cruelty may be designated a crime of domestic violence. We conclude that it may. The Washington Legislature passed the domestic violence act "to recognize the importance of domestic violence as a serious crime against society and to assure the victim of domestic violence the maximum protection from abuse which the law and those who enforce the law can provide." The domestic violence act allows certain crimes committed against an intimate partner to receive a domestic violence designation. Cases with domestic violence designations are given priority scheduling and courts may issue pretrial no-contact orders. At sentencing, courts may also "impose specialized no-contact orders, violation of which constitutes a separate crime."

The domestic violence act does not create new crimes, it simply emphasizes the need to enforce existing criminal statutes in such a way that victims of domestic violence are protected. Designating a crime as one of domestic violence " 'does not itself alter the elements of the underlying offense[,] rather, it signals [to] the court that the law is to be equitably and vigorously enforced.' " Further, a domestic violence designation itself does not increase a defendant's punishment.

To determine what crimes are eligible for a domestic violence designation, we first look to the domestic violence statute. The relevant portion reads:

> "Domestic violence" *includes but is not limited to* any of the following crimes when committed either by (a) one family or household member against another family or household member, or (b) one intimate partner against another intimate partner: [assault, drive-by shooting, reckless endangerment, coercion, burglary, trespass, malicious mischief, kidnapping, and unlawful imprisonment].

RCW 10.99.020(4) (emphasis added). Abdi-Issa is correct that animal cruelty is not listed in RCW 10.99.020. But the list of crimes is explicitly nonexclusive. Animal cruelty is sufficiently similar to the enumerated crimes that the trial court did not err in asking the jury whether, under these facts, it was a crime of domestic violence.

Abdi-Issa argues that animal cruelty is not sufficiently similar to the types of crimes listed in RCW 10.99.020 to be designated a crime of domestic violence because it does not involve a human victim. But many of the enumerated crimes, including burglary and malicious mischief, are against a victim's property. Pets, as a matter of law, are considered personal property. Here, Fairbanks was directly harmed as a result of Abdi-Issa's violent killing of her beloved pet and companion. She is plainly a victim of Abdi-Issa's crime.

Abdi-Issa contends that the prosecutors erred in charging animal cruelty instead of malicious mischief, where ownership is a clear element of the crime. But nothing required the prosecution to charge the lesser crime of malicious mischief.

Abdi-Issa also asserts that as a matter of law, animal cruelty is not a domestic violence offense because the victim of that offense is an animal, not a person. Abdi-Issa starts with the definition of family or household members, which includes " 'persons sixteen years of age or older with whom a person sixteen years of age or older has or has had a dating relationship.' " He notes that chapter 10.99 RCW states that a victim of domestic violence is "a family or household member who has been subjected to domestic violence." Abdi-Issa then concludes that the victim of domestic violence, for the purposes of RCW 10.99.020(4), is the victim of *a crime* of domestic violence and as a result, the offense of animal cruelty is not a crime of domestic violence.

This highly technical reading of the statutes ignores the plain language of the Sentencing Reform Act of 1981 (SRA), ch. 9.94A RCW, and

RCW 10.99.020(4). The general definition of "victim" under the SRA is "any person who has sustained emotional, psychological, physical, or financial injury to person or property as a direct result of the crime charged." The definition of "victim" under the SRA includes Fairbanks because she sustained an injury as a direct result of the crime charged.

This conclusion is consistent with the SRA's definition of a "victim of domestic violence":

> [A]n intimate partner or household member who has been subjected to the infliction of physical harm or sexual and psychological abuse by an intimate partner or household member as part of a pattern of assaultive, coercive, and controlling behaviors directed at achieving compliance from or control over that intimate partner or household member. Domestic violence includes, but is not limited to, the offenses listed in RCW 10.99.020 and * * * 26.50.010 committed by an intimate partner or household member against a victim who is an intimate partner or household member.

RCW 9.94A.030(55). Fairbanks' testimony suggests psychological abuse, which was a part of a larger pattern of assaultive, coercive, and controlling behavior, occurred. The SRA's broad definition of victim applies to any crime sentenced under the SRA, including animal cruelty. Fairbanks is a victim under the definitions set forth by the legislature. Under the plain language of RCW 10.99.020(4) and related statutes, animal cruelty may be designated a crime of domestic violence.

This conclusion is consistent with the legislature's categorization of domestic violence as a serious crime against society and its intent to ensure that victims have the maximum protection from abuse that the law can provide. In 2009, the legislature recognized that "considerable research shows a strong correlation between animal abuse, child abuse, and domestic violence." "The legislature intends that perpetrators of domestic violence not be allowed to further terrorize and manipulate their victims, or the children of their victims, by using the threat of violence toward pets." This shows that our legislature recognized the relationship between animal abuse and domestic violence.

This recognition is amply supported by research into domestic violence. Animal abuse is an indicator of domestic abuse in a relationship. Further, 50 percent of children living in homes with domestic violence report that the abuser threatened to harm or kill a pet, a mechanism domestic violence perpetrators use to maintain control over their victims.

Accordingly, we hold that the jury was properly instructed that it could find animal abuse was a crime of domestic violence. Thus, the trial court had the authority to enter a postconviction no-contact order under RCW 10.99.050.

[The Court also holds that it was proper to impose a longer sentence because the crime had an impact on Fairbanks, not just on Ludin, the human victim of the crime. Fairbanks testified that she had panic attacks, flashbacks, and trouble sleeping after witnessing this crime.]. . .

[Editor's Notes: 1. In People v. Kovacich, *201 CA App 4th 863 (2011), the defendant kicked the family dog in front of the wife and children so severely that the dog died at the veterinary clinic. The defendant was convicted of first-degree murder of the wife more than 26 years after she disappeared. Evidence regarding his animal abuse was correctly admitted as abuse against the wife and children. Since it fit the definition of abuse in CA Family Code §§ 6203 and 6211, it was admissible as propensity evidence under CA Evid Code § 1109.*

2. Because animal abuse is so prevalent in domestic violence cases, it is important to have safe places for pets or large animals like horses to stay when survivors of abuse go to domestic violence shelters, either at the shelter or nearby. And statutes should provide that animals can be included in domestic violence restraining orders.]

NETWORK FOR VICTIM RECOVERY OF D.C., NATIONAL CRIME VICTIM LAW INSTITUTE, PROJECT SAFEGUARD, NATIONAL FAMILY VIOLENCE LAW CENTER AT GEORGE WASHINGTON LAW SCHOOL, LESLIE MORGAN STEINER, AND BONNIE CARLSON, AMICUS BRIEF, *SHARKEY V. PETROCCO,* CO. CT. OF APP., FILED 12/27/22, 2023 WL 3794007

(cert. denied by Colorado Supreme Court (1/22/24) 2024 WL 289843)
(footnotes and citations omitted)

INTRODUCTION

On July 1, 2019 [Colorado] Governor Jared Polis signed into law HB–19–1324 entitled, "Strategic Lawsuits Against Public Participation—Concerning Motions to Dismiss Certain Civil Actions Involving Constitutional Rights." In passing the law, the General Assembly found that "it is in the public interest to encourage continued participation in matters of public significance and that this participation should not be chilled through abuse of the judicial process." C.R.S. § 13–20–1101(1)(a) (referred to hereinafter as the "anti-SLAPP statute"). [Strategic Lawsuits Against Public Participation.] The anti-SLAPP statute protects citizens who participate in public speech by allowing them to file a special motion to dismiss if sued for that conduct. If the plaintiff does not establish that their claim is reasonably likely to succeed, the motion must be granted.

All too often, abusers bring vexatious lawsuits against domestic violence survivors or their advocates to chill their free speech. Abusers may even use frivolous legal proceedings to threaten and silence "anyone who helps the survivor, including friends, family, advocates, lawyers, and law enforcement officials." Such tactics are recognized as an "effective way to isolate a survivor from support networks."

This case is the type that the Colorado legislature intended the anti-SLAPP statute address. Moira Sharkey ("Sharkey") is a public advocate against domestic violence. In 2020, she published Facebook posts discussing domestic violence and its devastating impact. Some of Sharkey's posts referenced David Petrocco ("Petrocco"), the former husband of Sharkey's deceased sister, while discussing her views on the domestic violence her sister suffered and the role that abuse played in her sister's death. In an effort to silence Sharkey and retaliate against her for her public comments about the dangers and consequences of domestic violence, Petrocco, a member of a wealthy family with extensive financial resources, sued Sharkey for defamation and "extreme and outrageous conduct," arguing that three statements made by Sharkey which allegedly accused Petrocco of killing his late wife were not entitled to Anti-SLAPP protection.

While the district court correctly recognized that Sharkey's statements discussing domestic violence constituted protected activity under the anti-SLAPP statute, the district court improperly concluded that Petrocco had carried his burden of demonstrating that he would likely prevail on his claims. In so doing, the district court failed to follow the procedure required under the statute and denied Sharkey's motion on grounds that, if upheld, would render the anti-SLAPP statute a worthless tool against the types of abusive litigation brought against domestic violence survivors and their advocates.

Because Colorado's anti-SLAPP statute was only recently enacted, this Court has had few occasions to examine and interpret it. It is therefore critical that the Court of Appeals provide clear guidance on how to interpret the statute so that it fulfills its purpose—protecting speech—and shields survivors of domestic violence and their advocates from abusive litigation.

ARGUMENT

Colorado's Anti-SLAPP Statute Protects Domestic Violence Survivors and Their Advocates from Abusive Lawsuits.

In resolving Sharkey's appeal, the Court should consider the Colorado legislature's objectives when designing the anti-SLAPP statute. At their core, anti-SLAPP statutes remedy a power imbalance, one where the threat of frightening and costly litigation is used as a cudgel to chill protected speech through harassment and intimidation. And while such misuse of the judicial process can arise in many contexts, few better illustrate the harm that the anti-SLAPP statute is meant to remedy than abusers who use litigation to threaten and silence domestic violence survivors or their advocates.

A. Vexatious Lawsuits and Threats of Litigation Are Frequently Used to Silence Individuals and Deter Public Participation

In passing the anti-SLAPP statute, the Colorado General Assembly sought to "encourage and safeguard the constitutional rights of persons to petition, speak freely, associate freely, and otherwise participate in government to the maximum extent permitted by law and, at the same time, to protect the rights of persons to file meritorious lawsuits for demonstrable injury." The law reflects the legislature's recognition that the judicial process can be abused to discourage individuals from speaking out on public issues. In fact, the harm that abusive litigation or "SLAPP suits" can cause has been recognized and discussed for decades.

SLAPP suits "forc[e] the target into the judicial arena" and "foist[ ] upon the target the expenses of a defense." "The longer the litigation can be stretched out, the more litigation that can be churned, the greater the expense that is inflicted and the closer the SLAPP filer moves to success." Even if the target of the suit ultimately succeeds, this "often amounts merely to a pyrrhic victory." As a result, "[p]ersons who have been outspoken on issues of public importance targeted in such suits or who have witnessed such suits will often choose in the future to stay silent."

Even the Supreme Court has recognized that SLAPP suits are burdensome for their targets: . . . As a New York judge once noted, "[s]hort of a gun to the head, a greater threat to First Amendment expression can scarcely be imagined."

B. Abusers Regularly Use Vexatious Lawsuits to Threaten and Silence Domestic Violence Survivors and Their Advocates

There may be no context in which the harm of SLAPP suits is more profound than when abusers use the courts to try to control domestic violence survivors and their advocates. A defining component of intimate partner violence is the power-control dynamic. One of an abuser's main goals is to "establish and maintain general control over one's partner." In fact, domestic violence is defined as "a pattern of behavior in a relationship by which the batterer attempts to control his victim through a variety of tactics."

Post-separation, domestic violence survivors often experience an escalation of threats and abuse as the abuser attempts to maintain or regain control over the survivor. A survivor's risk can increase by 75% or more after separation from an abusive intimate partner and this continuing threat of abuse can last for years.

SLAPP suits have become a common tool for abusers seeking to maintain power and control over domestic violence survivors. "Domestic violence survivors and their advocates have long known that abusers often use the legal system to continue to exert power and control over survivors years after a relationship has ended." "Abusive litigation" is thus understood within the field of domestic violence as something "abusers use in connection with court proceedings in order to control, harass, intimidate, coerce, and/or impoverish survivors."

C. Domestic Violence Survivors and Their Advocates Are Particularly Vulnerable to Abusive Litigation

For several reasons, the coercive effect of abusive litigation for domestic violence survivors can be quite powerful.

First, a lawsuit may force the survivor to see and interact with their abuser in court at a time when they are trying to distance themselves from their abuser. Such forced confrontations can be frightening and even lethal.

Second, the financial burden of fighting a SLAPP lawsuit—such as a defamation lawsuit—can be a powerful disincentive for a domestic violence survivor or advocate to report or speak out about abuse. The expense of defending litigation can be particularly coercive when the survivor is from a low-income background, has recently separated or divorced from their partner, or has been cut off from funds to hire a lawyer. The hardship of defending a lawsuit can be so significant that it forces the domestic violence survivor to return to their abuser.

Third, the public nature of the lawsuit, and the threat of intimate details about the domestic violence survivor's life becoming public, are yet another way in which the mere threat of litigation can coerce or intimidate a survivor into silence. Indeed, personal privacy concerns are frequently cited as a reason why domestic violence survivors forego reporting acts of abuse. Thus, SLAPP suits and vexatious litigation can profoundly discourage individuals from engaging in protected speech in the context of domestic violence. A means of quickly resolving such lawsuits is therefore essential.

D. Anti-SLAPP Laws Are an Essential Tool For Defending Abusive Litigation that Domestic Violence Survivors and Advocates Often Face

Anti-SLAPP statutes aim to prevent the judicial process from being a tool through which a party asserts power and control over another. They do so by providing an expedient means of terminating such lawsuits and mitigating the financial expense and other harms that may arise from the suit.

Colorado's anti-SLAPP statute works to protect the defendant of a SLAPP suit in two ways. First, defendants can obtain quicker relief from vexatious litigation by immediately filing a special motion to dismiss that is governed by distinct standards and procedures. The statute further bolsters SLAPP targets' rights by providing an avenue immediately [after] an anti-SLAPP motion denial. Second, victims obtain financial relief through a stay of discovery and an awarding of attorneys' fees upon a successful motion. As discussed above, this opportunity to terminate an abusive lawsuit before its financial, reputational, or psychological costs become too great is vital for domestic violence survivors.

II. Colorado's Anti-SLAPP Statute Protects Speech Concerning Domestic Violence, Including Sharkey's.

The anti-SLAPP statute should be broadly construed and liberally applied to ensure that survivors of domestic violence and their advocates can publicly discuss or report domestic violence without fear of reprisal in the form of costly, vexatious litigation. Colorado's anti-SLAPP statute was only recently enacted and the case law is still developing. It is therefore critical that the Court of Appeals provide clear guidance to the district courts that reading the statute too narrowly would undermine the General Assembly's goal of protecting public participation "to the maximum extent permitted by law."

To determine whether a plaintiff's case should be dismissed for infringing on the defendant's exercise of free speech and public participation, the anti-SLAPP statute establishes a two-prong inquiry. Under "Prong One," the court must determine whether the plaintiff's cause of action arises from an act in furtherance of the defendant's "right of petition or free speech under the United States constitution or the state constitution in connection with a public issue." Protected conduct under Prong One includes, among other things, public statements made "in connection with an issue of public interest." If the plaintiff's claim is based on conduct protected under the statute, the analysis moves to "Prong Two" where the court must dismiss the claim unless the plaintiff establishes a "reasonable likelihood" that they will prevail on the merits.

A proper application of both prongs is required to ensure that speaking out on issues of public concern—such as domestic violence—is not discouraged by abusive lawsuits aimed at silencing survivors or their advocates.

A. The Meaning of "In Connection with a Public Issue" Should Be Broadly Construed to Include Public Discussions Concerning Domestic Violence, Such As Sharkey's Facebook Statements. . .

B. The Court of Appeals Should Reject Petrocco's Restrictive Application of the Anti-SLAPP Statute and Affirm the District Court's Ruling on Prong One

The district court in this case properly concluded that "[i]t is indisputable that the issue of domestic violence and its effect on individuals is an issue of public interest, concern and significance." The district court also astutely recognized that the anti-SLAPP statute protects Sharkey's Facebook posts because they "inform[ed] the public of potential abuses of power by the judiciary and law enforcement and engender discussion about the public health crisis of deaths related to domestic violence." And significantly, the district court was also correct in acknowledging that domestic violence was once considered a private, "family matter," before becoming recognized as a topic of nationwide public concern. . .

III. Prong Two of the Anti-SLAPP Statute Should Be Meaningfully Applied to Ensure Abusive Lawsuits are Dismissed

Once it is determined that the plaintiff's claim is based on the defendant's exercise of free speech on a public issue, it becomes the plaintiff's burden to demonstrate that their claim is reasonably likely to prevail ("Prong Two"). In testing whether a plaintiff has carried their burden under Prong Two, it is imperative that district courts apply the proper standard and degree of scrutiny to the plaintiff's claims. Here, rather than test the merits of Petrocco's claims and his likelihood of success, the district court instead concluded that the anti-SLAPP motion should be denied because the case involved "issues of fact" and that "it is for a jury, not the Court, to be the ultimate trier of fact." But this is not the standard and simply observing the existence of fact issues is not a substitute for the searching analysis required under the statute.

When evaluating whether a plaintiff has demonstrated a "reasonable likelihood" of success, the trial court must do more than simply examine the sufficiency of the plaintiff's pleadings or look for "issues of fact." The statute expressly states that the court must consider "supporting and opposing affidavits stating the facts upon which the liability or defense is based." To merely look at the adequacy of the allegations in the complaint would render the anti-SLAPP statute little more than a motion to dismiss under C.R.C.P. 12(b)(5)—an outcome contrary to the General Assembly's goal of providing heightened protections for those exercising protected rights. . .

IV. Failure to Properly Apply the Anti-SLAPP Statute Will Result in Tangible Harm to Domestic Violence Survivors and their Advocates.

The stakes in this case are high. Domestic violence impacts more than ten million adults annually—approximately twenty people each minute. One in four women and one in ten men "experience sexual violence, physical violence and/or stalking by an intimate partner during their lifetime." And nearly half of domestic violence crimes are never reported—a statistic attributable at least in part due to fear of reprisals.

Domestic violence is not only pervasive, it is also often lethal. One in two "female murder victims. . .are killed by intimate partners." But the deadly costs of domestic violence cannot be measured only in homicides. Research suggests that it may be more common for victims of domestic violence to die from suicide than homicide. The emotional and psychological harm that arises from domestic violence and the power-control dynamic thus cannot be overstated.

Vexatious lawsuits contribute to dangers of harm to survivors by providing abusers a way to perpetuate or escalate their terrorizing behaviors. SLAPP lawsuits are a weapon for abusers to control domestic violence survivors, isolate them from their support structures, and silence those who would speak out on their behalf. It is therefore essential that the anti-SLAPP statute be applied in a robust, meaningful way to prevent such abusive, life-threatening conduct.

CONCLUSION

For the foregoing reasons, the Court should affirm the district court's ruling that Sharkey's Facebook statements constitute protected activity under the anti-SLAPP statute and reverse the district court's ruling that Petrocco carried his burden of demonstrating a reasonable likelihood of success on his claims against Sharkey.

[Editor's Notes: 1. 28(3) Domestic Violence Report (Feb/March 2023), pp 33–56 is a Special Issue on litigation abuse in domestic violence relationships, containing many good articles on this topic.

2. All federal courts and trial courts in some U.S. jurisdictions have authority to find litigants to be "vexatious litigants," requiring them to obtain permission from the court before filing any pleadings. California courts consider litigation filed in any state or in a federal court when making this finding. This finding is sometimes used in cases of domestic violence to stop abusers from using courts to abuse their former partners. It would be advisable for all states to adopt such legislation.

3. See also Robert Nonomura, Nick Bala, Kennedy McMillan, Andrew Au-Yeung, Peter Jaffe, Lisa Heslop, Katreena Scott, When the Family Court Becomes the Continuation of Family Violence After

Separation: Understanding Litigation Abuse, Alliance of Canadian Research Centres on Gender-Based Violence, in Chapter 12 below.]

B. ABUSERS

MICHAEL PAYMAR, VIOLENT NO MORE: HELPING MEN END DOMESTIC ABUSE

Hunter House 10–16 (2000)

ANDY'S STORY

Andy was born in Duluth, Minnesota. He, like some of the other men in this book, grew up with domestic violence in his family. He was arrested in 1982 for domestic assault and was ordered to attend our program. Andy has struggled to understand the roots of his violence. He has been violence-free for more than ten years and now works with men who, like himself, have been abusive to women.

I remember coming home from school and my father had my mother by the hair. It was obvious that she'd been crying because her mascara was smeared and her face was all puffy. He had a knife in his hand and he said to me, "Do you want me to kill this bitch? Because I will!" I was crying and begging him not to hurt her.

He battered her frequently and I never saw her fight back. She was always trying to accommodate him. Sometimes her attempts to appease him would work and sometimes they would piss him off more.

My brothers and I frequently got into fights, and my dad thought that was perfectly normal. If we complained or came to him, he would say we had to settle it like men.

I got a lot of my attitudes about girls and women from my father, but mostly I think society provided very negative messages about families in general. For me to get beat by a girl in a sports event was the ultimate in humiliation, and my father always told me you shouldn't hit girls, yet he beat my mother. He died when I was eleven.

I met Debra in 1980 and we started to live together. The worst violence I remember was when Debra said something about me at this party and I got embarrassed. When we got home, I grabbed her and threw her to the ground and started pounding her head on the sidewalk. She was screaming and there was terror in her eyes. My brother ran over and tried to get me off of her. He said, "Andy, you're going to kill her!" I'm not sure if I would have, but I stopped.

I thought Debra provoked my abuse. She would call me names or criticize my parenting abilities or say something she knew would piss me off, and I felt totally justified in letting her have it.

I usually blamed Debra for the violence. When she would come home late, I felt justified in hitting her. On some level I knew it was wrong to hit her, but I believed she brought it on herself. I always thought if she would just stop resisting me and do as I said, she wouldn't get hit.

After being violent, I would try to get her to see that what I did wasn't that bad. I'd say, "You don't have any marks on you," or, "Other men would have done worse." If I'd slapped her, I'd say, "Well, I didn't use a closed fist."

One time we got into a fight in the bedroom and I pushed her and she fell over the nightstand by the bed. She ended up with a broken arm and had to have a cast. A couple of weeks later, we were over at our friends' house, sitting around the table, and they asked what had happened to Debra's arm. She made up some story about tripping and falling. I was really uncomfortable and I got angry at her because I was embarrassed in front of our friends.

At the time, I never felt that Debra was afraid of me. If you had come into our house back then and asked me about her being afraid, I would have said, "Hell, no!" I mean, why would she sleep with me if she was afraid or why would she call me a fuckin' asshole if she was afraid? If she was afraid of me why would she say, "You're a sissy; go lay down by your fuckin' bowl by the dog. What are you going to do, hit a woman again?"

Debra was also violent with me. She was tough, and at the time both of us were into the bar scene. Sometimes she would throw things at me, slap me, or try to kick me. Actually, I was glad when she did that, because then I would feel totally justified in beating her up. There were times when I would goad her by getting in her face, calling her particular names so she would strike first. When she did, it would give me the green light to knock the hell out of her. After all, she hit me first. I was never afraid of her. Sometimes I would laugh at her after she hit me.

I rarely apologized unless the violence was really bad. When I apologized there was still this hint that it was her fault. I expected her to forgive me, and I would get really angry when she wouldn't. When she didn't accept my apology, I would say, "You fuckin' bitch. you started this stuff, and now look at you!"

I never thought she would leave me, but she did. The police came to our house three times but never arrested me. When they came, I would be real calm and wouldn't show them my anger, and Debra would be real agitated. I would tell the police it was her fault and she started the fight. They would go over to her and tell her not to provoke me.

Finally they did arrest me, because they had told me to leave the house after an incident and I had come back. I was charged with assault. I was really mad at the police, the justice system, and Debra. I felt no one was listening to my side of the story and everyone was blaming me when I thought Debra was just as much to blame. I threatened Debra, telling her if she didn't get the charges dropped I would really hurt her. She went to the city attorney, but they wouldn't drop the charges.

I was ordered into the counseling program and was really resistant at first. I didn't think I belonged there. I would say in group, "What about her violence? What am I supposed to do when she slaps me?" The counselors would challenge me to look at my violence and not to focus on her. It finally began to sink in and I realized that Debra didn't have to change for me to change.

After four or five groups something happened for me. It was actually freeing to take responsibility for my own behavior. It was challenging to examine my beliefs. I began to enjoy going to groups and talking about this stuff with other men. Even though I started making changes, it wasn't enough to save my relationship with Debra. I guess too much had happened between us—too much pain and too much of my violence—for us to heal as a couple.

I waited a long time before I decided to get involved in a new relationship. I wanted to be sure I had worked through my issues around wanting to control women. I also wanted to be absolutely sure I would be nonviolent in any future relationship.

I told Beth, my current partner, about my past. It was a risk, but I felt she should know that I had battered Debra. I think it's important to be honest and accountable. Today, I'm constantly challenging my beliefs about men and women. In my current relationship I try to be aware of my body language, because I'm a big guy and I have a loud voice. I need to be careful about how I respond to my partner when I'm angry. I'll always need to monitor myself.

In the past I was frightened at the prospect of being rejected by women, so I tended not to give too much, not to be too vulnerable, for fear I'd get hurt. I think part of it was my upbringing as a male. Men don't share feelings, men don't cry, men are supposed to be strong. It's an unfortunate attribute I see in the men I work with and it's something I need to work on.

When I was battering, it never occurred to me that I didn't need the tough-guy image or that relationships with women could be different. Since I've made these changes in my life, my relationships with women and men have changed. When I'm with men, I'm really aware of sexist comments and attitudes. I don't want superficial relationships with people.

I'm optimistic that men who batter can change. Some of the changes are small and the process is slow, but I believe it can happen. It's been more than ten years since I battered and I've been violence free. Yet I still take an inventory of what I'm doing in my life.

Men who come into our groups in Duluth are so angry, just like I was. They're angry at the police, the courts, and their partners. I know this will sound strange, but the best thing that ever happened to me was getting arrested, I finally had to look at my behavior. I had to stop conning everyone, including myself.

ANDY'S STORY FIVE YEARS LATER

I sat down with Andy five years after our initial interview. I wanted to find out what had changed in his life, whether he remained non-violent, and what advice he had for men in similar situations. Andy has been married for six years and continues to work with men who batter. He recently went back to college and earned a degree in psychology.

On His Past

An important element in my change process was the way people held me accountable when I got arrested. Equally important was that people believed I could change. When I was ordered into the Domestic Abuse Intervention Project, the group leaders and my probation officer all believed in me—that was important to a twenty-one-year-old who was going down the wrong track. When I began the group, I was kind of scared. I mean, I'd never talked to people about my feelings before, and I'd never been asked the kinds of questions they wanted me to answer. Group process? Bar stools were the closest I ever got to a group. But the process turned out to be comfortable—I wasn't told I was bad, but I did get challenged in a very respectful and helpful way.

On His Current Marriage

When I told Beth about my past use of violence, I think she was a little nervous about getting into a relationship with me, and for awhile I think she was rightly checking me out. We were in love, but our first two years of marriage were definitely rocky.

Our initial problems occurred when I moved into her house. Beth and her kids all had a certain way of doing things and I was thrust into their environment, with their rules. Beth thought that I was avoiding conflict and that I wasn't committed to the relationship because I was working long hours, so in her mind we couldn't work through our problems. We had some very big compatibility issues.

On Dealing With Conflict

During those first two years of marriage, when Beth and I would argue, I would sometimes get sarcastic, raise my voice, and at other times would just shut down and withdraw. I would usually apologize when I was acting in an inappropriate manner. This was a painful time for both of us.

It was at about this time that Beth told me there were times she was afraid of me. I couldn't believe it. She would say, "You know, you're a big guy, and when we get into an argument, and if you raise your voice, it makes me afraid sometimes." She would then qualify these statements by saying, "I don't believe you'll physically hurt me, but I still feel afraid." I never sensed she was afraid, because she wouldn't shut down or retreat from any conflicts we were having. When she confronted me about this, it really floored me. I didn't want to own it, I didn't want to entertain it, I didn't want to feel it, and I didn't want to hear it. I so desperately didn't want her to be afraid of me, but she was. Here I was, working with men who batter, and I'm very visible in the community because of my work, and here Beth is telling me that on some occasions she's afraid, It was really depressing. All I had ever wanted was to be a loving husband to Beth and a loving stepparent to the children—I wanted her to love me, approve of me, and think I'm somebody special. So when she told me about being scared, I felt like a monster—I hated it.

She would say things like, "You know you have this history," and I would really resent it, because I was not the same person I was back in 1982. I was angry she would put me in that framework. I felt she was playing the trump card and that was that—everything's over now. I can't do anything and I can't say anything.

On Working Through Problems in His Marriage

We were both determined to work things through. We went to marriage counseling and I went to individual counseling. We separated on two different occasions because we recognized we both needed to make some changes, or else we would wind up in divorce. The separation was helpful. We took the time to sort things out and find some better ways of communicating. We're a lot more honest with each other now. I don't walk away from conflicts anymore and we work through our problems. We've actually set up times for dealing with issues.

On His Childhood, Anger, and Healing

I was pretty severely damaged as a child. I experienced and witnessed a lot of abuse and pain, even though my memories of that time are a little hazy. I don't have as much anger inside me today about my family because I've done a lot of healing these past seven years. At the time Beth and I were having these problems, I decided I wanted to do some "family of origin" counseling and try to get in touch with what my childhood was all about. I interviewed several counselors until I found one I thought would be helpful. I think my separation from Beth was in part a catalyst for me to go back into therapy. It was also at this time that I started thinking about my dad—I finally got to the place where I could forgive him, and I miss him today. I asked my mother about my childhood, but she didn't want to talk about my dad's abusive behavior, so I let it go.

Working on improving yourself is so critical to personal growth. I have a men's group that meets every other week, which is really important to me—we talk about personal growth, relationships, and gender issues and I get strength from them. I've had a lot of healing experiences over the years and consequently a lot of my anger has diminished.

On Spirituality

I really think my faith in God has been important to my change process. I draw strength from God when I pray, and there's a lot of wisdom in the scriptures about love, trust, and respect. In my work with men who batter, I really stress the importance of being "plugged in" some way. Religion, spirituality, whatever—just do something for self-improvement.

On Talking to His Stepchildren About His Past

My three stepchildren know I went to jail and they know I'm an alcoholic. Telling them was a decision that Beth and I made together, and it was relatively easy. They know that, in part, the reason I do this work is because of my past violence. They are very accepting. My relationship with these kids has been just super.

On His Life Today

Beth and I have a good relationship today. She's my best friend. We have a level of intimacy that's very special. As I said, the first two years were a struggle, but we worked things through. I believe if those kinds of problems surfaced again we would recognize the signs and deal with the issues in a heartbeat. This comes from a deeper level of commitment to our relationship that simply wasn't there those first two years of our marriage. We often talk about our relationship and how far we've come. There have been times that we just hold each other, and we are brought to tears because of how deep our love and intimacy are today. We have created a process to check things out with each other. The love and respect we have for each other are very powerful.

ALYCE LAVIOLETTE, ASSESSING DANGEROUSNESS IN DOMESTIC VIOLENCE CASES

Founder, Alternatives to Violence, Long Beach, CA
California Statewide Dispute Resolution Institute, San Jose, CA (2016)

CONTINUUM of AGGRESSION and ABUSE *by Alyce LaViolette*

Exacerbating Factors: Family of Origin Issues - Substance Abuse - Age (Younger)
Previous Abusive Relationships - Psychological Issues

Common Couple Aggression	High Conflict	Separation or Loss Specific Aggression	Abuse	Battering	Terrorism
• Aberrant Act • Remorse • Does not cause fear, oppression or control • No injury • Comes from escalating arguments • Could happen in any family • Balance of power in a relationship	• Does not solve problems well • Anger is an issue in family • May have remorse • May have sporadic physical aggression and/or destruction of property • Can have emotional abuse • No fear • Balance of power in relationship	• Isolated act(s) of aggression • No prior context of domestic violence • Aggression fueled by stress of loss/grieving • May engender fear, particularly in women, based on vicarious trauma	• Sporadic physical aggression • Name calling, but not character assassination • Verbal abuse, but not psychological • May be remorseful • Threats of abandonment • Aggression takes place without witnesses	• Monopolization of perception • Generally more regular physical abuse, but may occur without physical • Threats to victim's support system • Jealousy • Putting down friends and family • Destruction of property • Self-absorbed • Sexual abuse • Change in victim's personality • More generally violent	• Stalking • Monopolization of perception • Insidious psychological abuse • Well thought-out threat to kill • Torturing pets • Extreme isolation • Generally more regular physical abuse, but may occur without physical • Sexual humiliation and degradation

Mediating Factors: Connection to community - Job that has meaning - Age (Older)
Participation in abuse intervention program
Participation in recovery program

By: Alyce LaViolette Copyright: 1998, 2005, 2011, 2016

JOAN ZORZA, THE NEW DOMESTIC VIOLENCE TYPOLOGIES: AN ACCURATE RECONCEPTUALIZATION OR ANOTHER TRIVIALIZATION?

3 Family & Intimate Partner Violence Quarterly 225 (2011)
(citations omitted)

There is a real move afoot to redefine domestic violence (DV) into several distinct typologies, with the claim that not only are there different types of DV, but that each of them should be dealt with completely differently. This trend resonates well with many different groups that currently deal with DV, indeed almost all of the groups (e.g., fathers' rights groups, custody evaluators, mediators, and others working with the family courts) except the majority of what we have known as the battered women's movement that deals daily with the overwhelming majority of its victims, and many feminists, namely most of us. Much of this new thinking is based on an awareness that some women do hit, that the Conflict Tactics Scales (CTS) and the many instruments largely based on it find that women are approximately as abusive as men. Countering that is all the evidence showing that it is women who are injured far more often and far more seriously, and that is almost always only women who are terrified of their abusers and who experience post-traumatic stress disorder (PTSD) and other serious effects, evidence that comes in large part from the criminal justice system, the health system, and DV programs. * * * This article will examine some of the new thinking and analysis and discuss what is probably true, and what may be wrong with the new approach, as well as some of its implications. As to the typologies, it will primarily look at Michael P. Johnson's new book, *A Typology of Domestic Violence: Intimate Terrorism, Violent Resistance, and Situational Couple Violence.* * * * In addition to intimate terrorism he also identifies three other types of violence: violent resistance, mutual violence, and situational couple violence.

JOHNSON'S FOUR TYPES OF ABUSE

Intimate Terrorism

In intimate terrorism (IT) the perpetrator uses violence to exercise power and impose control over his or her IP [intimate partner]. * * * Johnson [points to] the Power and Control Wheel[.] * * * To be effective, coercive control requires that the abuser make clear that he is both willing and able to impose the punishment, which he then does by intimidation. Furthermore, coercive control requires that the intimate terrorist must monitor his victim to know when to use punishment. In addition, he must wear down his partner's resistance by undermining her so she will believe she is worthless, or that his authority is legitimate. This is why he uses psychological attacks on her self-esteem and blames her for making him have to be violent. He supplements this by depriving her of any resources, be they social support or financial, that she would need to effectively resist.

Violent Resistance

Violent resistance happens to those terrorized battered women who do fight back physically, whether as an instinctive reaction to being attacked (often from the first attack) or in desperation trying to get her intimate terrorist partner to stop. * * * [A]s many women who resist have found, it often backfires and ends up escalating their abusers' violence. * * * Johnson cites a study of women who were court mandated into batterer treatment programs which found that 65% of them (nearly two-thirds) had been defending themselves. * * * Yet what he does not say is that the vast majority of those defending themselves should never have been in the criminal justice system in the first place[.] * * * [One study] find[s] * * * that females are 'the perpetrators in five percent or fewer of the cases,' suggesting that the remaining 35% of women who ostensibly abuse offensively in the study Johnson cites is much too high a figure. Yet, * * * [although there has been] a 71% decline from 1970 to 2006 in the number of men killed by their IPs, [this is not similarly] seen in the number of women killed by their IPs.

Situational Couple Violence (SCV)

* * * Johnson tells us situational couple violence [SCV] is far more common, is situationally provoked, but done without any attempt by either partner to control the other or the relationship. * * * Johnson does not minimize its severity * * * but he claims that it can be treated by couples counseling.

Mutual Violent Control

Mutual violence occurs only "in a very small number of cases" and happens when both partners are violent and controlling. Johnson admits we know almost nothing about these couples or the dynamics of their relationships except that both are attempting to control the relationship. * * *

STUDYING VIOLENCE

Coercive control does not explain all violence. Johnson notes that "[v]iolence is not always motivated by a desire to gain or resist control," but can also be "primarily an expression of anger or frustration . . . a matter of self-image . . . [or] simply a bid for attention." But he asserts that with intimate partner violence one is looking not at a single episode of violence but at a pattern over time that involves many situations. * * * To determine if abuse in a relationship is IT (intimate terrorism), Johnson "uses questions about threats, intimidation, surveillance," and reducing resistance to identify a pattern of coercive, controlling violence. He also asks about the partner to determine if the violence was IT or one of the other types of abuse. * * * Johnson also exposes problems that have been ignored in trying to figure out what type of violence one is dealing with and why different types of studies have come up with such different data, data that has resulted in men's and fathers' rights groups claiming that women are as violent as men. * * *

PROBLEMS WITH SOCIAL SCIENCE'S VIOLENCE TYPOLOGIES

* * * The Conflict Tactics Scale (CTS) is the first instrument developed with significant federal government input to measure DV, and it has assumed that it was indeed measuring what it was designed to do. * * * [A]ll versions of the CTS are both over- and under-inclusive. Context is everything in DV, but the CTS does not examine context. Thus, how severe an act is, and whether it causes injury or fear are totally irrelevant as far as the CTS is concerned which, as will be noted, adds to these problems.

Over-Inclusive

The CTS instruments are over-inclusive in that some of what is measured is not DV[, such as violent resistance *qua* self-defense, genuine accidents, and violent acts without an intent to harm.] * * * (It is also true that it is often very difficult to distinguish whether something is or is not DV, particularly since abusers often trivialize and deny their abusive behaviors by alleging that something they deliberately inflicted was done to save or protect their partner.) * * *

Under-Inclusive

* * * Even later versions of the CTS miss many abusive behaviors, including most stalking, suffocation, scratching, arson, denying needed medications or food, denying telephone access (particularly cruel and potentially devastating when a victim is seeking help), destroying or denying access to needed aids (e.g., wheelchair, hearing aids, seeing eye dog, eyeglasses), coercive control, and sexual coercion. In addition, the CTS does not count as IP abuse something that the abuser does by using someone or something else to do the abuse, e.g., training the dog to attack his IP on command or any time she tries to leave the home, or inviting other men to have sex with his partner and telling them that "she especially loves it when she is yelling 'Stop' or 'No!' " [Those last two examples were actual cases, the second one posted on the Internet and resulting in the woman being gang raped.] Similarly, the abuser beating or sexually abusing a child or animal until the woman agrees to have sex with him or to give him her paycheck will not be counted as DV on the CTS. In addition, abuse that destroys property is completely missed by the CTS[, as are] * * * humiliating acts [such] as spitting on a partner or driving her naked or scantily clad from the home. Yet all of these acts have been repeatedly committed by men against their IPs but seldom (if ever) done by women against their male lovers, with the result that the CTS undercounts men's violence against women, making women's abuse seem disproportionately greater than it actually is.

[The author further explains that the CTS counts only abuse occurring during the marriage, during arguments, and only in the last 12 months.] * * * Yet battered women tell us that half of all abuse happens at other times, often during silence, such as when they are awakened in the middle of the night to being beaten. * * * Many women may be afraid to report abuse, particularly as most CTS surveys are done over the telephone, and the home is perhaps the least safe place for women, particularly if they fear that their abuser is home or has bugged the home or phone.

REPORTER INFLUENCE BIASES THE RESULTS

The CTS assumes either party can report for not only themselves, but also for the other one, and many of the surveys using the CTS asked only one of the partners if either of them was abusive. [But men minimize and under-count their violence, and women do the same with the violence inflicted on them; women also over-count their own violence.] * * * Thus I have often heard women admit under oath in court or depositions they had been violent when they slapped and killed a mosquito on their partner's back, [or] tossed him the car keys when he asked for them[.] * * * I have also heard men far more often deny or minimize under oath their obviously violent acts, e.g., the man who twisted his wife's arm to the point that he fractured her bone and dislocated her elbow and when pushed under cross-examination, finally admitted it, claiming he had only done it to punish his wife for talking on the phone (to the police—most likely called only after his "punishment" had begun) without his permission. * * *

Almost all other indications of abuse show that it is overwhelmingly women who are injured and who sustain the more serious injuries, something that Johnson and even most men's rights people acknowledge. While many people claim (with little proof) that men are too embarrassed or ashamed to admit when they are battered by women, few mention that approximately half of men who are battered in intimate relationships are beaten by male lovers and that these men are far more likely to be reluctant to admit that they are being abused by men. * * * Yet * * * "available evidence finds that men are more likely to call the police, more likely to press charges and less likely to drop them" than women[; and] * * * when men are assaulted by women "the violence is not as prolonged and not as extreme, they are far less likely to be injured, they are less likely to fear for their own safety, they are less likely to be subject to violence by their ex-partners, and they are likely to have more financial and social independence." In contrast much of women's violence, as Johnson also admits, is in retaliation or self-defense, often only done after having been severely abused for many years.

IT OFTEN MISTYPED AS SCV

* * * While Johnson's IT description rings very true, his SCV category seems to be an oversimplification and trivialization of much DV, with much of it growing out of the CTS being the basis for the studies, as well as the possibility * * * that in many instances those studying the abuse may only be seeing the beginning of a pattern [by looking at the short-term violence after separation, but not following up years later]. * * * [Johnson categorizes violence stemming from arguments involving family life, such as cleaning, sex, and managing the money, as SCV, but] most abusive men use arguments and demands precisely as a tactic to terrify their partners and justify their use of terroristic violence. In fact, when these areas of dispute are actually examined, they look surprisingly like many of those reflected on the power and control wheel, and Evan Stark's (2007) study of coercive control over IPs' personal liberties and personal autonomy. * * *

IMPLICATIONS

It is really worrisome that SCV is being used by most of the mental health professionals involved with the family court system to completely excuse and trivialize much of men's violence. * * * [They] have used claims that abuse (particularly post-separation abuse) is only SCV to justify not exempting them from mediation, giving batterers shared parenting, and all the other ills that further empower abusive men and disempower and endanger their victims. * * * [Johnson further notes] that batterer treatment and intervention programs "have minimal success" so that 40% of those who complete the programs will be successfully nonviolent, vs. 35% of those who get no treatment * * * [H]e also thinks that the criminal justice system should be taking DV cases much more seriously, and correctly observes that its incident-based nature * * * poses a serious obstacle[, and many do not] * * * look at who is the "primary perpetrator."

* * * I suggest that SCV is far too broad a category, picking up some violence that is indeed not that serious, but missing some that needs to be taken far more seriously, as Johnson acknowledges, and treated like IT. * * * [U]ntil we move away from assuming that the CTS is accurately measuring DV, we will probably never get a handle on understanding or solving the major problem that DV poses[.]

C. DOMESTIC VIOLENCE IN OTHER CULTURES

JACQUELYN C. CAMPBELL, SANCTIONS AND SANCTUARY: WIFE-BATTERING WITHIN CULTURAL CONTEXTS

From To Have and To Hit: Cultural Perspectives on Wife Beating, 2nd ed., edited by Dorothy Ayers Counts, Judith K. Brown, and Jacquelyn C. Campbell, University of Illinois Press 277–279 (1999)
(footnotes and references omitted)

* * * EXPLANATORY THEORIES

Western social sciences have used a variety of theories to explain the occurrence of wife beating, and many schemes have been used for their classification. For this volume, we have divided the theories into the broad categories of psychological and sociological/cultural and concentrate on the latter as more appropriate for examination with anthropological evidence. Various forms of stress and trauma, social learning, and exchange theory have received the most empirical support and attention in psychology, although it is recognized that each has societal components as well as explanations within the individual psyche. Psychoanalytic and neuropsychological reasons for wife beating have also been explored but are less well accepted, partly because of the victim-blaming and perpetrator-excusing logical extensions of these perspectives and partly because of a lack of consistent empirical support. Sociobiological (or evolutionary psychological) theory has been used in connection with homicide of women, which can be conceptualized as the far end of the continuum of wife beating. This framework has been discussed by Draper. In this chapter I will concentrate on reviewing the theories, especially feminist, resource, subculture of violence, and systems theories, which use wider societal perspectives. The societal factors used in social learning and exchange theories will also be examined. * * *

CONCLUSIONS

The evidence from the small-scale societies presented in this volume does not fully support one of the theoretical models to the exclusion of the others but instead suggests that none of the Western social science theories explains all of the patterns of wife beating and battering that have been described. Thus, anthropological evidence has some important additions to make to the scholarly and practical formulations about the beating of wives. Specifically, the editors of this volume found only limited support for the cultural/subcultural, resource, and social learning theories as now articulated; were unable to evaluate the underlying premise of exchange theory; argued that systems theory, in order to work across cultures, needs either to separate wife and child abuse or differentiate between child beating and child battering; and postulated that feminist theory had considerable support but would need to differentiate among wife beating, wife battering, and mutual violence (and admit the latter exists) to be more explanatory.

This review has also helped to emphasize the importance of societal-level influences on violence, a premise that is important for policy and prevention initiatives. Individuals do not seem to vary much across cultures in terms of psychological imperatives; young adult and adolescent males seem to be struggling with defining their roles, with how to be a "real" man according to whatever norms their cultures or subcultures have established. For example, the young, married, male Ujelang who wishes he could enact an unmarried warrior role is similar to the young, married, working-class U.S. man who wishes he could be either a really tough guy or a very rich guy, both of which have significant power in this society. Each goes out to drink with his friends, many of whom are unmarried and project a sense of freedom, even though the unattached males have their own status problems. Each may go back home and attack his wife. We are not sure whether this individual act is because of a patriarchal, behavioral, ethnological or psychological (status inconsistency, low self-esteem, frustration) imperative, but it is in the society's response to the beating that we see differences. In the Ujelang village, the man will be chastised if he does more than hit once; in the United States, his actions usually will go unremarked and definitely unrebuked by any but his partner and will probably escalate. Among the Ujelang, there is community scrutiny and evaluation of both the husband's and the wife's action by political leaders. In both places we see the male blaming the female's behavior. Sexual jealousy and female role enactment proscriptions, whether issues of parental certainty or patriarchy, abound worldwide (although we see an exception among the Wape). However, community acceptance of these "excuses" occurs to varying degrees.

The idea of group solidarity is also very important among the Ujelang; thus, where we can add negative sanctions against battering to a sense of group honor based on nonviolence and decent treatment of women (as the Kaliai are attempting to establish), there is a chance that battering will be limited. It is also clear that options for women are necessary, including personal autonomy, economic opportunity, and the ability to form close linkages with other women. Actual female power, as well as community sanction, seems stronger than male dominance norms in decreasing the amount of battering otherwise expected among the Ujelang, Ecuadorian Indians, and Mayotte. It is useful if the cultural (or subcultural) definition of a "real" man excludes the idea of controlling women by force if necessary, but it is apparent that societal structures and anticipatory community mechanisms can overcome individual propensities to violence.

The calls from feminist and systems theory activists to change the societal structures that allow and facilitate battering are thus supported by the anthropological data presented here. Sanctuary for beaten women is a necessary cornerstone in all cultures and is provided by wife abuse shelters in most industrialized countries. In other countries, such as Nicaragua, there are female centers that address legal and employment issues for women but also provide opportunities for women to address battering collectively. Much more needs to be done to provide similar sanctuary and opportunities in Iran and Taiwan. Since the data for this volume were collected, there have been increasing community-level initiatives in India that are extremely heartening. There also need to be strong societal and international sanctions against wife beating and especially battering, though we have shown that small group realities can be stronger than official sanctions in either direction. Changing neighborhood- and community-level realities is also a more realistic strategy than changing the precepts of an ancient religion or the lineage, locality, and/or property exchanges associated with marriage.

The work reviewed here thus extends the premise of changing societal structures to a focus of action on the small community or neighborhood level. In the United States, the plight of battered women has been publicized nationally, resulting in laws and shelters and at least a moderate increase in the economic and political status of women. Although work in these arenas needs to continue, perhaps it is time to start applying sanctions at the neighborhood level. Let us make individual batterers known to their communities, their churches, their schools, and their job sites for public censure. Let us work toward forming community- and neighborhood-level groups of women, for economic solidarity and for solidarity against men who batter. When a woman is being beaten, her neighbors can call the police if they are made aware of the warning signs. In this way, we can mimic Wape women, the compadres of Ecuadorian Indians, the kin and community courts of the Nagovisi, the male friends and relatives in Abelam, and the !Kung neighbors. These are all widely divergent societies, yet they all have mechanisms to limit the harm from wife beating. By some measures, these cultures can be described as "primitive" or less "developed," but when it comes to the beating of wives, they have much to teach us.

PAUL J. FLEMING, JENNIFER MCCLEARY-SILL, MATTHEW MORTON, RUTI LEVTOV, BRIAN HEILMAN, GARY BARKER, RISK FACTORS FOR MEN'S LIFETIME PERPETRATION OF PHYSICAL VIOLENCE AGAINST INTIMATE PARTNERS: RESULTS FROM THE INTERNATIONAL MEN AND GENDER EQUALITY SURVEY (IMAGES) IN EIGHT COUNTRIES

PLoS ONE 10(3): e0118639. doi:10.1371/journal.pone.0118639 (2015)
(tables and references omitted)

Introduction

Men's perpetration of violence against women results from a complex, interconnected ecology of psychological, economic, and sociological factors. It is estimated that over 75% of violence against women is perpetrated by their male intimate partners. Intimate partner violence (IPV), also called domestic violence, is defined by the World Health Organization [WHO] as "any behavior within an intimate relationship that causes physical, psychological or sexual harm to those in the relationship." Physical IPV, the focus of this paper, includes acts such as punching, kicking, and slapping and is commonly accompanied by psychological (emotional) and sometimes, sexual abuse. The World Health Organization estimates that global prevalence of physical and sexual intimate partner violence (IPV) among ever-partnered women is 30.0%, ranging between 23.2% and 37.7% for different global regions. A meta-analysis conducted on men's perpetration of IPV (married or cohabiting partner) identifies key characteristics that are correlated with their perpetration of IPV: low marital satisfaction, illicit drug use, and attitudes condoning marital violence. Other important factors included inequitable gender attitudes and depression. Two separate meta-analyses identify witnessing abuse as a child as a moderate risk factor for abuse perpetration in adulthood.

Additionally, societal factors, such as gender inequalities and patriarchal family structures facilitate a social environment that allows IPV. Settings with unenforced or limited laws preventing violence against women can enable men's perpetration of IPV, and locations of conflict or post-conflict typically have much higher rates of IPV, especially sexual violence. These higher rates are partially due to the higher levels of impunity of perpetrators when social institutions that prevent IPV break down or become ineffective, along with increased social and economic stressors on the household. High rates of violence can continue in post-conflict settings if courts and institutions responsible for preventing violence are not established or repaired.

Men's perpetration of IPV is also enabled by prevailing norms related to masculinity and gender equality in most societies. A review of research on the role of masculinity in partner violence presented evidence on different domains of masculinity and male gender norms that influence perpetration. Reviewed articles indicate that men who hold more traditional gender role ideologies (i.e., distinct roles for men and women) are more likely to perpetrate violence. Additionally, men who feel stress about their ability to conform to normative ideas regarding what it means to be a man are more likely to perpetrate IPV. Societies with greater gender inequities are more likely to teach young men a traditional gender role ideology and increase pressure that men act in traditionally masculine ways, including by perpetrating violence.

Power inequalities are central to understanding gender, masculinity and violence perpetration and have been the focus of theoretical understandings of masculinity in the past two decades. West and Zimmerman conceptualize gender, including masculinity, as constructed through social interactions and put the focus on the actions of individuals. Thus, a man's masculinity depends on (a) his collection of behaviors and interactions, and (b) how his social environment judges them. Men are often obligated to project a masculine image, often emphasizing strength and power over women. Since power over others is such a critical element of traditionally-defined masculinity, men can sometimes feel a need to assert their power in relationships with women. Because of these normative power dynamics, some men use violence (including physical or other types of violence) to assert power over female partners and thus demonstrate their masculinity. In this way, men's behaviors, including violence perpetration, help them construct an outward image of power over women that is aligned with a socially constructed ideal of masculinity.

Most international survey research on IPV, women's rights, and gender equity focuses on women, or has limited data on men's attitudes and behaviors. Research that does focus on risk factors for men's IPV perpetration has mostly been conducted in high-income countries and it is very limited in low- and middle-income countries. One notable exception is the United Nations (UN) Multi-country Study on Men and Violence in Asia and the Pacific. The UN multi-country study was conducted in six different Asian countries. A recent report from the UN multi-country study examined men's physical IPV perpetration and found that between 11.5% (rural Indonesia) and 61.9% (Papua New Guinea) of ever-partnered men reported ever perpetrating violence against a partner. The UN multi-country study found that men's age category, attitudes towards gender equality, childhood experiences of abuse, depression, and history of fighting were all significantly associated with intimate partner violence perpetration. The UN study also analyzed food insecurity, substance abuse (alcohol and illicit drugs) and sexual behaviors and found them to be significantly associated with violence perpetration.

While the UN multi-country study report helps to address a gap in research on men's perpetration in low- and middle-income countries, it is limited to only six countries in one region of the world. There have been no published studies comparing correlates of men's lifetime physical IPV perpetration across countries in different continents and regions of the world. Despite the known importance of social and cultural norms for IPV, it is yet to be determined how risk and protective factors for physical IPV perpetration vary in different societies around the world. This paper aims to fill these gaps by analyzing data from eight low- and middle-income countries across five continents to answer three principal research questions: (1) What is the prevalence of self-reported male lifetime perpetration of physical IPV in each setting? (2) What are the main risk and protective factors for physical IPV perpetration across low- and middle-income countries? (3) How do the risk and protective factors for physical IPV perpetration differ among surveyed countries? * * *

Results

Of the 7,806 men in our analytic sample, 2415 (30.9%) report ever having perpetrated physical violence against a partner. The share of men who reported lifetime perpetration of physical violence was 17% in Mexico, 24% in Bosnia, 25% in Brazil, 29% in Chile, 32% in Croatia, 37% in India, 39% in Rwanda, and 45% in the Democratic Republic of the Congo (DRC). Demographic, attitudinal, and behavioral information for men in our sample ranged greatly for each country. . . * * *

Discussion

A quarter or more of participants in most of the countries had ever perpetrated physical violence against a partner. The estimates from this analysis are similar to those found in the 2013 WHO study related to IPV prevalence and from the recent UN Multi-country study. This analysis pointed to several modifiable risk and protective factors that may be able to decrease violence perpetration by men.

We found that, among those variables measured, the factors most strongly associated with self-reported physical IPV perpetration were witnessing intra-parental violence and having been involved in fights with a weapon—both were highly significant in the all-country sample and statistically significant in nearly every country. Having permissive attitudes towards violence against women (VAW), an inequitable Gender Equitable Men (GEM) score [The authors explain that this scale measures the extent to which men agree with gender equality or separate roles for men and women.], and older age were also significant risk factors in the all-country sample and some of the individual country samples. Reporting depression was significantly correlated with physical IPV perpetration in the countries where this was asked.

The strength and significance of the correlation between witnessing of inter-parental violence and perpetrating physical IPV suggests evidence of the intergenerational transmission of behaviors and gender norms. This supports previous evidence highlighting the importance of witnessing violence as a child for men's future aggression against women and reinforces its generalizability to a range of developing country contexts. A meta-analytic review of 39 published research studies on the intergenerational transmission of partner violence demonstrated that children who witness parental violence are themselves more likely to be involved in violent relationships in adulthood. This increased likelihood of violence among those who witness violence is in part driven by psychosocial concepts from the Social Learning Theory and its subsequent version, Social Cognitive Theory. These behavioral theories have established that individuals learn how to behave socially through observing and imitating important others in their social environment. This observation and imitation occurs throughout the lifespan, but can be particular important for children and youth. Interrupting this cycle is critical to reducing violence perpetration. Additionally, though our study did not examine experiences of child abuse, it often co-occurs with intimate partner violence and may also contribute to this cycle of violence and should be addressed in violence prevention efforts.

Reports of getting into fights was also an important factor associated with physical IPV perpetration for men in most but not all countries. This may be connected to the finding that men who are depressed were more likely to perpetrate physical IPV since they both relate to how men learn to express their emotions and anger. For example, a man suffering from depression may take out feelings of sadness and loneliness by using violence against a partner. Conversely, this finding could demonstrate the negative mental health effects of perpetration on men. In either case, efforts to improve mental health for men may help reduce IPV perpetration. The finding related to fighting also highlights the fact that violence between men is linked to violence against women. Kaufman refers to the interrelatedness of types of violence as men's "triad of violence," including violence against women, violence against other men, and violence against self. Efforts to prevent IPV may also need to address men's three types of violence perpetration and the masculine norms that support all forms. The findings imply that policy efforts which take a narrow view of specific types of violence may miss opportunities to address interconnected violent attitudes and behaviors more holistically.

Men with more inequitable gender attitudes—and those with more permissive attitudes towards violence against women—were more likely to have perpetrated IPV. The masculine norm in many societies is often characterized by being aggressive, unemotional, and dominant over women. * * *

We found that younger (ever-partnered) men were less likely to have perpetrated violence against a partner. Previous studies of the impact of age on lifetime physical violence perpetration have had mixed results. It is possible that our findings simply indicate that younger men have had fewer opportunities to perpetrate. Previous analyses with IMAGES data have shown that older men tend to have more permissive attitudes towards violence against women. This may represent an additional explanation of the higher prevalence of perpetration among older men. Thus, it is possible that younger men's perpetration, and attitudes, represent societal shifts in acceptability of violence against women. Future survey research should examine this question longitudinally and measure IPV exposure of the last 12 months as well as lifetime prevalence, as recommended by recent UN guidance on minimum gender indicators.

Though education level was non-significant in the all-country sample, we found some limited evidence in the country samples that increased schooling may have a protective effect where those with more schooling were less likely to perpetrate violence than those with less schooling. But, the opposite was true in the DRC and there was a non-significant relationship in most countries when controlling for other factors. * * *

While some risk factors were important in almost every country, countries with high violence perpetration such as DRC and India had slightly different patterns of risk factors than countries with lower perpetration. Pierotti argues that as communities and countries are increasingly exposed to global cultural scripts that are opposed to VAW, they adopt attitudes in opposition to VAW. Countries that have increased engagement with the global economy may create opportunities for their citizens to be more exposed to "global cultural scripts." Risk factors for IPV perpetration may be different in countries or settings where global cultural scripts in opposition to VAW have not been entrenched (as evidenced in our sample by high prevalence of permissive attitudes towards VAW in DRC and India). In those settings, there may be other factors that were not in our model that are contributing to violence perpetration. * * *

DAVID LEVINSON, SOCIETIES WITHOUT FAMILY VIOLENCE

Family Violence in Cross-Cultural Perspective 102–107
(Sage Publications, 1987)

As pointed out in Chapter 1, one of the major benefits of the cross-cultural comparative approach is that it enables us to examine ways of life that are different from our own. I rely on the comparative approach here to help provide us with a sociocultural profile of societies in which family life is free of violence. In Table 7.3, I list the 16 societies in our sample that are relatively free of family violence. Freedom from family violence is indicated by the family violence scale score in the second column of the table. This score, which ranges from 1.00 to 3.66, indicates the combined level of wife beating, husband beating, physical punishment of children, and sibling fighting that occurs in each society in the sample. Societies with a score of 1.00 have no or rare family violence. These 16 societies provide an interesting subsample of the full society sample on which this book is based. The 16 are representative of all seven major geographical regions of the world. However, South America is overrepresented with four societies (Ona, Siriona, Pemon, and Toba), while Africa (Bushmen) and Asia (Andamans and Central Thai) are underrepresented. Similarly, a broad range of economic systems (hunter-gatherers, horticulturalists, herders, agriculturalists) are covered, but hunter-gatherers (Ona, Andamans, Siriono, Bushmen) are overrepresented, perhaps because hunter-gatherers rarely mistreat their children (Rohner, 1986).

Table 7.3: Societies Without Family Violence

	FVS	1	2	3	4	5	6	7	8	9
Fox	1.25	2	*3*	*3*	1	1	*5*	1	1	2
Iroquois	1.00	2	2	2	1	1	*4*	1	1	
Papago	1.25	2	2	2	*2*	*2*	3	3	1	1
Ona	1.00	2	2	1	1	1	1	3	*3*	1
Siriona	1.25	*3*	—	*4*	1	1	1		1	1
Pemon	1.20	2	2	2	1	1	1	—	—	2
Toba	1.25	2	—	2	1	1	*4*	—	1	
Javanese	1.25	1	1	2	1	*2*	3	1	1	1
Ifugao	1.00	2	2	*4*	1	1	3	—	2	*4*
Trobriands	1.33	2	2	2	1	1	3	2	1	2
Bushmen	1.00	*3*	2	2	1	1	1	—	1	1
Andamans	1.33	2	2	2	1	1	1	1	2	1
Central Thai	1.00	2	2	2	1	1	3	4	1	2
Kurd	1.33	2	*3*	*3*	1	1	—	—	1	1
I. Bedouin	1.00	2	*3*	2	1	*2*	1	3	2	
Lapps	1.33	1	*3*	2	1	1	1		1	1

FVS = family violence scale
1 = domestic decision making
2 = control of fruits of family labor
3 = divorce freedom
4 = type of marriage
5 = premarital sex double standard
6 = divorce frequency
7 = intervention type
8 = male fighting
9 = husband/wife sleeping NOTE: Italicized codes deviate from the typical pattern across these societies.

The nine columns of numbers in the table are the ratings for nine factors that seem especially typical of societies without family violence (italicized codes are ones that deviate from the typical pattern across these societies). In general, it seems that in societies without family violence, husbands and wives share in domestic decision making, wives have some control over the fruits of family labor, wives can divorce their husbands as easily as their husbands can divorce them, marriage is monogamous, there is no premarital sex double standard, divorce is relatively infrequent, husbands and wives sleep together, men resolve disputes with other men peacefully, and intervention in wife beating incidents tends to be immediate. Some of these findings are as I would expect, since they are simply the reverse of our findings regarding the causes of family violence. One should not be surprised, for example, to find that shared decision making in the household predicts the absence of wife beating since we already know that male dominance in decision making predicts wife beating. However, some of these findings do not follow this pattern, and, in fact, our earlier analysis indicated that they were unrelated to family violence. The three factors of interest in this regard—premarital double standard, the divorce rate, and husband-wife sleeping—are especially significant since they suggest that equality and closeness in the marital relationship lead to low rates of family violence. The central conclusion I reach from these findings is that family violence does not occur in societies in which family life is characterized by cooperation, commitment, sharing and equality. While these factors do not ensure that wives will not be beaten or children physically punished, it is clear that if they guide family relationships, family violence will be less frequent.

It should be noted, however, that some factors have been left out of the table because they seem to predict the absence of only one form of violence and have little or even an adverse effect on other forms. The best example of this class of factors is household organization, with extended-family households associated with the nonphysical punishment of children but unrelated to wife beating. Thus while it is possible, as I have done here, to produce a list of sociocultural characteristics of a family violence-free society, these factors, as a group, may be of limited predictive value when applied to a specific form of family violence. * * *

When analyzed in the context of factors I have found linked to family violence, such as husband dominance in domestic decision making, sexual economic inequality, single-parent caretakers, mens' houses, and violent conflict resolution, the absence of a household division of labor by sex can tell us much about how to prevent family violence. First, it tells us that with two regular caretakers in the home, there will be regular relief from the pressures that often accompany caretaking and less chance that those pressures will boil over into violence directed at the children. Second, given our earlier finding that sibling violence is often modeled on parent-child violence, it tells us that alternative caretakers in the home will indirectly control fighting between siblings. Third, the absence of a clear division of labor by sex tells us that adult male and female roles are not rigidly defined. Thus manifestations of an unresolved male sex identity conflict both outside and within the family are unlikely. And, last, it tells us that since sexual equality accompanies the shared division of labor, each party will have the emotional and economic independence to withdraw from a potentially violent relationship.

The . . . central conclusion of this study [is that] family violence will be more common in societies in which men control women's lives, it is acceptable to resolve conflicts violently, and the mother bears the major responsibility for child rearing. [There is] living proof that it doesn't have to be this way.

[Editor's Note: Based on cross-cultural studies on violence against women, the World Bank found in 1994 that four factors predicted significant violence against women: (1) economic inequality between men and women; (2) male economic and decision-making authority in the family; (3) violent interpersonal conflict resolution; and (4) the masculine ideal of male dominance, toughness, and honor. Other factors predicted low violence against women: (1) female power outside the home; (2) presence of all-female work or solidarity groups; (3) active community intervention in violence; and (4) the presence of sanctuaries from violence. (See LORI L. HEISE, JACQUELINE PITANGUY, & ADRIENNE GERMAIN, WORLD BANK, VIOLENCE AGAINST WOMEN: THE HIDDEN HEALTH BURDEN 29 (Discussion Paper No. 255 1994).)]

WILLIAM E. MITCHELL, WHY WAPE MEN DON'T BEAT THEIR WIVES: CONSTRAINTS TOWARD DOMESTIC TRANQUILITY IN A NEW GUINEA SOCIETY

From To Have and To Hit: Cultural Perspectives on Wife Beating, 2nd ed., edited by D.A. Counts, J.K. Brown, and J.C. Campbell, University of Illinois Press 100–109 (1999) (footnotes and references omitted)

The West, as we know, is fascinated with violence. Western journalists, film makers, and anthropologists working in New Guinea have made the island famous with reports of head-hunting, cannibalism and male-female antagonism. The range of New Guinea societies, however, is great. While the gentler societies lack the riveting appeal of those that are more flamboyantly aggressive, they can be instructive nonetheless. The Wape of Papua New Guinea's Sandaun (formerly West Sepik) Province are a case in point. Like many other Melanesian peoples, the egalitarian Wape live in a mountainous tropical forest habitat in sedentary villages and are slash-and-burn horticulturalists. Marriage occurs through bridewealth payments, polygyny is allowed but rare, postmarital residence is generally virilocal, and patrilineal clans are ideally exogamous while patrilineages are strictly so. But the Wape differ from a number of the societies with whom they share these customs: Wape men do not beat their wives. This does not mean that conjugal relations are always harmonious, but it is unusual for a man to slap his wife and I know of no instances where a woman suffered an injurious beating from her husband.

Because wife-beating is an accepted custom in many parts of Papua New Guinea and considered by the government to be a serious public health problem, in this chapter I identify some of the factors or constraints that help explain the comparative tranquility of Wape domestic life. These constraints—located on various but intersecting sociocultural, psychological, historical, ecological and physiological levels of analysis—are inextricably bound together in a complex circular relationship. Our knowledge of this relationship does not warrant the postulating of constraints operating on one level as being more important than those on another, so the general tranquility of Wape domestic life cannot be explained by a simple "cause and effect" model favored by an experimental positivistic science. The explanatory model proposed here is an associational one, more descriptive than causal, whose very circularity is essential to the explanation.

The data for this study, including a review of relevant court records, were collected during an eighteen-month field trip in 1970–1972 and brief revisits in 1982 and 1989. Although I have visited many of the villages of the approximately 10,000 Wape during my three trips to Wapeland, my view of Wape society and culture is as seen from Taute village, my principal fieldwork site.

CORRELATES OF WAPE DOMESTIC TRANQUILITY

Ethos and Emotions

The ethos of Wape society is markedly pacific. Although the society is not without its points of stress and the people not without passion concerning their personal relationships, the overall affective thrust of social life is to keep emotions, especially those that might lead to violence, under control. Even before Western contact, when enemy villages engaged in pay-back killings, the attacks might be years apart. Some Wape villages, on learning that the invading whites had banned warfare, abandoned the custom even before government patrols could intervene. During my fieldwork, I never saw a physical fight between men, between women, or even between children. The preferred Wape response to potential violence is conciliatory, not confrontational. When dissension in village life does occur, as it inevitably does, quarrels tend to be defused before culminating in physical violence or, if someone does strike another, he or she does not strike back. As a stranger to Wapeland, I had the first of several personal lessons in their gentle interaction style a few days after I moved into Taute village. When I shouted at a group of children crowding onto the raised and rotting veranda of our temporary house to get off, a man who had befriended me said reprovingly, "Speak softly!" The Wape perceive expatriates, especially men, as unpredictable and potentially bellicose. To gain some control over expatriate emotions, villagers place magical ginger under the house ladder of a visiting patrol officer—and I imagine a visiting anthropologist as well—to soothe him as he climbs down into the village. Another time, when I rebuked a group of men during the building of our house for cutting down the ornamental shrubs that hid the outhouse, they simply turned and silently walked away.

Enculturating a resident anthropologist or Wape children is not always an easy task, but the methods are identical. Aggressive acts are met with disinterest. An enraged toddler is left alone to kick and scream on the ground until her or his reason returns. Children and anthropologists soon learn that public aggression is an embarrassing and non-rewarding activity. Consequently, the Wape restrain the expression of negative emotions toward others and are generally friendly in their everyday village activities. Antipathy toward another person is rarely expressed directly in public though it may be expressed privately to a confidant.

Still, there are times when adults feel so personally transgressed and furious that they must do something more drastic than confiding their anger to a friend. Several alternatives are available. An offended person may gossip openly to others about the offense or, as everyone knows some sorcery, privately execute a punitive ritual. If, for example, a man's dog attacks and cripples a woman's piglet and the man makes no attempt to correct the wrong, in desperation she might go to his house and, standing outside, deliver a self-righteous harangue heard by all the neighbors while the transgressor and his family sit silently within. If the problem escalates, a meeting of the entire village is called by one of the concerned parties and anyone remotely involved with the problem should attend; not to go is to compromise one's integrity or innocence. Gathered on the front verandas of the houses surrounding the central plaza, men, women, and even children have their say until finally, perhaps several hours later, a consensus is reached.

I have stressed here the pacific ethos of Wape culture as well as indicated some of the actions resorted to when an individual's emotions must be expressed outwardly, namely, gossiping, sorcery, haranguing, and public meetings. However, none of these actions—regardless of the degree of aggressive intent—usually involve direct physical violence. Later I will discuss two exceptions to this finding that document a darker side of Wape emotions.

The Gaze of the Ancestors

The Wape are not conciliatory solely because they have been socialized to believe that public anger is often unrewarding or humiliating. There is a powerful sanctioning agent that helps to keep their behavior in check:

the spirits of their dead ancestors. As Hollan has similarly observed for the Toraja of Indonesia, "fear of supernatural retribution and social disintegration motivate the control of anger and aggression." The Wape believe that at death an adult's spirit returns to lineage lands in the forest. The spirit is also believed to be a frequent visitor to the village, where it looks after its descendants by sending illness and bad luck to family enemies. There is a high incidence of illness in Wapeland, testimony enough to ancestral power.

One night while visiting on a neighbor's veranda, I idly inquired about a slight, unidentifiable sound and learned that it was my host's dead father benevolently signaling his presence. Ancestral spirits are believed to see and hear all. This strongly discourages arguments among villagers because a spirit may avenge a descendant by negatively influencing an opponent's hunting, gardening or personal health. For this reason also, individuals occasionally express their anger publicly in Tok Pisin, the region's lingua franca, so the older ancestors who never learned it cannot understand what is being said.

Frequent disagreements among family members or neighbors can jeopardize the welfare of the entire village. To appease the ancestors, a conciliatory ritual must be held where the opponents speak out to them, announcing that they are now friends and asking the spirits to desist in the punitive interventions. A husband also knows that his wife's agnates as well as her classificatory mother's brothers are concerned about her welfare and, if he mistreats her, may resort to their ancestors or sorcery.

Gender Proximics

Another important factor pertaining to the absence of wife-beating is that Wape society, while acknowledging male-female differences in terms of dress and division of labor, is organized not to polarize gender differences but to de-emphasize them. Husbands and wives use the same paths and sleep together in the same house with their children. Village boys and girls, including teenagers, play at ease with one another. The lightly constructed homes are close together so that aural privacy is at a minimum; even a modestly raised voice is heard by all the neighbors, who are also relatives. Menstruating mothers and daughters are not secluded in menstrual huts but remain at home where husbands, if they are not going hunting continue to eat their wives' food. At puberty, boys begin to sleep separately in a village bachelors' house but they still interact daily with their parents and siblings and usually take their meals with them at home. Nor are boys or youths secluded from their mothers and sisters for initiation into manhood as in some New Guinea societies, where, often brutally, they are cleansed of female contamination in preparation for a warrior's career.

Female Status and Strategies

This is also a society where women and girls do not provide all of the child care. My tape-recorded interviews with male informants are penetrated with a baby-sitting father's asides to his restless toddler or the hungry cries of his infant. Fathers, as well as sons, take an active part in the care of infants and toddlers, especially when the mother is in the forest processing sago or collecting firewood.

This brings us to another important factor to explain why Wape husbands do not beat their wives: Wape women produce most of the food eaten. A typical meal consists of sago jelly with boiled greens—both the result of women's labor—and, with luck, a scrap of meat. While hunting is of great ritual and social importance to men, the introduction of the shotgun has seriously, and in some areas ruinously, depleted wild game. Pigs, of which there are few, are killed primarily for ceremonial exchanges among kin. As monogamy, both in the known past and present, is the Wape norm, a husband is dependent upon a single wife to feed him.

Another point is that a young woman has considerable say in the choice of a husband, signaling a young man in whom she is interested by slipping him a small present of food or tobacco. If possible, women prefer to marry within their natal village and rarely marry into a village that is more than an hour or two by foot from their father and brothers. Throughout a wife's marriage—and divorce is unusual—she and her husband are in close contact with her agnatic kin through a continuing series of economic exchanges that necessitates back-and-forth visiting while her brothers hold special ritual sanctions over her children, members of her husband's lineage. By the same token, she is tied to her mother's lineage too, especially to her classificatory mother's brothers who, as already indicated, watch over her well-being and whose homes are available as a place of refuge. A woman who feels that her husband is abusing her does not hesitate to move in with relatives, where she may stay for a week or more until they return with her to her husband's house. In no case may a husband seek his wife's return. In the meantime, he becomes dependent on his agnates' wives to feed him or else he must find his own food. Neither choice is a pleasant one.

The women of a hamlet, or at least the one in which I lived, develop strong solidarity bonds, something I only learned through observation. In the unlikely event that a couple becomes so angry during a quarrel that they begin to shout at each other, women of the hamlet, a few sometimes armed with large sticks, descend on the house and stand around it until the woman joins them outside.

A factor that relates to the interaction style of women is that they usually do not act in ways to further provoke or escalate a husband's anger towards them but are able to terminate his abuse with a very dangerous and ritualized action. While both Wape men and women are highly sensitive to personal shaming, when a wife is deeply humiliated or shamed by her husband's behavior toward her, she usually does not return the insult but instead attempts suicide. While female suicide attempts are not uncommon in Papua New Guinea, in most communities they appear to be more frequently precipitated by a husband's brutal beatings, as among the Gainj and Kaliai, than by his shaming words.

Three young wives of our small hamlet unsuccessfully attempted suicide while I lived there by drinking poison made from the root of the deadly derris vine. Interestingly, in each case the woman lived in a household with her husband and one of his parents. In two of the cases a precipitating event was criticism by her husband for not supplying enough food for the family.

There are no reliable suicide statistics for Wape society. But, on the basis of my own data and that of Lynette Wark Murray, the experienced missionary physician who patrolled Wapeland during my initial fieldwork, suicide attempts by unhappy wives, although hushed up by the community, do occur and follow a definite cultural pattern. Because an in-marrying wife's suicide is deeply stigmatizing to the husband's lineage, a woman who survives an attempted suicide finds herself the center of solicitous community attention. It is a desperate way to "get even" with an overly critical or abusive husband but, in the cases I observed, a most effective one, with the added compensation that it generated a favorable change in his domestic demeanor.

Although Wape men do not often commit suicide (I heard of only one inexplicable case), there is a corresponding dark side to men's behavior. While in the field I observed two instances and learned of several others where a man, said to be temporarily possessed by a wandering ghost, attempted to attack fellow villagers with his bow and arrows. These amok attacks occur only to men and are episodic, often with long periods of lucidity between them. A man so possessed is considered "crazy" by other villagers and is not held completely responsible for his actions. Because the target of a man's attack is socially diffuse, he has the opportunity to direct part of his aggression toward his wife, but he never does so.

Diet and Drugs

While the use of drugs, including alcohol, alone cannot make wife-beaters out of husbands, it should be noted that the Wape do not have easy access to alcohol, as is true in some parts of Papua New Guinea where wife-beating is culturally accepted. The addictive substances that are available to the Wape, namely tobacco and betel nut, are not gender differentiated: men and women alike are heavy users of both substances.

Severe protein and caloric deficiency are characteristic of the Wape diet and may, in a highly generalized way, be related to their pacific temperament and domestic tranquility. Sago is notoriously low in nutrients and the mountain-dwelling Wape, unlike most sago eaters who live on the coast or along large rivers, cannot obtain adequate protein from fish. Wape soils are poor and, although sago is supplemented with seasonal garden produce, gardens are small, unfenced and poorly cultivated. Medical growth and development studies indicate the birth weight of the Wape infant is one of the lowest reported in the world, and subsequent growth in height and weight is slow, with the onset of secondary sex characters correspondingly delayed. For example, a girl's first menstrual period occurs at a mean age of 18.4 years. There also is a progressive and marked loss of weight with age in both male and female adults. Many villagers suffer from chronic upper respiratory infections and malaria is holoendemic and uncontrolled. Several studies indicate that the health problems of the Wape were still severe as recently as the mid-1980's. It is hardly surprising that Wape ceremonial life is centered upon curing festivals.

Christian Mores and Government Law

Finally, we must consider the influence of the Catholic and Protestant missionaries and local government officials in respect to the absence of wife-beating in Wapeland. All Wape villages are under the influence of either Christian Brethren or Franciscan missionaries, and an indigenous fundamentalist church, New Guinea Revival, has also gathered considerable support. All of these churches are strong advocates of a harmonious family life and marital amity. The laws of the country further support these values and government and health officials distribute literature and lecture to villagers about them. But, as we already have seen, "domestic peace" is not a new idea to the Wape people. The importance of the churches' and state's moral rhetoric and sanctions regarding domestic life is not one of innovation, but of the reinforcement on another level of the contemporary Wape society's own tradition of domestic tranquility.

CONCLUSIONS

To answer the question of why Wape men do not beat their wives in a country where wife-beating is a major public health problem, I have noted and discussed some of the implicated constraints. These can be summarized as follows:

- A pacific and conciliatory cultural ethos supported by churches and the state;
- Nonpolarization of gender differences;
- Punitive intervention by watchful ancestral spirits;
- Women instrumental in selecting their husbands;

- Monogamy;
- Married couples domiciled among watchful relatives;
- Wives as principal food providers;
- Near absence of alcohol;
- Nutritionally deficient diet;
- Solidarity bonds among hamlet women;
- Threat of a wife's suicide if her husband shames her; and
- Women's agnates and classificatory mother's brothers responsive to their welfare.

None of these constraints alone can explain the relatively tranquil nature of Wape domestic life. When viewed as an interrelated cluster, though, these constraints help us understand the absence of wife-beating. If a society has very poor nutrition, a pacific conciliatory ethos, low access to alcohol, watchful and succoring neighbors and relatives, vengeful ancestors, husbands dependent on a single wife for sustenance, non-polarization of the sexes, and the threat of a wife's suicide if shamed by her husband, it is difficult to conceive of a marital relationship progressing to a state where a wife is being beaten.

However, this inquiry into the absence of Wape wife-beating has uncovered another form of Wape domestic violence—attempted suicide by females—with a cultural scenario of its own. In desperation, wives humiliated by their husbands "beat up" on themselves and, indirectly, their spouses by attempting to poison themselves. The difference is that attempted suicide, unlike being beaten, is a self-empowering act of rectitude, an aggressive action against one's person that, if one survives, may reshape a damaged husband-wife relationship more equitably. To Wape men, the possibility of a wife's attempted suicide is a sobering symbol for the limits of oppression. To women, it is a desperate act fraught with peril, an act some know is worth the risk.

[Editor's Notes: 1. Susan Rose, author of Challenging Global Gender Violence: The Clothesline Project (2014) writes in Chapter 6: "Abuse is Not Traditional: Culture and Colonization," that "neither patriarchy nor violence against women and children is 'traditional,' if one considers the societies in which the vast majority of human history has been lived." She notes that in gathering and hunting societies women's and men's roles were relatively equally valued. As modes of production shifted, women's status declined, and violence against women increased. Rose focuses on two indigenous groups (Maoris and Native Americans) who formerly had low rates of domestic violence but became very violent within the family as a result of colonization. She describes how intergenerational trauma from oppression contributes to the current situation, and illustrates ways that

these indigenous groups are re-claiming their traditional cultures as a resource rather than an excuse in challenging gender violence within their communities.

2. In "A Comparative Survey of the Historic Civil, Common, and American Indian Tribal Law Responses to Domestic Violence," 23 Okla. City U. L. Rev. 433 (1998), Virginia Murray describes traditional responses to DV in three U.S. tribes, including practices that prevented abuse. Historically, Cheyennes had a very long courtship, DV was automatic grounds for divorce, wives could go back to their original families or her family could force the abuser to leave, after divorce the wife got the children, house, and furniture, polygamy could help protect wives, though wives had to have cause for divorce while husbands did not.

In the Navajo nation, first marriages were arranged, couples were given pre-marital counseling, including the message that husbands were not allowed to abuse their wives and that DV is illegal, wives had equal rights with husbands along with equal responsibilities, and there were strong family laws in terms of women's status. Couples lived near the wife's original family and could not live alone during the first year of marriage. If the wife left due to DV, her family had to take her in. The most important Navajo deity, who created the world, was female: Changing Woman.

Cherokees were matrilineal civil libertarians who believed in equality and individual freedom. The wife owned the house, its contents, and the family crops. If she left her partner, she might raise the marital children with her brothers. There was no formal marriage or divorce, merely cohabitation. DV was very uncommon, even in response to adultery, which was not a crime, but a private matter.

The author concludes that the way things were structured in these three societies helped to avoid DV as well as providing effective ways to respond to it.]

CHAPTER 3

CROSS-CULTURAL ISSUES: SURVIVORS OF DOMESTIC VIOLENCE IN THE U.S. WHO FACE MULTIPLE OPPRESSIONS

■ ■ ■

This chapter focuses on how domestic violence is experienced by particular groups in the U.S., including women of color/women of the global majority, non-white immigrants, Muslim women, Jewish women, and disabled women. It starts with a thought-provoking essay describing how racism distorts the ways that White U.S. culture perceives survivors of domestic violence based on their race. This is followed by a speech asking how we solve the problem of violence against women of color in the U.S., including domestic violence, when there are aspects of the State which perpetuate violence against people of color.

In the section on Asian American battered women, the materials describe the vast differences within this group, the influence of immigrant status, and barriers in accessing domestic violence services. This section also discusses the concept of a "cultural defense," which some immigrant men have asserted when charged with domestic violence crimes, and which raises complex questions, including the role of an expert witness, what culture is, who defines it, how static or changing it is, and whether it should be taken into account in the U.S. legal system.

The section on African American battered women starts with an account of one woman who ended up in prison for shooting her abusive boyfriend. A new article asks why Black women are so angry, discusses the history of how they have been treated in this country, and describes the ways that racist attitudes and policies based on that history impact legal decision-making and Black women's access to resources or lack thereof.

The article dealing with battered Latinas includes statistics, and covers help-seeking, needs, and barriers to services. Then comes an amicus brief to the Supreme Court about Native American women, who face the highest rates of intimate partner abuse, and the importance of honoring historic treaties that established tribal sovereignty, which allows tribes to prosecute non-Native abusers.

Jewish women in the U.S. also are in a minority status, and consequently deal with many of the same issues: their relationship to the majority culture's legal system, how this system interacts with religious law and practice, pressure to hide such problems from the majority community, and loyalty to the community. Another article focuses on similar issues regarding Muslim battered women in the U.S.

The chapter concludes with excerpts from an article looking at disabled women and domestic violence, comparing the abuse this population experiences with that of non-disabled women and making policy recommendations. Survivors with cognitive and psychological disabilities are included in the materials.

The fact that these materials are located in one chapter does not signify that this is intended to be the only time the reader thinks about these issues. The intent is that the reader will use the information from this chapter to continue to examine the issues raised in the rest of this book. In every area of law, it is important to ask how policies and practices affect all survivors of domestic violence and to make changes accordingly.

A. INTRODUCTION

LETI VOLPP, ON CULTURE, DIFFERENCE AND DOMESTIC VIOLENCE

11 Am U J Gender Social Policy & Law 393 (2003)
(citations and footnotes omitted)

How should we consider cultural difference when we think about domestic violence? Elizabeth Schneider's path-breaking representation of Yvonne Wanrow, described in her book, Battered Women and Feminist Lawmaking, gives us an important example of how one can contemplate this question in the context of legal representation. In arguing that Yvonne Wanrow's perspective as a Native American woman had been excluded from her claim of self defense, Elizabeth Schneider and other attorneys at the Center for Constitutional Rights successfully asserted that the way one's specific identity shapes experiences must be factored into the consideration of a defendant's state of mind. What was missing, they argued, was evidence that would have explained why Yvonne Wanrow would react as she did when an uninvited white man, who she believed had tried to molest one of her children, entered her babysitter's home. This evidence included information as to the general lack of police protection in such situations, the pervasiveness of violence against women and children, Wanrow's belief that the man was a child molester, Wanrow's lack of trust in the police, and her belief that she could successfully defend herself only with a weapon.

But I fear that this representation was exceptional in its careful attention to particularized detail. I am concerned that when attempts to represent a woman's difference are less careful, what can accompany or underlie culturally based advocacy can be quite problematic. Very often, discussions of cultural alterity rely upon invocations of culture that are little more than crass, group based stereotypes that may, in fact, be quite remote from the individual experiences at issue. Moreover, unlike in Wanrow's case where the failures of the police were pivotal to the argument, invocations of culture often suggest that culture somehow exists apart from the state.

This reflects outmoded, although popular, perceptions of culture. Culture is still fused with ethnicity, and not understood as a descriptor explaining all kinds of social interactions. Moreover, culture is generally thought of as a noun, a fixed and static thing, rather than conceived as an adjective modifying particular practices. Discussions of the way culture can shape domestic violence occur in a broader context of already existing stereotypes about culture, that reflect problematic notions as to how culture is believed to link to race.

Despite the valiant attempts of organizations such as the Family Violence Prevention Fund to inform the American public that domestic violence in the United States is a universal phenomenon occurring at epidemic rates, behavior that we condemn, such as domestic violence, is more often conceptualized as cultural for nonwhite communities. In fact, some have argued that it appears that many feminists and battered women's advocates suspect that "other" cultures actually support domestic violence—without turning to ask whether this may also be the case in their own communities. This tendency to describe domestic violence as "cultural" when occurring in communities of color, and not through the language of power and control used to describe domestic violence in "mainstream" communities, is linked to the uninterrogated assumption that devalued and less powerful groups are somehow more culturally determined. This description suggests that members of communities of color behave in certain ways, because they follow cultural dictates, as if they are encoded with culture.

We can see this in the reaction to the case of Andrea Yates. Her killing of her five children was primarily explained as a result of mental illness, with a diagnosis of postpartum psychosis. While there was some discussion suggesting Andrea Yates inhabited a particular cultural location due to her family's Christian beliefs, that engendered their living in a school bus left by a traveling preacher, or that led her to keep having children without using birth control because the children came from God, the primary lens through which her behavior was understood was psychological. We thus heard about her experience with the mental health system, medications she had stopped taking, and suicide attempts.

Psychology is used to explain why people positioned as Western subjects act irrationally. In contrast, culture is used to explain why those considered non-Western subjects act irrationally. We could thus compare the coverage of Andrea Yates with other cases involving mothers who killed their children. One such case involved Khoua Her, a Hmong immigrant, who in Minnesota in 1998 strangled her six children and then hanged herself in a failed suicide attempt. Police had been called to the family's home at least sixteen times in the previous two years, and there was a long history of domestic violence. In searching for explanations, the media invoked a "cultural clash," and "the American pull to be an individual versus the Hmong orientation of putting the group first." Described as the worst mass murder in Minnesota memory, the Her case was invoked—along with tales of animal cruelty, religious sacrifice of small dogs, the statistic that nearly half of the Hmong community was on state welfare, a string of gang rapes, and a thirteen year old who smothered her newborn—by a popular radio talk show host who said, "Those people should either assimilate or hit the road."

We see here the process of selective blaming of culture. The same act is understood as the product of Hmong culture in one case, but not white American culture in the other. Rather, Andrea Yates, whether she is condemned or pitied, is primarily depicted as a mother under enormous pressure, her life uninflected by a racialized culture. Khoua Her, in contrast, is described as if her life is completely circumscribed by a racialized culture.

A particular academic description of culture that reflects some of these problems is an article which appeared in a symposium issue of the Stanford Law Review, authored by Nilda Rimonte, who was once the director of a battered women's shelter in Los Angeles that serves Asian women and children. In the article, Rimonte points to a number of reasons for domestic violence in Asian immigrant communities: the Pacific-Asian family's traditionally patriarchal system and the attendant belief in the supremacy of the male; the socialization goals and processes which favor the family and community over the individual; the cultural emphasis on silent suffering versus open communication of needs and feelings; and the enormous adjustment pressures which test the limits of immigrants' and refugees' survival skills.

Rimonte also suggests that few Asian countries have woman's rights movements whose energy and goals might significantly influence the women in their society, asserts that Asians have a different sense of time, claims that the idea of choices and rights may not be appropriate for Asians, and states that, unlike the Western ideal of the healthy family, the Asian family is structured around male privilege, authority, and superiority. The article presents a frozen, monolithic description of culture for an enormous region of the world that elides any difference or heterogeneity. Rimonte's sweeping and inaccurate generalizations have allowed other writers to make blanket statements about gender subordination in "Asian cultures" and to assert that there is something more misogynistic about Asian immigrant communities than "our own."

In the face of this selective stereotyping, the appeal of universalist descriptions of domestic violence, to suggest that specific cultural formations have no impact, is understandable. Two examples that surfaced in discussions I recently had with Asian American and Pacific Islander domestic violence advocates come to mind. The first was the response of one advocate to the query of a "mainstream" women's shelter (meaning one not serving diverse populations), that inquired for advice about the "cultural shame" of an Indian immigrant who had been sexually assaulted; this cultural shame, said the shelter staff, prohibited the woman from using the shelter's public shower. The response of the advocate was to tell the shelter that any woman who had been sexually assaulted would have issues around privacy and bodily integrity. The second was the response of another advocate to the question as to what, specifically, were the issues for battered lesbians. The advocate's response was that a battered lesbian's experience of domestic violence will reflect her class position, whether she is disabled, whether she is an immigrant, or whether she lives in a rural area, like any other woman in those situations. She then reflected that perhaps the fear of being outed by the abusive partner, if the battered woman was not already out, was specific to lesbians—but then reflected that any battered woman fears being outed, as battered. This kind of approach, to shift attention away from a focus on particular assumptions about how cultural identities shape domestic violence, to examining how experiences are similar, seems necessary.

But then how do we describe the specifics of culture? One important shift would be to understand that cultural practices are imbricated with material and political forces. Usually when cultural explanations are given, a static and insular culture is blamed, detracting attention away from one's limited access to services, or from the policies of the state. Thus, part of what I am arguing for here is an understanding of culture that does not strip away the economic and the political from its content. Take, for example, the idea that Asian immigrants have difficulty gaining access to the Violence Against Women Act ("VAWA") self-petitioning process. When this is blamed on "cultural limitations" of Asian communities—such as passivity, or shame—it removes the onus from agencies or the government to try to make services more accessible. Thus, invocations of culture can erase the racism of agencies and entities that fail to provide appropriate services to battered women by hiring diverse staff who speak relevant languages or translate materials. Further, invocations of culture can detract attention away from the policies of the state: VAWA self-petitioning was only required as a remedy to fix U.S. immigration laws that gave batterers tools with which they could abuse partners, after Congress enacted the Marriage Fraud Act. For an example that foregrounds the importance of economic concerns, we could return to the case of Khoua Her. Recently, an article in the Hmong Times suggested that Her strangled her six children because she saw death as the only means of saving them from poverty, after she lost the low-paying job that had provided food and benefits for her family. Understanding Her's acts as solely the product of

"Hmong culture" completely subsumes the role material forces may have played in shaping her perceptions.

Another important shift was evident in the second advocate's response, described above, when she insisted on invoking class, disability, immigrant status, and geographical location as relevant to any particular battered lesbian's experience. Identities and experiences do shape perspectives, but we must be attentive to the way in which this transpires through a complex process that reflects an individual's specific position. Essentializing narratives about particular cultures can often serve to mask reality. For example, a battered woman who is an immigrant may have failed to call the police, not because her culture condones passivity on the part of women, but because her partner was a police officer in her country of origin, because she has witnessed a failure of police protection and practices of police brutality, and because the police in her present location do not speak her language. Granting explanatory power to essentialized depictions of "culture," as purportedly made up of unchanging rituals that cement the subordinate location of women in a fixed system of social practices, will inevitably fail to accurately describe the relationship of culture, difference, and domestic violence.

Yet I would agree with Sherene Razack, who, in examining narratives of sexual violence against South Asian women, cautions against a simple turn to universalist narratives. She argues that there are three problems with reacting against culturalist stereotypes through using universal arguments. Razack asserts that deculturalized narratives rarely have enough traction to displace orientalist fantasies that are believed in mainstream communities, are too abstract to use in conversations within communities that are the subject of description, and lastly, fail to grapple with the fact that violent acts are committed in culturally specific ways.

ANGELA DAVIS, THE COLOR OF VIOLENCE AGAINST WOMEN

3(3) ColorLines 4 (Fall 2000)

[Editor's Note: Angela Davis, a former political prisoner, long-time activist, author, and professor at the University of California at Santa Cruz, gave the keynote address and spoke with participants at the 2000 Color of Violence Conference there.]

I feel extremely honored to have been invited to deliver this keynote address. This conference deserves to be called "historic" on many accounts. It is the first of its kind, and this is precisely the right intellectual season for such a gathering. The breadth and complexity of its concerns show the contradictions and possibilities of this historical moment. And just such a gathering can help us to imagine ways of attending to the ubiquitous violence in the lives of women of color that also radically subvert the institutions and discourses within which we are compelled by necessity to think and work.

I predict that this conference will be remembered as a milestone for feminist scholars and activists, marking a new moment in the history of anti-violence scholarship and organizing.

Many years ago when I was a student in San Diego, I was driving down the freeway with a friend when we encountered a black woman wandering along the shoulder. Her story was extremely disturbing. Despite her uncontrollable weeping, we were able to surmise that she had been raped and dumped along the side of the road. After a while, she was able to wave down a police car, thinking that they would help her. However, when the white policeman picked her up, he did not comfort her, but rather seized upon the opportunity to rape her once more.

I relate this story not for its sensational value, but for its metaphorical power.

Given the racist and patriarchal patterns of the state, it is difficult to envision the state as the holder of solutions to the problem of violence against women of color. However, as the anti-violence movement has been institutionalized and professionalized, the state plays an increasingly dominant role in how we conceptualize and create strategies to minimize violence against women. One of the major tasks of this conference, and of the anti-violence movement as a whole, is to address this contradiction, especially as it presents itself to poor communities of color.

THE ADVENT OF "DOMESTIC VIOLENCE"

Violence is one of those words that is a powerful ideological conductor, one whose meaning constantly mutates. Before we do anything else, we need to pay tribute to the activists and scholars whose ideological critiques made it possible to apply the category of domestic violence to those concealed layers of aggression systematically directed at women. These acts were for so long relegated to secrecy or, worse, considered normal.

Many of us now take for granted that misogynist violence is a legitimate political issue, but let us remember that a little more than two decades ago, most people considered "domestic violence" to be a private concern and thus not a proper subject of public discourse or political intervention. Only one generation separates us from that era of silence. The first speak-out against rape occurred in the early 1970s, and the first national organization against domestic violence was founded toward the end of that decade.

We have since come to recognize the epidemic proportions of violence within intimate relationships and the pervasiveness of date and acquaintance rape, as well as violence within and against same-sex intimacy. But we must also learn how to oppose the racist fixation on people of color as the primary perpetrators of violence, including domestic and sexual violence, and at the same time to fiercely challenge the real violence that men of color inflict on women. These are precisely the men who are already reviled as the major purveyors of violence in our society: the gang members, the drug-dealers, the drive-by shooters, the burglars, and assailants. In short, the criminal is figured as a black or Latino man who must be locked into prison.

One of the major questions facing this conference is how to develop an analysis that furthers neither the conservative project of sequestering millions of men of color in accordance with the contemporary dictates of globalized capital and its prison-industrial complex, nor the equally conservative project of abandoning poor women of color to a continuum of violence that extends from the sweatshops through the prisons, to shelters, and into bedrooms at home.

How do we develop analyses and organizing strategies against violence against women that acknowledge the race of gender and the gender of race?

WOMEN OF COLOR ON THE FRONT LINES

Women of color have been active in the anti-violence movement since its beginnings. The first national organization addressing domestic violence was founded in 1978 when the United States Civil Rights Commission Consultation on Battered Women led to the founding of the National Coalition Against Domestic Violence. In 1980, the Washington, D.C. Rape Crisis Center sponsored the First National Conference on Third World Women and Violence. The following year a Women of Color Task Force was created within the National Coalition Against Domestic Violence. To make some historical connections, it is significant that the U.S. Third World Women's Caucus formed that same year within the National Women Studies Association, and the groundbreaking book This Bridge Called My Back was first published.

Many of these activists have helped to develop a more complex understanding about the overlapping, cross-cutting, and often contradictory relationships among race, class, gender, and sexuality that militate against a simplistic theory of privatized violence in women's lives. Clearly, the powerful slogan first initiated by the feminist movement—"the personal is political"—is far more complicated than it initially appeared to be.

The early feminist argument that violence against women is not inherently a private matter, but has been privatized by the sexist structures of the state, the economy, and the family has had a powerful impact on public consciousness.

Yet, the effort to incorporate an analysis that does not reify gender has not been so successful. The argument that sexual and domestic violence is the structural foundation of male dominance sometimes leads to a hierarchical notion that genital mutilation in Africa and sati, or wife-burning, in India are the most dreadful and extreme forms of the same violence against women which can be discovered in less appalling manifestations in Western cultures.

Other analyses emphasize a greater incidence of misogynist violence in poor communities and communities of color, without necessarily acknowledging the greater extent of police surveillance in these communities—directly and through social service agencies. In other words, precisely because the primary strategies for addressing violence against women rely on the state and on constructing gendered assaults on women as "crimes," the criminalization process further bolsters the racism of the courts and prisons. Those institutions, in turn, further contribute to violence against women.

On the one hand, we should applaud the courageous efforts of the many activists who are responsible for a new popular consciousness of violence against women, for a range of legal remedies, and for a network of shelters, crisis centers, and other sites where survivors are able to find support. But on the other hand, uncritical reliance on the government has resulted in serious problems. I suggest that we focus our thinking on this contradiction: Can a state that is thoroughly infused with racism, male dominance, class-bias, and homophobia and that constructs itself in and through violence act to minimize violence in the lives of women? Should we rely on the state as the answer to the problem of violence against women?

* * *

MILITARIZED VIOLENCE

How then can one expect the state to solve the problem of violence against women, when it constantly recapitulates its own history of colonialism, racism, and war? How can we ask the state to intervene when, in fact, its armed forces have always practiced rape and battery against "enemy" women? In fact, sexual and intimate violence against women has been a central military tactic of war and domination.

Yet the approach of the neoliberal state is to incorporate women into these agencies of violence—to integrate the armed forces and the police.

* * *

If we concede that something about the training structures and the operations they are expected to carry out makes the men (and perhaps also women) in these institutions more likely to engage in violence within their intimate relationships, why then is it so difficult to develop an analysis of violence against women that takes the violence of the state into account?

The major strategy relied on by the women's anti-violence movement of criminalizing violence against women will not put an end to violence against women—just as imprisonment has not put an end to "crime" in general.

I should say that this is one of the most vexing issues confronting feminists today. On the one hand, it is necessary to create legal remedies for women who are survivors of violence. But on the other hand, when the remedies rely on punishment within institutions that further promote violence—against women and men, how do we work with this contradiction?

How do we avoid the assumption that previously "private" modes of violence can only be rendered public within the context of the state's apparatus of violence?

THE CRIME BILL

It is significant that the 1994 Violence Against Women Act was passed by Congress as Title IV of the Violent Crime Control and Law Enforcement Act of 1994—the Crime Bill. This bill attempted to address violence against women within domestic contexts, but at the same time it facilitated the incarceration of more women—through Three Strikes and other provisions. The growth of police forces provided for by the Crime Bill will certainly increase the numbers of people subject to the brutality of police violence.

Prisons are violent institutions. Like the military, they render women vulnerable in an even more systematic way to the forms of violence they may have experienced in their homes and in their communities. Women's prison experiences point to a continuum of violence at the intersection of racism, patriarchy, and state power.

A Human Rights Watch report entitled "All Too Familiar: Sexual Abuse of Women in U.S. Prisons" says: "Our findings indicate that being a woman prisoner in U.S. state prisons can be a terrifying experience. If you are sexually abused, you cannot escape from your abuser. Grievance or investigatory procedures, where they exist, are often ineffectual, and correctional employees continue to engage in abuse because they believe they will rarely be held accountable, administratively or criminally. Few people outside the prison walls know what is going on or care if they do know. Fewer still do anything to address the problem."

* * *

There are no easy solutions to all the issues I have raised and that so many of you are working on. But what is clear is that we need to come together to work toward a far more nuanced framework and strategy than the anti-violence movement has ever yet been able to elaborate.

We want to continue to contest the neglect of domestic violence against women, the tendency to dismiss it as a private matter. We need to develop an approach that relies on political mobilization rather than legal remedies or social service delivery. We need to fight for temporary and long-term solutions to violence and simultaneously think about and link global capitalism, global colonialism, racism, and patriarchy—all the forces that shape violence against women of color. Can we, for example, link a strong demand for remedies for women of color who are targets of rape and domestic violence with a strategy that calls for the abolition of the prison system?

[Editor's Note: In "Against Hate and Self-Hate: VAWA Must Now Be Implemented Without Cultural Biases," Ms. Magazine online (4/4/2022), Mallika Kaur, founder and Executive Director of the Sikh Family Center, notes that in the U.S. cultural differences are often seen as disempowering rather than nuanced and potentially empowering. She says that "when one of those terrible tragedies [like a murder/suicide] occurs in minority groups like the Sikh community, there is often a rush to suggest that something about Sikh culture contributed to the violence," even though the rate of abuse in the Sikh community mirrors that in the larger society. She calls on all of us to honor the range of choices that survivors of domestic violence choose in addressing abuse and to remember that there are people in all faiths and cultural communities who are allies in ending domestic violence.

She concludes: "For the implementation of VAWA [2022, which promises to allocate more resources to historically underserved communities and 'culturally specific services' in order to address gender-based violence] to truly meet the challenges of all people affected by gendered violence in 2022, it must openly examine layered biases faced by minority and minoritized cultural groups and provide real support to grassroots initiatives."]

* * *

B. ASIAN AMERICAN WOMEN

GINA SZETO, THE ASIAN AMERICAN DOMESTIC VIOLENCE MOVEMENT

(unpublished) (2012)
(citations and footnotes omitted)

II. ASIAN AMERICAN WOMEN AND DOMESTIC VIOLENCE

Even though domestic violence is a pervasive problem in the Asian American community, traditional, gendered notions of women prevent Asian American women from discussing domestic violence in their home and community. In addition to culturally rooted norms that prevent Asian American women from speaking out, the term "Asian American" can frustrate real dialogue about domestic violence in the Asian American community because of the confusion the term engenders. Use of the term "Asian American" assumes that all Asian Americans have the same cultural, societal, and economic issues and experience domestic violence in the same way. This notion is inaccurate. The term "Asian American" was created by the U.S. government "from the need to make racial categorizations in racially divided society" and by Asian American activists to help unify different Asian ethnic groups. So while the term is imperfect and creates an illusion of a homogenous Asian identity, if used with those limitations in mind, the concept can be useful in scholarship that limits its analysis to those characteristics that Asian Americans do share. Several shared characteristics are instructive as they relate to domestic violence: 1) the overwhelmingly immigrant character of Asian American communities, 2) the existence of similar cultural patterns across most Asian American communities, 3) issues with accessing services, and 4) the existence of harmful stereotypes about Asian Americans collectively and Asian American women specifically.

A. Statistics for Different Asian Ethnicities: A Glimpse

While the precise definition of "Asian American" is both elusive and evolving, it is instructive for the purposes of this paper to provide a snap shot of the various Asian American and Pacific Islander ethnicities in the United States.

There is much diversity in the term Asian American, with over 40 Asian countries represented in the U.S. and more ethnicities than countries. The various Asian ethnicities include Central Asians, East Asians, Native Hawaiians and Pacific Islanders, Southeast Asians, South Asians, and West Asians. According to 2010 U.S. Census data, the Asian American (AA) population in the U.S. is larger than it has ever been, reaching 14.2 million in 2009 (or 4.6% of the U.S. population). Since 2000, the AA population has grown 27.9% from 10.6 to 13.2 million.

The ten Asian American groups with the largest populations are Chinese, Asian Indian, Filipino, Vietnamese, Korean, Japanese, Pakistani, Hmong, Laotian, and Thai. The states with the largest Asian American populations are: 1. California, 2. New York, 3. Texas, 4. New Jersey, 5. Hawaii, 6. Illinois, 7. Washington, 8. Florida, 9. Virginia, and 10. Massachusetts. The states with the largest percentage of Asian Americans populations are Hawai'i with 45.9%; California with 12.9%; New Jersey with 7.8%; New York and Washington with 7.1%; Massachusetts and Virginia with 5%; Illinois with 4.4%; Texas with 3.6%; and Florida with 2.4%.

A review of the literature points to a high prevalence of domestic violence rates in Asian American homes. In a compilation by the Asian Pacific Islander Institute on Domestic Violence of community-based studies, 41–61% of respondents reported experiencing intimate physical and/or sexual violence during their lifetime. This is higher than the rates in a national study in which those experiencing such violence broke down as follows: Whites (21.3%), African Americans (26.3%), Hispanics of any race (21.2%), people of mixed race (27.0%), American Indians and Alaskan

Natives (30.7%), and Asians and Pacific Islanders (12.8%). *[Editor's Note: other studies have found that the highest rates of these types of abuse are among Native Americans.]*

About 61% of Asian Americans are foreign born, the highest rate of any minority group in the country. Asians Americans as a predominantly immigrant population is a trend expected to continue through 2030. However, this pattern differs when country of origin is taken into consideration. For instance, the majority of Japanese Americans are U.S.-born, and many of them are third or fourth generation. Chinese Americans also have a higher than average share of older (3rd and 4th) generations in their population. But for most Asian Americans, the immigrant character of the Asian American population creates enormous legal and non-legal barriers for Asian American women who experience domestic violence.

The U.S. Census considers those who do not speak English "very well" to have Limited English Proficiency. Thirty-five percent of Asian Americans and 13.8% of Native Hawaiians and other Pacific Islanders have limited English proficiency, compared to 8.6% of the general population. The range of Asian Americans who speak English less than very well is great, for example 31.5% of Tagalog speakers speak English "less than very well," while 61% of Vietnamese speakers, 57% of Korean speakers, 55% of Chinese speakers and 52% of Thai speakers speak English less than "very well."

It is not lost on domestic violence advocates who serve immigrant communities that language is one of the most obvious barriers for immigrant women seeking domestic violence help. Unable to speak English fluently, many immigrant women find it difficult to seek help from law enforcement, domestic violence shelters, and attorneys and agencies that exist to help them.

They may avoid seeking help altogether because of inability to effectively or comfortably communicate such a private matter in a language they are not fluent in. Immigrant women will also experience difficulty in understanding their legal rights, or that they have any at all.

Mainstream domestic violence shelters also present obstacles for immigrant women. Many domestic violence shelters do not offer multi-lingual services and lack the cultural sensitivity to meaningfully serve the needs of immigrant women. Battered immigrant women must often find their own interpreters, which usually involves asking their children or other relatives, persons who are connected with their batterers. If interpreters are available, immigrant battered women are often still hesitant to be forthcoming because of fear that their private matters will not be kept confidential or worse, that the interpreters may contact the batterers and disclose their location. For some, the inability to speak English effectively has been interpreted to indicate dishonesty by some mainstream domestic violence advocates.

A domestic violence advocate who serves the Asian American population reported that one of the women who came to her shelter had first gone to a mainstream one but was not accepted. When the advocate called the mainstream shelter to ask why she was not accepted into their shelter, the mainstream shelter said that they thought the victim was lying. In fact, it was her inability to speak English and the fact that the victim was not looking the advocate in the eye, a sign of deference in Asian culture, that caused the mainstream advocate to deny the battered woman services.

More controversially, some shelters may even accept English-speaking victims over immigrant victims because they believe that English-speaking women will make better use of their services. This is largely because many immigrant women may not be eligible for government benefits. As we can see, even when immigrant women do find the courage to leave an abusive home, many of them face additional hurdles once they reach the shelters that are supposed to provide them with assistance.

U.S. immigration laws are another obstacle preventing battered immigrant women from seeking help. Historically, these laws inadvertently made it more difficult for abused immigrant women to leave violent relationships. Battered immigrant women's confinement to these relationships was based in immigration laws that placed control of a married immigrant's legal status in the hands of her U.S. citizen or legal permanent resident spouse. As a result, many Asian American women lived at the mercy of their abusive husbands because they were under constant fear of deportation. The battered immigrant spouse was therefore faced with a difficult decision: either remain in the abusive relationship, or leave, become an undocumented immigrant and be potentially deprived of home, livelihood and perhaps child custody. The fear of deportation is immense for immigrant women, especially those women who have fled persecution in their homeland. For some, deportation means returning to a country where they would experience torture, jail or death. In other cases, deportation could result in immigrant women returning to impoverished countries with poor health conditions and weak economies.

In response, in 1994, Congress attempted to provide more substantial relief to battered immigrant women through the enactment of certain immigration provisions in the Violence Against Women Act (VAWA I). * * *

[*Editor's Summary:* The author describes provisions in VAWA II, VAWA III, and other federal legislation addressing the needs of battered immigrant women. These provisions encompass various forms of relief to encourage these women to request help from the U.S. criminal justice system and to prevent their deportation. This topic is covered in Chapter 17 of the textbook.]

STATE V. CHIA JAMES VUE

606 N.W.2d 719 (Minn.App. 2000)
(citations and footnotes omitted)

SYLLABUS BY THE COURT

Expert testimony linking a defendant's ethnicity with a propensity to engage in conduct consistent with the crime charged is inherently prejudicial and inadmissible.

OPINION

A Dakota County jury found appellant Chia James Vue guilty of one count of first-degree criminal sexual conduct, three counts of third-degree criminal sexual conduct, four counts of violating an order for protection, and one count of engaging in a pattern of harassing conduct. Appellant challenges his convictions and sentence, claiming (1) the district court erred in admitting expert testimony on Hmong cultural practices, (2) prosecutorial misconduct, (3) insufficient evidence, (4) double jeopardy for multiple prosecutions and punishments for offenses arising out of the same conduct, and (5) the district court erred in refusing to make a downward dispositional departure. We reverse on the basis of improper expert testimony.

FACTS

Appellant and M.V. are Hmong immigrants who came to the United States from Laos in the late 1970s. They were never legally married, but lived as husband and wife from 1980 through the mid-to-late 1990s, when their relationship deteriorated. In February 1998, M.V. obtained an order for protection against appellant.

On June 5, 1998, M.V. reported appellant to the police, claiming he had raped her four times in four separate incidents occurring between February and May 1998. Appellant was arrested and charged with four counts of criminal sexual conduct, four counts of violating an order for protection, and one count of pattern of harassing conduct.

Before jury selection, the court and counsel had a preliminary discussion on the state's plan to introduce expert testimony on Hmong culture. The prosecutor noted that the jury pool's responses to questionnaires showed a poor understanding of Hmong culture. The prosecutor sought to introduce expert testimony to provide context for the jury's determinations of witness credibility, but said the expert would not comment on the case itself. The prosecutor described the scope of the proposed testimony and added that it could help explain M.V.'s delay in coming forward and rebut the defense theory that the allegations were rooted in M.V.'s jealousy of appellant's second wife. The defense objected to the proposed testimony, and the court took the matter under advisement.

At trial, M.V. testified about the clan structure of Hmong society, the hierarchy of leadership within the clan, and the role of Hmong women in choosing a husband. She said it was inappropriate in Hmong culture for individuals with family or clan-related problems to seek help from outside the clan and that she was being treated as an outcast for having reported her husband to the police. She claimed appellant had been threatening and abusive to her throughout their marriage and had forced her to have sex with him hundreds of times. She said she did not report the rapes earlier because of Hmong social pressure and because appellant said he would kill her if she did.

During a break in the state's case-in-chief, the court held a voir dire examination of the proposed expert witness, a white Minneapolis Park Police officer, and a hearing on the defense motion to exclude his testimony. On direct and cross-examination, the officer described his interest in and personal and professional exposure to Hmong culture.

The prosecutor said the officer would testify to the following: a general history of the Hmong in America; the clan system and the hierarchy within the clans; assimilation issues facing the Hmong in America; Hmong-Americans' attitudes toward the American criminal justice system; the traditional system for resolving family and clan-related problems; issues with going outside the clan for help; the role and position of women in Hmong culture; and male-female relations in traditional marriages.

In allowing the testimony, the court compared it to expert testimony on battered woman syndrome, noted it was being offered to promote a complete understanding of the evidence, and found it would be helpful to the jury.

As an example of a conflict between Hmong culture and the American legal system, the officer described a traditional marriage practice in which men "kidnap" young girls. Among other generalized statements, the state's expert testified that Southeast Asian victims are generally reluctant to report crimes. Speaking of Hmong culture, he testified in part:

> Well, as I indicated it is a male-dominated culture, very clearly. It's not the only culture that's male dominated, I might add, but it's very clear in Hmong culture. Women are to be obedient, to be silent, to suffer rather than to tell. Domestic abuse is a very private situation. I'm not even so sure if the abuse is shared with other women. I think it's kept very much internal.

On cross-examination, the officer stated that "male-dominance" was "fairly universal in the Hmong culture." In addition, the defense counsel asked and the expert responded as follows:

> Q: Are you suggesting that what male dominance really means is abuse?

A: I have seen evidence—secondhand, I might add, maybe third-hand, not firsthand or I would have to act as a police officer—of male aggression within the Hmong community to keep the female in her place.

Q: Are you saying that that is a general trait or are you saying that all Hmong traditional males are abusive?

A: I've been around long enough to know that you can never make a statement that says all of anything will happen all of the time. I think there are patterns that can be identified over time and that that pattern is disturbing in the Hmong culture.

ISSUE

Did the district court abuse its discretion in admitting expert testimony on aspects of Hmong culture?

ANALYSIS

Appellant argues the expert testimony was inadmissible cultural stereotyping calculated to appeal to cultural and racial prejudice. He claims it (1) lacked foundation, (2) was irrelevant and unduly prejudicial, and (3) violated public policy and his state and federal constitutional rights to a fair trial, the presumption of innocence, due process, and equal protection. We agree.

Generally, admission of expert testimony rests within the district court's discretion and will not be reversed absent clear error. Even where a defendant alleges a constitutional violation, we review evidentiary questions for abuse of discretion.

Minn. R. Evid. 702 sets the basic standard for admission of expert testimony:

> If scientific, technical, or other specialized knowledge will assist the trier of fact to understand the evidence or to determine a fact in issue, a witness qualified as an expert by knowledge, skill, experience, training, or education, may testify thereto in the form of an opinion or otherwise.

But, along with the bare bones provisions of Minn. R. Evid. 702, a district court may consider the offered expert testimony under a balancing test embodied in Minn. R. Evid. 403:

> Although relevant, evidence may be excluded if its probative value is substantially outweighed by the danger of unfair prejudice, confusion of the issues, or misleading the jury, or by considerations of undue delay, waste of time, or needless presentation of cumulative evidence.

In criminal trials in particular, courts must be cautious when ruling on the admissibility of expert testimony. This is necessary to guard against the expert's "potential to influence a jury unduly" with his court-recognized "special knowledge" and to "ensure that the defendant's presumption of innocence does not get lost in the flurry of expert testimony."

In this case, the primary issue at trial was whether M.V. consented to the sexual contact with appellant. Both sides addressed her delay in bringing the allegations. The prosecutor offered the testimony of a park policeman to bolster M.V.'s story by "explaining" why a Hmong immigrant who had been raped by her husband would be reluctant to go to the police.

There is little in this record suggesting cultural testimony was necessary. The complainant was a grown woman; she was bilingual and educated; and she had been in the United States for many years. A lay jury would not have had trouble understanding or believing her testimony simply because she was Hmong. It is patronizing to suggest otherwise. The expert testimony itself confirmed the lack of relevancy to this case and to this victim. The transcription shows the following questions and answers:

> Q: Are you saying then—and this is what I'm leading up to, Lieutenant—that all of the Hmong people in Minnesota are following the same cultural trends?
>
> A: I would not say that all Hmong follow the same cultural trends, but I would say that the Hmong culture that I've observed is slower to change than other cultures that I've observed.
>
> Q: Would you say that language is one reason why, at least in your observations, there has been a slower cultural change?
>
> A: I would strongly agree that, *particularly among older Hmong citizens where English is nonexistent or very difficult at best.* I would say that the isolation that comes from not being able to go to a mall and shop and exchange normal conversation with shopkeepers or other people in society has kept Hmong women, in particular older Hmong women, prisoners in their homes.

(Emphasis added.) Thus, the "expert's" cultural testimony emphasized the barriers on reporting "among older Hmong citizens where English is nonexistent or very difficult at best." This is not our case.

Further, the credentials of this Minneapolis Park Police officer to give expert opinions on Hmong culture are suspect. The record shows that the officer's contact with Hmong culture arose primarily from personal experience with family friends, that his exposure to Hmong culture as a police officer was limited, and that he had little or no academic training involving Hmong culture.

While we acknowledge there is no formal requirement to qualifying as an expert under Minn. R. Evid. 702, the informal nature of this officer's familiarity with Hmong culture brings his qualifications to be an expert into doubt.

We note that here, unlike *Lee*, the defense did not open the door to the testimony by attacking the complainant's credibility with its own expert.

The "expert" testimony was inherently prejudicial. It went far beyond describing Hmong cultural practices that would help explain the alleged victim's behavior, if such testimony was needed. The testimony included generic statements about "male-dominance" in Hmong culture and directly implied a generalized perceived pattern of abuse of Hmong females by Hmong males.

While some of these statements could conceivably be relevant to a complainant's reluctance to come forward, their probative value, if any, is based on generalizations that appellant is part of a "guilty class" of spouse-abusers, and the victim is part of a "victim class" of abused women. By asserting that Hmong men tend to abuse their wives, the expert testimony directly implied to the jury that because defendant was Hmong, he was more likely to have assaulted his wife. It is self-evident that this is highly prejudicial. It is impermissible to link a defendant's ethnicity to the likelihood of his guilt.

Our criminal code is supposed to be blind to the array of cultures present in the State of Minnesota. The state wants it that way when cultural testimony goes against them. The state conceded at oral argument that it would object, in a statutory rape case or a domestic abuse trial, if defense counsel attempted to introduce expert evidence showing the charged conduct was permissible in the defendant's culture (in Minnesota, intercourse with a young woman under the age of 14 is prohibited, whether consensual or not). For instance, marriage to young women under the age of 14 is acceptable in many cultures, including Hmong. The prosecutor stated she would object to that as irrelevant, if offered by a defense attorney. But here the state urges the *same kind of cultural evidence* be allowed to bolster a case against appellant.

We conclude the prejudicial effect of the expert testimony about Hmong males' tendency to dominate and abuse their wives, and the tendency of Hmong wives not to want to report assaults, far outweighed any probative value. We find the district court abused its discretion in qualifying the expert and admitting his testimony.

Reversal is not required when an erroneous admission of objected-to evidence is harmless beyond a reasonable doubt. The United States Supreme Court has long recognized that the state bears the burden of showing an evidentiary error is harmless. When the erroneous admission does not implicate constitutional rights, we will reverse if there is "a reasonable possibility that the wrongfully admitted evidence significantly affected the verdict."

Admitting expert testimony always risks that the expert's opinions will inordinately influence the jury. The record shows appellant's conviction was based on disputed testimonial evidence. The outcome of the trial depended on whom the jury believed. By implying appellant's Hmong descent made him a probable spouse-abuser, the improper testimony clearly implied a conviction should be forthcoming. In view of the severe risk of prejudice it posed, we cannot escape the conclusion that the improper testimony strongly influenced the jury's decision to convict.

We conclude that the state failed to meet its burden of proving harmless error. We reverse and remand for a new trial.

DECISION

The district court improperly allowed expert testimony on Hmong culture. The testimony was speculative, conjectural, and its prejudicial effect far outweighed any possible probative value.

[Editor's Note: Appellate courts have generally upheld the use of expert testimony on why victims of sexual assault or domestic violence in general may be reluctant to report the crime to law enforcement, as opposed to focusing on victims who are members of particular groups. See Chapter 11.]

C. AFRICAN AMERICAN WOMEN

NANCY K. D. LEMON, EXCERPT FROM EXPERT WITNESS REPORT

Habeas Corpus Petition for an African American Woman in Prison for Having Killed Her Batterer in 1986 (2004)

Moreover, Ms. X did not leave her home to escape Mr. Y because she was parenting her two younger brothers. She was very focused on making sure they had food, clothing, went to school, and did not get into dangerous situations. They lived in a neighborhood riddled with horrific levels of violence. Ms. X described to me the multiple homicides she witnessed as a child, including one in which the police shot a man who may have had a knife, and another in which a man beat his wife to death in public. One of the declarants states that the police often would not respond after dark to parts of South Central Los Angeles, due to their own fear. Ms. X stated that the police almost never came to help; as mentioned above, if it was a "domestic," they would just drive on.

Because of this environment, calling the police was not an option for Ms. X. She had seen them either refuse to help at all, or shoot people who had no guns. And on the one occasion when the police were involved, they assaulted Mr. Y, who later beat Ms. X. This incident happened when Ms. X was three or four months pregnant with her first pregnancy, and Mr. Y was the father. He was going to go buy drugs, and she tried to stop him by sitting on the hood of the car and clinging to it while he drove away. The Firestone police (off of 76th and Nadeau Streets) saw this, stopped the car, and slammed Mr. Y against a fence when they found out that Ms. X was pregnant. She begged them to stop hurting him. Even though she was afraid of Mr. Y, she still loved him and did not want him hurt. They took Mr. Y to jail overnight. When he got out the next morning, he called Ms. X and asked her to come to his parents' house so he could apologize. But as soon as she got there, he grabbed her neck with both hands and threatened to kill her if she ever caused him to go to jail again. Her neck was tender for a long time, and she believed this threat. Although Ms. X did not identify it as such, as an expert on battering I would identify Mr. Y's behavior as strangulation, which can quickly become lethal and could constitute attempted murder.

> This statement is supported by studies and legislative history: California Penal Code section 13700, Law Enforcement Response to Domestic Violence, was not even passed until 1984. Its provisions for mandatory training of all law enforcement officers on the topic of domestic violence were not implemented until a few years later. Even after that, there have been many lawsuits filed against California law enforcement agencies for failing to take domestic violence crimes seriously.

After this, Ms. X was determined not to get the police involved. Instead, she tried to do whatever she could on her own, as a minor and a female, to protect herself, her baby, and her two younger brothers from drive-by shootings, beatings, and other dire consequences of the neighborhood they lived in and of her relationship, without law enforcement involvement.

AMBER SIMMONS, WHY ARE WE SO MAD? THE TRUTH BEHIND ANGRY BLACK WOMEN AND THEIR LEGAL INVISIBILITY AS VICTIMS OF DOMESTIC VIOLENCE

36 Harv. BlackLetter L.J. 47 (2020)
(footnotes and citations omitted)

INTRODUCTION

Janay Palmer and Ray Rice met in typical American fashion, at a movie theater in their hometown of New Rochelle, New York at fourteen and fifteen years old, respectively. They became immediate friends, until summer 2007 when the friendship escalated into a relationship. By May 2012, Ray and Janay were engaged and expecting their first child. They had normal relationship disagreements, until one night in Atlantic City.

On February 1, 2014, a surveillance camera video surfaced of Ray punching Janay unconscious in the elevator of an Atlantic City, New Jersey casino. That night, both Ray and Janay were both arrested. Ray was charged with third-degree aggravated assault and, shortly thereafter, was terminated from the Baltimore Ravens. Ray never went to trial for the assault, and after a one-year rehabilitation class, the charges were eventually dropped.

This story paints an all too familiar picture in the United States. Black women experience intimate partner violence at disproportionately higher rates than other ethnic groups and races in the United States. Some studies link the higher rates to Black women's affinity for their culture and their unwillingness to betray their race, but this is an incomplete and dangerous assertion. Another explanation is the common sentiment in the Black community to rely on spiritual beliefs to solve problems of issues in the family. Both of these explanations seek to explain why Black women remain in abusive relationships. However, there is a much more important question: What happens to those who want to leave?

The most dangerous time in an abusive relationship, for any victim of any race or ethnicity, is leaving. Black women who want to escape face a myriad of obstacles. Black women are four times more likely to be killed by a boyfriend or girlfriend and twice as likely to be killed by a spouse than their white counterparts. This fact discourages Black women from leaving the abusive environment. Also, Black women are disproportionally exposed to the effects of poverty, which makes it even more difficult for them to leave abusive relationships Single Black women have an average of $100 in wealth. Once children are added, single Black women have no measurable wealth. While all of the above obstacles are at play, there is a plethora of academic work addressing these issues. An under-acknowledged part of this problem focuses on how Black women are directly and indirectly discouraged from reporting their abuse to the proper authorities due to stereotypes.

This article will focus on an overlooked aspect of Black women's fight for freedom from domestic violence: the effects of the "Angry Black Woman" stereotype. The main objective of the criminal justice system in the United States is to uphold the ideals of fairness and justice. These ideals can be perverted by the implicit bias of individuals carrying out the abstract notions of justice and fairness. The opinions and closely held stereotypes of police officers, prosecutors, and judges prevent these actors from seeing Black women as victims. . .

I. HISTORICAL CONTEXT OF THE "ANGRY BLACK WOMAN" STEREOTYPE AND ITS INTERGENERATIONAL EFFECT ON BLACK FEMALE VICTIMS OF DOMESTIC VIOLENCE

A. Origins of the stereotype

Control of Black women was a goal of slave owners. Black feminist Barbara Christian posits that, "the enslaved woman became the basis for the definition of our society's Other." Making Black women society's *other* made it easier during slavery to justify their oppression. Othering took many forms: The Jezebel, The Mammy, and The Sapphire.

Black women are "othered" by what is referred to as the "Angry Black Woman" stereotype. This stereotype can be traced to Sapphire, a character on the Amon 'N' Andy Show in 1951. Sapphire would routinely bicker with her husband, George "Kingfish" Stevens, kick him out of the home, and complain about trivial things. Audiences got to know Sapphire as the man-hating, ball-busting, wife of Kingfish but, more importantly, her attitude became synonymous with the attitude of all other Black women.

While most Black women would agree that Black women are strong and resilient like Sapphire; they would also agree that the Sapphire image is an exaggerated trope with perilous implications. Black women are taught by female elders in their family to be strong:

> "We young black girls had to learn to protect ourselves against physical hurt, to figure things out in order to maximize our safety within both private and public space. To cushion ourselves against physical mistreatment meant learning to fight to defend ourselves and to in. To cushion ourselves therefore meant that we could not expect any protection from black men or, especially, from the police. I was able to be on my own as a strong, independent black woman who could handle anything life threw at me."

This ability to be resilient in the face of adversity is an evolutionary skill that was developed because Black women have always fought back.

B. Negative Images of Black Women in Popular Media

The notion of a strong independent Black woman has been morphed into a crude joke in popular media. Television shows such as VH1's *Love & Hip-Hop* and Bravo's *Real Housewives of Atlanta* focus almost entirely on in-group fighting, public arguments, or physical altercations. Black women on these shows are depicted in stereotypical fashion as loud and ghetto and angry, frequently getting into physical altercations, hurling insults at one another, and exhibiting overall immoral behavior.

Hollywood has a similar problem and, oddly enough, a Black man is at the center of the revival of Angry Black female characters, Tyler Perry. . .

The transformation of the strong independent Black woman into sensationalized "Angry Black Woman" has massive societal impact because most White Americans' only contact with Black people, in general, is from popular media, through the Internet, movies and television programs. This phenomenon is due to the continued segregation of the average American's social circle. Ninety-one percent of White Americans' social circle consists of other White people. Among Black Americans, eighty-three percent of their core social circle is made up of other Black Americans. The variation of these facts is minimal when controlled for gender, religion, political affiliation, and even region of the United States. Race is still the most significant statistical factor when it comes to social segregation. If Black and White Americans are not interacting with one another, how can the negative image of the "Angry Black Woman" stereotype be remedied?

II. POLICE OFFICERS: IMPARTIAL INTERVENORS OR HURDLES TO JUSTICE

A. History of Law Enforcement and Black Women

The relationship between black women and police officers follows a long line of historical precedents that dehumanized Black women. Black slaves, both men and women, could be murdered or mutilated by their master, with no legal redress. Black female slaves, specifically, were routinely "bred" with slave owners or other male slaves against their will, with no legal redress. Furthermore, every state that adopted a rape statute defined the crime as one that occurs to White women only. Law enforcement during the slave era in the United States was not required to protect and serve Black slaves, especially not Black female slaves.

Although this particular regime of slavery has ended, these types of violations have continued. In fact, during Jim Crow, Black women were even more susceptible to rape and violence because, as according to sociologist Patricia Hill Collins, they were:

> No longer the property of a few White men, African American women became sexually available to all White men. As free women who belonged to nobody except themselves and in a climate of violence that meted out severe consequences for their either defending themselves or soliciting Black male protection, Black women could be raped.

The police almost never held the men that committed the countless acts of violence against Black women accountable. Additionally, those Black women that did report the crimes against them faced threats of death, physical violence, and destruction of their property.

In 1969, the National Commission on the Causes and Prevention of Violence created its final report, in which it analyzed different crimes and various aspects of those crimes. The Commission found that Black women were determined to be the typical victim of violent assaultive crime, especially rape. However, the Commission also found that police systematically ignored the crimes that were committed in what it calls the ghetto, places where Black Americans live.

B. Police Bias and Black Female Victims of Domestic Violence

The Angry Black Woman stereotype has helped to further the tradition of police ignoring Black women. Specifically with domestic violence, law enforcement has the tendency to hold on to two common stereotypes about Black women: 1) Black women are not credible and cannot be believed and

2) Black women must be mutual combatants and there is no possible way they are merely victims. Take *Conerly v. Town of Franklinton* as an example of what happens when officers act on their beliefs of Black women. Felicia Fox was repeatedly abused by her longtime boyfriend, Robert Toomer. . .[She repeatedly called the police, who did nothing. Then Toomer killed Fox and was arrested.]

The story of Felicia Fox is a common one among Black female domestic violence victims. Black female victims of intimate partner violence are twice as likely to be killed by spouses and four times as likely to be killed by significant others than White women. This is because police purposefully give a lower priority to Black female victims of intimate partner violence. Why is that? The answer may be heuristics, a type of mental shorthand that associates certain characteristics with certain groups of people. Some legal commentators argue that what police engage in is not intentional racial hatred, but rather horrible racial gambling. Furthermore, racial stereotyping by police officers has been blamed on their interactions with popular media, family, and friends. While this may explain their stereotyping of Black female victims of domestic violence, it does nothing to excuse it.

How does the "Angry Black Woman" stereotype affect a police officer's response to Black female victims of domestic violence? There are countless examples. Black women that have the courage to report are often met with dissatisfactory experiences. One victim, Lola, recounts how a police officer questioned her in the immediate presence of her abuser. Yet another victim explains how an officer claimed there was no evidence of abuse because he could not see bruises on her dark skin. Would an officer behave in these ways with a White female victim? The phenomenon of the "dual-arrest" has undoubtedly and directly affected Black female victims of domestic violence. Dual-arrest is when an officer arrests both people involved in a domestic violence dispute, without regard to who is the aggressor and who is the victim.

The Violence Against Women Act (VAWA) requires responding police officers to arrest the "primary aggressor" in a domestic violence situation. Black women are more likely to be stereotyped the aggressor, because of the "Angry Black Woman" stereotype, and are therefore more likely to be arrested, even if they are the person who called the police for help. The Office of Violence Against Women realized that this was not an effective policy because some officers were arresting both parties to avoid determining who the true aggressor was. To protect against this effect, police departments that want VAWA funding must prove women are not being arrested, "solely to avoid having to make a determination of who the aggressor was." Despite the progress, "dual arrest" policies around the U.S. still continue to disproportionately affect Black women; for example, in New York, seventy percent of women who were mandatorily arrested under "dual arrest" were Black or Latina. Nonetheless, the public is still convinced that mandatory arrest is proper.

C. Fighting Back

Marissa Alexander was routinely beaten by her husband. Marissa was cornered in the bathroom of their home, as he yelled insults through the door. He broke through the door and grabbed Marissa by the neck. After struggling for what felt like forever, she escaped from the bathroom and ran to the garage. Marissa tried to escape out of the garage door, but it was stuck. She instead ran to the car and grabbed the handgun in the glove compartment. Her husband spotted her with the gun and charged at her, yelling threats on her life. She raised the gun and fired a warning shot into the air. Marissa Alexander was found guilty of aggravated assault with a deadly weapon, for firing a warning shot, in the air, away from her abuser.

Marissa Alexander is an example of what happens when Black female victims of domestic violence fight back Women, in general, who fight back lose sympathy with police and all other actors in the criminal justice system This is because a woman that fights back defies their role as the weaker gender. This fact rings truer for Black women because they are the antithesis of what police are taught a "battered woman" is. Black women are viewed by most, especially police officers, as aggressive and not passive. "Authentic" victims are meant to fit that fragile, weak mold and, when that does not happen, police officers paint those women as deviants. Nothing could be farther from the truth.

Black women, overwhelmingly, fight back against their abusers more than White women do. *Why is that?* The obvious answer that most research relies on is the overused trope: Black women are angry and aggressive and problematic. Hillary Potter looks deeper at the actions of Black female victims and reasoned that these women were not just enacting their own form of retributive justice. Hillary Potter does this work as an Associate Professor of Ethnic Studies at the University of Colorado at Boulder. The women Potter interviewed presented several factors that led them to fight back. Of the women interviewed, those who were exposed to abuse in their childhood tended to fight back more than those who were not exposed to violence. Another reason Potter finds Black women tend to fight back is their self-perception as non-victims, based on society's definition of who a victim is and who a victim is not. Society's view of women that fight back is rooted in a contradiction. Women defending themselves against attacks from strangers is encouraged, evidenced by the amount of pink, bedazzled cans of mace on the market. If this is true, then why are women that fight back against their intimate partners stigmatized?

For Black women, the social stigma of fighting back is exacerbated by the stereotype of just being a Black woman in the U.S. Black women fight back because they believe the criminal justice system is unfair to them. Police intervention, for most, is the last alternative for several reasons, especially when one considers the implicit bias police have against Black female victims. With little to no help from police officers and no sympathy in self-defense, what options do "Angry Black Women" have? The effects of the "Angry Black Woman" stereotype do not stop with the police. As domestic violence progresses further into the criminal justice system, we see that prosecutors contribute to stifling justice.

III. PROSECUTORS

A. History of Prosecution of Domestic Violence in America

The next rung in the criminal justice ladder is the prosecution of the crime. The United States has recently embraced the prosecution of perpetrators of family violence in spite of its contrary history. In eighteenth and nineteenth-century America, the law favored the privacy of the home, and with that the husband's prerogative to domestically chastise his wife. Courts in various states structured policies that tended to not interfere with the private sphere.

Specifically, with Black female victims, in *Fulgham v. State* the Alabama Supreme Court in 1871 allowed the prosecution of a Black, freed slave for striking his wife, another Black, freed slave. Likewise, the Supreme Court of Mississippi also decided to prosecute a Black man for beating his wife. While these decisions seem like steps in the right direction, these decisions were more of a play to control Black men; Black women were not at the forefront of these decisions. Black women were less of a concern for the courts in the nineteenth-century, because the control of Black men was more important.

B. Prosecutorial Intervention

With the shift in the culture, prosecutors now treat domestic violence as a serious crime. This is important when one considers prosecutors, in upwards of ninety-three percent of cases, decide the fate of the accused via plea bargain. . . Luckily, cases of prosecutorial refusal to press criminal charges are now an uncommon occurrence in domestic violence cases. This is exemplified by "no-drop" prosecution policies adopted by many district attorney's offices around the country. . .

Hard "no-drop" policies force domestic violence victims to continue through the process with or without the victim's cooperation, assuming there is an adequate amount of evidence available. This type of "no drop" policy has been criticized of stripping the victims of their choice and autonomy. In spite of this criticism, most Black women are mostly on board for the prosecution of their batterers. Soft "no-drop" policies continue with the [prosecution] of the abuser but allow the victim to choose whether or not they want to be a part of the process Additionally, victims are offered counseling and other support services and are encouraged to be active part of the process. Generally, soft "no-drop" policies are praised for emphasizing "the importance of listening to women and their concerns before taking action against their batterers."

For Black women, being cooperative with prosecutors does not do much to quell the inherent biases of being a Black woman and a victim. Black women are coached by prosecutors to "look sad, to try to cry, to never look the jury in the eye." Prosecutors tend to fit domestic violence victims into this narrow mold in part due to the legal system's emphasis on the Battered Woman's Syndrome. In fact, one former prosecutor, Alafair Burke, suggests that "the theory is taught to counselors, police officers, prosecutors, parole board officials, and social-service providers to improve the quality of their responses to domestic violence."

Battered Women's Syndrome is a concept first laid out by Lenore Walker in her 1979 book, *The Battered Woman*. Walker [describes] victims of domestic violence as helpless, passive, scared women that do not leave the relationship for fear of shame and dependency on the abuser. Women who, unfortunately, never fit this image, women of color and Black women specifically, had their stories pushed further into the margins. There have been steps to create an alternative theory, Survivor Theory. This theory, created and advocated for by Edward Gondolf and Ellen Fisher, reshaped the battered woman from helpless to a survivor who protects herself and her children from the abuser. While this theory moves in the right direction, it does not account for the wide variety of experiences Black women face in violent relationships, such as the decision to fight back. Furthermore, the legal system has yet to accept any alternative theories, to include the Survivor Theory, as wholly as it has accepted Battered Woman's Syndrome.

C. The Failings of VAWA

In 1994, Congress enacted the Violence Against Women Act, or VAWA. In general, VAWA has four objectives: "change attitudes toward domestic violence, foster awareness of domestic violence, improve services and provisions for victims, and revise the manner in which the criminal justice system responds to domestic violence and sex crimes." With regard to the last goal, VAWA created several grant programs intended to help state, local, and even tribal law enforcement to investigate and prosecute crimes against women. Since its enactment in 1994, Congress has reauthorized VAWA in 2000, 2005, and 2013, three times total, and all times with bipartisan support. . .

VAWA is only as effective as the system that delivers its promises. In a system that has already systematically over-policed Black communities, VAWA exacerbated the problem. Kimberlé Crenshaw places this idea in the larger context of Black community sentiment:

> There is also a more generalized community ethic against public intervention, the product of a desire to create a private world free

> from the diverse assaults on the public lives of racially subordinated people. In this sense the home is not simply a man's castle in patriarchal terms, but it is also a safe haven from the indignities of life in a racist society.

. . . In the past, all three reauthorizations of VAWA had bipartisan support. Among the [proposed] changes, there is emphasis on alternative justice options, external to the traditional criminal justice system, an admission by Democratic proponents of VAWA that the heavy law enforcement presence in previous versions of this bill have overwhelmingly affected Black communities. . .*[Editor's Note: See Chapter 14 for description of the most recent reauthorization of VAWA, signed by President Biden in 2022.]*

IV. JUDGES AND THEIR ROLE IN PERPETUATING STEREOTYPES

A. History of Judicial Bias And Black Women

Black women have a tumultuous history with the judiciary. One reason for this could be what has always been the predominant make-up of the judiciary in the United States, White men. It was not until 1939 that the United States even had its first Black woman judge, Judge Jane Matilda Bolin. This lack of representation correlates directly with the unfortunately racist decisions of the late 19th and early 20th centuries surrounding Black women. For example, the Supreme Court of Florida in 1918 refused to extend the assumption of chastity of unmarried rape victims to Black women, because of the relative immorality of the Black women and their tendency to be unchaste. Many opinions, like this one from Florida's highest court, kept Black female victims of any type from reporting incidents of violence against them. While the make-up of the court is a problem, there is a bigger problem: judicial bias.

B. Judicial Bias

Judges retain their own personal biases in the courtroom. Unfortunately, for Black women these biases may include unconscious racist sentiments or stereotypes. While this unconscious form of racism is not intentionally causing harm, it renders that same amount of harm that old-fashioned, outright racism did. . . [Author describes a study that found that White judges were biased in favor of White people, while Black judges had no preference for White or Black people.]

In addition to the implicit racial bias, judges also hold biases against domestic violence victims. Judicial hostility toward victims of domestic violence stems from ignorance and lack of knowledge of the plight of the abused. . . [Author gives examples of this hostility and states that training on domestic violence in D.C. has had a positive effect.]

C. Due Process Argument for Black Female Victims of Domestic Violence

The Due Process clause in the Fourteenth Amendment of the U.S. Constitution is meant to ensure states do not deprive their citizenry of, "life, liberty, or property, without due process of law." All citizens are guaranteed equal protection in the eyes of the laws of the state. Judges, through common law, determine how these protections are to be carried out throughout the 50 states and beyond. In this respect, Black female victims of domestic violence are cut out of those promises. . .

[Author describes *Town of Castle Rock v. Gonzales*, in which the U.S. Supreme Court held that Jessica Gonzales had no constitutional Due Process right to enforcement of her domestic violence restraining order against the father of her children, who abducted and murdered them. After being told of the abduction by Ms. Gonzales, the police refused to enforce the restraining order. This case is also discussed in Chapter 17 in the section on international human rights issues.]

V. SOLUTIONS: WHAT CAN BE DONE?

A. Re-education: Positively Changing the Narrative

Battered Women's Syndrome (BWS) for years has taught the public and actors in the legal field that the "battered woman" should fit one specific list of characteristics and should react to abuse one specific way. This theory was largely based on White women and their behavior and reaction to abuse, with no woman of color in mind. There must be a massive shift in the thinking of the public, legal actors, and the like towards re-education. Organizations such as Women of Color Network and the National Coalition Against Domestic Violence are leading re-education efforts through various platforms for the general public. In the legal field, however, BWS is something that still taught in Family Law courses across the nation and because of that it is highly relied upon in domestic violence litigation. While it is not suggested that all education on this syndrome should cease, education of BWS should be followed with qualifying language, such as, not every victim fits this model or this model is based on stereotypes of White female victims of domestic violence.

Additionally, the pervasive media image of the Angry Black Woman had tainted in the minds of the public what a domestic violence victim can be. This issue, in recent years, has seen headway with impactful Black female roles in television and film to include Kerry Washington, Viola Davis, and Lupita Nyong'o. These roles are important to re-educate not only the public but also those figures integral in an abused women's fight for justice: judges, prosecutors, and police officers. . . [The author calls for re-education of prosecutors and judges about Survivor Theory rather than BWS.]

B. Resources for All, Not Just for the Few

Black women are four times more likely to be victimized by intimate partners in the United States than their White counterparts. Unfortunately, this statistic does not translate to the availability of resources available to women who have been victims of domestic violence. Shelter services are undoubtedly designed around the needs of middle-class White women. For example, in a study of shelters in the Southern U.S. it was found that the majority of publicly funded shelters were located in predominantly White areas of town. It was also found that these shelters employ predominantly White staff and that the rules and social norms within the shelter reflected mainly White middle-class norms and expectations. As a result of this flawed design, Black women are less likely to utilize publicly funded services like shelters when they exit abusive relationships, leaving them open to risk.

The resources that lower income Black female victims of domestic violence need are, undoubtedly, not the same resources that well-connected, middle class White woman might need to get out of a dangerous, abusive relationship. . .

CONCLUSION

This leads back to the question posed in the title of this piece: *why are we so angry?* (Emphasis in original) Black women are angry because they are not heard. They are labeled. They are continuously victimized. They are never part of the narrative. They are pushed into the margins of the domestic violence prototype and written off as a group of people that cannot possibly be victims and that, as a result, cannot possibly be believed or helped. Police officers are part of the problem. Prosecutors are part of the problem. Judges are part of the problem. Society as a whole is the problem.

So long as society continues to "other" Black women and their struggles, experiences, and stories, the status quo will remain. The status quo with regard to domestic violence is killing Black women. It is silencing Black women. It is keeping Black women in their designated "box" and not allowing for any variance in personality or appearance. As Audre Lorde put it, "If I didn't define myself for myself, I would be crunched into other people's fantasies for me and eaten alive." For the Black female victim of domestic violence, these factors and stereotypes combine and intersect to reveal an almost hopeless outlook for the future. The original question then becomes: Wouldn't you be angry, too?

D. LATINAS

ESPERANZA UNITED, LATINAS AND INTIMATE PARTNER VIOLENCE, EVIDENCE-BASED FACTS

(2021)
(footnotes omitted)

. . .About 1 in 3 Latinas (34.4 %) will experience IPV during her lifetime and 1 in 12 Latinas (8.6%) has experienced IPV in the previous 12 months.

- This rate is approximately the same as for women from other racial and ethnic communities once socioeconomic status is taken into consideration.
- Another study examining IPV among Latinas found that rates of IPV were lower for Mexican immigrants (13.4%) than for persons of Mexican descent born in the United States (16.7%).
- The strength of immigrant groups despite the social and economic challenges they often face has been labeled the immigrant paradox. There are also differences among Latinas based on their country of origin and level of acculturation; more years in the U.S. predicts poorer health outcomes. A review of 41 research studies found evidence for lower reported IPV among immigrant Latinas compared to U.S.- born Latinas. *[Editor's Note: This may be due to immigrant Latinas not knowing that IPV is a crime in the U.S. or how to report it, or maybe living in the U.S. increases rates of domestic violence.]*
- In a study of 6,818 female college students, almost half of whom identified as Latina, 31% reported experiencing IPV since enrollment. Correlations were observed between severity of IPV and extent of PTSD, depression, school disengagement, and academic impacts.
- In a sample of over 300 pregnant Latinas, IPV during pregnancy was reported at 10% for physical abuse and 19% for emotional abuse. Increased rates of IPV among young mothers were seen in another study in which 26% of Latina mothers with preschool-age children reported IPV in their current or most recent relationship.
- Research with Latinas living near the Mexico border found that 37.5% had experienced IPV over their lifetimes.
- In a national sample, 41% of Latina mothers involved in child welfare and whose children remained in the home reported

experiencing IPV in their lifetime, 33% of whom had experienced IPV in the last year with 27% reporting severe IPV. U.S.-born Latina mothers experienced more frequent episodes of violence in the past year when compared to immigrant Latina mothers (5.59% vs. 2.72%).

- A long-term study of high school Latino adolescents ages 13–17 found that a history of childhood abuse was the strongest predictor of intimate partner violence for Latina emerging adults as it resulted in higher odds of experiencing sexual IPV victimization among Latina women ages 21–24.
- IPV often includes economic or financial abuse and sexual and reproductive coercion and can co-occur with other forms of abuse, for example:
- A study of 2,000 Latinas found that 63.1% of women who identified being victimized in their lifetime (i.e., interpersonal victimization such as stalking, physical assaults, weapon assaults, physical assaults in childhood, threats, sexual assault, attempted sexual assault, etc.) reported having experienced more than one victimization, with an average of 2.56 victimizations.
- A national sample of Latinas examining the forms of victimization including physical assault, sexual violence, stalking, threat victimization, and witnessing violence found that more than half of the women surveyed (53.6%) reported at least one victimization over a lifetime, and about two-thirds (66.2%) of those women had more than one victimization.
- Among 362 Latinas seeking family planning services about half (51%) had experienced IPV and 34% reported reproductive coercion. Other studies have also reported a link between IPV, reproductive coercion and unintended pregnancies for Latina survivors. In fact one study found that 21% of pregnant Latinas experienced both reproductive coercion and IPV increasing their risk for an unplanned pregnancy.
- Research is beginning to document economic and work-related IPV among Latinas. For Latina survivors, physical and sexual IPV co-occurred with economic abuse. Economic control, i.e., when the abuser controls or limits the victims access to resources, was the most common form of economic abuse.

Help seeking

Low rates of reporting and self-help seeking among Latinas experiencing IPV may create the illusion that IPV services are not needed by this population. However, understanding the specifics of help seeking behavior among Latinas can create a more cohesive picture.

- In a current systemic review of over 40,000 survivors of IPV in North America, Latina and Black women were less likely to seek mental health services compared to White women.
- Like many survivors, Latinas prefer to tell family members, female friends, or neighbors about IPV (i.e., utilize informal resources for help). This is especially true for undocumented Latinas who were more likely to seek out informal support for IPV as compared to Latinas with resident or citizen status. However, for both groups, formal help-seeking was more likely when experiencing severe physical abuse.
- Nearly half of Latinas in one study did not report abuse to authorities. Reasons for underreporting may include fear and lack of confidence in the police, shame, guilt, loyalty and/or fear of partners, fear of deportation, and previous experience with childhood victimization.
- An integrated review found that self-blame, shame, and embarrassment were expressed as barriers to IPV disclosure by Latina women. Research shows that Latina IPV survivors are less likely to seek mental health services than non-Latinas. In a study of 94 Latina mother survivors of IPV (85% Mexican), Latinas with PTSD reported more physically forced rape than those without PTSD, while no significant difference was found between psychologically coerced rape and PTSD. Findings indicate that Latinas with children are more likely to seek help for IPV than those without children.
- Low-acculturated Latinas (both abused and non-abused) are less likely to seek and use formal social services than their more acculturated counterparts.
- Among Latinas receiving shelter for IPV, undocumented Latinas were less likely to know what an order of protection was as compared to Latinas with resident or citizen status (59% vs. 84%). However, undocumented Latinas were more likely than Latinas with resident or citizen status (57% vs. 22%) to believe that their partner would abide by an order of protection if provided.

Commentary: Latina survivors' help-seeking behaviors are closely tied to their level of acculturation and other cultural factors. More recent immigrant Latinas are usually unaware of the laws, options, and possibilities regarding their experience of abuse. Latina survivors who have been in the United States for a longer period of time or were born in this country have had the opportunity to learn about resources and are more likely to use them. However, where they seek help varies from other ethnic/racial groups. Latina survivors are more likely to depend on family members and friends, rather than health care workers, clergy, and police.

Needs

The needs identified by Latina survivors point to the importance of culturally appropriate resources and approaches to assist Latina families experiencing IPV. Below is a list of needs identified by Latina survivors and community advocates. Cultural and linguistically appropriate services should include responses that account for cultural differences among Latino ethnic groups. Latinas say they need information about rights as a survivor, legal services, IPV, help when going to court, English lessons, protection/safety, transportation, education for independence, a place to stay, and someone to talk to in private.

Resources and responses that:

- Are in their native language
- Incorporate culturally-specific spaces and providers
- Do not ask about immigration status *[Editor's Note: Of course if the survivor is seeking legal status in the U.S., it will be necessary to discuss her immigration status with a legal advocate or attorney and also in court.]*
- Include space and services for children and extended family
- Address all genders in the community

Commentary: Despite the focus on shelters as the preferred mainstream strategy to assist IPV survivors, Latina survivors did not mention shelters among their most urgent needs. This finding should be viewed in the context of not only the potential unawareness of the existence of shelters in this country but also the reluctance of Latina women to leave their community for a variety of reasons. This in no way negates the need for Latina survivors to have access to emergency shelters and housing to address their experience of IPV.

Contextual factors

IPV happens within the context of a family's daily life, which is deeply affected by numerous factors, both personal and systemic, that impact and are impacted by IPV. Some of these have been documented in the literature.

- Cultural values must be identified and understood to develop effective IPV interventions. Two values of particular importance in the occurrence and prevention of IPV in Latina communities are the importance of family (familismo) and strong gender role expectations.

- Familismo refers to the central place that the family has in most Latinas' lives. Strong family roles point to the father as the primary breadwinner (although this role is rapidly changing due to economic realities) and to the mother as the person responsible for the well-being and cohesiveness of the family.
- Gender role expectations change as Latina immigrants acculturate to their new environment. However, for many Latinas their role as mothers is still the most important aspect of their lives, a responsibility against which most of their decisions and actions are weighed. A study found that Latina survivors prioritized their children over themselves, protected them, and provided for them as best as they could.
- Religion often plays a strong role in Latinas' decisions on how—or if—to address IPV.
- Religious beliefs may stop some Latinas from using services because they believe that the "sanctity of marriage" precludes their taking steps that could result in divorce or separation.
- Negative and/or uninformed reactions of religious leaders to disclosures of IPV often result in Latina survivors feeling responsible for making their marriage work regardless of the violence they are experiencing.
- Findings indicate that religion is often a source of resilience among Latina survivors of violence, however some research has found that using religion as a negative coping mechanism to escape life's stressors is associated with increased symptoms of Post-Traumatic Stress Disorder.
- Economic factors (such as employment issues related to immigration status) were also identified by Latina survivors as important elements that affect IPV. In several studies examining the vulnerabilities of socioeconomic status in relation to IPV, women who were unhindered by these factors showed improved mental and economic prosperity.
- Research shows that the high rate of IPV in immigrant populations has more to do with socioeconomic marginalization than with culture. In several analyses, low socioeconomic status was a more common determinant of IPV than race and ethnicity. Financial concerns and lack of formal schooling among Latinas have shown to be predominant

barriers for seeking support and developing sustainable livelihoods.

- In one study focusing on socioeconomic status of diverse sexual minority women, household income more than $50,000 was associated with fewer reports of severe IPV compared with those reporting a household income of less than US $10,000. Results also showed that Black and Latina sexual minority participants reported higher rates of severe IPV than white women.

- Economic sabotage, such as when an abuser interferes with their partner's work outside the home, has also been documented. One study reported abusive strategies such as on the job surveillance, on the job harassment, and work disruption tactics. However, they also found unique strategies experienced by Latinas, such as denying access to a driver's license, lying about childcare arrangements, and sending the partner to their country of origin temporarily.

- Immigration is, for many Latinas, the most salient element of their lives. As a result, Latina survivors' decisions about IPV are deeply affected by their immigration status and the climate of their communities. As is discussed in the Barriers to Services section, this contextual factor is a prime barrier to their ability to access resources.

- Anti-immigrant environments created by strict immigration enforcement policies and increased rates of deportation have impacted many Latin communities. For example, immigrant Latina women affected by IPV have reported experiencing increased rates of harassment, including reports of being followed by strangers, called derogatory words and discrimination at work. Increased climate of fear due to the immigration enforcement environment was identified as a barrier to reporting or help-seeking by 78% of respondents in a national survey conducted by national domestic violence advocacy organizations.

- Acculturation has been the focus of multiple studies investigating how the process of adapting to cultural norms in the US might relate to immigrant Latinas experiences of IPV. Studies find that IPV is less prevalent among those with strong ties to traditional Latino cultural values and orientation. Similarly, increased orientation towards American non-Latin culture has been associated with poor mental health among Latina survivors.

- Sociocultural factors that include the intersection of immigration status and levels of acculturation influence victimization rates and mental health outcomes of Latina women.

Resilience and resistance strategies

Although the literature in the field has begun to highlight how IPV affects Latina survivors and their children in negative ways, a few studies have focused on the strengths and resistance strategies used by the women.

- Latina survivors report multiple strategies to survive abuse.

Among them:

- Avoiding (placating batterer, walking away, talking batterer down, and encouraging counseling for the batterer)
- Defending (protecting one's body, fighting back, locking self in room, and teaching children to call the police)
- Spiritual or psychological (joining a support group and maintaining a relationship with God)
- Social or familial (maintaining relationships with supportive people, not involving family members to protect them, and support/advice from other battered women)
- Escaping (moving to an undisclosed location, disguising themselves, and saving personal money)
- In one Latina study, the ability to cope in stressful situations was identified as a protective factor for people who witnessed IPV as a child. Addressing past trauma was identified as a promising intervention strategy to improve the mental health of Latina victims of IPV with a history of adverse childhood experiences.
- Strategies for staying safe used by Latina survivors have included: keeping important phone numbers nearby to use for help seeking, keeping extra supplies of basic necessities on hand, hiding important papers, and creating an escape plan.
- Other strategies reported by Latina survivors who had used violence against their partners: religion, dialoguing with partner, using threats, hobbies or studying, exercising, flight, calling police, and divorce.
- An in-depth study with Latina survivors living in a rural community identified multiple aspects of resiliency following IPV. In their stories of survival, they spoke of uncovering their internal strengths and courage, their love for their children and being in solidarity with other survivors of IPV.

- Children were a predominant source of resilience for mothers to seek support and heal from IPV in order to provide them with a future without violence.
- In solidarity with other women experiencing IPV, women noted the importance of providing support and sharing information with other survivors.
- An in-depth study that featured immigrant Latina survivors of IPV in the Midwest found that children were a common source of resilience. All participants talked about the importance of giving their children a better future. Despite struggles with help-seeking, participants demonstrated resilience through sharing their stories of survival and strength with other participants. . .

Barriers to services

- In light of recent immigration enforcement policies, the apprehension to call the police due to the fear of deportation has become more salient for many Latina survivors. Immigrant Latinas may fear deportation while seeking help from social services.
- Specifically, immigration status is often identified as a barrier for immigrant Latinas to seek services.
- In a recent study, immigrant Latina survivors reported a decrease in the likelihood of calling the police due to heightened immigration enforcement policies and increased fear of deportation.
- Latina survivors report that immigration status is often used as a control mechanism to ensure that they do not leave the abusive situation.
- The strength of this control tool is amplified by the current realities of heightened deportation and immigration enforcement.
- A survey of over 500 foreign born Latina women found that 14% of participants reported experiencing problems in accessing IPV services due to immigration issues, some reporting they were denied IPV services for lack of proper identification.
- Threatening Latina survivors to take away their children if they leave their partners was an especially powerful strategy used by men against undocumented, non-English speaking women.

In addition to immigration, studies have found that low awareness of resources for IPV, language and cultural differences act as significant barriers to Latina survivors' ability to access services.

- There is little awareness of IPV services and options among Latina survivors.
- Women report a lack of knowledge about available resources in the community as a common barrier to services.
- One study found that only 1 in 4 Latinas had heard of IPV protective orders.
- Another study with immigrant Latina survivors found that many women initially believed the abuse they were experiencing was a "normal" part of marriage. It was only after migrating to the US that they became aware of a way of life in which abuse was not the norm and felt empowered to seek help for ending their abuse.
- Lack of culturally and linguistically appropriate services is also a barrier for many Latina survivors, as it is for women from many other racial/ethnic groups.
- In a recent systemic review, Latina women showed a reduced rate of support-seeking from social services compared to white and black women. Findings in the review illustrated that migrant status and cultural stigma are barriers to formal help-seeking, however one study found that integrating cultural-specific practices into trauma-informed services showed higher levels of well-being among Latina survivors of IPV. . .
- Future national studies need to include sufficiently large Latin samples that permit teasing apart the relevant differences and commonalities of Latin subgroups.
- Many of the scales and methods used currently may not be appropriate for capturing information that accurately reflects the experiences of Latin populations. The relevance and appropriateness of current measures and methods should be explored, and new ones developed as needed.
- The direct voices of diverse Latin populations need to be incorporated into research to explore in greater depth the context in which violence occurs.
- In order to recognize the resilience of Latinas, studies of physical and mental health outcomes of Latinas should also incorporate a focus on the strength and protective factors of this population. . .

- Routes for prevention identified by Latin community members and service providers include using a community approach, education around teen dating violence, prevention focused programming, and empowering vulnerable populations. Other recommendations include building cross-sector advocacy relationships and strengthening funding streams as well as commitment to anti-oppressive services. . .

E. NATIVE AMERICAN WOMEN

NATIONAL INDIGENOUS WOMEN'S RESOURCE CENTER, TRIBAL NATIONS, AND ADDITIONAL ADVOCACY ORGANIZATIONS FOR SURVIVORS OF DOMESTIC VIOLENCE AND ASSAULT IN SUPPORT OF PETITIONER, AMICUS BRIEF, *MCGIRT V. OKLAHOMA*, U.S. SUPREME COURT (2020) 591 U.S. ___, 140 S.CT. 2452

(footnotes and citations omitted)

ARGUMENT

I. The Current Rates of Violence Against Native Women and Children Constitute a Crisis

A. Native Women and Children Suffer the Highest Rates of Violence.

Today Native people, and especially Native women, experience some of the highest rates of violent victimization in the United States. Multiple federal reports have confirmed this reality, and both Congress and the federal courts have acknowledged this disparity. More specifically, Native women face the highest rates of domestic violence and sexual assault in the United States.

The most recent reports from the National Institute of Justice ("NIJ") include facts that are sufficiently stunning as to be almost incomprehensible. They conclude that more than 4 in 5 Native people have been victims of violence. Furthermore, Native Americans are more likely to be victims of assault and rape/sexual assault committed by a stranger or acquaintance rather than an intimate partner or family member. Over half (56.1%) of Native women report being victims of sexual violence.

The crisis of violence against Native children cannot be underestimated. Native children experience higher-than-average rates of abuse. Native children have a high rate of victimization at 15.2 per 1,000 American Indian/Alaska Native children. Native youth are also 2.5 times more likely to experience trauma compared to their non-Native peers. The trauma in tribal communities is so significant that Native youth suffer Post-Traumatic Stress Disorder ("PTSD") at rates equivalent to soldiers returning from the wars in Afghanistan and Iraq.

Of all Natives who have suffered violence, nearly 90 percent have experienced violence perpetrated by a non-Indian. As detailed below, Congress has concluded that the inability of Tribal Nations to prosecute the non-Indians who commit the majority of violent crimes against tribal citizens has contributed significantly to the incredibly high levels of violence committed against Native women and children on tribal lands.

B. Native Women and Children are More Likely to be Murdered than any Other Population in the United States.

On some reservations, Native women experience homicide at a rate 10 times the national average. According to the Centers for Disease Control and Prevention ("CDC"), nationally, Native women are murdered at a rate of 4.3 percent, while their white counterparts experience homicide at a rate of 1.5 percent. The crisis has garnered the attention of both Congress and the Executive Branch, as the President recently announced his creation of a Task Force to address the crisis of Missing and Murdered Indigenous Women. *See* Executive Order 13898.

One of the largest barriers to addressing the crisis of missing and murdered indigenous women is that when a Native woman goes missing on tribal lands, there is more often than not a jurisdictional barrier to launching the investigation and search-and-rescue effort that could ensure her safety. This barrier hinges entirely on the determination as to whether the land where the victim was last seen constitutes "Indian country," as defined by 18 U.S.C. § 1151(a).

If a Native victim goes missing within the borders of a reservation that Congress has never disestablished, the Tribal Nation has jurisdiction to investigate the crime, and, hopefully, rescue the victim. But if that same reservation is judicially disestablished, suddenly, tribal law enforcement are required to undertake a lengthy legal analysis concerning the trust/restricted/fee status of the parcel of land where the victim went missing to determine whether that land constitutes "Indian country" under 18 USC § 1151(a) *before* determining whether the Tribe has the requisite jurisdiction to investigate the crime. The time lost to this analysis can cost a Native victim his or her life.

It is no answer to say, as Oklahoma does, that these crimes will be effectively prosecuted by the State. More often than not, State law enforcement fails even to investigate—let alone arrest—the perpetrators who murder Native women and children. As recent studies have shown, when jurisdiction over the crime has been assigned to a State, "1 in 4 alleged murderers of an Indigenous woman or girl were never held accountable, and over one third of murder cases were wrongfully classified as accidental, exposure, natural causes, overdose, or suicide without an adequate and thorough investigation." See *also United States v. Bryant*, 136 S.Ct. 1954, 1960 (2016), as revised (July 7, 2016). ("Even when capable of exercising jurisdiction, [ ] States have not devoted their limited criminal justice resources to crimes committed in Indian country.").

And although this is the rare case where the State chose to prosecute, the Court should not mistake this for the norm. According to the advocates working on the ground to secure prosecutions of these crimes, "[i]n Oklahoma, prosecution of sexual assault is last, least and left behind."

Judicially disestablishing reservations, therefore, threatens to place criminal jurisdiction over the crimes committed against the most vulnerable victims in the hands of the sovereign least likely to prosecute.

II. Congress Responded to this Crisis by Restoring Tribal Jurisdiction

In 2013, in direct response to this crisis, Congress restored the criminal jurisdiction of Tribal Nations to arrest and prosecute non-Indians who commit crimes of domestic violence, dating violence, or violations of protective orders on tribal lands. *See* 25 U.S.C. § 1304(c). The incredibly high rates of violence perpetrated against the citizens of Tribal Nations focused front and center in both the Senate and House discussions surrounding the 2012–2013 reauthorization of VAWA. For instance, the majority report for the Senate Committee on the Judiciary acknowledged that:

> Another significant focus of this reauthorization of VAWA is the crisis of violence against women in tribal communities. These women face rates of domestic violence and sexual assault far higher than the national average. A regional survey conducted by University of Oklahoma researchers showed that nearly three out of five Native American women had been assaulted by their spouses or intimate partners, and a nationwide survey found that one third of all American Indian women will be raped during their lifetime.

Congress identified the loss of tribal criminal jurisdiction over non-Indian crimes on tribal lands as a major contributing factor to these incredibly high rates of violence, stating that "[u]nfortunately, much of the violence against Indian women is perpetrated by non-Indian men. According to Census Bureau data, well over 50 percent of all Native American women are married to non-Indian men, and thousands of others are in intimate relationships with non-Indians."

As Representative Tom Cole of Oklahoma noted, Native women "in many ways [are] the most at-risk part of our population. One in three Native American women will be sexually assaulted in the course of her lifetime. The statistics on the failure to prosecute and hold accountable the perpetrators of those crimes are simply stunning." And as Representative Sheila Jackson Lee of Texas noted, VAWA was passed to "address[ ] a gaping jurisdictional hole by giving tribal courts concurrent jurisdiction over Indian and non-Indian defendants who commit domestic violence offenses against an Indian in Indian country."

In its 2013 re-authorization of VAWA, Congress explicitly cited *Oliphant* as recognizing Congress's constitutional authority to restore tribal criminal jurisdiction. But Congress could not restore this jurisdiction by merely defining the categories of covered crimes alone. Because of the complicated history and framework surrounding the intersections of criminal jurisdiction and tribal law, Congress took great care to define precisely *where* tribal criminal jurisdiction over non-Indian domestic violence offenders would be restored.

Congress defined the "where" to be "Indian country," as previously defined in 18 U.S.C. § 1151, "Indian country defined." VAWA § 904(a)(3) states that "[t]he term Indian country' has the meaning given the term in section 1151 of Title 18."

Congress selected the term "Indian country" to demarcate where a Tribal Nation could (and could not) exercise VAWA's restored jurisdiction because "Indian country" is a term that has "a precise meaning under Title 18 of the U.S. Code."

Thus, although Congress made clear that VAWA's restored tribal jurisdiction "would not cover off-reservation crimes," Congress selected the legal term "Indian country" to make certain that VAWA 2013 would restore tribal jurisdiction over domestic violence crimes occurring on "all private lands and rights-of-way within the limits of every Indian reservation."

If this Court were to adopt Oklahoma's argument and discard *Parker's* adherence to Congress's exclusive authority over the disestablishment of reservations, VAWA § 904's reference to "Indian country" would have a much narrower application now, in 2020, than it did when Congress reauthorized VAWA in 2013. Such a conclusion would undermine Congress's constitutional authority over Indian affairs, and ultimately, would bring dire consequences to Native women and the Tribal Nations who seek to protect them.

III. Tribes are Successfully Implementing VAWA § 904 across "Indian country" to Protect Native Women from Non-Indian-Perpetrated Violence

Currently, at least twenty-five Tribal Nations are implementing VAWA § 904's restored tribal criminal jurisdiction and now arrest and prosecute non-Indians who commit domestic violence crimes within their respective "Indian country" territorial boundaries.

A. The Creek Nation was One of the First Tribes to Implement VAWA § 904.

The Creek Nation was one of the first Tribes to implement VAWA § 904's restored tribal criminal jurisdiction. The Creek Nation's 2016 implementation of VAWA is deeply rooted in Creek culture, law, and tradition.

In the early 1800s, prior to the Creek Nation's forced removal, non-Indian desire for Creek land resulted in high levels of violence against Creek Nation citizens. As a result, the Creek Nation understood that it must exercise its inherent criminal jurisdiction over all perpetrators of violence on Creek lands, including non-Indians.

Long before Oklahoma came into existence, the Creek Nation codified its laws outlawing rape and sexual assault against women on Creek Nation lands. If a person raped a woman on Creek Nation lands regardless of whether that person was Indian or not the Creek Nation had authority to arrest and prosecute the individual who committed the crime. The resulting Creek Nation law read:

> And be it farther enacted if any person or persons should under take [sic] to force a woman and did it by force, it shall be left to the woman what punishment she Should [be] satisfied with to whip or pay what she say it be law.

As indicated by the use of the term "person" to refer to offenders, as opposed to "citizen," "Indian," or "Native," the law's application was not limited to Creek Nation citizens or American Indians. Moreover, the law stipulated that the victim was to be consulted regarding the proper punishment for the perpetrator who committed the crime against her. No state or federal law during that time period allowed a woman to participate in the legal system to fashion a remedy for the violent crime she endured.

Following forced removal to Indian Territory, the Creek Nation reconstituted its national and local governments and justice systems, rekindled its ceremonial fires, and continued its efforts to protect citizens from violence. After the Civil War, the Creek Nation ratified a constitution in 1867, creating six districts within the Reservation itself, extending to the external borders of the 1866 Treaty. Well into the late 19th century, the Creek Nation criminal courts maintained a healthy criminal docket, which included prosecutions for rape, battery, and other violent crimes.

In 2016, the National Council of the Creek Nation passed NCA Bill 16–038, the Protection from Domestic and Family Violence Act ("PDFVA"), to "offer victims the maximum protection from further violence that the law can provide." The PDFVA constitutes a comprehensive 67-page law that includes provisions implementing VAWA § 904's restored criminal jurisdiction. The legislative history embedded within the bill indicates that the Creek Nation worked on the legislation for two years prior to enactment.

The Creek Nation defined the scope of its restored "Indian country" jurisdiction as extending throughout its 1866 Treaty reservation boundary. Specifically, the PDFVA states that the Creek Nation's restored jurisdiction "shall extend to all the territory defined in the 1866 Treaty with the United States."

Thus, the PDFVA itself, facilitated by Congress's 2013 re-authorization of VAWA, contemplates a comprehensive reach of territorial jurisdiction, meaning that the Creek Nation has, in its implementation of VAWA 2013, interpreted VAWA's reference to § 1151's "Indian country" as including the entirety of the Creek Nation's Reservation—a reservation that has never been disestablished by Congress.

On December 18, 2018, the Creek Nation convicted its first non-Indian offender under the PDFVA. The offender was convicted of one count of Domestic Abuse in the Presence of a Child and one count of Violation of a Protective Order. To date, half of the Creek Nation's PDFVA prosecutions have involved crimes of domestic violence committed in the presence of a child. As is so often the case, when a woman is not safe in her home, neither are her children.

B. Other Tribal Nations Have Implemented VAWA § 904 with Great Success Throughout "Indian Country."

As of June 2019, the 25 Tribal Nations that have implemented SDVCJ have collectively reported 237 arrests of non-Indian abusers leading to 95 convictions. . . .

IV. Departure from the *Parker* Framework Would Undermine Congressional Certainty in Passing "Indian Country" Legislation and Would Undermine the Ability of Tribal Nations to Implement VAWA § 904

To date, the *Parker* framework has provided a predictable test for Tribes implementing VAWA § 904 and for Congress, as Congress continues to pass legislation that relies on "Indian country" to include extant reservations that Congress has never disestablished. Abandoning the *Parker* framework, therefore, would undermine Congress's exclusive authority regarding Indian affairs and the inherent sovereignty of Tribal Nations. . .

[Editor's Note: This brief was linked by the U.S. Supreme Court with Sharp v. Murphy, *140 S.Ct. 2412 (2020) since both cases presented the same legal issue. A similar amicus brief was filed in 2018 in* Sharp v. Murphy. *In these cases the Court held that the 1866 treaty between the U.S. government and the Creek/Muskogee tribe was still in effect since it had never been abrogated and the reservation created under it was thus never disestablished. This treaty and companion treaties gave the Five Civilized Tribes—Creek/Muskogee, Choctaw, Cherokee, Chickasaw, and Seminole, all of whom were forcibly removed from the southeast part of the U.S. in the 1820's and 1830's—half of what later became Oklahoma, including the city of Tulsa.*

Oklahoma argued that the treaties should not be honored, partly because they affected half the state, including 1.8 million non-Native U.S. residents, and because these five reservations were the most populous reservations in the country. They noted that the Creeks are the fourth largest tribe in the U.S. and that the decision was likely to apply to the other four Indian Nations in Oklahoma. The Supreme Court ruled against Oklahoma, holding that the Creeks still own the land in their treaty and may exercise jurisdiction over it as a sovereign nation, including prosecuting all people who commit crimes there.]

F. WOMEN FROM VARIOUS RELIGIOUS GROUPS

STACEY A. GUTHARTZ, DOMESTIC VIOLENCE AND THE JEWISH COMMUNITY

11 Mich. J. Gender & L. 27 (2004)
(citations and footnotes omitted)

INTRODUCTION

Over the past decade domestic violence has emerged not only as a subject studied by academics, but also as an epidemic that has gained recognition in society at large. It was not that long ago that the world chose to look away when the issue of domestic abuse was raised. The "not in my community" attitude that plagued much of American society was also prevalent in the Jewish community, where stereotypes of Jewish families as warm and caring and stereotypes of Jewish men as being non-violent perpetuated the myth that domestic violence did not exist among Jews. Fortunately for the thousands of Jewish women who are tormented by abuse each year, most Jews no longer refuse to recognize domestic violence as a Jewish issue.

Within the Jewish community, advancements have been made toward understanding domestic violence as a Jewish problem and towards finding Jewish solutions to domestic abuse. This effort is furthered through the realization of the unique challenges faced by Jewish victims of abuse as well as appreciating the non-homogenous characterization of Jewish victims. In order to best examine domestic violence from a Jewish perspective, one must understand who the Jewish victims are. "Jewish" implies both a religious distinction and a cultural identity, with the two categories often having little overlap. There is no more an "average" Jewish person than there is an "average" American person. * * *

I. DEFINING THE PROBLEM: HOW IS DOMESTIC VIOLENCE A JEWISH PROBLEM?

A. Text and History

Jewish texts and their rabbinic commentaries have developed over the almost six-thousand-year history of Judaism. These texts include not only the Torah and the Talmud but also other recorded rabbinic compilations of Jewish law and responsa that were put in writing. It is from these texts and commentaries that halakhah [basing every aspect of one's life in Jewish law] is derived. Spanning almost six thousand years, Jewish law rooted in ancient traditions is often difficult for present-day society to come to terms with because it may appear to be at odds with modern notions of equality and justice. In addition, various commentaries are often taken out of context and manipulated by individuals looking for justification for their actions. While seeking to understand domestic violence against a Jewish history backdrop, one must keep in mind that Judaism is not monolithic. That is to say, over the centuries, as Jewish society has changed, Jewish laws and interpretations have changed with it. Therefore, there are often conflicting laws that require debate, interpretation, and study.

Like all religions of Western society, Judaism is rooted in patriarchy. "[E]ven though Jewish law is often protective of women, it discriminates against and patronizes them. This is both because patriarchy is intrinsic to Judaism and because Judaism is influenced by other patriarchal systems." The dichotomy of Judaism, as both protecting women and relegating women to second-class status, exemplifies the non-monolithic nature of Judaism, which can be both perplexing and troublesome to the modern-day observer. It is from this dichotomous cultural matrix that halakhah has developed. * * *

Naomi Graetz, in her book concerning rabbinic responses to wife-beating throughout history, divides these rabbinic attitudes into five categories: acceptance, denial, apologetics, rejection, and evasiveness. Rabbis who "accept" wife-beating, according to Graetz, are those who know a husband beats his wife but permit it. Graetz points out specific rabbis whose commentaries indeed appear to take such a position. "Denial" of domestic violence is the "not in my community" attitude still prevalent to some degree today. "Denial" differs from "apologetics," who "justify [domestic violence] by maintaining that Jewish men who actually engage [in abuse] do so for a good reason and, in any case, do not really hurt their wives." "Rejection" is the category that modern-day society can most identify with as these commentaries "have declared that wife beating is unconditionally forbidden." "Evasiveness," perhaps the most frustrating category, reveals rabbinic commentary acknowledging that abuse is wrong, but claiming the rabbis themselves are powerless to do anything about it. Each of these categories is worthy of further study and understanding. Acknowledging the existence of the categories only exemplifies the non-monolithic nature of Judaism and the variety of rabbinic interpretations available concerning domestic violence. Graetz is not alone in highlighting these commentaries, and discussion and study of these commentaries should not disturb the modern-day reader. What is most troublesome is not the existence of these commentaries, but rather the refusal by some Jewish leaders and scholars to acknowledge their existence. Mere acknowledgment does not air the "dirty laundry" of Judaism creating a shondeh (disgrace). Nor does it point to a "problem" within Judaism that, once remedied, will put an end to domestic abuse in Jewish homes.

It is naive to believe that all or even most Jewish men who abuse their wives and girlfriends do so because they find justification within halakhah. Over time, however, halakhah has developed Jewish traditions that some abusers, and those who refuse to acknowledge the abuse, use to justify their action or inaction. These traditions include the concepts of shalom bayit (peace in the home), lashon hara (gossip), shondeh (disgrace), teshuvah (repentance), and the laws regarding Jewish divorce. The misuse of halakhah and its dangers are discussed by Rabbi Abraham Twerski in his book on spousal abuse in the Jewish community: * * *

Shalom Bayit, a seemingly beautiful concept of maintaining a peaceful home, gets turned on its head by abusive men, abused women, and Jewish communities alike through misunderstanding, manipulation, and distortion. Domestic abuse is about power and control. A man who abuses is seeking to control or dominate the woman. An abusive man may use shalom bayit as a means to achieve domination when he becomes enraged that his wife failed to have dinner ready upon his arrival home from work or the children are playing too noisily for him to hear his television program. Through misinterpretation of what shalom bayit means, the man justifies his actions as furthering what he perceives as peace (i.e., dinner ready when he comes home, quiet evenings, etc.), which he believes will be achieved when he is in control. Similarly, women who want to have a peaceful home will try to appease the demands of the man in order to maintain or re-establish tranquility. "The Jewish value 'shalom bayit'—peace in the home—often creates a sense of guilt for Jewish abuse victims." In many Jewish families, the woman is seen as setting the tone for family life. Thus, it is understandable how a woman would blame herself when there is not peace in the home.

The community in which the family lives also manipulates shalom bayit, often subconsciously, to reinforce the abuse. "Because shalom bayit has been such a powerful Jewish ideal, we fool ourselves into thinking domestic abuse 'can't happen to us.' " Rabbis who do not understand domestic abuse, but who are motivated to help the couple, will often counsel women to "work it out." Despite all they have learned about abuse and the need to leave mythologies about Jewish families aside, rabbinic students learning the dynamics of domestic abuse and what resources they can bring as future pastoral counselors often struggle with the urge to want to "fix" the family. These actions are not to be interpreted as malicious, but rather as misguided attempts to use a Jewish concept in order to help maintain the survival of Jewish families.

Domestic violence does not end at the battered woman's doorstep, but rather seeps into society, permeating the woman's community. Community plays a crucial role in Jewish lives since religious observance of holidays and daily events dictate what one eats, when one works, and what one wears. In this way, observant Jews in particular are bound together since they live within close proximity to the synagogue and kosher stores and, thus, to each other. The closeness of Jewish communities could translate into an environment ripe for gossip. There, are however, "many injunctions against slanderous speech and according to the Talmud, slander is worse than idolatry." The enormity of this statement is only understood when one takes into account the central tenet of Judaism: belief in one G-d. Lashon hara (gossip) is not merely looked down upon, but requires individuals to self-govern, quashing gossip before it begins. Many women who have revealed abuse (i.e., confiding in a neighbor that their husbands hit them) have been told they are committing lashon hara. Similarly, when individuals in the community suspect or become aware of abuse, they may remain silent for fear of committing lashon hara by openly discussing the abuse. Both community fear and the woman's fear of committing lashon hara work toward isolating the woman and making her an invisible member of the community. While isolation is used by batterers to control, and is a tool not restricted to the Jewish community, the self-imposed isolation that the woman believes lashon hara dictates is uniquely Jewish. In this same way, while secular communities often want to "mind their own business," Jewish communities believe, albeit incorrectly, that their religion forbids them from speaking out in the open about an abusive situation.

Another concept that contributes to abused women's isolation is shondeh, a disgrace. Both secular and Jewish women often experience a sense of shame from being abused. "The Jewish community reinforces battered women's embarrassment and self-blame by calling abuse a shanda, blaming women for causing or not preventing it in their own home." Shame as a Jewish concept is explained by Lipshutz, Kaufman and Setel:

> The issue of shame in the Jewish community is a complicated one. So vulnerable to the random violence of surrounding cultures for so long, Jews still have the fear of looking "bad" to others. Throughout our history, Jews have often dealt with community dysfunction by flatly denying that problems such as spousal abuse, addiction and incest even existed. We idealized our homes as refuges from a hostile, anti-Semitic world. For generations of Jewish women and children, the abuse suffered within those families was hidden or even viewed as acceptable. Now that victims and survivors have demanded these issues no longer be ignored, they are sometimes blamed for "airing dirty laundry" or bringing shame on the community. Sadly, women victims often have a similar experience: When they take the courageous step of

leaving an abusive relationship, they may be perceived as betraying the Jewish ideals of family and marital fidelity.

The notion of "airing dirty laundry" remains present today in such force that it can work to sabotage domestic violence agencies and outreach centers' efforts to combat domestic abuse. One agency attempted to reach abused Jewish women by hanging posters at the mikveh. [ritual bath for women] The posters were consistently torn down by individuals who do not want domestic violence discussed in the open.

A woman may not keep silent for her shame alone, as children are affected by the shondeh of domestic violence as well. These women know that exposing flaws comes with a certain amount of danger, including jeopardizing the children's chances of marriage. * * * Rabbis reinforce shondeh when they refuse to believe that domestic abuse exists. * * *

Much emphasis is placed on the woman as the person to blame—whether it is because she must maintain shalom bayit, she is committing lashon hara by speaking about the abuse, or she is creating a shondeh with her accusations. Teshuvah, commonly translated as "repentance," further burdens the women as it places her in a position where it is she who must correct things and make them right. Many Jews misunderstand teshuvah to mean forgiveness. In this way, an abusive man may seek forgiveness in the form of teshuvah from the battered woman. The abuser who minimizes his acts or seeks repentance for them through teshuvah feels he has done what he needs to do to repair the situation, placing the onus upon the battered woman to accept the man's forgiveness. "[T]he concept of teshuvah . . . is so ingrained in our collective psyche that Jewish women continue to forgive their spouses and offer them chance after chance to change." However, with domestic violence, behavioral change is not that simple. * * *

The myth that teshuvah heals the wounds of domestic violence can be further perpetuated by rabbis. If a woman is able to gather enough courage to go to her rabbi, the rabbi may still be of the mind that abuse does not happen in the Jewish community. In addition, if the rabbi confronts the man, who insists he has done teshuvah, the rabbi may view the matter as closed. * * *

Statistics show that Jewish women stay in abusive relationships longer than non-Jewish women. This difference is not surprising considering the religious traditions and mythology surrounding Jews and Jewish women in particular. A Jewish woman who seeks to divorce her husband may further entrap herself in the cycle of abuse, since according to Jewish law, a halachically valid marriage can generally only be dissolved in two ways: through the documented death of one of the partners, or by the husband issuing a get to his wife. The get, a document of divorce, releases the woman from the man. A wife cannot deliver the get to her husband, and much controversy exists as to whether a beit din, religious court, may terminate, dissolve, or annul a marriage. Though the wife must consent to a divorce, the get must be initiated by the husband. When a husband refuses to give his wife a get, or, if he is presumed dead but there is no proof of his death, the wife becomes an agunah.

An agunah is a "bound" woman: chained or anchored to the husband to whom she no longer wishes to be married. Agunot are not permitted to remarry under Jewish law. If an agunah were to remarry or cohabitate with another man, it would be considered an adulterous relationship. Any children born of such a relationship are mamzerim. Mamzerim, loosely translated as illegitimate, are severely stigmatized under Jewish law. For example, a mamzer is generally permitted to marry only another mamzer.

Often a husband will agree to a get in exchange for the woman giving up her rights to custody of the children, alimony, child support, the family home, etc. Because Jewish law does not recognize civil marriage or civil divorce, the woman is at the mercy of her husband and his extortive measures if she wants a religious end to her marriage.

Battering, as previously discussed, is a means of control. "The 'goal' of this abuse is to help one person achieve and maintain power and control over the other." Thus, Jewish divorce laws help an abuser to achieve his "goal" since under the Jewish laws of divorce, the batterer is in a position to ensure that a woman's fate remains in his hands. The decision to leave an abusive spouse is not an easy one. That decision increases in difficulty when the need for a get is present. If a husband withholds the get after the woman leaves, she is still not free from him. Similarly, if the woman believes the get will be withheld, she may not even try to leave—thus chaining the agunah not only to her husband, but to his abuse as well. * * *

[Editor's Note: In "Jewish Divorce Denial Serves as a Form of Domestic Abuse," 26(4) DVR 53 (April/May 2021), by Keshet Starr, the author states: "Get *refusal almost always follows a long history of abuse. Among Organization for the Resolution of Agunot (ORA) cases surveyed, 91% reported a prior history of spousal abuse. An additional research study looked closer at relationship dynamics prior to* get *refusal according to ORA callers. Out of over 150* agunot *surveyed, 47% reported experiencing three different types of physical abuse and 18% experienced choking [i.e., strangulation], a lethality risk consistent with a particularly dangerous relationship. Eighty-one percent of participants reported emotional abuse, nearly 70% noted a pattern of isolation, and 62% experienced sexual abuse. These statistics indicate that in cases of* get *refusal, there is an extremely high likelihood that the relationship was previously abusive.*

Not only is the get *a step along the continuum of abuse, it may be the final and most fraught chapter. After all other connections between the couple are severed—they are no longer living together, they are not married, they have no minor children in common—the* get *is the final source of control. A number of well-known and publicized* agunah *cases feature* get *refusal situations that have continued years, even decades, after the civil divorce was finalized or the couple is no longer living together."]*

C. Societal Views

In addition to the stereotypes that abused women face, Jewish women also face anti-Semitism from the non-Jewish world. "Stamped as an abrasive, emasculating, and overbearing mother or a pampered, demanding, and self-centered shrew, a Jewish woman hardly evokes sympathy from the public or a court of law." These preconceived notions about Jewish women are as restricting as the myths Jews themselves believe about Jewish families. They contribute to the difficulty of Jewish women leaving and getting help.

A Jewish woman who decides to leave her abusive partner may have special needs that limit where she can go. If the woman keeps kosher, she cannot prepare food in a shelter kitchen that is not a kosher kitchen. "Adhering to the dietary laws keeps the observant Jew apart from those who have rejected [her]." The same laws that set a dividing line for the observant Jewish woman between the Jewish and non-Jewish world serve as a barrier to her freedom since "for many Orthodox women who need to keep kosher and observe the Sabbath, there is nowhere to go." In shelters that have a kosher kitchen, anti-Semitism becomes an issue between the Jewish and non-Jewish women. The non-Jewish women may resent what they see as Jewish women as receiving special privileges. Similarly, Jewish women are commanded by their religious observance to light candles on Shabbat. Shelters often have rules prohibiting the lighting of candles for safety reasons. In addition to kashrut [keeping kosher] and Shabbat, the shelter's communal atmosphere is often difficult for observant women to accommodate. For example, television programs being watched by the non-Jewish women and their children in the shelter will likely be considered inappropriate by the observant Jewish woman for herself and her children. The discomfort Jewish women feel in shelters makes their overall stay shorter on the average than that of non-Jewish women.

II. EXPLORING SOLUTIONS: ARE THERE JEWISH SOLUTIONS TO DOMESTIC VIOLENCE?

A. Religious Law

* * * Rabbis must set an example for their community by not misusing or manipulating the concept of shalom bayit. Similarly, they must support individuals by recognizing that the best means of achieving peace may be to end the marriage or relationship.

Rabbis also have the ability to play a major role in bringing aid to abused women through their work on the beit din, the Jewish religious court. * * * While batei din in the United States are largely unregulated and often operate under different standards, with various practice styles and atmospheres, there is some uniformity among them. * * * When one party refuses to submit to arbitration before a beit din, or refuses to comply with the decision of the beit din, the beit din can issue a hazmanah, or summons. After three hazmanot have been issued, the beit din has the power to issue a seruv, or contempt citation. * * *

Despite the need for a woman to approach the beit din as an informed litigant, the abilities of the beit din with regard to aiding a victim of abuse should not be underestimated. Though Jewish divorce laws strongly favor the man, decisions of the beit din are binding on both parties. Domestic violence is often considered an insufficient cause for a husband to have to give a get, making the selection of which beit din to use crucial. A beit din that operates with fairness, competence, and integrity ensures that a woman receives justice and that the actual powers of the beit din are utilized.

Since Jewish divorce often heightens the web of entrapment in which a victim of abuse is caught, it is necessary to understand what can be done to help a woman avoid becoming an agunah. Throughout the Orthodox community and elsewhere within Judaism, premarital agreements are being used to place women on more equal footing with men in the event divorce should arise. * * * [However,] while a carefully worded prenuptial agreement may bring some relief to a battered woman or agunah, it often does not.

* * * In order to eradicate the problem of agunah, halakhic reform is necessary. Halakhic reform can be achieved by takkanah (rabbinic edict). "Takkanah is a very important tool in the system of halakha which, despite its centrality to the viability of the halakhic process, has fallen on disuse." A takkanah would put an end to the requirement that a husband give his wife a get and adopt in its place a mutual agreement arbitrated before a beit din. Proactive measures within halakhah would amend Jewish law, equalizing men and women's positions with regards to Jewish divorce. Fostering change within halakhah, however, is likely slow to come, and for this reason, other avenues available to rabbis to help bring women justice through community leadership should be explored. * * *

C. Civil Law

* * * In 1983, New York became the first state to address the agunah problem legislatively by adopting Domestic Relations Law § 253. The statute bars a plaintiff from obtaining a divorce until he or she has removed barriers to the other party's remarriage. More recently, in 1992, the New York Legislature amended the statute to allow a judge, where appropriate, to consider the potential effects of a woman's religious inability to remarry in dividing marital assets or setting maintenance.

The *get* statute has been highly controversial. Some believe it is an "unconstitutional intrusion into religious affairs." Rabbinic authorities agree, however, that the statute does not coerce a man into giving a *get*.

This is a critical point because under Jewish law a *get* that is coerced is invalid. By telling the plaintiff that, if he wants a civil divorce, he will have to give the *get*, the court is placing the decision upon the plaintiff, rather than ordering him to give the *get*. * * *

"The chief problem is that the law only helps if the recalcitrant spouse is the one who sues for divorce, but in the vast majority of divorce actions in which the *get* becomes an issue, women are the plaintiffs." This is particularly true for women who are victims of spousal abuse. Where a woman has been abused by her husband and initiates divorce on those grounds (or any other), the statute does not help her. Many rabbis and attorneys, however, say that the statute has been effective. They believe that the statute has a preemptive force since some men agree to a religious divorce after being counseled on the statute's impact on their ability to file for civil divorce. * * *

CONCLUSION

Both Jews and non-Jews alike recognize the existence of domestic violence. Resources have been developed and continue to be developed within the Jewish community for Jewish victims of abuse. Yet much remains to be done to ameliorate the problems caused by domestic violence within the Jewish community.

Rabbis must lead their communities toward an honest and realistic understanding of domestic abuse. They must be educated on how to address domestic violence from the pulpit and how best to educate others regarding abuse. Similarly, rabbis need to recognize shalom bayit as an ideal, not an absolute. Informed about the dynamics of abuse, rabbis will be better able to counsel women who approach them for help.

Rabbis and communities' linking themselves with domestic violence organizations and outreach centers is tantamount to overcoming the "not in my community" attitude. Solid networks, aligning the Jewish community with domestic violence resources, will help ensure the safety of Jewish women. The community itself must not ignore abuse when it sees or suspects it. Confronting abuse is not a shondeh or committing lashon hara. The shondeh occurs when a woman is abused and her neighbors stand by and watch. Similarly, domestic violence organizations whose programs are not specific to Jewish women must understand the sensitivities particular to Jewish victims of abuse. Such organizations must reach out to Jewish communities and rabbis, informing the Jewish community that the organizations are receptive to Jewish women's needs.

Jewish society, as well as domestic violence workers and activists, must recognize the *agunah* as a victim of abuse. Having one's abilities to be free from a marriage, to remarry, and to bear children held hostage by a recalcitrant husband are forms of abuse. Secular divorce lawyers must become educated on Jewish divorce laws, so they may better be able to counsel clients seeking a secular divorce. For a Jewish woman seeking a secular divorce, receiving the *get* first (or at the very least placing the *get* in escrow until the secular divorce is finalized) can be the difference between the woman becoming an *agunah* or being freed from her marriage both under the laws of the state and the Jewish law. Similarly, Jewish women must become informed litigants in *get* proceedings. They must be able to research the operations of a *beit din* before presenting themselves to the *beit din* in order to ensure an equitable outcome.

NOORIA FAIZI, DOMESTIC VIOLENCE IN THE MUSLIM COMMUNITY

10 Tex. J. Women & L. 209
(footnotes omitted)

I. Introduction

> And among His signs is that He created for you mates from among yourselves, that ye may dwell in tranquility with them, and He has put love and mercy between your (hearts) . . . [Qur'an]

Unfortunately not all Muslim households experience the tranquility described in this verse from the Qur'an. Domestic violence occurs in Muslim homes all around the world and is a significant problem in the United States. According to estimates by Muslim activists in the United States, approximately ten percent of Muslim women are abused emotionally, psychologically, sexually, and/or physically by their husbands. One Islamic community estimates that for every case of abuse reported, almost fifty are unreported and that less than two percent of victims actually seek help. In spite of the prevalence of domestic violence, very little research has been done specifically on the problem of domestic violence in the American Muslim community. . .

First, this paper will highlight women's rights in Islamic law. Islamic law is based primarily on the Holy Qur'an and secondarily on the Sunnah, or the ways of the Prophet Muhammad, peace be upon him (PBUH). . . . Ignorance of their Islamic rights is one of the leading reasons why Muslim women remain in abusive situations and accept violence as Islamically ordained behavior. . . .

II. Domestic Violence in the Muslim Community

Marriage and family are the bases of Muslim society, and Islam is said to bless, support, and aid these relationships. The peace and security offered by a stable home is considered to be essential for the spiritual growth of Muslim families. It is believed that Islam's family system brings the rights of the husband, wife, children, and relatives into an equilibrium. For this reason, violence shatters the very security Islam is supposed to maintain in the home.

Deviation from Islamic teachings is believed to be one of the major causes of domestic violence in Muslim families. . . .

Domestic violence in Muslim homes takes several different forms. A husband may threaten to divorce his wife, to remarry, or to take the children away if she does not submit to his will. He may tell her that her failure to submit and obey will send her to hell, or he may twist Islamic teachings to question her worth as a Muslim woman. He might restrict her freedom, isolating her from family and friends, or display extreme jealousy and possessiveness. . .

Unfortunately, the situation is made even more difficult for Muslim women and the Muslim community as a whole by the fact that Muslim men use Islam to justify their behavior. In the most abusive homes, the husband believes, and he socializes his wife and children to believe, that whatever he wants the family to do is the same as what Allah wants. Abusive Muslim men use the Qur'an and Sunnah as their tools, manipulating verses to keep their wives subservient and obedient and manipulating the women's spirituality and faith to reinforce the abuser's power and control.

The most misinterpreted verse is Sura (Chapter) 4, Verse 34, which is often used as a license for abuse:

> Men are the protectors and maintainers of women, because God has given the one more (strength) than the other, and because they support them from their means. Therefore the righteous women are devoutly obedient, and guard in (the husband's absence) what God would have them guard. As to those women on whose part ye fear disloyalty and ill-conduct, admonish them (first), (next), refuse to share their beds, (and last) beat them; but if they return to obedience, seek not against them means (of annoyance): for God is Most High, Great.

Most scholars have interpreted this translation as charging men with the responsibility of financially and physically protecting and caring for their wives and families. The reason stated for this belief is that Allah has made men physically stronger than women. However, some have noted that the Arabic word used in the Qur'an, qawwamun (meaning "protectors" and "maintainers"), refers to a person who takes the responsibility of safeguarding the interests of another and should not be taken to mean "that men are masters to be blindly obeyed or a police force giving orders, as most men interpret for their own benefit."

. . .Some believe that "hit" is not an accurate translation. This belief is based on the Prophet's abhorrence of hitting women, as found in his statement "never hit the handmaids of Allah." Furthermore, the Prophet (PBUH) disapproved of men hitting their wives, and he never hit any woman or child in his lifetime. In his last sermon, the Prophet (PBUH) emphasized to men that they must be kind to their women. He preached that wives have rights over their husbands in addition to husbands having rights over wives; that wives are to be treated well, for they are their husbands' partners and committed helpers. The Prophet (PBUH) has also been quoted as saying that "the strong man is not the one who can use the force of physical strength, but the one who controls his anger."

Given all the Islamic provisions against violent behavior toward others and those provisions mandating the proper, kind, and just treatment of women, it is ironic that so many men believe or attempt to convince others that it is their God-given right to mistreat and abuse their wives. It is even more unfortunate that so many women believe that their religion and their God would condone or prescribe such horrendous behavior. . .

Rights in Islam

. . .This passage from a book on women and Islam describes how a woman should be treated according to Islamic beliefs. A woman's protected status, according to some interpretations of Islamic law, is a status to which she is entitled as a basic right. Women have been deprived of this status by years of social and historical prejudices and injustices.

However, with the beginning of Islam came a social reform movement focusing on social and economic justice. The most significant changes were the heightening of the status of women and slaves. The introduction of Islam modified Arab practices, such as polygamy, free divorce, female infanticide, and marital violence, to the advantage of women, but patriarchal interpretations of Islam and the infusion of cultural elements have destroyed the progressive nature of women's rights provided by Islam. . .

Islam provides mutual rights for men and women. Husbands have rights over their wives, and wives have rights over their husbands. Typically, the wife's role is defined as the guardian of the house, and the husband's role is defined as the provider and maintainer. This does not mean that the woman is restricted to the house, as many have often interpreted. She has the right to work outside her home and the right to seek knowledge, including formal education. The right to an Islamic education is so important that some believe women should pursue formal education despite the potential disagreement of their husbands. The Prophet (PBUH) was quoted as saying, "[S]eeking knowledge is mandatory for every Muslim." He believed in this doctrine and practiced it. Women came freely to him posing questions and addressing inquiries on all matters, including social, religious, and economic matters, and he answered their queries and enlightened his questioners on all current issues.

. . . The importance of mutual kindness and mercy in the marriage clearly are expressed in this passage of the Qur'an; thus any form of domestic abuse is in clear violation of Islamic law. Women have a right to safety and security, as well as a right to kindness, equity, and freedom from harshness. Additionally, women are afforded the right to freedom from fear of any human being, freedom from all oppression, the right to justice, freedom from defamation, and the right to peacefulness even during divorce.

Divorce is another powerful tool used to maintain power and control over Muslim women. It is common knowledge among Muslims that divorce is the most hated thing to God. Many will avoid the option of divorce for fear of displeasing God or family and the community. Some women will seek divorce only when their relationships become life-threatening. Furthermore, some Muslims believe that divorce is the right of the man alone. However, women do have the right to seek divorce. They may seek the authorization for divorce in their marriage contracts, and this authorization is permissible at the time of the marriage contract or after it. Many women are unaware of this right and often remain in abusive relationships because they believe they do not have the right to seek divorces or to leave. Men rarely seek a divorce, because divorce would require them to voluntarily relinquish the control they assert over their wives.

In addition to increasing women's awareness of their Islamic rights, it is equally necessary for Muslim men to know their duties to their wives. It is obligatory for spouses to associate with one another with peace and grace. Islam dictates that a husband be a comrade to his wife, not simply a dictator. The Prophet (PBUH) was quoted as saying, "[T]he most perfect believers in faith are the best of them in creation, and the best of you, the best to their women" and "the honorable honors them and no one insults them but is wicked." Scholars of Islam have stated that honoring women is an indication of the perfect character and that insulting women is a sign of meanness and vanity. . .

Why do they stay?

[Summary: In addition to the reasons many women of all faiths stay in abusive relationships, Muslim women may stay because someone who has had a divorce is highly looked down on and shunned in the larger Muslim community, because they identify strongly with being a member of the Muslim community and want to continue being a member, because they fear the gossip that leaving would cause, because they are not aware that they are entitled under Islamic law to a divorce or to better treatment, because staying is protecting the image of Islam in the non-Muslim community, or because they think they will be damned to hell if they leave.]. . .

III. Resources: Muslim versus Non-Muslim, i.e., "Western"

Two types of resources are available to battered women to assist them in leaving abusive relationships: the "Western" system and the "Muslim" system. The Western system refers to shelters run by non-Muslims and to the American legal system, including law enforcement and attorneys. The Muslim system refers to the Muslim community and its resources, such as local Mosques, Muslim-run shelters, and Islamic arbitration councils. . .

[The big differences between Muslim women and non-Muslim women in domestic violence shelters can make Muslim women feel isolated and alienated from the other shelter residents, leading to their returning to their abusers. Non-Muslim domestic violence advocates and law enforcement need training on working with Muslim survivors of abuse. . . The author describes various domestic violence shelters in Georgia and Texas who frequently have Muslim residents.]

Imams and Masjids

Islamic arbitration is another option available to those who do not seek out the "Western" system. . . . This panel is a registered legal institution. The parties, who must agree to appear before the panel, have the right to select the judges, but the conditions and bylaws require the judges to have a background in Islamic jurisprudence, since rulings are to be based on the Qur'an and Sunnah.

It is estimated that of the approximately ten cases a week that appear before the panel, about half involve marital disputes and/or domestic violence. With each marriage contract over which the Imam presides, he recommends that the parties incorporate a clause in their contract that requires them to resort to Islamic arbitration before seeking a Western legal remedy. The Imam stated that the underlying basis for many, if not most, of the conflicts involved the parties' misunderstanding of each other's duties and rights as husband and wife [under Islamic law]. . . .

Rulings vary, depending upon the circumstances of the dispute. Divorce is never encouraged, and every measure will be taken to keep the family unit together. However, if the situation is life-threatening, rulings will recommend the dissolution of the marriage. The problem with the arbitration procedures is that the rulings are not legally binding; rather, they are only ethically and morally binding, and there is no enforcing authority. [Rulings also vary from one Muslim community to another.]

Sometimes, the individuals sitting on the arbitration panels, also known as the Masjid shura (consultation) councils, are men who have close connections to the husbands involved in the dispute, and their objectivity may be questionable. Consequently, women using these arbitration panels may start to feel that their disputes are not being handled fairly. To address these concerns, most Muslims recommend that Islamic solutions be easily substituted with Western adjudication when women start to feel that they are not treated justly.

Muslim women who do seek help often will turn to their Masjids and Imams. Unfortunately, they do not always find the help they need. They are often told by the Imams to be patient and pray for the abuse to end. Sometimes, women are blamed for the abuse and accused of not pleasing their husbands. At other times, Imams have been known to sincerely but wrongly advise the women to place the importance of family privacy above any harm that they might endure. . .

IV. Recommendations

[Author calls on Muslim men, Imams, and Mosques to take an active role in eradicating domestic violence. She states that non-Muslim shelter workers and criminal justice system professionals need training on how to work with Muslim survivors of abuse, that Imams need training on domestic violence, and that Mosques need to incorporate the subject of domestic violence into their Islamic education classes. Mosques and Imams should support survivors of domestic violence to leave their husbands, building networks of Islamic professionals and programs who can assist survivors and keeping updated lists of places to stay. Mosques could earmark a percentage of zakat (Islamic taxes) for the living expenses of survivors or for domestic violence agencies.]

[Editor's Notes: 1. In "Diminished Access to Islamic Divorce for Domestic Violence Survivors," 26(4) Domestic Violence Report 51 (April/May 2021), Veena Bhatia focuses on Muslim women in India, who are subject to Sharia law, the Islamic legal system:

> *"In Sharia law, Muslim men may divorce their wives by saying the word "divorce" three times consecutively ("talaq, talaq, talaq"), at any time and without cause. The practice is commonly called "triple-talaq" or "triple-divorce" and only men can perform it. Triple-talaq divorce may occur via phone, email, text, or any form. Notably, neither Sharia Islamic law nor the Quran mention triple-talaq. Nonetheless, the practice is a long-standing, highly controversial family law practice in India. Opponents of the practice contend that the law marginalizes Muslim women by forcing them to remain in a marriage with men who verbally and emotionally abuse them. . .*
>
> *The Indian Muslim Women Movement (BMMA) is a grassroots organization that works to educate and empower Muslim women in India to oppose instant divorce. . . BMMA surveyed about 5,000 Muslim women concerning their views of Muslim Personal Law. This study, conducted across 10 Indian states, was the first to solicit the views of so many Muslim women. BMMA found that oral divorce is an abusive practice that is strongly linked to the manipulation of dowry. Upon marriage, the woman's family pays more than 10 to 15 lakhs (about $14,500 USD), and the man gains that amount by virtue of the marriage. Unfortunately, many men spend only a short time with their wives, divorce them, kick them out, and then marry again to collect additional dowry."*

The author notes that husbands may also not tell their new wives that they are already married; polygamy is allowed under Sharia law.

It is possible that these issues arise in some Muslim marriages in the U.S. as well.

2. "3 Seconds Divorce" is a 2018 documentary in Hindi available on Netflix. Bhatia states that the practice of triple talaq continues in India in spite of a ban by the Indian Supreme Court in 2017 and India's Parliament making it a crime in 2019. She notes that many other Muslim countries have banned this practice, with successful campaigns in Pakistan, Bangladesh, Sri Lanka, Turkey, Cyprus, Tunisia, Algeria, Malaysia, Jordon, Egypt, Iran, Iraq, Brunei, the UAE, Indonesia, Libya, Sudan, Lebanon, Saudi Arabia, Morocco, and Kuwait.

3. Of course, women in conservative Christian communities may be similarly discouraged from reporting abuse or leaving their abusers, and the Bible may be misinterpreted by Christian clergy in similar ways as the ways the author describes the Qur'an being misinterpreted. To address this, there is now a national network of Christian clergy and other faith-based leaders working against domestic violence, from the Faith Trust Institute in Seattle, Washington, to the Black Church and Domestic Violence Institute in Atlanta, Georgia.]

G. DISABLED WOMEN

DOUG JONES, DOMESTIC VIOLENCE AGAINST WOMEN WITH DISABILITIES: A FEMINIST LEGAL THEORY ANALYSIS

2 Fla. A & M U L Rev 207 (2007)
(citations and footnotes omitted)

I. INTRODUCTION

Domestic violence against women with disabilities is disturbingly prevalent. A national survey of domestic violence service programs reveals that "ten percent of the women served by the programs had physical disabilities, seven percent had mental retardation or developmental disabilities ('MR/DD'), twenty-one percent had mental illness, two percent had visual impairments and three percent had hearing impairments." These figures may underestimate the true incidence of domestic violence against women with disabilities because the figures represent only those women who have sought domestic violence services; they do not include unreported incidents or those women who did not seek services.

Some commentators argue that a more accurate estimation of the incidence of domestic violence against women with disabilities is that "regardless of age, race, ethnicity, sexual orientation or class, women with disabilities are assaulted, raped and abused" more than twice as often than women without disabilities. According to this projection, half of all women with disabilities will experience domestic violence. Despite the prevalence of domestic violence against women with disabilities, many researchers and commentators agree that the conventional means of a woman's escape from domestic violence, protective orders and domestic violence shelters, have not evolved to meet the needs of women with disabilities. For example, many shelters are not accessible to women with physical disabilities and standard protective orders often do not meet the needs of a woman with disabilities who has come to rely upon her abuser for care and assistance.

The Americans with Disabilities Act ('ADA') defines a disability as "(a) a physical or mental impairment that substantially limits one or more of the major life activities of such individual; (b) a record of such an impairment; or (c) being regarded as having such an impairment." This broad definition is too imprecise to be useful in a careful discussion of disability because it lumps very different disabilities into the same category. A more workable definition for disability would create three sub-classifications: physical disability, developmental disability, and psychological disability. Physical disabilities affect the appearance or function of a person's body and include paralysis and sensory impairments. Developmental disabilities affect a person's cognition or development and generally fall into five categories: autism, cerebral palsy, epilepsy, neurological impairments, and mental retardation. Finally, a psychological disability is a persistent psychological or psychiatric disorder or emotional or mental illness, such as depression or schizophrenia.

A useful place to begin an analysis of domestic violence against women with disabilities is with examples of such violence. What follows are three fictional cases of women with disabilities who suffered domestic violence. Each case involves a woman with a different type of disability—physical, developmental, and psychological. These cases illustrate several issues that are unique to cases of domestic violence against women with disabilities.

Edna K. has a physical disability: she has late-stage AIDS. Due to AIDS related complications, she uses a motorized wheelchair for mobility. She has a boyfriend who hits her and who abuses her in ways that take advantage of her disability. One time after a fight, her boyfriend took the battery pack out of her wheelchair, rendering her immobile. Despite Edna's pleas for the return of the battery, her boyfriend left her immobile for several hours.

Months later, after a separate incident of abuse, Edna's boyfriend was arrested for harassment and for menacing her. While her boyfriend was in jail, and before his court date arrived, Edna went to the District Attorney's office and expressed her wish to drop the charges against her boyfriend. Edna was told that she could not drop the charges since the State, not

Edna, was prosecuting her boyfriend. Even though Edna was not able to drop the charges, she officially informed the District Attorney of her intent not to cooperate. Since she was the only witness in this case, this effectively halted the prosecution.

When Edna gave notice of her intent not to cooperate, she told the Assistant District Attorney her reasons for not wanting to proceed with the prosecution. Because both Edna and her boyfriend have AIDS, they rely on each other for assistance with day-to-day care. When Edna is sick, her boyfriend takes her to the doctor, and vice versa. Edna expressed that she needed her boyfriend and her boyfriend needed her; she did not want jail to separate them.

Edna's case demonstrates how women with physical disabilities are vulnerable to forms of abuse to which non-disabled women are not vulnerable. Because she uses a wheelchair, her boyfriend was able to abuse her by controlling her mobility. Furthermore, Edna's case illustrates (or demonstrates) the unique issues that arise when a disabled woman's abuser is also her primary caregiver.

The next example involves Marge S., who has a developmental disability—mild mental retardation. Marge met her boyfriend eight years ago. He was working as the driver of an ambulette, which Marge relies on for transportation. During their relationship, Marge's boyfriend would pressure her to engage in sexual acts in which she did not want to perform. He never physically forced her to do anything. Instead, he persuaded her into these sexual acts, and threatened to leave her if she did not do what he wanted. Whereas these tactics would not be successful on most non-disabled women, they were successful on Marge because of her mental retardation. Essentially, Marge's boyfriend took advantage of her cognitive impairment to make her do sexual things she did not want to do, without going so far as to rape her outright. Afterwards, Marge told her boyfriend that she did not want to "do things like that anymore." Her boyfriend was dismissive of this desire, pointing out that no one "forced" her to do anything. He then called her a slut.

Marge's boyfriend was involved with other women during his relationship with Marge. When Marge confronted him about this, he claimed that he was entitled to be with other women because she had been with another man during their threesome. Finally, fed up with the way she was treated, Marge broke up with her boyfriend. He did not take this well. He began harassing her, calling and text massaging her cell phone ten to fifteen times a day. Many of the messages said "I love you," "let's start over," or "I want to get married." Later, Marge's boyfriend was arrested for harassment. When she discussed her case with an Assistant District Attorney, she explained that she stayed with her boyfriend for eight years because he is aware of her disability and believes it is difficult for people with disabilities to find intimate partners.

Marge's case shows how women with developmental disabilities are vulnerable to forms of abuse that prey on their developmental disabilities. Her case also reveals the difficulties women with disabilities face in finding and sustaining intimate relationships. These difficulties may cause some women with disabilities to choose an abusive intimate relationship over no intimate relationship at all.

The last case involves Selma B., who has a psychological disorder—borderline personality disorder. Borderline personality disorder is a serious mental illness characterized by pervasive instability in moods, interpersonal relationships, self-image, and behavior. This instability often disrupts family and work life, long-term planning, and the individual's sense of self-identity.

Selma's ex-husband was physically and verbally abusive. Selma was involved in several criminal and family court cases regarding this abuse. Selma often expressed frustration with the court system, complaining that it does not resolve problems and moves too slowly. However, she also failed to follow through with her cases, often becoming uncooperative or missing appointments with attorneys or counselors. Attorneys assigned to work with Selma describe her as erratic and difficult to work with, and attribute this difficulty to her psychological disability.

Selma's case is an example of how the infrastructure that provides services to victims of domestic violence is frequently unable to effectively meet the needs of women with disabilities. Her case shows how this is especially true when a woman's disability effects her personal interactions or communication.

The incidence of domestic violence against women with disabilities is high. Edna, Marge, and Selma are but three of the millions of women with disabilities who have suffered domestic violence. However, despite this high incidence, little feminist legal scholarship has addressed the issue. The aim of this paper is to use the lens of feminist legal theory to examine this issue in depth. The domestic violence service infrastructure, which assists victims/survivors of domestic violence with escaping that violence, inadequately meets the needs of women with disabilities who suffer domestic violence. This infrastructure includes, but is not limited to, law enforcement, prosecution officers, the court system, and non-profit organizations that provide shelters and other services. * * *

III. UNIQUE MYTHS, UNIQUE EXPERIENCES, AND UNIQUE BARRIERS

Myths and misconceptions about disabled women abound. These myths are one of the reasons why disabled women experience domestic violence differently. Such myths include the following: women with disabilities are not abused because it is simply too low and cowardly to assault someone who cannot fight back; women with disabilities are asexual and do not form intimate relationships, and therefore cannot be victims of domestic violence; even if women with disabilities experience some domestic violence, the perpetrators deserve a little leeway because it is unreasonable to expect a man in such a difficult situation not to vent his frustrations once in a while; women with disabilities are child-like, and not to be believed.

Many forms of domestic violence touch the lives of even non-disabled women. Physical abuse is the most visible manifestation, but domestic violence also includes name-calling, isolating a woman from friends and family, forcing a woman to engage in unwanted or disliked sexual acts, and/or threatening to kill or harm pets. However, women with disabilities experience unique forms of domestic violence that prey on their disabilities. * * *

Accordingly, a disabled woman's experience of domestic violence can be completely different from a non-disabled woman's experience of domestic violence. A batterer may take away or disable a wheelchair, place a communication device out of reach, place a dangerous object in the path of a blind woman, withhold medication or over-medicate, or refuse basic care such as bathing, dressing, or using the toilet.

Many barriers keep women without disabilities from escaping domestic violence. For instance, in addition to fearing that escape will instigate further violence, "emotional pressures" may keep a woman in an abusive relationship. "Constant insults and criticisms from her batterer may make her feel helpless and unable to act independently . . ." Further, a woman "may believe that abuse is a normal, though not ideal, part of relationships, especially if she saw her mother battered by a spouse or boyfriend when she was a child." A religious woman's moral beliefs may preclude her from divorcing a battering spouse. "Th[ese] belief[s] may be encouraged by friends, family, and/or religious counselors, who urge her to save her marriage." Worse, if a batterer has isolated a woman from her friends and family, she may feel alone and that there is no one to help her escape.

Another reason women with disabilities have unique experiences with domestic violence is that they face barriers to escape from domestic violence that women without disabilities do not face. In the first place, a woman with disabilities, especially if she has a developmental disability, may not even realize she is experiencing abuse. More so than non-disabled women, women with disabilities may accept abuse as a normal part of their life.

Even if a woman with disabilities recognizes her abuse and has a subjective desire to escape, she may feel that there is little she can do to escape. Woman with mobility or visual impairments may not physically be able to escape, and women who cannot drive may depend on transportation services that require advance notice for a pickup. Further, a woman with disabilities who grew up in protected environments, where her independence was limited or non-existent, may feel incapable of making decisions on her own or may feel that submission to authority figures—i.e. people without disabilities—is a necessary part of life, or even a virtue. Some argue that this submissive and passive attitude, which results from the protected environment that women with disabilities inhabit, make women with disabilities particularly attractive to men who seek vulnerable women to control.

Barriers facing women with disabilities are also socially constructed. General social prejudice against people with disabilities, including the notion that they are asexual, may make these women feel that they should appreciate any kind of intimate attention, no matter how abusive. If a woman with disabilities suffers under this myth, she will be less likely to seek escape from domestic violence. Further, a woman may believe her batterer when he tells her that without his care she would find herself in an institution because no other man would want her.

It may seem that it would be easy for women with disabilities to obtain help escaping from domestic violence because they are seen as vulnerable and they may have more contact with state authorities because of their disabilities. However, this is not the case. Instead, the misconception that women with disabilities are childlike or asexual is so pervasive that people seem to reject the very idea of a woman with a disability in a relationship. If she cannot be in a relationship, then the faulty reasoning is that she cannot be a victim of domestic violence. This misconception is a barrier and leads to the fact that women with disabilities are less likely to be believed or taken seriously when they report incidents of abuse.

Yet another barrier faced by women with disabilities is that their batterers are often their primary caretakers. Even if a woman wishes to escape, she may not think that shelters will be able to accommodate her needs or she may not have a backup caregiver to call. A woman with disabilities may face the difficult and unenviable choice of staying with an abusive caregiver or escaping to the very distinct possibility of institutionalization.

Finally, financial considerations work as barriers to escape. Employment discrimination and the restraints of disability may make it difficult for a woman to work, leaving her financially dependent on her caregiver/batterer. The caregiver/batterer may also be dependent on the disabled woman's disability checks, thus making him particularly averse to her ending the relationship.

IV. PROPOSALS AND THEORY

A. Domestic Violence Service Infrastructure Reforms

The barriers lined up to keep a woman with disabilities from escaping domestic violence can seem insurmountable. Reforms must be made to remove these barriers. The most significant and most tangible barriers that women with disabilities face, when attempting to escape, are those that physically prevent her from escaping. These are the most tangible barriers because they can be seen, touched or observed, and therefore they are the most ripe for reform.

The classic method of securing escape from domestic violence is crisis intervention. For women who are in abusive situations, crisis intervention includes escaping temporarily to a woman's shelter, escaping permanently from the abuser, and having an escape plan ready in the event of imminent violence if the woman must remain with the perpetrator. These options may be problematic for women with disabilities if the shelter is inaccessible to women with physical disabilities, if there is no accessible transportation to the facility, if the shelter staff are unable or unwilling to communicate with deaf or speech-impaired women, if she depends primarily on the abuser for assistance with personal needs and has no family or friends to stay with, or if she is physically incapable of executing the tasks necessary to implement an escape plan, such as packing necessities and driving or arranging transportation to a shelter.

However, only one-third of all domestic violence programs offer safety plan information modified for use by women with disabilities or provide disability awareness training for program staff. Disabled women's physical access to the domestic violence service infrastructure must increase. All buildings must comply with the architectural requirements of the Americans with Disabilities Act, state laws, and local ordinances. Program staff should receive training on basic disability facts, ways to communicate with women with disabilities, and the unique vulnerabilities and reduced escape options faced by women with disabilities. In addition, women with disabilities should be hired as program staff and administrators. That will enable service providers to be more effective and sensitive to disability issues as counselors. * * *

B. Education and Non-Legal Advocacy

Increasing disabled women's access to the domestic violence service infrastructure involves tearing down physical barriers, like shelters that are inaccessible or fail to meet the needs of disabled women. However, there are also mental barriers that must be torn down. These mental barriers exist both in the minds of women with disabilities who suffer domestic violence and in the minds of the members of the domestic violence service infrastructure who are tasked with helping these women escape.

Mental barriers in the minds of the members of the domestic violence service infrastructure include the commonly held myths and misconceptions about women with disabilities. Perhaps the most significant myth is that women with disabilities are asexual, both in the sense that a woman with a disability never has sexual feelings or urges and that no one could ever have sexual feelings or urges directed at a women with a disability. There are many effects of this myth. It causes women with disabilities who report their abuse to be believed less often than non-disabled women. If one believes that a woman with a disability is incapable of forming an intimate relationship, then it follows that the woman cannot be a victim of domestic violence. In addition, it makes women with disabilities feel as if they should appreciate any sexual attention, even if it is abusive. This myth must be eradicated. * * *

Women with disabilities may also have myths and misconceptions about themselves, which act as barriers to escape from domestic violence. This may be especially true for women with developmental disabilities. Women with disabilities may believe that abuse is a normal part of the life of a person with a disability. They may also buy into the myth of their own asexuality. If these myths are accepted, a woman with disabilities is less likely to seek escape from abuse because she may think abuse is a normal part of life, or she may not want to leave her abuser for fear that she will never be able to find another intimate partner. * * *

C. Courtroom Accommodations

[The author argues that women with disabilities may not experience the more minor abuse they suffer as traumatic, which may make expert testimony about "battered woman syndrome" inapplicable in their cases. He urges courts to instead allow expert testimony explaining why a woman with a disability would stay in an abusive relationship. This is key not only when the woman is charged with a crime, but also in a case where her fitness to be a mother is in question.]

D. Allowing Women with Disabilities to Drop Charges against their Caretakers/Batterers

* * * If a woman is dependent on her caregiver/batterer as her only source of care, her choices are limited. Either she may remain with her abuser, or she may attempt to escape—with which goes the distinct possibility of institutionalization if no accessible shelter or permanent housing can be found. This is truly an unenviable choice, but faced with the loss of independence and less than desirable living conditions associated with institutionalization, some women may choose to stay with, or at least continue to be cared for, by their caregiver/batterer. Additionally, a woman with disabilities who requires assistance with every day life activities like bathing and using the bathroom may want her caregiver/batterer to continue caring for her because she simply might not be comfortable with someone else helping her bathe or use the bathroom. However, if the woman's batterer has begun to be prosecuted, state laws and prosecution office policies will often strip this choice from her. In many states, once a prosecution has begun, a victim is unable to drop the charges because it is the state, and not the victim that brought the charges in the first place. If the caretaker/batterer is in jail, the woman with disabilities will not be able to receive care from him.

West argued that women must insist on an acceptance of their difference. Here, women with disabilities must also insist on this. The relevant hedonic difference between women with and without disabilities is that some women with disabilities require care and these women might want to drop charges against caregiver/batterers. While a woman without disabilities may be able to conceptualize this desire, it is unlikely she will ever be able to feel it the way a women with disability would. If disabled women are unable to make the choice to drop criminal charges, the law will be ignoring their subjective hedonic lives and will not be accepting their difference. If one takes West's relational theory seriously, this different hedonic preference must be given real and actual legal effect, and every jurisdiction should allow women with disabilities to drop criminal charges against their caregiver/batterers.

Additionally, Kimberle Williams Crenshaw would argue that the theory of intersectionality calls for women with disabilities to be able to drop criminal charges against their caregiver/batterers. Briefly, the idea behind intersectionality is that people experience life multidimensionally; for example both as a women and as a person with disabilities. The problem is that the law tends to analyze problems from a single axis point of view. For example, the law tries to solve the problems of women and the problems of people with disabilities, but rarely if ever tries to solve the problems of women with disabilities. This single axis approach is problematic because the experiences of multidimensional people such as women with disabilities are marginalized or erased. Truly, this marginalization has occurred in a situation where a woman with a disability may want to drop the criminal charges against her caregiver/batterer so that he can continue to care for her. However, the law—taking a single axis approach and treating disabled women merely as women—disallows this choice because it is not the choice that women without disabilities would make. Therefore, both relational theory and the theory of intersectionality call for the demarginalization of women with disabilities and [supports the argument that] women with disabilities [should be allowed] to drop criminal charges against their caregiver/batterers. * * *

[Editor's Note: In "Help Seeking Among Deaf Female Survivors of IPV," 22(3) Domestic Violence Report 33 (Feb/March 2017), Michelle Ballan and Molly Freyer note that Deaf women are subject to higher rates of IPV than are hearing women. Perpetrators of Deaf survivors may restrict access to American Sign Language (ASL) instruction, a TTY (text telephone) or videophone [a smart phone with texting and video capability], or hearing aids. The authors note that some Deaf people communicate well in ASL and others need a certified deaf interpreter (CDI), a Deaf person who provides interpreting services to Deaf people who have impairments that prevent them from utilizing an ASL interpreter. The CDI works with a hearing ASL interpreter. The authors also note that DV service agencies may have non-working TTY numbers, may see ASL interpretation as prohibitively

expensive, and may not be trained to work with Deaf people. The authors call for training on IPV for agencies serving the Deaf community and training on Deaf issues for DV agencies.]

CHAPTER 4

ABUSE IN GAY, LESBIAN, BISEXUAL, TRANSGENDER, AND QUEER RELATIONSHIPS

■ ■ ■

This chapter is similar to Chapter 3 in that it focuses on a particular group in the U.S., here gay men, lesbians, bisexuals, transgender and queer people. Some of the same themes we saw in Chapter 3 are again seen here: an historically problematic relationship between the specific community and law enforcement in particular and the justice system generally; a community ethic of not airing one's dirty laundry in public, so as not to give the majority culture excuses for further oppression; and a lack of resources meeting the needs of particular groups of victims of domestic violence.

Starting with the LGBTQ version of the Power and Control Wheel, the first article examines how gendered laws increase harm to this population, since many state statutes exclude same-sex survivors of abuse. An article examines how restraining orders are often misused in same-sex relationships, misidentifying the abuse as mutual. A case interprets a state statute that is silent on this topic, and finds it violates the Equal Protection clause of the U.S. Constitution. Another case illustrates typical ways a man abused his male partner, including outing the partner, who was in the Marines. The next case illustrates law enforcement refusal to enforce a domestic violence restraining order that a woman obtained against her former girlfriend. Another piece points out the multiple issues and oppressions faced by battered lesbians of color. The final two articles focus on transgender women abused by partners, examining ways they face many barriers to obtaining help, including within some domestic violence shelters.

This chapter also returns to the question, "What causes domestic violence?," further demonstrating the complexity of this area of inquiry. The previous chapters tended to analyze domestic violence as primarily based on male and female conditioning, stressing the great differences between the sexes in that conditioning. The similarity of that sex-role conditioning across many different ethnic and cultural groups was noted. But that analysis does not fully explain the phenomenon of domestic violence in non-heterosexual relationships. To answer the question, "What causes domestic violence," when the parties are in a same-sex relationship may require that the reader re-examine previously held assumptions about the root causes of domestic violence generally.

NATIONAL CENTER ON DOMESTIC AND SEXUAL VIOLENCE, LGBTQ POWER AND CONTROL WHEEL

www.ncdsv.org; Developed by Roe & Jagodinsky, Inspired and adapted from Domestic Abuse Intervention Project, Duluth, MN

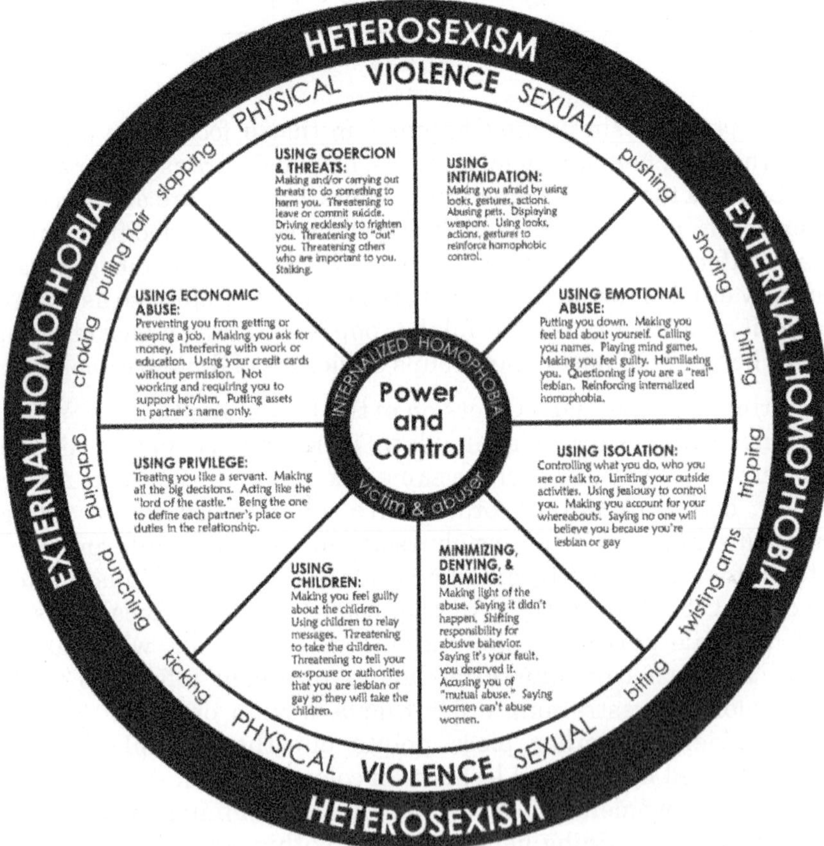

CAROLINE MORIN, RE-TRAUMATIZED: HOW GENDERED LAWS EXACERBATE THE HARM FOR SAME-SEX VICTIMS OF INTIMATE PARTNER VIOLENCE

40 New England J. Crim. & Civ. Confinement 477 (2014)
(footnotes omitted)

I. INTRODUCTION

* * * The first domestic violence legislation was passed in the [1970s]. * * * Unfortunately for some victims, most . . . [laws] were designed solely to benefit women in heterosexual relationships and not other similarly situated victims. For example, it is not unusual to encounter definitions of

IPV characterizing that conduct almost exclusively as a heterosexual woman's problem. Although the data varies, IPV occurs in same-sex couples with approximately the same frequency that it occurs among heterosexual couples, but many same-sex victims do not report the abuse for fear of homophobic reactions and biases from police, social services providers, and court personnel. Legislation tailored to same-sex couples differs from state-to-state, but in many jurisdictions IPV is narrowly defined in a way that incidentally, or even purposefully, excludes same-sex couples. * * *

Same-sex IPV is vastly underreported, unacknowledged, and is often reported as something other than intimate partner violence. * * * Delaware, Montana, and South Carolina explicitly exclude same-sex survivors of IPV from protection under criminal laws. * * * This Note criticizes the gendered approach to IPV legislation and enforcement[,] and recommends changes in legislation and the provision of social services that would significantly improve the equal treatment of victims of IPV. * * * Until the law is expressly extended to cover all victims of IPV equally, the problem will continue to worsen[.] * * *

II. BASIC FOUNDATION OF IPV LAWS AND TERMINOLOGY

A. Current Language Used to Address IPV

On average, twenty-four people per minute are victims of rape, physical violence, or stalking by an intimate partner in the United States. One in six women and one in thirty-three men have experienced at least one attempted or completed rape. In the United States alone, three women are killed every day by a current or former intimate partner. According to the National Center for Injury Prevention and Control, there were approximately 6,982,000 victims of rape, physical violence, or stalking in 2011. In comparison, the Federal Bureau of Investigation (FBI) reports that there were only an estimated 1,203,564 violent crimes in the United States in 2011, including murder, rape, and aggravated assault. This disparity demonstrates that the FBI does not consider IPV to be a violent crime. IPV is a significant and widespread public health problem in the United States but is not recognized by federal law enforcement in a way that signifies the danger it presents to thousands of citizens. This oversight minimizes the devastating effects of IPV on America.

A uniform vocabulary is both necessary and useful when discussing IPV. Accepted terms in the legal and social justice communities empower victims, avoid improper blame shifting, and help to ensure that the problem is addressed head on. A "victim" is commonly or properly defined as any person "who is the target of violence or abuse," regardless of their gender, sexual orientation, age, or any other characteristic. A perpetrator is a person who "inflicts the violence or abuse or causes the violence or abuse to be inflicted on the victim." An intimate partner includes: "current spouses (including common-law spouses), current non-marital partners, dating partners, including first date (heterosexual or same-sex), boyfriends/girlfriends (heterosexual or same-sex), former marital partners, divorced spouses, former common-law spouses, separated spouses, former non-marital partners, former dates (heterosexual or same-sex), [or] former boyfriends/girlfriends (heterosexual or same-sex)." It is not necessary for the relationship to be sexual or for partners to live together in order for the relationship to be considered intimate.

Violence is divided into four categories: threatening behavior, sexual violence, physical violence, and psychological or emotional abuse. * * * While women in heterosexual relationships account for a significant number of the individuals victimized by intimate abuse, the patterns of abusive behavior are very often the same as those practiced by abusive same-sex partners. * * * Additionally, the development of these patterns over time and the way they affect the victims are indistinguishable from the patterns in abusive relationships between heterosexual men and women. The power and control wheel used to understand IPV among heterosexual couples is only narrowly different than that used to explain the dynamics of same-sex IPV. * * *

B. Similarities and Differences Between Same-Sex IPV and Heterosexual IPV

* * * While LGBTQ IPV may be as prevalent as heterosexual IPV, it is not identical. LGBTQ abusers often utilize highly specific forms of abuse, including: "outing" or threatening to "out" a partner to friends, family, or employers; reinforcing fears that no one will help a partner because they are lesbian, gay, bisexual, or transgender; telling the partner that abusive behavior is a normal part of LGBTQ relationships, or that it cannot be IPV because it is within an LGBTQ relationship; and portraying the violence as mutual or consensual, especially if the partner attempts to defend against it.

Fortunately, a number of advocacy groups, legislators, and individual voters have taken the initiative to see that the LGBTQ community is afforded protection from partner abuse. Nationally, reporting of same-sex IPV is increasing: total reported cases of IPV between 2008 and 2009 increased from 3189 to 3658, a 15% rise in reporting. These numbers, however, are only part of the picture. There are still many barriers to providing equal protection of LGBTQ victims and survivors of partner abuse. Of the 3658 reporting LGBTQ survivors of IPV, only 380 reported accessing any form of institutional support. This limit on access and availability of services is due in large part to the lack of culturally competent programming for LGBTQ-identified survivors in IPV service provisions. ["In 2011, the National Coalition of Anti-Violence Programs (NCAVP) received 3930 reports of IPV. Excluding LA's reports, there was an 18.3% increase in reported instances of LGBTQ IPV nationwide. IPV homicides for same-sex couples increased greatly in 2011 to nineteen deaths—more than three times the number in 2010 and the highest ever recorded by NCAVP."]

Historically, LGBTQ individuals and communities have experienced discrimination and violence from law enforcement officers. *[Editor's Note: E.g., the Stonewall riot and other riots that are often considered the birth of the LGBTQ rights movement.]* The last remaining laws prohibiting private, consensual adult homosexual activity were only recently ruled unconstitutional [in *Lawrence v. Texas,* 539 US. 558 (2013)]. The history of criminalized LGBTQ identities and activities is still felt among many communities today, particularly "people of color, transgender people, youth populations, and immigrant communities." Transgender and gender non-conforming individuals frequently experience police profiling for engagement in prostitution or other illegal activities. The NCAVP's annual reports on hate violence against the LGBTQ communities continually count law enforcement among the primary categories of offenders. Police officers are generally more likely to view violence between LGBTQ individuals, especially partners of the same gender, as mutual or consensual abuse. Many police officers continue to express homophobia. Even among those who are educated about the dynamics of same-sex partner abuse, few police officers receive the training necessary to distinguish the actual abuser in most incidents of LGBTQ IPV. As a result, the arrest of the victim is not an infrequent occurrence. * * * In one study by the NCAVP, the police were called almost twice as many times as the prior year and arrests increased by 135%, but the reported cases of mis-arrest and police misconduct increased 144% and 74% respectively. The risk of mutual combat charges or dual arrests, particularly between gay men, is especially high. Police officers arriving on the scene, even those with a proper understanding of the dynamics, may not be able to easily distinguish the [primary or dominant] aggressor if both men are injured or deny that there is any danger to them if they remain. * * *

There are many circumstances that might additionally isolate an LGBTQ victim, including: a lack of community support for LGBTQ identifying individuals, a lack of social resources, and less likelihood of family support. Many LGBTQ survivors report facing additional obstacles that their straight counterparts do not confront in their attempts to access services. Abusive partners in LGBTQ relationships have most likely also experienced identity-based discrimination in the past. Victims may not want to expose their partners to additional bias or violence from homophobic, bi-phobic, and trans-phobic individuals or groups. * * *

Shelter services are a particular weakness for the LGBTQ community. Although there has been an increase in available shelters for heterosexual women in the United States, these shelters are not typically available to the LGBTQ community as lesbians and gay men in particular are often "screened out." Even when shelters do admit LGBTQ people, they may still perpetrate institutional biases ranging from subtle aggression, such as judgmental looks or making assumptions about sexual orientation or gender identity, to more severe institutional discrimination such as limiting the individuals' length of stay in the shelter. Some shelters also force transgender people to conform to assigned gender roles in order to be eligible for services or minimize the existence or impact of IPV in LGBTQ communities. Even where survivors of LGBTQ IPV can find LGBTQ-inclusive or LGBTQ-specific services, there may be limited options. The survivor's age, geographical location, financial status, or other characteristics may create restrictions within the shelter or program. * * * In some cases, survivors seeking to leave an abusive situation may resort to staying in less secure arrangements, such as homeless shelters, inexpensive hotels, or motels. These are weak alternatives for those individuals because their abusers are more able and more likely to find, harass, injure, or even kill them. * * * An added obstacle to same-sex partners with regard to shelter services is that the abuser may have access to the same shelter and shelter staff may not be adequately trained in screening for primary aggressors in LGBTQ relationships, so survivors run the risk of being housed with their abusive partner. Abusive partners may even pose as victims in order to prevent the actual survivor from accessing the limited available shelters or social services. For those who wish to leave their abusive relationship, alternatives like staying with friends or family are less likely to exist because an LGBTQ survivor may have been ostracized by his or her home community on the basis of sexual identity or disclosure of the IPV. * * *

Even where a survivor does have an informal support network, LGBTQ communities tend to be small and relatively tight-knit: confidential housing options of any kind may be limited or even non-existent. These factors often exacerbate a survivor's sense of isolation and the belief that they have nowhere else to go—a tactic of abuse that is used by violent partners regardless of sexual orientation. These issues are particularly pertinent in rural or small communities where there are fewer people, little or no known LGBTQ community, limited or no public transportation, and fewer resources for any IPV survivors.

Young members of the LGBTQ community are at a particularly high risk. Survivors under thirty made up 37.7% of those reporting IPV and the highest proportion of survivors were young adults (ages nineteen to twenty-nine at 30.3%), followed by youth ages fifteen to eighteen (at 6.1%) and fourteen years or younger (at 1.3%). These populations, already dealing with the stresses of school, puberty, and self-identity, are susceptible to bullying, family difficulties, and financial insecurity that make them additionally vulnerable to IPV. Unwilling or unable to report the abuse for fear that they will be abandoned by their parents or other family members and often unable to relocate to escape the abuse, younger LGBTQ people face an added level of danger. * * *

IV. SURVEY OF INTIMATE PARTNER VIOLENCE LAWS THAT DENY SAME-SEX VICTIMS COVERAGE

When a victim of IPV decides to seek protection under the law, there are two divergent paths available. One choice is a civil protection order, often called a restraining order, and the other is a criminal conviction. *[Editor's Note: In many jurisdictions, courts also issue criminal protective orders, requiring the defendant to stay away from the alleged victim pending trial and after conviction.]* * * * [S]ince a conviction may mandate little to no jail time, the victim may still be unable to escape the abuse. For these and other reasons, it is particularly vital that civil remedies, like civil protection orders, are available to same-sex partners.

A. Examination of State Statutes that Explicitly Deny Intimate Partner Violence Remedies for LGBTQ Victims

To the detriment of many LGBTQ-identifying individuals, a great number of jurisdictions prohibit same-sex partners from seeking protection under IPV statutes. *[Editor's Note: After* Obergefell v. Hodges, *135 S.Ct. 2584 (2015) and other decisions, these statutes likely would be held unconstitutional based on the right to equal protection. See, for instance,* Doe v. State of South Carolina, *808 S.E.2d 807 (2017), infra.]*

B. Examination of States' Gender-Neutral Intimate Partner Violence Statutes

The vast majority of jurisdictions have gender-neutral statutes that do not require partners to be of the opposite sex in order to be protected. * * * While gender or sexuality neutral statutes are clearly preferable to LGBTQ-exclusive statutes, they may still require a victim to satisfy the dating or cohabitation requirement to prove a relationship. Numerous other states have already interpreted the ambiguous language of the statutes and decided to extend IPV protection measures to same-sex couples. These states have implicitly recognized that there is no reason why LGBTQ individuals should be treated as second-class citizens. In addition, many courts have acknowledged that the intent of IPV protection statutes is to offer safety and security to victims of abuse in the community, and that this intention is gender-neutral and sexuality-blind. * * *

VI. HOW IPV LAWS THAT DENY SAME-SEX VICTIMS COVERAGE ARE VIOLATING EQUAL PROTECTION PRINCIPLES AND HOW TO SOLVE THIS PROBLEM

* * * A. Suggested Solutions

1. LGBTQ Inclusive Legislation

To solve the problem of exclusion of LGBTQ individuals from IPV laws, legislation should be modeled after states like Vermont and Massachusetts where an inclusive approach is utilized. The statutes in Arizona, Delaware, Montana, and North Carolina should be amended to remove reference to the gender or sexuality of the partners. By removing this language, the legislation will provide equal judicial remedies for LGBTQ individuals and provide a key step in stopping the cycle of IPV. In states with gender-neutral statutes, language that is more wholly inclusive should be added and judicial or legislative determinations should make it clear to state courts and law enforcement officers that the statutes apply equally to LGBTQ individuals.

2. Better Provision of LGBTQ Social Services

While there is an increasing awareness, and subsequently a growing responsiveness to the needs of LGBTQ IPV victims, there is still plenty of work to be done. In 2006, a total of 3534 incidents of IPV affecting LGBTQ individuals were reported to the thirty-three community-based, anti-violence programs that compose the NCAVP. In 2011, that number was 3930. Although quantitative data on LGBTQ victimization is still somewhat limited, available data clearly indicates that LGBTQ victimization is underreported and the response remains inadequate to address the need. * * * The passing of an LGBTQ-inclusive version of the Violence Against Women Act [in 2013] was a key step in improving access to services and legal remedies for LGBTQ survivors of IPV, sexual assault, and stalking nationwide. Local, state, and national funding for LGBTQ anti-violence programs should be a focus for policymakers and sponsors, particularly for survivor-led initiatives. Legislators should ensure that state and federal governments collect information on sexual orientation and gender identity whenever demographic data is requested in studies, surveys, and research dealing with IPV so that the scope and nature of the problem can be properly understood. Policymakers should specifically support and fund LGBTQ IPV training and assistance programs to increase the cultural competency of all victim service providers, from shelters to law enforcement. * * *

VII. CONCLUSION

* * * The gendered approach to IPV legislation and enforcement has had a greatly disparate effect on the treatment of LGBTQ IPV victims. LGBTQ IPV is vastly underreported and unacknowledged, slowing the development of statutes and laws to protect LGBTQ individuals in violent relationships. Until the law is expressly extended to cover all victims of IPV equally, the problem will continue to escalate, unnecessarily taxing the legal and social services of communities nationwide and damaging the lives of hundreds of thousands. A uniform national system of legislation that treats all victims equally under the law is the only way to break the cycle of IPV in America.

JACQUIE ANDREANO, THE DISPROPORTIONATE EFFECT OF MUTUAL RESTRAINING ORDERS ON SAME-SEX DOMESTIC VIOLENCE VICTIMS

108 Calif. L. Rev. 1047 (2020)
(footnotes omitted)

INTRODUCTION

Taylor and Michael were arguing over the phone bill the first time it happened. Michael had never been hit by anyone. Not his parents, not an intimate partner; he'd never even gotten in a bar fight or a schoolyard scuffle. As soon as it happened, Taylor was apologetic. While Michael stared in utter shock, Taylor began to cry, beg, and make promises. Michael would have never called the cops, but the neighbors must have heard, because before he could recover, officers were at the door. Taylor, not wanting to take the blame, told the cops that Michael had become physical. Michael showed the officers the red mark on his face, but before Michael knew what was happening, both men were cuffed and in the back of a patrol vehicle. Later, finding that the police had failed to identify the primary aggressor, a judge would sign off on a mutual restraining order, applying to both Taylor and Michael.

The situation described above is not particularly common among heterosexual couples. In general, dual arrests in domestic violence incidents, and the entering of mutual restraining orders that often follow, happen in about 1 percent of cases. This number, however, jumps to almost 30 percent in cases of same-sex domestic violence.

In recent decades, domestic violence has come to the forefront of the American social conscience. What was once considered a private issue between a man and his wife is now subject to massive government spending, criminal prosecution, and efforts by numerous local and national non-profit organizations. This focus is warranted: across the United States, more than one in three women will experience rape, physical violence, or stalking in her lifetime. Despite this national attention, many activists have routinely ignored the effects of our systemic approach to domestic violence in the lesbian, gay, bisexual, and transgender (LGBT) community. LGBT victims of domestic abuse are too often forgotten, not only by the criminal justice system but also by many within the LGBT community. This Note will discuss how the erasure of LGBT victims from the domestic violence narrative has perpetuated the overuse of dual arrest and mutual restraining orders in domestic violence cases with same-sex couples despite the minimal use of these legal tools in the general population. This overuse disadvantages both LGBT victims and the LGBT community as a whole. . .

I. ERASING QUEER VICTIMS, AGAIN

While domestic violence among same-sex couples is rarely discussed, this does not mean that such violence does not happen. In fact, numerous studies have suggested that domestic violence occurs in LGBT relationships at about the same rate, or higher, as in heterosexual relationships. And although the methods of abuse vary, the basic cycle of abuse is the same in both same-sex and heterosexual relationships. Abusers of LGBT victims employ similar tactics to gain power and control over their victim, often in combination with threats or explanations targeting the victim's sexual orientation or gender identity. For example, abusers may threaten to "out" their victim or convince the victim that abuse is normal in a same-sex relationship.

Despite the prevalence of abuse in same-sex relationships and the growing consciousness surrounding domestic violence in general, courts and activists have largely ignored LGBT domestic violence. The legal system's neglect of LGBT victims can be traced back to the common narrative about domestic violence: that of female victim and male abuser. Domestic violence and LGBT advocates' depictions of the phenomenon also contribute to this neglect.

As awareness about domestic violence increased, ideas about who could be a victim of domestic violence quickly formed. Activists, law enforcement officers, and others portrayed victims of this kind of violence as meek, helpless, and feminine. In some ways, this stereotyping galvanized support for domestic violence victims because it engendered an image of these victims as needing the state's protection. But the image of an "ideal" battered woman also served to alienate victims who do not fit squarely into the role. For example, for many years, domestic violence statutes only protected married women, ignoring entirely that men and unmarried women are also victims of domestic violence.

Experts have described the psychological effects of domestic abuse for many years as "Battered Women's Syndrome." Testimony about this "syndrome" has been instrumental in helping courts and juries understand the way that domestic abuse can cause victims to behave in ways that may seem counterintuitive to the average person. But the very title of the term suggests that only women can be victims of domestic abuse. This term frequently excludes LGBT victims because they "do not often fit the traditional stereotypes of dependent or weak females." While many domestic violence experts and advocates have begun using different terminology, such as "intimate partner battering and its effects," Battered Women's Syndrome has become well known and will likely require many years of undoing.

Popular misconceptions about victims of domestic violence have also gone hand-in-hand with misconceptions about the perpetrators of abuse. One explanation for this is the understanding of domestic violence as rooted in patriarchy that has served to further exclude LGBT victims of domestic violence. Domestic violence advocates have often described domestic abuse as a phenomenon that reflects the deep-rooted misogyny of our society. Early in the feminist movement, activists promulgated "an understanding of domestic violence as a product of patriarchy." In its most simplistic version, this understanding of domestic violence posited that men commit domestic violence because they are misogynistic, and that women are victims of domestic violence because they are oppressed by the patriarchal regime. This understanding was borne out by the fact that women do account for the largest percentage of victims of domestic violence, sustain more serious injuries than men overall, and are more likely to be killed by their partners. Further, abusers use power, control, and aggression—characteristics that are typically associated with masculinity. But this explanation of domestic violence left little room for victims who do not appear stereotypically feminine or abusers who are not stereotypically masculine. In this way, feminist domestic violence activists who sought to attribute the abuse to patriarchal biases may have in fact perpetuated those biases by excluding heterosexual male and LGBT victims.

Feminist theorists and domestic violence advocates are not the only activists that have played a role in keeping LGBT domestic abuse in the dark. Many LGBT activists themselves have shied away from discussing inter-partner violence within the community. LGBT activists may have political objections to acknowledging abuse between same-sex partners because such abuse derails the notion that there is a queer "utopia" or that the LGBT community is fully egalitarian. Furthermore, many in the LGBT community may believe that acknowledging abuse will reinforce commonly held negative stereotypes about same-sex relationships and deter efforts towards legal and social equality for LGBT people. For example, anti-LGBT groups often point to domestic abuse between same-sex couples as evidence that such relationships are inherently volatile, violent, and unnatural. LGBT activists may also subscribe to the conception of an "ideal victim" discussed above: that women are victims of abuse, not abusers, and that men are abusers, not victims. Although it was clearly not the goal of feminists and LGBT activists to disenfranchise victims of same-sex domestic violence, the narratives that these groups have bolstered have resulted in the erasure of victims who do not fit into the accepted paradigm.

However, the domestic violence movement need not divorce itself from these theories to be inclusive. In fact, the data on same-sex domestic violence fits squarely with the concept that domestic violence is a reflection of a society that promotes and values masculine aggression and dominance. A recent study concluded that men are more likely to perpetrate violence, regardless of whether they are in a same-sex or different-sex relationship. In general, it is true that men are more likely to be abusers than women are. But this also means that men in same-sex relationships are more likely to be abused than men in heterosexual relationships. Furthermore, women are most likely to be victimized by both men and women. This should signify that patriarchal gender bias does play a significant role in causing domestic violence, but that this does not dictate the gender of the abuser or the victim.

The deeply ingrained stereotypes about who can be a victim of domestic violence erase LGBT victims from the narrative. This erasure has dire consequences because it affects the way that police and courts treat LGBT victims. When government actors lack the proper statutory tools to evaluate domestic violence situations carefully, they rely heavily on their own biases and common understandings.

II. MUTUAL RESTRAINING ORDERS AND THEIR PREVALENCE AMONG SAME-SEX COUPLES

Because LGBT victims are not represented in the popular domestic violence narrative, police and courts fail to conceptualize them as "real victims." LGBT victims are thus subject to significantly higher rates of dual arrest and mutual restraining orders. This perpetuates a cycle of criminalization of LGBT victims, reinforces negative stereotypes, and disproportionately limits the freedom of queer victims. This Section first describes the common statutory schemes surrounding mutual restraining orders. Then it discusses the disparate rates of dual arrests and mutual restraining orders for same-sex domestic violence victims.

A. Statutory Schemes Addressing Mutual Restraining Orders

Today, restraining orders are an extremely common legal tool used to combat domestic violence. Restraining orders are relatively easy and inexpensive to obtain, they do not inherently trigger criminal prosecution, and they ostensibly provide victims with a measure of security against their assailants. For this reason, law enforcement and courts routinely respond to domestic violence issues by issuing restraining orders. When police officers respond to domestic violence incidents, *[Editor's Note: in states where this is an option,]* they often request an emergency protective order (EPO) from the on-call judge to protect the person that they deem to be the victim. A victim can then apply for a temporary restraining order (TRO). This results in a hearing where the court can enter a permanent *[Editor's Note: more accurately, a long-term]* protective order, which will typically be in effect for a specified number of years.

Restraining orders of this kind are particularly flexible. They are designed to allow a judge reviewing the motion to add or subtract terms of the order as they see fit in the particular situation. Beyond physical separation, restraining orders can also govern issues such as custody arrangements and financial issues, although courts can defer to the decision of a family court on custody matters if one is pending. While the flexibility of restraining orders is typically seen as one of their benefits, in some circumstances, this deference to judicial discretion allows judges to let their biases impact their decision-making.

One concern with judicial discretion is that judges can issue mutual restraining orders *sua sponte* even without request from the respondent. Mutual restraining orders prevent both the petitioner and the respondent from being in physical proximity or contacting one another. Judges may think that mutual restraining orders are not substantially different from regular restraining orders—after all, the goal is to keep the parties away from one another so that the violence will not continue. Judges may also feel that issuing a mutual restraining order saves time because they do not have to hear testimony and make a finding regarding which party is a primary aggressor or even that one party has committed domestic violence. These judicial assessments have often led to the issuance of unmerited mutual restraining orders, namely in situations where one party is the abuser and the other party is a victim.

Some state legislatures have enacted statutes to combat the overuse of mutual restraining orders. However, such legislation has been largely ineffective because it bans mutual restraining orders in name only, rather than in substance. According to a 2015 report detailing state laws regarding the use of mutual restraining orders, just four states have enacted laws prohibiting or limiting the use of mutual restraining orders and cross-orders without cause. Thirty-four states have adopted language that prohibits mutual restraining orders but explicitly permits courts to enter cross-orders, which are separate and identical restraining orders, upon the respondent's petition. While these statutes cure some of the issues that mutual restraining orders implicate, they fail to eradicate the end result, which is that both parties are restrained even if only one is an abuser.

Many state restraining order statutes also incorporate provisions required under the Violence Against Women Act (VAWA) Full Faith and Credit Clause. This clause requires that states give "full faith and credit" to restraining orders issued in other states only where each party has entered a formal request for an order and the court has made a finding that each party acted primarily as an aggressor. However, it is not clear that this provision has been enforced, and unjustified mutual restraining orders are likely enforced even in states with statutes that explicitly prohibit them.

Most state statutes that allow cross-orders make enforcement of justified orders more difficult. In these states, entering cross-orders may seem to be an expedient solution. While *sua sponte* mutual restraining orders are prohibited, the court can enter cross-orders, which are equivalent to mutual restraining orders, as long as the respondent requests it. Thus, if an abuser files his own petition for a restraining order in response to the victim's petition, the court can consider both petitions in the same hearing and grant them both. These state statutes often do not mandate that courts "clearly provide law enforcement with sufficient direction when determining if a violation of the order has occurred," giving law enforcement inadequate guidance on how to respond. Because these statutes do not require that the court specifically state prohibited behavior or instructions for enforcement, the court can easily grant cross-orders. In this way, state legislatures have done little to protect victims from being unjustly restrained, although they have required that the court use a separate piece of paper to do so.

Furthermore, in some states, such as New Hampshire, a court is justified in issuing a cross-order of restraint even if it does not make a specific finding that the other party has committed abuse. Courts can enter such orders if "[t]he court cannot determine who is the primary physical aggressor." This essentially renders the statute prohibiting mutual restraining orders useless, as the court can avoid the rule by finding that the primary aggressor is unclear and then entering cross-orders.

Finally, ten states have statutes that explicitly allow mutual restraining orders or are silent on the issue entirely. In these states, courts can issue mutual restraining orders *sua sponte*, often without any particular factual findings of abuse, in one combined order.

B. The Disparate Impact of Dual Arrest and Mutual Restraining Orders on Same-Sex Victims

Unmerited mutual restraining orders often exacerbate the problem of domestic violence rather than solve it. Domestic violence activists have recognized the problem of mutual restraining orders, and many states have passed statutes prohibiting such orders, if only in name. However, mutual restraining orders are not employed very often among the general population of domestic violence cases. Mutual restraining orders are largely prevalent in cases involving same-sex relationships. Notably, little research has been done to quantify the use of mutual restraining orders in situations of same-sex domestic violence. This is likely because such cases are not often appealed and thus not typically published.

In making determinations about primary aggressors, courts often rely on police reports and findings. Even if no police reports exist, in many states, courts use the same factors that police officers use in determining the primary aggressor. For this reason, data on police dual arrests can be a helpful proxy for understanding the difficulty that law enforcement and courts have in identifying primary aggressors, since dual arrest cases are similar to cases where mutual restraining orders are issued. In domestic violence cases, dual arrests most typically occur when law enforcement is unable to identify the primary aggressor in a given situation. In states with mandatory arrest laws, such arrests occur more frequently, especially when the state also provides no guidelines about identifying a primary aggressor.

While approximately 1.3 percent of all intimate partner violence cases involve dual arrests, 26–27 percent of domestic violence incidents involving same-sex couples result in dual arrest. Notably, this disproportionate use of dual arrests for same-sex couples is further differentiated among female and male couples. According to the National Criminal Justice Reference Service, dual arrests involving female couples occurred at twice the rate of those involving male couples. Furthermore, the dual arrest rate for all same-sex couples, regardless of gender, was ten times higher than the dual arrest rate for heterosexual couples with male victims, and thirty times higher than the rate for heterosexual couples with female victims. These figures shed light on how societal factors impact arrest rates: the lowest rates of dual arrest occur when the victim is a woman in a heterosexual relationship, where the situation fits the "ideal" victim narrative. The highest rates occur among female same-sex couples, where the narrative is broken on two different axes: first, the couple is "deviant" because it breaks the heteronormative mode, and second, the offender is "deviant" because she breaks the gender stereotype of females being victims, but not abusers.

Race also plays a factor in dual arrest rates. Dual arrests in all domestic violence cases decreased by 40 percent when the offender was white, indicating that officers may conceptualize people of color as inherently more violent and thus more likely to engage in "mutual abuse." These statistics show that law enforcement's preconceived notions of the domestic violence narrative significantly impact when they resort to mutual arrests.

II. EFFECTS OF MUTUAL RESTRAINING ORDERS

Although mutual restraining orders are relatively easy to invoke, they are exceedingly powerful tools. Restraining orders limit their subject's freedom immensely and create adverse consequences for large swaths of a person's life, impacting future employment, housing, and child custody arrangements. The disproportionate use of mutual restraining orders on LGBT couples, discussed above, may have a compounding effect on LGBT victims, who may already suffer stigma and prejudice. Furthermore, mutual restraining orders often counteract the purpose of the order itself, which is to protect the victim, because they render the order essentially ineffective. Mutual restraining orders can in fact create more danger for LGBT victims and can also have severe consequences for employment, housing, custody, and other areas where LGBT individuals are already at a disadvantage. Further, such orders frequently violate due process and perpetuate violence by sowing distrust for the justice system and perpetuating harmful homophobic stereotypes.

A. Lack of Enforcement

Perhaps the most obvious adverse effect of mutual restraining orders on LGBT victims of domestic violence is the difficulty they create for enforcement. Restraining orders are intended to protect the victim. But when a court enters a mutual restraining order, it legally restrains both victim and abuser from contacting one another. When the police are called for a violation of that mutual restraining order, officers are often uncertain how to proceed, since issuing courts are rarely required to provide guidance on how to enforce mutual restraining orders. Particularly if no violence has occurred, officers may be unable to tell who is in violation of the order and who is not. While identifying primary aggressors is already difficult in same-sex cases of mutual restraining order violations, the lack of training officers receive regarding LGBT domestic violence makes the challenge even harder. The result is a feedback loop in which dual arrests, caused by law enforcement's inability to identify a primary aggressor in same-sex couple situations, can lead to mutual restraining orders, which then lend themselves to either a second dual arrest or no arrest at all.

Mutual restraining orders also perpetuate the idea that same-sex couples are "just fighting," such that law enforcement may take calls about same-sex domestic violence less seriously. Because mutual restraining orders do not place responsibility on the primary aggressor, they indicate to future responding officers (and victims) that both parties are equally to blame. In turn, officers are more apt to view future violence as "mutual or consensual abuse" and to therefore downplay the seriousness of the situation. As we repeatedly see, downplaying domestic violence can eventually be fatal. For example, in *Town of Castle Rock, Colorado v. Gonzales*, police refused to enforce a woman's restraining order against her husband, despite multiple calls. The man subsequently murdered the woman's three daughters and opened fire on a police station.

Finally, victims who are subject to mutual restraining orders may face prosecution if the police do arrest them. This merely continues the cycle of control and abuse against the victim and leaves victims in worse situations than if they had not reported the abuse at all.

B. Custody Issues

Mutual restraining orders do not just implicate the physical safety of an LGBT victim but also have broader consequences in many parts of the victim's life. For example, a mutual restraining order may include an order for custody of a shared child. If the custody issue is deferred to a later decision in family court, the court may rely on the mutual restraining order to grant shared custody, giving the abuser both access to a child that they may have abused and continued access to their victim. Custody issues may be further complicated with LGBT parents because often one parent is not the biological or adoptive parent of the child. The non-biological parent's legal standing with relation to the child is therefore particularly tenuous. Abusers may use this to their advantage by threatening to take the child away from the victim unless the victim stays in the relationship. Although, after *Obergefell v. Hodges*, children born to married same-sex couples have a legal relationship with both parents, the decision did not create a legally recognized parent-child relationship for children of unmarried couples. This legal gap leaves many unmarried same-sex parents in fear of losing their child, particularly if the abuser will not allow them to adopt the child or they cannot adopt for another reason.

Mutual restraining orders exacerbate the difficulty of establishing custody arrangements after domestic violence has occurred. Courts in every state except Montana are required by state law to consider domestic violence when determining custody arrangements. *[Editor's Note: Montana requires that the court consider evidence of domestic violence as potentially detrimental to children.]* Approximately half of these state laws include a presumption against granting custody to an abuser. In cases where mutual restraining orders have been entered, however, this protection is inadequate, since a non-abusive parent will also have a restraining order on their record, providing little guidance to the court about which parent would be the most appropriate recipient of custody. Because courts typically prefer joint custody, custody is likely to be shared between the abuser and victim. At worst, the victim may have no legal access to their child if they do not have a legally recognized parent-child relationship. This could happen in cases where the victim is unmarried and is not the biological parent of the child.

Furthermore, homophobia can often impact custody decisions involving an LGBT parent, especially if the other parent is heterosexual. Family courts sometimes consider a parent's "moral fitness" as a factor in determining what custody arrangement is in the best interest of a child. This can include a parent's sexual conduct, which may be used to inject homophobic attitudes into the proceedings. For example, in *D.H. v. H.H., [in 2002]* the Alabama Supreme Court affirmed a trial court ruling that denied custody to a mother who identified as a lesbian. Chief Justice Roy Moore's concurring opinion described the mother's sexual orientation as an "inherent evil, and an act so heinous that it defies one's ability to describe it." Even in cases where there is no heterosexual biological parent, courts have expressed a belief that LGBT parents are inherently unfit. Mutual restraining orders reinforce these biases because they can indicate to judges that LGBT parents are violent, even if in reality they are victims.

C. Employment and Housing Access

Mutual restraining orders can also constrain the victim's access to necessities such as employment and housing. Typical background checks, like those used during hiring processes, will often note whether a person has ever been subject to a restraining order. This can create problems for victims who are seeking employment or whose workplaces frequently run background checks. Having a domestic violence restraining order can also prevent victims from receiving professional licenses or from entering universities and colleges. In states where restraining orders include provisions that prevent the restrained party from having a gun, victims with mutual restraining orders are immediately disqualified from any position that would require use of a weapon. *[Editor's Note: Federal law prohibits all people restrained by domestic violence protective orders from having firearms or ammunition. But see the Rahimi case in Chapter 14, currently pending before the U.S. Supreme Court, which may change this.]*

Mutual restraining orders also often adversely affect a victim's housing situation. *[In many states,]* Landlords can evict tenants with restraining orders because they fear the tenant may create a danger or nuisance to other residents. Further, victims who are subject to mutual restraining orders may be denied the housing protections designated for victims of domestic violence under VAWA. VAWA prevents public housing agencies from denying applicants or evicting tenants because of domestic violence perpetrated against them. However, these protections may not apply when the victim is subject to a mutual restraining order, because it is difficult to show that they are actually the victim in the situation. Problems in seeking employment and housing make it much more difficult for a victim to successfully leave their abuser, and a batterer may use the threat of showing others the restraining order to further control and intimidate the victim. The disproportionate issuance of mutual restraining orders thus compounds barriers to employment and housing for LGBT victims, who may already face discrimination in these areas.

D. Due Process

Unmerited mutual restraining orders may also violate a victim's right to due process. There is a constitutional right to be free from arbitrary restraint, and when a court issues an unmerited restraining order against a survivor of domestic violence, it unduly restricts that right. Professor Elizabeth Topliffe argues that "[b]ecause the states protect individuals from restraint absent an evidentiary showing, they have created a liberty interest in not being restrained unless there is a formal hearing that shows potential danger." In other words, mutual restraining orders that courts issue, either *sua sponte* or without sufficient findings of fact, violate a victim's due process right to freedom from restraint.

Indeed, the Supreme Court has held that due process requires findings of fact prior to imposing restrictions on an individual's liberty interest. Interpreting this requirement, appellate courts in California have consistently held that trial courts abuse their discretion when they issue mutual restraining orders without making requisite findings of fact that both of the individuals have committed abuse and were not acting in self-defense. Yet only a few states require family courts to make such findings, raising serious doubt that use of mutual restraining orders broadly adheres to due process principles.

E. Eroding Trust and Perpetuating Harmful Stereotypes and Homophobia

Mutual restraining orders issued against LGBT domestic violence victims also exacerbate law enforcement challenges facing the LGBT community. First, dual arrests and mutual restraining orders reinforce the LGBT community's distrust of both law enforcement and the courts. This distrust exists because the legal system has historically treated LGBT persons with brutality, homophobia, and unfairness. Mutual restraining orders indicate to LGBT victims that society believes they are responsible for the violence against them, or that the abuse they face is not important to law enforcement or the courts. As a result, same-sex victims are significantly less likely than different-sex victims to report incidences of violence or to seek legal recourse. This is particularly true because, when a victim is subject to a mutual restraining order, they put themselves at risk of re-arrest, fines, and even prosecution if they report another incident of domestic violence or a violation of the restraining order, since the police may consider them a co-perpetrator, rather than a victim.

Second, mutual restraining orders issued against LGBT victims of domestic violence reinforce harmful and homophobic stereotypes. These stereotypes, discussed in Part I, include perceptions that LGBT relationships are inherently violent, volatile, and unhealthy. Many homophobic organizations have used domestic violence among same-sex couples as evidence to bolster their arguments that same-sex relationships are undesirable and deviant. For example, The Family Research Council, an anti-gay conservative organization, has cited same-sex domestic violence rates to support its conclusion that "committed" same-sex relationships are radically different from heterosexual relationships, and thus not deserving of equal treatment under the law. Mutual restraining orders feed into these homophobic stereotypes by implying that both parties are equally violent. In this way, they create a feedback loop that perpetuates harmful anti-LGBT rhetoric.

Similarly, mutual restraining orders reinforce internalized homophobia. LGBT persons often feel that their sexual orientation is somehow wrong, bad, or criminal. Receiving a restraining order from a court of law can affirm the victim's self-doubt and guilt, or convince them that they are a batterer because they acted in self-defense. Batterers can also use mutual restraining orders to convince their victims that the behavior is not domestic violence because it is occurring in a same-sex relationship. And, as discussed above, the LGBT community may refuse to acknowledge abuse for fear that it perpetuates harmful stereotypes and detracts from efforts to gain acceptance and legal protections. Mutual restraining orders tell LGBT victims that they are not worth protecting. This contravenes the purpose of restraining orders and puts an already marginalized group at even greater risk of violence.

IV. FACTORS LEADING TO ISSUANCE OF MUTUAL RESTRAINING ORDERS

To combat the negative effects of mutual restraining orders on LGBT individuals, it is necessary to understand the factors that contribute to their disproportionate use in cases of same-sex domestic violence. First, statutes often provide insufficient guidance to police officers and judges, rarely requiring them to deliberate and make reasoned decisions when deciding who the primary aggressor is and issuing mutual restraining orders. Second, inadequate guidance leads decision-makers to fill the gaps using harmful stereotypes and narratives about who can be a victim of domestic violence. Finally, these harmful narratives reinforce homophobia and impact victims and abusers, who are also likely to be influenced by internalized homophobia.

A. Statutory Failures

One factor contributing to the prevalence of mutual restraining orders is law enforcement officers' lack of proper tools or statutory guidance to protect LGBT victims. Tasked with responding to volatile situations where there may be conflicting accounts, officers must make quick decisions and may let biases come into play if they lack sufficient guidance. Police officers must decide, typically based solely on information provided by those in the relationship, who, if anyone, has committed a crime. This lack of guidance stems, in part, from how states treat the determination of who is the primary aggressor: in thirty-one states, statutes explicitly task officers with identifying the "primary aggressor" in a domestic violence situation. About half of these statutes declare that the person who is not the primary aggressor need not be arrested, but do not mandate that officers only arrest the primary aggressor. This language offers broad discretion to police officers who may think of same-sex victims as equally culpable.

Nineteen states do not have specific primary aggressor language, although many use language indicating that the police should try to identify whom to arrest using particular factors. While states with no primary aggressor language or equivalent policy may have individual police departments that have adopted guidance directing officers how to respond to domestic violence incidents, police receive no statewide statutory guidance on how to approach a domestic violence situation appropriately.

Three states explicitly discourage mutual arrest, and four states have enacted statutory presumptions that arrest is not appropriate for the person who is not the primary aggressor. Only four states forbid officers from arresting someone who is not the primary aggressor. Nebraska and Massachusetts require that officers make a written report of their grounds for arrest if they make a dual arrest. These statutes, while clearly preferable to no guidance at all or entirely discretionary policies, still fall short because they direct action only *if* the responding officer has made a determination of the primary aggressor. In other words, when an officer fails to make an initial determination that one person is an abuser and the other person is a victim, any guidance about dual arrests is rendered ineffectual.

While there is some variation among statutes, it is clear that in most states police officers are, at most, asked to make a primary aggressor determination. While the most robust statutes indicate to officers that dual arrest should be a last resort, this kind of language is rare. The vast majority of states instead have provisions indicating that arrest of both parties is an acceptable solution, even when the officer has identified a primary aggressor, and especially if they are unable to do so. Such language may not make much of a difference in cases that fit the stereotypical narrative of a domestic violence situation, but as noted above, when same-sex couples are involved, officers are less sure of how to proceed. They may fall back on guidance from statutory policies to address the situation.

In same-sex domestic violence cases, statutory language that permits and perhaps even encourages dual arrest, or that does not require officers to identify the primary aggressor, can have dire consequences for victims subject to wrongful arrest. Arrest can put victims in immediate danger, for example, in "cases in which both parties were arrested and placed in the same jail cell, where the victim was subsequently reassaulted." The lack of guidance for mutual arrest can also interact with other policies *requiring* arrest. Connecticut, for example, has a mandatory arrest law for domestic violence incidents, but no law stating that officers should arrest only the primary aggressor. As a consequence, Connecticut has the highest dual arrest rate of any state, as officers unable to identify a primary aggressor are obligated to arrest both parties.

B. How Statutory Factors Can Create Bias Against Same-Sex Couples

Even when states provide policies to direct officers in identifying a primary aggressor, this guidance can still reflect harmful stereotypes. In states where statutory policies direct officers to determine a primary aggressor, the statute often provides a list of factors that the officer should consider in making this determination. Most states require police to consider some form of the following four factors:

1. Prior complaints of domestic violence;
2. Relative severity of injuries inflicted on each party;
3. Likelihood of future injury to each party; and
4. Whether one party used self-defense

However, several states include a fifth factor, which often encompasses a catchall phrase such as "any other relevant factor." At least one state explicitly includes the relative size and strength of each party and the appearance of fear as factors.

One factor resulting in dual arrest is that law enforcement may view same-sex partners as physical equals. This confuses the narrative of physical intimidation and overpowering that officers may associate with domestic violence. Officers often make assumptions about the identity of the primary aggressor in situations where they can rely on the stereotypical narrative of a female victim and male abuser. When a same-sex couple is involved, however, officers cannot fall back on this understanding of domestic violence, and thus find it harder to determine a presumed aggressor. Furthermore, studies have shown that both male and female same-sex victims of domestic violence are more likely than heterosexual women to use physical force to defend against their abusers. If victims admit to using force in self-defense, or if law enforcement finds evidence of injury to both parties, officers may be further misled or confused about which party was the primary aggressor. Due to this uncertainty, officers often arrest both individuals. If these individuals seek restraining orders, the court will need to decide which party is the primary aggressor—and will often have to do so with confusing and misleading information from police reports. Under these circumstances, the court may simply issue a mutual restraining order. Factors that implicate the size of victims, inquire into the severity and likelihood of injury, and allow for the full discretion of officers perpetuate the heteronormative domestic violence narrative because officers often have difficulty squaring these factors with situations in which same-sex victims may be more likely to both defend themselves and be seen as physically "equal" to their abuser. Furthermore, because same-sex victims are more likely to fight back, and may be closer in size and strength to their abuser, assessing the relative severity of the injuries can often be misleading.

These bias-invoking factors can carry over into courtrooms, where petitioners for restraining orders may be required to show that they are in fear in order to obtain favorable judgments. If the court does not believe that someone is in fear of their abuser, the victim may not be able to receive a restraining order.

C. False Narratives Reinforce Homophobia

The narrative of the "ideal" domestic violence victim casts a long shadow on LGBT victims, who, by definition, cannot fit the heterosexual mold. While statutory construction and advocates within the domestic violence community can perpetuate that narrative, it is also upheld by continued homophobia from law enforcement and courts. Scholars have suggested that, in many jurisdictions, officers are not required to identify a primary aggressor and may have little interest in doing so. Officers who harbor homophobic ideas may believe that domestic violence between same-sex couples is less severe, or perhaps that mutual physical violence is a natural or typical part of a "deviant" homosexual lifestyle. Homosexuality is often falsely equated with other types of social deviance, such as BDSM [bondage, discipline, and sado masochism]. Officers may consciously or subconsciously make heteronormative inferences and consequently give less attention to the nature of the specific situation when the altercation involves a same-sex couple.

A chilling example of this phenomenon is the case of 14-year-old Konerak Sinthasomphone. In this incident, Milwaukee police officers responded to a 911 call for domestic violence. When they arrived, they found Sinthasomphone, who appeared drunk. Despite the boy's age and clear intoxication, officers on the scene simply returned Sinthasomphone to his "sober boyfriend," Jeffrey Dahmer. If the police had taken the time to investigate Dahmer's apartment, they would have found the remains of Dahmer's twelfth victim. Instead, Dahmer went on to kill five more people before he was caught. Sinthasomphone was his thirteenth and youngest victim.

Further, the narrative of the "ideal" domestic violence victim damages the credibility of LGBT victims in court. In order to obtain a restraining order, victims are often required to testify about the abuse that occurred. But same-sex victims' testimony often deviates from the accepted narrative that domestic violence features a physically smaller female victim and a physically larger male abuser. Judges as well as police officers have internalized biases. A heterosexual judge who is presented with a same-sex couple that has already been subjected to dual arrest may categorize domestic violence accusations as "mutual abuse," a "cat fight," or rough-housing. These biases are particularly likely to occur when the victim fights back in self-defense, because self-defense contravenes the typical heteronormative narrative of passive victimhood. Furthermore, LGBT persons are already at a disadvantage in the courtroom because of homophobic perceptions that paint members of the LGBT community as less credible or trustworthy. Perceptions of LGBT persons as "untrustworthy, unsuited for long-term intimacy, self-absorbed, and hypersexual" may also influence the judge's ruling. A Lambda Legal survey reported that 19 percent of LGBT respondents involved in domestic violence court proceedings had heard negative comments about gender identity or gender expression from judges, attorneys, or court staff.

Judges and law enforcement may also fail to recognize situations of domestic violence entirely if the parties are unwilling to divulge their relationship status due to fear of homophobia and unfair treatment. Officers who are unaccustomed to the idea of same-sex relationships may be unable to identify domestic violence between two men or two women, and may treat the situation as one of mutual violence. The misidentification of same-sex relationships can lead to disproportionate dual arrests and mutual restraining orders in same-sex cases.

For example, in a 2001 Massachusetts case, the Appeals Court vacated mutual restraining orders against Richard Sommi and Samuel Ayer. Sommi and Ayer filed requests for restraining orders in separate courts. The first district court issued a restraining order against Ayer based on allegations of physical and emotional abuse. On the following day, the second court issued an order restraining Sommi. The court of appeals held that this was essentially a mutual restraining order, and thus required specific findings of fact and a detailed order sufficient to "apprise a law enforcement officer as to which party has violated the order in the event that a violation occurs." Although the court of appeals reversed the issuance of the mutual restraining order, the judge acknowledged that the record was sufficient to make a finding of abuse, which would merit two separate restraining orders. The court's decision might indicate that the appellate court perceived this as a case of "mutual abuse." Notably, the court failed to address the parties' relationship or the allegations of domestic violence at any time, simply calling them "co-habitants."

Finally, internalized homophobia on the part of both victims and abusers may contribute to the prevalence of mutual restraining orders in cases of same-sex domestic violence. In same-sex relationships that involve domestic violence, just as in heterosexual relationships, victims are often belittled and criticized by their partners. This psychological abuse can create feelings of shame, helplessness, and self-loathing. This individual abuse is combined with the socialized homophobia that is internalized by many LGBT persons. Abusers may convince victims that they are not deserving of help because they are living a deviant lifestyle, or that this kind of abuse is normal within same-sex relationships. In turn, victims are less likely to call police themselves, seek help, or trust a system that in all other aspects has oppressed them.

V. CHANGING THE NARRATIVE

Dual arrests and mutual restraining orders are a product of society's misunderstanding of who can be a victim of domestic violence. This misunderstanding is reflected both in the laws that instruct police and courts on how to proceed and in judicial and law enforcement attitudes towards LGBT victims of domestic violence. Thus, solving the problem of mutual restraining orders will require changes in many facets of our system, both legal and cultural. I propose that we begin these changes by creating clear statutory guidelines for both police and courts to follow. These guidelines should rely on objective characteristics, not on stereotypes, and should encourage reasoned deliberation. These guidelines should both address primary aggressor determinations and prohibit the issuance of mutual restraining orders without specific factual findings of mutual abuse. Along with statutory reform, we should educate judges and law enforcement so that they can properly use the statutory tools created to protect victims, regardless of the victim's gender or sexuality.

A. Primary Aggressor Law Reform

Primary aggressor factors carry considerable weight because courts often rely on police reports or statutorily defined factors when making determinations about domestic violence restraining orders. For this reason, states should be deliberate in ensuring that the factors included in legislation help to discourage dual arrest and reduce bias against same-sex couples. Current state laws do not adequately protect same-sex victims. Rather, states should adopt something similar to the model policy set forth by the International Association of Chiefs of Police (IACP). This policy defines the predominant aggressor as "[t]he individual who poses the most serious, ongoing threat, who might not necessarily be the initial aggressor in a specific incident." The policy also states that "[d]ual arrests are strongly discouraged. If an officer has probable cause to believe that two or more persons committed a crime and probable cause exists to arrest both parties, the arresting officer shall contact their supervisor before proceeding with the arrests." The ideal statute would adopt this language in large part. By explicitly stating that dual arrests are "strongly discouraged" and requiring officers to call their supervisor before making such a decision, the policy takes a hard stance against using dual arrest out of convenience. Finally, the policy states that "[i]n the event of a dual arrest, a separate report for each arrest should be written and filed and should include a detailed explanation indicating the probable cause for each arrest." States should make this language even stronger by requiring written findings related to each factor in the officer's primary aggressor analysis. While this may seem stringent, it is important that officers be required to spend time considering this decision. Scholars have suggested that the effects of implicit bias may be countered, or at least interrupted, when the individual is engaged in deliberate processing. By requiring that officers take extra steps to make dual arrests, including calling a superior and writing a report, this policy can help ensure that such decisions are not made on an improper basis.

One issue with the IACP's model policy is that it espouses a preferred arrest response policy. The provision states the following:

> *Preferred Arrest Response:* Law enforcement officers are *expected* to arrest *any* person who commits a crime related to domestic violence as defined by law, unless there is a clear and compelling reason not to arrest, such as self-defense or lack of probable cause, after a comprehensive investigation to identify the predominant aggressor.

The problem with this language is that it may give officers the impression that an arrest of someone who committed an act of violence is preferred, even if the individual is not the predominant aggressor. This seems to run contrary to the provision of the policy that discourages dual arrest. This language is similar to the language adopted by a number of states that says that the person who is not the primary aggressor need not be arrested. An ideal policy would reject this kind of language in favor of a provision that states that the victim or person who is not the primary aggressor must not be arrested. This language would reinforce the importance of treating victims as victims, regardless of whether they also used violence in self-defense.

An ideal policy would also list explicit factors that law enforcement and courts must consider when making a predominant aggressor determination. The IACP policy, along with many state statutes, fails to enumerate guidelines for such an analysis. Many states, while providing some factors as guides, also allow consideration of "any other relevant factor." These options leave too much room for homophobia and bias to play a role in these decisions. The ideal policy proposed here would enumerate the following factors that *shall* be considered:

1. The need to protect victims of domestic abuse
2. History of domestic abuse
3. Observable dynamics of power and control
4. Whether one person acted in self-defense
5. Statements of the parties and witnesses (e.g., whether one party is afraid of the other)

This set enumeration of factors would help decision-makers adequately assess domestic violence situations, without relying on biased narratives of who can, or cannot, be a domestic violence victim. The list eliminates factors that reinforce stereotypes of the ideal victim, such as severity of injury or relative size. This list also contains factors that are gender and orientation neutral, such as power and control dynamics and the history of abuse. It also prioritizes consideration of self-defense, which is more likely to occur among LGBT victims of domestic violence. Finally, the ideal policy would eliminate the "if" language used in many statutes, which implies that the rest of the mandate is dependent on the decision-maker's ability to discern the primary aggressor. This revision should indicate to law enforcement that dual arrest should almost always be avoided, even in cases where they cannot identify a primary aggressor.

B. Mutual Restraining Order Prohibitions

States and the federal government should update their statutes concerning the issuance and enforcement of mutual restraining orders. Currently, states take a wide variety of approaches to mutual restraining orders. Some states still allow mutual restraining orders to be issued *sua sponte*, while others allow "cross-orders" only if they are petitioned for separately and the court has made written findings on the record. At the federal level, the Violence Against Women Act (VAWA) requires that, for mutual restraining orders to be afforded "full faith and credit" among other states, the following conditions must be met:

1. The respondent filed a written pleading seeking a protection order from the tribunal of the issuing state.

2. The tribunal of the issuing state made specific findings in favor of the respondent.

While these provisions are a good start, they do not provide guidance for officers on how to enforce an order if and when a mutual restraining order is entered. Even at its best, the VAWA provision can only reach orders that are enforced in other states. For this reason, states must adopt comprehensive statutes that incorporate the VAWA provisions to ensure their enforcement. Alabama's statutes surrounding mutual restraining orders can serve as a model for ideal construction. They read in relevant part:

> The court shall not enter mutual orders. The court shall issue separate orders that specifically and independently state the prohibited behavior and relief granted in order to clearly provide law enforcement with sufficient direction when determining if a violation of the order has occurred. For the purpose of judicial economy, a court may consolidate two separately filed petitions into a single case.

The Alabama code sections also incorporate the VAWA provisions into their law. This kind of policy is effective for several reasons. First, the policy explicitly prohibits courts from issuing mutual restraining orders *sua sponte*. When mutual restraining orders (or more accurately, cross-orders) may only be entered into upon respondent's written request, courts are less likely to use such orders as a convenient solution if they are unmerited. Second, the policy requires that a judge give meaningful written direction to law enforcement officers on how to enforce a mutual restraining order once it is entered. This provision helps to break the self-perpetuating cycle of dual arrests that might otherwise occur in the rare case where a mutual restraining order is issued.

An ideal policy would also explicitly require a judge to make written findings of fact that each party had committed domestic violence and not acted in self-defense. This additional provision, as well as those already contained in the Alabama statute, requires a judge to take the time to deliberate and reason through each decision, which can be important in combatting implicit bias. Another benefit of requiring clear written reasons for issuing mutual restraining orders is that mutual restraining orders are more easily appealed when there is a robust record of factual findings. In cases in which a judge may still unjustly issue a mutual restraining order, this provision gives the victim a better chance of using the judicial system to correct the mistake. Finally, the Alabama code incorporates the VAWA provisions, which helps ensure their enforcement.

Adopting statutes that incorporate these provisions, as well as the provisions in VAWA, will go a long way toward protecting LGBT victims from the adverse effects of mutual restraining orders.

C. Education of Law Enforcement and Judges

Finally, additional education, training, and inclusivity among law enforcement and judges is needed to prevent the use of unmerited mutual restraining orders. As explored at length above, there are two major non-statutory factors that contribute to the disproportionate issuance of these orders to LGBT individuals. First, same-sex relationships do not fit the narrative of the "ideal" victim. And second, judges and law enforcement personnel may harbor explicit or implicit biases. Both of these factors lead courts and law enforcement to dismiss cases of LGBT domestic violence, or believe in the myth of "mutual battering" in same-sex relationships. Much of this false belief can be attributed to a lack of training on the dynamics of same-sex domestic violence and the ways in which this training compares to heterosexual domestic violence.

Although legal recognition of same-sex relationships has come a long way, there is still much to be done to convince the nation, and courts in particular, that such relationships are not only valid but also as genuine and healthy as heterosexual relationships. For this reason, Congress should amend VAWA so that a portion of the funding allocated to each state is directed towards education programs for judges and law enforcement. These programs should focus on the dynamics of same-sex domestic violence and appropriate responses to the problem. Furthermore, state and local governments should invest funding in providing services specifically for LGBT victims of domestic violence, including legal services that can help them navigate the judicial process. . .

DOE V. STATE

808 S.E.2d 807 (S.C. 2017)
(citations and footnotes omitted)

The Court granted Jane Doe's petition for original jurisdiction to . . . consider whether the definition of "household member" in South Carolina Code section 16–25–10(3) of the Domestic Violence Reform Act and section 20–4–20(b) of the Protection from Domestic Abuse Act (collectively "the Acts") is unconstitutional under the Due Process and Equal Protection Clauses of the Fourteenth Amendment to the United States Constitution. Specifically, Doe contends the provisions are unconstitutional because neither affords protection from domestic abuse for unmarried, same-sex individuals who are cohabiting or formerly have cohabited. In order to remain within the confines of our jurisdiction and preserve the validity of the Acts, we declare sections 16–25–10(3) and 20–4–20(b) unconstitutional as applied to Doe.

I. Factual / Procedural History

This case arises out of an alleged domestic dispute between a former same-sex couple. Doe claims that she and her [ex-fiancée] cohabited between 2010 and 2015. Following the dissolution of the relationship, Doe moved out of the shared residence and relocated to Columbia. * * * On August 6, 2015, Doe contacted police to report that she was assaulted by her [ex-fiancée] the day before as she was leaving a Columbia hotel. On August 10, 2015, law enforcement was summoned to Doe's workplace after someone called regarding a disturbance in the parking lot. When the officers arrived, Doe claimed that her [ex-fiancée] and another individual followed her from her apartment to work. While no physical confrontation took place, Doe claimed that she felt threatened by her [ex-fiancée's] actions. Law enforcement filed incident reports for both events, the first was identified as "simple assault" and the second was identified as "assault-intimidation."

On August 12, 2015, Doe sought an Order of Protection from the Richland County Family Court. The family court judge summarily denied Doe's request [since same-sex couples were not included as "household members" in the Protection from Domestic Abuse Act.]. * * * Doe filed * * * for declaratory judgment in this . . . Court to declare unconstitutional the statutory definition of "household member" because it "leaves unmarried, same-sex victims of abuse without the benefit of the same remedy afforded to their heterosexual counterparts." * * *

II. Discussion

Arguments

In essence, Doe maintains the South Carolina General Assembly intentionally excluded her from consideration for an Order of Protection in family court "because of her sexual orientation." As a result, Doe claims she was denied a remedy that is readily accessible to similarly situated opposite-sex couples. Doe explains that by purposefully defining "household member" as "a male and female who are cohabiting or formerly have cohabited" rather than in the disjunctive "male or female," the General Assembly enacted a statutory definition that violates the Due Process and Equal Protection Clauses of the Fourteenth Amendment to the United States Constitution. * * *

Although Doe acknowledges that an abuser in a same-sex relationship could be charged with criminal assault and battery and that she could obtain a Restraining Order in magistrate's court, she claims that these remedies are [less than those available in . . .] the Acts. * * * Doe points to the * * * Act that authorize[s] enhanced penalties for convicted abusers who commit additional acts of violence, restrictions on a convicted abuser's ability to carry a firearm, additional penalties for violations of protection orders, and more stringent expungement requirements.

To remedy the disparate treatment and avoid the invalidation of the Acts in their entirety, Doe advocates for this Court to: (1) construe the word "and" in sections 16–25–10(3)(d) and 20–4–20(b)(iv) to mean "or"; and (2) declare the definition of "household member" to include any person, male or female, who is currently cohabiting with someone or who has formerly cohabited with someone. * * * [T]he State contends * * * the Court [should]: (1) construes the phrase "male and female" as proposed by Doe; or (2) sever those words from the definition so that it reads only "cohabiting or formerly have cohabited." The State asserts that such a construction would be consistent with and effectuate the legislative purpose of the Acts, which is to protect against violence between members of the same household. * * *

B. Constitutional Analysis

1. Legislative History

* * * In 1984, the General Assembly enacted the Criminal Domestic Violence Act and the Protection from Domestic Abuse Act. * * * Over the course of the next thirty-one years, the General Assembly amended the Acts four times, the most extensive in 2015. * * * In 1994, the General Assembly amended sections 16–25–10 and 20–4–20 to delete "family or" preceding "household member," add "persons who have a child in common," and add/substitute "*a male and female who are cohabiting or formerly have cohabited*" for "*and persons cohabitating or formerly cohabitating.*" *[Emphasis in original.]* * *

In 2015, * * * it provided for, inter alia, enhanced penalties for one convicted of subsequent offenses of domestic violence, the offense of domestic violence of a high and aggravated nature, and the prohibition of possession of a firearm for one convicted of domestic violence. * * * Although a review of the statutory evolution is not dispositive * * *, it is conclusive evidence the General Assembly purposefully included the phrase "male and female" within the definition of "household member" in 1994 and has retained that definition.

2. Presumption of Constitutionality

* * * This general presumption of [constitutional] validity can be overcome only by a clear showing the act violates some provision of the constitution. * * *

3. Facial versus "As-Applied" Challenge

Cognizant of the presumption of constitutionality, we must first determine the type of constitutional challenge posed by Doe. * * * "The line between facial and as-applied relief is [a] fluid one, and many constitutional challenges may occupy an intermediate position on the spectrum between purely as-applied relief and complete facial invalidation." Further, * * * "[t]he distinction is both instructive and necessary, for it goes to the breadth of the remedy employed by the Court, not what must be pleaded in a complaint."

* * * One asserting a facial challenge claims that the law is "invalid *in toto*—and therefore incapable of any valid application." This type of challenge is "the most difficult challenge to mount successfully, since the challenger must establish that no set of circumstances exists under which the [statute] would be valid." * * *

In an "as-applied" challenge, the party challenging the constitutionality of the statute claims that the "application of the statute in the particular context in which he has acted, or in which he proposes to act, would be unconstitutional." However, "finding a statute or regulation unconstitutional as applied to a specific party does not affect the facial validity of that provision." Instead, "[t]he practical effect of holding a statute unconstitutional 'as applied' is to prevent its future application in a similar context, but not to render it utterly inoperative."

[The Court concluded the statutory definition is not facially unconstitutional "because it does not overtly discriminate based on sexual orientation," and "there are numerous valid applications of the definition of 'household member,' [so] it is not 'invalid *in toto*.'"] * * * Thus, the question becomes whether the statutory definition of "household member" as applied denied Doe equal protection of the laws.

4. Equal Protection

The Equal Protection Clauses of our federal and state constitutions declare that no person shall be denied the equal protection of the laws. Equal protection "requires that all persons be treated alike under like circumstances and conditions, both in privileges conferred and liabilities imposed." "The *sine qua non* of an equal protection claim is a showing that similarly situated persons received disparate treatment."

"Courts generally analyze equal protection challenges under one of three standards: (1) rational basis; (2) intermediate scrutiny; or, (3) strict scrutiny." "If the classification does not implicate a suspect class or abridge a fundamental right, the rational basis test is used." "Under the rational basis test, the requirements of equal protection are satisfied when: (1) the classification bears a reasonable relation to the legislative purpose sought to be affected; (2) the members of the class are treated alike under similar circumstances and conditions; and (3) the classification rests on some reasonable basis." "Those attacking the validity of legislation under the rational basis test of the Equal Protection Clause have the burden to negate every conceivable basis which might support it."

* * * Doe has met her burden of showing that similarly situated persons received disparate treatment. Doe suggests that this case should be subject to the intermediate level of scrutiny as a result of "gender

classification"; however, she seems to concede that the appropriate standard is the rational basis test. While there is some limited authority to support the application of intermediate scrutiny, we need not make that determination because the definition of "household member" as applied to Doe cannot even satisfy the rational basis test. *[Editor's Note: This is a very common move for trial and reviewing courts, unless a jurisdiction's court of last resort has already stated the level of scrutiny for sexual orientation discrimination. Until the U.S. Supreme Court decidedly states which level of review is appropriate, most courts use the rational basis test.]*

Defining "household member" to include "a male **and** female who are cohabiting or formerly have cohabited," yet exclude (1) a male and male and (2) a female and female who are cohabiting or formerly have cohabited," fails this low level of scrutiny. Specifically, we conclude the definition: (1) bears no relation to the legislative purpose of the Acts; (2) treats same-sex couples who live together or have lived together differently than all other couples; and (3) lacks a rational reason to justify this disparate treatment.

Based on our interpretation of the Acts, the overall legislative purpose is to protect victims from domestic violence that occurs within the home and between members of the home. * * * Statistics, as identified by the State, reveal that "women are far more at risk from domestic violence at the hands of men than vice versa." Thus, the State maintains the General Assembly defined "household member" as "a male *and* female who are cohabiting or formerly have cohabited" to address the primary problem of domestic violence within opposite-sex couples. * * * Without question, the statistics relied on by the State are accurate. However, a *victim* of domestic violence is not defined by gender, as the word is non-gender specific.

Moreover, although the Acts may have been originally enacted to address traditional findings of domestic violence, new research shows that individuals within same-sex couples experience a similar degree of domestic violence as those in opposite-sex couples.

Because the Acts are intended to provide protection for all victims of domestic violence, the definition of "household member," which eliminates Doe's relationship as a "qualifying relationship" for an Order of Protection, bears no relation to furthering the legislative purpose of Acts.

Additionally, the definition of "household member" treats unmarried, same-sex couples who live together or have lived together differently than all other couples. As we interpret the definition of "household member" a person, who fits within one of the following relationships, would be eligible for an Order of Protection: (1) a same-sex married or formerly married couple; (2) a same-sex couple, either married or unmarried, who have a child in common; (3) an opposite-sex married or formerly married couple; (4) an opposite-sex couple, either married or unmarried, who have a child in common; and (5) an unmarried opposite-sex couple who is living together or who has lived together.

Thus, while Doe and her [ex-fiancée] were similarly situated to other unmarried or formerly married couples, particularly unmarried opposite-sex couples who live together, Doe was precluded from seeking an Order of Protection based on the definition of "household member." We find there is no reasonable basis, and the State has offered none, to support a definition that results in disparate treatment of same-sex couples who are cohabiting or formerly have cohabited. * * * Because it is clear that the definition of "household member" violates the Equal Protection clauses of our state and federal constitutions, we must declare it unconstitutional.

5. Remedy

* * * Clearly, in the context of the statutory scheme of the Acts, this Court cannot construe and effectively amend the statutes to change the plain language of "and" to "or" as proposed by the State [and Doe]. * * * Also, even though the Acts include severability clauses, there is no reason to employ them as we have found the sections containing the definition of "household member" are not facially invalid. Rather, the constitutional infirmity is based on their application to Doe, i.e., not including unmarried same-sex couples in the definition of "household member." * * *

Further, even if we were to attempt to remedy the constitutional infirmity through severance, we find severance of the entire phrase "a male **and** female who are cohabiting or formerly have cohabited" to be unavailing since the constitutional infirmity would remain. Protection afforded by the Acts would still be elusive to Doe and would no longer be available to opposite-sex couples who are cohabiting or formerly have cohabited. Yet, it would be available to unmarried persons such as former spouses (same-sex or not) and persons (same-sex or not) with a child in common. * * * As a result, the Acts would be rendered useless. Such a drastic measure is neither necessary nor desired. Accordingly, we reject any suggestion to sever the Acts[.] * * * Finally, we decline to invalidate the Acts in their entirety. Such a decision would result in grave consequences for victims of domestic violence [and . . .] would be a great disservice to the citizens of South Carolina.

III. Conclusion

* * * [W]e declare [the Acts] unconstitutional as applied to Doe. Therefore, the family court may not utilize these statutory provisions to prevent Doe or those in similar same-sex relationships from seeking an Order of Protection.

FEW, J., concurring in part and dissenting in part.

[Everyone] agrees to this central point: if the Acts exclude unmarried, same-sex couples from the protections they provide all other citizens, they are obviously unconstitutional. * * * For two reasons, I would not declare the Acts unconstitutional. First, Doe and the State agree the * * * Act protects Doe, and thus, there is no controversy before this Court. Second, * * * ambiguity in both Acts—particularly in the definition of household member—requires this Court to construe [them] to provide Doe the same protections they provide all citizens, and thus, the Acts are not unconstitutional. * * *

M.G. v. R.D.

2003 WL 21129878 (unpublished)
Court of Appeal, Second District, Division 3, California
As Modified on Denial of Rehearing June 4, 2003
(citations omitted)

Defendant and appellant R.D. (defendant) appeals an order granting a petition by plaintiff and respondent M.G. (plaintiff) for an injunction prohibiting harassment. (Code Civ. Proc., § 527.6.)[1]

The essential issue presented is the sufficiency of the evidence to support the claim of harassment.

We conclude the trial court's decision is supported by substantial evidence and affirm the order.

FACTUAL AND PROCEDURAL BACKGROUND

Plaintiff and defendant are ex-boyfriends. Plaintiff serves in the Marine Corps and defendant is an L.A.P.D. officer.

On March 12, 2002, plaintiff filed a petition for an injunction prohibiting harassment and applied for a temporary restraining order. Plaintiff alleged in the petition, inter alia: defendant tried to rape him; defendant sent him harassing e-mails; and defendant made Internet viewable clips of two intimate videos they had made and dispensed this material to friends, family, plaintiff's colleagues at the university where he works, and to plaintiff's Marine Reserve unit.

On March 12, 2002, the trial court issued an order to show cause.

On May 10, 2002, the matter came on for trial. The witnesses included plaintiff and defendant. One of the chief issues at trial was whether defendant was the author of various offending e-mails received by plaintiff.

After hearing the matter, the trial court ruled as follows: "I really have no evidence or insufficient evidence to show the content of any videos. [¶] But I think that in looking at the various exhibits that are attached to the petition, the copies of the e-mails and, in particular the one that was previously marked as Exhibit 6 which bears the date of Tuesday, July the 3rd of 2001 sent at 5:30 a.m., it does seem to be a kind of threatening

---

[1] The circumstances herein make this an appropriate case for the protective nondisclosure of identity.

communication here. This came from . . . from [defendant's] computer. The court so finds Exhibit 1 and 2 are from the same computer, and this was traced back-it could be traced back to-again, to the computer, to the I.P. address utilized by [defendant]. [¶] It has language that says, and I quote directly from the document that: [¶] 'Hey, look what I found. Remember this? I must have about three dozen that I converted to digital quite some time ago, although the others have much better quality. Thought you might like it. . . . [¶] Then it goes on: 'I have all of the e-mail addresses of all of your friends.' [¶] And then it goes down to a couple of veiled threats about sending them out to all of the petitioner's friends. [¶] That is kind of the tenure [*sic*] of the thing. [¶] Again, that is what the court is directing its attention to, and that is what the court is considering to be . . . the allegations of harassment. [¶] Based on that, again, the court is not looking at and has not found any sexually explicit content of any videos. I'm going to grant the petition of [plaintiff] and order that [defendant] will be restrained. . . ."

The trial court then issued a Judicial Council form order prohibiting harassment as follows: "IT IS ORDERED THAT DEFENDANT [¶] a. shall not contact, molest, harass, attack, strike, threaten, sexually assault, batter, telephone, send any messages to, follow, stalk, destroy the personal property of, disturb the peace of, keep under surveillance, or block movements in public places or thoroughfares of [¶] the person seeking the order . . . [¶] b. shall stay at least . . . 100 yards away from the following protected persons and places: [¶] (1) Person seeking the order [¶] . . . [¶] (3) Residence of person seeking the order [¶] (4) Place of work of person seeking the order [¶] . . . [¶] (6) Other *(specify):* US MARINE CORP TROOP OF PERSON SEEKING ORDER."

Defendant filed a timely notice of appeal from the order.

CONTENTIONS

Defendant contends: plaintiff did not sustain his burden of proof of establishing by clear and convincing evidence that defendant was harassing him, or that plaintiff suffered severe emotional distress as a direct and proximate result of defendant's actions; and the injunction is overly broad insofar as it covers constitutionally protected free speech and assembly.

DISCUSSION

1. No merit to defendant's challenge to the sufficiency of the evidence.

a. Statutory scheme.

The controlling statute, section 527.6, provides in relevant part at subdivision (b): "For the purposes of this section, 'harassment' is unlawful violence, a credible threat of violence, or a knowing and willful course of conduct directed at a specific person that seriously alarms, annoys, or harasses the person, and that serves no legitimate purpose. The course of conduct must be such as would cause a reasonable person to suffer substantial emotional distress, and must actually cause substantial emotional distress to the plaintiff."

If the trial court finds "by clear and convincing evidence that unlawful harassment exists, an injunction shall issue prohibiting the harassment." (§ 527.6, subd. (d).)

b. Defendant's argument.

Defendant contends plaintiff failed to meet his burden to establish by clear and convincing evidence that defendant was harassing him and that plaintiff suffered substantial emotional distress as a result of defendant's actions.

c. Standard of appellate review.

Irrespective of the clear and convincing evidence standard which applied below, we review the trial court's decision under the substantial evidence standard.

d. Substantial evidence supports trial court's determination that defendant was harassing plaintiff.

The evidence at trial established that defendant engaged in a "knowing and willful course of conduct directed at a specific person that seriously alarm[ed], annoy[ed], or harasse[d] the person, and that serve[d] no legitimate purpose." (§ 527.6, subd. (b).)[3]

John L., a co-owner of two dot.com companies who has some expertise with computers, testified that he had examined 14 e-mail messages from defendant to plaintiff, and that based on their Internet provider address, all 14 messages originated from the same computer, from defendant's computer.

With respect to the content of those e-mails, a message dated July 3, 2001 is illustrative. Defendant wrote: "Hey, look what I found. Remember this? I must have made about 3-dozen that I converted to digital quite sometime ago. . . . The problem is I don't know what to do with [it] now[.] [¶] . . . I . . . have all of your friends' email addresses. Perhaps I will send them a copy or copies. . . . Or should I just post them on the net? . . . [¶] . . . How does it feel to be betrayed by someone you once love[d]?"

---

[3] The statute defines " '[c]ourse of conduct' " as "a pattern of conduct composed of a series of acts over a period of time, however short, evidencing a continuity of purpose, including following or stalking an individual, making harassing telephone calls to an individual, or sending harassing correspondence to an individual by any means, including, but not limited to, the use of public or private mails, interoffice mail, fax, or computer e-mail." (§ 527.6, subd. (b)(3).)

Defendant's position is that he did not author the e-mails in issue. Defendant testified his computer is not password protected, and that various people had access to his computer.

Because a reviewing court will not reweigh the evidence nor pass upon the credibility of witnesses, and the trier of fact is entitled to accept or reject all or any part of the testimony of any witness, defendant's arguments in this regard are unavailing. The trial court found the e-mails in question came from defendant's computer. The trial court also found there was no evidence that defendant actually prepared the e-mails. The logical import of that statement is that the trial court merely found no direct evidence that defendant authored the e-mails. However, there was abundant circumstantial evidence to that effect. Although defendant asserted his computer was not password protected and that various friends had access to his home computer, defendant did not specify who those persons were, nor did defendant explain how such persons had the intimate knowledge necessary to carry on this ongoing e-mail conversation with plaintiff. On this record, there is substantial evidence to support the trial court's determination that the e-mails originated from defendant's computer, and because there was no evidence that anyone else authored the e-mails, the trial court properly found that defendant engaged in a harassing course of conduct directed at plaintiff, so as to entitle plaintiff to injunctive relief.

e. Substantial evidence supports trial court's determination that defendants' actions caused plaintiff substantial emotional distress.

Plaintiff testified he was hurt by defendant's threats to discredit him by sending these e-mails to his friends and to the Marine Corps. Also, he feared going about his business, felt unsafe at home and had to move in with friends. He did not fear defendant would shoot him, but he did not know what defendant might do.

In view of the above, we find substantial evidence that defendant's conduct caused plaintiff substantial emotional distress within the meaning of section 527.6.

2. No merit to defendant's constitutional argument.

Defendant contends the injunction is overly broad insofar as it covers constitutionally protected free speech and/or assembly under the United States and California Constitutions. The argument is unavailing. The trial court's order simply enjoins defendant from harassing plaintiff and requires defendant to stay at least 100 yards away from certain specified locations. The order does not implicate defendant's rights of free speech and assembly.

DISPOSITION

The order is affirmed. As the prevailing party, plaintiff shall recover attorney fees pursuant to section 527.6, subdivision (i), as well as costs on appeal.

[Editor's Notes:

- *Many abusers, gay and heterosexual, assert their right to free speech under the 1st Amendment in justifying their abusive actions. Sometimes this is successful.*
- *In California, Civil Harassment Orders (CHOs) are more difficult to obtain than are DV Restraining Orders (DVROs), requiring at least two incidents of harassment rather than one act of abuse, and clear and convincing evidence rather than a preponderance of the evidence. In this case it is not clear why the plaintiff sought a CHO rather than a DVRO.*
- *Since federal law prohibits anyone subject to a DVRO from possessing a firearm, it is possible that the plaintiff in this case requested a CHO instead of a DVRO so that his ex-partner would not lose his job.]*

PRICE-CORNELISON V. BROOKS

524 F.3d 1103 (10th Cir. 2008)
(footnotes, citations and dissent omitted)

Defendant-Appellant Steve Brooks, the Undersheriff of Garvin County, Oklahoma, appeals the district court's decision denying him qualified immunity on Plaintiff-Appellee Dana L. Price-Cornelison's two constitutional claims that Brooks failed to enforce Price-Cornelison's protective orders because she is a lesbian victim of domestic violence. Price-Cornelison specifically alleged that, in refusing to enforce her protective orders, Brooks 1) denied her equal protection of the law; and 2) helped a private citizen unlawfully seize Price-Cornelison's property, contrary to the Fourth Amendment. We conclude that Brooks is entitled to qualified immunity on the equal protection claim, to the extent that that claim is based upon Brooks' refusal to enforce Price-Cornelison's emergency protective order on October 16, 2003, and therefore we reverse the district court on that portion of Price-Cornelison's equal protection claim. But we agree with the district court that Brooks is not entitled to qualified immunity on the equal protection claim, to the extent that claim is based upon Brooks' refusal to enforce Price-Cornelison's permanent protective order, on November 3, 2003. Nor is Brooks entitled to qualified immunity on the Fourth Amendment claim. Consequently we affirm these portions of the district court's ruling.

I. BACKGROUND

Viewing the evidence in the light most favorable to Price-Cornelison, the record establishes the following: Price-Cornelison had been involved in a homosexual relationship with Vickie Rogers since 1996. In 2003, the couple was living together at Price-Cornelison's farm, Lost Spring Farm ("the farm"), located near Pauls Valley, Garvin County, Oklahoma. Price-Cornelison, who is an anesthetist, worked an hour away, at a hospital in Muenster, Texas. She had an apartment in Muenster where she stayed overnight when she was on call at the hospital. Rogers stayed on the farm and took care of the couple's horses. Eventually Rogers grew tired of caring for the horses, so Price-Cornelison hired several farmhands to live on the farm to take care of the horses.

Price-Cornelison's and Roger's relationship deteriorated. On October 16, 2003, Price-Cornelison sought an emergency protective order from a Garvin County court, alleging that Rogers had threatened to shoot both Price-Cornelison and then herself and that Rogers had fired a gun over the telephone while making this threat. In her petition for the emergency protective order, Price-Cornelison asked the court to order Rogers to leave the residence "on or before" the following day, October 17, 2003. State Judge Tipton issued the emergency protective order that same day, October 16. That order directed Rogers "to immediately leave" her and Price-Cornelison's residence "or before 10–17–03."

After the state court issued the emergency protective order, Price-Cornelison went to work at the hospital in Muenster, Texas. A Garvin County sheriff's deputy served the emergency protective order on Rogers that same day, October 16. Rogers and some of her family and friends then began removing property from the farm. During this time, Price-Cornelison's farmhands called her in Texas to report that Rogers was taking "everything" from the farm. Price-Cornelison called the Garvin County sheriff's office and spoke to Undersheriff Brooks, who indicated that he had been assigned to handle her situation. When Price-Cornelison asked Brooks to go out to the farm and stop Rogers from removing Price-Cornelison's property, Brooks informed Price-Cornelison that Oklahoma is "a community property state and that [Rogers] could take anything she want[ed]." Price-Cornelison then asked Brooks to make a police report about the incident, but he refused, telling her that this was a civil matter. Price-Cornelison responded that she would have to leave work in Texas and drive back home to the farm to stop Rogers from taking Price-Cornelison's property. But Brooks informed Price-Cornelison that if she went to the farm, she would be arrested.

Price-Cornelison called the Garvin County sheriff's office several more times that day, to no avail. In addition, one of Price-Cornelison's friends, Mary Sanchez, called the sheriff's office and she, too, spoke to Brooks. Brooks told Sanchez the same thing he had told Price-Cornelison—

Oklahoma was a community property state; pursuant to the terms of the emergency protective order, Rogers could remove whatever property she wanted up until the next day, October 17, 2003; and, according to Brooks, Price-Cornelison could not be present at her own home at this time. During this conversation, Brooks also explained to Sanchez that Price-Cornelison had been "in one of those lesbian relationships. They have lived together for a long time, and they might as well have been like they were married."

Later that same day, Price-Cornelison called her attorney, whose office was in Oklahoma City. The attorney in turn called the Garvin County sheriff's office and also spoke to Brooks. According to Brooks, the attorney suggested Brooks get "off his doughnut-eating ass and do something." This suggestion was not well received; Brooks hung up on the attorney.

Brooks then went home, leaving instructions at the sheriff's office that if anyone called again about Price-Cornelison's emergency protective order, sheriff's personnel were to have the caller contact Brooks the next morning. According to Brooks, he left these instructions because he "did not want any of [the other deputies] to be negotiators as to who owned the property."

Heeding Brooks' warning, Price-Cornelison did not return home to the farm until she knew Rogers was no longer there. When Price-Cornelison did return home, late at night on October 16, she found that Rogers had taken many things belonging to Price-Cornelison, including appliances, furniture, electronics, pictures off the wall, tools, horse trailers and equipment, farm implements, and welding equipment, as well as all the horse and breeding records.

Two weeks later, on October 31, 2003, state Judge Blalock issued Price-Cornelison a permanent protective order against Rogers. That order required Rogers, among other things, "to remain away from" Price-Cornelison and away from her residence. Despite this permanent protective order, on November 3, 2003, Rogers returned to Lost Spring Farm with her sister, gaining access to the farm by crawling under a fence. Although at the time Price-Cornelison was in town buying supplies, one of her farmhands was at the farm and tried unsuccessfully to stop Rogers from entering onto the property. Rogers got into a verbal and physical confrontation with this farmhand. The farmhand called Price-Cornelison to tell her Rogers was at the farm. Still in town, Price-Cornelison called the Garvin County sheriff's office twice to report that Rogers was violating the protective order by being present at Price-Cornelison's farm. The woman who answered the phone at the sheriff's office, apparently Deputy Cricket Warren, told Price-Cornelison that "they" were "busy" and were not going to send anyone out to her farm.

After calling the Sheriff's office, Price-Cornelison drove back to her farm. When Rogers saw Price-Cornelison's car approaching, she and her sister left the property. No one from the sheriff's office ever came out to the farm in response to Price-Cornelison's calls about Rogers violating the protective order.

The next day, Price-Cornelison asked a local prosecutor how she could get her protective order enforced. The prosecutor indicated that it should be enforced and suggested that Price-Cornelison talk to Brooks. She did, that same day. Brooks told Price-Cornelison that everyone in the courthouse was laughing at her and that she should fire her attorney and obtain local counsel to represent her.

Price-Cornelison commenced this action in federal court in March 2004, asserting federal civil rights claims under 42 U.S.C. § 1983 and tort claims under Oklahoma law against the Garvin County Board of County Commissioners (the "County") and Undersheriff Brooks. The only two claims at issue in this appeal are Price-Cornelison's claims that Brooks, in his individual capacity, 1) deprived Price-Cornelison of equal protection of the law when he refused to enforce her protective orders because she is a lesbian victim of domestic violence; and 2) violated Price-Cornelison's Fourth Amendment right to be free from unreasonable seizures of her property by threatening to arrest Price-Cornelison if she returned to her home on October 16 and thus dissuading Price-Cornelison from preventing Rogers from removing Price-Cornelison's property from the farm. The district court denied Brooks qualified immunity on these two claims. He now appeals that decision. * * *

IV. ANALYSIS

A. Price's Equal Protection Claim.

1. Whether Price-Cornelison has asserted a constitutional violation.

The threshold qualified immunity question presented is whether, "[t]aken in the light most favorable to the party asserting the injury, do the facts alleged show the officer's conduct violated a constitutional right." In this case, Price-Cornelison alleges Brooks deprived her of equal protection of the law. * * *

Price-Cornelison alleges that Brooks deprived her of equal protection of the law when he refused to enforce both her emergency and permanent protective orders to the same extent that he enforced protective orders obtained by heterosexual victims of domestic violence. And it is clear that, "[a]lthough there is no general constitutional right to police protection, the state may not discriminate in providing such protection."

Relying on *Watson,* Price-Cornelison alleged that the County has a policy of providing less protection to lesbian victims of domestic violence than to heterosexual domestic violence victims. The district court held that Price-Cornelison had asserted sufficient evidence indicating that the County did have such a policy to go to trial on that issue. Because we cannot review that determination in the context of this appeal, we assume here that the County has such a policy.

To support her claim against Brooks, in his individual capacity, Price-Cornelison relies on the County's policy, plus Brooks' treatment of Amanda Chandler, a heterosexual domestic violence victim who requested that Brooks enforce her protective order against her former husband. The evidence, viewed in the light most favorable to Price-Cornelison, indicates the following: Amanda Chandler obtained a protective order requiring her former husband, Johnny Chandler, to stay away from her. On September 29, 2003, Amanda Chandler called the Garvin County Sheriff's office twice, reporting that her former husband was following her as she drove on the highway, and that he was trying to force her to pull over. Brooks advised Amanda Chandler to drive immediately to the Sheriff's office. Based upon Amanda Chandler's report, Brooks filed charges against Johnny Chandler for violating the protective order.

Price-Cornelison contrasts Brooks' enforcement of Amanda Chandler's protective order with his refusal to enforce both Price-Cornelison's emergency and permanent protective orders. But Brooks' refusal to enforce Price-Cornelison's *emergency* protective order, on October 16, 2003, by refusing to go to her farm and prevent Rogers from removing any property, is not sufficiently similar to Brooks' enforcing Amanda Chandler's protective order to provide support for Price-Cornelison's equal protection claim. Amanda Chandler's protective order was valid and enforceable on the day that she called seeking its enforcement. That was not the case with Price-Cornelison's emergency protective order. The express terms of the emergency protective order provided that Rogers did not have to vacate Price-Cornelison's farm until October 17, which was the day *after* Price-Cornelison called soliciting Brooks' help. The record further indicates that Brooks, on October 16, did call the Garvin County court to verify the dates that appeared on the emergency protective order and was told that they were correct; the state judge had given Rogers a day to gather her possessions together before leaving. Price-Cornelison has not asserted any evidence suggesting that, contrary to his treatment of Price-Cornelison, Brooks would have enforced a heterosexual domestic violence victim's protective order that was not yet effective under these same circumstances.

Price-Cornelison, however, did have an enforceable permanent protective order on November 3, 2003. We note here, at the outset of our discussion of Price-Cornelison's equal protection claim alleging that Brooks refused to enforce her permanent protective order, that the partial dissent takes issue with our reading of the facts relevant to these allegations. * * * If Price-Cornelison has alleged a constitutional violation, and for the reasons explained below we think she has, and if there is any evidence in the record to support the version of events averred by Price-Cornelison, we simply must affirm. In our judgment, there is evidence in this record to support her allegations and, thus, to require us to affirm the district court's decision denying Brooks' qualified immunity at this stage of the proceedings. * * *

Price-Cornelison's permanent protective order that was in effect on November 3, 2003, required Rogers, among other things, to remain away from Price-Cornelison's residence. Both Price-Cornelison and her hired farmhand, Tesh Morgan, called the sheriff's office several times on that day, reporting that Rogers had come onto Price-Cornelison's property in violation of the permanent protective order. Brooks spoke with Morgan. It appears that he may also have spoken to Price-Cornelison. Another deputy with whom Price-Cornelison spoke informed Price-Cornelison that "they weren't sending" anybody to investigate because "they were busy."

The next day, Price-Cornelison and Morgan spoke to Brooks about getting Price-Cornelison's permanent protective order enforced. They explained that they were afraid of Rogers, in light of her previous use of firearms to accentuate her threats to Price-Cornelison and Rogers' later confrontation with Morgan, and they were particularly concerned because two of Price-Cornelison's other hired hands lived on the farm with their child. * * * Despite these several reports that Rogers had violated the permanent protective order, Brooks declined to send any deputies to investigate, and no charges were ever filed against Rogers, even though there was an eyewitness to the violation.

Comparing Brooks' refusal to enforce Price-Cornelison's permanent protective order with the level of enforcement he provided to Amanda Chandler, and viewing this differing treatment in light of the County's policy of providing less police protection to lesbian victims of domestic violence than it provided to heterosexual domestic violence victims, Price-Cornelison has asserted sufficient evidence to show that Brooks himself treated Price-Cornelison less favorably than he treated other domestic violence victims.

Price-Cornelison next asserts that Brooks intentionally treated her differently because she is a lesbian and was a domestic violence victim. Because we must assume, for purposes of this appeal, that the County has a policy of providing lesbian victims of domestic violence with less police protection than other domestic violence victims, it is reasonable to infer, for purposes of Brooks' motion for summary judgment, that, in refusing to enforce Price-Cornelison's permanent protective order, Brooks was acting pursuant to that policy. In addition, it is undisputed that at the time Brooks refused to enforce Price-Cornelison's permanent protective order, Brooks was aware that she is a lesbian; he had previously mentioned this fact to several people. Price-Cornelison has, therefore, presented sufficient evidence to show that Brooks refused to enforce her permanent protective order because she is a lesbian domestic violence victim.

Price-Cornelison has, therefore, adequately alleged Brooks deprived her of equal protection of the law when he refused to enforce her permanent protective order on November 3, 2003. Price-Cornelison's claim, however, does not implicate a fundamental right—"there is no general constitutional right to police protection." Nor does it implicate a protected class, which would warrant heightened scrutiny. A government official can, therefore, distinguish between its citizens on the basis of sexual orientation, if that classification bears "a rational relation to some legitimate end." But Brooks has not asserted, and we cannot discern on this record, a rational reason to provide less protection to lesbian victims of domestic violence than to heterosexual domestic violence victims. Price-Cornelison, therefore, has sufficiently established that Brooks violated her constitutional rights.

2. Whether this constitutional right was clearly established at the time Brooks refused to enforce Price-Cornelison's permanent protective order.

* * * "The relevant, dispositive inquiry in determining whether a right is clearly established is whether it would be clear to a reasonable officer that his conduct was unlawful in the situation."

Brooks refused to enforce Price-Cornelison's permanent protective order on November 3, 2003. It was much earlier, in 1988, that *Watson* clearly established that, "[a]lthough there is no general constitutional right to police protection, the state may not discriminate in providing such protection." *Watson* reached this conclusion specifically in the context of addressing police protection afforded to domestic abuse victims. *Watson,* therefore, was sufficient to put Brooks on notice that providing Price-Cornelison less police protection than other domestic violence victims because she is a lesbian would deprive her of equal protection of the law, at least in the absence of an articulated rational governmental reason for such discrimination.

This is true even assuming that Brooks was acting according to a County policy of affording less police protection to lesbian victims of domestic violence, because *Watson* would have put Brooks on notice that applying such a policy could result in a constitutional violation. In any event, Brooks does not argue here that he is entitled to qualified immunity because he was following official policy, nor does he attempt to argue that there is a rational basis for such a policy; instead, he denies that there is such a policy. * * *

V. CONCLUSION

For these reasons, we REVERSE the district court's decision denying Brooks qualified immunity from Price-Cornelison's equal protection claim, to the extent that claim was based upon his refusal to enforce Price-Cornelison's emergency protective order on October 16, 2003. But we AFFIRM the district court's decision denying Brooks qualified immunity to the extent her equal protection claim was based upon Brooks' refusal to enforce Price-Cornelison's protective order November 3, 2003, and on her Fourth Amendment claim. We REMAND this case for further proceedings consistent with this opinion.

EDITOR'S SUMMARY OF VALLI KANUHA, COMPOUNDING THE TRIPLE JEOPARDY: BATTERING IN LESBIAN OF COLOR RELATIONSHIPS

From Diversity and Complexity in Feminist Therapy 176–184 (1990)

It can be very risky for lesbians of color to come out in various different communities. This is often even harder for lesbians of color who are also being abused, due to the historical difficulty many communities have had in dealing with "traditional," i.e., heterosexual domestic violence. The fact that there are lesbians of color who are battered or batterers forces us to look at the ongoing effects of racism, sexism, classism, and other oppressions.

It also means that feminists must face the fact that the larger women's movement has frequently not been successful in dealing with the intersections of gay oppression, abuse, sexism, and racism. The presence of battered lesbians (of color or white) means that activists against domestic violence must re-examine their analysis of the causes of domestic violence. Additionally, these activists need to be supportive of lesbians of color as clients, workers, and leaders in the anti-violence movement.

Within the lesbian community, recognizing the existence of battered lesbians of color highlights the need for more inclusion of lesbians of color generally. Given that many conservatives in the U.S. see homosexuality as pathological, lesbians of color who come out as abused or abusers will cause many gay and lesbian people to fear homophobic retaliation toward the entire LGBT community.

Many ethnic communities of color have focused on building pride and solidarity, but responding to the needs of battered lesbians of color within those communities will cause some racist people to blame those communities for the abuse, reinforcing racist stereotypes. Addressing the needs of abused lesbians of color will also force members of non-white ethnic communities to face their own sexism and anti-gay beliefs, which are hurtful to their own family members who are lesbians.

Battered lesbians of color often rightfully believe that their own ethnic communities will not protect them. Unlike heterosexual members of ethnic communities, who may experience the community as a refuge from racism, this is not the case for many battered lesbians of color. They may feel it necessary to hide the abuse in order not to trigger racism and homophobia from the larger society, targeting the entire community of color as well as themselves. These internal conflicts may cause many lesbians of color to stay in abusive relationships. Therapists working with this population need to address the many issues their clients face in coming out as battered lesbians of color.

Battering relationships between white lesbians and lesbians of color can sometimes reflect the differences in power due to race, e.g., a white woman using racist slurs as part of the abuse, or S & M turning into a master-slave scenario which is no longer consensual. There are no studies on how racism plays out within domestically violent relationships where one partner is white and one is not, nor any basis to assume that there are higher rates of abuse in biracial relationships. However, it is possible that white lesbians battered by lesbians of color may excuse the abuse as an attempt to bring more equality to the relationship. Conversely, when the abuse is from the white partner, the partner of color may feel she somehow deserves this, due to internalized racism.

Workers in the institutions dealing with domestic violence such as the criminal justice system and social services often have insufficient training about or understanding of the needs of women generally, women of color, and lesbians, which jeopardizes battered lesbians of color. Because they are aware of this, many abused lesbians of color will not seek help from the criminal justice system or the courts due to the retaliation they fear from these institutions. Clinicians who assist their clients to do this need to become advocates as well as good counselors, and consider the drawbacks to lesbians of color utilizing traditional anti-violence approaches. Of course, respect for the client's decisions whether or not to pursue traditional remedies is paramount.

Therapy as part of the response to domestic violence is controversial, given the history of the male-dominated mental health profession blaming female victims of abuse for having been abused. This controversy has started to change, due to increased training for therapists specializing in abuse. But there is a great need for more training about racism, lesbians of color, and abuse in lesbian relationships within the mental health field. This is a complex area, in which therapists need to have great sensitivity and understanding in order to assist battered lesbians of color to come forward and get help to end the abuse.

[Editor's Note: In a report by Truman and Morgan, Victimization by Sexual Orientation and Gender Identity, 2017-2020, published by Bureau of Justice Statistics (2022), summarizing the National Crime Victimization Survey, the rates of IPV victimization of people 16 and older who identified as lesbian, gay, or transgender were more than twice as high as rates among those who identified as heterosexual. Rates among bisexual people were more than 8 times higher than among heterosexuals. (https://bjs.ojp.gov/content/pub/pdf/vvsogi1720.pdf) This is consistent with prior studies about the greater vulnerability of bisexual people to DV, such as the 2010 National Intimate Partner and Sexual Violence Survey.]

KAE GREENBERG, STILL HIDDEN IN THE CLOSET: TRANS WOMEN AND DOMESTIC VIOLENCE

27 Berk. J. Gender, Law & Justice 198 (2012)
(most footnotes omitted)

INTRODUCTION

You have endured years of physical and psychological abuse from your partner. Your partner taunts you, claiming no one will believe you; besides, you are not even a real woman. Although you fear for your life and safety if you stay, you fear that the threat is worse if you go. But at last, gathering all of your courage, you leave your abusive partner and flee to a battered woman's shelter, hoping to disappear. In an attempt to figure out if you belong, the intake worker asks you a few awkward questions and then, finally, asks, "What's between your legs?"

Domestic violence committed against cisgender women[2] is widespread in the United States. Feminists of all stripes, from the radical to the essentialist, have fought to direct attention to this issue for decades. Their efforts have resulted in domestic violence shelters across the country, criminal statutes that target domestic violence, and a focus on domestic violence in national discourse. * * *

Although relatively few studies exist on domestic violence in LGB relationships, one large study by the UCLA Center for Health and Policy Research shows that domestic violence within LGB relationships is twice as prevalent as in heterosexual relationships. In relationships where one or both partners are trans, instances of domestic violence are possibly more prevalent. However, less data is available pertaining to trans victims of domestic violence than for cisgender LGB domestic violence victims. Often in studies addressing domestic violence in LGBT communities, the "T" is tacked on at the end as an afterthought. Even so, some data specifically addressing trans individuals is available. In the Gender, Violence and Resource Access Survey, fifty percent of trans respondents stated that they had been assaulted or raped by a partner; thirty-one percent identified themselves as domestic violence survivors. The comprehensive National Transgender Discrimination Survey (NTDS), which compiled the responses of over six thousand trans and gender nonconforming people, found that nineteen percent of respondents had been subjected to domestic violence specifically because they were trans or gender non-conforming.

Traditionally, domestic violence has been characterized by invisibility. Domestic violence has previously gone unregulated or unsanctioned because it occurs in the home, where privacy is supposed to reign supreme against the reach of the state. Trans people have unique issues that increase the likelihood that domestic violence committed against them will

[2] I use "cisgender" to describe people whose assignment of sex at birth is congruent with their current gender identity. This is not meant to imply that cisgender women must be "feminine" and cisgender men "masculine" in their gender presentations.

thrive in silence. Many trans people exist in a "legal limbo." They may be unable to get the "legal gender" on their identification to match their gender identity, forcing them to utilize an ID with gender markers that do not match their gender presentation. Their legal gender can have an impact on the state-recognized legitimacy of their identity and relationships as well as their access to services and benefits. For example, they may risk being fired because of the absence of protections that would be found in trans-inclusive antidiscrimination laws.

This legal limbo leaves many trans people in a precarious position in society. Many trans people are underemployed or work at jobs for which they are underpaid relative to their credentials. Others are simply unemployed because they could not access necessary education. The [NTDS] found that trans people are nearly four times as likely to have an income under $10,000 as the general population. This may lead trans people to be more susceptible to the economic control that abusers often utilize. These issues are further complicated by the intersection of other marginalized identities trans people might have, such as being people of color. The NTDS found that while trans people in general had twice the rate of unemployment as the general population, trans people of color had up to four times the national rate.

This hostile legal environment is compounded by societal transphobia which abusers can use to isolate and deprecate their partners. Transphobia represents an extra "tool" in the abuser's arsenal. This can be true in relationships during which a person transitions as well as in those in which the individual has already transitioned. In both relationships, the abuser can use threats of "outing" to establish and retain control over the partner.

The inadequacy of services available for abused trans people due to societal transphobia also helps the abusers maintain coercive control over their partners. Besides having access to few services, abused trans people may be unwilling to call on transphobic police for help because they fear that the police will not believe them or will abuse them too. Also, trans people may be barred from battered women's shelters because of shelter policies. Finally, their abusers may threaten trans parents with the loss of their children, a very real possibility for a trans person whose child custody is challenged in court. * * *

I. TRAPPED BETWEEN A ROCK AND A HARD PLACE: THE MECHANICS OF DOMESTIC VIOLENCE

The question "Why didn't you leave?" hangs heavily over many abuse victims as they prepare to separate themselves from their abusers, possibly after years of mistreatment. This question is asked by judges, friends, family, and by the victims themselves over and over again. * * * Social entrapment has an impact on anyone in an abusive relationship, but this entrapment acutely affects trans women in a number of ways. * * * The stigma resulting from transphobia in the larger community, a lack of trans-competent services for abused women, and other factors combine to exacerbate the effects of an abuser's coercive behaviors toward trans women. Those who wish to escape their partners have few options for recourse, even when they actively advocate for themselves.

A. Overview of Social Entrapment and Battered Women's Syndrome

* * * Three elements common to social entrapment are "1) a focus on the social isolation, fear and coercion that men's violence creates in women's lives; 2) attention to the indifference of powerful institutions to women's suffering; and 3) identification of the ways that men's coercive control can be aggravated by structural inequalities of gender, class, and racism." The theory of social entrapment explains how the abuser maintains control through the use of societal stereotypes and constructs and the ways in which the structural inequities "collude" with the abuser to maintain hir relationship. *[Editor's Note: "Hir," like "zir" or "zer," is a gender neutral pronoun used instead of "his or her," though it is more common to use "they" and "their."]* * * *

II. SOCIAL ENTRAPMENT AND TRANS WOMEN

* * * B. Stigmatization

Moreover, trans people who successfully navigate the medical waters and receive a diagnosis of Gender Identity Disorder (GID) must then grapple with the stigma that continues to attach to mental illness. As one researcher states, "[t]he shame and self-doubt often experienced by survivors may be compounded by the stigma of mental illness attached to the diagnoses of 'gender identity disorder.' " This stigma affects many trans people's sense of self-esteem. The medical community doubts a trans person's identity and sense of self, and so trans people are forced to conform to certain medical models to receive necessary treatment. ["Due to this medicalization and their relationship with health care providers, trans people may be unlikely to go to a hospital, which is one place where they may be screened for domestic violence and connected to services."] * * *

Trans women face the additional stigma of transmisogyny. Writer Julia Serano defines transmisogyny as occurring "[w]hen a trans person is ridiculed or dismissed not merely for failing to live up to gender norms, but for their expressions of femaleness or femininity." Whereas mainstream society can be forgiving, to an extent, of cisgender women displaying traits that are traditionally coded as masculine, it is quick to condemn the same trait exhibited by a trans woman, using it as proof that she is not a "real woman." The general societal acceptance of transmisogyny makes it a very powerful tool for abusers.

This social stigmatization can have deadly effects for trans people, and abusers can utilize it to isolate victims. Research indicates that most trans people will be the victim of a hate crime during their lives. For many, harassment and maltreatment is a common occurrence. For some, it can have lethal consequences. * * * [An] average of one trans person is murdered per month because they are trans. * * * People who commit crimes against trans people sometimes attempt to use the stigma against them in their defense. For example, people who have attacked or murdered trans people have attempted to use "trans panic" to defend their actions. * * * The stigmatization of trans people manifests itself in discrimination, which has negative consequences in areas such as employment and allows abusers to economically abuse their trans partner. Statistically, trans people with higher degrees are underemployed, earning significantly less than cisgender people with the same academic credentials. Trans people are also vulnerable to job termination if their status is revealed. * * *

Many trans people turn to survival crimes such as theft, drugs, or sex work as their only income option (or, in some cases, as the only way to access medical treatment such as hormones). Furthermore, involvement in criminalized industries means trans people are more likely to have interactions with the police. And for a trans person, interactions with the police can range from humiliating to downright dangerous. Many trans women, especially trans women of color, are profiled as sex workers and picked up for "walking while trans" in moral sweeps by the police. * * * Trans status can cause friction between a youth and hir family and a young trans person may choose to leave the home as a result. Or, hir parents may reject their child for being trans and kick the youth out of the home. After leaving home or being evicted, the youth may head to urban areas with larger trans populations. Many homeless youth also turn to survival crimes, which can lead to early engagements with the police and legal system. Or, they may end up in the foster care system, which has its own attendant risks for trans youth. * * *

D. Internalized Transphobia

The victim may herself believe that this is the kind of relationship she deserves, a factor that the abuser can take advantage of. * * * Combined with stories of dating violence (such as that of Chanelle Picket, a [Male-to-Female] trans woman who was recently murdered by a date enraged at the revelation of her trans status), these "warnings" can convince trans and intersex survivors that they are lucky just to have a partner who doesn't kill them. * * * The abuser can exploit the fact that a trans woman coming out or contemplating transition is in a very vulnerable position. Or an abuser can turn her internalized transphobia against a trans woman who has transitioned. The abuser can insult her, claiming that she is not a "real woman," that this is the best that she deserves, or that she will not have a better relationship. * * * A Scottish survey found that a third of the trans domestic violence survivors had partners who had either restricted or stopped them from expressing their gender identity through their clothing choices or through what name or pronouns they selected. An additional way that abusers dominate trans women is by controlling their access to medical care in one of two ways. Some abusers may try to deny their trans partners access to gender-affirming medical care, such as hormones. Conversely, others might try to coerce their trans partners into undergoing medical intervention that they may not desire.

E. Small Communities, Small Networks

Trans women also may find their ability to leave their abuser hampered by the fact that the LGBT community in their town is small and insular (and the trans community even smaller) and that there are not many service providers, even in cities with large trans populations such as New York or San Francisco. * * * Also, the community may discourage disclosure of one's "dirty laundry," fearing that it would increase negative perceptions of the LGBT community. * * * A trans woman may fear that her network of friends and acquaintances, especially if they are part of the LGBT community, will "take the side of the abusive partner." * * *

F. Outing

Another effective weapon that an abuser can use against a trans woman victim is to threaten to "out" her. The victim may be perceived within her circle of friends or at work as cisgender and therefore may be at risk of losing either her friends or her job if her trans status is revealed.

III. NOWHERE TO RUN: THE TRANSPHOBIA OF SOCIETY

* * * [A]s examined in the second element of [Evan] Stark's classic model of coercive control, entities that should help victims of domestic violence often further alienate them. Trans women can be made to acutely feel the "indifference of powerful institutions to women's suffering" when organizations like the police and battered women's shelters contribute to their isolation by refusing to offer them adequate services. Finally, as described in Stark's third element, the structural inequalities caused by transphobia, such as restricted access to housing and insured employment, enhance an abuser's ability to coercively control hir partner. * * *

A. Legal Genders and Gender Markers on Identity Documents

The legal landscape and current law governing the "legal gender" of trans people contribute to trans women's difficulties in safely leaving their abusers. A great number of sometimes-conflicting rules govern legal gender recognition. * * * Each administrative body responsible for issuing identification documents sets its own rules regarding what documentation and physical alterations are required for an individual to change the gender marker. * * * Not having identification that matches one's gender expression can have a significant impact on one's daily life. The NTDS found that "[f]orty percent (40%) of those who presented ID (when it was required in the ordinary course of life) that did not match their gender identity/expression reported being harassed and 3% reported being attacked or assaulted." * * *

B. Employment

* * * Trans people consistently face harassment and discrimination in the workplace. Forty-seven percent of respondents to the NTDS reported adverse job consequences (defined as "being fired, not hired, or denied a promotion") due to their trans status. The unemployment rates for black and Latino trans people were between two and four times the national average. However, courts have not been particularly helpful in remedying this inequality. * * *

C. Housing

A trans woman's ability to leave her abuser may also be constricted by limited housing options. Trans women may experience housing discrimination in a number of ways. * * * Once trans people secure housing, domestic violence can cause them to be evicted, especially if an abusive partner outs them to a transphobic landlord. * * * Due to the hypersexualization and perception of trans women, especially trans women of color, the sexual harassment of trans women in public housing is a very plausible, though perhaps under-examined, concern. Recent changes to the HUD policies guaranteeing equal access to housing regardless of gender identity may provide some protections to trans women in public housing. * * *

IV. AN UPHILL BATTLE: THE TRANSPHOBIA OF SERVICE PROVIDERS

The most dangerous point in an abusive relationship comes when the victim attempts to leave hir abuser. * * * To leave, the victim must be very courageous and must also have some form of safety net. For trans women, however, as discussed above, the safety net may range from inadequate to nonexistent. Rampant discrimination in the services that are supposed to assist an abused person in getting away from hir abuser—medical services, law enforcement, shelters, and the courts—may actually cause a trans woman to stay with her abuser rather than expose herself to their transphobia. Indeed, a trans woman may prefer "the devil she knows." * * *

B. Law Enforcement

* * * Trans people of color may be especially slow to involve the police in their personal affairs because they may not wish to give the police a reason to enter their community. Indeed, past experience with and fear of the police may cause trans women to identify more with their abusers than with the state. As one study has stated, "[s]ome [LGBT people] felt that, even though they needed help to escape abuse, they did not want to subject their partner to potentially discriminatory or dangerous interactions with police." * * * Police responding to domestic violence calls from trans women

also have been known to profile them as sex workers and refuse to help. * * * Therefore, past experiences with the police may cause a trans woman not to call them for fear of additional mistreatment. * * * Further compounding this issue, the police may decide to characterize the situation as mutual combat. * * * The police may similarly believe that a larger person is automatically the abuser since she should be able to defend herself against a physical assault. But, as The Network/La Red's literature points out, "Partner abuse is about control, not size or strength. There is no way to tell by looking at a couple who is the abuser and who is being abused." A focus on size ignores the fact that domestic violence is about control and not just about physical dominance.

* * * [A]n immigrant trans woman may hesitate to call the police given the current close ties between U.S. Immigration and Customs Enforcement (ICE) and the police. Involving the police in her affairs could put her immigration status at risk. She may summon the police for assistance, only to find herself put into removal proceedings. Furthermore, if she calls the police and is not an English speaker, she may even find herself in a situation where the police use her abuser as a translator! * * *

"Pat down searches rarely seem to be about weapons or safety and more often seem to be about 'gender checks.' They usually involve the officer groping a person's groin and/or breasts in an effort to 'figure things out.' Some male cops are curious or fascinated about transgender women." This interest with trans women may not stop at pat downs, and, as discussed above, can devolve into physical violence or a sexual assault. If a trans woman is incarcerated, she will most likely be placed in a sex-segregated facility according to her assigned gender at birth. * * *

C. No Shelter from the Storm: Domestic Violence Shelters

* * * Domestic violence shelters do vital work, providing a place of refuge for women and children fleeing abusive situations. Their policies on access for trans women are varied. * * * The reasons given for policies that exclude trans women typically center on the safety and comfort of the other residents, which means that their exclusion is for the comfort of cisgender women. * * * First, * * * there is a concern that transgender women who have not had genital surgery pose a threat to the women in the shelter and might physically or sexually assault a resident. Second, shelters claim that if they were to admit trans women, the shelters could be faced with situations in which male abusers dress as women in order to access the facility. Both these arguments are based on the belief that trans women are not "real women." * * * In a study done in Massachusetts, housing options available to LGBT survivors were often limited to short-term stays in the homes of shelter workers or in hotels, rather than the ninety-day accommodations available to cisgender heterosexual survivors. * * *

Those facilities that have integrated trans women do not report any assaults by or issues with trans residents that are different from those they report that involve cisgender residents. In fact, there is a higher risk that a cisgender resident will attack a trans resident. * * * The arguments dealing with the fear that trans women may threaten cisgender women's safety are "eerily similar" to the arguments that used to be made to exclude lesbians from shelters. There have been no reported incidents of men dressing as women to gain access to a shelter and track down their victim. However, there have been cases of a lesbian abuser pretending to be a victim to gain access. This dichotomy shows that the fear of men trying to pass is just an excuse, a belief that "privileges male attributes over female ones." * * * Trans women may have been raised as males, but many of them have never felt like males. * * *

D. The Courts

Bigotry in the legal system, both as experienced and as feared, can impact a trans woman's ability to leave her abuser. * * * Access to both civil orders of protection and child custody determinations can involve the courts making judgments about a trans woman's "legal gender." These determinations can provide a place in which a court's transphobia will have an impact on a trans woman's ability to leave her abuser. As some attorneys point out, "transgender people 'continue to experience more overt and unabashed bigotry within the legal system than almost any other group' and are routinely denied basic humanity when referred to by judges as 'it.' " * * * Furthermore, abusers can, in general, use threats regarding child custody as a way of controlling their partners. * * * Sometimes, abusers have engaged their partners in protracted custody battles as a way of continuing their control over a partner who has left. * * * Although courts have generally shied away from ruling that a person's trans status is a per se reason to deny custody, trans status has been a negative factor in custody determinations. Thirteen percent of respondents to the NTDS survey whose relationship with their children was ended stated that their relationships with their children had been ended or curtailed due to their trans or gender nonconforming identity. * * *

CONCLUSION

* * * The scheduled 2011 reauthorization [of VAWA] was stymied owing to several controversial changes, one of which was the addition to S. 1925 of "gender identity" and "sexual orientation" to the nondiscrimination clause. This is the first time that proposed changes have resulted in voting along party lines. * * * *[Editor's Note: The federal Office on Violence Against Women (OVW), part of the U.S. Department of Justice, posted on its website April 19, 2014: "And for the first time in a federal funding statute, VAWA 2013 explicitly bars discrimination based on actual or perceived gender identity or sexual orientation." OVW and the DOJ have issued various guidance documents to ensure grantees can operate sex-segregated services without violating the law by discriminating against trans victims.]* Regardless of their legal gender, trans women, and their relationships,

have always been covered by VAWA. * * * Although titled the "Violence Against Women Act," the law's actual language is primarily gender neutral, referring to intimate partner violence. Therefore, whether or not the state recognizes a trans woman's gender as female, she should still have been able to claim protection under VAWA. * * *

[Editor's Notes: 1. Currently, most states and municipalities do not have any explicit protections for trans people who are discriminated against in employment, housing, and other areas of life; and there is no uniform federal law on the matter, as federal courts are split on whether laws like Title VII of the 1964 Civil Rights Act banning employment discrimination "because of sex" cover gender identity. (This also applies, to some extent, to sexual orientation discrimination.) The author notes that passage of the Employment Non-Discrimination Act, which has been introduced in almost every Congress since 1994 and which explicitly includes gender identity and sexual orientation as protected characteristics—among other laws—would help remedy these issues.

2. In LGBTQ Intimate Partner Violence: Lessons for Policy, Practice, and Research *(UC Press, 2017), Adam M. Messinger "offers a thematically organized and engaging overview of nearly every English-language journal article, book chapter, and book on LGBTQ IPV, supplemented by a number of research reports from well-known organizations." (p. x.) Messinger does a fine job covering LGBTQ IPV, as well as DV generally and LGBTQ rights generally, in the U.S. and around the world, and, importantly, takes the time in his explanations to differentiate between the various combinations of sexual and gender minorities within the LGBTQ populations—including how other intersecting identities like class, race, and disability, play a role in the prevalence of, and response to, LGBTQ IPV.]*

RISHITA APSANI, ARE WOMEN'S SPACES TRANSGENDER SPACES? SINGLE-SEX DOMESTIC VIOLENCE SHELTERS, TRANSGENDER INCLUSION, AND THE EQUAL PROTECTION CLAUSE

106 Calif. L. Rev. 1689 (2018)
(footnotes omitted)

INTRODUCTION

"I once worked with a woman who was transgender, and whose partner had almost killed her. She had finally made the decision to leave the relationship and she went to a shelter in Massachusetts. When she got there, the counsellors were confused about her gender even though she had previously explained to them that she was transgender, and what that meant. The shelter staff asked her a set of intensive and grueling questions about her body including, 'What is between your legs?'. . .after this humiliating treatment, they told her that she could not be housed there because they decided that she was really a man. After being denied shelter, this woman went back to her batterer because she had no family, no friends and nowhere else to go."—Emily Pitt, Director, Fenway Community Health's Violence Recovery Program

Feminist movements from the turn of the twentieth century have made essential reforms to domestic violence law and policy. But women of color and lesbian, gay, bisexual, and transgender ("LGBT") activists have long called attention to the limitations of a movement that primarily focused on the needs of cisgender, white women. These critics advocate for a more intersectional feminist approach to IPV that takes into account the multiple sources of oppression faced by marginalized groups—including transgender women. This tension reverberates in debates on how best to structure anti-violence shelters that house those seeking reprieve from abusive relationships. Domestic violence shelters are often marked "women-only" with the goal of creating spaces for female empowerment, wherein women learn feminist principles of liberation, engage with theories of male domination, and find a "sisterhood" of support by forging healthy female relationships. However, as a result, shelters frequently deny transgender women access because shelter staff perceive them to be a threat to survivor comfort and to be disruptive to shelters' female-empowerment model. Consequently, though transgender women face similar gender-based oppression and a relatively higher risk of violence as compared to cisgender women, shelters commonly deny transgender women equal protection.

Federal agency policy and some state statutory provisions address this discrimination, but the Equal Protection Clause of the Fourteenth Amendment also presents a key opportunity to break down barriers to transgender inclusion. This Note conceptualizes how an equal protection challenge to women-only shelters might proceed in federal courts. By situating transgender identity within the Supreme Court's broader equal protection jurisprudence, it outlines three ways that the Court could analyze a transgender equal protection challenge: as an issue of first impression, as a sex-based discrimination claim, or as a sexual orientation claim. . .

II. DOMESTIC VIOLENCE SHELTERS & THE CASE FOR TRANSGENDER INCLUSION

IPV shelters are more than just temporary housing spaces. The typical shelter allows women to stay for thirty to sixty days, conceals their locations from abusive partners, and provides counselling and referrals that respond to women's help-seeking behaviors. Most shelters offer services that include accompanying a survivor to a hospital, helping her find a new apartment, applying for welfare, or getting a civil protection order. Because IPV shelters represent such an integral part of IPV services, it is especially important for transgender litigants to gain constitutional protections that ensure more equitable access to these spaces. . . .

CONCLUSION

This Note has exposed the limits of second wave feminist approaches to domestic violence law and policy making. Reviewing the tensions between dominance feminism and intersectional feminism, it has argued that earlier strains of the domestic violence movement, informed by dominance feminism, unfortunately tend to lapse into a gender essentialism that marginalizes women at the intersections of multiple oppressions. In particular, earlier strains of the domestic violence movement regarded IPV as an outgrowth of male dominance over biological females who had been socially trained to be helpless. Those earlier strains of the movement used this vision of the unequal male-female dyad to inform their interventions, and they largely overlooked the needs of LGBT populations. To overcome this lapse into gender essentialism, the domestic violence movement must decenter the cisgender woman and instead structure interventions to focus on the diverse needs of each survivor. Reforming domestic violence law and policy in a manner inclusive of transgender women represents a key step forward in this regard.

The Note has also analyzed the rationales that scholars and some domestic violence service providers have used to exclude transgender women from women-only domestic violence shelters. The concerns that emerge closely parallel those used in legal battles to exclude cisgender men from domestic violence shelters: first, that transgender women have "male privilege" that disrupts the feminist education offered at most shelters; second, that survivors will be retraumatized by having transgender women that present as male in close proximity; third, that allowing transgender women threatens survivors' safety because male batterers, posing as transgender women, will stalk and kill the survivors; fourth, that because resources are already very slim, they should not be taken away from the cisgender women in need. Although these rationales carry weight when applied to the exclusion of cisgender men, they do not hold up as justifications to exclude transgender women survivors. Many transgender women grow up presenting as female and, thus, face similar gender-based oppressions as cisgender women. Privacy and security concerns have not proven to be a problem in shelters that already include transgender women, which have successfully made reasonable alterations to accommodate survivor discomfort and fear. Finally, the gender asymmetry between cisgender men and women that justifies privileging resources for cisgender women does not carry over to the transgender women context, as transgender women face far higher rates of abuse than do cisgender women. Resource-saving rationales therefore also do withstand scrutiny. Ultimately, this analysis shows that justifications provided in favor of exclusion often rest on stereotypes of transgender survivors as inherently threatening on one hand and cisgender women as inherently vulnerable on the other. Not only do these stereotypes fail to cohere with reality, but the critical material need for shelter space among transgender women far outweighs the discomfort female survivors may feel as a result of including transgender women.

Legal and policy responses must be swift, uniform, and long lasting. In this regard, the Equal Protection Clause represents a key a tool to encourage women-exclusive, state-sponsored shelters to make reasonable accommodations to bring transgender women into their ranks. This Note has outlined three possible paths that such a claim might take. First, the Court could decide that transgender people are sufficiently unique that they constitute a category unto themselves. Under this approach, because petitioners will not likely gain suspect class status, the Court will review the exclusion of transgender women under a highly deferential rational basis review test, likely upholding the exclusion of transgender women from women-only shelters. Second, the Court could, in line with prior precedent, attempt to fit transgender people into bifurcated categories of "man" and "woman" based on biology or dominant gender expression. Within this framework, the Court would most likely strike down shelter policies excluding transgender women because transexclusionary policies rest on impermissible stereotypes of what it means to be a woman, and many reasonable gender-neutral alternatives have proven workable for domestic violence shelters. Finally, the Court could conceive of transgender people as part of the "LGBT" grouping, and consider transgender claims as it does those involving sexual orientation, that is, by invoking the "animus" principle. But the Court's conception of animus has vacillated. If it understands animus to be merely a condemnation of rank hatred, then it will uphold the transexclusionary shelter policies because domestic violence shelters are unlikely to exclude transgender women based on hatred. If, on the other hand, the Court adopts an expansive conception of animus that condemns implicit biases and structural discrimination, irrespective of the intent of those doing the excluding, the Court will likely strike down exclusionary shelters that ban transgender women. . .

CHAPTER 5

SUING BATTERERS IN TORT ACTIONS

■ ■ ■

Moving away from an overview, introduction, and examining some of the particular groups affected by domestic violence, this chapter begins the exploration of how the civil part of the legal system has dealt with domestic violence through a focus on interspousal torts.

The chapter starts with an old U.S. Supreme Court case describing the history of interspousal immunity laws and their impact on suits between victims and perpetrators of domestic violence. Then comes an article on the importance of tort claims for survivors of domestic violence, including their advantages and disadvantages, and why there are so few of these claims filed. Statutes of limitations are often a bar in domestic violence tort cases; the materials discuss how courts should handle this, including the possibility of defining domestic violence as a continuing tort.

The materials then raise the issue of joinder with divorce actions—i.e., should tort and divorce cases sometimes or always be joined, and if so, under what conditions, or should they always be separate? Two cases demonstrate the differing approaches state courts have taken on this issue.

The next article notes that the definition of "outrage" in marital relationships is inconsistently defined and based in sexist beliefs. The author proposes that violation of a restraining order should be grounds for finding that the violator has acted outrageously, the basis for a claim of intentional infliction of emotional distress.

The chapter ends with a case examining what happens when a tortfeasor in a domestic violence case attempts to discharge an award of tort damages in bankruptcy.

A. HISTORY, OVERVIEW, INTERSPOUSAL IMMUNITY

THOMPSON V. THOMPSON

218 U.S. 611 (1910)

This case presents a single question, which is involved in the construction of the statutes governing the District of Columbia. That question is, Under that statute may a wife bring an action to recover damages for an assault and battery upon her person by the husband?

The declaration of the plaintiff is in the ordinary form, and in seven counts charges divers assaults upon her person by her husband, the defendant, for which the wife seeks to recover damages in the sum of $70,000. An issue of law being made by demurrer to the defendant's pleas, the supreme court of the District of Columbia held that such action would not lie under the statute. Upon writ of error to the court of appeals of the District of Columbia, the judgment of the supreme court was affirmed.

At the common law the husband and wife were regarded as one,—the legal existence of the wife during coverture being merged in that of the husband; and, generally speaking, the wife was incapable of making contracts, of acquiring property or disposing of the same without her husband's consent. They could not enter into contracts with each other, nor were they liable for torts committed by one against the other. In pursuance of a more liberal policy in favor of the wife, statutes have been passed in many of the states looking to the relief of a married woman from the disabilities imposed upon her as a feme covert by the common law. Under these laws she has been empowered to control and dispose of her own property free from the constraint of the husband, in many instances to carry on trade and business, and to deal with third persons as though she were a single woman. The wife has further been enabled by the passage of such statutes to sue for trespass upon her rights in property, and to protect the security of her person against the wrongs and assaults of other.

It is unnecessary to review these statutes in detail. Their obvious purpose is, in some respects, to treat the wife as a feme sole, and to a large extent to alter the common-law theory of the unity of husband and wife. These statutes, passed in pursuance of the general policy of emancipation of the wife from the husband's control, differ in terms, and are to be construed with a view to effectuate the legislative purpose which led to their enactment.

It is insisted that the Code of the District of Columbia has gone so far in the direction of modifying the common-law relation of husband and wife as to give to her an action against him for torts committed by him upon her person or property. The answer to this contention depends upon a construction of § 1155 of the District of Columbia Code. That section provides:

> Sec. 1155. power of wife to trade and to sue and be sued.—Married women shall have power to engage in any business, and to contract, whether engaged in business or not, and to sue separately upon their contracts, and also to sue separately for the recovery, security, or protection of their property, and for torts committed against them, as fully and freely as if they were unmarried; contracts may also be made with them, and they may also be sued separately upon their contracts, whether made before or during marriage, and for wrongs independent of contract,

> committed by them before or during their marriage, as fully as if they were unmarried; and upon judgments recovered against them execution may be issued as if they were unmarried; nor shall any husband be liable upon any contract made by his wife in her own name and upon her own responsibility, nor for any tort committed separately by her out of his presence, without his participation or sanction: Provided, that no married woman shall have power to make any contract as surety or guarantor, or as accommodation drawer, acceptor, maker, or indorser.

In construing a statute the courts are to have in mind the old law and the change intended to be effected by the passage of the new. Reading this section, it is apparent that its purposes, among others, were to enable a married woman to engage in business and to make contracts free from the intervention or control of the husband, and to maintain actions separately for the recovery, security, and protection of her property. At the common law, with certain exceptions, not necessary to notice in this connection, the wife could not maintain an action at law except she be joined by her husband. For injuries suffered by the wife in her person or property, such as would give rise to a cause of action in favor of a feme sole, a suit could be instituted only in the joint name of herself and husband.

By this District of Columbia statute the common law was changed, and, in view of the additional rights conferred upon married women in § 1155 and other sections of the Code, she is given the right to sue separately for redress of wrongs concerning the same. That this was the purpose of the statute, when attention is given to the very question under consideration, is apparent from the consideration of its terms. Married women are authorized to sue separately for "the recovery, security, or protection of their property, and for torts committed against them as fully and freely as if they were unmarried." That is, the limitation upon her right of action imposed in the requirement of the common law that the husband should join her was removed by the statute, and she was permitted to recover separately for such torts, as freely as if she were still unmarried. The statute was not intended to give a right of action as against the husband, but to allow the wife, in her own name, to maintain actions of tort which, at common law, must be brought in the joint names of herself and husband.

This construction we think is obvious from a reading of the statute in the light of the purpose sought to be accomplished. It gives a reasonable effect to the terms used, and accomplishes, as we believe, the legislative intent, which is the primary object of all construction of statutes.

It is suggested that the liberal construction insisted for in behalf of the plaintiff in error in this case might well be given, in view of the legislative intent to provide remedies for grievous wrongs to the wife; and an instance is suggested in the wrong to a wife rendered unable to follow the avocation of a seamstress by a cruel assault which might destroy the use of hand or arm; and the justice is suggested of giving a remedy to an artist who might be maimed and suffer great pecuniary damages as the result of injuries inflicted by a brutal husband.

Apart from the consideration that the perpetration of such atrocious wrongs affords adequate grounds for relief under the statutes of divorce and alimony, this construction would, at the same time, open the doors of the courts to accusations of all sorts of one spouse against the other, and bring into public notice complaints for assault, slander, and libel, and alleged injuries to property of the one or the other, by husband against wife, or wife against husband. Whether the exercise of such jurisdiction would be promotive of the public welfare and domestic harmony is at least a debatable question. The possible evils of such legislation might well make the lawmaking power hesitate to enact it. But these and kindred considerations are addressed to the legislative, not the judicial, branch of the government. In cases like the present, interpretation of the law is the only function of the courts.

An examination of this class of legislation will show that it has gone much further in the direction of giving rights to the wife in the management and control of her separate property than it has in giving rights of action directly against the husband. In no act called to our attention has the right of the wife been carried to the extent of opening the courts to complaints of the character of the one here involved.

It must be presumed that the legislators who enacted this statute were familiar with the long-established policy of the common law, and were not unmindful of the radical changes in the policy of centuries which such legislation as is here suggested would bring about. Conceding it to be within the power of the legislature to make this alteration in the law, if it saw fit to do so, nevertheless such radical and far-reaching changes should only be wrought by language so clear and plain as to be unmistakable evidence of the legislative intention. Had it been the legislative purpose not only to permit the wife to bring suits free from her husband's participation and control, but to bring actions against him also for injuries to person or property as though they were strangers, thus emphasizing and publishing differences which otherwise might not be serious, it would have been easy to have expressed that intent in terms of irresistible clearness.

We can but regard this case as another of many attempts which have failed, to obtain by construction radical and far-reaching changes in the policy of the common law, not declared in the terms of the legislation under consideration. * * *

Nor is the wife left without remedy for such wrongs. She may resort to the criminal courts, which, it is to be presumed, will inflict punishment commensurate with the offense committed. She may sue for divorce or separation and for alimony. The court, in protecting her rights and awarding relief in such cases, may consider, and, so far as possible, redress her wrongs and protect her rights.

She may resort to the chancery court for the protection of her separate property rights. Whether the wife alone may now bring actions against the husband to protect her separate property, such as are cognizable in a suit in equity when brought through the medium of a next friend, is a question not made or decided in this case.

We do not believe it was the intention of Congress, in the enactment of the District of Columbia Code, to revolutionize the law governing the relation of husband and wife as between themselves. We think the construction we have given the statute is in harmony with its language, and is the only one consistent with its purpose.

The judgment of the Court of Appeals of the District of Columbia will be affirmed.

MR. JUSTICE HARLAN, dissenting:

This is an action by a wife against her husband to recover damages for assault and battery. The declaration contains seven counts. The first, second, and third charge assault by the husband upon the wife on three several days. The remaining counts charge assaults by him upon her on different days named,—she being at the time pregnant, as the husband then well knew.

The defendant filed two pleas,—the first that he was not guilty, the second that, at the time of the causes of action mentioned, the plaintiff and defendant were husband and wife, and living together as such.

The plaintiff demurred to the second plea, and the demurrer was overruled. She stood by the demurrer, and the action was dismissed.

The action is based upon §§ 1151 and 1155 of the Code of the District, which are as follows:

> Sec. 1151. All the property, real, personal, and mixed, belonging to a woman at the time of her marriage, and all such property which she may acquire or receive after her marriage from any person whomsoever, by purchase, gift, grant, devise, bequest, descent, in the course of distribution, by her own skill, labor, or personal exertions, or as proceeds of a judgment at law or decree in equity, or in any other manner, shall be her own property as absolutely as if she were unmarried, and shall be protected from the debts of the husband, and shall not in any way be liable for the payment thereof: Provided, That no acquisition of property passing to the wife from the husband after coverture shall be valid if the same has been made or granted to her in prejudice of the rights of his subsisting creditors.
>
> [dissent quotes Sec. 1155.] * * *

The court below held that these provisions did not authorize an action for tort committed by the husband against the wife.

In my opinion these statutory provisions, properly construed, embrace such a case as the present one. If the words used by Congress lead to such a result, and if, as suggested, that result be undesirable on grounds of public policy, it is not within the functions of the court to ward off the dangers feared or the evils threatened simply by a judicial construction that will defeat the plainly-expressed will of the legislative department. With the mere policy, expediency, or justice of legislation the courts, in our system of government, have no rightful concern. Their duty is only to declare what the law is, not what, in their judgment, it ought to be, leaving the responsibility for legislation where it exclusively belongs; that is, with the legislative department, so long as it keeps within constitutional limits. Now, there is not here, as I think, any room whatever for mere construction, so explicit are the words of Congress. Let us follow the clauses of the statute in their order. The statute enables the married woman to take, as her own, property of any kind, no matter how acquired by her, as well as the avails of her skill, labor, or personal exertions, "as absolutely as if she were unmarried." It then confers upon married women the power to engage in any business, no matter what, and to enter into contracts, whether engaged in business or not, and to sue separately upon those contracts. If the statute stopped here, there would be ground for holding that it did not authorize this suit. But the statute goes much farther. It proceeds to authorize married women "also" to sue separately for the recovery, security, or protection of their property; still more, they may sue separately "for torts committed against them, as fully and freely as if they were unmarried." No discrimination is made, in either case, between the persons charged with committing the tort. No exception is made in reference to the husband, if he happens to be the party charged with transgressing the rights conferred upon the wife by the statute. In other words, Congress, by these statutory provisions, destroys the unity of the marriage association as it had previously existed. It makes a radical change in the relations of man and wife as those relations were at common law in this District. In respect of business and property, the married woman is given absolute control; in respect of the recovery, security, and protection of her property, she may sue separately in tort, as if she were unmarried; and in respect of herself, that is, of her person, she may sue separately as fully and freely as if she were unmarried, "for torts committed against her." So the statute expressly reads. But my brethren think that, notwithstanding the destruction by the statute of the unity of the married relation, it could not have been intended to open the doors of the courts to accusations of all sorts by husband and wife against each other; and therefore they are moved to add, by construction, to the provision that married women may "sue separately. . . . for torts committed against them, as fully and freely as if they were unmarried," these words: "Provided, however, that the wife shall not be entitled, in any case, to sue her husband separately for a tort committed against her person." If the husband violently takes possession of his wife's property and withholds it from her, she may, under the statute, sue him, separately, for its recovery. But such a civil action will be one in tort. If he injures or destroys her property, she may, under the statute, sue him, separately, for damages. That action would also be one in tort. If these propositions are disputed, what becomes of the words in the statute to the effect that she may "sue separately for the recovery, security, and protection" of her property? But if they are conceded,—as I think they must be,—then Congress, under the construction now placed by the court on the statute, is put in the anomalous position of allowing a married woman to sue her husband separately, in tort, for the recovery of her property, but denying her the right or privilege to sue him separately, in tort, for damages arising from his brutal assaults upon her person. I will not assume that Congress intended to bring about any such result. I cannot believe that it intended to permit the wife to sue the husband separately, in tort, for the recovery, including damages for the detention, of her property, and at the same time deny her the right to sue him, separately, for a tort committed against her person.

I repeat that with the policy, wisdom, or justice of the legislation in question this court can have no rightful concern. It must take the law as it has been established by competent legislative authority. It cannot, in any legal sense, make law, but only declare what the law is, as established by competent authority.

My brethren feel constrained to say that the present case illustrates the attempt, often made, to effect radical changes in the common law by mere construction. On the contrary, the judgment just rendered will have, as I think, the effect to defeat the clearly expressed will of the legislature by a construction of its words that cannot be reconciled with their ordinary meaning.

I dissent from the opinion and judgment of the court, and am authorized to say that Mr. Justice Holmes and Mr. Justice Hughes concur in this dissent.

[Editor's Note: In "Judicial Patriarchy and Domestic Violence: A Challenge to the Conventional Family Privacy Narrative," 21 Wm. Mary J. Women & L. 379 (2015), historian Elizabeth Katz asks why, "given judges' patriarchal inclination to protect abused women in the divorce and criminal contexts, did the majority Justices in Thompson (and some state supreme court judges) refuse to allow interspousal tort suits?" She gives several answers: while some judges may have believed that the Married Women's Acts did not permit such tort suits, it is more likely they saw practical reasons to deny them: "The rapid increase in divorce and the perception that women were able to obtain sufficient alimony may have led judges to conclude that tort was simply a redundant remedy," and might lead to

double recovery. Furthermore, alimony gave judges ongoing power in the case, and "In the criminal context, an abused wife relied on the police and judges to physically protect her and to punish her husband for his unacceptable conduct." Both alimony and the criminal system left male judges in control, while a one-time tort award meant the wife no longer needed judicial involvement and might become financially self-sufficient. "Tort was the aggressive legal option for the New Woman. This realization may have caused the male legal elite to become severely uncomfortable. In a world in which women appeared to be radically advancing in work and politics, the male judiciary was willing to strongly and publicly address domestic violence but only in ways that left men in control."]

JESSICA DAYTON, THE INTERSECTION OF FAMILY LAW AND TORTS IN DOMESTIC ABUSE CASES

California Family Law Specialist (summer 2021, no. 3, p.1)
(footnotes omitted)

I. Introduction

Our traditional notions of the legal system have siloed areas of practice and systems of justice. The criminal justice system and the civil courts exist independently of each other and do not integrate seamlessly. Attorneys generally practice in one specialty of law and are not competent to meet all the legal needs of all clients. In the process of freeing themselves from a toxic relationship, a survivor of domestic abuse may interface with different court systems and various types of attorneys. For example, the district attorney represents the state's interest in accountability and justice; the defense attorney or victim's rights attorney represents a victim in criminal case, which one depends on whether the victim realizes they can have their own representation independent of their batterer's defense team; the family law attorney, who is likely to have little knowledge of tort remedies; and the personal injury attorney, who is often less interested in the "messy details" of the relationship as the emotions involved in domestic abuse are foreign to the typical practitioner of slip and fall injuries. If we are to support survivors in their quest for freedom and justice, we should not promote a system that requires a survivor to navigate so many different systems and maintain separate cases each for accountability, safety, dissolution, and damages, while making connections with four or more different specialty attorneys.

The tort of domestic violence is a subset of personal injury law. Indeed, it is the most personal of injuries a victim can suffer. A victim's injuries are compounded by the fact that they were committed by the person with whom they shared their life; a person they trusted; a person they loved. I have long believed domestic violence law is its own specialty area of practice. The legal needs of victims span criminal, civil, family, and all areas of practice. When attorneys have a discreet approach to their practice, the legal needs of domestic abuse victims are often overlooked. Domestic violence law is a subset of knowledge that is particular to the experiences and dynamics of power and control as it plays out in every aspect of life. Because domestic abuse victims have needs and rights that transcend all areas of practice, if you are only knowledgeable in one area, you are likely doing a disservice to your client.

While of course as attorneys we would never want to disadvantage our client, we also have the personal incentive not to violate the Rules of Professional Conduct. We have an ethical obligation to inform clients of potential causes of action. This can be found in our duties of competence, diligence, and communication. If you are representing a victim of domestic abuse in a family law case, it is incumbent upon you that you also explore, or refer for consultation, the possibilities of tort remedies.

II. Available Tort Remedies

Domestic Violence

The Statute

The tort of domestic violence requires the infliction of injury from abuse caused by a person having a relationship with the victim. "Abuse" is defined both by the [Ca.] penal code and the [Ca.] family code. The relationship requirement is as defined by the family code. From a personal injury perspective, physical abuse is easily identifiable and easily provable. Of note, the reference to Family Code section 6320 creates liability for coercive control, a pattern of behavior that unreasonably interferes with a person's free will and personal liberty. Codified examples include: isolation, deprivation of basic necessities, and controlling movements, communications or finances. The reality is that suing someone for emotional harm, without accompanying physical harm, is complicated by issues of causation and proving damages.

Legislative History

California was the first state in the country to recognize a unique tort of domestic violence. Prior to the inception of Civil Code section 1708.6, Californians would pursue domestic violence tort remedies through general assault and battery claims. Indeed, in many states, this is still the only option for victims to redress civil claims of domestic violence. Nine states still uphold interspousal tort immunity, a concept abolished by California in 1962. However, even those states that bar intentional torts between spouses during marriage, permit such actions after dissolution for tortious abuse during the marriage.

In enacting Civil Code section 1708.6 in 2002, the California legislature made the following findings:

(a) Acts of violence occurring in a domestic context are increasingly widespread.

(b) These acts merit special consideration as torts, because the elements of trust, physical proximity, and emotional intimacy necessary to domestic relationships in a healthy society makes participants in those relationships particularly vulnerable to physical attack by their partners.

(c) It is the purpose of this act to enhance the civil remedies available to victims of domestic violence in order to underscore society's condemnation of these acts, to ensure complete recovery to victims, and to impose significant financial consequences upon perpetrators.

California's enactment of Civil Code 1708.6 followed the action of the United States Supreme Court in striking down the federal civil remedy for victims of violence against women, contained in the Violence Against Women Act of 1994. Accordingly, it became the responsibility of individual states to address civil remedies for victims of domestic violence. The enactment of Civil Code 1708.6 just two years later shows California's clear intent to fulfill the promise of more complete remedies to victims of domestic violence.

[Ca.] Assembly Bill 1933 analysis states "this bill strengthens and clarifies the relief available to victims of domestic violence in two ways. First, this bill offers a clear statement of the state's policy that victims of domestic violence be able to bring suit against their abusers and recover damages. By creating a specific tort of domestic violence, this bill gives victims and the courts a clear statement of the rights and remedies of victims in these cases. Second, this bill allows an award of attorney's fees in a case based on domestic violence, a remedy not available under existing law."

Continuing Tort Doctrine

In *Pugliese v. Superior Court*, the [Ca.] Court of Appeal addressed the question of whether a domestic violence victim could recover for acts of domestic violence occurring prior to the three-year statute of limitations prescribed by [Ca.] Code of Civil Procedure section 340.15. The plaintiff in *Pugliese* alleged a course of conduct of domestic violence occurring over a fifteen-year period, the last act of which occurred within three years of the filing of the Complaint. The plaintiff sought damages for all acts of abuse, even those occurring prior to the three-year statute of limitations. The Court of Appeals agreed, holding, "we believe the Legislature adopted by statute the continuing tort theory, thus allowing domestic violence victims to recover damages for all acts of domestic violence occurring during the marriage, provided the victim proves a continuing course of abusive conduct and files suit within three years of the 'last act of domestic violence.' "

The continuing tort doctrine is applicable to domestic violence as a "continuing wrong." And "where a tort involves a continuing wrong, the statute of limitations does not begin to run until the date of the last injury or when the tortious acts cease. Defendant attempted to argue the domestic violence consisted of discrete acts. However, the Court rejected this notion recognizing, "Domestic violence is the physical, sexual, psychological, and/or emotional abuse of a victim by his or her intimate partner, with the goal of asserting and maintaining power and control over the victim. Most domestic violence victims are subjected to 'an ongoing strategy of intimidation, isolation, and control that extends to all areas of a woman's life, including sexuality; material necessities; relations with family, children, and friends; and work.' "

Sexual Battery

As described above, domestic abuse is not limited to physical violence. Many victims of domestic abuse are also experiencing sexual assault by their partners. The tort of sexual battery is available both to those who do not intimately know their assailant and those who do. California Civil Code § 1708.5 provides a cause of action for acts with intent to cause a harmful or offensive contact with the intimate parts of another, or by use of his or her intimate part, and a sexually offensive contact with that person directly or indirectly results. The statute of limitations is the latter of 10 years or from 3 years from discovery of the harm.

Gender Violence

Gender Violence encompasses acts that would constitute a criminal offense under state law that has an element of use, attempted use, or threatened use of physical force committed at least in part based on the gender of the victim, regardless of whether those acts resulted in prosecution. Gender Violence is also a physical intrusion of a sexual nature under coercive conditions. By definition, domestic abuse is also gender violence.

Sexually Transmitted Diseases

Case law is settled that an individual has a duty not to transmit a STD [Sexually Transmitted Disease] if that person knows or should know that he or she is infected. There are numerous possible causes of action for the transmission of sexually transmitted diseases. One could plead battery, intentional or negligent infliction of emotional distress, fraud by concealment, fraud by misrepresentation, or negligent misrepresentation. Depending on your theory of liability, actual or constructive knowledge is required.

These cases are challenging and carry the reality of diminished privacy, and complex issues of proof and causation. The statute of limitations [SOL] will depend on the legal theory; negligence-based theories carry a two-year SOL, whereas fraud-based theories are three years.

Human Trafficking

The reality is that some dissolution clients are in fact victims of human trafficking. They are escaping an environment of forced labor or services. The elements of a human trafficking cause of action require the deprivation or violation of the personal liberty of a person by substantially restricting their liberty. This is accomplished by force, fear, fraud, deceit, coercion, violence, duress, menace, or threat of unlawful injury, under circumstances where the victim reasonably believed that it was likely that the person making the threats would carry them out. These cases require a sharp eye and assessment of the true living situation of the parties. Where dynamics of control and coercion overrode your client's freedom, it is imperative to think if human trafficking is present.

Stalking

Stalking can be present during the relationship or after. The image of an obsessive outcast leaving a flower on the car of a stranger is not the norm. Stalking happens whenever a person engages in conduct intending to follow, alarm, or harass a plaintiff, and the plaintiff reasonably feared for their safety or suffered substantial emotional distress. This dynamic happens when abusive partners attempt to maintain control within the relationship and most commonly when the survivor client attempts to leave the relationship.

Distribution of Sexually Explicit Materials

This is more commonly referred to as "revenge porn" but please do rethink your use of that terminology. "Revenge" suggests the target of the crime has done something wrong and is therefore deserving of some retaliation. The word "porn" has consent inherent within it. This is image based sexual abuse. It is a crime and it is also a tort. The elements require: the intentional distribution by any means of the image of another without the other's consent if the defendant knew the plaintiff had a reasonable expectation that the material would remain private and the image exposes an intimate body part of the other person or shows them engaging in a sexual act.

Unlawful Recordings

There is a civil cause of action for unlawful recordings. As California is a two-party consent state, there is a cause of action for the willful eavesdropping or recording of confidential communication. Note this must not be pursuant to any exception in a restraining order or for the purposes of collecting evidence to obtain a domestic violence restraining order.

III. What is At Stake—Damages

There is no financial amount that will compensate a survivor for the abuse they have suffered. However, financial recovery can go a long way to helping a survivor rebuild their life and hold their abuser accountable. In addition to the compensation for injuries, a civil tort claim may provide a victim the forum for justice that they were denied in the criminal court. It can also provide the accountability that can be lost in the dissolution in our no-fault state.

As in any personal injury case, there are special and general damages. Some torts, addressed above, specifically also provide for statutory attorney fees. Calculation of damages is an art, not a science. Of course you can quantify medical costs, lost wages, and damaged property. The calculation of emotional and psychological damages is more nuanced. Experts can be used to value items such as future therapy or the value of the impact on relationships and ability to work. Once you have these concrete numbers, the discussion on valuation is that which a client feels can make them whole. Importantly, one must also consider the assets of the defendant. It provides little leverage for settlement to demand in excess of what a defendant has. That will only serve to motivate the defendant to litigate. Similarly, a judgment in excess of what a defendant has provides no tangible relief to a survivor. The domestic violence tort remedy is complicated by the lack of insurance coverage availability. Exclusions for intentional torts require that recovery be out of the defendant's assets rather than insurance coverage.

The act of valuing your case is one that must be done in conjunction with your client in consideration of their goals and the overall strategy of all open and potential cases.

IV. Litigating the Civil Financial Settlement Within the Existing Family Law or Restraining Order Case

It is not always necessary to bring a separate tort action when you are representing a victim of domestic abuse in their dissolution or restraining order case. The DVPA [Domestic Violence Prevention Act] provides for prevailing party fees as well as payment for costs and services. Your client's needs may be met by pursuing their damages amount within these categories.

A global settlement in a dissolution can include civil damages. The tort claim can be resolved whereby the tortfeasor spouse agrees to an unequal division of community property in compensation for their tortious actions. This has the added tax benefit to the injured spouse in that the equalization amount is part of the dissolution and thereby tax exempt as a transfer incident to divorce. Certainly knowledge of potential tort claims can stall divorce settlement too. The abusive spouse will no doubt want confirmation that a Marital Settlement Agreement includes a provision that it resolves all claims between the parties. You very well may have to file a separate tort action in order to address those claims. Be aware, agreeing to a "waiver of all claims" or "resolving all claims" without a knowing and informed waiver by the client of their tort claims is in fact not an informed waiver. Do not foreclose your client's options with an uninformed settlement.

If you are litigating a dissolution and civil case simultaneously, California Rule of Court Rule 5.2 gives the family court discretion to take jurisdiction over related matters. A dissolution proceeding may be consolidated with a civil action in certain instances. However, given the right to trial by jury in a civil case, the family law judge may require a jury trial waiver as a condition of consolidation. Or the judge would decide nonjury matters and submit the other issues to a jury.

V. CONCLUSION

When practitioners have tunnel vision about their area of practice, it is the client who is hurt. If you are not prepared to advise your client on all of their options, seek competent counsel. No attorney knowingly wants to revictimize a survivor of domestic abuse, and by foreclosing options for a survivor without their knowledge, you are depriving the survivor of agency in their process of healing and justice.

CALIFORNIA CIVIL CODE SECTION 1708.5

(as amended 2022)

THE PEOPLE OF THE STATE OF CALIFORNIA
DO ENACT AS FOLLOWS:

Section 1708.5 of the Civil Code is amended to read [*Editor's Note: the new language is in italics, and is popularly called "stealthing"*]:

(a) A person commits a sexual battery who does any of the following:

(1) Acts with the intent to cause a harmful or offensive contact with an intimate part of another, and a sexually offensive contact with that person directly or indirectly results.

(2) Acts with the intent to cause a harmful or offensive contact with another by use of the person's intimate part, and a sexually offensive contact with that person directly or indirectly results.

(3) Acts to cause an imminent apprehension of the conduct described in paragraph (1) or (2), and a sexually offensive contact with that person directly or indirectly results.

(4) Causes contact between a sexual organ, from which a condom has been removed, and the intimate part of another who did not verbally consent to the condom being removed.

(5) Causes contact between an intimate part of the person and a sexual organ of another from which the person removed a condom without verbal consent.

(b) A person who commits a sexual battery upon another is liable to that person for damages, including, but not limited to, general damages, special damages, and punitive damages.

(c) The court in an action pursuant to this section may award equitable relief, including, but not limited to, an injunction, costs, and any other relief the court deems proper.

(d) For the purposes of this section:

(1) "Intimate part" means the sexual organ, anus, groin, or buttocks of any person, or the breast of a female.

(2) "Offensive contact" means contact that offends a reasonable sense of personal dignity.

(e) The rights and remedies provided in this section are in addition to any other rights and remedies provided by law. (emphasis added)

[Editor's Note: VAWA 2022 created a new federal civil cause of action for non-consensual distribution of sexual images (often called revenge porn). Damages can be as high as $150,000 plus attorney's fees. The Department of Justice is directed to raise awareness among victim advocates about this option.

Since this behavior is also a crime, the U.S. Attorney General will develop a strategy to prevent it and cyberstalking. The FBI is directed to improve data collection regarding these crimes. VAWA 2022 also defines technology abuse, and describes how it intersects with DV, sexual assault, dating violence and stalking.]

B. DOMESTIC VIOLENCE AS A CONTINUING TORT AND NEW CAUSE OF ACTION

PUGLIESE V. SUPERIOR COURT

146 Cal.App.4th 1444 (2007)
(citations omitted)

I. INTRODUCTION

Petitioner Michele Noel Pugliese (Michele) seeks a writ directing the superior court to set aside an order granting real party Dante J. Pugliese's (Dante) in limine motion to exclude all references to acts of domestic violence alleged to have occurred three years prior to the date Michele filed her domestic violence complaint. We conclude that domestic violence litigants are entitled to seek recovery for all acts of domestic abuse occurring during the domestic relationship, so long as the litigant proves a continuing course of abusive conduct. Accordingly, we grant the writ of mandate and direct the superior court to set aside its order granting Dante's in limine motion.

II. FACTUAL AND PROCEDURAL BACKGROUND

Michele and Dante were married in January 1989. Michele filed a petition for dissolution of that marriage on April 22, 2002.[1] On April 2, 2004, Michele sued Dante for assault, battery, intentional infliction of emotional distress and violation of civil rights. Michele alleged Dante had engaged in a pattern of domestic abuse, both physical and mental, which began within a few months of the marriage. Although the physical acts allegedly ceased in April 2001, Michele claims the emotional abuse continued until April 2004. In September 2005, Dante filed a motion in limine to exclude evidence of any assaults and batteries alleged to have occurred more than three years prior to the filing of the complaint, claiming that Michele could not recover damages for acts occurring prior to that time because the statute of limitations set forth in Code of Civil Procedure section 340.15 barred such recovery. The trial court granted Dante's in limine motion, and this petition followed.

III. ISSUE

The issue presented is whether Michele is barred, pursuant to the three-year limitations period set forth in Code of Civil Procedure section 340.15, subdivision (a), from recovering damages for acts of domestic violence occurring prior to April 2001.

IV. DISCUSSION

* * * B. Standard of review

It is a question of law whether a case or a portion of a case is barred by the statute of limitations, and we are not bound by the trial court's determination and instead conduct a de novo review.

C. Michele's Civil Code section 1708.6 domestic violence claim was timely filed

Spouses are permitted to pursue appropriate civil remedies against each other, including lawsuits asserting the tort of domestic violence.

Civil Code section 1708.6, subdivision (a) provides: "A person is liable for the tort of domestic violence if the plaintiff proves both of the following elements: [¶] (1) The infliction of injury upon the plaintiff resulting from abuse, as defined in subdivision (a) of Section 13700 of the Penal Code. [¶] (2) The abuse was committed by the defendant, a person having a relationship with the plaintiff as defined in subdivision (b) of Section 13700 of the Penal Code."[2]

---

[1] It is unclear whether the parties' divorce has been finalized.

[2] Penal Code section 13700 provides in pertinent part: " 'Domestic violence' means abuse committed against an adult or a minor who is a spouse, former spouse, cohabitant, [or] former cohabitant. . . ." (Pen.Code, § 13700, subd. (b).)

The time for commencement of an action under Civil Code section 1708.6 is governed by Code of Civil Procedure section 340.15, which provides:

"(a) In any civil action for recovery of damages suffered as a result of domestic violence, the time for commencement of the action shall be the later of the following:

"(1) Within three years from the date of the last act of domestic violence by the defendant against the plaintiff.

"(2) Within three years from the date the plaintiff discovers or reasonably should have discovered that an injury or illness resulted from an act of domestic violence by the defendant against the plaintiff.

"(b) As used in this section, 'domestic violence' has the same meaning as defined in Section 6211 of the Family Code."

Family Code section 6211 defines "domestic violence" as "abuse perpetrated against . . . [a] spouse or former spouse." (Fam.Code, § 6211, subd. (a).)

"Abuse" is defined as any of the following: "(a) Intentionally or recklessly to cause or attempt to cause bodily injury. [¶] (b) Sexual assault. [¶] (c) To place a person in reasonable apprehension of imminent serious bodily injury to that person or to another. [¶] (d) To engage in any behavior that has been or could be enjoined pursuant to Section 6320."[3] (Fam.Code, § 6203.)

The rights and remedies provided in Civil Code section 1708.6 are in addition to any other rights and remedies provided by law. (Civ.Code, § 1708.6, subd. (d).) Thus, spouses and ex-spouses are entitled to allege, as did Michele, causes of action for assault, battery and intentional infliction of emotional distress.[4] When such counts are alleged, we look to the limitations period applicable to each of these causes of action to determine if they are barred by the statute of limitations. Causes of action for assault, battery and intentional infliction of emotional distress are governed by the two-year statute of limitations set forth in Code of Civil Procedure section

[3] Section 6320 permits a court to enjoin a party from "molesting, attacking, striking, stalking, threatening, sexually assaulting, battering, harassing, telephoning, including, but not limited to, annoying telephone calls as described in Section 653m of the Penal Code, destroying personal property, contacting, either directly or indirectly, by mail or otherwise, coming within a specified distance of, or disturbing the peace of the other party. . . ." (Fam.Code, § 6320.)

[4] Michele also alleged a violation of her civil rights pursuant to Civil Code sections 51.7 and 52.1, subdivision (b). A civil rights violation cause of action does not have its own limitation period, but rather depends on the nature of the underlying act upon which the claim is predicated. Assuming Michele has adequately pled a cause of action for a violation of civil rights, we conclude the three-year limitation period set forth in Code of Civil Procedure section 340.15 would apply.

335.1.[5] Michele alleges the last physical act of abuse occurred in April 2001. Thus, her assault and battery causes of action are barred by Code of Civil Procedure section 335.1. As for Michele's intentional infliction of emotional distress claim, she alleges the last act of emotional abuse occurred in April 2004, less than two years prior to the filing of the complaint. Thus, her intentional infliction of emotional distress claim was timely filed pursuant to Code of Civil Procedure section 335.1.

Although the assault and battery causes of action are barred by the applicable statute of limitations, the complaint, taken as a whole, alleges a violation of Civil Code section 1708.6. Michele claims that during the period June 1989 to April 2004, Dante shoved, pushed, kicked, hit, slapped, shook, choked and sexually abused her. She also alleges he pulled her hair, pinched and twisted her flesh, threatened to kill her, threatened her with bodily harm, confined her in the family car while driving erratically and drunkenly and infected her with sexually transmitted diseases. Clearly, Michele has alleged that Dante intentionally or recklessly caused or attempted to cause her bodily injury, sexually assaulted her, placed her in reasonable apprehension of imminent serious bodily injury and engaged in behavior that could have been enjoined pursuant to Family Code section 6320. We therefore conclude Michele has set forth a cognizable claim for domestic violence. Accordingly, the three-year limitations period set forth in section 340.15 applies.[6] (Code Civ. Proc., § 340.15.)

Because Michele alleges the last physical act of abuse occurred in April 2001 and the last act of emotional abuse occurred in April 2004, and because the complaint was filed within three years of these dates, Michelle' Civil Code section 1708.6 domestic violence claim was timely filed.

D. The plain language of Code of Civil Procedure section 340.15 entitles Michele to seek damages for acts of domestic abuse occurring prior to April 2001

Michele contends she is entitled to seek damages for acts of domestic abuse occurring beyond the three-year limitations period set forth in Code of Civil Procedure section 340.15, subdivision (a). We agree.

"The fundamental purpose of statutory construction is to ascertain the intent of the lawmakers so as to effectuate the purpose of the law." To determine the intent, the court turns first to the words, attempting to give effect to the usual, ordinary import of the language and to avoid making any language mere surplusage. In the absence of "a compelling reason for

[5] Code of Civil Procedure section 335.1 provides that "[a]n action for assault, battery, or injury to, or for the death of, an individual caused by the wrongful act or neglect of another" must be commenced within two years.

[6] Although Michele referenced Code of Civil Procedure section 340.15, she did not specifically allege a violation of Civil Code section 1708.6 within her complaint. However, the allegations of battery, assault and intentional infliction of emotional distress meet the definition of abuse set forth in Family Code section 6203.

doing otherwise," a statute of limitation is to be construed in accordance with its plain language.

Code of Civil Procedure section 335.1, the statute setting forth the limitations period for assault and battery between *nondomestic* partners, views each incident of abuse separately and the limitations period commences at the time the incident occurs. By contrast, section 340.15 provides that domestic violence lawsuits must be commenced within three years "from the date of the *last act* of domestic violence. . . ." (Code Civ. Proc., § 340.15, subd. (a)(1), italics added.) The words "last act" are superfluous if they have no meaning. By adding these words, we believe the Legislature adopted by statute the continuing tort theory, thus allowing domestic violence victims to recover damages for all acts of domestic violence occurring during the marriage, provided the victim proves a continuing course of abusive conduct and files suit within three years of the "last act of domestic violence."[7]

Dante makes little attempt to explain the Legislature's use of the words "last act," focusing instead on the purpose of statutes of limitations, which is to "prevent the resurgence of stale claims after the lapse of long periods of time as a result of which loss of papers, disappearance of witnesses, and feeble recollections make ineffectual or extremely difficult a fair presentation of the case." Dante concludes the situation at hand is precisely the sort in which statutes of limitations must be strictly enforced; otherwise he will be forced to combat evidence that has long since faded in amount, potency, reliability, and relevance.

While we recognize the difficulty a spouse or ex-spouse may have in defending against domestic violence cases, the continuing tort doctrine seems especially applicable in such cases. Generally, a limitations period begins to run upon the occurrence of the last fact essential to the cause of action. However, where a tort involves a continuing wrong, the statute of limitations does not begin to run until the date of the last injury or when the tortuous acts cease.

Dante contends that the continuing tort doctrine should not be applied to violations of Civil Code section 1708.6. He claims, in essence, that the tort of domestic violence is made up of essentially three separate torts, i.e., assault, battery and the infliction of emotional distress. According to Dante, because a victim knows she or he has been injured at the time of the assault, battery or infliction of emotional distress occurs, the victim must file suit against the abuser within two years of the act or forever lose the right to do so. However, the tort of domestic violence is more complex than Dante concedes. Domestic violence is the physical, sexual,

[7] We can envision facts which may lead a court to exclude references to prior acts of domestic violence and to bar recovery for these acts. However, here it is alleged the acts of physical violence began shortly after the marriage and continued until April 2001, without any break in the cycle of violence.

psychological, and/or emotional abuse of a victim by his or her intimate partner, with the goal of asserting and maintaining power and control over the victim. Most domestic violence victims are subjected to "an *ongoing* strategy of intimidation, isolation, and control that extends to all areas of a woman's life, including sexuality; material necessities; relations with family, children, and friends; and work." Pursuing a remedy, criminal or civil, while in such an environment defies the abuser's control, thus exposing the victim to considerable risk of violence.

We have found no California case applying the continuing tort doctrine to the tort of domestic violence. However, an Illinois case, *Feltmeier v. Feltmeier* (2003) 798 N.E.2d 75, is instructive. In that case, an ex-wife (Lynn) brought an action against her ex-husband (Robert) for intentional infliction of emotional distress, alleging that she was a battered wife and that for over a 12-year period Robert had engaged in a pattern of domestic abuse, both physical and mental in nature, which began shortly after the marriage and did not cease even after its dissolution. Robert moved to dismiss the lawsuit, asserting that portions of Lynn's claim were barred by the applicable statute of limitations, which required claims for intentional infliction of emotional distress to be filed within two years of the date of the injury. Robert claimed that each separate act of abuse triggered a new statute of limitations so that all claims occurring two years prior to the filing of the complaint were time-barred. Lynn responded that Robert's actions constituted a "continuing tort" for purposes of the statute of limitations and that her complaint, "filed within two years of the occurrence of the last such tortious act," was therefore timely. The Illinois Supreme Court agreed with Lynn, noting that "[a] continuing tort . . . does not involve tolling the statute of limitations because of delayed or continuing injuries, but instead involves viewing the defendant's conduct as a continuous whole for prescriptive purposes." The Court held: "While it is true that the conduct set forth in Lynn's complaint could be considered separate acts constituting separate offenses of, *inter alia,* assault, defamation and battery, Lynn has alleged, and we have found, that Robert's conduct *as a whole* states a cause of action for intentional infliction of emotional distress." In reaching its conclusion, the Court noted the difference between the delayed discovery rule and the continuing tort rule. "The discovery rule, like the continuing tort rule, is an equitable exception to the statute of limitations. However, under the discovery rule, a cause of action accrues, and the limitations period begins to run, when the party seeking relief knows or reasonably should know of any injury and that it was wrongfully caused. By contrast, in the case of a continuing tort, such as the one at bar, a plaintiff's cause of action accrues, and the statute of limitations begins to run, at the time the last injurious act occurs or the conduct is abated. Thus, as previously stated, a continuing tort does not involve tolling the statute of limitations because of delayed or continuing injuries, but instead involves viewing the defendant's conduct as a continuous whole for prescriptive purposes."

The conduct set forth in Michele's complaint could be considered separate offenses of assault, battery and intentional infliction of emotional distress. However, Michele has alleged continual domestic abuse over a 15-year period,[8] and that Dante's tortious conduct did not completely cease until April 2004. Accordingly, Michele's Civil Code section 1708.6 cause of action did not accrue until April 2004 and she is entitled to seek recovery of damages for acts occurring prior to that time.

E. The legislative history of Civil Code section 1708.6 supports our conclusion that the Legislature intended the tort of domestic violence to be considered a continuing wrong

A considerable portion of Dante's brief is devoted to a discussion of the legislative history of Code of Civil Procedure section 340.15. While it is clear the Legislature, in adopting the three-year limitations period, understood that victims of domestic violence need additional time within which to file suit, nothing contained in the legislative history conclusively establishes whether the Legislature intended courts to treat a Civil Code section 1708.6 tort as a continuing wrong. The legislative history of Civil Code section 1708.6 is more enlightening.

Civil Code section 1708.6 was modeled after the Violence Against Women Act of 1994 (VAWA), which provided a federal civil remedy for victims of gender-motivated violence. Subsection (b) of the VAWA stated that "[a]ll persons within the United States shall have the right to be free from crimes of violence motivated by gender. To enforce that right, subsection (c) declared: "A person . . . who commits a crime of violence motivated by gender and thus deprives another of the right declared in subsection (b) of this section shall be liable to the party injured, in an action for the recovery of compensatory and punitive damages, injunctive and declaratory relief, and such other relief as a court may deem appropriate." A " 'crime of violence motivated by gender' " was defined as "a crime of violence committed because of gender or on the basis of gender, and due, at least in part, to an animus based on the victim's gender. . . ." The term " 'crime of violence' " was defined as: "(A) an act or series of acts that would constitute a felony against the person or that would constitute a felony against property if the conduct presents a serious risk of physical injury to another, and that would come within the meaning of State or Federal offenses described in section 16 of Title 18, whether or not those acts have actually resulted in criminal charges, prosecution, or conviction and whether or not those acts were committed in the special maritime, territorial, or prison jurisdiction of the United States." The definition

[8] Dante contends that Michele has not alleged that she was a battered spouse. We are not convinced that such an allegation is required. However, liberally read, the allegations of the complaint make this claim.

included "an act or series of acts that would constitute a felony described in subparagraph (A) but for the relationship between the person who takes such action and the individual against whom such action is taken."

In 2000, the United States Supreme Court declared [this section of] the VAWA unconstitutional, holding that "Congress' effort in § 13981 to provide a federal civil remedy can be sustained neither under the Commerce Clause nor under . . . the Fourteenth Amendment." (*United States v. Morrison* (2000) 529 U.S. 598, 627.) As a result, it became the responsibility of individual states to institute civil remedies for victims of rape and domestic violence. In 2002, California enacted Civil Code section 1708.6. Because California already had statutory torts providing the sort of civil remedies referred to in *Morrison* in the areas of sexual battery (which includes rape) and stalking, Civil Code section 1708.6 focused solely on domestic violence.

In adopting Civil Code section 1708.6, our Legislature declared: "(a) Acts of violence occurring in a domestic context are increasingly widespread. [¶] (b) These acts merit special consideration as torts, because the elements of trust, physical proximity, and emotional intimacy necessary to domestic relationships in a healthy society make participants in those relationships particularly vulnerable to physical attack by their partners. [¶] (c) It is the purpose of this act to enhance the civil remedies available to victims of domestic violence in order to underscore society's condemnation of these acts, to ensure *complete* recovery to victims, and to impose significant financial consequences upon perpetrators." (italics added.)

Clearly our Legislature, like the authors of the VAWA, understood that domestic violence encompasses a series of acts, including assault, battery and intentional infliction of emotional distress, and that when these acts are coupled with an oppressive atmosphere of control, the continuing tort of domestic violence results.

The legislative history of Civil Code section 1708.6 and the plain language of Code of Civil Procedure section 340.15 convince us that damages are available to victims of domestic violence, not just for the "last act" of abuse, but for acts occurring prior to the date of the "last act." Accordingly, we conclude the trial court erred in granting Dante's in limine motion to exclude all references to acts of domestic violence alleged to have occurred three years prior to the date Michele filed her domestic violence complaint.

IV. DISPOSITION

Let a writ issue directing respondent superior court to set aside its order granting real party's in limine motion and to issue a new and different order denying the motion. The temporary stay is vacated. Petitioner is to recover the costs of this petition.

[Editor's Note: In Doe v. Damron, *70 Cal.App.5th 684 (2021), the former wife sued the former husband, who both resided in Georgia, for domestic violence, sexual battery, and gender violence in California, alleging that the husband raped, battered, and strangled her while they were traveling two times in California. She also stated that the husband had abused her physically many times in Georgia but she abandoned those allegations in the tort suit. The trial court granted the husband's motion to dismiss for lack of personal jurisdiction, and the wife appealed. The appellate court reversed and remanded, holding that the husband's actions satisfied the minimum contacts requirement under due process for California to exercise specific personal jurisdiction, and that the exercise of specific personal jurisdiction over the husband was reasonable under the due process clause. This is a significant case due to its holding that a tort such as a domestic violence assault gives rise to jurisdiction even though the tortfeasor was visiting the state only briefly. Damron was also criminally prosecuted for the same conduct.*

The appellate court stated, "Damron's actions easily satisfy the minimum contacts requirement. If a negligent car accident or dog bite suffices [as prior caselaw held], surely an assault does, too. In no way could Damron's intentional tort in California be described as a ' " 'random,' 'fortuitous,' or 'attenuated' " ' basis for jurisdiction that falls short of the minimum contacts." It is hoped that appellate courts in other states will issue similar decisions.]

C. RELATIONSHIP TO DIVORCE

BOBLITT V. BOBLITT

190 Cal.App.4th 603 (2010)
(citations omitted)

In the proceeding to dissolve the marriage between Linda A. Boblitt and Steven B. Boblitt, the family court judge considered Linda's claims that Steven had committed acts of domestic violence against her before and during the marriage (and during the dissolution proceeding) in determining whether to award Linda spousal support. (See Fam.Code, § 4320, subd. (i).) Subsequently, in this tort action for damages based on Steven's alleged domestic violence against Linda (see Civ.Code, § 1708.6 [recognizing tort of domestic violence]), the trial court concluded Steven was entitled to judgment on the pleadings because the judgment in the dissolution proceeding (which was then on appeal) precluded Linda from further litigating the domestic violence issues under the doctrines of *res judicata* (claim preclusion) and *collateral estoppel* (issue preclusion).

We conclude the trial court erred in granting Steven's motion for judgment on the pleadings for two reasons. First, a judgment that is on appeal is not "final" for purposes of applying the doctrines of claim and issue preclusion. Second, a request for spousal support in a marital dissolution proceeding is not based on the same primary right as a tort action based on domestic violence and therefore a party is not necessarily precluded from seeking damages for alleged acts of domestic violence and also asking a family law court to consider those same acts of domestic violence in awarding spousal support.

Because this tort action for domestic violence was not precluded by the judgment in the dissolution proceeding, we will reverse the judgment in this action and remand the case with instructions to the trial court to deny Steven's motion for judgment on the pleadings.

FACTUAL AND PROCEDURAL BACKGROUND

We take the following facts from Linda's first amended complaint and from documents in the dissolution proceeding that are subject to judicial notice.[2]

Linda and Steven began cohabiting in February 1983. His verbal abuse of her began that day. It later escalated to physical abuse. In December 1984, he broke her jaw. His physical and verbal abuse of her continued off and on for the next 23 years.

Meanwhile, in December 1989, the parties married. Eventually, Linda filed for dissolution of the marriage in January 2004. Even after that, however, Steven continued to verbally harass and physically abuse her, up through January 28, 2008.

In January 2007, Linda filed a statement of issues in the dissolution proceeding in which she described in some detail Steven's "long history of physical and emotional abuse" of her and asserted that her injuries from the abuse, both physical and psychological, had impaired her ability to work.

Just three days later, Linda commenced this action by filing a complaint for damages against Steven, alleging a cause of action for domestic violence and assault and battery, a cause of action for breach of fiduciary obligations, and causes of action for negligent and intentional infliction of emotional distress. In March 2008, Linda filed her first amended complaint in the action; it contained the same causes of action as the original complaint.

In April 2008, a judgment on reserved issues was entered in the dissolution proceeding. In the statement of decision supporting that judgment, the family court judge (Judge James Mize) stated that "[i]n ordering spousal support" he had "considered all of the circumstances set forth in Family Code [section] 4320," which include "[d]ocumented evidence

[2] " ' "A motion for judgment on the pleadings performs the same function as a general demurrer, and hence attacks only defects disclosed on the face of the pleadings or by matters that can be judicially noticed." ' Accordingly, '[w]e accept as true the complaint's factual allegations and give them a liberal construction.' "

of any history of domestic violence, as defined in Section 6211, between the parties, including, but not limited to, consideration of emotional distress resulting from domestic violence perpetrated against the supported party by the supporting party, and consideration of any history of violence against the supporting party by the supported party."

Judge Mize also included a separate section in the statement of decision entitled "DOMESTIC VIOLENCE AND CREDIBILITY OF THE PARTIES," in which he described that "[o]ne of the principal questions at trial for the Court was the determination of whether there had been domestic violence and whether descriptions of domestic violence were truthful." The judge asserted that Linda "was permitted to testify as to every allegation of domestic violence up to the date of trial," which occurred in July 2007. It is not clear, however, whether, or to what extent, Judge Mize found domestic violence. He stated that some of Linda's "allegations of physical domestic violence . . . were simply not credible." In particular, he concluded that Linda's "allegations that she was sexually assaulted by [Steven] are simply unbelievable." But he also noted that Steven's "behavior during the marriage and post-separation could be described as intimidating" and that Steven "did and said some things that he should not be proud of or that were not appropriate." The judge explained that, to the extent Steven's behavior interfered with Linda's business, he was remedying that behavior "by making a spousal support award for [Linda] in the amount of $2,000.00 for eight months," with the reduction to zero at the end of that period conditioned on the parties having no contact with each other in the interim. Judge Mize asserted that Linda had "requested repayment for past medical bills, future medical bills, counseling and alleged pain and suffering," but he found "[n]o award to [Linda] other than the support ordered here is appropriate."

In July 2008, after an unsuccessful new trial motion, Linda appealed the judgment in the dissolution proceeding.[3]

In late November or early December 2008, Steven moved for judgment on the pleadings in this action, asserting that "each and every claim (cause of action) alleged in the Amended Complaint w[as] or could have been tried in the [dissolution proceeding,] thus barring relitigation of the claims herein." As to the allegations of physical and verbal abuse, Steven asserted that the court in the dissolution proceeding "consider[ed] domestic violence in the context of seeking relief by way of spousal support." He also noted that the court in the dissolution proceeding had rejected Linda's request for "repayment for past medical bills, future medical bills, counseling and alleged pain and suffering."[4]

---

[3] On our own motion, we take judicial notice of Linda's appeal in the dissolution proceeding.

[4] In moving for judgment on the pleadings, Steven argued with respect to Linda's cause of action for breach of fiduciary obligations that Linda was seeking "relief based upon orders, facts, and the judgment from the [dissolution proceeding]." In granting Steven's motion, the trial court observed that "the same facts [involved in Linda's cause of action for breach of fiduciary

In opposing the motion, Linda argued that the judgment in the dissolution proceeding was "not a final judgment . . . on the merits," noting that the judgment was on appeal. She also argued her domestic violence cause of action was "not tried in the dissolution action."

The trial court (Judge Michael Virga) granted Steven's motion without leave to amend "on the grounds of *res judicata* or *collateral estoppel*,"[5] concluding Linda either raised, or could have raised, all of her claims against Steven in the dissolution proceeding. From the resulting judgment of dismissal, Linda timely appealed.

DISCUSSION

On appeal, Linda contends the trial court erred in granting Steven's motion for judgment on the pleadings because the judgment in the dissolution proceeding was not final and "[t]he dissolution proceeding did not encompass [Linda's] spousal abuse injury claims." We agree on both points.

I. Waiver

First, however, we pause to address Steven's claim that Linda "has waived all of the arguments now presented to this Court as a result of not raising them before the trial court."

Steven acknowledges that Linda asserted in her papers in the trial court that the judgment in the dissolution proceeding was not final, but he claims she provided "no analysis as to why this might be important [and] no citation to any case that describes what a final judgment is." As to Linda's other argument, Steven contends it "appears nowhere in the underlying law suit. It simply cannot be found."

To the extent Steven complains that Linda raised one of her arguments in the trial court but did not support it with analysis or citation

---

obligations] were argued in the [dissolution] action" and "Judge Mize addressed all these issues in his Statement of Decision and judgment."

On appeal, Linda offers no argument relating to the trial court's ruling on her cause of action for breach of fiduciary obligations. Accordingly, our decision does not address that cause of action.

Linda's cause of action for negligent infliction of emotional distress was coextensive with her cause of action for breach of fiduciary obligations because it was based on "economic actions [Steven allegedly took] during the course of the parties' dissolution proceeding, many of which [we]re identified in the [cause of action for breach of fiduciary obligations]." In turn, Linda's cause of action for intentional infliction of emotional distress was coextensive with her cause of action for domestic violence and assault and battery because it was based on "[t]he intentional actions of [Steven]" that were alleged in the other causes of action.

Because Linda offers no argument on appeal specifically relating to her cause of action for negligent infliction of emotional distress and because that cause of action was based on the same allegations as her cause of action for breach of fiduciary obligations, which we do not address, we also do not address the cause of action for negligent infliction of emotional distress.

As for Linda's cause of action for intentional infliction of emotional distress, to the extent that cause of action was premised on the same allegations as her cause of action for domestic violence, our discussion regarding the latter cause of action applies with equal force to the former.

5 Mistakenly, the court ruled it was "sustain[ing]" Steven's "demurrer."

to authority, a similar complaint could be levied at Steven in this court, because while he asserts waiver based on Linda's alleged failure to raise in the trial court the arguments she now makes, he does not cite any case or other authority regarding the doctrine of waiver or supporting his assertion that a finding of waiver would be appropriate here. These omissions would justify us treating Steven's waiver argument as waived because " '[e]very brief should contain a legal argument with citation of authorities on the points made. If none is furnished on a particular point, the court may treat it as waived, and pass it without consideration.' " " 'Contentions supported neither by argument nor by citation of authority are deemed to be without foundation, and to have been abandoned.' "

Despite the foregoing, we elect to consider all of the arguments before us, and doing so we find no merit in Steven's waiver argument. "[E]ven assuming the arguments [Linda now makes] were not tendered in the trial court, they present questions of law that do not turn on disputed facts," and we may thus consider them. * * *

IV. The Dissolution Proceeding Did Not Encompass Linda's Cause Of Action For Domestic Violence

Rather than rely on the lack of finality of the dissolution proceeding alone to reverse the judgment of dismissal—given that the judgment in that proceeding may soon be final and this issue could arise again—we also address Linda's second argument, which is that the dissolution proceeding did not encompass her domestic abuse claims against Steven. Again, we agree.

" '*Res judicata*' describes the preclusive effect of a final judgment on the merits. *Res judicata*, or claim preclusion, prevents relitigation of the same cause of action in a second suit between the same parties or parties in privity with them. *Collateral estoppel*, or issue preclusion, 'precludes relitigation of issues argued and decided in prior proceedings.' Under the doctrine of *res judicata*, if a plaintiff prevails in an action, the cause is merged into the judgment and may not be asserted in a subsequent lawsuit; a judgment for the defendant serves as a bar to further litigation of the same cause of action."

"For purposes of *res judicata*, California applies the primary right theory to define cause of action as: (1) a primary right possessed by the plaintiff, (2) a corresponding duty imposed upon the defendant, and (3) a wrong done by the defendant which is a breach of such primary right and duty. Thus, a single cause of action is based on the harm suffered, rather than on the particular legal theory asserted or relief sought by the plaintiff."

In the trial court, Steven argued that Linda's cause of action for domestic violence was premised on the breach of her primary right "to be free from domestic violence, assault and battery," and "this primary right ha[d] already been litigated" in the dissolution proceeding. According to Steven, "It is of no moment what new or different legal theories or relief are sought. The 'primary right' is the same in both actions."

We have found little California case law that is helpful on the question of the claim preclusive effect of a judgment in a marital dissolution proceeding in a later tort action, but *Nicholson v. Fazeli* (2003) 113 Cal.App.4th 1091, 6 Cal.Rptr.3d 881 turns out to rest on reasoning that is persuasive here.

In *Nicholson,* the appellate court confronted (among other things) whether a "wife's malicious prosecution action [was] precluded by the family court's prior ruling on her motion for attorney's fees and costs" in her marital dissolution proceeding. The husband's trust had been joined as a party in the dissolution proceeding, and the wife had "filed a complaint against the Trust . . . seeking declaratory relief and imposition of a constructive trust" relating to certain property. A "court order temporarily partially removed [the husband] as trustee of the Trust and replaced him with his sons . . . as trustees *ad litem* for the sole purpose of defending the Trust against [the wife]'s complaint. . . . [An] attorney for [the sons] filed a cross-complaint in the dissolution action against [the wife] and [the husband] seeking possession of [various property] alleged to be Trust property in [the wife]'s possession." Ultimately, "the Trust voluntarily dismissed its cross-complaint without prejudice." [citation omitted] The wife then "filed a motion in the dissolution action seeking attorney's fees and costs under Family Code sections 271 and 2030 from [the husband and his sons] and the Trust," "assert[ing] that [the husband and his sons], the Trust and [the attorney] had filed and prosecuted a frivolous cross-complaint out of spite." "[T]he judge in the dissolution action awarded [the wife] $50,000 in attorney's fees and costs under Family Code sections 271 and 2030 against [the husband] and the Trust. The judge denied her request that [the sons] should be ordered to pay her fees and costs."

The wife then "filed a malicious prosecution action against [the husband], [his sons] and [the attorney]," "alleg[ing] that the cross-complaint filed by [the attorney] on behalf of [the sons] against her and [the husband] had been procured by [the husband] and that they lacked probable cause for their allegations in the cross-complaint." The trial court ultimately granted the defendants' motion for judgment on the pleadings without leave to amend.

On the wife's appeal, the appellate court ultimately turned to the defendants' "claim that the *res judicata* effect of the family court's ruling on [the wife]'s request for attorney's fees and costs in the family law proceedings preclude[d] her from bringing an action for malicious prosecution." Noting the "primary right" theory used in California to define a cause of action, the appellate court concluded as follows:

"Clearly the primary right intended to be vindicated by Family Code sections 271 and 2030 is the right of a party to a family law proceeding to an adequate opportunity to litigate, notwithstanding a disparity in the parties' income and assets. Indeed, [the wife] brought her motion while the dissolution action was still ongoing, and her need to litigate the dissolution issues continued to require her to pay for attorney's fees and costs. A malicious prosecution action, on the other hand, is brought to vindicate one's right to be free from malicious and unmeritorious litigation. The corresponding duties are also distinct. A party to a dissolution action has a duty, under Family Code section 2030, to provide funds for the party's adversary's litigation costs where the adversary's need and party's means justify such a provision. The duty imposed by Family Code section 271 requires a party to a dissolution action to be cooperative and work toward settlement of the litigation on pain of being required to share the party's adversary's litigation costs. The duty involved in a malicious prosecution action, on the other hand, is the obligation to refrain from maintaining a malicious and unmerited lawsuit. [¶] As both the primary rights and corresponding duties are different, [the wife]'s malicious prosecution action was not barred by the claim preclusion aspect of res judicata."

We find a similar reasoning persuasive here. A tort action like the present one is based on "the primary right to be free from personal injury" (no matter how many different tort theories may be alleged). "It is clearly established that '. . . there is but one cause of action for one personal injury [which is incurred] by reason of one wrongful act.' " There is no sound basis, however, for concluding that a claim for spousal support in a marital dissolution proceeding is also based on "the primary right to be free from personal injury," even if one of the circumstances the family court considers in adjudicating that claim is domestic violence between the parties.

The Family Code recognizes that a person has a right to spousal support from his or her former spouse under certain circumstances. Specifically, subdivision (a) of Family Code section 4330 provides that "[i]n a judgment of dissolution of marriage or legal separation of the parties, the court may order a party to pay for the support of the other party an amount, for a period of time, that the court determines is just and reasonable, based on the standard of living established during the marriage, taking into consideration the circumstances as provided in Chapter 2 (commencing with Section 4320)." One of the many circumstances set forth in Family Code section 4320 is "[d]ocumented evidence of any history of domestic violence . . . between the parties."

In our view, this provision, which requires a family court to consider evidence of domestic violence in determining whether an award of spousal support is appropriate, and if so, how much support is just and reasonable, does not seek to vindicate the primary right to be free from personal injury, as a tort action for domestic violence does. Rather, subdivision (i) of Family

Code section 4320 is just one of many provisions that exist to vindicate the primary right of a party in a marital dissolution (or legal separation) proceeding to obtain spousal support from the other party if the circumstances justify such support.

Because the same primary right does not underlie a request for spousal support in a marital dissolution proceeding and a tort action for damages, the doctrine of claim preclusion does not preclude a person from offering evidence of domestic violence in connection with a request for spousal support in a dissolution proceeding, then suing for damages for domestic violence, or vice versa. Accordingly, a judgment in a dissolution proceeding where claims of domestic violence were (or could have been) litigated with relation to a claim for spousal support does not preclude a later tort action for domestic violence.

This conclusion is not altered by the fact that in the dissolution proceeding Linda may have (as Judge Mize stated) "requested repayment for past medical bills, future medical bills, counseling and alleged pain and suffering," which Judge Mize declined to award her. "Given finite family law jurisdiction, a tort action claiming damages cannot be joined with or pleaded in a dissolution proceeding." Thus, Judge Mize had no power in the dissolution proceeding to award Linda damages for her "past medical bills, future medical bills, counseling and alleged pain and suffering," even if she did request them. And because Judge Mize had no power to award damages, his refusal to do so has no preclusive effect.

Of course, a judgment in a dissolution proceeding where claims of domestic violence were, in fact, litigated still may have preclusive effect under the doctrine of *issue* preclusion, which " 'precludes relitigation of issues argued and decided in prior proceedings' " even if it does not have preclusive effect under the doctrine of *claim* preclusion. But here, the doctrine of issue preclusion did not justify judgment on the pleadings in favor of Steven. If there had been a final judgment in the dissolution proceeding when Steven moved for judgment on the pleadings, and if Steven had shown that all of the allegations of domestic violence on which Linda's current tort action is based were, in fact, litigated and decided against her in the dissolution proceeding, leaving nothing new for decision in this case, then it might have been proper to grant his motion. As it was, however, there *was* no final judgment in the dissolution proceeding when Steven moved for judgment on the pleadings. Moreover, Steven did not carry his burden [citation omitted] of showing that the parties litigated in the dissolution proceeding all of the allegations of domestic violence Linda seeks to raise in this case, or that Judge Mize resolved all of those allegations against her. Without the actual evidence introduced in the dissolution proceeding, which Steven did not put before the trial court or this court, Judge Mize's statement that Linda "was permitted to testify as to every allegation of domestic violence up to the date of trial" in July 2007 does not establish which incidents of domestic violence actually were litigated in the dissolution proceeding. Further, Judge Mize's statement of decision was not specific on whether he found domestic violence, or which alleged incidents of domestic violence he found were not proven because Linda was "not credible," as Judge Mize referred only generally to "[o]ther allegations of physical domestic violence." Under these circumstances, the doctrine of issue preclusion cannot support the judgment on the pleadings in favor of Steven.

Because the judgment in the dissolution proceeding did not preclude Linda from pursuing her tort action for domestic violence against Steven (or her cause of action for intentional infliction of emotional distress, to the extent that cause of action was based on the same allegations as the domestic violence cause of action), the trial court erred in granting Steven's motion for judgment on the pleadings.

DISPOSITION

The judgment of dismissal is reversed, and the case is remanded to the trial court with directions to vacate the order granting the motion for judgment on the pleadings and enter a new order denying that motion. Linda shall recover her costs on appeal.

[Editor's Note: California is a no-fault divorce state, while the next case is from New York, a state where at the time of the decision one had to prove fault to obtain a divorce.]

XIAO YANG CHEN V. IAN IRA FISCHER

6 N.Y.3d 94 (2005)
(citations and some footnotes omitted)

OPINION OF THE COURT

Plaintiff Xiao Yang Chen and defendant Ian Ira Fischer were married on March 11, 2001. Shortly thereafter, Fischer commenced an action for divorce on the ground of cruel and inhuman treatment. Chen counterclaimed for divorce—also alleging cruel and inhuman treatment—and asserted an additional cause of action for fraudulent inducement. Specifically, as grounds for divorce, Chen alleged that on May 6, 2001, Fischer "grabbed [her] and violently slapped her across the face and ear causing [her] to suffer bruising, pain and swelling" and that he threw her on the ground and attempted to suffocate her. As a result of that incident, each party filed a family offense petition against the other in Family Court and received a temporary order of protection. The parties agreed to consolidate these petitions with the matrimonial action. At the conclusion of the matrimonial trial, they further agreed to withdraw the petitions without prejudice on the record in open court.

On October 15, 2001, prior to trial of the matrimonial action, the parties entered into a stipulation on the issue of fault. "[I]n satisfaction of the stipulation," the parties agreed to withdraw all their fault allegations—including those related to the May 6 incident—save one. After trial on the remaining issues—including equitable distribution and a fraudulent inducement cause of action—on May 8, 2002 a dual judgment of divorce was granted on the ground of cruel and inhuman treatment based on each party's sole remaining fault allegation.

Chen allegedly commenced the instant personal injury action on January 18, 2002, while the matrimonial action was pending. The complaint asserted two causes of action—one for intentional infliction of emotional distress and a second for assault and battery. As to the second cause of action, the complaint alleged that on May 6, 2001, Fischer slapped her in the face and ear, causing permanent injury, necessitating continuing medical treatment and rendering her unable to perform her usual and customary activities. Fischer answered, raising several affirmative defenses, including res judicata and various theories of estoppel.

Fischer moved to dismiss the complaint pursuant to CPLR 3211(a)(5) and Chen cross-moved to dismiss several of Fischer's affirmative defenses. Supreme Court granted Fischer's motion and denied Chen's cross motion. The court found that the allegations in Chen's personal injury action were "virtually identical" to those in her counterclaim for divorce and arose out of the same transaction or series of transactions. Thus, the court determined that the tort action was barred by res judicata.

The Appellate Division affirmed, agreeing that the action was barred because the tort claim could have been litigated with the divorce action and Chen did not expressly reserve the right to bring that claim when she withdrew her fault allegations for purposes of the stipulation. The Court extended the rule we set forth in *Boronow v. Boronow*, 71 N.Y.2d 284, 290, 525 N.Y.S.2d 179, 519 N.E.2d 1375 [1988]—that issues relating to marital property be decided with the matrimonial action—to interspousal tort actions. Specifically, the Court found that "[s]ocietal needs, logic, and the desirability of bringing spousal litigation to finality now compel us to . . . hold that an interspousal tort action seeking to recover damages for personal injuries commenced subsequent to, and separate from, an action for divorce is . . . barred by claim preclusion".[2] We granted Chen leave to appeal and now reverse.

Typically, principles of res judicata require that "once a claim is brought to a final conclusion, all other claims arising out of the same transaction or series of transactions are barred, even if based upon different theories or if seeking a different remedy." In the context of a matrimonial action, this Court has recognized that a final judgment of

[2] The Appellate Division, citing *Weicker v. Weicker*, 237 N.E.2d 876 [1968], held that "New York does not recognize a cause of action to recover damages for intentional infliction of emotional distress between spouses such as the one asserted by Chen in her first cause of action against Fischer." We agree and limit our discussion to Chen's cause of action to recover damages for assault and battery.

divorce settles the parties' rights pertaining not only to those issues that were actually litigated, but also to those that could have been litigated. The primary purposes of res judicata are grounded in public policy concerns and are intended to ensure finality, prevent vexatious litigation and promote judicial economy. However, unfairness may result if the doctrine is applied too harshly; thus "[i]n properly seeking to deny a litigant two 'days in court', courts must be careful not to deprive [the litigant] of one."

It is not always clear whether particular claims are part of the same transaction for res judicata purposes. A "pragmatic" test has been applied to make this determination—analyzing "whether the facts are related in time, space, origin, or motivation, whether they form a convenient trial unit, and whether their treatment as a unit conforms to the parties' expectation or business understanding or usage."

Applying these principles, it is apparent that personal injury tort actions and divorce actions do not constitute a convenient trial unit. The purposes behind the two are quite different. They seek different types of relief and require different types of proof. Moreover, a personal injury action is usually tried by a jury, in contrast to a matrimonial action, which is typically decided by a judge when the issue of fault is not contested. Further, personal injury attorneys are compensated by contingency fee, whereas matrimonial attorneys are prohibited from entering into fee arrangements that are contingent upon the granting of a divorce or a particular property settlement or distributive award.

This case is distinguishable from the situation presented by *Boronow*. There, we noted that title issues are "intertwined" with the dissolution of the marriage relationship and could usually "be fairly and efficiently resolved" along with the matrimonial action. Typically, however, a personal injury action is not sufficiently intertwined with the dissolution of the marriage relationship as to allow for its efficient resolution. Thus, the interspousal tort action does not form a convenient trial unit with the divorce proceeding, and it would not be within the parties' reasonable expectations that the two would be tried together.

Significant policy considerations also support this conclusion. To require joinder of interspousal personal injury claims with the matrimonial action would complicate and prolong the divorce proceeding. This would be contrary to the goal of expediting these proceedings and minimizing the emotional damage to the parties and their families. Delaying resolution of vital matters such as child support and custody or the distribution of assets to await the outcome of a personal injury action could result in extreme hardship and injustice to the families involved, especially for victims of domestic violence. In addition, parties should be encouraged to stipulate to, rather than litigate, the issue of fault.

Unlike the Appellate Division, we decline to adopt the reasoning of the New Jersey Supreme Court in *Tevis v. Tevis*, 400 A.2d 1189 [1979]. In

Tevis, the court held that under that State's "single controversy" rule, the interspousal personal injury claim should have been brought with the matrimonial action so that the issues between the parties could be decided in one proceeding in order to prevent protracted litigation. However, that view is decidedly the minority view and the New Jersey Supreme Court has recently acknowledged the potential drawbacks to litigating an interspousal tort claim prior to the divorce proceeding—noting that it "may have a negative psychological impact on parties by prolonging the uncertainty of their marital status." Indeed, other states to address the issue have reached the conclusion we reach today, emphasizing the fundamental differences between the two types of actions and noting the complications that could result from the rigid application of res judicata principles.

Here, although the personal injury claim could have been litigated with the matrimonial action—as the facts arose from the same transaction or series of events—it was not, as all of Chen's fault allegations, save one, were withdrawn by stipulation for the salutary purpose of expediting the matrimonial action. She is therefore not precluded from litigating that claim in a separate action.

Parties are free, of course, to join their interspousal tort claims with the matrimonial action and the trial court retains discretion to sever the claims in the interest of convenience, if necessary. If a separate interspousal tort action is contemplated, however, or has been commenced, the better practice would be to include a reservation of rights in the judgment of divorce. Finally, if fault allegations are actually litigated in a matrimonial action, res judicata or some form of issue preclusion would bar a subsequent action in tort based on the same allegations.

Accordingly, the order of the Appellate Division should be reversed, with costs, and the case remitted to Supreme Court for further proceedings in accordance with this opinion. * * *

D. INTENTIONAL INFLICTION OF EMOTIONAL DISTRESS

MERLE H. WEINER, DOMESTIC VIOLENCE AND THE *PER SE* STANDARD OF OUTRAGE

54 Md. L. Rev. 188–195, 213, 219–224 (1995)
(footnotes and citations omitted)

INTRODUCTION

This Article . . . inquires whether the tort of intentional infliction of emotional distress can provide a viable remedy for domestic violence victims. The Article begins by analyzing the current state of the law. The success of suits for intentional infliction of emotional distress generally turns on the plaintiff's ability to demonstrate that the defendant's conduct was "outrageous." In theory, such a showing should not be difficult for a domestic violence victim. Under traditional doctrine, there are four factors that arguably support a finding of outrageousness in cases involving domestic violence: a special relationship exists between the parties; domestic violence typically involves a pattern of harassment; an abuser usually exploits a known hypersensitivity of his victim; and a historic and gendered distinction between public and private spheres persists, which should make violence in the private sphere seem particularly outrageous.

Notwithstanding these considerations, the use of the tort by domestic violence victims is problematic under current law. Courts have applied the tort inconsistently in domestic violence cases. The meaning of the term "outrageous" is highly subjective, and allows courts to hold that domestic violence does not qualify. If fact, the ubiquity of domestic violence in our society presents a major barrier to labelling such violence "outrageous" under existing doctrine. Further, current law creates a dilemma for feminists who are reluctant to invoke various arguments that underscore the outrageousness of domestic violence—for example, traditional stereotypes of women's role in the home.

This Article argues for a *per se* standard of outrage whereby the defendant's conduct would be outrageous as a matter of law if he violated an injunction issued for a woman's protection. Such a rule would avoid the need for a subjective, ad hoc inquiry into the outrageousness of domestic violence. Upon proving that the defendant had in fact willfully violated a civil protection order, the plaintiff would establish conclusively the most important element of the tort.

By proposing a solution to the tort's current limitations for domestic violence victims, this Article hopes to provide a useful remedy to women who find the existing remedies (including the tort) inadequate. In general, the proposal may help victims shut out of the criminal justice system, either because the abuser's conduct is not criminal, or because the criminal process is ineffective for domestic violence victims. As a plaintiff can recover punitive damages for the tort of intentional infliction of emotional distress, the tort's punitive component can function like the criminal law, thereby discouraging violence. As one author wrote, "[P]unishment is a central feature of outrageousness. Defendants may be punished—stigmatized by the label 'outrageous' and made to pay damages—because of the obnoxious quality of their behavior alone. In this respect, the tort functions like the criminal law." Yet the tort of intentional infliction of emotional distress also provides benefits beyond the punitive function of the criminal law, as it allows victims to receive compensatory damages. The tort can even be useful for a woman who has obtained a civil protection order and whose abuser has committed criminal contempt or another criminal offense by violating the order. The police often do not obtain an arrest warrant if the batterer has fled, and prosecutors and judges treat private complaints for contempt "less seriously." Even if the woman prosecutes the action for criminal contempt herself, she is faced with a more difficult burden of proof than in an ordinary civil action. She must prove every element of the offense beyond a reasonable doubt, and the successful criminal contempt prosecution will not provide her with compensation for her injuries or punitive damages. Nor will she receive the additional benefit of society labeling her abuser's conduct "outrageous," although a criminal contempt proceeding undoubtedly provides some form of censure.

The proposal similarly may assist women who otherwise would lack a civil remedy. This Article is less concerned with the domestic violence victim who can establish a battery (aided, perhaps by compelling physical evidence), than with the woman who cannot, for whatever reason, establish that she has been harmed in that manner. This Article focuses on the woman who has obtained a civil protection order, i.e., injunctive relief through a domestic violence remedial scheme, and yet continues to be abused, although perhaps not in a way that is readily actionable under current tort law. For example, the proposal would be useful to the woman who is not "assaulted" because she suffers only verbal threats of future bodily harm, or a woman who misses the statute of limitations for assault or battery. The proposal even benefits the woman who could successfully prosecute a civil contempt action for the violation of her civil protection order. The tort of intentional infliction of emotional distress affords her the opportunity to obtain punitive damages unavailable in a civil contempt action. It also guarantees her compensatory damages for her emotional distress, often not recoverable in a civil contempt action. In addition, it allows her to prove her case by a preponderance of the evidence, an easier evidentiary burden than the "clear and convincing evidence" standard which exists in a civil contempt proceeding.

The proposal provides the indirect victims of domestic violence with a civil remedy as well. The impact of domestic violence on children is often ignored. Yet, as one court has acknowledged, "In a large percentage of families, children have been present when the abuse occurred. . . . Even if the child is not physically injured, he [or she] likely will suffer emotional trauma from witnessing violence between his [or her] parents." The child who witnesses an outrageous act could recover under the tort (and be benefitted by the proposal herein) because the child, a third party, is a close relative of the intended victim of the outrageous act. Similarly, other friends and relatives of the victim also may have a cause of action.

Finally, the proposal hopes to move society towards a recognition that all domestic violence is outrageous. A Comment to the Second Restatement, written over a quarter of a century ago, is still true: the law "is still in a state of development, and the ultimate limits of this tort are not yet determined." By adopting the rule that violating a restraining order is per se outrageous conduct, the legal system would validate domestic violence victims' experiences of harm, and move closer to a recognition that domestic violence is itself "outrageous" conduct.

> Law is a language of power, a particularly authoritative discourse. Law can pronounce definitively what something is or is not and how a situation or event is to be understood. . . . Legal language does more than express thoughts. It reinforces certain world views and understandings of events.

Tort law generally, and the tort of intentional infliction of emotional distress in particular, frames what interests we value as a society and prescribes how human beings should treat each other. Within the known and comfortable contours of the law, the *per se* standard of outrage for violation of a civil protection order will help mold society's thinking about domestic violence. The proposed standard takes the first step towards making all domestic violence *per se* outrageous. * * *

II. THE INADEQUACIES OF THE PRESENT APPROACH

A. Inconsistencies Exist

Courts that have addressed the tort of intentional infliction of emotional distress in the context of domestic violence have taken inconsistent approaches that have resulted in inconsistent outcomes. A brief examination of six cases illustrates the various approaches, and illustrates that there is no consensus on at least one key issue: how to analyze the element of "outrageousness" in a domestic violence situation.

* * *

B. Domestic Violence Is the Norm

As is evident from the above cases, some judges do not characterize domestic violence as outrageous conduct. Struggling with whether a defendant's conduct is "truly outrageous," judges have applied the tort to the domestic context in a manner that has been described as "somewhat controversial." The prevalence of domestic violence in our society explains, in part, the inconsistent case outcomes and presents a major obstacle for domestic violence victims who seek redress through use of the tort. Domestic violence is incredibly common, as is society's tolerance of it. Murray Straus has written, "[F]or many people a marriage license is a hitting license [and] physical violence between family members is probably as common as love and affection between family members. . . ." A survey conducted for the U.S. National Commission on the Causes and Prevention of Violence found that about twenty-five percent of the people interviewed approved of a spouse hitting the other spouse under certain circumstances. This figure is probably conservative due to underreporting. When one includes emotional abuse, domestic violence, as well as society's acceptance of it, is virtually epidemic. At least one court has acknowledged explicitly that the prevalence of domestic violence makes the tort's application problematic. The court in *Hakkila* stated, "Conduct intentionally or recklessly causing emotional distress to one's spouse is prevalent in our society. Thus, if the tort of outrage is construed loosely or broadly, claims of outrage may be tacked on in the typical marital disputes, taxing judicial resources."

It appears that male judges exemplify and perpetuate, to some extent, society's tolerance of domestic violence, and this tolerance poses an obstacle for plaintiffs seeking to establish the outrageousness of the abuse. The New Jersey Supreme Court Task Force on Women in the Courts, while examining judicial attitudes in the context of the implementation of the Prevention of Domestic Violence Act, found that judges exhibited "gender-based biases, stereotypical attitudes and . . . well intentioned ignorance." In particular, judges were insensitive to the "dependency factors present in the abusive relationship." They also often "trivialized the plight of the female as victim" because it was a "domestic problem," and considered "what [the woman] did to earn her beating." Furthermore, they failed to punish violations of domestic violence orders in situations that "clearly would not be tolerated except in the domestic context." The offending judges' conduct supports one critic's opinion that "[t]here is a general belief [among judges] that if the woman was seriously abused, then she would leave; if she stays, then the abuse did not occur." Anecdotal evidence indicates that judicial insensitivity is rampant. To make matters even worse, "[i]n the judicial system dominated by men, emotional distress claims have historically been marginalized: 'The law of torts values physical security and property more highly than emotional security and physical relationships.' " Even if a case survives pretrial adjudication, the judge may give the issue of outrage to the jury, subjecting the domestic violence victim to lay misconceptions about domestic violence. The judge may also give a jury instruction on outrage that is potentially detrimental to domestic violence victims. In sum, the male-dominated judiciary is predisposed to disfavor civil claims by victims of domestic violence: "The legal system is dominated by members of the same group engaged in the aggression. The practice is formally illegal but seldom found to be against the law. The atrocity is *de jure* illegal but *de facto* permitted."

C. The Current Doctrinal Approach Is Problematic for Feminism

Feminists face a dilemma when invoking the tort of intentional infliction of emotional distress as a remedy for domestic violence. We may find it strategically advantageous to portray the plight of victims in terms of traditional gender roles in order to emphasize the outrageousness of abusers' misconduct and enhance the chances for recovery. On the other hand, such stereotypes help to perpetuate legal and social disadvantages.

By stressing women's moral purity, for example, society can justify keeping women out of some rough-and-tumble areas of the workforce. More insidiously, "lingering stereotypes reinforce gender hierarchy by obscuring its dynamics. The result is that sex-based subordination appears natural and necessary, rather than a consequence of societal construction and a subject for societal challenge." Stereotypes also perpetuate a world view that does not comport with the reality of most women's lives. For instance, many women are single heads of households, and a vast majority of women participate in both the private and public spheres. The traditional public/private sphere dichotomy ignores this reality, and allows courts to rationalize staying out of domestic violence issues altogether. It is similarly problematic to rely on doctrine that defines domestic violence victims as hypersensitive, evoking the stigma of abnormality that the prefix "hyper" implies. Additionally, the current doctrine creates perverse incentives for a victim who wants to increase her chances for recovery: A domestic violence victim is more likely to recover under current doctrine if she experiences repeated harassment or learned helplessness, rather than leaving an abusive relationship.

III. A NEW STANDARD FOR THE DOMESTIC VIOLENCE CONTEXT: *PER SE* OUTRAGE

A. A Description of the Standard

As noted above, almost all states have statutes authorizing civil protection orders for domestic abuse, and protective orders are also available in criminal cases. This Article's modest proposal is that a willful violation of a civil protection order should constitute outrage *per se*. Whenever a woman, or the state on her behalf, has obtained a judgment for criminal contempt or a conviction for the violation of a civil protection order, that conviction or finding of contempt should suffice to establish the outrage element of the tort of intentional infliction of emotional distress. Alternatively, a woman should be able to prove to a civil court, without first having obtained an order of criminal contempt or a conviction, that the defendant willfully violated her civil protection order. This proposal would simplify the determination of outrage and reduce the plaintiff's burden in proving intent to inflict severe emotional distress, but would leave intact the elements of severe emotional distress and causation. Adoption of the *per se* standard would ensure that "the circumstances in which the tort is recognized [are] described precisely enough . . . that the social good from recognizing the tort will not be outweighed by the unseemly and invasive litigation of meritless claims."

This approach has an analogy in the tort law of negligence. The doctrine of *per se* negligence exists in most American jurisdictions and allows a court to use the violation of a safety statute to assist it in deciding one element of the tort. Negligence *per se* applies

> Where a statute or municipal ordinance imposes upon any person a specific duty for the protection or benefit of others, if he [or she] neglects to perform that duty he [or she] is liable to those for whose protection or benefit it was imposed for any injuries of the character which the statute or ordinance was designed to prevent, and which were proximately caused by such neglect.

Under a negligence *per se* rule, a defendant can be liable for certain acts or omissions that might not qualify as negligence under the ordinary reasonable person test, and the issue of reasonable conduct need not go to the jury. Negligence *per se* is a bright-line rule. It supplants the jury's subjective determination of reasonableness with an objective standard. While negligence *per se* establishes the existence of the defendant's breach of a legally cognizable duty owed to the plaintiff, it does not establish liability. The plaintiff must still show that such negligence was a proximate cause of the injury or damage sustained. * * *

E. RELATIONSHIP TO BANKRUPTCY

HERMOSILLA V. HERMOSILLA

447 B.R. 661 (D. Mass. 2011)
(citations omitted)

I. INTRODUCTION

Defendant/appellant Alex Hermosilla ("Alex") appeals the Bankruptcy Court's decision that an unliquidated personal injury claim owed to his former spouse, plaintiff/appellee Hilda Cristina Hermosilla ("Cristina"), is exempt from discharge pursuant to 11 U.S.C. § 523(a)(6).

Alex's appeal presents four main arguments: First, he argues that the Bankruptcy Court lacked subject matter jurisdiction to determine the dischargeability of his debt to Cristina for her unliquidated personal injury claims. Second, he contends that the statute of limitations on her tort claims had run before she filed. Third, he asserts that Cristina waived her tort claims in a stipulation to their divorce judgment and/or that the claims are barred by res judicata because the Probate Court took Cristina's injuries into consideration when awarding alimony. Fourth, Alex argues that it was improper for the Bankruptcy Court to grant summary judgment because there still remained genuine disputes as to material facts, namely whether Cristina was actually injured and, if so, whether Alex intended to cause those injuries.

In conjunction with Alex's appeal, Cristina has submitted three motions that are now pending. First, she moves to strike Alex's appeal on the grounds that it was not timely filed as required by Federal Rule of Bankruptcy Procedure 8009. Second, she filed a motion to dismiss Alex's appeal entirely for being procedurally defaulted and/or substantively meritless. Third, Cristina requests sanctions for damages and costs incurred defending against Alex's frivolous appeal.

I agree that Alex's appeal is procedurally barred for failure to comply with Bankruptcy Rule 8009. Accordingly, I GRANT Cristina's motions to strike Alex's brief and dismiss Alex's appeal for failure to comply with Bankruptcy Rule 8009. But while this is a procedural finding, I do have to address the merits in connection with Cristina's motion for sanctions. That motion requires that I determine whether Alex's appeal is frivolous and whether Cristina is deserving of remuneration for having to defend against it. I so find and GRANT Cristina's motion for sanctions and remand the matter to the Bankruptcy court to determine the amount.

II. FACTUAL BACKGROUND

A. The Events Prior to the Underlying Bankruptcy Proceeding

Cristina and Alex were married on May 15, 2001. On July 20, 2003, the pair got into an argument, and Alex severely beat Cristina (the "Assault"). As a result of the Assault, the government filed a criminal complaint against Alex for assault and battery with a dangerous weapon. On August 5, 2004, Alex pled sufficient facts to be found guilty; a guilty finding was entered on that same date. Alex received, among other things, a suspended sentence of nine months in the Essex County House of Correction.

On August 18, 2003, Cristina filed for a divorce from Alex in the Probate and Family Court Department of Essex Court Superior. The Probate Court entered a judgment of divorce nisi on September 15, 2005, which became final on December 14, 2005. On February 22, 2007, the Probate Court amended the September 15, 2005, judgment to include a stipulation of the parties (the "Stipulation"), which provided in relevant part that: 1) Cristina waived all future claims to alimony and spousal support; and 2) Cristina and Alex waived "any and all claims which could have been or were presented in these divorce proceedings and post divorce proceedings in [the Probate Court]."

B. The Bankruptcy Proceeding

On February 16, 2005, Alex filed a voluntary Chapter 7 bankruptcy petition. Cristina, in turn, commenced the underlying bankruptcy proceeding on May 20, 2005. Cristina's complaint contained three counts seeking a judgment that the following debts allegedly owed to her by Alex were exempted from discharge: (1) spousal support pursuant to 11 U.S.C. § 523(a)(5); (2) attorney's fees and health premiums pursuant to 11 U.S.C. § 523(a)(15); and (3) unliquidated damages owed to Cristina by Alex for "willful and malicious injury" (the Assault) pursuant to 11 U.S.C. § 523(a)(6). At the time Alex had filed for bankruptcy, Cristina had not yet filed a civil claim against him seeking damages for the injuries she sustained during the Assault. Under 11 U.S.C. § 362(c)(2), Cristina was therefore barred from filing her civil action during the pendency of Alex's bankruptcy action.

On March 11, 2010, at the direction of the Bankruptcy Court, Alex and Cristina submitted an Amended Joint Pretrial Statement, which included a statement of admitted facts requiring no proof, and which expressly acknowledged that the Amended Joint Pretrial Statement would supersede the pleadings. The Statement provided that the following facts were admitted:

> During [the Assault], Alex purposefully struck Cristina with great force, grabbed Cristina by the throat and struck her head repeatedly against the interior wall of the premises at which Alex and Cristina then resided and threw Cristina with such force onto a table that the table was caused to be broken.
>
> At the time Alex committed the physical acts referenced above, he intended to cause and did cause Cristina physical harm and pain and emotional fright and did cause Cristina such physical harm that she was caused to seek and obtain medical care for her injuries and did cause her such emotional harm that she was cased [sic] to seek and obtain care for her emotional condition.
>
> Cristina became indebted for services rendered to her for her physical and emotional injuries for which Alex is liable to Cristina together with the physical and emotional damages Alex caused Cristina.
>
> On July 21, 2003 a Criminal Complaint issued out of the Lynn District Court against Alex for assault and battery with a dangerous weapon and assault and battery as a result of Alex's beating of Cristina on July 20, 2003.
>
> On August 5, 2004, Alex responded to the charges and admitted sufficient facts to support a finding of guilt on the charges of assault and battery with a dangerous weapon and assault and battery . . . a guilty finding [was] entered on those findings on August 5, 2004.

The Statement identified only one issue of fact remaining to be litigated, specifically: "Whether Alex willfully and maliciously injured Cristina and as a result owes her a debt." Among the issues of law remaining to be litigated, the Statement included: "Whether Alex's conduct [i.e., the Assault] set forth above constitute 'willful and malicious injury' to Cristina resulting in a debt for personal injury which is non-dischargeable under § 523(a)(6)."

On March 15, 2010, a few days before trial was set to commence, Cristina waived Count I (spousal support) and Count II (attorney's fees and health premiums) because they were prohibited by the facts established in her and Alex's divorce Stipulation. Thus, the Bankruptcy Court was left to determine only the dischargeability of her unliquidated personal injury claim under 11 U.S.C. § 523(a)(6). When the bankruptcy trial began on March 17, 2010, in lieu of opening statements, Cristina instead argued that she was entitled to summary judgment on Count III. Alex responded that summary judgment was inappropriate for two reasons: First, he contended that there remained facts in dispute regarding the alleged Assault, namely whether he intended to cause Cristina injury and whether an injury did in fact result. Second, he argued that he could not be liable in tort to Cristina because she had waived all such claims in the Stipulation, and therefore there was no debt that the Bankruptcy Court could discharge.

At the hearing, the Bankruptcy Court decided that, based upon the admissions of the parties, Alex did intend to injure Cristina and did in fact injure her. However, the Bankruptcy Court reserved judgment on the issue of whether the Stipulation to the divorce judgment waived Cristina's right to later file a personal injury claim for injuries she sustained in the Assault. The Bankruptcy Court instructed the parties to submit briefings on the issue. On May 26, 2010, the Bankruptcy Court granted summary judgment in favor of Cristina. Alex then filed the instant appeal from the Bankruptcy Court's decision on June 7, 2010.

C. The Bankruptcy Court's Decision

The Bankruptcy Court's order granting summary judgment for Cristina on Count III of her complaint held that Alex's unliquidated debt to Cristina for her personal injury claim is excepted from discharge pursuant to 11 U.S.C. § 523(a)(6). In its decision, the Bankruptcy Court squarely rejected all of the arguments that Alex submitted in his brief opposing Cristina's motion for summary judgment.

First, the Bankruptcy Court observed that Alex's argument that the statute of limitations for Cristina's tort action had run was completely contradicted by a provision of the Bankruptcy Code that expressly calls for tolling during the pendency of a debtor's bankruptcy. Next, the Bankruptcy Court dismissed Alex's assertion that Cristina's tort claims were barred by res judicata and/or waived by the Stipulation, noting that the Supreme Judicial Court of Massachusetts ("SJC") had rejected the exact argument that Alex set forth. Finally, the Bankruptcy Court rejected Alex's contention that the pleadings were insufficient to support a grant of summary judgment, finding that the facts admitted in the Statement established all the elements necessary for discharge under section 523(a) of the Bankruptcy Code. The Bankruptcy Court therefore granted Cristina's motion for summary judgment.

Having addressed each of Alex's arguments in turn, the Bankruptcy Court commented that Alex's defenses had no basis in fact or law and likely warranted sanctions pursuant to Federal Rule of Bankruptcy Procedure 9011(b). However, the Bankruptcy Court was barred from imposing such sanctions without first providing Attorney Baker, Alex's counsel, notice and a reasonable opportunity to respond. Therefore, the Bankruptcy Court instructed Attorney Baker to submit a brief explaining why he should not be sanctioned. Ultimately, the Bankruptcy Court suspended consideration of the Order to Show Cause pending the resolution of Alex's appeal in this Court. * * *

IV. DISCUSSION

Alex's appeal is subject to dismissal because he did not submit his supporting brief within fourteen days of when his appeal was docketed, as required by Federal Rule of Bankruptcy Procedure 8009. Moreover, Alex's appeal is so divorced from proper factual or legal support that it warrants the imposition of sanctions pursuant to Federal Rule of Bankruptcy Procedure 8020. First, Alex argues that the Bankruptcy Court lacked subject matter jurisdiction to determine the dischargeability of his debt to Cristina because she has not yet reduced her personal injury claims to judgment. Second, Alex contends that he could not possibly be indebted to Cristina because the statute of limitations on her tort claims has run. Third, Alex asserts that Cristina waived her tort claims in the Stipulation to the divorce judgment, and/or that the claims are barred by the doctrine of res judicata because the Probate Court took Cristina's injuries into consideration when awarding alimony. Fourth, Alex claims that it was improper for the Bankruptcy Court to grant summary judgment, because there still remained genuine disputes as to material facts, specifically, whether Cristina was injured and, if so, whether Alex intended to cause those injuries. As will be explained below, each of these arguments is completely erroneous, as the Bankruptcy Court already found. * * *

B. Frivolous Appeal

In addition to seeking dismissal of Alex's appeal, Cristina also asks for sanctions. Federal Rule of Bankruptcy Procedure 8020 ("Rule 8020") permits a district court to award just damages and single or double costs to the appellee if it determines that an appeal from a Bankruptcy Court decision is frivolous. While there is no set formula for determining whether an appeal is frivolous, courts in the First Circuit generally consider whether the appellant acted in bad faith, and whether the argument presented on appeal is meritless in toto or only in part. Other factors to be considered are whether the appellant's argument effectively addresses the issues on appeal, fails to cite any authority, cites inapplicable authority, makes unsubstantiated factual assertions, asserts bare legal conclusions, or misrepresents the record. In particular, the court may impose sanctions if the appellant raises issues that are contradicted by long-established precedent or by a case decided while the appeal is pending.

In the present case, Alex's appeal is frivolous *in toto,* as each and every one of the arguments he presents is completely unsupported by fact or law.

1. Subject Matter Jurisdiction

Alex claims the Bankruptcy Court lacked subject matter jurisdiction to determine the dischargeability of his debt to Cristina as a result of the Assault because Cristina has not yet reduced her tort claims against Alex to a judgment. This argument ignores the plain, unambiguous meaning the Bankruptcy Code assigns to the word "claim" in 11 U.S.C. § 101(5)(A).

The governing federal statute and Bankruptcy Code define a "debt" as a "liability on a claim," which in turn is defined as a "right to payment, whether or not such right is reduced to judgment, liquidated, unliquidated, fixed, contingent, matured, unmatured, disputed, undisputed, legal, equitable, secured, or unsecured." * * *

Second, his argument that the statute of limitations on Cristina's tort claims had run also ignores the express provisions of the Bankruptcy Code. Alex is correct that ordinarily there is a three-year statute of limitations on tort actions. However, as the Bankruptcy Court noted, sections 108(c) and 362(c)(2) of the Bankruptcy Code toll the statute of limitations for such actions during the pendency of a debtor's bankruptcy proceedings. Because the dischargeability of Alex's debt to Cristina is still being litigated, the statute of limitations for the underlying tort claims giving rise to that debt continue to be tolled, and therefore Cristina is not yet barred from bringing those claims.

Third, Alex's contentions that Cristina's tort claims were waived via the Stipulation and/or barred by res judicata is based on a distinction that has no bearing on the case at bar. He argues that Cristina's "tort-based issues" were presented to the Probate Court during the divorce proceedings, and that the judge took them into consideration when awarding spousal support, such that he "compensated her for them." However, the Probate Court is a court of limited jurisdiction, which does not have the authority to decide tort claims. In fact, the SJC has already rejected Alex's argument in a case quite similar to the one at bar. * * *

Moreover, nothing in the Stipulation waives the instant issues. First, Alex takes issue with the fact that the Statement "was prepared by [Cristina's] attorney, who was not particularly open to modification of his work, and the 'admissions' made in it all were taken from the amended complaint, not from depositions (there were none) or other discovery." He continues by saying that the facts admitted in the Statement are in conflict with the triable issues of fact and law also set forth in the Statement, and with Alex's answer to the original complaint. This argument is unpersuasive. If counsel was concerned that the material contained in the Statement was inaccurate in any way, or that contrary information could be revealed via depositions or other discovery, he should not have signed the Statement on behalf of his client. He cannot now argue that the Statement is not binding against his client simply because at the time he signed it he was uneasy about doing so. Alex's counsel knew, or certainly should have known, that the stipulated facts contained in the Statement were deemed admitted, and that those admissions would supersede the pleadings. In fact, the Statement contained a section setting forth as much.

Second, Alex contends that Cristina has not shown that she has actually suffered an injury because "[p]aragraphs 9 through 12 of the complaint do not allege any injury physical or otherwise—only that there was an affray" and that "the joint pre-trial statement seems merely to quote the amended complaint, the material allegations of which, in answer to the original complaint were denied." However, the Statement clearly sets forth that "[Alex] intended to cause and *did cause Cristina physical harm and pain and emotional fright* and did cause Cristina such physical harm that she was caused to seek and obtain medical care for her injuries and did cause her such emotional harm that she was cased [sic] to seek and obtain care for her emotional condition." (emphasis added). If that is not an admission of injury, it is hard to imagine what could be.

Third, Alex claims that the admissions contained in the Statement do not necessarily establish that Cristina's injuries were willfully or maliciously inflicted. He argues that the fact that he admitted to having pled sufficient facts to be found guilty of assault and battery with a dangerous weapon and assault and battery does not prove that he acted willfully or maliciously; he asserts that reckless or negligent behavior could also have triggered his conviction. However, Alex admitted that he *"purposefully struck* Cristina with great force, *grabbed Cristina by the throat and struck her head repeatedly* against the interior wall of the premises . . . and *threw Cristina with such force onto a table that the table was caused to be broken."* (emphasis added). These are willful actions.

Alternatively, Alex argues that "there are other possible explanations" for Cristina's injuries; he imagines, for example, "it is possible that Alex believed he was defending himself." However, Alex never affirmatively argued at the hearing before the Bankruptcy Court or in the memorandum opposing summary judgment that he submitted to the Bankruptcy Court that Alex was acting in self-defense. He claims only that it "is not beyond the realm of possibility." Nothing in the record suggests that Alex was acting in self-defense. Alex cannot now avoid summary judgment by offering "conclusory allegations, improbable inferences, [or] unsupported speculation in the place of genuine, trialworthy issues." Summary judgment was warranted.

In addition, he asserts that the admissions contained in the Statement are insufficient to establish willfulness or maliciousness. All of these arguments fail.

Fourth, Alex's absurd assertion that the admissions contained in the Stipulation were insufficient grounds for summary judgment are so ridiculous that one can only imagine that they were made in bad faith. It boggles the mind to think that Alex could admit, as a fact not requiring proof, that he "intended to cause and did cause Cristina physical harm and pain," and then later argue that there were questions as to injury and intent precluding summary judgment. If there was ever a case to impose sanctions, this would be the one.

* * * Cristina contends that "Alex's appeal is utterly baseless and has caused Cristina to incur significant unwarranted expenses." Specifically, Cristina asserts that she has spent $23,629.75 on legal services in connection with this appeal. She requests no less than $16,221.00 in sanctions. I agree and remand the case back to the Bankruptcy Court for the determination. * * *

[Editor's Note: On remand, the Bankruptcy Court upheld sanctions of $9,000 against Alex's attorney. See Hermosilla v. Hermosilla, *450 B.R. 276, June 2011. The sanctions were upheld at 2011 WL 6034487, to "deter future misconduct." The court noted that some of the attorney's statements were "patently false," and stated that this was not the first time he had been sanctioned in this case—he had been sanctioned $1585.70 for filing a motion "wholly without merit," and he had turned this straightforward matter into a five-year litigation. This is an example of litigation abuse, discussed in Chapters 2 and 12.]*

CHAPTER 6

CIVIL RESTRAINING ORDERS

■ ■ ■

This chapter continues the exploration of civil remedies for domestic violence, focusing on protective orders issued by civil courts, also called restraining orders, orders of protection, or civil protective orders. The first article calls for such orders to last indefinitely, since they have been found to be generally effective. A commentator argues that survivors of abuse should be allowed to obtain orders that protect them but do not require that they end the abusive relationship. Another commentator focuses on teen survivors of intimate partner abuse, an often-overlooked and important group at great risk for abuse as noted earlier in this book.

This chapter also illustrates some non-violent tactics of batterers as they seek to continue to control their ex-partners, including during visitation or custody exchanges, and the ways some courts and legislatures have responded. Another case holds that even if the abused ex-partner has temporarily relocated for safety, the court can still order the abuser to leave the former joint residence so the survivor can return and live there safely. A third case examines what the court should do when the restrained party seeks to terminate the restraining order early.

Two cases look at the relationship between restraining orders and divorces, in terms of whether the doctrine of *res judicata* precludes a later filing for a protective order after the divorce is final, and whether the request for a protective order can be used by a divorce court to lower the protected party's share of the marital assets.

Two new cases focus on mutual restraining orders, which can be very problematic in domestic violence cases. They illustrate how such orders come to be issued, why they are problematic, their effect on child custody decisions, and how some courts and legislatures have dealt with this issue. The second case states that the restrained party exercised "dominion and control" over the other party, essentially the same concept as coercive control, a term first introduced in Chapter 2.

Enforcement has been called "the Achilles heel" of the civil protective order system, since issuance of an order without enforcement may actually put the survivor in a worse position. An article by a team of international researchers analyzes multiple studies regarding effectiveness of restraining orders. A case illustrates how a criminal court handled multiple violations of the same order in an extremely dangerous situation.

An editor's note summarizes a case dealing with the issue of the protected party being prosecuted for aiding the batterer in violating the order, and concludes that this is not allowed.

Restraining orders also may be enforced interstate, under each states' "long-arm statutes," as was the legal issue in an interstate case in the Torts chapter. One case involves threats posted on YouTube, a form of abuse that is becoming more common in this age of the Internet. Another case involves threats communicated via calls and letters that crossed state lines.

The chapter concludes with a description of interstate enforcement of such orders mandated under the first Violence Against Women Act, based on full faith and credit, a long-standing constitutional principle.

A. OVERVIEW

JANE K. STOEVER, ENJOINING ABUSE: THE CASE FOR INDEFINITE DOMESTIC VIOLENCE PROTECTION ORDERS

67 Vand. L. Rev. 1015 (2014)
(footnotes and table omitted)

I. Introduction

* * * The state's response to domestic violence is relatively recent. Historically, courts vested husbands with the right of chastisement over their wives, who were considered their property; courts later characterized marriage as existing in a domain beyond law and in a "sphere separate from civil society." Both the property approach and the romantic notion of the companionate relationship, however, had the effect of condoning domestic violence. This lack of governmental response persisted until recent decades, when the criminal and civil justice systems began responding to intimate partner violence. From 1970 to 1993, state legislatures created special laws and proceedings for domestic violence protection orders, a type of injunction intended to intervene in abusive relationships and prevent further violence. *[Editor's Note: Actually, the first U.S. jurisdiction to enact a domestic violence restraining order statute was New York, in 1962 (N.Y. Fam.Ct. Act §§ 811–846).]* The Uniform Interstate Enforcement of Domestic Violence Protection Orders Act defines "protection orders" as injunctions issued by a court under the domestic violence, family violence, or anti-stalking laws of the issuing state to prevent an individual from engaging in violent or threatening acts, harassment, contact, communication, or physical proximity to another person. Protection orders are now the most widely used legal remedy against domestic violence, with more survivors utilizing this civil justice system remedy than seeking tort remedies or having involvement with the criminal justice system.

Domestic violence survivors apply for civil protection orders in pursuit of safety. Many of these individuals have experienced high levels of violence. They have been punched, choked *[Editor's Note: i.e., strangled]*, beaten, kicked, burned, set on fire, and raped. They have suffered emotional, psychological, and economic harm, and have been threatened with weapons and words promising lethality. Rather than these being isolated incidents, as with stranger violence, the abusive partner targets the victim, and the abuser's efforts to exert power and control over the survivor pervade the survivor's experience. Abuse is recurrent and typically escalates in frequency and severity over time, with past intimate partner violence being the "best predictor of future violence." A survivor, thus, is often unable to feel secure at home, the supposedly safest place in the world.

The protection order remedy has proven to be highly effective in preventing future violence, but in most states, this remedy is only available for one year or for a similarly limited duration. If an abusive partner threatens to kill an intimate partner, will that danger terminate when the yearlong domestic violence protection order expires? The legal construction suggests that it does, but social science data and the lived experiences of domestic violence survivors prove otherwise. At the end of the year, petitioners may generally seek the extension of the order through a motion and adversarial hearing. Some jurisdictions permit only one brief extension, while others require violence or threats to have occurred during the duration of the order rather than interpreting the absence of violence as proof of the court order's effectiveness and reason for it to remain in place. Given the persistent and potentially fatal nature of domestic violence, granting judicial protection in the form of indefinite protection orders could increase survivors' safety and autonomy while saving them from having to reengage with an abusive partner each year, which poses substantial safety risks.

The brief timeframe for orders regarding human safety can be juxtaposed with long-term or truly permanent injunctions issued in many other areas of the law to prevent "irreparable harm" to property, copyrights, trademarks, employment, and other tax and business interests. These readily available indefinite orders stand in stark contrast to the short-lived domestic violence orders that are supposed to prevent bodily harm. Given the historic lack of response to domestic violence, the differential and exceptional treatment of domestic violence is not surprising. Short-term statutory injunctions against domestic violence problematically give the appearance of remedying domestic abuse while permitting domestic violence to continue. This is a form of what Reva Siegel has termed "preservation through transformation," in which legal change gives the appearance of correcting a wrong but, in fact, perpetuates the status quo. * * *

II. The Recurrent and Dangerous Nature of Domestic Violence

* * *

A. Re-Victimization and Separation Assault

Domestic violence is different from other crimes in ways that make past acts highly relevant and predictive of future danger. Intimate partner abuse rarely consists only of a single, isolated event; instead, the abusive partner more commonly engages in an ongoing process of violence and control. * * *

Judges may assume that the danger is over if the parties have separated, but domestic violence survivors face the greatest risk of acute violence and lethality during the actual separation from an abusive partner and the ensuing years. Rather than ensuring safety, leaving or attempting to leave often escalates and intensifies the violence. Martha Mahoney coined the phrase "separation assault" to describe the increase in the batterer's quest for control when the survivor seeks to leave the relationship and the subsequent "attack on the woman's body and volition in which her partner seeks to prevent her from leaving, retaliate for the separation, or force her to return." * * *

Further quantitative and qualitative research confirms that high-level violence is often the result of the abuse survivor's departure from the relationship, not the survivor's failure to leave. Studies have shown that an abuse survivor's risk increases by seventy-five percent upon leaving and that this level of danger continues for two years. Approximately two-thirds of all women who separate from their abusive partners are revictimized by them. In one study, researchers found that seventy-five percent of reported domestic violence incidents involved women who were already separated from their batterers. In a qualitative study on attempted homicides by intimate partners, the femicide attempts typically occurred as the abused women were attempting to leave their relationships. * * * Another study revealed that the proximity of an abusive partner to the victim is a key factor in post-separation assaults.

In addition to the immediate threat of separation assault, continued abuse can happen over lengthy periods of time with prolonged gaps between incidents. While at least one-third of abusers reabuse in a short timeframe, more do so when examining longer periods of time, with longitudinal studies showing gaps of several years between abusive incidents for some abusers.

B. Courthouse Dangers

The short-term nature of most states' protection orders fails to account for the risk the courthouse itself poses to victims and the danger of repeatedly engaging the abusive partner in litigation about the violence. Abuse survivors go to court seeking protection, but returning to court every year to seek extensions of the court's protection is a physically and psychologically dangerous prospect. Regarding the psychological risk, one scholar notes, "If one set out by design to devise a system for provoking intrusive post-traumatic symptoms, one could not do better than a court of law." * * *

Domestic violence courts are more dangerous than any other type of court. A court hearing provides an abusive party with a precise date and time where the abuser will find his or her target of abuse. Attorneys who specialize in representing abuse survivors are well aware of the frequency of courthouse assaults and insist that "[b]attered women not only need good laws, they need safe courthouses so they will not be killed, abused, or followed home by their abusers." * * *

III. The Widespread Availability of Permanent Injunctions

[The author describes laws allowing for injunctions in general and argues that domestic violence restraining orders, a type of injunction, often meet the standards for permanent injunctions.] * * *

IV. History Reveals the Law's Differential Treatment of Domestic Violence

* * *

A. The Right of Chastisement and Family Privacy Theory

The historical context in which domestic violence laws evolved is important to understanding the current limited duration of civil protection orders. Laws in the United States were constructed to exclude marital relations from an otherwise comprehensive scope, with the family deemed private and exempt from legal scrutiny. Because family law pertains to intimate and emotional relationships and is rooted in "sacred command," law defining and regulating the family has traditionally been treated as exceptional in comparison to the market.

The exceptionalism of family law and the legal rules that apply to violence in the family is a historically driven phenomenon. Historically, the doctrine of family privacy shielded abusive partners from judicial reach and prevented abuse survivors from receiving protection. * * * [The author describes the common law right of husbands to chastise their wives, interspousal immunity, and the limitations of the Married Women's Property Acts.] Multiple other vestiges of coverture persisted throughout the twentieth century, such as the marital rape exception.

While family privacy theory has traditionally condoned family violence, this theory has also influenced the whole of family law in a variety of noteworthy ways. During the twentieth and twenty-first centuries, the Supreme Court developed a robust doctrine of family privacy, setting national norms in many areas affecting families. * * * In sum, much of recent family law has grown from rights developed under the family privacy theory, which positively permits pluralism and a diversity of family forms to flourish. An ongoing theme in family law is the tension between family privacy and the need for the state to intervene to further the fundamental function of government to protect citizens from harm—for example, in cases of child abuse or intimate partner violence.

Regarding the state's response to family violence, in the early 1900s, state legislatures created family and juvenile courts to handle criminal acts committed against spouses and children outside of the traditional criminal system. Rather than punishing the perpetrator and criminalizing violence against a family member, family courts encouraged reconciliation, sought to preserve family unity, and resulted in keeping family violence private. Thus, the legal treatment of domestic assault only shifted in structure and rationale from marital prerogative to marital privacy; the discourse of forgiveness and altruism toward this affective bond continued.

Prior to the 1970s, the only civil remedy available to domestic violence survivors was to seek a restraining order in the context of a divorce. At that time, divorce was difficult to obtain without an attorney and required grounds, fees, and extensive proceedings. Divorce also necessarily meant that the parties were in a marital relationship and the petitioner had decided to dissolve the marriage. Emergency ex parte orders in the divorce required proof beyond a reasonable doubt, and the penalty for violating the restraining order was civil contempt, which typically only amounted to a "verbal slap on the hand." This route that demanded divorce was not expeditious or appealing to many married women, and the relief was insufficient to actually end violence, especially given the weak enforcement mechanisms. An alternative legal remedy was needed.

B. The Creation of the Domestic Violence Protection Order

Laws against domestic violence grew out of the work of the battered women's movement of the 1960s and 1970s. During this period, feminists created the first domestic violence shelters and organized support groups for abused women based on a feminist-theory approach centered on contextual responses to individual women's needs. Battered-women's activists and scholars then undertook the substantial task of revolutionizing domestic violence laws. They sought to transform domestic violence from a private matter into a public one by creating legal mechanisms to enhance women's safety and independence.

Because of historic failures of police to respond appropriately to domestic violence and of prosecutors to treat intimate partner violence as a crime, significant energy went into developing aggressive criminal justice responses to domestic violence, with most states creating mandatory arrest laws and "no-drop" prosecution policies. * * * Alongside the development of mandatory criminal justice system responses to domestic violence, reformers developed the civil justice remedy of the protection order.

While traditional civil injunctions have historical roots that date back to the Court of Chancery in England, the first domestic violence protection order legislation [in the U.S.] was passed in 1970, when advocates recognized that injunctive relief could "radically alter the balance of power between abusers and their victims." By 1993, each state had enacted a protection order statute. This survivor-initiated remedy was intended to be autonomy enhancing while also enabling survivors to further invoke protections of the criminal justice system. In light of the deeply entrenched laws and practices that condoned violence and the abject failure of police and prosecutors to respond to domestic violence, statutes providing for yearlong domestic violence protection orders offered significant remedies that were heretofore unavailable.

As with most legal issues related to family relationships, including the issuance of divorce and custody decrees, state law largely governs protection orders and thus varies by state. As states enacted domestic violence protection order statutes to protect victims of domestic violence and their children from further harm, each state determined the types of relationships covered, how to define domestic violence, the relief available, and the length of the orders. While early statutes addressed "wife abuse," these statutes are now gender-neutral and generally cover relationships involving marriage, dating, relatives, or household members. Domestic violence is commonly defined as an actual or threatened criminal offense against an intimate partner or family member. * * *

States have developed their protection order statutes over the past few decades to include a wide array of injunctive relief that extends beyond relief available through criminal restraining orders. Protection orders may prohibit the respondent from abusing, threatening, harassing, contacting, or coming near the petitioner; require the respondent to vacate a shared residence; order him or her to complete counseling for domestic violence, drug abuse, alcohol abuse, or parenting skills; and award temporary child custody and visitation, along with attorney's fees. Some jurisdictions permit monetary awards for child support, maintenance, housing payments, property destruction, or medical expenses due to violence. Select states allow courts to order global positioning system tracking of a respondent using a system that has victim-notification capabilities. Statutes typically also contain a provision that allows a judge to enter additional relief that is tailored to the unique safety needs presented in the case. These survivor-initiated proceedings carry the weight of enforcement by the criminal justice system or through a separate contempt action.

Domestic violence protection order laws are developing as legislators, judges, academics, and advocates gain greater understanding of the dynamics of domestic violence, the needs of abuse survivors, and the means to prevent further abuse. For example, statutes have evolved over the past four decades to protect unmarried women and men in heterosexual or homosexual relationships, and many states have expanded relief to address teen dating violence and the abuse of pets. On a national level, the Violence Against Women Act requires states to give full faith and credit to protection orders issued in other states. The generally limited duration of protection orders, however, persists, as detailed in Part V. Making it possible to permanently enjoin abuse is a needed part of the evolution of the protection order remedy. * * *

The examination of states' statutes reveals that protection orders are often curtailed when the parties have children in common. * * * These practices should be viewed alongside social science findings that women with children are more likely to experience violence following the entry of a restraining order or protection order than women without children. The statutory treatment of abused parents is thus contrary to the need to protect survivors with children. * * *

2. The Efficacy of Protection Orders

Beyond consideration of the difficulty of putting a price on past violence and future safety, evidence of the efficacy of domestic violence protection orders reveals the unique value of these injunctions. Multiple studies have shown that protection orders are effective both at eliminating or substantially decreasing violence and at helping survivors feel safer and more empowered. Social scientists have concluded that protection orders "appear to be one of the few widely available interventions for victims of [intimate partner violence] that has demonstrated effectiveness." Furthermore, lengthier orders have been found to produce greater safety outcomes. While protection orders considerably reduce violence, studies also reveal that abusive partners frequently violate the orders, which demonstrates the ongoing danger that survivors face and the need for extended court protection.

Regarding the efficacy of protection orders, a study of nearly 2,700 women who had reported domestic violence to the police found that those who obtained civil protection orders experienced an eighty percent decrease in subsequent police-reported physical violence. Overall, these women experienced a significantly decreased likelihood of physical and non-physical intimate partner violence, including decreased risk of contact by the abusive partner, weapon threats, injuries, and abuse-related medical treatment. An interview-based study found a seventy percent decrease in physical abuse among women who maintained their protection orders. Similarly, in another study, eighty-six percent of the women who received a protection order stated that the abuse either stopped or was greatly reduced. * * *

Of particular importance to the argument in favor of long-term protection orders, social scientists have found that lengthier orders produce more substantial safety outcomes. Multiple studies have now found a correlation between the duration of the protection order and the survivor's safety, which researchers have described as a "dose-response relationship according to the duration of the [civil protection order]." Maintaining the court's protection over time, therefore, is key to significantly decreasing future violence and sustaining an end to all forms of abuse.

In conjunction with their length, additional factors can contribute to the effectiveness of protection orders. For example, orders that contain more comprehensive and specified relief are more likely to provide protection to survivors. Research has shown that survivors who are not awarded relief they have sought are more likely to be re-abused, a conclusion that supports the importance of listening to a survivor's identification of what will make him or her safe. Differences in communities' implementation and enforcement of orders and in the availability of confidential shelters and other safety resources in a geographic region can also affect the efficacy of orders.

Another measure of effectiveness is abuse survivors' perceptions of the value of orders, and studies show that they perceive protection orders to be effective and crucial to their safety. In a study of women who had recently obtained temporary protection orders, ninety-eight percent felt more in control of their lives, ninety-one percent felt that obtaining the order was a good decision, and eighty-nine percent felt more in control of their relationship as a result of the court order. A majority of women report feeling safer after obtaining protection orders; in a recent study of seven hundred women with protection orders, forty-three percent felt "extremely safe," thirty-four percent felt "fairly safe," while ten percent did not feel safe, and twelve percent were unsure about how they felt. Abuse survivors also report that the orders help document that the abuse occurred and convey to the abusive partner that physical violence is wrong.

Although protection order holders generally experience an overall decrease in violence, multiple studies have still found high rates of protection order violations by abusive partners. A review of thirty-two studies concluded that approximately forty percent of protection orders are violated. Violations are particularly likely when the respondent stalks the petitioner prior to or following the issuance of the protection order, or when the parties remain in a relationship. Other factors that predict especially high rates of domestic violence recidivism include the abuser's use of a weapon, the number of criminal charges filed against the perpetrator, the presence of an arrest record for domestic violence and nondomestic violence crimes, and the history of protection order violations. The overall decrease in violence positively demonstrates the value and potential of protection orders, while the reabuse rates show the need for continued court protection through long-term or indefinite orders.

The protection order remedy is the legal remedy that most abuse survivors choose to utilize, but it is not the right path for every individual. Formal state intervention, either criminal or civil, can bring unexpected, complicated consequences. In some jurisdictions, the report of children being abused or witnessing abuse will trigger a Child Protective Services investigation and prompt a "failure to protect" case to be filed against the abuse survivor. A survivor may also weigh the potential for facing discrimination in housing; employment; and health, life, and homeowner's insurance even when such discrimination is illegal—along with the loss of welfare benefits and potential immigration consequences. The psychological impact of the court process is an additional material factor for many survivors. Protection orders are not a panacea for every abuse survivor, but where a survivor desires long-term court-ordered protection through a civil protection order, such a remedy should be available.

[The author explains why criminal alternatives, including criminal protective orders, are insufficient to stop domestic violence, and why civil protective orders meet the constitutional standards required to comply with both procedural and substantive due process. She also describes the public interest in stopping domestic violence, one of the prongs required when a court issues a permanent injunction.] * * *

Costs related to experiencing domestic violence and to ending violence are substantial. In the United States, the annual cost of medical care, mental health services, and time away from work due to intimate partner violence is estimated to be $8.3 billion (in 2003 dollars). Every year, survivors of intimate partner violence lose nearly 8 million days of paid work, which amounts to more than 32,000 full-time jobs. They also lose approximately 5.6 million days of household productivity due to domestic violence, and there are significant costs for services to children exposed to domestic violence. * * *

Protection orders serve the public interest by producing widespread economic and safety benefits. According to a recent study on the costs and benefits of domestic violence protection orders, every dollar spent on protection order interventions produced $30.75 in avoided costs to society. * * *

Making indefinite protection orders available in each state would be a meaningful advancement alone. Some states could even choose to enact a presumption of permanent protection orders. * * *

HAWAII REV. STAT. § 586–1

* * * "Domestic abuse" means:

(1) Physical harm, bodily injury, assault, or the threat of imminent physical harm, bodily injury, or assault, extreme psychological abuse or malicious property damage between family or household members; or

(2) Any act which would constitute an offense under section 709–906 [physical abuse], or under part V or VI of chapter 707 committed

against a minor family or household member by an adult family or household member.

"Extreme psychological abuse" means an intentional or knowing course of conduct directed at an individual that seriously alarms or disturbs consistently or continually bothers the individual, and that serves no legitimate purpose; provided that such course of conduct would cause a reasonable person to suffer extreme emotional distress. * * *

ILL. STAT. CH 750 § 60–103

§ 103. Definitions. For the purposes of this Act, the following terms shall have the following meanings: * * *

(9) "Interference with personal liberty" means committing or threatening physical abuse, harassment, intimidation or willful deprivation so as to compel another to engage in conduct from which she or he has a right to abstain or to refrain from conduct in which she or he has a right to engage.

[Editor's Notes: 1. In "Toward a Uniform Domestic Violence Civil Protection Order Law," 48 Seton Hall L. Rev. 897 (2018), Ashley Hahn notes that the definition of domestic violence in many state civil protection order (CPO) statutes is narrower than that used by the U.S. DOJ, many legal scholars, advocates and psychologists. This leaves many survivors without legal protection. Furthermore, available relief is very limited in some states. Stating that domestic violence is a national concern warranting a national response, Hahn proposes a uniform DV CPO law for all U.S. jurisdictions, though she does not provide a suggested model. She calls on Congress to use its spending power, conditioning states' receipt of federal funds on adopting such a law.

2. In "Behind the Screen: The Constitutionality of Remote Testimony for Survivors of Domestic Violence," 49 (2) Hastings Constitutional Law Quarterly 178 (2022), Rachel Harris notes that the court response to the COVID pandemic enabled many survivors of domestic violence to testify remotely in protection order cases as well as filing petitions electronically. She argues that these procedures made such orders more accessible to survivors and that remote testimony greatly diminished physical and emotional danger from abusers. She also maintains that survivors are more likely to testify truthfully if they are not in fear of the abusers and retraumatized with respect to PTSD. Harris examines the constitutionality of remote testimony and concludes that it complies with constitutional requirements. She concludes that courts should continue to offer this option and e-filing even when the pandemic is greatly diminished.]

SALLY F. GOLDFARB, RECONCEIVING CIVIL PROTECTION ORDERS FOR DOMESTIC VIOLENCE: CAN LAW HELP END THE ABUSE WITHOUT ENDING THE RELATIONSHIP?

29 Cardozo L. Rev. 1487 (2008)

> Sylvia did not see Michael [her abusive partner] as a monster. She saw him as the product of a lousy childhood. She also saw him as a good provider and . . . as the father of their two daughters. Nor did she see herself as defenseless but rather . . . as a self-reliant working woman and as someone who stood her ground. She never wanted Michael locked up; she wanted him to change. She wanted to rehabilitate her family, not to break it up.

INTRODUCTION

* * * During the past three decades, as a consequence of feminist advocacy, legal remedies for domestic violence have for the first time become widely available. However, most of these remedies extract a price that is, for many women, unacceptably high. The most prevalent remedies for domestic violence—including access to battered women's shelters, arrest and prosecution of offenders, and civil protection orders—usually require that the victim separate from the batterer. Yet many women in abusive relationships do not want to separate. Like Sylvia, they want the relationship to continue but the violence to stop. Current domestic violence law does not sufficiently meet the needs of these women. On the contrary, remedies for domestic violence too often protect a woman's right to safety only if she is willing to leave her partner, thereby sacrificing her right of autonomy as expressed through her decision to stay in an intimate relationship. The law has moved from placing too much emphasis on relationships to placing too little emphasis on them.

The fact that many women do not want to leave their abusive partners is not surprising. Adults commonly find their deepest satisfaction and fullest self-realization in intimate relationships, and women are more likely than men to regard the formation and preservation of relationships as a paramount value. In addition, leaving the batterer can actually increase the risks to a battered woman. Despite the common assumption that domestic violence will continue unless the victim leaves, empirical research shows that violent relationships can become non-violent and that legal intervention can assist in bringing about that change. Until domestic violence law recognizes and accommodates the desire of many battered women to remain in their relationships, it cannot be considered truly successful. * * *

In this effort to reconceive domestic violence law, it is fitting to focus on civil protection orders, since they are the single most commonly used legal remedy for domestic violence. To members of the general public, as well as many lawyers, judges, and scholars, protection orders are synonymous with "stay-away" orders, which are designed to protect the victim by ending her relationship with the abuser. Indeed, the overwhelming majority of civil protection orders for domestic violence take this form. However, there is another type of civil protection order for domestic violence, one that is currently prohibited in some jurisdictions, underutilized in others, and largely ignored in discussions of domestic violence law. Unlike a stay-away order, these orders prohibit future abuse but permit ongoing contact between the parties. Protection orders permitting ongoing contact are a valuable option for many women who are unwilling to leave their relationships and therefore would not seek a stay-away order. By customizing each order to express the victim's preferences for how much and what kinds of contact should be allowed, these orders can put the force of law behind the individual woman's choices. Through the use of careful screening mechanisms and other safeguards, this system can also protect women's safety. While not all battered women would be suitable candidates for orders permitting continuing contact, many would benefit from the availability of a legally enforceable order that requires an end to the violence without requiring an end to the relationship.

* * * Although these types of orders are currently available in some courts and under some circumstances, they should be consistently and prominently offered in all jurisdictions—not as a replacement for stay-away orders, but as an additional component of the legal response to domestic violence. * * *

5. Violations and Enforcement

While every effort should be made to ensure that protection orders are structured so that they are not violated, further abuse by the batterer is always a possibility. The fact that an order is violated does not necessarily mean that it is worthless or that obtaining it was a mistake. The process of obtaining a protection order can be a valuable experience and prepare the woman to take additional actions on her own behalf.

If the protection order is violated, this may paradoxically be helpful to the victim by providing her with a fuller understanding of her situation. It may even lead her to change her mind about remaining in the relationship. For many battered women, deciding to separate from an abuser is an incremental process. Many women cling to the hope that the partner will stop being abusive; only when that dream dies, usually as the result of some turning point or significant incident, is the woman finally able to decide to leave. By getting a protection order before she feels ready to separate from her partner, and then seeing that he is unwilling or unable to comply with a direct judicial mandate to stop the abuse, the victim might reach the point of deciding to end the relationship sooner than she otherwise would.

If a limited protection order is violated, effective enforcement procedures should be available, just as for any other order. As a legal matter, the abuser would be subject to criminal prosecution and/or contempt proceedings for violating the order, in addition to the legal consequences, if any, that would otherwise attach to his misconduct. As a practical matter, a number of factors make enforcement of limited protection orders particularly challenging. If a woman is reluctant to jeopardize her relationship or if she is intimidated by the batterer, she may be unwilling to report that the order has been violated. On the other hand, the fact that a limited order was crafted to reflect her preferences may increase her commitment to seeing it enforced. Furthermore, a limited order avoids the enforcement problems that result when a stay-away order is violated after the victim voluntarily contacts the abuser. If abuse does occur, the prospects for holding the abuser accountable are better if the victim has a limited order than if there is no order in place.

* * * Battered women's advocacy organizations can play a valuable role in this process by maintaining contact with victims who have obtained protection orders and offering them support and assistance if they want to report violations and pursue enforcement remedies. * * *

If a violation is reported, effective enforcement requires that police, prosecutors, and judges respond vigorously. In comparison to a batterer who violates a stay-away order by contacting the victim or coming to her home, a violation of an order permitting ongoing contact may seem less clear-cut. Nevertheless, it should not be assumed that evidence of violation of an order lacking stay-away provisions is impossible to obtain. Depending on the circumstances, the evidence might include physical injuries, property damage, and testimony by the victim and other witnesses. For violations that involve threats, harassment, or other types of psychological abuse, orders that describe the prohibited acts with specificity can facilitate enforcement. Some states already recognize psychological abuse in their criminal law and/or among the grounds for issuing a protection order; in those jurisdictions, police, prosecutors, and judges are especially likely to be familiar with psychological abuse. * * *

Perhaps the biggest obstacle to enforcement will be the attitude that if a victim is not willing to separate from her partner, she must not really be in danger, so a violation of the protection order is trivial, particularly if it does not involve physical violence. This attitude reflects the widespread but erroneous belief that the only rational response to domestic violence is separation, as well as the tendency to underestimate the significance of psychological abuse. With adequate training and increased experience, police, prosecutors, and judges may gain a better understanding of the dynamics of domestic violence and learn to treat violations of limited orders seriously. By way of analogy, many police officers have learned to take seriously violations of protection order provisions prohibiting the offender's presence in the victim's home, even in the absence of actual violence. Until recently, police tended to regard this type of protection order violation as a mere technicality and undeserving of arrest; in the past few years, the criminal justice system has increasingly come to think of the abuser's presence in the victim's home in violation of a protection order as a valid proxy for domestic violence itself. Similarly, police, prosecutors, and judges who are not already familiar with psychological abuse will need to learn that such abuse is deeply damaging, that it plays a central role in coercive control of the victim by the batterer, and that it may be a precursor to physical violence.

One way to sidestep problems with police and prosecutors is by allowing battered women to bring their own criminal contempt actions for protection order violations, as some states now do. Criminal contempt proceedings have a number of advantages over prosecuting a protection order violation as a separate crime, including the fact that they are faster and that judges are inclined to look unfavorably on people who violate a court order. However, pursuing a criminal contempt remedy pro se can be difficult, especially when the defendant is represented by counsel. Providing appointed counsel to battered women in contempt proceedings would mitigate these difficulties. *[Editor's Note: See note below regarding* Robertson v. U.S., *a case involving criminal contempt for violating a civil protection order.]*

Another step that the victim can take without the assistance of police or prosecutors is to request modification of the order. After a limited order has been violated, the victim should be able to return to court to add stay-away provisions if she wishes.

Inevitably, establishing effective enforcement methods for limited orders will be a painstaking and at times frustrating process, as it has proven to be for protection orders in general. As limited protection orders become more widespread, there will be more opportunities to study what enforcement practices do and do not work. The effort to improve enforcement will need to be a focus of continuing attention. * * *

LISA VOLLENDORF MARTIN, WHAT'S LOVE GOT TO DO WITH IT: SECURING ACCESS TO JUSTICE FOR TEENS

61 Cath. U. L. Rev. 457 (2012)
(citations and footnotes omitted)

In 2005, seventeen-year-old Regina Howard went to the Superior Court of the District of Columbia to file a petition for a civil protection order against her ex-boyfriend and the father of her child, Marcus James. Marcus and Regina constantly fought after their daughter was born, and those fights escalated into Marcus beating Regina on a weekly basis. Regina decided to seek a protection order after Marcus punched, kicked, and strangled Regina until she passed out in front of their daughter. When she attempted to file her petition, however, the clerk turned Regina away and told her that she was not permitted to file without a parent. At the time,

D.C. law did not address whether or under what circumstances a minor could obtain a protection order. Regina's friend told her that she obtained a protection order in D.C. before she turned eighteen without parental involvement, so Regina decided to try again. It was only after her third attempt—and after a lawyer heard about her case and offered to assist her—that Regina was able to file her petition and obtain a protection order. If Regina had not possessed unshakable determination, she would have remained unprotected.

In 2009, fourteen-year-old Karen Carson sought a civil protection order with her mother's assistance against her seventeen year-old boyfriend, John Brown, after he beat and raped her. It was undisputed that the parties shared a dating relationship. The trial court concluded that John's conduct amounted to domestic violence and issued a civil protection order for Karen's safety, which, among other things, ordered John to transfer to a new high school. The Washington Court of Appeals vacated the order, holding that John's conduct could not qualify as domestic violence under Washington law until Karen was at least sixteen years old. Being only fourteen, Karen had no right to legal protection.

Since its emergence in the late 1970s, domestic-violence law has evolved considerably. Due to the tireless work of activists, courts' and communities' views of whether men have a right to beat women and whether the law has a role to play in addressing intimate partner violence have seismically shifted. Systems have been developed to make courts more accessible and legal protections more readily available to persons subjected to abuse.

The issue of teen dating violence emerged against this backdrop. Activists, researchers, and scholars demonstrated the prevalence of abuse in teens' intimate relationships and argued that the same legal protections and social services developed to assist adults should also be extended to teens. Several state legislatures and courts responded by enacting laws that enhance the protections available to abused teens. Despite these positive advances, teens still face substantial obstacles when they seek legal protection from abuse, especially when they approach the courts unaccompanied by a parent or guardian. States must do more to recognize the issue of teen dating violence and guarantee teens the same access to justice that states have accorded adults subjected to domestic violence. * * *

VI. CONCLUSION

To offer teens meaningful legal protection from abuse, state legislatures must draft statutes in a manner that facilitates teens' access to civil protection orders. Protection-order statutes must clearly and unconditionally grant abused teens standing and legal capacity to seek protection orders, without requiring parent notification or involvement. At a minimum, protection-order statutes must specifically articulate the circumstances under which minors have standing and capacity to seek protection orders. To best protect teens, protection-order statutes should confer standing without regard to age, and legal capacity on persons ages twelve and older. Furthermore, states should extend protection-order statutes to encompass individuals in romantic, dating, or sexual relationships, as well as to individuals subjected to sexual assault or stalking. Moreover, courts should be authorized to appoint attorneys to represent minor petitioners who need assistance pursuing their claims. Adults should be accorded standing to seek protection orders on behalf of minors who they know are or fear to be experiencing abuse, and courts should be required to consider the wishes of minor petitioners when adults seek protections on their behalf. Protection orders should be available against minor perpetrators ages twelve and older, and safeguards should be put in place to ensure that courts treat minor respondents in an age-appropriate manner at hearings and in any subsequent enforcement proceedings. * * *

TEXAS FAMILY CODE § 82.010— CONFIDENTIALITY OF APPLICATION

(a) This section applies only in a county with a population of 3.4 million or more.

(b) Except as otherwise provided by law, an application for a protective order is confidential, is excepted from required public disclosure under Chapter 552, Government Code, and may not be released to a person who is not a respondent to the application until after the date of service of notice of the application or the date of the hearing on the application, whichever date is sooner.

(c) Except as otherwise provided by law, an application requesting the issuance of a temporary ex parte order under Chapter 83 is confidential, is excepted from required public disclosure under Chapter 552, Government Code, and may not be released to a person who is not a respondent to the application until after the date that the court or law enforcement informs the respondent of the court's order.

ILLINOIS CODE § 22/204.3— APPOINTMENT OF COUNSEL

§ 204.3. Appointment of counsel. The court may appoint counsel to represent the petitioner if the respondent is represented by counsel.

[Editor's Note: See also Note: Madison Morton, Someone in Their Corner: Protecting Pennsylvania's Domestic Violence Victims with a Civil Right to Counsel in Family Court Proceedings, 15 Drexel L. Rev. 709 (2023)]

IN RE MARRIAGE OF F.M. AND M.M.

65 Cal.App.5th 106 (Cal App 2021)
(footnotes and citations omitted)

F.M. (mother) appeals the trial court's denial of her application for a domestic violence restraining order (DVRO) against her former husband M.M. (father). Mother alleges that the trial court erroneously refused to consider evidence of abuse committed following the filing of her application, failed to properly evaluate the evidence of domestic violence that the court did agree to hear, and improperly found that physical separation alone could substitute for the legal protections afforded by a restraining order. We agree the court erred in all of these respects, and reverse.

I. FACTUAL AND PROCEDURAL BACKGROUND

A. Dissolution Proceedings Are Filed

Mother and father married in June 2002. The parties are originally from Nigeria. In August 2018, mother filed a petition for dissolution of the parties' marriage, listing June 7, 2017, as the date of separation. At the time of filing, the parties resided together with their six children, who were between the ages of 3 and 13. Throughout the marriage, mother was a stay-at-home parent and the primary caregiver for the children.

In December 2018, mother filed a request for child and spousal support. In her moving papers, she stated that father had abused her throughout their marriage. Over the next six months, the dissolution proceeded without resolution through a series of status conferences. During this time mother, father, and their children continued to reside together.

B. Mother's DVRO Request

On August 15, 2019, mother filed in pro. per. a DVRO application seeking protection from father for herself and their children under the Domestic Violence Prevention Act. She requested orders forbidding father from committing abuse, compelling him to stay away and to move out of their shared residence, and to be restrained from travelling with their children. In support of her request, she claimed that on four occasions during the previous two months father had called her vulgar names in front of their children, seized her cell phone, demanded that she leave the house, thrown her belongings outside, and tried to strike her with his hands. She also stated that father had made multiple threats to kill her. According to mother's declaration, she had suffered no physical injury from these incidents but had been beaten by father in the past. She also alleged that father had moved their eldest daughter to another location without her permission.

The trial court granted mother's application, in part, and issued a temporary restraining order (TRO). Father was ordered not to abuse mother and to stay at least five yards away from her. The court denied mother's other requests pending a September 2019 hearing, including her requests to add the children as protected parties, to require father to move out of their shared residence, and to prevent father from traveling with the children. In denying these requests, the court explained that mother had not described the alleged abuse in sufficient detail and had failed to provide a legal basis for a move-out order. The court also noted that parenting orders would be issued after the parties met with family court services.

Before the scheduled hearing, father filed a response to mother's DVRO application. He stated that he was financially supporting the family without any contribution from mother. He reported that mother was verbally abusive towards him and the children, and that she would threaten to call the police whenever he asked her for help in paying household expenses. According to father, their oldest daughter was so upset at mother's treatment of her that she had asked to move out. He denied committing any acts of violence, claiming that when mother harassed him he would not respond and would try to avoid her.

C. DVRO Hearings

The DVRO matter was heard over several days in the latter part of 2019. Before the first hearing, mother and father met with a child custody counselor who recommended that mother be given sole legal and physical custody of the parties' children. The counselor's report noted that mother and father had argued during the entire meeting and were unable to make good use of mediation. The report also detailed father's unilateral decision to send their eldest daughter to live in Elk Grove with the mother of his other child. Mother said she had not seen her daughter for almost a month and that father would not disclose their daughter's exact location. The counselor opined that father's decision to relocate the child was "peculiar" and "unusually controlling."

1. September 2019 DVRO Hearing

At the September 5, 2019 hearing, the trial court adopted the child custody counselor's recommendations. Regarding mother's DVRO application, the court stated, "[C]learly, you two do not need to be living together. I think that's the big issue." The court continued, "[T]he problem is you are living together, and if you were just living in separate households, you wouldn't be encountering each other—[¶]. . .[¶]. . . and there wouldn't be problems." Mother responded that she was looking for an apartment and would move out as soon as she found one. The court replied that it wanted to set a date certain for mother's move-out, saying the court was "not as much concerned with this request for this restraining order because I think the allegations you've made in this request have to do with the fact that the two of you are living together." Mother said she would move out by the end of the month.

The trial court asked mother whether she thought a restraining order would still be necessary once the parties had separate residences. Mother expressed concern about father being around her and the children because "[h]is behavior, it's not good." As an example, mother said that father calls her a "motherfucker bitch" in the presence of the children. The court decided to continue the hearing for two months to allow the parties' oldest daughter to be interviewed by the family court counselor since both parents had alleged the other was manipulating the child. Mother was directed to present a court order to the Elk Grove police to obtain a standby and retrieve the child. Even though father had not filed a request for a DVRO, the court ordered mother to move out of the parties' home by the end of the month. The court granted mother's request to reissue the TRO. Father was denied visitation.

In October 2019, mother attended her scheduled custody counselor meeting, but father missed his own appointment. The counselor's report noted that mother had moved out of the family home and was temporarily living in a motel. She also described a recent incident in which father had pushed her when she returned to their former shared residence to collect some of her personal belongings. Mother called the police, who arrested and jailed father. Additionally, mother had attempted to retrieve their eldest daughter but was unsuccessful because her court paperwork lacked the trial court's signature and stamp. The report also noted that the parties' second eldest daughter was refusing to relocate with mother.

2. November 2019 DVRO Hearing

On November 6, 2019, the court held the second hearing on mother's DVRO request. When asked by the court about the October incident, father admitted he had been arrested and jailed but denied having pushed mother and said that no criminal charges were filed against him. Mother responded that father had beaten her, leaving a bruise on her hand, and that she intended to press charges. The court again continued the hearing and encouraged mother to contact the district attorney's office no later than November 15, 2019. The TRO was reissued.

As the hearing was concluding, father mentioned that his arrest occurred after mother came to his home without a police standby in order to pick up clothes for the children and to try to take their second eldest daughter from the home. The trial court asked mother if she had gone to father's home by herself. When she said she had, the court admonished her: "[T]hat doesn't show very good judgment on your part. [¶] You had this restraining order; you say you're afraid of him. I don't know under what circumstances it would be a good idea for you to do that. [¶] . . . [¶] . . . I'm just saying that when we ultimately have a hearing on this request for a domestic violence restraining order, that's a factor I'm going to look at, because when someone is truly in fear of another person, they don't go to their house." Mother explained that father had told her she could come, but the court replied: "No, ma'am, you do not go to his house. If there's something that you need to do there, you need to have a civil standby. That does not show good judgment."

Ahead of the final hearing, mother filed a declaration asking the trial court to order father to move out of their former shared residence so she could return with their children. She explained that she had not found an apartment and was living out of her car with the children.

3. December 2019 DVRO Hearing

At the December 16, 2019 hearing, the trial court began by asking mother to put forth evidence in support of her DVRO request. Mother responded: "Now, he's threatening—[¶] . . . [¶] . . . [h]e's going to kill me, because I went to our joint account and we have joint $23,000, and I took $3,000 from it, and he's telling everybody he's going to kill me, and I'm so scared of my life." The court refused to consider this evidence because the incident had occurred the previous Friday, stating: "You need to support this request with what took place *before* you filed this request. What happened Friday *is not relevant* to this request." (Italics added.)

Mother then explained that father was refusing to give her their children. The trial court also rejected this evidence because it related to the parenting order, not domestic violence. The court then asked her, "You are living separately and apart, correct? [¶] . . . [¶] . . . So, you don't have the conflict with living with each other. [¶] . . . [¶] . . . So what is the basis for your continued request for the restraining order?" Mother responded by referring to threats father had made in November and December 2019. The court cut her off, repeating that she could not rely on events that occurred after she filed her DVRO request.

Mother then explained that in August 2019 father would beat her and call her "bitch" and "motherfucker" in front of the children. She said the abuse started in 2017, when father went to Nigeria "to get married to a new wife." Father told her he did not want her and threatened to kill her if she did not leave their house. When mother referred to the incident leading to father's recent arrest, the court interrupted and said that the arrest came after mother filed her request for the restraining order. The court asked father for his response, cutting him off as well when he began relating events that happened after August 2019. Father then denied that he had abused mother and accused her of repeatedly coming to his house and causing him distress.

The trial court asked mother if she had any additional evidence, and she replied she wanted her daughters back because they were not doing well in school and because father was a "party man." The court interrupted her again, telling her that the issue was irrelevant to the DVRO request. Mother then said her additional evidence was "[j]ust the beating he has been giving me." She also said that she had tried to press criminal charges against father but had not yet received a response from the authorities.

D. Trial Court Findings and Ruling

The trial court summarized its findings at the close of the December 2019 hearing:

"THE COURT: Well, you haven't provided any corroborating evidence to me that that, in fact, took place. All I have is your say so if that's what happened, and I have [father]'s testimony that that didn't happen. You have the burden of proof, not him; you do." [The court stated that it did not find sufficient evidence to grant the DVRO, though the parties needed a lot of help with their parenting issues. The court then told the parties they needed to stay away from each other.]

Following a brief discussion of child custody issues, the trial court denied mother's DVRO request after finding that mother had not met her burden of proof to establish that a restraining order was necessary. The court explained: "[Mother] provided no corroborating evidence for her statements as to what took place in the past. [¶] The court finds they are too general in nature and lack [the] specificity required to support the request." This appeal followed.

II. DISCUSSION

On appeal, mother argues that the trial court erred in denying her request for a restraining order because the court refused to hear her testimony regarding acts of domestic violence that father committed against her after she filed her DVRO application and obtained the TRO. She also faults the court for failing to properly credit and consider the evidence it did agree to consider, and for misapplying the law by determining that physical separation alone could substitute for the legal protections afforded by the DVPA.

A. General Principles

As relevant here, the DVPA defines domestic violence as abuse of a spouse or the child of a party. "Abuse" includes intentionally or recklessly causing or attempting to cause bodily injury, placing a person in reasonable apprehension of imminent serious bodily injury, or engaging in behavior that could be enjoined under section 6320. Section 6320 includes "molesting, attacking, striking, stalking, threatening, sexually assaulting, [and] battering . . . harassing, telephoning, . . . contacting, either directly or indirectly, by mail or otherwise, coming within a specified distance of, or disturbing the peace of the other party."

Under the DVPA, a court may issue a protective order " 'to restrain any person for the purpose of preventing a recurrence of domestic violence and ensuring a period of separation of the persons involved' upon 'reasonable proof of a past act or acts of abuse.' " The statute should "be broadly construed in order to accomplish [its] purpose" of preventing acts of domestic violence.

We review the trial court's grant or denial of a DVPA restraining order request for an abuse of discretion. We likewise review a trial court's failure to consider evidence in issuing a DVRO for an abuse of discretion. " To the extent that we are called upon to review the trial court's factual findings, we apply a substantial evidence standard of review.'

"Judicial discretion to grant or deny an application for a protective order is not unfettered. The scope of discretion always resides in the particular law being applied by the court, i.e., in the ' "legal principles governing the subject of [the] action. . . ." ' " Thus, "we consider whether the trial court's exercise of discretion is consistent with the statute's intended purpose." " 'If the court's decision is influenced by an erroneous understanding of applicable law or reflects an unawareness of the full scope of its discretion, the court has not properly exercised its discretion under the law. Therefore, a discretionary order based on an application of improper criteria or incorrect legal assumptions is not an exercise of informed discretion and is subject to reversal.' The question of whether a trial court applied the correct legal standard to an issue in exercising its discretion is a question of law requiring de novo review."

B. The Trial Court's Refusal to Consider Evidence of Postfiling Abuse Was Prejudicial Error

During the December 2019 hearing, the trial court repeatedly refused to consider evidence regarding alleged acts of domestic violence committed by father after mother filed her DVRO request, deeming such evidence irrelevant to whether a permanent *[i.e., long-term]* restraining order should issue. Mother contends this was error, asserting that "[n]othing in the plain language of the DVPA restricts courts when ruling on a DVRO request to hearing evidence of abuse that occurred only before the request was filed." We agree.

"The DVPA requires a showing of past abuse by a preponderance of the evidence." Section 6300 subdivision (a) provides, in part: "An order may be issued under this part to restrain any person . . . if an affidavit or testimony and any additional information provided to the court . . . shows, to the satisfaction of the court, *reasonable proof of a past act or acts of abuse*." (Italics added.) Mother correctly observes that the DVPA does not "provide that the 'past act or acts of abuse' must have occurred only before the petitioner filed the request, or that a court is barred from considering any abuse occurring thereafter."

While a trial court should, of course, hear and evaluate the evidence relating to incidents set forth in a petitioner's request, evidence of postfiling abuse is also relevant, particularly when that abuse occurs after a temporary restraining order has been issued, as was the case here. The purpose of a domestic violence restraining order is not to punish past conduct, but to "prevent acts of domestic violence [and] abuse" from occurring in the future. Evidence of recent abuse or violation of a TRO is plainly relevant to whether a petitioner should be granted a protective order. Evidence Code section 210 defines "relevant evidence," in part, as "evidence . . . having any tendency in reason to prove or disprove any disputed fact that is of consequence to the determination of the action." Evidence Code section 351 provides: "Except as otherwise provided by statute, all relevant evidence is admissible."

Postfiling abusive conduct is clearly relevant in cases in which a TRO has been granted pending a hearing on a permanent restraining order. As noted above, section 6320 allows a court to enjoin, among other things, attacking, striking, threatening, harassing, contacting directly or indirectly, or disturbing the peace of the protected party. Section 6203, subdivision (a)(4) specifically provides that engaging in behavior that "has been . . . enjoined pursuant to Section 6320" constitutes abuse for purposes of the DVPA. The probative value of postfiling evidence is even more apparent in cases such as this one where the trial court's final ruling was delayed by several months.

In this case, the August 2019 TRO forbade father from attacking or threatening mother, disturbing mother's peace, or contacting her directly or indirectly apart from "peaceful contact" required for visitation with the children. Mother offered admissible evidence that father violated these prohibitions after she obtained the TRO. For example, she testified that father threatened to kill her a few days before the December 2019 hearing after he learned that she had withdrawn $3,000 from their joint bank account. She also testified about an altercation in October 2019 at father's home in which she was physically attacked by him, resulting in his arrest.

The trial court's categorical refusal to consider postfiling evidence of father's alleged abuse and violation of the TRO, based solely on the ground that the conduct had occurred after mother filed her DVRO application, was legal error and therefore constituted an abuse of the court's discretion. The court's evidentiary cut-off violated the DVPA's mandate that a court "shall" consider the "totality of the circumstances" in determining whether to issue a restraining order.

The error was prejudicial. To establish prejudice, an appellant must demonstrate that there was a " ' "reasonable probability that in the absence of . . . error, a result more favorable to the appealing party would have been reached." ' " If mother's testimony regarding father's postfiling conduct had been credited, the evidence could have established abuse sufficient to support the issuance of a DVRO under the proper legal standard. Accordingly, we reverse the order denying mother's request for a DVRO and remand this matter to the trial court for a new hearing to be conducted consistent with this opinion. We address mother's remaining arguments to provide further guidance on remand.

C. Sufficiency of Mother's Evidence of Prefiling Abuse

In denying mother's DVRO request, the court found her testimony lacked specificity and corroboration. According to the court, mother "need[ed] to tell [the court] specific dates." The court also faulted her for failing to provide corroborating evidence: "Well, you haven't provided any corroborating evidence to me that [domestic violence], in fact, took place. All I have is your say so if that's what happened, and I have [father]'s testimony that that didn't happen. You have the burden of proof, not him; you do. [¶] . . . [¶] . . . And I just don't find that there's sufficient evidence to grant this domestic violence restraining order." The court concluded that mother "provided no corroborating evidence for her statements as to what took place in the past. [¶] The Court finds they are too general in nature and lack [the] specificity required to support the request."

We agree with mother that the DVPA does not impose a heightened standard for specificity, nor does it contain any corroboration requirement. Instead, it provides that a court may issue a DVRO "if an affidavit or testimony and any additional information provided to the court . . . shows, to the satisfaction of the court, *reasonable proof* of a past act or acts of abuse." (italics added.) The DVPA also expressly provides that a court may issue a restraining order "based *solely* on the affidavit or testimony of the person requesting the restraining order." (italics added.)

Our review of the evidence does not reveal a fatal lack of specificity in mother's evidence. Mother's request for a restraining order documented specific acts of domestic violence and described father's ongoing abusive behavior. For example, she alleged that father had threatened her life and had specifically threatened to kill her if she called the police for help. He had allegedly called her father in Nigeria and made the same threats. She alleged that father repeatedly called her a "motherfucker," "bitch," and "prostitute" in front of their children. In her DVRO request, mother referenced four specific dates on which these incidents occurred, and she also testified that these kinds of acts occurred with regularity. Mother also alleged that father had beaten her and hit her with his hands, and had taken her phone away from her. Threats on a person's life, demeaning a person in front of their children with vulgar and degrading language, physically beating a person, and seeking to exercise control over a person by taking away their phone, are all actionable forms of abuse under the DVPA.

Of course, "[a] trier of fact is free to disbelieve a witness . . . if there is any rational ground for doing so." Here, the trial court did not indicate on the record that mother lacked credibility as a witness, and indeed, the court must have credited her testimony because it issued and reissued the TRO several times. Instead, the court found mother failed to meet her burden of proof because she did not offer corroborating evidence. In many domestic violence cases, however, the sole evidence of abuse will be the survivor's own testimony which, standing alone, can be sufficient to establish a fact: "The testimony of one witness, even that of a party, may constitute substantial evidence." On remand, the trial court is directed to weigh this evidence without a corroboration or heightened specificity requirement.

D. Physical Separation Is Not a Substitute for the Protections of a Restraining Order

Mother correctly argues that the trial court erred insofar as it relied on the fact that she no longer lives with father as a basis for denying her DVRO request. Section 6301, subdivision (b) expressly provides, in relevant part: "The right to petition for relief shall not be denied because the petitioner has vacated the household to avoid abuse. . . ." As mother states: "In light of the recognized seriousness of domestic abuse, domestic violence survivors must not be denied critical protection under the DVPA merely [because] they have succeeded in extracting themselves from the immediate risks posed by living with their abuser."

Here, the trial court repeatedly stated on the record that mother's protection from abuse could be accomplished simply by having her and the parties' six children move out of the house. For example, at the September 2019 hearing, the court stated that it was "not as much concerned" about the allegations that father had threatened to kill mother and had verbally abused her in front of their children, because those behaviors were, in the court's view, simply a function of them living together. At the same time, the court repeatedly stated that the parties needed to stay away from each other, which the court presumably believed they could do without a court order in place. This was error.

The trial court's use of residential separation as a substitute for a DVRO was inappropriate given that the parties still have to coparent. Because the parties have six children together, further interactions between the two are unavoidable. The record shows that even with separate residences, continuing interaction between the parties has resulted in ongoing conflict. On remand, the trial court may not deny mother's petition for a restraining order on the basis that she no longer lives in the same residence with father.

[Editor's Note: See also Nicole G. v. Brathwaite, *49 Cal.App.5th 990 (2020), in which the court denied the abusive boyfriend's request for a domestic violence restraining order and granted one to Nicole, the girlfriend. The court also ordered the boyfriend, a convicted felon, to move out of the condo they lived in which Nicole had vacated to protect herself. This order allowed her to move back in. Even though she had moved out, Nicole had continued to pay the mortgage and property taxes on the condo. On appeal the boyfriend argued that the family law trial court should not have ordered him to move out in the restraining order, since there was a*

partition suit pending in another court that would decide ownership and possession of the condo. The appellate court held that the trial court had not abused its discretion in ordering the boyfriend to move out as part of the restraining order, since the statute allows this, even though title to the condo would be decided in the partition suit. This case stands for the proposition that domestic violence survivors do not lose the right to live in their homes if they need to temporarily vacate the home for safety.]

MACDONALD V. CARUSO

5 N.E.3d 831 (Mass. 2014)
(citations and most footnotes omitted)

The central issue in this case is the standard to be applied when a defendant seeks to terminate a permanent abuse prevention order under G.L. c. 209A, § 3. We conclude that a defendant who seeks to terminate such an order must show by clear and convincing evidence that, as a result of a significant change in circumstances, it is no longer equitable for the order to continue because the protected party no longer has a reasonable fear of imminent serious physical harm. Having considered the evidence presented here in support of the defendant's motion to terminate the permanent order, in light of the totality of the circumstances, we conclude that the judge did not abuse her discretion in denying the motion.

Background. According to the complaint and affidavit filed by the plaintiff, Tracy MacDonald, on June 25, 1999, in support of her application for an ex parte temporary restraining order under G.L. c. 209A, § 4, against the defendant, Kevin James Caruso, the plaintiff had obtained an "order of protection" in the State of New York against the defendant in March, 1994. She left New York, where she had resided, on November 6, 1995, because the defendant threatened to kill her, and she has not lived in New York since that date.[2] On June 1, 1999, she began receiving "odd mail" in Massachusetts, where she resided, postmarked in the region where the defendant then resided, stating that she had inquired about numerous products; one bore the defendant's handwriting. The defendant also used her social security number and forged her signature to acquire a credit card in her name, and she received a telephone call from the credit card company claiming that she was in default for failing to pay the $2,000 due on the card. On June 20, 1999, the plaintiff saw the defendant when she was on a boat ramp in Plymouth, near where she lived.

A Probate and Family Court judge issued a temporary abuse prevention order directing the defendant to refrain from abusing or contacting the plaintiff, to stay away from her residence in Halifax, and to surrender any firearms or ammunition to the police department in Highland, New York, where the defendant resided. The judge scheduled an

---

2 The plaintiff asserted that the defendant owned seven handguns.

adversary hearing for July 9, 1999, the date the temporary order was scheduled to expire. The defendant did not appear at the adversary hearing, and another Probate and Family Court judge issued an initial abuse prevention order for one year, to expire on July 9, 2000.

The defendant was present for the hearing on July 7, 2000, the next designated hearing date, but the order was further extended for one year, to July 6, 2001, with a new hearing scheduled for that expiration date. The defendant again appeared at that hearing, where a permanent order entered, with the judge noting that the surrender of firearms to the police department should also be extended because the defendant presented a likelihood of abuse to the plaintiff. The defendant did not challenge the permanent order on direct appeal.

In May, 2011, the defendant moved to terminate the permanent abuse prevention order. In his verified motion, he attested:

> "[T]here is no further need for the order, because it is now twelve years old, with no alleged or proven violations. He has moved from New York to Park City, Utah, and [p]laintiff now resides in Massachusetts, a separation distance of more than 2,100 miles. He is married since 2004, and happily so. He has retired from the business world, and now seeks to pass his time with various recreational activities that are available to him in his new home, as well as with travel. He has clearly moved on with his life. . . ."

The defendant also noted that the abuse prevention order "continues to affect his life in ways that have nothing to do with [the] [p]laintiff." The collateral consequences he described included extra scrutiny at airports, his disqualification from charitable pursuits that require record checks, and his inability to hunt and to obtain a pistol permit for self-protection. After a hearing, at which the plaintiff did not appear, the judge (who was the same judge who had ordered the second one-year extension after an adversary hearing) denied the defendant's motion, concluding that the defendant had not met his burden of proving, by clear and convincing evidence, that there has been a significant change of circumstances and that the order was unnecessary to protect the plaintiff from harm or the reasonable fear of harm.

The defendant appealed, and in an unpublished memorandum and order pursuant to its rule 1:28, the Appeals Court affirmed the denial of the defendant's motion. The court declined the defendant's invitation to modify the standard established in *Mitchell v. Mitchell,* 62 Mass.App.Ct. 769, 781, 821 N.E.2d 79 (2005), that an abuse prevention order "should be set aside only in the most extraordinary circumstances and where it has been clearly and convincingly established that the order is no longer needed to protect the victim from harm or the reasonable fear of serious harm." Applying that standard, the court concluded that the judge did not err in finding that the defendant failed to meet this burden. We granted the defendant's application for further appellate review.

Discussion. General Laws c. 209A provides "a statutory mechanism by which victims of family or household abuse can enlist the aid of the State to prevent further abuse" through orders prohibiting a defendant from abusing or contacting the victim, or requiring a defendant to stay away from the victim's home or workplace. The statute, with other abuse prevention statutes, reflects "the Commonwealth's public policy against domestic abuse—preservation of the fundamental human right to be protected from the devastating impact of family violence."

A temporary abuse prevention order may issue ex parte for up to ten court business days where a plaintiff shows a "substantial likelihood of immediate danger of abuse." After hearing, the temporary order may be extended for no more than one year if the plaintiff proves, by a preponderance of the evidence, that the defendant has caused or attempted to cause physical harm, committed a sexual assault, or placed the plaintiff in reasonable fear of imminent serious physical harm. On or about the date the initial order expires, the plaintiff may seek to extend the duration of the order "for any additional time necessary to protect the plaintiff" or obtain a permanent order. The standard for obtaining an extension of an abuse prevention order is the same as for an initial order—"most commonly, the plaintiff will need to show a reasonable fear of imminent serious physical harm at the time that relief . . . is sought." No presumption arises from the initial order; "it is the plaintiff's burden to establish that the facts that exist at the time extension of the order is sought justify relief." Therefore, a permanent order may not enter unless the plaintiff has twice proved by a preponderance of the evidence a reasonable fear of imminent serious physical harm. And where the initial order was one year in duration, the plaintiff must show that the fear of imminent serious physical harm remains reasonable approximately one year after the event that triggered the filing of the c. 209A complaint.

Where, as here, the defendant does not challenge on direct appeal the entry of a permanent abuse prevention order under G.L. c. 209A, it becomes a final equitable order. But relief from the order may still be obtained where it is "no longer equitable that the judgment should have prospective application." In determining what standard to apply to determine when it is "no longer equitable" that a permanent c. 209A order continue to have prospective application, we note that G.L. c. 209A, § 3, provides that a "court may modify its order at any subsequent time upon motion by either party." In doing so, the Legislature recognized that, given the complicated and dynamic nature of the relationships among "family or household members," and the complex web of personal ties and responsibilities that may still connect them even where there is an order, especially the parenting of children, even a carefully crafted abuse prevention order may require modification as circumstances change. The Legislature also recognized that modification may be sought by a plaintiff, by a defendant, or jointly by all parties, and that a motion to modify may seek to revise the terms of an abuse prevention order or to terminate the order itself. We decide here only the standard to apply where a defendant seeks to terminate an order, recognizing that the standard appropriate for such a motion may not be the same where the motion to terminate is brought by the plaintiff or jointly by all parties, or where the motion seeks only to modify the terms of an order.

A defendant's motion to terminate an order is not a motion to reconsider the entry of a final order, and does not provide an opportunity for a defendant to challenge the underlying basis for the order or to obtain relief from errors correctable on appeal. Therefore, a defendant bringing such a motion bears the burden of proving a significant change in circumstances since the entry of the order that justifies termination of the order.

The significant change in circumstances must involve more than the mere passage of time, because a judge who issues a permanent order knows that time will pass. Compliance by the defendant with the order is also not sufficient alone to constitute a significant change in circumstances, because a judge who issues a permanent order is entitled to expect that the defendant will comply with the order. However, if there is a significant change in circumstances not foreseen when the last order was issued, the passage of time and compliance with the order may be considered in determining whether, under the totality of circumstances, a defendant no longer poses a reasonable threat of imminent serious physical harm to the plaintiff.

The defendant contends that his burden should only be to prove by a preponderance of the evidence that the plaintiff no longer has a reasonable fear of imminent serious physical harm from the defendant. We conclude that, where a defendant seeks to terminate an abuse prevention order, the defendant must prove by clear and convincing evidence that the protected party no longer has a reasonable fear of imminent serious physical harm from the defendant, and that continuation of the order would therefore not be equitable.

Where the order a defendant seeks to terminate is only one year in duration, as it was in *Mitchell v. Mitchell,* 62 Mass.App.Ct. at 770, 821 N.E.2d 79, the defendant will have the opportunity within one year to challenge the continuation of the order at a hearing where the plaintiff will bear the burden of proving a continued reasonable fear of imminent serious physical harm. A motion prematurely to terminate such an order must be supported by more than a preponderance of the evidence to justify the burden, both on the plaintiff and the court, to revisit the order before its expiration. See *id.* at 781 n.22, 821 N.E.2d 79 ("Unwarranted requests to modify may themselves be a form of abuse and create a burden on the courts as well as on the opposing party").

Where the order is permanent, as it is here, a defendant has been found at least twice (here, three times) to pose a reasonable threat of imminent serious physical harm to the plaintiff, and the judge who issued the permanent order found (at least implicitly) that the defendant poses a permanent threat to the safety of the plaintiff. The standard of proof "serves as 'a societal judgment about how the risk of error should be distributed between the litigants.' " Where a defendant has been found over an extended period of time to pose this level of danger to a plaintiff, we conclude that the risk of error should be on the side of the plaintiff and that something more than proof by a preponderance of the evidence is necessary to ensure the plaintiff's safety.

The clear and convincing evidence standard is more demanding than the preponderance standard, but we do not accept the defendant's characterization that it is either "amorphous" or "an enormously heavy burden of proof." Clear and convincing evidence is required to hold a litigant in civil contempt; to find libel against a public official or public figure; and to terminate parental rights. It is applied every day in our courts and the burden, while demanding, is often met. The standard is less demanding than the proof beyond a reasonable doubt standard required to justify an involuntary civil commitment, either because the respondent poses a danger to himself or to others, or because of sexual dangerousness.

In determining whether a defendant has met the clear and convincing evidence standard, a judge must determine whether the defendant has proven a significant change in circumstances since the order was issued, and whether, under the totality of the circumstances, the plaintiff, without the protection of an order of abuse prevention, would no longer reasonably fear imminent serious physical harm from the defendant. Here, the defendant has identified five changes in circumstances that he contends justify termination of the order: (1) he has moved from New York to Utah, (2) he has been happily married since 2004, (3) he has retired from the "business world," (4) more than twelve years have passed since the issuance of the permanent order, and (5) there have been no "alleged or proven violations" of the order. We have already noted that the fourth and fifth alleged changes do not suffice alone to constitute a significant change of circumstances. As to the third alleged change, we are not persuaded that retirement from employment constitutes a relevant change in circumstances that reasonably may affect the risk posed by a defendant. The first and second alleged changes, however, may support a finding of a significant change of circumstances, in that the defendant's relocation from New York to Utah increases the cost and effort required for the defendant to see the plaintiff in Massachusetts, and his long-standing marriage may suggest that, as he contends, he has "moved on with his life" and no longer is so emotionally connected to the plaintiff as to pose a risk to her.

Assuming that the defendant has met his burden of proving a significant change in circumstances, we turn to whether the judge abused her discretion in finding that the defendant failed to meet his burden of proving by clear and convincing evidence that he no longer poses a reasonable threat of imminent serious physical harm to the plaintiff. The defendant asks us to give meaning to the plaintiff's failure to appear at the hearing or otherwise to object to his motion to terminate. We decline to do so. A judge should certainly give serious consideration to the plaintiff's position regarding a defendant's motion to terminate, regardless of whether the plaintiff opposes or supports the motion, but a judge may not give meaning to a plaintiff's silence or failure to appear, because a judge cannot know whether silence reflects acquiescence in the termination or continued fear of the defendant. Moreover, a plaintiff shoulders no burden at a termination hearing and is entitled to rest on the finality of the order.

The defendant also asks us to consider the collateral consequences that a defendant may suffer from an abuse prevention order, including his inability to obtain a permit to carry firearms. We decline to do so. Where a defendant has failed to meet his burden to terminate an abuse prevention order, the order shall not be terminated, regardless of how onerous the collateral consequences, because the only relevant issue is the safety of the plaintiff. Where that burden has been met, the order should be terminated, because its prospective application is no longer needed to protect the plaintiff, and even if there were no collateral consequences, it is no longer equitable for the order to remain in force. Therefore, the collateral consequences arising from the order are not relevant to the judge's decision regarding termination of the order.

Addressing the relevant changes of circumstances, the additional distance between the defendant's and the plaintiff's residences may significantly diminish the reasonable fear of imminent serious physical harm if the abuse prevention order had issued when the plaintiff and defendant worked or resided in close proximity to each other, and the defendant had harmed or threatened harm to the plaintiff when their paths crossed. But the orders in this case issued when the plaintiff resided in Massachusetts and the defendant resided in New York, so there was already considerable distance between the two. That the defendant would now need to travel approximately six hours by airplane rather than approximately six hours by car to see the plaintiff bears on the likelihood of his seeing her, and the expense and effort to do so, but by itself does not mean that he could not engage in the same conduct from afar that triggered issuance of the initial order.

The most significant change of circumstance in this case is the defendant's marriage to another woman since 2004, considered together with his undisputed compliance with the abuse prevention orders, which corroborates his contention that he has "moved on with his life." But the defendant rested his motion to terminate solely on his own attestations in his verified motion. He did not submit an affidavit from the chief of police or the keeper of the records of his city in Utah attesting that the police had no record of any allegations of domestic abuse, or submit the New York and Utah equivalents of the Massachusetts criminal offender record information (CORI) and Statewide registry of civil restraining orders records to show the absence of arrests or convictions or other restraining orders. To prove that he had truly "moved on with his life," the defendant in this case needed to demonstrate not only that he has moved on to another relationship but also that he has "moved on" from his history of domestic abuse and retaliation. Because the defendant bears the burden of demonstrating, by clear and convincing evidence, that he no longer reasonably poses a threat to the plaintiff, the judge did not abuse her discretion in finding that the defendant's attestations alone fell short of meeting this burden.

Although we conclude that the judge here, on this record, did not abuse her discretion in denying the defendant's motion to terminate the abuse prevention order, we leave open the possibility that the defendant might be able to meet his burden if he were to renew his motion with a stronger evidentiary foundation. The standard of clear and convincing evidence in these matters is properly demanding, but not insurmountable if supported by a persuasive evidentiary record demonstrating that a defendant no longer poses a reasonable risk of committing serious physical harm. Because we do not believe that a defendant's possibility of winning a motion to terminate an abuse prevention order is illusory, or that a judge can never abuse her discretion by denying such a motion, we direct judges to place their findings of fact regarding such motions on the record, regardless of whether the motion is allowed or denied, to assist an appellate court in reviewing the determination on appeal. * * *

COLORADO CODE § 13–14–100.2—LEGISLATIVE DECLARATION

(1) The general assembly hereby finds that the issuance and enforcement of protection orders are of paramount importance in the state of Colorado because protection orders promote safety, reduce violence and other types of abuse, and prevent serious harm and death. In order to improve the public's access to protection orders and to ensure careful judicial consideration of requests and effective law enforcement, there shall be two processes for obtaining protection orders within the state of Colorado, a simplified civil process and a mandatory criminal process.

(2) The general assembly further finds and declares that domestic abuse is not limited to physical threats of violence and harm but also

includes mental and emotional abuse, financial control, document control, property control, and other types of control that make a victim more likely to return to an abuser due to fear of retaliation or inability to meet basic needs. Many victims of domestic abuse are unable to access the resources necessary to seek lasting safety options. Victims need additional provisions in protection orders so that they can meet their immediate needs of food, shelter, transportation, medical care, and childcare for their appearance at protection order hearings. These needs may exist not only in cases that may end in dissolution of marriage but also in other circumstances, including cases in which reconciliation may occur. * * *

COLORADO CODE § 13–14–106—PROCEDURE FOR PERMANENT CIVIL PROTECTION ORDERS

* * * (c)(3) A court shall not grant a mutual protection order to prevent domestic abuse for the protection of opposing parties unless each party has met his or her burden of proof as described in section 13–14–104.5(7) and the court makes separate and sufficient findings of fact to support the issuance of the mutual protection order to prevent domestic abuse for the protection of opposing parties. A party may not waive the requirements set forth in this subsection (3).

COLORADO CODE § 13–14–108—MODIFICATION AND TERMINATION OF CIVIL PROTECTION ORDERS

* * * (2)(a) Nothing in this article precludes the protected party from applying to the court at any time for modification, including but not limited to a modification of the duration of a protection order or dismissal of a temporary or permanent protection order issued pursuant to this section.

(b) The restrained party may apply to the court for modification, including but not limited to a modification of the duration of the protection order or dismissal of a permanent protection order pursuant to this section. However, if a permanent protection order has been issued or if a motion for modification or dismissal of a permanent protection order has been filed by the restrained party, whether or not it was granted, no motion to modify or dismiss may be filed by the restrained party within two years after issuance of the permanent order or after disposition of the prior motion.

(3)(a)(I) Notwithstanding any provision of subsection (2) of this section to the contrary, after issuance of the permanent protection order, if the restrained party has been convicted of or pled guilty to any misdemeanor or any felony against the protected person, other than the original offense, if any, that formed the basis for the issuance of the protection order, then the protection order remains permanent and must not be modified or dismissed by the court.

(II) Notwithstanding the prohibition in subparagraph (I) of this paragraph (a), a protection order may be modified or dismissed on the motion of the protected person, or the person's attorney, parent or legal guardian if a minor, or conservator or legal guardian if one has been appointed; except that this paragraph (a) does not apply if the parent, legal guardian, or conservator is the restrained person.

(b) A court shall not consider a motion to modify a protection order filed by a restrained party pursuant to paragraph (a) of this subsection (3) unless the court receives the results of a fingerprint-based criminal history record check of the restrained party that is conducted within ninety days prior to the filing of the motion. The fingerprint-based criminal history record check must include a review of the state and federal criminal history records maintained by the Colorado bureau of investigation and federal bureau of investigation. The restrained party shall be responsible for supplying fingerprints to the Colorado bureau of investigation and to the federal bureau of investigation and paying the costs of the record checks. The restrained party may be required by the court to provide certified copies of any criminal dispositions that are not reflected in the state or federal records and any other dispositions that are unknown. * * *

(5) The court shall hear any motion filed pursuant to subsection (2) of this section. The party moving for a modification or dismissal of a temporary or permanent protection order pursuant to subsection (2) of this section shall affect personal service on the other party with a copy of the motion and notice of the hearing on the motion, as provided by rule 4(e) of the Colorado rules of civil procedure. The moving party shall bear the burden of proof to show, by a preponderance of the evidence, that the modification is appropriate or that a dismissal is appropriate because the protection order is no longer necessary. If the protected party has requested that his or her address be kept confidential, the court shall not disclose such information to the restrained party or any other person, except as otherwise authorized by law.

(6) In considering whether to modify or dismiss a protection order issued pursuant to this section, the court shall consider all relevant factors, including but not limited to:

(a) Whether the restrained party has complied with the terms of the protection order;

(b) Whether the restrained party has met the conditions associated with the protection order, if any;

(c) Whether the restrained party has been ordered to participate in and has completed a domestic violence offender treatment program provided by an entity approved pursuant to section 16–11.8–103,

C.R.S., or has been ordered to participate in and has either successfully completed a sex offender treatment program provided by an entity approved pursuant to section 16–11.7–103, C.R.S., or has made significant progress in a sex offender treatment program as reported by the sex offender treatment provider;

(d) Whether the restrained party has voluntarily participated in any domestic violence offender treatment program provided by an entity approved pursuant to section 16–11.8–103, C.R.S., or any sex offender treatment program provided by an entity approved pursuant to section 16–11.7–103, C.R.S.;

(e) The time that has lapsed since the protection order was issued;

(f) When the last incident of abuse or threat of harm occurred or other relevant information concerning the safety and protection of the protected person;

(g) Whether, since the issuance of the protection order, the restrained person has been convicted of or pled guilty to any misdemeanor or any felony against the protected person, other than the original offense, if any, that formed the basis for the issuance of the protection order;

(h) Whether any other restraining orders, protective orders, or protection orders have been subsequently issued against the restrained person pursuant to this section or any other law of this state or any other state;

(i) The circumstances of the parties, including the relative proximity of the parties' residences and schools or work places and whether the parties have minor children together; and

(j) Whether the continued safety of the protected person depends upon the protection order remaining in place because the order has been successful in preventing further harm to the protected person.

B. RELATIONSHIP TO DIVORCE

BRENDA L. WALTON v. PHILIP M. WALTON

2004 WL 3017265 (slip copy) (Ohio App.) (unpublished)
(citations and footnotes omitted)

DECISION AND JUDGMENT ENTRY

This is an appeal from a judgment of the Wood County Court of Common Pleas that issued a civil protection order based on appellee's allegations of domestic violence. For the reasons that follow, this court affirms the judgment of the trial court.

Appellant Philip Walton sets forth the following assignments of error:

"I. The trial court committed error in permitting petitioner-appellant to relitigate in a domestic violence case allegations of abuse that had been litigated and rejected in a pending domestic relations case.

"II. The trial court's finding that domestic violence occurred is against the manifest weight of the evidence."

In July 2003, appellant Philip Walton filed a complaint for divorce against appellee Brenda Walton in the Wood County Court of Common Pleas, Domestic Relations Division. During October, November and December 2003, three days of hearings were held on the parties' motions, including appellee's request for temporary custody of their two minor children and exclusive occupancy of the marital residence. On January 6, 2004, the domestic relations magistrate issued a decision rejecting appellee's requests and ordering the parties to rotate in and out of the marital home while the children remained there. On January 15, 2004, appellee filed a petition for a civil protection order in the Wood County Court of Common Pleas, General Division. The trial court issued an ex parte protection order that same day on the basis of appellee's affidavit and testimony. On January 20, 2004, appellant filed a motion asking the trial court to reconsider the necessity for and scope of the ex parte order, and on January 22, 2004, an evidentiary hearing was held on appellee's petition. At the hearing, the parties stipulated to the admission of certain exhibits that had been entered into evidence at the temporary motions hearings in the domestic relations case.

On February 5, 2004, the trial court filed a judgment entry in case no. 04–DV–003 finding that domestic violence had occurred. The trial court issued a civil protection order but stressed that the domestic violence order did not in any way modify the January 6, 2004 magistrate's order in case no. 03–DR–138. It is from the judgment issuing the civil protection order that appellant appeals.

In his first assignment of error, appellant asserts that, by hearing the allegations of abuse raised in appellee's petition for a civil protection order, the trial court relitigated issues that had been heard and rejected in the parties' pending domestic relations case. In support of his argument, appellant cites the doctrine of res judicata. Appellant argues that, while the mere filing of a divorce action is not a basis upon which to deny a civil protection order, the fact that a civil protection order is available as an additional remedy to domestic relations proceedings is not a license to relitigate in an attempt to obtain relief previously denied a party in the domestic relations court.

The doctrine of res judicata acts to bar claims previously adjudicated in full (historically called estoppel by judgment in Ohio) as well as issues that have been previously adjudicated between the same parties (generally known as collateral estoppel). Appellant argues that the proceedings in domestic relations court centered primarily on whether appellee had been abused by appellant, thereby precluding the issue of abuse from being litigated again in the action brought for a civil protection order. This court disagrees.

The Supreme Court of Ohio has recognized that there can be times when the circumstances surrounding a pending divorce may necessitate protective action more stringent than the general prohibition set forth in Civ.R. 75 which is incidental to the filing of any divorce action. In *Felton v. Felton*, 1997–Ohio–302, the court held at syllabus that "[a] court is not precluded by statute or public policy reasons from issuing a protection order pursuant to Ohio's civil domestic violence statute, R.C. 3113.31, where the parties' dissolution or divorce decree already prohibits the parties from harassing each other." While the facts in *Felton* differ slightly from those of this case, what is significant is the *Felton* court's holding that there are times when the general civil remedy available through a protection order issued pursuant to R.C. 3113.31 is necessary during the pendency of a divorce.

Because the magistrate's January 6, 2004 report in case no. 03–DR–138 is a part of the record herein, we know that the court heard appellee testify that appellant had physically abused her. That evidence was presented, however, in the context of a hearing on appellee's motion for exclusive use of the marital residence. While the magistrate's order makes reference to appellee's claims that appellant physically abused her, the issue before that court clearly was that of residence in the marital home. The relief requested by appellee was exclusive use of the home. In the instant case, the issue was possible physical abuse and the relief requested was a civil protection order. After several days of testimony, the domestic relations magistrate denied appellee's motion.

Upon consideration of the foregoing, this court finds that appellee's petition for a civil protection order was not barred by res judicata and, accordingly, appellant's first assignment of error is not well-taken.

In his second assignment of error, appellant asserts that appellee's claims were contrived and that the trial court's finding that domestic violence occurred was against the manifest weight of the evidence. As set forth in R.C. 3113.31(A)(1), "[d]omestic violence means the occurrence of one or more of the following acts against a family or household member: (a) [a]ttempting to cause or recklessly causing bodily injury; (b) [p]lacing another person by the threat of force in fear of imminent serious physical harm * * *."

Pursuant to *Felton, supra*, at 42, "when granting a protection order, the trial court must find that petitioner has shown by a preponderance of the evidence that petitioner or petitioner's family or household members are in danger of domestic violence." The decision whether to grant a civil protection order lies within the sound discretion of the trial court, and an appellate court should not reverse the judgment of the trial court absent an abuse of that discretion. An abuse of discretion "connotes more than an error of law or judgment; it implies that the court's attitude is unreasonable, arbitrary or unconscionable."

Upon review of the transcript of the January 22, 2004 hearing, we conclude that the issuance of the civil protection order was neither an abuse of discretion nor against the manifest weight of the evidence. Appellee testified that she filed the petition for a protection order because she was afraid of her husband and had been for quite some time because he had abused her physically and emotionally for most of their 22-year marriage. Appellee described specific instances of physical abuse inflicted on her by appellant and estimated that appellant had been physically abusive to her 50 times over the years. She also offered into evidence several photographs depicting bruises on her body which she testified were caused by appellant. Appellee described steps she took to protect herself from her husband on numerous occasions.

The trial court chose to believe appellee's testimony that appellant had physically abused her and that his actions put her in fear of physical harm. Because the trier of fact sees and hears the witnesses and is particularly competent to decide "whether, and to what extent, to credit the testimony of particular witnesses," we must afford substantial deference to its determinations of credibility. Although the trial court could have chosen to credit appellant's testimony that there had never been any mental or physical abuse, we find that its determination that appellee showed by a preponderance of the evidence that she was in danger of domestic violence was neither an abuse of discretion nor against the manifest weight of the evidence and, accordingly, appellant's second assignment of error is not well-taken.

On consideration whereof, this court finds that substantial justice was done the party complaining and the judgment of the Wood County Court of Common Pleas is affirmed. Pursuant to App.R. 24, costs of this appeal are assessed to appellant.

C. MUTUAL RESTRAINING ORDERS

K.L. v. R.H.

70 Cal.App.5th 965 (Cal. App. 2021)
(footnotes and citations omitted)
(Note: The facts described may be upsetting to some readers.)

The purpose of the [Ca.] Domestic Violence Prevention Act (DVPA) "is to prevent acts of domestic violence, abuse, and sexual abuse and to provide for a separation of the persons involved in the domestic violence for a period sufficient to enable these persons to seek a resolution of the causes of the violence." To achieve this purpose, the DVPA authorizes the court to issue orders enjoining a party from, among other things, "molesting, attacking, striking, stalking, threatening, sexually assaulting, battering, . . . harassing, . . . destroying personal property, . . . coming within a specified distance of, or disturbing the peace of the other party, and, in the discretion of the court, on a showing of good cause, of other named family or household members."

The DVPA prohibits mutual orders enjoining both parties from the foregoing behavior unless "[t]he court makes detailed findings of fact indicating that both parties acted as a primary aggressor and that neither party acted primarily in self-defense." (Fam. Code, § 6305, subd. (a)(2).) In determining whether a party was a primary aggressor or acted in self-defense, the trial court must consider the factors set forth in Penal Code section 836, subdivision (c)(3).

K.L. and R.H. are the parents of Z.L.; their year-long relationship was defined by multiple acts of abuse by K.L., and the complete inability of either party to effectively communicate with the other. After their domestic relationship ended, both filed requests for DVPA orders against the other in December 2019. In February 2020, after an evidentiary hearing, the trial court found that both K.L. and R.H. had acted as a primary aggressor against the other, and that neither had acted in self-defense. The court therefore issued mutual orders against both parties, and also issued orders granting joint physical and legal custody of Z.L. to both parties.

The trial court erred by issuing mutual restraining orders without considering and following the relevant statutory authority. Because there was more than sufficient evidence supporting a DVPA order protecting R.H. and her child H.H. from K.L., that order shall be affirmed. We reverse the orders regarding child custody. If, after the trial court regains jurisdiction following the resolution of the dependency proceedings involving Z.L., either party files a request for order concerning custody, the trial court shall consider and apply the rebuttable presumption of Family Code section 3044 and the factors that may overcome that presumption.

STATEMENT OF FACTS

R.H. and K.L. began dating in the fall of 2017, and ended their relationship in December 2018. R.H. had a child before meeting K.L.; H.H. is now about seven years old. R.H. and K.L.'s child, Z.L., was born in November 2018.

Soon after they started dating, on November 23, 2017, K.L. appeared on R.H.'s doorstep after an argument and pointed a gun at her chest and then at her forehead. R.H. was terrified. K.L. ordered R.H. to calm down and be quiet and hit her in the face, but she could not stop crying. When K.L. allowed R.H. to go to her bedroom, she was shaking so badly she could not stand. K.L. laughed at R.H. and held out the gun to show her there were no bullets in it.

R.H. locked herself in her bedroom that night, and did not answer when K.L. knocked on the door in the middle of the night. The next morning, when R.H. would not let him in, K.L. broke down the locked door. When R.H. asked him to leave, K.L. punched her in the face several times. He grabbed her and slammed her head into the nightstand about six times. K.L. also tore out R.H.'s braids, which were sewn into her scalp. He also tried to rip off her tube top and take pictures of her naked body.

A neighbor heard R.H. screaming and called 911. The police came and K.L. admitted to "forcibly" pulling off her wig with the intention of taking pictures of her and posting them on social media. K.L. was detained on a charge of inflicting corporal injury on a cohabitant, but R.H. chose not to press charges because K.L. apologized and they were still in a relationship. . .

[*Editor's Summary:* There were many more incidents of physical abuse from April 2018 through end of 2019, some involving K.L. sexually assaulting R.H. while she was unconscious, tearing out braids sewn into her scalp, and repeatedly strangling R.H. During some of the incidents R.H. was pregnant with Z.L. or one of the parties was holding Z.L., who was bruised by K.L. H.H. was also injured in some of the assaults by K.L. R.H. and the children resided in a domestic violence shelter at one point; K.L. came to the shelter, so the staff immediately moved R.H. and the children to a motel. At another point K.L. and R.H. reconciled, then R.H. left again with the children. R.H. made several police reports. Some incidents occurred at custody exchanges of Z.L. Several of these incidents are briefly summarized below in the trial court's findings after hearing the evidence.]

On December 21, 2019, after the court had granted temporary restraining orders to both parties, K.L. punched R.H. in the head at a visitation exchange in front of the Westminster Police Station. R.H. felt a sharp pain and was frightened. K.L. claimed he had a video showing the incident did not occur, but did not introduce the video at the hearing.

K.L. and R.H. used the Talking Parents app to communicate regarding Z.L. Talking Parents is a court-mandated, online coparenting communication tool that records the time messages are sent and read, prevents messages from being altered or deleted, and is admissible in court. As part of K.L.'s request for a DVPA order, the following communications from R.H. on Talking Parents were read into the record: July 29, 2019: "Also, being sick doesn't mean I can't take care of my kids, you dick." September 9, 2019: "You like being a dick." The court also read into the record several exchanges between K.L. and R.H. involving R.H.'s failure to show up on time for custody exchanges.

R.H. also had read into the record messages from K.L. to her on Talking Parents: "I guess Z[.L.] being raised by African bitches and all you guys from [*sic*] and your grandmother you still need public assistance for the rest of your life or take care of a man. You claim I beat you up. Wait until you marry a white man and beat your ass all the time and no one will believe you. I know your dad turning in his grave seeing his daughter suck dick for a living, but you'll probably lie how you got there, too, about your dad. Go bleach your skin like your mom, you ugly bitch. Once you go get your boobs done, they look saggy, old Sponge Bob body ass. You look stupid living in the house. One day you won't be able to afford to live nowhere and you'll have to bounce from program to program."

The court also considered evidence that R.H. had pleaded guilty to misdemeanor child endangerment and misdemeanor commercial burglary in 2014, and had suffered several probation violations before being dismissed early from probation in January 2020. R.H. was also convicted of providing false identification to a peace officer, and detained but not arrested or charged with child cruelty and battery on a spouse in June 2019.

[Editor's Note: The amicus brief explains that R.H.'s misdemeanor convictions arose from an incident in which she was shopping at Kohl's department store with her child and took some clothes, hardly an example of actual child endangerment.]

PROCEDURAL HISTORY

On June 28, 2019, K.L. filed a request for a DVPA order, seeking protection for himself and Z.L. from R.H. At the hearing on July 19, 2019, the court found "there is insufficient evidence to substantiate by a preponderance of the evidence that domestic violence has occurred," and denied K.L.'s request for a DVPA order.

On December 3, 2019, K.L. filed a new request for a restraining order against R.H. When R.H. arrived at the courthouse that same day, her conversation with court staff led her to believe she could not file a restraining order that day. She left and the following day—December 4, 2019—filed her request for a DVPA order against K.L.

During his examination of R.H., K.L. acknowledged that his request for a DVPA order was based solely on claims that R.H. threatened him. K.L. specifically acknowledged that R.H. had never caused or attempted to cause him bodily harm, had never sexually assaulted him, and had never placed him in reasonable apprehension of imminent serious bodily injury to himself or anyone else.

During R.H.'s presentation of evidence supporting her request for a DVPA order, the trial court stated that evidence of three incidents of domestic violence was enough, and more would be repetitive. When R.H.

requested that she be permitted to present evidence of more acts of violence, the court denied the request.

On February 5, 2020, the court issued DVPA orders in favor of both K.L. and R.H. The court also issued a child custody and visitation order in connection with each DVPA order, granting K.L. and R.H. joint legal and physical custody of Z.L.

The trial court heard the two competing requests as "two separate trials." It first considered K.L.'s request against R.H. and found there was substantial evidence that (1) domestic violence or abuse by R.H. occurred within the meaning of Family Code sections 6203 and 6320; (2) R.H. was the perpetrator and K.L. was the victim of the violence or abuse; (3) the violence or abuse did not occur in self-defense; (4) the safety of K.L. and Z.L. would be jeopardized if the court did not issue the requested restraining order and (5) a restraining order lasting three years was necessary to separate R.H. and K.L. for a sufficient period to enable them to seek resolution of the causes of the violence or abuse. The court identified the following facts supporting its finding that R.H. committed domestic violence against K.L.: (1) R.H. threatened K.L. at the December 2, 2019 custody exchange; (2) R.H. disturbed K.L.'s peace as set forth in the Talking Parents app exchanges submitted by K.L.; and (3) R.H. had previous criminal convictions that were "violent in nature." Given the court's previous ruling that the earlier denial of K.L.'s request for a DVPA order in July 2019 precluded the admission of evidence of R.H.'s alleged violence or abuse before that date, we presume that the court considered only the Talking Parents exchanges occurring after July 19, 2019; any reliance by the court on Talking Parents exchanges before that date in support of K.L.'s request for a DVPA order would be error.

The trial court also granted R.H.'s request for a restraining order against K.L. based on the "litany of issues and incidents," particularly those occurring in November 2017, April 2018, October 2018, November 2018, March 2019, October 2019, and December 2019. The court specifically found that R.H.'s mother, J.A., was a credible and reliable witness.

In connection with the issuance of mutual restraining orders, the court found that R.H. and K.L. "were both primary aggressors, neither one acted primarily out of self-defense."

After issuing the mutual restraining orders, the trial court addressed child custody. The court acknowledged that its findings of domestic violence and abuse by both R.H. and K.L. brought the rebuttable presumption of Family Code section 3044 into play. The court also acknowledged it did not "have time to address" all the factors to overcome the presumption. The court ordered that the parties would have joint legal and physical custody, with one week on and one week off.

R.H. filed a notice of appeal.

DISCUSSION

I. STANDARDS FOR ISSUANCE OF MUTUAL RESTRAINING ORDERS

"Under the DVPA, a court may issue a restraining order to prevent domestic violence or abuse if the party seeking the order 'shows, to the satisfaction of the court, reasonable proof of a past act or acts of abuse.' " "Abuse" includes intentionally or recklessly causing or attempting to cause bodily injury to, sexual assault, placing a person in reasonable apprehension of imminent serious bodily injury, attacking, striking, stalking, threatening, battering, harassing, destroying personal property, or disturbing the peace of the other party.

The issuance of a mutual restraining order is governed by Family Code section 6305:

> "(a) The court shall not issue a mutual order enjoining the parties from specific acts of abuse described in Section 6320 unless . . .: [¶] . . . [¶]
>
> "(2) The court makes detailed findings of fact indicating that both parties acted as a primary aggressor and that neither party acted primarily in self-defense.
>
> "(b) For purposes of subdivision (a), in determining if both parties acted primarily as aggressors, the court shall consider the provisions concerning dominant aggressors set forth in paragraph (3) of subdivision (c) of Section 836 of the Penal Code." " '[D]etailed findings of fact' " under this statute "require sufficient factual findings or analysis for a reviewing court to assess the factual or legal basis for the trial court's decision."
>
> Penal Code section 836, subdivision (c)(3), provides as follows:
>
> "The dominant aggressor is the person determined to be the most significant, rather than the first, aggressor. In identifying the dominant aggressor, [the court] shall consider (A) the intent of the law to protect victims of domestic violence from continuing abuse, (B) the threats creating fear of physical injury, (C) the history of domestic violence between the persons involved, and (D) whether either person involved acted in self-defense." . . .

III. THE TRIAL COURT ERRED BY ISSUING A MUTUAL RESTRAINING ORDER WITHOUT CONSIDERING THE STATUTORY REQUIREMENTS

Family Code section 6305 permits trial courts to issue mutual restraining order, but limits them to specific circumstances that are not present in the record before us. Indeed, the language of the statute makes clear that mutual restraining orders are the exception, and "shall not issue" unless the trial court makes specific findings, and that in making those findings the court "shall consider" both the intent of the law protecting domestic violence victims and the specific circumstances of the history of domestic violence in the case before it. Specifically, the statute mandates that the court determine which of the parties is the "most significant" aggressor. Such a determination requires that the acts of the parties be weighed against each other. As a result, in deciding whether mutual restraining orders should issue, the trial court must consider the parties' respective alleged acts of domestic violence in concert, and not separately, as the court did here.

In this case, the trial court failed to properly apply the statutory factors to the evidence before it.

The trial court found that the following acts by K.L. had been established by a preponderance of the evidence: (1) the November 2017 incident in which K.L. pointed a gun at R.H., punched her in the face, slammed her head into the nightstand, tore out her braids, and broke down a locked door; (2) the April 2018 incident where K.L. threw a microwave toward R.H. and H.H.; (3) the October 2018 incident where K.L. pushed R.H., who was then pregnant, off the bed, causing her to suffer an antepartum hemorrhage; (4) the November 2018 incident where K.L. hit R.H.'s mother in the nose; (5) the March 2019 incident in which K.L. drugged and sexually assaulted R.H.; (6) the October 2019 incident in which K.L. pulled R.H. off the bed, causing her to hit her head on the floor, kicked her out of his apartment, caused her to bang heads with year-old Z.L., strangled her, destroyed her phone, and smashed her head into a metal area of her car; and (7) the December 2019 incident in which K.L. punched R.H. in the head after the trial court had granted a temporary restraining order protecting R.H. from K.L.

The trial court also found by a preponderance of the evidence that R.H.: (1) threatened K.L. at the December 2, 2019 custody exchange by saying she was going to "fuck him up" and threatening to kill him; (2) disturbed K.L.'s peace as set forth in the Talking Parents app exchanges submitted by K.L.; and (3) had previous criminal convictions that were "violent in nature."

Based on the foregoing evidence of the parties' acts of domestic violence, the trial court found that both K.L. and R.H. acted as primary aggressors and that neither acted primarily in self-defense. In making these findings, however, the trial court failed to consider the mandatory factors of Penal Code section 836, subdivision (c)(3). Specifically, the trial court failed to consider the intent of the DVPA and other laws protecting victims of domestic violence from continuing abuse, whether either party made the threats to the other creating fear of physical injury, and the history of domestic violence between K.L. and R.H.

The evidence before the trial court regarding the parties' behavior at the December 2 custody exchange does not rise to the level of threats by R.H. sufficient to justify the issuance of a restraining order. K.L. admitted at the hearing that R.H. had never placed him in reasonable apprehension of imminent serious bodily injury to himself or anyone else. This testimony should have been relevant to the trial court's analysis under Penal Code section 836, subdivision (c)(3)(B). R.H. said she would "fuck up" K.L. and kill him *after* she had observed the bruise on Z.L.'s head, seeing that K.L. had shaved Z.L.'s head against the doctor's recommendation, and having K.L. state that he had shaved Z.L.'s head as a means of punishing R.H. Moreover, R.H.'s words came after more than two years of substantiated physical, emotional, and sexual abuse of R.H. by K.L. The trial court failed to consider this history of domestic violence under Penal Code section 836, subdivision (c)(3)(C).

The statements by R.H. to K.L. on Talking Parents, while evidencing a lack of ability between these two people to communicate, do not reach the level of disturbing K.L.'s peace. " '[T]he plain meaning of the phrase "disturbing the peace of the other party" in section 6320 may be properly understood as conduct that destroys the mental or emotional calm of the other party.' " What disturbs the peace of a person differs in each case. *[The court gives examples from other cases of facts that did or did not disturb the other person's peace.]*

In this case, calling K.L. a "dick" and failing to show up for custody exchanges is not sufficient to disturb anyone's peace, especially if that person has been physically and emotionally abusing the other person for almost two years. Pursuant to Penal Code section 836, subdivision (c)(3)(A), (B), and (C), these words and actions do not justify a finding that R.H. was the dominant aggressor or that R.H. was not acting in self-defense. This conclusion does not condone or approve R.H.'s words or actions, but recognizes they simply do not rise to the level required by the law.

Finally, the trial court erred as a matter of law by relying on R.H.'s previous criminal convictions in ordering the issuance of a mutual restraining order. Family Code section 6306, which the trial court cited in explaining why it was considering R.H.'s convictions, provides, in relevant part: "(1) Prior to deciding whether to issue an order under this part or when determining appropriate temporary custody and visitation orders, the court shall consider the following . . .: any conviction for a violent felony specified in Section 667.5 of the Penal Code or a serious felony specified in Section 1192.7 of the Penal Code; any misdemeanor conviction involving domestic violence, weapons, or other violence; any outstanding warrant; parole or probation status; any prior restraining order; and any violation of a prior restraining order. [¶] (2) Information . . . that does not involve a conviction described in this subdivision shall not be considered by the court in making a determination regarding the issuance of an order pursuant to this part. That information shall be destroyed and shall not become part of the public file in this or any other civil proceeding."

R.H.'s misdemeanor convictions for child endangerment and second degree burglary are neither felony convictions nor misdemeanors involving violence; nor are they within the categories specified in Family Code section 6306, subdivision (b)(2). Therefore, the court should not have considered them in deciding whether to issue mutual restraining orders, or in connection with the issue of custody.

While the trial court defined R.H.'s crimes of child endangerment and second degree burglary as "violent," they are not listed as "violent" felonies under Penal Code section 667.5, subdivision (c), or as "serious" felonies under Penal Code section 1192.7, subdivision (c). More importantly, these crimes do not meet the definition of "violent." Violent crimes involve "physical force, sexual contact, physical injury or destruction of property, fear, coercion, or duress." Nothing in the record shows these crimes were violent under the *In re Febbo* definition. Moreover, these crimes had no connection to the acts of violence between K.L. and R.H.; they were committed before these two individuals even began a dating relationship, and were not committed against K.L.

"It is essential in a case such as this that the court rigorously evaluate the evidence to ensure that the moving party has, in fact, been victimized. This is so, particularly, where, as here, the trial court is aware that the acts *committed* by the moving party . . . are significantly more violent than the acts *alleged* by the moving party." The acts committed by K.L. against R.H. were significantly more violent than the acts committed against K.L. by R.H. The trial court failed to evaluate the evidence before it in light of the Penal Code section 836, subdivision (c)(3) factors, and therefore erred in finding that R.H. was an aggressor who did not act in self-defense. The mutual restraining order therefore cannot stand. . .

[The court reverses the joint custody order in light of California's rebuttable presumption against custody to a person who has committed domestic violence against the other party, which the trial court did not find was rebutted. It orders the parties to give a copy of this decision to the juvenile court, since Z.L. is a dependent of that court. It awards R.H. her costs on appeal.]

Footnote 11. Recently, in the context of a juvenile dependency case, we cautioned against the danger of implicit bias affecting the judiciary's perception of victims of domestic abuse. "We are also mindful of society's preconceptions that often damage the 'credibility of victim-witnesses who present on the stand in atypical and non paradigmatic fashions.' We expect such victims to be 'sweet, kind, demure, blameless, frightened, and helpless' and 'not a multi-faceted woman who may or may not experience fear or anger.' 'These are the preconceptions that judges and jurors bring with them into the courtroom when they assess the veracity of a victim-witness's story.' We encourage continued diligence and education to guard against such preconceptions. While not directly applicable to our analysis, we encourage the trial court to keep this in mind in this and other matters.

[Editor's Note: An amicus brief filed by LLS Anti-Racism Center and several other anti-racist legal groups argued that implicit bias and unconscious stereotyping can affect how Black women are perceived when they seek protection in family court, since victims of domestic violence are stereotyped as passive and demure, and Black women are less likely to fit this mold than are White women. The appellate court's footnote 11 is based in part on this section of the brief.

Similarly, the brief argues that preconceptions about domestic violence victims can lead Black women who express anger and frustration to be seen as less credible than White women, who are more likely to be stereotyped as expressing only fear. The brief notes that the trial court equated R.H.'s negative verbal statements toward K.L. with his repeated severe violence toward her, then held R.H. responsible for her own abuse, labeling her a primary aggressor and issuing a mutual restraining order.

Third, the brief cites data showing that 1 in 18 Black women born in 2001 [in the U.S.] will be incarcerated sometime in her life, compared to 1 in 111 White women. It notes that studies show that prosecutors are more likely to charge Black women than White women with crimes and to disproportionately overcharge those crimes, including charging crimes with high minimum sentences, leading to disproportionate outcomes for Black women in plea negotiations. Furthermore, the authors point out that the trial judge in this case characterized R.H.'s shoplifting conviction as "violent," which was incorrect, and used the conviction to wrongly find that she was a primary aggressor in her relationship with K.L.]

MCCORD V. SMITH

51 Cal.App.5th 358 (CA App 2020)
(footnotes and citations omitted)

After the end of their relationship, former domestic partners [and fiances] Keith McCord and Celeste Smith each asked the trial court for a domestic violence restraining order (DVRO) against the other. The court granted Smith's request and denied McCord's request. . . . McCord appealed from the court's order. We affirm.

Substantial evidence supported the trial court's findings underlying the issuance of the DVRO in favor of Smith and against McCord. There weas no evidence supporting the issuance of a DVRO in favor of McCord and against Smith, and McCord makes no specific argument on appeal regarding this portion of the trial court's order.

. . . Smith broke up with McCord on November 2, 2018. She testified that McCord tried to talk her out of it, hugged her, and ultimately restrained her on her bed with his hand over her mouth. After he let go of her, Smith ran outside to her driveway; at that time, she did not call the police.

McCord sent Smith e-mails throughout November, after she had stated her intention to break up with him. Dawn Sheldon, another friend of Smith, testified that the breakup was very volatile and Smith was afraid. Sheldon was scared for Smith because McCord was being "forceful," and she kept telling Smith to get a restraining order. [There was testimony that McCord repeatedly contacted Smith after being served with the Temporary Restraining Order, showed up at her house, her workplace and her church, sent her flowers, bruised her wrist, etc.]

. . . A DVRO may be issued to prevent, among other things, "stalking, threatening, . . . harassing, telephoning, . . . contacting, either directly or indirectly, by mail or otherwise, coming within a specified distance of, or disturbing the peace of the other party." Acts that disturb the peace of a party have been held to include those that destroy the party's mental or emotional calm. The trial court's findings that McCord's statements and actions were a means of exercising control and dominion over Smith and threatening her were amply supported by the evidence. Those acts were sufficient to constitute a disturbance of her peace, as well as stalking, threatening, and harassing. McCord correctly notes that with respect to at least one incident—his texting the photo of Smith's nursing license—there was "[n]o profanity, no shouting, no threats"; this is not the relevant standard, however. The trial court did not err in issuing the DVRO in favor of Smith and her minor daughter, and against McCord.

. . . McCord also argues that he did not coerce Smith by sending her a photo of her nursing license with the text message, "Is this yours?" The trial court found the text message was a part of an overall series of actions by McCord that threatened Smith's peace of mind: "Mr. McCord's behavior and continually following up, visiting Ms. Smith's house, text messaging her, sending her photographs of herself and of her nursing license, asking a fairly rhetorical question, 'Is this yours?' when he knew full well the nursing license was hers . . . shows that he did intend to exercise some form of dominion and control." Ample evidence supported the trial court's findings. Whether one single act by McCord would have been sufficient to justify the issuance of the DVRO is not the question—the trial court considers whether the totality of the circumstances supports the issuance of the DVRO.

[Editor's Notes: 1. This is an example of a court applying the concepts of "dominion and control" and "coercion" as the basis for a restraining order. Note that it was decided before California amended its restraining order statute to specifically include coercive control.

2. In J.J. v. M.F., *223 Cal.App.4th 968 (2014), the appellate court reversed the trial court's spontaneous issuance of a mutual restraining order. Ca. Family Code section 6305 requires that before a court issues a mutual restraining order, it must attempt to determine if either party acted primarily as the dominant aggressor, rather than in self-defense, which this court had not done. The appellate court noted that the boyfriend had a long history of physically abusing the girlfriend, and when she pushed him he grabbed her by the neck, "choking," [i.e., strangling] her. The trial court had characterized this as "mutual combat," and said the girlfriend had harassed the boyfriend when she called several times asking him to return their son's jacket.*

The appellate court disagreed: "Given this dispute [over the jacket], [the boyfriend's] history of physical abuse, and his threats to harm her, [the girlfriend] reasonably believed he might do her harm when he came at her and yelled at her to hand over their son. The force she used to push him away was not excessive. . ." "Nor did [the girlfriend's] calls about the jacket support a finding that she was acting primarily as an aggressor," as she made them in good faith. "Her very young son was ill, the weather was cold. . . and the child had only the one warm jacket." Furthermore, the boyfriend never indicated that he felt threatened by the girlfriend or wanted a restraining order against her. The appellate court reversed the part of the order protecting the boyfriend and upheld the part protecting the girlfriend. Later, the legislature amended the statute to clarify that an additional requirement for a mutual order is that each party must file a separate request for a restraining order.]

ALABAMA CODE 1975 § 30–5–5

(d) The court shall not enter mutual orders. The court shall issue separate orders that specifically and independently state the prohibited behavior and relief granted in order to protect the victim and the victim's immediate family and to clearly provide law enforcement with sufficient directives. . .

(f)(1) The following information shall not be contained on any court document made available to the public and the defendant by the circuit clerk's office: The plaintiff's home address and, if applicable, business address; a plaintiff's home telephone number and, if applicable, business telephone number; the home or business address or telephone number of any member of the plaintiff's family or household; or an address that would reveal the confidential location of a shelter for victims of domestic violence as defined in Section 30–6–1.

(2) If disclosure of the plaintiff's address, the address of any member of the plaintiff's family or household, or an address that would reveal the confidential location of a shelter for victims of domestic violence is necessary to determine jurisdiction or to consider a venue issue, it shall be made orally and in camera.

(3) If the plaintiff has not disclosed an address or telephone number under this section, the plaintiff shall satisfy one of the following requirements:

a. Designate and provide to the court an alternative address.

b. Elect to substitute the business address and telephone number of his or her attorney of record in place of the address of the plaintiff on any court document.

(g) No court costs and fees shall be assessed for the filing and service of a petition for a protection order, for the issuance or registration of a protection order, or for the issuance of a witness subpoena under this chapter. Costs and fees may be assessed against the defendant at the discretion of the court.

D. ENFORCEMENT/EFFECTIVENESS

REINIE CORDIER, DONNA CHUNG, SARAH WILKES-GILLAN, AND RENEE SPEYER, THE EFFECTIVENESS OF PROTECTION ORDERS IN REDUCING RECIDIVISM IN DOMESTIC VIOLENCE: A SYSTEMATIC REVIEW AND META-ANALYSIS

22(4) Trauma, Violence, & Abuse 804 (2021)
(citations omitted)

. . . Internationally, the most commonly available justice strategy to intervene in situations of domestic violence is a civil law protection order (PO). Varying terms are used for POs, such as civil POs, restraining orders, peace bonds, or apprehended violence order. Varying types of POs and processes for obtaining POs also exist worldwide. However, they are most commonly issued and policed by law enforcement and the justice system, with the aim of stopping perpetrators from using further domestic violence, coercion, harassment, and stalking of a partner or ex-partner. While POs are relatively accessible, evaluating the effectiveness of POs is complex and remains under investigation.

Challenges of Evaluating Effectiveness of POs

The first challenge to evaluating the effectiveness of POs is the varying definitions of effectiveness across the literature. There is currently no consensus on what types or degrees of reabuse would indicate a level of effectiveness. One view is that any reported violation of a PO indicates ineffectiveness, while differing views consider a reduction in physical or psychological reabuse as evidence of success. Most commonly, effectiveness of POs has been based on deterrent effects and revictimization, which aim to determine whether POs facilitate victim safety. A further complexity in examining PO effectiveness is violence may continue and the PO violated, but it is not reported to authorities so is not recorded in any administrative data sets. Another important indicator of success is whether victims report being safer and less fearful as a result of a PO being in place.

A historical complication about effectiveness is the varied outcome data used in reports of PO effectiveness. Many studies have used existing archival data (i.e., police reports and court documentation) or victim data (i.e., surveys/interviews with women who obtained the PO). Commonly, there is variation between victim report surveys of PO violations and studies relying solely on violation reporting data from police or court sources; victim studies are more likely to show higher rates of reported reabuse. This is unsurprising as lower level or hard to evidence PO violations are unlikely to result in contacting police, and more generally, most incidents of domestic violence are not reported to police and/or police do not necessarily record all breaches. Another confound in researching the effectiveness of POs is differences in legislation and policing associated with POs internationally. The definitions of domestic violence, procedures for obtaining a PO, conditions of POs, enforcement of violations and penalties for PO violations differ between jurisdictions (states or territories) within a country, and differ between countries. Countries with federal systems of government, such as the United States of America, Canada, and Australia, have state- or territory-based legislation for POs, which adds to the complexity of comparing effectiveness within a country and between countries. These variations may impact the differences in outcomes using the same measures.

While studies with control groups, in particular randomized controlled trials, are considered to be the strongest type of evidence, this methodological approach may not be feasible or ethical in determining the effectiveness of POs. These real-life considerations when researching PO effectiveness, combined with variations in definitions and outcomes of effectiveness across existing studies, add to the challenge of evaluating the effectiveness of POs. As such, this review only focuses on the measures of effectiveness available in the literature, including recidivism and violation rates.

Besides the uncertainty surrounding the overall effectiveness of POs, there are also challenges in accounting for the many confounding factors that may increase or decrease PO violations and future reoffending which results in later POs, including which offenders' characteristics yield better responses to POs. Another variation pertains to the characteristics, relationship type, and motivations of the victims seeking a PO. Some victims seek out POs due to fear for their child's safety, while others are currently dating the aggressor or in the process of ending a relationship. Variations in the type of PO and PO processes may also influence the effectiveness of POs, such as the eligibility of those receiving POs, the likelihood POs will be enforced by law, the consequences of PO violation, and the nature of the offense(s).

Effectiveness of POs

. . . Individually, some large-scale, rigorous studies have reported a decrease in abuse after receiving a PO. Some studies indicate the effectiveness of POs in reducing further incidents of domestic violence varies depending on multiple contextual factors. There have been attempts to consolidate the research through literature reviews. However, many of the reviews were not robust systematic reviews, and the individual studies contained within the reviews were not always rigorous designs. . .To date, no systematic review has been conducted to examine the effectiveness of POs or factors related to increased risk of continuing to use domestic violence. . .

The purpose of this study was to add to the existing evidence in regard to evaluating the effectiveness of POs by conducting a systematic review and meta-analysis of the existing literature on the effectiveness of POs in reducing violation rates and reoffense more generally in the longer term, as well as individual and contextual factors associated with increased risk of future reoffense. The characteristics of the included studies were categorized by victim-reported data and police/court-reported data to analyze differences in PO violation rates. This systematic review therefore aimed to answer the following research questions:

1. Based on PO violation rates, what is the effectiveness of POs in reducing reoffense rates of domestic violence?

2. Based on a meta-analysis of reoffense rates following the issuance of a PO, what are the weighted average rates of reoffense as reported by victims and police and is there is significant difference between victim reports of reoffense rates and police reports (with and without arrests)? and

3. What are the factors associated with an increased risk of reoffending following a PO being issued?

. . .A total of 4,821 articles were identified. . .This [selection process] resulted in a total of 25 included studies [that met the criteria]. . .

Study Participants

Most of the studies (n 1/4 16) included female victim participants. Of the 25 studies, 3 included male offenders, 4 described the participants as cases containing male and female offenders, 1 included couples, and 1 study reported the sample as domestic violence cases without further description. The total number of participants across the 25 included studies was 31,586. Most offenders were male and all participants were aged over 17 years. All of the studies were conducted in the United States, with one exception; a study conducted in Sweden. . .

Data Type and Measures Collected by Studies

. . . The samples of most studies (21) solely involved the issuing of a PO to the offender. Two studies included samples where the offender was issued with a PO, as well as being arrested at the time of the incident. In the sample of one study, the offender was issued a PO, and there was a simultaneous victim-directed intervention consisting of education to collect evidence and report violations. One study compared violation rates from those issued with PO in specialist domestic violence courts (DVCs) and those issued with a PO from non-specialist DVCs.

Reported Definitions of Recidivism

Eight of the 25 included studies did not report a definition of recidivism. Of the 17 studies that reported a definition of recidivism, 4 defined recidivism as a violation of a PO, 4 defined recidivism in terms of rearrest, subsequent police contact, or committing a new crime, 4 used a definition of recidivism focused around physical violence and 5 studies used a definition of recidivism that considered either physical and psychological abuse or victimization.

Sources and Time Points of PO Violation Rates

All 25 studies reported PO violation rates. A majority of the studies (15) used victim sources to report PO violation rates. Seven studies used police report data and 3 studies used combined data (PO and police report data). Collection of PO violation data occurred at various time points, ranging from 40 days to 4 years. . .

Qualitative Evaluations of Effectiveness

Although the included studies reported individual violation rates of between 20.5% (police reports) and 65.3% (victim reports), many studies reported that victims experienced the PO as effective, helpful, or made them feel safer. This finding suggests that while the reoccurrence of violence persists to some extent, having a PO can be perceived as beneficial by the victim and have a positive impact on their sense of safety. As highlighted in previous literature, there are an array of reasons why victims perceived POs to be effective. For many victims, a PO can assist in deterring, monitoring, and reporting violating behaviors that would otherwise not warrant an arrest or punishment, thus giving the victim and police power to prevent these behaviors and increasing the victim's sense of safety. Importantly, self-reported safety and well-being have been associated with successful separation from the offender and access to resources and assistance. Future policy and program planning should recognize the importance of this finding to promote safety following domestic violence, as it signposts that systems of response are required, not stand-alone interventions.

Quantitative Evaluations of Effectiveness

All studies evaluating the effectiveness of POs within groups found that POs significantly reduced negative outcomes. However, results at an individual study level were different for between-group differences when the issuance of POs were compared to no PO being issued or were compared to another form of intervention, with none of the studies reporting issuing POs to be significantly more effective than no POs or other interventions (arrest, DVC, treatment) in reducing recidivism. However, it is interesting to note that our meta-analysis findings indicated that when data from multiple studies are combined, the issuance of POs and simultaneous arrest for the offense produced a significantly lower reoffense rate compared to issuing POs without an arrest at the time of the incident. These findings suggest that a combination of law enforcement strategies may be more effective in deterring reoffense and highlights the importance of exploring ways to enhance the implementation and efficacy of law enforcement strategies.

At an individual study level, existing psychosocial intervention approaches are yet to establish effectiveness in reducing domestic violence. However, the findings might also be an artefact of victims being more willing to report violations to police when the victim is connected to support and the perpetrator [is] in a treatment program. Given the reoffense rates even after the issuance of a PO and small proportion of existing studies that include an intervention, an important area for further research is to develop a range of interventions that may be effective for use in combination with law enforcement strategies in further reducing the reoccurrence of domestic violence.

Challenges With the Conceptualization of Effectiveness

Our findings about effectiveness collectively demonstrate the lack of consensus in the literature surrounding how to best define if a PO has been effective. Russell identified in a literature review that none of the studies reviewed attempted to determine what constitutes an acceptable rate of PO violation to be deemed effective. While most included studies provided a definition of how they measured effectiveness of PO orders, none of the studies acknowledged and/or explicitly addressed the variability of definitions between studies. There is great variation between jurisdictions regarding the definition, policing, recording, and enforcement of violations of POs. These also vary over time due to changes in legislation and practice. Despite this variation, the used definition of violation is not well defined or described in many of the included studies and would also vary across jurisdictions based on their legislation. Foundational to any future research into the effectiveness of POs is careful consideration of what constitutes PO effectiveness, including violation rate, severity and type of violation, and possible responses to violations, all of which also differ between jurisdictions. To more accurately understand effectiveness, comprehensive reporting from both the victim perspective and other data sources needs to be available for triangulation.

This is important in developing responses to domestic violence. As the findings of this systematic review demonstrate, the level of reported continuing violence differs markedly. The dynamics of domestic violence are such that perpetrators minimize and conceal their violence and victims often find it difficult to report all violations. Therefore, women's reports of continued violence can offer insights into those violations most and least likely to be reported, which can be used to develop more effective responses by police, courts, and advocates. Combining perpetrator and practitioners' reports of behavioral change, administrative data, such as police or court records with victim reports of reoffense and sense of safety can provide a more accurate evaluation of effectiveness. Relying on more than one data source may help to provide a more accurate account of violation rates. . .

Violation Rates of POs as a Function of Different Data Sources

Our second main finding was that mean weighted PO violation rates varied based on the data source used to report the PO violation, with victim-reported PO violations significantly higher (34.3%) than police reports (28.2%). Given that none of the included studies reported that POs prevented any violations indicates that, unequivocally, POs do not completely prevent violation. However, as several studies showed that the issuing of a PO reduced the percentage of violations, we can conclude that POs can reduce the occurrence to violation to some extent. This review found that, according to police reports, POs were most effective when used in combination with arrests (23.4%). However, it is currently unknown whether the combination of POs and arrests presents a similar reduction in reoffending rates when measured by victim report. These results related to the confounding nature of reporting source are consistent with the mixed findings reported in previous research. The confounding nature of reporting contributes to the complexity of synthesizing the findings from various studies. For example, it is likely that the sample of many of the studies included in this review did include those who had also been arrested for the index incident that led to the PO, but it simply wasn't differentiated in the reported sample. Thus, it isn't that none were arrested necessarily but that the studies did not parse these differences. Future research should consider parsing and reporting on both PO and report data to provide a more accurate account of PO effectiveness.

Reasons for Differences between Data Sources

Definitional differences. There are several explanations as to why such variance exists. One reason for the commonly reported variation in PO violation rates is likely due to the varying definitions of violations used among studies (e.g., a complete cessation or a decrease in violence). Many studies limited a violation to physical or sexual violence, while others included verbal abuse, harassment, and stalking. This definitional difference may affect what is recorded as a violation, possibly excluding a large amount of data that may be considered a violation by other perspectives.

Enforcement of POs. For POs to be effective, there must be a law enforcement response to a reported violation and consequence to the perpetrator. Enforcement of PO violations, including follow-up by police and arrest, is postulated to contribute to variation in rates of PO violations. Police enforcement of a violation relies on victims first reporting the violation and the report being recorded by authorities. If a violation is not then enforced by police, the PO is less likely to be perceived as effective by the victim and less likely to deter the perpetrator from further violations. Previous research has found only a proportion of reported violations resulted in arrest. Further, police are reportedly less inclined to arrest a perpetrator in the absence of any physical injury to the victim. If violations are not recorded and enforced by police, it can further discrepancies between victim experiences and police records. Enforcement of POs also differs between jurisdictions and within and between countries. Further, enforcement may change across time as policies are updated. These differences may also impact the ability to accurately capture and compare PO enforcement and effectiveness.

Victim reporting of violations. Furthermore, victims may not report violations or only report some violations. Women have reported embarrassment, blame, lack of confidentiality, fear of perpetrator retaliation, and dissatisfaction with previous police response as barriers to reporting PO violations to the police. Findings suggest that future program development and research should focus on interventions that respond effectively to offender risk and maintain a victim's sense of safety and trust in law enforcement. To more accurately capture violations and effectiveness, comprehensive reporting from the victim's perspective, perpetrator and practitioner report of behavioral change, and court/police sources needs to be available to triangulate.

Factors Influencing Violation

Our third main finding was that stalking, offender prior arrests and violence, relationship characteristics, and demographics of the victim are the most frequently reported factors that influence the effectiveness of POs. All five studies investigating stalking reported stalking to be a significant predictive factor for ongoing PO violations and increased physical, psychological, and sexual violence to victims, as well as poorer mental health and a lower sense of safety. Stalking may be particularly challenging to address, as it is often difficult to provide evidence of stalking behaviors compared with other forms of violations. As a result, stalking can be treated with less urgency by law enforcement and service providers, with reports of stalking rarely resulting in incident reports or arrests. More research is needed to improve ways to protect against stalking behavior and the resulting negative outcomes. Given the lower levels of safety and well-being reported by stalking victims even with a PO, effectiveness of POs may only be achieved for this subgroup of victims when POs are combined with community-based interventions that offer further education, support, and resources to victims together with greater surveillance of offenders.

Evidence from the meta-analysis indicates offenders with prior arrests and higher levels of violence were significantly more likely to violate POs and continue the use of violence and abuse. These findings suggest that POs are likely to be less effective in reducing revictimization where the perpetrator has a history of arrests and violent behavior. In the instances where offenders pose a high risk of further violence, the application of criminal charges and greater surveillance may be more likely to reduce violence, particularly in combination with a PO. Screening offenders for their risk of violence, including past arrests, may be essential when considering the most effective form of response to reduce the likelihood of reoffense. It may be that such offenders require more targeted and intensive treatments or surveillance in order to reduce reoffense. There is emerging evidence that electronic monitoring may be of use in combination with POs. However, evaluation research in this area confronts similar challenge to PO research where differing systems and concurrent interventions influence outcomes and make comparisons difficult. Some studies have relied solely on administrative data, while others have used multiple data sources. As technology advances, it is worth consideration of use in combination with PO to increase targeted intervention and surveillance. Victims also report concerns that the application of POs and having charges laid may incite the perpetrator to commit further violence.

Another factor that influenced the effectiveness of POs was relationship status. Two of three studies in this review found that continuing the relationship with the perpetrator decreased the effectiveness of POs keeping victims safe. While separating has also been identified as a risk factor for increased violence in the literature, the issuance of a PO can provide relief from postseparation violence and harassment. A PO can also be part of the process that facilitates leaving a violent partner. In this stage, it is proposed that women begin to engage in activities that will help them to leave, including building social support, help-seeking, and setting limits in the relationship. Seeking formal help, such as POs, may indicate a commitment to separating from the perpetrator. Thus, separation in combination with a PO provides consequences for the perpetrator, decreasing contact and potentially increasing the effectiveness of the PO.

Victims from low socioeconomic backgrounds, particularly victims who were unemployed or who had low or very low median family income reported more PO violations. This finding demonstrates the importance of future policy and program developments being inclusive of multifaceted responses that take account of the response required to contain the perpetrator's risk. The victims' financial and other circumstances may impact their safety from the perpetrator; thus, supports are needed from the point of crisis and in the longer term.

. . .designs that include a shorter follow-up time with offenders or victims may report a lower reoffense rate. . .

Conclusions

This systematic review found that overall the reporting of the effectiveness of POs was mixed. POs were not effective in completely stopping or preventing the continuing use of violence and abuse toward the victims seeking protection. However, there is emerging evidence of reduced subsequent violence to some extent and even more so for some groups. These groups include victims who were not stalked by their partner, victims whose partner did not have a prior history of arrests or high levels of violence, victims who discontinued their relationship with their partner, and victims with medium to high median family incomes. In order to increase the effectiveness of POs for these subgroups, future research is required to identify the best combinations of legal and treatment responses for perpetrators of varying levels of risk and the optimal types of support required for victims to establish their safety. . .

[Editor's Note: Years ago, when I was representing survivors of domestic violence obtaining restraining orders, I advised them to report any violations to the police, and I sometimes called the District Attorney's office to urge them to prosecute certain violations. I also told the survivors that if the DA would not prosecute, they could file for contempt. A few brave women did this, representing themselves at the hearing while their abusers had court-appointed public defenders. The agencies I worked for could not afford to have me represent the women at these hearings. This is typical today as well. My clients rarely filed for contempt, partly because in California the penalty for each contempt is only five days in jail. But it was still important for them to know that they had this option for enforcing the order, and they could also have a private attorney represent them if they could afford this.

In Robertson v. U.S., *a case from the District of Columbia, the U.S. Supreme Court partially addressed this issue in 2010:*

Mr. Robertson violated a Civil Protective Order (CPO) protecting his girlfriend after he seriously assaulted her. He demanded that she drop criminal charges, again assaulting her, and throwing lye at her, for which she was hospitalized. The criminal complaint was not amended to add the second assault. He pled guilty to a felony for the first assault in exchange for no prosecution by the U.S. Attorney for DC for the second assault and was ordered to prison.

A few months later the girlfriend filed criminal contempt against Robertson. He was found guilty of three counts, ordered to pay $10,000 for her medical bills, and sentenced to 180 days jail for each count. Years later Robertson filed a motion to vacate these convictions, arguing that his plea agreement precluded the contempt convictions. The court denied the motion. When he appealed, amicus briefs from the Solicitor General, the DC AG, and domestic violence groups argued that private parties can enforce CPO's through contempt. The Court of Appeal affirmed the denial, holding that the girlfriend acted as a private party in the contempt action even though the Attorney General for DC assisted her, and that this was legal.

Robertson again appealed, and the U.S. Supreme Court granted certiorari, over the objection of then-Solicitor General Elena Kagan. One of the amicus briefs cited the U.S. Supreme Court's decision in Gonzales v. City of Castle Rock, Co., *where the husband kidnapped and murdered the three daughters of the parties. The Court held that Ms. Gonzales had no due process right to enforcement of her CPO, as they said that arrest for its violation was discretionary rather than mandatory. The Court noted that she could have filed a private action for the violation even if the police refused to arrest her husband. These amicus authors in the* Robertson *case cited this quote in their argument that eliminating a victim's right to enforce her CPO would eviscerate the CPO remedy.*

*After oral argument the Supreme Court decided that certiorari was improvidently granted, and allowed the lower court decision to stand. (*Robertson v. U.S. ex rel. Watson, *560 U.S. 272 (2010)) Four Justices dissented: Roberts, Scalia, Kennedy, and Sotomayor. Without explaining their reasoning, they equated all criminal contempt actions with criminal prosecution, stating that the fundamental question is whether a criminal prosecution can be brought on behalf of and in the interest of a private party. They also wrote, "The terrifying force of the criminal justice system may only be brought to bear against an individual by society as a whole, through a prosecution brought on behalf of the government." The dissent stated that* U.S. v. Dixon *(1993) was dispositive of this case. It held that a private party's prosecution for criminal contempt barred the government's subsequent prosecution of the contemnor for the same criminal offense due to double jeopardy.*

This issue is sure to arise again, given the huge numbers of CPO's that are violated each year in the U.S. Hopefully the Supreme Court will uphold the right of protected parties to enforce their orders through contempt actions.]

DAVID TRIGGS, JR. V. STATE OF MARYLAND

852 A.2d 114 (Md. 2004)
(citations and footnotes omitted)

We are called upon in this case to determine whether it was error for the trial judge to impose eighteen consecutive sentences when the defendant was convicted for making eighteen threatening calls to his wife in violation of a protective order requiring that he have "no contact" with his wife. We find no error in the sentence.

I. INTRODUCTION

A. Facts

On Sunday morning, September 16, 2001, David Triggs (hereinafter "Petitioner") made the first of dozens of calls to his ex-wife, Pamela Triggs (hereinafter "Mrs. Triggs"), who lived in Montgomery County, in violation of a protective order prohibiting him from having any contact with her. When he made many of the calls, which continued over a four-day period, Petitioner threatened to rape and murder his ex-wife and murder their three children, who were with him during a scheduled visitation when he called.

Petitioner and Mrs. Triggs were married for almost seven and a half years when they divorced on March 1, 2002. They had three children together, who were eight, six, and four at the time of their divorce. Petitioner's four-day "reign of terror" . . . was the culmination of a long history of a troubled relationship filled with domestic abuse. * * * [This included repeated sexual abuse, verbal abuse, extreme control, financial abuse, shooting at his wife, not letting her sleep, threats to kill her and her co-workers and friends, causing her to lose her job, using the children to relay death threats, etc. She obtained two protective orders. Mr. Triggs was arrested for violating the second order and sent threatening letters to the children from jail. He was convicted, given probation for a year, and ordered again to have no contact with Ms. Triggs.

A warrant was issued for his arrest but was not served before he picked up his children for his scheduled two-week visitation. During the two weeks he had the children, he made more than fifty calls over a four-day period to Mrs. Triggs, in which he insisted on talking to her and threatened to kill the children if she did not call him back. The police listened to the messages and obtained an arrest warrant. Mr. Triggs continued to call Mrs. Triggs repeatedly, and to threaten to torture and kill the children and her, while the police attempted to locate and arrest him. Finally the police apprehended him and returned the children to Mrs. Triggs physically unharmed. Mr. Triggs had also been calling and threatening his mother, grandmother, sisters, nieces, and nephews, who were escorted to the police department for their own safety. After his arrest, while he was in custody, he again sent disturbing letters.]

B. Procedural History

* * * Following a jury trial, Petitioner was convicted of thirty of the forty-three counts: one count of telephone misuse, four counts of harassment, seven counts of telephone threats, and eighteen counts of violating a protective order. At the sentencing hearing, conducted about two months after the trial, the court sentenced Petitioner to three-years imprisonment for the telephone misuse conviction, consecutive six-month sentences for each of the harassment and telephone threat convictions, and consecutive one-year sentences totaling eighteen years for each violation of a protective order conviction. The sentences resulted in a term of imprisonment totaling twenty-six years and six months. * * *

In an unreported opinion, the Court of Special Appeals vacated the sentences for harassment and telephone threats and affirmed the eighteen convictions and sentences for violating a protective order. With respect to the harassment and telephone threats, the court concluded that Petitioner was punished for the same conduct under Section 32–19A of the Montgomery County Code, regarding harassment, and Section 555A of Article 27 of the Maryland Code, regarding telephone threats. . . .[The] intermediate appellate court determined that the sentences for harassment and telephone threats merged under the rule of lenity because the county ordinance did not "clearly indicate an intent of cumulative punishment when the conduct also violated another statute."

With respect to the eighteen counts of violating a protective order, the Court of Special Appeals observed that Section 4–509 of the Family Law Article provides penalties "for each offense" of violating a protective order. "Because each call constituted a separate 'offense,' " the court affirmed Petitioner's eighteen convictions for violating a protective order.

We granted Petitioner's petition for a writ of certiorari, which presented the following question for our review:

Where Petitioner was convicted of harassing and threatening his wife, by telephone, over a period of two days, was it error to impose separate, one-year, consecutive sentences as to each of eighteen convictions under the Family Law statute?

Although Petitioner frames his question in terms of the multiple sentences only and does not address the multiple offenses and convictions, he maintained at oral argument, and the State likewise conceded this point, that his argument necessarily implicates what we have called the "unit of prosecution," which arises in the context of determining whether the charging of multiple offenses is appropriate. Our focus in this opinion, thus, is the unit of prosecution the General Assembly intended in order to trigger the penalty provisions for violating a protective order. When a protective order requires an abuser to have "no contact" with a victim, we conclude that repeated calls constitute separate acts and therefore separate offenses for the purposes of the sentencing provisions requiring penalties "for each offense" in Section 4–509 of the Family Law Article. * * *

[Editor's Note: In Patterson v. State, *979 N.E.2d 1066 (Ind. 2012), a case of first impression in that state, the appellate court considered the question of whether a protected person who is the subject of a no-contact order can be held criminally liable for aiding, inducing, or causing another person to violate that order. The court held that the answer was no and reversed the denial of Ms. Patterson's motion to dismiss the charges. After she obtained a no-contact order against her abusive fiancé, a sheriff's deputy served a subpoena on her and her daughter at her fiance's residence. The fiancé was arrested for violating the order and Patterson was arrested for aiding in violating it. A few weeks later, she and her fiancé were again arrested as Ms. Patterson was at that residence.*

In an interlocutory appeal, the appellate court held that the legislature did not intend to criminalize parties who did not follow orders issued to protect them. They reasoned that when the legislature provided that a warning must be included on the restraining order form directed to the restrained party that even if the protected party invited the restrained party to enter the protected zone, it was still a crime for the restrained party to do so, this meant the legislature did not intend to criminalize the protected party's behavior. The dissent argued that the statute did allow prosecution of a protected person if they deliberately seek to aid another to disobey a court order for protection and that it is up to the legislature to explicitly exclude such prosecutions if that is their intent.]

E. INTERSTATE ISSUES

HEMENWAY V. HEMENWAY

992 A.2d 575 (N.H. 2010)
(citations and footnotes omitted)

The defendant, Edmund J. Hemenway, Jr., appeals a final order of protection issued by the Derry Family Division, arguing that the trial court lacked subject matter and personal jurisdiction. We affirm in part and reverse in part and remand.

The record reveals the following facts. The plaintiff, Michelle Hemenway, and the defendant were married and have four children. They had lived together in Florida until July 16, 2008, when the wife left Florida with their children and moved to New Hampshire. They reached a mediated divorce settlement in Florida on May 14, 2009.

At the beginning of August 2008, the wife applied for, and received, a temporary restraining order against her husband in Massachusetts. In late August, the wife filed a domestic violence petition pursuant to RSA chapter

173–B in the Derry Family Division and obtained a temporary restraining order against him. In her petition, the wife alleged that he committed two acts of criminal threatening, to wit, on July 16, 2008, in Florida, he "became verbally abusive and threatened" her and their children, and, on August 2, 2008, he threatened her at her parents' house in Dracut, Massachusetts.

The family division held a hearing on the petition. The husband did not appear but instead through counsel filed a special appearance to contest jurisdiction. The family division found that it had jurisdiction, and concluded that the two incidents constituted criminal threatening and therefore domestic abuse. The family division issued a final protective order prohibiting the husband from threatening or abusing his wife or her family members, contacting her absent special authorization by the family division, coming within a certain distance of her, going to her home or workplace, or taking, converting or damaging her property. The family division also ordered the husband to "relinquish all deadly weapons as defined in RSA 625:11, V which may have been used, intended to be used, threatened to be used, or could be used incident to the abuse," "all concealed weapons permits and hunting licenses," and prohibited the husband from "purchasing . . . any firearms or ammunition during the pendency of this order." Finally, the family division awarded custody of the children to the wife, and prohibited visitation with the husband pending further hearing. The husband moved to reconsider, which the family division denied. This appeal followed.

The husband argues that the family division lacked subject matter jurisdiction over him because the incidents alleged in the petition occurred in Massachusetts and Florida. He also contends that the family division lacked personal jurisdiction over him under our long-arm statute, RSA 510:4 (1997), and under the Due Process Clause of the Federal Constitution. The wife argues that we should follow other jurisdictions and hold that a protective order that does not impose affirmative obligations on a defendant is valid even absent personal jurisdiction. Alternatively, she argues that the family division had personal jurisdiction over the husband because he flew to Manchester-Boston Regional Airport and, while she was in New Hampshire, made threatening telephone calls and wrote her a threatening letter. She also contends that RSA chapter 173–B, by its plain language, provided subject matter jurisdiction over the petition.

I. Subject Matter Jurisdiction

We first consider the husband's argument that the family division lacked subject matter jurisdiction. * * * The plain language of RSA 173–B:2, IV and RSA 490–D:2, VI granted subject matter jurisdiction to the family division. RSA 173–B:2, IV states that the family division has "jurisdiction over domestic violence cases." RSA 173–B:3, I, provides that "[a]ny person may seek relief pursuant to RSA 173–B:5 by filing a petition, in the county or district where the [wife or husband] resides, alleging abuse by the [husband]." Moreover, a person who "has left the household or premises to avoid further abuse" may "commence proceedings . . . in the county or district where [he or she] temporarily resides." RSA 173–B:2, II. "The fundamental logic of that statutory provision is unassailable: a victim of domestic abuse who seeks a place of refuge must be able to engage the protections of the law of the jurisdiction in which she is sheltered." * * *

II. Personal Jurisdiction

We next consider the husband's argument that the family division lacked personal jurisdiction. "[T]he plaintiff bears the burden of demonstrating facts sufficient to establish personal jurisdiction over the defendant." We utilize a two-part test to determine whether the wife has met her burden. "First, the State's long-arm statute must authorize such jurisdiction. Second, the requirements of the federal Due Process Clause must be satisfied." Our long-arm statute provides that New Hampshire courts have personal jurisdiction over a non-resident defendant "who, in person or through an agent, transacts any business within the state, commits a tortious act within this state, or has the ownership, use, or possession of any real or personal property situated in this state . . . as to any cause of action arising from or growing out of the acts enumerated above." RSA 510:4, I. "Pursuant to the Federal Due Process Clause, a court may exercise personal jurisdiction over a non-resident [husband] if the [husband] has minimum contacts with the forum, such that the maintenance of the suit does not offend traditional notions of fair play and substantial justice." "[W]e construe the State's long-arm statute as permitting the exercise of jurisdiction to the extent permissible under the Federal Due Process Clause."

We first address the wife's argument that the family division had personal jurisdiction because the husband flew to Manchester-Boston Regional Airport, made threatening telephone calls and mailed her a threatening letter while she was in New Hampshire. The wife, in her petition, alleged only that the husband threatened her in Florida and Massachusetts, and made no reference to threatening telephone calls or letters in New Hampshire. Although she alleged in the petition that friends warned her that her husband was coming to New Hampshire, the family division struck that allegation. Indeed, the family division correctly prohibited the wife from introducing additional instances of abuse not contained in the domestic violence petition.

* * * Because it would be error to rely on allegations not contained in the petition and considered by the family division, we conclude that, on the record before us, the wife has failed to "demonstrate facts sufficient to establish personal jurisdiction over the defendant." Therefore, we need not consider "whether the exercise of personal jurisdiction over the [husband] would fall within the minimum contacts standard required by the due

process clause of the United States Constitution." However, this "conclusion . . . does not end the inquiry."

Courts in several states that have considered the validity of a protective order granted without personal jurisdiction over a non-resident defendant have applied an exception to the personal jurisdiction requirement. These courts reason that an order that prohibits abuse but does not require affirmative action by a defendant is valid even without personal jurisdiction. * * *

Similarly, in *Williams v. North Carolina,* 317 U.S. 287, 298–99 (1942), the Supreme Court determined that:

> Domicil creates a relationship to the state which is adequate for numerous exercises of state power. Each state as a sovereign has a rightful and legitimate concern in the marital status of persons domiciled within its borders. The marriage relation creates problems of large social importance. Protection of offspring, property interests, and the enforcement of marital responsibilities are but a few of commanding problems in the field of domestic relations with which the state must deal. Thus it is plain that each state, by virtue of its command over its domiciliaries and its large interest in the institution of marriage, can alter within its own borders the marriage status of the spouse domiciled there, even though the other spouse is absent. * * *

Thus, "a court may adjudicate matters involving the status of the relationship between multiple parties even where personal jurisdiction over all of the parties is not established," and "a State court may grant a divorce to a spouse domiciled within that State without violating the due process rights of an absent spouse over whom it does not have jurisdiction."

A protective order which "prohibits the defendant from abusing the plaintiff and orders him to have no contact with and to stay away from her . . . serves a role analogous to custody or marital determinations, except that the order focuses on the plaintiff's protected status rather than [the plaintiff's] marital or parental status." Accordingly, an order that prohibits abuse but does not "impose any personal obligations on a defendant" is valid even without personal jurisdiction over the defendant.

A protective order "prohibit[s] acts of domestic violence," providing "the victim with the very protection the law specifically allows," while preventing "the defendant from engaging in behavior already specifically outlawed." A contrary ruling would present a domestic violence victim with two "unpalatable choices . . . either to . . . return to the State in which the abuse occurred . . . or, alternatively, to wait for the abuser to follow the victim to [New Hampshire] and, in the event of a new incident of abuse, seek an order from a [New Hampshire] court." Such a result is at odds with the purpose of RSA chapter 173–B and New Hampshire's "strong interest in providing protection to victims of domestic violence within this State."

Accordingly, we affirm the family division's final protective order to the extent that it protects the wife from abuse, but reverse to the extent that the order requires affirmative action from the defendant. We remand to allow the trial court to modify its order in accordance with the opinion.

STACY ELENA RIOS V. CHRISTOPHER FERGUSAN

978 A.2d 592 (Conn.Super. 2008)
(citations and footnotes omitted)

The internet has transformed our ways of communicating and sharing information, but content on the internet that some find offensive or harmful has also created new and challenging issues. Everyday the news brings reports about users posting controversial or disturbing content on social networking web sites such as MySpace, Facebook, and YouTube that are accessible worldwide. This case asks whether a person who is threatened with physical harm by an internet posting can obtain judicial relief in the form of a restraining order to protect her from the threatened harm. More precisely, it presents the issue of whether a Connecticut court has jurisdiction to enter a restraining order under General Statutes § 46b–15 against a North Carolina resident who created and disseminated a recording on the internet on YouTube threatening a resident of this state with physical harm. Although courts in this state and beyond have repeatedly wrestled in recent years with jurisdictional issues in cases involving the internet, the extension of jurisdiction to threatening behavior communicated over the internet on YouTube is apparently an issue of first impression. For the reasons stated below, the court finds that it has personal jurisdiction for purposes of entering such an order. The restraining order previously granted on a temporary and provisional basis is granted for six months, subject to further extension as available at law.

On September 16, 2008, the applicant, Stacy Rios, filed an application for a restraining order under General Statutes § 46b–15 against Christopher Fergusan, a resident of North Carolina who is the father of her four-year-old child. An ex parte restraining [order] was granted by the court, which scheduled a hearing for two weeks hence. On September 30, the applicant appeared for the hearing, but, no service having been made on respondent, the court heard brief testimony and then continued the ex parte order for three weeks to give Rios additional time to serve Fergusan. She appeared again on October 21, when she presented satisfactory proof of personal service on Fergusan in North Carolina by a process server authorized to serve him there although he was not in court that day. The court then heard additional evidence and found that Fergusan had subjected Rios to a continuing threat of present physical harm to her. The evidence established that Fergusan has threatened her with physical violence in the past and that she resided for a while in North Carolina but left there and returned to Connecticut earlier this year, after which he posted a video on YouTube in which he brandished a firearm in a rap song in which he says that he wants to hurt the applicant, to shoot her, and to "put her face on the dirt until she can't breathe no more." He temporarily took the video off YouTube but then placed another video there that again threatened her. Concerned about the court's jurisdiction over Fergusan, however, the court granted the restraining order application for an additional unspecified temporary interval while the court considered the issue.

An application for relief from abuse pursuant to § 46b–15 is a civil action. Although the courts of several states have held that restraining orders may be issued without personal jurisdiction over a respondent, the Connecticut restraining order statute explicitly requires a finding of personal jurisdiction for such an order. Section 46b–15(e) provides that "[e]very order of the court made in accordance with this section after notice and hearing shall contain the following language: 'This court had *jurisdiction over the parties* and the subject matter when it issued this protection order.'" (Emphasis added.) The court, therefore, must have personal jurisdiction over the respondent in order to issue a restraining order after notice and hearing. In determining whether personal jurisdiction can be exercised over a nonresident defendant, "[the court] must first decide whether the applicable state long-arm statute authorizes the assertion of jurisdiction over the [defendant]. If the statutory requirements [are] met, its second obligation [is] then to decide whether the exercise of jurisdiction over the [defendant] would violate constitutional principles of due process."

The Connecticut long arm statute that is applicable to § 46b–15 is codified in § 52–59b, which provides in relevant part: * * *

The portions of § 52–59b most likely to be applicable in the present case are subsections (a)(2)—committing a tortious act within the state, and (a)(3)—engaging in a persistent course of conduct. Under § 52–59b (a)(2) the court can exercise personal jurisdiction over a nonresident individual who "commits a tortious act within the state." Several Connecticut courts have held that a nonresident "commits a tortious act within the state" for purposes of § 52–59b (a)(2) by sending a communication whose content may be considered tortious directly into Connecticut. * * *

This court concludes, therefore, that a nonresident defendant does not need to be physically present in Connecticut at the time of the commission of the alleged tortious act for him to have "commit[ted] a tortious act within the state" for purposes of § 52–59b(a)(2).

Unlike the letter or email cases, however, "an internet posting . . . is not 'sent' anywhere in particular, but rather can be accessed from anywhere in the world." There is no Connecticut authority addressing the exercise of personal jurisdiction over nonresident individuals premised upon internet postings. "Courts in other jurisdictions, [however], when confronted with jurisdictional questions in the context of posting messages upon . . . a listserve or newsgroup, have concluded that the mere posting of messages upon such an open forum by a resident of one state that could be read in a second state was not sufficient to confer jurisdiction upon the latter." * * *

As the *Young* court noted, moreover, premising personal jurisdiction on "[i]nternet activity directed at [the forum state] and causing injury that gives rise to a potential claim cognizable in [that state] . . . is consistent with the [standard] used by the Supreme Court in *Calder v. Jones*, 465 U.S. 783 (1984)." In *Calder* a California actress brought suit there against a reporter and an editor in Florida who wrote and edited in that state a National Enquirer article claiming that the actress had a drinking problem. The Supreme Court held that California could exercise personal jurisdiction over the Florida residents because "California [was] the focal point both of the story and of the harm suffered." The writers' "actions were expressly aimed at California," the Court said, "[a]nd they knew that the brunt of [the potentially devastating] injury would be felt by [the actress] in the State in which she lives and works and in which the National Enquirer has its largest circulation."

The evidence establishes in this case that Fergusan's YouTube video is more than the mere posting of a message upon an open internet forum by a resident of one state that could be seen by someone in a second state. The evidence shows here that he specifically targeted his message at Rios by threatening her life and safety. * * * The court concludes that the evidence here establishes a sufficient basis to find personal jurisdiction under § 52–59b(a)(2).

By specifically targeting a Connecticut resident with its threats to the applicant's life and safety and thereby creating in her a fear for her well-being, the YouTube video created by the respondent can be deemed a tortious act committed in this state.

Since § 52–59b(a)(2) permits the exercise of personal jurisdiction over Fergusan, the court must next determine "whether the exercise of jurisdiction over the [defendant] would violate constitutional principles of due process." "As articulated in the seminal case of *International Shoe Co. v. Washington*, 326 U.S. 310, 316 (1945), the constitutional due process standard requires that, 'in order to subject a defendant to a judgment in personam, if he be not present within the territory of the forum, he have certain minimum contacts with it such that the maintenance of the suit does not offend traditional notions of fair play and substantial justice.' "

"The due process test for personal jurisdiction has two related components: the 'minimum contacts' inquiry and the 'reasonableness' inquiry. The court must first determine whether the defendant has sufficient contacts with the forum state to justify the court's exercise of personal jurisdiction." "The twin touchstones of due process analysis under the minimum contacts doctrine are foreseeability and fairness. '[T]he foreseeability that is critical to due process analysis . . . is that the defendant's conduct and connection with the forum State are such that he should reasonably anticipate being haled into court there.' " "Whether sufficient minimum contacts exist for a court to have jurisdiction is clearly dependent on the facts of each particular case." "Once minimum contacts have been established, [t]he second stage of the due process inquiry asks whether the assertion of personal jurisdiction comports with 'traditional notions of fair play and substantial justice'—that is, whether is reasonable under the circumstances of the particular case."

Even though there is no allegation that Fergusan ever stepped foot in Connecticut, the court can exercise personal jurisdiction over him without violating the principles of due process. Rios's application for a restraining order arises from Fergusan's purposeful action of creating and posting a YouTube video that threatens her life and safety. He posted the video on an internet medium that can be disseminated worldwide, but the content of the video establishes that he was purposefully directing it to the applicant in Connecticut. In this context, his posting of the video constitutes sufficient "minimum contacts" to justify the exercise of personal jurisdiction over him. Moreover, the exercise of personal jurisdiction over him does not offend traditional notions of fairness. It should have been foreseeable to Fergusan that by placing a video on YouTube threatening Rios in Connecticut he could be haled into this state to answer an application seeking a restraining order against him.

Furthermore, Connecticut has a strong interest in protecting its citizens from domestic abuse, and the plaintiff has an obvious interest in obtaining convenient and effective relief in Connecticut. If the court cannot exercise personal jurisdiction in this case, "the unpalatable choices remaining are either to require the victim of abuse to return to the State in which the abuse occurred in order to obtain an effective abuse prevention order or, alternatively, to wait for the abuser to follow the victim to [Connecticut] and, in the event of a new incident of abuse, seek an order from a [Connecticut] court." Accordingly, the plaintiff's interest in obtaining and the state's interest in providing relief and protection from domestic abuse outweigh any burden Fergusan may face in defending this case in Connecticut. Exercising personal jurisdiction over him is neither unjust nor otherwise violates the constitutional principles of due process. The court therefore concludes that it has jurisdiction over the respondent to enter a restraining order protecting the applicant. The restraining order previously entered on a temporary basis is granted for six months, subject to further extension as may be allowed by law.

[Editor's Note: See also Hogue v. Hogue, *16 Cal.App.5th 833 (2017), in which the California Court of Appeal held, inter alia, that an out-of-state abuser's acts of domestic violence directed at a survivor then residing in California—e.g., via social media or other electronic means—subjected that abuser to the "special regulation" that is the Domestic Violence Prevention Act (Cal. Fam. Code, § 6200 et seq.), thus granting the California courts jurisdiction over the out-of-state abuser, and therefore allowing the trial court to issue a restraining order against him.*

In Dobos v. Dobos, *901 N.E.2d 248 (Ohio App. 2008), the court of appeal held that Ohio's long-arm statute could give the trial court authority to issue a long term protective order against a Hungarian citizen who was in that country. The husband's physical abuse allegedly spanned the length of the marriage, while the parties lived in Hungary two years, then in Ohio three years, and again in Hungary three years. The Hungarian police refused to help the wife since she had no broken bones or puncture wounds, so she fled back to Ohio with the children and sought a protective order. The court granted the husband's motion to dismiss, holding it lacked personal jurisdiction over him. The appellate court reversed: the husband's prior abuse of the wife in Ohio, coupled with his calls from Hungary to her and others in Ohio, attempting to find her and threatening her that he would come to Ohio to force her and the children to return to Hungary, could give the trial court jurisdiction over him. The matter was remanded for an evidentiary hearing, including determining whether the husband had sufficient minimum contacts with Ohio that exercising jurisdiction would comply with due process.*

But see Anderson v. Deas, *615 S.E.2d 859 (Ga. App. 2005), in which the Georgia Court of Appeals held that Mr. Deas' allegedly threatening calls to Ms. Anderson from another state to Georgia were not sufficient to give Georgia personal jurisdiction over Mr. Deas, as the state's long-arm statute required that he come to Georgia to commit a tortious act. The order of protection was denied by the trial court, Ms. Anderson appealed the denial, and the appellate court affirmed.*

In "The Stream of Violence: A New Approach to Domestic Violence Personal Jurisdiction," 64 UCLA L. Rev. 684 (2017), Cody J. Jacobs addresses the split among state courts about whether personal jurisdiction over an alleged domestic violence perpetrator is required in order to obtain a civil protection order preventing the defendant from contacting the victim. The author argues that courts should reframe the way they look at personal jurisdiction in these cases by applying the principles embedded in the stream of commerce doctrine and the effects test, the test used when intentional tortfeasors "engage in tortious conduct that they know will have an effect in another forum, even if the tortfeasor never set foot in that forum." Jacobs proposes a test for jurisdiction in interstate protection order cases based on whether the defendant knew the victim's likely destination if the victim were forced to flee to another state. The author explains that this test "hold[s] the defendant responsible for the knowledge he possesses about the likely results of his actions," and demonstrates how this test will be consistent with due process principles.]

CODE OF ALABAMA § 30–5B–3— JUDICIAL ENFORCEMENT OF ORDER

(a) A person authorized by the law of this state to seek enforcement of a protection order may seek enforcement of a valid foreign protection order in a court of this state. * * *

(h) A court of this state may enforce provisions of a mutual foreign protection order which favor a respondent only if both of the following criteria are met:

(1) The respondent filed a written pleading seeking a protection order from the tribunal of the issuing state.

(2) The tribunal of the issuing state made specific findings in favor of the respondent.

BATTERED WOMEN'S JUSTICE PROJECT, NATIONAL CENTER ON PROTECTION ORDERS AND FULL FAITH AND CREDIT, A PROSECUTOR'S GUIDE TO FULL FAITH AND CREDIT FOR PROTECTION ORDERS: PROTECTING VICTIMS OF DOMESTIC VIOLENCE

(2011)

WHAT IS FULL FAITH AND CREDIT?

The federal Violence Against Women Act (VAWA) requires states, tribes, and territories to give full faith and credit to protection orders issued by other jurisdictions. 18 U.S.C. § 2265 (2006). Full faith and credit means that jurisdictions must honor and enforce criminal and civil protection orders issued in other states, tribes, and territories.

"Any protection order issued that is consistent with subsection (b) of this section by the court of one State, Indian tribe, or territory (the issuing State, Indian tribe, or territory) shall be accorded full faith and credit by the court of another State, Indian tribe, or territory (the enforcing State, Indian tribe, or territory) and enforced by the court and law enforcement personnel of the other State, Indian tribal government or Territory as if it were the order of the enforcing State or tribe." 18 U.S.C. § 2265(a).

The statute requires that the issuing court have personal and subject matter jurisdiction, and that the respondent have reasonable notice and an opportunity to be heard sufficient to protect due process. See 18 U.S.C. § 2265(b).

The Violence Against Women Act of 2005 (effective January 5, 2006) amended the full faith and credit provision to clarify that § 2265 applies to territories. The statute now clearly states that law enforcement personnel and the courts must enforce protection orders issued in other jurisdictions. The definition of "protection order" (18 U.S.C. § 2266(5)(A)) was modified to include "restraining orders or any other order issued by a civil or criminal court" and to add "sexual violence" to the enumeration of conduct these orders are designed to prevent. The prior language on support, child custody, and visitation was clarified. 18 U.S.C. § 2266(5)(B). In addition, the new language prohibits a state, Indian tribe, or territory from making publicly available on the Internet any information regarding the registration or filing of a protection order, restraining order, or injunction in the issuing or enforcing state, tribe, or territory, if such publication would be likely to publicly reveal the identity or location of the party protected under such an order. 18 U.S.C. § 2265(d)(3). This language sharply limits the information government agencies may maintain in public postings or databases of protection orders on the Internet.

The full faith and credit provision also provides that:

- A protection order that is otherwise consistent with the requirements of § 2265 must be given full faith and credit even if the enforcing jurisdiction requires the filing or registration of the order, and the order has not been filed or registered. 18 U.S.C. § 2265(d)(2).
- An enforcing jurisdiction may not notify the respondent upon the filing or registration of a protection order issued in another jurisdiction, unless the protected person requests it. 18 U.S.C. § 2265(d)(1).
- Tribal courts have full civil jurisdiction to enforce protection orders, including authority to enforce any orders through civil contempt proceedings, exclusion of violators from Indian lands, and other appropriate mechanisms. 18 U.S.C. § 2265(e). * * *

PROTECTION ORDERS COVERED BY THE FEDERAL FULL FAITH AND CREDIT PROVISION

The full faith and credit provision applies to enforceable civil and criminal protection orders, injunctions, or restraining orders issued by tribes, territories, or states, whether ex parte, after a hearing, or by agreement. Orders may differ from jurisdiction to jurisdiction in form, content, length, layout, or name (e.g., protection from abuse order, no contact order, stay away order, harassment order, restraining order, permanent order, juvenile court protection order, conditions of release order, and conditions of probation order).

For a protection order to be enforceable, it must meet the following conditions:

- The court that issued the order must have had personal and subject matter jurisdiction. 18 U.S.C. § 2265(b)(1).
- The respondent must have had reasonable notice and an opportunity to be heard sufficient to protect the respondent's right to due process. 18 U.S.C. § 2265(b)(2).

If the protection order is ex parte, notice and opportunity to be heard must be provided within the time required by the law of the issuing jurisdiction, and within a reasonable period of time after the order is issued, sufficient to protect the respondent's due process rights. 18 U.S.C. § 2265(b)(2). This means that the protection order is enforceable as long as there will be an opportunity to be heard within a reasonable period of time before a final order is issued.

In a single protection order issued against both parties, provisions against the petitioner are not entitled to full faith and credit if:

- No cross or counter petition, complaint, or other written pleading was filed by the respondent seeking such a protection order; or
- A cross or counter petition was filed and the court did not make specific findings that each party was entitled to such an order. 18 U.S.C. § 2265(c). * * *

[Editor's Note: In "Cross-Border Domestic Violence: The Global Pandemic and the Call for Uniform Enforcement of Civil Protection Orders," 40 Suffolk Transnat'l L. Rev. 35 (2017), Angelica Feldman notes that very few countries or regions of the world have policies covering international enforcement of restraining orders. Given the high rates of migration due to abuse, this is a major gap. She calls for the creation of bilateral or multilateral treaties, led by the Hague Conference on Private International Law, as such policies can save lives.

Effective 1/1/2018, California enacted Fam. Code section 6453(c), providing that it will enforce Canadaian restraining orders, the first U.S. state to pass such legislation.]

CHAPTER 7

CHILDREN IN HOMES WHERE DOMESTIC VIOLENCE TAKES PLACE

■ ■ ■

This chapter focuses on children involved in domestic violence situations. The first section deals with substantive custody and visitation decisions, including the effects on children of living with batterers and the overlap between partner abuse and child abuse. The section starts with a new article on the failure of family courts to take domestic violence into account in crafting custody orders, and instead the courts often believing abusers' false claims that the survivors are alienating the children from them. An editor's note summarizes a new study finding that the decisions of many actors in the family court system further endanger children rather than protecting them.

The materials also address how legislatures and courts can best protect such children while dealing fairly with their parents and the need for domestic violence training for child custody evaluators. An article discusses the importance of understanding the ways that adverse childhood experiences (ACEs) play key roles in cases in family court. Two other articles and two cases deal with statutory rebuttable presumptions against custody to abusers, found in about half of U.S. states, and how these are working. Another case discusses the proper judicial response when a teenage girl says she wants to live with her father, who has abused her mother.

An article discusses supervised visitation in these cases and argues that courts should not order any visitation when the non-custodial parent is dangerous and disruptive.

The second section looks at what courts should do when either the battered parent or the batterer takes the children to another location, sometimes crossing state or international lines. In some instances this is done as part of an abduction, in which case both the civil and the criminal aspects of the legal system may be implicated. Frequently the battered parent and the children are fleeing from the abuse and requesting protection from courts in the new state or country, triggering the Uniform Child Custody Jurisdiction and Enforcement Act, the Parental Kidnapping Prevention Act, and/or the Hague Convention on the Civil Aspects of International Child Abduction. A new Supreme Court case discusses the proper standard to be applied under the Hague Convention where the abused parent has brought the child to the U.S. to protect herself and the child and the abuser is seeking custody in his home country.

Next come guidelines from the National Council of Juvenile and Family Court Judges for cases in which the battered parent has been granted a custody order and is now petitioning the court for permission to relocate to a more distant location, which impacts the visitation rights of the batterer.

The third section focuses on the response of juvenile courts and the child welfare system to children who have witnessed domestic violence or may have themselves been physically hurt in the context of a parent's being abused. A new article calls for breaking down silos between three different parts of the court system: domestic violence, child welfare, and custody, arguing that siloing these interrelated matters causes great detriment. Next, an appellate court decision reverses the juvenile court after it denies a battered mother the right to parent her child even though she complied with all the conditions the court required of her.

The chapter ends with an article looking at batterers as fathers, and suggesting ways these men can be helped to understand the impact of their behavior on their children and to change.

A. CUSTODY AND VISITATION

DEBRA POGRUND STARK, JESSICA M. CHOPLIN, AND SARAH ELIZABETH WELLARD, PROPERLY ACCOUNTING FOR DOMESTIC VIOLENCE IN CHILD CUSTODY CASES: AN EVIDENCE-BASED ANALYSIS AND REFORM PROPOSAL

26(1) Michigan J of Gender & Law 1 (2019)
(footnotes omitted)

Introduction

There is substantial evidence that family law judges, child representatives, guardians ad litem, and other family law professionals are not adequately taking domestic violence into account in child custody determinations. Survivors of domestic violence are often either not believed or are viewed as being alienating rather than protective of their children. When a father claims that the mother is alienating him from his children, that father is much more likely to obtain the custody order they are seeking (joint or sole custody of their children), even when the courts are aware that the father has committed domestic violence or direct abuse of the children. Mothers are much less likely to obtain the custody order they are seeking (sole custody and protective restrictions on the parenting time of the other parent) when they allege domestic violence or direct abuse of their children and the father alleges alienation. An estimated 58,000 children a year in the United States are court ordered into unsupervised contact with physically or sexually abusive parents following divorce. The failure to protect children and domestic violence survivors continues even when one parent has been convicted beyond a reasonable doubt of domestic violence against the other parent. According to one study, joint legal custody orders (for shared decision-making by the parents) are the most common custody outcome—[and] primary physical custody (physical placement) is given to the domestic abuse victim in only 60 percent of the cases. There are no explicit provisions for the safety of the victim or children (such as ordering that placement exchange occur in a protected setting) in 70 percent of these cases. These results are particularly problematic since there is strong evidence that exposure to domestic violence often causes long-term, serious harm to children, but can be mitigated when protective factors are present or pursued.

As discussed in Section I, to reduce the harms to children from further exposure to domestic violence, courts need to grant custody orders that empower the non-abusive parent to protect their children from further harm. As explained in Sections I and II, when the domestic violence is based upon a pattern of coercive abuse, the custody orders should provide sole legal custody (i.e., decision-making) and primary physical custody (i.e., parenting time) to the non-abusive parent, unless that parent is not fit to parent. In addition, the custody orders should contain other protective measures, such as supervised exchanges of the children, attending and completing partner abuse intervention programs, and, in some cases, supervision or suspension of parenting time.

So why are guardians ad litem and child representatives recommending, and courts ordering, sole or joint custody and unrestricted parenting time to parents when there is evidence those parents have been engaging in a pattern of coercive abuse of the other parent that seriously endangers their children's health, safety, and wellbeing? To what extent is this due to gender bias and a lack of training on the dynamics of domestic violence? To what extent are judges failing to order protective conditions on parenting time because they are unaware of the danger of serious harm to children when one parent engages in domestic violence against the other parent? To what extent is it due to a failure to screen for and make findings on domestic violence? How do the various custody laws among the fifty states contribute to judges failing to order necessary protections?

As discussed in Section II, the presence of domestic violence is a factor in determining the "best interests of the child" in virtually every state's custody laws. . .

Fathers' rights groups, on the other hand, view the situation very differently. They claim that courts favor mothers over fathers, that mothers routinely falsely allege domestic violence or child abuse as part of a "gamesmanship of divorce" to gain an economic advantage in the divorce or parentage case, to get custody, or to alienate the father from the child.

Fathers' rights groups also claim that children are harmed when they are separated from their father. Furthermore, over the past few years, fathers' rights groups such as the National Parents Organization and Stop Abusive and Violent Environments have used these arguments to mount a national push for law reform that would create rebuttable presumptions of equal or shared parenting time and shared decision-making, without adding an exception for situations where one parent has engaged in domestic violence or direct child abuse. *[Editor's Note: The former Joint Custody Association also pushed nationally for such policies in the 1980's and 1990's.]* To what extent are these claims valid and these policy proscriptions prudent or reckless? . . .

Section I of this Article contains a literature review of the harms to children when one parent engages in domestic violence against the other parent; ways to mitigate this harm and reduce the likelihood of co-occurrence of domestic violence and child abuse; and other best practices for taking domestic violence into account in child custody cases. Section I also includes an evidence-based analysis of fathers' rights groups' claims relating to domestic violence and child custody decisions. Section II explores the extent to which best practices have been implemented by state legislatures and state supreme courts. It also identifies gaps in mandating such best practices. In Section III, this Article proposes specific reforms to the laws among the 50 states and the District of Columbia relating to child custody that implement evidence-based best practices to better protect children and survivors of domestic violence from the danger of further serious harm. Among these best practices would be distinguishing "situational couple violence" [i.e., mutual abuse in which coercion does not pervade the entire relationship] from a "pattern of coercive abuse" [i.e., one-way coercion is pervasive in the relationship], with different kinds and levels of protections to be put in place for each. . . .

Common misconceptions include the notions (1) that domestic violence is typically not an issue for couples who are in the process of divorce and are disputing child custody because once they are separated the violence will not continue; (2) that amongst women who are victims, domestic violence results in eventual separation; (3) that children exposed to domestic violence are not harmed so long as they are not directly injured; (4) that domestic violence is exclusively between adults and should not play a role in deciding child custody; (5) that assessment of needs of abused women and their children, and the effects caused by the perpetrator, can be satisfactorily conducted by family courts, attorneys, and mediation or other court services; (6) that legal and mental health services for female victims and their children who are separating from the perpetrator are readily available; and (7) that solutions and community assistance when separating from the perpetrator are limited for victims of domestic violence and their children.

. . . [C]ontrary to current practices, reducing children's exposure to domestic violence within a home needs to be one of the most important goals in determining custody. In determining what is in the best interests of the child, this should come first when considering whether to require protective measures that restrict or deny parenting time based upon a judgment that it would cause "serious endangerment" to the child's welfare. Courts are not doing this well within the United States or internationally. . .

Gender bias often takes place in custody dispute resolutions due to the belief that women are more likely to make false allegations of child abuse and domestic violence in order to alienate children from their fathers. These stereotypes are associated with sexist beliefs, the notion that the world is a just place, and the tendency to disbelieve, minimize, or disregard evidence of abuse. As a result of these beliefs, evaluators often recommend that abusive fathers be given sole or joint custody or unsupervised visits with the children. Mothers are often punished for reporting abuse and are held to stricter standards than are fathers. . .[D]ata do not support the claims that women often make up allegations of abuse and that courts favor women over men in custody cases. The data collected reflects the contrary. Judges place too much weight on alienation claims and fail to credit or place proper weight on evidence of domestic violence and child abuse. . .

[T]here is a strong co-occurrence of child abuse/neglect and domestic violence; it has been found that among approximately 30 percent to 60 percent of families where domestic violence or child maltreatment has been identified, there is a significant likelihood that both forms of abuse occur. . .According to recent findings, households in which domestic violence occurs have a 41 percent correlation with households also experiencing critical injuries or deaths due to child abuse and neglect. . .

[Studies have shown that] [c]ustody and visitation conclusions were influenced more by the evaluator's knowledge of domestic violence than the facts of the individual cases. . . As another important evidence-based recommendation in assessing whether a family suffers from domestic violence, evaluators should look for patterns of controlling and coercive behavior, rather than emphasizing isolated incidences of physical violence. Studies have documented the fact that when evaluators conduct assessments that place particular focus on coercive-controlling violence, the parenting plans that result from those assessments provide a higher level of safety against domestic violence. In addition, such emphasis typically results in a grant of custody to domestic violence-surviving mothers. . .

Conclusion

. . . This Article presented a literature review to assess treatment of domestic violence and best practices for taking domestic violence into account in child custody cases. Our key findings include:

(i) domestic violence can cause serious, long-term harm to children, and there is a strong co-occurrence of domestic violence with physical injury to children, and child abuse;

(ii) judges favor fathers over mothers in custody cases (granting the custody in the fashion the fathers seek over what the mothers seek) by placing greater weight upon claims of alienation by fathers over claims of domestic violence by mothers, especially when the judges are not trained on domestic violence and hold traditional gender norms and believe the world is a just place;

(iii) the long-term harms to children from domestic violence can be mitigated when protective factors are present or pursued, which include supporting the non-abusive parents in their efforts to protect themselves and their children from further domestic violence;

(iv) to effectuate this support, family law professionals must be thoroughly trained on both the basics of domestic violence and the many counter-intuitive nuances of domestic violence, with custody evaluators, guardians ad litem, and child representatives needing to screen for domestic violence in all of their custody cases;

(v) a key component of this training is learning how to distinguish situational couple violence, which might be able to be safely addressed through "parallel parenting" type custody orders, from situations where there has been a pattern of coercive abuse based upon a general goal of control in all matters, and which will likely continue and escalate after separation; and

(vi) in cases with a pattern of coercive abuse there should be a rebuttable presumption that courts order sole decisionmaking and primary parenting to the non-abusive parent, and protective conditions and restrictions being placed on the parenting time of the coercively abusive parent.

The review of state custody laws in the United States reflects substantial gaps between the practices and rules that evidence-based policies suggest, and the actual laws in place in most states. Only one state requires custody evaluators, guardians ad litem, or child representatives to screen for domestic violence. Only 11 states clearly require without waiver that family law judges—and only 13 states clearly require without waiver that custody evaluators, guardians ad litem, or child representatives—receive training on domestic violence. Only 21 states and the District of Columbia created in their custody statutes a rebuttable presumption against sole or joint custody to a parent who has engaged in domestic violence as defined in their statutes. *[Editor's Note: According to the National Council of Juvenile and Family Court Judges, there were 28*

U.S. states plus Washington, D.C. with such laws as of 2018.] And, while 34 states clearly and explicitly refer to domestic violence (or domestic abuse or family violence against the other parent) as a basis to condition or restrict parenting time of a non-custodial parent, some of these states' statutes that create rebuttable presumptions, or refer to domestic violence as a basis to condition or restrict parenting time, narrowly define domestic violence or do not require, but only permit, the court to order any conditions or restrictions. These gaps in the law, and in requiring domestic violence screening and training, contribute to poor custody decision-making by judges to the detriment of the safety and welfare of domestic violence survivors and their children. Nuanced and balanced law reforms would align the laws with evidence-based best practices for taking domestic violence into account in child custody cases. If enacted and implemented, these law reforms should lead to safer, healthier, and better outcomes in child custody cases for families throughout the United States.

[Editor's Notes: 1. See Lisa A. Tucker, "Domestic Violence as a Factor in Child Custody Determinations: Considering Coercive Control," 90 Fordham L. Rev 2673 (2022), in which the author argues that even though courts should adopt a coercive control lens in determining child custody orders in domestic violence cases, abusers are likely to retaliate against their partners for asserting this approach in court. "At issue is how family courts might effectively recognize and analyze the coercive control behaviors of parents seeking custody in a way that is fair, objective, and grounded in social science. Given gender dynamics, the interplay between domestic violence and sustained litigation, and the heavy responsibility and complexity of the task of identifying coercive control, courts will undoubtedly encounter substantial difficulties in applying new domestic violence definitions to real families." Thus, Tucker states that while well-intentioned, statutes incorporating coercive control as a factor in custody decisions may actually put abused mothers and children in more danger. She calls on domestic violence advocates and attorneys to continue to push for legal changes, while recognizing the dangers presented by the current system and advising their clients accordingly.

2. See also "Protective Mothers, Endangered Children: Tracing System Failure for Children of Divorce and Separation," Geraldine Butts Stahly, Connie Valentine, and Veronica York, 14(2) Fam & Intimate Partner Violence Quarterly 7 (2021), reporting results of a national study involving 400 respondents regarding court responses to children in homes with domestic violence. The findings demonstrate that in general children of divorce and separation across the nation were frequently not protected. This lack of safety was more pronounced in California, as California mothers lost custody of their children to identified abusers significantly more often than did mothers in other states.

The authors conclude: "Based on this study, nearly all current systems in place are failing to protect children of divorce and separation. The vast majority of interventions by law enforcement, child welfare services, children's attorneys, mediators, evaluators and judicial officers led ultimately to risky outcomes. Rather than work in a collaborative manner to protect this group of children, professionals appeared to work in concert to endanger them. California mothers lost primary custody at a higher rate (85.3%) than non-California mothers (74.6%) and a majority of children in both groups reported further injury (73% versus 60.7%) after being placed in unsupervised or full custody of their accused perpetrators. It is of great concern that state actors are placing children in danger."]

JAN JESKE AND MARY LOUISE KLAS, ADVERSE CHILDHOOD EXPERIENCES: IMPLICATIONS FOR FAMILY LAW PRACTICE AND THE FAMILY COURT SYSTEM

50 Fam. L. Q. 123 (2016)
(footnotes omitted)

I Introduction

"Everyone has the right to a future that is not dictated by the past."

Children are impacted throughout their lives by what happens to them in childhood. When those childhood experiences are traumatic, the child may have lifelong consequences. Recent research studies on Adverse Childhood Experiences (ACEs) have demonstrated how ACEs impact the physical and mental health and social well-being of both children and adults. Whenever a family interacts with the court system—whether family court, child protection, juvenile delinquency, domestic violence, or paternity court—the system should endeavor to mitigate the harm already done and do no further harm.

This might best be accomplished by ensuring that lawyers, judicial officers, court staff and other stakeholders with whom the family comes in contact understands the effects of ACEs and performs his or her responsibilities with the goal of mitigating and preventing harm. These professionals should take trauma-informed measures to work more effectively with parties who suffer from the negative impact of ACEs so as to construct the future to do no more harm. This requires meaningful information on the past, present, and future parenting behavior of those who have influenced and may influence the child's environment. A national task force found that sixty percent of American children can expect to have their lives touched by violence, crime, psychological abuse, or trauma. Present efforts to understand the longstanding effects of adverse childhood experiences may only expose the tip of the iceberg. * * *

Traumatic stress is a deeper harm that encompasses child abuse, domestic violence, divorce, and high-conflict or other household dysfunction that may last well beyond childhood. It may interfere with a parent's ability to interact with his or her attorney. Trauma affects what the client needs from an attorney and how the attorney will interact with the client who may be reluctant to reveal critical information that could be outcome determinative. Further, a history of traumatic stress may inhibit the client's ability to form trusting relationships with others, such as their own children or court service workers. * * *

II. What Are ACEs?

"Adverse Childhood Experiences" (ACEs) are stressful or traumatic experiences, including abuse, neglect, and a range of household dysfunctions. The cumulative impact of ACEs on adult health outcomes had not been previously examined until Kaiser Permanente and the Center for Disease Control and Prevention undertook a study to examine the relationship of health risk behavior and disease in adulthood to the breadth of childhood exposure to ten categories of trauma. The ten categories encompassed: emotional abuse, physical abuse, sexual abuse, emotional neglect, physical neglect, an incarcerated household member, parental separation or divorce, domestic violence where mother or stepmother was treated violently, household dysfunction such as substance abuse, and household dysfunction such as mental illness. * * *

A. What Is the ACEs Study?

The ACEs Study is ongoing collaborative research between the Centers for Disease Control and Prevention and Kaiser Permanente. Over 17,000 Kaiser Permanente patients involved in routine health screenings volunteered to participate in the ACEs study. * * * The study used questions related to three categories of childhood abuse: psychological abuse (two questions), physical abuse (two questions), and contact sexual abuse (four questions). There were also questions on four categories of exposure to household dysfunction during childhood: exposure to substance abuse (two questions), mental illness (two questions), violent treatment of mother or stepmother (four questions), and criminal behavior (one question). If a respondent answered yes to one or more questions within a category, they were defined as exposed to that category of ACEs.

Although the data continues to be analyzed, it reveals staggering proof of the health, social, and economic risks that result from childhood trauma. Notably, the study participants are middle class, college educated, and mostly white. As a rule, participants had jobs and access to good health care. * * *

B. Importance of ACEs Study for Family Law

Those who work with families in the court system need to be aware of the ACEs studies. The fact that more than 500 articles discuss the adverse childhood experiences (ACEs) research findings suggests the importance of this information, including developments in epidemiology, neurobiology, and biomedical and epigenetic consequences of toxic stress. Professionals, organizations, agencies, and communities are implementing best practices based on the ACEs research in family law, education, juvenile justice, criminal justice, public health, medicine, mental health, social services, and in municipalities and states. ACEs research can lead to recommendations on how to implement trauma-informed best practices. This information may help family law practitioners, judicial officers, guardians *ad litem*, court staff and other stakeholders in the family court system to work more efficiently and increase the likelihood of better case outcomes. * * *

The ACEs Study became even more significant with the publication of parallel research of neuroscientists and pediatricians at Harvard and the Child Trauma Academy that provided the link between why traumatic childhood experiences could have adverse health consequences throughout all of adulthood. The stress of severe, chronic childhood trauma, such as being constantly belittled, berated, slapped or punched, or watching father inflict physical violence on mother releases flight, fight, or freeze hormones that physically damage a child's developing brain because they become toxic when they are turned on too long. A San Francisco pediatrician found that for her patients who had four or more categories of adverse childhood experiences "their odds of having learning or behavior problems in school were thirty-two times as high as kids who had no adverse childhood experiences." * * *

2. THE MINNESOTA ACE STUDY AND INITIATIVES

* * * A Hennepin County judge points to the Kaiser-CDC ACEs study correlation between adult behavior and childhood adversity showing that people with four or more ACEs are five times as likely to engage in sexual intercourse by age fifteen and seven times more likely to perpetuate domestic violence than those with no ACEs. * * *

EDITOR'S SUMMARY, NATIONAL COUNCIL OF JUVENILE AND FAMILY COURT JUDGES, REVISED CHAPTER 4, FAMILIES AND CHILDREN, MODEL CODE ON DOMESTIC AND FAMILY VIOLENCE

(2022)

After three years of extensive work, the original Model Code on Domestic and Family Violence was released in 1994 by the National Council of Juvenile and Family Court Judges. This comprehensive Model Code provides a statutory framework for promoting effective responses to domestic violence by the criminal, civil, and family courts, and it encourages consistency across the country. Its five chapters address general provisions, criminal penalties and procedures, civil orders for protection, family and children, and prevention and treatment.

After almost three decades, Chapter 4, Family and Children, was found most in need of revisions to update current knowledge about domestic violence and to better address how courts can best protect children. The NCJFCJ found that there have been persistent poor outcomes in many family courts for children and survivor parents in domestic abuse situations. The focus of the revised Chapter 4 is on an approach that requires a careful analysis and tailored response, which means that adequate information is obtained (safely and ethically) and provided to the court, allowing for a comprehensive assessment of the context, nature, and effects of domestic abuse on the abused parent and children who experienced abuse. Due process and procedural fairness are also key, including in the work of non-judicial actors such as child custody evaluators and guardians ad litem. The revisions also incorporate the concept of coercive control, an important aspect of non-physical abuse, and its effects on children and abused parents.

Because the parent who is abusive and whose children resist contact with them may allege in family court that the parent who is abused is engaging in "parental alienation," the revised Chapter's definition of domestic abuse explicitly prohibits courts from adversely considering the actions of parents who are abused that are intended to protect themselves or their children from the risk of harm posed by the other parent.

The sections in the revised Chapter include: definitions, best interest of the child, rebuttable presumption against custody to abusive parents (in applicable jurisdictions), parenting time/visitation, use of experts to assist decision-making, alternative dispute resolution, relocation, modification and enforcement of parenting orders, child-related relief in civil protection orders, and education for family court judges, staff, and practitioners. NCJFCJ is offering training and technical assistance on the new Chapter. It is hoped that many state legislators, judges, attorneys, child custody evaluators, and others will implement these revisions and that the results will better protect children and abused parents.

CITY AND CO. OF SAN FRANCISCO V. H.H.

76 Cal.App.5th 531 (2022)
(citations and footnotes omitted)

Family Code section 3044 creates a rebuttable presumption that an award of sole or joint physical or legal custody of a child to a person who has perpetrated domestic violence against the other party seeking custody within the past five years is detrimental to the child. If the court determines the presumption has been overcome, it must state its reasons in writing or on the record. Here, the trial court issued a restraining order protecting a mother from the father of a young child and, citing the statute, granted the mother sole legal and physical custody, but left intact a visitation schedule under which the child lived with each parent approximately half time. Mother argues this schedule amounted to joint physical custody and therefore violated the statute. She also contends the trial court erred in refusing her request for a statement of decision. We agree with mother and reverse the visitation order.

BACKGROUND

The parties are the parents of a son, D.H., who was born in September 2015. The following description of the facts leading to mother's request for a domestic violence restraining order and sole legal and physical custody of the child are taken from mother's declaration and the court orders included in the record. Father did not file a respondent's brief on appeal.

According to mother's declaration, when she told father she was pregnant, he got "so angry, he kicked [her] in the stomach." She did not call the police because she was scared of what he would do. In March or April of 2015, mother saw father downtown with another woman. He got upset and slapped her, and she heard him tell the woman "it wasn't his baby." Father grabbed mother by her hair and yanked so hard he tore out two big braids and left a bald spot on her scalp. Mother called the police but father left before they arrived. Thereafter, mother tried to avoid father. The woman started to taunt mother, saying she wanted to fight mother and telling her, " 'Bitch, you are having this baby for me.' "

The birth was difficult and both D.H. and mother ended up in critical care. D.H. remained in the hospital for a month, during which time father visited once. Around the end of 2015, a paternity test father had requested confirmed he was the father and mother filed for child support. Father was furious and called mother many times, calling her a bitch.

In early 2016, when mother went to her car to drive to a child support hearing, she found her tires punctured and flat. Later that day, people in her building told her they had seen father flattening the tires.

At the hearing, father was angry and aggressive with mother. He came up behind her when she went to the bathroom and yelled, " 'Bitch, I am going to beat the fuck out of you!' " Mother was so scared she went into the wrong courtroom. Father was arrested.

In 2016, father sought custody orders. After hearings and mediation, in August 2016, the court granted mother temporary sole physical and legal custody. In October 2016, mother filed a request for a restraining order against father, which was denied. Father then sought a restraining order against mother, the hearing on which was continued to January 11, 2017. Meanwhile, at a hearing in December 2016, the court granted father visitation from 10:00 a.m. to 3:00 p.m. on Thursdays and Saturdays, with exchanges on Thursdays at the San Francisco Police Department's central station and exchanges on Saturdays at Rally Visitation Services (Rally). A review hearing was set for January 11, 2017, together with the hearing on father's restraining order request.

Father did not appear at the hearing on January 11, 2017, and the restraining order request was taken off calendar. Although she was present, mother did not know the custody portion of the hearing was continued to February 23, 2017, and, as a result, did not go to the February hearing. At that hearing, the court ordered joint legal and physical custody of D.H. and increased father's parenting time, ordering weekly visits running from Tuesday morning to Friday morning or afternoon (depending on the availability of supervision at Rally, where the exchanges were to occur). Mother filed a request to return to sole legal and physical custody but was not able to serve father.

Problems escalated when the parties started the new schedule. Father would yell at mother in front of D.H. during exchanges, insult her and tell her he was going to hurt her, and he frequently returned D.H. late after his visits. Mother was scared to ask the court to change the custody order because father was "so angry and intimidating," including threating to "try to kill [mother] if [she] took him to court."

In 2018, on multiple occasions, father called the police or Child Protective Services (CPS), accusing mother of threatening him or hurting the baby, both of which mother denied. Mother was interviewed by CPS repeatedly, as were her older children from a prior relationship, and each time the case was closed.

On one occasion in December 2018, father returned D.H. with "so many scratches and bruises that [mother] took him to the doctor, and the doctor reported it to CPS." Mother spoke with CPS and the case was closed.

In January 2019, mother received a call from a doctor saying father had taken D.H. to urgent care and accused mother of burning the child with a cigarette. Father then refused to return D.H. for "many weeks" and filed an ex parte request for sole custody. According to her declaration, mother does not smoke, and she denied hurting D.H. in any way. The court denied the emergency orders at a hearing on February 1, 2019, but father still refused to return D.H. Mother worked with the San Francisco County District Attorney's Child Abduction Unit but did not get D.H. back until March 18, 2019.

After a hearing on April 2, 2019, the court found it was in D.H.'s best interests to continue the existing custody and visitation orders. The court noted that CPS found the allegations of neglect by mother unfounded and closed the case, and found there was "no credible evidence" supporting mother's request for sole custody and termination of father's visitation. The court ordered both parties to participate in the Kids Turn co-parenting program within six months and file proof of completion with the court no later than October 31, 2019.

On September 30, 2019, mother received about 30 phone calls from a private number in which a woman asked if she was D.H.'s mother and mother could hear a man's voice in the background. The next day, the same woman called and said, " 'Bitch, you sucking his dick? I've been beating your son.' " Mother could hear father in the background saying things including that "they were going to blow up my car and my house with my kids in it," he was going to "beat my ass and tear my car up," and he had a gun. Father and the woman were laughing, and both sounded drunk. Mother called 911 and the police helped her get an emergency protective order against father's girlfriend.

Father continued to insult or threaten mother during exchanges when other people were not present, and told her on three occasions that he had a gun. In May 2020, he told her he would "beat [her] ass" if she called the police again, and on two or three other occasions that he was going to hurt or kill her. Mother was "scared for [her] life, and always watching over [her] back." She was also scared father or his girlfriend were hurting D.H. D.H. told her "over 100 times" that father, the girlfriend, or his older brother (father also has older children) hit him, and on July 6, 2020, when D.H. returned to mother, he had "big red bags under his eyes" and said father had punched him in the chest. On a number of occasions, D.H. returned from visits displaying violent behavior (strangling mother, pushing her, and yelling " 'fuck you!' ") and, on one occasion saying, " '[y]ou weren't supposed to have me, I wasn't supposed to be here.' " Around July 16, 2020, mother found the driver's side door of her car "smashed in," a scratch and a dent on the passenger side, a light "coming off" the car, and a tire punctured.

Problems with father not returning D.H. to mother at the court-ordered time also continued, with father sometimes making excuses and sometimes failing to respond to mother's texts asking about the child. On one occasion in 2020, father kept D.H. for several days beyond the end of his scheduled visit, even after calls from the police.

Mother's declaration concluded, "I fear for my life and for our son's safety. [H.H.] is torturing me. I don't trust him. I am scared that he is going to kill me. Living with this kind of fear is hard on me and my children, including our son. I really need someone to help me."

Mother's request for a domestic violence restraining order was filed on July 24, 2020, seeking protection from father for mother, her two older children, and D.H. Mother also requested sole legal and physical custody of D.H. The court issued a temporary restraining order and set a hearing for August 12, 2020. Temporary orders pending the hearing gave mother legal and physical custody of D.H. with no visitation for father.

In the declaration accompanying father's response to the requests for orders, father denied all of mother's factual assertions and stated that mother continuously makes up lies about him. He stated that mother knew about the February 2017 hearing at which his visitation was increased and chose not to attend "because she had been caught in a series of lies after filing a false police report about me." He further stated that a CPS investigation was opened in January 2019, when he took D.H. to the doctor because the child appeared to have been burned by a cigarette, and that he called CPS in April 2020 because D.H. had "a large knot" on his head and scratches on his body when father picked him up from mother's home. Father believed mother was addicted to prescription pills and "a lot of the issues [she] and I have in communicating about our son are derived from her narcotics abuse," and asked that she be required to undergo drug testing. He stated that he had completed the parenting program previously ordered by the court, and his girlfriend had also completed the program. Father requested modification of the custody order to give him physical custody during school days and every other weekend, with alternate weekend visits for mother.

On August 12, 2020, the court granted mother's request to review father's response and continued the hearing to August 26, extending the temporary restraining order to that date, but reinstating father's custodial time with D.H. from 4:30 p.m. on Tuesdays until 6:30 p.m. on Fridays, with exchanges inside the San Francisco Police Department's central station. The parties were ordered to communicate only by text message and only regarding the child, and reminded of the order to provide the court with proof of completion of the Kids' Turn program.

At the August 26 hearing, mother testified that in May 2020, father threatened to "kill me with a gun" while standing about a foot away from her at the gate to her apartment complex, and "he looked like he was going to do it to me." On the phone in May 2020, he said he was going to "beat me and kick my ass if he knew he wasn't going to go to jail." Mother also testified that father pulled out her braids from the roots in 2016, punched her in the stomach, and slapped her. She described the incident related in her declaration in which father followed and threatened her in court, and was arrested, and testified that her tires were punctured on two occasions before court hearings in this case. Mother testified, "I fear for my life. . . .I mean, you know, he has two strikes. I fear for my life. I'm scared, and I feel like I need a restraining order from him."

Father's attorney declined to have him testify, saying she would rely on his sworn declaration "basically denying all of [mother's] unfounded and uncorroborated statements." Counsel pointed out there were no police reports, phone records, or other evidence to support any of mother's assertions. Counsel noted that father and his girlfriend were providing certificates to prove completion of a parenting program equivalent to the specific one the court had earlier ordered the parties to complete, while mother had not provided any proof of having completed a parenting program.

Mother's attorney, after noting that mother was prepared to testify about her concerns that D.H. was being abused, argued, "in the event the court finds my client's testimony credible that a single past act of abuse has occurred and enters this restraining order based on that alone, then joint custody of the children is not appropriate until [section] 3044 is rebutted." Father's attorney did not suggest the presumption would be rebutted or otherwise address this issue. Mother's attorney also requested a statement of decision, to which the court replied, "I'm not going to issue a statement of decision on this case."

The court found sufficient evidence to grant a three-year restraining order protecting mother and her two older children. It removed D.H. from the scope of the order, stating, "[i]f there is abuse of the minor—and I know from the history of this case that there's been cross-allegations of abuse—each parent should immediately report it to CPS and have them deal with the abuse issues."

The court gave mother temporary sole legal and physical custody "pursuant to Family Code section 3044." It found good cause to maintain the existing visitation schedule, however, and ordered that father have parenting time from 4:30 p.m. on Tuesdays until 6:30 p.m. on Fridays. Mother's attorney objected that leaving this schedule in place violated section 3044 because the "essentially 50/50" time share was a "de facto joint custody order." The court noted the objection and stated, "I think this is in the best interest of the minor. I think that this is the schedule that the child has had for a number of years now."

The court ordered both parents to refrain from speaking negatively about the other in front of the child, all exchanges to occur inside the San Francisco Police Department's central station, and all communications between the parties to be through text or email, with phone, video, or in person communication only in case of emergencies. The court further specified parameters under which father would forfeit a visit for which he was late to pick up, and warned it would consider moving the exchange date if there was a pattern of late pick-ups.

Father's counsel asked the court to order mother to submit proof that she completed the court-ordered parenting program and the court noted that order was outstanding, and "to the extent that [mother] wants to seek any change, that is something that I took into consideration. So if she hasn't done what the court ordered, the court is not likely to change the visitation schedule. [¶] So please have that done; okay?"

Mother filed a timely notice of appeal.

DISCUSSION

As relevant here, section 3044, subdivision (a), provides: "Upon a finding by the court that a party seeking custody of a child has perpetrated domestic violence within the previous five years against the other party seeking custody of the child . . ., there is a rebuttable presumption that an award of sole or joint physical or legal custody of a child to a person who has perpetrated domestic violence is detrimental to the best interest of the child. . . .This presumption may only be rebutted by a preponderance of the evidence."

"This presumption is mandatory and the trial court has no discretion in deciding whether to apply it: '[T]he court *must* apply the presumption in any situation in which a finding of domestic violence has been made. A court may not " 'call . . . into play' the presumption contained in section 3044 only when the court believes it is appropriate." '

To overcome the presumption, the court must find "[t]he perpetrator of domestic violence has demonstrated that giving sole or joint physical or legal custody of a child to the perpetrator is in the best interest of the child." This determination must be made without consideration of the statutory preference for "frequent and continuing contact with both parents" set forth in sections 3020 and 3040; this statutory preference "may not be used to rebut the presumption, in whole or in part."

The court must also find that certain factors enumerated in section 3044, subdivision (b)(2), "on balance, support the legislative findings in Section 3020." Section 3020, subdivision (a), provides: "The Legislature finds and declares that it is the public policy of this state to ensure that the health, safety, and welfare of children shall be the court's primary concern in determining the best interests of children when making any orders regarding the physical or legal custody or visitation of children. The Legislature further finds and declares that children have the right to be safe and free from abuse, and that the perpetration of child abuse or domestic violence in a household where a child resides is detrimental to the health, safety, and welfare of the child."

The specific factors the court must consider are as follows:

"(A) The perpetrator has successfully completed a batterer's treatment program that meets the criteria outlined in subdivision (c) of Section 1203.097 of the Penal Code.

"(B) The perpetrator has successfully completed a program of alcohol or drug abuse counseling, if the court determines that counseling is appropriate.

"(C) The perpetrator has successfully completed a parenting class, if the court determines the class to be appropriate.

"(D) The perpetrator is on probation or parole, and has or has not complied with the terms and conditions of probation or parole.

"(E) The perpetrator is restrained by a protective order or restraining order, and has or has not complied with its terms and conditions.

"(F) The perpetrator of domestic violence has committed further acts of domestic violence."

Section 3044 expressly requires a court to explain its reasons in writing or on the record if it finds the presumption of detriment has been overcome, including specific findings on each of the factors in subdivision (b). "It is the intent of the Legislature that this subdivision be interpreted consistently with the decision in *Jaime G.* [citation] which requires that the court, in determining that the presumption in subdivision (a) has been overcome, make specific findings on each of the factors in subdivision (b). [¶] (2) If the court determines that the presumption in subdivision (a) has been overcome, the court shall state its reasons in writing or on the record as to why paragraph (1) of subdivision (b) is satisfied and why the factors in paragraph (2) of subdivision (b), on balance, support the legislative findings in Section 3020."

In the present case, the trial court found section 3044 applied and therefore granted sole legal and physical custody to mother. Its order, however, maintained the schedule under which D.H. was with father from Tuesday to Friday each week. The court was not swayed by mother's argument that this was in essence a 50/50 time share that violated section 3044 despite the court's formal award of sole physical and legal custody to mother.

Celia S. held the trial court violated section 3044 where, after finding the father's domestic violence against the mother triggered the section 3044 presumption and awarding sole legal and physical custody of the children to the mother, the court ordered visitation for the father in the form of a previously existing 50/50 timeshare custody arrangement. Explaining that "in determining the true nature of the court's order, we must consider the legal effect of the order, not the label the court attached to it," the *Celia S.* court agreed with the mother's contention that "the trial court may not circumvent section 3044 by characterizing its order as merely an award of visitation."

Celia S. explained, "Under the Family Code, ' "[j]oint physical custody" means that each of the parents shall have significant periods of physical custody.' While there is no statutory definition of " 'significant' time" for purposes of "identifying a joint physical custody arrangement," *Celia S.* cited cases establishing guidelines: " 'Where children "shuttle[ ] back and forth between two parents" so that they spend nearly equal times with each parent, or where the parent with whom the child does not reside sees the child four or five times a week, this amounts to joint physical custody.' In contrast, where 'a father has a child only 20 percent of the time, on alternate weekends and one or two nights a week, this amounts to sole physical custody for the mother with "liberal visitation rights' for the father.' "

The visitation schedule here, three days with father and four with mother, clearly amounted to joint physical custody. The court obviously did not make any finding that the section 3044 presumption was overcome, as it granted mother sole legal and physical custody pursuant to section 3044. To order visitation that was effectively joint physical custody, the court would have had to find the presumption overcome by a preponderance of the evidence showing the order was in the child's best interest—without consideration of the statutory preference for "frequent and continuing contact with both parents"—and to find the factors in section 3044, subdivision (b)(2), "on balance, support the legislative findings in Section 3020." And the court would have had to state its reasons for making these findings "in writing or on the record," including "specific findings on each of the factors in subdivision (b)."

None of these requirements were met. The trial court simply stated that it believed its order was in D.H.'s best interest and "this is the schedule that the child has had for a number of years now." We have no choice but to conclude the court failed to comply with section 3044.

Mother further argues that the trial court violated section 3022.3 by denying her request for a statement of decision. This statute provides: "Upon the trial of a question of fact in a proceeding to determine the custody of a minor child, the court shall, upon the request of either party, issue a statement of the decision explaining the factual and legal basis for its decision pursuant to Section 632 of the Code of Civil Procedure."

Code of Civil Procedure section 632 requires the court to "issue a statement of decision explaining the factual and legal basis for its decision as to each of the principal controverted issues at trial upon the request of any party appearing at the trial." The statement of decision must be in writing unless the parties agree otherwise or unless the trial is concluded within one calendar or less than eight hours over more than one day, in which case the statement of decision may be made orally on the record in the presence of the parties.

In general, Code of Civil Procedure section 632, and therefore section 3022.3, "applies when there has been a trial followed by a judgment. This is true even if the motion involves an evidentiary hearing and the order is appealable. But "[e]xceptions to the general rule have been created for special proceedings. In determining whether an exception should be created, the courts balance ' "(1) the importance of the issues at stake in the proceeding, including the significance of the rights affected and the magnitude of the potential adverse effect on those rights; and (2) whether appellate review can be effectively accomplished even in the absence of express findings." '

"[W]here the issues are sufficiently important, as in a child custody case, formal findings of fact and conclusions of law are required upon the request of a party, regardless of the nature of the proceedings."

The importance of issues bearing on child custody and visitation orders are obvious. As we have said, the Legislature has declared it the "public policy of this state to ensure that the health, safety, and welfare of children shall be the court's primary concern in determining the best interests of children when making any orders regarding the physical or legal custody or visitation of children," that "children have the right to be safe and free from abuse," and that "the perpetration of child abuse or domestic violence in a household where a child resides is detrimental to the health, safety, and welfare of the child." The Legislature has also stated that when these policies conflict with the additional public policy of ensuring that children "have frequent and continuing contact with both parents after the parents have . . . ended their relationship," "a court's order regarding physical or legal custody or visitation shall be made in a manner that ensures the health, safety, and welfare of the child and the safety of all family members."

Jaime G. v. H.L., supra, 25 Cal.App.5th at pages 805–807, 236 Cal.Rptr.3d 209 discussed at some length the particular importance of specific findings in the context of section 3044. "The purpose of the rebuttable presumption statute is to move family courts, in making custody determinations, to consider properly and to give heavier weight to the existence of domestic violence." "Presumptions are used in this context because courts have historically failed to take sufficiently seriously evidence of domestic abuse"; they address the problem of it being " 'too easy for courts to ignore evidence of domestic abuse or to assume that it will not happen again' " and " 'function to counteract the proven tendency of some courts to make judgments based on ignorance or stereotypes.' " "Mandatory checklists," as *Jaime G.* described the factors in section 3044, subdivision (b)(2), "can improve professional decisionmaking for professionals as diverse as surgeons and pilots," and while they "can seem bothersome to experienced professionals," the "Legislature's intent was to require family courts to give due weight to the issue of domestic violence" and "the requirement that courts make specific findings 'in writing or on the record' further this legislative goal." Written findings facilitate meaningful appellate review grounded on the "policies set forth in the governing law," which is "essential to the creation of the body of precedent necessary for the system of rebuttable presumptions to produce consistent and predictable results."

The need for clear and specific findings to facilitate appellate review, as well as to inform the parties and ensure consideration of the proper factors in the first instance, is illustrated by the present case. The trial court awarded mother sole legal and physical custody pursuant to the statutory presumption that awarding custody to father, who the court found to have committed domestic violence against mother, would be detrimental to D.H. The court made no determination that father proved by a preponderance of the evidence that an award of custody to him would be in the child's best interest with respect to the considerations and policies contained in sections 3011 and 3020, and that the section 3044, subdivision (b)(2), factors "on balance, support the legislative findings in section 3020." Had the court made such a determination, the presumption would have been overcome and the court would have been required to explain its reasons in writing or on the record. Yet the trial court kept in place an arrangement under which D.H. was with father three days of the week—a nearly equal timeshare that amounted to joint custody. This order is irreconcilable with the custody order under section 3044, and the only explanation the trial court provided, other than a conclusory statement that it was in the child's best interests, was that "this is the schedule that the child has had for a number of years now."

The trial court abused its discretion in ordering a visitation schedule that amounted to joint custody after finding father committed domestic violence against mother and awarding sole legal and physical custody to mother pursuant to the section 3044. It further erred in refusing mother's request for a statement of decision. The errors are prejudicial, as the record offers no explanation to reconcile the orders and demonstrate the court found the presumption rebutted. Reversal of the visitation order is required.

On remand, the court may award father visitation that does not amount to joint custody. "In doing so, however, the court must comply with statutory provisions governing a visitation award in proceedings involving allegations of domestic violence. (See, e.g., § 3031, subd. (c) ['When making an order for custody or visitation in a case in which domestic violence is alleged and an emergency protective order, protective order, or other restraining order has been issued, the court shall consider whether the best interest of the child, based upon the circumstances of the case, requires that any custody or visitation arrangement shall be limited to situations in which a third person, specified by the court, is present, or whether custody or visitation shall be suspended or denied']; § 3100.) The court also may hear a request from [father] to modify custody subject to section 3044's presumption." . . .

VALADEZ V. VALADEZ

969 N.W.2d 770 (Wis.App., 2021)
(footnotes and citations omitted)

Julie C. Valadez appeals from a judgment of divorce terminating her marriage to her former husband, Ricardo Valadez. As relevant to our disposition of this appeal, Julie argues that the circuit court erred in awarding sole legal custody of their children to Ricardo based on its erroneous conclusion that Ricardo overcame the statutory presumption against custody by proving that he received batterer's treatment from a certified treatment program or a certified treatment provider. Because of the court's finding that Ricardo engaged in a pattern of domestic abuse against Julie, she similarly takes issue with the court's decision granting the parties shared placement without making the safety of Julie and the children the court's paramount concern, as required by § 767.41(5)(bm). For the reasons stated, we reverse and remand with the directions specified below.

BACKGROUND

The following facts were found by the circuit court after a five-day trial. We recite here only the findings that pertain to our analysis on appeal.

Julie and Ricardo were married in 2004 and had been married for approximately sixteen years at the time of their divorce trial. They have four minor children together, two of whom have been diagnosed with autism.

In late 2017, Ricardo was arrested and charged with a misdemeanor for domestic abuse against Julie. Julie petitioned for divorce a few months after Ricardo's arrest and subsequently sought a domestic abuse injunction. Ricardo stipulated to the entry of a four-year injunction, which prohibited him from contacting Julie or entering the marital home, where Julie and the kids were living at the time. After the injunction was issued, the circuit court entered a temporary order which, among other things, gave Julie sole legal custody and primary placement of the children and awarded Ricardo periods of supervised placement.

At some point after the injunction was issued, Ricardo entered the marital home in contravention of the injunction. After the incident, Julie moved out of the house and enrolled in the Wisconsin Department of Justice's "Safe at Home" program, which offers victims of domestic abuse and other crimes a legal substitute address that can be used for public and private purposes.

In early 2019, the state agreed to amend Ricardo's misdemeanor domestic abuse charge to disorderly conduct upon payment of restitution and successful completion of alcohol and other drug abuse and domestic abuse treatment. Julie was present at the sentencing hearing and objected to the amendment of the charge because she did not believe that the counseling Ricardo had completed with his licensed professional counselor, Tyler Loomis, was specific to domestic violence. Nonetheless, the court (not the same judge who presided over the injunction and divorce hearings) approved the amended charge, accepted Ricardo's plea of no contest thereto, and sentenced Ricardo accordingly.

While the divorce was pending and after the resolution of the domestic abuse case, the guardian ad litem (GAL) submitted a proposed temporary order modifying placement. The GAL believed that it was in the best interest of the children to modify the existing order to allow Ricardo longer periods of placement with the children. The court approved of the modification over Julie's objection. A couple of months before trial, the GAL submitted another proposed order to modify placement, this time proposing equal placement, which the court again granted over Julie's objection.

Both Julie and Ricardo testified and presented arguments to the court at their divorce trial. Julie argued at trial that the court should not award custody to Ricardo due to his history of domestic abuse against Julie. Julie asserted that Ricardo failed to prove that he successfully completed a certified treatment program aimed at combatting domestic abuse or saw a certified batterer's treatment provider such that he was able to overcome the presumption against custody. Ricardo argued that he received counseling from Loomis that was aimed at dealing with Ricardo's abuse issue and that this was sufficient to overcome the presumption against custody. The GAL agreed with Ricardo and asked the court to award Ricardo sole legal custody.

The circuit court determined that Ricardo had engaged in a pattern of domestic abuse and therefore the statutory presumption against awarding him custody applied. Notwithstanding, the court concluded Ricardo had rebutted the statutory presumption because he "successfully completed domestic abuse treatment[,]" explaining as follows:

Although he did not complete a certified treatment program, § 767.41(2)(d)1. expressly contemplates equivalent treatment from a certified treatment provider. Based on a review of the treatment he received in [the domestic abuse case], the Court finds that Mr. Valadez obtained equivalent treatment from Tyler Loomis, who as a licensed professional counselor ("LPC") qualifies as a certified treatment provider. In fact, the State in that case itself recognized that this treatment was equivalent and satisfactory in accepting the treatment and amending the charge.

The court awarded sole legal custody of all four children to Ricardo. The court further ordered "equal shared [physical] placement, with a weekly rotating schedule."

Julie appeals. We include additional facts as necessary below.

DISCUSSION

The Circuit Court Erred in Concluding Ricardo Rebutted the Presumption Against Awarding Him Sole or Joint Custody

. . .Child custody and placement determinations are committed to the sound discretion of the circuit court. We will sustain a discretionary decision if the court examined the relevant facts, applied a proper standard of law, and using a demonstrated rational process, reached a conclusion that a reasonable judge could reach. In addition, we affirm the circuit court's findings of fact unless they are clearly erroneous, but we independently review any questions of law. A court erroneously exercises its discretion if it applies the wrong legal standard.

WISCONSIN STAT. § 767.41(2)(d)1. creates a rebuttable presumption that a parent who commits domestic violence against the other parent is not entitled to joint or sole custody of the children. It provides in relevant part as follows:

> [I]f the court finds by a preponderance of the evidence that a party has engaged in a pattern or serious incident of interspousal battery, . . . or domestic abuse, . . . there is a rebuttable presumption that it is detrimental to the child and contrary to the best interest of the child to award joint or sole legal custody to that party. The presumption under this subdivision may be rebutted only by a preponderance of evidence of all of the following:
>
> a. The party who committed the battery or abuse has successfully completed treatment for batterers provided through a certified treatment program or by a certified treatment provider and is not abusing alcohol or any other drug.
>
> b. It is in the best interest of the child for the party who committed the battery or abuse to be awarded joint or sole legal custody based on a consideration of the factors under sub. (5)(am).

None of the parties to this appeal challenges the circuit court's finding that Ricardo engaged in a pattern of domestic abuse such that the presumption against custody applies to him. Where they disagree is whether Ricardo rebutted the statutory presumption by proving that he successfully completed "a certified treatment program" or other "treatment for batterers . . . by a certified treatment provider."

The resolution of this issue requires us to interpret WIS. STAT. § 767.41(2)(d)1. The "purpose of statutory interpretation is to determine what the statute means so that it may be given its full, proper, and intended effect." Statutory interpretation begins with the language of the statute. If the meaning of the words are plain and unambiguous, a court's inquiry ends and there is no need to consult extrinsic sources of interpretation, such as legislative history. Statutory language is given its "common, ordinary, and accepted meaning, except that technical or specially-defined words or phrases are given their technical or special definitional meaning."

Statutes are "read where possible to give reasonable effect to every word, in order to avoid surplusage." When courts interpret a statute, they are not at liberty "to disregard the plain, clear words of the statute." "If the meaning of the statute is plain," courts "ordinarily stop the inquiry and give the language its 'common, ordinary, and accepted meaning.' " "A dictionary may be utilized to guide the common, ordinary meaning of words."

Ricardo testified that as part of the plea deal in his criminal case, he received "counseling for domestic abuse, anger and drinking through my counselor, Tyler [Loomis]." But Loomis did not testify, and Ricardo offered no other information about his counselor or the nature of his treatment. As we now explain, that is not enough evidence to establish that Ricardo received "treatment for batterers provided through a certified treatment program or by a certified treatment provider."

In finding that Ricardo had "successfully completed domestic abuse treatment," the circuit court took "judicial notice" of the amended criminal charge. The court reasoned that because the state had "accepted" Ricardo's treatment in a criminal plea deal, that same treatment sufficed to rebut WIS. STAT. § 767.41(2)(d)'s presumption against awarding custody to an abuser. Ricardo suggests that we, like the circuit court, should review the CCAP entries in Ricardo's criminal case and rely on the fact that the district attorney's office approved Ricardo's treatment to conclude that he has met his burden of presenting evidence sufficient to overcome the presumption against custody. However, Ricardo fails to explain why it matters in this case that a prosecutor accepted his treatment for purposes of entering a plea agreement in a case that did not have a statute with the same requirements as § 767.41, which requires "treatment for batterers provided through a certified treatment program or by a certified treatment provider" to rebut the presumption. Whether Loomis' counseling and credentials met that standard is a statutory interpretation question that cannot be answered by looking to a plea deal in a separate criminal case involving a different set of statutes and different considerations, when nothing suggests it met the statutory requirements at issue here.

In accepting Ricardo's argument that if the treatment was sufficient for the plea deal, it is sufficient under the custody statutes, the circuit court specifically acknowledged that Ricardo did not participate in a certified treatment program. However, without citing to any controlling cases or other legal support, the court determined that WIS. STAT. § 767.41(2)(d) allows for something other than *certified* programs or providers, concluding that any licensed professional counselor can be considered a "certified" provider for purposes of rebutting the statutory presumption. As defined in our statute addressing licensed professionals, professional counseling covers a wide range of methods and models aimed at "achiev[ing] mental, emotional, physical, social, moral, educational, spiritual, vocational or career development and adjustment." Section 767.41(2)(d), on the other hand, is aimed at something more specific: "treatment for batterers provided through a certified treatment program or by a certified treatment provider." In that context, "certified" would imply a certification to treat batterers, not the more generalized work of a licensed professional counselor.

In rendering its decision here, the circuit court read words into the statute that are not there, indicating that the statute "expressly contemplates equivalent treatment" and ignored words that are there—"treatment for batterers provided through a certified treatment program or by a certified treatment provider." Courts "are bound to apply the plain language of the statute enacted by the legislature." As a fundamental tenet of statutory interpretation, where possible, we render no word in a statute surplusage, but instead give meaning *to every word.*

We see nothing in the statute indicating that it contemplates treatment that is not aimed at batterers and provided by a *certified* program or provider. We must assume that the legislature chose to specify certified programs and providers by design and for a reason. We cannot ignore these words or assume that the legislature included them without assigning any meaning to them.

Wisconsin Stat. § 767.41 does not define "certified treatment program" or "certified treatment provider" or even "certified." As such, we may look to the common meaning of the term. "Certified" commonly means "endorsed authoritatively: guaranteed or attested as to quality, qualifications, fitness or validity." To provide an example of when "certified" may be properly used in the context of a profession, Webster's defines a "certified public accountant" in relevant part as "an accountant . . . who has met the requirements of a state law and has been granted a state certificate." It follows from these definitions that a certified treatment provider for batterers would be a treatment provider "who has met [certain] requirements" to justify granting him or her "a certificate" indicating that he or she has been "endorsed authoritatively" as qualified and fit to treat batterers.

Applying these principles and common definitions, we conclude that the words enacted by the legislature mean that one may only overcome the presumption against sole or joint custody set forth in WIS. STAT. § 767.41(2)(d)1. by successfully completing treatment designed for batterers and provided by a certified program or provider. We cannot ignore the plain language of the statute that so requires, nor can we assume that the words are mere surplusage. We therefore conclude that the circuit court erred in deciding that Ricardo overcame the presumption against custody on this ground and remand to the court because § 767.41 does not allow Ricardo to be awarded custody until he has successfully completed the proper treatment. We note that the court ordered many conditions when awarding custody, such as requiring Ricardo to maintain absolute sobriety, identifying required communications regarding custody decisions, input on custody decisions, keeping the children in and with their same schools and doctors, and therefore we remand to the circuit court to reconsider its custody decision in light of our decision.

Given Ricardo's Pattern of Domestic Abuse, the Circuit Court Failed to Address the Applicable Statutory Requirement When Ordering Placement

As with custody determinations, we review a circuit court's decisions regarding physical placement under an erroneous exercise of discretion standard and "affirm the circuit court's decisions when the court applies the correct legal standard and reaches a reasonable result." Julie argues that here the circuit court erroneously exercised its discretion by failing to consider, or even mention, the standard set forth in WIS. STAT. § 767.41(5)(bm), which applies when a court finds that one parent has engaged in a pattern of domestic abuse, when ordering shared placement of the children for Julie and Ricardo. Ricardo fails to even refer to § 767.41(5)(bm) when attempting to defend the circuit court's placement decision in direct response to Julie's criticism thereof, thereby conceding Julie's argument on this point.

"Courts . . . have no power in awarding placement other than that provided by statute." WISCONSIN STAT. § 767.41(5)(bm) provides that when a court finds a pattern of domestic abuse, "the safety and well-being of the child and the safety of the parent who was the victim of the . . . abuse shall be the paramount concerns in determining legal custody and periods of physical placement." This is not a rebuttable presumption, like the one addressing legal custody. The court's finding that Ricardo engaged in a pattern of domestic abuse against Julie automatically makes the safety of Julie and her children the most important factor in any physical placement determination.

The circuit court made no mention of WIS. STAT. § 767.41(5)(bm) when it ordered "equal shared placement." As stated above, Ricardo effectively concedes this failure by the court. Given our reversal based on the court's erroneous conclusion that Ricardo overcame the statutory presumption that he successfully completed the proper treatment, we decline to search the record to support the circuit court's decision. While the court made extensive findings regarding the parties' allegations and credibility, and placed various conditions in its order designed to ensure safety, we would be speculating as to the role the court's erroneous custody decision had in its placement decision. Thus, we remand to the court to reconsider its placement determination. . .

WISSINK V. WISSINK

301 A.D.2d 36 (N.Y. 2002)
(citations and footnotes omitted)

This appeal presents a vexing custody dispute over a teenaged girl who has expressed a clear preference to live with her father. While both parents are seemingly fit custodians, the father has a history of domestic violence directed at the mother; yet he has never posed a direct threat to the child.

Because of this circumstance, we hold that the Family Court erred in awarding custody to the father without first ordering comprehensive psychological evaluations to ensure that this award of custody was truly in the child's best interest.

The child in controversy, Andrea, born June 21, 1986, is the biological child of the mother and father; the mother also has a daughter, Karin, by a prior marriage. The parties have had a tumultuous relationship marked by numerous episodes of heated arguments, physical violence, police intervention and Family Court orders of protection. It is apparent that when it comes to his dealings with the mother, the father is a batterer whose temper gets the better of him. When it comes to Andrea, however, the father is the favored parent; he has never directly mistreated Andrea.

The parties have lived apart at various times during their marriage, and separated most recently in 1999 following yet another physical altercation. The mother commenced a family offense proceeding and a proceeding for custody of Andrea. The father cross-petitioned for custody. The Family Court assigned a law guardian and ordered a mental health study which was clearly deficient. A hearing was held at which the parties, Karin, and other witnesses testified, and the court examined Andrea in camera; she downplayed the father's culpability and expressed her clear preference for living with him.

The order appealed from awarded custody to the father. In separate orders, the Family Court dismissed the mother's custody petition and sustained the mother's family offense petitions, directing, inter alia, that the father enter and complete a domestic violence program. We now reverse the order awarding custody to the father and remit for a new custody hearing following an in-depth forensic examination of the parties and child.

Andrea's preference for her father and her closely bonded relationship to him were confirmed by her law guardian and the "mental health professional" social worker who interviewed her. Indeed, putting aside the established fact of his abusive conduct toward her mother, Andrea's father appears a truly model parent. He is significantly involved in her school work and her extracurricular activities. They enjoy many pleasurable activities, including movies, shopping, building a barn, and horseback riding. He provides her with material benefits—a television set, clothing, a horse, a trip to Europe. He is loving and affectionate. She is his "princess," his "best girl." In contrast, Andrea's mother has not been significantly involved in her school work or her extracurricular activities, and Andrea does not enjoy her company or their relationship.

Were it not for the documented history of domestic violence confirmed by the court after a hearing, we would have unanimously affirmed the Family Court's award of custody to the father in accordance with Andrea's expressed preference and the evidence documenting their positive relationship. However, the fact of domestic violence should have been considered more than superficially, particularly in this case where Andrea expressed her unequivocal preference for the abuser, while denying the very existence of the domestic violence that the court found she witnessed.

The record is replete with incidents of domestic violence reported by the mother, and by evidence supporting her testimony. The earliest incident that the mother reported was perpetrated when Andrea was merely an infant in 1986. In a fit of anger the father hit and kicked the mother and pulled out chunks of her hair. In the course of the attack she heard him say, "Oh well, she's going to die." On Super Bowl Sunday in 1995, he attacked her, throwing her on the floor, kicking, hitting, and choking her. She sustained marks on her neck and a sore throat causing pain while speaking and inhibiting her ability to swallow.

In March 1995, she obtained an order of protection from the Village Court of Montgomery. In the fall of that year the father allegedly held a knife, approximately 8 to 10 inches long, to the mother's throat while Andrea, then nine, sat on her lap. In February 1996 the mother again obtained an order of protection from the Village Court of Montgomery.

In 1997, the father attacked the mother, hit and kicked her, resulting in her obtaining a permanent order of protection from the Orange County Family Court. The severity of her injuries are documented by a photograph, entered in evidence, showing a large black and blue bruise on her left hip.

In June 1999, the mother left the marital home with Andrea and moved into a shelter where they remained for five days. Upon their return home the father blocked her car in the driveway, yelled at the mother and punched her.

On June 24, 1999, a few days after her return from the shelter, during a dispute over tax returns, the father tried to wrest papers the mother held in her teeth by squeezing her face in his hands, leaving marks and even enlisting the assistance of Andrea; he allegedly directed the child to "hold [the mother's] nose so she can't breathe."

On December 20, 1999, while Andrea was at home, the father attacked the mother, choking her. She had marks on her neck for days.

The latter two incidents were the subjects of the mother's most recent Family Offense petition, which the court sustained. In doing so, the Family Court also noted that a final order of protection had been entered in 1997, stating "based upon the proceeding [of 1997] as well as the succeeding [incidents] * * * Mr. Wissink is guilty of incidents of domestic violence occurring on June 24, [1999] and December 20, [1999]."

Domestic Relations Law § 240(1) provides that in any action concerning custody or visitation where domestic violence is alleged, "the court must consider" the effect of such domestic violence upon the best interest of the child, together with other factors and circumstances as the court deems relevant in making an award of custody. In this case the Family Court did not entirely ignore that legislative mandate, and specifically noted that it had considered the effect of domestic violence in rendering its custody determination. However, the "consideration" afforded the effect of domestic violence in this case was, in our view, sorely inadequate.

The court-ordered mental health evaluation consisted of the social worker's interview of Andrea on two occasions (about 45 minutes each) and each parent once (about one hour each). These interviews resulted in the social worker's clearly foreseeable conclusion that Andrea was far more comfortable and involved with her father than her mother, that she did not relate well to her mother, and that she preferred living with her father.

In a case such as this, where the record reveals years of domestic violence, which is denied by the child who witnessed it, and the child has expressed her preference to live with the abuser, the court should have ordered a comprehensive psychological evaluation. Such an evaluation would likely include a clinical evaluation, psychological testing, and review of records and information from collateral sources. The forensic evaluator would be concerned with such issues as the nature of the psychopathology of the abuser and of the victim; whether the child might be in danger of becoming a future victim, or a witness to the abuse of some other victim; the child's developmental needs given the fact that she has lived in the polluted environment of domestic violence all of her life and the remedial efforts that should be undertaken in regard to all parties concerned.

The devastating consequences of domestic violence have been recognized by our courts, by law enforcement, and by society as a whole. The effect of such violence on children exposed to it has also been established. There is overwhelming authority that a child living in a home where there has been abuse between the adults becomes a secondary victim and is likely to suffer psychological injury.

Moreover, that child learns a dangerous and morally depraved lesson that abusive behavior is not only acceptable, but may even be rewarded.

In many states a rebuttable presumption that perpetrators of domestic violence should not be eligible for legal or physical custody has been accepted and the courts of those states are required to specify why custody should be granted to an offender and how such an order is in the best interest of the child. We in New York have not gone that far, but the legislature, in enacting Domestic Relations Law § 240, has recognized that domestic violence is a factor which the court must consider among others in awarding custody or visitation.

Moreover, the court also erred in limiting the mother's inquiry regarding the father's failure to comply with child support obligations and in finding financial consideration "not relevant at all" to the custody proceeding. The Family Court was required to consider the parties' support obligations and their compliance with court orders. If, as the mother alleged, the father violated the child support order, and if he terminated the telephone and electrical services in the marital residence after he had been ordered to stay away pursuant to an order of protection, these facts would clearly be relevant to the court's custody determination.

Only after considering the complex nature of the issues and the relative merits and deficiencies of the alternatives can the court attempt to determine the difficult issue of the best interest of the child in a case such as this.

For the above reasons we thus reverse the custody order and direct a new custody hearing to be conducted after completion of a comprehensive psychological evaluation of the parties and the child. However, we stay Andrea's return to her mother, permitting her continued residence with her father, pending a final custody determination.

We note that the foregoing is without prejudice to the mother renewing her petition for custody, which was dismissed by an order from which no appeal was taken.

ORDERED that the order is reversed insofar as appealed from, on the law and as a matter of discretion in the interest of justice, without costs or disbursements, the petition is denied, and the matter is remitted to the Family Court, Orange County, for further proceedings in accordance herewith; and it is further,

ORDERED that pending the final custody determination, the father shall have temporary custody of the child, Andrea, with visitation to the mother pursuant to the terms of the order appealed from.

[Editor's Note: In "Coercive Control: Update and Review," by Evan Stark and M. Hester, 25(1) Violence Against Women 81 (2019), they note: "Children may appear to be passive instruments of the abuser's control, as in a custody fight, or, at the other extreme, a child may openly align with the abusive parent or join his coercive control. In either case, as [other researchers] show, they are striving to retain their agency within a process of victimization, an example of what Stark calls 'control in the context of no control.' "]

ELIZABETH BARKER BRANDT, CONCERNS AT THE MARGINS OF SUPERVISED ACCESS TO CHILDREN

9 J. L. & Fam. Stud. 201 (2007)
(citations and footnotes omitted)

I. INTRODUCTION

Supervised access has emerged as an important tool for managing child-custody matters. In the past fifteen years, formal supervised access programs have become increasingly common throughout the country. Supervised access encompasses a number of different situations ranging from the supervision of custody exchanges between parents, to the supervision of all of a parent's contact with her or his child. Supervision may be provided by trained supervisors, by volunteers, by professionals who also provide therapeutic services in the context of supervision, or by family members. Supervision may take place in locations specially dedicated for supervision, in the offices of professional supervisors, in neutral public locations, or even in private homes.

While parents may voluntarily utilize supervised access services, supervision is most often ordered by courts. The circumstances leading to court-ordered supervised access to children are varied. Supervised exchanges may be ordered for safety reasons because one or both parents pose a danger to each other or to the child or have a history of acting inappropriately when in the presence of each other or the child. Temporary supervision of a parent's contact with a child may be ordered where the parent and child have previously not had a relationship or where there has been a long interruption in the parent-child relationship; in such situations, supervision is ordered to facilitate the re-establishment of the parent-child relationship. A parent's contact with his or her child also may be supervised temporarily when allegations are pending that he or she subjected the child to dangerous, abusive, threatening or inappropriate behaviors or situations. Often the goals of such temporary supervision are not only to protect the child until an accurate assessment of threat to the child can be undertaken, but also to deliver services to the child and parent with the goal that supervision may no longer be necessary at some future point in time. If a court finds that a parent subjected his or her child to such conduct or circumstances, longer term supervision may be ordered to continue the contact of the child with the parent even where there is no realistic possibility that ordinary access will be possible.

The growth of supervised access to children reflects larger trends in custody law. The absence of clear judicial rules in the area of custody has contributed to an increase in conflict and in strategic litigation behavior by parents. In highly conflicted cases, supervised access is a tool that can protect children from some aspects of parental conflict. However, supervised access can also be used as part of a litigation strategy by parents who seek to gain an advantage and to exercise dominion over the other parent. Furthermore, courts may award supervised visitation in high-conflict cases to provide a perceived buffer for the children when the court cannot or does not get to the bottom of the dispute. Second, the move of courts toward a paradigm of post-divorce shared parenting and custody determinations resulting from compromise and settlement has made it increasingly difficult to eliminate a parent's custodial contact with children. Together, these considerations have made many courts reluctant to eliminate custodial contact between parents and children. Supervised visitation is a mechanism that enables courts to continue parental custody in cases even where one parent is a threat to the child or to the other parent.

Orders requiring some form of shared parenting after divorce are increasingly common. The support for this conclusion is largely anecdotal. There is little quantitative research on custody outcomes. The most important study—by Eleanor Macoby and Robert Mnookin—was conducted in 1990 and is thus fairly dated. In that study of California custody cases, joint physical custody of children was common. Even when neither parent requested joint physical custody, courts awarded it in more than a third of the cases. The study established that the higher the level of conflict the more likely the imposition of joint custody was (resulting from pressure to compromise). Not only is joint custody used as a mechanism for settling high-conflict custody cases, this result is pushed by the law in a number of jurisdictions that impose a statutory presumption in favor of joint custody. Even where sole custody is ordered, the non-custodial parent is given significant visitation in most instances. The West Virginia Supreme Court articulated the prevailing view: "[e]ven where there are allegations of abuse and/or neglect, parents whose rights have not been terminated generally have a right to continued contact with the child, although such visitation may be supervised for the protection of the child." To be sure, the research seems to indicate that, on the whole, joint physical custody is good for children. This movement towards the continuing involvement of both parents has overshadowed the question of when continuing contact with a parent should be eliminated. Supervised access is often the vehicle by which potentially dangerous and disruptive parental involvement with children is perpetuated.

Despite the growing frequency with which supervised access is ordered by courts, little research on the impact of supervision on children has been undertaken. A growing body of research details the role of supervised access in reducing the level of conflict between parents and decreasing the frequency of parental interaction with the courts. Research also documents parents' perceptions of their children's adjustment during supervised access. Certainly, to the extent this research indicates that supervised access reduces levels of conflict, improves parenting behavior, and leads to more realistic expectations of parents, we can infer that supervised access is beneficial to children. Yet, we know little about children's perceptions of supervised access, how or whether supervised access alters a child's relationship with parents, or whether children are able to emerge from supervised access with the possibility of a normal relationship with parents. Most importantly, we do not know whether supervised access actually protects the best interests of children who have continued contact with an abusive, manipulative and/or threatening parent. Nor have we examined the impact of supervised access to a child on the ability of the other parent to build a new family unit and move past the custody dispute.

These questions are especially important in situations in which the parent-child interactions will be supervised over a long period of time or the child resists the court-ordered supervised contact with a parent.

Also missing from our approach to supervised access is a coherent set of principles regarding when and under what conditions supervised access should be ordered by courts. This absence of substantive standards may be a direct reflection of our lack of understanding of supervised access. Many jurisdictions have adopted detailed standards for the provision of supervised access services. Yet few have articulated substantive guidelines for the imposition of supervised access beyond the physical safety or best interests of the child.

Our lack of understanding of the impact of supervision on children and the absence of coherent guidelines for courts raises two pragmatic concerns. First, courts may order supervised access under circumstances in which parent-child contact should be suspended. Second, courts may be continuing parent-child contact because of the perceived buffer it provides under circumstances in which contact is detrimental to the child(ren) involved. Thus, my central question is under what circumstances should supervised access be ordered? Given that the central legal command in all states is to fashion a custody arrangement that is in the child's best interests, what considerations should warrant the intervention of a court-appointed supervisor in the parent-child relationship, and what considerations should warrant the continuation of contact between a child and a parent who threatens a child's health, well-being or safety? As part of these questions, I will also examine whether supervised access provisions contain adequate safeguards to accomplish their objectives of protecting children. * * *

It is simply not clear what purpose is served by holding the children and custodial parents in cases such as *Suttles* and *M.A.* hostage to continuing contact, or the possibility of such contact, by the abusive parent. The appellate court in *Suttles* gave no consideration to the relationship between the child and the father, if any. In *M.A.* the child was an infant at the time of the sexual abuse and does not appear to have had a well-established relationship with the father. The court does not appear to have considered the impact of abuse or the effect of witnessing violence on the children in either case. Nor did the courts in either case consider the difficulty the mothers and children might experience in building a new family life together when confronted with the specter of ongoing communication from the fathers, and the possibility of future, court-ordered contact between the children and their fathers.

More startling is that if the children in these cases had been removed from their respective homes in an abuse and neglect action based on the abusive parent's conduct, aggravated circumstances would have existed that would have relieved the public agency of any responsibility to reunify the abusive parent and child. Since the children in *Suttles* and *M.A.* had one appropriate parent, however, no such state intervention took place. Thus, the presence of one appropriate parent in combination with supervised access ensures that these children will have to continue contact with the bad parent. This is a perverse result. Apparently the only way for the appropriate parent to avoid further contact with an abuser, or to protect the child from continued contact with the abusive parent, is to petition to terminate parental rights—an action that could likely prove difficult, expensive and unsuccessful. * * *

[Editor's Note: See also Lenore Walker, "Nonjudicial Influence on Family Violence Court Cases," 64(12) American Behavioral Scientist 1749 (2020), arguing that family courts' great dependence on professionals such as guardians ad litem and child custody evaluators, who often disbelieve abuse allegations, has led to serious risk of harm to women and children by minimizing domestic violence and child abuse. She states that these professionals often use unproven and unscientific theories as an excuse not to recommend that the court protect them. The author describes a possible solution: family therapeutic jurisprudence courts in these cases, where children have a voice and there is rarely a role for a child custody evaluator or guardian ad litem.]

B. LEAVING WITH THE CHILDREN: ABDUCTION, RELOCATION, UCCJEA, HAGUE CONVENTION

DEBORAH M. GOELMAN, SHELTER FROM THE STORM: USING JURISDICTIONAL STATUTES TO PROTECT VICTIMS OF DOMESTIC VIOLENCE AFTER THE VIOLENCE AGAINST WOMEN ACT OF 2000

13 Columbia J. Gender & L. 101 (2004)
(citations and footnotes omitted)

III. JURISDICTIONAL STATUTES

* * * Child custody cases conceivably implicate a web of jurisdictional statutes, including the Uniform Child Custody Jurisdiction Act (UCCJA), the Uniform Child Custody Jurisdiction and Enforcement Act (UCCJEA), the Parental Kidnapping Prevention Act (PKPA), the VAWA, the Violence Against Women Act of 2000 (VAWA 2000), and the Indian Child Welfare Act (ICWA), among others. When these laws were enacted, the degree to which domestic violence was taken into account varied. However, courts can utilize each of these laws to protect victims. * * *

6. Judicial Communication

Several provisions in the UCCJEA encourage or require communication and cooperation between courts in different jurisdictions. Such communication is vital in domestic violence cases to ensure that courts have accurate information about the history of violence. Without judicial communication, the court that receives information only from the perpetrator is unlikely to have an accurate picture of what has happened.

When perpetrators file immediately for custody in the home state, victims should receive notice of the proceedings; however, because of their flight, they may never receive personal notice or notice by publication. In other cases, victims may receive notice but prefer to remain in the refuge state rather than return to a dangerous home state. If a victim does receive notice and is able to obtain legal representation in the home state, the attorney may appear on her behalf. The court in the home state is unlikely to learn from the abuser that the victim fled due to domestic violence; rather, the court may hear allegations from the abuser that the victim abducted or abused the children. However, if a court in the refuge state assumes emergency jurisdiction, this court will understand the history of domestic violence and be able to communicate with the home state court to resolve safely the jurisdictional question. This type of judicial communication will ensure that the home state court can make a jurisdictional decision based on a fuller record, including evidence that one party has perpetrated domestic violence against another.

The UCCJEA provides the following structure for communication between courts. First, it encourages courts to communicate concerning proceedings arising under the UCCJEA. The law generally requires a record to be made of the communication, and it requires courts to give parties the opportunity to present facts and legal arguments before a jurisdictional decision is made. In addition, the parties must be informed about the communication and granted access to the record.

Second, in addition to providing discretionary standards for judicial communication, the UCCJEA requires courts to communicate under certain circumstances. When a court has been asked to exercise emergency jurisdiction and has been informed that a child custody proceeding has been commenced in another forum with initial, continuing, or modification jurisdiction—or that an order has already been made—the court must immediately communicate with the other court. Conversely, a court that is exercising initial, continuing, or modification jurisdiction, upon being informed that another court is exercising emergency jurisdiction, must immediately communicate with that court. The purpose of judicial communication is to resolve the emergency, protect the safety of the parties and the child, and determine a period for the duration of the temporary order.

The requirement that courts in different jurisdictions communicate when emergency jurisdiction is at issue establishes a template for communication in cases involving domestic violence. Despite this mandate, however, perpetrators of domestic violence frequently fail to inform courts that custody proceedings are pending in other jurisdictions. Courts should not reward this type of manipulation, but should decline jurisdiction based on misconduct when abusers fail to inform them of proceedings pending in other jurisdictions.

The UCCJEA also contains a provision that requires a court to determine whether a child custody proceeding has been commenced in a court in another state having jurisdiction substantially in accordance with the UCCJEA prior to exercising jurisdiction. A court is prohibited from exercising jurisdiction if a proceeding is pending elsewhere unless the first proceeding is terminated or stayed based on inconvenient forum. Similarly, if a proceeding for enforcement of a custody order is commenced in one state and the court determines that a modification proceeding is pending elsewhere, judicial communication is mandated.

The UCCJEA provisions requiring judicial communication may be used to assist victims in interstate custody cases. Judicial communication, when used properly, will ensure that the courts have input from both parties. This will prevent courts from relying solely on information provided by domestic violence perpetrators.

7. Interstate Discovery

The UCCJEA also contains provisions regarding interstate discovery that may be useful in domestic violence cases. A party may offer testimony of witnesses located in another state or a court on its own motion may order that the testimony of a person be taken in another state. These procedures allow a victim to avoid physically returning to a home state even if the custody proceeding is taking place in the home state. Technological advances such as telephones, audiovisual equipment, or other electronic means may be utilized, and courts must cooperate to designate an appropriate location for a deposition or testimony.

A court may request that a court in another state take the following action:

- Hold an evidentiary hearing;
- Order a person to produce or give evidence;
- Order that an evaluation be made with respect to the custody of a child involved in a pending proceeding;
- Forward a certified copy of the transcript of the record of the hearing, the evidence otherwise produced, and any evaluation prepared in compliance with the request;
- Order a party to appear in the proceeding with or without the child.

All pertinent records related to custody proceedings must be preserved until the child turns eighteen years old.

These tools can be used to protect the safety of victims of domestic violence in interstate child custody cases. For example, if the home state retains jurisdiction, it can obtain the testimony of the victim through telephonic deposition without requiring the victim to leave the refuge state. If the home state declines jurisdiction based on inconvenient forum and the refuge state assumes jurisdiction based on significant connection, the refuge state can request that the home state forward transcripts of any related court proceedings or order that an evaluation of the abuser's home in the home state take place. Courts for the most part have not utilized these technological advances to obtain information from other states even though they can do so without requiring the parties to appear personally.

[Editor's Note: In "Criminalizing Battered Mothers," 2018 Utah L.Rev. 259 (2018), Courtney Cross describes a no-win situation in which many battered mothers are trapped: if they stay with their abusers, the mothers risk losing custody and being convicted of failing to protect the children, but if they leave with the children, which the state pressures them to do—thus putting them in danger of separation abuse—they may risk losing custody and be convicted of parental child abduction.

Many states' statutes do not acknowledge that frequently mothers who leave with their children are fleeing abuse, instead lumping them together with fathers, whose motivation for child abduction is often to exert power and control over the mothers. Cross calls for large scale systemic change to enhance survivors' independence, starting with amending parental kidnapping laws to protect survivors of abuse who are seeking safety [e.g., Ca. Penal Code section 278.7]. Additionally, attorneys and domestic violence advocates must become aware of all relevant civil and criminal laws dealing with parental abduction and advocate for all survivors, both across and outside of the legal system. This includes lobbying for alternatives to incarceration, advocating for free or low cost visitation supervision centers, educating judges and child custody evaluators about domestic violence dynamics, pushing for more social services, and helping develop jobs for low income survivors and abusers.

Cross concludes, "Such wide ranging advocacy would necessitate coalition building outside of the victims' rights movement and would illuminate often overlooked commonalities between the domestic violence movement and the criminal justice reform movement."]

GOLAN V. SAADA

596 U.S. 666 (2022)
(footnotes and citations omitted)

JUSTICE SOTOMAYOR delivered the unanimous opinion of the Court.

Under the Hague Convention on the Civil Aspects of International Child Abduction, Mar. 26, 1986, T. I. A. S. No. 11670, S. Treaty Doc. No.

99–11 (Treaty Doc.), if a court finds that a child was wrongfully removed from the child's country of habitual residence, the court ordinarily must order the child's return. There are, however, exceptions to that rule. As relevant here, a court is not bound to order a child's return if it finds that return would put the child at a grave risk of physical or psychological harm. In such a circumstance, a court has discretion to determine whether to deny return.

In exercising this discretion, courts often consider whether any "ameliorative measures," undertaken either "by the parents" or "by the authorities of the state having jurisdiction over the question of custody," could "reduce whatever risk might otherwise be associated with a child's repatriation." The Second Circuit has made such consideration a requirement, mandating that district courts independently "examine the full range of options that might make possible the safe return of a child" before denying return due to grave risk, even if the party petitioning for the child's return has not identified or argued for imposition of ameliorative measures.

The Second Circuit's categorical requirement to consider all ameliorative measures is inconsistent with the text and other express requirements of the Hague Convention.

I. A

The Hague Convention "was adopted in 1980 in response to the problem of international child abductions during domestic disputes." One hundred and one countries, including the United States and Italy, are signatories. Hague Conference on Private Int'l Law, Convention of 25 Oct. 1980 on the Civil Aspects of Int'l Child Abduction, Status Table, https://www.hcch.net/en/instruments/conventions/status-table/?cid=24.

The Convention's "core premise" is that " 'the interests of children . . . in matters relating to their custody' are best served when custody decisions are made in the child's country of 'habitual residence.' " Accordingly, the Convention generally requires the "prompt return" of a child to the child's country of habitual residence when the child has been wrongfully removed to or retained in another country. This requirement "ensure[s] that rights of custody and of access under the law of one Contracting State are effectively respected in the other Contracting States."

Return of the child is, however, a general rule, and there are exceptions. As relevant here, the Convention provides that return is not required if "[t]here is a grave risk that . . . return would expose the child to physical or psychological harm or otherwise place the child in an intolerable situation." Because return is merely "a 'provisional' remedy that fixes the forum for custody proceedings," the Convention requires that the determination as to whether to order return should be made "us[ing] the most expeditious procedures available," (citation providing that the party petitioning for return has "the right to request a statement of the reasons for the delay" if the court "has not reached a decision within six weeks from the date of commencement of the proceedings").

Congress implemented the Convention in the International Child Abduction Remedies Act (ICARA). ICARA permits a parent (or other individual or institution) seeking relief under the Convention to file a petition for return of a child in state or federal court, and directs courts to "decide the[se] case[s] in accordance with the Convention." Consistent with the Convention, ICARA "empower[s] courts in the United States to determine only rights under the Convention and not the merits of any underlying child custody claims."

Under ICARA, the party petitioning for the child's return bears the burden of establishing by a preponderance of the evidence that the child was wrongfully removed or retained. If the court finds the child was wrongfully removed or retained, the respondent opposing return of the child has the burden of establishing that an exception to the return requirement applies. A respondent arguing that return would expose the child to a grave risk of harm must establish that this exception applies by "clear and convincing evidence." Absent a finding that an exception applies, a child determined to be wrongfully removed or retained must be "promptly returned" to the child's country of habitual residence.

B

Petitioner Narkis Golan is a citizen of the United States. She met respondent Isacco Saada, an Italian citizen, while attending a wedding in Milan, Italy, in 2014. Golan soon moved to Milan, and the two wed in August 2015. Their son, B. A. S., was born the next summer in Milan, where the family lived for the first two years of B. A. S.' life.

The following facts, as found by the District Court, are not in dispute. Saada and Golan's relationship was characterized by violence from the beginning. The two fought on an almost daily basis and, during their arguments, Saada would sometimes push, slap, and grab Golan and pull her hair. Saada also yelled and swore at Golan and frequently insulted her and called her names, often in front of other people. Saada once told Golan's family that he would kill her. Much of Saada's abuse of Golan occurred in front of his son.

In July 2018, Golan flew with B. A. S. to the United States to attend her brother's wedding. Rather than return as scheduled in August, however, Golan moved into a domestic violence shelter with B. A. S. In September, Saada filed in Italy a criminal complaint for kidnapping and initiated a civil proceeding seeking sole custody of B. A. S.

Saada also filed a petition under the Convention and ICARA in the U. S. District Court for the Eastern District of New York, seeking an order for B. A. S.' return to Italy. The District Court granted Saada's petition after a 9-day bench trial. As a threshold matter, the court determined that Italy was B. A. S.' habitual residence and that Golan had wrongfully retained B. A. S. in the United States in violation of Saada's rights of custody. The court concluded, however, that returning B. A. S. to Italy would expose him to a grave risk of harm. The court observed that there was "no dispute" that Saada was "violent—physically, psychologically, emotionally, and verbally—to" Golan and that "B. A. S. was present for much of it." The court described some of the incidents B. A. S. had witnessed as "chilling." While B. A. S. was not "the target of violence," undisputed expert testimony established that "domestic violence disrupts a child's cognitive and social-emotional development, and affects the structure and organization of the child's brain." Records indicated that Italian social services, who had been involved with the couple while they lived in Italy, had also concluded that " 'the family situation entails a developmental danger' for B. A. S." The court found that Saada had demonstrated no "capacity to change his behavior," explaining that Saada "minimized or tried to excuse his violent conduct" during his testimony and that Saada's "own expert said . . . that [Saada] could not control his anger or take responsibility for his behavior."

The court nonetheless ordered B. A. S.' return to Italy based on Second Circuit precedent obligating it to " 'examine the full range of options that might make possible the safe return of a child to the home country' " before it could " 'deny repatriation on the ground that a grave risk of harm exists.' " The Second Circuit based this rule on its view that the Convention requires return "if at all possible." To comply with these precedents, the District Court had required the parties to propose " 'ameliorative measures' " that could enable B. A. S.' safe return. *[Editor's Note: These measures are also called "undertakings."]* Saada had proposed that he would provide Golan with $30,000 for expenses pending a decision in Italian courts as to financial support, stay away from Golan until the custody dispute was resolved, pursue dismissal of the criminal charges he had filed against Golan, begin cognitive behavioral therapy, and waive any right to legal fees or expenses under the Convention. The court concluded that these measures, combined with the fact that Saada and Golan would be living separately, would "reduce the occasions for violence," thereby ameliorating the grave risk to B. A. S. sufficiently to require his return.

On Golan's appeal of this return order, the Second Circuit vacated the order, finding the District Court's measures insufficient to mitigate the risk of harm to B. A. S. Emphasizing that the District Court's factual findings provided "ample reason to doubt that Mr. Saada will comply with these conditions," the Second Circuit concluded that "the District Court erred in granting the petition subject to (largely) unenforceable undertakings" without "sufficient guarantees of performance." Because the record did "not support the conclusion that there exist *no* protective measures sufficient to ameliorate the grave risk of harm B. A. S. faces if repatriated," the court remanded for the District Court to "consider whether there exist alternative ameliorative measures that are either enforceable by the District Court or supported by other sufficient guarantees of performance."

To comply with the Second Circuit's directive, over the course of nine months, the District Court conducted "an extensive examination of the measures available to ensure B. A. S.'s safe return to Italy." The District Court directed the parties to appear for status conferences and to submit status reports and supplemental briefs, and the court corresponded with the U. S. Department of State and the Italian Ministry of Justice. At the court's instruction, the parties petitioned the Italian courts for a protective order, and the Italian court overseeing the underlying custody dispute issued a protective order barring Saada from approaching Golan for one year. In addition, the Italian court ordered that an Italian social services agency oversee Saada's parenting classes and therapy and that visits between Saada and B. A. S. be supervised.

The District Court concluded that these measures were sufficient to ameliorate the harm to B. A. S. and again granted Saada's petition for B. A. S.' return. It rejected Golan's argument that Saada could not be trusted to comply with a court order, expressing confidence in the Italian courts' abilities to enforce the protective order. The District Court additionally ordered Saada to pay Golan $150,000 to facilitate B. A. S.' return to Italy and to cover Golan's and B. A. S.' living costs while they resettled. The Second Circuit affirmed, concluding that the District Court did not clearly err in determining that Saada likely would comply with the Italian protective order, given his compliance with other court orders and the threat of enforcement by Italian authorities of its order.

This Court granted certiorari to decide whether the Second Circuit properly required the District Court, after making a grave-risk finding, to examine a full range of possible ameliorative measures before reaching a decision as to whether to deny return, and to resolve a division in the lower courts regarding whether ameliorative measures must be considered after a grave-risk finding.

II. A

"The interpretation of a treaty, like the interpretation of a statute, begins with its text." As described above, when "a child has been wrongfully removed or retained" from his country of habitual residence, Article 12 of the Hague Convention generally requires the deciding authority (here, a district court) to "order the return of the child." Under Article 13(b) of the Convention, however, a court "is not bound to order the return of the child" if the court finds that the party opposing return has established that return would expose the child to a "grave risk" of physical or psychological harm. By providing that a court "is not bound" to order return upon making a grave-risk finding, Article 13(b) lifts the Convention's return requirement, leaving a court with the discretion to grant or deny return.

Nothing in the Convention's text either forbids or requires consideration of ameliorative measures in exercising this discretion. The Convention itself nowhere mentions ameliorative measures. Nor does ICARA, which, as relevant, instructs courts to "decide the case in accordance with the Convention" and accordingly leaves undisturbed the discretion recognized in the Convention. The longstanding interpretation of the Department of State offers further support for the view that the Convention vests a court with discretion to determine whether to order return if an exception to the return mandate applies. (citation explaining that "a court in its discretion need not order a child returned" upon a finding of grave risk).

Unable to point to any explicit textual mandate that courts consider ameliorative measures, Saada's primary argument is that this requirement is implicit in the Convention's command that the court make a determination as to whether a grave risk of harm exists. Essentially, Saada argues that determining whether a grave risk of harm exists necessarily requires considering whether any ameliorative measures are available.

The question whether there is a grave risk, however, is separate from the question whether there are ameliorative measures that could mitigate that risk. That said, the question whether ameliorative measures would be appropriate or effective will often overlap considerably with the inquiry into whether a grave risk exists. In many instances, a court may find it appropriate to consider both questions at once. For example, a finding of grave risk as to a part of a country where an epidemic rages may naturally lead a court simultaneously to consider whether return to another part of the country is feasible. The fact that a court may consider ameliorative measures concurrent with the grave-risk determination, however, does not mean that the Convention imposes a categorical requirement on a court to consider any or all ameliorative measures before denying return once it finds that a grave risk exists.

Under the Convention and ICARA, district courts' discretion to determine whether to return a child where doing so would pose a grave risk to the child includes the discretion whether to consider ameliorative measures that could ensure the child's safe return. The Second Circuit's rule, "in practice, rewrite[s] the treaty," by imposing an atextual, categorical requirement that courts consider all possible ameliorative measures in exercising this discretion, regardless of whether such consideration is consistent with the Convention's objectives (and, seemingly, regardless of whether the parties offered them for the court's consideration in the first place).

B

While consideration of ameliorative measures is within a district court's discretion, "[d]iscretion is not whim." A "motion to a court's discretion is a motion, not to its inclination, but to its judgment; and its judgment is to be guided by sound legal principles." As a threshold matter, a district court exercising its discretion is still responsible for addressing and responding to nonfrivolous arguments timely raised by the parties before it. While a district court has no obligation under the Convention to consider ameliorative measures that have not been raised by the parties, it ordinarily should address ameliorative measures raised by the parties or obviously suggested by the circumstances of the case, such as in the example of the localized epidemic.

In addition, the court's consideration of ameliorative measures must be guided by the legal principles and other requirements set forth in the Convention and ICARA. The Second Circuit's rule, by instructing district courts to order return "if at all possible," improperly elevated return above the Convention's other objectives. The Convention does not pursue return exclusively or at all costs. Rather, the Convention "is designed to protect the interests of children and their parents," and children's interests may point against return in some circumstances. Courts must remain conscious of this purpose, as well as the Convention's other objectives and requirements, which constrain courts' discretion to consider ameliorative measures in at least three ways.

First, any consideration of ameliorative measures must prioritize the child's physical and psychological safety. The Convention explicitly recognizes that the child's interest in avoiding physical or psychological harm, in addition to other interests, "may overcome the return remedy." A court may therefore decline to consider imposing ameliorative measures where it is clear that they would not work because the risk is so grave. Sexual abuse of a child is one example of an intolerable situation. Other physical or psychological abuse, serious neglect, and domestic violence in the home may also constitute an obvious grave risk to the child's safety that could not readily be ameliorated. A court may also decline to consider imposing ameliorative measures where it reasonably expects that they will not be followed. (providing example of parent with history of violating court orders).

Second, consideration of ameliorative measures should abide by the Convention's requirement that courts addressing return petitions do not usurp the role of the court that will adjudicate the underlying custody dispute. The Convention and ICARA prohibit courts from resolving any underlying custody dispute in adjudicating a return petition. Accordingly, a court ordering ameliorative measures in making a return determination should limit those measures in time and scope to conditions that would permit safe return, without purporting to decide subsequent custody matters or weighing in on permanent arrangements.

Third, any consideration of ameliorative measures must accord with the Convention's requirement that courts "act expeditiously in proceedings for the return of children." Timely resolution of return petitions is important in part because return is a "provisional" remedy to enable final custody determinations to proceed. The Convention also prioritizes expeditious determinations as being in the best interests of the child because "[e]xpedition will help minimize the extent to which uncertainty adds to the challenges confronting both parents and child." A requirement to "examine the full range of options that might make possible the safe return of a child" is in tension with this focus on expeditious resolution. In this case, for example, it took the District Court nine months to comply with the Second Circuit's directive on remand. Remember, the Convention requires courts to resolve return petitions "us[ing] the most expeditious procedures available," and to provide parties that request it with an explanation if proceedings extend longer than six weeks. Courts should structure return proceedings with these instructions in mind. Consideration of ameliorative measures should not cause undue delay in resolution of return petitions.

To summarize, although nothing in the Convention prohibits a district court from considering ameliorative measures, and such consideration often may be appropriate, a district court reasonably may decline to consider ameliorative measures that have not been raised by the parties, are unworkable, draw the court into determinations properly resolved in custodial proceedings, or risk overly prolonging return proceedings. The court may also find the grave risk so unequivocal, or the potential harm so severe, that ameliorative measures would be inappropriate. Ultimately, a district court must exercise its discretion to consider ameliorative measures in a manner consistent with its general obligation to address the parties' substantive arguments and its specific obligations under the Convention. A district court's compliance with these requirements is subject to review under an ordinary abuse-of-discretion standard.

III

The question now becomes how to resolve the instant case. Golan urges that this Court reverse, arguing that the ameliorative measures adopted by the District Court are inadequate for B. A. S.' protection and otherwise improper. The United States, as *amicus curiae*, suggests remanding to allow the District Court to exercise its discretion in the first instance under the correct legal standard.

Under the circumstances of this case, this Court concludes that remand is appropriate. The Convention requires courts to make a discretionary determination as to whether to order return after making a finding of grave risk. The District Court made a finding of grave risk, but never had the opportunity to engage in the discretionary inquiry as to whether to order or deny return under the correct legal standard. This Court cannot know whether the District Court would have exercised its discretion to order B. A. S.' return absent the Second Circuit's rule, which improperly weighted the scales in favor of return. Accordingly, it is appropriate to follow the ordinary course and allow the District Court to apply the proper legal standard in the first instance.

Remand will as a matter of course add further delay to a proceeding that has already spanned years longer than it should have. The delay that has already occurred, however, cannot be undone. This Court trusts that the District Court will move as expeditiously as possible to reach a final decision without further unnecessary delay. The District Court has ample evidence before it from the prior proceedings and has made extensive factual findings concerning the risks at issue. Golan argues that the ameliorative measures ordered intrude too greatly on custodial determinations and that they are inadequate to protect B. A. S.' safety given the District Court's findings that Saada is unable to control or take responsibility for his behavior. The District Court should determine whether the measures in question are adequate to order return in light of its factual findings concerning the risk to B. A. S., bearing in mind that the Convention sets as a primary goal the safety of the child.

The judgment of the United States Court of Appeals for the Second Circuit is vacated, and the case is remanded for further proceedings consistent with this opinion.

[Editor's Note: On remand, the trial court again ordered the return of B.A.S. to Italy, stating that Italy was his "habitual residence" even though he had lived in the U.S. for 4 of his 6 years, and that the Italian courts could adequately protect him. Ms. Golan again appealed to the 2nd Circuit, who stayed the trial court order; briefing was due to be completed 10/31/22. Ms. Golan was advocating for other mothers in similar situations. Sadly, on 10/18/22, she was found dead in her New York apartment. There were no signs of trauma, and as of summer 2023 there has been no determination of the cause of death. Ms. Golan's sister was awarded temporary custody of B.A.S. in New York and obtained a restraining order against Mr. Saada which also protects B.A.S. It is not known if there has been a permanent custody decision.

After her death, in In re B.A.S., *2022 WL 16936205 (Nov. 10, 2022) the 2nd Circuit dismissed Ms. Golan's appeal as moot, vacated the District Court's order, and remanded the case to that court to address the Hague Convention petition in light of the changed circumstances.*

See also Nicole Fidler (one of Ms. Golan's attorneys), In Memory of Narkis Golan, 56 Fam. L. Q. 271 (2023).]

NATIONAL COUNCIL OF JUVENILE AND FAMILY COURT JUDGES, RELOCATING AFTER DISSOLUTION IN DOMESTIC VIOLENCE CASES

15(1) Synergy 10 (Winter 2011)

When one parent seeks to relocate after a divorce or dissolution case has been decided, the court must perform a difficult balancing act to preserve the interests of all parties. These interests include the right of one parent to move freely and benefit from additional economic and social opportunities in a new location, the right of the other parent to continue meaningful contact with the children, and the best interests of the children, which must be foremost in the court's consideration. While this balancing act presents challenges in many cases, the risks may be highest in relocation cases involving a parent who is also a victim of domestic violence. Recent cases and statutory amendments demonstrate mixed results to the relocation issue across states and highlight how some states are managing the challenge.

In October 2010, the New York appellate court allowed a mother to relocate with her child to South Carolina over the objections of the father. (*Sara ZZ v. Matthew A*, 909 N.Y.S.2d 212 (NY Supreme Ct, App. Div. 2010) In reaching its decision, the court found that the mother was motivated by a desire to escape the "intimidation" of the father, and that the father was motivated to oppose relocation out of a desire to "continue exercising control over the mother and her life." While the court noted several other factors supporting relocation, including family support in South Carolina and the mother's willingness to travel to support visitation, the appellate opinion devotes significant attention to the trial court's findings regarding the advantage of relocating for this victim of domestic violence. The opinion suggests that when relocation is motivated by a victim's desire to live free from violence and is opposed by a batterer as a means of exerting control, the balance of interest favors allowing relocation.

In April 2010, the Arizona appellate court considered the impact of domestic violence in a relocation case, but the Arizona court reached a markedly different conclusion. (*Hurd v. Hurd*, 219 P3d 258 (AZ App. 2009)). Initially, the trial court allowed relocation after finding both "a significant history of domestic violence" against the mother, which often occurred in the presence of the children, and indications that the father had abused the children. The level of abuse indicated in *Hurd* appears more significant than the level in the New York case. However, the appellate court disagreed with the trial court because the trial record focused on the benefits to the mother of relocating and did not include findings specifically regarding the beneficial impact to the children. The *Hurd* decision suggests that even if a victimized parent clearly benefits from relocation, unless the court explicitly finds the move to be in the best interest of the children, relocations should not be allowed.

State legislatures struggle with finding an appropriate balance in relocation cases. For example, in 2009, North Dakota enacted a new law to prevent one parent with equal residential responsibility from moving out of the state unless the other parent consents. (ND Cent. Code § 14–09–07) The new law empowers a non-moving parent to exert significant control over the other parent's ability to relocate. An existing law that requires courts to consider domestic violence protection orders when determining parenting responsibilities may impact the new law; however, the relationship between these two laws is not explicit in the statutes and will depend on whether the court applies the new law. *[Editor's Note: North Dakota has also had a statutory presumption against awarding custody to batterers for many years, so courts deciding relocation requests should also consider the impact of that statute.]*

By contrast, Texas amended § 153.502 of its family code to require courts to consider motives related to escaping domestic violence, regardless of whether a parent obtained a protective order, if it finds that one parent has engaged in activities that suggest an intent to relocate internationally.

Relocation cases are described as the "San Andreas Fault of family law" and both statutory and case law reflects the struggle to balance the interests of all members of a family. One way to alleviate the legal seismic shifts is articulated by the National Council of Juvenile and Family Court Judges in *Family Violence: A Model State Code* (Model Code). The *Model Code* states it is in the best interest of the child to live with a non-abusive parent, wherever that parent chooses to live. The *Model Code* recognizes that "the enhanced safety, personal and social supports, and the economic opportunity available to the abused parent in another jurisdiction" may both be in the parent's best interest and "likewise and concomitantly, in the best interest of the child."

C. RESPONSE OF JUVENILE AND CRIMINAL COURTS TO "FAILURE TO PROTECT"

JOAN MEIER AND VIVEK SANKARAN, BREAKING DOWN THE SILOS THAT HARM CHILDREN: A CALL TO CHILD WELFARE, DOMESTIC VIOLENCE, AND FAMILY COURT PROFESSIONALS

28 Va. J. Soc. Policy & L 275 (2021)
(footnotes and citations omitted)

INTRODUCTION

The fields of domestic violence and child welfare have historically functioned as completely separate. They emerged from different social sensibilities and at different times, operate within distinct parts of the legal system (child welfare in government agencies and juvenile courts;

domestic violence in private organizations and civil and criminal courts), receive largely distinct and non-intersecting professional education and training, and are driven by substantially different philosophies and value systems. The problems that stem from these disjunctions have been recognized, but only in part. For instance, as Part I below describes, researchers and reformers have worked with child welfare agencies to remedy their lack of understanding of domestic violence which too often triggers removal of children from loving, safe parents who are co-victims of the other parent. But until quite recently, there has been little attention to the fact that family courts adjudicating private custody litigation also regularly decide child placements in cases involving domestic violence and child maltreatment. Moreover, the often-unfavorable reception given to mothers making such allegations, and surprisingly common awards of custody to parents accused of abuse—even child abuse—is not widely recognized.

This Article, authored by two law professors, one specializing in domestic violence and the other in child welfare, suggests that custody courts may actually be the *most significant* system responding to adult and child abuse. This is because custody courts regularly hear both types of allegations (often within the same families), and they are mandated to determine children's "best interests." But the siloing of domestic violence, child welfare, and custody courts has undermined such courts' willingness and capacity to engage with the risks to children from a parent.

Our collaboration has surfaced two interlocking problems in child welfare agencies and family courts, which compel correction: First, grave problems with the foster care system have led reformers to encourage agencies to encourage safe parents to seek child custody in civil court as a means of sidestepping foster care. The hope has been that this would protect children from the problems with foster care and keep them safe with one of their parents. However, as detailed below, qualitative and quantitative research indicate that family courts surprisingly often fail to assure a child's safety from an unsafe parent. In this regard, dedicated child welfare reformers' lack of knowledge about what is happening in family courts may be increasing—rather than decreasing—harms to children.

At the same time, the gulf between family court and child welfare systems contributes to the negative outcomes for mothers alleging child maltreatment in family courts. Family court judges may understandably but mistakenly believe that if there was true child abuse it would have been dealt with in the child welfare system. When child welfare agencies have not investigated or validated child abuse claims by one parent against the other, many family courts mistakenly conclude that the child abuse claims are false, and that the protective parent is the problem parent and should not have custody of the children.

This Article first describes the historic and current siloing of domestic violence, child welfare, and family court practices in response to domestic violence and child maltreatment. It then summarizes the qualitative and quantitative critiques of family courts' unfavorable responses to mothers' allegations of family violence, including frequent custody removals. It also explores some of the reasons family courts may be skeptical of child maltreatment allegations and resistant to assuming a child-protective role. Turning to child welfare agency practices, the authors note a parallel skepticism from even these agencies toward custody litigants' claims of child abuse. Moreover, recent advocacy by well-intended reformers to rely on civil custody litigation instead of foster care where there is one safe parent, has emerged without awareness of these realities of custody litigation, which often increase rather than decrease children's risks from a parent.

In response to these dynamics and problems, this Article proposes three specific reforms. By and large, it is not law that needs to change, but attitudes and practices. The remedies include cross-training and education aimed at opening up both systems' ideologies, assumptions and practices. A key proposal is the recruitment of child welfare agencies themselves to advocate for children's safety *within the parents' custody case.* This and other strategies could save many children from both the trauma of removal from a safe and loving parent and the danger and trauma of being forced to live either with an unsafe parent or in foster care, which can be traumatic even at its best.

I. SILOED YET INTERSECTING: CHILD WELFARE, DOMESTIC VIOLENCE, AND CUSTODY COURTS

The separation of social and legal interventions for child welfare and domestic violence has deep historical roots. Both fields emerged only after the erosion of the pre-existing patriarchal legal framework which treated the use of violence as a father's right and duty to discipline and control wives and children. Each field developed separately and with a differing sensibility—child maltreatment was ultimately addressed by state agencies, and domestic violence through criminal or civil legal action initiated by victims. Significant efforts were made at the turn of the 21st century to break down the silos between domestic violence and child welfare, in part to better address families in which both were occurring. These initiatives, however, did not include civil courts adjudicating child custody. And, while child custody law has incorporated domestic violence reforms, no parallel reforms have focused on child maltreatment. Thus civil family courts, which have a checkered record in responding even to adult domestic violence, have lacked any scrutiny of their responses to child maltreatment.

A. Evolution of System Responses

Although a Martian, or in fact many humans, might presume that one person's abuse of different victims within the family would be treated as a single problem, the reality on planet Earth is that domestic violence and child abuse have long been addressed entirely separately. This continues today, despite the now widespread understanding that a substantial number of families and cases involve both forms of victimization; and that at least a significant portion of child maltreatment cases involve similar power and control dynamics to domestic violence.

1. Child Protection

Child protection first became a matter of public concern in the late 1800s; over the next 40 years, 494 private charitable Societies for the Prevention of Cruelty to Children (SPCCs) arose across the country. By the 1930s, the federal government had created a governmental child protection program, and by the 1960s most states had converted their private charities into state-funded and -governed child welfare agencies. While child welfare professionals' mission targeted children's health and safety, "wife-beating" was often part of the early case narratives; as is true today, the same man often abused both mother and children. However, domestic violence was, at best, a secondary concern for the "child-savers." Rather, child protection agencies looked to mothers as the responsible and blameworthy parent, in part because they were more accessible and responsive—even when the father was victimizing the children. And, while views of child maltreatment and its causes have ebbed and flowed with the times, a coherent understanding or view of "family violence" involving the same perpetrator of abuse against both adult and child victims has never really emerged. Instead, child maltreatment as a field has become synonymous with maternal failures, and within that field, fathers' abuse of children has been shadowy at best.

Two entirely separate federal funding streams and programs have powerfully reinforced the legal separation of society's responses to adult partner violence and child maltreatment. The Child Abuse Prevention and Treatment Act (CAPTA), adopted in 1974, targeted child maltreatment, and the Family Violence Prevention and Services Act (FVPSA) in 1984, and later, in 1994, by the Violence Against Women Act (VAWA), targeted partner violence. It was not until 2013 that federal grants under VAWA even permitted domestic violence legal representation to extend to child maltreatment cases. VAWA still only supports work on child sexual—but not child physical—abuse.

One fundamental obstacle to better integration between child welfare and domestic violence systems has been women's rational fear of losing their children if reports of child abuse (or even domestic violence) are shared with the child welfare agency. Agencies have long used "failure to protect" charges against mothers whose children are victimized by an abusive father, often removing the children from their mother and home. This has fueled a deep resistance of domestic violence advocates and survivors toward collaboration with the child welfare system.

In the 1990s, a pioneering effort by two leading domestic violence and child welfare experts challenged the bifurcation of adult domestic violence and child maltreatment. Susan Schechter and Jeffrey Edleson, along with others, pointed out the links between domestic violence and child maltreatment, the harm to children exposed to adult abuse, the risks batterers pose for children, and the importance of supporting rather than blaming the adult victim. Subsequently, the federally supported "Greenbook Initiative" brought together professionals from child welfare agencies, domestic violence non-profits, and dependency courts to develop a set of principles for best practices across the domestic violence and child welfare silos. The Greenbook principles were put to work in six separate pilot projects around the country, with varying reports of success from the three collaborating groups regarding improved practices. For instance, many agencies adopted screening for domestic violence, and referrals of battered women for services increased. The Greenbook Evaluation Report does not, however, provide data or qualitative information on how these changes affected children. The Greenbook's spotlighting of the need for systems to collaborate to address the co-occurrence of adult and child abuse also spurred halting but incomplete efforts at the federal level to merge some of the funding and programs addressing each.

Building on the Greenbook's pioneering work, domestic violence expert David Mandel developed the Safe and Together Institute, whose "mission is to create, nurture and sustain a global network of domestic violence-informed child welfare professionals, communities and systems." The Institute's trainings, concrete and teachable "perpetrator pattern-based approach," and valuable educational and follow-up resources for child welfare agencies have increased such professionals' awareness of the multi-faceted ways that a perpetrator of intimate partner violence impacts the whole family, including the children. While the organization's mission has focused on child welfare agencies, it has also begun some work with civil family courts.

2. Domestic Violence

Unlike the child maltreatment field, which was primarily driven by a charitable impulse to protect presumptively innocent, helpless children, activism against wife-beating or domestic violence evolved primarily out of advocacy for women's rights. Not until the 1970s, when the first lasting movement against domestic violence emerged, did concrete legal remedies for intimate partner violence develop. In 1970, the District of Columbia invented the civil protection order, which allowed abused women to seek an equitable injunction against abuse. Over the following two decades, comparable equitable protection order remedies were adopted across the country.

Since then, domestic violence awareness has spread to numerous fields, including criminal law, employment, health care, housing, insurance, and others. Of particular relevance for this Article, concerted advocacy by domestic violence experts and advocates in the 1980s and 1990s succeeded in creating statutory requirements that custody courts must consider domestic violence, either as a factor in determining children's best interests, or as the basis for a presumption against custody to a perpetrator. The effectiveness of these legislated reforms, however, has been questioned by myriad domestic violence lawyers, experts, and litigants, who have found family courts remarkably unreceptive to domestic violence evidence and concerns.

B. Custody Courts' Resistance to Addressing Child Maltreatment

While the Greenbook Initiative and the Safe and Together Institute have, with mixed results, sought to pioneer paradigm shifts within child welfare agencies regarding domestic violence, these efforts have not incorporated civil courts adjudicating child custody. The Greenbook focused on "co-occurring" domestic violence and child abuse, and asserted that "the three primary systems that serve these families [are] the child welfare system, the dependency courts, and domestic violence service providers." However, given that custody courts must determine children's "best interests" and are legally mandated in all states to consider family violence, it is likely that it is family courts which are actually the *primary* system responding to both types of allegations. Unfortunately, civil family courts do not widely share this capacious view. Rather, as is described below, many judges deem themselves incompetent to hear child maltreatment allegations and seem to believe that such information should be siloed solely within child welfare agencies. As is described, in subsequent sections, this perspective does not lead to child protective court decisions.

One can see judges' resistance to hearing about child maltreatment in one 2018 protection order case heard in a city's dedicated domestic violence court. The judge, after listening to a mother (who had testified about her own victimization) described the abuser's attacks on their children, burst out angrily, saying the equivalent of: "*Why is this here?! Why hasn't DCFS addressed this?! We are not suited for this—we don't have training in child abuse!*" Similarly, in a custody case which the first author and a law student handled many years ago, the highly-regarded and domestic-violence-trained judge exploded and started berating the client (the mother) and her representatives when the student started to detail the father's hurling of a child across a room. These volatile responses may have been triggered by a strong negative reaction to this disturbing material—

even though in both cases the judge was sitting on a domestic violence docket. One would hope that it would not surprise judges on a domestic violence docket if they are presented with information about child abuse—but the strength of this reaction is emblematic of many courts' reactivity and resistance to hearing about child abuse.

This resistance has likewise been reported by advocates in several states. Some assert that family court personnel sometimes refuse altogether to consider any information about child maltreatment or even child welfare investigations. One advocate described a conversation in which a judge leading a commission on reform of the state's child custody statute, angrily refused to also include a child abuse expert on the expert body, despite including domestic violence experts, and despite the custody statute's inclusion of child abuse as a factor courts must consider. While these stories undoubtedly do not represent all judges sitting on civil domestic violence or domestic relations dockets, the national data discussed in Section II.B below strengthen the indications that many family courts harbor negative attitudes toward child maltreatment allegations.

How is it that not only domestic relations—but even *domestic violence* civil courts—perceive child abuse as an inappropriate topic for their dockets? This Article submits that this is the most concrete manifestation of the historically distinct development of society's responses to domestic violence and child maltreatment. But the historical silos are also contemporaneously reinforced. For instance, the battered women's movement's focus on women's rights has meant that advocacy for domestic violence reforms has centered on victimization of women, not children. Domestic violence custody law reforms thus far have focused solely on adult abuse. While child abuse is typically referenced in passing in protection order or custody statutes, such statutes typically import a definition from child welfare statutes or the criminal code, with little additional guidance to courts. And while reformers have developed domestic violence trainings for domestic violence and family court judges, it is rare—if ever—that such a training will also address how courts should understand and assess child abuse allegations.

In short, while domestic violence law reformers have endeavored to awaken the civil and criminal legal systems to the reality and dynamics of adult domestic violence, no comparable systematic efforts have focused on child maltreatment, whether co-occurring with domestic violence or not.

Today, the fact that there is a separate state agency designed to address child maltreatment provides an easy structural argument for why judges hearing cases between parents, as opposed to involving the State, might believe their jurisdiction does not extend to child maltreatment, even though it is statutorily relevant to custody. Some child welfare system proponents have voiced a similar attitude. In a recent discussion of a proposal for custody courts to adjudicate child maltreatment and domestic violence in an up-front hearing, a self-described child welfare expert argued that child maltreatment was solely child welfare agencies' job, not custody courts'.

1. Lack of Intersectional Professional Education

These silos begin, to some degree, in the professional schools. While law schools may have domestic violence classes or clinics, those courses rarely address child abuse to a meaningful degree, although they may refer to child protection practices and laws, or to the impact of domestic violence on children. This is true even now in the first author's own clinical domestic violence course. And while other law school courses may address the child protection system, they focus, understandably, on law and policy more than on child abuse itself, let alone the links between child abuse and domestic violence. Among mental health professions, as of 2002 and 2012 no family violence curriculum was required in social work and clinical psychology graduate programs, and most clinical psychologists rated their education in child maltreatment as poor.

The majority of legal and mental health professionals who find their way into family law and child custody litigation thus lack meaningful education or training in domestic violence, child maltreatment, and especially, both. Nor is continuing education likely to make up for that insufficiency. Limited 1–3-hour trainings are not capable of engendering critical or deep thinking that could challenge an attendee's personal beliefs about families and child custody.

Finally, despite the ubiquity of family courts' reliance on court-appointed neutral evaluators, only six states (Alaska, Arizona, California, Louisiana, Oklahoma and Texas) require training on domestic violence. Roughly 75% of contested custody cases in court involve allegations of some kind of family abuse, often involving both child and adult victims. Therefore the lack of basic professional education for court-affiliated professionals on domestic violence, child maltreatment, and the links between them—and the absence of any *requirement* of such education for most court-affiliated professionals—surely contributes to courts' ignoring of the elephant in the living room.

2. Judicial Systemic Siloing

Like the professions themselves, courts are internally siloed. In most states and the District of Columbia, there is a separate "child abuse and neglect" ("CAN") or "dependency" docket which hears cases brought by the child protection agency. Child abuse is thus assumed to be handled "over there" in the agency cases. While it's not entirely logical, this feeds the unstated belief that child abuse does not belong—or exist—in the other civil dockets., such as "domestic relations" or custody.

A parallel type of siloing is apparent among specialized domestic violence courts. For instance, in the District of Columbia, the new domestic violence court was forward-thinking in 1996 because it brought together criminal and civil dockets handling domestic violence cases, prioritized communication about the same families by judges across dockets, and to some extent assigned one family to one judge. But more than twenty years later, custody cases involving domestic violence continue to be heard only in the separate Domestic Relations Unit. In general, regardless of whether states possess a domestic violence court, separate court dockets for civil protection orders, child abuse and neglect, and custody are the norm.

Invariably, when courts assign child abuse and neglect or domestic violence cases to separate dockets, it sends the message to court personnel that those cases are to be handled *there*. The unstated corollary is that, if a case is not in the Child Abuse and Neglect ("CAN") court or the domestic violence ("DV") Unit, it's assumed *not to be a case of child abuse or domestic violence*, respectively. [emphasis in original] Such bureaucratic siloing reinforces—and may even generate—family court professionals' assumption that domestic violence, and especially child maltreatment, is not an intrinsic part of a custody adjudication.

II. CUSTODY COURT RESPONSES TO MOTHERS ALLEGING CHILD ABUSE

The siloing of child maltreatment and domestic violence, and the separation of child welfare agencies and family courts, would not necessarily be a problem if both agencies fulfilled their mandates effectively and adequately protected at-risk children. However, a vast literature and a growing body of empirical data describe domestic relations courts' resistance and even punitive responses to mothers' allegations of family violence, especially child abuse. Custody or unsafe visitation awards to allegedly abusive parents are not uncommon; and a growing body of child homicide cases documents the most severe outcomes of these errors.

A. Substantive Critiques

Legal and psychological scholars have extensively criticized family courts, both in the United States and internationally for disbelief—and even hostility—toward women in custody battles alleging that a father is abusive. They have observed that custody courts commonly do not acknowledge domestic violence or child abuse, are driven by myths and misconceptions about perpetrators and victims, and often fail to understand the implications of domestic violence for children and parenting, resulting in awards of unfettered access or custody to abusive fathers. They have described a growing number of cases in which courts deem the mothers' allegations to be signs of malevolence or a toxic psychology, and some which cut children completely off from their protective mothers. These drastic responses to mothers' abuse allegations appear to be most pronounced in cases of alleged child sexual abuse.

B. Empirical Data

These substantive critiques have been supported by a small number of empirical studies of custody courts' handling of adult domestic violence or minimization of adult domestic violence. A recent Wisconsin study found that half of all custody courts failed to mention domestic violence even when the perpetrator had been criminally convicted. Another national study analyzed 27 "turned-around" cases, in which a first court rejected abuse claims and placed a child at risk with an abusive parent, but a second court validated abuse and (belatedly) protected the child. Consistent with extensive anecdotal reports in the literature and social media, the researchers found courts and neutral professionals at the first proceeding were suspicious of mothers' allegations of abuse, and tended to pathologize or label such mothers as "parental alienators."

The above scholarship has shed light on family court trends, but none of these empirical studies examined a national picture, nor addressed courts' responses to child abuse as distinct from or in conjunction with domestic violence. Recently a first-ever empirical study of family court outcomes nationwide, led by the first author, has produced objective data documenting family courts' decisions in cases where one parent alleges either adult or child abuse by the other. The federally-funded *Child Custody Outcomes in Cases Involving Parental Alienation and Abuse Allegations* study (the "Study") is described in more detail elsewhere. The Study of all relevant custody opinions within a 10-year period powerfully confirms the qualitative critiques in the literature. In addition, to the authors' knowledge, this study provides the only existing credible data on family courts' responses to child abuse—as distinct from intimate partner violence—allegations.

In brief, courts rejected mothers' allegations of any type of family abuse, on average, approximately 2/3 of the time. Seventy-nine percent of child physical abuse claims and 81% of child sexual abuse allegations were rejected. When an allegedly abusive father cross-accused the mother of parental alienation, rejection rates were highest. Only *one* child sexual abuse claim out of 51 (2%) was accepted by a court in that circumstance.

Courts' rejections of mothers' allegations had severe consequences: Approximately one-third of mothers alleging child abuse lost custody to the alleged abuser. When they alleged both types of physical and sexual child abuse, the penalties escalated: These mothers lost custody 56% of the time. Even when courts deemed the father abusive, 13% were able to remove custody from the mother with an even higher percentage of custody removals for mothers alleging child abuse. As is discussed in the Study, these patterns do not appear when genders are reversed.

While the Study did not and could not know whether trial courts' factual findings and rejections of abuse allegations were wrong or right, when paired with the qualitative, anecdotal reports and surveys of allegedly protective mothers' outcomes in court, the data are sobering. And while some may argue that courts could be correct to disbelieve the vast majority of child sexual abuse claims in custody litigation, independent research consistently finds that 50–75% of child abuse allegations in context of custody litigation are considered credible.

Overall, the Study's new data powerfully reinforces the extensive critiques in the literature and social media of mothers who report having disclosed true abuse and losing custody to the abuser. It should now be clear that family courts set an extremely high bar for proof of child physical—and particularly child sexual—abuse allegations against fathers. The data and reports confirm that the pattern is deeply gendered. This should be troubling to all who care for children's safety and well-being.

C. Why?

The foregoing reports and data beg a two-part question: Why are family courts so resistant to mothers' allegations of fathers' abuse, and why especially to child abuse? While these questions deserve a study of their own, the authors of this Article propose that the siloing discussed above plays a role in courts' rejection of child maltreatment allegations: To the extent that family courts relegate—implicitly or explicitly—child abuse to child welfare agencies, as noted above, they can be expected to believe that "those issues belong there, not here." This leads to a skeptical and critical response when such allegations arise where they "do not belong." But the reality is that legitimate child abuse allegations often arise in family court first. This is for many reasons, not least of which is that much child abuse only begins—or is disclosed by the child—after the parents separate, which is when custody proceedings are often initiated. Unfortunately, courts have been known to reject child abuse allegations on the ground that they were raised for the first time in custody court.

More generally, some scholars have posited that courts' skepticism toward mothers' abuse allegations stems from a lack of knowledge about how domestic violence and trauma affect families, and implicit or explicit gender bias. Another hypothesis turns on the natural human inclination to avoid psychological and emotionally traumatic material such as child sexual abuse. Professionals experiencing vicarious trauma—the psychological tendency to numb and avoid traumatic abuse material when one is overloaded, causing the brain to shut down in response to it—may appear uninterested in child abuse or inclined to "shoot the messenger" rather than accept such allegations and take action to protect a child.

While these phenomena likely play a role, the fact that courts' negative responses are aimed more at mothers than fathers necessitates, at least in part, a gender-specific explanation. Nor does that explanation need to stop at overt or implicit gender bias against women or favoring men. Rather, the over-riding and superficially gender-neutral value driving family courts—shared parenting—is itself implicitly but deeply gendered.

Regardless of whether a court orders equal shared parenting, most courts consider shared parenting the pre-eminent value in custody litigation, and the crucial value by which they judge parents. Given that most primary caregivers are mothers, they naturally oppose shared parenting more often than fathers do; and are accordingly disadvantaged in court. Another source of implicit bias in custody adjudications is the tendency for courts and systems to expect relatively little of men as parents before deeming them worthy of custody, in contrast to expectations of mothers.

These background disadvantages for mothers in custody court are compounded when they allege that a father is dangerous. As the 2020 United Kingdom Ministry of Justice-sponsored study of "harm" from family courts concluded, "respondents [litigants] felt that courts placed undue priority on ensuring contact with the non-resident parent, which resulted in systemic minimization of allegations of domestic abuse." Rather than inferring that women are reluctant to share parenting *because* of family violence, judges and other professionals committed to shared parenting often see mothers' family violence allegations as merely a strategy for undermining the father's parenting time. This dynamic is accentuated by courts' focus on "parental alienation," a concept which treats children's resistance to one parent as evidence that the other parent has undermined that relationship, either deliberately and malevolently, or because of pathology. While the parental alienation concept theoretically also applies in non-abuse cases and to any gender, both the UK hearings and the first author's Study found it to be more powerful when utilized against mothers accusing fathers of abuse. In short, the #MeToo movement may have catalyzed a new social reckoning with the reality of men's abuse of women in the larger world, but it has yet to do the same for legal attitudes toward abuse in the family.

Thus, there are many reasons family courts might marginalize and reject mothers' abuse allegations, especially child abuse, which is intuitively more horrifying and harder to accept than partner violence. Structurally, courts are reinforced in believing that child abuse is handled elsewhere, by the child protection agency and/or dependency court. Judges and other neutral professionals, such as evaluators and Guardians Ad Litem, often lack meaningful expertise in domestic violence and especially child sexual abuse. While they may be trained to some extent on domestic violence, the same is not true for child maltreatment. And courts' resistance to mothers' claims of child abuse is also powerfully fueled by their priority to shared parenting and fathers' rights—which theories like parental alienation reinforce. In the eyes of many courts, child abuse poses more of an obstacle to shared custody than does partner violence.

Unfortunately, despite the fairly extensive literature describing the dynamics in family courts, awareness of the negative reception which awaits mothers alleging family violence in court has not penetrated the child welfare field. Simply put, the domestic violence and child welfare fields generally read different journals, use different listservs, and attend different conferences. One consequence of this lack of integration is that both child welfare agencies and their reformers have trusted family courts to protect children, not realizing that such courts often fail to see themselves—or to act—as child protectors.

III. CHILD WELFARE AGENCIES' TREATMENT OF CUSTODY LITIGANTS

A. Turfing and Discounting

Ironically, while as noted above, custody courts look to child welfare agencies to handle child abuse, child welfare agencies also often defer their investigations to the civil courts—often assuming that they will "sort out" the truth. At the same time, agencies share courts' deep skepticism toward allegations of child abuse that arise in the context of custody litigation. Some agency personnel refer disdainfully to the influx of reports they receive on Sunday nights, after children return from visitation with their non-custodial parents, as "custody night." Others are advised—or believe—that the presence of custody litigation is grounds for serious skepticism of a child abuse report. And even where such views are not explicitly stated, in our experience from cases we have handled, they are implicitly held by many agency professionals. The many reasons such beliefs are incorrect cannot be addressed in this Article, but are discussed elsewhere.

Thus, like the scarecrow in The Wizard of Oz, whose arms were crossed and pointing in opposite directions, civil courts and child welfare agencies each seem to expect the other to handle child abuse allegations in shared cases, thereby leaving many children and protective parents altogether without systemic support. The net effect of both systems' excess skepticism and unwillingness to address child abuse where there is custody litigation, is that children are left unprotected—at best—by each part of the system which is responsible for their welfare. And where courts order children into unprotected parenting time with an allegedly abusive father, many children suffer.

B. Double-Edged Reforms

Compounding the legal system's failure to genuinely protect children is the harm inflicted on abused children by state agencies' reliance on foster care to keep some children safe. While foster care is not typically a first-line strategy, it is common in cases involving serious domestic violence. The problems with foster care have caused reformers to encourage agencies to send non-offending, protective parents to obtain legal custody as a safe and better alternative. But, in the second author's experience, this reform focus developed without understanding that family courts often not only fail to protect children from—but even force them into the care of—a dangerous or abusive parent.

1. Harms of Foster Care

While foster care is presumably used to protect children from an abusive or neglectful parent, frequently children are removed from both parents, even when one is non-offending and safe. Unfortunately, research demonstrates that removing children from safe and loving parents is profoundly harmful. Separating children from their safe parents can cause both emotional and psychological trauma to a child that can last a lifetime. The harm that can occur as a result of removal results in a "monsoon of stress hormones . . . flooding the brain and body." The evidence about the harm of involuntarily separating children from their safe parents is so overwhelming that a professor of Pediatrics at Harvard Medical School concluded: "There's so much research on this that if people paid attention at all to the science, they would never unnecessarily separate children from parents."

Such harms can be exacerbated when the removal is abrupt. Children are sometimes removed suddenly and without warning, intensifying the psychological trauma of a separation. Children in foster care often raise issues of ambiguity, loss, and trauma when talking about the experience of being removed—even describing the removal as kidnapping.

Once in foster care, children's experiences may be no better, and can, in some ways, be worse. Foster children experience high rates of maltreatment, routinely change placement, and sometimes receive inappropriate and inadequate medical, educational and mental health services. Children in cases who had experienced maltreatment that were placed in foster care had higher rates of juvenile delinquency and criminal activity as adults than similarly situated children who remained at home. Additionally, some research has found no significant outcome differences for maltreated children who were and were not placed in foster care, regarding cognitive and language outcomes, academic achievement, mental health outcomes or suicide risk. Children who "age out" of foster care experience high rates of homelessness, incarceration, unemployment, and other negative outcomes. Given these poor outcomes, it is unsurprising that *every state* has failed to meet federal standards to ensure the well-being of children in foster care, which has contributed to many states' systems being put under federal oversight pursuant to consent decrees.

In short, research suggests that foster care can be a toxic intervention for children. Given that it is often used when moderate/severe domestic violence is present, it is especially concerning that the domestic violence context renders it even more traumatic for children to be removed from their safe parent. In one prominent study of foster care alumni, 25% percent of foster care alumni still experienced post-traumatic stress disorder, a rate which is nearly twice as high as the rate for U.S. war veterans.

2. Reform Efforts—Keeping Children with Protective Parents

Given the harms to children from removal to foster care, many child welfare advocates have turned their focus to trying to divert cases with one safe parent out of the foster care system. Federal law requires child welfare agencies to make "reasonable efforts" to prevent children from being removed from their parents. As part of this obligation, agencies must explore whether a child has a non-offending parent who can safely care for a child. For example, in cases involving domestic violence, the Michigan Department of Health and Human Services instructs its caseworkers "to assist the adult victim of DV in the planning for his/her safety and the safety of the child." Its policy manual requires caseworkers to be "coordinating" with family court, though it does not define what that entails. Similarly, Pennsylvania and Maryland have actually prohibited child welfare agencies from involving juvenile courts when there is a nonoffending parent who can and will safely care for the child. As the Maryland Court of Special Appeals explains, "[a] child who has at least one parent willing and able to provide the child with proper care and attention should not be taken from both parents and be made a ward of the court." Before dismissing juvenile court jurisdiction, courts must inquire whether the non-offending parent is keeping the child safe, which may require obtaining a custody (or protective) order in court.

In recognition of the critical importance of allowing children to stay with their safe parent, several innovative legal centers have been formed to support the efforts of non-offending parents to retain custody of their children and prevent them from entering the foster care system. The first of these—the Detroit Center for Family Advocacy, which the second author co-founded—provided parents with the assistance of a lawyer, social worker and parent mentor, to resolve any safety concerns that the child welfare agency identifies. The Center received case referrals directly from the child welfare agency and worked collaboratively with agency investigators to address the factors creating a risk to the child. A quarter of cases that the Center handled involved child custody issues. In these cases, Center advocates focused on seeking custody orders that would prevent the offending parent from having unfettered access to the child. The multidisciplinary team would work with the non-offending parents, file for custody (or seek modification of an existing custody order), and help the parent navigate the court process. The Center ended its work in 2016 due to a lack of funding, but the model has been replicated in New Jersey, Washington, Iowa, and Oklahoma, among other jurisdictions.

The Center received case referrals directly from the child welfare agency and worked collaboratively with agency investigators to address the factors creating a risk to the child. A quarter of cases that the Center handled involved child custody issues. In these cases, Center advocates focused on seeking custody orders that would prevent the offending parent from having unfettered access to the child. The multidisciplinary team would work with the non-offending parents, file for custody (or seek modification of an existing custody order), and help the parent navigate the court process.

While these creative interventions hold promise, in the vast majority of cases, non-offending parents must navigate this process on their own or with a family lawyer who may lack familiarity with child welfare processes. Most child custody litigants are purely *pro se*. And while many child welfare investigators instruct the non-offending parent that they must get a custody order to avoid removal of the child, agencies typically provide little or no assistance to help the parent in doing so. It is also rare for child welfare investigators to appear in a custody proceeding to support the non-offending parent. Additionally, to complicate matters, when child welfare personnel choose not to substantiate a finding of abuse or neglect in part because they know a case is in custody litigation matters (as described in Section III.A. *supra*), this inaction can be seen by the custody judge as a signal that the abuse claims are false. Such courts appear unaware that "un-substantiation" usually means only that an allegation's validity is unknown.

Given the anecdotal and empirical reports described above, these processes create a perfect storm for parents and children seeking safety from an abusive other parent. Not only might the protective parent have to navigate the court process on her own—once in court, there is a significant risk that her claims of abuse and domestic violence will be rejected by the judge, engendering a cascade of further harms. And such courts may not only fail to protect the children from a potentially abusive parent, they may even "shoot the messenger" by reversing custody. Moreover, due to agencies' lack of understanding of family court processes, child welfare investigators might treat that court's decision as a failure of the *non-offending parent* to protect the child. Such blame can flow in part from the child protective system's history of treating mothers as "failing to protect" children from a father's abuse, as well as a mistaken faith in family courts' commitment to thoroughly and objectively vetting family violence allegations and protecting children. In short, both systems' misperceptions of the other can contribute to parallel refusals to protect children.

The authors of this Article believe that serious work is needed to eliminate the cross-cutting misconceptions between civil family courts and child welfare agencies. These misconceptions involve (i) who should and can adjudicate child maltreatment; (ii) what an un-substantiated finding means and when it is or is not appropriate; (iii) why *valid* child abuse concerns frequently arise in custody cases; and (iv) trends and structural biases within each system. The next section turns to the Authors' proposed systemic reforms to address these important concerns. They propose that each of these reforms is firmly within reach, with the right investment of expert support, training, and policy advocacy.

IV. THREE PRACTICABLE SYSTEM REFORMS

There are three over-arching mechanisms that could help to correct the systemic failures leading to the troubling outcomes for children described above: (i) participation of child welfare professionals in support of protective parents' private custody litigation; (ii) use of agencies' foster care funds to support attorneys to represent non-offending (safe) domestic violence victims; and (iii) several simple policy changes and accompanying trainings for both agencies and courts addressing how each should approach cases of mutual concern.

A. Child Welfare Agency Participation in Private Custody Litigation

Arguably the single most significant obstacle to protection of at-risk children in custody litigation is family courts' reluctance to engage seriously with such allegations, as is described in Section II, *supra*. A simple yet potentially powerful mechanism for countering this reluctance would be for child welfare agencies to support a non-offending protective parent's position in custody litigation, by participating in the litigation and potentially testifying about their findings. While such intervention is unlikely where the agency firmly believes the allegations are false, in the majority of cases (where they either substantiate or un-substantiate the allegations due to lack of information or systemic triage) the allegations are often still credible enough to signal potential risk to a child. In these cases, agency practice should be to offer ongoing assistance to a protective parent—especially in court—to further their shared goal of ensuring children's safety and welfare. In some cases, testimony from the caseworker or supervisor could usefully explain that allegations were not substantiated merely because they lacked sufficient evidence, because their rules are restrictive in ways that do not constrain the court, or even because it was believed that the custody judge would appropriately determine their validity.

The idea of child welfare agencies supporting protective mothers in custody litigation was first proposed as a "thought experiment" by the first author in 2003. While agencies working with Safe and Together have occasionally engaged in this way, society must move further to systematize such supportive interventions by child welfare agencies. The authors of this Article believe this could be accomplished through either legislative or rulemaking changes in federal and state-level policies governing child protection agency procedures.

B. Using Foster Care Funds to Support Safety with a Non-Offending Parent

In addition to requiring caseworkers to stay involved in the custody litigation to support the safe parent in keeping the child safe, child welfare agencies should use their federal foster care funds to support the provision of legal services to non-offending parents. As noted above, most domestic violence victims appear *pro se* in child custody cases, which makes them especially vulnerable to family courts' disbelief of their allegations of child abuse. They may not know what evidence to present to support the allegations, how to gather it, how to testify about the allegations, or how to question opposing witnesses. It is in these situations that lawyers can make a real difference.

Thanks to action by the federal Children's Bureau in 2018, foster care expenditures under Title IV-E of the Social Security Act may now be used to support lawyers in representing parents involved with child welfare. This includes lawyers seeking to help prevent "candidates for foster care" from entering care. Federal foster care funds can thus now be used to support programs like the Detroit Center for Family Advocacy (and others) that provide legal assistance to keep kids safely out of foster care. Child welfare agencies can also request matching federal funds to support legal representation for child-welfare-involved families. Given the critical need for lawyers to represent protective parents in custody litigation, agencies should use these funds to support these legal services. Such funds could support local legal aid organizations, public defenders, or low-fee private practitioners. Formal state policies, in addition to advocates and reformers, should encourage this practice. Such a shift might also help child welfare agencies move away from thinking in terms of parents' pathologies and realign around recognizing and supporting safe parents—consistent with the philosophy of the Greenbook and Safe and Together Institute's reform efforts.

C. Policy Reforms and Substantive Trainings

There are three areas in which policy development and education/training can help to reverse the misconceptions which are leading to courts' and agencies' failures to keep children safe even when there is a non-offending, safe, caring parent.

First, both agencies and courts should be prohibited from using the mere fact that the parents are battling over custody as a reason to downgrade the credibility of abuse allegations. On the contrary, there are multiple reasons why custody litigation should be expected when one parent abuses others in the family. Such a prohibition could draw on precedent from early domestic violence reforms involving arrest policies: For instance, the original D.C. Police pro-arrest policy stated explicitly that the fact that a 911 call relates to violence within the family may not be counted against probable cause. Similarly here, policies and statutes should make clear the fact that parent's involvement in custody litigation may not be counted against the credibility of child maltreatment allegations. Such a policy could be embodied in states' custody statutes, court rules and/or agency policy manuals. While this could make it slightly harder for agencies to reject some genuinely false allegations, it would, on balance, allow proportionally more children to benefit from such a policy.

Second, both agencies and courts should be encouraged to adopt new policies and practices for indeterminate cases. Both systems should recognize the reality that many "unsubstantiated" cases may in fact entail risk to a child, despite a lack of clear proof. Child welfare agencies should make clear in their investigations why an allegation was not substantiated, and should clearly document situations in which the lack of substantiation does not reflect a finding of no abuse. Additionally, agencies should adopt a new category of findings for cases where allegations are not yet substantiated but a risk to the child may still exist. In these cases, where possible, agencies should work with the non-offending parent to keep the child safe through custody litigation, as discussed above.

Unlike agencies, courts *must* issue parenting orders. In indeterminate cases, therefore, courts would be well-considered to take measured action and to avoid defaulting to the view that the allegations are false. Indeterminate findings would ideally be followed by recruitment of a skilled child therapist to work with the child, and a therapist with expertise in the relevant type of family violence to work with the accused adult. Such therapeutic work is likely to produce greater clarity about the truth over time. In turn, this would lead to both better protection for children *and* greater potential for healing negative parent-child relationships.

Finally, substantial, systematic expert trainings on child maltreatment and system practices should be mandated for both family courts and child welfare agencies. Trainings should address both systems' complementary misconceptions about each other, and shared misconceptions about child maltreatment allegations by parents in custody litigation. Such trainings should, of course, address the two policy changes above. They should also explain why custody litigation is not *per se* evidence of false allegations, why child abuse often does not come to light until after parties separate, why mothers often avoid reporting to child welfare agencies, and how and why agencies and courts, respectively, see their own and the other's roles. Some of these trainings should be joint, for both family court and agency personnel, and include high-level staff so they may discuss their perceptions regarding who should do what, why, and how. For instance, courts may benefit from hearing that agencies often choose not to bring cases to juvenile court for reasons that do not mean there is no danger to a child. And agencies may benefit from understanding that simply filing an action in family court does not always ensure adequate review of abuse evidence and protection of children. Skillfully handled, such meetings could generate new understandings and improved procedures and collaborations, in the interests of at-risk children.

Such trainings must also challenge the widespread social and legal skepticism toward mothers' reports of abuse by fathers, educating participants on the research showing that intentional false child abuse allegations are exceedingly rare and most often brought by *noncustodial* parents, and on implicit gender biases which may fuel undue and inappropriate skepticism and hostility toward mothers alleging abuse. Incorporation of the Safe and Together Institute's "perpetrator pattern-based approach" may be foundational to shifting both systems' responses to mothers who accuse fathers of abuse, reducing both the gender-bias and underestimating of risk to children which currently permeates both systems in cross-system cases.

CONCLUSION

In the course of the Authors' collaboration on this Article, both learned a great deal from each other about family court and child welfare system practices and potential reforms. Each believe that the same will be true for child welfare, child custody, and domestic violence professionals who come together to address the lacunae in the legal system's responses to child maltreatment which intersects with custody litigation. The authors do not claim to be the first to point out the gulfs between civil courts, child welfare, and domestic violence systems. We believe, however, that this Article's proposed reforms are new—building on all that has gone before. Nor are they any more unrealistic than many previous reforms regarding domestic violence in the child welfare caseload or child custody laws' inclusion of domestic violence. Clarity and quality of trainings—and mandates to participate—will be critical for such reforms to succeed. But the existence of resources such as the Safe and Together Institute, and the many experts in child welfare and family violence we have cited throughout, as well as increasingly concerned lawmakers, provide reason for optimism that real change can and will be accomplished. It must.

[Editor's Notes: 1. In March 2022, President Biden signed the Violence Against Women Act Reauthorization Act (VAWA), including Title XV Section 1501 et seq, inspired by the murder of 7-year old Kayden Mancuso in 2018 by her father during court ordered unsupervised visitation. The father later killed himself. Kayden's Law strengthens how state courts handle custody proceedings and increases funding for grants for states to implement domestic violence programs. It contains extensive Congressional findings about the overlap between domestic violence, child sexual abuse, and other child abuse. The goal is to strengthen state courts' abilities to recognize and adjudicate domestic violence and child abuse allegations based on valid, admissible evidence so that courts can enter orders that protect and minimize the risk of harm to children. Some states are passing similar laws so they can qualify for federal grant funds.

2. Inappropriate allegations of Parental Alienation in custody cases involving domestic violence are an international problem. See Reem Alsalem, "Custody, violence against women and violence against children, Report of the Special Rapporteur on violence against women and girls, its causes and consequences," UN Human Rights Council, 53rd session, summer 2023—"The report addresses the link between custody cases, violence against women and violence against children, with a focus on the abuse of the term 'parental alienation' and similar pseudo-concepts."]

IN RE J.M.

50 Cal.App.5th 833 (2020)
(footnotes and citations omitted)

In two separate appeals, Y.C. (Mother) challenges three juvenile court orders regarding her son, J.M., Jr. (J.M.). In her first appeal, Mother challenges the court's denial of a January 19, 2019 Welfare and Institutions Code section 388 petition for modification—joined by J.M.—through which Mother sought to have J.M. placed with her or, in the alternative, further reunification services. We conclude that the trial court abused its discretion in denying this petition and reverse.

Following termination of her reunification services, Mother addressed the domestic violence issues that comprised the entire basis for the sustained dependency petition regarding J.M. She also addressed various additional concerns the court and respondent Los Angeles County Department of Children and Family Services (DCFS) raised throughout the proceedings. Specifically, the court required efforts from Mother wholly unrelated to domestic violence, such as improving her living conditions, completing drug testing, and receiving mental health services. Mother complied. Thus, since termination of her reunification services, Mother not only successfully completed all programs to address domestic violence issues, but did everything else the court asked of her.

That Mother ameliorated all concerns leading to dependency court jurisdiction constitutes a substantial change in circumstances. Moreover, Mother presented evidence that, in light of this change in circumstances and the record as a whole, it was in J.M.'s best interests to be placed with her. Namely, Mother provided evidence—including testimony of a DCFS social worker—that she was ready, willing, and able to care for her son, that they had a growing bond, and that she posed no danger to him. The court's primary reason for denying the petition was a concern that Mother had not provided sufficient evidence to address the court's concern that she was not capable of caring for J.M.'s special needs, such as evidence reflecting she had been "trained" on how to do so. That concern, however, was unsupported by the record and was based on unwarranted speculation. The record contains no evidence suggesting Mother could not appropriately care for her son. Rather, it reflects only that J.M.'s long-term foster caregivers had more experience with doing so—and had done so without first receiving any "training." Accordingly, the court abused its discretion in not granting Mother's petition.

Even after the termination of reunification services, at which point a juvenile court focuses primarily on stability and permanency for the child, the court's analysis must be more nuanced than simply comparing a parent's home and abilities with those of a long-term caregiver and deciding which the court deems preferable. Although, at this stage, a *parent's* interest in maintaining a relationship with his or her biological child is no longer the focus, the court must still consider the benefits to *a child* of remaining connected with his or her biological parent and extended family. Here, the benefits to J.M. of remaining connected with a biological parent who has made the kind of "reformation" for which section 388 creates an "escape mechanism," overcome the presumption that her son remaining in a stable and potentially permanent foster home is in his best interests. The juvenile court erred in concluding otherwise. Accordingly, we reverse the court's May 15, 2019 order denying Mother's section 388 petition, and instruct the court to place J.M. with Mother.

This disposition of Mother's first appeal necessarily requires reversal of the September 30, 2019 orders that are the subject of Mother's second appeal—namely, an order denying an August 13, 2019 section 388 petition in which Mother, joined by J.M., again sought reunification services or placement, and the order terminating her parental rights.

BACKGROUND

I. Factual and Procedural History Relevant to Mother's First Appeal

A. Initial Referral and Petition

On March 13, 2017, DCFS received a referral alleging general neglect of J.M. (born Jan 2017) by Mother and J.M.'s father, J.M., Sr. (Father), due to domestic violence. The referral alleged that the prior evening Mother sent messages to a relative stating that Father had hit her and threatened to stab her with a knife. When the police responded, Mother was uncooperative and denied that there had been domestic violence, even though she had bruises on her forehead and arm. J.M. was asleep in the home during the domestic violence incident. He appeared healthy and clean and had no marks or bruises.

The initial petition DCFS filed on behalf of J.M. sought jurisdiction over the child based on Mother and Father having a history of engaging in violent altercations, the March 12, 2017 incident, Father's conviction for battery, Mother's failure to protect J.M., and allegations that Mother had a diagnosis of bipolar disorder and had failed to seek mental health treatment or take psychotropic medication as prescribed. Crucially, the court sustained the petition based on the allegations related to domestic violence only; it struck all other allegations in the petition.

The court removed J.M., then two months old, from Mother and Father, and placed him in foster care with M.F. (Caregiver) and her husband (collectively, Caregivers), with whom J.M. remains placed. The court granted Mother monitored visitation with the option for DCFS to permit Mother unmonitored visits at DCFS's offices. Mother was granted family reunification services, including domestic violence and parenting classes and individual counseling. Her case plan further required that she submit to a psychiatric evaluation and take any psychotropic medications prescribed.

B. Mother Is Granted, Then Loses, Overnight Visitation with J.M.

Mother visited J.M. consistently over the next several months. She was very attentive during visits, hugging, holding and taking pictures of J.M. She expressed that she missed her son and wanted him to be returned to her care.

In November 2017, she reported that she had moved out of Father's home and was renting a room on her own. It was not until this point in the proceedings that Mother acknowledged there had been domestic violence issues with Father.

November 2017 progress notes from the County of Los Angeles Department of Mental Health (DMH) reflect that Mother had consulted with a DMH psychiatrist about her lack of bipolar symptoms and her desire to discontinue her medications. The psychiatrist indicated Mother could try weaning off her medications gradually, and Mother agreed to resume all her medications, should she start feeling emotionally unstable.

In December 2017, after Mother had completed three successful unmonitored daytime visits, the court ordered DCFS to assess her home for overnight visits. On January 19, 2018, the juvenile court granted Mother a 29-day visit with J.M. at her home. The court did so despite DCFS objections to the size and condition of Mother's home, a very small room in a converted garage with no crawl or play space for the baby and no kitchen for Mother to cook food, and in which Mother also kept a small dog. Although the court permitted the 29-day visit, it also ordered DCFS to confirm Mother's home was properly permitted. The court further directed Mother to find a more suitable place for an infant.

As of January 31, 2018, per DMH progress notes, Mother's bipolar disorder was "on remission," and, at her request, Mother was not being prescribed any medication.

In February 2018, DCFS asked the court to terminate Mother's 29-day visit. It reported that Mother's unit violated zoning laws and that Mother was resistant to and no longer participating in domestic violence training, had discontinued individual therapy, and was not taking psychotropic medication. DCFS also reported that Mother had repeatedly denied her lack of compliance and insisted she did not need medication. DCFS noted further concerns that Mother maintained her home in a manner that was unsafe for an infant; for example, it noted concerns that J.M. was observed sleeping in a crib that contained a mechanical pencil and medication. Mother contested these reports and accused social workers of fabricating the hazards they identified. Mother also reported her efforts to work additional hours so she could earn enough money to afford a new home.

On February 16, 2018, the court rescinded Mother's 29-day visit and returned J.M. to Caregiver. The court explained that Mother had indicated a month prior that she would move into safe, permitted housing, but failed to do so, and that living in an unpermitted home could result in her summarily losing her housing at any point, should the violation be reported. The court further expressed concern that Mother might be in contact with Father, given a DCFS report that, during a surprise visit, a social worker had observed a man "approaching the back where [M]other's room was located" but "when he noticed [the social worker], he immediately turned around and walked away" "fast" and "[Mother's] dog followed the individual." The court ordered Mother to stay 100 yards away from and have no contact with Father. The court granted Mother monitored visitation with DCFS discretion to authorize overnight visits or release J.M. to Mother if she moved into a more suitable home and complied with other court orders. The court further ordered Mother to submit to weekly and on-demand drug tests.

The court acknowledged that Mother had "consistently, regularly contacted and visited and made significant progress in resolving the problems that led to the removal and ha[d] demonstrated the capacity and ability to complete the objectives of the treatment plan." The court therefore ordered six months of further reunification services (in addition to the approximately nine months Mother already received), but granted DCFS's request that Mother submit to a mental health evaluation.

C. Termination of Reunification Services

In the reunification period that followed, Mother made some positive progress with her case plan and maintained continuous, positive visits with her son. By all accounts, Mother was caring, attentive, protective, and loving during her weekly monitored visits with J.M., and brought J.M. toys, clothing, shoes, and bottles. DCFS reported no concerns regarding Mother's conduct during visits. Mother completed all required courses and counseling, and started a new job as a truck dispatcher, which allowed her to work at night from home, using a computer and cellular phone. She had participated consistently in individual therapy since February 2018, and was cooperative and engaged in sessions, openly sharing her history of trauma. According to a letter from Mother's therapist during this period, Mother demonstrated an increased insight into how past events had led up to her current situation and involvement with DCFS, and was working on identifying environmental stressors that have affected her mental health and behaviors. Mother had also learned strategies to help effectively respond to stressors. Although not required to do so by the court, and although DCFS did not report any problems or concerns with respect to anger management, Mother also participated in anger management training.

Also during this period, however, Mother violated the court's no-contact order regarding Father, which came to the attention of DCFS because Mother was arrested while traveling with Father on a train and charged with obstructing a police officer. This incident occurred two days after the court issued its no-contact order.

Mother also had not complied with the court's order to complete a mental health evaluation, although she stated that she had an appointment for the evaluation. As a result, DCFS reported it was "unknown whether or not [M]other ha[d] any unresolved mental health issues." DCFS did not, however, report any facts suggesting Mother's mental state or mental health presented a current risk to J.M., or that it had previously presented such a risk. Mother was largely compliant with her drug testing, but had tested positive for marijuana on five occasions.

On September 19, 2018, the court terminated family reunification services for Mother, consistent with DCFS's recommendation. Mother thus received a total of 16 months of reunification services, from May 2017 to September 2018. The court explained that, although Mother had completed most of her reunification requirements, she had violated the stay-away order by being arrested with Father, that she was still living in an illegal unit from which she could be summarily evicted, and that the presumptive statutory duration of reunification services for a child as young as J.M. had expired. The court said it would consider whether to reinstate reunification services if Mother moved to a domestic violence shelter or other appropriate housing, had no contact with Father, and complied with all other court orders. The court provided Mother with information on government-assisted affordable housing that could be made available within a short period of time. The court set a section 366.26 permanency planning hearing and granted Mother unmonitored visits with J.M. once a week with DCFS discretion to liberalize.

Mother filed a petition for extraordinary writ challenging the juvenile court's orders terminating family reunification services and declining to return J.M. to her custody. This court summarily denied the petition on December 12, 2018. . .

[Summary: J.M. was diagnosed with autism and developmental issues, started treatment for them, and continued to have positive visits with

Mother. However, the court terminated reunification services for Mother. Three months after services were terminated, Jan. 2019, Mother sought placement of J.M. with her, or further reunification services with overnight visits, arguing that she had addressed all of the court's stated concerns when it terminated services: a new home, no contact with Father, negative drug tests, and no mental health issues. She was working at night from home and had childcare to cover her daytime sleeping hours. However, the court still was concerned about Mother not having special training regarding J.M.'s special needs. DCFS continued to deny overnight visits and the court continued to deny Mother's requests to have J.M. live with her or stay overnight or to have additional reunification services. The court terminated Mother's parental rights, finding that it was in J.M.'s best interests to be adopted.

The appellate court held that Mother had established a substantial change in circumstances, which is required in order to reverse termination of parental rights.] Namely, she offered substantial evidence that she had resolved the domestic violence underlying the initial dependency petition: She had not been in contact with Father for over a year, had completed all required domestic violence training, and nothing suggested Mother was or had been in another potentially violent or abusive relationship.

Moreover, Mother offered evidence that she had also addressed the myriad of other concerns—completely unrelated to any risk of domestic violence—that the court raised in terminating her reunification services. Namely, she offered uncontroverted evidence that she had stable and permitted housing, participated in individual therapy, completed parenting and anger management programs [even though anger management had not been ordered by the court], and no longer needed any psychotropic medications or mental health services. The court made no findings to the contrary. [The trial court abused its discretion in concluding that Mother had not shown a substantial change.] . . .

Domestic violence certainly poses a serious threat to the well-being and safety of children in the home, but J.M. was never physically harmed, nor did he witness any such violence. Mother was initially unwilling to acknowledge the issue and initially struggled to stay away from Father. But denying J.M. the benefit of being raised by his biological mother based on her mistakes early in the proceedings—particularly when she no longer posed a risk to him—would be to make the perfect the enemy of the good. The goal of dependency court proceedings is not to engineer perfect parents, but to protect children from harm. Moreover, a [Welfare & Institutions Code] section 388 petition seeking reinstatement of reunification services or return of the child will necessarily involve a parent who has made mistakes sufficient to support termination of services at some point in the past. The question must be whether the changes the parent made since then are substantial enough to overshadow that prior determination, such that reunification is now in the child's best interests. That Mother did not immediately break free from the cycle of abuse does not render it in J.M.'s best interests to deny him the opportunity to be raised with his biological mother and extended family, with all the benefits courts recognize this could offer him, particularly when, at the time of the hearing on her petition, Mother had for over a year avoided contact with Father and maintained stable, appropriate housing and gainful employment. . .[The appellate court also noted that J.M. was never at risk due to Mother's psychological issues, which had subsided.]

Although J.M. came within the jurisdiction of the court based on domestic violence issues with Father that placed J.M. at risk, the court devised a list of ways, wholly unrelated to any risk of domestic violence, in which Mother needed to prove herself as a parent in order for her to earn back her child—obtain permitted housing, keep her home neat, or do some unidentified "training" regarding how to care for him. Failure to correct these purported problems would not have created a risk to J.M. independently sufficient to support juvenile court jurisdiction. Nevertheless, Mother did what the court asked of her (the court never ordered Mother to take any training regarding J.M.'s special needs; it merely faulted her after the fact for failing to do so). All the while, Mother never stopped visiting her son, never stopped asking for overnight visits and placement in her home. This shows a tremendous level of initiative and dedication, and suggests that it would be in J.M.'s best interests to be placed with her.

The court was certainly entitled to disbelieve Mother's testimony on various topics; after all, Mother had lied and been otherwise untruthful in the past. But the court did not have discretion to write off Mother as a parent entirely, or to force her to prove an above average level of parental ability in order to meet her burden of establishing it was in her son's best interests to have a chance of being raised by his biological mother.

For all the reasons discussed above, we conclude the juvenile court abused its discretion in determining the substantial changes since termination of Mother's reunification services did not render placement of J.M. with Mother in his best interests. We therefore reverse the court's denial of Mother's January 2019 petition for modification. This necessarily requires reversal of the court's denial of a similar petition Mother filed on August 13, 2019, as well as the court's termination of Mother's parental rights. . .

The court is instructed to enter a new order granting Mother's January 14, 2019 section 388 petition and immediately placing J.M. with Mother. Whether to implement a plan of family maintenance or terminate juvenile dependency altogether is a matter properly left to the juvenile court at this stage, and we express no opinion thereon.

[Editor's Notes: 1. See also In re Ma. V., *64 Cal.App.5th 11 (2021), another case in which the juvenile court's order removing children from their abused mother was reversed by the appellate court. That court noted that the mother had broken up with her abusive partner 10 months earlier, had no contact with him, and was not in a new relationship. The trial court stated that one of its reasons for removing the children was that the mother might get into another abusive relationship in the future; the appellate court held that this was error since the court is supposed to base its order on the current situation.*

It went on to comment: "We note in closing this court has observed a recent, and troubling trend, of what we perceive as mothers being punished as victims of domestic violence. We recognize issues of domestic violence often put children at risk. The cases we refer to, however, are akin to this one, where children are brought into the dependency system because of domestic violence between the mother and a romantic partner. Even after a mother manages to distance herself from the abuser, however, SSA [Social Services Administration] and the juvenile court continue to use the history of domestic violence as a basis to remove the children. Indeed, it seems as if once a woman is battered, she will forever be faced with losing her children. This is not the legal test. 'When evaluating the complexity of domestic violence relationships, not every case will be the same. Unlike drug and alcohol addiction, there are no Alcoholics Anonymous (AA) meeting cards, coins, or clean tests to measure success [as a victim of domestic abuse].'

We are also mindful of society's preconceptions that often damage the 'credibility of victim-witnesses who present on the stand in atypical and non-paradigmatic fashions.' We expect such victims to be 'sweet, kind, demure, blameless, frightened, and helpless' and 'not a multi-faceted woman who may or may not experience fear or anger.' 'These are the preconceptions that judges and jurors bring with them into the courtroom when they assess the veracity of a victim-witness's story.' We encourage continued diligence and education to guard against such preconceptions."

2. In "Blaming the Victim? The Intersection of Race, Domestic Violence, and Child Neglect Laws," 8 Geo. J. L. & Mod. Critical Race Persp. 355 (2016), Jacqueline Mabatah describes a case in which an abused black woman was sentenced to 45 years in prison for "failing to protect" her young son from being killed by her abuser. She was granted parole in 2016 after serving 9 years. The author explains that courts often fail to consider the abuse toward the mother, the great lengths battered mothers often go to in order to protect their children, and instead focus on the fact that the mother "chose" to stay with the abuser. The author focuses on poor black mothers, and states that "through a critical race feminist analysis we can better understand that a battered woman's choices and behavior are not pathological, but are instead reasonable reactions to the circumstances in which she lives. . .By tackling domestic violence against women, we can reduce the exposure to criminal liability for truly non-neglectful or abusive women."]

DARLA SPENCE COFFEY, PARENTING AFTER VIOLENCE: A GUIDE FOR PRACTITIONERS

Institute for Safe Families, Health Federation of Philadelphia (2009)

* * *Fathering After Violence

Fathering After Violence (FAV) is a national initiative pioneered by Juan Carlos Areán and Ann Fleck Henderson and developed by the Family Violence Prevention Fund (FVPF) [now Futures Without Violence] and its partners to enhance the safety and well-being of women and children by motivating men to renounce their violence and become better fathers (or father figures) and more supportive parenting partners. (Fleck-Henderson & Arean, 2004). FAV is not a program per se or a quick solution to a complex problem. Rather, it is a conceptual framework to help end violence against women by using fatherhood as a leading approach. Using this framework as a starting point, the FVPF and other practitioners have developed culturally appropriate practical tools, prevention and intervention strategies, and policy and practice recommendations. FAV proposes engaging abusive fathers by helping them develop empathy for their children and using this empathy as a motivator to change their behavior. It uses an assessment framework to help practitioners discern which fathers might be appropriate to work with to repair their relationships with their children. The FAV initiative is described in some detail below. This information is taken from the website www.endabuse.org [now www.futureswithoutviolence.org] * * *

Guiding Principles for Fathering After Violence

The Fathering After Violence initiative provides the following guiding principles for the work of Fathering After Violence. It is suggested that any provider adopt these principles when engaging abusers in a process to focus on parenting and their relationship with their children.

- The safety of women and children is always the first priority.
- This initiative must be continually informed and guided by the experiences of battered women and their children.
- This initiative does not endorse nor encourage automatic contact between the offending fathers and their children or parenting partners.
- In any domestic violence intervention, there must be critical awareness of the cultural context in which parenting happens.

- Violence against women and children is a tool of domination and control used primarily by men and rooted in sexism and male entitlement.
- Abuse is a deliberate choice and a learned behavior and therefore can be unlearned.
- Some men choose to change their abusive behavior and heal their relationships; others continue to choose violence.
- Working with fathers is an essential piece of ending violence against women and children.
- Fathers who have used violence need close observation to prevent further harm.
- Work with fathers must embrace notions of non-violence broadly.
- Service coordination among providers of domestic violence services is essential.
- The reparative process between abusive fathers and their children often is long and complex and is not appropriate for all men.

Fathering After Violence: The Reparative Framework

The reparative framework proposed by the Fathering After Violence Initiative is intended to guide FAV work with those fathers who are in the position to start healing their relationships with their children in a safe and constructive way. This framework was conceptualized by research with men who had stopped their violence and started to heal their relationships with their children and, in many ways, parallels the "stages of change" model discussed earlier. A key emphasis is on identifying the readiness of an abusive father to accept responsibility for the violence and repair his relationship with his children, letting the children set the "pace."

The Reparative Framework:

[This includes changing abusive behavior; modeling constructive behavior; stopping denial, blaming and justification; accepting all consequences for one's behavior; acknowledging damage; supporting and respecting the mother's parenting; listening and validating; and not forcing the process nor trying to "turn the page."] * * *

The Fathering After Violence initiative is an important first step in identifying ways to engage fathers in restorative parenting. They have found that many men are able to develop empathy toward their children more easily than toward their partners. Understanding the effects that domestic violence has had on their children can be a strong motivator for some men to change their behavior. Finally, recent research suggests that some mothers who have suffered abuse want their children to have safer and healthier contact with their fathers and that positive involvement with a father figure can be very beneficial to children's development. There is good reason for doing this work. * * *

What Children Need To Hear From The Abuser

Abusers need to be prepared to talk with their children about the violence. This is a difficult conversation to have, but in the same way that children need to hear certain messages from their non-abusing parent, they need to hear from the abusing parent that violence is not okay, and that the children are not responsible for the violence. Specific messages could include: [List includes taking responsibility for the abuser's behavior, saying s/he is sorry the child had to see or hear the violence, that violence is not ok and not the child's fault, abuser will listen to the child, it's ok if the child is angry or sad, abuser is getting help so child can feel safer, etc.].

Supporting Accountability

Abusers need to learn to be accountable for their behavior, and that means being accountable to their children. If an abuser maintains an attitude of treating his children as possessions and/or an unwillingness to relinquish an authoritarian parenting style, he will not be able to accept that a part of the healing process for the children includes having conversations with the children that reflect his "owning" his behavior.

Such a conversation, or series of conversations, with children needs preparation and forethought. Abusers should be encouraged to spend time reflecting on what they need to say to their children. They need to be conscious about choosing a peaceful time to talk to the children. Abusers should be as specific as possible in acknowledging the wrongness of their violent, abusive, and controlling behavior—without rationalizing or blaming anyone else. Finally, such a conversation is not a true conversation unless the abuser commits to listening to the children's reactions. Children may or not be ready to respond. They may still feel very fearful. They may also have denial about the domestic violence, blame their mother (taking a page from the abuser's book), and/or be too angry at the abuser to be able to respond.

Abusers should be directed that, just because they are ready for this conversation, does not mean that the children are ready. They cannot demand a response from their children. And they certainly should not demand, or expect, "forgiveness."

What an abuser does will always "speak much louder" that what he says. Therefore, part of being accountable to the children is behaving in a nonviolent way in all future interactions with the children's mother and demonstrating to the children that he is safe to be around. The abuser needs to make a commitment to speak positively to others about the children's mother. (Talking badly about their other parent is a form of abusiveness to the children.) It is important for the children to observe that the abuser can get angry without being frightening. If applicable, the abuser demonstrates accountability by paying child support regularly. An abuser needs to be prepared for the kind of response that his children may have towards him when he initiates a conversation about the domestic violence.

Respectful Parenting with the Other Parent

A commitment to nonviolence includes communicating and interacting with the other parent in a respectful manner. This is extremely important for the children as it is a way to demonstrate changed behavior and model for the children how to respect their parent. This can go a long way in correcting the disrespect victims are often shown by their children after there has been violence and abusiveness directed at them by the children's other parent.

Respectful parenting includes: [List includes showing respect to the other parent as a parent, sharing decision-making about raising the children, discussing disagreements in a respectful way and only when children are not present, compromising and negotiating about the care and discipline of the children, etc.]

Respect of the other parent continues when the other parent is not around. Any discussions about the other parent need to be confined to saying positive things, with no triangulation with the children or interrogation of the children about their mother's activities. Some issues that abusers should not discuss with the children include: [List includes talking about child support, abuser's anger with the mother, questioning children about who she's seeing, where she lives, abuser's feelings about mother's new partner, etc.] * * *

CHAPTER 8

ALTERNATIVE DISPUTE RESOLUTION

■ ■ ■

This chapter looks at alternative dispute resolution in the context of domestic violence. It starts with a description of the debate about the appropriateness of court-based mediation when parents are disputing custody or visitation and there has been a history of partner abuse and calls for studies to measure its effectiveness. Then come statutory guidelines for mediators dealing with custody cases involving domestic violence. Next is an alarming study finding that alleging domestic violence during such court-based mediation sessions may lead to survivors of abuse losing custody to abusers due to mediators' recommendations to the court.

The second half of the chapter focuses on how restorative justice may be used in domestic violence situations. The first article lays out the principles of restorative justice, describes five models using these principles, and analyzes each model's effectiveness for victims and perpetrators of domestic violence crimes. Another examines the usefulness of community-based justice forums as an alternative to the criminal justice system in these cases. The materials then look at several traditional types of restorative justice, asking how these practices are being utilized to address intimate partner violence. These traditional practices include Navajo peacemaking as well as religion-based arbitration panels in the Muslim community. Whether these types of alternative dispute resolution may be more useful than a traditional U.S. legal approach, particularly in communities marginalized by mainstream U.S. society, is an ongoing question.

A. COURT-BASED MEDIATION

SUSAN LANDRUM, THE ONGOING DEBATE ABOUT MEDIATION IN THE CONTEXT OF DOMESTIC VIOLENCE: A CALL FOR EMPIRICAL STUDIES OF MEDIATION EFFECTIVENESS

12 Cardozo J. Conflict Resol. 425 (2011)
(citations and footnotes omitted)

INTRODUCTION

Several schools of thought exist as to whether mediation is appropriate when the underlying relationship involves domestic violence. Some argue that mediation is always inappropriate when a couple has a history of domestic violence. Others believe that, while mediation in cases of domestic violence should not be barred, it should generally not be encouraged. Yet a third group focuses on mandatory mediation and argues that mandatory mediation should never occur when the relationship has a history of domestic violence, unless the victim wishes to go through mediation. Another significant group believes that each situation should be evaluated individually through screening to determine whether mediation is appropriate, and that there could be many situations where mediation could be appropriate even when there has been a history of domestic violence. Finally, there is a small group that argues that mediation can be effective in almost any family law case, even those in which domestic violence is a factor.

State legislatures, courts, and mediation programs have responded to these arguments in a variety of ways. Some states have approached the issue by exempting from family mediations situations where there has been domestic violence, while other state statutes do not provide for such an exemption. Court-sponsored and community-based mediation programs also differ in their approaches to domestic violence issues. Most programs have instituted a screening process to evaluate whether disputes are appropriate for mediation and whether the parties have a history of domestic violence that could affect the mediation. Many mediation programs provide training for mediators to recognize signs of domestic violence and be able to manage situations where it becomes an issue, but not all programs do.

In spite of the fact that scholars and mediators still debate these issues and legislatures and courts have developed a variety of "solutions," very few empirical studies have evaluated the effectiveness of mediation in cases where there is a history of domestic violence. Those studies that have been done are very limited, involving only a small number of subjects. Scholars rely mostly on anecdotal evidence to support their arguments. Although many of their claims seem intuitive, more needs to be done to evaluate how effective mediation programs are in handling disputes involving domestic violence because of the large number of those disputes that end up in mediation. In addition, because of the variations in how programs address screening and mediator training issues, empirical data is necessary to evaluate which approach(es) are better at addressing domestic violence issues in family mediations and, most importantly, which ones help to improve fairness of mediation outcomes and reduce future incidents of domestic violence.

Regardless of the ongoing debate concerning its appropriateness for domestic violence victims, mediation has become the norm in family law cases involving custody disputes, divorces, and property disputes. As a result, an increasing number of cases utilizing mediation involve victims of domestic violence. * * *

I. POTENTIAL PROBLEMS WITH FAMILY MEDIATION WHEN THE COUPLE HAS A HISTORY OF DOMESTIC VIOLENCE

Legal scholars, mediation advocates, and domestic violence victims' advocates have long debated whether mediation is appropriate for parties that have a history of domestic violence. Their concerns generally fall into four basic categories. First, there are challenges about how to define "domestic violence" when determining whether cases are appropriate for mediation. Second there are concerns about whether the mediation process can be fair, voluntary, safe, and neutral when the parties have a history of domestic violence. Third, there are concerns about potential outcomes of such mediations and whether those outcomes can be fair and safe for victims. Finally, there are public policy concerns that are interwoven with the debates about mediation when there is a history of domestic violence. The following subsections develop these potential problems with family mediation when the parties have a history of domestic violence.

A. The Challenge of Defining "Domestic Violence"

One of the most immediate problems with determining when it is appropriate to mediate family law cases where there is a history of domestic violence is that there are a number of challenges in determining how to even define "domestic violence" in this context. First, because legislatures have passed laws to address domestic violence, there are legal definitions of "domestic violence." Those definitions may or may not reflect definitions of "domestic violence" or "domestic abuse," as understood by society, victims' rights advocates, or scholars. Second, although "domestic violence" has historically been used to refer specifically to physical abuse, most experts today recognize that there are other forms of abuse that may fit into this category as well, including emotional or verbal abuse, extreme levels of control over actions or finances, etc. Third, mediation proponents have begun to recognize that not only violent acts but also threats of violence may have a negative impact on the mediation process. Fourth, although many mediation advocates would agree that mediation should not be used where there are allegations of "serious" domestic violence, most are not in agreement about how to define "seriousness." Finally, mediation experts recognize that there are additional factors that influence how "domestic violence" should be defined when determining which parties are capable of mediating, including timing issues and the specific context in which the domestic violence has occurred.

Loretta M. Frederick, senior legal and policy advisor of the Battered Women's Justice Project, has raised an important issue that courts and other mediation programs should consider in designing screening processes. For example, how a mediation program defines "domestic violence" can be relevant to whether the screening process is effective in discovering whether domestic violence exists in a relationship and therefore how the court or mediation program should treat that situation.

When state laws specify what programs should be available based on whether there is a history of domestic violence, the legal definition of domestic violence will be relevant. At the same time, there can also be "contextual" definitions of domestic violence. In other words, how one evaluates the potential influence of domestic violence in a specific situation with a couple may depend on:

> (1) the perpetrator's intent in using violence and abuse against a partner, with implications for his or her approach to parenting; (2) the meaning which the victim and children take from the violence; and (3) the effect of the abuse on the adult victim and children, including the harm done and the risk of physical and other forms of violence.

Scholars have also begun to differentiate between different types of domestic violence and to argue that the type may matter when determining whether a couple can effectively mediate. For example, Joan Kelly and Michael Johnson have defined four different types of domestic violence: coercive controlling violence, violent resistance, situational couple violence, and separation-instigated violence. Kelly and Johnson define coercive controlling violence, also sometimes called "intimate terrorism," as "a pattern of emotionally abusive intimidation, coercion, and control coupled with physical violence against partners." Coercive controlling violence is what most people typically associate with domestic violence. The second type of domestic violence, violent resistance, has also been defined as "female resistance," "resistive/reactive violence," and "self-defense." Situational couple violence is a "type of partner violence that does not have its basis in the dynamic of power and control." Finally, separation-instigated violence is a term used to describe violence that does not occur until a couple is in the process of ending their relationship. Kelly and Johnson believe that an understanding of the different types of domestic violence can lead to better screening processes. *[Editor's Note: This typology of abuse is controversial in the field of domestic violence.]*

Applying these different definitions, it is possible to see how many cases involving situational couple violence might still be possible to mediate, because that history would not necessarily signal potential problems with power imbalances or intimidation. On the other hand, many cases involving coercive controlling violence would most likely not be appropriate for mediation. Cases involving separation-instigated violence would most likely have to be evaluated on a case-by-case basis to determine whether the victim is capable of mediating, but those cases would certainly emphasize the need to have protocols in place before, during, and after the mediation to protect the victim from additional violence.

Ohio provides an example of how some states have chosen to define domestic violence more broadly than the statutory term. The Ohio Supreme Court's domestic violence training program for mediators focuses on detecting and addressing "domestic abuse" rather than "domestic violence," because "domestic abuse" "connote[s] a broader range of behaviors that should be of concern to mediators and their stakeholders when assessing an individual's capacity to negotiate on his or her own behalf and on behalf of his or her children." In contrast, the term "domestic violence" is a statutory term in Ohio, and the court was concerned that its use "may result in a narrowed understanding of the dynamics at play in these situations."

For example, the Ohio Supreme Court's training materials set out the following definition of "domestic violence," as defined by the National Council of Juvenile and Family Court Judges (NCJFCJ) Model Code on Domestic and Family Violence: * * * [requires physical or sexual harm or attempts at those, and excludes self-defense]. In contrast, the training materials also provide the American Bar Association Commission on Domestic Violence's broader definition of "domestic abuse":

> A pattern of abusive and controlling behaviors that one current or former intimate partner or spouse exerts over another as a means of control, generally resulting in the other partner changing his or her behavior in response.

* * * [The author argues for a broad definition of domestic abuse in the screening process.]

Because most mediation advocates agree that cases involving a "serious" history of domestic violence should be excluded from family law mediations, it is important to think about how "seriousness" should be defined. "Seriousness" is often a factor in determining which cases are appropriate for mediation, and definitions which are either too broad or too narrow may include cases that are really not appropriate for mediation or exclude cases that could be successfully mediated. For example, one way to evaluate whether cases involving domestic violence could be mediated would be to measure how serious the injury is, while another way would be to look at the number of incidents involved.

A few hypothetical examples illustrate this debate. Imagine a case where the abuser had sent the victim to the hospital one time with several broken bones, a concussion, and bruising over much of her body. If the mediation program applied the first definition of seriousness, serious of injury, to the screening, then this couple would be excluded from mediation. However, one could easily imagine situations in which the victim would be fully capable of participating in mediation in spite of the severity of that past incident. Maybe this single incident occurred several years ago and has not had the kind of psychological effect on the victim that would prevent her from mediating effectively. Maybe the victim filed charges against her abuser and moved out, seeking counseling. There are many potential situations in which the victim may be fully capable of protecting her own interests in mediation, depending on the circumstances.

In contrast, one could imagine a case where the physical injuries from the abuse were very slight or even nonexistent but the psychological effect on the victim was very significant because of the repetitive nature of the abuse. * * * This discussion of "serious" domestic violence clearly illustrates the importance of evaluating whether couples should mediate on a case-by-case basis.

In addition, the consideration of context is also important. Some scholars argue that, even where there is a history of domestic violence, there may be some cases where mediation is still appropriate based on the timing of past incidents and other contexts. For example, Sandra Zaher has argued that categorical exclusion of cases involving domestic violence from mediation would deprive "those women who make a free and informed choice to use a convenient and inexpensive service . . . of that choice." In contrast to some feminist critiques of mediation in this context, Zaher believes that "there are some women who are capable of comprehending the mediation process, who understand the alternatives, and who are no longer adversely affected by the violence of their partners, and who therefore are capable of voicing their own rights and interests, as well as those of their children." The effect of past violence on the victim is a determining factor in whether he or she could effectively mediate.

David Chandler observes that whether or not a victim can effectively mediate with her abuser may depend on individual circumstances. [These include how strong the victim's support system is, how recent the abuse was, and whether the victim has had counseling about the abuse.] * * *

This discussion of the challenges of defining "domestic violence" for purposes of family law mediations emphasizes the true value of considering whether parties are capable of mediating on a case-by-case basis. Rigid definitions do not take into account subtle variations in individual circumstances that could be a factor in whether a couple is capable of mediating their differences. This shortcoming could lead to broad-scale inclusion of cases that should not be mediated or exclusion of cases that could, in fact, be successfully mediated. At the same time, the debate over how to define domestic violence also emphasizes the importance of having well-developed screening protocols and well-trained mediators in these situations—if programs are to consider the appropriateness of mediation on a case-by-case basis, the mediator or screener must have a significant understanding of the complexity of domestic violence issues and an ability to make determinations about which cases can be safely, effectively, and fairly mediated.

B. Concerns About the Mediation Process When the Parties Have a History of Domestic Violence

Both mediation advocates and victims' advocates have significant concerns about the mediation process where the parties have a history of domestic violence. Although the mediation process is designed to manage the power imbalances that often exist in mediations, a history of domestic violence has the potential to create insurmountable power imbalances. In fact, an abuser may use intimidation, e.g., either verbal or nonverbal threats of future violence, as a way to create power imbalances that act to his or her advantage. Even without actual threats, a victim may feel intimidated to the point that he or she feels incapable of standing up for his or her interests in the mediation.

In addition, one hopes that parties voluntarily participate in mediations. However, some states require parties to mediate family law issues, and not all provide exceptions for cases with a history of domestic violence. Even if victims can "opt out" of mediation, many victims' advocates are concerned that victims feel pressured to participate, thus undermining the voluntary nature of the process. Further, there are concerns about how to ensure that the mediation process is safe for victims. These issues create further challenges for mediators, who must balance their professional responsibility to remain neutral in mediations with the need to rectify power imbalances, ensure fairness, and maintain safety.

1. The Potential for Power Imbalances and Concerns About Intimidation

Some victims' rights advocates argue that it is never appropriate to mediate a family law dispute, such as divorce, division of property, or child custody, where there is a history of domestic violence. These advocates argue that mediation places the victim in an impossible situation where he or she is more likely to feel pressured and, because of unequal bargaining power, end up with an agreement that does not protect his or her interests. The assumption is that those power imbalances lead to results in mediation that would not have happened in an adversarial setting.

Barbara J. Hart argues that mediation of child custody disputes should not be mandatory in situations where the mother has been battered. Because battered women do not feel like they have power in the abusive relationship, Hart argues that they are likely to not be strong advocates for themselves in custody mediations and end up with an agreement that puts both themselves and their children in further danger. Other scholars have also voiced serious concerns about the power imbalances that can exist in a mediation where there has been domestic violence and believe that mediation is often not appropriate, or at least should be handled very carefully, in that context. As one writer has observed, "[O]ne can [not] expect a victim of abuse to voluntarily want or be able to sit safely at the negotiating table with their abusive partner." The victim is inclined to give in on issues that she should not give in to because she wants to get out of the room as quickly as possible or because she fears retaliation if she stands up to her abuser.

Mediators are always concerned about the potential for unfair power imbalances in mediation and seek to create an environment in which parties who do not have as much power can have their interests met through the process. In the case of family mediations where there is a history of domestic violence, programs have done much to address the potential problem with power imbalances. Studies that have looked at mediation outcomes in this context provide limited, conflicting data about whether such efforts have been successful, pointing to a need for further studies on the subject.

2. Can Mediation in this Context Really Be Voluntary?

One of the underlying principles of mediation is that it is a voluntary process that can be terminated by any participant at any time. As discussed previously, some states, however, mandate mediation in family law cases. States like California do not have an exception for cases involving domestic violence, meaning that even where the parties have such a history, they will still be referred to mediation. Regardless of whether mediation is mandatory or not, there are some scholars and victims' advocates who believe that there is no voluntary participation in mediation for a victim of domestic violence. They observe that victims may feel that they cannot refuse to mediate because of either pressure from the court or from the abuser. Victims' advocates also believe that the process cannot be viewed as voluntary when the victim is intimidated to accept an agreement during a mediation that is not in her best interests, because of force or manipulation. Mandatory mediation does not mean mandatory settlement, but victims' advocates are concerned that power imbalances and fears of future violence may lead victims to believe that they have no choice but to agree to their abusers' demands.

3. Safety: The Potential for Violence During Mediation

Even assuming that appropriate screening will filter out the vast majority of cases that should not be mediated, it does not mean that mediators can feel assured of the victim's safety both during and after the mediation takes place. As a couple moves through the mediation process or other legal proceedings, the situation could quickly change. There may be subtle indicators—or sometimes overt signs—that the abuser is still intimidating the victim to get what he or she wants from the mediation, and if the mediator is not vigilant he or she will miss those signals. Rather than viewing screening as a one-time process, one scholar has argued that the mediator needs to think of screening as an ongoing need. In addition, there are many ways to approach the mediation process in order to reduce the potential threat of violence either during or immediately after a mediation session, including shuttle mediation, caucusing, and telephone mediation.

4. Concerns About Mediator Neutrality

Another potential problem in mediations with parties who have a history of domestic violence is mediator neutrality. In theory, what makes mediation unique—and therefore effective—is the fact that a neutral third party acts as a facilitator for the process of negotiating a settlement. But in mediations where the participants have a history of domestic violence, the mediator is tasked with managing power imbalances and remaining vigilant against threats, intimidation, and potential violence. As one scholar has observed, this can be a delicate, difficult balance for the mediator to maintain. * * *

Another scholar agrees that mediator neutrality can be almost impossible to maintain in the face of power imbalances, even when there is no history of domestic violence: "[w]hen a mediator analyzes and attempts to correct a power imbalance, she can no longer claim to be simply a facilitator of the couple's process; rather, she is taking an active role in affecting the outcome of that process." How does the mediator maintain neutrality while at the same time ensuring safety, managing power imbalances, and encouraging fair settlements? Programs have taken a variety of approaches to this challenge, but more needs to be done to assess their effectiveness.

Some victims' advocates take a more extreme stance about the role that the mediator should play in these mediations, arguing that the mediator should not really be neutral at all—instead, the mediator should be responsible for ensuring that the victim gets a fair settlement. One of the problems with this approach is that it puts the mediator in a difficult position. On the one hand, one can see the obvious benefits of focusing on the needs of the victim of violence in mediations, but at the same time the mediator no longer functions as a neutral party. * * * [The author notes that one scholar calls for the mediator being the ongoing monitor of whether the abuser complies with the agreement, and discusses problems with this approach.]

C. Concerns About How a History of Domestic Violence Might Affect Mediation Outcomes

Because of the potential for problems with the mediation process that relate to a couple's history of domestic violence, there are also concerns about mediation outcomes in this context. If the couple is able to come to an agreement as a result of the mediation, that agreement may not reflect the needs or legal rights of the victim. Victims may be so intimidated by their abusers in the mediation that they end up with unfair agreements. Additionally, victims' advocates are concerned that either the mediation or the agreement could increase the chance for further violence.

1. Fairness of Agreements

Victims' advocates and feminist scholars have also expressed concerns that a history of domestic violence can so taint a mediation session that any agreement arrived at is likely to be unfair to the victim. For example, Sarah Buel has argued that "[t]hreats made prior to the session, or one look inside, can force victims to give up rights and remedies to which they are entitled, in exchange for the illusion of safety."

In addition, it may be difficult in a particular situation to determine what constitutes a "fair" agreement. Trina Grillo has observed that a mediator's own personal beliefs about "fairness" have the potential to color the outcomes of mediations. Among possible definitions of a fair agreement, as Grillo lays them out, is "one that closely resembles what the court would have ordered had the case gone to trial." Other mediators "look for an intuitive conception of fairness shared by the parties and, at least to a limited extent, by the mediator." Grillo recognizes the difficulties inherent in this latter definition, as the parties—as well as the mediator—may have differing concepts of fairness. A third approach uses "law not primarily as a set of necessary applied rules, but providing a relevant reference point, both in terms of a practical alternative and as an expression of societal norms and, perhaps, some underlying principles." What the range of definitions of "fairness" reflects is the difficulty of determining what is actually a "fair" outcome of mediation—"fairness" may be in the eye of the beholder.

2. Potential for Future Violence

One concern about mediating cases where the couple has a history of domestic violence is whether the mediation process has the potential to exacerbate or escalate the potential for future violence. Some victims' advocates believe that, as a result of participating in mediation, the victim has a much greater chance of being battered again in the future. Others feel that the risk of future violence is no greater in mediation than it is in the adversarial process, and may in fact be less.

Victims' rights advocates who oppose mediation where domestic violence is at issue are often advocates of the law enforcement model. As described by one scholar, "the law enforcement model advocates formal legal action combined with punishment or rehabilitation of wife abusers," in order to "ensure the safety of the victim and to give the abuser a clear message that society will not tolerate his continued violence against his mate." Law enforcement model advocates argue that the only way to prevent future domestic violence is to use legal processes, such as criminal prosecution of the abuser and civil protection orders for the victims. They believe that the only way to protect the victim is by prosecuting the abuser.

It is undisputable that mediators, mediation program administrators, and court personnel need to be aware of the potential for future violence. One way to reduce the potential for future violence is to focus on the mediation process and train mediators in how to handle the dynamics of family law mediations in this context. Through screening, it seems likely that the more volatile cases that really have a significant threat of future violence would not be scheduled for mediation.

D. Public Policy Concerns

Scholars and victims' advocates are divided about the potential public policy implications of mediating family law cases where there is a history of domestic violence. Some domestic violence victims' advocates argue that mediation, as a matter of public policy, sends the wrong message about domestic violence. They argue that, because domestic violence does not require the abuser to take responsibility for the abusive acts, it "sends a message to both the participants and to society in general that domestic violence is either tolerable, or that both parties are responsible for domestic violence." Others stress the potential positive effects of mediation for the victims, and the possibility that mediation may empower those women to have more of a voice in what happens to their future.

1. Mediation May Put Domestic Violence "in the Shadows"

Because mediation is a private process, victims' advocates are concerned that mediation has the potential to hide domestic violence in the shadows, where it will not be addressed, and creates more potential for violence against victims in the future. As a result, the law enforcement model does not contemplate using mediation to solve family disputes involving domestic violence, because critics feel that mediation "covers up" potential violence and potentially re-victimizes the victims.

Probably the article most cited for arguing against mediation in the context of domestic violence is Lisa G. Lerman's Mediation of Wife Abuse Cases: The Adverse Impact of Informal Dispute Resolution on Women. Lerman, a supporter of the law enforcement model, argues that cases involving domestic violence are never appropriate for mediation and instead should be referred to the courts. Lerman focuses on cases where women are seeking help with domestic violence issues specifically and are directed into mediation as a way to resolve their problems. She believes that mediators avoided dealing with the issue of violence in those mediations, preferring to focus on issues that are simpler to resolve, such as "visitation schedules, financial problems, or time spent with other friends or lovers." Because mediators usually focused on the issues that were easiest to negotiate, mediation agreements tended to address these subsidiary issues rather than addressing the larger issue of domestic violence. In addition, Lerman believes that many mediators view the victims as partially to blame for the violence targeted towards them, thus skewing the mediation even further by encouraging women to accept part of the responsibility for the violence.

The real question is whether Lerman's assumptions hold true in situations where abused women enter into the mediation process for other reasons, for example, to resolve child custody issues or issues related to separation or divorce. Does mediation always have the kind of impact that she assumes it does in these types of situations? Does proper training of mediators help to ensure that the problems that Lerman views within mediation in this context result in a different type of outcome? Or, has even the passage of time made enough difference in public perceptions of domestic violence that what was true when Lerman voiced her initial criticism in 1984 is no longer the case in 2010?

2. Can Mediation Empower Domestic Violence Victims?

In direct contrast to the preceding view, some mediation advocates argue that the mediation process has the potential to empower victims of domestic violence, giving them the tools that they need to create agreements that support their interests and enhance their safety, rather than further victimize them. Sandra Zaher has explained that "mediation can empower the powerless by enabling them to speak in their own voice and assert their own interests, perhaps for the first time." Supporters of this view stress the necessity of having quality mediators involved in a mediation process that safeguards victims' interests and physical safety. In fact, John Haynes, the founding president of the Academy of Family Mediators, has argued that mediation can encourage the victim (and the abuser as well) "to focus . . . on where they are going in their lives as separate, whole, independent people." Some authors have found that such a process can have the effect of empowering the victim in the mediation, rather than solely defining him or her as someone who has been abused.

Of course, not all victims' advocates and scholars agree that mediation can empower victims of domestic violence. Tina Grillo agrees generally that mediation has the ability to empower participants by "permit[ting] persons to speak for themselves and make their own decisions," but not when there is a history of domestic violence. Instead of being empowering, Grillo argues that mediation "would surely be psychologically traumatizing" for a woman to be in a "direct confrontation with [an abusive] husband, with the safety of herself and her children at stake."

II. APPROACHES TO MEDIATION PROGRAM DESIGN TO ADDRESS CONCERNS ABOUT DOMESTIC VIOLENCE

Mediation programs have taken into account many, if not all, of the preceding considerations in their design of mediator training programs, screening protocols, mediation program policies, and approaches to mediations where couples have a history of domestic violence. As a result, many scholars and mediation advocates today believe that mediation can be an effective way to resolve family disputes regarding issues such as divorce proceedings, property allocation, and child custody, even when the parties have a history of domestic violence. The following section analyzes some of the approaches to addressing the potential challenges for mediating in this context.

A. Approaches to Family Mediation Program Design: Pre-Mediation

1. Screening

In response to concerns about inappropriate cases, i.e., cases involving domestic violence, making their way into the mediation process, most mediation programs have developed screening protocols to ensure that cases are appropriate for mediation. Screening can involve written questionnaires and/or interviews, and its purpose is to determine whether there has been domestic violence in the relationship that could interfere with the effectiveness, fairness, or safety of the mediation process for the victim. The Model Code, the Model Standards, and the American Law Institute all require screening of possible family conflict mediation cases for a history of domestic violence, although they do not mandate a particular approach to screening.

Screening requires a thoughtful and careful approach, and the screening process must be confidential. Many victims of domestic violence are reluctant to disclose the violent acts, so screeners must ask questions that go deeper than the surface level. Screeners must be flexible in how they ask questions to anticipate potential problems with mediation, and screenings must occur in a private place that allows victims to feel safe.

Screening programs have come a long way in the past couple of decades. In the early 1980s, there were mediation scholars who advocated screening to determine whether cases involving domestic violence were appropriate for mediation, but Lerman criticized screening because she felt that "screening standards are often amorphous and are not consistently applied." In particular, Lerman criticized Bethel and Singer who, rather than developing specific guidelines for screening, instead stated vague recommendations that " '[w]hatever case intake method is used must provide careful screening of complaints. Those cases suitable for mediation should be identified and preserved, and others should be referred to appropriate legal or social agencies.' " She argued that screening of potential parties for mediation should be much more carefully implemented in the context of domestic violence, and that more carefully defined, specific criteria should be used to determine whether mediation is appropriate. At the outset, the screening process should include questions about potential past violence in disputes between couples or family members. In addition, Lerman believes that those screening for mediation appropriateness should make clear to alleged domestic violence victims that there are other alternatives to mediation. In general, it seems that the vast majority of screening processes today have heeded Lerman's concerns about the need to determine whether domestic violence currently is or has been present in the relationship, although fewer screeners may notify alleged victims of other alternatives to mediation.

[The author discusses written vs. face to face screening, the need to screen all parties regardless of gender for being victims or abusers, what questions should be asked, and specific screening tools being used such as the Conflict Assessment Protocol and the Domestic Violence Evaluation (DOVE) protocol. She notes that DOVE was designed to predict future abuse rather than to assess capability of a survivor of domestic violence to mediate with the abuser.] * * *

2. Mediator Training

[The author outlines need for mediator training on domestic violence dynamics and issues, and the Model Standards of Practice for Divorce and Family Mediators promulgated by the Association of Family and Conciliation Courts, which require such training. She notes that a study showed that only 70% of mediators had domestic violence training on a regular basis, and discusses the California and Ohio approaches to training for mediators on domestic violence.] * * *

Family mediators, without a doubt, should go through some form of domestic violence training in order to be able to recognize cases involving domestic violence and manage the mediation process in a safe and fair manner. At a minimum, that training should include education about how to recognize signs of domestic violence, the power dynamics involved in a relationship in which there is domestic violence, and the psychological effect of violence on the victim. Additionally, mediators must be trained to properly screen for domestic violence, how to use different techniques such as caucusing to manage power imbalances, and how to plan for safety prior to, during, and after mediation sessions. Finally, mediators should receive substantive training in the legal issues associated with domestic violence and what resources are available for victims in the community. To understand more fully how much training is needed, how often mediators should be required to undergo training, and specifically what topics should be included in training sessions, there is a need to study the effectiveness of mediator training programs that already exist.

3. Attorney Training

Although the focus is usually on the need for mediator training programs, some mediators and attorneys also argue that family law attorneys need better training in order to more effectively represent domestic violence victims in mediation—and for that matter, in litigation as well. Most attorneys have not undergone any special training to be able to recognize when family law cases involve domestic violence. This lack of training is significant because most clients do not volunteer that information to their attorneys. Because those same attorneys often request that the court send their clients to mediation, such training could be valuable in helping them to better represent their clients' interests and plan for their clients' safety. In fact, one report has found that "attorneys and judges mishandle an array of domestic violence cases, in part because they lack basic education and knowledge on the issue." In order to provide adequate training, victims' advocates argue that law school courses should incorporate domestic violence issues more often and should sponsor more clinical programs offering legal services for abuse victims.

Family law attorneys should have training in both domestic violence issues and mediation in order to most effectively counsel and advocate for clients who are victims of domestic violence. In particular, appropriate training can help the attorney to act as a screener throughout the process to ensure that the client's safety and interests are protected. Prior to mediation, a well-trained attorney can evaluate whether the case is even appropriate for mediation and can advise clients about other possible legal strategies or remedies. If lawyers are able to recognize their clients' needs, lawyers can also "act as power enhancers and equalizers" during mediation sessions.

4. Mediator-Domestic Violence Professional Collaboration

Scholars have also advocated more collaboration between mediators and domestic violence professionals. One of the key ways that collaboration has occurred has been through mediator training programs. Training organizers now regularly bring in domestic violence advocates to do components of their training, thus improving the level of communication between these two groups of professionals. Very recently, the call for collaboration was renewed once again, with a warning that a failure to collaborate may lead to the mediation community and the domestic violence community sending mixed messages. In some locations, the victims' advocates, family courts, and mediation programs have successfully collaborated to accomplish a number of goals, such as developing screening protocols and coordinating community responses to domestic violence issues. At the same time, the two communities still face significant obstacles to increased collaboration, such as differences in how each defines domestic violence, a mutual lack of trust, and resistance to change.

B. Approaches to Family Mediation Program Design: Mediation Process

Although much of the focus of family mediation specialists and victims' advocates has been on what happens prior to the mediation, such as the development of and use of screening protocols and mediator and attorney training programs, they have also stressed the importance of designing appropriate mediation processes in order to minimize the potential for power imbalances, intimidation, unfair agreements, and further violence or abuse. Much of the attention on the mediation process has been focused on two areas in particular: (1) the form of the mediation session; and (2) the presence of attorneys or support persons in the mediation session. An appropriate mediation process can reduce the potential for future violence and lead to more fair results that protect the legal interests of the victim.

1. Different Approaches to Form

[The author describes mediators meeting with the victim privately before mediation to learn information victim is not comfortable revealing in abuser's presence; caucusing with the parties separately during joint mediation; "shuttle mediation," in which the mediator goes back and forth between the parties who are in separate rooms; and having attorneys in a separate room from each party.] * * *

2. The Role of Attorneys, Support Persons, and Victims' Advocates

Many scholars believe that victims should have the opportunity to be represented by advocates, either by an attorney or by some other person trained in domestic violence victim advocacy. One practitioner has advocated that "each time the court referred a victim to mediation or a mediator discovered domestic violence through screening, a pro bono attorney could be called upon to assist financially indigent victims through the mediation process." In fact, an attorney or another support person in mediations with the victim could help "balance negotiating power and eliminate intimidation and fears of underrepresentation." In addition, an attorney, victims' rights advocate, or other representative could help the victim to articulate his or her concerns within the mediation and provide advice about whether a proposed agreement is actually in the victim's interest.

The Model Standards also stress the value of having parties represented by attorneys in mediation, both in situations in which the couples have a history of domestic violence and those that do not include such a history. Although the Standards state that "[t]he mediator should allow counsel for the parties to be present at the mediation sessions," the Standards also allow the mediator to exclude an attorney from the session if only one party is represented by counsel. In Standard XI, which specifically covers domestic violence issues, the mediator is to "strongly encourage the parties to be represented by counsel or an advocate throughout the mediation process if they are not already," and to "allow[ ] a friend, representative, advocate, or attorney to attend the mediation sessions to support the victim of domestic violence."

The Uniform Mediation Act ("UMA") requires mediators to allow parties to any mediation to bring a support person with them, and thus states that have adopted that provision of the UMA already have that right in place. States that have not adopted the UMA or another statutory provision similar to the support person provision should consider the reasoning behind the provision and institute their own versions of that right, as an attorney or victim's advocate may be necessary to safeguard the legal interests of domestic violence victims. The right to bring a support person is just another way of assuring that procedural safeguards will be maintained throughout the mediation process.

C. Approaches to Family Mediation Program Design: Other Considerations

* * * [The author states that victims can utilize mediation of family issues while also obtaining a protective order and/or proceeding with prosecution in criminal court.]

Additionally, knowledgeable mediators and mediation program administrators may also introduce both victims and abusers to other community and professional resources available to them. For example, some mediation proponents believe that the mediation process, because of its privacy and the role of the neutral mediator, actually encourages the abuser to admit his actions and seek help. Mediators can educate participants about a variety of options that may be available, including:

> batterers' treatment and anger management programs; alcohol and drug treatment; dual-diagnosis consultants and treatment; victim support and treatment; posttraumatic stress groups; therapy; . . . supervised access and exchange facilities; reunification therapists; parenting coordination; assistance in implementing court-ordered parenting plans; treatment for traumatized children; parenting without violence classes; parenting education, skills training, and coaching; custody evaluation; child protection services; protective orders; removal of weapons; criminal penalties; court orders with triggers; suspended or supervised visitation; case management; interpreter services; housing and employment assistance; immigration services; establishing child support and paternity; child care; and advocacy.

Being in a position to offer information about these types of resources requires that mediation programs, supervisors, and mediators be prepared and educated about those resources beforehand. Screeners and mediators should have simple pamphlets and other forms of information readily available for parties, and mediator training programs should educate mediators about the range of resources that are available and how to put victims and their abusers in contact with those resources.

III. STUDIES OF MEDIATION EFFECTIVENESS IN THE DOMESTIC VIOLENCE CONTEXT

* * * No studies thus far have sought to expand the scope of their inquiry into the full range of issues discussed in this Article, including: the connection between mediator training and effective, safe, and fair mediation screening, processes, and outcomes; whether particular types of screening are more effective at identifying cases that should not be mediated or need special protocols in place; what perceptions mediation participants have of the mediator, mediation process, and mediation outcome and how those perceptions correlate, if at all, to mediator training

and process design; comparisons between different programs that have different approaches to these issues; and whether other factors such as the race, ethnicity, income, educational background, etc. of the mediation participants have any influence on what works and does not work in this context. * * *

WISCONSIN CODE § 767.405—FAMILY COURT SERVICES

(2021)

(5) Mediation referrals. (a) Except as provided in sub. (8)(b), in any action affecting the family, including a revision of judgment or order under s. 767.451 or 767.59, in which it appears that legal custody or physical placement is contested, the court shall refer the parties to the director of family court services for possible mediation of those contested issues. The court shall inform the parties of all of the following:. . .

2. That the court may waive the requirement to attend at least one mediation session if the court determines that attending the session will cause undue hardship or would endanger the health or safety of one of the parties and the bases on which the court may make its determination. . . .

(8) Initial session of mediation required. (a) Except as provided in par. (b), in any action affecting the family, including an action for revision of judgment or order under s. 767.451 or 767.59, in which it appears that legal custody or physical placement is contested, the parties shall attend at least one session with a mediator assigned under sub. (6)(a) or contracted with under sub. (7) and, if the parties and the mediator determine that continued mediation is appropriate, no court may hold a trial of or a final hearing on legal custody or physical placement until after mediation is completed or terminated.

(b) A court may, in its discretion, hold a trial or hearing without requiring attendance at the session under par. (a) if the court finds that attending the session will cause undue hardship or would endanger the health or safety of one of the parties. In making its determination of whether attendance at the session would endanger the health or safety of one of the parties, the court shall consider evidence of the following:

1. That a party engaged in abuse, as defined in s. 813.122(1)(a), of the child, as defined in s. 813.122(1)(b).

2. Interspousal battery as described under s. 940.19 or 940.20(1m) or domestic abuse as defined in s. 813.12(1)(am).

3. That either party has a significant problem with alcohol or drug abuse.

4. Any other evidence indicating that a party's health or safety will be endangered by attending the session.

(c) The initial session under par. (a) shall be a screening and evaluation mediation session to determine whether mediation is appropriate and whether both parties wish to continue in mediation. At the initial session, the mediator shall discuss with each of the parties information included in proposed parenting plans under s. 767.41(1m). . .

(10) Powers and duties of mediator. A mediator assigned under sub. (6)(a) shall be guided by the best interest of the child and may do any of the following, at his or her discretion:

(a) Include the counsel of any party or any appointed guardian ad litem in the mediation.

(b) Interview any child of the parties, with or without a party present.

(c) Require a party to provide written disclosure of facts relating to any legal custody or physical placement issue addressed in mediation, including any financial issue permitted to be considered.

(d) Suspend mediation when necessary to enable a party to obtain an appropriate court order or appropriate therapy.

(e) Terminate mediation if a party does not cooperate or if mediation is not appropriate or if any of the following facts exist:

1. There is evidence that a party engaged in abuse, as defined in s. 813.122(1)(a), of the child, as defined in s. 813.122(1)(b).

2. There is evidence of interspousal battery as described under s. 940.19 or 940.20(1m) or domestic abuse as defined in s. 813.12(1)(am).

3. Either party has a significant problem with alcohol or drug abuse.

4. Other evidence which indicates one of the parties' health or safety will be endangered if mediation is not terminated.

[Editor's Note: In "Till Death Do Us Part?!: Online Mediation as an Answer to Divorce Cases Involving Violence," 16 N.C. J. L. & Tech. 253 (2015), Dafna Lavi argues that e-mediation, through emails or video conferencing, is a potentially useful option for resolving disputes between an abusive spouse and a victimized spouse when chosen voluntarily by the parties. She notes that online mediation can be safer than in-person meetings since the parties are not face to face, and that the mediator can screen emails, sending back any that are abusive before the other party sees them. Lavi argues that people tend to be more thoughtful when they communicate in writing, though she admits that some people are more hostile when using email than they would be in person and that emails do not convey feelings particularly well, which can be a disadvantage for the mediator in assessing and managing the parties' communication. She also states that in emails the abuser will not be able to interrupt and control the

other party through using subtle but threatening body language. If parties want to communicate directly through video conferencing, the mediator can caucus with each party separately as needed to maintain a non-abusive interaction. While e-mediation in divorces began in 1996, the author concedes that its use in domestic violence cases has not yet been evaluated. The author calls for specialized training and the development of standards for e-mediators in violent divorce cases, who should already be experienced in face to face mediation. Lavi recommends that online mediation in these cases be examined as an option, using a "reasoned, gradual model," and that independent researchers evaluate this type of e-mediation, based on feedback from parties and mediators.]

NANCY E. JOHNSON, DENNIS P. SACCUZZO, AND WENDY J. KOEN, CHILD CUSTODY MEDIATION IN CASES OF DOMESTIC VIOLENCE: EMPIRICAL EVIDENCE OF A FAILURE TO PROTECT

11(8) Violence Against Women 1022–1053 (2005)
(citations, references, tables, and footnotes omitted)

* * * The issue is whether mediation results in better or poorer outcomes for children when there is domestic violence (DV) than when there is none.

In sum, before mandated child custody mediation can be accepted as an appropriate means for settling disputes, three basic issues must be addressed. First, there is great need for empirical studies examining how well mediators and screening systems recognize and acknowledge DV during the mediation process and what factors are associated with a greater likelihood of acknowledgement. Second, custody and visitation outcomes of mediations and what drives those outcomes need to be evaluated. Finally, it must be ascertained how well mediation addresses child safety and health factors relevant to custody decisions.

METHOD

Materials

San Diego, California was chosen as the site for the study because it is believed to represent one of the best models in the country for sensitivity to issues and handling of DV. The starting point for the study was every single action filed in the Family Court in one Southern California jurisdiction (San Diego) during the calendar year 1996. Every seventh filing was examined. If there was a custody dispute in that filing, it was selected for further study. If there was no custody dispute, the researchers examined each subsequent filing sequentially and selected the first custody dispute that could be identified. From the resultant 948 files cases were eliminated in which the parties resolved the dispute either before or during mediation. All remaining cases were those in which there was a mediation that failed to resolve the dispute, either in full or in part. Each of these 512 mediations therefore resulted in a formal report with custody recommendations by the mediator.

Every one of the 512 non-agreement mediation reports and their associated Court Screening Forms were scanned in their entirety and subsequently printed. These 512 mediation reports were the raw data that were categorized and content analyzed.

The Court Screening Form provided the initial indicators of DV. The form arises out of a number of legislative mandates for the court to screen in areas such as child abuse, DV, and special needs (e.g., language interpreters). The questions relevant to this study included:

1. Does either parent allege domestic violence?
2. Will either parent request to be seen separately?
3. Are there any domestic violence restraining orders?
4. Are there allegations of child abuse?
5. Is Child Protective Services involved with your family?

These five questions meet the letter of the legislative mandate for the court to screen for DV, but fail to identify DV in a number of cases in which there has been no prior involvement with the court, law enforcement, or social services. If the victim chooses not to self-identify as a DV victim, then the screening will be entirely ineffective.

Mediation reports ranged from 2 to 11 pages in length and in general, contained two sections: in one, the mediator made detailed recommendations about custody and visitation. In the other, the mediator wrote a narrative describing the mediation process and the rationale for any recommendations given. Each report also contained an appended page, containing a detailed parenting plan in which the mediator summarized the percentage of physical custody recommended for each parent. The reports in this sample represent the work of at least twenty-five mediators, each of whom completed mandatory training in DV as required by California court rules and the California Judicial Council. * * *

DISCUSSION

Present results provide data in terms of baseline frequencies and insights into the process and outcome of mediation in general and mediated DV custody disputes in particular. Strong evidence was found indicating that mediators often failed to recognize and report DV even when there were clear indicators of DV. In addition, the court screening form very often failed in signaling the existence of abuse. To the extent that the court relies on the mediator's report, the intent of the legislature that the court assess and address DV is not well served.

It would appear that evidence of criminal justice involvement and other clear indicators of DV do increase the odds that DV will be acknowledged. Moreover, the general finding was that when the mediator documented an independent DV indicator such as police involvement, the mediator was more likely to document the DV than not. Nevertheless, the DV was ignored in an alarming number of these cases.

The findings in which the mediator reported substance abuse or psychiatric treatment but failed to acknowledge or address the DV are consistent with the hypothesis that the mediator anchored on some problem other than the DV. Such an interpretation is consistent with decision theory applied to criminal justice system choice points. Under such a view, the mediator may lose sight of DV because of the saliency of substance abuse or psychiatric treatment. It appeared in several cases that the enormity of the disintegration of one parent obliterated all other factors. Whether the disintegration was due to the schizophrenia of the mother or the alcohol addiction of the father, this disintegration became the focus, and the safety risks associated with DV were not adequately considered. In addition, the presence of DV often serves to obscure the relevance of other risk factors that might alert the system to potential risks to victims.

Mediator recommendations for custody and visitation are critical to evaluating the outcome of the custody mediation, especially as it relates to safety protections for DV victims and their children. Overall, legal and physical custody arrangements stemming from mediation resulted in poor outcomes for victims of DV. In spite of the known dangers of joint custody arrangement in cases involving DV, joint legal custody was recommended in the overwhelming majority of DV cases, in fact even more so than in non-DV. It is important to note that our sample represents mediated non-agreement cases only, and represents the mediators' recommendations rather than the final orders of the judge. Nevertheless, it is interesting that the mediators in fact recommended joint custody far more often than they believed based on their stated estimates.

The physical custody arrangements were no more encouraging. Based on the mediator's estimates, the mediator recommended primary physical custody for the mother and joint physical custody with the same frequency in DV and non-DV cases. Fathers who were perpetrators of DV were awarded custody at an alarming rate, and even more disheartening, based on the mediators' estimates reported to the court, mediators recommended primary physical custody for the father significantly more often in DV cases than in non-DV cases. The most frequently expressed reason for the recommendation was that custody with a violent father would be less disruptive to the children. This explanation does not adequately justify the risky decision. In addition, results concerning the mediators' reports of their estimated time sharing arrangements indicate gender bias as well as a propensity to underestimate time given to batterer fathers. This supports previous findings that gender bias frequently has been an element in custody disputes.

These findings also cast doubt on the likelihood that the safety of DV victims and their children can be adequately addressed through the process of child custody mediation, even in cases in which DV is acknowledged by the mediator. It is distressing that documented concerns about the mother's safety had essentially no bearing on the likelihood that the mediator would recommend supervised visitation and that there is a higher percentage of protected child exchanges when there are no indicators of DV.

Present findings offer evidence that the children may be placed in greater jeopardy when DV is alleged at all. For instance, when there were no DV indicators but the mediator documented police involvement, supervised visitation was recommended more often compared to cases with any DV indicators. The least likely to be protected by supervised visitation were the cases with a DV indicator not acknowledged by the mediator. A second example is when the mediator documented concerns for the child's safety. In such cases, supervised visitation was recommended 50% of the time when there were no DV indicators, 38.8% of the time when there were DV indicators, and only 31.3% of the time when there were DV indicators but the mediator did not acknowledge them. Because victim-acknowledged DV that is not reported by mediators has such a damaging effect on safety precautions for victims and their children, it appears essential to implement strategies to ensure that DV is not only routinely accounted for in mediation reports, but that it is explicitly taken into account in visitation and exchange recommendations.

The increased odds of supervised visitation in the presence of documented child safety concerns and parental drug use are in the direction we would hope to see to provide protection for the child against an abusive or incompetent parent. In contrast, when the mediator acknowledged difficulties with child exchanges, the recommendation was only about one fifth as likely to contain supervised visitation as when no child exchange difficulties were raised. This is not what one would expect. Assuming that difficulties with child exchanges are relevant primarily to protect the DV victim during the exchange, we would expect to see supervised visitation recommended at least equally as often when there are exchange difficulties as when there are not. However, this was not the case. The mediator's acknowledgement of child exchange difficulties greatly lowered the likelihood of supervised visitation. It would seem that within the context of DV, when the mediator finds child exchange difficulties relevant enough to acknowledge, then protection of the child during visitation is for the most part lost, as revealed in the marked reduction in the chances of supervised visitation when such difficulties are noted.

Our findings on supervised visitation are consistent with a general pattern observed throughout our analyses: the presence of DV does not increase protections for the victim, whether child or parent. In fact at best, victims get a comparable level of protection; at worst, they get less protection. At this point, there are a few hypotheses. One would be that mediators become so focused on the need to protect the parent victim during difficult child exchanges that they lose sight of the need to protect the child from abusive or incompetent non-custodial parents. Another hypothesis is that when the DV rises to a certain level of relevance in the mediator's attention, it tends to obscure other considerations. For example, when mediators acknowledged DV as well as parental drug use, they were less likely to recommend supervised visitation than when they acknowledged only drug abuse and not the DV. Finally, the mediator may erroneously assume that violence on the part of one parent against the other does not signify any risk for the children (the idea that spousal violence says nothing about parenting). More extensive training in domestic violence and its co-occurrence with child abuse might assist these mediators to recognize the dangers to children and to keep them salient in the decision process.

According to the present results, the ability of mediators to focus on the best interest of the children is called into question. What mediators recall in post hoc retrospective studies and what they clearly communicate in their formal reports to the court are two different things. For example, a report of mediator retrospective descriptions of the topics addressed in mediation indicated the main topics discussed in "each mediation session." According to the report, common themes discussed in each mediation session included such factors as the child's adjustment, developmental needs, or special needs. Results indicate that these topics are hardly covered in the majority of mediation reports. Although demographic information about the children appeared to be gathered consistently, it is of great concern that child health and safety concerns were addressed minimally. Clearly, these topics are of vital importance, as confirmed by Whiteside and others. Based on our findings, we must conclude that either the reports are not an accurate reflection of what was actually discussed or the topics are simply not covered with anywhere near the frequency needed. In either case, the result is an inadequate communication to the court.

It must be acknowledged that the known variables related to a child's adjustment are incorporated by most mediation reports in an inconsistent and haphazard manner. This finding suggests that the best interests of the child are frequently glossed over or ignored. Steps are needed to ensure that topics regarding child health and safety are discussed in all cases, including those that do not reach agreement. One such step would be the use of a standardized format for custody mediation.

It is becoming clear that mediation is not effective in custody disputes involving families with histories of DV. Although post hoc satisfaction surveys have indicated positive outcomes for families who have mediated, these surveys fail to capture the true picture. Assessment and screening systems are inadequate to identify DV victims. Even when properly identified, DV victims were not adequately protected through mediation. Victims of DV should not be mandated to comply with a process that greatly disadvantages them and results in life-altering agreements that put them and their children at greater risk for further abuse.

*[Editor's Note: In "Intimate Partner Violence and Family Dispute Resolution: 1-Year Follow-up Findings From a Randomized Controlled Trial Comparing Shuttle Mediation, Videoconferencing Mediation, and Litigation," 27(4) Psychology, Pub Pol & L 581 (2021), Holtzworth-Munroe et al report that they compared three different processes in **196** cases with high levels of intimate partner violence: shuttle mediation (in which the mediator goes back and forth between the parents), videoconferencing, and litigation. They were able to contact 50% of the original participants by phone. There were no significant differences across conditions in parent reports of satisfaction with the process, level of continuing IPV or interparental conflict, parenting quality, parent functioning, child functioning, relitigation rates in family or criminal court, or study-related IPV incidents.*

They found that parents in videoconferencing, versus those in shuttle mediation, reported more PTSD symptoms from IPV, which is concerning, and that parents in traditional litigation reported significantly more social support (people coming with them) when they went to court than those in mediation. The researchers concluded that the 1-year outcomes do not clearly favor mediation or litigation, and that if both parents are willing to mediate and there are IPV safety protocols, a protected environment and well-trained staff, mediation may be an appropriate alternative to traditional litigation.]

B. RESTORATIVE AND TRANSFORMATIVE JUSTICE

JUDGE BENNETT BURKEMPER & NINA BALSAM, EXAMINING THE USE OF RESTORATIVE JUSTICE PRACTICES IN DOMESTIC VIOLENCE CASES

27 St. Louis U. Pub. L. Rev. 121 (2007)
(citations and footnotes omitted)

I. INTRODUCTION

Restorative Justice is a way of looking at crime that focuses on identifying and healing the harm to the victim, holding the offender accountable, and involving the community of people affected by the crime. Despite the fact that restorative justice practices have proven quite beneficial to victims who choose to participate, advocates against domestic violence have been justifiably wary about their use with victims/survivors. This Comment will explore the use of restorative justice practices in domestic violence situations and argues that at least some of these practices can be safely and beneficially used given an understanding of the dynamics of domestic violence, careful planning, and responsiveness to the needs of domestic violence victims/survivors. Sections II and III provide an overview of restorative justice principles and practices while Section IV examines how these principles and practices apply to victims and Section V explains why victims might want to engage in restorative justice practices. Section VI covers those special considerations that should be taken into account when using restorative justice in domestic violence cases because of the particular dynamics of domestic violence. Section VII describes how practices that account for these considerations should be constructed. Section VIII describes actual practices that have successfully taken these considerations into account. Finally, Section IX describes an emerging project in Missouri that takes these considerations into account.

II. RESTORATIVE JUSTICE PRINCIPLES

Although restorative justice practices have been increasingly utilized in the adult and juvenile justice systems, restorative justice remains a relatively unknown concept in the United States.

Commonly defined as a "process to involve, to the extent possible, those who have a stake in a specific offense and to collectively identify and address harms, needs, and obligations, in order to heal and put things as right as possible," restorative justice differs widely from the traditional retributive philosophy that underlies most criminal justice systems. While the central focus in traditional criminal courts is that a crime is a violation of the law for which the state imposes punishment, restorative justice focuses on the harm to the victim most affected by the crime and how to make that person whole. In the traditional system, the offender may be held "accountable" by the imposition of punishment; through restorative justice, however, the offender may be held accountable not only by taking responsibility but also by making amends. Unlike the traditional justice system, restorative practices involve not only the offender and the victim but the community as well. The community is integral in addressing harm to victims and holding offenders accountable.

Victims given an opportunity to meet their offenders through restorative justice processes are generally more satisfied with the criminal justice system and less fearful of being re-victimized. Further, offenders who participated in a restorative justice have a personal connection with, and understand the impact of the crime on, their victims and, as a result, comply with agreements at a higher rate than with court orders in which they have little or no input. Offenders recidivate at lower rates than those who do not go through a restorative justice process. In addition to lowering recidivism rates, restorative processes save time and money. The community benefits by providing an increased sense of involvement in the methods by which crime is addressed in that there is greater collaboration among community members and greater satisfaction for and increased confidence within the criminal justice system.

III. RESTORATIVE JUSTICE PRACTICES

Various models of restorative justice are being utilized in the United States and throughout the world. This section presents the most widely used Restorative Justice Models which include: Victim Offender Dialogue; Family Group Conferences; Community Accountability Boards; Restorative Justice Circles; and Victim Impact Panels.

A. Victim Offender Dialogue

Victim Offender Dialogue (VOD) is the form of restorative justice most commonly used in the United States. As its name indicates, the victim and the offender are the primary actors in a conference that is facilitated by a trained mediator. The goal of a VOD model is to allow the victim and the offender to meet, for the victim to be able to explain the effects of the crime on him/her, and to hold the offender accountable. VOD generally results in a mutual agreement, the terms of which focus on healing the harm to the victim and holding the offender accountable. Agreements are reached and complied with in the vast majority of these cases. Dialogues can be used at any point in the criminal justice system, including as a diversion from prosecution, as an alternative to trying the case, as a condition of probation, or even after the offender has been incarcerated. The use of these dialogues was endorsed by the American Bar Association in 1994.

B. Family Group Conferences

Family Group Conferences (FGC) are similar to VODs in structure and purpose but FGCs include a larger group of conference participants by including family members of both the victim and the offender, members of the community and any other interested parties. The FGC model recognizes the empowerment of the family and its impact on the healing process after a crime is committed. Conferences are used, to a large extent, in juvenile cases.

C. Community Accountability Boards

Community Accountability Boards involve community members who make up the Board, and offenders and victims and their families and supporters. The Board, along with the other participants, decides how an offense will be addressed and most board meetings end with reparation agreements comprised of restitution, if applicable, and community service. Similar to the FGC model, Boards are often used in juvenile cases, but can be used in adult probation settings.

D. Restorative Justice Circles

The Restorative Justice Circles model, similar to the FGC model, includes victims, offenders, other interested parties and members of the community. Participants are arranged in a circle and a "talking piece" is passed from person to person to ensure each participant has an opportunity to speak to the individualized effects of the offense, the conditions leading to the offense, and appropriate ways to address healing for the victim and the community. In the criminal context, the circles model is employed to address sentencing and may even include the judge and prosecutor. Circles are also used in school settings for discipline cases and have been used in other settings, such as workplace disputes, to resolve conflict or provide support for participants.

E. Victim Impact Panels

Victim Impact Panels involve victims meeting with offenders with whom they have not had previous contact so that the victims can explain the impact of the crime on them. These panels help victims heal by allowing victims to explain the harm caused to them and help offenders develop an understanding of the impact on victims so they are less likely to recidivate. * * *

V. WHY A VICTIM MIGHT WANT TO ENGAGE IN RESTORATIVE JUSTICE

* * * As for domestic violence cases, three National Institute of Justice (NIJ) grant reports found significant dissatisfaction among victims having gone through the traditional court system. Satisfaction was directly related to whether the victim felt she had some control of the process and the outcome. Consequently, dissatisfaction led to reluctance to report incidents to the police in the future. One study found that some victims did not want to separate from their abuser or want their abuser to go to jail; they just wanted the abuse to stop. * * *

VI. SPECIAL CONSIDERATIONS IN DOMESTIC VIOLENCE CASES

While all crime victims are emotionally affected by the trauma of the event and might find it difficult to interact with the offender, these effects hold particularly true in cases of domestic violence. Because abuse is often part of the historical and intimate relationship, victims/survivors are traditionally afraid of, and intimidated by, the offender. A victim/survivor may believe, quite accurately in some cases, that the offender may try to intimidate or even harm her if she is part of a process that holds him accountable.

However, because of the benefits that restorative justice can bring to victims, some domestic violence victims/survivors may want to engage in such a process, and that engagement may very well benefit them. So, the question is, how should a process be constructed that takes into account the aforementioned special considerations and is most potentially beneficial to the victim/survivor?

VII. CONSTRUCT CONSIDERATIONS

In any construct, attention must be paid to a number of issues. First, the stage at which the restorative justice encounter occurs can be of utmost importance. If the victim/survivor is afraid of being hurt by the offender, she will not be comfortable meeting with him without protections being available. She also may not be able to encounter him if he is not in custody. This might militate against the encounter occurring outside of a prison setting.

Second, the circumstances in which the process occurs should be carefully considered. For example, a victim/survivor who is afraid of being hurt by the offender and still feels intimidated by him might not want to meet with him at all, which militates in favor of a surrogate process. This surrogate process provides for a victim/survivor to meet with an offender, but not the perpetrator of the crime against her.

Third, the preparation that both the victim/survivor and the offender receive prior to engagement is critical. Ideally, victims/survivors should be supported through the restorative justice process by a victim advocate who is aware of and trained in the dynamics of domestic violence. The victim/survivor should undergo a screening assessment to determine whether she is emotionally ready for the encounter and will be safe during the process. The screening should also assess whether the victim's/survivor's reasons for wanting to be involved are realistic and appropriate. Offenders should also be screened to minimize the risk of re-victimization. They must be ready to take responsibility for their actions and want to stop their abusive behavior. Thereafter, each party should receive an orientation to the restorative process in which they will engage and be prepared to talk about the issues of importance. Each party should also be informed of the issues that may be brought up by the other party.

Fourth, persons who facilitate restorative justice practices with victims/survivors and offenders must be well-trained in both the dynamics of domestic violence and facilitation of restorative justice encounters. Mediation training is insufficient because the format, assumptions, and desired results are often very different in a restorative justice process. In addition, the facilitator must be skilled enough to pick up nuances that might indicate that the victim is no longer safe or comfortable and either re-direct or stop the proceedings.

Fifth, support for the victim/survivor through the process is also essential. In addition to the numerous factors warranting support discussed above, victims/survivors often do not get support for their experience due to victim-blaming by their families, communities, and some members of the criminal justice system. Therefore, it is important that an advocate accompany the victim/survivor through the process and that she has access to a support system of both peers and professionals who will validate her experience.

Finally, offenders need support for accepting responsibility for their actions and changing their beliefs and behaviors. Again, their family, community, and some members of the criminal justice system may serve to reinforce their beliefs and their abusive behavior. Therefore, it is important for offenders to have a community of people who encourage and support change.

VIII. CONSTRUCTS THAT WORK

Three widely differing models show promise in leading to greater healing for victims/survivors and transformation of offenders. Each of these models has been in existence long enough to have quantitative outcomes or anecdotal evidence demonstrating that the process benefits the victim/survivor and the offender.

The Surrogate Victim/Offender Dialogue Program (SVODP) is a model operating in Washington County, Oregon and is co-sponsored by Washington County Community Corrections and the Center for Victim Services. The program is driven by victims/survivors requesting to participate who are referred by a local shelter or from another referral source. These victims/survivors meet with perpetrators of domestic violence who are in prison and with whom they have had no previous relationship.

Victims/survivors who participate in the SVODP project are carefully screened for readiness based on whether the victim: attended counseling through a shelter or a domestic violence counseling program; expressed a desire to talk to an offender as part of her journey toward healing; has a clear personal outcome goal for the session; and has been warned by her counselor of the possible outcomes of the dialogue. To increase the victim's sense of safety and control in the situation, she may terminate participation in the session at any time.

Offenders are also carefully screened and prepared for the dialogue. Among other criteria, the offender must have: accepted responsibility for his actions; a desire to make a change in his life; consistently attended a batterers intervention program; talked with his counselor about feelings of anger that might occur during the session; and a clear personal outcome goal for the session.

Outcomes from the Surrogate Victim/Offender Dialogue Program are anecdotal as it is currently a pilot project. However, victims report they experience both empowerment and increased healing through involvement; one measure of this is the waiting list of victims interested in participating.

The second model is Family Group Conferencing (FGC) used in child maltreatment cases that include the co-occurrence of domestic violence. The cases are referred by Child Welfare, Adult (Parole and Probation), and Youth Corrections. The program, called the Family Group Decision Making Project, was started and administered by Dr. Joan Pennell, Ph.D. in Newfoundland and Labrador, Canada and has been continued by Dr. Pennell at North Carolina State University.

The foundation position for the program is: 1) domestic violence and child maltreatment often happen in the same family; 2) family violence isolates child and adult victims from their support and breeds secrecy; 3) even after batterers leave, women and children may suffer post-traumatic stress disorder; and 4) FGC helps build or rebuild informal and formal supports to keep family members safe. In order to have safe conferencing, the program needs to: 1) build partnerships with women's advocates, children's advocates, and the legal system; 2) perform safety assessment for each referral and then decide whether to hold the FGC; 3) determine safety measures for holding an FGC by consulting with survivors and other support; 4) proceed with caution; and 5) respect the strengths of family members.

A great deal of time is spent on safety planning and preparing the victim/survivor for the conference through developing a support system of family and friends, some of whom will be present at the conference. Many hours are also spent on building a support system that encourages the offender to take responsibility for his actions and commit to stopping the abuse. The conference is attended by the victim/survivor, the offender, and their family and friends. Institutional representatives are also present, but the family meets separately to develop a plan. The plan focuses on how the family will help the victim take care of the children, support the victim in living violence-free, and support the offender in transforming. The plan must then be approved by the institutional representatives.

Outcomes from The Family Group Decision Making Project are quite promising in terms of reducing child maltreatment and domestic violence and, no conference has reported any violence. Further, in interviews with 115 participating families, 66% believed they were better off after the conference. According to a review of Child Welfare files, child protection events were reduced from 233 pre-conference to 117 post-conference versus an increase in the comparison group of 129 before and 165 after. Child welfare files showed a reduction from 84 to 34 events in mother/wife abuse versus an increase in the comparison group from 45 to 52.

Even more significant are the outcomes that relate to beliefs about male domination in relationships that may lead to domestic violence, and the behaviors beyond abuse that reflect power and control in the relationship. The study measured family dynamics, including the abuser's domination of the conversation and control of economic resources. In interviews, participants revealed that domination of the conversation was reduced from four to two these incidents pre versus post conference and control of economic resources was reduced from four to zero incidents. For the comparison group, domination of the conversation remained at two incidents pre versus post study and control of economic resources increased from three to four incidents. In terms of emotional abuse, men in the study belittled their partners in five incidents pre-study versus three post-study while these incidents increased in the comparison group. The study also measured the batterer's minimization of violence, transference of responsibility for the violence to the victim, and refusal to accept responsibility for the abuse. For families involved in the study, these incidents were reduced from eight pre-study to three post-study while incidents in the comparison group increased from four to six. Finally, the study measured the batterer's rigid adherence to sex roles, including expecting or demanding that his partner serve him, and noted a reduction in these beliefs from three to one in participating families while remaining constant in the control group.

The third model, Circle Sentencing (CS), is used in selective domestic violence cases at the Tubman Family Alliance in Minnesota. Circle Sentencing is employed in criminal cases where the victim wishes to participate and the offender admits guilt and articulates a desire to change. Generally, the victim, offender, family, friends of both the victim and offender, and members of the criminal justice system are involved in the CS process. The group mutually determines the offender's sentence and what the offender needs to do to repair the harm to the victim. Follow-up meetings are held to oversee compliance with the agreement reached. Additionally, Healing Circles are offered for support of victims. Twenty domestic violence cases have been handled through CS since 1998, and 95% of those offenders have not re-offended. * * *

[The authors describe using Victim Impact Panels in domestic violence cases in Missouri, with victims who are not related to the offenders talking to them about the impact of the crime. Panels include a family member and grown child of a survivor, a family member of an offender, a prior rehabilitated offender, and community members such as law enforcement, business leaders, elected officials, and faith leaders. Because it uses community members, it is similar to the Family Group Conferencing Model.]

Perpetrators who attend the Panels come from the Court's Order of Protection docket where they are initially ordered to participate in a batterer's intervention program. After sufficient progress in the batterer's intervention program and thorough screening, they attend a Victim Impact Panel. Those perpetrators deemed not ready to be personally involved in the Panels due to the danger of them re-victimizing will be able to watch a video tape that will be made of one of the panels.

One panel has been held so far, with outcomes showing increased understanding by perpetrators of the impact of their crime. Victims also show greater healing and empowerment, which seems to increase with time.

X. CONCLUSION

Restorative Justice Practices have been used in domestic violence situations and have resulted in greater victim healing and changes in offender beliefs and behaviors. While not all victims will want to engage in restorative justice practices, those that desire to participate should be given the opportunity. However, to help to ensure victim safety, programs should be developed by individuals with an understanding of the dynamics of domestic violence who will keep the special considerations articulated in this Comment in mind as they create the protocols for the program.

[Editor's Note: Domestic Violence Restorative Circles, offered by Men As Peacemakers in Minnesota, include men who have been incarcerated for DV and are on probation as well as 4–5 community volunteers trained in DV dynamics. The circles meet weekly for 7–8 months and focus on the abuser's taking responsibility for his past actions, repairing harm, committing himself to not using violence in the future, etc. The survivor of DV is not directly involved though is invited to be in a separate Support Circle to obtain various types of support; most survivors decline this offer. No data nor an evaluation of the outcomes of the restorative circles was provided on the website, menaspeacemakers.org, last visited 1/26/24.]

LEIGH GOODMARK, "LAW AND JUSTICE ARE NOT ALWAYS THE SAME": CREATING COMMUNITY-BASED JUSTICE FORUMS FOR PEOPLE SUBJECTED TO INTIMATE PARTNER ABUSE

42 Fla. St. U. L. Rev. 707 (2015)
(footnotes omitted)

* * * I. B. Restorative Justice

* * * While feminist antiviolence efforts and restorative justice share a number of principles, feminists have expressed concern about using restorative justice in cases of intimate partner abuse. Sociologist James Ptacek groups those concerns into three general categories: safety, accountability, and political concerns. First, feminists are concerned that restorative justice practitioners fail to understand and respect the unique characteristics of, and challenges posed by, intimate partner abuse and, as a result, do not account for the dangers such cases can present in their program design. Second, feminists express skepticism that offenders will actually be held accountable for their actions through restorative justice, viewing such initiatives as "cheap-justice." Third, feminists fear that turning to restorative justice and other alternatives to the criminal justice system risks obscuring the fact that intimate partner abuse is a crime and decreases the power of women to demand action from the criminal justice system.

Nonetheless, restorative justice could provide an alternative to what some characterize as an ineffectual criminal justice system response in cases involving intimate partner abuse. Sociologist Lawrence Sherman, who published some of the earliest research on arrest policy in cases involving intimate partner abuse, points out, "Since there is no evidence that standard justice is any more effective than doing nothing in response to an incident of domestic violence, the only challenge to restorative justice is to do better than doing nothing." Moreover, studies suggest that restorative justice processes may provide greater procedural justice for people subjected to intimate partner abuse than the traditional criminal justice system.

C. Transformative Justice

Concerned about the application of restorative justice to cases involving intimate partner abuse but interested in looking beyond the criminal justice system for responses to such cases, law professor Donna Coker articulated a vision for deploying what some scholars have called transformative justice. Transformative justice shares some of the core beliefs of restorative justice: skepticism about the effectiveness of the criminal justice system and a commitment to the idea that harm, not crime, should be the touchstone for intervention. Law professor Angela Harris notes two crucial differences between the two, however. First, transformative justice is explicitly centered on principles of antisubordination. As Harris writes, "The aim of transformative justice is to recognize and grapple with the complicated ways in which race, gender, and other modes of domination are mutually entwined . . . . [E]ach incident of personal violence should be understood in a larger context of structural violence." Second, Harris explains, transformative justice recognizes that restorative justice's reliance on the state and on institutions like "community" or "family" may be problematic, given the power imbalances that inhere in these institutions. While transformative justice is focused on security, it recognizes that no one vision of security will address the needs of all who suffer harm. Law professor Erin Daly has suggested that transformative justice must be contextual—transformative justice is deeply rooted in the time, place, and particular circumstances of the community seeking justice.

In the context of intimate partner abuse cases, transformative justice is concerned with creating and empowering communities, defined not through traditional institutions, but by people subjected to abuse. Those communities are charged with supporting the autonomy of people subjected to abuse. While reintegration of abusers into the community may be a goal, that goal is secondary to the restoration of their partners' autonomy. Transformative justice projects consider the relationship between abusers' own oppression and their use of abusive tactics but do not excuse such behavior as a result of economics, racism, heterosexism, or other indicia of oppression. Law professor Donna Coker sees transformative justice as expanding the range of responses available to people subjected to abuse without exposing them to the dangers inherent in the criminal justice system and traditional restorative justice practices. Transformative justice recognizes that communities share accountability for intimate partner abuse when they fail to prevent harm from occurring or when they promote harm, but it focuses on the community's capacity to safeguard those who experience intimate partner abuse.

Transformative justice seeks to improve the community's ability to respond to intimate partner abuse. Transformative justice projects provide community members with the skills to address intimate partner abuse and assess accountability on both the individual and the community levels. Creative Interventions, a transformative justice project in Oakland, California, has developed a number of tools and projects to address intimate partner abuse, including the Storytelling and Organizing Project (STOP) and the Community-Based Intervention Project. STOP collects stories of community engagement around incidents of intimate partner abuse, using the stories to inform others about how those interventions were carried out and what lessons were learned. Mimi Kim, the founder of Creative Interventions, explains that using such stories subverts the dominant paradigm of intervention by state actors "by privileging stories of violence intervention carried out within the spheres of home, family, friendships, work, and community." In partnership with a number of other organizations working to end gender violence, Creative Interventions created the Community-Based Intervention Project, a community-organizing model focused on recruiting allies and training community facilitators—not professionals, but individuals who are from the community, familiar with the parties, understand the contextual dynamics of intimate partner abuse, and are removed from the crisis itself—to respond to discrete incidents of abuse.

* * * Another possibility for bringing transformative justice to life is through the creation of community-based justice forums centered on certain key principles. * * *

Conclusion

* * * "Prosecutions will never be enough on their own .... [M]any women will not seek justice in this way." People subjected to abuse need not be limited to the systems of justice currently available to them through the state. We can design justice, and we can, through the creation of alternative justice systems, design it in ways that specifically address their needs. Community-based alternative justice mechanisms could provide people subjected to intimate partner abuse with the kind of individualized justice they seek, justice that is attentive to the need for voice, validation, and vindication. Such systems need not displace the state response to intimate partner abuse but could provide an alternative forum for those who are unwilling to engage with the state or who cannot meet their justice goals through retributive state-based systems. At the very least, thinking about the development of alternatives to the criminal justice response to intimate partner abuse should highlight the ways in which the retributive system fails to meet the needs of some people subjected to abuse for justice. Moreover, designing alternative systems of justice suggests alterations that could be made within the criminal justice system—for example, greater input into decisions about arrest, prosecution, and sentencing—that would better meet the individualized justice goals of people subjected to abuse. Around the world, in a variety of contexts and communities, people are seeking and finding justice outside of state-annexed criminal justice systems. Why not make those same opportunities available to people subjected to abuse in the United States?

DONNA COKER, ENHANCING AUTONOMY FOR BATTERED WOMEN: LESSONS FROM NAVAJO PEACEMAKING

47 UCLA L. Rev. 32–38, 101–107 (1999)
(citations and footnotes omitted)

I. DOMESTIC VIOLENCE CASES IN PEACEMAKING

* * * B. Peacemaking: Theory and Practice

Ultimately ... the greater necessity is that [tribal court] decisionmaking craft a jurisprudence reflecting the aspiration and wisdom of traditional cultures seeking a future of liberation and self-realization in which age-old values may continue to flourish in contemporary circumstances.

Though the Peacemaker Courts were first established in 1982, they were largely ignored until 1991, when the Supreme Court of the Navajo Nation began a push to reinvigorate modern Navajo law with Navajo common law. In an endeavor to bring about cultural and social reform as well as legal reform, the Navajo Supreme Court is attempting to integrate traditional Navajo law into all adjudicatory functions. The general premise is that Anglo justice, described as hierarchal and "win-lose," has failed the Navajo. They argue that the only hope for Navajo people is a return to the problem-solving methods that worked in early Navajo history. *[Editor's Note: Many members of this tribe prefer to use their original name, Dine, rather than Navajo, since Navajo was a pejorative name assigned to them by another tribe.]*

The Honorable Robert Yazzie, Chief Justice for the Supreme Court of the Navajo Nation, contrasts the Navajo concept of "horizontal" justice with the Anglo "vertical" system of justice. The latter uses coercion and power, focuses on finding "truth," and limits standing to parties who claim direct injury, and its criminal law focuses on establishing guilt. In contrast, horizontal justice systems have a much wider "zone of dispute" and rely on moral suasion rather than coercion and power. The emphasis in horizontal justice systems is on healing rather than on guilt. Yazzie argues that the term " 'guilt' implies a moral fault which commands retribution," but the end goal of Navajo law is not fault finding but "integration with the group" accomplished through "nourishing ongoing relationships with the immediate and extended family, relatives, neighbors and community." Thus, Peacemaking is premised on traditional Navajo jurisprudence in which "law is not a process to punish or penalize people, but to teach them how to live a better life. It is a healing process that either restores good relationships among people or, if they do not have good relations to begin with, fosters and nourishes a healthy environment."

Traditional Navajo thinking does not separate religious and secular life; rather, all of life is sacred and imbued with spiritual meaning. The concept of *k'e*, fundamental to Navajo common law, expresses an interdependence and respect for relationships between humans, the natural world, individuals and family, and individuals and clan members. This interdependence operates to define Navajo common law, which derives from relational frameworks in which "responsibilities to clan members are part of a sophisticated system that defines rights, duties, and mutual obligations." "The individual and the community are part of the kinship that exists among all life forms and the environmental elements. Harmony is the desired result of the relationship with all life forms, including humans, animals, and plants." Relational justice does not necessitate the subordination of the individual, however. Traditional Navajo thought and law are radically egalitarian and eschew coercion. Individuals do not speak for others, not even for members of their own family.

These concepts of relational justice provide the foundation for the practice of Peacemaking. In Peacemaking, parties meet with a peacemaker and others who have either a special relationship to the parties (e.g., family and friends) or relevant expertise (e.g., alcohol treatment counselors and hospital social workers). Each participant is given a chance to describe the problem that the petitioner has identified as the reason for the session. The peacemaker then leads the group in developing recommendations and agreements designed to ameliorate or solve the problem.

Peacemaking is structured around procedural steps. It begins with an opening prayer in both Navajo and English. After the peacemaker has explained the rules, the petitioner is allowed to explain his or her complaint. The respondent is then asked to respond to the petitioner's complaint. Next, the peacemaker provides a "[b]rief overview of the problem as presented by the disputants." Family members and other participants, including traditional teachers, may then join the discussion, providing their description or explanation of the problem(s).

The peacemaker, usually chosen by his or her chapter, is a respected person with a demonstrated knowledge of traditional Navajo stories. He or she must be someone who possesses the power of persuasion, because peacemakers do not judge or decide cases. Their power lies in their words and their influence. Peacemakers "show a lot of love, they use encouraging words, [when you] use [Navajo] teaching to lift [participants] up you can accomplish a lot, [if you] are very patient."

Peacemaking may be hard for outside observers to understand, because it seems to combine so many different things: mediation, restorative justice, therapeutic intervention, family counseling, and Navajo teaching. Understanding is also made more difficult because of the significant differences in the practice of various peacemakers and the different approaches used for different kinds of problems. Peacemaking practice is fluid, flexible, and thoroughly practical, fitting the process to the situation. As Phil Bluehouse, coordinator for the Peacemaker Division, relates:

> [I]f there's no flexibility [in peacemaking], we'll be doing a disservice. . . . [I] prefer [the] middle ground leaning more towards flexibility, because to me, that's the nature of the human being. . . . I encouraged fluidity over the process. Be dynamic, be explorative. . . . The court[s] compartmentalize, it's this kind of case or that kind of case. I say, we're dealing with human beings. . . .

The Peacemaker Court Manual also stresses the need for flexibility:

> It cannot be stressed, repeated or urged enough that the Peacemaker Court . . . is not frozen in its present form forever. As an experiment which has been carefully built upon Navajo custom and tradition, we will have to see whether it meets the needs of the Navajo people . . ., and we will have to see what changes need to be made.

Peacemaking is a formal part of the Navajo legal system, developed and overseen by the Navajo Nation judiciary. There are two primary routes by which cases reach Peacemaking: court referral and self-referral. Criminal cases may be referred by the court as the result of diversion or as a condition of probation. The Domestic Abuse Protection Act creates special rules for domestic violence protection order cases: A referral to Peacemaking must be approved by the petitioner, and the peacemaker must have received special domestic violence training. In all other civil cases, the rules allow courts to refer cases to Peacemaking over a party's objection, but in practice judges seldom refer civil cases involving allegations of domestic violence unless both parties agree to the referral. In addition to court referral, Peacemaking may be initiated by a petitioner on a claim that he or she has been "injured, hurt or aggrieved by the actions of another." Self-referred cases make up the majority of Peacemaking cases. In a self-referred case, the peacemaker liaison seeks authorization from the district court to subpoena the respondent and all other necessary parties identified by the petitioner. * * *

Conclusion: Lessons From Navajo Peacemaking

This Article moves back and forth between a study of the specifics of Navajo Peacemaking in domestic violence cases and an exploration of Peacemaking's theory of adjudication and its lessons for intervention strategies in domestic violence more generally—even when those possibilities are imperfectly realized in current Navajo practice.

In the struggle for greater autonomy and for some measure of safety against male violence, women choose methods and resources, discarding those that fail to work and refining those that, while not perfect, provide some advantage. Women's experiences of battering are framed by their experiences of other subordinating experiences: racism, childhood abuse, and economic deprivation. These experiences are also framed by women's political and cultural ideals and commitments. While there is no one intervention strategy that will work for all women, one critical measure of the effectiveness of any strategy is its capacity for placing resources—material, emotional, spiritual—in the hands of battered women. In some locales, this may best be accomplished through informal mechanisms that engage intentional communities, such as churches or civic organizations, in assisting battered women.

As developed in this Article, the Navajo Peacemaking model may increase a woman's material resources through *nalyeeh* and referrals to social services. It may increase her familial, emotional, and spiritual resources through its assistance in reconnecting her with family, redefining for her in-laws her relationship with their abusive son, providing referrals to counseling (both secular and spiritual), and through demonstrating care and support.

Peacemaking offers other potential benefits for some women. It may assist in disrupting familial supports for battering because family members are subpoenaed and peacemakers confront familial denial and minimizing. Peacemaking may directly address the abuser's victim blaming, excusing, or minimizing statements. Peacemaking may allow for the recognition of the impact of oppressive systems in the lives of men who batter without resort to excuse or victim blaming. Peacemaking thus avoids the "responsibility versus description" dichotomy of formal adjudication that limits its ability to address the complexity of battering behavior.

Peacemakers value relationships, even relationships with a batterer. Because peacemakers do not presume that separation is the best course of action, women are free to see Peacemaking as their last hope for saving a marriage. Peacemaking may provide women with tools to change the balance of power within their relationships.

Peacemaking also provides partial remedies for the problems that plague other informal adjudication. Rather than mediation's neutral ideal, peacemakers see themselves as fair but interested intervenors whose role is to instruct and to guide. Thus, Peacemaking has the potential to operate with a clear and overt antimisogyny norm. This antimisogyny norm may be strengthened by the use of traditional Navajo stories that emphasize the importance of gender balance and complementariness.

The Navajo Peacemaking experience underscores the necessity of an antimisogyny norm. Peacemakers who equate battering with a conflict or disagreement may domesticate the abuse. When peacemakers are clear that the abuse is an important object of intervention and that it is harmful and the responsibility of the abuser, it provides the possibility for real change in the batterer's thinking. It can reframe the battering. It may force the batterer to listen to " 'his family tell of the ordeal and . . . what they went through during this time of terror.' "

Despite these potential benefits, Peacemaking is no more ideal at meeting the goal of promoting women's autonomy than are other imperfect interventions. Indeed, as described in this Article in some detail, Peacemaking's current practice creates real dangers for some women, primarily because it coerces participation in self-referred cases. Additionally, safety is compromised because Peacemaking does not routinely provide battered women with the information they need to make an informed decision about whether to enter Peacemaking. Some peacemakers appear biased against divorce, thus sandwiching women between the separation focus of formal adjudication and a stay-married focus in Peacemaking. But this is not always the case. Some peacemakers routinely assist women in obtaining a divorce, some women come to Peacemaking expressly to use the process to gain a divorce, and a significant number of women take their case to family court when they are unhappy with Peacemaking's results (or with their partners' failure to change).

What are the lessons of Navajo Peacemaking for designing informal domestic violence intervention strategies? First, such a process must have safeguards to limit the abuser's ability to use the process to locate and continue to abuse the woman. Cases should be screened to identify battering. Respondent victims should be able to opt out. They should be given full information regarding the pros and cons of the process (as compared with others), and should be assisted with safety planning. Such a process would borrow from Navajo Peacemaking the understanding that fairness need not mean neutrality. This is particularly true with regard to the facilitator's understanding of violence and controlling behavior. The facilitator should use not only an antiviolence norm but also an antimisogyny norm. Peacemaking demonstrates the power of stories used in the furtherance of such a norm. In pluralistic American culture, stories compete. The facilitator in the informal process I imagine would, much as the most common batterer's treatment programs now do, support a story that values women's autonomy.

Like Peacemaking, this process should allow for a description of the oppressive structures that operate in the life of the batterer without reinforcing his sense of "victimhood" or entitlement. This underscores the process's link to social justice, spirituality, and the capacity for individual change. It allows women to affirm cultural and political identity—their solidarity with men in antiracist, anticolonialist work—without sacrificing their right to be free of gender-related violence. Such a process should value connection and relationships but should equally value choice—enlarging women's ability to choose by increasing women's resources.

The remedies available might include those currently available in restraining-order processes. For those who are separating, this might include such remedies as stay-away provisions, child custody and visitation, and child support. For those who live together, it might include prohibitions against violence, harassment, stalking, and phone calls at work. It might also include affirmative agreements to share housework or childcare, to express anger in non-controlling and non-threatening ways, to seek alcohol and batterer's treatment, and to cease certain battering-supporting friendships. As proposed by Braithwaite and Daly, it should include changes in the distribution of family assets so as to provide the woman with greater economic independence.

Without a sense of clan and familial responsibility, it may be difficult to persuade an abuser's family to provide the victim with goods and services. However, agreements involving victim reparations will often, in actuality, draw on familial assets. The process should encourage the attendance of the victim's family members as well, which will sometimes strengthen frayed family relationships.

Drawing on Yamamoto's work on intergroup race apologies as well as Navajo Peacemaking theory, such a process should encourage the batterer and his family and other support systems to recognize the harm caused by his behavior. Peacemaking supports this recognition through the use of the victim's stories and those of her family and friends. It also supports this recognition through the peacemaker's confrontation of denying and minimizing statements made by the batterer and his family. Yamamoto's second step, "taking responsibility," will often require more extensive inquiry into the various tactics used by a batterer to control, intimidate, and harm his partner or ex-partner. This requires confrontation not only of statements that deny or minimize the violence, but also of statements that attempt to excuse or blame the violence on the victim's bad behavior. It requires a cataloguing of controlling behaviors. This process cannot be accomplished solely through the use of an informal process, but it can begin there. Referrals to batterer's treatment, alcohol treatment, and spiritual healers or counselors must continue the process. The third step, "reconstruction," requires the concrete measures described above. *Nalyeeh*, or reparations after this thorough searching process, is much more than victim compensation. Reparations should include the resources, within the limits of availability, required to broaden the victim's autonomy. More than a therapeutic intervention, such a process would seek to restructure the power relationships between a man who batters and the woman he batters.

The Navajo "art and science of dealing with crime" provides some valuable lessons for thinking about the future of anti-domestic violence work. Intervention strategies that broaden women's choices, that address their material and context-specific needs, are the strategies that will be most effective. Peacemaking is not perfect—no domestic violence intervention is perfect—but Peacemaking offers possibilities for women that are largely unavailable in other intervention strategies.

[Editor's Note: In Culture: A Double-Edged Sword, Ending Violence Against Women: Population Reports, Vol. XXVII, No. 4 (1999) Series L, No. 11—Issues in World Health, page 10, the author notes that:

> *"Although culture can aggravate women's vulnerability, it can also serve as a creative resource for intervention. Many traditional cultures have mechanisms, such as public shaming or community healing, that can be mobilized as resources to confront abuse. Activists from Canada's Yukon Territory, for example, have developed Circle Sentencing, an updated version of the traditional*

sanctioning and healing practices of the Canadian aboriginal peoples. Within the 'circle,' crime victims, offenders, justice and social service personnel, as well as community residents, listen to the victim's story and deliberate about how best to 'restore justice' to the victim and the community. Sentencing often includes reparation, community service, jail time, treatment requirements, and community healing rituals.

Activists in India and Bangladesh likewise have adapted the salishe, *a traditional system of local justice, to address domestic violence. For example, when a woman is beaten, the West Bengali NGO Shramajibee Mahila Samity sends a female organizer to the village to consult with the individuals and families involved. The organizer then facilitates a* salishe, *attempting to steer the discussion in a pro-woman direction. Collectively, the community arrives at a proposed solution, which is formalized in writing and monitored by a local committee."]*

NOORIA FAIZI, DOMESTIC VIOLENCE IN THE MUSLIM COMMUNITY, PART II

10 Tex. J. of Women & the L. 209 (2001)
(citations and footnotes omitted)

* * *

IMAMS AND MASJIDS

Islamic arbitration is another option available to those who do not seek out the "Western" system. One such example exists in the Dallas/Fort Worth area, where Imam Moujahed Bakhach, Imam of the Fort Worth Mosque, is the main judge of the local arbitration panel. The panel was established around 1989 in response to problems within the Muslim community involving the misunderstanding or lack of knowledge involving Islamic rights and duties. This panel is a registered legal institution. The parties, who must agree to appear before the panel, have the right to select the judges, but the conditions and bylaws require the judges to have a background in Islamic jurisprudence, since rulings are to be based on the Qur'an and Sunnah.

It is estimated that of the approximately ten cases a week that appear before the panel, about half involve marital disputes and/or domestic violence. With each marriage contract over which the Imam presides, he recommends that the parties incorporate a clause in their contract that requires them to resort to Islamic arbitration before seeking a Western legal remedy.

The Imam stated that the underlying basis for many, if not most, of the conflicts involved the parties' misunderstanding of each other's duties and rights as husband and wife. In one dispute before the panel, a wife complained that her husband never helped with the housework, among other things. The husband did not believe it was his duty and thought that housework was strictly her responsibility. The Imam informed the husband that the Prophet (PBUH) did housework and that there was no reason why the husband should feel that he did not have to do it. The man was unaware of that information and that housework is not strictly the wife's responsibility. This is just one minor example of how lack of Islamic education contributes to marital disputes and abusive households. Too many times, misunderstanding and ignorance is based on particular family and cultural traditions that are mistaken as Islamic teachings.

Rulings vary, depending upon the circumstances of the dispute. Divorce is never encouraged, and every measure will be taken to keep the family unit together. However, if the situation is life-threatening, rulings will recommend the dissolution of the marriage. The problem with the arbitration procedures is that the rulings are not legally binding; rather, they are only ethically and morally binding, and there is no enforcing authority.

Islamic arbitrations are further limited by the values and standards of each local community, which introduces a problem with the "Islamic" system of handling domestic violence cases. Each Muslim community differs across the United States in both cultural and educational make-up. These differences factor into the degree of communication between the community and its women. In areas with is more open communication about rights and duties and where women can be heard and taken seriously, women have a better chance of receiving a satisfactory ruling in arbitration. Where there are problems with communication and oppressive cultural practices, the ruling is less likely to be favorable to the woman.

Sometimes, the individuals sitting on the arbitration panels, also known as the Masjid shura (consultation) councils, are men who have close connections to the husbands involved in the dispute, and their objectivity may be questionable. Consequently, women using these arbitration panels may start to feel that their disputes are not being handled fairly. To address these concerns, most Muslims recommend that Islamic solutions be easily substituted with Western adjudication when women start to feel that they are not treated justly.

Muslim women who do seek help often will turn to their Masjids and Imams. Unfortunately, they do not always find the help they need. They are often told by the Imams to be patient and pray for the abuse to end. Sometimes, women are blamed for the abuse and accused of not pleasing their husbands. At other times, Imams have been known to sincerely but wrongly advise the women to place the importance of family privacy above any harm that they might endure.

[Editor's Note: Some commentators have asked whether restorative justice could offer a better alternative to non-White victims of domestic

violence in the U.S., given that many restorative justice practices originally come from indigenous populations, and that these practices are based in the community, so may be more flexible and more able to reflect community standards. These commentators note that restorative justice could create a "separate but more equal justice system" for communities of the global majority (a term now being used in lieu of "minority" within the U.S.). "Community" would be defined as whoever the parties invite to the meeting. It is hoped that this community would condemn domestic violence without state intervention, and would more readily understand the pressures facing the particular survivor of abuse than would judges in traditional court settings. Additionally, this method of dispute resolution would not require survivors to disclose the abuse to outsiders, avoiding reinforcing negative stereotypes about their culture and race, and also avoiding problems arising from involving the state, a major concern for many survivors of color as well as undocumented survivors.]

CHAPTER 9

RAPE OF INTIMATE PARTNERS

■ ■ ■

This chapter begins the next section of the textbook, an examination of how the criminal justice system treats domestic violence. The topic of the chapter, intimate partner rape, sometimes falls "between the cracks" of sexual assault laws, policies, and programs on the one hand, and domestic violence laws, policies, and programs on the other. However, it belongs in both areas, as rape and sexual assault are frequent aspects of domestic violence.

The chapter begins with the history of the marital rape exemption in criminal law, which lasted for centuries in Anglo-American law. The materials discuss the rationales for this exception, as well as its recent demise. They also note that even though all U.S. jurisdictions now criminalize marital rape, there are still major problems in terms of identifying these cases, reporting marital rape, charging it, and obtaining convictions. Some of the problems are based in statutes still exhibiting antiquated approaches to marital rape, while others stem from victims' emotional hurdles, unresponsive prosecutors, and a lack of understanding by the larger society regarding how serious intimate partner rape is.

A new article focuses on coercive control and its role in sexual coercion where the parties have been in a romantic relationship. Several sections from the current Model Penal Code illustrate the above-described antiquated approach and lack of understanding regarding rape of intimate partners.

A case in which a victim of marital rape recanted at trial discusses the inappropriateness of expert testimony for the defense on "make-up sex." Another case focuses on whether a state's rape shield law can be used to exclude evidence of a wife's alleged prior sexual history with her husband when he is charged with raping her. A third case holds that marital sex was not consensual when the husband forced the wife to exchange sex for food and money, after not allowing her to work outside the home.

JESSICA KLARFELD, A STRIKING DISCONNECT: MARITAL RAPE LAW'S FAILURE TO KEEP UP WITH DOMESTIC VIOLENCE LAW

48 Am. Crim. L. Rev. 1819 (2011)
(citations and footnotes omitted)

INTRODUCTION

Until the late twentieth century, a husband could compel his wife to have sex with him without fear of consequence. Although the criminal justice system could punish a man who forced a woman to have nonconsensual sexual intercourse, marriage served as an absolute defense to rape, and a marital rape exemption existed in the statutory laws of every state. The common law also recognized the existence of a marital rape exemption, and, in order to bring a recognized charge of rape, a woman had to allege that she was not the wife of the defendant. Regardless of how brutal or evil the spousal rape, courts did not consider it a crime.

Beginning in 1976, states began to dissolve their marital rape exemptions, and by 1993, spousal rape, just like nonmarital rape, was a crime in all fifty states and the District of Columbia. State legislatures and courts came to understand that the marital rape exemption was "employed to justify the subjugation of women in English and American law and society during the past," but that there was no room for such a doctrine in modern American law and society. They finally recognized that married women should have the same right to control their bodies as unmarried women and, therefore, that the various justifications previously used to uphold the marital rape exemption should no longer hold any weight.

Although every state legislature has formally abolished its marital rape exemption, reminders of the exemption still remain in the statutory law of several states. These additional hurdles are found in decreased sentences for the accused, proof of force and/or resistance, and shorter time frames by which a woman has to report a rape by her husband, ultimately making spousal rape more difficult to prosecute. Even in states that do not have these increased requirements, successful prosecution of marital rape cases is still extremely difficult.

Domestic violence law, on the other hand, has seen huge advances over the past few decades. Of particular importance are the mandatory arrest and no-drop prosecution laws that legislatures in every state have enacted to increase police response and decrease batterer relapse. Although these laws are criticized, it is significant that legislatures have implemented policies that seek to decrease spousal battery and alert society to the harms of domestic violence. Unquestionably, domestic violence law has its own problems and differs from marital rape. However, the progress that society, state legislatures, and the judicial system have made regarding domestic violence should serve as a model for marital rape law. This Note will argue that to advance marital rape law to the same level as domestic violence law, two crucial changes must occur: first, those states whose statutes do not treat marital rape and nonmarital rape exactly the same must enact statutes that do not distinguish between the two crimes; and second, legislatures must institute policies aimed at the more effective prosecution of marital rape. * * *

I. DOMESTIC VIOLENCE LAW: A SHIFT FROM THE PRIVATE HOME TO THE PUBLIC SPHERE

Domestic violence is defined as violence between members of a household, most commonly spouses. The United Nations defines domestic violence as "[a]ny act of gender-based violence that results in, or is likely to result in, physical, sexual, or psychological harm or suffering to women, including threats of such acts, coercion or arbitrary deprivation of liberty, whether occurring in public or private life." Such gender-based violence is extremely common. In fact, in the United States, more than two million women are battered by an intimate partner each year.

Domestic violence was once a private matter only managed by women individually in the seclusion of their homes. Now, domestic violence is a public offense that state authorities can target through the criminal justice system. Beginning in the early 1990s, state legislatures introduced law reforms targeting domestic violence, thereby bringing domestic violence into the public sphere. These reforms, which were aimed at reshaping law enforcement officials' views on domestic violence, changed the nature of domestic violence by treating it as a crime instead of an intrafamilial private dispute. Two particular reforms—mandatory arrest laws, which require police to arrest domestic violence suspects upon probable cause, and no-drop prosecution policies, which compel prosecution even if victims are uncooperative—are "the clearest manifestations" of how the view of domestic abuse has changed in recent years. * * *

II. MARITAL RAPE IN THE CONTEXT OF DOMESTIC VIOLENCE

Most marital sex is consensual. However, marital rape pervades our society, and it is widely recognized that women can be raped by their husbands, as well as by strangers. Marital rape scholars and activists disagree on the extent to which marital rape and domestic violence are similar. Some locate marital rape within the domestic violence context; others believe that such rape cannot occur without other forms of domestic violence; and still others assert that marital rape poses a distinct threat. One scholar, Diana Russell, in her study of women in San Francisco, found that ten percent were victims of both marital rape and battering, four percent were victims of marital rape only, and twelve percent were victims of battering only. Russell has asserted that treating marital rape as merely a subset of domestic violence excludes too many women who are victims of marital rape, but not of domestic violence. According to her, although a substantial percentage of men who physically batter their wives also sexually assault them, and although both rape and domestic violence are forms of violence by which the husband asserts control over his wife, spousal rape may exist on its own in a marriage. Other research and policy on domestic violence largely ignores marital rape. Instead, it focuses primarily on non-sexual physical aggression, such as assault and battery, further supporting the notion that marital rape is not just a type of domestic violence.

Today, there are three recognized forms of marital rape: battering rape, force-only rape, and obsessive rape. Battering rape, which is often motivated by anger, involves forced sex combined with beatings; the rape itself is either part of the entire physical abuse incident or is a result of the husband asking his wife to prove that she forgives him for the beating by having sex with him. The link between domestic violence and rape is clearest in this category of marital rape. In fact, husbands who commit battering rape may be among the most dangerous perpetrators of domestic violence. In force-only rape—which is the most common form of marital rape—the husband uses only as much force as is necessary to coerce his wife into having sex with him. Force-only rape is primarily motivated by the need for control, and relationships that involve such rape tend to be characterized by intense power struggles over issues of money, children, and sex. * * * Lastly, obsessive rape, which is the least common of the three forms, occurs when the husband uses force to carry out strange, perverse sexual interests.

III. THE MARITAL RAPE EXEMPTION

Although it has always been a crime for a man to force an unmarried woman to have sexual intercourse against her will, it was not always a crime for a husband to force his wife to have intercourse. In fact, rape was traditionally defined as "nonconsensual sexual intercourse, by force, with a woman other than the defendant's wife." The marital rape exemption originated at common law; in *Commonwealth v. Fogerty*, the first United States case to recognize the existence of a marital rape exemption, the Supreme Judicial Court of Massachusetts held [in 1857] that marriage to the victim was a defense to rape. State legislatures later incorporated the exemption into their own laws.

A. Traditional Justifications

Originally, three main justifications existed for the marital rape exemption. The first justification for the marital rape exemption was based on implied consent and contract theory. This justification originated from Sir Matthew Hale's notion that a marriage constitutes a contract, the terms of which include a wife's irrevocable consent to have sexual intercourse with her husband whenever he wants—essentially that the husband has a "marital right" to sexual intercourse.

According to Hale, "the husband cannot be guilty of a rape committed by himself upon his lawful wife, for by their mutual matrimonial consent and contract the wife hath given up herself in this kind unto her husband, which she cannot retract." Under this theory, the wife's consent did not have to be proven for each sex act; rather, consent to sexual relations with one's husband was ongoing and implied by marital vows.

The implied consent rationale is no longer a valid justification for the marital rape exemption. The theory is inconsistent with the concept of consent in all other areas of criminal law. Because the law does not allow someone to consent to serious bodily harm or injury inflicted on oneself or another, and because the states have a compelling interest in protecting their citizens from serious bodily harm, it follows that this compelling interest bars the states from recognizing a theory of implied consent to the harms resulting from rape within a marriage. Moreover, the implied consent theory does not exist outside of rape law; under domestic relations law, a woman may withhold consent to sexual intercourse with her husband in several circumstances.

Second, proponents of the marital rape exemption justified the exemption on the basis of coverture and property rights. Under this doctrine, a woman's identity was merged into that of her husband upon their marriage. Because husband and wife were one entity, a husband could not be charged with raping his wife, as that would equate to raping himself. Furthermore, because women were regarded as property, rape was not a crime against a woman; rather, it was a crime against a man's property interest. This rationale continued to support the marital rape exemption into the nineteenth century. However, the Married Women's Property Act dissolved this rationale by granting women the rights to incur personal legal obligations and to own property independent of their husbands. No recent case has recognized this rationale as valid.

Under the third original justification for the marital rape exemption, the preservation of marital privacy and domestic harmony required that the law stay out of the relationship between husband and wife. The concept of privacy stemmed from the idea of a "curtain . . . closing off [a couple's] private troubles from public view." According to this theory, if laws could intrude on family relations and the private sphere of the family, the possibility of reconciliation and restoration of marital harmony would be unlikely.

Supporters of the exemption continue to use the marital privacy justification in the modern era; however its legitimacy has declined drastically. As stated by the Supreme Court of Virginia in *Weishaupt v. Commonwealth*:

> It is hard to imagine how charging a husband with the violent crime of rape can be more disruptive of a marriage than the violent act itself. Moreover, if the marriage has already deteriorated to the point where intercourse must be commanded

at the price of violence we doubt that there is anything left to reconcile.

In other words, the justification—which was based on the premise that a marriage in which a husband raped his wife was worth saving and that a marriage should be kept intact at all costs—does not make sense in a marriage subject to rape and abuse.

B. Modern Justifications

With decreased reliance on the original justifications for the marital rape exemption, defenders of the exemption have propounded other rationales. First, supporters have argued that marital rape does not occur often enough in society to be recognized as a serious problem and that it is not as serious as nonmarital rape. However, such arguments are unreasonable, as studies show that up to fourteen percent of married women have been raped by their husbands at least once in their lives. Furthermore, even if the percentage of women raped by their husbands was much smaller, criminality should not depend on the number of people affected. Proponents have also argued that the damage to a woman from rape in marriage is less severe than the damage caused to a victim of nonmarital rape. However, marital rape may indeed be the most traumatic form of rape. Women who are raped in marriage likely suffer more psychological damage because the rape results in a sense of betrayal, the destruction of the marriage, and the possibility that such rape will continue over many years. Women will also likely suffer greater physical consequences, for they are more likely to resist the force of their husbands than that of a stranger.

Second, proponents of the marital rape exemption have claimed that it is too difficult to prove lack of consent of the wife during the "rape episode" because the couple likely had consensual sex hundreds of times before. However, this justification also lacks merit, for the "difficulty of proof has never been a proper criterion for deciding what behavior should be officially censured by society."

The third justification holds that a marital rape victim can pursue other legal remedies, such as assault and battery, instead of a rape charge. Advocates of this justification believe it is unnecessary to subject marriages to the intense pressure of a rape prosecution when other less invasive alternatives exist. However, there is a difference between assault and rape; unlike battery and assault laws, rape laws recognize rape as both a psychological and a physical crime. Furthermore, not all women who are raped by their husbands are subject to physical assault as well.

The fourth justification is that a husband should have the right to sexual relations with his wife without fear of prosecution. This rationale is reminiscent of the traditional marital privacy and domestic harmony justification. Such a rationale, though, "simply confuses marital sex with marital rape" and is unacceptable in modern day society.

The last modern justification for the marital rape exemption involves protection for the husband, where the exemption shields a husband from a wife's false accusation of rape. This "lying woman" justification, premised on the idea that women are vindictive liars, posits that criminalizing marital rape results in women filing false rape charges to gain leverage against their husbands in divorce and custody proceedings. Essentially, it promotes the "stereotype of women as liars, schemers, troublemakers and homebreakers who want to ruin innocent men to suit their own vindictive or irrational ends." Similar to the other justifications, the "lying woman" justification is not valid, because the criminal justice system is designed to handle false claims.

No matter what the justification, though, the marital rape exemption denies married women equal protection against the violent crime of rape solely on the basis of gender and marital status.

IV. ONE STEP FORWARD: THE DISSOLUTION OF THE MARITAL RAPE EXEMPTION

Today, forced sex between husband and wife is considered rape and is illegal in every jurisdiction in the United States. Progress toward this modern doctrine began in the mid-1970s, as state legislatures and society began to recognize that the marital rape exemption differentiated between women who were raped by their spouses and women who were raped by strangers. Such a distinction rested solely on the unquestionably incorrect assumption that married women, unlike other persons, had no interest in being protected by the states from violence and sexual assault. Moreover, the marital rape exemption resulted in extremely harmful effects to all women, not just those that were the subject of spousal rape. According to one scholar:

> The irrationality of the marital rape exemptions is not their fundamental flaw. The evil flaw of these exemptions is not that they irrationally treat . . . married women different from unmarried women, or husbands different from rapists unacquainted with their victims . . . . The evil is that they legalize, and hence legitimate, a form of violence that does inestimable damage to all women, not only to those who are raped. In addition to the obvious violence, brutality, and terror marital rape exemptions facilitate, . . . [they], like the rapes they legalize, sever the central connection to selfhood that links a woman's pleasure with her desires, will, and actions. The will of the married woman who learns to accept routinized rape is no longer ruled by or even connected to her desires . . . . [S]he sacrifices the ability to control her own will and to determine her own actions, pleasures, and

desires free from external influence. In short, she sacrifices selfhood.

Despite the fundamental inequity of the marital rape exemption, it was not until 1976 that Nebraska became the first state to overturn its exemption. Even after Nebraska eliminated its provision granting immunity for marital rape, it took seventeen years for all states to recognize the crime of marital rape by no longer excluding sexual spousal assault from the definition of rape in their respective statutes. The next change in marital rape law came in 1977, when Oregon became the first state to charge a husband with rape while he and his wife were still married and living together. Several early cases in other states upheld the state legislatures' revised statutes removing the marital rape exemption.

In 1984, New York became the first state to remove its marital rape exemption through the judicial process; the New York Court of Appeals found the state's marital rape exemption unconstitutional. In *People v. Liberta,* the husband-defendant lived separate from his wife pursuant to a restraining order that required the defendant to move out, to remain away from the family home, and to stay away from his wife. Three days after missing a visit with his son, the defendant called his wife to see if he could visit his son that day. Although the defendant's wife did not allow him to come into the house, she agreed to allow him to pick up her and their son and take them both back to his motel, under the assurance that the defendant's friend would be with them at all times. After arriving at the hotel, the friend left, and the defendant attacked his wife, threatened to kill her, and forcibly raped and sodomized her. *[Editor's Note: This was in the son's presence].* Although New York's rape statute contained a marital exemption, the state prosecuted the husband under the provision that considered him unmarried because the defendant and his wife were "living apart pursuant to a valid and effective . . . order issued by a court of competent jurisdiction which by its terms or in its effect requires such living apart." The defendant appealed the application of the exemption, claiming that he and his wife were still married and, therefore, that he should be subject to the exemption and that both the rape and sodomy statutes violated the equal protection rights of unmarried men under the Fourteenth Amendment.

The New York Court of Appeals, the state's highest court, held that "there is no rational basis for distinguishing between marital rape and nonmarital rape," and thus "declare[d] the marital exemption for rape in the New York statute to be unconstitutional." The court noted that "a marriage license should not be viewed as a license for a husband to forcibly rape his wife with impunity. A married woman has the same right to control her own body as does an unmarried woman." The court rejected the various justifications for the marital rape exemption, most notably observing that the marital rape exemption does not further marital privacy because the right of privacy only protects consensual acts, not violent rape.

Following *Liberta*, courts in other jurisdictions reached similar conclusions on the unconstitutionality of the marital rape exemption in their states' statutes. Such cases largely focused on the lack of a rational basis for a statutory scheme protecting a woman from rape by someone other than her husband, but not protecting the same woman from rape by her husband. For example, in *People v. M.D.*, the Appellate Court of Illinois, like the court in *Liberta*, summarized and rejected the justifications for the marital rape exemption, holding that the state's marital rape exemption violated the Equal Protection and Due Process Clauses of the United States and Illinois Constitutions.

In *In re Estate of Peters*, the Supreme Court of Vermont "reject[ed] entirely the notion that marriage creates a kind of implied 'blanket consent to sexual contact' " and noted that any "distinction between marital and nonmarital criminal rape is based on archaic 'common-law doctrines that a woman [i]s the property of her husband.' " The court held that marital status makes no difference under Vermont's criminal provision for sexual assault, remarking that the statute was specifically amended in 1985 to remove the exemption for those who commit sexual assault against their spouses. The court concluded that the statute now expressly prohibits nonconsensual sex, regardless of the marital status between the parties.

Even in the twenty-first century, courts are still addressing the concept of a marital rape exemption. In the 2010 case *Mayo v. Commonwealth*, the Supreme Court of Kentucky affirmed the trial court's judgment, convicting the defendant of first-degree rape and sodomy of his wife from whom he had been separated for approximately two weeks before the acts in question occurred. The court noted that a spouse can be guilty of raping and sodomizing his wife. Furthermore, the court observed that:

> [T]he fact that the victim and [the defendant] may have had consensual anal sex in the past does not make it more or less likely that she consented to having any type of sex . . . with [the defendant] at the time in question, especially since [the defendant] was permitted to testify repeatedly that he had had consensual sex with the victim multiple times in the hours preceding the rape.

State legislatures and the courts have effectively abolished the formal marital rape exemption in all fifty states and the District of Columbia. While it took almost two decades to reach this result, it marks a great initial achievement for married women and society as a whole.

V. TWO STEPS BACK?: BARRIERS TO CONVICTING MARITAL RAPISTS

Although marital rape is illegal in all states today, convicting perpetrators of the crime is still difficult for two reasons. First, several states have statutes that still distinguish marital rape from nonmarital rape through shorter waiting periods, reduced sentences, and a required mental state. Second, prosecution of marital rape has proven extremely difficult as a result of the social stigma attached to the crime, overburdened prosecutors, and disbelieving juries.

A. State Statutes Reminiscent of the Marital Rape Exemption

Every state legislature has formally eliminated its marital rape exemption, but several states still retain barriers to marital rape prosecution in their reformed statutes. Failure to wholly criminalize such conduct sends the message that marital rape is still tolerated under certain circumstances. Today, states can be divided into two categories based on their statutes' treatment of marital rape. The first category consists of states that do not have any marital rape exemption. These states' statutes make no distinction between marital rape and nonmarital rape and are more advanced, judged by their recognition of the utter illegitimacy of any sort of marital rape exemption.

The second category consists of states whose statutes distinguish between marital rape and nonmarital rape. Such states either allow for prosecution of marital rape only in certain circumstances, or impose extra requirements on victims of marital rape that are not required of victims of nonmarital rape. Some states' statutes require the victim of marital rape to bring a rape charge within a much shorter time period than a victim of nonmarital rape. South Carolina, for example, requires that a victim report marital rape within thirty days; however, the state has no reporting requirements for victims of nonmarital rape. Given the social stigma attached to rape, the emotional effects felt by a victim of spousal rape, and the fact that a victim may not be aware of the reduced statute of limitations, these time restrictions often prevent prosecution. Some jurisdictions have statutes that afford lower sentences for marital-rape defendants than for defendants who commit nonmarital rape. In Virginia, nonmarital rape and marital rape are subject to sentences ranging from five years to life imprisonment; however, in marital rape cases, a judge may dismiss charges against the defendant, if both the victim and the prosecuting attorney agree to such dismissal, in exchange for the defendant completing counseling [while] on probation. Several states also exempt a spouse from prosecution when the victim was mentally incapacitated or physically helpless during the rape. Lastly, a few states require an added element of force or resistance, such that even if cases go to trial, prosecutors are more likely to face problems of winning convictions. Unlike the more reformed states of the first category that do not recognize any difference between marital and nonmarital rape, states that require additional elements of proof continue to promote the classical idea that rape in marriage is not as bad as rape outside of marriage and that women who are subject to marital rape are "second class victims not worthy of equal protection." According to one constitutional scholar,

> No congressional action, or any Supreme Court analogue to *Brown v. Board of Education*, has enshrined in the country's fundamental law the political judgment that "equal protection of the laws" minimally guarantees an equal protection from the states' criminal codes and enforcement agencies against violent sexual assault, regardless of marital status. In other words, no fundamental legal reform exists to bring these laws into line with what is perceived by commentators to be a constitutional mandate. Thus, the change in social consciousness that often follows constitutionally mandated legal reform has not come to fruition.

B. Prosecution Hurdles

Even in those states in which the marital rape exemption has been completely eliminated, prosecution of marital rape has been uncommon and difficult. Like victims of domestic violence, victims of marital rape face emotional hurdles, unresponsive prosecutors, and a general lack of understanding regarding the seriousness of the situation. Because of the social stigma attached to rape, women may often be unwilling to report an incident of rape to the police. This stigma may be even stronger in the case of marital rape. In fact, one study found that less than one-fifth of women raped by an intimate partner reported the rape to the police. Women who are raped by their husbands also may fail to realize that they have the right to refuse sex with an intimate partner.

Even in cases in which women overcome the stigma and report the rape, such women face overburdened prosecutors, disbelieving juries, and frustrated judges. While courts have been more accepting of recognizing domestic violence in recent years, there is still a sense of reluctance to delve into cases of marital rape. Prosecution remains infrequent and conviction rates are low in marital rape cases; only approximately 7.5% of marital rapes are prosecuted, and, of those, 58.1% do not result in conviction. Marital rape cases present the same difficulties as other rape cases for prosecutors, but to a greater degree. Prosecutors often think that such cases will not result in convictions as a result of potentially disbelieving juries. When the victim's testimony is the sole evidence of the rape, prosecutors fear the defense will easily create reasonable doubt in the minds of jurors. The trauma of marital rape is not necessarily physically apparent in a courtroom, and the prosecutor cannot easily prove, outside the victim's testimony, the chief effects of marital rape, which are the violation of self-determination and a breach of marital trust. Jurors can also misinterpret a lack of physical evidence as a sign of consent to sexual intercourse, thus undercutting the rape charge. Furthermore, the defense's argument may include remnants of the "lying woman" justification—that the victim has something to gain, either in divorce, custody, or finance, in making the rape charge and, therefore, that the victim is bringing a false claim to attain that goal. Because of these significant prosecution and court obstacles, prosecutors often avoid pursuing marital rape cases, and victims seldom report charges so as not to endure a trial that they will likely lose.

VI. BRINGING MARITAL RAPE LAW IN LINE WITH DOMESTIC VIOLENCE LAW

While changes in domestic violence policy—most prominently, the enactment of mandatory arrest and no-drop prosecution laws—have faced significant controversy and backlash, such changes represent significant progress in the recognition, understanding, and prosecution of domestic violence. Marital rape law, on the other hand, has not seen the same amount of progress. Although the marital rape exemption, which was the original formal barrier to prosecution, no longer exists in any state, the legal obstacles and informal barriers to full prosecution of marital rape make it a much less developed body of law than domestic violence law. While the problem of domestic violence has gained increased recognition over the past two decades in both our culture and the criminal law, largely as the result of the feminist and battered women's movements, domestic sexual violence has been slow to reform. In recent years, even date rape and acquaintance rape—which, like marital rape, do not fit into the "stranger rape" profile—have garnered increasing attention; marital rape, though, has failed to attract the same attention and support. * * *

B. Bringing Marital Rape Law and Prosecution Up to Speed

To bring society's and the criminal justice system's acknowledgment and understanding of marital rape in line with that of domestic violence, there needs to be a change at both the statutory and the prosecutorial levels.

> Legislative and prosecutorial efforts to combat marital rape will not succeed until pervasive myths about sex, rape, and marriage are eradicated .... Legislatures must affirmatively negate the marital exemption from rape statutes, and prosecutors must become educators, not only in the courtroom, but also in society at large, communicating the realities of marital rape through effective use of the media.

From a statutory perspective, states that have statutes that make absolutely no distinction between marital rape and nonmarital rape, in terms of elements of the crime, statute of limitations, and length of the sentence should be viewed as the "ideal." States that do not already have these statutes should model theirs after those that do, so that they too officially recognize the gravity of marital rape and do not just consider it as a lesser form of rape. Force and resistance should not be required in any statute because requiring proof of such elements would likely deny many women the right to bring rape charges against their husbands. Further, the timeframe victims have to report marital rape and the sentences for marital rape should equal the timeframes and sentences for nonmarital rape in that state. Maintaining different time limits and sentences for marital and nonmarital rape leads legislatures, courts, and the public to view marital rape as less harmful than nonmarital rape. An ideal rape statute would not make any distinction whatsoever between marital and nonmarital rape. Framing statutes as such would result in the acknowledgment that the crime of marital rape is equal in severity to that of nonmarital rape.

Despite the difficulties in proving a marital rape charge, prosecutors must pursue criminal charges in the same manner that they would in a "stranger rape" case. "The very notion of prosecutorial discretion recognizes the opportunity for a prosecutor's personal biases about spousal rape to affect his or her decision of whether to prosecute." Thus, similar to how states have no-drop prosecution laws, adoption of similar sorts of laws or guidelines for the prosecution of marital rape could be effective. While no-drop prosecution laws have their weaknesses and laws advocating or mandating prosecution for marital rape probably would as well, such policies likely would have the effect of increasing attention to the seriousness of marital rape and better targeting it. Prosecutors could not refuse to file based on their own preconceived notions regarding marital rape. Prosecutors could also introduce evidence about marital rape and domestic relationships to buttress the victim's testimony, which might help counter jurors' skepticism regarding a marital rape charge when there is a lack of physical evidence. Moreover, prosecution is essential for men to recognize that marital rape is a crime and that the system will hold them accountable if they rape their wives. * * *

JENNY E. MITCHELL AND CHITRA RAGHAVAN, THE IMPACT OF COERCIVE CONTROL ON USE OF SPECIFIC SEXUAL COERCION TACTICS

27(2) Violence Against Women 1 (2019)
(footnotes and citations omitted)

. . .

Sexual Coercion

Historically, discussion of sexual coercion has been complicated by societal uncertainty and disagreement about the definition of rape and other types of sexual violence within consensual intimate relationships. Sexual coercion refers to the persuasion of an unwilling partner to comply with nonconsensual sex through nonviolent means. Nonconsent entails the unwilling partner's absence of consent, resistance to sex, or compliance under duress from a partner. Most often, sexual coercion has been grouped together with violent and forcible sexual assault.

Typically, sexual coercion involves ostensibly nonaggressive tactics such as verbal coercion, manipulation of guilt or obligation, continuing to sexually touch or seduce a partner after she has displayed signs of nonconsent, and incapacitation of a partner via substances. Moreover, the tactics may not occur immediately before an instance of unwanted sex, and can affect subsequent sexual compliance. Even if nonconsensual sex was not obtained at the time a partner uses the tactic, repeated negative relationship experiences that occur after declining requests for sex can affect a victim's capacity for refusing sex or hopelessness for resisting over time. In addition, immediate partner pressure is unnecessary for sexual coercion to occur due to the strength of contextual pressure of societal norms condoning of gendered sexual obligation.

The incidence of sexual coercion may be informed by pervasive societal norms that perpetuate an imbalance of power and sexual expectations between individuals in male and female roles. According to sexual scripting theory, culture constructs gendered norms as to what behavior and attitudes are acceptable within sexual and romantic relationships. For male-assigned individuals, what is accepted generally includes objectification of females, asserting intense sexual needs, insistent focus on sexual pleasure, and relentless pursuit of partners. Acceptance of sexual scripting norms has been shown to be related to perpetration of emotional abuse as well as males' intentions to use sexual coercion. Some studies suggest that, in the context of societal scripts, male sexual abusers demonstrate cognitive distortions that justify their actions and are formed as long-term attitudes, motivated cognitions proximal to an incident, and dissonance resolving strategies after an incident. Research shows that female-centric sexual scripting (related to sexual passivity and subordination of own needs vs. males' needs) also contributes to females' continued victimization by unwanted sex. These scripts influence cultural denial of the existence of and invalidation of the severity of nonviolent rape/sexual coercion within an intimate partnership, making it extremely difficult for females to identify their own experience or access resources to change their ongoing experiences. It is also important to note that studies support the centrality of females' sense of autonomy to satisfying sexual scenarios, as well as the weighty impact of societally ingrained barriers that prevent females from experiencing actualization of autonomy. Dutcher and McClelland (2019) conceptualize a vigilance surrounding "good" and "careful" sexual behavior common among females, which requires energy and effort but may be so normative that it is beneath conscious awareness. In addition, studies support the existence of cognitive methods that females use to cope with widespread sexual disparities including justification of the unimportance of sexual equality, attributing disparities to biology, and procrastination of actualizing needs. It is very common to feign pleasure to end or escape from unwanted sex. These coping mechanisms are hypothesized to normalize or distance from distressing feelings.

Because sexual coercion occurs in the most private realm of one's life and does not leave a tangible mark, this type of abuse can serve to silence, isolate, or make invisible the victim similarly to other forms of coercive abuse. The successful use of sexual coercion may lead to a very particular type of entrapment for women. Women may be less likely to report or identify coercion because lower levels of force are associated with decreased acknowledgment of sexual violation. Furthermore, women experiencing unwanted sex in a relationship context are already less likely to label themselves as victims despite the harmful effects of the experience, making this area critical to study. It may also be that tactics are tailored to fit a specific victim's particular vulnerabilities. Rather than simply being used more frequently, they may be used in a manner targeted for effectiveness with a particular victim.

Linking Coercive Control and Sexual Coercion

Although a relationship between sexual coercion and intimate partner violence (IPV) is commonly acknowledged, how these two abusive dynamics interrelate has not been expressly defined. Raghavan et al. have proposed that sexual coercion may exist as an extension of a coercive controlling dynamic in an intimate partnership, and some preliminary support for the relationship between sexual coercion and coercive control currently exists. Specifically, Marshall and Holtzworth-Munroe's findings demonstrate that psychological aggression (this definition overlapped with the current understanding of coercive control) may be more related to the perpetration of sexual coercion than physically forced sex, whereas general physical aggression in relationships relates to perpetration of both sexual coercion and physically forced sex. In line with the coercive control framework, these results lend some credence to the idea that those who use more psychologically manipulative abuse commonly use tactics that act more covertly and receive little acknowledgment. Also consistent with a coercion framework, DeGue, DiLillo, and Scalora's results showed that partners who used sexual coercion as opposed to sexual assault were more able to predict others' emotional responses and manipulate others, while being less likely to have impulsive traits and a history of childhood emotional abuse. These results imply that those who used sexual coercion used it in controlling and intentional ways, as opposed to in the moment without understanding the way their behaviors influenced others. In addition, two studies demonstrated an association between a pattern of psychological abuse (many tactics of which would meet the definition of coercive controlling behaviors) and routine insulting of victims' worth with the use of sexual coercion. Finally, partners' sexually coercive behavior predicted victims' subsequent compliance with unwanted sex, suggesting that immediate partner physical or nonphysical pressure is not necessary for sexual compliance and that a dynamic of control might be implicated from other aspects of the relationship. . .

The Impact of Sexual Coercion

A growing body of evidence documents the widespread nature of sexual coercion and that victims experience serious negative consequences. In the context of a relationship, unwanted sexual contact with a partner has been linked to long-term harm to mental and physical health, including higher levels of stress and dissociation than reported when abused by a stranger or acquaintance. Even in the absence of violence, unwanted sex with a partner has been shown to be harmful and was related to self-blame, sadness, and guilt; major depression; sexually transmitted infection risk behavior; and, in one study, more severe posttraumatic stress disorder (PTSD) symptomology than physically forced rape. . .

Sexual Coercion Tactics

. . .In a sample of incarcerated, mainly unmarried heterosexual males convicted mostly of nonviolent offenses, the majority used nonviolent sexual coercion tactics that were similar to college samples (i.e., breakup threats, persistent arguments, lies, persisting despite nonconsent cues, and intoxication of partners). This is consistent with evidence supporting that, at domestic violence crime scenes, more victims report experiencing sexual coercion than forced sex. Unfortunately, it is unclear what kinds of sexual coercion strategies were used in this sample, because items were categorically grouped as physically forced or nonphysically forced. In addition, one of the items classified as physical was worded ambiguously: "Has your partner ever forced you to have sex when you did not wish to?" More clarification is needed in this population to comprehend the use of specific tactics, such as those identified by Raghavan et al. who specified eight tactics of sexual coercion: threats of/physical force, exploitation, humiliation/intimidation, pressure, relational threats, hopelessness, helplessness, and bullying. Exploitation intimates that deception or manipulation of a power imbalance may be used to obtain sex. Humiliation and intimidation employ shame to coerce the victim into unwanted sex. Pressure encompasses what has previously been denoted as verbal tactics, such as persistent arguments, nagging, and begging, whereas relational threats emphasize societal perception of obligation surrounding sex in a relationship or manipulate fear of the relationship ending as a consequence of refusing sex. Related to historical instead of immediate pressure, hopelessness tactics involve the victim feeling that the consequences of denying their partner sex are more aversive than suffering through unwanted sex, whereas helplessness entails a learned response in which resistance to sex has been futile and ignored in the past. Lastly, bullying involves blackmailing behaviors or accusations against victims' character.

In a population of court-referred partner-violent men, more than 40% admitted use of these specific sexually coercive tactics, with more than 60% of these men admitting frequent use of such behaviors.

There seems to be a consensus in the literature that among college students and among samples involved with the legal system, use of physical force to obtain sex is less frequent, or at least less frequently endorsed, than the use of nonviolent psychological tactics. . . .

[Editor's Notes: 1. In "Mommy, Baby and Rapist Makes Three? Amid Abortion Bans, the Pressing Need for a Nationwide Lower Standard to Strip Parental Rights, Regardless of a Rape Conviction," 27(3) William & Mary J of Race, Gender & Soc. Justice 963 (2021), Melanie Dostis notes that the federal Rape Survivor Child Custody Act (2015) made it easier to terminate parental rights of rapists, but many states require a rape conviction rather than clear and convincing evidence of rape, and make termination of parental rights discretionary rather than mandatory. Dostis states that much more needs to be done to protect pregnant rape survivors—e.g., allowing them to obtain legal abortions without notifying the rapist, exempting them from appearing at adoption or child support hearings where they may have to see their assailants, ensuring that the rapist cannot block an adoption, and clarifying that rapists are by definition unfit parents.

2. See also Judith Lewis, "The Stability Paradox: The Two-Parent Paradigm and the Perpetuation of Violence Against Women in Termination of Parental Rights and Custody Cases," 27(2) Michigan J of Gender & Law 311 (2021), in which she argues that courts' assumption that children need two parents to have stability based on their glorification of the nuclear family is a "dangerous fallacy. When rape or intimate partner violence (IPV), is present, or the re-occurrence of violence remains a threat, the family unit is far from stable." This paradigm promotes violence against children and adult survivors of abuse: she cites a recent Pennsylvania case in which the abusive boyfriend of the mother was given in loco parentis standing after the mother separated from him even though he was not the children's biological or adoptive father. Lewis proposes a model statute to terminate parental rights of rapists and IPV abusers.]

MODEL PENAL CODE § 213.1—RAPE AND RELATED OFFENSES

(1) Rape. A male who has sexual intercourse with a female not his wife is guilty of rape if:

(a) he compels her to submit by force or by threat of imminent death, serious bodily injury, extreme pain or kidnapping, to be inflicted on anyone; or

(b) he has substantially impaired her power to appraise or control her conduct by administering or employing without her knowledge drugs, intoxicants or other means for the purpose of preventing resistance; or

(c) the female is unconscious; or

(d) the female is less than 10 years old.

Rape is a felony of the second degree unless (i) in the course thereof the actor inflicts serious bodily injury upon anyone, or (ii) the victim was not a voluntary social companion of the actor upon the occasion of the crime and had not previously permitted him sexual liberties, in which cases the offense is a felony of the first degree.

(2) Gross Sexual Imposition. A male who has sexual intercourse with a female not his wife commits a felony of the third degree if:

(a) he compels her to submit by any threat that would prevent resistance by a woman of ordinary resolution; or

(b) he knows that she suffers from a mental disease or defect which renders her incapable of appraising the nature of her conduct; or

(c) he knows that she is unaware that a sexual act is being committed upon her or that she submits because she mistakenly supposes that he is her husband.

MODEL PENAL CODE § 213.4—SEXUAL ASSAULT

A person who has sexual contact with another not his spouse, or causes such other to have sexual contact with him, is guilty of sexual assault, a misdemeanor, if:

(1) he knows that the contact is offensive to the other person; or

(2) he knows that the other person suffers from a mental disease or defect which renders him or her incapable of appraising the nature of his or her conduct; or

(3) he knows that the other person is unaware that a sexual act is being committed; or * * *

(5) he has substantially impaired the other person's power to appraise or control his or her conduct, by administering or employing without the other's knowledge drugs, intoxicants or other means for the purpose of preventing resistance; * * *

MODEL PENAL CODE § 213.6—PROVISIONS GENERALLY APPLICABLE TO ARTICLE 213

* * * (2) Spouse Relationships. Whenever in this Article the definition of an offense excludes conduct with a spouse, the exclusion shall be deemed to extend to persons living as man and wife, regardless of the legal status

of their relationship. The exclusion shall be inoperative as respects spouses living apart under a decree of judicial separation. Where the definition of an offense excludes conduct with a spouse or conduct by a woman, this shall not preclude conviction of a spouse or woman as accomplice in a sexual act which he or she causes another person, not within the exclusion, to perform.

(3) Sexually Promiscuous Complainants. It is a defense to prosecution under Section 213.3 and paragraphs (6), (7) and (8) of Section 213.4 for the actor to prove by a preponderance of the evidence that the alleged victim had, prior to the time of the offense charged, engaged promiscuously in sexual relations with others.

(4) Prompt Complaint. No prosecution may be instituted or maintained under this Article unless the alleged offense was brought to the notice of public authority within [3] months of its occurrence or, where the alleged victim was less than [16] years old or otherwise incompetent to make complaint, within [3] months after a parent, guardian or other competent person specially interested in the victim learns of the offense.

(5) Testimony of Complainants. No person shall be convicted of any felony under this Article upon the uncorroborated testimony of the alleged victim. Corroboration may be circumstantial. In any prosecution before a jury for an offense under this Article, the jury shall be instructed to evaluate the testimony of a victim or complaining witness with special care in view of the emotional involvement of the witness and the difficulty of determining the truth with respect to alleged sexual activities carried out in private.

Explanatory Note for Sections 213.1–213.6

* * * Section 213.1(1) retains the traditional limitation of rape to the case of male aggression against a female who is not his wife. * * *

[Editor's Note: See Deborah W. Denno, "Why the Model Penal Code's Sexual Offense Provisions Should Be Pulled and Replaced, 1 Ohio St. J. Crim.L. 207 (Fall 2003). As of January 2024, twenty-one years later, they had not been changed.]

PEOPLE V. SANDOVAL

164 Cal.App.4th 994 (2008)
(citations and some footnotes omitted)

A jury convicted defendant Isaias Sandoval of spousal rape with force (Pen.Code, § 262, subd. (a)(1)—count one), corporal injury to a spouse (§ 273.5, subd. (a)—count two), felony false imprisonment (§ 236—count three), criminal threats (§ 422—count four) and damaging a wireless communication device, a misdemeanor (§ 591.5—count five).

Sentenced to state prison for an aggregate term of six years, defendant appeals contending (1) the trial court prejudicially erred in excluding the testimony of a defense expert, (2) the trial court failed to instruct the jury to find each element true beyond a reasonable doubt, (3) Evidence Code section 1109 is unconstitutional, and (4) the trial court abused its discretion in allowing the prosecution to introduce evidence of prior domestic violence. We reject defendant's contentions and will affirm the judgment.

FACTS

A.G. and defendant had been married to each other for 11 years; during the last three years they were separated. After their separation, A.G. moved to Sacramento with the children in February 2006, leaving defendant behind and not telling him where she was going. Nonetheless, defendant found her and arrived in Sacramento in May or June 2006. In September 2006, A.G. was again living with defendant and their two children.

About 9:00 a.m. on September 21, 2006, A.G. and defendant argued about defendant's lack of employment. A.G. told defendant that their relationship was not working and he needed to move out. A.G.'s testimony about what happened next differed from her earlier statements to the police.

At trial, A.G. testified that defendant asked her not to evict him, grabbing her upper arms and pushing her in the back with one hand. She did not fall down but instead threw herself to the ground so he would get scared and leave, thinking she was going to call the police. He agreed to leave but she changed her mind and did not want him to leave because he had no place to go and would end up using drugs, so she tried to call the police to report that he hit her. She used her cell phone but defendant took it and broke it. Angry, she broke the phone more. She went to the bedroom. Defendant followed A.G. into the bedroom where they had consensual sex. At first, she did not want to have sex. After he asked for forgiveness and she forgave him, they had consensual sex. She described the sex as gentle. About noon, A.G. left defendant in their apartment and ran to the complex office where she called the police. She was crying. The 911 tape was played for the jury.

A.G. admitted that she had previously reported the following to the police. Defendant threw her to the floor and hit her in the face two times with his fist. He took his belt off, made a loop with it and threatened to strangle her with it. He took her cell phone and broke it, preventing her from calling the police. He also threatened to stab her to death with a knife if she called the police. He placed a towel over her nose and mouth and pulled her underpants down. She pleaded with him to stop, telling him she did not want to have sexual intercourse, and tried to push him off. He bit her hand. She continued to struggle but he penetrated her vagina with his penis and ejaculated. She went to the bathroom. Defendant made her return to the bedroom and stay for about an hour and then told her he would leave. She called 911 from the apartment office, reporting that she could not use her cell phone because defendant had broken it, that he had hit her, thrown her to the floor, struck her in the head, forced her to have sexual intercourse, and locked her up in a room.

At trial, A.G. denied that defendant hit her, threatened to kill her or her sister, or threatened to stab her. A.G. explained away her scratches on her hand as caused by cleaning. Although defendant bit her on the hand and back, he had done so before during sex. She bit herself on the inside of her lip and her ear injury was an old one. She had no explanation for the bruise over her right eye. She had a fingernail mark on her nose.

A.G. claimed at trial that defendant had pushed her, but only once, days before the incident on September 21. She denied that he had beaten her three years before and had threatened to hurt her if she called the police. A.G. admitted at trial that she told Ann Tran on September 26, five days after the current incident, that defendant had a history of domestic violence, and that A.G. was afraid defendant might hurt family members if released from jail. She admitted she told Tran that defendant hit her, threw her on the bed, covered her mouth with a towel and raped her, and that three years before, defendant had beaten her and threatened to hurt her if she reported it.

At trial, A.G. admitted that when she was examined at a hospital, she told a nurse practitioner and a domestic violence advocate who was present that defendant had threatened to hit her with a belt and to cut her up with a knife and threatened to kill her and her sister. She also admitted that defendant punched A.G. in the face, dragged her by her hair, grabbed her by her arms and wrists, pinched her lips together to keep her quiet, put a towel over her nose and mouth, broke her cell phone and forced her to have sexual intercourse.

About 2:00 p.m. on September 21, 2006, the apartment complex's security guard, Jose Hernandez, went to the complex office and saw A.G. She was crying. She needed an interpreter when the police arrived. She told Hernandez that she had a domestic violence problem at home. At trial, A.G. denied discussing the September 21 incident with the complex's security guard prior to the arrival of the police.

When Sacramento Deputy Sheriff Kenny Lee arrived at the apartment complex office, Hernandez interpreted for Lee and A.G. A.G. had bruising and redness on her forehead, scratches on her nose and back, redness on the inside of her leg, abrasions on her elbow and wrist and a bite mark on her hand. At her apartment, A.G. showed the officer the belt in the bathroom and broken cell phone pieces. A.G. told the officer that she was married to defendant, that they had moved from Mexico, and that she had moved the previous year to Sacramento from the Bay Area to get away from defendant and did not tell him she was moving. Defendant found her three months before the September 21 incident and she let him move in provided that he obtain employment and assist around the house. On September 21, they argued because he had done neither and she told him to move out. She then recounted the incident.

The sexual assault examination revealed non-motile sperm in A.G.'s vagina which was consistent with a sexual assault earlier in the day and a small tear in A.G.'s vaginal opening which was a new injury and very unusual for someone who does not report a sexual assault.

When interviewed by detectives on September 25, 2006, defendant admitted that he had argued with A.G., broke her cell phone because she was going to call the police, bit her hand and her back, and hit her once with the belt. He admitted he grabbed her, taking her to bed where they had sexual intercourse even though she said no. He claimed that she liked him to bite her. He also claimed that he had been using "crystal" the day of the incident.

On October 11, 2006, defendant's telephone call from jail to a woman named "Sonia" was monitored. He stated that the sexual abuse charge was "screwing" him up and if "she take[s] off the charges" he would not bother A.G.

On December 20, 2006, defendant's telephone call from jail was monitored. He claimed he received a letter and "she says that . . . she'll help me. That I tell her how. That she was told that she can't take away the charges." Defendant said she could help him by "not appearing at trial."

On February 5, 2007, Sonia Orozco-Gutierrez visited defendant at the jail. Defendant told her that "if they don't [ ] find her this time the case will close" and "the case closes if—if she doesn't appear."

DISCUSSION

I.

Defendant first contends that the trial court prejudicially erred in excluding defense expert testimony on marital relationships and sex. We conclude there was no error.

Background

Prior to presentation of defense evidence, defense counsel sought to call Deborah Davis as an expert and the trial court conducted an Evidence Code section 402 hearing at the prosecutor's request. Davis was a psychology professor at the University of Nevada and had taught psychology classes for 34 years. She had taught seminars pertaining to romantic relationships for 16 years, which included the topic of handling conflict. She had also published research on sex in relationships, which included research on rape and consent. She also owned Sierra Trial and Opinion Consultants, a corporation. Defense counsel offered Davis as an expert on marital relations and sex.

The prosecutor questioned Davis. Davis admitted that she had never qualified to testify in court on the topic of marital relations and sex; she had "never been asked to serve as one." She had served as a consultant on the topic in a civil case and three criminal cases, all for the defense. She had previously qualified as an expert on the topic of eyewitness accuracy and interrogations and confessions, each time for the defense. With respect to the current case, Davis had reviewed the preliminary hearing transcript and defendant's statement to the police. She planned to testify about couples, conflict and sex, and the theory colloquially referred to as "make-up sex," which she described as a "phenomena of sex being more arousing after a fight in some circumstances," as a pattern of behavior and why it occurs. She explained that the make-up sex in literature was "investigated" under other theories, that is, "attachment theory, excitation transfer theory, and so on." She planned to inform the jury about things they did not know in order to come to their own conclusions, "not to come to a conclusion [herself]."

Defense counsel argued Davis's opinion was relevant to the issue of consent and defendant and A.G.'s pattern of interaction. Defense counsel planned to ask Davis a hypothetical question about make-up sex. The prosecutor opposed Davis's testimony arguing that it was not outside the scope of common knowledge and experience and that Davis lacked expertise.

The trial court precluded the testimony, finding that the testimony would not assist the jury "in any way," that Davis's proffered testimony was not beyond the jury's common experience and not relevant to any defense since Davis stated that she was not reaching a conclusion herself and that her general testimony would not address the issue of whether defendant actually and reasonably believed that A.G. consented. The court noted that Davis had never qualified as an expert in marital relations and sex, commenting that it was "probably because" the testimony "simply would not assist the trier of fact and/or it's not necessarily beyond the common experience of the jurors." The court also noted that Davis had never interviewed defendant or A.G.

Analysis

Defendant contends that the trial court abused its discretion in excluding Davis's proffered testimony. Defendant claims the trial court's erroneous ruling also violated his right to due process and to present a defense. Defendant argues that Davis was fully qualified to testify as an expert on the topics of marital relations and sex and her testimony was relevant to consent. With respect to Davis's qualifications, defendant asserts that it was undisputed that she had extensive experience. Citing *McCleery v. City of Bakersfield* (1985) 170 Cal.App.3d 1059, defendant claims that the practice should not be to exclude for lack of prior testimony because there would never be any experts. With respect to the relevance of

Davis's testimony, defendant cites nothing on point but argues Davis's testimony on "make-up" sex would "disabuse jurors regarding misconceptions about the likelihood of consensual sexual relations immediately after a heated and physical argument." Citing *People v. Wells* (2004) 118 Cal.App.4th 179, he claims such testimony is analogous to expert testimony on child sexual abuse accommodation syndrome (CSAAS). We find no error.

"A person is qualified to testify as an expert if he has special knowledge, skill, experience, training, or education sufficient to qualify him as an expert on the subject to which his testimony relates. . . ." Expert opinion is appropriate if it is "(a) [r]elated to a subject that is sufficiently beyond common experience that the opinion of an expert would assist the trier of fact; and [¶] (b) [b]ased on matter (including his special knowledge . . .) . . . that is of a type that reasonably may be relied upon by an expert in forming an opinion upon the subject. . . ."

A trial court's determination as to whether an expert should be allowed to opine about a particular subject is reviewed on appeal for abuse of discretion.

CSAAS cases involve expert testimony regarding the responses of a child molestation victim. Expert testimony on the common reactions of a child molestation victim is not admissible to prove the sex crime charged actually occurred. However, CSAAS testimony "is admissible to rehabilitate [the molestation victim's] credibility when the defendant suggests that the child's conduct after the incident—e.g., a delay in reporting—is inconsistent with his or her testimony claiming molestation." "For instance, where a child delays a significant period of time before reporting an incident or pattern of abuse, an expert could testify that such delayed reporting is not inconsistent with the secretive environment often created by an abuser who occupies a position of trust. Where an alleged victim recants his story in whole or in part, a psychologist could testify on the basis of past research that such behavior is not an uncommon response for an abused child who is seeking to remove himself or herself from the pressure created by police investigations and subsequent court proceedings. In the typical criminal case, however, it is the People's burden to identify the myth or misconception the evidence is designed to rebut. Where there is no danger of jury confusion, there is simply no need for the expert testimony."[2]

---

[2] Faced with the question of the admissibility of expert testimony concerning "rape trauma syndrome," *People v. Bledsoe* (1984) 36 Cal.3d 236, observed, "In a number of the cases in which the issue has arisen, the alleged rapist has suggested to the jury that some conduct of the victim after the incident—for example, a delay in reporting the sexual assault—is inconsistent with her claim of having been raped, and evidence on rape trauma syndrome has been introduced to rebut such an inference by providing the jury with recent findings of professional research on the subject of a victim's reaction to sexual assault. As a number of decisions have recognized, in such a context expert testimony on rape trauma syndrome may play a particularly useful role by disabusing the jury of some widely held misconceptions about rape and rape victims, so that it may evaluate the

We reject defendant's argument that Davis's testimony is akin to CSAAS testimony. First, the evidence was not proffered to rehabilitate the complaining witness; it was offered to explain her consent and to bolster her recantation at trial. Second, the proffered evidence did not relate to any behavior of the complaining witness, subsequent to the criminal conduct, that was inconsistent with the crime. Finally, the defense identified no myth or misconception held by the jury that needed to be addressed. Defense counsel's argument was simply that not everyone may be aware of make-up sex. As the Attorney General argues, the concept of "make-up" sex was within the common knowledge and experience of the jurors, was not relevant to the issue of consent and would not have assisted the jury on the issue of consent. We conclude the proffered expert testimony would not have assisted the jury in understanding the concept of make-up consensual sex. Nor would it have assisted the jury in determining the complaining witness's credibility—the primary issue at trial. There was simply no need for expert testimony.

The trial court's statement that Davis had never qualified before to testify on marital relations and sex, particularly make-up sex, was simply part of the trial court's observation that the testimony would not assist the trier of fact. The trial court did not abuse its discretion in excluding Davis's testimony. Defendant's constitutional claims likewise lack merit for the reasons stated. * * *

MAYO V. COMMONWEALTH

322 S.W.3d 41 (Ky. 2010)
(citations and some footnotes omitted)

A circuit court jury convicted H. Drew Mayo of one count of first-degree rape, one count of first-degree sodomy, and of being a second-degree persistent felony offender (PFO 2). Mayo now appeals from the resulting judgment as a matter of right. Finding no reversible error, we affirm.

I. FACTUAL AND PROCEDURAL HISTORY

The grand jury indicted Mayo for raping and sodomizing his estranged wife by forcible compulsion and for being a PFO 2. The charges proceeded to jury trial. At trial, the victim testified that she and Mayo had been separated for about two weeks before the acts in question occurred. According to the victim, she brought Mayo to her home—the former marital home that Mayo had vacated—to talk. The victim testified that an argument ensued and that Mayo became angry and forcibly raped her and forced her to perform oral sex on him. The victim testified that she did not want to have sex of any kind with Mayo at that time, but she engaged in the oral and vaginal copulation because Mayo threatened her with anal sex

evidence free of the constraints of popular myths." *Bledsoe* concluded that rape trauma syndrome testimony is inadmissible to prove the victim was in fact raped.

if she did not comply. The victim also testified that Mayo threatened to "bust" her in the mouth if she did not comply.

Mayo's version of events was different. Mayo agreed that he and the victim had been separated; but Mayo testified at trial that he and the victim had spent time together in the day or so preceding the alleged rape, and he believed they were going to repair their relationship. According to Mayo, he and the victim had consensual sexual intercourse several times in the hours preceding the alleged rape.

Obviously disbelieving Mayo, the jury convicted him of first-degree rape, first-degree sodomy, and being a PFO 2. The jury recommended ten years' imprisonment for the rape to be served consecutively to ten years' imprisonment for the sodomy. In lieu of these sentences, the jury recommended that Mayo be sentenced to twenty years' imprisonment for the PFO 2 conviction. The trial court sentenced Mayo in accordance with the jury's verdict and recommended sentences, after which Mayo filed this appeal.

II. ANALYSIS

Mayo raises several interconnected issues, some of which we will combine in this opinion. Mayo contends the trial court erred by [ ] granting the Commonwealth's motion in limine to prevent testimony of past anal intercourse between Mayo and the victim; * * * We find no reversible error as to any of Mayo's arguments.

A. No Error in Excluding Evidence of Past Consensual Anal Intercourse.

On the morning the trial was scheduled to begin, the trial court conducted an in-chambers hearing on motions in limine, including an oral motion by the Commonwealth to prohibit evidence of the victim's sexual history. At the conclusion of that lengthy hearing, the trial court seemed to rule that Kentucky Rules of Evidence (KRE) 412, commonly known as the rape shield law, prevented testimony about the victim's sexual history because Mayo had not provided the Commonwealth with the fourteen-day notice required by KRE 412(c)(1)(A). During the trial, however, the trial court orally amended its ruling to permit questioning regarding prior sexual relations between Mayo and the victim near the time of the alleged rape. But the trial court did not allow testimony regarding prior anal intercourse between Mayo and the victim.

On appeal, Mayo contends the trial court committed reversible error by excluding testimony of alleged consensual anal intercourse between him and the victim. Mayo admitted to having had sexual relations with the victim on the day in question and was, thus, relying on a consent defense. So Mayo contends that the trial court should have allowed testimony about prior anal intercourse to show that the alleged threat he made to the victim—submit to oral and vaginal intercourse under threat of anal intercourse—was not really a threat because anal intercourse had previously been a consensual act between Mayo and the victim. We disagree that the trial court erred in its ruling.

Our analysis must begin with a recitation of the relevant provisions of KRE 412. That rule provides, in relevant part:

> (a) Evidence generally inadmissible. The following evidence is not admissible in any civil or criminal proceeding involving alleged sexual misconduct except as provided in subdivisions (b) and (c):
>
> > (1) Evidence offered to prove that any alleged victim engaged in other sexual behavior.
> >
> > (2) Evidence offered to prove any alleged victim's sexual predisposition.
>
> (b) Exceptions:
>
> > (1) In a criminal case, the following evidence is admissible, if otherwise admissible under these rules: . . . .
> >
> > > (B) evidence of specific instances of sexual behavior by the alleged victim with respect to the person accused of the sexual misconduct offered by the accused to prove consent or by the prosecution. . . .
>
> (c) Procedure to determine admissibility.
>
> > (1) A party intending to offer evidence under subdivision (b) must:
> >
> > > (A) file a written motion at least fourteen (14) days before trial specifically describing the evidence and stating the purpose for which it is offered unless the court, for good cause requires a different time for filing or permits filing during trial; and
> > >
> > > (B) serve the motion on all parties and notify the alleged victim or, when appropriate, the alleged victim's guardian or representative.
> >
> > (2) Before admitting evidence under this rule the court must conduct a hearing in camera and afford the victim and parties a right to attend and be heard. The motion, related papers, and the record of the hearing must be sealed and remain under seal unless the court orders otherwise.

Although the general thrust of KRE 412 is toward exclusion of evidence regarding an alleged victim's sexual history, the rule makes an exception for evidence of past sexual behavior of the alleged victim with the accused if offered by the accused to prove consent or if offered by the prosecution. Certainly, we have interpreted KRE 412(b)(1)(B) in an earlier unpublished case to mean that "past sexual behavior between the alleged victim and the defendant is relevant and is generally admissible on the issue of consent" because "evidence of consensual sex or the desire to have consensual sex after an allegation of rape would tend to prove that consent may have in fact been given and that no rape occurred." Mayo relies upon this exception to argue that the trial court should not have excluded evidence regarding prior consensual anal intercourse Mayo allegedly had with the victim.

Before we delve into whether the trial court properly excluded this evidence, we must address some general principles. Mayo argued to the trial court, and seems to argue similarly before us, that sexual relationships between a husband and wife fall outside the protections of KRE 412 primarily because of a general assumption that spouses engage in sexual relations with each other. So Mayo's argument goes: any stigma associated with revealing a victim's sexual history would not apply when the alleged victim was the spouse of the alleged perpetrator because no juror would think less of a victim after learning that the victim had engaged in sexual relations with a spouse. But before we can address whether sex crimes committed against a spouse fall outside the protections of KRE 412, we must determine whether a spouse can even commit an inter-spousal sexual offense.

Former Kentucky law defined rape and sodomy in such a way as to preclude one spouse from raping or sodomizing the other spouse.[3] Under modern Kentucky law, however, it is clear that "[s]exual intercourse and deviate sexual intercourse can constitute rape or sodomy, even though the defendant and victim are married to one another." So having determined that it is possible for a spouse to be guilty of raping or illegally—that is, without consent—sodomizing a spouse, we move on to the question of whether evidence of inter-spousal sexual relations is outside the scope of KRE 412.

Mayo argues that evidence of sexual relations between a victim and spouse is outside the scope of KRE 412 because "[t]he obvious purpose of KRE 412 was to prevent unfair and unforeseen attack by a defendant upon the character of the victim"; but "[t]he husband/wife relationship is clearly not the type of evidence that would be [unforeseen] by the victim to be used at trial." But Mayo is unable to cite to *any* authority to support his contention that KRE 412 does not apply to inter-spousal sexual relations. The rule contains no such exception, and we decline to create one in this

---

[3] See ROBERT G. LAWSON & WILLIAM H. FORTUNE, *KENTUCKY CRIMINAL LAW* § 11–2(e) (1998) ("Kentucky historically defined rape and sodomy as acts with someone other than a spouse, a definition in accord with both the common law and the Model Penal Code.") (internal footnotes omitted). For a convincing rejection of the reasons underlying the antiquated theory that a husband could not be guilty of raping his wife, see Warren v. State, 255 Ga. 151, 336 S.E.2d 221 (1985).

case. In short, KRE 412 is not rendered inapplicable simply because the victim is the spouse of the accused.

Having cleared away the procedural underbrush, we now may focus on the merits of the trial court's decision to exclude evidence of alleged past consensual anal intercourse between Mayo and the victim. At the hearing on the Commonwealth's motion in limine, the trial court focused upon the lack of notice given by Mayo of his intent to introduce evidence of his past sexual relations with the victim under the rape shield exception codified at KRE 412(b)(1)(B). Since there was admittedly insufficient notice given to comply with the requirements of KRE 412(c)(1)(A), the trial court had the discretion to rely upon the lack of notice alone to exclude testimony about the victim's sexual history with Mayo.

But the trial court did not ultimately rely upon the lack of notice. Instead, the trial court permitted testimony about the sexual relations Mayo claims to have had with the victim in the day or so before the rape; and Mayo repeatedly—and usually without objection—testified on both direct and cross-examination about those purported sexual encounters.

The trial court really only excluded evidence of past alleged anal intercourse between Mayo and the victim, seemingly because it believed that such evidence would prejudice the victim in the eyes of the jury. Although it did not frame it as such, the trial court essentially barred the testimony regarding anal intercourse by applying KRE 403, which permits exclusion of otherwise relevant evidence if the probative value of that evidence is "substantially outweighed by the danger of undue prejudice. . . ."

The probative value of the evidence regarding a history of anal sex was low. Solely for the sake of analysis, we shall assume that the victim did have consensual anal sex with Mayo in the past. That does not mean, however, that she consented to having anal sex—or any other type of sex—with Mayo on the date in question. And the only real issue in Mayo's trial was whether the victim consented to the intercourse in question, or whether that intercourse was rape by forcible compulsion.

At most, evidence of past anal sex with Mayo would show a slight lessening of the fear suffered by the victim when Mayo threatened her with anal sex if she did not consent to oral and vaginal intercourse. In other words, because the only real issue was whether the sex in question between Mayo and the victim was consensual, the fact that the victim and Mayo may have had consensual anal sex in the past does not make it more or less likely that she consented to having any type of sex—anal or otherwise—with Mayo at the time in question, especially since Mayo was permitted to testify repeatedly that he had had consensual sex with the victim multiple times in the hours preceding the rape. Adding a detail that those sexual encounters or other more temporally remote past sexual encounters involved anal intercourse did not materially add to Mayo's consent defense.

On the other hand, evidence that the victim had engaged in past anal intercourse with Mayo would have had the potential to embarrass the victim. Mayo has pointed to nothing concrete to contradict the trial court's conclusion that the victim would have been unduly prejudiced in the minds of the jurors if evidence were presented regarding the victim's alleged affinity for, and history of, anal intercourse. * * *

Of course, evidence is not necessarily inadmissible if it has a stigmatizing effect. But the stigma that may have been associated with a history of anal intercourse is not the only reason to exclude the evidence. As stated before, the probative value of that evidence in this case was low because it had little bearing on whether the victim consented to have intercourse with Mayo at the time in question, especially since Mayo was permitted to testify about his alleged sexual encounters with the victim in the hours leading up to the rape. So permitting testimony about a history of anal intercourse was unnecessary and could have distracted the jury from its task of determining whether the victim consented to oral and vaginal intercourse at the time in question.

Determining whether proposed evidence's prejudicial effects substantially outweigh its probative value under KRE 403 is a delicate, fact-intensive inquiry. As an appellate court, we may only disturb a trial court's reasoned decision in this area if that decision is an abuse of the trial court's discretion. On balance, we cannot find that the trial court abused its discretion when it ruled that the prejudicial effects of the anal intercourse testimony substantially outweighed that evidence's probative value, nor do we conclude that the trial court's exclusion of this evidence improperly abridged Mayo's rights to cross-examine witnesses and to present a defense to the charges against him.

BOYKAI V. YOUNG

83 A.3d 1043 (P.A. Super. 2014)
(some footnotes and citations omitted)

Ted Young ("Appellant" or "Husband") appeals from the protection from abuse (PFA) order entered on March 20, 2013, which provided for the protection of Geraldine Boykai ("Appellee" or "Wife") for a period of one year. On appeal, Husband asserts that the trial court erred as a matter of law in concluding that the evidence established "abuse" under the Protection From Abuse Act, 23 Pa.C.S. § 6101, *et seq.* We affirm.

The trial court provided the following procedural and factual history:

> Both parties are originally from Liberia, Africa. Wife . . . came to the United States in 2004. Husband . . . came in 2005. The parties met in November, 2010 and moved in together. After Wife became pregnant, the parties married on November 8, 2011. Their child, [T.], was born [in April of 2012].

> Wife filed a [petition for a] PFA [order] on January 29, 2013. On February 6, 2013, the Honorable Alan Rubenstein entered a temporary order and continued the case. On February 27, 2013, the undersigned continued the matter, entered a temporary order, and the parties reached a custody agreement. On March 20, 2013, the undersigned conducted a hearing. Wife's principal allegation was that Husband forced her on numerous occasions to have sex against her will. * * *
>
> Wife testified that Husband only began to force himself on her if she declined after the parties were married. This included the time when she was very pregnant. She testified in some detail how he physically would overpower her. She stated he wanted intercourse three times a day, seven days a week. She stated it hurt at times. After the baby was born in April, 2012, the obstetrician told Wife not to have relations with her Husband for six weeks, but Husband still insisted at least once. Then, after the six weeks were up, Husband resumed his frequent daily demands.
>
> Finally, Wife began to oppose Husband's actions. Husband became very angry and stopped giving Wife money for herself and the child. Husband still tried to force himself on her. * * *
>
> Husband claimed he never forced himself on his wife. Husband claimed that he did not have any relations with his Wife after the baby was born because he was very happy with his child. But then[,] in response to his lawyer's continued questioning, [Husband] revised his testimony to state he only had sex with his wife when they both agreed. However, he did say that he told his Wife "it is only sex[,]" implying that they were having a disagreement.
>
> Husband produced a witness, a neighbor, who inadvertently corroborated Wife's testimony on the core issue of forcing sex. On cross, she stated that when she asked Wife "How are you and Ted," on several occasions Wife responded "Ted likes too much sex[."] She testified that Wife told her this when the baby was two or three months old.

The court entered a PFA order on March 20, 2013, which it summarized as follows:

> At the conclusion of the hearing, we entered a PFA Order in favor of Wife. The Order stated that Husband shall not abuse, stalk, harass, threaten or attempt to use physical force against Wife. It excluded Husband from the marital residence, prohibited Husband from having any contact with Wife, and proscribed him from possessing, transferring, or acquiring firearms for the

> duration of the order. The PFA Order is for one year; [i]t will expire on March 19, 2014.

Husband timely appealed. On appeal, Husband raises one issue for our review:

> Whether the Lower Court erred when it entered an Order under the Protection From Abuse Act against [Husband] where [Wife] failed to establish that she sustained "abuse" as that term is defined in the Act and, as a collateral question, whether this issue has not been waived where it was raised in [Husband's] Statement of Matters Complained of on Appeal and was not so vague or overbroad as to leave the Lower Court guessing at the exact argument raised on appeal?

"Our standard of review for PFA orders is well settled. 'In the context of a PFA order, we review the trial court's legal conclusions for an error of law or abuse of discretion.' "

Section 6102 of the Protection From Abuse Act provides the following definition of "abuse":

> "Abuse." The occurrence of one or more of the following acts between family or household members, sexual or intimate partners or persons who share biological parenthood:
>
> > (1) Attempting to cause or intentionally, knowingly or recklessly causing bodily injury, serious bodily injury, rape, involuntary deviate sexual intercourse, sexual assault, statutory sexual assault, aggravated indecent assault, indecent assault or incest with or without a deadly weapon.

In the instant case, Husband's sexual assaults began after the parties were married in 2011 and continued at least until the filing of the PFA petition in early 2013. During this time, Wife did not report the assaults to police or doctors. In January of 2013, Wife sought to file for child and spousal support in Bucks County. At that time, she told a filing clerk that she needed protection from her husband, and she was referred to Legal Aid of Southeastern Pennsylvania. Subsequently, Wife petitioned for a PFA order, based on Husband's assaults. In March of 2013, the trial court held a hearing on the petition. At the hearing, when asked why she did not report the assaults to police or doctors, she testified, verbatim:

> I never thought that you can call the police that your husband rape you. Because we're from Africa—I'm sorry for me bringing in another topic—Africa is like—he is trying to bring Africa rules in America. Like wives are slaves to men in Africa. So he was trying to bring that on me.[2]

---

[2] Although Wife attributes Husband's actions to their shared foreign culture, Pennsylvania, too, permitted these types of rapes less than thirty years ago. *See generally* Abigail Andrews

Over the past thirty years, our Legislature has endeavored to modernize Pennsylvania's sexual offenses statute. In addition to the repeal of the marital rape exemption in the 1980s, the Legislature has amended the definition of the "forcible compulsion" element of rape. While the crime previously required a showing of physical force, today, intellectual, moral, emotional, or psychological force all suffice to establish "forcible compulsion." Additionally, the Legislature codified a new offense, the crime of "sexual assault," which assigns culpability for sexual intercourse that occurs without the victim's consent, thereby precluding any need for a showing of force to establish that offense.[4] Still, some anticipate continuing legislative reform in the future. *See generally* Susan Estrich, *Rape,* 95 YALE L.J. 1087, 1182–83 (1986) (arguing against terming non-consensual sex as less than "rape," *e.g.* "sexual assault," and acknowledging that rape involving serious bodily injury merits aggravated treatment).

Turning to the case before us, Husband's argument implicates the trial court's use of the word "rape" in characterizing its finding of abuse. He argues that without physical force, there can be no finding of abuse under the PFA Act. Additionally, he contends that Wife's use of the word "force" in her testimony stems from her "good, yet limited, grasp of the English language." Specifically, he observes,

> The record reflects that Husband never struck her and, indeed, it appears as if she rather easily warded him off when she wished to. When she didn't want to engage in sexual relations, she simply pushed him away. * * * When Wife used the word "force" she was talking about something very different from the kind of physical coercion contemplated by the Lower Court. "Force" to her was Husband's purported refusal to support her if she did not agree to sexual relations." * * * Exchanging sex for support, while unseemly, is not "force" and, consequently, is not "abuse" as that term is used in the PFA [Act].[5]

Appellant misinterprets the meaning of the word "force" in the context of rape in Pennsylvania. To the extent that the trial court concluded that Husband abused Wife by means of exchanging sex for financial support,

---

Tierney, Comment, *Spousal Sexual Assault: Pennsylvania's Place on the Sliding Scale of Protection from Marital Rape,* 90 DICK. L.REV. 777, 793–94 (1986). Then-Governor Richard Thornburgh described rapes that occur within marital homes as something less than "real" rape, and vetoed at least one attempt to repeal Pennsylvania's marital rape exemption. *Id.* Ultimately, the Legislature repealed the marital rape exemption in Pennsylvania.

[4] Section 3124.1, Sexual Assault, provides as follows: "[A] person commits a felony of the second degree when that person engages in sexual intercourse or deviate sexual intercourse with a complainant without the complainant's consent."

[5] Although the trial court made no specific finding as to what "support" Husband withheld, Wife testified as follows, verbatim: "That's when he start punishing me because he—he stopped feeding me. He stopped supporting me. He stopped paying my bills. Because he wanted to have sex seven days a week and I said, no, three days a week and he said no. Because he say he the breadwinner in the family and that he stopped supporting the home." Wife also testified that Husband would not permit her to seek work. The trial court found Wife's testimony credible.

such compulsion amounts to intellectual or psychological force, thus establishing the elements of forcible rape. *see, e.g., Commonwealth v. Eckrote,* 12 A.3d 383, 387 (Pa.Super.2010) (threatening suicide amounted to psychological force, which established "forcible compulsion" element of rape).

Moreover, despite Husband's assertions, "force" is not required to establish "abuse" under the PFA Act. Here, the trial court's conclusion that the facts at issue establish "abuse" under the PFA Act was based on its determination that "Husband's conduct rose to the level of marital rape *or* sexual assault." (emphasis added). Even if it were not the case that Husband's actions amounted to forcible rape, the testimony adduced at the hearing also supports the conclusion that Husband engaged in sexual intercourse with Wife without Wife's consent, *i.e.,* the crime of sexual assault, which, like all forms of rape, constitutes "abuse" under the PFA Act.

As a practical matter, the relevant question is whether the alleged victim consented to sexual intercourse. To that end, the PFA Act supports a finding of abuse regardless of whether the sexual intercourse at issue is the result of forcible compulsion, or is simply non-consensual. Accordingly, we find no error of law or abuse of discretion in the trial court's conclusion that Husband abused Wife, and we affirm the trial court's order.

[Editor's Note: In "The Right to No: The Crime of Marital Rape, Women's Human Rights, and International Law," 41 Brooklyn J. Intl L. 153 (2015), Canadian law Professors Melanie Randall and Vasanthi Venkatesh note that many countries around the world do not criminalize marital rape, or treat it as a second class crime. Some even have a statutory "marital right of intercourse." The authors state that "this is a human rights problem, calling out for redress, both legally and socially." They argue that state failures to criminalize sexual assault in marriage or between unmarried intimate partners do not comply with international human rights norms, including equality, liberty, and security of the person. These rights are guaranteed in the Universal Declaration of Human Rights, the International Covenant on Civil and Political Rights, the International Covenant on Economic, Social, and Cultural Rights, the Convention on the Elimination of All Forms of Discrimination Against Women (CEDAW), and the Convention Against Torture, as well as the Convention of Belem do Para (Organization of American States), the Istanbul Convention (European nations), and the African Charter on Human Rights.

The authors state that allowing men to rape their female partners with impunity is also a breach of the due diligence standard required by States with regard to violence against women, since this failure violates rights that are legally guaranteed. In fact, they note that States are obligated to prevent violations of the rights of women under CEDAW, as well as punishing rapists and providing compensation to victims. The authors concede that criminalization alone will not solve this problem, and acknowledge the limitations of using criminal laws to stop domestic violence. Nevertheless, they argue that "the use of criminal law is a necessary, if incomplete, part of the strategy to end this form of gendered violence," a strategy that "must be part of a broader challenge to gender inequality in general."]

CHAPTER 10

LAW ENFORCEMENT RESPONSE

■ ■ ■

This chapter opens with a paper by the International Association of Chiefs of Police (IACP) outlining the history of law enforcement's response in domestic violence cases and describing what this response should entail. Then come pieces about the Maryland Lethality Assessment Program for domestic violence calls to law enforcement, and one focusing on stalking and domestic violence.

The next piece was written in 2020 response to the murder of George Floyd and argues that police should not be involved in responding to domestic violence, among other crimes, due to the history of law enforcement targeting people of the global majority/people of color unfairly. This is followed by an article cautioning that domestic violence policies should be based on the wishes and needs of survivors, who may want police involved.

The next piece argues that local law enforcement's compliance with the federal Secure Communities program results in immigrant victims of domestic violence staying silent about abuse.

Two long-time activists note that in domestic violence cases mandatory arrest policies often led to abused women being inappropriately arrested, or arrests of both parties. The authors describe the process of working with local law enforcement to change their policies and reduce numbers of dual arrests, partly by stressing the need to determine the primary or dominant aggressor. Then comes a summary of research examining the effect of primary/dominant aggressor policies in domestic violence cases, finding that the policies led to lowered rates of dual arrest of non-White people, increased dual arrest for LGBTQ couples, and had no effect on rates of arrest of heterosexual white people in domestic violence situations.

The next part of the chapter focuses on police liability for failure to arrest batterers, sometimes resulting in the deaths of partners or children. The materials start with an article examining possible legal grounds for liability given Supreme Court jurisprudence that has cut off several possible avenues of relief. This is followed by cases attempting to hold law enforcement responsible using approaches based on constitutional and statutory grounds, such as denial of equal protection or due process, the existence of a special relationship between law enforcement and the victim leading to a duty to protect, liability for failure to train officers properly, and whether the state actually increased the danger to the victim through indifference communicated to the abuser. This section concludes with a case in which a man arrested for domestic violence sued the city for false arrest, based in part on alleged discrimination against men.

The final section deals with "batterers in blue," meaning abusers who are themselves law enforcement officers. An article describes why law enforcement officers are significantly more dangerous than other batterers, and why their victims are virtually unprotected. A policy paper from the IACP outlines the particular dangers faced by victims of these batterers, what is expected of such officers, and what the official response should be when they become abusive to their partners. The chapter ends with a summary of a news article describing a police officer being arrested for domestic violence and losing possession of his gun based on a Gun Violence Restraining Order.

A. ARREST ISSUES

INTERNATIONAL ASSOCIATION OF CHIEFS OF POLICE, INTIMATE PARTNER VIOLENCE RESPONSE POLICY AND TRAINING GUIDELINES

(2017)

http://www.theiacp.org/MPDomesticViolence

Executive Summary

The complexities of intimate partner violence warrant the full attention of law enforcement and the criminal justice system. Law enforcement professionals have the ability to support victims, hold offenders accountable, and prevent future acts of violence. In order to be successful, law enforcement agencies must articulate their priorities concerning intimate partner violence and ensure that this message, as well as officer expectations, is outlined for all members. Creating, implementing, and developing training on an intimate partner violence department policy ensures that an agency is prepared to effectively respond to and successfully prepare these complex cases and reinforces the safety of the community it serves.

For the purposes of this document, the term "intimate partner violence" is defined as a pattern of abusive behavior in any relationship that is used by one partner to gain or maintain power and control over or to harm another intimate partner. Intimate partner violence can include physical, sexual, emotional, economic, or psychological actions or threats of actions that are intended to control and/or harm another person. This includes any behaviors that intimidate, manipulate, humiliate, isolate, frighten, terrorize, coerce, threaten, blame, hurt, injure, or wound someone. [emphasis in original]

A comprehensive intimate partner violence policy provides agency members with direction and support; helps ensure the safety of victims, agency members, and community members; and aims to hold perpetrators accountable. This resource provides law enforcement with issues, procedures, and recommendations to consider when developing an intimate partner violence policy as well as suggestions for developing training content. The IACP recommends departments take a preferred arrest response to intimate partner violence cases after effectively identifying the predominant aggressor. Therefore, any intimate partner violence policy should have a three-pronged focus—with victim safety and empowerment, officer safety, and perpetrator accountability being at the forefront. Departments should ensure that all other related policies are updated to be consistent with the provisions of this new or updated policy and that other forms of family violence, including elder and child abuse, are addressed in a parallel manner.

Knowledge and understanding about the crime of intimate partner violence, including promising practices for responding to and investigating the crimes of intimate partner violence, has expanded over the past decade, yet many misperceptions about intimate partner violence exist. In small communities and rural areas, reporting may be even more difficult as victims in these communities often find themselves located at great distances from law enforcement agencies, social services, and medical care facilities.

The policy elements set forth in this document aim to strengthen the investigation and prosecution of intimate partner violence crimes. This document encourages thorough police investigations, comprehensive interview techniques, a focus on the offender's actions, and diligent work to establish rapport and trust with victims. Responding officers and investigators must take a professional, victim-centered approach to the crimes of intimate partner violence. This approach can restore the victim's dignity and sense of control, while decreasing the victim's anxiety and increasing their understanding of the criminal justice system and process. Through following a comprehensive policy and robust up-to-date training, responding officers and investigators have the power to help a person heal from intimate partner violence.

Document Overview

This policy and training document provides essential background material, supporting details, and suggested policy elements on intimate partner violence. It also addresses investigative procedures and promising practices for working with victims of this form of violence. A comprehensive intimate partner violence policy aims to enhance public confidence in the reporting and investigative processes, thereby encouraging all intimate partner violence victims to report the crime. The topics in this guide were designed to assist law enforcement leaders in tailoring a policy that meets the requirements and circumstances of their own communities and agencies.

The primary objectives of an intimate partner violence policy are to do the following:

- Identify procedure and practice guidelines for a victim-centered, multidisciplinary response to intimate partner violence cases and thorough investigation of this crime
- Articulate the significant role and responsibilities of all department members throughout the intimate partner violence response and investigation
- Present appropriate action for and response to any violation of permanent, temporary, or emergency orders of protection
- Highlight methods to minimize further physical and psychological trauma to victims of intimate partner violence by creating a respectful, objective response
- Foster the safety of law enforcement responding to calls for intimate partner violence
- Present details on identifying and documenting stalking, and other co-occurring crimes, where applicable
- Encourage a coordinated community response and ensure all victims are supported and offered free and confidential support, social service referrals, and information from a trained intimate partner violence victim advocate
- Identify strategies to identify the predominant aggressor and hold suspects accountable by keeping the investigation focused on their behavior and actions

When creating any policy and/or training curriculum on intimate partner violence, it is imperative that law enforcement understands this is a serious crime that hurts both individuals as well as the larger community. Agencies must respond appropriately and consider populations that have particular needs including children; older adults; male victims; individuals with disabilities (physical, developmental, intellectual, or communicative); individuals living in rural communities; lesbian, gay, bisexual, or transgender individuals; non-native English speakers; individuals affiliated with gangs; economically disadvantaged individuals; individuals with HIV/AIDS; trafficked individuals; and others. These community members and populations may need additional or special assistance that might not be outlined in this document. Departments are encouraged to collaborate with local community organizations to develop culturally competent protocols to effectively and thoroughly address the needs of their various community populations.

[The Table of Contents includes: Facts about Intimate Partner Violence, Definitions, Training and Personnel Selection, Telecommunicator Response, Initial Officer Response, On-Scene Investigation, Identifying Evidence of Co-Occurrring and Interrelated Crimes, Supervisor Involvement, Protection Order Enforcement, Predominant Aggressor Determination, Arrest Decision and Procedures, Victim Safety and Protection, Post-Incident Investigation and Follow-Up, and Coordinated Community Responses to Intimate Partner Violence, including campus public safety and law enforcement agencies.]

Facts About Intimate Partner Violence

[*Editor's Note: "Nearly one in every three adult women experiences at least one physical assault by a partner during adulthood. Approximately four million American women experience a serious assault by an intimate partner during a 12-month period."*[1]] On average, nearly 20 people per minute are physically abused by an intimate partner in the United States. During one year, this equates to more than 10 million women and men.[2] It is a problem of epidemic proportions. Crimes classified as intimate partner violence are unlike most crimes due to the intimate relationship between the victim and the accused. Traditionally, this distinction led authorities to treat these crimes as though they were not crimes but private family matters.

Through increased awareness and education, society, including law enforcement, has a greater understanding of the dynamics and issues involved in intimate partner violence, fully recognizing it as a crime. In the past, police culture and training discouraged arrests in intimate partner violence incidents, and officers were expected to mediate and defuse the situation, and at times, law enforcement were reluctant to intervene.

The response of law enforcement to the crime of intimate partner violence, however, varies widely from jurisdiction to jurisdiction and officer to officer. There are instances when intimate partner violence calls are assigned low priority, when officers fail to make arrests or make unwarranted dual arrests, and when assaults involving extensive physical injury and weapons are treated as misdemeanors. An effective law enforcement response to intimate partner violence must include the adoption of a comprehensive policy that (1) holds perpetrators accountable, (2) supports victims, and (3) is consistently applied. Any comprehensive policy must be part of a developed, coordinated community infrastructure that can provide support to maximize victim safety,

---

1 C. J. Newton, MA, Domestic Violence: An Overview, FindCounseling.com, Mental Health Journal, Feb. 2001, reprinted by American Academy of Experts in Traumatic Stress, http://www.aaets.org/article145.htm (last visited Jan. 22, 2018).

2 Michele C. Black et al., *The National Intimate Partner and Sexual Violence Survey (NISVS): 2010 Summary Report* (Atlanta, GA: National Center for Injury Prevention and Control, Centers for Disease Control and Prevention, 2011), http://www.cdc.gov/violenceprevention/pdf/nisvs_report2010-a.pdf (last visited November 9, 2016).

implement sanctions against perpetrators, and offer rehabilitation opportunities for perpetrators.

To accomplish an effective law enforcement response, every agency member should understand the following:

- Intimate partner violence accounts for 15 percent of all violent crime.[3]
- The presence of a gun in an intimate partner violence situation increases the risk of homicide by 500 percent.[4]
- Nineteen percent of intimate partner violence involves a weapon.[5]
- Calls related to intimate partner violence represented the highest number of fatal calls for service for officers.[6]* * *

Body-Worn Cameras and Other Recording Devices

Policies and procedures for the use of body-worn cameras should clearly articulate how members should use cameras with victims of domestic violence, sexual assault, and stalking in order to maintain safety, privacy, and confidentiality.

A multidisciplinary team of community and criminal justice partners should be consulted in order to provide input regarding the complexities of responding to victims of domestic violence, sexual assault, and stalking and the impact cameras and recording may have on these individuals.

The decision to audio and/or videotape responses should be done with knowledge and understanding of applicable federal and state laws, especially pertaining to retention, release, and viewing and in consultation with a prosecutor in order to weigh the advantages and disadvantages of the practice.

Department policy should also address how confidential conversations with advocates on scene will be handled, as well as discussions with victims regarding safety planning.

[Editor's Note: see "Deliberations from the IACP National Forum on Body-Worn Cameras and Violence Against Women," available at http://

---

[3] Jennifer L. Truman and Rachel E. Morgan, *Nonfatal Domestic Violence, 2003–2012* (U.S. Department of Justice, Office of Justice Programs, Bureau of Justice Statistics), http://www.bjs.gov/content/pub/pdf/ndv0312.pdf (last visited November 9, 2016).

[4] Jacquelyn C. Campbell et al., "Risk Factors for Femicide in Abusive Relationships: Results from a Multisite Case Control Study," *American Journal of Public Health* 93, no. 7 (July 2003): 1089–1097, http://www.ncbi.nlm.nih.gov/pmc/articles/PMC1447915 (last visited November 9, 2016).

[5] Truman and Morgan, *Nonfatal Domestic Violence.*

[6] Nick Breul and Mike Keith, *Deadly Calls and Fatal Encounters: Analysis of U. S. law enforcement line of duty deaths when officers responded to dispatched calls for service and conducted enforcement (2010–2014)*, http://www.nleomf.org/programs/cops/cops-report.html (last visited November 9, 2016).

www.theiacp.org/Police-Response-to-Violence-Against-Women. See also Connecticut statute § 29–6d, enacted in 2015, providing that any records from such cameras in domestic violence or sexual assault cases are not subject to disclosure, to the extent that this could constitute an invasion of privacy.] * * *

Strangulation

Non-visible injuries

- Difficulty breathing/unable to breathe, hyperventilation
- Raspy voice, hoarse voice, coughing, unable to speak
- Trouble swallowing, painful swallowing
- Neck pain
- Nausea, vomiting
- Involuntary urination and/or defecation
- Fainting/light-headedness
- Headaches, head "rush," ears ringing
- Disorientation, memory loss, "spaced out"

Visible injuries

- Petechiae (pinpoint red spots about the area of constriction)
- Hemorrhaging, bruising
- Scratch marks, scrapes, abrasions
- Bloody nose, broken nose
- Fingernail impressions
- Swelling of neck or face
- Pulled/missing hair, bumps on head
- Skull fracture/head injuries
- Swollen tongue, swollen lips

* * *

Predominant Aggressor Determination

The officer should utilize the totality of information gained from a thorough and comprehensive investigation to make a determination of predominant aggressor. When trying to determine which person poses the most serious ongoing threat to whom, officers should consider the following:

1. Who uses threats and intimidation in the relationship?

2. Does either individual in the relationship isolate their partner?
3. Who is emotionally abusive (uses degrading names, humiliating comments, etc.)?
4. How are minimization, blame, and denial being used by the victim and/or the suspect?
5. Who utilizes the children to get their way in the relationship?
6. Who has forced sexual contact or used sexual acts as a way to control the other?
7. Who has control of money and finances or uses them as a way to control the other?
8. Who utilizes coercion and threats?
9. Have any threats been carried out or steps taken to carry them out?
10. Does either party have a history of committing violent crimes?
11. What does the premise history tell you about calls for service to the residence?
12. Is there a history of intimate partner violence between the parties?
13. Is there a physical size difference between the parties?
14. Does either party have a protection order against them or a history of protection orders against them?
15. Who appears to be more capable of assaulting the other?
16. What is the severity of the injuries to the parties?
17. Did either party utilize self-defense?
18. Is there potential for violence in the future? If so, by whom?
19. Which party has access to firearms or other weapons?
20. What types of injuries do the parties have? Are they offensive or defensive in nature?
21. Does either party express fear of the other?
22. Is there evidence from witnesses?

Following a thorough investigation that factors in the context within which the incident occurred, if the officer determines that in fact both parties have utilized equal violence, that there was no self-defense involved, and that there was no predominant aggressor, the officer should notify a supervisor.

If the officer determines probable cause exists to arrest both parties, the arresting officer should write and file a separate report for each arrest and include a detailed explanation as to the probable cause for each arrest.

The investigating officer(s) <u>*should not*</u> consider the following factors in making arrest decisions in interpersonal violence cases:

- Marital status of the parties
- The ownership or tenancy rights of either party or living arrangements
- Verbal assurances that the violence will stop
- The victim's emotional status
- The victim's initial reluctance regarding an officer-initiated arrest
- Whether or not physical injuries suffered by the victim can be personally observed at the time of the law enforcement response
- A claim by the suspect that the victim provoked or perpetuated the violence.
- Denial by either party that the violence or crime occurred when there is evidence of intimate partner violence
- Whether or not there have been arrests on previous calls
- Whether or not the victim has a criminal background
- Belief that the arrest might not lead to a conviction
- Whether or not a current protection order exists
- Adverse financial consequences that might result from the arrest
- That the incident occurred in a private place
- The racial, cultural, social, political, or professional position, age, gender, or the sexual orientation of either the victim or the suspect
- Immigration status of the victim or the suspect
- The use of alcohol and/or drugs by either or both parties
- Whether or not there were witnesses
- Whether or not the police witnessed the incident
- Whether the suspect is a law enforcement officer
- The investigating officer's perception of the willingness of the victim or of a witness to the domestic abuse to testify or participate in a judicial proceeding

While the above facts may be used as background information to complete a thorough intimate partner violence investigation for prosecution, they should not be part of an officer's determination to arrest.

[Editor's Note: See also "Breaking the cycle: Help came to her door to finally end the grip of domestic violence," by Cameron Knight, Cincinnati Enquirer, (10/27/21), about the Domestic Violence Response Team (DVRT) from Women Helping Women in Cincinnati, Ohio, which since 2018 has responded with police to domestic violence calls. Advocates speak with the survivor, and connect them with services, arranging for whatever the DV survivor needs: a place to stay, a protection order, creating a safety plan, child care, groceries, having someone accompany them to court hearings, counseling. In 2020 they responded to over 1000 calls. The police are supportive as they see that this program is effective, helping officers not just respond over and over to the same situation with the same family. The University of Cincinnati School of Criminal Justice is conducting a five-year evaluation of the program, but in the meantime it seems to be making a significant difference. The City of Los Angeles has also had an effective DVRT for decades.]

MARYLAND NETWORK AGAINST DOMESTIC VIOLENCE, POSITION PAPER: EFFECTIVENESS OF THE LETHALITY ASSESSMENT PROGRAM

(2022)(footnotes omitted)

The Lethality Assessment Program-Maryland Model (LAP), created by the MNADV, is an innovative, award-winning, nationally recognized practice to prevent intimate partner homicides and serious injuries. The LAP has also been identified as a "supported intervention" according to the Center for Disease Control's (CDC) Continuum of Evidence Effectiveness, and as a "leading promising practice" by the Office on Violence Against Women (OVW). . .

Understanding that Intimate Partner Homicide (IPH) is often preventable, the Maryland Network Against Domestic Violence (MNADV) promotes public health solutions that encourage better screening, identification, and service provision to those most at risk.

Partnering with Dr. Jacquelyn Campbell of Johns Hopkins University, the MNADV led an extensive and comprehensive multi-disciplinary research and development project to adapt the Danger Assessment (DA), an empirically developed risk assessment tool, into a screening and service provision protocol for first responders to incorporate in violence prevention. Through these efforts, the lethality screen and protocol were created and implemented in 2005.

The Lethality Assessment Program—Maryland Model (LAP) is an innovative, multi-pronged strategy to prevent domestic violence homicides. Law enforcement officers and other community professionals trained in the LAP use the evidence-based lethality assessment instrument to easily and effectively identify victims of intimate partner violence who are in highest risk of being killed or seriously injured by their intimate partners. Once a

High-Danger victim has been identified, the first responder immediately connects the victim via a hotline call to the local domestic violence service program (DVSP) for emergency safety planning and enhanced service provision. This warm handoff to a service provider in the immediate aftermath of the event distinguishes the LAP from other homicide prevention models and is a key to its effectiveness.

Before the LAP, the need for quality risk assessment tools was clear. Research at the time showed that for 28–33% of victims, the homicidal incident was the first act of violence. This demonstrates that when assessing homicide risk, first responders must be prepared to identify non-physical risk factors for abuse escalation.

Research also showed a startling trend of missed opportunities for intervention: a 2001 study of previous femicides in 11 US cities found that more than 44% of abusers were arrested, and almost one-third of victims had contacted the police, in the year preceding the homicide. Meanwhile, only 4% of those experiencing partner abuse had used a domestic violence hotline or shelter within the year prior to being killed by their partner. This evidence demonstrated that most people at risk of IPH were coming into contact with police rather than self-initiating contact with a service provider.

The LAP created a new mode of intervention: meet victims where they are—in front of law enforcement—but do not leave them there. By connecting victims to sustainable safety planning resources and assistance, the LAP closes the gap between victims and the services they need.

Response #1 When the victim chooses to speak with the hotline advocate. The advocate conducts a brief (no more than 10 minutes), structured conversation with the victim to safety-plan for the next 24 hours. Depending on the courses of action discussed in the telephone conversation between the victim and advocate, the first responder may work with the advocate and victim to assist in the victim's safety-plan (e.g., transporting the victim to shelter, or to a precinct to take out an emergency restraining order).

Response #2 As the LAP is an empowerment-based model, it is always the victim's choice to speak directly with an advocate. Even victims who are assessed as "Non-High Danger" at the time of the call for service, and those who are not ready to seek help, receive valuable information from the Lethality Screen; it affords them insight into the warning signs that could indicate that an abusive relationship is escalating in severity.

Now, nearly 20 years later, the LAP has a body of research behind it which speaks to the effectiveness and value of this model. The Lethality Assessment, honored as a "promising practice" by the U.S. Department of Justice, is evidence informed and empirically validated. . . [The authors state that the LAP is also predictive of which DV situations are likely to result in child homicides.]

[*Editor's Summary:* The LAP has been tested and found effective in many jurisdictions: Between 2008 and 2013, Maryland saw a 32% drop in domestic violence-related deaths. While this effect cannot be directly attributed to the LAP, increasing participation in the LAP certainly contributed. A study evaluating MD data found that the LAP reduced female homicides by males by 35–45% because it prompts at-risk victims to take protective actions.

In another study of 7 Oklahoma jurisdictions using the LAP, this tool was found to accurately predict both domestic violence homicides and those survivors at low risk of homicide or severe violence. Additionally, participants in the LAP study in OK experienced less severe violence than domestic violence victims who did not participate. This is likely due to a key component of the LAP: immediate, on-site connection to a service provider. Victims who were in the LAP were more likely to hide their partner's weapons, access formal domestic violence services, seek a protection order, establish a help code with loved ones, etc. Additionally, participants in the LAP were significantly more satisfied with the police response than those in the comparison group.

Domestic violence advocates in Pennsylvania, Connecticut and Virginia also reported positive results of the LAP in educating victims and law enforcement, reaching DV victims who would not otherwise have been connected to DV services, providing immediate and long-term help, and building more collaboration between law enforcement and DV agencies.]

STALKING AWARENESS, PREVENTION AND RESOURCE CENTER, ADDRESSING STALKING

(no date; footnotes omitted)

Stalking is a prevalent, dangerous crime requiring a thorough law enforcement response. Too often, stalking goes unrecognized and uncharged, and offenders are not held accountable for the extent of their crime(s).

Stalkers are persistent and often dangerous offenders who must be stopped.

- Stalkers are often violent:1 in 5 use weapons to threaten or harm their victims, and stalking often intersects with physical and sexual violence.
- Stalking preceded the attack in 76% of completed and 85% of attempted intimate partner femicides.
- Stalking increases the risk of intimate partner homicide by 3 times.

- The most common use of the criminal justice system prior to attempted or completed intimate partner homicide was reporting partner stalking.

Victims report experiencing stalking at much higher rates than legal systems identify it.

- In the U.S., 1 in 3 women and 1 in 6 men experience stalking in their lifetimes.
- Fewer than 40% of stalking victims report to law enforcement.

When victims do report, law enforcement may not identify and/or charge stalking.

. . .Legal systems may focus on one specific incident that resulted in a law enforcement response (e.g., an assault, an isolated threat, an act of vandalism) without realizing that the incident is not isolated, but is merely one piece of a larger course of conduct the offender has been engaging in.

. . .Proving the charge requires evidence of the acts constituting the stalking course of conduct, which is a series of incidents over a period of time that would cause a reasonable person fear or emotional distress. This means that the charge of stalking permits admission of a wide range of evidence without the need to file a motion to admit evidence of "other bad acts" under Evid. R. 404(b) (or its equivalent).

Such evidence provides context, shedding light on the defendant's purpose, motive, and intent and helping to explain the victim's behavior. It provides the judge and jury with the fullest possible picture of the relationship between the parties and of the offender-victim dynamics that permeate that relationship, allowing better understanding of how and why the crimes were committed.

Charging stalking may support important safety conditions for bail or probation, a lengthier prison sentence, and future prosecution if the offender later resumes stalking the same victim—or, as often happens, another one.

Does your agency have a shared understanding of and approach to stalking charges with your prosecutor's office?

In addition to the physical and/or sexual violence they experience, many stalking victims lose time from work, experience significant mental health impacts, and/or relocate. They may be eligible for a variety of services. . .

[A checklist with many details follows to help assess a law enforcement agency's response to stalking, along with citations to websites for SPARC and the International Assoc of Chiefs of Police. Topics include:

1. Policies and Protocols

2. Setting the Tone
3. Case Data
4. Training and Response
5. Staff Conduct
6. Leadership to Reduce Stalking and Interconnected Crimes
7. Website Information
8. Social Media]

KATE MCCORD (VIRGINIA SEXUAL & DOMESTIC VIOLENCE ACTION ALLIANCE), KELLY MILLER (IDAHO COALITION AGAINST SEXUAL AND DOMESTIC VIOLENCE), AND NAN STOOPS (WASHINGTON COALITION AGAINST DOMESTIC VIOLENCE), MOMENT OF TRUTH: STATEMENT OF COMMITMENT TO BLACK LIVES

(6/30/20)

[Editor's Note: In the wake of George Floyd's murder in May 2020, 46 sexual assault and domestic violence coalitions signed on to the following statement.]

This is a moment of reckoning. The murder of George Floyd broke the collective heart of this country, and now, finally, millions of people are saying their names: George Floyd, Breonna Taylor, Tony McDade, Ahmaud Arbery—an endless list of Black Lives stolen at the hands and knees of police. The legacies of slavery and unfulfilled civil rights, colonialism and erasure, hatred and violence, have always been in full view. Turning away is no longer an option. Superficial reform is not enough.

We, the undersigned sexual assault and domestic violence state coalitions call ourselves to account for the ways in which this movement, and particularly the white leadership within this movement, has repeatedly failed Black, Indigenous, and people of color (BIPOC) survivors, leaders, organizations, and movements:

- We have failed to listen to Black feminist liberationists and other colleagues of color in the movement who cautioned us against the consequences of choosing increased policing, prosecution, and imprisonment as the primary solution to gender-based violence.
- We have promoted false solutions of reforming systems that are designed to control people, rather than real community-based solutions that support healing and liberation.
- We have invested significantly in the criminal legal system, despite knowing that the vast majority of survivors choose

not to engage with it and that those who do are often re-traumatized by it.

- We have held up calls for "victim safety" to justify imprisonment and ignored the fact that prisons hold some of the densest per-capita populations of trauma survivors in the world.
- We have ignored and dismissed transformative justice approaches to healing, accountability, and repair, approaches created by BIPOC leaders and used successfully in BIPOC communities.

We acknowledge BIPOC's historical trauma and lived experiences of violence and center those traumas and experiences in our commitments to move forward. We affirm that BIPOC communities are not homogeneous and that opinions on what is necessary now vary in both substance and degree. We stand with the Black Women leaders in our movement, for whom isolation, risk, and hardship are now particularly acute. And we are grateful to the Black Women, Indigenous Women, and Women of Color—past and present—who have contributed mightily to our collective body of work, even as it has compromised their own health and well-being.

This moment has long been coming. We must be responsible for the ways in which our movement work directly contradicts our values. We espouse nonviolence, self-determination, freedom for all people and the right to bodily autonomy as we simultaneously contribute to a pro-arrest and oppressive system that is designed to isolate, control, and punish. We promote the ideas of equity and freedom as we ignore and minimize the real risks faced by BIPOC survivors who interact with a policing system that threatens the safety of their families and their very existence. We seek to uproot the core drivers of gender-based violence yet treat colonialism, white supremacy, racism, and transphobia as disconnected or separate from our core work.

A better world is within reach. It is being remembered and imagined in BIPOC communities around the world, and it is calling us to be a part of it. In this world:

- all human beings have inherent value, even when they cause harm;
- people have what they need—adequate and nutritious food, housing, quality education and healthcare, meaningful work, and time with family and friends; and
- all sentient beings are connected, including Mother Earth.

It is time to transform not only oppressive institutions, but also ourselves. Divestment and reallocation must be accompanied by rigorous commitment to and participation in the community solutions and supports that are being recommended by multiple organizations and platforms.

We are listening to and centering BIPOC-led groups, organizations, and communities. We join their vision of liberation and support the following:

- **Reframe the idea of "public safety"**—*to promote and utilize emerging community-based practices that resist abuse and oppression and encourage safety, support, and accountability*
- **Remove police from schools**—*and support educational environments that are safe, equitable, and productive for all students*
- **Decriminalize survival**—*and address mandatory arrest, failure to protect, bail (fines and fees), and the criminalization of homelessness and street economies (sex work, drug trades, etc.)*
- **Provide safe housing for everyone**—*to increase affordable, quality housing, particularly for adult and youth survivors of violence, and in disenfranchised communities*
- **Invest in care, not cops**—*to shift the work, resourcing, and responsibility of care into local communities*

The undersigned coalitions agree that the above actions are both aspirational and essential. While timing and strategy may differ across communities, states, and sovereign nations, we commit to supporting and partnering with BIPOC leaders and organizations. We commit to standing in solidarity with sovereignty, land and water protection, and human rights. And we say resoundingly and unequivocally: BLACK LIVES MATTER!

The Coronavirus pandemic, unchecked and increased police violence, political and economic upheaval, and stay-at-home isolation have produced the "perfect storm." We have a choice to make: run from the storm or into it. We choose to run into it and through it. We choose to come out the other side better, whole, loving, just, and more human.

We have spent decades building our movement's voice and power. How we use them now will define us in the years ahead. Let our actions show that we did not stand idly by. Let them show that we learned, changed, and will continue to demonstrate that Black Lives Matter is a centering practice for our work.

[Editor's Notes: 1. See Leigh Goodmark, "Should Domestic Violence Be Decriminalized?", 40 Harvard J of Law and Gender 53 (2017), in which the author argues that the criminal justice system should target habitual domestic violence offenders rather than all DV offenders, and that there

should be graduated responses with first offenders being offered restorative justice programs rather than jail, and responses increasing in severity if the violence is repeated. She also calls on anti-violence advocates to play an active role in movements to address the structural causes of violence and crime, working for racial, economic, and social justice in addition to gender justice.

2. See also Rhea Shinde, "Black Women, Police Brutality, and the Violence Against Women Act: How Pro-Arrest Policies Facilitate Racialized and Gendered Police Violence," 22(2) Georgetown J of Gender & Law [online, no page numbers] (2021), arguing that VAWA's policies supporting mandatory arrest and pro-arrest as well as aggressive prosecution exposed Black girls and women to more arrest, brutality, and involvement with the justice system.

3. Beth Richie discussed this letter in the book she co-authored with Angela Davis, Gina Dent, and Erica Meiner, "Abolition. Feminism. Now."]

MALLIKA KAUR, VICTIMS MUST NOT BE LOST IN DOMESTIC VIOLENCE & POLICING DEBATES

Ms. Magazine, 10/06/2020 (online)

California Governor Newsom just signed a bill expanding the legal definition of domestic violence to include "coercive control": a series of behaviors that attempt to deprive another of "free will and personal liberty." Amidst 2020's debates about policing domestic violence, those speaking for victim-survivors must also re-commit to prioritizing victims' free will and liberty to choose from a range of options. Some victim-survivors may want alternatives to police, courts, even traditional shelters. All want alternatives to domestic violence.

If this year is about exposing hard truths, here's another: we have too easily outsourced our domestic violence problem. Instead of responding and taking a stand in our families and communities, we have, over time relegated it to police and government systems. Now, reenergized by [Black Lives Matter] BLM protests, serious attention is being paid to alternate approaches. A decade after co-creating an immigrant community-based organization providing such alternatives, I welcome this attention. Still, I dread trading any romanticization of "police" for any romanticization of "community."

Leading up to this October's Domestic Violence Awareness Month, there has on the one hand already been necessary attention to the pandemic's disastrous, and worsening effects of domestic violence. On the other hand, debates rage in light of the racial justice movement: how does "defund the police" envision responding to domestic violence, currently the single largest category of calls received by police?

Working with victims, survivors, advocates, and experts over 17 years, I carry countless stories of police chauvinism and racism in response to survivors—even too many cases of victims being arrested or even incarcerated. But I also hold stories of women, and children, who attribute their lives and wellness to police who responded to very dangerous situations when no one else would. To me this hardly proves there are "a few bad apples" in law enforcement. It does prove that not all domestic violence is the same; not all victimized by domestic violence are identical, not even all within a certain race or ethnicity (some in fact don't even prefer the label "survivor" that was preached when I first started this work). One size fits only one.

That's precisely why when it comes to policing domestic violence, it's not all or nothing.

Policing is not the answer. "Community" is not the answer either. Victim-survivors need and demand several combinations, to have an expanded set of options from which to freely choose. And many of those closest to domestic violence survivors—their crisis counselors and advocates—have for long already been employing exactly such creative combinations. They have trained to offer many options and to accept different choices. Not all abuse is the same. Abuse runs the gamut from coercive control, to battering, to murder. Every day, on helplines across the country, advocates—crisis counselors, shelter workers, therapists, lawyers—support people in assessing the dangerousness of the abuse they are facing. We know the only experts about the lethality of a situation are the victim-survivors themselves. Heavily armed (often with a doomsday arsenal) abusive men are unfortunately not uncommon. But also the slight, meek-seeming, well-employed, privileged abusive person may well be more murderous than someone who more fully performs hypermasculinity. After all, even a few seconds of pressure to someone's neck—colloquially "choking"—can cause brain injury if not death. We believe someone when they say they fear they will be killed.

Not all victims are alike. 1 in 4 women in this country have experienced victimization by an intimate partner. Clearly, every fourth woman in this country is not alike: in privilege, in preference, in personality. Not even all victims within any racial or ethnic group are identical. Fully knowing the legal system often doesn't do justice and its pace is consistently out-of-step with the pace of trauma recovery, some will choose a long and hard fight, employing the police and the courts. The notion that this is a choice only by "rich, white women" is false. It invisiblizes the immigrant woman who tells me that she didn't flee one lawless country to settle for no semblance of justice in this one. It dismisses the woman who is convinced that only the threat of greater violence will curb her partner's threat. It ignores the many women who have none of the "community," often promised as the alternative to policing.

Not all community responses are alike or preferred. Ten years ago I co-founded a community-based organization, Sikh Family Center, the only organization focused on gendered violence in the Sikh American population. We have had strangers step up and provide shelter; friends pack courts during emotional hearings; elders have simple but essential conversations: "I know what's happening, I'll keep checking on her daily, and I will come over if I suspect you've hurt her again." There is a lot of beauty in these responses: they are not only individual interventions, they propel the culture change to prevent domestic violence in the first place. A prominent non-Sikh family lawyer took one of our complicated cases pro bono a few years ago, waving aside the money we had raised for representation: she was stunned by the community's support for a stranger on a cross-country run from her abusive husband. Within our community often marginalized—especially post 9/11, for its turbaned and bearded men—this White attorney realized there was much progressiveness to be celebrated. Like other community organizations, ours too seeks to cultivate what's best in the community. Yet, at the same time, we wrestle with the reality of community members who conspire with the abusive person because of their family ties; their economic worth; or other shared experience—at times as shamefully simple as "she's complaining about what every wife goes through." We have also grappled with the community members unable to comprehend how even after all the help and support they extended, she has not left an abusive situation. And community members who make it impossible (psychologically, emotionally, even physically) for a survivor to seek safety, within the relationship or outside of it.

Our experience at Sikh Family Center is not unique. On the condition of anonymity the director of a large women of color organization told me this month: "The only people thinking this is the answer, have not tried engaging the community on domestic violence. Even the most well meaning folks have little staying power in these long and complicated and often dangerous scenarios."

It was in the context of an even more intractable and apologist community—with much lesser support for abuse victims—that feminists of the 1970s did push for increased police response to domestic violence. They have repeatedly been rebuked for this in recent months. But anyone familiar with countries that still have the near-zero police response to gender violence that the U.S. had then is hard pressed to agree the 1970s movement a "failure." Undoubtedly white feminist voices were privileged. And the movement was eventually effectively coopted: a justification for the Violence Against Women Act prioritizing 85% of the dollars to policing and punishing.

But the feminists championing the movement and "survivors" were not entirely separate categories. They have never been, in the anti-violence movement. The movement in the 2020s now needs to take heed from survivors, including those being victimized today. They cannot be asked to curtail their choices, even endanger their lives, even for the urgent purpose of correcting the U.S. police and prison complex.

Not all police response should be alike. Making the response more scenario-specific is essential. This nuance can only be provided through knowledge from community and advocates. And the labor lent by advocates cannot be undervalued: it should cost the police, not be built-into their budgets. The faces of George Floyd, Breonna Taylor, Trayvon Martin—and indeed generations of unnamed, and certainly unfilmed, Black people before them—make it difficult to again propose more "training" and "reform" for the policing system that is racist in its origin and praxis. Yet, the faces of the many endangered and embattled women also make it impossible to propose we never call on police. When a person is in a deathly rage, ready to kill their partner, there are few community members who will stand in the way. When we are living in a world where it is apparently too hard for too many to wear a weightless face mask for the health of others (as well as themselves), it requires little imagination to forecast bystander action in the face of brutality against someone else. Broken police and prison systems are the result of a broken social contract.

The social contract will take time to repair. That doesn't mean we stop trying. But in the meantime, if we as a society are going to continue outsourcing our domestic violence problem, let's do so to those trained and committed to standing with survivors, no matter what choices they make, no matter how many times they change their minds. Shifting a few percentage points of massive police budgets would better equip direct services advocates and boost the social services they provide to those victimized. If that is still too large an ask, the feminists will keep marching, for everyone's liberty.

[Editor's Notes: 1. See Chan M. Hellman, Casey Gwinn, and Gael Strack, "Criminal Justice Reform and Interactions with Law Enforcement: Perspectives from Survivors of Domestic Violence," 26(2) DV Report 17, (Dec/Jan 2021), describing results of a 2020 national survey of 153 survivors of domestic violence, 60% of whom had received services from a Family Justice Center. 56% were Black, Indigenous or People of Color. 57% of total respondents reported positive experiences with police, including 54% of the non-White respondents. 48% of the overall respondents reported negative experiences with police; 51.4% of BIPOC victims had negative experiences. 72% of respondents stated that they did not support efforts to reduce the use of criminal justice in DV cases and 80% opposed diversion for DV offenders. 91.5% supported domestic violence advocates or community members responding with police; most were in favor of anti-bias training for police. 96% opposed bail reform that would allow their offenders to get out of jail more quickly, and most said they want more

engagement from law enforcement, though survivors of color were more open than Whites to efforts to reduce the use of the criminal system. Only 28% of respondents supported reallocating part of the police budget to community agencies.

2. See also "Another Perspective on 'The Moment of Truth,'" Casey Gwinn, and Gael Strack, 26(2) DV Report 17 (Dec/Jan 2021), in which the authors acknowledge the structural racism in the criminal justice system. They note that prior to VAWA, domestic violence was essentially decriminalized, with very few arrests and high numbers of homicides, and cite statistics showing that VAWA's emphasis on using the criminal justice system to address domestic violence saved lives, especially Black women's and men's lives, and reduced domestic violence across the U.S. The authors also emphasize the need for prevention of abuse, stating that they run the largest camping and mentoring program in the country, Camp HOPE America, designed for children impacted by domestic violence, which is effective in keeping them out of jail and prison.

3. And see Jacquelyn Campbell, "We Must Not Forget Racial Injustice Nor Can We Forget Dangers Facing Women," 26(3) DV Report 33 (Feb/March 2021) describing the "playing field" for Black women and their partners as "distinctly tilted in the direction of injustice," and advocating for a rehauling of the family and criminal courts so that instead of focusing only on punishment, they also act as "agents of healing and hope."]

RADHA VISHNUVAJJALA, INSECURE COMMUNITIES: HOW AN IMMIGRATION ENFORCEMENT PROGRAM ENCOURAGES BATTERED WOMEN TO STAY SILENT

32 B.C. J. L. & Soc. Just. 185 (2012)
(citations and footnotes omitted)

INTRODUCTION

When Maria Bolanos called the police during a fight with her partner, she never imagined that a call for help could lead to her own deportation. A police officer responded to the call from the twenty-eight-year-old Salvadoran undocumented immigrant, but ended up charging her with illegally selling a phone card to a neighbor. The police later dropped the charge, but not before fingerprinting Bolanos. Under the Secure Communities program, officers cross-referenced her fingerprints with a federal immigration database maintained by Immigration and Customs Enforcement (ICE). Because Bolanos had been previously fingerprinted after customs officials caught her illegally entering the United States, she was flagged for deportation.

Secure Communities was designed to improve public safety by identifying and removing criminal aliens. ICE claims that Secure Communities "prioritiz[es] the removal of criminal aliens, those who pose a threat to public safety, and repeat immigration violators," but Bolanos' current predicament may prove otherwise. Even though police later dropped the phone card charge, Bolanos' fingerprints were the first step toward deportation proceedings. Bolanos' story demonstrates how Secure Communities not only removes dangerous criminals from communities, but also is used as a widespread immigration enforcement tool.

Using Secure Communities as a broad enforcement mechanism undermines the relationship between undocumented immigrants and local law enforcement by making victims of crime hesitant to ask for help. In instances of domestic violence, the risk of contacting the police is further compounded by barriers of language, culture, and dependency on documented, abusive partners. Undocumented domestic violence victims—mostly women—are less likely to report abuse than documented or non-immigrant victims because they fear being reported to immigration authorities. Undocumented women are especially vulnerable when their abusive partners are documented because a documented abuser has no fear of deportation and therefore has another element of power. Abusers may exert their control by threatening deportation or blocking their victims from obtaining lawful status.

This Note argues that Secure Communities should only crosscheck fingerprints of those accused of serious crimes, thereby preserving the relationship between police and undocumented victims of domestic violence. * * *

III. A PROPOSED SOLUTION FOR ICE

Secure Communities undermines protections for domestic violence victims by encouraging silence through fear of deportation. Because domestic violence perpetrators often use their partners' undocumented status as a means of control, victims will be less likely to call for help if they know that police will share their biometric data with immigration enforcement. Undocumented women are further deterred from calling for help because any arrest, regardless of whether the charge is later dropped, may allow local law enforcement to obtain their fingerprints.

ICE should therefore modify Secure Communities to allow for adequate protections of domestic violence victims in three distinct steps. First, the program should mandate delayed reporting until after those arrested during domestic violence incidents are convicted. Second, ICE should limit the program to sharing only those fingerprints obtained through felony charges and misdemeanor convictions. Finally, ICE should encourage local officials to communicate these changes to the public.

The benefits to these changes are two-fold: protecting vulnerable women from violence and preserving the relationship between undocumented immigrants and local police. The Bolanos incident, like others, underscores how the program has departed from its alleged original intent of removing dangerous criminals from communities. ICE and the states should narrowly tailor Secure Communities to protect victims of domestic violence while still removing dangerous criminals.

A. ICE's Attempt to Acknowledge the Problem

ICE changed Secure Communities in the summer of 2011. John Morton, the Director of ICE, sent a memorandum to Field Office Directors, Special Agents in Charge, and Chief Counsel to outline the revised policy on prosecutorial discretion. In his memorandum, Morton sets forth a new policy regarding prosecutorial discretion in "cases involving the victims and witnesses of crime, including domestic violence . . . ." Morton claims:

> The vast majority of state and local law enforcement agencies do not generally arrest victims or witnesses of crime as part of an investigation. However, ICE regularly hears concerns that in some instances a state or local law enforcement officer may arrest and book multiple people at the scene of alleged domestic violence. In these cases, an arrested victim or witness of domestic violence may be booked and fingerprinted and, through the operation of the Secure Communities program or another ICE enforcement program, may come to the attention of ICE.

Morton then advises officers, agents, and attorneys "to exercise all appropriate discretion on a case-by-case basis when making detention and enforcement decisions in the cases of victims of crime . . . ."

While attempting to recognize the domestic violence issue, this aspirational memorandum does not ensure that immigrant victims of domestic violence will not be subjected to racial profiling or subsequent removal proceedings. * * * ICE should therefore establish clear guidance to fully protect victims of domestic violence because, without it, "prosecutorial discretion" may further enable pretextual arrests.

B. A Three-Step Process to Protecting Victims of Domestic Violence and Increasing Community Safely

Discretion alone will likely not solve the problem of pretextual arrests that prevent abused women from calling for help. Instead, ICE should implement three specific changes to protect victims of domestic violence. First, ICE should modify Secure Communities to specify that reporting of arrestees pursuant to domestic violence incidents is not required until conviction. Second, ICE should limit the program to felony charges and misdemeanor convictions. Third, ICE should work with states and localities to implement a public relations campaign that communicates these changes. This final step would ensure that all residents—documented and undocumented—understand the program's scope and that they can contact law enforcement without fear of deportation. * * *

[Editor's Notes: 1. While the Secure Communities program was suspended from 2015–2017 under President Obama in favor of the Priority Enforcement Program (PEP), in January 2017, President Trump reinstated the Secure Communities program. In February 2017, an undocumented survivor of domestic violence staying at a shelter was arrested by ICE agents inside the El Paso, Texas courthouse just after she obtained a restraining order. While President Joe Biden revoked the Executive Order regarding the Secure Communities Program in 2021, the ICE Criminal Apprehension Program continues to share data regarding immigrants between law enforcement agencies and ICE in some circumstances.

2. In "The Effects of Arrest on Intimate Partner Violence: New Evidence from the Spousal Assault Replication Program," (National Institute of Justice, 2001), Christopher D. Maxwell, Joel H. Garner, and Jeffrey A. Fagan reported on their re-evaluation of the six replication studies carried out between 1981 and 1991 to test whether arrests deterred subsequent violence in IPV cases better than less formal alternatives. Contrary to Sherman's analysis, these authors stated that the results were inconsistent, and there were many differences between sites that made findings harder to analyze. However, they found that arresting male batterers was consistently related to lower recidivism against female intimate partners, and that most cases had no repeat violence regardless of the type of intervention. There was no correlation between arrest and higher risk to victims. The batterer's prior criminal record, younger age, and intoxication during the incident were predictive of future violence. Victim interviews indicated that older nonwhite men were less aggressive, while police reports showed lower levels of repeat violence if the abuser was white and employed. The length of time the abuser was detained was not significant, so arrest alone was a deterrent._Of course, some batterers were not deterred; the authors noted that we need to develop policies that help partners of those people.]

Mandatory arrest laws got a further boost from the Violence Against Women Act of 1994. This Act required states to certify that they had adopted either pro-or mandatory arrest policies in order to be eligible for federal funding under the Grants To Encourage Arrests program—a program that provided $120 million over three years to state and local police departments. Eager to ensure that they would be able to access this important funding, states that had not already adopted such laws quickly did so. Today, every state has some form of pro-arrest policy and, as of 2004, at least twenty states and the District of Columbia mandated arrest in cases involving domestic violence. * * *

VI. FROM DOMINANCE TO ANTI-ESSENTIALIST FEMINISM

Mandatory policies reflect the influence of dominance feminism, a strand of feminism prevalent in the 1980s and 90s, the same time that domestic violence law and policy was being created and implemented.

Dominance feminists, led by Catherine MacKinnon, contended that male domination of women in the sexual sphere was the primary vehicle for the continued subordination of women. MacKinnon argued that "our male-dominated society, aided by male-dominated laws, had constructed women as sexual objects for the use of men." Using this theory, dominance feminists cast the unwillingness of the law to confront issues of sexual harassment and rape as the manifestation of male assertions of dominion over the sexuality of women. * * *

Mandatory arrest, no-drop prosecution, and policies banning mediation are consistent with a dominance feminist view of the law. Dominance feminism facilitated the enactment of mandatory policies by suggesting that by virtue of their subordinated status, women were incapable of making rational choices in the face of abuse and instead were in need of the substituted judgment of the legal system. Such policies fail to acknowledge that women can be battered and nonetheless be actors with the ability to determine the course of their lives. Dominance feminism provided an ideological justification for domestic violence policies that stereotyped all women who had been battered as a particular type of victim, denied them agency, and dictated what their response to the violence should be.

Critics of dominance feminism have given it a different label: victim feminism. Dominance feminism rests upon the idea that every woman is a victim or a potential victim of male subordination, acted upon rather than acting. That perspective has been challenged by a new wave of feminist theorists who argue that the experiences of individual women, rather than a stereotyped "universal" woman or victim, must be at the center of feminist theorizing and policymaking. Anti-essentialist feminists argue that there is no unitary women's experience; the experiences of black women may be vastly different than those of white women, for example, or those of poor women distinct from those with greater means.

The attempt to shoehorn all women's experiences into that of the ber-woman, anti-essentialist feminists contend, has privileged the experiences of white, middle class, straight women over those of others. Anti-essentialists argue that we must instead see women at the intersections of the various identities that construct them: race, sexual orientation, class, disability, and any other characteristic that shapes the woman. Only then can policies be responsive to the needs of all women. While some have argued that third-wave feminism is pre-legal, anti-essentialism may, in fact, be the legal manifestation of third-wave feminism, embracing third-wave feminism's rejection of early versions of feminist theory and focusing on the "multiple nature of personal identity."

Mandatory policies in cases involving domestic violence are inconsistent with anti-essentialist feminism. Mandatory policies assume that all women who have been battered are "victims," stereotyping them as meek, afraid, and easily manipulated and controlled, rather than seeing the complexity of and differences among them. These policies deny women the ability to define themselves, distilling every woman down to the stereotypical victim in need of the system's protection, unable to make rational choices. Mandatory policies ignore that women experiencing violence may have multiple goals, assuming instead that all women prioritize safety and accountability.

Defining all women as victims allowed the legal system to narrow the available options, depriving women who had been battered of the ability to pursue possibilities beyond the range of those deemed acceptable by the legal system. Anti-essentialist feminism requires that women who have been battered be treated as individuals with different identities and capacities, and that they be given the opportunity to make choices consistent with their own goals and priorities. In a third-wave feminist world, women who have been battered should not be told by the state that they have no choice about arrest, prosecution, or mediation. Instead, domestic violence law and policy should respect the rights of individual women to choose whether and how to use the criminal and civil legal systems. Such a shift would be consistent both with anti-essentialist feminist theory and with the focus on autonomy and agency that characterized the early battered women's movement.

Critics of anti-essentialist feminism have argued that its focus on the individual creates a fragmentation of interests that can render policymaking impossible. But focusing on an individual's autonomy—her right to make her own decisions—creates a clear path for policymakers. Domestic violence law and policy should not act on individuals, but rather should be available to be deployed by them as they see fit. Domestic violence law and policy need not address each individual's personal concerns; it need only give her the ability to choose whether, when, and how to utilize tools like arrest, prosecution, and mediation. Creating space for choice honors the differences between women, recognizing that race, class, sexual orientation, disability status, and a multiplicity of other variables color how a particular woman might want to respond to a particular incidence of violence at a particular moment in time. Enabling women who have been battered to decide how they will engage with the legal system respects their autonomy and agency and allows individual women to craft the solutions that they perceive are most likely to meet their goals, whether those goals are safety, accountability, economic stability, or maintenance of their intimate relationships.

The choices made by women who have been battered will certainly have consequences, sometimes overwhelmingly negative consequences. Some women who choose not to have their partners arrested will be battered again; some will die. Some offenders will be free to abuse again as a result of dismissed prosecutions. Some women will strike bad deals in mediation or experience revictimization in the process. Creating space for individuals to exercise their ability to choose, regardless of the outcomes of those choices, is a hallmark of autonomy. But many other women will be empowered by the ability to make these choices for themselves in the contexts of their own lives, rather than having the legal system impose decisions upon them based on what they "should" want. If empowerment is still the goal of the battered women's movement, we must accept that women who have been battered have the right to make choices that we might disagree with, dislike, or fear.

Although many of the advocates who originally endorsed them have come to question mandatory policies, that reevaluation may have come too late. The state, which has embraced these mandatory policies, has very different goals for its interventions than advocates do. The state has put substantial resources behind policies like mandatory arrest and no-drop prosecution, and an entire generation of police and prosecutors has been schooled in both the theory underlying these policies and the techniques for instituting them. * * *

Mandatory interventions, particularly in the criminal justice system, are the rule, not the exception, and new mandatory interventions are being proposed to address perceived shortcomings in the system. Changing the legal system's culture to foster autonomy for women who have been battered will be significantly more difficult than getting the legal system to embrace those changes in the first instance. The experience with mandatory policies should serve as a cautionary tale, though, prompting advocates and policy makers to think carefully before enacting laws and policies that bind all women who have been battered, notwithstanding those women's own goals, beliefs, choices, and situations. Mandatory interventions in cases involving domestic violence are a second-wave relic that feminists should shed as we move into a third-wave world.

MARTHA MCMAHON AND ELLEN PENCE, MAKING SOCIAL CHANGE: REFLECTIONS ON INDIVIDUAL AND INSTITUTIONAL ADVOCACY WITH WOMEN ARRESTED FOR DOMESTIC VIOLENCE

9(1) Violence Against Women 47 (2003)
(citations and footnotes omitted)

* * * Thus, the criminal justice system has always been a "player" in domestic violence, visible or invisible. Activists pursued an agenda of criminalization because many believed that men would not stop battering women until the community thought of it as a crime and treated it as such. Pursuing an agenda to criminalize domestic violence meant using individual cases to make a social point in order to protect women by making social change. Criminalization was never intended to be the only or major

response. Criminalization was not an end in itself; it was one means to an end. * * *

This is not to say that there are no possible gains but to argue that activists and advocates need to be continually reflective about how institutions such as the criminal justice system continuously reproduce relations of domination in society, whether gendered, racialized, or classed. And the workings of power are often far more visible to women on the margins of society or those situated in the intersections of different relations of inequality than to those nearer the center. * * *

We began the first part of this article by writing that the arrests of women for domestic violence tell us more about the complexities of criminalizing domestic violence than they do about women's use of violence. We argued that the social and legal understandings of women's use of domestic violence are profoundly inadequate, with dangerous consequences for women. We also discussed the need to analyze the intersections of race and class, rather than focusing primarily on gender, to understand domestic violence and the legal system's responses to it. We asked whether the high rates of arrest of women for domestic violence implied that the anti-domestic violence movement had been misguided in its reliance on criminalization and in the institutionalization of the anti-domestic violence movement. Women of color in the United States and Canada were often the first to question the reliance on criminalization. Some of their reasons were the same as those of feminist critics in addition to reasons of particular risks posed to members of marginalized communities, men, women, and children. Questions about the anti-domestic violence movement's strategies prompted us to (a) analyze the movement as a social movement with challenges common to all movements, (b) attempt to understand the broader political and historical context of the movement's strategies and choices, and (c) reflect on the complexities of making social change.

In the meantime, women who are not batterers are being arrested under laws originally designed for men who are. In the second part of the article, we turn to strategies for responding concretely to this problem.

STRATEGIES FOR ADVOCACY

Today, advocates are faced with a number of challenges to adapt to the unintended consequence of battered women being arrested for assaulting their abusers. In this section, we limit our discussion to the efforts of the advocates and their allies in the legal system in the city of Duluth, Minnesota. It is a local effort and focused on the application of the law rather than changing the law itself. The latter discussion is outside the scope of this article, but it should not be outside the scope of our advocacy agenda. In Duluth, five strategies are used to respond to the problem of battered women being arrested for using violence. These strategies express a critically reflective and historically situated engagement of the criminal justice system rather than a "reliance or dependence" on it to protect women. The Duluth strategies are drawn widely from those used in other communities, although the particular combination of these five strategies is unique to Duluth.

FIRST STRATEGY: REDUCING THE NUMBER OF ARRESTS

Duluth's women's advocates approached the task of reducing the number of women arrested for assault in two ways. First, through institutional advocacy with the police, advocates succeeded in introducing the expectation that arresting officers determine whether either party in a domestic violence case is acting in self-defense. After reviewing the reports of every arrested woman over a 2-year period, police administrators were convinced that officers needed specialized training in making self-defense determinations at the scene. In some cities, including Duluth, one third to one half of the women arrested for domestic-related assaults have a legitimate, direct claim of self-defense. Under the new procedures and training programs, the number of cases in which officers determine that a woman assaulted her partner has dropped dramatically.

The second approach was to discourage the growing practice of dual arrests when both parties assault each other but one party is clearly more dangerous and dominant in his or her use of force. This was accomplished through requiring the investigating officers making the decision to arrest to apply a new test to the case under consideration, that of determining who is the "predominant aggressor." A simple rule of thumb, for example, might be for the intervening officer to ask himself or herself, "If I were to walk away from here without doing anything, who would be most at risk?" The new concept of predominant aggressor was tested first in Washington state, then in Wisconsin, and now in a growing number of states with strong preferred or mandatory arrest statutes. * * *

In the 41 cases mentioned above, it was the male suspect who fit the category of predominant aggressor, using the single criterion of who caused the most harm. Yet the woman involved was also arrested. Women fit the predominant aggressor category in only a small minority of arrest reports describing situations in which both parties used force. In 5 reports from the original 75, it was difficult to determine a predominant aggressor based on the incident under investigation or the history of violence between the parties. A well-trained police department, using a predominant aggressor policy and monitoring compliance among arresting officers, would eliminate well more than 50% of arrests of women and show them to be problematic toward the goal of securing public safety.

At the urging of advocacy groups, Duluth officers are now instructed to arrest only the predominant aggressor and write a full report for prosecutorial review regarding the secondary aggressor's actions. We argue that women's advocates' campaign for zero tolerance for violence is inappropriate to the reality of many women's lives and needs to be reformulated as one of conditional tolerance and contextual sensitivity. * * *

It would be a mistake to read the new strategies simply as evidence of the battered women's movement having gotten things wrong in the past and now trying to patch up flawed work. Such a conclusion teaches us little about the situationally grounded, dynamic, and often contradictory nature of making social change, and it provides little guidance for further organizing. The cautions about working with the criminal justice system and institutionalizing the struggle against violence are not misplaced, but the social change accomplished by those years of organizing has also opened new opportunities. For example, the predominant-aggressor test, as we argue below, is not one that could have been introduced in Duluth 20 years ago. If working with the criminal justice system to get domestic violence publicly and legally recognized as a crime has come at a price, it has also moved the battered women's movement to a new place from which to work.

SECOND STRATEGY: WORKING WITH DEFENSE ATTORNEYS

In a number of cities, including Duluth, women's advocacy programs now work with defense attorneys to more aggressively defend women who are charged with assaulting their abusers. This is not always an easy task because women defendants in these cases tend to readily confess to the police that they hit their partners, how hard, and why. Women, Joan Zorza explained, are more likely than men to volunteer information about using violence simply because they are not socialized to respond with violence. Abusers, on the other hand, will frequently deny their use of violence and demand a vigorous defense by their court-appointed or privately funded attorneys. This is not necessarily so with women defendants. Although Duluth advocacy groups understand the strategic importance of working with defense attorneys, there has been little innovative local work done in this area. The Duluth City Attorney's office has shown the most interest in addressing the public safety and social justice issues created by prosecuting battered women who fight back.

THIRD STRATEGY: WORKING WITH PROSECUTORS

A strong notion of the social or public good inspired the original changes in the criminal justice system to better protect women from violence. Using the same argument that court interventions should serve the public good, women's advocates in Duluth encourage prosecutors to defer cases in which women have used violence but were clearly not battering their partners. They argue that public safety is not enhanced by pursuing a prosecution simply because it is technically possible. This, advocates point out, is not the spirit or intent of the legal traditions granting prosecutors broad authority to determine how to charge and prosecute in the interest of justice and the public good. Is there a public interest, advocates ask, in prosecuting women who are being beaten, refuse to take it, and hit back? Given the gendered nature of violence, should prosecutors not take into account the difference in risks to such a woman and to her partner?

To prosecute victims of battering, whether they are men or women, exposes victims to new risks on top of those they already face from violent partners. Based on these arguments, the prosecutor's office in Duluth convened an ad hoc committee to study the problem and provided the leadership to craft a program that gave defense attorneys and victims of ongoing abuse the option of asking for a conditional deferral of the case. The prosecutor's office faced significant criticism from individuals in the police and court system for agreeing to defer cases that could easily be successfully prosecuted. The prosecutor's office argued that they are charged with seeking justice, not convictions. They established a process in which victims of ongoing abuse, regardless of their gender, who are charged with misdemeanor offenses against their abusers can, by agreeing to admit to the facts of the case, be sidetracked into an educational program and put on a quasi-probation status for a year.

The educational program is significantly different from that offered to persons convicted of assaulting their partners who are engaged in a pattern of intimidation, coercion, and violence. The program was designed by an advocate with years of experience working with women as victims of abuse. She challenged women's use of retaliatory violence pragmatically: Although it might serve to immediately slow down or even stop his violence, as a long-term strategy for coping with battering, her violence has potentially dangerous consequences. In the educational classes, women receive training on the legal definition of self-defense in comparison to retaliatory, or even defensive, violence. Group members map out the history and pattern of their abusers' violence and discuss its implications in their lives and the lives of their children. They explore available methods of stopping the violence and evaluate these, given their personal circumstances. They discuss the nature of their attachment to their abusers and the long-term consequences of continuing the relationship if their abusers do not stop battering. The members examine their economic, emotional, spiritual, and physical needs and spend a great deal of time problem solving and assisting each other as advocates. The facilitator spends considerable time advocating for women in the group as they negotiate complicated problems with the courts, child protection, landlords, employers, and others. * * * When women are battering their female partners or are engaging in a pattern of abuse against men who are not abusing them, it is important to challenge them as one would men in abusers' programs. * * *

FOURTH STRATEGY: SENTENCING AND REHABILITATION

A fourth strategy employed in Duluth was to challenge sentencing practices that treated a person who assaulted an abusive partner the same way they treated the abuser. The courts tend to homogenize the meaning of violence, to see quite different actions as "equivalent," and therefore to apply the same remedies to quite different uses of violence. As an alternative, women's advocates and probation officers in Duluth developed a "sentencing recommendation matrix" that attempts to contextualize violence and make recommendations based on the severity, frequency, and impact of the violence. This matrix is designed to require that sentencing recommendations put less emphasis on past unrelated criminal activity or on the absence of previous convictions. Instead, recommendations should be based on an understanding of the pattern, severity, and frequency of the abuse. In essence, it is a shift from determining a sentence based on the defendant's relationship to the state to one based on understanding his or her relationship to the victim.

Advocates and probation officers successfully argued that mandating battered women who hit back, or refuse to simply take it, to a year's probation and a batterers' group was inappropriate. Not only were these women not batterers, but the process also distracted the criminal justice system and the community from providing battered women with what they really needed. In cases in which battered women are not eligible for the deferral program (e.g., they have committed a felony assault against their abuser or a second assault against their abuser) and are convicted, the use of the new matrix will likely result in a sentence tailored to their specific circumstances.

In conjunction with the probation-sentencing matrix, probation officers and staff of the batterers educational program agreed that the women's advocacy program should design a special group for victims of abuse who are convicted of assaulting their partners or who are deferred for an alleged assault (see description above).

FIFTH STRATEGY: CONFRONTING CRITICISM

Finally, women arrested for domestic violence require an aggressive advocacy program to take up the cause of women who fight back. Today, increasing numbers of advocacy programs are using gender-neutral language to describe their services. When battered women are arrested, advocates are told they cannot advocate for these women because they are not victims but offenders. In a culture in which dominant understandings of equity and fairness rely on the denial of the reality of differences, the strategies we advocate will initially be perceived as unfair or as expressing a double standard. Women's advocates will need to become sophisticated and adept at explaining the gendered nature of violence and the meaning of pursuing equality in social contexts in which people are clearly not equal in power or social resources.

But even the best arguments will be countered by accusations of reverse sexism. Although it is important not to ignore perceptions of unfairness, it is equally important not to capitulate to reactionary forces resisting our goal to provide a community response that protects women from ongoing abuse. Women who fight back become increasingly vulnerable to their abusers if the advocacy community does not recognize their actions as legitimate responses to being beaten. The idealized image of the perfect victim and the naive notion that there is a healthy or proper way of being abused makes women who fight back, women who are prostituted, women who have become addicted to drugs or alcohol, and women who are homeless more vulnerable to both the abuser and the institutions to which they turn for help.

The leadership in women's advocacy programs that is White, middle class, and oriented toward a predominantly Western view of social relationships can learn much from the struggles of marginalized groups and Third World women, whose demands for equity are falsely represented as demands for special privileges or cultural exceptions. As demonstrated in these struggles, it is important to resist seeing advocacy for women who use violence as an issue of bias or special treatment. It should be remembered that much of the battered women's movement's work has been to challenge the social sanctioning of male violence in the private sphere and to end the protections afforded such male privilege by the criminal justice system and other institutions. Every effort we have made has met with resistance and claims that we seek to establish a double standard. We have consistently fought against such efforts to obscure women's realities. Battered women who use violence to protect themselves from brutal partners deserve no less from us.

EDITOR'S SUMMARY OF "A 10-YEAR STUDY OF THE IMPACT OF INTIMATE PARTNER VIOLENCE PRIMARY AGGRESSOR LAWS ON SINGLE AND DUAL ARREST" BY DAVID HIRSCHEL, PHILIP D. MCCORMACK, AND EVE BUZAWA

36 (3–4) Journal of Interpersonal Violence 1356 (2021)

The adoption of policies mandating arrest in Intimate Partner Violence (IPV) cases in many US jurisdictions has resulted in more arrests, now averaging approximately 50% of IPV-related police calls. Mandatory arrest and preferred arrest policies also led to more cases in which both parties are arrested (dual arrests), averaging 2.4% of cases. Concern that victims were being wrongly arrested along with perpetrators led to policies requiring law enforcement officers to determine the primary or dominant aggressor and to arrest only that party. Washington state adopted the first such law in 1985, and now approximately 35 states have done so, as have many counties and cities. Some older studies found that adopting these statutes resulted in fewer dual arrests compared to states without such statutes. Findings in older studies were mixed with regard to the race of couples and arrest rates, with some finding that in jurisdictions with primary aggressor laws White people were more likely to be arrested for IPV, and others finding that IPV arrest rates were higher for Black people.

Hirschel et al conducted a study of 10 years of data from 36 states and Washington DC examining the effect of primary or dominant aggressor policies in IPV cases. They concluded that such policies reduced the incidence of dual arrests as a percentage of all IPV arrests. However, they also found that in states that had both preferred arrest statutes and primary aggressor statutes, officers tended to make fewer IPV arrests, with an average decrease of almost 25% compared to jurisdictions without such statutes. The authors stated that this may be because officers are not able to determine the primary aggressor, so make no arrest, or perhaps they are appropriately weeding out cases which lack probable cause for arrest. Also notable was that over the 10 years studied, rates of single arrest increased while dual arrests decreased. Seriousness of injury was a key factor in IPV arrest rates, as one would expect.

The researchers also noted that there are differences in the wording of state statutes and local policies (e.g., being "encouraged" to determine the primary aggressor vs. a mandate, and criteria for determining the primary aggressor), and differences in the content of police training on these topics, which could lead to different outcomes.

Hirschel et al found that dual arrests in IPV cases were significantly higher for same sex couples than for heterosexual couples, concluding that officers need specific training on identifying the primary aggressor in same sex cases. Notably, in primary aggressor states there was a 40.6% decrease in arrest rates of Black people for IPV, as well as lower rates of dual arrest in the Black community. Other non-white couples were even less likely to be arrested singly or dually in such states. However, overall, the researchers concluded that primary aggressor laws produced no statistically significant difference in the rate of dual arrests.

B. SUING THE POLICE

LISA SNEAD, DOMESTIC VIOLENCE LITIGATION IN THE WAKE OF *DESHANEY* AND *CASTLE ROCK*

18 Tex. J. Women & L. 305 (2009)
(citations and most footnotes omitted)

I. INTRODUCTION

In the last two decades, the United States Supreme Court has eviscerated federal remedies available to survivors of domestic violence when police officers refuse to enforce protective orders. *DeShaney v. Winnebago County Department of Social Services* [489 U.S. 189 (1989)], (hereinafter "*DeShaney*") has essentially eliminated substantive due process as a viable remedy while *City of Castle Rock v. Gonzales* [545 U.S.

748 (2005)] (hereinafter "*Castle Rock*") has done the same with procedural due process. The remaining equal protection claims are rarely a realistic remedy for survivors as the elements of a prima facie equal protection case require that the plaintiff-survivor prove an actual intent to discriminate.

Survivors of domestic violence need legal remedies in order to encourage police officers to enforce their protective orders. Damages, like the two million dollars awarded to Dina Sorichetti and her mother when the New York Police Department (NYPD) failed to enforce their protective order, [*Sorichetti v. City of New York*, 482 N.E.2d 70, 72 (N.Y. 1985)] can (and will) motivate police departments to clarify and update their domestic violence policies. In the wake of this case, the NYPD re-wrote its arrest policies to include mandatory arrests in domestic violence cases. As Professor Kristian Miccio noted, the change was not the result of lobbying, guilt, or good will; instead, the change was a direct result of the police department's liability for the two million dollar damage award. If police officers learn there are no legal consequences for failing to enforce protective orders, there will be little incentive for officers to enforce orders, particularly if "mandatory" no longer means "mandatory."[8] If, on the other hand, survivors are able to hold state actors accountable for their actions, then police officers will be more willing to enforce protection orders rather than risk being sued.

State courts must recognize remedies for survivors in order to provide victims with recourse now. Survivors in many states still need legislation that will provide them with the means to ensure police officers enforce domestic violence protective orders. At the same time, domestic violence victims cannot wait for legislators to recognize the need for remedies and then begin the long process of drafting and passing legislation. Until state legislators codify remedies, courts, particularly state courts, must find alternative means to ensure domestic violence victims are not left without remedies when their protective orders are not enforced. The state-created danger and special relationship doctrines are both viable legal doctrines that can provide survivors with recourse when municipalities and individual police officers fail to enforce protective orders.

II. CURRENT DOMESTIC VIOLENCE REMEDIES ARE INADEQUATE FOR THE VAST MAJORITY OF DOMESTIC VIOLENCE VICTIMS

Where state actors have investigated allegations of abuse and returned a child to a perpetrator of violence, substantive due process does not provide that child with an entitlement to state protection, even when state actors are aware of the dangers posed to the victim by the third party. In *DeShaney*, the citizen who was not entitled to state protection was four year-old Joshua DeShaney, whose father abused him so severely that he is

[8] In addition to denying Jessica Gonzales's claim for relief under the Due Process Clause, the United States Supreme Court noted that "mandatory" does not really mean "mandatory" in the context of domestic violence arrest policies. *Castle Rock*, 545 U.S. at 760.

now in a permanent, semi-vegetative state. The Winnebago County Department of Social Services investigated reports of child abuse committed against Joshua by his father for over two years. Despite multiple reports of abuse and medical evidence of Joshua's repeated injuries, Social Services allowed the young boy to remain in the care of his father. In the suit brought on Joshua's behalf against the Department of Social Services, the United States Supreme Court held that the department was not liable for the injuries to Joshua since social workers had not left him in a worse position than before the state's involvement. The Due Process Clause did not require Winnebago County Department of Social Services to protect Joshua from acts of violence committed by his father.[16] In dicta, the Court indicated that state actors still owe a duty of care to victims of third-party violence if a special relationship exists between the victim and the state actor. In this instance, the state would owe a duty to Joshua under the special relationship doctrine if he had still been in the physical custody of the state.

Almost two decades after its decision in *DeShaney*, the United States Supreme Court held that procedural due process likewise does not provide a victim with an entitlement to state protection, even when the victim has a valid restraining order. In this case, the citizens who were not entitled to protection were Jessica Gonzales and her three daughters, Rebecca, Katheryn, and Leslie. On June 22, 1999, Gonzales's ex-husband abducted his daughters in direct violation of a restraining order and, after spending the evening with them at an amusement park, murdered the three little girls. During this almost eight-hour ordeal, Gonzales called the police repeatedly, telling them she had a restraining order and that her husband had the girls in a nearby amusement park in clear violation of the order. The Castle Rock police officers on duty did not contact security at the amusement park or issue any kind of alert for the missing girls; instead, they repeatedly told Jessica Gonzales that they could do nothing about the restraining order and that she should wait a few more hours to see if her ex-husband brought the girls home. The night ended when Gonzales's ex-husband drove to the Castle Rock Police Department and opened fire. After the police killed him with return fire, they found the dead bodies of Rebecca, Katheryn, and Leslie Gonzales in his truck. Jessica Gonzales sued the police officers and the City of Castle Rock for failure to enforce her restraining order, alleging procedural due process and 42 U.S.C. § 1983 violations. Gonzales claimed that Title 18, Article 6, Section 803.5 of the Colorado Revised Code required the officers to enforce her protective order and that the officers violated her civil rights when they refused to do so.[25]

---

16 The Court went on to note that if Joshua were removed from his home, placed in foster care, and then abused, the state might be liable. As long as Joshua was abused at home, he was in no worse a position than before, and Social Services was immune from liability.

25 The language printed on the back of the restraining order, pursuant to title 18, article 6, section 803.5(3) of the Colorado Revised Statutes, stated, "A peace officer *shall* use every reasonable means to enforce a restraining order. (b) A peace officer *shall* arrest, or . . . seek a

The United States Supreme Court ultimately disagreed with Gonzales and held that victims of domestic violence do not have a property interest in having their protective orders enforced, even when the legislature has mandated arrest.

In a limited number of cases, domestic violence survivors have successfully litigated equal protection claims under the Fifth and Fourteenth Amendments; however, these claims are inadequate remedies for most domestic violence survivors. In order to make a prima facie case for an equal protection violation, a survivor of domestic violence must establish discriminatory purpose or intent; it is not enough to demonstrate that there is a disproportionate effect of a policy. A survivor must therefore point to specific facts beyond her own experience that show a policy or custom to provide less protection to domestic violence victims than to victims of similar crimes. In addition to proving there is a discriminatory policy, the victim must also provide evidence that "discrimination was the motivating factor" behind the policy.

In *Watson v. City of Kansas City, Kansas* [857 F.2d 690 (10th Cir. 1988)], the Tenth Circuit found that police officers violated Nancy Watson's equal protection rights only after she presented extensive evidence about police officer training and statistics that demonstrated that domestic violence crimes were systematically treated differently than other similar assault crimes in Kansas City. *[Editor's Note: Ms. Watson, the wife of a police officer, was subjected to many instances of domestic violence, and told if she called the police again they would arrest her and she would never see her children again. The district court granted defendant's motion for summary judgment, but the Court of Appeals reversed.]* Similarly, the domestic violence survivor in *Thurman v. City of Torrington* [595 F. Supp. 1521 (D. Conn. 1984)] provided evidence gathered over an eight-month period to demonstrate that the city systematically provided domestic violence victims with inadequate protection. *[Editor's Note: The district court sustained her § 1983 complaint that the department violated her and her son's equal protection rights by consistently affording lesser protection in domestic violence cases than in stranger assault cases.]* These cases are the exception rather than the rule as most victims will not have sufficient evidence to prove that there is an official custom or policy to discriminate against domestic violence victims, much less prove that the intent to discriminate was the motivating factor behind implementing the policy. While lawyers whose clients meet the exacting prima facie requirements of an equal protection claim should use this remedy, equal protection is, in general, too difficult to prove for the vast majority of victims.

---

warrant for the arrest of a restrained person when the peace officer has information amounting to probable cause that: (I) The restrained person has violated or attempted to violate any provision of a restraining order," cited in *Castle Rock*, 545 U.S. at 759 (emphasis added).

III. THE STATE-CREATED DANGER AND SPECIAL RELATIONSHIP DOCTRINES PROVIDE COURTS WITH A MEANS TO RECOGNIZE REMEDIES FOR DOMESTIC VIOLENCE VICTIMS

The "no duty" rule, whereby police officers do not have a general duty to protect individual members of the public from acts of violence committed by third parties, prevents domestic violence survivors from recovering damages when police officers fail to enforce their protective orders. In suing their respective municipalities, both Joshua DeShaney and Jessica Gonzales were attempting to create exceptions to the "no duty" rule. If they had been successful, then state actors could be liable for harms caused by third parties if the actors failed to act consistently with the demands of the Due Process Clause. Unless an exception to the "no duty" rule exists, state actors are essentially immune to suits.

The state-created danger doctrine and the special relationship doctrine remain viable exceptions to the general "no duty" rule. Many courts recognize at least one of the doctrines and apply them in other areas of the law. While neither doctrine as currently applied in domestic violence cases is an ideal solution, both doctrines are promising remedies for survivors. Courts must be willing to adopt these doctrines and apply them within the specific context of domestic violence litigation. Doing so can create recourse for domestic violence victims whose protective orders are not enforced by state actors.

A. The State-Created Danger Doctrine

Under the state-created danger doctrine, state actors can be liable for harm caused by their affirmative acts if they place a victim in a more dangerous position. Under this doctrine, police officers can be liable for refusing to enforce protective orders if this failure to enforce places the victim in greater danger than she faced before. The elements of the exception vary slightly from state to state and circuit to circuit, but in general, the court must find that a relationship existed such that the survivor was a foreseeable victim of the state actor's actions and that the state actor affirmatively used his or her authority in a way that rendered the citizen more vulnerable to the danger. Many courts have added the requirement that the actions be "shocking to the conscience."

Victims of domestic violence have historically used the state-created danger doctrine with limited success. * * *

B. The Special Relationship Doctrine

Though limited to use in state courts, the special relationship doctrine is another exception to the general no-duty rule that can provide survivors with causes of action against officers who fail to enforce protective orders. The United States Supreme Court's interpretation of the Due Process Clause is not binding on state courts' interpretations of their own constitutions; therefore, courts are free to recognize a special relationship exception where the victim was not in actual physical custody of a state actor. * * *

3. "Justifiable Reliance" and the Problems Created by Domestic Violence

The requirement that reliance on the state actor be "justifiable" creates a problem for victims of domestic violence since at least one court has held that repeated or prolonged contacts with police officers render reliance unjustified. The line between justified and unjustified reliance is unclear. Under this standard, it is possible that reliance is never justified unless police have responded before and enforced an order. On the other hand, reliance may always be justified unless police have failed to enforce a victim's protective order in the past. * * *

WASHBURN V. CITY OF FEDERAL WAY

310 P.3d 1275 (Wash. 2013)
(citations and footnotes omitted)

This case presents questions about the tort liability of a municipal corporation. Paul Chan Kim murdered his partner, Baerbel K. Roznowski, after officer Andrew Hensing of the Federal Way Police Department (Department) served Kim with an antiharassment order forbidding him to contact or remain near Roznowski. Roznowski's two daughters filed suit against the city of Federal Way (City), alleging that Hensing's negligent service of the order resulted in Roznowski's death at Kim's hands. The parties tried the case to a jury, which returned a verdict against the City.

The City claims the trial court erred in denying its CR 56(c) motion for summary judgment and its CR 50(a) motion for judgment as a matter of law because it owed Roznowski no duty under the public duty doctrine, foreclosing any tort liability. We disagree. The City had a duty to serve the antiharassment order on Kim, and because it had a duty to act, it had a duty to act with reasonable care in serving the order. We therefore affirm the trial court's denial of the City's motions, although we do so on different grounds than those relied on by the Court of Appeals.

I. FACTUAL BACKGROUND AND PROCEDURAL HISTORY

Roznowski and Kim began a troubled relationship in the 1990s. In 2008, Roznowski decided to end the relationship and move to California to live near her adult daughters. To move, Roznowski needed to sell her house. Kim stood in the way of the sale because, although he owned his own home, he resided at Roznowski's house and her home was filled with his belongings. Readying her property for sale therefore required ousting Kim and his possessions.

In late April 2008, Roznowski and Kim argued about her demands that he remove his belongings from her property. This fight escalated and Roznowski called 911 because she feared Kim might assault her. Officers from the Department responded to the call and met with both Kim and Roznowski. Neither Roznowski nor Kim appeared harmed, and the officers did not detect any evidence of physical violence. Nonetheless, the officers told Kim to "take a walk" and collect himself. With Kim out of the house, one of the officers discussed the situation with Roznowski and told her she could attempt to obtain a no-contact order against Kim.

Roznowski decided to seek court-ordered protection against Kim. She went to the King County Regional Justice Center, met with a domestic violence advocate, discussed her options, and then sought and obtained a "Temporary Protection Order and Notice of Hearing—AH" (hereinafter antiharassment order) from the King County Superior Court. The antiharassment order prohibited Kim from surveilling Roznowski, contacting her, or entering or being within 500 feet of her residence.

Roznowski asked the Department to serve the antiharassment order. The Department's service file included Roznowski's petition for the antiharassment order, the order, and a law enforcement information sheet (LEIS). The LEIS allows petitioners to provide law enforcement with information related to serving the court orders. Roznowski's LEIS informed the officers that Kim was her domestic partner, Kim did not know she had obtained an antiharassment order, Kim did not know the antiharassment order would force him out of Roznowski's home, and that Kim would likely react violently to service of the order. In the field marked "Hazard Information," Roznowski noted that Kim had a history of assault. The LEIS also asked that a Korean interpreter help serve the antiharassment order based on Kim's limited proficiency in English.

Officer Hensing served the antiharassment order two days later, early on a Saturday morning. Hensing offered contradictory testimony regarding his preparation for service, indicating that he either did not read the order or the LEIS, or, at best, gave them a cursory glance. Either way, he did not bring an interpreter.

When Hensing knocked on the door, Kim answered. Hensing saw Roznowski in the background inside the house while serving the antiharassment order, but he did not interact with her or inquire as to her safety. Hensing confirmed Kim's identity, handed him the antiharassment order, informed him he needed to appear in court, and left. Roznowski was left to explain to Kim what had happened—she had restrained him from contacting her and he needed to vacate the home. Another argument ensued, and Kim eventually left to run an errand.

Kim finished his errand, returned to the house, and attacked Roznowski with a knife before attempting to take his own life. Medical personnel arrived to find Roznowski bleeding to death, with Kim lying beside her. Medical intervention failed to save Roznowski, who died from blood loss from the multiple stab wounds Kim inflicted.

Roznowski's daughters, Carola Washburn and Janet Loh (hereinafter collectively Washburn), filed suit against the City for Roznowski's wrongful death. The suit alleged various theories of negligence and sought damages for the daughters in their individual capacities and on behalf of Roznowski's estate.

The City moved for summary judgment, claiming that it owed Roznowski no duty under the public duty doctrine. The trial court denied the motion, finding that the antiharassment order required Kim to remain more than 500 feet away from Roznowski and that Hensing had failed in his duty to enforce the antiharassment order by leaving Kim in the house with Roznowski after serving the antiharassment order. The City moved for reconsideration of this decision, which the trial court denied. The City then sought discretionary review of the denial of summary judgment at the Court of Appeals, Division One, but the court commissioner denied the motion, and a panel of the court denied a motion to modify the commissioner's order.

At trial, much of the testimony offered by Washburn concerned the importance of proper service of an antiharassment order. Expert testimony from Karil Klingbeil, a family violence counselor, informed the jury about the point of separation between the abuser and victim. Klingbeil testified that the point of separation is a "very volatile and dangerous period" because the abuser learns that he or she has lost control of the victim. Another expert, Dr. Anne Ganley, a psychologist focusing on domestic violence, testified that at the point of separation, the batterer can "explode." Roznowski's LEIS informed Hensing that Kim did not know she had sought protection, meaning that the point of separation occurred when Hensing served the antiharassment order.

The former police chief of the city of Bellevue, Donald Van Blaricom, testified that Hensing's service of the antiharassment order did nothing to minimize the danger Kim posed to Roznowski as a result of service of the antiharassment order. Van Blaricom stressed that proper service required four things: (1) reading the petition, antiharassment order, and LEIS because the officer needed to know how the recipient would likely react to service to prepare for a violent outburst; (2) ensuring that the recipient understood the contents and effect of the antiharassment order, which might require the officer to bring a translator; (3) contacting the petitioner to verify his or her safety and health as part of effective service; and (4) enforcing the antiharassment order, which, in this case, required at a minimum that Hensing tell Kim that Kim needed to leave.

Norman Stamper, former chief of the Seattle Police Department, largely echoed Van Blaricom's analysis and ultimate conclusion. In particular, Stamper stated it was "astonishing" that Hensing had not read the LEIS because it provided information critical to "prevent murder." Stamper found it "hugely significant" that Hensing did not contact

Roznowski after seeing her in the background, but instead left after serving the antiharassment order, essentially setting Roznowski up for a "horrible crime."

Washburn introduced testimony stating that Hensing's improper service of the antiharassment order led to Roznowski's death. Ganley testified that offenders with Kim's psychological profile, individuals "highly compliant to outside authority, particularly to law enforcement," would not have returned to kill a victim in the face of proper service by police. * * * Klingbeil and Van Blaricom concurred that proper service of the antiharassment order would have minimized danger to Roznowski.

At the close of Washburn's case-in-chief, the City moved for judgment as a matter of law under CR 50(a). The City argued that Washburn failed to present evidence sufficient to prove the City owed Roznowski any actionable duty. The trial court denied the motion.

In its defense, the City offered an expert who testified that Hensing acted reasonably in serving the antiharassment order. The expert, Seattle Police Department Sergeant Thomas Ovens, testified that Hensing had appropriately prepared himself by reviewing the antiharassment order and serving it; Ovens stated Hensing did not need to read every word on the LEIS, only to generally familiarize himself with it.

Ovens' testimony and the City's cross-examination of Washburn's witnesses focused on the differences between an antiharassment order and a domestic violence protection order. A domestic violence protection order requires police to help the protected party obtain exclusive control of the residence, and police must arrest the restrained party for a violation of the order. Antiharassment orders have neither of these features. Ovens testified that based on the type of antiharassment order Hensing served, Hensing could not immediately enforce it because he needed to give Kim time to remove his belongings. Given the characteristics of the antiharassment order at issue in this case, Ovens testified that Hensing acted reasonably in his service of the antiharassment order.

The jury instruction conference involved extensive discussions as to whether to give an instruction stating that the City owed Roznowski a duty of ordinary care in serving the antiharassment order. The City had "strenuous" objections to any such instruction based on its public duty doctrine argument. [The trial court gave the instruction.] * * *

After deliberations, the jury returned a verdict for Washburn. * * * The Court of Appeals affirmed in a published opinion. * * *

III. ANALYSIS

* * * C. The trial court properly denied the City's CR 56(c) and CR 50(a) motions because the City owed Roznowski two duties in serving the antiharassment order on Kim

* * * We hold that the City owed two different duties to Roznowski—a legal duty to serve the antiharassment order and a duty to act reasonably in doing so. We hold that this duty to act with reasonable care, under these facts, meant taking reasonable steps to guard against the possibility that Kim would harm Roznowski as a result of the service of the antiharassment order. * * *

(a) Chapter 10.14 RCW imposed a legal duty on the Department to serve the antiharassment order on Kim

One of the exceptions to the public duty doctrine is the legislative intent exception. * * * While chapter 10.14 RCW imposes no duty to guarantee the safety of citizens like Roznowski, it does impose on police officers a duty to serve antiharassment orders. The City concedes that RCW 10.14.100 required officers of the Department to serve Kim with the antiharassment order.

Under the legislative intent exception, if the City's discharge of this duty to act, service of the order, constituted "culpable neglect," it bears liability in tort.

(b) The City owed Roznowski a duty to guard against the danger she faced at Kim's hands because Hensing's actions created that danger

* * * We hold that, under the facts of this case, Hensing, as part of his duty to act reasonably, owed Roznowski a duty to guard against the criminal conduct of Kim. We find several factors created this duty.

First, Hensing knew, or should have known, that Kim could or would react violently to the service of the antiharassment order for several reasons. The LEIS itself alerted Hensing to this fact. Roznowski filled out the LEIS by noting that Kim had a history of assault and would likely react violently to service of the antiharassment order. Further, the police are generally aware of the problem of separation violence. The testimony of Van Blaricom, Stamper, and Ovens all reflect this, as does the very existence of the LEIS itself, which police departments created to help alert officers serving these types of orders to the risks they faced.

Second, Hensing knew, or should have known, that he was serving Kim at Roznowski's house. The LEIS and service file indicated as much. Hensing also knew, or should have known, that the woman he saw in the background was Roznowski given that he served Kim at her house.

Given the first two factors—danger and Roznowski's presence—plus the possible need for a translator, when Hensing handed Kim the antiharassment order and walked away, Hensing created a situation that left Roznowski alone with Kim as Kim realized, or was about to realize, that Roznowski had ended their relationship. Hensing should have realized that, * * * he had created a new and very real risk to Roznowski's safety based on Kim's likely violent response to the antiharassment order and his access to Roznowski.

The jury heard extensive testimony on the simple steps Hensing could have taken to eliminate the risk to Roznowski. He could have ordered Kim to leave the house and stood by to make sure Kim did so without harming Roznowski. Ganley and Van Blaricom testified that doing so would have prevented Kim from murdering Roznowski. Hensing, however, did neither of these things. He walked away, leaving Roznowski alone in her house with Kim and the reaction from the service of the antiharassment order. * * *

The City's other argument against imposing a duty under *Restatement* § 302B is that doing so runs counter to the justification for the public duty doctrine. The City notes that it has a statutory duty to serve orders like the one at issue here, and that imposing liability will deter beneficial services such as this. The City equates the existence of a duty with liability. As we have noted, governmental entities are not liable if they act reasonably. Nor are governmental entities liable if their negligence does not proximately cause the plaintiff's injuries. * * *

IV. CONCLUSION

* * * The City had a duty to act here, and this duty required the City to act in a reasonable manner. Hensing knew or should have known that Roznowski and Kim were both present and that his service of the antiharassment order might trigger Kim to act violently. Given this knowledge or constructive knowledge and Kim's proximity to Roznowski when Hensing served Kim, Hensing's duty to act reasonably required him to take steps to guard Roznowski against Kim's criminal acts. Because we find the City owed Roznowski both a duty to act and a duty to act reasonably, we affirm the trial court's decision to deny the City's CR 56(c) and CR 50(a) motions. * * *

TURCZYN EX REL. MCGREGOR V. CITY OF UTICA

2014 WL 6685476 (N.D.N.Y.) (unpublished)
(most citations omitted)

I. Introduction

Plaintiff Kylie Ann Turczyn, deceased, by and through Barbara McGregor, as administratrix of the estate of Kylie Ann Turczyn, commenced this action against defendants City of Utica, City of Utica Police Dept., and Elizabeth Shanley alleging substantive due process claims pursuant to 42 U.S.C. § 1983 and separate state law causes of action. Pending is defendants' motion to dismiss for failure to state a claim. For the reasons that follow, the motion is granted in part and denied in part.

II. Background

A. Facts[1]

Shanley, an Oneida County domestic violence investigator, was at all relevant times assigned by the Police Department to accomplish the goals of reducing "occurrence[s] of domestic violence by increasing reporting and by identifying and tracking repeat victims and/or offenders," and "increas[ing] victims' access to supportive services by encouraging [them] to report their abuse, thereby increasing arrest rates for domestic offenders." On June 22, 2012, Thomas Anderson, Turczyn's former boyfriend and the father of her daughter, broke into Turczyn's home armed with a 9 mm rifle. Anderson repeatedly shot Turczyn, taking her life in view of their four-year-old daughter, G.T. Anderson then dispatched himself.

In the twelve months preceding this horrific event, Turczyn made between five and ten complaints to Utica police officers, "including informing them of a specific threat by Anderson to kill her." Turczyn specifically told Shanley "that Anderson was armed and had threatened to kill her." Despite their knowledge of domestic violence between Turczyn and Anderson, neither Shanley, New York State Police, nor Utica Police took any steps to arrest Anderson, investigate Turczyn's complaints, or follow-up with Anderson "as is the policy and protocol of the domestic violence unit."

On June 18, 2012, Shanley told Turczyn to seek an order of protection, which she attempted to do, but was told by an unknown person at the Oneida County Family Court to return the following day because the court was " 'too busy.' " The following day, Turczyn left a voice message for Shanley, explaining that she was unable to obtain an order of protection and that Anderson had a gun and planned to kill her that week. Despite her knowledge, "Shanley took no action." Shanley also mistakenly believed that Turczyn's issues with Anderson were outside of the purview of Utica Police and should, instead, be dealt with by New York State Police; however, "she did not inform any other police agency or take any action herself."

B. Procedural History

Turczyn commenced this action by filing a complaint on October 31, 2013. Defendants thereafter moved to dismiss. In response, Turczyn filed an amended complaint as of right, which is now the operative pleading. In her amended complaint, Turczyn alleges the following causes of action: (1)

---

[1] The facts are presented in the light most favorable to plaintiff.

a denial of substantive due process rights under the Fifth and Fourteenth Amendments due to deliberate indifference; (2) a *Monell*[2] claim against the City; (3) negligence; (4) a "derivative action" on behalf of G.T.; and (5) negligent infliction of emotional distress. Defendants now move to dismiss the amended pleading pursuant to Rules 8(a)(2) and 12(b)(6) of the Federal Rules of Civil Procedure. * * *

IV. Discussion

A. Preliminary Matters

At the outset, it is noted that some of Turczyn's claims are deemed abandoned by her failure to oppose their dismissal. In particular, Turczyn squarely opposed dismissal of her substantive due process claim as against Shanley, and scarcely, but sufficiently to save the claim from dismissal for abandonment, offered reasons why her substantive due process claim as against the City should survive defendants' motion. Aside from the substantive due process claim, Turczyn failed to offer any opposition to defendants' motion, which also sought dismissal of her pendant causes of action. Accordingly, Turczyn's pendant state law claims are dismissed.

Additionally, it is clear that the Police Department must be dismissed as urged by defendants, because "a department of a municipal entity is merely a subdivision of the municipality and has no separate legal existence." As such, all claims as against the Police Department are dismissed. * * *

B. Rule 8

First, defendants argue that Turczyn's § 1983 due process claim is subject to dismissal under the Rule 8 plausibility analysis—specifically because of Turczyn's failure to allege facts supportive of a sufficient nexus between Shanley's omissions and Turczyn's death. The court disagrees. The amended complaint plausibly alleges a causal connection between the conduct of defendants—their alleged conscience-shocking failure to protect Turczyn—and her injuries, *i.e.*, the allegations plausibly suggest that defendants' acts were a substantial factor in bringing about Turczyn's injuries. Accordingly, this argument is rejected.

C. Rule 12(b)(6)

Defendants argue that Turczyn has failed to state a substantive due process claim as against Shanley or the City. Defendants contend that Turczyn alleges only passive conduct on the part of Shanley that does not give rise to a substantive due process violation. More generally, defendants assert that Turczyn has failed to plead facts to show "implicit prior assurances through repeated sustained inaction," and that, even if she did, the state action alleged does not rise to the level of conscience-shocking

[2] See *Monell v. Dep't of Soc. Servs. of N.Y.*, 436 U.S. 658, 98 S.Ct. 2018, 56 L.Ed.2d 611 (1978).

behavior. Alternatively, defendants argue that Shanley is entitled to qualified immunity. With respect to the City, defendants contend that Turczyn has failed to allege facts that support a claim of municipal liability. For reasons explained below, defendants' motion is denied with respect to Turczyn's substantive due process claim against Shanley, but granted with respect to her *Monell* claim against the City.

Only one relevant exception to the general rule that no substantive due process claim lies for a state's failure to protect an individual from private violence, *see DeShaney v. Winnebago Cnty. Dep't of Soc. Servs.,* 489 U.S. 189, 197, 109 S.Ct. 998, 103 L.Ed.2d 249 (1989), potentially applies in this case. That exception imposes liability for failure to protect where state actors in some way affirmatively assist "in creating or increasing the danger to the victim." *Okin v. Vill. of Cornwall-On-Hudson Police Dep't,* 577 F.3d 415, 428 (2d Cir.2009); *see Pena v. DePrisco,* 432 F.3d 98, 110 (2d Cir.2005). "[R]epeated, sustained inaction by government officials, in the face of potential acts of violence, might constitute 'prior assurances,' rising to the level of an affirmative condoning of private violence, even if there is no explicit approval or encouragement." *Okin,* 577 F.3d at 428. Moreover, when "state officials communicate to a private person that he . . . will not be arrested, punished, or otherwise interfered with while engaging in misconduct that is likely to endanger the life, liberty or property of others, those officials can be held liable under section 1983 for injury caused by the misconduct" "even though none of the defendants [is] alleged to have communicated the approval explicitly." *Id.* at 428–29 (quoting *Pena,* 432 F.3d at 111)). In a nutshell, "[t]he affirmative conduct of a government official may give rise to an actionable due process violation if it communicates, explicitly or implicitly, official sanction of private violence."

A successful substantive due process claim also requires that the plaintiff show "that the state action was 'so egregious, so outrageous, that it may fairly be said to shock the contemporary conscience.' " A hierarchy of intent provides guidance on the likelihood that a particular harm rises to the necessary level. Intentionally inflicted harms are most likely to meet the standard, while reckless and negligent inflictions of harm are each less likely, in graduated downward steps, to show conscience-shocking state action. As for recklessly inflicted injuries, " '[d]eliberate indifference that shocks in one environment may not be so patently egregious in another.' " Accordingly, the inquiry is highly fact specific.

Unlike *Town of Castle Rock v. Gonzales,* 545 U.S. 748 (2005), or *Neal v. Lee County,* 2010 WL 582437 (N.D.Miss.)—cases in which police had limited interaction with either the victim or killer prior to the victim's demise, and upon which defendants rely for dismissal of the claim against Shanley—the allegations here go substantially farther. Turczyn alleges several occasions[3] when Shanley knew of Anderson's threatening acts and did nothing, which arguably communicated to him prior assurances that there would be no penalty to pay for his conduct. "This is so even though none of the defendants are alleged to have communicated the approval explicitly." *Pena,* 432 F.3d at 111. *Okin* has specifically recognized the liability that may arise under these circumstances. *See* 577 F.3d at 428–29 (explaining that liability under § 1983 attaches when "state officials communicate to a private person that he . . . will not be arrested, punished, or otherwise interfered with while engaging in misconduct that is likely to endanger the life, liberty or property of others").

The amended complaint also pleads facts that demonstrate, at this juncture, egregious behavior that shocks the contemporary conscience. As in *Okin,* the allegations here tend to show that Shanley, who was tasked with accomplishing certain goals related to curbing domestic violence, was deliberately indifferent as to whether or not Anderson would make good on his multiple threats against Turczyn's life over a twelve-month-period. These allegations sufficiently support that Shanley's affirmative conduct was the product of deliberate indifference that shocks the conscience, and would provide a reasonable jury with a valid basis to so find.

Finally, Shanley is not entitled to qualified immunity at this juncture. Her argument on this issue is two-fold. First, Shanley asserts that no constitutional violation occurred, and, second, she claims that, even if a constitutional violation occurred, the right was not clearly established. The first prong of the argument is easily swept aside by reference to the preceding paragraphs that explain that the amended complaint alleges a cognizable substantive due process violation. As for whether or not the right was clearly established, which is a prerequisite to qualified immunity, this question has been resolved by the Second Circuit. On the issue, the court has explained that it is "clearly established," under the state-created danger theory, "that police officers are prohibited from affirmatively contributing to the vulnerability of a known victim by engaging in conduct, whether explicit or implicit, that encourages *intentional* violence against the victim, and as that is the substantive due process violation alleged here, qualified immunity does not apply." *Okin,* 577 F.3d at 434. Accordingly, Shanley is not entitled to qualified immunity at this time.

As for the City, defendants assert that Turczyn has failed to plead a *Monell* claim because the amended complaint merely alleges legal conclusions. With respect to Turczyn's allegation that the City failed to properly train or supervise its employees, defendants contend that the amended complaint is too conclusory, but that, even if adequately pleaded,

[3] In fact, Turczyn claims that she lodged five to ten complaints—of which Shanley was aware—with the Utica Police within the twelve months preceding the murder. So many occurrences may amount to "repeated [and] sustained inaction . . . in the face of potential acts of violence." *Okin,* 577 F.3d at 428.

Turczyn's municipal liability claim must nonetheless fail because she has not alleged deliberate indifference.

It is well settled that "the inadequacy of police training may serve as the basis for § 1983 liability . . . where the failure to train amounts to deliberate indifference to the rights of persons with whom the police come into contact." *City of Canton, Oh. v. Harris,* 489 U.S. 378, 380, 388, 109 S.Ct. 1197, 103 L.Ed.2d 412 (1989). The deliberate indifference standard is "stringent" and requires "proof that a municipal actor disregarded a known or obvious consequence of his action." A showing of deliberate indifference requires that: (1) "a policymaker knows 'to a moral certainty' that her employees will confront a given situation"; (2) "the situation either presents the employee with a difficult choice of the sort that training or supervision will make less difficult or that there is a history of employees mishandling the situation"; and (3) "the wrong choice by the . . . employee will frequently cause the deprivation of a citizen's constitutional rights."

Here, because Turczyn has failed to adequately plead that the City's failure to train and supervise amounted to deliberate indifference, she has failed to state a claim of municipal liability. The amended complaint uses the label "deliberate indifference" in reference to Turczyn's municipal liability claim and generically references the City's failure to properly train and supervise, but it fails to allege facts that support either conclusory notion. Turczyn's pleading failure mandates dismissal of her *Monell* claim against the City.

[Shanley, the sole remaining defendant, was ordered to file an appropriate responsive pleading.]

COLESON V. CITY OF NEW YORK

24 N.Y.3d 476 (2014)
(citations omitted)

OPINION OF THE COURT

In this negligence action, we must determine whether the evidence submitted by plaintiffs in opposition to the City of New York's summary judgment motion was sufficient to raise a triable issue of fact as to the existence of a special relationship between plaintiffs and the City. We hold that the evidence presented in this case was sufficient to defeat the motion, and we therefore reverse the order of the Appellate Division.

I.

Commencing in the year 2000, plaintiff Jandy Coleson suffered both verbal and physical abuse at the hands of her husband Samuel Coleson. As a result, Coleson was jailed on a number of occasions and plaintiff obtained numerous orders of protection against him. In May 2004, following an incident where Coleson was abusing drugs, plaintiff ordered Coleson to leave the apartment and she changed the locks. On June 23, 2004, Coleson tried to force himself into the building and threatened to kill plaintiff and stab her with a screwdriver he was carrying. Plaintiff called the New York City Police Department (NYPD), but when they arrived on the scene, Coleson had already fled. The officers, including one Officer Reyes, searched for Coleson with plaintiff's assistance. Coleson was apprehended shortly before 10:00 a.m.

On the same date, plaintiff applied for another order of protection and was later transported by the police to the local precinct with her son. Plaintiff testified in her deposition that while at the precinct, an officer told her that "they had arrested [Coleson], he's going to be in prison for a while, [and that she should not] worry, [she] was going to be given protection." She was escorted by the police to Safe Horizon, a nonprofit organization that provides services to domestic violence victims, to meet with a counselor and receive other assistance. That evening, at approximately 11:00 p.m., plaintiff received a follow-up phone call from Officer Reyes, who told her that Coleson "was in front of the judge" and that he was going to be "sentence[d]." Reyes also "told [plaintiff] that everything was okay, that everything was in . . . process, [and] that she was going to keep in contact with [her]." This phone call lasted for approximately two hours.

Two days later, plaintiff went to pick up her son from his school, which was across from a car wash, when she saw Coleson. Coleson approached her, stating that he wanted to speak with her. He took out a knife and stabbed plaintiff in the back. The child, who was seven years old at the time, testified at his deposition that he saw Coleson chasing plaintiff with a knife while plaintiff screamed for help. The child hid behind a car, and a man who worked at the car wash took the child and locked him in a broom closet. About 5 to 10 minutes later the child came out of the closet and saw his mother on the ground in a pool of blood.

Plaintiff, on behalf of herself and her son, commenced this negligence action against the City of New York and the NYPD (collectively the City). Plaintiffs also asserted a claim for negligent infliction of emotional distress, arguing that the child was in the zone of danger during the incident.

The City moved for summary judgment dismissing the complaint, arguing that the statements Officer Reyes allegedly made to plaintiff were not definite enough to create justifiable reliance in order to establish a special relationship in satisfaction of the duty prong of plaintiffs' negligence cause of action. Further, the City argued that the child was not in the zone of danger because he did not witness the attack on his mother. In opposition, plaintiffs argued that a special duty existed between plaintiff and the City based on the NYPD's agreement to provide protection to her. They also asserted that the child did witness the assault because he observed Coleson approach his mother with a knife, and although he was placed in a broom closet, he could hear what was occurring.

Supreme Court granted the City's motion for summary judgment. The court held that plaintiffs failed to establish the requirements for a special relationship because they failed "to demonstrate that the verbal assurance of protection at the precinct was followed by any visible police protection" and "fail[ed] to show any post arraignment promise of protection." The court also determined that the child was not in the zone of danger because he was locked in a broom closet at the time of the incident.

The Appellate Division affirmed, holding that "[i]n the absence of any evidence that defendants assumed an affirmative duty to protect plaintiff from attacks by her husband, [the City does] not owe a duty of care to plaintiff." The court stated that the statements of the officers which plaintiff relied upon "were too vague to constitute promises giving rise to a duty of care." Finally, the court concluded that based on the lack of a special relationship, the child's claim for negligent infliction of emotional distress should also be dismissed.

In a concurring opinion, two justices noted that although the majority's ruling is mandated under *Valdez,* "[i]f the City's statements in this case are not specific enough to find that [the City] assumed an affirmative duty to protect plaintiff, it is difficult to imagine any statements that could ever be specific enough" and "it seems likely that no court of this State will ever find a municipality to have a special duty toward a plaintiff unless the municipality affirmatively consents to assume such a duty."

The Appellate Division granted plaintiffs' motion for leave to appeal to this Court and certified the question of whether the order was properly made.

II.

Liability for a claim that a municipality negligently exercised a governmental function "turns upon the existence of a special duty to the injured person, in contrast to a general duty owed to the public." "[A] duty to exercise reasonable care toward [a] plaintiff" is "born of a special relationship between the plaintiff and the governmental entity." This Court has determined that a special relationship can be formed in three ways:

> "(1) when the municipality violates a statutory duty enacted for the benefit of a particular class of persons; (2) when it voluntarily assumes a duty that generates justifiable reliance by the person who benefits from the duty; or (3) when the municipality assumes positive direction and control in the face of a known, blatant and dangerous safety violation."

In *Cuffy v. City of New York,* 69 N.Y.2d 255, 513 N.Y.S.2d 372, 505 N.E.2d 937 (1987), we listed the requisite elements for a duty voluntarily assumed:

> "(1) an assumption by the municipality, through promises or actions, of an affirmative duty to act on behalf of the party who was injured; (2) knowledge on the part of the municipality's agents that inaction could lead to harm; (3) some form of direct contact between the municipality's agents and the injured party; and (4) that party's justifiable reliance on the municipality's affirmative undertaking."

We noted that "the injured party's reliance is . . . critical."

Applying the *Cuffy* factors here, we conclude that plaintiffs raised a triable issue of fact as to whether a special relationship existed. With regard to the first factor, a jury could conclude that the police officers made promises to protect plaintiff. Plaintiff was notified by the police that Coleson was arrested, that he was in front of a judge to be sentenced, would be in jail for a while, and that the police would be in contact with her. As to the second factor, the police officers conceivably knew that Coleson would harm plaintiff if he was not apprehended, as evidenced by his arrest and the issuance of an order of protection to plaintiff. Given that plaintiff was told by Officer Reyes that everything was in process and she would keep in contact, there is an issue of fact as to whether the police knew that their inaction could lead to harm. The third factor is easily met, as plaintiff had direct contact with the police, by the police responding to her call about Coleson's threats, making an arrest, escorting her to the police precinct, and plaintiff's phone call with Officer Reyes. Finally, regarding a party's justifiable reliance on the municipality's affirmative undertaking, given the assurances that plaintiff received from Officer Reyes that Coleson was in jail and that he would be there for a while, a jury could find that it was reasonable for plaintiff to believe that Coleson would be jailed for the foreseeable future, and that the police would contact her if that turned out not to be the case.

The conduct of the police here was more substantial, involved, and interactive than the police conduct in *Valdez*. In *Valdez v. City of New York*, 18 N.Y.3d 69, 936 N.Y.S.2d 587, 960 N.E.2d 356 (2011), the plaintiff was shot by her estranged boyfriend, after, in an attempt to flee, she was advised by officers that she should go back into her apartment and that the police would locate and arrest her boyfriend. This Court concluded that the officer's statements to the plaintiff did not create a special relationship because "[i]t was not reasonable for [the plaintiff] to conclude, based on nothing more than the officer's statement that the police were going to arrest [her boyfriend] 'immediately,' that she could relax her vigilance indefinitely."

Unlike in *Valdez*, plaintiff was told by the police that Coleson was going to be in prison for a while and that they would stay in contact with plaintiff. Contrary to the City's and the dissent's contention, these particular assertions were not vague. This Court has stated that

> "at the heart of most of these 'special duty' cases is the unfairness that the courts have perceived in precluding recovery when a municipality's voluntary undertaking has lulled the injured party into a false sense of security and has thereby induced him [or her] either to relax his [or her] own vigilance or to forego other available avenues of protection" (*Cuffy*).

The role that police officers play when responding to domestic violence victims is critical in allowing victims to feel consoled and supported. We do not, as the dissent suggests, seek to discourage the police from being responsive to crime victims. Rather, the police should make assurances only to the extent that they have an actual basis for such assurances, and to the extent that such assurances will not lull a victim into a false sense of security. The statements made by Officer Reyes to plaintiff may have lulled her into believing that she could relax her vigilance for a reasonable period of time, certainly more than two days.

Whether a special relationship exists is generally a question for the jury. On this record, plaintiffs raised a triable issue of fact as to whether a special relationship existed that should be decided by a jury.

As the Appellate Division only addressed the issue of special relationship, remittal to that court to review the City's claim of governmental immunity is warranted.

III.

Plaintiffs argue that the child was in the zone of danger because, although he was in a closet at the time his mother was stabbed, he saw Coleson with the knife and while in the closet heard his mother's screams. The City argues that the child was not in the zone of danger because he was in the closet and did not see his mother being stabbed. "In order to recover for an alleged emotional injury based on the zone of danger theory . . ., a plaintiff must establish that he suffered serious emotional distress that was proximately caused by the observation of a family member's death or serious injury while in the zone of danger." We conclude that the child was not in the zone of danger because he was in a broom closet while his mother was stabbed, and thus neither saw the incident nor was immediately aware of the incident at the time it occurred.

IV.

In sum, the acts of the police officers in this case were sufficient to raise a triable issue of fact as to justifiable reliance. Accordingly, the order of the Appellate Division should be modified in accordance with this opinion, without costs, the case remitted to the Appellate Division for consideration of issues raised but not determined on appeal to that court, and as so modified, affirmed and the certified question not answered upon the ground that it is unnecessary.

PIGOTT, J. (dissenting in part).

The majority's opinion creates a paradox. Under the guise of protecting victims of domestic violence by allowing them to recover in tort against a municipality for a police officer's vague promises and assurances during an emotionally charged and dangerous situation, the opinion encourages the police to forgo any meaningful communication or action that could be even *remotely* construed as creating a special relationship between the complainant and police.* In doing so, the majority retreats from our recent decisions in *Valdez, Dinardo,* and *McLean* where we reiterated the well-established rule that only an "affirmative undertaking" that creates justifiable reliance can justify holding a municipality liable for negligence in performing a governmental function (*Cuffy*).

According to the majority, the police did four things that now expose the City to potential liability: (1) they made promises to protect plaintiff; (2) they "conceivably knew" that plaintiff's husband, Samuel Coleson, would harm her if he was not apprehended because they had arrested him and the court issued an order of protection to the plaintiff; (3) plaintiff had direct contact with police because Officer Christine Reyes spoke with plaintiff on the telephone and advised her that everything was in process and she, Officer Reyes, would keep in contact; and (4) Officer Reyes advised the plaintiff that Coleson was in jail and that he would be there for a while, thus allowing plaintiff, who had a tumultuous and violent history with this man, to justifiably rely on this assurance to go about her daily life. The majority now says that in doing these four things, the police may be exposing the City to liability.

Had the police actually made specific assurances as to how plaintiff would be protected, then certainly a question of fact would have been presented. Here, however, plaintiff claims that a police officer told her at the station, after Coleson's arrest, that Coleson was "going to be in prison for a while, not to worry, [she] was going to be given protection." When asked at her deposition, she was unable to state what, if any, protection the police had promised to provide, nor did she ask. Assuming, as we must, plaintiff's testimony to be true, it cannot be said that such a vaguely-worded statement, i.e., that plaintiff would be provided protection, without any indication as to the type of protection to be provided, constituted an action by police "that would lull a plaintiff into a false sense of security or otherwise generate justifiable reliance" (*Dinardo*; *cf. Mastroianni v. County of Suffolk*, 668 N.Y.S.2d 542, [1997] [after responding to a call at the victim's residence upon a complaint that her estranged husband had allegedly been inside her home, police remained across the street for an hour after having assured her that they would "do whatever (they) could"

* I do not suggest, as the majority asserts, that the majority "seek[s] to discourage the police from being responsive to crime victims." My point is that the majority's holding will have that *effect*.

if she had further problems with him]; *De Long v. County of Erie,* 469 N.Y.S.2d 611 [1983] [assurance by 911 operator employed by the county that help would be at victim's home "right away," in response to victim's burglary-in-progress complaint, potentially played a part in victim's decision to remain in her home as opposed to seeking other assistance]). The majority does not explain how this plaintiff could have justifiably relied upon such a vague offer of "protection," or how such a question could be answered by a jury without engaging in speculation, absent any specific assurances as to *how* that "protection" would have been provided.

Equally troubling is that the majority appears to have added to the justifiable reliance prong of the *Cuffy* test, namely, that police may make assurances "only to the extent that they have an *actual basis* for such assurances." Is it possible to make these situations any more difficult for the police and those they are called on to protect? Not only must the police watch what they say, they must also be prepared to back up what they say, no matter how vague the assurances may be. For example, statements such as, "It's going to be okay," or "We'll send him away so he doesn't hurt you again" will undoubtedly be utilized in potential civil suits as examples of assurances that the police made that had no "actual basis." Such statements are on the same spectrum as the vague promises of "protection" and to "keep in contact" that were made in this case. The end result, of course, is that police will be deterred from providing any assurances to victims of domestic violence, those victims will be less than willing to cooperate in the prosecution of their significant others (or family members), and the cycle will continue, with victims in all likelihood returning to their abusers, all because the police were (justifiably) wary about making any comment that could be considered a promise of safety.

The majority claims that the 11:00 p.m. phone call that plaintiff received from Officer Reyes on the night of Coleson's arrest, when Officer Reyes allegedly told plaintiff that Coleson "was in front of [a] judge" and was going to be "sentence[d]" and that police would "keep in contact with [plaintiff]," raised a triable issue of fact on the issue of justifiable reliance. This conclusion construes statements made by police apprising the victim of the status of the victim's complaint as potential assurances of protection upon which the majority claims a plaintiff may justifiably rely. Under the majority's holding, any status report akin to the one given in this case will expose a municipality to liability, even if, as in this case, the municipality has not made an affirmative undertaking. Thus, the majority's holding will encourage law enforcement to provide victims of domestic violence, or any victim of violent crime, with as little information as possible out of concern that anything they say can and will be used against them (and their employer) in a potential civil suit.

According to the majority, the fact that Officer Reyes told plaintiff that her husband would be in prison for "a while" and that police would stay in contact with her distinguishes this case from *Valdez,* but there is little distinction since neither the plaintiff here nor the plaintiff in *Valdez* had reason to believe, based on statements by police, that she could relax her vigilance. The officers in *Valdez* promised the plaintiff that the estranged boyfriend would be arrested "immediately," and we held that the plaintiff could not have justifiably relied on that statement in light of the fact that neither the police nor the plaintiff knew the boyfriend's whereabouts. Here, the police did not mention how long Coleson would be detained, and it cannot be said that Officer Reyes's statement that she would "keep in contact" meant that Officer Reyes would contact plaintiff if and when Coleson was released, nor does plaintiff make that claim, so Officer Reyes's statement could not have lulled her into inaction.

I would therefore answer the certified question in the negative.

MOTLEY V. SMITH

2016 WL 6988597 (US Dist. Ct. E.D. Cal.) (unpublished)
(citations and some footnotes omitted)

ORDER GRANTING IN PART AND DENYING IN PART DEFENDANTS' MOTION TO DISMISS

* * * BACKGROUND

A. Factual Background

As noted above, Pamela Motley and Cindy Raygoza[1] (collectively, "plaintiffs") filed their Second Amended Complaint (SAC) on July 7, 2016. The SAC largely repeats the allegations plaintiffs levied in their First Amended Complaint (FAC) against the Fresno Police Department ("FPD"), a number of its individual officers ("officer defendants"), and the City of Fresno ("Fresno") (collectively, "defendants"). * * *

Pamela Motely and Cindy Raygoza are both victims of domestic violence. Between early March and mid-April 2014, Pamela Motley was stalked and harassed—and on at least one occasion assaulted—by her estranged husband, Paul Motley. Pamela Motley sought a restraining order against Paul and called the FPD on multiple occasions to complain of Paul's threatening behavior. According to plaintiffs, when various officer defendants responded to these calls, they were often rude and insensitive. The officers also failed to provide Pamela Motley with information regarding domestic violence and citizen's arrest rights as required by California Penal Code §§ 679.05 and 836(b). Lastly, despite his alleged violations of the restraining order, the FPD and the officer defendants did

---

[1] Plaintiff Cindy Raygoza—who is deceased—pursues this action by and through the legal representative and administrator of her estate. In addition, as the court noted in its previous order, Cindy Raygoza's adult children are pursuing their own claims for deprivation of rights to familial association under 42 U.S.C. § 1983 and wrongful death under California Code of Civil Procedure § 377.60 *et seq.*

not seek out and arrest Paul. On April 12, 2014, Paul shot Pamela Motley in the face, rendering her blind in one eye and quadriplegic.

In February 2014, Cindy Raygoza was beaten by Michael Reams, a man she was dating. Officer Engum responded to the incident after Cindy Raygoza called 9-1-1. According to plaintiffs' allegations, Officer Engum proceeded to berate Cindy Raygoza for her choice in men; he also failed to provide her with the requisite information mandated by California Penal Code §§ 679.05 and 836(b). Plaintiffs allege Officer Engum's words re-victimized Cindy Raygoza and caused her to become weary of seeking help from the FPD in the future. Plaintiffs also allege the FPD failed to pursue and arrest Reams for the February 2014 incident. Reams returned to Cindy Raygoza's apartment on July 14, 2014 and stabbed her to death.

B. Procedural Background

On June 20, 2016, the court dismissed portions of plaintiffs' FAC with leave to amend.[3] First, the court dismissed plaintiffs' § 1983 claim to the extent it was based on allegations that defendants violated plaintiffs' Fourteenth Amendment substantive due process rights, noting "a State's failure to protect an individual against private violence simply does not constitute a violation of the Due Process clause." (quoting *DeShaney v. Winnebago Cty. Dep't of Soc. Servs.*, 489 U.S. 189, 197 (1989)). Second, the court dismissed Pamela Motley's claim that defendants violated her equal protection rights, characterizing the claim as one alleging gender-based discrimination and then noting Pamela Motley had failed to plead any facts supporting a reasonable inference of gender animus on the part of the defendants. Third, the court dismissed plaintiffs' various state law claims. The court dismissed plaintiffs' negligence claims stemming from the defendants' alleged failure to arrest Paul Motley and Michael Reams, noting the plaintiffs had failed to adequately plead that the officer defendants owed them a duty to perform such an action. The court found the same was true with respect to plaintiffs' state law claims based on the officer defendants' alleged failure to protect them. Finally, the court dismissed plaintiffs' state law negligence claims regarding the officer defendants' failure to provide plaintiffs with domestic violence information as mandated by California Penal Code § 836(b).

As mentioned above, plaintiffs filed their SAC on July 6, 2016. In it, plaintiffs clarify they are pursuing equal protection claims for both gender-based discrimination as well as discrimination based on their status as

[3] In that order, the court also dismissed two of plaintiffs' claims with prejudice. Specifically, the court dismissed with prejudice Cindy Raygoza's claim for injunctive relief and any negligence claim brought by plaintiffs predicated on a violation of the Violence Against Women Act. However, the court also denied defendants' earlier motion to dismiss in part, concluding that Cindy Raygoza had adequately pled an equal protection claim based on allegations that defendant Engum made misogynistic comments to her. The court also concluded that Cindy Raygoza could pursue a *Monell* claim against defendant City of Fresno based on the alleged custom or practice on its part of discriminating against female victims of domestic violence.

victims of domestic violence. In the SAC, plaintiffs also re-allege their negligence claims as well as Cindy Raygoza's wrongful death claim.

* * * DEFENDANT'S MOTION TO DISMISS

A. Pamela Motley's Gender-Based Equal Protection & *Monell* Claims

In their motion to dismiss, defendants challenge only Pamela Motley's gender-based equal protection claim. As the court noted in its previous order:

> "The Equal Protection Clause of the Fourteenth Amendment commands that no state shall 'deny to any person within its jurisdiction the equal protection of the laws,' which is essentially a direction that all persons similarly situated should be treated alike." In order to state a claim under § 1983 for "a violation of the Equal Protection Clause of the Fourteenth Amendment a plaintiff must show that the defendants acted with an intent or purpose to discriminate against the plaintiff based upon membership in a protected class." * * *
>
> The denial of police protection to disfavored persons stemming from discriminatory intent or motive violates the Equal Protection Clause. However, "in police failure-to-serve cases, the courts consistently have required more evidence of discriminatory intent than a simple failure of diligence, perception, or persistence in a single case involving [members of a protected class]."

Defendants argue that in their SAC plaintiffs have failed to plead any specific facts indicating Pamela Motley was denied police protection based on her gender. The court disagrees. Plaintiffs' supplementation of their original allegations in their SAC consists of allegations that various defendant officers behaved in a rude, aggressive, insensitive, or disinterested manner when responding to Pamela Motley's complaints about Paul. These allegations—consisting largely of subjective interpretations of nonverbal behavior—contain no indication of any gender animus. However, plaintiffs also now allege in their SAC that on at least one occasion an officer defendant—Officer Urton—provided Pamela Motley with " 'fatherly advice' that if Pamela were his daughter he would suggest that she just leave town if she were worried." While perhaps not as potent as the language discussed by the court in *Balistreri*, Officer Urton's alleged statement is still derogatory and demeaning and hints at "an animus against abused women." Furthermore, because the court must construe the allegations of the SAC in the light most favorable to plaintiffs, this language is sufficient to give rise to an equal protection claim by plaintiff Pamela Motley based on gender discrimination. * * *

D. State Law Claims

1. Failure to Arrest Paul Motley

In their SAC plaintiffs allege defendants were negligent *per se* for failing to arrest Paul Motley. Defendants seek to dismiss this claim, arguing they did not owe plaintiffs a duty of care.

In California, the violation of a statute or ordinance can create a presumption of negligence. A plaintiff must allege and ultimately establish "four 'basic facts'. . . for this presumption to apply." These include: (1) the violation; (2) the violation as a proximate cause of the injury; (3) an injury resulting from an occurrence of the nature which the statute was designed to prevent; and (4) the injured party being a member of the class of persons for whose protection the statute was adopted.

In their SAC, plaintiffs allege that the officer defendants were mandated by California Penal Code §§ 836(c)(1) and 13701(b) to arrest Paul Motley. California Penal Code § 836(c)(1) states:

> When a peace officer is responding to a call alleging a violation of a domestic violence protective order or restraining order. . .and the peace officer has probable cause to believe that the person against whom the order is issued has notice of the order and has committed an act in violation of the order, the officer shall, consistent with [California Penal Code § 13701(b)], make a lawful arrest of the person without a warrant and take that person into custody whether or not the violation occurred in the presence of the arresting officer.

Section 13701(b) repeats the mandate contained in § 836(c)(1) and also instructs officers to avoid dual arrests and to use "reasonable efforts to identify the dominant aggressor in any incident." The cited statutes do appear to impose a mandatory duty to arrest in certain situations. Nonetheless, plaintiffs' claim as alleged in the SAC is defective because it fails to plead the first "basic fact" of a negligence *per se* claim: a violation of the statute. Under § 836(c)(1), the mandatory duty to arrest is not triggered until after the violator has notice of the domestic violence protective order or restraining order. According to the allegations of plaintiffs' SAC, the officer defendants did not encounter Paul Motley after he was notified of the restraining order. Thus, based on the factual allegations of the SAC, a statutory violation never occurred.

Moreover, to the extent plaintiffs contend defendants should have dedicated more resources to apprehending Paul, defendants are shielded from such a claim pursuant to California Government Code § 845, which provides: "Neither a public entity nor a public employee is liable for failure to. . . provide police protection service or, if police protection service is provided, for failure to provide sufficient police protection service."

2. Failure to Protect

Defendants also move to dismiss plaintiffs' claim that defendants were negligent in failing to protect Pamela Motley. The court previously dismissed this claim with leave to amend, noting (1) that "police officers. . .generally may not be held liable in damages for failing to take affirmative steps to come to the aid of, or prevent an injury to, another person," and (2) that plaintiffs had failed to plead facts establishing an exception to this general rule.

In the pending motion to dismiss, defendants argue plaintiffs have failed to allege any new or additional facts in their SAC with respect to this claim. Defendants' argument appears to be well-taken and plaintiffs do not dispute the assertion on which it is based. Accordingly, the court will dismiss plaintiffs' failure to protect claim.

3. Failure to Provide Information

In their SAC, plaintiffs allege that the officer defendants were negligent *per se* because they failed to provide Pamela Motley and Cindy Raygoza with informational materials regarding domestic violence or to inform them of their citizen's arrest rights as mandated by California Penal Code §§ 679.05 and 836(b). Plaintiffs allege the failure to comply with these statutes "changed the risk of injury" to Pamela Motley and Cindy Raygoza because they were left unaware of preventative measures they could have taken to mitigate the dangers they faced from their abusers. Defendants argue plaintiffs' allegations are too speculative to establish causation, and thus fail under federal pleading standards.

California Penal Code § 836(b) states:

> Any time a peace officer is called out on a domestic violence call, it shall be mandatory that the officer make a good faith effort to inform the victim of his or her right to make a citizen's arrest. . . .This information shall include advising the victim how to safely execute the arrest.

Under California Penal Code § 679.05(a), a domestic violence victim has "the right to have a domestic violence advocate and a support person of the victim's choosing present at any interview by law enforcement authorities, prosecutors, or defense attorneys." * * *

The court notes that, given the allegations of the SAC, § 679.05 does not appear to apply to either Pamela Motley or Cindy Raygoza. Neither ever attended an interview by law enforcement authorities, prosecutors, or defense attorneys. Instead, their encounters with law enforcement were limited to officers' responses to their 9-1-1 calls. These responses are akin to the "initial investigation[s]" specifically excluded under § 679.05(c) and, thus, that statute cannot serve as the basis for a cognizable claim by plaintiffs here.

However, plaintiffs do appear to have stated a cognizable negligence *per se* claim with respect to the defendant officers' alleged failure to adhere to the requirements of California Penal Code § 836(b). In this regard, plaintiffs allege in their SAC that the officer defendants failed to provide them with the required information, the information would have negated the dangers they faced, and the statute mandating the dispensation of this information was designed to protect a class of which they were members; i.e., domestic violence victims. In moving to dismiss this claim, defendants argue that these allegations are "speculative" and that "proof of causation cannot be based on mere speculation, conjecture and inferences drawn from other inferences to reach a conclusion unsupported by any real evidence. . . ." However, the case is now before the court on a motion to dismiss and proof is not yet demanded. Rather, all that is required at this stage of the litigation are factual allegations sufficient to support "a reasonable inference that the defendant is liable for the misconduct alleged." Moreover, of course, in considering a motion to dismiss, the court is obligated to treat factual allegations made by the plaintiff as true. The SAC adequately alleges that Pamela Motley and Cindy Raygoza would have been able to protect themselves if the officer defendants had adhered to § 836(b). Such an allegation is sufficient to survive a motion to dismiss.

Defendants also argue that plaintiffs' claim against the City of Fresno based upon the officers failure to provide the information required by § 836(b) must be dismissed because "plaintiffs have failed to allege facts that would establish the alleged acts or omissions of any of the defendant officers proximately resulted in their injuries." However, because the officers' alleged negligence occurred within the scope of their employment, plaintiffs may pursue a claim for vicarious liability against Fresno.

Finally, defendants contend that they are immune from liability because California Government Code §§ 821 and 845 exempts public employees for "failure to provide police services." However, it appears that defendants are not entitled to immunity with respect to this claim pursuant to those provisions because the duty to provide the required information was mandatory rather than discretionary.

E. Leave to Amend

The court has carefully considered whether plaintiffs could further amend their complaint to remedy the defects noted above. "Valid reasons for denying leave to amend include undue delay, bad faith, prejudice, and futility." Plaintiffs have amended their complaint twice. Additionally, through the court's order granting in part and denying in part defendants' previous motion to dismiss the first amended complaint, plaintiffs have received guidance with respect to the deficiencies of that complaint. Therefore, the court concludes that granting further leave to amend with respect to the dismissed claims would be futile in this case. . .

[Editor's Note: The court dismissed the plaintiffs' claim re rights to familial association/relations and their negligence claims for failure to arrest Paul Motley and failing to protect both plaintiffs. It allowed Motley's claims regarding denial of equal protection and municipal liability, both plaintiffs' claims re failure to provide information, and Raygoza's claim for wrongful death to go forward.]

GIRALDO V. CITY OF HOLLYWOOD, FLORIDA

142 F.Supp.3d 1292 (S.D. Fla. 2015)
(footnotes and citations omitted)

* * *I. Background

Plaintiff, Christian Fernando Giraldo, commenced this action on August 5, 2014. The operative complaint is the Third Amended Complaint (the "TAC"), which names four defendants: City of Hollywood, Florida ("Hollywood"); Officer Raul Toledo, in his individual capacity; Officer Michael Malone, in his individual capacity; and Officer Brittany Schendel, in her individual capacity. Plaintiff alleges violations of the First Amendment, Fourth Amendment, and Fourteenth Amendment arising from his arrest on September 29, 2013 by the Officers. * * *

On September 29, 2013, Giraldo called 911, requesting that officers come to his home to respond to a domestic dispute between himself and his girlfriend, Aurora Hernandez-Calvino ("Calvino"). Officers Malone, Toledo, Schendel, and Mendez responded to the scene. In domestic violence situations, it is protocol to interview individuals separately. Officers Schendel and Malone interviewed Giraldo while Officers Toledo and Mendez interviewed Calvino. Calvino told Officer Toledo that she and Giraldo's verbal argument escalated to a physical argument and that she had been pinned on the bed. Overhearing Calvino tell the police officers that Giraldo had a concealed weapons permit, was a martial arts instructor, and was a marine, Giraldo interrupted Schendel as she was questioning him and went over to the officers speaking to Calvino to explain himself. Giraldo testified in deposition that as he tried to provide the weapons permit to Toledo, Toledo "shrugged [him] off" and said "I'm not asking you the f*cking question, give it to her." Giraldo provided Schendel with his license, and she resumed questioning him, saying "[c]ome on, I'm talking to you. Pay attention to me. Let me hear your side of the story. You can talk to them later. They need to discuss what she wants to say, and I'm discussing what you want to say." The parties dispute the events that unfolded at this point; it is uncontroverted that ultimately Giraldo was removed from the apartment. Schendel then spoke to Calvino, who told her that she and Giraldo had an argument. During the argument, Giraldo threw the remote and broke it, removed the light bulbs from the ceiling and put them very high up to where she could not reach them, pushed her on the bed and climbed on top of her as she fought to get away.

Calvino pointed out the bed that she was held down on, the smashed remote, and the light bulbs that had been removed. Calvino then filled out a Complaint Affidavit, writing down her version of events. That sworn affidavit states that Giraldo removed the light bulbs so Calvino could not see as she tried to pack, that he threw and broke a remote, grabbed her from behind, and that he threw her on the bed. It further states that Giraldo used force with his head onto Calvino's so she pulled his t-shirt until it ripped and he got off of her.

Officer Malone testified in deposition that he does not remember seeing any red marks or bruises on Giraldo. Officer Schendel testified in deposition that she does not recall seeing any red marks on Giraldo. According to Officer Schendel's testimony, only she and Officer Malone composed the police report. The Police Report, which is signed by Malone, as the Officer/Affiant, and Schendel, as the Notary, states that "this Officer did observe the remote in the bathroom to be smashed. This Officer did not see any physical marks on either party." Only Officer Toledo testified in deposition that he saw a "little tear on the collar" of Giraldo's shirt and "some red marks on his neck"; Officer Toledo does not remember sharing that observation with Malone or Schendel. * * *

III. Discussion

A. Count I and Count II: Qualified Immunity

Count I alleges unlawful seizure in violation of the Fourth Amendment because the seizure was unreasonable and Count II alleges unlawful arrest in violation of the Fourteenth Amendment because the arrest was unsupported by probable cause or a valid warrant. The Officers argue that they are entitled to qualified immunity, and so Counts I and II should be dismissed.

When analyzing qualified immunity at summary judgment, courts "may not resolve genuine disputes of fact in favor of the party seeking summary judgment" and must view the evidence in the light most favorable to the opposing party in determining whether genuine issues of material fact exist. "The defense of qualified immunity completely protects government officials performing discretionary functions from suit in their individual capacities unless their conduct violates clearly established statutory or constitutional rights of which a reasonable person would have known." * * *

Plaintiff does not dispute that all Defendants acted within their discretion; thus, the burden shifts to Plaintiff to show that a violation of a constitutional right has been alleged, and that the right is clearly established. The Court need not decide these two prongs sequentially. * * * Where the officers had arguable probable cause for an alleged unlawful arrest, that is, where "reasonable officers in the same circumstances and possessing the same knowledge as the [officer] *could have believed* that probable cause existed to arrest," the officer is entitled to qualified immunity.

Based on the undisputed facts, the Officers responding to the scene had arguable probable cause to arrest Giraldo. Calvino's sworn complaint is itself sufficient to support arguable probable cause. Plaintiff stresses that officers may rely on a victim's complaint only "absent allegations indicating that their reliance was unreasonable." * * *

The record does not reveal circumstances suggesting that the Officers should have doubted the veracity of Calvino's statement or that relying on her statement would have been unreasonable. To the contrary, the Officers have shown that they encountered evidence corroborating her statements. Consistent with Calvino's story, there was a bed in disarray, a broken remote, and light bulbs removed from their sockets. Even assuming that Calvino fabricated her story, the evidence presented to the Court by the Officers establishes that reasonable officers in the same circumstances and possessing the same knowledge as they did could have believed that probable cause existed to arrest Giraldo. * * * Plaintiff contends that the Officers unreasonably disregarded or failed to obtain Giraldo's side of the story. It is uncontroverted, however, that Officer Schendel specifically attempted to obtain Giraldo's story, explicitly urging him to "[l]et me hear your side of the story" despite Giraldo's attempts to engage Officer Toledo as Toledo spoke with Calvino. While the Police Report states that there were no physical marks on either party, the two officers who contributed to the report, Schendel and Malone, testified that they did not observe any marks. It is mere speculation that Schendel and Malone actually did observe marks on Giraldo, yet deliberately chose to exclude that information from the Report in order to establish probable cause to arrest. Plaintiff also points to the testimony of Dr. Kirkham, a criminologist, that a reasonably competent officer would have arrested Calvino instead of Giraldo. The Court has not considered Dr. Kirkham's testimony as to the legal issue of whether arguable probable cause existed.

Thus, the Court finds that Officers Schendel, Malone, and Toledo are entitled to qualified immunity and will grant summary judgment in their favor as to Counts I and II.

B. Count IV: Gender Discrimination in Violation of the Fourteenth Amendment

Count IV alleges that Defendant Officers engaged in intentional discrimination against Plaintiff in violation of the Fourteenth Amendment. Plaintiff opines that it is clearly established that gender discrimination is an infringement of the equal protection clause, and alleges that the Officers engaged in intentional discrimination in determining that Giraldo was the aggressor and arresting him.

To state a claim under the Equal Protection Clause of the Fourteenth Amendment, Plaintiff must allege that: "(1) he is similarly situated with other persons who received more favorable treatment; and (2) his discriminatory treatment was based on some constitutionally protected interest such as race or gender." Plaintiff must also allege that the Defendants acted with intent to discriminate against him; "[c]onclusory allegations or assertions of personal belief of disparate treatment or discriminatory intent are insufficient."

The Officers argue that Plaintiff has failed to allege the first prong. Giraldo avers that he has alleged that those similarly situated are other victims who called for police assistance following a domestic disturbance. The Officers next argue that Giraldo has failed to provide any evidence that the Officers intentionally discriminated against him. In response, Plaintiff asserts that he has alleged that the Officers intentionally discriminated against him, and points to deposition testimony by Schendel. Schendel testified that she was a victim of domestic violence at the hands of her ex-boyfriend, who lied to the police officers that responded to the domestic violence call. Schendel also answered "no" when asked whether anything could have changed her mind as to whether to arrest Giraldo from the time she "walked from the apartment until the time [she] got to Mr. Giraldo." Plaintiff offers nothing as to the other officers. Officer Schendel's deposition testimony that she was once a victim of domestic violence is attenuated and is not sufficient to create a genuine issue of material fact as to whether the officers improperly acted on the basis of Giraldo's gender. Rather, Plaintiff has extended only mere conjecture that discriminatory intent based on his gender motivated his arrest and the events leading up to it. * * * The Court finds that the Officers are entitled to summary judgment in their favor as to the intentional discrimination claim.

C. Hollywood's *Daubert* Motion

In its *Daubert* Motion, Hollywood argues for the exclusion of testimony by Plaintiff's expert, George Kirkham, on a number of different topics. As the Court has already determined that the Officers are entitled to summary judgment, the Court will now discuss only the portions of the Daubert Motion that are relevant to deciding Hollywood's Motion for Summary Judgment; the remaining portions are moot.

* * * Under the third prong [of *Daubert*], "expert testimony is admissible if it concerns matters that are beyond the understanding of the average lay person." * * *

In the Response to Hollywood's Motion for Summary Judgment, Plaintiff invokes the following deposition testimony from Kirkham:

- That "consider[ing] the physical size, relative size of two people [ ] just translates blatantly into gender.";

- That the combination of Standard Operating Procedure (SOP) 250, which does not include gender in a list of what factors should *not* be considered when determining whether an arrest should be made in the context of domestic/dating violence, and the size training would lead to a "de facto" custom and practice.;
- That a reasonably competent police department would not leave the word "gender" out of their domestic violence policy.

In the Daubert Motion, Hollywood argues that Kirkham's opinions about the physical size factor should be striken, as there is no apparent methodology underlying them. Kirkham testifies that the factor of "physical size" might be held to predominate over any other factors; Kirkham gives in support of this the fact that men more often times are the assailant in domestic violence situations. Plaintiff argues that while "it is simply common sense that training officers to arrest the bigger individual implicates arresting men, [ ] Kirkham's testimony is still needed to explain to the jury how that can interact with the various police policies/procedures on the scene." The Court disagrees. Kirkham's opinions amount to just that, that training officers to arrest the bigger individual implicates arresting men, and is gender biased. His opinions on the topic fail to go beyond the understanding of the average lay person and have no reliable underlying methodology, other than generally Kirkham's own experience as a criminologist and former law enforcement officer. Similarly, Kirkham's testimony about SOP 250's omission of the word "gender" and the combination of size training and SOP 250 leading to a "de facto" custom and practice" are not admissible. * * *

D. Counts I, II, and III: Municipal Liability under Section 1983

In Counts I and II, Plaintiff alleges that Hollywood has a widespread and persistent policy, custom, or practice of engaging in gender discrimination when responding to domestic disturbance calls as is evidenced by their SOPS. In support of this, Plaintiff alleges that when training officers on the factors to consider in determining who the primary aggressor in a domestic incident is, Hollywood instructs its officers to "consider the physical size of the parties." Plaintiff also points a list of factors in SOP 250 that should *not* be considered when determining whether an arrest should be made in the context of domestic/dating violence; the list does not include gender or sex. In Count III, Plaintiff alleges that Hollywood engages in a pattern and practice of discrimination and profiling when determining who should be arrested when responding to domestic disturbance calls. In support, Plaintiff points to the training materials and SOP 250 outlined in Counts I and II, as well as statistical evidence. Specifically, in the City of Hollywood, during a three month period, 130 males were arrested as compared to only 38 females; that of the females arrested, only 25 were arrested when the victim was a male; and that less than 15% of domestic violence arrests involved female on male violence. * * *

Hollywood argues that it is entitled to summary judgment in its favor because Plaintiff has failed to identify any specific instances of discrimination other than his own. Indeed, Plaintiff cites no other specific instance. Plaintiff instead relies on SOP 250, the training module's reference to "physical size," and the training module's repeated suggestions that a domestic violence aggressor would be male (e.g., referencing "male privilege" and male pronoun usage such as "[a] victim may believe *his* threats"). Plaintiff contends that these materials, in combination, support the existence of either an official policy of arresting males in domestic violence contexts, or in the alternative, that they led to an unofficial custom or practice of gender discrimination. The Court disagrees.

It is undisputed that Hollywood's Police Department (the "Department") had a standard operating procedure entitled "Biased Based Profiling," known as SOP 121, in effect at the time of the arrest. SOP 121 is an overarching policy applying to all members of the Department. SOP 121 defines bias based profiling as "[t]he selection of an individual(s) based solely on a trait common to a group for enforcement action. This includes but is not limited to . . . gender." At the relevant time SOP 121 was (and still is) a mandatory orientation topic for all then-active officers and new officers. SOP 121 states that officers shall not consider gender in establishing probable cause. In its Motion, Hollywood argues that SOP 250 must be read in conjunction with SOP 121 and that when read together, the omission of "gender" from SOP 250 and the inclusion of "physical size" as one of multiple non-exclusive factors considered by Department officers in determining probable cause in domestic violence situations are not sufficient to create a genuine issue of material fact. In response, Plaintiff asserts that the existence of SOP 121 is not dispositive, and suggests that, in fact, the inclusion of gender in other SOPs, but not in the SOP relating to domestic disputes, is probative of discriminatory intent.

The fact that SOP 250 does not include gender in its non-exhaustive list of factors not to be considered does not necessarily mean, as Plaintiff asserts, that the Department actively encouraged its officers to consider it. This is especially so where SOP 121 states that gender shall not be considered when establishing probable cause. * * *

Plaintiff proffers arrest statistics procured from Hollywood during discovery; namely, that 78% of domestic violence arrestees are men, and that while only 11% of women who call the police on a man for domestic violence are themselves arrested instead, the number is nearly 40% for men who call the police on women for domestic violence. With respect to the arrest statistics, Hollywood argues that there is nothing about them that is noteworthy such that it suggests that a policy or custom of gender discrimination was present at the time of Giraldo's arrest. In its Motion, Hollywood, citing statewide statistics, argues that the Department statistics are consistent with statewide trends.

* * * Even taken on their own, without making a statewide comparison, the bare statistics are not sufficient to support a jury finding that there is an official policy, or an unofficial policy or custom, of gender discrimination. * * *

E. Count VI: Failure to Train

Count VI alleges that Hollywood failed to train its officers regarding dating and domestic violence, leading to the violations of Giraldo's constitutional rights. * * * Such a policy of inadequate training may be proven by showing that the failure to train evidenced a "deliberate indifference" to the rights of a municipality's citizens. * * * A plaintiff can establish that a municipality was on notice of a need to train by showing a widespread pattern or "even a single earlier constitutional violation" if the plaintiff also demonstrates "that constitutional violations were likely to recur without training." In some cases, the need for training is so obvious that deliberate indifference can be established even without an earlier violation or pattern of abuse.

Hollywood argues that Plaintiff cannot show the requisite notice for deliberate indifference through either avenue. * * * The Court agrees with Hollywood that Plaintiff has not made a sufficient showing to defeat summary judgment in this regard. Plaintiff next argues that the need to train is so obvious in this case that Plaintiff need not establish a pattern of abuse. * * * The record in this case does not amount to evidence of "obviousness" such as that described in *Canton* and Plaintiff has failed to cite any other relevant caselaw in support. The Court finds that Hollywood is entitled to summary judgment on the failure to train claim.

F. Count V: First Amendment Retaliation Claim

[Plaintiff filed a complaint with the Internal Affairs Unit regarding his arrest, and alleges that the intake form and form letter he received in response led him to believe that he could not speak to the media, a violation of his First Amendment rights.] * * * The court finds that even when construing the record evidence in the light most favorable to Plaintiff, a reasonable jury could not find that the language on the two forms would likely deter an ordinary person from the exercise of First Amendment rights. * * *

C. BATTERERS IN BLUE

JACQUELINE M. MAZZOLA, HONEY I'M HOME: ADDRESSING THE PROBLEM OF OFFICER DOMESTIC VIOLENCE

27 J. Civ. Rts. & Econ. Dev. 347 (2014)
(footnotes omitted)

Introduction

"Kristin—don't worry. We're all over this. We were on it as soon as you called." This was not the first time a supervisor at the Utica Police Department reassured Kristin. Kristin received this response sometime in the late summer of 2009. A few weeks later, on September 28, Kristin's eight-year-old son returned home from school, walked into his home, and found his mother dead and his father near death. Joseph A. Longo, a thirteen-year veteran of the Utica Police Department, had taken a kitchen knife and brutally stabbed Kristin thirteen times in her back and upper chest, killing her and then turning the knife on himself.

Kristin suffered extensive verbal, physical, and mental abuse by Longo throughout their marriage. Longo also physically, verbally, and emotionally abused his four children. On August 13, 2009, Longo stood in front of his children and wife, held his service revolver, and told them, "[t]oday is the day I go postal on all of you." Before this incident, supervisors at the Utica Police Department discouraged Kristin from seeking an order of protection against Longo and from reporting anything serious to the police because Longo could be suspended or he could lose his job. One day after this incident, Kristin reported what had happened to the Utica Police Department and told the supervisor that she feared for her life and her children's lives. She also notified Longo's supervisor that Longo was emotionally unstable and needed counseling. The supervisor's response was, "I know he is not ok."

While Longo's supervisors did meet with Longo shortly after this incident, it was to no avail. The same day as that meeting, Longo returned home while still on police duty with his service revolver and forced Kristin to flee her own home. Once again, she reported this incident, and Longo's supervisor reassured her that Longo's gun would be confiscated. However, the gun was not confiscated.

On September 14, 2009, in front of his youngest child and Kristin, Longo put the barrel of his service revolver in his mouth and threatened again to kill himself. Kristin relayed her fears to Longo's supervisor, who in turn reassured her that the police department was aware of the situation and would protect her and her children. Longo was disciplined, however it was for an unrelated incident where he pointed his gun at a woman while working as a high school security guard. Fellow officers were concerned about Longo's behavior, and one officer even urged the police chief to confiscate Longo's weapons. Contrarily, the police chief, who was one of Longo's close friends and Longo's ex-partner, affirmatively ordered Longo to keep his weapons and remain on duty. One of the chief's subordinates overrode the chief's order and took away Longo's weapons. On September 28, 2009, Kristin and Longo were in court together for their divorce. Kristin was awarded exclusive possession of the family home. Less than four hours later, Kristin was found dead in that home. * * *

A. Double the Trouble for Victims of Officer Domestic Violence

Domestic violence crosses all socioeconomic classifications and professions, including doctors, lawyers, and even police officers. However, victims of officer domestic violence face numerous dangers that victims in the general population do not face. For example, "[f] ear dominates a victim of domestic violence; when the abuser is a police officer, that fear is compounded." Officer abusers are tougher and more dangerous, and "[t]hey have training, a badge, a gun and the weight of the police culture behind them." In fact, domestic violence in police officer families may be as much as four times as prevalent when compared to the ten percent of families in the general population who experience domestic violence. Even assuming that domestic violence occurs in police families at the same rate as it does in the general population, approximately 60,000 to 180,000 police families are affected.

Officer domestic violence is not only devastating for the direct victims of the abuse, but it also has an indirect devastating effect on the entire community. Domestic violence by just one officer questions the credibility and effectiveness of the entire police precinct. If officers are supposed to protect the community and stop acts of domestic violence, officers must first respond to the domestic violence present within the precinct. If an officer is not responding to domestic violence within the precinct, that officer's ability to perform his police duties may be compromised because that officer may be unable to think rationally on the scene. For example, if an officer abuser goes on a domestic violence call, he may not adequately protect the victim for various reasons; he may think that she is lying, or he may believe that the restraining order should not be enforced. Also, if the officer abuser is called to testify in a case of domestic violence, that testimony may be filled with personal bias.

The discrepancy between the number of families in the general population affected by domestic violence and the number of police families affected by domestic violence may be attributed to the very nature of being a police officer. When some civilians become police officers, they change and develop a "command presence." At work, officers need to be in control. They give and take orders daily. When these orders are not complied with, officers are taught to use physical force and verbal intimidation. Officers are issued handguns, batons, and handcuffs and receive special training on how to use these, and their own fists, as weapons. Officers are also trained to use certain techniques to incapacitate someone. Most injuries caused by these techniques are not easily observable. These same control tactics are often incorporated into an officer's home life. For example, officer abusers know how and where to hit a domestic violence victim so that bruises are not visible. Thus, when a victim complains of injury, she often will not have any physical evidence of injury to support her claim.

Officers also have privileges that civilians do not have. For example, officers can legitimately access records of confidential and personal information. Officers have access to information including locations of shelters and community support groups, and officers receive training in surveillance and investigation. Officers can use these privileges for personal reasons, such as tracking the victim and identifying any visitors the victim may have over, including fellow officers who may stop by to take a statement, therapists who are needed to develop safety plans with the victim, and lawyers who may visit with the victim to discuss divorce or other legal courses of actions. Thus, hiding from an officer is nearly impossible. Advocates from a battered women's shelter state that when a victim of officer domestic violence seeks help, "[i]t's a frightening feeling, even for the domestic violence advocates. That's because officers know the locations of confidential shelters, or can easily find out, posing a risk to everyone."

B. Hush Hush: The Code of Silence and Underreporting

The "code of silence" that pervades police precincts is another significant factor that contributes to the higher incidents of domestic violence seen in police families. The code of silence "is an unofficial acknowledgment that no officer blames or implicates another officer who is accused of a wrongdoing." The code of silence severely limits a victim's access to helpful networks. Because officers face daily life-or-death situations together, a culture of solidarity and loyalty is fostered among the officers. This solidarity leads to the unspoken code of silence.

The officers that maintain a conspiracy of silence may persuade the victim that the loss of her abuser's job would devastate her family. Officers may also fear that they will be ostracized or will be abandoned by other officers if they break this code of silence. As a result, at trial some officers may cover up for another officer and may commit perjury instead of telling the truth about a fellow officer. The code of silence applies to all wrongdoings, including domestic violence allegations and may be "the greatest single barrier to the effective investigation and adjudication of complaints against police officers."

This "code of silence" may even extend beyond the police precinct because officers work with and form relationships with members of the criminal justice system, such as dispatchers, victim advocates, fellow officers, attorneys, judges, and corrections personnel. Officers can exploit these relationships to manipulate the system. This exploitation in turn severely limits the victim's ability to seek help. This close relationship with other professionals may also leave a victim, or a victim's family, weary of proceeding against an officer abuser because a victim may fear that the officer has special insight into how the criminal justice system works. As one survivor put it, "I knew they'd cover up for him like they did for each other." Not only does a victim fear that if she presses charges against the officer abuser those charges will be dropped, but a victim also fears that the officer will find a way to fabricate charges against her. For example, a victim may fear that the officer may plant drugs or stolen property on her, or even worse, "she may know that he is capable of rigging her car to cause an auto 'accident' or running her off the road."

Compounding all of these factors is yet another obstacle: victims of officer domestic violence are not only unlikely to receive help, but are also unlikely to report domestic violence. Between 1998 and 2002, approximately sixty percent of domestic violence in the general population was reported to the police. The most common reason victims of domestic violence cited for not reporting the abuse was that the incident was a "private/personal matter." Another reason for the non-reporting was to "protect the offender." For victims of officer domestic violence, this fear is even greater because in order to report an incident of domestic violence, the victim would have to open up to her abuser's colleagues. Those who do report incidents of officer domestic violence have seen very few results because the abusers were supported by a system that gave the officer abusers more credibility than the victims, that failed to fully investigate officer domestic violence allegations, and that may have even supported the officer abusers. Thus, there is a hushing effect on both sides—the reporting of the abuse and the following through with an allegation against a fellow officer. * * *

Conclusion

Police officers still inadequately respond to domestic disturbances and under-enforce the laws regarding domestic violence. When the domestic violence abuser is an officer, this response may be even worse. Victims of officer domestic violence face heightened risks and inadequate remedies. To protect the victims, police precincts must adopt strict policies regarding officer domestic violence. If these policies are not followed, the entire police precinct will be subject to tort liability to compensate victims for a police precinct's failure to protect and respond properly to officer domestic violence. Legislation must be passed to encourage officers to work with officer domestic violence victims and to prevent future harms to the victim, the abuser, and the community. As one survivor points out, "[a]s a victim of police abuse, the last place I would have gone to report [the abuse] was to an advocate who worked in the same building as my husband." This fear to report must be changed through legislation.

[Editor's Note: In Muhammad v. Muhammad, *108 P.3d 779 (WA, 2005), the wife, who was working outside the home, obtained a domestic violence protective order against the husband, a deputy sheriff. The husband was also arrested and charged with domestic violence harassment and intimidation with a deadly weapon after he brandished a gun at the wife and her sister. As a result of the restraining order, he lost his job since he was automatically barred from possessing a firearm. In the divorce, the trial court awarded significantly more than half of the marital property to the husband, stating that the wife had to know that the husband would lose his job and could not pay the bills if she obtained a protective order, and since she was at fault, her share would be smaller.*

The appellate court affirmed this division, but the state supreme court reversed, holding that Washington courts are statutorily prohibited from considering fault in division of community property. The dissent stated that the trial court's division was based on the economic realities of the case, not on the fault of the parties, and that courts can divide property equitably. It opined that even though the husband's worth after the separation was over 5 times what the wife's was after the trial court's division of property and debts, each party was in approximately the same economic position they were in before marriage.]

INTERNATIONAL ASSOCIATION OF CHIEFS OF POLICE, DISCUSSION PAPER ON IACP'S POLICY ON DOMESTIC VIOLENCE BY POLICE OFFICERS

(2003)

* * * C. Incident Response Protocols

A department's response to 911 calls where officers are involved immediately sets the tone for how a situation will be handled throughout the remainder of the continuum. A range of trained personnel is critical to the effective management of an incident.

1. Department-Wide Response. When handling a report of domestic violence involving a police officer, all actions must be documented and forwarded to the chief through the chain of command.

2. Communications Officer / Dispatcher Documentation. When a call or report of domestic violence involves a police officer, the dispatcher should have a standing directive to document the call and immediately notify both the supervisor on duty and the dispatch supervisor. This directive ensures that command personnel receive the information and prevents the call from being handled informally.

3. Patrol Response. In a domestic violence situation involving an officer, the dynamics between the responding patrol officer and the accused officer (i.e., collegiality, rank differential) have the potential for making the on-scene decisions additionally difficult. Therefore, the responding patrol

officer shall immediately request that a supervisor on-duty who is of higher rank than the involved officer report to the scene, regardless of the involved officer's jurisdiction.

4. On-Scene Supervisor Response. The on-scene supervisor must respond to the call and assume responsibility for all on-scene decision making to include:

- Securing the scene and collecting evidence
- Ensuring an arrest is made where probable cause exists
- Attempting to locate the alleged offender if he/she has fled
- Removing firearms
- Addressing issues of victim safety
- Notifying the chief in the accused officer's jurisdiction

a. Crime Scene Documentation. * * *

b. Arrest Decisions. * * * In all cases, responding officers should base arrest decisions on probable cause. * * * Officers must make every effort to determine which party is the dominant aggressor in order to avoid the arrest of victims.

c. Weapon Removal. When an arrest is made, the on-scene supervisor shall relieve the accused officer of all service weapons. Where multiple firearms are present (officers may own recreational firearms that they keep at home), removing only the service weapons may leave the victim vulnerable to further violence. While federal, state, and local laws vary on how and when firearms can be removed, police have broad powers to remove them in certain circumstances, particularly if an arrest is being made. The on-scene supervisor may suggest that the accused officer voluntarily relinquish all firearms. The supervisor can also ask the victim about the removal of firearms from the home for safekeeping by the department. In situations where an arrest is not made, the on-scene supervisor may consider removing the accused officer's firearm(s) as a safety consideration and to reduce department liability.

After firearms are removed, decisions need to be made about how long they will be or can be held. Where court orders of protection are in place, these orders may affect decisions on the return or seizure of firearms. * * * A department may choose to be more restrictive that federal law by prohibiting officers from possessing service weapons when subject to protective orders or under criminal and/or administrative investigations. * * *

5. Additional Critical Considerations. Although a domestic violence incident involving an officer from another jurisdiction could present a department with compounding complications, a policy that addresses such circumstances can minimize confusion and liability. Of equal importance

is the need for department policy to address employees involved in domestic violence who live outside the department's jurisdiction. It is recommended that neighboring jurisdictions prepare written Memoranda of Understanding so that departments can be assured that they will receive mutually agreed upon, timely notification of an incident's occurrence.

It is important that the department's policy addresses the possibility that the accused officer is the chief/director/supervisor of the department in order to affirm the department's commitment to zero-tolerance. In such a situation, notification would be made to the individual with direct oversight.

Departments may be faced with a domestic violence incident where the victim is a police officer or both victim and offender are police officers. If this occurs, standard domestic violence response and investigative procedures should be followed. Safety of the victim should be the paramount concern. The department should take steps to protect the privacy of the officer who has been abused, and make referrals to confidential domestic violence services. The department should not allow the reported incident to impact negatively upon the assignments and evaluation of the victimized officer. In the event that an order of protection has been issued, a department will need to make careful decisions concerning work assignments for accused officers pending administrative and criminal investigations. Firearm removal in this situation becomes additionally complex. In the development of the policy, individual departments should seek legal guidance to protect the rights of all concerned.

6. Department Follow Up. The policy requires officers to report to their supervisor if they become the subject of a criminal investigation or protective order proceeding, however departments should not rely on self-reporting. It is recommended that departments establish a mechanism such as annual/periodic checks of protective order databases for names of officers. The chief should require a debriefing of all officers including communications officers/dispatch involved in response to a police officer domestic violence case and should use the opportunity to review with personnel the department's confidentiality guidelines. In addition, a command-level critical incident management review of every domestic violence case involving an officer should be conducted.

The department must select a danger assessment tool to be used to determine the potential for further violence on the part of an accused officer and provide training on the use of the tool to a designated member of the command staff. In addition, the assessment should be supplemented by interviews with the victim, witnesses, and family members. Information gathered should be used to settle on appropriate sanctions, administrative actions, and referrals. Danger assessment findings may be shared with the judge, while the officer is in custody, prior to arraignment. The command officer assigned as the victim's principal contact should discuss the findings with the victim as part of safety planning. All victims shall be informed of the possibility of danger regardless of the outcome of the assessment.

Another tool which supervisors and chiefs are encouraged to use when a pattern of abusive behavior is detected is an administrative order of protection. This is a directive from a supervisor ordering an officer to refrain from particular conduct toward a particular person as a condition of continued employment. The use of administrative orders of protection are helpful in that they may enhance victim safety, and punishment for violations of an order can proceed quickly reducing department liability and eliminating the time a department may need to continue to pay an officer on administrative leave or suspension for the duration of a lengthy criminal case.

D. Victim Safety and Protection

IACP efforts within this project have clearly identified victims of police officers as especially vulnerable. Police officers are usually well known within the criminal justice community and may be well respected in law enforcement circles. Victims in these circumstances may feel powerless. They face formidable obstacles in seeking police assistance. Therefore, the department must be actively engaged in outreach to families of officers and connected to the range of services within the community.

1. Advocacy Resources. * * *

2. Designated Principal Contact. Promptly following the report of the incident, the department shall assign a member of the command staff as the victim's principal contact for case information. This connection is essential for addressing safety and informing victims about all aspects of department protocols and policies and applicable laws. As a matter of safety, the victim's whereabouts and any communication with victims must be kept confidential. The principal contact must inform the victim of department confidentiality policies and their limitations.

3. Victim Safety. Departments must recognize that as the consequences of being held responsible for his/her behavior (the potential loss of employment coupled with the loss of control over the intimate partner) become apparent, an abusive officer may escalate behavior to extreme acts of violence such as abducting the victim, taking hostages, and committing homicide and/or suicide. The victim's principal contact must ensure that the victim is offered the opportunity to create a safety plan and discuss stalking. Information learned through the danger assessment tools are critical for alerting the department and the victim to the potential for additional violence and for developing strategies in an attempt to cope with the situation.

E. Post-Incident Administrative and Criminal Decisions

Once an arrest has been made or an incident has otherwise been documented, careful attention must be devoted to the proper handling of the case. The department should conduct two separate but parallel investigations. The chief may ask an outside law enforcement agency to handle the administrative or criminal investigation for reasons of limited resources or to avoid the appearance of a conflict of interest. Simultaneous investigations will prevent a department from continuing to employ an officer who has violated department policy while the outcome of a criminal investigation and prosecution may take considerably longer to conclude. In order to ensure that an accused officer's departmental and legal rights are upheld during the administrative and criminal investigations, the department should seek legal guidance.

1. *Administrative Investigations and Decisions*. The chief shall appoint an investigator within the internal affairs division of the department to conduct the administrative investigation. If a department does not have an internal affairs division, the chief should appoint an investigator. Based on the report of an incident the department must undertake a comprehensive administrative investigation of the accused officer and take steps to reduce the potential for further violence by seizing firearms and using administrative orders of protection. The investigating body/officer must have the authority to make decisions about arrest, access to all pertinent case information, and experience conducting case analysis. Decisions on administrative actions should not be contingent on anticipated outcomes of the criminal procedure. Departments have a broad range of administrative options; employing these options in a timely manner is crucial to victim and community safety as well as the well-being of the officer and the efficient operation of the department. With respect to seized firearms, departments need to establish policy governing the length of time firearms can be held and the protocol used for their return. Departments need to take responsibility for notifying victims prior to the return of firearms. Court orders of protection may affect the terms of firearm seizure and return. The department may employ the full range of administrative sanctions against an officer who has violated department policy.

Any officer determined through an administrative investigation to have committed domestic violence shall be terminated from the department.

2. *Criminal Investigations and Decision*. The chief shall appoint an investigator within the domestic violence unit to conduct the criminal investigation. If a department does not have a domestic violence unit, the criminal investigations unit or the detective division should handle the criminal investigation. * * *

Upon the conclusion of a criminal investigation, all information pertaining to the incident and all necessary charging paperwork must be forwarded directly to the prosecutor's office. The quality and quantity of information transferred should be thorough, including documentation of earlier calls to the agency, photo documentation of on-scene damage and injuries, previous concerns about officer behavior, danger assessment findings, etc.

Any officer convicted through criminal proceedings of domestic violence shall be terminated from the department. Federal law prohibits anyone convicted of a misdemeanor domestic violence crime from possessing firearms or ammunition. The chief shall ensure the department seizes all firearms owned by the department or possessed by the convicted officer as allowable under state law.

3. *Termination Procedures*. Once the administrative and/or criminal investigations conclude with the decision to terminate an officer, the chief is responsible for notifying the officer in person and in writing. Because of the heightened risk for violence at the point of termination, it is critical that the officer be given information on available support services and that the victim be notified immediately of the department's intended course of action and offered all available assistance, to include safety planning. The department should take extra precautions to protect against violence in the workplace. The chief is responsible for notifying the state licensing body about the decision to terminate the officer. * * *

EDITOR'S SUMMARY OF "MORGAN HILL POLICE DEPARTMENT FILES GUN VIOLENCE RESTRAINING ORDER AGAINST SAN JOSE OFFICER: FILING STEMS FROM FEB. 13 INCIDENT AT MORGAN HILL RESIDENCE"

by Michael Moore
March 2, 2022, Morgan Hill Times

On Feb. 13, 2022, according to court records, a woman called the Morgan Hill Police Department, saying that Bruce Barthelemy, an off-duty police officer who had worked for the San Jose Police Department for 14 years, had pushed her and would not let her leave, causing her to be afraid for her family. She said both parties were intoxicated. The court records stated that when police arrived, Barthelemy met them in front of the home with a loaded gun, threatening to shoot himself if they arrested him.

The officers arrested Barthelemy and called Judge Daniel Nishigaya, who issued a temporary Gun Violence Restraining Order, ordering Barthelemy to surrender any guns, ammunition or magazines in his possession and not possess any of these while the order was in effect.

[Editor's Note: The court records indicate that the protective order was extended multiple times, until in 2023 the court granted the Police

Department's request to dismiss it since there was another restraining order by then prohibiting Barthelemy from possessing any firearms or ammunition. It is not known who issued that other order: criminal court, family court, or another court. Court records show that the defendant was charged with contempt of court and misdemeanor domestic battery but it is not known if he was convicted of either crime or if he is still employed as a police officer.]

CHAPTER 11

PROSECUTORIAL RESPONSE

■ ■ ■

This chapter starts by looking at the role of the prosecutor in domestic violence cases. It opens with a discussion of the arguments for and against "no-drop" prosecution policies in domestic violence cases, under which prosecutorial decisions to proceed are based on the evidence and likelihood of conviction rather than on the stated wishes of the victim. The author of that article argues in favor of supporting the autonomy of victims of domestic violence. The next piece describes a Family Justice Center in Buffalo, New York; these centers are found across the country and internationally and are designed to be "one-stop shopping" for survivors of domestic violence to receive various types of services.

The second part of the chapter looks at tools being used by prosecutors in obtaining convictions of batterers. In well-functioning jurisdictions, these include ensuring that strangulation, common in domestic violence cases, is identified early and properly documented and that victims receive appropriate medical help. Then comes a summary of an article arguing that prosecutors should consider charging domestic violence as a hate crime in jurisdictions that define crimes motivated by gender bias as hate crimes, since domestic violence is often based on misogyny.

Several cases cover how prosecutors introduce various types of evidence to corroborate the victim's testimony, to substitute for such testimony if the victim is unavailable or unwilling to testify, or to explain the testimony if the victim recants. Given the U.S. Supreme Court's decision in *Crawford v. Washington*, as well as its decisions in *Davis/Hammon* and *Giles v. California*, all of which implicate the Confrontation Clause in the U.S. Constitution's Sixth Amendment, prosecutors face major hurdles in introducing prior statements when the victim is unavailable. The first case analyzes the use of such statements when the defendant claims the deceased victim provoked him. The second case deals with the use of expert testimony for the prosecution when the victim recants. The third upholds prosecutorial use of prior uncharged domestic violence incidents against the same victim to convict the defendant for serious violence against his partner. The fourth case illustrates the rule of forfeiture by wrongdoing, whereby a victim's hearsay statements may become admissible if the defendant intentionally prevents the victim from testifying at the trial. This section concludes with a commentator arguing that there should be a doctrinal exception in domestic violence cases to the usual rules regarding the Confrontation Clause.

The chapter ends with an editor's note summarizing the amicus brief in the case mentioned above in which a man who killed his partner after years of abusing her used a provocation defense, based on "heat of passion." The brief argues that abusers like this one are in fact exercising the ultimate control, rather than losing control, and notes that the rationales advanced by these defendants are often the all-too-familiar refrains used by batterers to justify their behavior. The closing article discusses the concept of a "cultural defense," which some immigrant men have asserted when charged with domestic violence crimes, and which raises complex questions, including what culture is, who defines it, how static or changing it is, and whether and how it should be taken into account in the U.S. legal system.

A. OVERVIEW

LEIGH GOODMARK, AUTONOMY FEMINISM: AN ANTI-ESSENTIALIST CRITIQUE OF MANDATORY INTERVENTIONS IN DOMESTIC VIOLENCE CASES

37 Florida State U. L. Rev. 1 (2009)
(citations and footnotes omitted)

Part II

* * * Once advocates had convinced states to enact mandatory arrest laws, they turned to the next obstacle in ensuring batterer accountability using the criminal system: prosecutors. Just as police officers historically had used their discretion to refuse to arrest perpetrators of domestic violence, prosecutors had also routinely chosen not to pursue cases against the few perpetrators of violence who police had actually arrested. Ironically, prosecutors' failure to pursue cases involving domestic violence has been cited as yet another reason police declined to make arrests.

Scholars have posited a number of reasons for the low rate of prosecution in domestic violence cases: the lack of evidence, the patriarchal views of prosecutors, skepticism about the seriousness of the crimes involved, and prosecutors' perceptions that judges were not interested in entertaining such cases. The justification most frequently offered by prosecutors for their reluctance to pursue domestic violence cases was their inability to rely on their star witnesses—the wives and girlfriends of the men they were prosecuting. The unwillingness of victims to testify to the abuse they had suffered deprived prosecutors of their best, and often their only, witnesses and hamstrung prosecutions in which the testimony of the involved parties was the only available evidence.

The failure of women who had been battered to participate in prosecutions was widely attributed to the victims' fear of repercussions at the hands of their abusers, a credible fear given that, even after successful prosecution, sentences for domestic violence offenses were ridiculously light and jail time was rarely imposed in misdemeanor cases. Prosecutors began to look for ways to ensure that cases could be brought successfully even if victims chose not to participate in the process—a method that has come to be known as victimless prosecution.

The success of victimless prosecution hinges on the willingness of police officers to respond to cases involving domestic violence differently and more thoroughly than they would ordinary assault cases. Police officers were trained to carefully investigate crime scenes, make detailed reports, and collect evidence that would allow prosecutors to pursue cases even when the victims were unwilling to testify-much as police would investigate homicide cases. Prosecutors relied on physical evidence, photographs of both the victim and the perpetrator (to show his demeanor at the time of arrest and any injuries, defensive or otherwise), recordings of 9-1-1 tapes, statements made to police, medical records, and other witness statements to secure convictions in cases that would have been impossible to successfully prosecute without such careful attention to gathering evidence.

Victimless prosecution allowed prosecutors to circumvent the wishes of the victim by replacing her testimony, which had previously been viewed as essential, with other evidence sufficient to persuade a finder of fact beyond a reasonable doubt that the charged crime had actually been committed. Victimless prosecution also enabled prosecutors to undermine the testimony of victims who appeared on behalf of their partners, impeaching them with prior inconsistent statements to police, or confronting them with photographs of injuries and their own words on 9-1-1 tapes.

Despite the implementation of these increasingly sophisticated methods of preparing domestic violence cases, prosecutorial reluctance to bring domestic violence cases and victim unwillingness to testify continued to hamper successful prosecutions. The adoption of no-drop prosecution was meant to address both of these issues. No-drop means exactly what it says—prosecutors would not dismiss criminal charges in otherwise winnable cases simply because the victim was not interested in, or was even adamantly opposed to, pursuing the case.

Advocates of no-drop prosecution strategies offer three justifications for the policies. First, they argue that no-drop prosecution in domestic violence cases is good for society in that the purpose of the criminal system is not to bend to the wishes of individual victims, but rather to punish offenders and to deter others from committing similar crimes. The role of the prosecutor in the American criminal system is to reinforce the state's conception of the boundaries of acceptable behavior by ensuring compliance with the laws that define and regulate what individuals are and are not permitted to do. The failure to prosecute domestic violence cases, whether attributable to prosecutorial diffidence or victim unwillingness, sends the message that violence against one's intimate partner is acceptable, in direct contravention of the criminal laws. Consistent enforcement of the law is essential in ensuring respect for that law. Allowing intimate partners to continue to flout those laws without fear of repercussion enabled perpetrators of domestic violence to believe that the laws against abusing one's intimate partner could be taken as seriously as most individuals take speed laws on major highways—which is to say, not seriously at all.

The second justification proffered for no-drop prosecution is victim safety. Prosecuting those who commit domestic violence increases safety both for the individual victim by removing the immediate threat to her, and for future victims of the same perpetrator. The victim's inability to thwart the process is a particularly important guarantor of her safety. Because the victim no longer has the ability to stop the prosecutor from bringing the case to court, her abuser has no motivation to pressure her to do so. Shifting the burden of deciding whether to prosecute the abuser from the victim to the prosecutor was thought to significantly safeguard the victim from further coercion and violence.

The final justification for no-drop prosecution policies was, ironically, victim empowerment. Women who had been battered, the argument went, would derive strength and validation from the experience of participating in the prosecution. This argument assumed successful prosecution of the case and positive treatment of the victim throughout the process.

One important distinction in the realm of prosecution policy is between "hard" and "soft" no-drop policies. In "soft" no-drop jurisdictions, victim testimony is not compelled; instead, prosecutors work with women who have been battered to help them feel comfortable with the system and offer them resources and support that will make compliance with the prosecutor's requests to assist in the prosecution possible. If the woman who has been battered is ultimately unwilling, unable, or uninterested in assisting prosecutors, she will not be forced to do so (although the services and support the woman may be relying on may no longer be available if she chooses not to cooperate with prosecutors).

"Hard" no-drop policies, in contrast, are the purest form of these policies—prosecutors pursue their cases regardless of the victim's wishes so long as sufficient evidence to prosecute exists. In a hard no-drop jurisdiction, when a victim is unwilling to appear voluntarily, prosecutors might subpoena her to testify or, in the most extreme cases, issue a warrant for her arrest and/or have her incarcerated in order to compel her testimony. Law professor Cheryl Hanna, a former prosecutor, explains the necessity for such actions: "No-drop policies that do not compel victim cooperation lack credibility." If both the perpetrator and victim are aware that the prosecutor will not follow through on the threat to force the victim's compliance, there is little incentive for the perpetrator to refrain from pressuring the victim to withdraw her support for prosecution and even less for the reluctant victim to comply voluntarily.

At their core, these policies reflect a struggle over who will control the woman who has been battered—if the state does not exercise its control over her by compelling her testimony, the batterer will, by preventing her from testifying. Hard no-drop policies express the state's belief that it has a superior right to intervene on behalf of the woman who has been battered in service of both the woman's needs and the state's objectives. Using Barbara Hart's hierarchy of the goals of legal interventions in domestic violence cases, hard no-drop policies clearly prioritize safety over all other aims, including fostering the agency of the woman who has been battered. * * *

The arguments made by those who support mandatory interventions beg the conclusion that women who have been battered can rarely, if ever, act autonomously, a problematic assertion given the primacy of autonomy in the American political and legal systems. Accepting that women who have been battered are incapable of engaging in independent deliberation devalues these women as members of the political society and invites and justifies what some might characterize as paternalism on their behalf. Paternalism reflects a lack of respect for autonomy and for the individual as a person. A number of the policies adopted to address domestic violence—policies championed by many advocates for women who have been battered—are guided by what seems to be patently paternalistic views of these women as powerless, limited individuals incapable of acting on their own behalf.

A better way to characterize the spirit motivating these policy choices, at least on the part of advocates for women who have been battered, is that they exemplify maternalism. These policies come from a well-meaning place—the desire to protect women who have been battered from further intimidation and violence, from their own inability to invoke the legal system given their fear of retaliation from their abusers, from losing their children or economic benefits in unfair mediations. This maternalism is born of and needs of women who have been battered and their belief that mandatory interventions are instrumental in ensuring that the system treats cases of domestic violence seriously.

But maternalism is no better than paternalism in that it assumes that women who have been battered are incapable of considering the full range of possibilities and deprives them of the ability to make choices for themselves, based on their own goals, values, beliefs, and understanding of their situations. Maternalism undermines the autonomy of women who have been battered. Exercises of maternalism to justify the implementation of mandatory policies are fundamentally at odds with one of the foundational goals of the battered women's movement—empowerment. * * *

FAMILY JUSTICE CENTER, BUFFALO, NEW YORK

https://fjcsafe.org

The Family Justice Center (FJC) [in Buffalo, NY, one of many FJC's around the U.S.] provides comprehensive crisis intervention and support. Our services are trauma-informed and guided by 5 principles: safety, trust, choice, collaboration, and empowerment. Advocates work closely with clients to determine a personalized service plan based on needs and client-identified goals.

- **Counseling:** Crisis intervention, emotional support, and linkage to trauma assessments and trauma counseling is available for children and adults.
- **Needs Assessment:** Advocates complete assessments to identify needs, the level of danger, and stalking behaviors.
- **Safety Planning:** In collaboration with the client, advocates create an individualized plan to help increase safety.
- **Case Management:** Client-defined goals are identified. A plan to achieve these goals is developed and advocates follow up to provide support.
- **Resources & Referrals:** Linkage to community resources occurs, based on identified needs.
- **Forensic Medical Unit:** Clients can have their injuries assessed and documented, including a strangulation assessment and a traumatic brain injury assessment. This documentation can be helpful in criminal prosecution and family law matters.
- **Pressing Criminal Charges:** Buffalo Police are on-site at the Downtown location for clients to file a report and/or press charges. Police from other jurisdictions may come on-site to complete a police report when available.
- **Web Conferencing with Family Court:** Clients can obtain emergency orders of protection from Family Court via web-conferencing at an FJC location.
- **Connection to Legal Services:** Clients are connected to local legal services providers as needed.

- **Interfaith Spiritual Support**: Qualified volunteers and community partners provide spiritual support to people of all faiths.
- **Language Interpretation:** Spanish-speaking victim advocates available. Interpreters are available for non English-speaking clients, or those in need of other accommodations.
- **On-site Childcare:** Each location houses a playroom for children while their parent/guardian is meeting with an advocate.
- **Pet Therapy:** SPCA Paws for Love Pet Therapy dogs are regularly on-site with their handlers.
- **Patient Navigator/Health Home Worker:** Both a patient navigator and health home worker are on-call and can provide medical case management services.
- **Financial Reimbursement:** Advocates provide Office of Victim's Services (OVS) application assistance for victim compensation where eligible.
- **Pantry:** The FJC has a small essential needs pantry to assist clients with hygiene products and other personal care items.
- **Short-term & Transitional Housing:** In collaboration with Community Services for Every1, the FJC is able to assist clients with housing needs when clients meet eligibility requirements.
- **Address Confidentiality Program:** The FJC is an Application Assistance Provider in Erie County. This program can help keep a new address confidential.
- **Support Groups:** Peer support and psychoeducational groups are offered.
- **Support for Family & Friends:** Advocates are available to discuss how to provide support to a co-worker, family member, or friend that may be in an unhealthy relationship. The Reachout WNY web site is useful when someone is trying to help a teen.
- **Support for Family & Friends of someone lost to DV Homicide:** The FJC hosts a Bereavement Group and honors those lost to homicide due to domestic violence during our annual Vigil.
- **Educational and Training Presentations:** Area businesses, agencies, the general public, schools, and community-based organizations. Advocate is able to provide

offsite services for students. For presentations or training, please complete our online form

[Editor's Notes: 1. Five directors of Family Justice Centers (FJCs) from across the U.S. published an article to discuss the history and efficacy of FJCs and the international FJC Alliance: Gwinn et al., The Family Justice Center Collaborative Model, 27 St. Louis U. Pub. L. Rev. 79 (2007). The authors described the FJC collaborative model as one that "seeks to put the victim and her children first by bringing as many professionals and services as possible under one roof[,]" to assist with "her criminal case," any civil issues (such as a restraining order or a dependency proceeding), and social service resources like counseling and advocacy. They stated that implementing FJCs has produced both a decrease in expenses by reducing redundancies, and an increase in the number of victims willing and able to seek services.

In the 2013 Final Statewide Evaluation of the California Family Justice Initiative, the authors noted that client "[c]oncerns and misinformation about immigration [were] a noted barrier before coming to the Family Justice Center, but not afterwards." Survivor concerns included fear of deportation, fear of having children removed, and a lack of awareness of legal services to address immigration and citizenship. One of the most significant benefits of Family Justice Center services noted by survivors was receiving immigration services that helped them become legal residents.

The Six Year Evaluation Report 2014–2019 (2020) about the Contra Costa County Ca. Family Justice Alliance concluded: "100% of families experienced an increase in safety. 80% reported an increase in empowerment related to their ability to advocate for themselves, make informed choices, and to navigate complex systems; and 75% of families experienced an increase in protective factors and resilience in the prevention of secondary assault or re-assault."

A 2018 study reported that the Milwaukee Sojourner Family Peace Center found 96% of clients were satisfied or quite satisfied with services in one of the largest Family Justice Centers in America with statistically significant increases in survivor-defined goal attainment, empowerment, and hope.

In a 2010 study of the San Diego FJC, the first one to open in the US, 86% of clients identified positive change in their lives because of services at the FJC, and 56% said they were emotionally stronger.

A 2010 publication stated that "The FJC framework contributed to a 90% drop in domestic violence homicides in the city of San Diego, a 75% reduction in domestic violence homicides in Alameda County, CA, and a 51% drop in Brooklyn, NY City."

This data is from Family Justice Center Framework Impacts, Published Findings and Outcomes, Family Justice Center Alliance. Their website lists 53 affiliated programs around the U.S., one in Canada, and a program in Europe.

2. In Criminal Orders of Protection for Domestic Violence: Associated Revictimization, Mental Health, and Well-being Among Victims, 36 (21–22) Journal of Interpersonal Violence (2021) 10198, Tami P. Sullivan, Nicole H. Weiss, Jacqueline Woerner, Janan Wyatt, and Camille Carey report on a study measuring the effect of orders of protection issued by criminal courts in domestic violence cases, also known as CPOs. These are issued in all U.S. states. They surveyed almost 300 victims at two points during the criminal case, comparing orders with limited restrictions on the defendant, orders that contained a residential stay-away order, and orders where the court prohibited contact with the victim. Each person interviewed was paid $50 and provided with a list of community resources relevant to DV, mental health and substance use, social services, employment, and economic stability. In addition, they were offered an opportunity to develop a detailed, individualized safety plan.

The researchers found that all three types of orders generally reduced physical, sexual, and psychological abuse of the victim, "unwanted pursuit behavior" (i.e., stalking), victim symptoms of PTSD/depression, stress and fear of revictimization. But some victims reported increased revictimization and problems with mental health along with lower levels of well-being, since court orders do not deter all offenders and may cause some to retaliate. The authors conclude that criminal courts and orders may reach domestic violence victims who might not otherwise access services to improve their safety and resilience, an example of therapeutic jurisprudence.]

B. EVIDENTIARY ISSUES

SANTA CLARA COUNTY, CALIFORNIA, CALIFORNIA PROTOCOL FOR INTIMATE PARTNER VIOLENCE STRANGULATION RESPONSE

(2021)

Background

Over the last decade, a host of new research and training on the injuries from intimate partner violence (IPV) strangulation, the effects of non-fatal strangulation (NFS), and the linkages between non-fatal strangulation and the risks of homicide have changed the way strangulation cases are investigated and prosecuted. No longer are cases where a person was "choked out" and "blacked out" but shows no visible injuries on the outside of their neck treated as misdemeanor conduct. More often these cases are now both investigated by law enforcement and prosecuted by the Office of the District Attorney for what they really are, felonies where a person was strangled to the point that they lost consciousness and were made susceptible to further injury, with both short- and long-term consequences.

Sexual assault forensic exam (SAFE) teams in California have reported that 18% of survivors who seek medical forensic exams after sexual assault have also been strangled. Sadly, this includes survivors who are minors. In response, SAFE teams, including Santa Clara County's, led the recent legislative change that established medical forensic exams for intimate partner violence and defined the age of consent for those exams at 12 years and older (Fam. Code § 6930). The SCVMC SAFE team developed new non-fatal strangulation exam guidelines and training to improve healthcare response and support for use in any medical exam involving strangulation. Victim services agencies like [names], as well as the DA's Office's Victim Services Unit, have trained their teams and worked with survivors to provide better services. Lethality assessments conducted by police at the scene of domestic violence crimes now always include asking survivors about their history of strangulation, and a recent study by Community Solutions of their clients found that more survivors have suffered a history of strangulation than report such to the police.

Community Solutions reviewed over 400 police reports taken between August 2018 and June 2019; roughly 13% of the survivors reported to the police that they had been strangled by their partner/former partner. The agency also examined 100 Danger Assessments administered during the same period by confidential victim advocates at Community Solutions, and 42% of survivors reported that they had been strangled by their partner/former partner.

There is a crucial piece of this work that is missing—medical forensic examinations. In sexual assault cases, survivors go to Santa Clara Valley Medical Center for a medical forensic examination both to identify their injuries for medical treatment and support, and to document their injuries as part of a criminal investigation. <u>In intimate partner violence strangulation cases, where no disclosure of sexual assault is made and the injuries are largely internal to the head and neck, no such medical forensic examinations happen at all.</u> Survivors are not getting the urgent medical help they need, and crucial evidence to support their statement that they have been strangled is lost and cannot be presented in court.

Moreover, in sexual assault cases the State of California reimburses police agencies for the cost incurred by forensic nurse examiners in conducting medical forensic examinations, but no such funding exists to do medical forensic strangulation examinations in intimate partner violence cases. Conducting a pilot project in our County to see how such examinations could work, assess the value to the survivors and the community, and identify the costs is a key first step in making these examinations part of the County's Law Enforcement Protocol on Domestic Violence, and in securing long-term funding for these examinations from the State of California and the County of Santa Clara. This effort will also increase the awareness of law enforcement about the dangers of strangulation cases to the survivors, and also the danger to officers in investigating cases where a suspect has strangled the survivor. Lastly, the benefit of these examinations as an entry point to getting the survivor needed medical care cannot be overstated. We expect that these survivors will get vital medical care as a result of this pilot, at no cost to them, that they otherwise never would have received. . .

[Editor's Notes: 1. According to CBS SF, the pilot program launched in Jan. 2020, though at first only 20% of victims offered an exam participated. A domestic violence advocate stated this was likely because law enforcement did not encourage exams and victims may not understand the benefits. She suggested that law enforcement refer victims directly to domestic violence agencies, who can screen for strangulation and discuss the exams with victims. On 3/24/21, the Santa Clara Co. Board of Supervisors expanded the program to cover the whole county and included children in child abuse cases. CBS SF reported: "In cases where medical forensic exams were conducted, the criminal case supported the filing of more serious felony charges over misdemeanor charges 86.6 percent of the time during the pilot program. In comparison, the felony rate for cases of intimate partner violence was 28.8 percent in 2019, before the county started its testing program, according to a recent report by the Office of Gender-Based Violence Prevention." The board also approved that the county and the District Attorney's Office partner with the San Diego-based Training Institute on Strangulation Prevention to request an assessment of the county's response and prevention system and get advice on how to improve it.

On 3/8/22, the Santa Clara County DA sent it first annual report to the Board of Supervisors on how the Strangulation Response program was working. Costs to county and city agencies were incorporated into existing budgets. In 2021, 83 victims received the exams, more than doubling the number in the pilot year, 2020 (30 victims); in 2021, 47 returned for follow up care. The examinations made case investigations and prosecutions stronger: 83% resulted in charged cases (compared to 58% in 2020), and 74% of cases were charged as felonies (compared to 20% in 2020). 50% of the perpetrators had a prior history of domestic violence convictions. Of the 25 victims accompanied to the exam by a community domestic violence advocate, 21 continued with agency services. Further training for law enforcement and EMS was in progress. There appear to be no follow up reports from 2022 or 2023.

2. Ca. AB 2185, passed in 2022, amended Ca. Penal Code § 11161.2 to require health care providers to offer free forensic medical evidentiary exams in domestic violence cases, including a separate supplemental form where there is evidence of recent or past strangulation. The bill states that additional diagnostic testing may be necessary in cases of suspected strangulation. Patients have the right to the presence of a social worker, victim advocate or support person of their own choosing during the exam. Exams may be conducted by members of the Sexual Assault Response Team or Sexual Assault Forensic Examiner Team. Costs will be paid by the state.

Strangulation can be the cause of brain injury, as can other abuse involving the victim's head. In "PINK Concussions Task Force Brings Together Brain Injury and DV/IPV Experts,"15(1) Family & Intimate Partner Violence Quarterly 83 (2022), Katherine Snedekar writes: "The numbers of women who have brain injury inflicted by a violent partner are estimated to be staggeringly high—higher than NFL players or those who are injured in military service. As brain injury from domestic violence/intimate partner violence (DV/IPV) had been rarely discussed in medical conferences or in news stories, an international taskforce was launched in 2019 by the non-profit, PINK Concussions, to change the status quo." Through this taskforce, experts in brain injury and domestic violence advocates are starting to work together to research and educate professionals and the public about the overlap between these two areas.

Snedegar states: "Historically, it has been assumed by the medical community that symptoms observed in and reported by women who experienced domestic violence were solely the result of psychological trauma; however, now the experts in this field are discovering the signs and symptoms to be more associated with TBI [Traumatic Brain Injury]. Brain injury had not been considered by survivors and professionals working with survivors as a possible impact of the violence; and the 'life difficulties' these women faced were chalked up to either a mental health issue or the result of trauma and the experience of DV."

3. See also E. M. Valera, "Increasing our understanding of an overlooked public health epidemic: Traumatic brain injuries in women subjected to intimate partner violence," 27(6) Journal of Women's Health 735 (2018), https://doi.org/10.1089/jwh.2017.6838.

4. Domestic violence advocates are starting to screen clients for possible concussion/brain injury and to refer them to appropriate medical care. Presumably the medical examinations provided through AB 2185 include screening for brain injury and referrals to treatment as well as documentation for possible prosecution of the abuser.]

EDITOR'S SUMMARY OF "THE CASE FOR THE INCREASED USE OF HATE CRIME LAWS TO PROSECUTE VIOLENCE AGAINST WOMEN" BY JESSICA MITTEN

22 Geo. J. Gender & L. (2021) (no page numbers—online)

Hate crime laws, which commonly apply to cases involving the defendant's bias based on race, religion, and ethnicity, are starting to include gender, which can be used to prosecute those who are violent toward women. From only 10 states in 1990, there are now 35 that include gender in their hate crime laws, and the federal government has done so since 2009.

However, hate crime laws motivated by gender are vastly underutilized, due to conceptions of law enforcement and prosecutors who often do not see violence against women as a hate crime. In 2019, only 80 hate crimes motivated by gender were reported to the FBI by law enforcement agencies, which is only 1% of the total hate crimes reported. In contrast, victims reported that over 27% of hate crimes were motivated by gender in the Bureau of Justice Statistics' National Crime Victimization Survey, conducted between 2013 and 2017.

Nearly half of all female murder victims are killed by a current or former intimate partner who is male, and the vast majority of rapes are perpetrated toward women by a man the victim knows. But these are seldom charged as hate crimes, since law enforcement and prosecutors tend to see violence against women committed by a partner or acquaintance as personal, not motivated by bias. However, a personal connection does not preclude a hate crime. Nor does a motivation of power and control, which often underlies rapes [and domestic violence], preclude a hate crime since women are frequently targeted because of their gender.

The rationales for hate crime laws include the fact that these crimes victimize not only the direct target but others like them and entire communities. Even though men are more likely to be victims of crime in general, gender-based crimes like rape make women as a group more afraid of crime, especially rape, than men are. *[Editor's Note: High profile domestic violence crimes can also terrorize women throughout the community, who fear their partners or ex partners will do the same to them.]*

While rapes are generally under-charged by prosecutors, use of hate crime laws in sexual assault [and domestic violence] cases as penalty enhancements can result in longer sentences and redefine violence against women as political rather than private. This helps the focus of the case to shift from blaming the victim to blaming the offender.

NORTH DAKOTA CODE § 29–01–16—WHEN MISDEMEANOR OR INFRACTION MAY BE COMPROMISED

When a defendant is held to answer on a charge constituting a misdemeanor or infraction, for which a person injured by the act constituting the offense has a remedy by a civil action, the offense may be compromised as provided in section 29–01–17, except:

1. If the offense was committed by or upon a judge of any court in this state, or in any city in this state, or a peace officer, while in the execution of the duties of the person's office;

2. If the offense was committed with an intent to commit a felony; or

3. If the offense involves a crime of domestic violence as defined in section 14–07.1–01 or is a violation of section 12.1–20–05, 12.1–20–07, 12.1–20–12.1, or 12.1–20–12.2.

BELTRAN V. WARDEN

2015 WL 7874326 (No. Dist. Cal.) (unpublished)
(citations omitted)

ORDER DENYING PETITION FOR WRIT OF HABEAS CORPUS; DENYING CERTIFICATE OF APPEALABILITY

Before the Court is the above-titled petition for a writ of habeas corpus, filed pursuant to 28 U.S.C. § 2254 by Petitioner Tare Nicholas Beltran, challenging the validity of his state court sentence. Respondent has filed an answer to the petition. Petitioner has filed a traverse. For the reasons set forth below, the Court will deny the petition.

I. PROCEDURAL HISTORY

By information filed November 21, 2007, the San Francisco District Attorney charged Petitioner with willful, deliberate, premeditated murder [of Claire Joyce Tempongko, his ex-girlfriend]. The information further alleged that Petitioner used a deadly weapon, a knife, in the commission of the crime.

On September 30, 2008, the jury acquitted Petitioner of first-degree murder, but found him guilty of second-degree murder. The jury also found true the weapon use allegation. On December 12, 2008, the trial court sentenced Petitioner to fifteen years to life in state prison, with an added one-year term for the use of the knife.

On March 30, 2011, the California Court of Appeal reversed Petitioner's judgment in an unpublished decision. The California Supreme Court granted Respondent's petition for review of the court of appeal decision. On review, in a published decision issued June 3, 2013, and modified on denial of rehearing on August 28, 2013, the California Supreme Court reversed the state appellate court's decision and remanded to that court for further proceedings. December 11, 2013, on remand from the California Supreme Court, the California Court of Appeal affirmed Petitioner's judgment in an unpublished decision. The California Supreme Court denied review on March 19, 2014.

On July 2, 2014, Petitioner filed the instant federal petition. On October 22, 2014, the Court issued an order to show cause. * * *

1. Confrontation Clause claims

Petitioner argues that his rights under the Confrontation Clause were violated when the trial court admitted the following: (1) the autopsy report and related evidence; (2) Tempongko's statements to Officers Dharmani and Lack; and (3) Tempongko's statements to Houtz [the man she was currently dating].

The Confrontation Clause of the Sixth Amendment provides that in criminal cases the accused has the right to "be confronted with the witnesses against him." The federal confrontation right applies to the states through the Fourteenth Amendment.

The ultimate goal of the Confrontation Clause is to ensure reliability of evidence, but it is a procedural rather than a substantive guarantee. *Crawford v. Washington*, 541 U.S. 36, 61 (2004). It does not command that evidence be reliable, but rather that reliability be assessed in a particular manner: by testing in the crucible of cross-examination.

The Confrontation Clause applies to all "testimonial" statements. *See Crawford*, 541 U.S. at 50–51. "Testimony. . .is typically a solemn declaration or affirmation made for the purpose of establishing or proving some fact." *Id.* at 51 (quoting Webster, An American Dictionary of the English Language (1828)); *see id.* ("An accuser who makes a formal statement to government officers bears testimony in a sense that a person who makes a casual remark to an acquaintance does not."). The Confrontation Clause applies not only to in-court testimony but also to out-of-court statements introduced at trial, regardless of the admissibility of the statements under state laws of evidence. For purposes of federal habeas corpus review, the standard applicable to violations of the Confrontation Clause is whether the violation had an actual and prejudicial effect upon the jury. * * *

b. Tempongko's statements to police officers Dharmani and Lack

Petitioner argues that his rights under the Confrontation Clause were violated when the trial court admitted Tempongko's statements to police officers Dharmani and Lack. The state appellate court rejected this claim on remand as follows:

> While appellant was still at large after Tempongko's killing, the United States Supreme Court held in *Crawford v. Washington*

that the admission of testimonial out-of-court statements, even if authorized by an exception to the hearsay rule, violates the confrontation clause. In ruling on the prosecution's proffer of Tempongko's out-of-court statements to police in the wake of appellant's acts of domestic violence, the trial court correctly understood that it was bound by *Crawford*'s holding. Nonetheless, appellant now argues that the trial court erred in applying that holding to the present case.

In *Davis v. Washington* (2006) 547 U.S. 813 (*Davis*), the court clarified the term "testimonial," as used in this context, as follows: "Statements are nontestimonial when made in the course of police interrogation under circumstances objectively indicating that the primary purpose of the interrogation is to enable police assistance to meet an ongoing emergency. They are testimonial when the circumstances objectively indicate that there is no such ongoing emergency, and that the primary purpose of the interrogation is to establish or prove past events potentially relevant to later criminal prosecution." At the same time, the court noted that it was not "attempting to produce an exhaustive classification of all conceivable statements" as testimonial or nontestimonial.

Davis was decided together with a consolidated companion case, *Hammon v. Indiana*. In *Davis*, the Supreme Court held nontestimonial, and therefore admissible, tape recorded statements made by a domestic violence victim during a 911 call, in which the victim responded to the 911 operator's questions by identifying her assailant as the defendant, and describing what he was doing to her as the call progressed. In *Hammon*, police officers responding to a domestic violence call encountered the victim alone on the front porch of her home, appearing frightened, but denying that anything was wrong. After the officers entered the home, one of them questioned the victim outside the defendant's presence, asking her what had happened. She responded that the defendant had thrown her down onto broken glass and punched her in the chest. The Supreme Court held that because there was no ongoing emergency at the time, and no continuing immediate threat to the victim, the statements were obtained for the purpose of investigating a past crime, rather than to guide police who were intervening in an ongoing emergency. Thus, the statements were testimonial, and their admission was barred by the confrontation clause.

In analyzing application of *Davis* and *Hammon* to the facts of the present case, we must be guided by our own Supreme Court's interpretation of *Davis* in *People v. Cage* (2007) 40 Cal.4th 965. In that case, the court noted that in order for an unsworn statement to be testimonial, "it must have occurred under circumstances that imparted, to some degree, the formality and solemnity characteristic of testimony." The statement also "must have been given and taken primarily for the purpose. . .[of] establish[ing] or prov[ing] some past fact for possible use in a criminal trial," an issue that is "to be determined 'objectively,' considering all the circumstances that might reasonably bear on the intent of the participants." Consistent with these principles, responding to questions from police "in a nonemergency situation, . . . where deliberate falsehoods might be criminal offenses," is testimonial; however, "statements elicited by law enforcement officials are not testimonial if the primary purpose in giving and receiving them is to deal with a contemporaneous emergency, rather than to produce evidence about past events for possible use at a criminal trial."

In the present case, appellant contends that the trial court erred in concluding that some of the statements Tempongko made to the police who came in response to her calls about appellant's domestic violence were not testimonial as that term was clarified in *Davis*. Specifically, appellant argues that the following evidence should have been excluded: (1) police officer Dharmani's testimony that after he responded to Tempongko's 911 call on April 28, 1999, she told him that appellant had broken a window in her apartment after she refused to let him in; that when she finally let him in, he threw her to the ground, pulled her by her hair, and then left; and that he later left a telephone message threatening to return; and (2) police officer Tack's testimony that when he responded to Tempongko's mother's call to the police on November 18, 1999, and forced open the door to Tempongko's bedroom, Tempongko told him that appellant had grabbed her by the hair and pulled her head back, causing her to leave the apartment to get her mother and stepfather, and that when she returned with them, appellant forced her into the bedroom and locked the door. Appellant argues that because there was no ongoing emergency at the time these statements were made, and the statements concerned past events rather than a currently developing situation, the statements were testimonial in nature.

Respondent counters by arguing that the facts of this case are more similar to those in *Davis* than to those in *Hammon,* and by citing two post-*Davis* California Court of Appeal cases involving similar facts. In one, *People v. Saracoglu* (2007) 152 Cal.App.4th 1584, a woman and her child came to a police station and spoke to two officers there. The woman was nervous, crying, upset, and scared, and had visible cuts and bruises. She told the police that about 30 minutes earlier, the defendant had choked, pushed, hit, and threatened her, and told her he would shoot her if she went to the police. She explained that she had come to the police station because she was afraid of the defendant, and accepted the officers' offer to get her an emergency protective order. The officers then went to her home and arrested the defendant.

The woman failed to appear to testify at the defendant's trial, so the trial court permitted one of the police officers to testify at trial about what the woman told him at the police station. The Court of Appeal upheld the trial court's ruling. In so doing, the court rejected not only the defendant's contention, but also the Attorney General's concession that the woman's statements were testimonial because they described events that had already occurred. Rather, the court concluded that "[o]bjectively viewed, the primary purpose of [the woman]'s initial interrogation by [the officer] was 'to deal with a contemporaneous emergency, rather than to produce evidence about past events. . . .' " The court noted that the woman told the police that the defendant had threatened to kill her if she went to them. This implied that she could not return home without facing that threat; thus, her visit to the police station constituted part of an ongoing emergency situation. In short, the woman's "primary purpose for making her initial statements to [the officer] was to gain police protection," rather than to report a past crime.

The second case on which respondent relies, *People v. Banos* (2009) 178 Cal.App.4th 483, involved a defendant who was accused of killing his ex-girlfriend after a history of domestic violence. The prosecution offered evidence of statements that the victim made to police on five occasions: (1) during a meeting with a police officer in the victim's apartment, in which she related that the defendant had punched and threatened her earlier that day, and then called while she was waiting for the police to arrive and threatened to kill her; (2) during another meeting with the same police officer later the same day, in which the victim told the officer that the defendant had come back to her apartment after the officer left, and had hit her and threatened her again; (4) during a 911 call in March 2004, in which the victim told the dispatcher that the defendant was inside the victim's apartment, in violation of a restraining order, and that she was afraid he would attack her; and (5) during a conversation with the officer who responded to the same 911 call, in which the victim reiterated what she had told the dispatcher.

The *Banos* court held that the victim's statements during the March 2004 call to 911, and her statements to the officer who responded to the call, were admissible as non-testimonial because the victim's "primary purpose for making the statements to the 911 dispatch officer was to gain police protection" in the context of an "ongoing emergency." The court held that the other three statements were testimonial for confrontation clause purposes, however, because on each occasion, the victim was reporting past events at a time when there was no ongoing emergency. On the first occasion, the victim was home, the defendant was not present, and the victim was upset, but not distraught. On the other two occasions, the defendant had already been detained by the police when the victim gave them her version of the events.*

Applying the principles set forth in the cases discussed above to the facts of the present case, we conclude that Tempongko's statements to Tack on November 18, 1999, were properly admitted. The police arrived to intervene in what they were told was an ongoing episode of domestic violence, and had to force open the door to Tempongko's bedroom. Tempongko's statements to them were made moments after the police arrived, and while appellant was still present in Tempongko's apartment. When the police spoke with Tempongko, they were in the process of determining what action they needed to take in order to protect her from possible harm. Accordingly, objectively viewed, Tempongko's statements were made primarily to inform the police in their efforts to deal with an ongoing emergency, and thus were not testimonial.

In contrast, Tempongko's statements to Dharmani on April 28, 1999, were made after appellant's assault on Tempongko had already concluded, and he had left her apartment. Tempongko was standing on a public street when she spoke to Dharmani, and presumably was free to go from there to any place of safety she chose, but told Dharmani she would be more comfortable going back to her apartment. Thus, Tempongko's statements were not made primarily to obtain police assistance in a present, ongoing emergency, but rather to report an earlier, already completed assault. Accordingly, the statements were testimonial in nature, and should have been excluded under *Crawford* and its progeny.

Nonetheless, we decline to reverse appellant's conviction based on the error in admitting these statements. There was ample other evidence, which (as discussed *post*) was properly admitted, demonstrating appellant's history of domestic violence toward Tempongko prior to the murder, and her resulting fear of him. Moreover, appellant's behavior during the May 17, 1999 and November 18, 1999 incidents was more violent than the window

* The court held that the statements were nonetheless admissible under the forfeiture by wrongdoing exception to the confrontation clause. That issue is not presented in this case.

breaking and hair pulling that Tempongko described to Dharmani on April 28, 1999. Thus, the hearsay evidence of Tempongko's statements to Dharmani was merely cumulative with regard to appellant's history of domestic violence, and not independently prejudicial because it was less serious than the other incidents. Accordingly, the trial court's error in admitting this evidence was harmless beyond a reasonable doubt.

The record does not support Petitioner's argument that the events on November 18, 1999 more closely resemble the facts in *Hammon* because the incident in question had been "completed," and that Petitioner's arrest that day was for "past behavior" and based on "historical information" supplied by Tempongko. The incident in question was ongoing when Lack arrived on the scene. Although the incident started with Petitioner's alleged fight with Tempongko, the incident continued after Tempongko's mother left to call the police when Petitioner grabbed Tempongko by the shoulders, physically pushed her back into the bedroom, and kept her there against her will. Tempongko did not exit the bedroom until after Lack and other police officers arrived and pulled Petitioner out of the bedroom. Contrary to Petitioner's assertion, the events of November 18, 1999 more closely resemble the facts in *Davis,* in that the questions asked by Officer Lack and the statements elicited from Tempongko "were necessary to be able to resolve the present emergency, rather than simply to learn (as in *Crawford*) what had happened in the past." Tempongko described the events of that day in order to explain the situation at hand and to explain her state of mind regarding being in the bedroom with Petitioner, and not simply to "establish past conduct relevant to future criminal prosecution," as Petitioner alleges. Moreover, the trial court only admitted the statements that Tempongko made to Officer Lack when she was released from the room, but excluded other statements relating to prior acts and the officer's recollection of a previous encounter with Petitioner. Accordingly, the state court's denial of this claim correctly applied Supreme Court precedent as set forth in *Davis* and was a reasonable determination of the facts in light of the evidence presented in the state court proceeding.

In addition, the record does not support a finding that the admission of Tempongko's statements to Officers Lack or Dharmani[4] had a "substantial and injurious effect or influence in determining the jury's verdict." Tempongko's November 18, 1999 statements to Officer Lack were not the only evidence regarding Petitioner's prior instances of domestic violence. Petitioner admitted that he had a felony domestic violence conviction from 1999. The prosecution presented evidence that there was an emergency protective order requiring Petitioner to stay away from Tempongko's apartment, and that he violated that order on September 7,

---

[4] This Court presumes correct the state court's finding that Tempongko's statements to Officer Dharmani violated the Confrontation Clause.

2000. The prosecution also presented evidence that Petitioner forcefully restrained Tempongko on May 17, 1999, and would not release her until police arrived in response to a 911 call made by Teofilo Miranda. With respect to the April 28, 1999 statements to Officer Dharmani, the record supports the state court's determination that Tempongko's statements to Officer Dharmani were cumulative to other evidence of Petitioner's history of domestic violence, including the above-referenced evidence regarding the November 18, 1999 incident and a 1999 felony domestic violence conviction, as well as evidence regarding the incident on May 17, 1999.

Moreover, Petitioner does not dispute that he killed Tempongko. Petitioner's defense was that he killed Tempongko because she provoked him rather than out of malice. However, the prosecution presented significant evidence undermining Petitioner's account of provocation, independent of Tempongko's statements to Officers Dharmani and Lack. Petitioner claimed that Tempongko called him the night of her death and asked him to come over. However, Michael Houtz testified that Tempongko did not plan on meeting anyone the night of her death, and Tempongko's son, Justin Nguyen, testified that she did not expect or want Petitioner to come over that evening. There was also evidence that Tempongko received phone calls from Petitioner that day which made her anxious, and that when Houtz dropped her and her children off that night, she fled his car because she feared that Petitioner might be near her home. Petitioner claimed that Tempongko spontaneously provoked him by insulting him and his family, and by claiming that she had aborted his child. However, Nguyen testified that Petitioner entered the apartment in an argumentative manner, and immediately began berating Tempongko and asking her where she had been all day. Nguyen also testified that he did not recall Tempongko threatening or cursing Petitioner. Finally, there was evidence indicating consciousness of guilt: Petitioner deliberately discarded in the trash the bloody sweatshirt he had been wearing when he stabbed Tempongko; Petitioner asked a club owner for a clean shirt; Petitioner took the time to say good-bye to his sister, Petitioner left for Mexico, staying there for six years, and Petitioner did not return voluntarily to the United States and returned only pursuant to being arrested in Mexico pursuant to a warrant related to this case. Any error in introducing Tempongko's statements to Officers Dharmani and Lack regarding Petitioner's prior acts of domestic violence did not have a substantial or injurious effect or influence in determining the jury's verdict. This habeas claim is denied. * * *

BYRD V. BROWN

2010 WL 6764702 (S.D.N.Y.) (unpublished)
(citations and footnotes omitted)

REPORT AND RECOMMENDATION

Jimmy Byrd brings this petition for a writ of habeas corpus pursuant to 28 U.S.C. § 2254, challenging his conviction for assault in the first and second degrees under New York state law. He contends that * * * (2) the admission of expert testimony on the topic of Battered Woman's Syndrome violated his rights under the Due Process Clauses of the Fifth and Fourteenth Amendments; * * * For the reasons that follow, I recommend that his petition be denied. *[Editor's Note: The term "Battered Woman's Syndrome" has been disfavored for many years, as discussed in more depth in Chapter 13. Some jurisdictions are now replacing this with "intimate partner battering and its effects." See, e.g., Ca. Evidence Code section 1107.]*

Background

A. The Incident

At approximately one a.m. on Friday, July 26, 2002, Mr. Byrd and his registered domestic partner, Jill Johnson, were at home in the apartment that Ms. Johnson owned. Ms. Johnson and the petitioner had lived together for ten years and had a daughter who was nine. The petitioner started a fight with Ms. Johnson over what he perceived as her failure to adequately clean a dirty jar. In the course of the fight, the petitioner struck Ms. Johnson three times in the back of the head with his hand, after which she tried to move away from him into another room. He followed her into the next room, pulled her, punched her in the abdomen, grabbed her by the neck, and pushed her to the floor, which was made of hard ceramic tiles. Then, while wearing plastic sandals, he repeatedly stomped on her abdomen. At the same time, he grabbed her head and slammed it against the floor two or three times. He may also have kicked and punched Ms. Johnson while she was on the floor. He hit her once more in the back as she tried to get up off the floor, so hard that it caused her hands to tingle with pain. After the beating ended, Ms. Johnson got up and resumed cleaning the jar.

B. The Aftermath

That night, Ms. Johnson was unable to sleep; she experienced intense pain, saw flashes, and vomited repeatedly. The next day her pain became worse and she was unable to stand up straight. Mr. Byrd encouraged her to eat, but when she did, she was unable to keep the food down.

Within two days of the incident, Ms. Johnson's pain was so severe that she suggested to petitioner that she needed to go to the hospital. He dismissed that suggestion, noting that she had not "pass[ed] any blood," and asserted that she was not badly hurt. He told Ms. Johnson, "I know I hurt you but I could have done worse, I could have killed you. I know what I'm doing. . . . I didn't hurt you[ ] as bad as I could have." He warned that to go to the hospital would "open Pandora's box" and "change [their] lives forever." Ms. Johnson decided not to seek treatment because she "didn't want to get [the petitioner] into trouble." When she brought it up again the next day, he smacked her head and told her he did not "want to hear anymore about hospital," although he said he would take her to the hospital if they saw any blood in her urine or vomit. Ms. Johnson continued to vomit and her pain worsened. By Wednesday, July 31, the pain had become excruciating, so that when the petitioner took their daughter out for a walk, Ms. Johnson left a $200 check and a note for Mr. Byrd explaining her whereabouts, "straightened up as much as [she] could," and took a taxi to the hospital.

When she arrived at the hospital, Ms. Johnson initially told the doctors that she had instigated a fight with her husband by attempting to stab him with a knife because she "still didn't want to do anything to get [Mr. Byrd] in trouble," was "doing all [she] could to not get him in trouble," and was "not going to press charges" or "do things to upset him." Ultimately, the doctors were able to get Ms. Johnson to explain what had actually happened and informed her that she had to talk to a social worker and report the assault. Ms. Johnson "didn't want to" because she "was scared he would get upset" and felt she was "ruining everything for [her] daughter."

When she arrived at the hospital, Ms. Johnson's pain was so severe that it affected her breathing, and her abdomen was tender and distended. X-rays revealed that she had several fractured ribs, while a CAT scan showed that Ms. Johnson's pancreas had been split in two by the force of the kicks, pushing it into her spine. Doctors at the hospital determined that Ms. Johnson needed emergency surgery; indeed, she was already beginning to go into shock when she arrived in the emergency room and might have died had she waited longer to receive treatment.

When the doctors performed surgery, they discovered that Ms. Johnson's abdomen was full of pancreatic fluid, which had started to digest some of the tissues in her abdomen, and the part of her pancreas that had been severed from the rest of the organ had died. It was therefore necessary during surgery to remove the dead portion of Ms. Johnson's pancreas as well as her spleen, which normally would receive blood from that section of the pancreas. As a result of these amputations, Ms. Johnson's ability to fight infection and her capacity to digest food were permanently diminished.

On the day that Ms. Johnson was admitted, the police were called to the hospital in order to investigate whether she had been the victim of domestic violence. During her recuperation from her injuries, Ms. Johnson cooperated with the police by answering their questions and turning over belongings that served as evidence of her assault. On August 12, 2002, she gave testimony to a Grand Jury from her hospital bed by video. Additionally, a social worker at the hospital called the Administration for Children's Services ("ACS") regarding Ms. Johnson's daughter, and an investigation was opened into both Mr. Byrd and Ms. Johnson. Ms. Johnson cooperated with the investigation. During this time, Ms. Johnson admitted to investigators that she was "afraid she would be abused further" by the petitioner, that she had known "she would be in the hospital one day like this from the injuries" the petitioner caused her, and was "still scared of him retaliating."

Mr. Byrd repeatedly visited Ms. Johnson in the hospital following her surgery, often bringing the couple's daughter with him. During the petitioner's visits to the hospital, he apologized repeatedly to Ms. Johnson, promised to change, and professed his love to her. He apologized as well to Ms. Johnson's mother, who had come to be with her while she was recovering in the hospital. While Ms. Johnson was in the hospital, he called her several times a day, and they had long conversations. Indeed, during one meeting with a social worker that lasted about an hour and a half, Ms. Johnson received approximately five phone calls from Mr. Byrd and answered each one. The petitioner also exhibited angry behavior towards Ms. Johnson while she was in the hospital, in particular screaming at her once he learned that ACS had opened an investigation regarding their daughter.

Although Ms. Johnson had initially cooperated with investigators, she stopped doing so some time after she was released from the hospital. She began to assert that she was unsure whether she wanted to press charges and that she would not testify against the petitioner at trial. She indicated to investigators that some of Mr. Byrd's family members had contacted her and told her not to move forward with prosecution.

C. *Sirois* Hearing and Trial

Because the prosecution feared Ms. Johnson was no longer willing to testify in the case against the petitioner, a *Sirois* hearing was held before the Honorable James A. Yates in order to determine whether there was convincing evidence that "a criminal defendant's misconduct has induced a witness' unlawful refusal to testify at trial."

On March 25, 2003, Ms. Johnson testified at the hearing pursuant to a subpoena. She attributed her earlier cooperation with the prosecutor to a threat by ACS that the agency would take away her daughter if she did not cooperate with the prosecution of the petitioner. She proceeded to limit her prior testimony, claiming that her injuries had not been overly severe and minimizing her fear of Mr. Byrd.

At the hearing, Dr. Ann Burgess testified as an expert on Battered Woman's Syndrome ("BWS"). She testified that BWS had been identified and studied for approximately thirty years, and that women who exhibit symptoms of BWS are often under the "coercive control" of their abusers such that they feel compelled to do everything the abuser demands in order to avoid provoking his disfavor. Dr. Burgess also described how a victim of domestic violence might initiate prosecution against the abuser and then recant after time has passed because she doubts herself and wants to avoid angering or upsetting the abuser. She testified that, in order to convince a victim not to move forward with prosecution against him, a batterer might use several indirect means, including apologizing, threatening, and blaming the woman for his abuse. She also noted that these tactics could be effective even when the batterer is incarcerated and thus separated from the victim.

Dr. Burgess concluded that Ms. Johnson was "a battered woman" who was "in a coercive controlled relationship with the defendant." This opinion was based on a review of transcripts and other exhibits and testimony related to the case, but was formed without having interviewed Ms. Johnson. Dr. Burgess concluded that Mr. Byrd's frequent visits to Ms. Johnson in the hospital, his apologies, and his constant checking up on her were a means of exerting control, as was an episode in which he forced their daughter to strip down to her underwear in Ms. Johnson's hospital room in order to demonstrate to Ms. Johnson and her mother that she had not been abused.

At the hearing, the prosecution also introduced evidence that approximately 450 phone calls had been made from Rikers Island, while the petitioner was detained there, to Ms. Johnson's home. Dr. Burgess testified that Mr. Byrd's control over Ms. Johnson could have continued even when he was out of contact with her, since his threats and apologies would continue to be effective and would only have been intensified by his extensive telephone contact with Ms. Johnson while he was incarcerated. In Dr. Burgess' opinion, these telephone calls were a "premeditated" exertion of control because the petitioner knew that his behavior had allowed him to control Ms. Johnson in the past. Evidence introduced at the hearing further established that the calls made from the jail to Ms. Johnson's home were accomplished with personal identification codes borrowed from other inmates in order to circumvent an order of protection that prohibited Mr. Byrd from contacting Ms. Johnson; according to Dr. Burgess, this demonstrated to Ms. Johnson that the petitioner "[was]n't going to play by the rules."

Ultimately, Dr. Burgess concluded that it was Ms. Johnson's fear of the petitioner that caused her not to testify against the petitioner and that he "played a major role in her refusal to go forward." Although she cited the "constant pressure" that he put on Ms. Johnson in drawing this conclusion, it was also her opinion that the petitioner was in control of Ms. Johnson "without engaging in any conduct whatsoever." Dr. Burgess testified that Ms. Johnson's attempts to minimize her testimony when she appeared before the court in March of 2003 were consistent with this conclusion.

As the trial began on January 8, 2004, Justice Yates had deferred any determination on whether Ms. Johnson's refusal to testify was a result of the petitioner's misconduct, because he still held out hope that she would testify in full. However, when Ms. Johnson took the witness stand at trial she refused to answer any questions, although she had been granted full transactional immunity. The judge admonished her that she could be charged with contempt for refusing to testify and that her silence was "increasing his chances that [Mr. Byrd] go to prison, not decreasing it." Ultimately, Justice Yates ruled that the prosecution had shown by clear and convincing evidence that Ms. Johnson was unavailable to testify as a result of Mr. Byrd's intentional misconduct, citing the petitioner's repeated phone calls to Ms. Johnson from jail notwithstanding the order of protection and the petitioner's visits to the hospital when Ms. Johnson was recovering from surgery, which he viewed in the context of a "long history of abuse" by the petitioner, including his preventing Ms. Johnson from seeking medical treatment following the incident. The judge found that the phone calls and hospital visits were "clearly intended" to prevent her from testifying, and therefore held that the videotape of Ms. Johnson's testimony to the grand jury could be admitted as evidence at the trial. Justice Yates also ruled that no testimony related to prior acts of violence in the relationship between the petitioner and Ms. Johnson would be admitted because its prejudicial effect would outweigh its probative value.

Mr. Byrd's trial went forward on January 8, 12, 13, 14, 15, 20, and 21, 2004. The prosecution presented testimony from . . . Dr. Burgess. . . . Dr. Burgess' testimony at trial was limited to her general expert knowledge of relationship violence and did not address the petitioner's specific case. Dr. Burgess testified that it is fairly common for victims of relationship violence to refuse to move forward with prosecution, particularly when they are being contacted by their abuser. * * *

On January 21, 2004, Mr. Byrd was found guilty of assault in the first degree for intentionally causing serious physical injury to Ms. Johnson by means of a dangerous instrument—a shod foot—and assault in the second degree for intending to and causing physical injury to the victim by means of a dangerous instrument—the tile floor against which he had struck her head. On February 26, 2004, he was given determinate sentences of twenty-five years and seven years respectively, the sentences to run concurrently.

D. Subsequent Proceedings

The petitioner appealed his conviction, arguing that: (1) the trial court erroneously admitted Ms. Johnson's grand jury testimony; (2) the court wrongly admitted Dr. Burgess' expert testimony; (3) statements made by the prosecutor during her summation deprived the petitioner of a fair trial; and (4) his conviction for assault in the first degree was erroneous because sandals do not constitute a dangerous instrument under the law and the conviction was against the weight of the evidence.

On April 15, 2008, the Appellate Division, First Department, affirmed the judgment of conviction. The court concluded that Ms. Johnson's grand jury testimony was properly admitted at trial because the prosecution "proved by clear and convincing evidence that defendant's misconduct induced her unavailability to testify." The Appellate Division cited the petitioner's "hostility and abusiveness" in his visits to Ms. Johnson in the hospital, the "hundreds of calls" made in violation of the order of protection, and attempts by Mr. Byrd's relatives to convince Ms. Johnson not to testify, all of which it evaluated "in the context of a relationship with a long history of physical and mental abuse." The court found that Dr. Burgess' testimony was proper because expert evidence on BWS has been accepted by New York courts since 1985, and a relatively novel factual application of such evidence—demonstrating that a defendant's actions rendered a witness unavailable to testify at trial—did not require a fresh evaluation of the scientific validity of that testimony. * * *

On July 24, 2008, the New York Court of Appeals denied Mr. Byrd's application for leave to appeal. The petitioner commenced the instant proceeding on May 29, 2009. * * *

As on appeal to the Appellate Division, Mr. Byrd argues here that his conviction should be overturned because: (1) the admission of Ms. Johnson's grand jury testimony was in error; (2) Dr. Burgess' expert testimony was improperly admitted at trial; (3) statements made by the prosecutor during her summation deprived him of a fair trial; and (4) his conviction for assault in the first degree was unwarranted because a sandal is not a dangerous instrument under the law, there was insufficient evidence that his sandal was a dangerous instrument, and the conviction was against the weight of the evidence.

1. Expert Testimony at Evidentiary Hearing

Expert testimony describing BWS is admissible in federal as well as New York courts. There was no need to hold a hearing to determine its scientific reliability, since BWS has been widely accepted as a valid theory upon which to base expert testimony by federal and New York courts for many years.

However, "expert testimony on [BWS] should be admissible only to address an issue that is inherently confusing to the jury and when there is no other evidence to address it." The testimony is admissible when "[i]t is aimed at an area where the purported common knowledge of the jury may be very much mistaken, an area where jurors' logic, drawn from their own experience, may lead to a wholly incorrect conclusion." Just as BWS testimony has been admitted in order to allow a jury to understand why a battered woman might, contrary to the instincts or assumptions of the average person, refuse to prosecute her batterer, there is no reason why it may not be admitted to allow the court to understand why seemingly innocuous acts—such as telephone calls, visits, and apologies—may act to intimidate or coerce a battered woman.

Contrary to the petitioner's contention, allowing expert testimony for this purpose does not constitute reliance on that testimony to prove the defendant's misconduct. It is not because Ms. Johnson exhibits symptoms of BWS that the petitioner is responsible for her unavailability at trial, but rather because the petitioner prevented Ms. Johnson from seeking medical help for the injuries he inflicted upon her; called and visited her constantly while she was recuperating from those injuries; and then called her hundreds of times from prison, in violation of an order of protection. When viewed in the context of BWS—context provided by the expert testimony of Dr. Burgess—these actions may be understood as wrongdoing on the part of the petitioner. * * *

B. Expert Testimony at Trial

The petitioner next argues that the admission of Dr. Burgess' testimony regarding BWS at trial was erroneous and deprived him of a fair trial. * * *

As discussed above, expert testimony concerning BWS is plainly admissible in order to establish why a complainant may be reluctant to testify at trial. "[E]xpert testimony on battered woman syndrome should be admissible only to address an issue that is inherently confusing to the jury and when there is no other evidence to address it," but is properly admitted "to explain the victim's behavior after [an] assault" where "[t]he expert did not testify, or suggest, that the victim should be believed or that defendant was guilty."

At trial, the testimony of Dr. Burgess was limited in scope. She did not testify about the facts of the instant case and drew only the conclusion that "[i]t is common for [battered women] to refuse to cooperate if they are being contacted by the abuser." The judge used limiting instructions to help the jury understand the purpose for which the testimony was admissible. This is the same purpose for which it has been introduced in previous trials under New York law. *See People v. Smith,* 779 N.Y.S.2d 853, 854 (3d Dep't 2004) ("The testimony in question was elicited to provide the jury with an explanation of the victim's behaviors surrounding the underlying incidents, which otherwise may have appeared unusual to a jury, a purpose that the courts have long condoned."); *Ellis,* 650 N.Y.S.2d at 505–06 ("The actions of a woman suffering from BWS are subject to many misconceptions or myths. . . . The nature of a battered woman's behavior is such that an often drawn 'common sense' conclusion is that the abuse has not in fact happened."); *see also Arcoren v. United States,* 929 F.2d 1235, 1241 (8th

Cir.1991) ("[The expert witness] expressed no opinion on whether [the victim] suffered from battered woman syndrome or which of her conflicting statements were more credible. [The expert witness] merely provided expert information to aid the jury in evaluating the evidence. [The expert witness]'s testimony did not interfere with or impinge upon the jury's role in determining the credibility of witnesses."). Furthermore, the testimony was introduced in this case at least in part simply to counteract the explanation for Ms. Johnson's failure to testify at the trial adduced by the defense, namely that she had only testified for the grand jury in response to threats by ACS that if she did not do so, her child would be taken away from her. Thus, admission of Dr. Burgess' testimony was not improper, and it certainly did not rise to the level of a constitutional error. * * *

ALLEN V. BARNES

2015 WL 1999820 (E.D. Cal.) (unpublished)
(most citations and footnotes omitted)

FINDINGS AND RECOMMENDATIONS

Petitioner is a state prisoner proceeding pro se with a petition for a writ of habeas corpus pursuant to 28 U.S.C. § 2254. He challenges a judgment of conviction entered against him in 2010 in the Solano County Superior Court on charges of attempted involuntary manslaughter, corporal injury to a cohabitant, assault with a firearm, and mayhem. He seeks federal habeas relief on the following grounds: (1) the trial court's admission into evidence of his prior acts of domestic violence violated his right to due process; * * * Upon careful consideration of the record and the applicable law, it is recommended that petitioner's application for habeas corpus relief be denied.

Background

In its unpublished memorandum and opinion affirming petitioner's judgment of conviction on appeal, the California Court of Appeal for the First Appellate District provided the following factual summary of petitioner's crimes of conviction:

Defendant Kelvin Menjeryl Allen was convicted of several charges and related enhancements after he shot and seriously injured his girlfriend, Mickey Kentra. The trial court sentenced defendant to 19 years in prison. On appeal, defendant contends the court erred by: (1) admitting evidence of his prior acts of domestic violence against Kentra, * * *.

We reject defendant's arguments. However, we modify the judgment to correct the implementation of section 654 as to some of the charges against defendant, and to correct one other discrepancy in the sentence. We affirm the judgment as modified.

I. FACTUAL AND PROCEDURAL BACKGROUND

A. The Charges Against Defendant

An information charged defendant with: (1) attempted deliberate, premeditated murder; (2) inflicting corporal injury on a cohabitant; (3) assault with a firearm; and (4) mayhem. As to all counts, the information alleged defendant personally used a firearm and inflicted great bodily injury under circumstances involving domestic violence.

B. The Evidence Presented at Trial

Kentra and defendant began dating a few years before the October 15, 2009, shooting. They began living together at defendant's mother's house, where they stayed for about a year and a half. In January 2009, Kentra moved into a two-bedroom apartment at 1513 Alamo Drive in Vacaville. A few months later, defendant moved into the apartment with Kentra's permission. Kentra and defendant shared a bedroom and slept in the same bed. From January to October 2009, Kentra worked at a gas station and paid the bills.

A few months prior to October 2009, defendant acquired a shotgun, which he kept by his side of the bed. He kept shotgun shells in the bedroom and in their car. He sometimes kept the gun loaded. He had a lock for the gun, but rarely if ever used it. When defendant walked his dog, which he did most days, he took the shotgun with him. Defendant generally took the shotgun with him when he left the apartment.

Kentra and defendant had a turbulent relationship, and defendant frequently accused Kentra of having sexual relations with men she met at work. Defendant drove Kentra to and from work. Defendant sometimes sat in the car and watched Kentra work, and he became jealous because of her interactions with male customers. Toward the end of their relationship, Kentra told defendant (about once or twice per month) that she wanted to leave him and did not want to be with him anymore. About four to six times prior to October 15, 2009, defendant threatened to kill Kentra.

Defendant and Kentra had physical altercations during which he punched and kicked her. In December 2007, while they were living with defendant's mother, defendant kicked Kentra's arm and broke it. Kentra did not report the incident to the police. When she went to the hospital for treatment, she told the staff she fell down the stairs, because she did not want to get defendant in trouble. On a different occasion at defendant's mother's house, defendant shot Kentra with a pellet gun. Once when Kentra returned from work, defendant accused her of cheating on him and hit her. When Kentra fell down, defendant kicked her. Although she had "a bunch of bruises," Kentra did not call the police or tell anyone about the incident because she was afraid. * * * [Defendant eventually shot Kentra in the arm, wounding her badly but not killing her. He claimed he pointed the shotgun at her but did not expect it to go off, so the shooting was an accident.]

C. The Verdicts and Sentence

* * * After a retrial on count one, defendant was acquitted of attempted murder, but convicted of the lesser offense of attempted voluntary manslaughter. The jury found true the related enhancement allegations as to firearm use and great bodily injury/domestic violence. * * *

III. PETITIONER'S CLAIMS

A. Erroneous Admission of Evidence

In his first ground for relief, petitioner claims that the trial court's admission into evidence of his prior acts of domestic violence against Kentra violated his right to due process. He argues that this evidence was improperly admitted as to three of the counts against him (attempted murder, mayhem and assault with a deadly weapon) because those counts did not involve domestic violence. He contends the evidence was irrelevant and unduly inflammatory as to those three counts. Petitioner specifically complains that evidence of his prior acts of domestic violence was admitted at his retrial on the sole count of attempted murder, which "did not involve domestic violence as an essential element." Petitioner argues that the evidence of prior crimes should have been restricted to the corporal injury count at his first trial. Petitioner also argues that the trial [court] erred in instructing the jurors that they could consider the evidence of prior domestic violence in connection with all of the counts against him, instead of limiting the applicability of this evidence to just the corporal injury count.

The California Court of Appeal rejected these arguments, reasoning as follows:

> A. Prior Acts of Domestic Violence
>
> 1. Background
>
> Prior to both trials, defendant moved in limine to exclude evidence of his prior domestic violence, arguing it constituted inadmissible character evidence under Evidence Code section 1101, was irrelevant and unduly prejudicial, and would violate his due process rights. In both instances, the trial court excluded evidence that defendant committed an act of domestic violence against his former wife in 1995, but admitted evidence of defendant's prior domestic violence against Kentra under Evidence Code section 1109. The court instructed the jury it could consider the uncharged acts in determining whether defendant was "disposed or inclined" to commit domestic violence, and whether he committed the charged offenses. *[Editor's Note: Section 1109 does allow evidence of abuse against former partners, including*

uncharged acts, as long as the judge finds it more probative than prejudicial under Evidence Code section 352, which is similar to Federal Rule of Evidence 403. And admission of the evidence must not violate the hearsay rule.]

2. Analysis

Evidence of a person's past conduct generally is inadmissible to show his or her propensity to commit the charged crime, but is admissible to prove facts other than propensity, such as motive, opportunity, intent, preparation, plan, knowledge, identity, or absence of mistake or accident. Under Evidence Code section 1109, in "a criminal action in which the defendant is accused of *an offense involving domestic violence,* "evidence of other acts of domestic violence is admissible to show propensity." (italics added.) Defendant contends three of the charges against him—attempted murder, assault with a firearm, and mayhem—were not offenses involving domestic violence within the meaning of the statute, because those crimes do not "inherently" involve domestic violence. Defendant argues it is not sufficient that the evidence established his crimes in fact involved domestic violence. * * *

Evidence Code section 1109 does not include a list of offenses that involve domestic violence. Instead, the statute incorporates the definition of domestic violence in [Penal Code] section 13700 (and, under certain circumstances, the broader definition in Family Code section 6211). Section 13700 defines "domestic violence" as "abuse committed against an adult or a minor who is a . . . cohabitant . . . or person with whom the suspect . . . is having or has had a dating or engagement relationship"; "[a]buse" means "intentionally or recklessly causing or attempting to cause bodily injury, or placing another person in reasonable apprehension of imminent serious bodily injury to himself or herself, or another." Applying these definitions, the evidence at trial clearly established that defendant's crimes involved domestic violence. Kentra was defendant's cohabitant and was a person with whom he was in a dating relationship. Defendant intentionally or recklessly caused Kentra to suffer bodily injury, and placed her in reasonable apprehension of imminent serious bodily injury, when he threatened to kill her and then shot her. * * *

Defendant contends this court should adopt an interpretation of Evidence Code section 1109 similar to *Walker'* s interpretation of Evidence Code section 1108, *[Editor's Note: section 1108 is almost identical to section 1109 but applies to sexual assault rather than domestic violence cases.]* and hold that attempted murder, assault with a firearm, and mayhem are not "offense[s] involving domestic violence," because domestic violence is not an essential element of

> those offenses. We reject this argument. First, assuming *Walker* correctly interpreted Evidence Code section 1108, defendant has not established that interpretation should be extended to Evidence Code section 1109. To the contrary, in *People v. Brown* (2011) 192 Cal.App.4th 1222, the appellate court expressly declined to extend *Walker* to Evidence Code section 1109, and concluded that the circumstances of a crime may establish it is an offense involving domestic violence, even if domestic violence is not an essential element of the crime. In *Brown,* the defendant was charged and convicted of first degree murder in the homicide of his former girlfriend. The trial court admitted evidence of the defendant's prior acts of domestic violence under Evidence Code section 1109, holding that murder was an offense " 'involving domestic violence.' " The appellate court affirmed, stating: "Given the legislative history and the language of [Evidence Code] section 1109, we agree with the trial court's observation in this case that murder is 'the ultimate form of domestic violence,' and that defendant's prior acts of domestic violence were admissible based on the nature and circumstances of his relationship with and conduct toward Bridget. Defendant was charged with first degree murder based on strangling Bridget, his former girlfriend, after a lengthy period in which he tried to intimidate her because she chose to break up with him. He was clearly 'accused of an offense involving domestic violence' within the meaning of [Evidence Code] section 1109." * * *
>
> Applying *Brown* here, defendant's prior acts of domestic violence were admissible because, as discussed above, the evidence established the charged offenses involved domestic violence.
>
> A second basis for rejecting defendant's argument is that, even under the *Walker* approach, defendant's prior acts of domestic violence would be admissible to show propensity as to all four charges. Under *Walker,* the specified misconduct must be an element of the charged offense or *"alleged in the information as an enhancement or aggravating factor."* The information here alleged that, in the commission of all four offenses, defendant *"personally inflicted great bodily injury upon [Kentra], under circumstances involving domestic violence,"* within the meaning of section 12022.7, subdivision (e). (Italics added.) Accordingly, defendant was, in each count, "accused of an offense involving domestic violence [.]"

The question whether evidence of petitioner's prior acts of domestic violence against Kentra was properly admitted under California law is not cognizable in this federal habeas corpus proceeding. The only question before this court is whether the trial court committed an error that rendered the trial so arbitrary and fundamentally unfair that it violated federal due process.

The United States Supreme Court "has never expressly held that it violates due process to admit other crimes evidence for the purpose of showing conduct in conformity therewith, or that it violates due process to admit other crimes evidence for other purposes without an instruction limiting the jury's consideration of the evidence to such purposes." In fact, the Supreme Court has expressly left open this question. Accordingly, the state court's rejection of petitioner's due process claim is not contrary to United States Supreme Court precedent.

In any event, any error in admitting evidence of petitioner's prior acts of domestic violence did not have "a substantial and injurious effect or influence in determining the jury's verdict." Petitioner was found guilty of attempted manslaughter, which requires a jury finding that the defendant took at least one direct but ineffective step toward killing a person and intended to kill that person, but was provoked and acted rashly and without due deliberation. As noted by respondent, the evidence that petitioner took at least one direct step toward killing Kentra and intended to kill her is overwhelming, given that he shot her at close range with a shotgun. Although the prior crimes evidence was potentially powerful, "[the fact] that prior acts evidence is inflammatory is not dispositive in and of itself." Evidence that petitioner had committed prior acts of domestic violence against Kentra would not have had a substantial effect on the verdict under these facts.

The court also notes that the jury instructions in this case did not compel the jury to draw an inference of propensity from evidence of petitioner's prior acts of domestic violence. Rather, the trial court instructed the jury at the close of the evidence that if they found petitioner had committed the prior acts of domestic violence they could, but were not required to, "conclude from that evidence that the defendant was disposed or inclined to commit domestic violence." The jury was also instructed that if they found that petitioner had such a disposition, they could, but were not required to, infer that he was likely to have committed the charged offenses. The jury was further instructed that if they concluded that petitioner committed the prior acts, that conclusion was "only one factor to consider" and was "not sufficient by itself to prove that [petitioner] is guilty of [the crimes charged]." In addition, the jury was instructed that the prosecution had the burden of proving all charges against petitioner beyond a reasonable doubt. The jury is presumed to have followed all of these instructions.

In sum, the admission of petitioner's prior acts of domestic violence did not violate any right clearly established by United States Supreme Court precedent or result in prejudice under the circumstances of this case.

Accordingly, petitioner is not entitled to relief on this due process claim.
* * *

[Editor's Note: Ca. Evidence Code sections 1108 and 1109 are atypical among U.S. jurisdictions in allowing prior acts of sexual assault or domestic violence, including uncharged acts against other victims or survivors, to be introduced in prosecutions for similar crimes.]

ELEANOR SIMON, CONFRONTATION AND DOMESTIC VIOLENCE POST-*DAVIS*: IS THERE AND SHOULD THERE BE A DOCTRINAL EXCEPTION?

17 Mich. J. Gender & L. 175 (2011)
(citations and footnotes omitted)

IV. SHOULD THERE BE A DOMESTIC VIOLENCE "EXCEPTION"?

The last section explored the results of the state domestic violence cases engaging *Crawford/Davis* to evaluate the predictability of testimonial classifications and to determine whether courts routinely widely construed or expanded *Davis*. This section will engage the normative consideration of whether there should be a "domestic violence exception" in confrontation doctrine. It will be argued that there should be such a doctrinal exception in the confrontation framework so as to allow our criminal justice system to more fully prosecute batterers and to help alleviate the classification unpredictability in such cases. This exception would not entail revision of any Federal Rule of Evidence, as the right of confrontation is a constitutional right. Instead, the exception would be a common law, Supreme Court-created exception to the doctrine.

The Supreme Court affirmatively believes there should not be a doctrinal domestic violence exception to confrontation. The Court in *Crawford* emphasized that its history demonstrates that the Sixth Amendment confrontation right is a procedural rather than substantive right, such that it must be equally and consistently applied in all cases. Thus, as Justice Scalia asserted, "dispensing with confrontation because testimony is obviously reliable is akin to dispensing with jury trial because a defendant is obviously guilty." It is not done. In *Davis*, the Court affirmed the conception of the right as procedural. While the Court did acknowledge that there are particular difficulties in domestic violence prosecutions, by noting the susceptibility of victims to coercion and the possibility of giving the defendant a "windfall," it refused to treat such cases differently. Justice Scalia stated, "[w]e may not . . . vitiate constitutional guarantees when they have the effect of allowing the guilty to go free." He pointed out that the rule of forfeiture does provide some protection to domestic violence victims because "one who obtains the absence of a witness by wrongdoing forfeits the constitutional right to confrontation." However, as discussed in Part I above, two years later, in *Giles*, the Court made proving such forfeiture difficult, requiring proof of the specific intent of the defendant to prevent the testimony. In *Giles*, the Court also expressly acknowledged the prosecutorial difficulties presented by domestic violence but again specifically rejected the notion of an exception or different rule: "[d]omestic violence is an intolerable offense . . . [b]ut for that serious crime, as for others, abridging the constitutional rights of criminal defendants is not in the State's arsenal [of means to combat domestic violence]." In its recent confrontation cases, then, the Supreme Court has recognized the inherent differences in domestic violence prosecutions but has refused to make any exceptions to the defendant's (procedural) right of confrontation.

Apart from the Supreme Court doctrine and its historical-procedural rationale, there are additional reasons why there should not be a domestic violence exception. First, perhaps there is no need for such a doctrinal exception. As demonstrated by the results of state court decisions, much hearsay evidence necessary to domestic violence prosecutions is being admitted. Much evidence is being judged non-testimonial (sixty-three percent of all statements analyzed), and even if some is judged testimonial, it is ultimately judged admissible through harmless error or forfeiture (eighty-five percent of cases found at least some of the statements ultimately admissible). Thus, if the purpose of such a domestic violence exception is to ensure that prosecutors are able to introduce hearsay statements crucial to their domestic violence prosecutions, the *Davis* framework as implemented by state court judges may be said to be functioning sufficiently.

Second, the current framework enables judicial discretion in determining the admissibility of statements, which is an aspect that is important to our system's evidentiary structure and appropriate here. The Federal Rules of Evidence confer enormous discretion to the trial court judge as the ultimate decider on admissibility issues. The Federal Rules include this type of discretion because admissibility decisions are often incredibly contextual and dependent on a number of variables in the trial and in the evidence; accordingly, the trial judge is often in the best position to make the decision. This rationale applies equally to Confrontation Clause decisions. In many instances, the right to confront is arguably more important than in others, and in these instances, the judge can find the statements to be testimonial, while in others, non-testimonial. For instance, in cases where the declarant has filed false claims before or the context of the statement seems particularly unreliable, the judge can insist on confrontation (or no evidence) by deeming the statement testimonial. Through this judicial discretion, then, both the defendant's right to confront and the victim's justice in prosecution are protected. In creating a doctrinal exception for all domestic violence cases, some judicial discretion is necessarily removed.

Third, perhaps there is no need for such an exception because actors within the system can change and adapt to the *Davis* framework so as to ensure admissible evidence in the future. As discussed above, it is possible that judges have already adapted to the new framework by admitting evidence they have judged to be reliable by framing their reliability considerations as *Crawford/Davis* evaluations of primary purpose, ongoing emergency, and testimonial or not. Prosecutors and police, as other system actors, may also alter their behavior, if they have not already begun doing so, to utilize the current framework to its fullest. Prosecutors have the ability to structure their prosecutions around the type of non-testimonial statements that the Court has made clearly admissible. For example, *Davis* protected excited utterances made during 911 calls and thus "maintained a large tool in the prosecutor's repertoire." Further, in *Giles*, the Court clarified that "[s]tatements to friends and neighbors about abuse and intimidation, and statements to physicians in the course of receiving treatment" are non-testimonial. Thus, under the current framework, several types of victim statements may be admitted and prosecutors should attempt to introduce those as much as possible. Prosecutors should also decline to concede that a certain statement is testimonial, for as noted above, there is much room for debate within the *Davis* structure; prosecutors may take advantage of that lack of clarity by arguing that seemingly testimonial statements may actually be non-testimonial. Additionally, prosecutors could increase their use of experts in domestic violence trials to ensure that the jury is knowledgeable about the particularities of such a crime, to explain the lack of victim presence and testimony, to clarify contradictions and misconceptions that may exist about domestic violence, and to opine the effects abuse can have on a person and a relationship. Finally, prosecutors may also engage in strategies to increase victim cooperation and therefore provide in-court testimony, avoiding *Crawford/Davis* problems completely. Certain states have specialized prosecution programs, increased victim advocacy, and specialized domestic violence courts, structures which they have found effective in reducing victim fear and therefore increasing victim testimony. Increased prosecutorial communication and contact with the victim as well as minimization of the burden on the victim are crucial in increasing the likelihood of victim testimony. While victims refuse to testify for a number of reasons, as discussed above, these types of programs may help to overcome at least some of the obstacles.

Of all the actors involved in establishing evidence in domestic violence cases, police have the most limited capacity to increase the amount of admissible evidence. As stated in *Davis*, "[w]hile prosecutors may hope that inculpatory 'non-testimonial' evidence is gathered, this is essentially beyond police control. Their saying that an emergency exists cannot make it be so." That acknowledged, as prosecutors rely more on other sources of evidence, the burden shifts to law enforcement to find many of those sources. Police accordingly should ensure that they "gather as much evidence as possible and accurately identify all potential witnesses and ways to contact them, or identify third parties who will remain in touch with them." Police may also function as an additional communication tool with the victim, so as to increase the chances of victim cooperation.

Even acknowledging the validity of the above outlined reasons to keep the current conception of the confrontation right, it is clear that the results under the current conception have been inconsistent and unpredictable and therefore unsatisfactory. The results indicate that lower court judges have been forced to engage in somewhat of a dishonest exercise, admitting what they find to be reliable evidence by labeling it "non-testimonial" and/or admitting such evidence through harmless error. Thus while the current structure does provide for judicial discretion, it is somewhat of a fictional and limited discretion. The arguable "discretion" may actually be an impediment, for judges are forced to couch their actual (reliability) assessments in testimonial versus non-testimonial considerations: "[n]o doubt many state courts view [*Crawford*] as interference of their evidentiary sovereignty." Additionally, even if system actors have altered (or can alter) their behaviors, there are significant costs in doing so. The types of evidence upon which prosecutors are forced to rely, and that police are forced to collect, still often leave insufficient evidence for prosecution and conviction. News reports indicated that nearly fifty percent of domestic violence cases were being dropped in some jurisdictions post-*Crawford* because of the lack of evidence. Domestic violence continues to be perpetrated in the privacy of the home, with few witnesses and little cooperation from the victim. Thus even if prosecutors rely more heavily on experts and statements to non-police, they still have very little upon which they may rest their case. Finally, even if prosecutors are able to increase victim cooperation, many argue that forcing a victim to testify constitutes a type of re-victimization of the victim and accordingly something that should not be forced.

For the above listed reasons, it is evident that the *Davis* framework has proved, if not unworkable, then at least heavily flawed within the context of domestic violence cases. The creation of a doctrinal domestic violence exception in the confrontation right of defendants would do much to rectify the current major problems. While it does appear that in many ways lower courts have engaged in a type of expansion of *Davis* in domestic violence cases already, the creation of a clear, bright-line exception has several benefits. In general, bright-line rules enable courts to function with more consistency: they send clear messages to the public about the law and behavior in the particular area, enhancing the expressive function of the law. Additionally they enable practitioners and parties to more fully and reliably assess the strengths and weaknesses of their cases. Applied in this context, a domestic violence exception would rectify the inconsistency and unpredictability detailed above. In creating such an exception, the law would be sending a clear and powerful message about the unacceptability both of domestic violence and of intimidating victims in advance of trial—

a message that the general public embraces and yet one that is not reflected in confrontation doctrine. Moreover, the exception would help practitioners better evaluate the strength of the case before them, for often the piece of evidence of least certain admissibility is also the piece of evidence most important to the case: the victim's statements.

As an initial conceptualization, such a doctrinal exception would use the *Davis* framework of testimonial versus non-testimonial statements but would broaden the concepts of "ongoing emergency" and "primary purpose" in domestic violence cases such that any statements made by a victim in an abusive relationship, whether to law enforcement or non-law enforcement, would be deemed non-testimonial. The prosecutor would be required to show to the judge's satisfaction that the defendant imposed upon the victim a "classic abusive relationship, which is meant to isolate the victim from outside help . . ." Upon such a showing, the statements would be judged non-testimonial and admissible if satisfying the other applicable evidentiary rules.

The theoretical rationale for such a reclassification of battering victims' statements is the cyclical and patterned nature of domestic violence. Domestic violence is a "pattern of harm in both a quantitative and qualitative sense." Both the frequency and duration of domestic violence turn it into a pattern of harm quantitatively, consisting of "repeated acts by the same offender against the same victim." Studies have shown that over sixty percent of men who batter their wives do so repeatedly; nearly twenty percent of women were victims of abuse by the same partner ten or more times; and nearly seventy percent of women who had been assaulted by an intimate partner reported that their victimization lasted more than one year. The importance of both power and control in domestic violence turns it into a pattern of harm qualitatively, such that the ensuing harm comes not only from the violence: physical battering is "just one method of inflicting . . . trauma" within a relationship characterized by numerous other forms. Thus a domestic violence victim exists in a relationship defined by long-term, ongoing, powerful, and continuous abuse. It is accordingly clear that it is illogical and impractical to attempt to find the beginning and end of an "emergency" in such a context. Determining the contours of an "emergency" can be arbitrary even in non-domestic violence contexts, but it is even more arbitrary in the context of an abusive relationship, where a victim is under constant threat of assault or maltreatment. Creating a doctrinal exception in domestic violence cases means that judges would no longer have to engage in such a capricious and ultimately unhelpful exercise.

A domestic violence exception would deprive the defendant charged with domestic violence of some of his right of confrontation, for he would not always have the opportunity to confront all of his accusers, even if the statement was (under the current framework) testimonial. Being deprived of any portion of a right in the criminal justice system is not a trivial concern. But this type of trade-off (less confrontation for the defendant, more hearsay evidence for the prosecution) mirrors the trade-offs that exist throughout criminal justice system and the Federal Rules of Evidence. The Federal Rules and the Constitution involve delicate balancing acts of disparate and often opposing concerns. Here, while the defendant's right to confrontation is narrowed in specific contexts (i.e. the abuse victim's unconfronted hearsay may be deemed admissible), the defendant still maintains significant protections provided to him by various parts of the criminal justice system and the U.S. Constitution. The defendant still has the opportunity to cross-examine the police officers or government officials who are witnesses in court and thus subject their testimony to the "crucible of cross-examination." The defendant still has the opportunity to present any testimony, including his own, to rebut any hearsay statements of the victim introduced under the exception. The defendant is still protected by the hearsay rule, which is a separate limitation on out-of-court statements, unaffected by any exception in the confrontation right. Further, the trial judge retains significant discretion under the Federal Rules to exclude evidence deemed not relevant, unreliable, not probative or too prejudicial, always providing a protection to the defense. Finally, the U.S. Constitution further protects the defendant's rights through the Fifth Amendment guarantees against self-incrimination and against double jeopardy, and the Sixth Amendment guarantees to a speedy and fair trial and to counsel.

While creating such a domestic violence exception is undoubtedly a significant change in confrontation doctrine, it is not entirely unimaginable. The judicial conception of the confrontation right has been completely reconfigured in the last six years and remains a live issue for the court. Moving from *Crawford* to *Davis* to *Giles*, the Court has engaged in a continual refining and sharpening of the confrontation right—a process which has grown out of the previous decisions and subsequent effects of those decisions. Creating a doctrinal domestic violence exception such as the one suggested above would simply constitute a further refinement of the confrontation right, not any substantial break in judicial precedent.

Additionally, the Court has proved that it is not blind to domestic violence as a serious issue within the confrontation right. As mentioned above, both the *Davis* and *Giles* majorities recognized the inherent difficulties and obstacles particular to domestic violence prosecutions. For example, in *Davis*, the majority stated that domestic violence is a crime "notoriously susceptible to intimidation or coercion of the victim to ensure that she does not testify at trial." And in *Giles*, the Court noted that "[a]cts of domestic violence often are intended to dissuade a victim from resorting to outside help, and include conduct designed to prevent testimony to police officers or cooperation in criminal prosecution." Further, while the majority in *Giles* does not create a separate rule for domestic violence cases, it appears that a majority of the Court, based on the various concurrences and dissents produced, may in fact support a "softer" intent rule for proof of forfeiture in domestic violence cases. This softer, "inferred intent" was discussed by Justice Souter in his concurrence and consists of a standard wherein intent may be inferred from defendant's knowledge that his conduct would prevent the victim's testimony. While no such rule in forfeiture cases was imposed (and while the composition of the Court has since changed), it is still an indication of a willingness of at least some justices to potentially treat domestic violence cases differently in the context of confrontation issues. This willingness suggests that a doctrinal exception to confrontation doctrine for these cases is not out of reach.

CONCLUSION

> "We concur . . . that much of this law is archaic, paradoxical and full of compromises and compensations . . . But somehow it has proven a workable even if clumsy system . . . To pull one misshapen stone out of the grotesque structure is more likely simply to upset its present balance between adverse interests than to establish a rational edifice."

The above quote is from the 1948 Supreme Court decision *Michelson v. United States*, a decision concerning the use of character evidence by the prosecution, but is a quote that in fact is appropriate here. The quote reflects the idea that our system of criminal justice and the rules that govern that system constantly engage in delicate balancing and intricate trade-offs that only appear logical or justifiable when viewed as an overall cohesive framework. To examine one portion of the arrangement in isolation may create the appearance of unfairness or inequity. Only when that one piece of the structure is examined in conjunction with another piece does the system become workable and justifiable. Thus in isolation, it may appear unfair to carve out a domestic violence exception to the Confrontation Clause, for such an exception unquestionably infringes upon a defendant's constitutional right to confront his accuser. But as detailed in this Article, once one considers the nature of the crime of domestic violence, the particular challenges faced by prosecutors, and the protections that still exist unaffected for the defendant, it appears that such an exception in fact fits into the "grotesque structure" of our system.

[Editor's Note: This issue continues to be key in criminal domestic violence cases when victim/survivors initially tell first responders the name of the abuser and what happened, but do not appear for trial. See, e.g., State v. William Johnson, *208 N.E.3d 949 (Ohio Ct. App. 2023)(911 recording admitted in violation of Confrontation Clause, since emergency was over as victim no longer in home, and a few minutes had passed; conviction reversed);* State v. Smith, *209 N.E.3d 883 (Ohio Ct. App. 2023 (Statements to police and EMS made in back of ambulance as victim was treated for injuries wrongly admitted because emergency was over since suspect no*

longer on scene. Amicus brief from domestic violence organizations argued court's analysis was "divorced from the realities of domestic violence." Ohio Supreme Court granted review Jan. 2024.]

PEOPLE V. MERCHANT

40 Cal.App.5th 1179 (2019)
(footnotes and citations omitted)

A jury convicted Jecarr Franswa Merchant of kidnapping, battery, and dissuading a witness after he careened down the freeway refusing girlfriend Lisa R.'s pleas to stop or let her out, pulled Lisa's hair, and flung her cell phone out the window as she tried to call 911. Lisa did not appear at trial. Applying the forfeiture-by-wrongdoing exception to the Sixth Amendment right to confrontation, the court admitted her statements to law enforcement on the day of the incident. It further allowed the prosecution to introduce evidence of Merchant's prior acts of domestic violence against Lisa and his former girlfriend, J.C. Merchant challenges the admission of both categories of evidence. Finding no error, we affirm the judgment.

FACTUAL AND PROCEDURAL BACKGROUND

Merchant and Lisa started dating in January 2014. On December 22, Lisa agreed to accompany him on a drive from Lancaster to a point near the junction with the Interstate 210 (I-210) freeway. When Merchant continued going south past I-210, Lisa asked to be dropped off, saying she had things to do. Merchant became angry and began driving recklessly. Concerned, Lisa asked to be dropped off at the shoulder. She tried to make eye contact with other drivers in hopes that someone might call for help. She managed to call 911 herself, further enraging Merchant.

As Lisa spoke to the emergency dispatcher, Merchant grabbed her by the hair and jacket. He swerved and sped at 90 to 100 miles per hour down the freeway, going on the shoulder and nearly hitting several cars. Lisa felt something bad was going to happen to her; she feared Merchant would drive to a deserted spot and beat her. Caltrans live feed cameras captured Merchant's vehicle "going crazy" on the right shoulder of the freeway while a woman passenger screamed for help and tried to get out of the moving vehicle.

Lisa told the dispatcher, "my boyfriend – he is kidnapping me. He's in my Ford Excursion. And he won't pull over. He's on [Interstate] 15 headed to San Diego, please somebody help me." She tried to convey their location and direction of travel. Furious, Merchant told her, "You're makin' me go to jail bitch. Whatever, I already got a charge like this and shit . . . I don't need this. I'll go to jail for life." At some point the 911 call dropped. When Lisa tried to call back, Merchant ripped the phone out of her hand and threw it out the window.

Merchant exited the highway and drove over a center island. Lisa tried to open the door to escape. Law enforcement caught up just as Lisa managed to shift the gear into park. Merchant's vehicle was low on gas and would not restart. A California Highway Patrol officer interviewed Lisa at the scene. She described what happened in detail and estimated Merchant drove for 10 or 12 minutes as she begged to be let out.

The Riverside County District Attorney (D.A.) filed an amended information charging Merchant with kidnapping, willful infliction of corporal injury, dissuading a witness, and robbery. The information alleged Merchant had served three prior prison terms, was previously convicted of a serious felony, and had a prior strike conviction.

The case proceeded to trial in May 2017. The court allowed the prosecution to introduce Merchant's past acts of domestic violence—two directed at Lisa and six directed at his former girlfriend, J.C.—to show his propensity for domestic violence and his intent and common plan. Lisa never appeared for trial, and the parties stipulated she was unavailable. Over defense objection, the court relied on a series of jail calls between Merchant and Lisa to apply the forfeiture-by-wrongdoing exception to the Sixth Amendment right to confrontation. Based on this ruling, the prosecution introduced Lisa's statements to the highway patrol officer on December 22.

Merchant did not testify. His primary defense was that there was no kidnapping—"What kidnapper allows his victim to call 911 and talk for ten minutes?" Counsel labeled her recorded statements a "hysterical, unbelievable version of what happened" and argued Lisa invented the kidnapping allegation because she was angry at Merchant.

The jury found Merchant guilty as charged on counts 1 and 3. On count 2, it convicted him of the lesser included offense of misdemeanor battery against a spouse or cohabitant; on count 4 it acquitted him of robbery. Merchant admitted his prior conviction allegations. In November 2017, the court sentenced him to a total term of 29 years, consisting of the eight-year upper term for count 1, doubled for the strike; a consecutive three-year middle term on count 3, doubled for the strike; two years for two of the prison priors; and a five-year enhancement for the prior serious felony conviction.

DISCUSSION

Merchant raises two claims of evidentiary error. First, he argues Lisa's hearsay statements to law enforcement were admitted in violation of his constitutional right to confront adverse witnesses. Second, he challenges the admission of prior domestic violence evidence. We find no error as to either claim.

1. Lisa's Hearsay Statements Were Properly Admitted.

With Lisa unavailable, her hearsay statements to the responding highway patrol officer were central to the prosecution's case. In addition, the prosecution relied on law enforcement witnesses to describe Lisa's past domestic violence reports. This evidence was admitted under the forfeiture-by-wrongdoing exception to Merchant's Sixth Amendment right to confrontation.

Merchant argues the court erred in applying the forfeiture-by-wrongdoing doctrine. He claims his actions in exhorting Lisa not to come to court fell short of the "wrongdoing" required to trigger the exception. Although he may have attempted to make Lisa feel guilty about attending trial, Merchant contends he did not threaten her in any of the jail calls. He further maintains that jail calls to Lisa made 16 months before trial were too remote in time to permit a nonspeculative inference that those calls secured Lisa's unavailability. We disagree. Because substantial evidence supports the court's finding that Merchant engaged in wrongdoing designed to prevent Lisa from testifying at trial, admitting Lisa's statements to law enforcement did not violate Merchant's constitutional right to confront her.

a. Legal Principles

A criminal defendant has a Sixth Amendment right "to be confronted with the witnesses against him." A court may not admit a witness's testimonial hearsay statements against a defendant unless the witness is unavailable and the defendant had a prior opportunity for cross-examination. Nonetheless, in narrow circumstances a defendant may forfeit his right to confrontation by his own wrongdoing. For the forfeiture-by-wrongdoing exception to apply, a defendant must have engaged in wrongful conduct *designed* to prevent a witness from testifying. Said differently, a defendant must "engag[e] in wrongdoing that renders the declarant unavailable with an intent to prevent that declarant's in-court testimony."

"[W]rongdoing" need not rise to the level of murder. "The common-law forfeiture rule was aimed at removing the otherwise powerful incentive for defendants to intimidate, bribe, and kill the witnesses against them—in other words, it is grounded in 'the ability of courts to protect the integrity of their proceedings.' " Thus in *Jones*, the defendant forfeited his right to confrontation when during phone calls from jail he dissuaded his ex-girlfriend from testifying by implying he had friends on the outside available to do "whatever [was] necessary."

The Supreme Court declined in *Davis* to decide what *procedure* courts must follow to find forfeiture by wrongdoing. But it observed that federal courts generally utilize a preponderance-of-the-evidence standard when applying a parallel hearsay exception. California courts have since adopted a preponderance standard for evaluating forfeiture by wrongdoing. We evaluate whether there is sufficient evidence from which the trial court could make its finding on a preponderance standard.

b. Application

Before trial, the prosecution filed a motion seeking to admit Lisa's out-of-court statements to law enforcement. It proffered her statements to officers on December 22, 2014 describing the charged offense as well as her statements to officers earlier that year describing domestic violence incidents on March 8 and November 21. According to the prosecution, Merchant's statements to Lisa during recorded jail calls supported application of the forfeiture-by-wrongdoing doctrine.

The court determined Lisa's statements were testimonial in nature, implicating Merchant's right to confrontation. Nevertheless, reviewing Merchant's recorded jail calls, it determined he intentionally secured Lisa's unavailability at trial and thereby forfeited his confrontation right. The judge acknowledged the case was "a lot weaker" than the usual forfeiture by wrongdoing case because Lisa was not killed or expressly threatened with harm to make her stay away. Merchant instead engaged in "more of a passive coercion." Yet there was enough evidence from the jail calls and Merchant's pattern of abuse to find by a preponderance that his actions intended to and succeeded in keeping Lisa away.

Sufficient evidence supports the trial court's finding. A criminal protective order was entered two days after the offense on December 24, 2014, precluding Merchant from any contact with Lisa. On January 6, Merchant called his friends "Groove," "Buck," and "Snake." Groove said the D.A. was in the area searching for Lisa. Buck told Merchant, "As long as she don't come in to court you could be all right." Merchant asked Groove or Snake to check in on Lisa and "keep her away for six months." Groove agreed.

On January 7, Merchant called Lisa. He told her the D.A. had offered him 15 years, but if he proceeded to trial he faced 28. He claimed his counsel recommended that Lisa "stay away for six months." Merchant said he was "scared to fuckin' go to trial 'cause if you pop up, I'm gone, like no ifs, ands, and buts—my life is gone." He told her he had asked Buck to "[g]o over there and tell my girl what's up." Although Buck had purportedly told him that Lisa would not show up, Merchant said he needed to hear it from her directly. He pressed Lisa, " "[Y]ou know I didn't kidnap[ ] you babe. You know what I'm sayin'? You know that, babe. You hear me?" and told her how stressed he was that someone could find her. Merchant told Lisa not to write him letters because she might be located. Finally, Lisa acquiesced: "Okay. I'm not." [¶] . . . [¶] "I'm not goin' over, babe. I'm with you." "Don't worry about it," she assured him, "I'm [sticking] by your side." Merchant expressed relief and thanked her. He asked, ""[S]o you want me to go through with the trial?" Lisa replied, "Yeah. 'Cause I'm not going to babe." The couple exchanged "I love you['s]" and ended the call.

Merchant called later that day to remind Lisa to stay under the radar. He told her he knew she would be there for him and reconfirmed whether he should "[g]o all the way to trial with this?" Lisa again assured him that she was not going anywhere. Merchant seemed satisfied. The call ended shortly after with an exchange of "I love you['s]."

On January 8, Merchant called Lisa to say the D.A. would have to drop charges if she did not appear for two months. Lisa assured Merchant that she was hiding from the D.A., and not to worry. Seemingly placated, Merchant instructed her to stay by the phone.

The next day, Merchant called and told Lisa not to leave the house without telling him. He told her he felt stressed, but his "homie" told him to calm down because Lisa was not going anywhere and had just been "talkin' good." Lisa told him, " "[C]alm down 'cause I ain't going nowhere"; Merchant emphasized that she needed to "lay low." Later that day, he called Lisa again and convinced her not to leave the house, even for a job interview. Two hours later, Merchant called to warn Lisa not to invite guests over.

On January 10, Lisa told Merchant she caught Snake staring at her when she went to the store. Merchant explained that Snake was just worried that Lisa would show up, and she should reassure him otherwise.

In all, Merchant called Lisa 167 times between January and May 2015. Although he made no direct threat to harm her, Lisa's friend told the D.A.'s office weeks before trial that Lisa remained terrified of what might happen to her if she came to court. Sufficient evidence supports the court's finding that Merchant engaged in wrongdoing designed to prevent Lisa from testifying. Through obsessive, repeated calls, he begged Lisa to lay low, stay at home, and not invite company, venture out, or write correspondence. He told her charges would be dismissed if she evaded detection, whereas his life would be over if she came forward. Lisa was made aware that though he was incarcerated, Merchant had friends on the outside watching her. When she equivocated that she was *trying* to stick by him, Merchant immediately responded, "You better. What the fuck you mean, you're trying to? You better." Gratitude and expressions of love followed each time Lisa promised not to appear. In the context of an abusive relationship with its dynamics of control, the trial court could reasonably find that Merchant intended to, and did, secure Lisa's nonappearance.

Jones is analogous. There, the defendant was on trial for choking *[i.e., strangling]* someone who told his ex-girlfriend that he was seeing another woman. The ex-girlfriend told detectives that she had ended her five-year relationship with the defendant because of physical violence, and that on the date of the charged offense, he had called her with the victim's cell phone to say, " 'I just choked [sic] your homegirl out and I have her phone.' " The ex-girlfriend failed to appear at trial, and jail records showed the defendant had called her a dozen times to dissuade her from testifying. Based on these calls, the trial court properly applied the forfeiture-by-wrongdoing doctrine to admit the ex-girlfriend's statements to detectives. As the court explained, applying the doctrine on these facts advanced its objective of helping courts maintain the integrity of judicial proceedings and removing incentives for defendants to intimidate, bribe, or kill witnesses who might appear against them.

Merchant attempts to distinguish *Jones*, arguing his jail calls to Lisa were more remote in time and did not so clearly cause her failure to appear. According to Merchant, "[t]here is an extremely significant difference from contacting a witness and discouraging [her] attendance at trial one week before trial, as in *Jones*, and in doing so nearly a year and a half prior to trial, as in this case." But while there may be a distinction, it is not as stark as Merchant suggests. Merchant made 167 calls over a five-month period soon after his arrest, locking in Lisa's nonappearance before he decided to reject the plea offer. Viewed in context of an abusive relationship, his pleading, cajoling, and careful monitoring of Lisa's whereabouts could reasonably be taken as a threat to induce her nonappearance at trial a year later. According to Lisa's friend, who spoke with a D.A. investigator just two weeks before trial, Lisa remained "terrified" to come forward.

The facts are sufficiently analogous to *Jones* to justify the same outcome under a preponderance-of-the-evidence standard. There was no error in applying forfeiture by wrongdoing, and admitting Lisa's statements to law enforcement at trial did not violate Merchant's constitutional right to confront her.

2. The Trial Court Did Not Err in Admitting Merchant's Prior Acts of Domestic Violence.

Merchant contends the trial court abused its discretion in admitting evidence of prior acts of domestic violence against Lisa and former girlfriend J.C. under sections 1109 and 1101, subdivision (b). Among other claims, he argues the prior act evidence should have been excluded under section 352.

a. Additional Background

Merchant had an on-and-off relationship with J.C. starting in 2005; their daughter was born in November 2013. He began dating Lisa in January 2014, 11 months before being charged in this case. Prior to trial, the prosecution filed a motion in limine to admit Merchant's prior acts of physical violence against Lisa and J.C. According to the prosecution, the 11 prior acts against the women and a 12th act against Merchant's stepfather tended to show Merchant's propensity to commit domestic violence under section 1109, and/or shed light on his intent or common plan as to the charged crimes under section 1101, subdivision (b). Merchant objected to the entirety of the prior act evidence. The court addressed each piece of evidence individually, admitting only eight of the 12. It excluded the remaining evidence as minimally relevant or cumulative.

Specifically, the court found two prior acts involving Lisa admissible:

- On March 8, 2014, Merchant was upset that Lisa was not ready for bed and pushed her several times in the face and chest. Charges for this incident were separately pending at trial. The trial court found this evidence admissible under section 1109 to show propensity and concluded that because Lisa would not testify, its presentation would consume little time for purposes of [Evidence Code] section 352.
- On November 21, 2014, Lisa and Merchant got into an argument while she was driving a vehicle. He punched her in the side of the head and pulled her hair. When she stopped for gas, he drove away and left her stranded. Charges for this incident were separately pending at trial. This evidence was found admissible under section 1109. In addition, given the similarities to the charges, it was admissible to show that Merchant acted pursuant to a common plan and not by mistake or accident under section 1101, subdivision (b). Section 352 did not require exclusion given the high probative value and minimal consumption of time.

Likewise, the court found six events concerning J.C. admissible:

- In April or May 2008, while J.C. was driving on the freeway with Merchant in the passenger seat, he punched her in the stomach and shoulder and threw her cell phone in the backseat. When J.C. stopped the car, he retrieved the phone, called a friend, and said he wanted to kill J.C. but did not want to go to jail. He then threatened J.C. that he could kill her if he wanted and proceeded to throw her cell phone outside the car. This court found this evidence admissible to show propensity under section 1109 and common plan and intent under section 1101, subdivision (b).
- On an unspecified date, Merchant asked J.C. to perform a sexual act. She refused and wanted to go home. Merchant prevented her from leaving, pushing her onto the bed. As she reached across the bed for her phone to call the police, he grabbed her hard by the hair and threatened to shoot her. The court found this evidence admissible to show propensity under section 1109 and intent under section 1101, subdivision (b).

- On August 11, 2008, Merchant pushed J.C. and hit her in the ear and thigh. When she stepped outside to leave, he grabbed her belongings and took them inside. She tried to retrieve them, but Merchant kicked her. This evidence was admissible to show propensity under section 1109 and intent under section 1101, subdivision (b).
- On July 25, 2009, while Merchant was driving on the freeway, J.C. tried to end their relationship. Merchant punched her and refused to take her home. He instead drove J.C. to his house and took away her keys to prevent her from leaving. J.C. eventually managed to grab her keys and leave. This evidence was admissible under section 1109 and under 1101, subdivision (b) to show common plan and intent.
- Merchant called J.C. nearly 100 times over a two-week period in November 2010, in violation of a criminal protective order. When J.C. asked to be left alone, Merchant threatened that they would remain together "til death." This evidence was admissible under section 1109 and under 1101, subdivision (b) to show common plan and intent. Section 352 narrowed how this "100 calls" evidence could be presented. As the trial court explained: "The fact that it happened over a hundred times is one thing. But the fact that all the calls are played would be another."
- In May 2011, Merchant pleaded guilty to false imprisonment of J.C. in connection with the July 25, 2009 incident. This evidence was admissible under section 1109 to show propensity and under section 1101, subdivision (b) to show common plan and intent.

By contrast, the court excluded the following four acts as minimally probative or cumulative:

- In early 2008, when J.C. tried to break up with Merchant, he became angry and would not let her leave. He grabbed her necklace and broke it. When J.C. got in her car to drive away, Merchant threw a jewelry box at the car, damaging the rear tail light. This evidence was inadmissible under sections 1109 and 1101, subdivision (b) because the extent of physical violence was "minimally relevant." The court also excluded it under section 352 explaining, "there's a cumulative nature to these," and "[a]t some point, the number of incidents becomes . . . more prejudicial than probative."
- In August 2009, Merchant threatened J.C., who was then on probation, that he could make her life miserable and put her back in jail. The court found this inadmissible under sections

1109 and 1101, subdivision (b) because "there's no physical violence," and the evidence did not tend to show a common plan. It also found the evidence cumulative under section 352.

- In 2011, while awaiting trial in another case, Merchant relentlessly called J.C. and threatened to hurt her unless she sent him nude pictures. Once she did so, he threatened to share the pictures with her family and coworkers, stating he was not going to jail for no bitch. The court deemed this evidence cumulative under section 352, since it was encompassed within the "100 calls" evidence admitted above. And to the extent it was offered just to show that Merchant had made threats, it was inadmissible under sections 1109 or 1101, subdivision (b).
- In January 2006, Merchant threatened his stepfather at gunpoint not to touch his property. He was convicted for criminal threats and imprisoned for four years, eight months. This was inadmissible under section 1109 and minimally relevant for a noncharacter purpose under section 1101, subdivision (b) because the victim was not in a dating relationship with Merchant.

b. Legal Principles

Character evidence is generally inadmissible to prove a defendant's conduct on a specific occasion. But specific acts of prior misconduct may be offered for a noncharacter purpose, such as to show intent, common plan, or identity. When other act evidence is introduced under section 1101, subdivision (b), the degree of similarity required with the charged offense depends on the purpose for which it is offered. "The least degree of similarity between the uncharged act and the charged offense is required to support a rational inference of intent; a greater degree of similarity is required for common design or plan; the greatest degree of similarity is required for identity."

In addition, the Legislature has carved out specific exceptions to the ban on propensity evidence for defendants charged with sex crimes (§ 1108, subd. (a)) and domestic violence (§ 1109, subd. (a)). Subject to conditions not relevant here, "in a criminal action in which the defendant is accused of an offense involving domestic violence, evidence of the defendant's commission of other domestic violence is not made inadmissible by Section 1101 if the evidence is not inadmissible pursuant to Section 352." The statute reflects the Legislature's determination that in domestic violence cases, similar prior offenses are uniquely probative of a defendant's guilt on a later occasion. "Domestic violence" includes abuse against a girlfriend or former girlfriend.

Even if other act evidence is relevant and admissible under section 1101, subdivision (b) or section 1109, it must be excluded under section 352 where its probative value is substantially outweighed by the probability that its admission will consume too much time, cause undue prejudice, confuse the issues, or mislead the jury. The prejudice that section 352 is designed to avoid is not the damage that naturally results from highly probative evidence, but rather the prospect of leading the jury to prejudge a person or focus on extraneous factors. We review the admission of other act evidence for abuse of discretion.

c. Analysis

We readily conclude that the trial court did not err in admitting eight items of other act evidence under sections 1109 and 1101, subdivision (b). Merchant was accused of kidnapping Lisa, inflicting physical abuse, dissuading her from seeking assistance, and robbing her during the chaotic car ride. Prior act evidence admitted by the court was highly probative because it shared broad similarities with the charged conduct. Three of the prior acts involved Merchant hitting or punching his then-girlfriend in a moving vehicle. Two involved Merchant preventing J.C. from using her cell phone to call for help. In three instances, Merchant prevented J.C. from leaving or grabbed her belongings as she tried to leave. Two prior acts showed Merchant's propensity for engaging in physical violence against Lisa, the victim in this case. That Merchant incessantly called J.C. from jail in violation of a criminal protective order bolstered evidence at trial that he had done the same to Lisa. None of the prior acts occurred more than 10 years before the charged offenses [as required by 1109].

Taken together, the prior act evidence demonstrated Merchant's pattern of control in romantic relationships. He tended to convert verbal disagreements with his girlfriend into physical abuse, inflict physical violence (including in a moving vehicle), prevent her from leaving, and block her attempts to call for help. This pattern was highly probative of his propensity to engage in similar conduct on December 22 as charged. It was also highly probative of his intent (lack of mistake) and common plan or pattern of behavior in committing the charged offenses. Given the nature of the evidence, the court reasonably found that the probative value of admission outweighed its prejudicial effect.

It is significant that the court excluded four items of prior act evidence. In three of the excluded incidents, Merchant merely threatened J.C. or caused property damage. The extent of physical violence in these incidents was found minimally probative to the case. The court further reasoned that at some point, domestic violence evidence concerning J.C. became cumulative and more prejudicial than probative. It excluded Merchant's criminal threat against his stepfather—the victim was not someone Merchant had dated, and the act was minimally probative of his intent or common plan.

As we read the record, the trial court carefully weighed relevant factors to admit acts that bore a reasonable similarity to the charged offenses and exclude those deemed cumulative or minimally probative. The admitted domestic violence evidence was highly probative and not *unduly* prejudicial, as it did not invite the jury to prejudge Merchant or consider extraneous factors. Merchant complains of the "sheer volume of incidents introduced," but the court's decision to admit eight out of 12 items, rather than just five or three fell squarely within its purview. Simply put, we cannot say the court abused the discretion it so clearly exercised.

We reject each of Merchant's arguments to the contrary. He claims the incidents involving J.C. had no probative value. But the fact that Merchant engaged in domestic violence against two different women *strengthens* its probative value on propensity. Courts have consistently rejected his next claim—that the admission of propensity evidence under section 1109 violates due process. Proper application of section 1101, subdivision (b) likewise does not implicate due process.

Merchant argues the instruction on propensity evidence invited the jury to convict him under a lower standard of proof. The jury was told to evaluate whether prior acts of domestic violence occurred under a preponderance standard. The instruction explained that a finding that abuse occurred was a single factor to consider and insufficient standing alone to prove guilt. It also made clear that even if past domestic violence occurred, the prosecution still had to prove each charge and allegation beyond a reasonable doubt. As Merchant concedes, courts have consistently rejected the claim he makes.

Finally, Merchant argues his 2011 conviction for false imprisonment was inadmissible under section 1109 because it was not a qualifying act of domestic violence. Domestic violence includes "abuse" directed against a girlfriend, which in turn "means intentionally or recklessly causing or attempting to cause bodily injury, or placing another person in reasonable apprehension of imminent serious bodily injury to himself or herself, or another." The 2011 conviction stemmed from a July 2009 incident in which Merchant punched J.C. while driving on the freeway, refused to take her home, and prevented her from leaving when they reached his house. This qualified as domestic violence because his acts placed J.C. in reasonable apprehension of serious bodily injury. Our conclusion does not turn on whether there was evidence "about how J.C. felt" during the incident.

3. Sufficiency of the Evidence

Merchant makes a two-sentence argument that his convictions must be reversed for insufficient evidence. This contention turns entirely on his two claims of evidentiary error. Absent improperly admitted hearsay and propensity evidence, Merchant maintains there is insufficient evidence to sustain the convictions. Because we find no error in the admission of Lisa's unconfronted statements, or in the admission of prior domestic violence evidence, we likewise reject his insufficiency-of-the-evidence claim.

Defenses

[Editor's Note: Domestic abusers have claimed many defenses when they are charged with assaulting or killing their partners. In Allen v. Barnes, *excerpted above, the defendant claimed that even though he intentionally pointed a shotgun at his girlfriend, the shooting was accidental as he did not expect or intend for it to go off.*

In Giles v. California, *discussed in* Beltran v. Warden, *excerpted above, the defendant claimed he shot his girlfriend in self-defense even though she had no weapon and was lying on the ground.*

Another defense often used by domestic abusers is provocation. In the amicus brief submitted to the California Supreme Court in 2012 as part of the Beltran *case, amici Ca. Partnership to End Domestic Violence and others argued that the provocation defense is often used by men who habitually abused their victims before killing them, stating that the victims "made them do it." The brief urged the court to "reevaluate its precedents holding that perceived intimate partner disputes may constitute legally adequate provocation—that is, provocation that might cause a 'reasonable man' to lose control . . . The provocation defense should not shield habitual domestic abusers because, contrary to the assumptions underlying the defense, they do not kill in a tragic momentary loss of self-control. The empirical evidence shows that habitual abusers consciously and intentionally deploy a campaign of violence to control their intimate partners. The evidence in this case shows that the defendant here typifies this profile."*

As is clear from the 2015 habeas decision, neither the jury nor the appellate courts gave credence to Beltran's defense that the victim provoked him. However, the provocation defense is still employed in some homicide cases where there has been a history of the defendant abusing the victim.

Some people have suggested that there should be a statutory provision allowing survivors of abuse, but not abusers, to claim provocation in appropriate cases. This can be complicated to prove, since the survivor may have had a restraining order issued against her (or him) for self-defensive conduct, or the abuser might have called the police on the survivor.]

VICTORIA AJAYI, VIOLENCE AGAINST WOMEN: THE ETHICS OF INCORPORATING THE CULTURAL DEFENSE IN LEGAL NARRATIVE

25 Geo. J. Legal Ethics 401 (2012)
(footnotes omitted)

INTRODUCTION

The cultural defense is a defense that is sometimes used by immigrants in domestic violence cases to argue a lack of mens rea, or the requisite intent to commit a crime. The crime committed might be an action condoned in the immigrant's foreign culture, or something might have happened that was so shocking and contrary to the immigrant's cultural norms that he committed a crime in the heat of passion.

Because the cultural defense can apply in a variety of cases, it is difficult to establish a bright-line rule concerning the cultural defense as a whole. In some cases it seems both natural and laudable to apply the cultural defense. Advocates of the cultural defense argue that it upholds American standards of individualized justice and cultural pluralism. For example, in Yemen, chewing khat leaves is a common practice. In the United States, khat is seen as a harmful drug akin to heroin or LSD. Thus, people have suffered prosecution for illegal actions when their violation of the law can be attributed to their cultural background. In another sympathetic example, a Sikh priest needed to wear a blade in public because of his religion, but doing so violated a city ordinance. While the court found that the city ordinance did not violate the priest's freedom of religion, it still dismissed the case under judicial discretion. Here laudable principles of tolerance and cultural pluralism rationalize the use of the cultural defense.

However, in domestic violence cases where men harm women, the use of the cultural defense echoes damaging ideas about women in the American psyche. The theory of cultural convergence suggests that the cultural defense is most successful when the underlying cultural norms represented by the different culture are reflected in American cultural norms. Principles of right and wrong and the determination of what is an accepted practice vary by culture, and the United States is a country of many cultures. Where the cultural defense is used to mitigate harsh sentencing for men who have abused women, it takes advantage of a poor American cultural narrative: the subjugation and abuse of women. The abuse of women is not the dusty and remote observation of feminist scholars; it is discernable to the average citizen through repeated images and suggestion in popular culture. * * *

Rather, the *Model Rules* should mandate that a lawyer first provide client counseling and in the absence of the client's willingness to use an alternative argument, excuse herself from the case. With regard to cases of violence against women, the availability of the cultural defense is an argument so dangerous that, when successfully used, it can have fatal consequences, inasmuch as it sends the message that immigrant men can be tried for killing their wives and escape serving time in jail. After hearing about a case where a man used the cultural defense to avoid a jail sentence for killing an unfaithful wife, an immigrant man told his wife, "I could do anything to you. I have money for a good attorney." Thus, to avoid the danger of reinforcing a harmful cultural narrative and to promote the safety of all women, the use of the cultural defense in domestic violence cases should be avoided whenever possible. * * *

III. THE APPLICATION OF THE CULTURAL DEFENSE

An overly strict application of ethical relativism can produce undesirable results in practice. In a landmark cultural defense case, *People v. Chen*, Dong Lu Chen was sentenced to five years of probation after murdering his wife with a hammer. The judge presiding over his case, Justice Edward Pincus, found that the traditional Chinese horror of cuckoldry led Chen to murder his wife. Burton Pasternak, a white anthropologist, testified about Chinese cultural norms.

Chen lived and worked in Maryland, and his wife and three children lived in New York. On one visit to New York, Chen discovered that his wife was unfaithful. He reportedly became disoriented, picked up an object and struck her in the head several times. Pasternak testified that a normal Chinese person would have acted in the same violent way. Pasternak testified that in comparison to the American community, the Chinese community has heightened social control over its members. Chen had earlier claimed to hear voices in his head; Pasternak's suggestion was that the voices Chen heard were the voices of Chinese society.

Professor Leti Volpp asserts that Pasternak's testimony was "bizarre" and a representation of an American fantasy of Chinese society rather than an accurate representation of Chinese society. For example, Pasternak was unable to recount an example of when a Chinese man actually killed his wife in the face of adultery. Instead he based his testimony on the idea that a Chinese man would have difficulty remarrying because his wife's adultery would have exposed him as a man unable to control his family. In delivering the sentence, Justice Pincus referred to Chen as a victim. Society had failed him by not stopping him from killing his wife in time, and society's failure to stop Chen was the result of the chasm between American and Chinese culture. According to Volpp:

> The defense presented a narrative that relied on her invisibility as an Asian woman for its logical coherence . . . manifest through the absence of Jian Wan Chen as a subject, a void that was filled only by stereotypes of the sexual relationships of "Chinese women" . . . [and] also a remnant of the indifference with which many in the United States treat the epidemic of violence against women.

IV. CULTURAL CONVERGENCE AND THE NARRATIVE OF VIOLENCE AGAINST WOMEN

Cynthia Lee posits that cultural convergence may have influenced the outcome in *Chen*. Cultural convergence theory asserts that cultural defense arguments are more successful when the cultural norms of the different culture converge with American cultural norms. With regard to *Chen*, Lee takes note of a history of pardoning American men who kill their wives. "The reason behind the success of the Asian immigrant man's provocation claim may not so much be because of his immigrant status, but rather because his underlying claim is familiar and resonates with the judge and jury."

Thus, although Justice Pincus stated otherwise, Lee asserts that the ruling was influenced by the American cultural norm of sympathy for a man driven to kill after the adultery of his wife. Feminists, however, acknowledge that, while individualized justice and cultural plurality are proper goals of the criminal justice system, the call for multiculturalism must not strengthen sex-based stereotypes that promote violence against women.

Lee's theory of cultural convergence with regard to violence against women is important because it combats the use of ethical relativism as a support system for the cultural defense. With respect to violence against women, the cultural defense can serve as a way to reinforce American cultural notions of violence against women rather than a way to respect the disparate traditions of our pluralistic society. While the cultural defense has been successfully used by women, it is "far more often used by immigrant men who abuse, rape or kill immigrant women." Allowing the cultural defense in cases of abuse against women takes advantage of an American cultural narrative where women are to blame for their own abuse. For example, in the case of Mr. Chen, his wife was culpable in her own murder because she acted outside of Chinese cultural norms by cheating on her husband.

The idea that the female victim of domestic violence is culpable for her own abuse is something of a motif in cases where the cultural defense converges with domestic violence. For example, in *People v. Aphaylath*, the court held that the lower court should have included cultural evidence where a Cambodian man murdered his wife for taking a phone call from another man. Using the cultural defense in this case suggests that the wife—the victim—was culpable in her own murder because she accepted a phone call from a man who was not her husband.

If the man had been an American without influences from another culture, could he have replaced evidence of his disparate culture with evidence of his love for his wife? Perhaps he loved his wife so deeply that when she received a phone call from another man (presumed to be her lover) he lost his mind and killed her in the heat of passion. Allowing the cultural defense as a mitigating factor in cases of abuse against women reinforces ideas of womankind as property, as properly submissive, and disposable. * * *

After the ruling in *Chen*, one man informed his wife that if that was the outcome of murdering your wife in America, she had better be careful because he had the option of murdering her as well.

In American culture, there is a narrative of women as weak, dominated, submissive, abused, and helpless. Even outside of the perhaps esoteric annals of American case law, the cultural acceptance of violence against women is prevalent. Popular culture commonly promotes and exploits the subjugation and objectification of women. Using the cultural defense in cases of violence against women accesses that narrative and reinforces a derogatory idea in the American psyche, the idea that women are to blame when men abuse them. For example, a study of femicide in the news found that women explicitly and implicitly received the blame for their own murders. Female victims were described with negative language, and narratives showcased the woman's own failure to report instances of abuse before her death. Killers were described with sympathetic language, their mental and economic weaknesses highlighted, and the murder of the woman was depicted as an event in which the woman and her murderer evenly divided the blame between them. * * *

When the norms of another culture reflect American cultural norms, that disparate culture is more likely to be understood. Thus, where the cultural defense is successfully used, it reflects an American cultural narrative in which women are objectified, abused, and blamed for their own abuse. Rather than advancing this harmful narrative through use of the cultural defense, a lawyer should refrain from using it because the social costs are too high.

CHAPTER 12

JUDGES, COURTS AND SENTENCING BATTERERS

■ ■ ■

In this chapter, we examine the role of the court in domestic violence cases. The first two articles focus on domestic violence courts. While these courts can be very beneficial in reducing recidivism and protecting victims, the materials stress that courts alone cannot stop domestic violence, but must be part of a larger coordinated community response. A third article notes the importance of family courts identifying and stopping litigation abuse by batterers, a common post-separation tactic. Next comes a piece about how COVID has impacted domestic violence courts.

The following article looks at why many of the players in the legal system, including judges, have so little attention for domestic violence cases. It suggests that part of the solution is "compassionate witnessing," which encompasses becoming aware of the impact of this work on everyone involved, including judges, attorneys, ourselves, and others, and reaching for connection and healing in ourselves and in those around us.

The second half of the chapter examines sentencing practices with regard to batterers. A leading researcher summarizes what we know about the effectiveness of court-mandated batterer's intervention programs around the country and explains best practices to probation officers supervising people convicted of abusing their partners. Next is a short piece about how domestic violence courts should monitor batterers for compliance with probation conditions.

The chapter concludes with state statutes mandating the publication of domestic violence convictions, providing treatment programs for batterers in custody, and looking closely at batterers with criminal records if they apply to facilitate government-based programs for abusers.

A. ROLE OF COURTS, DOMESTIC VIOLENCE COURTS, IMPACT OF DOMESTIC VIOLENCE ON JUDGES

MELISSA LABRIOLA, SARAH BRADLEY, CHRIS S. O'SULLIVAN, MICHAEL REMPEL, AND SAMANTHA MOORE, A NATIONAL PORTRAIT OF DOMESTIC VIOLENCE COURTS

Center for Court Innovation (2010)
(now Center for Justice Innovation)
(citations omitted)

Executive Summary * * * Conclusions

The number of specialized domestic violence courts is continuing to grow nationwide. We identified 208 courts that have specialized dockets or dedicated judges, an increase of more than 150 courts since the last national study a decade ago identified only 42 domestic violence courts. Specialized domestic violence courts can be found in 32 states across the Northeast, South, Midwest, and West, as well as in the territory of Guam. It is notable, however, that California and New York account for nearly half the total.

We found consensus among court stakeholders with respect to the primary rationales for creating a domestic violence court: increased victim safety, offender accountability, and deterring of future violence. Qualitative data, however, revealed differing expectations of which policies and practices would achieve these aspirations. Moreover, we found substantial divergence in the importance assigned to other goals, such as fostering judicial expertise, correctly applying state statutes, and achieving a coordinated response to domestic violence. We also found diversity in the structure of today's domestic violence courts and in the practices adopted across many domains. These domains included the availability of victim services and safety measures (such as safe spaces and escorts in the court), the use of offender assessments and programs, and practices related to offender accountability (such as sanctions for noncompliant offenders).

These findings highlight an important distinction between domestic violence courts and other problem-solving models, particularly drug and mental health courts, which have a more clearly delineated structure and widely shared set of core goals, policies, and practices. We hope that these results constitute a useful first step in stimulating the field to engage in greater information exchange and collaboration, perhaps leading to the development of a more consistent set of policies and practices, or at least fostering greater mutual understanding of the alternative goals, policies, and models that exist today. * * *

Chapter 1

* * * The multiplicity of goals of domestic violence court is a natural consequence of their disparate origins. As early as the 1970s, the feminist and battered women's movements began to reshape many aspects of the criminal justice response to domestic violence. Activists promoted the recognition of domestic violence not as a private matter but as a crime, spawning the passage of federal and state laws requiring consistent enforcement and greater attention to the safety of abused women. Pro-arrest policies, evidence-based prosecution, and specialized police and prosecution units all emerged as a result. Change accelerated with the passage of the Violence Against Women Act in 1994, which established federal pro-arrest laws and funding mechanisms for victim services and other innovations.

These reforms led to a massive influx of domestic violence cases into criminal courts nationwide. Whether to provide a more intensive focus on the unique problems posed by domestic violence cases, to enforce new domestic violence laws with a consistent approach, or to cope more efficiently with the ballooning case volume, the results provided a number of reasons to handle domestic violence cases in a specialized courtroom.

During the 1990s and early 2000s, jurisdictions began to create *specialized* courts to handle cases that share a common underlying problem. Generally known as "problem-solving courts" (or "collaborative justice courts" in California), more than 3,000 have been established nationwide, including drug courts, mental health courts, community courts, and domestic violence courts. Each model tackles a different set of issues, from drug addiction to mental illness to community disorganization, but they all seek improved outcomes for defendants, litigants, victims, and communities by addressing the underlying issue that led the offender to commit the crime.

Most problem-solving courts also share a number of common practices, such as referral to community-based programs, ongoing compliance monitoring, and collaboration among multiple justice and community partners. To provide centralized oversight spanning the different models, more than a dozen states have established a statewide problem-solving court coordinator.

Even though they emerged concurrently with the broader problem-solving court movement, domestic violence courts do not reflect all the movement's principles and practices as just summarized. Most problem-solving courts focus on victimless crimes. Drug and mental health courts, for instance, deal with nonviolent offenses and can focus their attention on the defendant. In domestic violence cases, not only is there a victim but also the same victim is at ongoing risk of being assaulted by the same offender. Domestic violence courts have a responsibility to the victim, and often provide services for them in addition to addressing the criminal behavior of the defendant. At the same time, victim advocates have argued that the criminal justice system has not treated assaults by intimate partners as seriously as similar crimes committed against strangers or acquaintances.

Perhaps more critically, most problem-solving court models operate under the assumption that the defendant's criminal behavior stems from underlying problems that treatment or services can resolve. Although many if not most domestic violence courts subscribe to this analysis as well, the premise is controversial in regard to domestic violence offenders. Many agencies that work with victims of domestic violence argue that the underlying problem is not an aberration or treatable illness of individual offenders but of societal values. Furthermore, among researchers, there is considerable doubt over whether court-mandated programs can succeed at rehabilitation in this area.

In some states, statutes and policies have influenced the planning and operations of domestic violence courts. For example, California, Florida, and North Carolina have statutes specifying mandatory sentences and monitoring requirements for those convicted of domestic violence crimes. In these states, domestic violence courts may be seen as a logical mechanism to promote the proper execution of statutes, such as mandatory sentences to probation and batterer programs. In other states that allow greater discretion in charging and sentencing, domestic violence court models may be more variable and depend on the goals and resources of the individual court.

For all of the above reasons, domestic violence courts reflect neither unified origins nor a unified approach, but they do share common goals. Domestic violence courts also lack a single information clearinghouse as exists with drug courts (National Association of Drug Court Professionals), leading many such courts to reflect specific local or statewide approaches. Thus, a comprehensive list of the country's domestic violence courts did not exist until its collection as part of this study, an undertaking that was fraught with difficulties, described in chapter 3. It remains to be seen whether such a list will be routinely updated and whether cross-fertilization among domestic violence courts will become the norm.

Domestic Violence Courts Today

Variations in Definitions of Domestic Violence Courts

One important distinction among domestic violence courts is that some are criminal courts and some are civil courts. Several states, however, including New York and Florida, are experimenting with "integrated" domestic violence courts that combine civil and criminal functions so that a single court can hear both types of cases involving the same defendant or family members. * * *

History and Evolution of Domestic Violence Courts

In 2000, the National Center for State Courts surveyed 160 courts that seemed to have implemented some type of specialized case management for domestic violence cases. These practices ranged from a specialized intake unit dedicated to domestic violence cases or defined set of policies and practices for monitoring compliance among domestic violence offenders to a full specialized court with a dedicated judge and calendar. Of the 103 responding courts, 42 indicated that they had in fact established a criminal domestic violence court. This survey provided the first source of information on domestic violence court policies. It revealed consensus in regard to the goals of assisting victims, enhancing victim safety, and increasing defendant accountability but great diversity with regard to court practice and structure. Keilitz (2001) suggested that many of the courts lacked the supporting practices and service linkages necessary to achieve their goals.

Most of the courts reported having specialized mechanisms in place for handling domestic violence cases, such as case screening and identification, intake units, and court-ordered batterer programs or, as mentioned above, dedicated calendars and judges. Few courts, however, reported using all of these practices together, and Keilitz was unable to detect a common configuration or strategy for the application of these practices. Keilitz concluded that "the concept of a domestic violence court is not yet well developed or defined among the court community."

This conclusion was reinforced in Shelton's 2007 report that attempted to update Keilitz's catalog of specialized courts within the United States. Using the internet, Shelton identified what were believed to be 51 additional domestic violence courts. Shelton confirmed Keilitz's impression that domestic violence courts continued to be developed in a "piecemeal fashion" and speculated that "the crucial infusion of federal funds for the establishment of such courts was done in a way that resulted in the development of alternative models in various locales."

Goals and Outcome Assessments

Since domestic violence courts lack a common vision or set of practices, it is not surprising that attempts to assess the impact of domestic violence courts have different findings. Approximately a dozen studies have tested the impact of domestic violence courts on overlapping outcomes. The following discussion reviews the findings related to court efficiency, interagency coordination, informed decision making, victim services, offender accountability, and recidivism. * * *

A reduction in recidivism could be a result of therapeutic treatment or deterrence mechanisms. The most recent reviews conclude that batterer programs, the primary treatment mechanism used by domestic violence courts, produce no or extremely modest effects. Domestic violence courts might still reduce recidivism through the deterrent effects of increased monitoring and consequences for noncompliance, however. Few studies have been conducted regarding the effectiveness of these mechanisms, and even fewer have used an experimental or rigorous quasi-experimental design. A quasi-experiment conducted in the Bronx found no significant difference in re-offending rates between offenders who were mandated to judicial monitoring and those who were not. The authors noted, however, that the Bronx court did not implement a strong form of judicial monitoring, that court appearances were monthly at most, that judicial interactions with the offenders were neither clear nor probing, and that sanctions were not consistently imposed for noncompliance. They interpret the findings to indicate that mere "surveillance" does not appear to reduce recidivism, leaving open the question of whether a truly rigorous form of judicial supervision might have positive effects.

Summary

* * * The literature does suggest that domestic violence courts expedite processing of misdemeanor cases. Findings suggest that victims are more satisfied and more likely to access services if a case is heard in a domestic violence court rather than a traditional court. These courts also appear to make greater use than non-specialized courts of several potential accountability mechanisms: program mandates, judicial monitoring, intensive probation, and penalties for noncompliance with court orders to programs. Yet, only a handful of studies have rigorously examined any of these features of domestic violence courts. * * *

ANAT MAYTAL, SPECIALIZED DOMESTIC VIOLENCE COURTS: ARE THEY WORTH THE TROUBLE IN MASSACHUSETTS?

18 B.U. Pub. Int. L. J. 197 (2008)
(footnotes omitted)

* * * III. Specialized Domestic Violence Courts—In Depth

* * * A. Initial Roots in New York

As domestic violence courts gain recognition across the country, many jurisdictions are reevaluating their own judicial response to cases of domestic violence, debating whether to institute similar courts, and if so, determining how to administer these courts most effectively. For guidance, many turn to the state where the specialized domestic violence court first originated—New York.

The first New York domestic violence court opened in Brooklyn in 1996 and handled felony-level domestic violence cases. The model court featured a single presiding judge, a fixed prosecutorial team, and a court staff who received special training in domestic violence issues. The model incorporated computer technology allowing judges to closely monitor defendants to ensure their compliance with court orders; probation programs that bring defendants back into court for "post-disposition monitoring;" and a wide range of support services for victims including "counseling, safety planning, and links to housing."

The court also launched a public education campaign to "change the way the criminal justice community viewed domestic violence." Through educational programs and partnerships, the court aimed to "stimulate a more coordinated response to domestic violence" that went beyond the interiors of the courtrooms. As a result, the court established a "court partners' meeting," which included judges, court personnel, victim advocates, prosecutors, defense attorneys, probation and parole officers, representatives from batterers programs, and social service agencies. The court partners meeting convened every six weeks to allow the various agencies to "exchange information and ideas on the most effective way to respond to domestic violence." For example, discussions at these meetings revealed that many offenders left prison without knowing that the original order of protection for their victims was still in effect. To ensure offenders were well-informed, the domestic violence court established a procedure requiring parolees to return to court for a formal review of their order of protection.

A study in 2001 by the Urban Institute Justice Police Center demonstrated that the Brooklyn model has produced promising results only five years after its initial launch in 1996. Virtually every victim with a case pending was offered extensive services, such as housing, job training, and safety-planning. Prior to the court's opening, only about 55 percent of domestic violence victims were assigned to a victim advocate. But after the court opened, the percentage increased to virtually 100 percent. The percentage of protection orders issued in these cases increased from 87 percent to 98 percent and the court helped cut the dismissal rate in half—from 8 percent to 4 percent. Furthermore, while conviction rates increased only slightly (from 87 to 94 percent), plea bargaining was utilized more often and "convictions by guilty pleas were more common and trials were less common," which represented "a cost-savings to the court system."

The success in Brooklyn served as a model for nearly thirty other domestic violence courts in other New York jurisdictions. More recently, the state court system has launched "integrated" domestic violence courts on a trial basis. These multi-jurisdictional courts allow a single judge to oversee criminal cases, orders of protection, custody, visitation, and divorce matters for one family. These courts are viewed as a practical solution to simplify the court process for families in distress, "creating an environment where litigants no longer have to navigate multiple courts systems simultaneously and reducing the risk they will receive conflicting orders." * * *

2. The Quincy Domestic Violence Prevention Program

To ensure that abused women have access to the full protection of the law, the Commonwealth has implemented several model programs, starting with the 1987 launch of Quincy District Court's Domestic Violence Prevention Program (hereinafter "Quincy Program"). The Quincy Program was "the first of its kind in Massachusetts to integrate the traditionally separate roles of clerks, judges, district attorneys, probation officers, police officers, and batterers' treatment counselors."

A key goal of the Quincy Program is to "empower victims" of domestic violence and provide maximum support to them. To assist plaintiffs seeking protections, the Quincy District Court provides trained clerks to help victims fill out forms necessary to obtain retraining orders and to accompany them to court. In addition, to ensure abused women are familiar with the system, the district attorney's office holds daily briefing sessions to explain to victims their rights, the court process, community resources, criminal complaint options, and safety planning. In addition, the court offers two special sessions each day to expedite protection order hearings.

The Quincy Program also "cracks down on abusers" by confiscating weapons and enforcing orders prohibiting the use of alcohol or drugs, "using random testing to monitor compliance." The Quincy Program has a regular probation revocation session during which judges review complaints of restraining order violations and "may revoke probation without waiting for a new criminal trial and conviction." This accelerated enforcement procedure was incorporated into the Quincy Program "because probation violators [can] pose tremendous safety risks to their victims." Offenders who violate restraining orders may be sentenced to incarceration, but more often they are sent to specialized treatment programs for substance abuse, anger management, and rehabilitation. *[Editor's Note: As Andrew Klein notes later in this chapter, studies have found that anger management is largely ineffective with partner-batterers, while batterer's intervention programs may be effective.]*

As a direct result of Quincy's more integrated approach, "more and more women [have been] seeking help, appearing at court hearings, entering support groups, and taking out criminal charges." Between 1987 and 1992, there was a twofold increase in the number of women seeking restraining orders from the Quincy Court, and these victims persevered in pressing their cases two to three times more often than women in other jurisdictions. But the most significant measure of success for the Quincy Program has been the decline in deaths from battering. In 1991, the Quincy District Court had no domestic homicides, while nearby Essex County, which has a similar population and size, experienced fifteen domestic murders. * * *

i. Combined Civil-Criminal Jurisdictions

The disjunction between civil and criminal jurisdictions is a critical issue and one that many models of specialized domestic violence courts address. These specialized courts are structured to integrate jurisdiction for domestic violence-related criminal cases (both misdemeanors and felonies) and civil protection order dockets. Combining these jurisdictions not only results in efficient adjudication of domestic violence but also encourages the court and prosecutors to take any and all domestic violence incidents seriously, rather than dismissing what would be labeled as minor domestic bickering.

* * * Also in place is a new post-conviction compliance process, known as "judicial review hearings." The judges schedule review hearings at 30, 60, and 120 days after sentencing to better monitor offender compliance and use "graduated sanctions and rewards to motivate offender compliance with probation officers and the terms and conditions of probation."

The Clark County Domestic Violence Court in Vancouver, Washington illustrates effectively the structure of a system which combines criminal and civil jurisdictions. * * * Furthermore, the streamlining has shortened excessive time delays in processing domestic violence cases, making it an administrative advantage for specialized courts.

ii. Judicial Insensitivity

The Dorchester Court has considered proposals for more and improved judicial training and historically has worked to develop a coordinated response to domestic violence. Beginning in 1991, a Dorchester Court judge initiated the Dorchester Court Roundtable, allowing judges to come together "to share knowledge, discuss areas of concern, brainstorm about potential solutions and spark experimentation." The roundtables take place more than once a year and usually begin with a panel or presentation by judges. The afternoon sessions usually include discussions by experts on relevant issues, such as "offender accountability, innovations in high volume domestic violence court models, engaging the defense bar, judicial ethics and leadership."

In addition, the Dorchester Court judges were active participants of the Massachusetts District Court Professional Development Group for Abuse Prevention Proceedings, which developed the "Trial Courts' Guidelines for Judicial Practice in Abuse Prevention Proceedings." All judges assigned to the Dorchester Domestic Violence Court have since adhered to these guidelines and routinely emphasize to offenders that "domestic violence is a serious crime, and not a personal problem or lesser matter." Judges often sanction offenders with jail or probation with conditions that include the successful completion of a Massachusetts Department of Public Health certified batterer intervention program and, if needed, substance abuse treatment. The Trial Court also began conducting, in 1994, two-day training programs for all Massachusetts District Court judges and has provided similar training for all new judges since then.

c. Results of Specialization

Available data on the impact of the specialized Dorchester Court shows that its results are very positive. In a 2001–2003 comparison study, the Urban Institute evaluated the three specialized domestic violence courts the JOD Initiative developed in (1) Dorchester, Massachusetts (2) Milwaukee, Wisconsin, and (3) Washtenaw County, Michigan.

i. Victim Services

All abuse victims that participated in the study via surveys and focus groups were "generally satisfied with the response of police, prosecutors, and the court and rated their fairness and impact on future violence positively." More victims were able to receive individualized attention and guidance as they navigated the civil and criminal court systems. In both Dorchester and Washtenaw County, victim advocates in prosecutors' offices or the court contacted at least 80 percent of victims in criminal cases and "provided an average of four or more different types of services to those contacted." In addition, two-thirds to three-quarters of victims in Dorchester and Washtenaw County reported contact with probation officers, which was "about two to three times the number of comparison victims reporting such contact" from non-specialized court systems in other states.

ii. Offender Accountability

The specialized court system also increased offender accountability in Dorchester. Offenders in Dorchester were more likely than offenders in other states to be ordered to attend a treatment program, abstain from drug and alcohol use, undergo substance abuse testing, and be assigned longer terms in batterer intervention programs. In addition, since offenders in Dorchester were more likely to be convicted and sentenced—and more likely to be sent to jail or probation—they were correspondingly more likely to comply. Given the seriousness of the sentences, Dorchester experienced a dramatic increase in probation compliance from 221 offenders in 2001 to 602 in 2003, making up 90 percent of all offenders that year alone. Offenders were more likely to attend all batterer treatment program sessions and report to probation in the first two months than comparison offenders. In addition, they were significantly less likely to be re-arrested for domestic violence during their first year of probation.

* * * A. Judicial opposition

Judges may be opposed to the creation of specialized criminal domestic violence courts. For example, elected judges in Washington State have a tendency to believe they have a mandate from the people and "a right to conduct their court as if it were their own kingdom." This predisposition, when combined with "the desire to protect their own self-contained courtrooms, creates resistance to change among judges." * * *

1. Increased Workload

Many judges are also concerned that "any change which expands the duties of judges will substantially increase their workload." This is largely true since in most domestic violence courts, the role of the judge is "a departure from standard judicial practice" in that he or she is more engaged with the community and required to "develop an understanding of the realities and limitations of service[s] . . . to victims, offenders, and children in order to sentence appropriately and to make appropriate [court] orders." The judge in the domestic violence court is likely to "adopt a more inquisitorial style by making inquiries from the bench to better inform the course of action to be taken," which is similarly the case in other problem-solving courts, such as juvenile, mental-health, and drug courts.

2. Emotional Toll and Frustration

In addition to increased workloads, judges prefer not to deal exclusively with domestic violence matters since domestic violence cases are "intensely emotional and can lead to great frustration" for judges as well as prosecutors in domestic violence units. Judges get increasingly aggravated with victims they perceive as "refusing" to leave abusive relationships. One prosecutor explained that it is "very hard to deal with individuals who don't want to help themselves." In fact, some judges have gone so far as to make insensitive comments in open court towards domestic violence petitioners who have previously dropped charges. For example, some judges have said, "oh, it's you again," or "how long are you going to stay this time," or "you want to go back and get beat up again."

Unfortunately, judges can lose sight of the fact that "dealing with the criminal process is just a small piece of what the victim must cope with because of the violence in the victim's life." Victims of domestic violence often face other issues like homelessness, unemployment, and uninsured medical concerns—all of which are "beyond the expertise and duty" of a domestic violence court judge.

3. Infringing on Separation of Powers

Some judges oppose specialization because of concerns that expanded duties within the domestic violence court will infringe on the legislature's responsibilities. * * *

However, domestic violence courts are "not entirely dissociated from the polity." District and Municipal Courts are, "by their nature, connected to the community they serve, and respond to pressures from that community." The Dorchester Court in Massachusetts received the tacit approval to launch its domestic violence courtroom through organized community roundtables and approved federal grants. Furthermore, separation of powers concerns may be unwarranted because they "confus[e] making new law with creating a new organizational structure to enforce existing laws more effectively." To the extent that domestic violence court judges collaborate with other agencies to develop new procedures or "solutions to common problems, this enhances—not usurps—the authority of the other branches of government." * * *

These factors, together with "fear of the unknown and concern that another judge may obtain some political advantage," make it difficult to embark upon a major court project like a specialized domestic violence court. * * *

V. Conclusion

" 'There's no silver bullet to solve [the] problem' of domestic violence," as Judge Fritzler of the Clark County District Court stated. In Massachusetts, there have been many efforts to address domestic violence, and specialized domestic violence courts are only one possible step for communities to take—but it is a step that more communities should take. Many are reluctant to change their court system, but this resistance can be overcome by emphasizing the benefits of specialization. A domestic violence court will not only enhance the operations of the courtrooms, but also improve procedures in police stations, provide more resources in prosecutor's offices, and garner more offender compliance within probation departments. Across the country, abuse victims have found that greater specialization provides them easier access to the system and the help they need. Simultaneously, offenders are finding it harder to get away with violent behavior. They are forced to recognize their battering for what it is: a criminal act and an act for which they must be punished. Specialized courts are highly valuable and can be credited with finally bringing genuine support and, more importantly, real justice to victims of abuse who are largely ignored by traditional court systems.

[Editor's Note: In "Legal system 'silos' are harming domestic violence victims" (SF and LA Daily Journals, 12/27/21), after 20 years on the bench, retired Superior Court Judge Eugene Hyman notes that victims of domestic violence are expected to speak to dozens of players up and down the chain of our various legal systems, from doctors and police officers to social workers and judges. He states that the system does the victim a disservice by not requiring these public servants to talk to one another. While Hyman acknowledges that the silos are well-intentioned roadblocks put in place to prohibit misuse of sensitive material, he cautions that they can make systems deaf to potential cries for help. He notes that in some cases the systems are discouraged from sharing information, which can result in abusers escaping punishment and victims and children having to repeat over and over their stories of trauma while many are being abused again. He calls for first responders, prosecutors, criminal courts, probation, social

services, family courts, dependency courts and immigration courts to re-envision themselves as collaborative partners, asking about prior abuse, receiving cross-training, and sharing information with each other.]

ROBERT NONOMURA, NICK BALA, KENNEDY MCMILLAN, ANDREW AU-YEUNG, PETER JAFFE, LISA HESLOP, KATREENA SCOTT, WHEN THE FAMILY COURT BECOMES THE CONTINUATION OF FAMILY VIOLENCE AFTER SEPARATION: UNDERSTANDING LITIGATION ABUSE

Alliance of Canadian Research Centres on Gender-Based Violence
Family Violence & Family Law Brief (# 15, July 2022)
(citations omitted)

. . .Litigation Abuse as Coercive Control

Separation and divorce are psychologically, emotionally, and financially straining though many separating couples can make reasonable and fair arrangements for economic and parenting issues without involving the courts.

If there has been violence in a relationship, however, court and professional involvement will generally be needed to protect the vulnerable and allow for a fair resolution of issues. When there has been coercive control during a relationship, after separation the perpetrator will often use the family litigation process in an abusive way not simply to gain the upper hand in negotiations or court proceedings, but to continue to dominate their target.

Litigation abuse can be understood as "an enactment of coercive control through legal processes." When coercive control is manifested in the form of litigation abuse, it is difficult to address because the abuser uses aspects of the legal system that are central to its functioning. Litigation abuse exploits the principles of due process, access to justice, and adversarial court proceedings as a way to weaponize the power of the legal system against an ex-partner.

Like other forms of family violence, litigation abuse is a gendered phenomenon. Women may misuse the court process or take unreasonable positions in settlement discussions and may, for example, make unfounded allegations of abuse against fathers though unfounded allegations of abuse are often the result of misperception or misunderstanding rather than deliberate fabrication. However, litigation abuse as an aspect of a post-separation pattern of coercive control that started during cohabitation is more commonly perpetrated by men. Men are, for example, more likely than women to decide to self-represent because they want to have the opportunity to cross-examine their former partner.

The family law system presents opportunities for coercive control to continue through court proceedings themselves. The emotional, precarious, and high-stakes circumstances of separation and divorce mean that legal proceedings provide an expedient—and "legally permissible"—means of amplifying distress and maintaining control over an ex-partner. By recognizing the contextual factors of power and control that motivate litigation abuse, courts stand a better chance of not becoming a vehicle for the coercive and controlling tactics of an abuser.

If it is identified, there are a number of potential legal responses to litigation abuse. Perhaps the most significant is that the court may regard this as a form of family violence to consider in making decisions about parenting time and responsibilities, or, as a factor in allowing the victim to relocate with the children. If a court finds that litigation abuse has occurred, this may affect an award for "costs," requiring a party who has behaved "unreasonably" in the course of litigation to pay part or all of the legal fees and litigation costs of the other party. A person who has been the subject of repeated, unmerited court applications may make an application to have another person declared a "vexatious litigant," preventing the person who has abused the legal process from bringing further court proceedings. In limited circumstances the courts may make a restraining order to prohibit certain types of behaviours associated with the court process, such as a prohibition on posting abusive information related to the proceedings on the internet.

Most of these legal responses are retrospective, in that they can be invoked only after there has been litigation abuse and generally do not directly prevent on-going litigation abuse. However, justice system professionals can have an important role in warning those who are engaging in litigation abuse that their conduct may have future consequences. Lawyers for victims may do this in correspondence, and judges may give warnings at cases conferences. Judges may also take abusive litigation conduct into account in making cost orders at interim proceedings, sending a clear message to those abusing the litigation process. Lawyers for abusers can also have a significant role in warning their clients that they may forfeit parenting rights or suffer financial consequences if they do not change their behaviour.

Douglas reported on a study based on interviews with 65 mothers who experienced FV (family violence) in Australia that highlights the many ways in which the family court system is used to further FV. . . *[Note: These behaviors and suggested solutions are relevant in many countries, including the U.S.]* Tactics intended to prolong litigation, such as unreasonable adjournment requests, were experienced by many participants. For example, an abuser would request a 6-month adjournment to drag out litigation and mediation processes, only to arrive unprepared (or seek additional adjournment) once the date arrived. Understood within the context of FV, it is important to recognize when these behaviours are not merely the result of carelessness or ineptitude. Rather, they are strategies that impose psychological, financial, and emotional distress and to maintain an omnipresence in the lives of survivors.

Likewise, spurious and dishonest claims served not only to prolong litigation, they also stymied the mothers' efforts to move forward from an abusive relationship. Adding the partner's relatives as parties to litigation added unnecessary financial stress on them, strained the survivor's family relationships and/or humiliated the survivor. Douglas's research also noted that abusers will sometimes include their own relatives in the conflict, with each one filing separate, spurious claims against the survivor to overwhelm and financially exhaust her.

Responding to a survivor's application with a counter-claim is an especially potent form of litigation abuse because of the ways they can further magnify the marginalization and burdens faced by FV survivors. One example is when a mother seeks child support, or retroactive child support, the father seeks sole or shared parenting time even though he has had little role in caring for the child. Another example is when abused mothers applying for restraining orders encounter cross-applications by their abusers alleging that the violence was bi-directional. These allegations derail legal proceedings and create unnecessary financial costs that survivors must then defend. Allegations of "parental alienation" may have similar impacts of intimidating survivors into withdrawing their own applications for restraining orders, especially if they already fear not being believed.

Ultimately, abusive litigation tactics can overwhelm a survivor's capacity to cope. What bears emphasizing is how vulnerabilities present within the specific context of the case; and these often involve disproportionate power and financial resources. As with other coercive and controlling strategies, litigation abuse is part of a pattern of behaviours that undermine, discredit, harass, and intimidate survivors—as well as disrupt their relationship with their children. With litigation abuse the "entrapment" of coercive control is also buttressed by the power of law itself: survivors find themselves (1) compelled by law to interact with their abusers; (2) subjected to the secondary victimization of invasive questioning (or false counter-allegations); and (3) rebuked for attempting to protect their children from a coercive and controlling co-parent.

Relatedly, it is essential to recognize how conventions and deeply ingrained beliefs about gender, culture, class, ethnicity, religion, and disability can lead to variance in how litigants' credibility, parental competency, or risks of harm are perceived. These forms of social marginalization are targeted and magnified in the context of FV. And both abusers and survivors are aware that these systemic biases exist, with abusers often exploiting them to discourage an ex-partner's resistance (by, for instance by threatening retaliatory false reports of child maltreatment or immigration services). Against the backdrop of the Millennial Scoop and the "disproportionately high incidences of Indigenous and Black children in admissions into care at many [children's aid societies]" in Ontario [Canada], these threats can instill a high degree of intimidation. . .

- Survivors benefit from having good advocates who can help synthesize their stories. . .
- "Winning" is not always enough: Many survivors report that the pursuit of costs was ultimately not worth the continued stress and manipulation of fighting for them. . .
- A family law case may involve different judges hearing different aspects of the litigation, and this can obscure patterns of litigation abuse. . .
- Litigation abuse extends to institutions and services beyond the family courts [e.g., false reports to child protective services, police, immigration authorities]. . .
- There is need for more research on the identification of litigation abuse. . .
- All legal professionals have a responsibility to obtain relevant information about FV including social context education. . .

[Editor's Note: In "Coercive Control in the Courtroom: The Legal Abuse Scale (LAS)," Journal of Family Violence (published online May 19, 2022), Ellen R. Gutowski and Lisa A. Goodman describe the first author's research with 222 mothers throughout the U.S. who were survivors of Intimate Partner Violence and had been involved in family law proceedings. She created a list of 27 potential items, and after testing, analyses yielded the 14-item Legal Abuse Scale (LAS), "a tool that will enable systemic assessment of legal abuse in family court and other legal proceedings, expansion of research on this form of coercive control, and further development of policy and practice that recognizes and responds to it." The LAS items include: threatened to use court to take custody away, took you to court for this, threatened to use court to get unsafe access to children, took you to court for this, threatened to use court to punish you, took you to court repeatedly, took you to court only to cause you distress, was dishonest about your character or mental health to professionals on your case, told professionals you are trying to harm the other parent's relationship with children, threatened to withhold financial support, actually did this, threatened to take control of all assets, and took you to court to do this.]

NEW JERSEY STATUTES 2C: 25–20. TRAINING COURSE AND CURRICULUM; DOMESTIC CRISIS TEAMS

(effective 1/18/22)

b. (1) The Administrative Director of the Courts shall develop and approve a training course and a curriculum for all municipal court judges,

Superior Court judges responsible for the adjudication of domestic violence matters, and judicial personnel involved with the intake and processing of domestic violence complaints. All judges and judicial personnel identified in this section shall participate in core training regarding issues such as the dynamics of domestic violence, the impact of domestic violence on children, trauma-informed danger assessments, batterer intervention programs, and domestic violence risk factors and lethality. In addition, municipal court judges shall receive specific training related to the issuance of temporary restraining orders in emergent situations. Superior Court judges responsible for the adjudication of domestic violence matters shall receive supplemental training related to the issuance and enforcement of temporary and final restraining orders, including factors considered when determining if a final restraining order should be issued, child custody and parenting plans, the setting of child support, distribution of property and ongoing housing expenses, and counseling. The core curriculum and individualized training programs shall be reviewed at least every two years and modified by the Administrative Director of the Courts from time to time as need may require.

(2) The Administrative Director of the Courts shall be responsible for ensuring that all municipal court judges, Superior Court judges responsible for the adjudication of domestic violence matters, and judicial personnel involved with the intake and processing of domestic violence complaints attend initial training within 90 days of appointment or transfer and annual in-service training as described in this section.

(3) The Attorney General and the Administrative Director of the Courts shall provide that all training on the handling of domestic violence matters required under this subsection shall include information concerning the impact of domestic violence on society, and include topics regarding the dynamics of domestic violence, the impact of domestic violence on children, the impact of trauma on survivors, risks for lethality in domestic violence cases, safety planning and services for survivors of domestic violence, the impact of racial bias and discrimination on survivors and marginalized communities, the statutory and case law concerning domestic violence, the necessary elements of a protection order, the guidelines regarding when domestic violence incidents trigger mandatory or discretionary arrest, policies and procedures as promulgated or ordered by the Attorney General or the Supreme Court, and the use of available community resources, support services, available sanctions and treatment options.

EDITOR'S SUMMARY OF JENNA SMITH, BRITTANY DAVIS, AND NIDA ABBASI, COVID-19 AND DV: LESSONS FROM COURT RESPONSES

Center for Court Innovation (now Center for Justice Innovation) (2022)

While the COVID 19 pandemic created many difficulties for litigants and courts, there were lessons learned that will be useful from now on. For example, virtual hearings make courts more accessible to the public and build trust, so courts should plan on hybrid hearings, with some litigants and witnesses in person and some appearing virtually. Also, courts can work with others to address the digital divide, e.g., by establishing places for litigants to participate in remote hearings if they do not have access to technology. Remote interpretation is best done with video rather than just over the telephone. Virtual hearings can improve safety for survivors, especially if they have a video safety plan (e.g., using virtual backgrounds to hide their true location).

The Center for Court Innovation also recommends using regular online meetings for coordinating among courts, attorneys, domestic violence agencies, probation, CPS, etc. And allowing service of legal papers via phone, email, text, or US mail; there are ways to document receipt. Batterer's programs may need to meet virtually, and some use virtual daily check ins. Probation officers may also monitor high risk defendants virtually.

Finally, courts and communities must do more to address trauma and inequity as part of responding to domestic violence, including training staff on trauma-informed practices and vicarious trauma, screening for risk of increasing violence/lethality, connecting litigants to additional resources, and conducting outreach as part of building relationships with survivors.

ANN E. FREEDMAN, FACT-FINDING IN CIVIL DOMESTIC VIOLENCE CASES: SECONDARY TRAUMATIC STRESS AND THE NEED FOR COMPASSIONATE WITNESSES

11 Am U. J. Gender Soc. Pol'y & L. 567 (2003)
(citations and footnotes omitted)

INTRODUCTION

This symposium . . . is an excellent occasion for drawing attention to two striking features of domestic violence law and practice. The first is the troubling inadequacy of fact-finding resources in civil domestic violence proceedings, particularly in cases involving children. This inadequacy means that even with progressive laws and promising remedies, justice and assistance for victims of domestic violence and their children are often out of reach.

The second striking feature is the high proportion of civil domestic violence cases that are murky and difficult, in part as a result of these cases' high degree of particularity. By the latter phrase, I mean that domestic violence family cases include a strikingly diverse variety of life circumstances, patterns of behavior, and needs for social support and legal intervention. This variety is coupled with unusual challenges in the gathering, presentation, and sifting of evidence. Finally, domestic violence cases, like many family matters, are primarily concerned with shaping and predicting the future on the basis of evidence about the past and the present. For this and other reasons, the correct outcome is more difficult to discern and may be more uncertain than in most other court cases. Even the concept of "outcome" is more ambiguous in these cases. While court judgments mark the end point of many legal disputes, both domestic violence and child maltreatment cases often require longer term judicial oversight and extended social services. As one litigator remarked, in effect, these cases begin rather than end with a judge's ruling. The result is that many cases pose significant fact-finding challenges.

When cases are complex, the deficiencies of fact-finding resources have even more devastating consequences, because there is a sharp decrease in the odds of getting the accurate results that facilitate constructive support to adults and children who need it. Thus, the more difficult and confusing the cases, the more elusive the goal of providing appropriate civil remedies and other social assistance to victims and their children. * * *

This Article suggests another critical factor in understanding both the fact-finding gap and its relative obscurity in domestic violence discourse: the largely unacknowledged problem of secondary traumatic stress, and an associated lack of interdisciplinary collaboration to address this problem. Secondary traumatic stress has the potential to affect everyone who has any contact with trauma, who are collectively described as "observers" or "bystanders." Among the traumatic experiences whose vicarious impact on bystanders has been documented are rape, child abuse and domestic violence, as well as war, solitary confinement, torture, and natural and environmental disasters. Prolonged, repeated interpersonal victimization, such as that which can occur in the context of domestic violence, child abuse, prisons, concentration camps and slave labor camps, is most likely to produce more serious forms of traumatic stress, both in survivors of trauma and in bystanders who have extensive contact with them. This Article suggests that the practice of compassionate witnessing can assist bystanders, particularly people on the front lines in the legal system, to respond more effectively to individuals experiencing or recovering from family-related trauma, particularly when prolonged and repeated victimization is involved. It also concludes that improving societal responses to both domestic violence and child maltreatment depends primarily on the formation of interdisciplinary communities of support, bringing together participants in the legal system and others with different training and perspectives who also work with people experiencing domestic violence and child maltreatment. Finally, this Article contends that compassionate witnessing, if widely practiced within the legal system, will provide new clarity about the link between the fact-finding role of family courts and the rights of both adults and children to be protected from intimate violence and patterns of domination and control. * * *

Part IV explores likely interconnections between the painful subject matter involved in civil domestic violence proceedings and the disheartening conditions in many family courts. Family court personnel experience first hand the reality that violent and controlling behavior in family and intimate relationships is prevalent, largely uncontrolled, poorly understood and often devastating in its consequences. Because of this exposure, system participants necessarily experience powerful emotional responses. Given the dispiriting circumstances in most family courts, the detrimental effects of secondary traumatic stress are especially likely.

Unfortunately, most people are unaware of the nature and extent of secondary traumatic stress, lack access to supportive resources, and have little or no training about how to recognize reactivity in themselves and others or how to respond to the resulting distress. As a result, people are likely to adopt coping mechanisms and engage in self-protective defensive maneuvers to create distance and reduce to tolerable levels their own entirely understandable discomfort, anxiety, and, in some circumstances, pain. * * *

IV. COMPASSIONATE WITNESSING AS A RESOURCE FOR CHANGE

One aspect of the problem of domestic violence and child maltreatment that makes effective responses hard to create and sustain—particularly responses that depend on fact-finding—is the great difficulty most people experience in confronting the inhuman treatment that people inflict on each other. * * *

Learning to respond to trauma effectively involves developing the capacity to be aware of our deep connections to the situations and people with whom we work without becoming overwhelmed by our own defensive thinking and losing track of our roles and responsibilities. This challenge operates on us individually, and in all human systems. The ability to identify who has taken a particular action and respond appropriately with further action is a central feature of legal practice (and of human social intercourse in general). Yet we are constantly at risk of defending ourselves from our own emotional responses to the proceedings (and shock at the power of legal judgments) by reducing the human beings who appear in court to two-dimensional figures called "perpetrators" or "batterers;" "victims," "battered women" or "children of batterers;" or even "bystanders." When we treat these categories as accurate, comprehensive and mutually exclusive descriptions of actual people, we may experience some temporary relief from the discomfort of our own ambivalent feelings about the drama to which we are bystanders. Unfortunately, when we are treating our categories as if they fully captured reality and fail to recognize other dimensions that are operating simultaneously, we lose the open heartedness that is necessary to engage effectively with humans in distress. Moreover, we will lack the clarity and groundedness necessary to make and implement the required judgments, which the other participants (and we) understandably find so shocking. * * *

A. Compassionate Witnessing and the Problem of Bystander Reactivity

2. An Introduction to the Concept of Compassionate Witnessing

Compassionate witnessing takes the constructs of psychotherapy and simplifies and extends them. Not simply a professional tool, compassionate witnessing is one name for a more conscious and practiced version of a capacity all human beings share, and all use in our relationships. In essence, compassionate witnessing allows bystanders to recognize our reactivity as a sign of the truth of our shared humanity: while we are individually quite different, we simultaneously all have the same basic needs and the same repertoire of emotional responses. Rather than acting out that reactivity, compassionate witnesses make the conscious choice to stay present to this truth of connectedness and similarity, while using various techniques that allow them to simultaneously acknowledge and own their own reactive feelings. Staying present has some important correlates. For example, from a perspective of our common humanity, we cannot cast someone else out without in some sense casting ourselves out too. Similarly, the practice of staying present to our common humanity with others we encounter entails finding effective ways to respond to suffering. Our openheartedness allows us to recognize and understand the suffering of others, because it is similar to our own. Our own suffering, combined with our ability to find comfort in the face of our suffering, leads us to see the importance of responding to the suffering of others. As a result, compassionate witnesses both experience and create a sense of commonality and shared purpose in addressing sources of trauma. * * *

It is helpful to realize that compassionate witnessing involves a more conscious use of the skills people use to create intimacy and connection with each other in daily life. Intimacy between people depends on each person's willingness to be in touch with her or his own feelings and wants, which are expressions of that person's life force. Compassionate witnesses are able to acknowledge their own feelings and wants—a personal sense of self—while in relationship with another, who also has distinct feelings, wants and selfhood. None of us grow to adulthood with these capacities for intimacy fully intact. The work of adulthood (and not only of psychotherapy) is to restore that capacity, which is necessary to a full life and satisfying relationships. All of us spend some of our time mired in the defensive strategies developed in childhood (and perhaps intensified as a result of painful adult experiences), and, in consequence, disown parts of ourselves. The more we attempt to separate ourselves from our distress, the more disoriented, vulnerable to upset, and disconnected we become, and the more maintaining our defenses seems a matter of life and death. A downward spiral of defense meeting defense keeps people feeling isolated, lonely and increasingly desperate for connection. Yet with connection comes the certainty that blocked material and aspects of ourselves we learned long ago to view as dangerous to our well-being will be brought to the fore.

All of us suffer from this dilemma, as it is part of the human condition, and all of us move in and out of connection as we navigate through our lives. Some people are more sensitive to this dilemma, or have been exposed to more traumatic experiences, and for them, this dilemma can become excruciating. People engaging in violence and efforts at coercion and control are acting out this dilemma in particularly dangerous and destructive ways. * * *

3. Components of Compassionate Witnessing Practice

Compassionate witnessing can enable bystanders, including lawyers, judges, court personnel, advocates, and others, to remain present to the painful truths of the experiences of victims and perpetrators of violence in intimate relationships and family settings. What is more important, this practice is profoundly beneficial to everyone who undertakes it, whatever their chosen work, because, to use Byron Katie's phrase, it is a practice of "loving what is." Nine components of compassionate witnessing practice, which can also be understood as requirements for adopting this stance, are discussed here. These include: (1) conscious choice; (2) adopting a moral stance as a witness; (3) acknowledgment of the particular challenges of work with trauma (that is, the problem of secondary or vicarious traumatic stress); (4) integrated use of reason and emotion; (5) maintenance of appropriate boundaries; and (6) a willingness to explore one's personal connections to the experiences and situations one encounters as a witness. The three final, and perhaps most important, components are: (7) active self-care; (8) participation in creating an interdisciplinary community of support for one's work and for victims and perpetrators of violence; and (9) a commitment to being present and participating in remedial engagement moment to moment under conditions of uncertainty.

The core of the practice of compassionate witnessing, a thread that runs through and links all nine elements, is a sense of integrity, based on an understanding of what it means to be human, that leads to actions guided by kindness and care for ourselves and others.

* * * [First, it] is the choice to engage that is key. From the exercise of conscious choice comes a host of other resources, including passion, curiosity, excitement, creativity, patience, persistence and a willingness to take risks and make change. These are some of the resources needed for remedial engagement with trauma.

A second requirement is adopting a moral stance as a witness. * * * A compassionate witness in any professional role is one who, consistent with her or his professional relationship to the person or people involved, is present to the human realities of the circumstances presented, including any traumatic material, stays in relationship to the situation and all of the people involved (including herself or himself), attends responsibly to both intellectual and emotional aspects of issues that are raised, and takes appropriate action in light of governing norms.

The difference between compassionate witnessing and traditional professional norms has to do with the ideas of presence and relationship embedded in this statement. Tradition suggests that therapists, judges and lawyers can operate in disconnected, distant and resolutely intellectual ways, and simultaneously be present to people and their often complex, ambiguous and painful experiences. Recent work in psychology and trauma studies challenges these notions, suggesting that human connections are essential to professional work of this kind. Thus, the idea of compassionate witnessing invites professionals to find a new middle ground of engagement, consciously maintaining a healthy sense of both self and other in relationship. Compassionate witnesses are conscious of the twin temptations to withdraw and to become over-involved, and commit themselves simply to do the best they can under the circumstances, simultaneously acknowledging both the power that society and the people who seek their assistance have invested in them and the limits of what they are able to do. * * *

The next several elements that compassionate witnessing practice adds to traditional thinking about judging and lawyering flow very directly from a commitment to be kind to ourselves and others, and thus maintain our integrity as witnesses. * * * Like therapists who work with survivors of severe trauma, judges, attorneys, advocates, neutral evaluators and other system personnel must acknowledge the possible effects of secondary traumatic stress. A compassionate witness is conscious of this phenomenon and attentive to the possible impact of vicarious distress on her or his own functioning and that of others involved in responding to traumatic situations. Ignoring this issue or denying possible effects has painful consequences for people working with traumatic material, because it supports problematic coping mechanisms and creates isolation rather than community.

The fourth requirement, which is closely related to the third, is a different perspective on how professionals (in common with other human beings) can best respond in situations where they are bystanders and witnesses to trauma. Professional training often teaches lawyers, judges, psychologists and other professionals to handle their emotions by using the tools of a well-developed intellect, putting their emotions in second place, or even ignoring them altogether. However, in dealing with trauma, no one can successfully and consistently function effectively without using both reason and emotion, and without some tools to handle the personal identifications that trauma often evokes in bystanders. By developing the capacity to use reason and emotion in an integrated way, professionals who choose to function as compassionate witnesses are able to use their own emotional responses as resources in carrying out their other professional responsibilities, including remaining present in the face of the disturbing and painful material to which they are exposed, and maintaining appropriate boundaries, neither over-involved nor disengaged from the human complexities of the situation. * * *

Indeed, our willingness to be real with ourselves about our own experiences challenges false dichotomies between us as professionals and the clients and litigants with whom we work. * * * Professionals who are able to acknowledge their own resistance to facing painful experiences will find it much easier to be understanding of the similar feelings and behavior of clients and litigants. * * *

Rather, everyone oscillates between consciousness and unconsciousness. The practice of compassionate witnessing simply facilitates the process of recognizing when we have become unconscious, and moving back toward consciousness. It is also helpful to recognize that we are the ones who reap the greatest benefits of developing our own capacities for conscious living. Compassionate witnessing is a practice people adopt out of self-love, not out of altruism.

Maintaining appropriate boundaries is essential to successful functioning in one's professional role, and also to serving as a compassionate witness. Boundaries promote the well-being of the client, who needs to be able to seek specific kinds of support from outside observers, free of the mutual responsibilities that friends or family members undertake with each other. Boundaries also protect the bystander who has become a witness from taking on personal responsibility for rescuing, changing or befriending a client or litigant. * * *

People who work in the field of domestic violence can both protect themselves from burnout and help bring about systemic change by committing themselves to active self-care, which includes recognizing and owning our own responses as we do this work, and taking responsibility for reaching out for the support each of us needs. As each of us cares for ourselves, we become better able to make recognition of our common humanity an operating principle in our professional work. We will also enthusiastically join efforts to create the interdisciplinary communities of support necessary for systemic reform. To use a well-worn phrase, it is by changing our own behavior that we become part of the solution, not part of the problem.

The role of a compassionate witness also entails efforts to create community and a commitment to operating in the present, without ever knowing what will happen next. * * *

2. The Transformative Potential of Compassionate Witnessing in the Legal System

When individuals who make up the legal system practice compassionate witnessing, critical needs of litigants and their children begin to be met. * * *

Just as lawyers who incorporate compassionate witnessing into their work find that the change benefits both lawyers and clients, many judges now recognize the value of compassionate witnessing in their work with victims of violence, including domestic violence.

In fact, Herman's work is one of the resources James Ptacek used in his thoughtful study of domestic violence judges in Massachusetts. These were judges who had chosen to work in specialized domestic violence courts, which had been established after many years of struggle to reform the legal system's response to domestic violence. Ptacek observed the ways eighteen judges in two of these courts interacted with women seeking restraining orders and men alleged to be batterers, arguing that judges' demeanor in the courtroom, an aspect of the "emotional labor" of judging, can empower or re-victimize women seeking to stop abuse in their intimate relationships. Ptacek found that ten of the eighteen judges he observed usually used what he characterized as a "good-natured" demeanor in their interactions with battered women. "The judges who exhibited this kind of demeanor used their authority to make women feel welcome in court, to express concern for their suffering, and to mobilize resources on their behalf."

If demeanor is an image of authority, the image [good-natured] judges wanted to communicate is one of empathy and support. They want to use their power to make women feel welcome in the court and to facilitate their requests for judicial remedies. There is an awareness by these judges that this demeanor is communicated by the design of court processes, by their patience, by open expressions of concern, through their listening to both parties, and by serious attention to the criminal nature of violence and abuse.

This demeanor contrasted with several alternative forms of self-presentation, including bureaucratic (formal and distancing), firm, condescending or harsh. Advocates for battered women have long contended that the attitudes and behavior of law enforcement personnel, including police officers, prosecutors, court personnel and judges are a critical factor in the effectiveness of legal remedies for domestic violence. * * *

Ptacek's work also confirms the relevance of other elements of compassionate witnessing practice to judges' ability to engage supportively with litigants experiencing domestic violence.

> * * * Truly engaging with a woman seeking an order requires more than merely pretending empathy. To really reach someone who has been assaulted and who may be intimidated and upset, a judge is more effective if he or she genuinely feels empathetic. * * * Empathetic engagement with women who are suffering from terrorizing violence can be exhausting. "Trauma is contagious," according to Judith Lewis Herman. . . . Herman states that in the role of witness to a violent crime, the therapist "experiences, to a lesser degree, the same terror, rage, and despair" as the survivor. This is called "vicarious traumatization." Judges who are willing to recognize women's experience of victimization will also feel this, as will advocates, shelter workers, and other feminist activists. * * * One judge spoke of how she dealt with the personal strain of working with women who had been abused. She described the restraining order hearings as a "terrible emotional burden":
>
> "I think that two things help me with the stress. One, I talk about it. . . . I try not to make it identifiable, and I'm careful about confidences. But the things that are most traumatic, I do talk about. Both with friends and in terms of public speaking, as examples. And I do a lot of committee work. . . . I find that that gives me a sense of contributing in a way that dealing with the case by miniscule case-as much as I enjoy that, and I take each case very seriously, I think that if you feel like you are having some long effect, or short-term effect, anyway, on the system as a whole, it's easier to deal with the grind."

By talking about traumatic events, and engaging in work on battering that is less isolating and individualized than sitting on criminal cases, this judge seeks to create a social environment that will strengthen her ability to stand as witness to such violence. * * *

2. Honoring and Challenging Strategies of Disconnection

* * * Miller and Stiver devote an entire chapter of *The Healing Connection*, their paradigm-shifting book arguing for a relational approach to psychotherapy, to the radical notion of "Honoring the Strategies of Disconnection." They note:

> We want to emphasize our belief in the great importance of respecting [people's] strategies of disconnection . . .
>
> . . . [O]ne's strategies for staying out of authentic connection . . . are in some sense adaptive. . . . [T]hey arise when the only relationships that are available are in some fundamental way

> disconnecting or even destructive: at some point in a person's history there was good reason to develop these strategies . . .
>
> Instead of labeling such behaviors in therapy as resistance [or as defenses], we think of them as lifesaving- or mind-saving-strategies that people have developed for a reason. . . .
>
> Thinking about strategies of staying out of connection [empathetically] can make a big difference in our whole attitude and approach. We can feel a new kind of respect and honoring-even admiration-for some of the strategies patients have developed even as we believe these strategies are making problems for the patients themselves, and for the therapist. . . . * * *

Developing Coordinated Community Responses

Advocates who have developed coordinated community responses to domestic violence have also pointed out the greater practical efficacy of looking at the handling of domestic violence matters in each community from a systems perspective rather than in terms of the functioning of particular individuals. Legal systems must be designed to promote and reward the desired behavior of system participants, so that appropriate responses to domestic violence do not depend on heroic actions by individual workers. This is one of several ways compassionate witnessing and coordinated community response initiatives overlap conceptually and practically. * * *

3. The Eighth and Ninth Components of Compassionate Witnessing: Creating Community and Confronting the Unknown

[The author also explains that the last element of compassionate witnessing is confronting the unknown: "The practice of compassionate witnessing opens the heart simultaneously to the power of each moment of our lives, and our inability to know the future."]

CONCLUSION

A chapter titled "Remembrance and Mourning," in the second half of Judith Lewis Herman's book, *Trauma and Recovery*, begins as follows, "In the second stage of recovery, the survivor tells the story of the trauma. She tells it completely, in depth and in detail. This work of reconstruction actually transforms the traumatic memory, so that it can be integrated into the survivor's life story." This Article argues that the fact-finding gap in civil domestic violence proceedings deprives victims and also everyone else—their children, perpetrators, and bystanders—of an essential resource: a forum in which people can tell the stories of trauma and have those stories witnessed by others, so that the traumatic memories can be transformed and integrated into people's life stories, into the web of their intimate relationships, and into the life of the society. * * *

* * * The legal system has a distinctive role in the process of preventing and healing from trauma: creating a sustained capacity for finding facts accurately when there are allegations of violent and coercively controlling behavior, applying governing norms fairly, creating the conditions for due process and the respect for human rights in the legal process, and cooperating with other social institutions to respond effectively and humanely to the needs of people caught up in the drama of violence and coercion and control. Adopting the practice of compassionate witnessing ourselves has the advantage of bringing immediate comfort. Extending the practice to a wider audience in the legal system is one pathway between the difficulties of our present situation and a more hopeful future.

As the body of the Article illustrates, the intellectual underpinnings and societal implications of the practice of compassionate witnessing are complex, while the practice itself is both simple and profound. In each area of small or large deficiency that we encounter, the challenge is to mobilize human creativity to make change possible. The holistic nature of the practice of compassionate witnessing plays an essential role. The desire to turn away from suffering is powerful. Yet, as Herman points out, the force of secrecy and denial is matched by the yearning for openness and recovery. When people practice compassionate witnessing, there is a synergistic effect both on people around them, and on the resources available to support change. No one can or needs to become a compassionate witness in isolation, because small shifts in a new direction call forth similar impulses that everyone shares to some degree. Likewise, no one can or needs to take responsibility for discerning all the steps necessary to bring about the changes required. We engage most deeply with reality when we form the intention to be guided by kindness, integrity and compassion in our work, inquire into distortions in our thinking that cause unnecessary suffering to ourselves and others, find other like-minded people, and proceed with caution and curiosity into the unknown.

[Editor's Notes: 1. See also Jennifer Brobst, The Impact of Secondary Traumatic Stress Among Family Attorneys Working With Trauma-Exposed Clients: Implications for Practice and Professional Responsibility, 10 J. Health & Biomed. L. 1 (2014).

2. As mentioned in Chapter 1, one of the ways that some advocates, attorneys, and law teachers have dealt with the secondary trauma of this work is by participating in Re-Evaluation Counseling (RC), a form of peer counseling practiced in many countries. The sessions are free and the classes are low cost. For more information, go to www.reevaluationcounseling.org. I have been involved with this organization since 1975 and have found this resource extremely valuable in being able to keep working in the domestic violence field, while keeping an open heart and aiming for a joyful life.]

B. SENTENCING BATTERERS

[Editor's Note: In "Court-Mandated Interventions for Individu Convicted of Domestic Violence," Campbell Systematic Reviews 2008:1 (2008), Lynette Feder, David B. Wilson, and Sabrina Austin provide the following background to court-mandated batterer programs.

"The idea of counseling male domestic violence offenders developed directly out of the women's shelter movement where advocates, working with battered women, realized that the only way to stop the cycle of violence was to change the behavior of the abuser. It is not surprising, therefore, that these programs borrowed heavily from a feminist orientation. Typically, the various programs encouraged men to confront their sexist beliefs and accept responsibility for their past abuse, while teaching them alternative behaviors and reactions (e.g., anger management, assertiveness, relaxation techniques and communication skills).

The greatest growth in these different batterer intervention programs (BIPs) was brought about by the rise in pro-arrest domestic violence laws in the late 1980s. As police increased their rates of arrest for these offenses, pressure was placed on courts to deal with these offenders. Given this population's high rates of attrition from treatment programs, court-mandated BIPs were viewed as one method to ensure greater compliance while simultaneously serving as an alternative to over-crowded jails."]

ANDREW R. KLEIN, PRACTICAL IMPLICATIONS OF CURRENT DOMESTIC VIOLENCE RESEARCH FOR PROBATION OFFICERS AND ADMINISTRATORS

Battered Women's Justice Project (2015)

V. What does the research tell probation about batterer intervention programs?

1. Do batterer intervention programs prevent reabuse?

Batterer programs, in and of themselves, are not likely to protect the most vulnerable victims from further harm from higher risk abusers. Consequently, if mandated or utilized, batterer intervention programs should be supplemented by other measures to assure victim safety from these abusers.

Commonly, whether diverted, placed on probation or jailed, many Intimate Partner Violence (IPV) offenders are required to attend batterer intervention programs. These programs have increased dramatically over the past several decades. There have been more than 35 evaluations of batterer intervention programs, but they have yielded inconsistent results. Two meta-analyses of the more rigorous studies find the programs have, at best, a "modest" treatment effect, producing a minimal reduction in re-arrests for domestic violence. In one of the meta-analyses, the treatment effect translated to a 5% improvement rate in cessation of reassaults due to the treatment. In the other, it ranged from none to 0.26, roughly representing a reduction in recidivism from 13 to 20%.

On the other hand, a few studies have found that batterer intervention programs make abusers more likely to reabuse or have found no reduction in abuse at all.

The multistate study of four batterer programs concludes that approximately a quarter of batterers appear unresponsive and resistant to batterer intervention. In this long-term study, based on victim and/or abuser interviews and/or police arrests, approximately half of the batterers reassaulted their initial or new partners sometime during the study's 30-month follow-up. Most of the reassaults occurred within the first six months of program intake. Nearly a quarter of the batterers repeatedly assaulted their partners during the follow-up and accounted for nearly all of the severe assaults and injuries.

2. Does the type or length of batterer intervention program make a difference?

Several studies have found that the type of batterer intervention program, whether feminist, psycho-educational, or cognitive-behavioral, does not affect reabuse. One study also found that a "culturally focused" program specifically designed for black male abusers did no better than the program offered to all abusers. In fact, those assigned to a conventional, racially mixed group were half as likely to be arrested for reassaults compared to those assigned to a black culturally focused counseling group or a conventional group of all blacks.

However, a rigorous study based in New York City found the length of the program (26 weeks compared to 8 weeks) may make a difference, with the longer program proving more effective at deterring reabuse. The researchers suggest that the longer program's increased effectiveness was due to its longer suppression effect while abusers were mandated to attend, whether or not they actually attended. On the other hand, a multistate study of four programs ranging in length from 3 to 9 months found no difference in subsequent reabuse.

3. Do couples counseling or anger management treatment programs prevent rebabuse?

As long as the batterer intervention program is focused on preventing reabuse, the type of program makes no difference. However, longer batterer programs may be better than shorter programs, like the batterer program mandated for convicted abusers in California (Penal Code § 1203.097(A)(6)) that must be conducted for two hours each week and for a minimum of 52 consecutive weeks.

[Editor's Note: However, see Ca. Penal Code section 1203.099 which creates a pilot program in six counties until 2026, allowing them to offer BIPs for a shorter time period and requiring an evaluation of their effectiveness.]

Probation should not recommend couple counseling or anger management programs for abusers and if such programs are imposed alert victims that these programs have not been found to be protective for victims.

There has been little recent research on the application of couples counseling involving batterers and their victims as most batterer treatment standards prohibit couples counseling. While an early study in 1985 found it ineffective, with half of the couples reporting new violence within six weeks of couples counseling, other studies found lower reabuse rates. A small study suggests that couples counseling ***after*** separate counseling for batterers and victims may be safe and beneficial for couples who want to remain together.

Although anger management is often part of batterer intervention programs based on cognitive psychology, most state batterer treatment standards prohibit generic anger management programs or couples counseling as alternative forms of treatment on their own. In one of the largest studies to date, the Office of the Commissioner of Probation in Massachusetts studied a sample of 945 defendants arraigned for violating a protective order. As part of their subsequent disposition, they were ordered into a certified batterer intervention program, anger management program, and/or a mental health treatment or substance abuse treatment program; 13% were sent to multiple programs. The study found that those referred to 12- to 20-week anger management programs had a higher completion rate than those referred to the much longer 40-week batterer intervention programs. Higher completion rates notwithstanding, there was no difference in rearrest rates for those who completed anger management programs and those who failed to complete one. Furthermore, those who completed anger management programs recidivated at higher rates than those who completed batterer intervention programs, even though those referred to batterer intervention programs had significantly more criminal history, including more past order violations, more long-standing substance abuse histories, and less education than those referred to anger management programs.

An earlier study of a program in Pittsburgh found that abusers who relied on anger management control techniques were more likely to reabuse their partners than those who relied on increased empathy, a redefinition of their manhood, and more cooperative decision making as a means to ending their abuse.

4. Does alcohol and drug treatment prevent reabuse?

Incorporating alcohol and/or drug treatment as a standard component of batterer intervention programs adds to the likelihood of reductions in reabuse among batterers.

Effective treatment should include abstinence testing to assure sobriety and no drug use. Abusers who cannot maintain sobriety should be ordered into more intensive treatment, including inpatient, or medicated assisted treatment for their own well being and that of their victims.

The correlation between alcohol and drug treatment has been confirmed in numerous studies cited previously. These studies find substance abuse treatment can be effective in reducing domestic violence. In one such study, for example, researchers found that among 301 alcoholic male partner abusers, of whom 56 % had physically abused their partners the year before treatment, partner violence significantly decreased for half a year after alcohol treatments but still was not as low as the nonalcoholic control group. Among those patients who remained sober, reabuse dropped to 15%, the same as the nonalcoholic control group and half that of treated alcoholics who failed to maintain sobriety. As this study suggests, however, alcohol and drug treatment, in and of itself, may not be sufficient for all abusers. Supporting this is a Massachusetts probation study of 945 defendants convicted of violating protective orders and subsequently ordered into a program. The study found that those who completed a variety of alcohol and drug treatment programs had higher rates of rearraignment over six years, for any crime or for violations of protective orders, than those who completed batterer intervention programs (57.9 vs. 47.7% for any crime, and 21.1 vs. 17.4% for violation of protective orders). Furthermore, there was no significant difference in rearraignment rates between those who completed the substance abuse treatment and those who did not.

On the other hand, studies suggest alcohol and drug treatment may be a necessary component of successful intervention to prevent reabuse. The multistate study of four batterer programs found that, among those who completed the program, those who became intoxicated within a three-month period were three times more likely to reassault their partners than those who did not.

5. Are court-referred batterers likely to complete batterer programs?

Probation should take all appropriate steps to ensure that court conditions are enforced, violators are returned to court promptly, and violation cases (i.e., revocation hearings) are heard expeditiously and violators appropriately sanctioned. The lack of immediate proportional sanctions for technical violations sends the wrong message to the specific defendant, all abuser defendants, not to mention victims who are depending upon probation to further their safety.

Multiple studies of disparate programs around the country have found high non-completion rates ranging from 25 to 89%, with most at around 50%. Rates vary because different programs have different standards for monitoring attendance as well as different policies regarding re-enrollment, missed meetings, and so on. A study in California found that, of 10 counties examined, only one maintained a database to track offender participation in the mandated batterer intervention program; it reported that 89% did not complete the program.

Not surprisingly, adding on additional treatment programs increases non-completion. For example, although 42% of the referred batterers in the Bronx court study failed to complete the batterer intervention program, that number increased to 67% for those also required to complete drug treatment. For those required to complete drug treatment alone, the non-completion rate was 60%.

High rates of technical violations are common for probationers sentenced for domestic violence, including violations of no-contact orders and drug abstinence, and failure to attend batterer intervention programs. Various probation studies found technical violation (non-crime) rates ranging from 34 % of those sentenced in the Brooklyn felony domestic violence court, 41 % in Colorado, 61 % in Champaign County, Ill. and 25 to 44 % in Rhode Island (regular vs. specialized domestic violence supervision).

6. Do those who complete batterer programs do better than those who fail?

Compliance with mandated batterer intervention programs provides probation with a dynamic risk instrument based on a defendant's ongoing current behavior. Reabuse can be prevented if probation responds appropriately and expeditiously to batterers who fail to attend or to comply with court-referred batterer intervention programs.

Abusers who complete batterer programs are less likely to reabuse than those who fail to attend, are noncompliant, or drop out. The differences can be substantial.

A Chicago study of more than 500 court-referred batterers referred to 30 different programs found that recidivism after an average of 2.4 years was 14.3 % for those who completed the program, whereas recidivism for those who did not complete the programs was more than twice that (34.6 %). Those who did not complete their program mandate in the Bronx court study were four times more likely to recidivate than those who completed their program.

The multistate study of four programs found that abusers who completed the programs reduced their risk of reassault in a range of 46 to 66 %. A Florida study found that the odds that abusers who completed the program would be rearrested were half those of a control group not assigned to the program, whereas the odds of rearrest for those who failed to attend were two and one-half times higher than the control group. A Massachusetts study found that, over a six-year period, those who completed a certified batterer intervention program were significantly less likely to be re-arraigned for any type of offense, a violent offense or a protection order violation. (Massachusetts does not have a domestic violence statute, so researchers could not differentiate domestic from nondomestic violence offenses.) The rate differences for these offenses, between those who completed a program and those who did not, was as follows: 47.7 vs. 83.6 % for any crime, 33.7 vs. 64.2 % for a violent crime, and 17.4 vs. 41.8 % for violation of a protective order. The Dallas study found that twice as many program dropouts as program completers were rearrested within 13 months: 39.7 vs. 17.9 % for any charge, and 8.1 vs. 2.8 % for assault arrests. An Alexandria, Va., study of almost 2,000 domestic violence defendants found that noncompliance with court-ordered treatment was associated significantly with being a repeat offender.

While some studies have found reduced reabuse for abusers who completed treatment programs, a few studies have found less dramatic reductions, for example, in Broward County, where the difference was only 4 vs. 5%, and in Brooklyn, where it was 16 vs. 26%.

7. Which batterers are likely to fail to attend mandated batterer intervention treatment?

Screening referrals based on the common variables found to correlate with successful completion—age, prior criminal history and substance abuse—can reduce program failure. Alternatively, supplemental conditions targeting abusers with these characteristics may be necessary to assure successful program participation.

Researchers generally agree that there are a number of variables associated with failure to complete programs. They include being younger, having less education, having greater criminal histories and violence in their family of origin, being less often employed and less motivated to change, having substance abuse problems, having children, and lacking court sanctions for noncompliance. A number of studies emphasize the positive correlation between program completion and "stakes in conformity," including the variables of age (being older), marital status (being married) and employment (being employed).

Studies also find that many of the same variables that predict non-completion also predict reabuse and general recidivism. In the Florida probation study, an examination of court-referred batterers found that the same characteristics that predicted rearrest (including prior criminal history and stakes in conformity) also predicted missing at least one court-mandated program session. Other studies, including a study of two Brooklyn batterer intervention programs, also found that employment correlated both positively with completion and negatively with rearrest.

However, prior criminal history remains the strongest and most consistent predictor of non-completion and new arrests. In the Brooklyn study, defendants with a prior arrest history were found to be four times more likely to fail to complete programs than defendants without prior arrests. The Bronx court study similarly found that prior arrests as well as a history of drug abuse predicted both non-completion and recidivism and found background demographics to be less important.

8. When are noncompliant abusers likely to drop out of batterer programs?

To safeguard victims and/or new partners, probation officers should respond immediately to an abuser's first failure to enroll in or attend a court-mandated batterer intervention program.

Several studies have found that batterers who do not complete batterer intervention programs are likely to be non-compliant from the start. Furthermore, these studies found that non-compliance at the first court monitoring predicted both program failure and recidivism. In the Brooklyn study, the strongest predictor of program failure was early non-compliance. Defendants who had not enrolled in a program by the time of their first compliance hearing were significantly less likely to complete the program than those enrolled by the first hearing. These findings are similar to those found in the Bronx study. Defendants who were not in compliance at their first monitoring appearance were six times more likely to fail to complete the program than those in compliance at that time. These findings are consistent with extensive research indicating that the largest proportion of court-identified abusers who reabuse are likely to reabuse sooner rather than later.

9. What should probation's response be if court-referred abusers are non-compliant with programs?

Probation officers should return probationers to court for non-compliance and explain to the judge that this technical violation constitutes a red flag and danger for the victim, not to be ignored or treated lightly.

The Rhode Island probation study that compared probationers in specialized probation supervision caseloads with those in less stringent general caseloads found that the former committed significantly less reabuse over one year. The difference, however, applied only to what researchers called "lower risk" probationers, those without prior arrest histories. Although there were several differences in how the two caseloads were supervised, enforcement of batterer intervention program attendance was one of the major differences. The specialized group's program was more rigidly enforced, as measured by significantly more violations for nonattendance. As a result of the court violation hearings, most of the noncompliant probationers were required to attend weekly compliance court sessions until they completed the program.

An evaluation of two model domestic violence courts found that victims in the court [whose abusers had] significantly more probation revocations for noncompliance (12 % vs. only 1 % in the other court) reported significantly less reabuse than in the comparison court. In the court with more revocations, victims reported a lower frequency of physical assaults for up to 11 months after the study incident. The defendants in the court with the higher revocation rates had a significantly higher number of prior arrests than the defendants in the comparison court (8.3 vs. 3.7 %). Researchers posited that lower domestic violence arrests were obtained primarily through early detection and incarceration of probationers who either continued to reabuse or failed to comply with conditions.

Broward County probation study researchers concluded the following correlation between program noncompliance and reabuse: If abusers are not afraid of violating their court orders, they are also not afraid of the consequences of committing new offenses.

10. What should Probation's response be to abusers who reoffend while on probation, enrolled or after completing a batterer intervention program?

Probation officers should advocate incarceration for any probationers who reabuse while on probation, enrolled in batterer programs or after having completed the programs. Due to their limited "treatment effect," simply re-enrolling high-risk abusers in batterer programs endangers victims. Those abusers who reabuse are likely to continue doing so if left on their own.

Batterers rearrested while enrolled or after completing a batterer intervention program are, not surprisingly, at high risk for reabusing. The multistate batterer intervention program study found, for example, that the majority of court-referred batterers who reassaulted did so more than once. Similarly, a Rhode Island probation study found that batterers who were arrested for domestic violence while their prior arrest was still pending, or while they were still on probation for an earlier offense (domestic or nondomestic), had one of the highest reabuse rates of any probated abuser, averaging over 50%.

11. What effect do batterer intervention program referrals have on victims?

Probation officers have an affirmative obligation to warn the victims of their probationers that batterers' attendance at batterer programs does not ensure the cessation of abuse during or after the program. On the whole, unless batterer intervention programs are closely monitored and program compliance is rigorously enforced, batterer intervention programs may be ineffective for most abusers and give victims false hope, encouraging them to remain with dangerous abusers.

Studies find that most victims are satisfied with their abusers' referral to a batterer intervention program. In the Bronx study, 77% of victims were satisfied with the case outcome if the abuser was ordered to attend a program, compared to only 55% of victims who were satisfied when the abuser was not required to attend a program. A survey of victims of men attending batterer intervention programs throughout Rhode Island found most female victims enthusiastic about the batterer programs. Some victims who were enthusiastic were reassaulted but still felt that the program improved their situation. Program enrollment may also influence victims to remain with their abusers. Victims are more likely to remain with their abusers if their abusers are in treatment programs and are hopeful that the abusers will "get better."

BILL S. 493—NORTH CAROLINA

(2019)

. . .Requires a defendant ordered to attend an abuser treatment program pursuant to subdivision (a)(12) to begin regular attendance of the program within 60 days of the entry of the order. Requires the court to specify the date and time for a review hearing with the court to assess whether the defendant has complied as soon as practicable after 60 days from the entry of the original order. Requires that date and time to be set when entering the original order, and requires the clerk to issue a Notice of Hearing for the compliance review to be given to or served, as appropriate, upon the defendant and filed with the court on the same day as entry of the original order. Permits the plaintiff to attend the review hearing. Provides for the defendant to give the clerk a written statement showing compliance with the order prior to the review hearing, at which time the clerk must remove the hearing from the court docket and notify the plaintiff of the defendant's compliance and that no review hearing will occur.

GEORGIA CODE § 16–5–26—NOTICE OF CONVICTION; PUBLICATION

(a) The clerk of the court in which a person is convicted of a second or subsequent violation of Code Section 16–5–20 [simple assault] and is sentenced pursuant to subsection (d) of such Code section [domestic violence], Code Section 16–5–23 [simple battery] and is sentenced pursuant to subsection (f) of such Code section [domestic violence], or Code Section 16–5–23.1 [battery with visible or substantial bodily harm] shall cause to be published a notice of conviction for such person. Such notice of conviction shall be published in the manner of legal notices in the legal organ of the county in which such person resides or, in the case of nonresidents, in the legal organ of the county in which the person was convicted. Such notice of conviction shall be one column wide by two inches long and shall contain the photograph taken by the arresting law enforcement agency at the time of arrest, the name and address of the convicted person, and the date, time, place of arrest, and disposition of the case and shall be published once in the legal organ of the appropriate county in the second week following such conviction or as soon thereafter as publication may be made.

(b) The convicted person for which a notice of conviction is published pursuant to this Code section shall be assessed $25.00 for the cost of publication of such notice and such assessment shall be imposed at the time of conviction in addition to any other fine imposed.

(c) The clerk of the court, the publisher of any legal organ which publishes a notice of conviction, and any other person involved in the publication of an erroneous notice of conviction shall be immune from civil or criminal liability for such erroneous publication, provided that such publication was made in good faith.

[Editor's Note: In "Pursuing Accountability for Perpetrators of IPV: The Peril (and Utility?) of Shame," 98 B.U. L. Rev. 1677 (2018), A. Rachel Camp cites instances where judges have sentenced batterers to stand outside the courthouse holding a sign reading "This is the face of domestic violence." She states that while some people may see this sort of sentence as holding perpetrators of IPV accountable, it can actually be counterproductive, leading to more abuse of the partners, since batterers are often shame-prone themselves and may be survivors of trauma who respond to feelings of humiliation with violence. She calls for all victims and perpetrators to be treated with dignity rather than shaming and stresses the need to focus on changing the systemic conditions that contribute to IPV perpetration in order to reduce domestic violence.]

CENTER FOR JUSTICE INNOVATION (FORMERLY CENTER FOR COURT INNOVATION), FACT SHEET: DOMESTIC VIOLENCE COURT COMPLIANCE MONITORING

(2013) (footnote omitted)

Judicial monitoring is one of the cornerstones of the domestic violence court model and can help courts work toward victim safety and offender accountability, including compliance with court orders. Research indicates that on-going judicial supervision, in conjunction with specialized probation supervision of offenders in the community, can positively affect the behavior of batterers and keep them from re-offending, at least during the pendency of the case.

How Compliance Monitoring Works

Typically, compliance monitoring involves bringing defendants back to court post-plea/ post-disposition to ensure adherence to court-ordered conditions, such as orders of protection or batterer program mandates. Consequences for failure to comply with these conditions are explained to the defendant at the time of plea/ disposition and at all subsequent compliance dates. In addition, some domestic violence courts require defendants to appear for compliance hearings during the pendency of their cases as a condition of bail. It should be noted that courts may monitor defendants that are not sentenced to a program. For example, judges can bring defendants back to court to check for any new arrests and assess compliance with the order of protection.

Consistency and Accountability

Holding regular compliance hearings sends the message to defendants that the court takes domestic violence crimes seriously and is informed about defendants' behavior, and that non-compliance with court orders and mandated programs will be met with swift sanctions. Communicating to each defendant, through words and actions, that the court will not tolerate battering and that the court is watching is important to promoting the principle of accountability. Judges can further this goal by maintaining a formal judicial demeanor and acknowledging compliance with court mandates without offering congratulations.

Frequency

Compliance monitoring can take several forms depending on court caseload. In certain high volume courts, a separate compliance court is held a few days a week and is presided over by a Judicial Hearing Officer, in some cases a retired judge or magistrate. Courts with medium volume may dedicate a half day, once a week, to the compliance calendar, which is overseen by the domestic violence court judge. Courts with lower caseloads might hold the compliance calendar twice a month at the beginning of the general domestic violence court calendar.

Defendants who are not in compliance are often scheduled to appear at the beginning of the compliance calendar, which allows other defendants to observe the imposition of sanctions such as brief jail sentences and defendants being required to sit in the courtroom. Noncompliant defendants are also asked to appear for monitoring more frequently, perhaps weekly. Defendants who are in compliance with all conditions for several months may be permitted to come to court less frequently tailoring the frequency of court appearances to a defendant's compliance is called graduated monitoring, and is an effective sanction and reward for the court.

Planning for Effective Compliance Monitoring

Domestic violence court planning groups are encouraged to discuss compliance monitoring with stakeholders (especially probation), create interagency compliance monitoring protocols and procedures, and incorporate these into their domestic violence court planning documents and operations. At a minimum, each domestic violence court should:

- Identify appropriate program mandates, such as batterer intervention and substance abuse treatment programs. *Anger management and couples counseling programs are inappropriate for domestic violence cases and should not be ordered by the court*; [emphasis added]
- Ensure that batterer programs have appropriate consequences in place for non- compliance, and that alternate sanctions (such as jail) are used in response to attendance policy non-compliance to ensure that the defendant is not being sent back to a program from which he was expelled;
- Cultivate relationships with local service providers, and ask each program to designate a liaison to the court. If possible, invite a representative from each program to be present when domestic violence court is in session, in order to directly report on defendants' compliance and meet with newly-mandated defendants;
- Create protocols to ensure that programs and probation report accurate information to domestic violence court on a timely basis, including when offenders fail to attend programs or are terminated from programs, as well as violations of probation conditions;
- Establish regular, frequent monitoring dates for all defendants post-conviction, starting within two weeks if possible;
- Develop a sanctioning plan, including the use of graduated sanctions (such as increased frequency of appearances, remand, probation, more stringent probation conditions, or sitting in the jury box); and
- Determine which types of compliance information the resource coordinator will gather in preparation for each compliance hearing, such as reports from probation and mandated programs, drug test results, information from the victim advocate, and any new police reports or court cases.

Holding Compliance Hearings

At disposition, it is recommended that the judge conduct a detailed allocution and review all conditions of the plea agreement, including the order of protection, any program mandates, and the requisite compliance monitoring. Potential consequences for non-compliance should be clearly delineated, and the message conveyed that the judge and court are watching the defendant closely. Subsequent hearings should entail reviewing each defendant's compliance information and imposing sanctions for non- compliance as indicated, according to the sanctioning plan created by the domestic violence court planning team, as well as restating all plea conditions and reiterating that the court is closely monitoring the defendant.

Examples of compliance monitoring protocols, scripts, forms, and monitoring/sanctioning plans can be obtained from the Center for Court Innovation.

[Editor's Notes: 1. In "Are Interventions with Batterers Effective? A Meta-analytical Review," 29(3) Psychosocial Intervention 153 (2020), Ramon Arce, Esther Arias, Mercedes Novo, and Francisca Farina report on results of 25 studies in various countries that included over 20,000 batterers. They distinguished between recidivism reported by official records (ORs) and by couple reports (CRs), finding a significantly higher rate of recidivism measured in CRs than in ORs. Based on CRs, batterers intervention programs had no effect on recidivism, while ORs found a significant reduction in recidivism.

Overall, both the Duluth Model and cognitive-behavioral treatment programs were found useful, but there were some studies showing an increase in recidivism after batterers completed Duluth Model programs, so the authors recommended using the CBT approach. Interventions lasting over four months were found generally useful, while shorter ones sometimes increased recidivism or had no effect. The authors stressed the importance of conducting follow up studies at least one year after completion of the batterers program since recidivism may occur long after the program ends.

2. In "A multimodal approach to reduce attrition, recidivism, and denial in abuser intervention programs," 61(8) J of Offender Rehab 426, Bruce D. Friedman, Nada J. Yorke, Katya Compian, and Deanna Arner Lazaro describe the results of a 52-week batterer's intervention program involving 47 men ages 18–66. 45 were court ordered, 2 volunteered. 12 identified as African American, 26 as Hispanic, and 10 as Caucasian. Only 6 had no prior criminal record. Only 19 were employed when they began. Of the 15 who did not complete the program, 5 were rearrested for new domestic violence charges in the 30 months post-intake, while only 1 of the 32 completers was arrested and this was for non-IPV related violence.

The program used a multi-modal curriculum designed with evidence-based clinical interventions, adult learning strategies, and Risk/Needs/ Responsivity principles. The study also measured cognitive changes and acceptance of personal responsibility in the participants through self-assessments and victim feedback during and after completion. This program had higher than usual retention and lower than usual recidivism; the authors state that this was probably in part because it was free and in part because of the curriculum design. There was a marked change between the lack of significant cognitive shift in denial and acceptance of personal responsibility at 14 weeks into the program and these scores upon completion, supporting the importance of a long program. While the study was small, hopefully this model will be further tested and then replicated more widely.]

NORTH CAROLINA CODE § 143B–1454—DIVISION OF ADULT CORRECTION OF THE DEPARTMENT OF PUBLIC SAFETY—FUNCTIONS

* * * (d) The Division shall establish an alcoholism and chemical dependency treatment program. The program shall consist of a continuum of treatment and intervention services for male and female inmates, established in medium and minimum custody prison facilities, and for male and female probationers and parolees, established in community-based residential treatment facilities.

(e) The Department, in consultation with the Domestic Violence Commission, and in accordance with established best practices, shall establish a domestic violence treatment program for offenders sentenced to a term of imprisonment in the custody of the Department and whose official record includes a finding by the court that the offender committed acts of domestic violence.

The Department shall ensure that inmates, whose record includes a finding by the court that the offender committed acts of domestic violence, complete a domestic violence treatment program prior to the completion of the period of incarceration, unless other requirements, deemed critical by the Department, prevent program completion. In the event an inmate does not complete the program during the period of incarceration, the Department shall document, in the inmate's official record, specific reasons why that particular inmate did not or was not able to complete the program.

COLORADO CODE § 16–11.8–104—DOMESTIC VIOLENCE OFFENDER TREATMENT—CONTRACTS WITH PROVIDERS—FUND CREATED

(1) On and after January 1, 2001, the department of corrections, the judicial department, the division of criminal justice within the department of public safety, or the department of human services shall not employ or contract with and shall not allow a domestic violence offender to employ or contract with any individual or entity to provide domestic violence offender treatment evaluation or treatment services pursuant to this article unless the individual or entity appears on the approved list developed pursuant to section 16–11.8–103(4).

(2)(a) The board shall require any person who applies for placement, including any person who applies for continued placement, on the approved list developed pursuant to section 16–11.8–103(4) to submit to a current background investigation that goes beyond the scope of the criminal history record check described in section 16–11.8–103(4)(b)(III)(A). In conducting the current background investigation, the board shall obtain reference and criminal history information and recommendations that may be relevant to the applicant's fitness to provide domestic violence offender treatment evaluation or treatment services pursuant to this article.

* * *

CHAPTER 13

SURVIVORS OF DOMESTIC VIOLENCE AS CRIMINAL DEFENDANTS

■ ■ ■

This chapter concludes the section of this book which focuses on the criminal justice system's response to domestic violence, and looks at survivors of domestic violence who are charged with crimes (other than "failure to protect" their children, dealt with in Chapter 7).

The chapter starts with an overview of the many crimes victims of domestic violence tend to commit besides killing their abusers, and the reasons for their commission. The next piece argues that our societal stereotypes of victims of domestic violence often wrongly exclude victims who fight back and are charged with crimes, and that such victims may be disproportionately people of the global majority (i.e., non-whites). Another commentator argues for "VAWA diversion" for immigrant survivors of abuse who are wrongly charged with assaulting their partners.

An excerpt from an amicus brief critiques the term "battered woman syndrome" and argues that it is antiquated and inaccurate; instead the preferred term is "intimate partner battering and its effects." The next article examines "stand your ground" laws, and how they have often been misapplied when survivors of domestic violence fight back. A new case reverses the manslaughter conviction of a battered woman who killed her abuser, based on incorrect jury instructions. Another case reverses the conviction of a woman who argued that when she extorted money from a former boyfriend, she did so under duress from her abusive partner. The last article in this section, by a domestic violence expert witness (the author of this textbook), describes how this work is transformative, not only for the clients, but for the expert.

The other section in this chapter focuses on post-conviction issues, including sentencing of abused women in domestic violence criminal cases and battered women in prison. A new case applies the New York Domestic Violence Survivors Act for the first time, lowering the life sentence of an abused woman who killed her batterer to 7.5 years.

The materials then examine issues of parole and habeas corpus relief, starting with an article maintaining that such women are double victims, first from their abusers and then from the state. A case reverses a state parole board, as it relied on improper factors in denying a battered woman parole. The chapter ends with an article focusing on issues facing convicted survivors of abuse when they re-enter society and calls on domestic violence agencies to advocate for these people and to work for appropriate changes in the legal system.

A. OVERVIEW, PRE-CONVICTION ISSUES

SHELBY A. D. MOORE, UNDERSTANDING THE CONNECTION BETWEEN DOMESTIC VIOLENCE, CRIME, AND POVERTY: HOW WELFARE REFORM MAY KEEP BATTERED WOMEN FROM LEAVING ABUSIVE RELATIONSHIPS

12 Tex. J. Women L. 451 (2003)
(citations and footnotes omitted)

II. FACING REALITY: WOMEN IN ABUSIVE RELATIONSHIPS COMMIT CRIMES OTHER THAN HOMICIDE

Women, in general, commit crimes for a number of reasons. Notably, recent studies indicate that as many as forty percent of women in prison have been victims of domestic violence. Scholars and those engaged in battered women's defense work are beginning to document that many battered women are accused of crimes relating directly or indirectly to an abusive relationship. Battered women are often charged with child abuse or child endangerment because their status as mothers requires them to protect their children even when they are unable to protect themselves from abusive partners.

As a general notion, criminal law tends to treat female offenders more leniently because of their status or potential status as mothers. Not only is this role central to women's position in society, it is also important in the criminal law's assessment of which women are worthy of a court's decision to use its discretion to treat women with leniency. The system with its tendency toward leniency is dismantled when women are charged with crimes against children, particularly in cases involving passive crimes such as failure to protect. The criminal law reinforces the image of mothers as selfless beings and makes few allowances, even for women who are in violent relationships. Unfortunately, present writings ignore the structural factors that shape the lives of battered women as criminal defendants, particularly when they are poor. Instead, they "[focus] myopically on 'personal responsibility,' individual 'choice,' or the problem of drug addiction—as though all of these existed in a social vacuum." * * *

B. Drug Offenses and Family Violence

There is a dearth of information concerning battered women who abuse drugs or commit drug offenses. The reason, quite simply, is that lawyers and legal scholars have given little attention to the connection between domestic violence and the prosecution of women for the use or sale of narcotics. Few articles have been written about the legal attempts to prosecute crack-addicted mothers who give birth to drug-addicted babies. A small number of other writings analyze the disparate impact of federal and state sentencing guidelines, especially on women trapped in violent relationships with drug-dealing men. Even fewer legal commentators and lawyers examine the complexities of the situations of female criminals in the context of women who sell or use crack cocaine, particularly women who have been abused. However, recent statistics indicate that the percentage of women arrested and prosecuted for drug offenses has dramatically increased above all other crimes. They are being imprisoned in both the state and federal systems for drug offenses at an alarming rate, most often for drug possession.

Attention has been given, however, to domestic violence and substance abuse as it relates to child welfare. Indeed, some scholars indicate that there is clearly a nexus between substance abuse and domestic violence. Where domestic violence is present in the home, battered women self-medicate—resorting to drug and alcohol abuse to cope with their depression, pain, and fear. These substances impair battered women's ability to care for either themselves or their children. Accordingly, they make "particularly unsympathetic parties in abuse and neglect proceedings."

For some time, social scientists have recognized that abused women either sell or use drugs as a means of psychological and physical escape. Beth E. Richie has detailed stories of battered women who were incarcerated for drug offenses. In one case, she presents the story of a twenty-one year old woman detained for drug use. She had been battered by her boyfriend for four years prior to her arrest. * * *

Michelle Jacobs also asserts that we should understand the connection between economic status and a woman's inability to move beyond a violent relationship. She argues that "[w]e cannot ignore the fact that women may sell drugs at the insistence of their abuser, as a coping mechanism, or simply to support themselves when they are trapped in a violent relationship."

They are not always immobilized by their own drug addiction, however. Instead, they may sell drugs as a means of getting money to escape the abuse. The following story demonstrates the measures women may take to leave their batterer:

> There is one and only one reason I am here . . . I sold drugs to try to get an apartment. The undercovers who busted me knew that I was not an addict, but I guess they didn't care. They need a certain number of arrests before they can go home. I had lots of drugs on me, and I was about to cop lots of money. . . . That's all they needed to know. I tried working, but my husband found out, beat me up, and took my money. There were lots of drugs in our neighborhood, and so it wasn't hard to find customers and

suppliers. I never had an identity as a dealer, but I was starting to save enough to move out. No one, so far, has believed me that I only did it as a way to get away from him.

By recognizing that battered women sell or use drugs, we do not have to endorse these activities. But we must understand the full range of and the circumstances surrounding the crimes they commit. One commentator notes, "If we are going to advocate an end to violence against women, we must understand more about all types of violence women experience as well as the range of coping mechanisms women develop." Further, if we cannot envision that it is even plausible that battered women engage in the sale or use of narcotics as a means of coping with or escaping violent relationships, it is difficult to see how we can effectively represent them. We, quite simply, cannot provide complete or adequate representation.

C. Property Crimes and Domestic Violence

Consistent with the harsh treatment of abused women who commit drug offenses, little attention has been given to the connection between women, poverty, and the other types of crimes women commit. Even more unsettling, however, is that there is little discussion as to how domestic abuse is connected with or contributes to the circumstances under which battered women commit crime.

In addition to detailing the burdens faced by battered women prosecuted for narcotics offenses, Beth E. Richie has also given thoughtful attention to women who commit property crimes, including arson, burglary, and theft. She presents the stories of abused women incarcerated in Rikers Island for crimes they committed or are alleged to have committed as a result of abusive relationships. She recounts the story of a woman charged with arson for an accidental fire started while fending off a beating by her husband. Her neighbors heard her threatening to kill her husband if he did not stop beating her. Police used this information to arrest her for arson after she and her husband knocked over a candle during the struggle. She did not intend to start a fire. And although she and her husband escaped the apartment without injury, the police arrested her, even after observing her black eyes and scarred face.

Richie also tells the story of a woman trapped in a violent marriage for seven years. She was detained for burglary after stealing from her employer for whom she worked as a maid. She states:

> The abuse got so bad that it was getting hard for me to keep going to work. Since we needed the money, this only made him more upset, and I was getting really desperate. I started working for a white family who had more than enough things, so I started lifting food and clothes. They would just leave money around, and once he came there to finish an attack he started the night before and he saw the money and took it and some jewelry. He said he had

> no respect for me for being a maid and all, and that he'd think more of me if I put my "slave work" to use for us. So I began to move from job to job every few months to steal stuff. He'd sell it and keep the money. He was beating me and harassing me and teasing me all the while, unless I made a good boost. It was like we were working together for the first time. The only time I felt really good was when he was spotting for me. It was like he was acting like a real husband for the first time, and I got sucked into feeling protected and taken care of. Since I was the one stealing, I've served time twice before for possession of stolen property and burglary. But he was the one who set it up. He was the one who beat me if I didn't get the goods.

This scenario is not presented to suggest that all battered women commit crimes because their abusers compelled them to do so. As one scholar states, there are times when the situation is more complicated, including when the abused woman engages in crime with her abuser because it presents an opportunity for mutuality and shared power. Indeed, she notes, "The more complicated the facts, the more difficult it becomes for us to decipher where the abuse creates entry into criminal activity and where the battered woman's own agency has taken over." This is a particularly difficult question, yet it cannot erase those circumstances where battered women commit crimes in the company of or in fear of their batterers. It is a question which must be explored, not only by feminist legal theorists, but also by defense attorneys who have undertaken the onerous task of representing battered women defendants who commit crimes other than homicide or related offenses.

Estimates are that as many as fifty percent of women will be victims of violence during their lifetimes. As a result, it is critical that attorneys explore domestic violence issues with their female clients. This inquiry should also include whether there has been emotional and verbal abuse. Attorneys experienced with representing battered women defendants indicate that victims of abuse are often reluctant to talk about abuse and private family matters they believe are irrelevant to the present reason for consulting an attorney. However, the information may be critical to the attorney's ability to thoroughly perform her responsibilities. Just as important, screening all female defendants for domestic violence is, quite simply, an ethical responsibility. Indeed, we must become comfortable exploring with female defendants questions regarding control over finances, isolation, fighting patterns between spouses, whether their partner monitors their actions, and other issues that might reveal that female defendants have been abused and, further, whether such abuse had any impact on the crime for which they are accused. * * *

[Editor's Note: According to Victoria Law, in "Awareness of the Criminalization of Survivors Is Increasing—Has it Entered the

Courtroom?," Truthout 7/4/17, "The exact numbers of women imprisoned [in the U.S.] for defending themselves against domestic violence—or for abuse-related convictions—remain unknown. As reported previously on Truthout, no government agency tracks the number of abuse survivors behind bars.

In 1999, the U.S. Department of Justice found that nearly half of all women in local jails and state prisons had experienced abuse before their arrests. That is the most recent nationwide data available. More recent smaller studies indicate that the prevalence of abuse has not abated—a 2012 study found that 90 percent of the 102 incarcerated women interviewed reported physical and sexual violence from their partners in the year before their incarceration. * * *

[An] attorney who often works with domestic violence survivors, including those imprisoned for self-defense, [told Truthout] 'I never talked to a survivor who killed her abusive partner who didn't try every other path available first.' She has heard numerous stories from survivors who called police only to have their complaints not taken seriously; in some instances, especially for Black women, the police label the victim as the aggressor. She's also worked with abuse survivors who did not call the police because their partner was a police officer, because they were using substances or because, though they wanted the violence to stop, they did not want their partner to be arrested. Many tried to access shelters or other resources and, because of under-funding, were turned away. For abuse survivors who are also immigrants, fears of detention and deportation, particularly under the Trump administration, have stopped them from seeking assistance.

The National Network to End Domestic Violence (NNEDV) found that, in a single day in 2016, nearly 73,000 abuse victims were served. However, nearly 12,000 others made requests for services, including emergency shelter, housing, transportation, child care and legal services, that could not be met because of agencies' lack of resources.

[NNEDV found similar statistics in its 2022 national survey of domestic violence programs: over 79,000 adult and child victims were served but programs were unable to meet 12,692 requests for services primarily for housing and emergency shelter, due to lack of resources. nnedv.org]

When services come up short, the blame often falls on survivors. Sue Osthoff is the co-founder and [former] director of the National Clearinghouse for the Defense of Battered Women [now the National Defense Center for Criminalized Survivors], a [more than] 30-year-old organization that provides support to survivor-defendants. 'However the system can blame women for her experiences, it will,' she told Truthout. The response from the legal system—from police to prosecutors to juries—is often, 'Why didn't she get help?' If a survivor did not tell someone about the abuse, the violence can be dismissed as 'not that bad.' If she did, then the survivor is blamed for knowing that she should leave but failing to do so."]

LEIGH GOODMARK, WHEN IS A BATTERED WOMAN NOT A BATTERED WOMAN? WHEN SHE FIGHTS BACK

20 Yale J. L. & Feminism 75 (2008)
(citations and footnotes omitted)

II. THE PARADIGMATIC VICTIM AND HER SILENCED SISTERS

The dilemma for women who fight back is that a stock narrative already exists for victims of domestic violence. That narrative has been shaped by the work of Lenore Walker, who first introduced the ideas that came to be known as battered woman syndrome, as well as by political choices the battered women's movement made in attempting to secure support, resources, and legislative and systemic change. That narrative is drastically different from the narratives of women who fight back.

A. The Paradigmatic Victim Is Passive

[The author asserts that the paradigmatic victim is passive, submissive, weak, and powerless. She ascribes this to Lenore Walker's characterization of battered women as suffering from learned helplessness, which she contrasts with Gondolf and Fisher's "recast[ing] the battered woman as a survivor who actively takes measures to protect herself and her children from within the relationship."] * * * While survivor theory provides an alternative narrative to Walker's helpless victim, it similarly fails to capture the experiences of women who fight back. * * * The stories of battered women are too complex to be shunted into the overarching categories of "victim" and "survivor." Creating such categories has the unintended but nonetheless harmful consequence of penalizing those victims whose stories do not fit neatly within them.

B. The Paradigmatic Victim Is White

* * * Simply by virtue of their race, women of color face an uphill battle in having their victimization recognized and rectified, even when they attempt to conform their behavior to that of a stereotypical victim. April, an African American battered woman, described her experience:

> I was told to act like a little white girl . . . to look sad, to try to cry, to never look the jury in the eye. It didn't really work for me because the judge took one look at me and said, "You look pretty mean; I bet you could really hurt a man." * * *

As sociologist Beth Richie points out, "In the end, the assumed race and class neutrality of gender violence led to the erasure of low-income women and women of color from the dominant view." * * *

C. The Paradigmatic Victim Is Straight

* * * The combination of battered woman syndrome, historical representations of victimhood, gender essentialism, and political expediency as endorsed by the media and popular culture have combined to create the prevailing narrative for victims of domestic violence: Battered women are weak, dependent, passive, fearful, white, straight women who need the court's assistance because they are not able to take positive action to stop the violence against them. * * *

III. THE STORIES OF WOMEN WHO FIGHT BACK

Studies of women who use force against their partners indicate that overwhelmingly large numbers of those women have been battered. In her recent study of women arrested for domestic assaults, sociologist Susan Miller found that ninety-five percent of the women had used violence in reaction to a partner's violence. As Miller explains, "Typically, women's use of force is in response to their current or former partner's violence or can be characterized as a reaction that results from past abuses and their relative powerlessness in the relationship."

Researchers agree that the vast majority of women who use violence do so to defend themselves or their children or to prevent an impending attack. But women cite other reasons as well: to stand up for themselves in an attempt to salvage their self-worth, to get their partners' attention, to earn their partners' respect, to retaliate for threats against their families, and to retaliate for their partners' abusive behavior. Sociologist and battered women's advocate Evan Stark argues that women use violence in order to express their identities as beings independent of their controlling partners. * * *

Ironically, women's use of force may lead to escalation of the violence and make women who fight back more vulnerable to serious injury. * * * Women who use violence experience higher levels of depression and fear or anxiety than violent men and often feel guilty about their actions. * * *

"[S]ocieties that believe in the stereotype of feminine passivity and tolerance . . . may perceive a woman who uses violence against her intimate partner as 'unnatural,' 'freakish,' and 'criminal by nature' and deal with her accordingly." Once a battered woman uses violence, her status as "victim" is imperiled. * * *

Social science research suggests that two groups of women are particularly likely to fight back against their abusers: African American women and lesbians. * * *

A. African American Women Who Fight Back

* * * One very basic and concrete reason that African American women are more likely to fight back may be their perception that no outside assistance is available. * * * Particularly for poor African American women

living in depressed urban areas, simply reaching the available social services may be impossible. * * *

African American women may feel that to break the silence is to bring further shame and disapprobation on African American men from the wider society. * * * Marilyn Yarbrough and Crystal Bennett describe "three common stereotypes ascribed particularly to African American women": Mammy, Jezebel, and Sapphire. Mammy, derived from the historical depictions of female domestic slaves, is a nurturer, "ready to soothe everyone's hurt, envelop them in her always ample bosom, and wipe away their tears." Jezebel, "the bad-black-girl," uses her sexuality to entrap men and to extract what she wants from them. Yarbrough and Bennett describe Sapphire as "the wise-cracking, balls-crushing, emasculating woman" who "lets everyone know she is in charge." * * * A victim who judges stereotype as a "Jezebel," for example, might find the credibility of her claims of abuse questioned. The historical link between Jezebel's promiscuity and dishonesty has meant that "African American women were not, and often are not, portrayed as being truthful and, therefore, they could not be trusted." * * *A victim labeled a Sapphire-like woman would have a difficult time convincing the legal system of her need for protection even if she took no defensive action; if she fights back, she may have no chance at all. * * *

Given that the legal system is the primary means for responding to domestic violence in American society, the unavailability of that system as a real option for African American women may leave them grasping for other alternatives to address the violence they face. Forced to choose between continuing to be battered and seeking help through a racist system that might find them culpable for the violence against them, African American women may see fighting back as a more attractive alternative. * * *

In describing her relationship with her abuser, for example, Johnetta stressed her sense of herself as an atypical victim of violence because she fought back.

> Part of my problem is that I am a strong Black woman. I am angry, and some people think I am too loud. So even though he beat me almost to death, I beat him too. If I had been as strong as he was, we'd both be in trouble. But since I wasn't as strong, he got away with almost murdering me. It's as simple as that. The broken bones, the scar where he cut my face . . . all of those are because he was stronger outside, and I was stronger inside. By that I mean I'm not a regular battered woman, because he got his share of licks. It wasn't until he started playing the mind games on me that I was really vulnerable to him. * * *

One African American woman who did not fight back felt that she had failed to "live up to" her "birthright" because she did not have a story of retaliating against her partner; her "image of African American women was that they stood up for themselves." * * *

African American women are also more economically independent of their partners than white women. With less financial impetus to remain in their relationships, African American women may be less willing to tolerate physical violence and more likely to fight back.

The long history of oppression and violence against black women informs their need to be prepared to protect themselves, but it may also have prompted some to assume "more assertive, more confident . . . more positive . . . and more resilient" personas than they actually feel. * * * Ironically, that perception of strength—and the sense that therefore these women are not "victims"—may be what prevents African American women from receiving help from these systems; when African American women are seen as too assertive or not sufficiently afraid of their abusers, the doors of shelters and other service providers remain closed. * * *

For women who believe they are responsible for maintaining family integrity despite the violence done to them, leaving an abusive relationship is not a viable option; "[t]o break up their families would just add to the problems of both their own families and the problems of the black community." Maintaining the family structure may be important not only to challenge outsider perceptions of the weakness of black family ties, but may also be essential to the family's economic viability. * * *Faced with the choice of breaking up their families or enduring abuse, African American women, particularly poor women, may look to a third option—fighting back.

B. Lesbians Who Fight Back

Lesbians may also be more likely to fight back against their abusers than are heterosexual women, but theories about why these women fight back are scarce. The narratives of battered lesbians suggest three types of explanations for why they may be more likely to fight back: because they are unwilling to seek outside assistance to address the violence against them, because they are unlikely to be believed when they do seek assistance, and because resources to address the violence against them are not as readily available. * * *

1. Why Battered Lesbians Don't Ask Outsiders for Help

Battered lesbians may be reluctant to seek outside assistance—from family, friends, the lesbian community, or the larger community—to end the violence against them. As a result, they may find themselves trapped within violent relationships, in which fighting back may be the only viable option to attempt to stop the violence. * * * [The author explains reasons why battered lesbians may be reluctant to seek help from outsiders, including shattering the "lesbian utopia" myth, pressure within the lesbian community to appear strong and unafraid, seeing fighting as normal in relationships, pressure from other lesbians not to look like a victim, fear that reporting abuse will trigger more homophobia from outsiders, threats by the batterer to disclose that the victim is a lesbian, internalized homophobia in which the victim feels that being a lesbian is bad so she deserves abuse, isolation due to homophobia from friends and family, or isolation from other lesbians.]

2. Battered Lesbians Are Unlikely To Be Believed

[The author states that battered lesbians may be met with disbelief when they report the abuse, due to societal beliefs that only heterosexual women are victims of domestic violence, so they may resort to fighting back to abate the violence.] * * * Despite research to the contrary, battering in lesbian relationships is frequently described as mutual violence, with both partners being equally powerful and equally culpable. * * *

> A [lesbian] victim's inability to see herself as a victim because she has used violence may prevent her from conveying the kind of coherent narrative that the court wants to hear.

* * * Bluntly put, batterers are not always butch. (Nor are butch women always large and strong.) * * * Judges [and juries] assessing the credibility of parties appearing before them may find it difficult to believe that butch women could ever be the victims of violence—let alone of violence done by their femme partners—especially in instances where the victims are larger and tougher looking than the batterers.

3. Access to Resources To End the Violence

* * * Fighting back may further jeopardize the battered lesbian's ability to access services. Admitting to the use of violence may lead to the recharacterization of the victim as a batterer, rendering her ineligible for shelter, counseling, and other assistance.

4. The Legal System and Battered Lesbians

* * * Because of most courts' unfamiliarity and discomfort with same-sex domestic violence, judges may demand more evidence of the violence, proof that may be impossible to provide given the private nature of battering. * * *

IV. THE IMPORTANCE OF OWNING NARRATIVES

* * * Judicial doubt intensifies when women describe how they fight back against their abusers. While the stories that clients tell their lawyers "reveal a broad spectrum of human character," stories that challenge judicial pre-existing understandings of victim behavior are likely to raise doubts about the victim's credibility. Women who fight back enter the courtroom with their credibility in question by virtue of their failure to comply with the prevailing victim stereotype. As evidenced by the stories told above, women who fight back are not seen as needing protection, and

their claims are routinely downplayed (particularly in the cases of lesbian victims) or dismissed.

In heterosexual couples, arguments about similarities in the rates of violence among men and women may be at play as well. An entire literature disputing the prevalence of men as perpetrators of interpersonal violence has emerged; some see this literature as a backlash against the gains that the battered women's movement has made over the past thirty years. Backlash or no, doubters have succeeded in pressing the public case for proportionality—the proposition that within relationships, men and women are equally violent. Despite the reasoned responses to these claims (that men's violence is more serious, more damaging, and more likely to be a means of controlling their victims), those preaching proportionality have made some inroads into society's understanding of what interpersonal violence is. When judges with whom the proportionality argument resonates hear that women have fought back, they may be likely to simply categorize those women as violent, rather than exploring the context for women's violence and the justification for its use. * * *

Attorneys have tremendous power in shaping the stories of their clients; even if the lawyer hews closely to the story told by the client (and not all do), it is the lawyer's voice, the lawyer's choice of words, the lawyer's tone and inflection and pacing that structure the narrative heard by the court [and jury]. Lawyers can misuse that power in a number of ways: by silencing client voices, by omitting particular kinds of narratives, by presenting only narratives that are acceptable to the legal system, and by requiring client obedience to the lawyer's translation of the story. When lawyers rewrite client stories without client input or approval, they take from clients the power to decide how they want to be presented and exclude the client from the strategic choices that will shape her case. * * *

What is clear is that judicial education has made an impact in helping to create and maintain the rigid stereotypes of battered women that judges continue to expect. The essentializing of battered women is a byproduct of the indoctrination of judges in learned helplessness and the battered woman syndrome; no "Domestic Violence 101" training is complete without some coverage of these concepts. Trainings tend to generalize and simplify for the sake of brevity and understanding; by distilling the discourse down in this way, judges are offered only the most basic, easily digested understanding of what domestic violence is and how a vast range of women experience it. * * *

Beyond formal training programs, then, how can advocates for battered women educate judges to look beyond the paradigmatic victim? [The author encourages attorneys to educate judges and juries by telling the real stories of women who fight back, explaining why even though they used violence they are victims of abuse by their partners.] * * * They can create "disorienting moments" for judges, prompting them to question what they think they know about domestic violence and who victims of violence are. Telling counterstories is the kind of education that might actually create a more hospitable environment for women who fight back. * * *

The lawyer must also recognize that the client may not yet have found her voice. Traumatized, defiant, angry, grieving the loss of the relationship, ashamed of her action or inaction, the client's story may change depending on the emotions she feels and the acceptance or resistance she meets as she begins to articulate her narrative. Her story may be in transition, and may remain in flux over the life of the case. Professor Leslie Espinoza cautions, "[L]awyer interaction with a client who has been abused should allow the client the space to construct a story in her own time." The lawyer must avoid the temptation to make the initial client story the "one 'true' story" and adhere to that narrative regardless of how the client's understanding of her story evolves over time. * * *

[Editor's Note: In "Evil Women And Innocent Victims: The Effect Of Gender On California Sentences For Domestic Homicide," 22 Hastings Women's L. J. 113 (2011), Ryan Elias Newby states that when women use weapons such as guns and knives in both defensive and aggressive interpersonal violence, they are disproportionately affected by weapons enhancements statutes, such as those in place in California. Notably, a woman is less likely to use fists, hands, and feet or weapons that otherwise require use of superior physical force against her partner than she is to have such weapons used against her. Newby also notes that women who kill their partners are more likely to use weapons than men are because they are less able to commit homicide using fists, hands, or feet compared to men.

On the other hand, Newby found that those women who kill their male partners who are able to show prior aggression by their partners may receive lesser sentences even when they are unable to prove perfect self-defense. This may be because their stories comport with more traditionally acceptable notions of victimhood. Women who cannot show physical harm but can show the undesirability of their male partners as well as their own attempts to be a good wife and mother may also be accorded sympathy in court. Newby also found that women who kill for gain will be accorded severe punishments, particularly if that gain is financial.

Of course the prosecution may characterize the killing as done for financial gain when there are life insurance proceeds, even though the actual motivation for the killing is to stop the abuse. See, e.g., the case of Deborah Peagler, memorialized in the documentary Crime After Crime.]

ZELDA B. HARRIS, THE PREDICAMENT OF THE IMMIGRANT VICTIM/DEFENDANT: "VAWA DIVERSION" AND OTHER CONSIDERATIONS IN SUPPORT OF BATTERED WOMEN

23 St. Louis U. Pub. L. Rev. 49 (2004)
(citations and footnotes omitted)

The struggle to combat domestic violence has sustained a modern feminist movement that began over thirty years ago. The push to prioritize domestic violence on the feminist agenda has yielded far-reaching and tangible results in a relatively short period. The passage of the Violence Against Women Act of 1994 ("VAWA") and the Battered Immigrant Women Protection Act of 2000 ("VAWA II") is a testament to this fact. VAWA and VAWA II are a culmination of efforts and collaborations made between and across members of the feminist and civil rights movement. However, as the fanfare over the collective rewards fades, serious concerns remain regarding the impact of the policies and laws on non-white women who have been subjected to historical oppression based on race or national origin. Unfortunately, poor women of color have been left to bear the expense and debts owed from waging a war against gender inequality.

One example of the damage is the effect of mandatory misdemeanor domestic violence prosecution policies on women who have immigrated to the United States with abusive U.S. citizen or legal permanent resident spouses. The mandatory policies, lobbied for by anti-domestic violence advocates, have effectively disabled immigrant women from securing the personal freedom needed to gain the very safety for themselves and their children that the movement promised.

The following essay seeks to shed light on some of the unintended consequences of mandatory prosecution policies as gleaned from my experience representing battered women in the Domestic Violence Law Clinic in Tucson, Arizona. Tucson is located in close proximity to the border of Mexico. Consequently, many of the clients served by the Clinic are recent immigrants from Mexico and other Latin American countries.

Any interaction with the criminal justice system can have permanent consequences for immigrants seeking permanent residence or citizenship in this country. The current domestic violence laws and policies, in an effort to effectuate color-and gender-blind justice, treat the female immigrant defendant the same as the male, non-immigrant defendant. The imposition of mandatory prosecution policies on battered immigrant women who find themselves defendants in criminal court has overly harsh and unwarranted results. The typical criminal defendant represented by the Clinic is a poor, recently immigrated, non-English speaking woman with children. That typical client is a survivor of domestic violence at the hands of the person who stands as a "victim" in criminal court. * * *

VIII. VAWA DIVERSION AND OTHER CONSIDERATIONS

Rather than a wholesale elimination of all mandatory policies and laws outlined in this article, I propose the implementation of discretionary prosecution under select circumstances as warranted by identified case facts. The approach necessarily requires a level of trust by and between criminal justice system actors, anti-domestic violence advocates, and members of historically oppressed groups that has heretofore been unrealized. The alternative leaves victims like Rosa in the cross hairs of intersecting policies enacted to address domestic violence as a serious public concern without regard to the consequences that leave devastated victims in their wake. I argue for the imposition of this discretionary model for immigrant victims of domestic violence who are also facing charges of misdemeanor domestic violence. The proposal attempts to address two concerns: (1) that victims of domestic violence are identified as early as possible by the prosecutor's office, even when the victims enter the system as defendants; and (2) that victim/defendants in domestic violence cases progress through the criminal justice system in a manner that renders them more capable of ending the violence in their lives rather than keeping them trapped in a cycle of violence.

A. Individualized Case Assessment by Prosecutorial Staff Specifically Trained in Identification of Domestic Violence Victims

To the extent that agreement exists between advocates and state actors that domestic violence is a crime requiring particular attention, resources should be devoted to specially train prosecutors to identify and recognize the particular forms of coercive control that abusive spouses use against immigrant victims of domestic violence. Early identification of these cases will allow for the provision of appropriate case disposition alternatives that do not yield the unintended consequences discussed above.

B. VAWA Diversion and Other Case Disposition Options for Victim/Defendants in Domestic Violence Cases

Once identified, prosecutors should be given discretion to offer an array of case disposition alternatives that will allow the victim/defendant to address the violence in her life in a safe and responsible manner, but do not render her deported, childless, and unemployed. An alternative that has proved successful in the Clinic service area is commonly referred to as VAWA diversion. The VAWA diversion alternative is really a misnomer because the victim/defendant is not required to admit facts sufficient to sustain a conviction for a domestic violence offense. Instead, the case is held open in the pre-trial phase while the victim/defendant completes counseling. The number of hours of counseling required is determined by the prosecutor, and the counseling must be obtained through a program that is appropriate for the needs of a victim of domestic violence. After the requisite number of counseling hours has been completed, the case is voluntarily dismissed by the prosecutor, and the victim/defendant is allowed to exit the system without a conviction or the resulting negative immigration law consequences. Any concerns about repeat offenders can be relieved by the official recognition of the VAWA diversion as a legitimate case disposition. Accordingly, the prosecutor's office may want to implement a policy that a defendant may only participate in one VAWA diversion program in her lifetime.

Other options such as creative plea bargaining should be explored. Creative approaches to plea bargaining may include carefully drafted plea agreements that reduce the charge to a non-domestic violence offense and a non-violent offense with a maximum term of probation that does not exceed one year.

In Rosa's case, a reduction of the assault charge to a class three misdemeanor would provide greater assurance against deportation on the grounds of conviction for a crime of violence. Similarly, basing the disorderly conduct charge on something other than fighting (i.e., unreasonable noise) could aid in preventing deportation. Accordingly, an attractive prosecution offer for Rosa might include an outright dismissal of the contributing to the delinquency or dependency of a minor charge and a plea of guilty to the reduced charges of assault and disorderly conduct.

C. Referral to Immigration Legal Assistance Programs and Appointment of Public Defense Counsel

Immigrant victim/defendants involved in domestic violence cases should be provided with referrals to immigration legal assistance programs so that appropriate remedies may be sought under the VAWA provisions of the INA. Further, resources must be made available so that victim/defendants can be afforded representation through the public defender's office as the case outcome can have a substantial impact on their immigration status and rights in this country.

D. Referral to Culturally-Specific Advocacy and Counseling Services

Immigrant victim/defendants should be identified early and referred immediately to culturally-sensitive, anti-domestic violence advocacy service providers. These agencies can provide counseling and other supportive services in a manner that recognizes the multiple identities of race, gender, and national origin of victim/defendants like Rosa.

E. Community Education and "Rosa's Rights"

The above-suggested proposals contemplate action after the initiation of a prosecution. However, community education could lessen the potential for cases similar to Rosa's from being referred for prosecution in the first instance. Agencies providing services to recently immigrated women are in a unique position to educate potential victim/defendants about their rights. In Tucson, social service providers routinely hand out a card, in English and Spanish, which lists community resources available to victims of domestic violence. A similar card can be created and distributed to the same population of victims informing them of their rights upon state intervention in a case of domestic violence. The rights, "Rosa's Rights," should include: (1) the right to request a language interpreter at the scene; (2) the right to assert self-defense; (3) the right to report prior abuse; (4) the right to request medical attention; and (5) the right to request documentation of injuries. * * *

ERIN SMITH, AMICUS BRIEF, PEOPLE V. CORNELL BROWN, 33 CAL.4TH 892 (2004)

for the California Alliance Against Domestic Violence et al,
under the supervision of Nancy K. D. Lemon
(citations and footnotes omitted)

III. "BATTERED WOMEN'S SYNDROME" IS NOT AN APPROPRIATE TERM TO DESCRIBE THE EXPERIENCE AND EFFECTS OF BATTERING

First conceptualized in the 1970s, the term "battered women's syndrome" (hereinafter "BWS") is often used to describe common reactions that victims have to domestic violence. BWS has been used as a shorthand reference to the body of scientific and clinical research that is relevant in domestic violence cases.

A. The Term Is Descriptively Inaccurate and Misleading to the Trier of Fact

Due to the extensive knowledge developed in the last twenty-five years with respect to battering and its effects, the term "BWS" is imprecise. Id. The term no longer adequately reflects "the breadth or nature of the scientific knowledge now available concerning battering and its effects."

An additional limitation of the term BWS is that it implies that the victim suffers from a psychological impairment or pathology. The pathological implication sends a message that the victim is passive or helpless in the face of abuse. This assumption is, however, contrary to current knowledge.

Moreover, BWS implies that all victims of domestic violence experience one common set of effects from battering. This implication is at odds with our current understanding of the complexity and variability of individuals' responses to violence. Rather than there being a set of uniform responses to violence, "scientific and clinical literature has documented a broad range of emotional, cognitive, physiological, and behavioral sequelae to traumatic events such as battering." The variability in responses to violence is not captured by a term that purports to label just one "syndrome."

What is more, by using the word "woman," the term ignores male victims of domestic violence. Approximately 8% of men are victims of domestic violence in their lifetimes. Men are victims of domestic violence both in heterosexual relationships and homosexual relationships.

In addition to the descriptive inadequacy of the term itself, the term potentially distorts the administration of justice by the criminal justice system. The term's limitations can be misleading to the trier of fact, who may make the assumptions described above. Furthermore, the term turns the attention away from the batterer's behavior, which is the prosecuted conduct, and to the mental state of the victim. As a result, the trier of fact may be misled into thinking that the determinative issue in the case is whether the victim has BWS, and not whether the alleged conduct occurred.

Additionally, a limited definition of BWS may prevent the trier of fact from obtaining relevant information. For example, one construction of BWS limited the mental effects of battering to include only Post-Traumatic Stress Disorder (hereinafter "PTSD"). Since victims' psychological responses to battering are not limited to PTSD, using this narrow understanding of the psychological responses that constitute BWS "excludes other potentially relevant and important information necessary for the factfinders in their deliberations."

Moreover, courts can misconstrue the common reactions that victims have to battering as a checklist of elements, each of which must be present in order for the victim to be considered a "battered woman" with the "syndrome." For example, since recantation is commonly associated with current understandings of BWS, a court may think that a victim who does not recant does not have BWS and is, therefore, not a "battered woman." This approach is incorrect since, as discussed above, victims have widely variable reactions to battering.

Furthermore, it would undermine the achievements of domestic violence advocates, who sought to assist others in understanding domestic violence and how it fits into the law by outlining common experiences in battering relationships, if those common experiences were now misconstrued as an absolute checklist that can be used to deny victims of domestic violence the benefit of expert testimony at their trials.

B. The Statewide and National Trend Is to Abandon the Term "Battered Women's Syndrome"

In California, the statewide trend has been to attempt to abandon the term BWS. First, in 1996, this Court correctly noted that many experts preferred to use "battering and its effects" or "battered women's experiences" instead of "BWS." This Court recognized several critiques of the phrase BWS:

> (1) [I]t implies that there is one syndrome which all battered women develop, (2) it has pathological connotations which suggest that battered women suffer from some sort of sickness, (3) expert testimony on domestic violence refers to more than women's psychological reactions to violence, (4) it focuses attention on the battered woman rather than on the batterer's coercive and controlling behavior and (5) it creates an image of battered women as suffering victims rather than as active survivors.

* * * In addition to the courts, the [California] state legislature has indicated its intent to move away from the term BWS. In 2000, Evidence Code section 1107(e) was added to change the title of section 1107 to "Expert Witness Testimony on Battered Women's Experiences" instead of "Expert Witness Testimony on Battered Women's Syndrome." Following this Court's recognition in *Humphrey* of the problems associated with the term BWS, this amendment indicates the legislature's acknowledgment of the harms of BWS.

There is a similar trend on the national level to move away from the term BWS. In 1996, the U.S. Department of Justice, the National Institute of Justice, the U.S. Department of Health and Human Services, and the National Institute of Mental Health, in conjunction with the State Justice Institute and the National Association of Women Judges, prepared a report titled *The Validity and Use of Evidence Concerning Battering and Its Effects in Criminal Trials: Report Responding to Section 40507 of the Violence Against Women Act.*

This report compiled three papers on the subject and concluded that there is a "strong consensus among the researchers, and also among the judges, prosecutors, and defense attorneys interviewed for the assessment [of the effects of BWS evidence on criminal trials], that the term 'battered woman syndrome' " does not reflect the scientific knowledge now available regarding battering and its effects, implies a psychological impairment, and suggests a single pattern of response to battering. Therefore, "the term 'battered woman syndrome' is no longer useful or appropriate." Report at vii. "[A] more accurate and appropriate reference is 'evidence concerning battering and its effects.' "

Amici respectfully encourage this Court to follow this national and statewide trend away from the term "BWS" by using "battering and its effects" or, as in Evidence Code section 1107(e), "battered women's experiences," in the Court's opinions.

[Editor's Note: In 2004, the California Legislature amended Evidence Code section 1107 to delete all references to Battered Woman Syndrome. Instead, the section now refers to "intimate partner battering and its effects." The majority opinion in People v. Cornell Brown *almost completely avoided using the term BWS, instead referring to "expert testimony about the*

behavior of victims of domestic violence victims," or "evidence on domestic violence."]

BRANDI L. JACKSON, NO GROUND ON WHICH TO STAND: REVISE STAND YOUR GROUND LAWS SO SURVIVORS OF DOMESTIC VIOLENCE ARE NO LONGER INCARCERATED FOR DEFENDING THEIR LIVES

30 Berkeley J. Gender L. & Just. 154 (2015)
(footnotes omitted)

INTRODUCTION

A few years ago, a young woman named Natasha shot and killed her boyfriend in the apartment they were sharing. He had trapped her in the bedroom and was about to launch into another of what had become weekly "beatdowns," where he would hit her with a closed fist. Prior to the killing, the beatings had become more severe and more frequent, as were the threats that he was going to kill her. As to whether there were other options available to her to escape, Natasha said, "At the time I pulled the trigger, I didn't think so. He'd cornered me in a small bedroom with no way out except maybe jumping out a glass window or simply undergoing yet another beatdown. He was fond of beating me, then forcing me to perform oral sex on him right away. If my lips were bloody, he'd force himself into my rectum." Natasha was charged with second-degree murder and criminal possession of a firearm (which belonged to her boyfriend). She was convicted of manslaughter and sentenced to fifteen years in prison.

In February 2012, George Zimmerman, a resident of a gated community and a neighborhood watch volunteer, called 911 to report a young teen (later identified as Trayvon Martin). Zimmerman said Martin "looks like he's up to no good, or he's on drugs or something. It's raining and he's just walking around, looking about." The dispatcher told Zimmerman, "just tell me if he does anything," to which Zimmerman responded, "[t]hese assholes they always get away . . . ." Martin started running, and Zimmerman started following him. The dispatcher told Zimmerman not to follow Martin, and that the police were on their way. At some point, Martin was out of sight. Yet, Zimmerman tracked him down, got out of his car, and approached Martin. The facts related to the altercation cannot be reliably determined, but it ended with Zimmerman fatally shooting Martin. Fifty-four days later, Zimmerman was charged with second-degree murder. He was acquitted.

While the circumstances of the above situations differ greatly, the charges in both cases were acutely affected by similar laws that allow one to "Stand Your Ground" (SYG) and meet force with force if attacked in one's own home or where one is legally authorized to be, even if there is opportunity for safe retreat. The above cases demonstrate how varying implementation of these laws creates disparate and unjust results. The

SYG doctrine is arguably responsible for allowing Zimmerman—who voluntarily removed himself from the safety of his vehicle to chase down the young black teen whom he eventually fatally shot "in self-defense"—to walk free, while imposing a fifteen-year prison sentence on Natasha, who killed her extremely abusive and threatening boyfriend when he trapped her in the bedroom.

Public outrage regarding both the delay in Zimmerman's arrest and his subsequent acquittal of murder charges put Florida's SYG statute under national scrutiny. Numerous organizations began advocating for the repeal of these laws based on the common belief that they "undermine public safety, senselessly put people at risk, and enable the kind of tragedy we've witnessed in the case of Trayvon Martin." This article does not intend to undermine these serious and very real concerns that SYG laws may legally excuse abhorrent misconduct, as was the case with George Zimmerman. * * * This article argues that lawmakers should consider the impact these laws have on women who survive abusive relationships before eagerly repealing all forms of SYG laws. For women like Natasha who kill their abusers in self-defense after years of sustaining physical, emotional, sexual, and/or financial abuse, permitting a small category of legally justifiable violence via SYG protection could more adequately preserve justice for certain oppressed populations.

This article examines the effect of SYG laws on domestic violence survivors, whose situations differ from others in which a person feels threatened by a stranger. Given the circumstances of the abusive relationship, when a battered woman feels threatened, she does not usually have a reasonable opportunity to retreat from an episode of domestic violence. Part I examines background information on the theories explaining the dynamics of domestic abuse, as well as the birth and evolution of SYG laws. This Part provides a backdrop for understanding the situation in which a survivor finds herself prior to using deadly force, and explains the various SYG statutes that may affect her case. Part II analyzes the problems that SYG laws (versus the duty to retreat) create for battered defendants, namely, whether they are in fact protected by SYG immunity from prosecution. This Part also examines how fact finders' gender biases and misperceptions about domestic violence cause them to inappropriately apply SYG laws. Lastly, Part III proposes the following solutions: (1) retain affirmative SYG laws in a limited capacity; (2) limit SYG privilege so that it is available only while inside the home; and (3) create a statutory presumption of reasonable fear where there is a history of abuse between a dominant aggressor and a more vulnerable person. These legislative changes most closely comport with a balanced system of justice, taking into account a woman's right to self-defense when faced with lethal force from an abusive partner, while avoiding potentially adverse effects of expanding a doctrine that justifies violence. * * *

[Editor's Notes: 1. Marissa Alexander's case is another example of how SYG laws have not been applied fairly to survivors of domestic violence. She spent almost six years either in prison or confined to home detention after she was convicted of aggravated assault in 2012 for firing a warning shot at her husband, who admitted having previously abused her. The shooting happened nine days after she gave birth to their child when Marissa was cornered and threatened by her husband. She was freed early in 2017 and is advocating that the Florida SYG law be amended to take the burden of proof off defendants who have to demonstrate in pre-trial hearings that they acted in self-defense; instead, prosecutors would have to prove the absence of self-defense. Even though the law says there is no duty to retreat, Marissa's judge ruled that the SYG law did not apply in her case when he sentenced her to 20 years in prison even though her husband was not harmed. Approximately half the states in the U.S. have SYG laws. Survived and Punished, an organization working to end the criminalization of survivors of domestic and sexual violence, advocates for the release of women like Marissa Alexander.

2. In "Between the Hammer and the Anvil: Battered Women Claiming Self-Defense and a Legislative Proposal to Amend Section 3.04(2)(b) of the U.S. Model Penal Code," 52 Harv. J. on Legis. 17 (2015), Israeli law professors Dayan and Gross note that "the American doctrine relating to battered women who act in self-defense is inconsistent and incomplete," leading to "tragic legal consequences." They propose establishing "a legal presumption that circumstances of prolonged and severe violence in the family poses a real danger to the victim's body and life." They also propose altering the MPC language regarding the duty to retreat and the duty to comply with the abuser's demands; victims of abuse would have to meet these new requirements before resorting to deadly protective force. The authors also call for criminalizing marital rape in the MPC, a change that is long overdue, and that in some cases is directly related to survivors of abuse killing their abusers in self-defense. See chapter 9 above for MPC language, which does not criminalize marital rape.]

STATE V. ELZEY

472 Md. 84 (Md. 2021)
(footnotes and citations omitted)

Latoya Bonte Elzey grabbed a butcher knife during a heated argument with her boyfriend, Migail Hunter. A few minutes later, Hunter fell to the floor with a knife wound to his heart. By the time an ambulance arrived, Hunter was dead.

At her murder trial in the Circuit Court for Wicomico County, Elzey did not dispute that she killed Hunter, but claimed that she did so in self-defense. To support her theory of self-defense, Elzey introduced expert testimony from a psychiatrist concerning Battered Spouse Syndrome (sometimes referred to in this opinion as the "Syndrome"). The expert testified that Elzey suffered from Battered Spouse Syndrome at the time of Hunter's killing as a result of her history of abusive relationships, including her relationship with Hunter.

The jury acquitted Elzey of the murder charges, but convicted her of voluntary manslaughter. On appeal, Elzey argued that the trial judge's instruction to the jury concerning Battered Spouse Syndrome was erroneous. The Court of Special Appeals agreed with Elzey, holding that the instruction incorrectly required the jury to make a predicate finding that Hunter repeatedly abused Elzey, before the jury could consider the evidence of past abuse and the expert testimony Elzey had presented. The court also concluded that the instruction gave the jury "mixed messages" about how it should evaluate the evidence of past abuse in relation to the Syndrome and Elzey's claim of self-defense. Because it determined that the erroneous instruction was not harmless beyond a reasonable doubt, the court ordered a new trial. The State then sought further review in this Court.

For the reasons discussed below, we agree with the Court of Special Appeals and Elzey that the trial court erred in its formulation of the jury instruction on Battered Spouse Syndrome, and that this error was not harmless beyond a reasonable doubt.

I

Background

The Killing of Migail Hunter

In May 2017, Elzey and Hunter had been together for approximately one year. Hunter was six feet, two inches tall and 41 years old. Elzey was 26 years old and five feet, six inches tall.

Elzey and Hunter were homeless in May 2017. Elzey's friend, Shatoria Hope, allowed Elzey and Hunter to stay temporarily in her small apartment in Salisbury, Maryland, which Ms. Hope shared with her children. Around midnight on May 21, 2017, after an afternoon and evening of drinking on May 20, Elzey and Hunter began to argue in the living room of Ms. Hope's apartment. Ms. Hope was cooking in the adjoining kitchen at the time, and heard Elzey and Hunter arguing. Hunter was angry about something he had seen on Elzey's phone. After yelling at Hunter to keep his hands off her, Elzey came into the kitchen and grabbed a knife. Ms. Hope persuaded Elzey to put the knife back, and Elzey returned to the living room, where she and Hunter resumed their argument. Elzey tried to explain to Hunter what he had seen on her phone. Ms. Hope then heard a loud slapping sound, followed immediately by Elzey telling Hunter to stop hitting her. Soon after that, Elzey came back into the kitchen. She was crying and yelling that she was tired of Hunter putting his hands on her. Elzey again grabbed a knife. This time, Elzey left the kitchen with the knife—specifically, a large butcher knife—and went back into the living room.

Elzey and Hunter continued arguing for several minutes. Ms. Hope heard Elzey repeatedly yell at Hunter about his putting his hands on her. Ms. Hope also heard Hunter repeatedly say, "go ahead, go ahead and do it," or "do what you got to do." Ms. Hope turned from the stove and looked into the living room. Although she had an obstructed view due to a partial wall that separated the kitchen and living room, Ms. Hope saw Hunter walk up toward Elzey, as he said, "do it, do it, if you're going to stab me." Ms. Hope did not see what then occurred between Elzey and Hunter, but she heard a loud "boom" come from the living room. When Ms. Hope went into the living room to find out what had caused the noise, she saw Hunter on the floor. Ms. Hope asked Elzey what had happened. Elzey told her that Hunter had walked into the knife.

Hunter died a few minutes later as a result of a stab wound that punctured his aorta. The knife also injured one of Hunter's ribs. The wound was one inch long and two inches deep; its path was right to left and upward.

A grand jury in Wicomico County subsequently returned an indictment against Elzey, charging her with murder and related offenses.

Trial

I. Evidence Relating to Elzey's Claim of Self-Defense

Elzey's trial began on June 25, 2018. Ms. Hope testified to what she heard and saw, as summarized above. The State also played a videotaped statement that Elzey gave to the Maryland State Police in the early morning hours of May 21, 2017. In that statement, Elzey told the officers that Hunter physically abused her, and that, at one point, Hunter's abuse had led her to seek refuge at a relative's home.

Elzey testified in her own defense. She told the jury that she had no vehicle on the night of May 20–21 and nowhere to go. She testified that Hunter had her ID card, Social Security card, food stamp card, and other personal items of hers in his wallet. Elzey claimed that Hunter kept those items because "[h]e was very possessive" and "would not allow me to carry my own items."

Elzey also testified about physical abuse that Hunter inflicted on her, which she said began within two months of the start of their relationship. According to Elzey, Hunter frequently would choke her or would force her to perform oral sex. Elzey testified that Hunter's bouts of rage were often sparked by jealousy involving other men's interest in Elzey. Elzey told the jury that, despite Hunter's abuse, she stayed with Hunter "because I loved him, and I . . . believed that he was going to change." Elzey further testified that she and Hunter were not staying with her family members in the area because her relatives "were not accepting the fact that I was with a man that was beating on me."

Over the State's objection, the trial court allowed Elzey to provide the jurors with details concerning abuse by other intimate partners before her relationship with Hunter. Elzey told the jurors about a past boyfriend who punched her in the face on a weekly basis, giving her multiple black eyes. She said she went to the hospital twice for treatment following that boyfriend's assaults. Elzey also testified about another prior relationship in which her then-boyfriend (who was also the father of one of her children) broke her jaw, requiring doctors to wire her mouth shut.

Elzey testified that, during the few days that she and Hunter stayed at Ms. Hope's house, there was a point when Elzey and Hunter were the only adults in the apartment because Ms. Hope was at a hospital. After Ms. Hope's children went to bed, Hunter became angry at Elzey when she would not have sex with him. According to Elzey, Hunter then choked her to the point that she could not breathe.

At midnight on May 21, according to Elzey, Hunter had her phone and was going through it. Hunter saw that a man had pictures of Elzey in the man's Facebook account, which caused Hunter to "go[ ] off." According to Elzey, Hunter "was steady arguing with me, steady yelling at me, steady cussing at me." Elzey said that, as the argument escalated, Hunter was "approaching me in my space," "push[ing] me in my head," and "making me feel threatened for my life."

Elzey told the jury that she grabbed the knife "as a scare away, to keep you away from me, like do not come nowhere near me. I have this. I'm not trying to use it against you. I'm just telling you to stay away from me." Elzey described Hunter's response after she reappeared in the living room with the knife: "He just said, excuse my language, he said, fuck that, bitch. You're going to have to do something. You're going to have to use that knife. That knife does not scare me." Elzey testified that Hunter "continued to come and approach me. . . He was in my face . . . I could feel his spit, he was pretty close to me." Elzey stated that she was "holding the knife up" as Hunter approached her. She claimed that she turned her head away from Hunter, because "I don't want to look at him, and he's steady coming towards me, and I'm just not looking at him. And then all a sudden, he collapsed."

The defense called Dr. Neil Blumberg, a psychiatrist, to testify as an expert witness. Dr. Blumberg told the jury that he had conducted a psychiatric evaluation of Elzey to determine her mental state at the time of the alleged offense. Dr. Blumberg concluded that, at the time of Hunter's death, Elzey was suffering from a number of mental disorders, including severe Post-Traumatic Stress Disorder ("PTSD"), Unspecified Depressive Disorder, moderate Alcohol Use Disorder, and mild Cannabis Use Disorder. Dr. Blumberg opined that Elzey's PTSD and depression were the direct result of the domestic violence she had suffered at the hands of several intimate partners and severe physical abuse that her grandmother inflicted on her during childhood. According to Dr. Blumberg, Elzey's constellation of mental disorders was consistent with what he often sees in someone who suffers from Battered Spouse Syndrome.

Dr. Blumberg described Battered Spouse Syndrome as a psychological condition in which a person experiences repeated episodes of abuse by an intimate partner, becomes depressed, and, because she feels she cannot leave the relationship, convinces herself that the abuser will change. Dr. Blumberg explained that women with the Syndrome develop "learned helplessness," in which they feel unable to change their situation. He described the cycles of abuse that are indicative of the Syndrome and how victims of abuse are able to sense that a confrontation is escalating and, therefore, that "things are going to happen."

Dr. Blumberg's opinion that Elzey suffered from Battered Spouse Syndrome was based on the totality of Elzey's past relationships and the pattern of abuse she suffered at the hands of three intimate partners, including Hunter. Dr. Blumberg first described Elzey's relationship with the boyfriend who broke her jaw. That relationship began when Elzey was 18 and lasted five years:

> They began arguing more primarily after she began spending more time with their child. He, apparently, felt ignored, and he began physically abusing her. She said he was smacking her, emotionally abusing her, putting her down, becoming increasingly controlling.

"He would explode and hit her. . . . And she described over this extended period of about five years going through what is generally referred to as a cycle of violence. Things would kind of escalate. There would be more arguing. There would be an explosive outburst where she would be beaten in some way.

He then would tend to be apologetic. I'm sorry. It's never going to happen again, and they'd go through a period in which things were really positive before the next irritant and escalation and explosive outburst where she was the one who generally got injured."

Dr. Blumberg explained that, after the relationship with that boyfriend ended, Elzey was in another abusive relationship in 2015–16. In this next relationship, Dr. Blumberg noted, "[e]verything was fine for the first six months, and then he started to become abusive." The boyfriend had "[p]roblems with anger." There would be physical outbursts, in which he "blackened her eyes, . . . busted her lip, created a gash on her head. He would beat her if she wouldn't give him money." Elzey was "too afraid to leave him," but when this boyfriend left the state, Elzey "basically escaped and moved away."

Almost immediately after that relationship ended, Elzey became involved with Hunter, who began to abuse her within two months. In light of Elzey's prior abusive relationships, Dr. Blumberg described Elzey's relationship with Hunter as "the same old, same old . . . [S]he has just escaped from an abusive relationship. Here's a guy who takes her in. Everything is fine, initially. And then they become homeless. They're drinking. He's using cocaine. And they begin to have these increasingly verbal abusive interactions that ultimately result in physically abusive actions."

2. The Jury Instruction on Battered Spouse Syndrome

Defense counsel proposed the following jury instruction on Battered Spouse Syndrome (which she referred to as Battered Woman's Syndrome):

> If you find, based on the testimony presented, that the defendant suffered from Battered Woman's Syndrome, you may consider how the effects of this condition may have altered the defendant's mental state. Specifically, you may consider this evidence in deciding whether the defendant actually believed that she needed to defend herself against an imminent threat and whether that belief was reasonable based on all the facts and circumstances as they have been made known to you by the evidence and the testimony in this case.
>
> You may consider whether the presence of Battered Woman's Syndrome altered the defendant's perceptions and beliefs, including her perceptions and beliefs about the danger of the threat posed to her and that the danger was imminent.
>
> You must determine the reasonableness of the defendant's belief[s] and actions based on those beliefs in light of the circumstances as they appeared to the defendant at the time of the killing, and as they are evaluated by you now. Reasonableness is based both on the defendant's beliefs and on your evaluation as to their reasonableness.
>
> If the defendant presents credible evidence of self[-]defense, the State must prove beyond a reasonable doubt that the defendant did not act in self-defense. If you have a reasonable doubt as to whether or not the defendant acted in self-defense, your verdict must be not guilty.

The trial court declined to give the Battered Spouse Syndrome instruction suggested by the defense. Rather, the court indicated it was inclined to model its instruction on instruction 8.13(G) in David E. Aaronson, *Maryland Criminal Jury Instructions and Commentary* (2014–15 ed.). Aaronson's model instruction provides, in pertinent part:

> You have heard evidence that the defendant was a victim of repeated physical and psychological abuse by __________ (*insert name of victim*). You have also heard from an expert witness that a person who is a victim of repeated physical and psychological abuse by a [spouse] [former spouse] [child] [(cohabitant) (co-occupant)] [former (co-habitant) (co-occupant)] may suffer from a psychological condition called "Battered [Spouse] [Woman] [Child] Syndrome." [Also, you heard expert testimony that the defendant exhibits the characteristics consistent with "battered [spouse] [woman] [child] syndrome".]
>
> You must determine based on a consideration of all of the evidence whether the defendant was a victim of repeated physical and psychological abuse by __________ (insert name of victim), and if so, whether [she] [he] suffered from "Battered [Spouse] [Woman] [Child] Syndrome."
>
> If you determine that __________ (*insert name of defendant*) suffered from battered [spouse] [woman] [child] syndrome, then you should consider this evidence for the purpose of explaining ______________'s (*insert name of defendant*) motive or state of mind, or both, and [her] [his] beliefs and perceptions at the time of the commission of the alleged offense in order to determine whether the requirements of self-defense exist.

Defense counsel objected to the court's proposed instruction:

> Your Honor, the only . . . change that the defense was planning to suggest was the language with regard to abuse by the victim. Because of *Wallace-Bey v. State*, . . . we offered . . . two suggested . . . instructions, one of which would indicate ["]by the victim and others,["] but the other would just say, ["]repeated physical and psychological abuse["] period, without indicating specifically as to by whom.

The trial court responded:

> Well, would it be necessary under your understanding of the law that [the jury] be convinced that there was repeated physical and psychological abuse by the victim? Because it seems to me that that's a requirement. It's also true that . . . it could be ["]and others.["]

Although the trial court, thus, initially seemed amenable to changing the language in the proposed instruction so that it referred to abuse by "the victim and others," the court quickly changed course. Referring to Aaronson's model instruction, the court stated:

> Actually, it says, ["Y]ou must determine based on [a] consideration of all the evidence whether the defendant was a

> victim of repeated physical and psychological abuse by["] the victim, in the second paragraph. And I believe that they would have to so find. . . . I'm not hearing the case law to be that you may use the Battered Spouse Syndrome to justify the killing of anyone. You know, you have to be using it to just . . . mitigate or excuse. . . . [I]f the individual who has died didn't abuse you in any way, I don't think that you're allowed to invoke the defense.

As the discussion continued, defense counsel again did not take issue with the inclusion of the reference to the "victim" in the second paragraph of the instruction, but reiterated her request that the instruction refer in that spot to "the victim and others." . . .

After the close of the evidence, the trial court instructed the jury on the concepts of perfect self-defense (which the trial court referred to as "complete" self-defense) and imperfect self-defense (which the court called "partial" self-defense):. . .

The court then gave its Battered Spouse Syndrome instruction, modifying the Aaronson language slightly:

> Ladies and gentlemen, you have heard evidence that the Defendant was a victim of repeated physical and psychological abuse. You have also heard from an expert witness that a person who is a victim of repeated physical and psychological abuse by a victim may suffer from a psychological condition called battered spouse syndrome. You have also heard expert testimony that the Defendant exhibits the characteristics consistent with battered spouse syndrome.
>
> You must determine, based upon a consideration of all the evidence, whether the Defendant was a victim of repeated physical and psychological abuse by the victim, and if so[,] whether she suffered from battered spouse syndrome.
>
> If you determine that the Defendant suffered from battered spouse syndrome[,] then you should consider this evidence for the purpose of explaining the Defendant's motive or state of mind, or both, and her beliefs and perceptions at the time of the commission of the alleged offense in order to determine whether the requirements of self-defense exist.

After the trial court instructed the jury, Elzey's counsel excepted to the instruction on Battered Spouse Syndrome, [reminding the court that they believed the instruction should include abuse from others, not just from the victim, and the court's response that the defense can include abuse from others in closing argument]. . .

In her closing argument, the prosecutor provided the jury with her interpretation of the court's Battered Spouse Syndrome instruction [i.e., that there must be repeated physical and psychological abuse of the defendant by the decedent alone to qualify the defendant's condition as battered spouse syndrome].

The jury acquitted Elzey of first-degree murder, second-degree murder, and first-degree assault. The jury convicted Elzey of voluntary manslaughter, second-degree assault, and reckless endangerment. The circuit court merged the second-degree assault and reckless endangerment convictions into the voluntary manslaughter conviction for sentencing and imposed a sentence of 10 years of imprisonment.

C. Appeal

On appeal, Elzey raised several claims of error. Pertinent here, Elzey argued that the trial judge erred in instructing the jury on Battered Spouse Syndrome in two respects. First, according to Elzey, the instruction confused the jury concerning the relevance of abuse by others besides Hunter with respect to Battered Spouse Syndrome (the "juror confusion issue"). Second, Elzey contended that the instruction erroneously directed the jury to make a predicate factual finding that Hunter repeatedly abused Elzey before it could consider the evidence of abuse by others and Dr. Blumberg's expert testimony on the Syndrome (the "predicate finding issue"). The State argued that the instruction was correct in all respects, and that the trial court acted within its discretion in delivering it.

The Court of Special Appeals agreed with Elzey that the Battered Spouse Syndrome jury instruction was erroneous, both because it improperly required the jury to make a predicate finding that Hunter repeatedly abused Elzey, and because it was confusing as to the relevance of Elzey's past abuse by others. The court further held that the instructional error was not harmless beyond a reasonable doubt, and therefore ordered a new trial.

On January 8, 2020, the State filed a petition for *certiorari* seeking review of the following question: "Was the Court of Special Appeals wrong in holding that a jury may not be instructed to find that the victim abused the defendant and the defendant suffers from Battered Spouse Syndrome before considering expert testimony on the syndrome?" On March 11, 2020, we granted the State's petition.

II. Standard of Review

We review a trial court's giving of a jury instruction for abuse of discretion. . . We review *de novo* whether a jury instruction was a correct statement of the law. This is the case because "even in areas where a trial court has discretion, no discretion is afforded to trial courts to act upon an erroneous conclusion of law." Similarly, a trial court lacks discretion to give an instruction that is "ambiguous, misleading, or confusing to jurors." Reversal of a conviction and a new trial are warranted where the State does not show that an instructional error was harmless beyond a reasonable doubt. To meet this burden, the State must show that the error did not play any role in the jury's verdict. "To say that an error did not contribute to the verdict is . . . to find that error unimportant in relation to everything else the jury considered on the issue in question, as revealed by the record."

III. Discussion

A. The Trial Court Erred in Its Instruction on Battered Spouse Syndrome.

1. The Use of Battered Spouse Syndrome Evidence in Criminal Cases

"Battered Spouse Syndrome" has been officially recognized in Maryland law since 1991, when the General Assembly approved House Bill 49, which was codified at section 10–916 of the Courts and Judicial Proceedings Article.

In the medical and scientific communities, the Syndrome is considered a subcategory of PTSD. PTSD is "a collection of thoughts, feelings, and actions that logically follow a frightening experience that one expects could be repeated." Women in abusive relationships who suffer from Battered Spouse Syndrome "respond to the repeated abuse in a manner similar to others who have been repeatedly exposed to different kinds of trauma." Over the past three decades, courts and legislatures have come to understand that evidence concerning the Syndrome can shed light on the effects of repeated physical, sexual, and psychological abuse on a person's state of mind, and thereby provide support for claims of self-defense, insanity, and duress.

The plain text of the Battered Spouse Syndrome statute, CJP § 10–916, permits the trial court to admit expert testimony regarding the Syndrome to explain the state of mind of a defendant at the time of the alleged criminal offense. The General Assembly has recognized the Syndrome as both a medical and psychological condition. In enacting the statute, the General Assembly recognized that expert testimony may be necessary to explain the complexity of the Syndrome and how it may cause a battered person to act in ways that are counter-intuitive to the average lay person.

In several cases, the Court of Special Appeals and this Court have addressed the relevance of the Syndrome in criminal cases. In the earliest case following the statute's enactment, *Banks v. State*, the Court of Special Appeals clarified that CJP § 10–916 did not "create a new defense to murder." "Rather, evidence of the Battered Spouse Syndrome is offered in support of the state of mind element of perfect or imperfect self-defense, *i.e.*, it is offered to prove the honesty and reasonableness of the defendant's belief that he or she was in imminent danger at the time of the offense."

. . .

Wallace-Bey v. State is the most recent appellate case interpreting CJP § 10–916 and how Syndrome evidence is to be used during a criminal trial. There, the Court of Special Appeals considered whether the trial court impermissibly limited the testimony of the defendant (Wallace-Bey) and the defense expert.

Wallace-Bey killed her boyfriend while he was lying in bed after having allegedly raped her. At trial, Wallace-Bey asserted a self-defense theory as her sole defense to a first-degree murder charge. The trial court excluded evidence of prior abuse by anyone other than the decedent.

The intermediate appellate court held that the trial court's ruling on the evidence of prior abuse was erroneous, because CJP § 10–916 "is silent as to whether the court may admit evidence of abuse of the defendant by persons other than the [decedent]," and evidence of that sort "could still be admissible under some other provision or theory of relevance." The court concluded that information about prior abuse "could have assisted the jury in evaluating the validity and probative value" of the defense expert's opinion. The court pointed to a report prepared by Wallace-Bey's expert (Dr. McGraw), which made clear that Wallace-Bey's exposure to traumatic experiences, including childhood sexual abuse, was a cornerstone of Dr. McGraw's conclusion about how battered spouse syndrome affected Wallace-Bey's actions during the shooting. Citing published research, Dr. McGraw opined that Wallace-Bey's history of abuse made her vulnerable to being in a relationship in which she "re-experienced the pattern of domestic violence she had been exposed to in childhood." According to Dr. McGraw, medical literature indicates that a history of being battered can have a "direct effect" on a battered woman's "state of mind and her appraisal of danger[.]" Dr. McGraw added that persons with long histories of trauma respond to threats "in the context of the sum total of their total traumatic life experiences" and that the "cumulative effect of violence" can "severely alter[ ]" a person's "ability to cope with a threat[.]"

The court held that, "[b]y linking the evidence of Wallace-Bey's history of abuse to the basis for Dr. McGraw's expert opinion," Wallace-Bey sufficiently established the relevance of that evidence. The court continued:

> Indeed, the components of Dr. McGraw's report that discuss Wallace-Bey's history of other abuse pertain to the two aspects of battered spouse syndrome (learned helplessness and heightened sensitivity) that are most probative to the elements of perfect and imperfect self-defense. Information about that prior abuse could have assisted the jury in evaluating the validity and probative value of Dr. McGraw's opinion.

The intermediate appellate court remanded for a new trial.

With these precedents in mind, we consider whether the trial court's instruction to Elzey's jury concerning Battered Spouse Syndrome was erroneous.

3. The Predicate Finding Issue

The Court of Special Appeals held that the trial court erred in interpreting CJP § 10–916 to require the jury to find that Hunter repeatedly abused Elzey before it could consider all the evidence admitted (including Dr. Blumberg's expert testimony) to prove that Elzey suffered from Battered Spouse Syndrome. We agree that the trial court erred in instructing the jury to conduct this preliminary inquiry. . .

In sum, in a case where there is evidence that the defendant was abused by one or more third parties before the decedent allegedly abused her, and an expert opines that all of the defendant's abusive relationships contributed to her development of Battered Spouse Syndrome, a trial court may not instruct the jury to make a predicate finding that the decedent repeatedly abused the defendant, before the jury may consider all the evidence that goes to whether the defendant was suffering from the Syndrome at the time of the alleged offense. Because the trial court's instruction told Elzey's jury to make such a predicate finding before considering all the evidence bearing on whether Elzey suffered from the Syndrome, it was erroneous.

4. The Juror Confusion Issue

In addition to discerning error in the trial court's predicate finding requirement, the Court of Special Appeals held that the Syndrome instruction also was erroneous for a second reason: it "sent mixed messages to the jury." Specifically, the instruction "was unclear and potentially misleading as to what, if any effect past abuse may have had on [Elzey's] state of mind, even though the court had admitted [Dr. Blumberg's] testimony on her past abuse and its effect on her state of mind." We agree with the Court of Special Appeals that the instruction was fatally ambiguous. . .

As discussed above, under *Wallace-Bey*, the trial court properly admitted evidence of Elzey's past abuse, as well as Dr. Blumberg's expert opinions, which were based, in significant part, on that past abuse. All of the alleged abuse was relevant to the jury's determination whether Elzey suffered from the Syndrome and, if so, how that psychological condition affected her perception of the threat that Hunter presented and, ultimately, the viability of her self-defense claim. However, as the Court of Special Appeals aptly stated, the trial court gave the jury "mixed messages" about the relevance of Elzey's prior abuse to its deliberations. This was error.

B. The Erroneous Jury Instruction Was Not Harmless Beyond a Reasonable Doubt.

The Court of Special Appeals held that the two errors in the jury instruction on Battered Spouse Syndrome were not harmless beyond a reasonable doubt. The State disagrees, arguing that any instructional error was necessarily harmless because the jury acquitted Elzey of the murder and first-degree assault charges and convicted her only of the manslaughter, second-degree assault, and reckless endangerment charges. The State contends that, because the jury's verdict shows that it concluded Elzey acted in imperfect self-defense, any error in the Syndrome instruction regarding how the jury was to factor in evidence of prior abuse must have had no effect on the verdict:. . .

We disagree with the State. Although it does appear from the verdict that the jury concluded Elzey acted in imperfect self-defense, the State has not convinced us that, if the jury had received a proper jury instruction on the Syndrome, the jury necessarily would have reached the same verdict. We can imagine at least two possible scenarios in which the jury would have found that Elzey acted in perfect self-defense if the trial court had properly instructed the jury.

First, without any consideration of the Syndrome evidence, the jury might have found that Elzey did not initially intend to harm Hunter when she brought the knife back into the living room during her argument with the six-foot, two-inch Hunter. The jury further could have found that, after Hunter approached Elzey despite seeing the knife, and told her, "[y]ou're going to have to use that knife," and "[t]hat knife does not scare me," Elzey honestly (but unreasonably) believed that Hunter was about to try to disarm her and then use the knife on her, or otherwise seriously harm her. In this scenario, Elzey's intentional moving of the knife upward when Hunter came within arm's length could form the basis for a voluntary manslaughter conviction. If the jury had been properly instructed, it might have considered and credited Dr. Blumberg's testimony that Elzey suffered from the Syndrome, and concluded that Elzey had a heightened ability to sense that the confrontation with Hunter was escalating and, therefore, that she reasonably believed that "things [were about] to happen." If it so concluded, the jury might have determined that Elzey's belief that she was in imminent danger was not only honest, but also was reasonable.

Second, the jury might have found that Elzey suffered from the Syndrome, but only after considering Hunter's abuse, and disregarding evidence of Elzey's history of prior abuse. If so, the jury apparently concluded that her yearlong abusive relationship with Hunter led Elzey honestly to believe that Hunter posed a serious threat to her, but that Elzey unreasonably gauged the seriousness of that threat. However, if the jury had been properly instructed, it would have considered Dr. Blumberg's testimony about Elzey's long history of abuse and factored that into its assessment of Elzey's mental state and her ability to perceive when "things are going to happen." In that scenario, the jury might have concluded, based on Dr. Blumberg's testimony, that Elzey's long history of trauma at the hands of multiple intimate partners enabled her to interpret Hunter's intentions accurately, as he approached her and told her she would need to use the knife.

In sum, we are unable to say that the instructional error in this case "in no way influenced the verdict." Thus, we must reverse Elzey's convictions and remand for a new trial. . .

U.S. v. NWOYE

824 F.3d 1129 (D.C. Cir. 2016)
(citations and most footnotes omitted)

* * * Nwoye [has] moved to vacate the conviction [for the crime of extortion] based on alleged ineffective assistance of trial counsel. A claim of ineffective assistance of counsel requires the defendant to show (i) that counsel's performance was constitutionally deficient and (ii) that the ineffective assistance prejudiced the defendant. On the first prong, the deficiency prong, Nwoye claimed that competent trial counsel would have introduced expert testimony on battered woman syndrome. On the second prong, the prejudice prong, Nwoye claimed that such expert testimony would have led the District Court to instruct the jury on duress. And Nwoye further argued that the combination of the expert testimony and the duress instruction would have created a reasonable doubt respecting her guilt. * * * The District Court denied Nwoye's ineffective-assistance-of-counsel claim [on the second prong, and did not reach the first]. * * *Although the prejudice question is close, we * * * conclude that Nwoye was prejudiced by trial counsel's failure to introduce expert testimony on battered woman syndrome. * * *

I

A

In January 2007, a woman named Queen Nwoye was indicted for conspiring with her then-boyfriend, Adriane Osuagwu, to extort money from Ikemba Iweala[,] a prominent doctor. He and Nwoye had previously had an affair. Over the course of 49 days in 2006, Osuagwu and Nwoye repeatedly threatened Iweala that they would publicize his prior relationship with Nwoye unless Iweala paid them. Their threats were effective. Iweala made six separate payments to Osuagwu and Nwoye, totaling almost $200,000.

At Nwoye's trial, Nwoye admitted to engaging in the alleged extortion but testified that Osuagwu had coerced her participation through his physically abusive and controlling behavior. According to Nwoye, her relationship with Osuagwu turned abusive shortly after they started dating in 2005. Osuagwu would frequently slap Nwoye with his hand, hit her with his shoe, and beat her on her face and body. Later, Osuagwu's physical violence escalated. Osuagwu beat Nwoye when she initially refused to introduce him to Iweala. Whenever she objected to the extortion, Osuagwu would beat her "like a drum." And on one occasion when Nwoye did not play her part in the extortion scheme, Osuagwu slapped Nwoye and threatened to "strangle" and "kill" her if the scheme were exposed.

Nwoye further testified that Osuagwu exerted financial and psychological control over her. Osuagwu forced Nwoye to hand over her ATM card and PIN. In addition, Nwoye and her children lived with Osuagwu at Osuagwu's home in Maryland. Nwoye testified that Osuagwu—the only person who knew that she lived at the house—would often threaten to kill Nwoye and bury her inside the house. Nwoye also testified that she was afraid to report Osuagwu to the police because Osuagwu had told her that he was a former FBI agent.

At the same time, Nwoye's testimony revealed that Osuagwu did not have direct physical control over Nwoye at all times. While Nwoye attended nursing school or worked at a hospital for three days a week, she was apart from Osuagwu. And Osuagwu spent at least a few days in California while Nwoye remained in Maryland. * * * But even while they were apart, Osuagwu constantly monitored Nwoye. He forced Nwoye to keep her phone with her and demanded that she answer promptly, even going so far as to require Nwoye to wear a Bluetooth earpiece during class at nursing school.

B

Despite the significant evidence of Nwoye's abusive relationship with Osuagwu, Nwoye's trial counsel did not seek to introduce expert testimony on battered woman syndrome. * * * Battered woman syndrome is a term that was coined by Dr. Lenore Walker in the late 1970s to describe the psychological and behavioral traits common to women who are exposed to severe, repeated domestic abuse. Dr. Walker's theory was that women subject to cyclical domestic abuse develop psychological paralysis—or "learned helplessness"—that renders them unable to escape abusive relationships.[1] * * *

C

At Nwoye's trial, Nwoye's counsel did not present expert testimony on battered woman syndrome. Counsel instead staked Nwoye's duress defense entirely on Nwoye's own trial testimony. * * * To be entitled to an instruction on duress, Nwoye had to present sufficient evidence (i) that she acted under an unlawful threat of imminent death or serious bodily injury

[1] Although the majority of domestic violence victims are women, some cases involve victims who are men. Some scholars have advocated abandoning the term "battered woman syndrome" in favor of the label "battering and its effects." We use the term "battered woman syndrome" in this opinion because the term is commonly used by courts and because it describes the alleged circumstances in this case.

and (ii) that there was no reasonable alternative to participating in the extortion scheme.

The District Court ruled that Nwoye had not presented sufficient evidence on the second prong of duress—the no-reasonable-alternative prong—and therefore declined to give the duress instruction. The jury then convicted Nwoye of conspiracy to commit extortion, and the District Court sentenced Nwoye to 20 months in prison, followed by three years of supervised release.[2]

Nwoye appealed, challenging the District Court's decision not to give the duress instruction. This Court affirmed. The Court explained that Nwoye had a number of reasonable alternatives to participating in the extortion scheme, including reporting Osuagwu to police or to friends and co-workers when she was at school or work, away from Osuagwu. * * * The Court also stressed that although Nwoye had testified about the abuse she suffered, she failed to present "other usual indicia supporting a BWS defense—expert witnesses testifying to the effects of isolation, financial dependence, or estrangement from family members." Therefore, the Court concluded that Nwoye was not entitled to a jury instruction on duress. * * * Judge Tatel dissented. In his view, Nwoye's testimony concerning Osuagwu's threats and abuse amounted to "more than enough evidence to have warranted a duress instruction."

D

In 2013, after the termination of her supervised release, Nwoye filed a motion to vacate her conviction. Nwoye claimed that her trial counsel was constitutionally ineffective because counsel failed to call an expert witness to testify about battered woman syndrome. * * * At the [evidentiary] hearing, Nwoye's expert—Dr. Carole Giunta—testified extensively about battered woman syndrome in general. Dr. Giunta also opined that Nwoye's relationship with Osuagwu exhibited the "classic dynamics" of a battering relationship. * * * After considering this new evidence, * * * the District Court decided that Nwoye was, in any event, not prejudiced by the lack of expert testimony on battered woman syndrome. The District Court reasoned that such testimony still would not have satisfied the second prong of duress—the no-reasonable-alternative prong—and that the testimony therefore would not have entitled Nwoye to a jury instruction on duress. * * *

II

* * * On appeal, therefore, the only issue for us to decide is whether the failure of Nwoye's trial counsel to present expert testimony on battered woman syndrome was prejudicial. * * * To establish prejudice, Nwoye must demonstrate "a reasonable probability that, absent the errors, the factfinder would have had a reasonable doubt respecting guilt." To

[2] For his part, Osuagwu pled guilty to conspiracy and was sentenced to 22 months in prison.

demonstrate a reasonable probability, Nwoye "need not show that counsel's deficient conduct more likely than not altered the outcome in the case." She must demonstrate only "a probability sufficient to undermine confidence" in the verdict.

* * * First, Nwoye argues that expert testimony on battered woman syndrome would have entitled her to a jury instruction on the defense of duress. Second, she claims that a duress instruction, together with the expert testimony on battered woman syndrome, would have created a "reasonable probability" that the jury "would have had a reasonable doubt respecting guilt." [We agree.] * * *

A

* * * The question, put simply, is whether expert testimony on battered woman syndrome would have moved the evidentiary needle enough to entitle Nwoye to a duress instruction. To answer that question, we must initially assess whether, in general, expert testimony on battered woman syndrome can be admissible to prove duress—that is, whether it can be reliable and can be relevant to the duress defense. If so, then we next must assess whether the particular expert testimony proffered by Nwoye in her post-conviction proceeding was reliable and would have provided relevant evidence at Nwoye's trial. Finally, * * * we must determine whether the introduction of such testimony at Nwoye's trial would have entitled her to a jury instruction on duress.

1

* * * Given the history of expert testimony on this subject [allowed in litigation] and the extensive literature, we too agree that expert testimony on battered woman syndrome can be reliable, assuming of course that the expert can demonstrate sufficient expertise to meet the usual requirements for experts to testify on a subject.

To be admissible in support of a duress defense, expert testimony on battered woman syndrome must also be *relevant* to proving duress. * * * We agree with the majority of the courts that expert testimony on battered woman syndrome can be relevant to the duress defense. The reason, put simply, is that the duress defense requires a defendant to have acted reasonably under the circumstances, and expert testimony can help a jury assess whether a battered woman's actions were reasonable.

Reasonableness is the touchstone of a duress defense. To satisfy the first prong of the duress defense, the defendant must have acted under the influence of a *reasonable* fear of imminent death or serious bodily harm at the time of the alleged crime. And to satisfy the second prong of the defense, there must have been no "*reasonable*, legal alternative to committing the crime." Whether an alternative is reasonable turns on whether a reasonable person would have availed herself of it. * * * [W]hether expert testimony on battered woman syndrome is relevant to the duress defense turns on whether such testimony can identify any aspects of the defendant's "particular circumstances" that can help the jury assess the reasonableness of her actions. * * *

With respect to * * * the imminent-harm prong[,] women in battering relationships are often "hypervigilant to cues of impending danger and accurately perceive the seriousness of the situation before another person who had not been repeatedly abused might recognize the danger." Remarks or gestures that may seem harmless to the average observer might be reasonably understood to presage imminent and severe violence when viewed against the backdrop of the batterer's particular pattern of violence. As our colleague Judge Brown stated while on the California Supreme Court: "Although a jury might not find the *appearances* sufficient to provoke a reasonable person's fear, they might conclude otherwise as to a reasonable person's perception of the *reality* when enlightened by expert testimony on the concept of hypervigilance." [emphasis in original]

Regarding the second prong of the duress defense—the no-reasonable-alternative prong—battered women face significant impediments to leaving abusive relationships. Most importantly, battered women who leave their abusers risk a retaliatory escalation in violence against themselves or those close to them—sometimes termed "separation abuse." For example, studies have suggested that women in battering relationships are more likely to be killed by their batterers after separating from them. In addition, batterers often isolate their victims and exert financial control over them, rendering separation a significant burden. Expert testimony on those impediments to separation can help explain why a battered woman did not take advantage of an otherwise reasonable-sounding opportunity to avoid committing the alleged crime. * * *

2

The next question is whether expert testimony on battered woman syndrome would have been reliable and relevant *in Nwoye's case*. We conclude that it would have been. * * * And we have no reason to question its reliability. * * * Nwoye's expert testimony, moreover, would certainly have been relevant to Nwoye's defense. This Court suggested as much on Nwoye's direct appeal by noting the conspicuous absence of expert testimony on battered woman syndrome at Nwoye's trial. And the Government does not dispute that Nwoye's trial testimony strongly suggested that she had been a victim of a battering relationship. An expert on battered woman syndrome could therefore have helped the jury assess the reasonableness of Nwoye's actions, as we described above.

3

The next question is whether expert testimony on battered woman syndrome would have entitled Nwoye to a duress instruction in this case. On Nwoye's direct appeal, when we rejected Nwoye's claim that she was entitled to a duress instruction, we pointed specifically to the absence of "expert witnesses testifying to the effects of isolation, financial dependence, or estrangement from family members." We now conclude that the introduction of such testimony at Nwoye's trial would have entitled Nwoye to a duress instruction.

Perhaps most critically, expert testimony on the likelihood of retaliatory violence upon separation could have provided a plausible explanation for why Nwoye failed to extricate herself from the extortion scheme. * * * Moreover, Nwoye may have reasonably believed that reporting Osuagwu to the police (or others) would have been unlikely to result in his immediate arrest and would have therefore placed her at greater risk in the interim. Thus, Nwoye's testimony concerning Osuagwu's abuse, supplemented by expert testimony on battered woman syndrome, would have constituted "sufficient evidence from which a reasonable jury could find" for Nwoye on a theory of duress. * * * The concept of battered woman syndrome fits this case to a T. A woman was beaten repeatedly by her boyfriend. Some outsiders may question why she didn't just leave her boyfriend. But the expert testimony would help explain why. * * *

B

* * * [T]he failure of Nwoye's counsel to present expert testimony on battered woman syndrome deprived Nwoye of any viable legal avenue to acquittal. * * * Jurors faced with testimony from a battered woman concerning her abuse and its effects may doubt the testimony because they do not believe that a woman subject to such abuse would stay with her abuser without alerting police or others. Expert testimony on battered woman syndrome could have helped Nwoye "dispel the ordinary lay person's perception that a woman in a battering relationship is free to leave at any time."

* * * The jury of course could still have convicted Nwoye; for example, the jury could have disbelieved that Nwoye was telling the truth about the abuse in the first place or could have been unpersuaded by the expert testimony. But for present purposes on appeal, we have no basis to question that Nwoye has told the truth about being abused by Osuagwu or to question the expert testimony. * * * Nwoye was prejudiced by her counsel's failure to present expert testimony on battered woman syndrome.

* * * Because we have concluded that Nwoye was prejudiced by the failure of her trial counsel to introduce expert testimony on battered woman syndrome, we [reverse and] remand for the District Court to consider in the first instance the other prong of the ineffective-assistance-of-counsel standard: whether the performance of Nwoye's counsel fell below an objective standard of reasonableness. If counsel's performance was constitutionally deficient, then Nwoye will have established ineffective assistance of counsel and will be entitled to have her conviction vacated. * * *

DISSENT

[The dissent notes there was evidence that Nwoye left Osuagwu and returned to her husband in the summer of 2006 without incident, and that she eventually contacted the Nigerian security services regarding Osuagwu's criminal behavior.] * * * [Furthermore,] Ms. Nwoye regularly left her home to attend nursing school classes and to work at the hospital and was thus "physically separated" from Osuagwu. She also met alone with Dr. Iweala and did not tell him that she was being forced to extort money from him. Most importantly, the court of appeals emphasized that "Osuagwu spent nearly two weeks in California, thousands of miles away from Nwoye," giving her more than enough opportunity to notify law enforcement. "[A] defendant with such 'countless opportunities to contact law enforcement authorities or [to] escape the perceived threats' cannot as a matter of law avail herself of the duress defense." [The dissent notes that Nwoye was not isolated, financially dependent on Osuagwu, or estranged from family. Thus, she did not show she had no reasonable legal alternative, and no expert testimony could remedy this, so Nwoye was not entitled to a jury instruction regarding duress.] * * *

[Editor's Note: Just as Nwoye was required to prove that her actions were reasonable in order to prevail in her duress defense, survivors of abuse who claim self-defense after assaulting or killing their abusers must convince the judge or jury that their actions and beliefs were reasonable. This is often difficult to achieve, given that battered women who defend themselves tend to be seen as unreasonable. It is also often difficult for these defendants to prove that the abuse they faced was "imminent," a second element of proving self-defense in most state statutes, as it may be that the only time the survivor may be able to act without being beaten or killed is when the abuser has his back turned, is asleep, or is passed out from the effects of drugs or alcohol.]

NANCY K. D. LEMON, A TRANSFORMATIVE PROCESS: WORKING AS A DOMESTIC VIOLENCE EXPERT WITNESS

21 Berkeley J. Gender L. & Just. 208 (2009)
(citations and most footnotes omitted)

"We engage most deeply with reality when we form the intention to be guided by kindness, integrity, and compassion in our work, inquire into distortions in our thinking that cause unnecessary suffering to ourselves and others, find other like-minded people, and proceed with caution and curiosity into the unknown."[1]

I will always remember some of the life stories battered women [and men] have told me over the last thirty years. Stories of nightmarish events,

[1] Ann Freedman, Fact-Finding in Civil Domestic Violence Cases: Secondary Traumatic Stress and the Need for Compassionate Witnesses, 11 Am. U. J. Gender Soc. Pol'y & L. 567, 653 (2003). [excerpted in Chapter 12 of this textbook]

of deep grief and terror, of amazing resilience and courage and ingenuity. Stories sometimes humorous, and occasionally with happy endings. Often it is clear that telling the story with my attention is transformative for the speaker; listening is often transformative for me as well.

I first testified as a domestic violence expert witness in 1994. I received a call from a survivor named Virginia with whom I had consulted previously on domestic violence issues. She explained that she was going through a custody fight with her ex-boyfriend Robert, the father of one of her children, and that he was abusive to her. She filed for a restraining order against Robert and requested custody of their mutual daughter. He responded by filing a paternity suit, claiming he was the father not only of that daughter but also of her older daughter. The older daughter, however, had been fathered by another man, as Virginia was already pregnant when she met Robert. Robert knew this, but sought joint custody of both children and child support from Virginia.

The Family Court Services (FCS) worker in the case, who recommended that Robert be given joint legal custody and visitation with both children, claimed that she was an expert on domestic violence issues. She testified that her expertise was based in part on her having been a guest speaker one time in my Domestic Violence Law class. Virginia asked if I could testify on her behalf regarding the inadvisability of awarding custody to an abuser. She stated that if the FCS worker's expertise included speaking in my class, then surely I was at least as qualified to testify on domestic violence issues.

Having never testified as an expert before, I was apprehensive as to whether I would qualify. I agreed, however, to try. When I was sworn in and took the stand, Virginia's attorney started to ask me about my credentials and work history. After a few minutes the judge interrupted, asking if the attorney was trying to qualify me as an expert on domestic violence. She replied in the affirmative. The judge then stated, "Well everyone knows Nancy Lemon is an expert on domestic violence! I'll stipulate to that!" I breathed a huge sigh of relief and went on to testify about the issues in the case, including the fact that perpetrating domestic violence is relevant to a determination of parental fitness. Robert's attorney, who had apparently never heard of me, was taken aback by the judge's stipulation but had to accept me as an expert.

Though the judge awarded Robert visitation with both children over Virginia's objection, this award was reversed on appeal with regard to Virginia's older daughter, since technically there was no relationship between Robert and this child. I saw that my expertise could potentially be useful to survivors of domestic violence who were caught up in the legal system, and found testifying anxiety-producing but exciting. There is nothing like testifying in court, especially being subjected to rigorous cross-examination, to sharpen one's wits. I learned a great deal from that first expert experience, and realized I would like to do more expert work in the future.

This comment will cover the statutes and reported cases in California related to domestic violence expert testimony, the development of standards of practice for this new profession, and some of the challenges we experts face. I will discuss of some of the cases I have worked on over the course of my thirty years of work with domestic violence survivors and insights I have gleaned from this line of work. * * *

Sometimes doing this work can be uplifting. In one case, the battered female defendant who was out of jail pending trial on her own recognizance, told my assistant and me that for the first time in a very long time she was happy, and was no longer interested in taking illegal drugs. * * * When I interviewed her, she was not allowed to leave the jurisdiction to be with her children because of the pending trial, nor could she work or go to school. She was, however, happy. She had ended her relationship with her boyfriend, who was in custody awaiting trial. Although she was homeless, she had acquired a big tent, a bed, a table, and a beautiful place to camp. She was able to eat and shower at the local homeless shelter. I realized that this was virtually the first time in her life when she was able to take a break. For the time being, she was free from abuse, neglect, parental responsibilities, and the need to work or go to school. She was able to focus on herself, her needs, her dreams, and her wishes. It was a pleasure being with her as she emerged like a butterfly before our very eyes, figuring out who she really was and what she wanted for her life. Ironically, by taking her away from her normal life and engaging her in his crimes, her boyfriend had potentially opened her up to a new lease on life.

INTERVIEWS AS TRANSFORMATIVE

At times, of course, even with my best efforts, the side I am on loses the case. This can be a very frustrating experience, especially when I believe that the judgment was in error. The first homicide case in which I testified resulted in a second-degree murder conviction for the battered woman defendant. Based on my interactions with the defendant, during which she disclosed a long history of abuse by the husband, his threats to kill her with his bare hands, and her belief that he would have killed her if she had not shot him, I had been sure the jury would find her not guilty based on self-defense. Given our current criminal justice system, it is unlikely that she will ever be released on parole. She is not eligible for domestic violence habeas relief because two domestic violence experts testified at her trial. She has exhausted all her avenues of appeal, both state and federal. I have stayed in touch with this woman for years, and have often wondered if there was anything I could have done differently or better to help prevent this injustice. This was the first case in which I felt the legal system was truly unjust, though there have been many more since then. It is painful sometimes to be a participant in a legal system that, in my experience, is often far from perfect. I often spend time in my co-counseling sessions reflecting on what it is like for me to do this work, and expressing the frustration and grief it brings up.

Over the years, I have come to realize that no matter what happens in the courtroom or in plea negotiations, and whether or not I even see a given person again, the interviews with the clients can be transformative in themselves. Asking someone to relay their life story, for as many hours as is necessary while giving them undivided and supportive attention, can be a life-changing experience for them. Because I usually invite a therapist colleague who I am training to participate in the interviews, the client gets attention from two experienced listeners. The clients almost always cry at least once during the interview, which I see as a sign that they feel safe and heard. My over thirty years of experience with co-counseling has made me quite comfortable with the expression of emotions. I have found that although my role is not to provide therapy, my paying supportive attention to the survivors enables them to feel safe enough to tell me things that they have never told anyone else (for example, how bad the abuse really was). These revelations are often key to their legal cases.

An incident that illustrates how transformative interviews can be occurred a few months ago. In 1999, I interviewed a young woman who was awaiting trial for the homicide of her stepmother. She had not intended the victim to die. Her abusive boyfriend, who was her co-defendant, had pressured her to participate in the crime leading to the death. I wrote a lengthy report in the case, but the case resolved before trial when she pled guilty. She has been in prison now for ten years. I send her Christmas cards. She wrote to me last year, asking for a copy of my report, as it could be helpful to her when she becomes eligible for parole. She referred in her letter to the "therapy sessions" with me, and said, "I've been evaluated by different psychologists but I feel that you spent enough time with me to have an accurate perception of who I am as a person and a patient/client." She asked if I would be willing to go see her. I am unable to go to visit or offer more sessions, as I was hired just to meet with her before trial, the prison is three hours by car from where I live, and the prison authorities may not allow me to see her since I am no longer officially connected to her case. I continue, however, to be in mail communication with her.

Similarly, a year or so ago, one of my expert witness colleagues, a therapist who conducts interviews with me, the client's attorney, and I were visiting a battered woman who had been in prison for over twenty years for killing a man who had taken advantage of her sexually. My colleague was the primary interviewer this time, and I was present as a legal consultant for the firm representing the woman. The woman related the many years of abuse she had endured from virtually every man in her life, including her stepfather, father, numerous boyfriends, and the decedent. Her memory, however, was sometimes spotty and she did not see the connections between all of this abuse, or its effect on her. After several hours of listening and asking questions, the interviewer described what she was hearing: that the cumulative effect of so much abuse over so many years led to the homicide, where the client experienced flashbacks of the men who had beaten and raped her as she stabbed the decedent. The client burst into deep sobs, and continued crying for a long time. She said this was the first time she had felt sane while thinking about the killing. Suddenly it all made sense to her. She was extremely grateful to all of us present that day for truly understanding what had happened to her, and helping her regain a sense of herself.

It is not only the clients who are transformed by these interactions; everyone involved in abuse cases is affected by the stories heard, whether we are judges, attorneys, social workers, expert witnesses, court employees, or in other roles. In response, some people become numb to this pain, while others are able to develop a sense of compassion for the victims or even the perpetrators. It is important to develop this sense of compassion, and to practice compassion for ourselves and for our colleagues. My goal is to connect with each survivor I work with, and to communicate to them that I know she or he did the best they could, often under horrific circumstances, which is an integral part of eliciting the information needed for their defense.

Doing this work has been challenging for me, both personally and professionally. It has also been extremely rewarding. I am constantly learning about new areas of law. Fears that I used to have of "criminals" and "murderers" are gone. As I stated in the Preface and Acknowledgments to the 2009 edition of my textbook, Domestic Violence Law:

> I am . . . grateful to all the survivors of domestic violence whose stories I have had the honor of listening to as an expert witness. Many of these interviews last five or six hours, and people often share parts of their lives they have never spoken of to anyone else. I usually leave these interactions with a deeper sense of compassion, and admiration for the strength and resourcefulness of survivors. The more I do this work, the more clear it is to me that all of us are more alike than we are different, and that I am simply fortunate not to be struggling with abuse in my own life. It is not that I am somehow better, smarter, or more deserving than my clients, friends, colleagues, and family members who have been abused, but that I have been luckier.

I look forward to a future where this work will no longer be necessary.

[Editor's Note: Several of the women I wrote about in this article were granted parole and a couple have spoken at Berkeley Law School. One of them worked for Justice Now, a non-profit agency in Oakland, CA providing legal and supportive services to CA's incarcerated women,

including healthcare access, defense of parental rights and sentencing mitigation.]

B. POST-CONVICTION ISSUES

PEOPLE V. ADDIMANDO

197 A.D.3d 106, 152 N.Y.S.3d 33
(Supreme Court, Appellate Division, 2021)
(citations and footnote omitted)
(Note: This opinion contains graphic descriptions of physical abuse.)

On the instant appeal, this Court is presented, inter alia, with the question of whether the County Court properly applied the Domestic Violence Survivors Justice Act (L 2019, ch 31; L 2019, ch 55, § 1, part WW), effective May 14, 2019, which amended Penal Law § 60.12 (hereinafter the DV Survivors Act or Penal Law § 60.12). The DV Survivors Act permits courts to impose reduced alternative sentences in certain cases involving defendants who are victims of domestic violence. This case appears to be the first time that an appellate court has the opportunity to address the DV Survivors Act.

For the reasons now set forth, we hold that the County Court did not properly apply the DV Survivors Act when sentencing the defendant. Upon considering the plain language of the DV Survivors Act, the legislative history of the statute, and the particular circumstances of this case, we modify the judgment, on the facts and as a matter of discretion in the interest of justice, by reducing (1) the term of imprisonment imposed on the conviction of murder in the second degree from an indeterminate term of imprisonment of 19 years to life to a determinate term of imprisonment of 7½ years to be followed by five years of postrelease supervision, and (2) the term of imprisonment imposed on the conviction of criminal possession of a weapon in the second degree from a determinate term of imprisonment of 15 years to be followed by five years of postrelease supervision to a determinate term of imprisonment of 3½ years to be followed by five years of postrelease supervision, which terms shall run concurrently with each other.

Sometime during the night of September 27, 2017, and the morning of September 28, 2017, the defendant fatally shot Christopher Grover, who was her domestic partner and the father of her two children. According to the defendant and several others who testified at the approximately one-month jury trial, the defendant had been repeatedly subjected to brutal physical and sexual abuse at the hands of Grover for many years. The jury rejected the defendant's battered women's syndrome justification defense, and found her guilty of murder in the second degree and criminal possession of a weapon in the second degree. The defendant moved to be sentenced under the DV Survivors Act. Following a hearing at which the defendant adduced additional evidence that she had been abused, the County Court denied her motion and sentenced the defendant to an indeterminate term of imprisonment of 19 years to life on the conviction of murder in the second degree and a concurrent determinate term of imprisonment of 15 years to be followed by five years of postrelease supervision on the conviction of criminal possession of a weapon in the second degree.

I. The DV Survivors Act/Penal Law § 60.12

. . .Penal Law § 60.12 (1) provides:

> "the court, upon a determination following a hearing that (a) at the time of the instant offense, the defendant was a victim of domestic violence subjected to substantial physical, sexual or psychological abuse inflicted by a member of the same family or household as the defendant as such term is defined in subdivision one of section 530.11 of the criminal procedure law; (b) such abuse was a significant contributing factor to the defendant's criminal behavior; (c) having regard for the nature and circumstances of the crime and the history, character and condition of the defendant, that a sentence of imprisonment pursuant to section 70.00, 70.02, 70.06 or subdivision two or three of section 70.71 [of the Penal Law] would be unduly harsh may instead impose a sentence in accordance with this section."

The language of the DV Survivors Act clearly and unambiguously sets forth three factors for a court to consider, namely: (1) whether the defendant was a victim of domestic violence inflicted by a member of the same family or household; (2) whether the abuse was a significant contributing factor to the defendant's criminal behavior; and (3) whether, having regard for the nature and circumstances of the crime and the history, character, and condition of the defendant, a sentence in accordance with the customary statutory sentencing guidelines would be unduly harsh.

(1) The statute does not expressly set forth the standard of proof or the appropriate evidentiary burden that must be borne by the defendant, as the movant. Utilizing as comparison the evidentiary standard applicable on a motion to vacate a judgment and set aside a sentence, we apply the preponderance of the evidence standard to our review and analysis herein. At the commencement of the subject hearing, the parties agreed that this was the appropriate standard of proof, and the County Court applied this standard. The preponderance of the evidence standard requires enough evidence to "produce a reasonable belief in the truth of the facts asserted." "A party who has the burden of proof by a preponderance of the evidence must prove his or her contention by the greater weight of evidence."

Although the strongest indication of the statute's meaning is in its plain language, "the legislative history of an enactment may also be relevant and is not to be ignored, even if words be clear." The legislative history reveals that the statute sought to address harsh punishment received by victims of domestic violence who commit crimes against their abusers. "[A]ll too often in our court system when women are defending themselves against domestic violence, instead of being met with a judge with compassion and assistance and help, the judge is just putting forth punishment."

The sponsors of this law intended for a sentencing court to exercise discretion in its analysis of the aforementioned three factors: "We are not saying that you throw out what they've done out of the window in the sentencing. The judge still has the discretion. We're asking the judge to take into consideration what they have gone through, what they were living with." . . .

Significantly, the exercise of discretion of a sentencing court does not translate into unfettered judgment. Our role as an intermediate appellate court in reviewing sentences imposed is "an important responsibility to assure that sentences in given cases are not 'unduly harsh or severe under the circumstances.' " CPL 470.15 (3) confers upon this Court the authority to modify sentences in the exercise of discretion in the interest of justice.

Against this backdrop, we evaluate the determination of the County Court to deny the defendant's motion for sentencing under Penal Law § 60.12. The County Court authored a decision, purporting to apply the three-part factors and reviewing aspects of the evidence presented at the trial which it deemed significant. Upon doing so, the court ultimately determined that the defendant failed to sustain her burden of proof pursuant to Penal Law § 60.12 and thus, denied the defendant's motion pursuant to that statute.

The County Court recognized that the "defendant present[ed] a compelling story of abuse, with horrific allegations that include repeated, sadistic sexual violence and physical abuse, complete with pictures and eyewitnesses viewing the results of her abuse" Nevertheless, the court indicated that the People raised "critical questions about the defendant's testimony regarding her alleged abuse, the identity of her abuser and her violent acts and decisions on September 27, 2017."

The County Court identified "four factual bases" to support its decision. First, it found that the abuse history presented by the defendant was "undetermined and inconsistent regarding the extent of the abuse, as well as the identity of her abuser(s)." Second, it stated that the "nature" of the alleged abusive relationship between the defendant and Grover was "undetermined," based on the demeanor and behavior of Grover on the day of and prior to his death. Third, it concluded that the defendant had "a tremendous amount of advice, assistance, support, and opportunities to escape her alleged abusive situation," and thereby could have "avoid[ed]" the decision to take Grover's life. Fourth, the court considered "most importantly" the specific facts of the homicidal act itself, where the defendant shot Grover "point-blank" in his temple as he laid "supine, with his eyes closed."

Essentially, the County Court found that while it was presumed the defendant may have been abused in her life, the choice she made that night and the manner in which the murder occurred outweighed what the court referred to as the defendant's "undetermined abusive history."

Upon our extensive review of the evidence, we reject the County Court's methodology, approach, application, and analysis of the three factors, as set forth under Penal Law § 60.12 (1).

First, contrary to the County Court's determination, the abuse history was *not* "undetermined." Instead, the defendant established, through her lengthy testimony, photographs, and other evidence that Grover repeatedly abused her physically and sexually. The defendant testified that Grover burned her with a metal spoon that he heated on the stove. In December 2014, Grover forced her to have sex by strangling her with the belt of her bathrobe. A photograph taken in February 2015, the day after the defendant's second child was born, depicted a visible bruise on her breast. According to the defendant, Grover watched violent pornography and demanded that the defendant reenact the scenes that he viewed. During 2016 and 2017, Grover burned her numerous times, "always in the kitchen and always from a spoon," hit her leaving bruises, and forcibly penetrated her vaginally and anally with a wine bottle and "fake knives" made of PVC.

Second, the County Court's determination that there was insufficient proof that the abuse was a significant contributing factor in the defendant's acts is unfounded. Specifically, the court found that the "choices the defendant made on September 27, 2017, and the choices the defendant did not make on or before September 27, 2017, combined with the undetermined abuse history and the decedent's personality profile, provide insufficient evidence to sustain the defendant's burden that her act was caused by abuse that was a 'significant contributing factor.' "

The court stated that "[t]he factual scenario surrounding the homicide and the events within several days therein create a question as to whether the purported abuse was a significant contributing factor. In other words, because the defendant had numerous opportunities to avoid any further abuse and was capable of communicating 'direct' sentiments to. . . . Grover, it is unknown what motive compelled the defendant."

Basically, the court premised its analysis on a presumption or notion that the defendant could have avoided further abuse at the hands of Grover. We will not engage in any such presupposition. The evidence, which included a detailed history of repeated sexual, physical, and psychological abuse by Grover against the defendant, expert testimony regarding the impact of that abuse on the defendant, and the defendant's testimony regarding the events prior to the subject shooting, established that the abuse was a significant contributing factor to the defendant's criminal behavior. Among other things, the defendant testified that she was "pretty sure [Grover] was going to kill" her. On the night of the subject shooting, Grover told the defendant that "he could kill [her] in [her] sleep," asking whether "someone would wake up first or just die right away." According to the defendant, Grover then showed her diagrams of a human brain on his telephone, stating "I could shoot you in this part and you would die right away. But if I killed you in this part, you wouldn't be able to talk or remember things." When the defendant retreated to the bathroom, Grover followed her and threatened that he "could shoot [her] in the shower, but it would echo." Thereafter, according to the defendant, Grover pushed her down, shoved his penis into her mouth, pulled her by her throat, and raped her, causing her to bleed vaginally. Further, just prior to the subject shooting, Grover menaced, "I'm going to kill you, I'm going to kill myself, and then your kids have no one." The defendant described that, "[a]s soon as he said that," she "took one last step towards him, . . . lunged, and . . . pulled the trigger."

Third, we disagree with the County Court's finding that "having regard for the nature and circumstances of the crime and . . . history, character and condition of the defendant," a sentence within the normal statutory sentencing guidelines would not be "unduly harsh." In effect, the court engaged in a weight of the evidence analysis. The court again based this finding on, inter alia, an arcane belief/suggestion that the defendant could have avoided the murder by withdrawing from her apartment, which are antiquated impressions of how domestic violence survivors should behave. It appears that the court found that because the defendant could have withdrawn from her apartment or escaped from Grover, a reduced sentence under Penal Law § 60.12 was unwarranted. Clearly, if the defendant had not committed the fatal shooting, or had she escaped prior thereto, or had her actions been found to be legally justified, Penal Law § 60.12 would have no application or effect in this case. When assessing this factor, the court failed to fully take into account the impact of physical, sexual, and/or psychological abuse on the defendant as a domestic violence survivor. In fact, it all but discounted the defendant's evidence and proof, repeatedly referring to the abuse the defendant and others testified to as "undetermined." This approach simply runs afoul of the spirit and intent of the statute. It is unacceptable that, in reflecting the views of a more enlightened society, the legislature saw fit to enact the DV Survivors Act, only to have the court frustrate that legislative intent by applying outdated notions regarding domestic violence issues.

Upon consideration of the nature and circumstances of the crime, as well as the history, character, and condition of the defendant, we conclude that a sentence in accordance with the DV Survivors Act is warranted. The defendant is a 32-year-old mother of two young children, and has no known prior arrests or convictions. The defendant testified that she was repeatedly physically and sexually abused by Grover, as well as by other men in her past, and reportedly was sexually assaulted at the age of five. However, our examination under this factor does not end there. We also consider, among other things, the details of the crimes, including that the defendant shot Grover in the head as he was lying on the couch. Grover's fatal injury was described as a hard contact wound in which the gun fired by the defendant was pressed against Grover's skin, leaving a muzzle imprint.

Based on the foregoing, we modify the judgment, on the facts and as a matter of discretion in the interest of justice, to the extent indicated herein. . .

III. Conclusion

The DV Survivors Act/Penal Law § 60.12 was passed in recognition that less harsh sentences may be imposed in certain appropriate cases involving domestic violence survivors. We are persuaded that the instant case is such an appropriate case. Accordingly, we give the DV Survivors Act its intended effect, consistent with the reasons for its implementation, and reduce the sentences imposed accordingly.

Ordered that the judgment is modified, on the facts and as a matter of discretion in the interest of justice, by reducing the sentence imposed on the conviction of murder in the second degree from an indeterminate term of imprisonment of 19 years to life to a determinate term of imprisonment of 7½ years to be followed by five years of postrelease supervision, and the sentence imposed on the conviction of criminal possession of a weapon in the second degree from a determinate term of imprisonment of 15 years to be followed by five years of postrelease supervision to a determinate term of imprisonment of 3½ years to be followed by five years of postrelease supervision, which sentences shall run concurrently; as so modified, the judgment is affirmed.

[Editor's Notes: 1. An award winning documentary about three survivors of domestic violence including Nikki Addimando, "And So I Stayed" by Daniel A. Nelson and Natalie Portillo, was played for the judge and prosecutor at the resentencing hearing. The film humanized Ms. Addimando and helped result in her reduced sentence of 7.5 years and credit for time served. The film is available to stream for a fee via GoodDocs.net.

2. People v. S.M., *72 Misc.3d 809 (NY County Court, 2021), decided before* Addimando, *also applied the Domestic Violence Survivors Justice Act in a resentencing case involving a survivor of repeated physical domestic violence. S.M. was beaten by her abuser into driving him one day while he committed many robberies and a murder. She served over 7 years in prison for participating in the robberies. When she applied for resentencing under the new law she was out of prison and was on five years postrelease supervision. The court held that S.M. was eligible for resentencing even though she was out of custody. It noted that she had completed many programs in prison and had positive progress reports, plus she was now working full time and raising her child. It stated that her original sentence of 9.5 years plus 5 years postrelease supervision was unduly harsh in light of having been forced to participate in the crimes. The court shortened her sentence to 4 years prison plus 2.5 years postrelease supervision. Since she had served 7 years, she had completed the entire sentence and was no longer subject to supervision.*

3. As of 2022, only California (Penal Code section 236.15, effective 1/1/22) and Illinois had similar laws to the Domestic Violence Survivors Justice Act, allowing courts to resentence domestic violence survivors convicted of certain crimes related to their being victimized by an intimate partner. California's AB 1497, effective 1/1/24, expanded this relief to abuse survivors convicted of violent crimes. It is hoped that more states will enact such laws.]

ERIN LIOTTA, DOUBLE VICTIMS: ENDING THE INCARCERATION OF CALIFORNIA'S BATTERED WOMEN

26 Berkeley J. Gender L. & Just. 253 (2011)
(citations and footnotes omitted)

INTRODUCTION

Who is a double victim? She has survived abuse at the hands of an intimate partner, and her reward for this survival is further abuse by the criminal justice system. She has survived twenty-five years of abuse from her husband, her boyfriend, her father, or her brother. She is now living through an additional twenty-five years of abuse in the form of prison walls and all the control and violence those walls exercise over her. She is white, she is black, she is Asian, Latina, Native American. She can be any age, though she is likely now well into her forties. She probably has at least a high school diploma and may have a graduate degree. Abused by her husband, the double victim now serves time for his death. Abused by her boyfriend, she now sits in prison for a crime he forced her to commit. A survivor of abuse, she is now serving time for sitting in the car with their baby while her husband, ten yards away, killed another man. She is serving fifteen years to life, twenty-five years to life, life without parole, or a death sentence.

There are at least one hundred double victims in California prisons, and likely more, who have received life sentences for crimes related to the effects of intimate partner battering, but who did not have the full benefit of the protective laws available today. Thanks to hard-fought efforts of advocates, legislators, and incarcerated women themselves, these women can now obtain a second chance at justice in California through a special habeas corpus statute, Penal Code section 1473.5. The women who can utilize this statute form the focus of this Comment, though their experiences frequently will speak for incarcerated battered women as a whole.

This Comment will examine the two paths that most often lead to the release of a battered woman serving a life sentence for a crime related to her experience as a survivor of abuse: (1) release upon parole or (2) release through a petition for writ of habeas corpus pursuant to California Penal Code section 1473.5. * * * The habeas statute came to be after the 1991 enactment of the California Evidence Code section expressly permitting expert witness testimony on intimate partner battering and its effects. Such testimony can prove critical for a battered woman on trial as a criminal defendant. California Penal Code section 1473.5 recognizes the plight of battered victims convicted before the change in law and permits women meeting certain requirements to file writs of habeas corpus "on the basis that expert witness testimony relating to intimate partner battering and its effects . . . was not received in evidence at the trial court proceedings . . ." * * *

I. THE DILEMMA OF IMPRISONED BATTERED WOMEN AND ITS IMPACT ON THE STATE

As of 2011, California has several laws that address the plight of women convicted of crimes related to their experiences of intimate partner battering; these laws represent initial steps in remedying the wrongs already experienced at the hands of various branches of the state. In most cases, these women ended up in prison because the system failed them at multiple points: police did not respond to 911 calls; shelters with few resources turned away women and their children; judges did not issue restraining orders; prosecutors failed to charge the batterers; or defense attorneys, for a variety of reasons, did not present evidence about the abuse history. Injustice and sex-based discrimination plague the experiences of these women as they navigate the justice system. Women who kill their abusers receive harsher sentences on average for their crimes than either men who kill their female partners or men who kill in self-defense. * * *

A cruel irony thus exists for victims of intimate partner violence: when courts ignore these women's experiences, the legal system risks replacing the abuse endured at the hands of a batterer with new abuses inflicted by the prison system. * * *

Valley State Prison for Women—which houses roughly 37 percent of California's female prisoners—has one of the highest reported rates of sexual victimization overall (10.3%) and one of the highest rates of sexual victimization by other prisoners (7.9%). Additionally, California law continues to allow male guards to watch female prisoners at all times, even while showering or going to the bathroom. These invasive practices mimic the total control wielded by abusive partners and reinforce victims' experiences of abuse. * * *

Beyond the prison walls, the incarceration of battered women impacts communities through its devastating effects on the family. Nearly 80 percent of women in California prisons are mothers with two or more children, and two-thirds of women living with their children at the time of arrest were raising these children as single parents. One study at the University of California, Berkeley, found that "incarcerating a mother is significantly more likely to disrupt the children's lives than the incarceration of a father." Children with incarcerated mothers, far more so than those with incarcerated fathers, are likely to be sent to live with another relative, to live alone, or to enter into the foster care system. * * *

Between 1979 and 2007, the number of female prisoners in California increased nearly ten-fold from 1,232 to 11,416. Incarcerating just one person now costs the state around $46,000 per year. *[Editor's Note: As of July 2017, this figure in California is over $75,500.]* The health care costs of incarcerating older female prisoners, who make up a large part of the population affected by the laws discussed in this Comment, typically total three times this amount. Not only does it make ethical sense to free these women, it makes economic sense as well. However, for these women, the routes to freedom under California law contain many obstacles.

II. ROUTES TO FREEDOM: A BRIEF OVERVIEW

On paper, battered women imprisoned in California for a life sentence may have up to six routes available for release. In addition to the habeas route laid out in Penal Code section 1473.5, there are possibilities of release via parole, clemency, resentencing, compassionate release, and a writ of error coram nobis or vobis. Statistics from the California-based advocacy group Free Battered Women (FBW) indicate the near futility of all the options except habeas and parole. Of the forty-three convicted battered women released from prison under FBW's watch between 1997 and 2010, thirty of those women obtained release through parole, eleven through 1473.5 habeas petitions, and two on other legal grounds. This Part explores paths other than parole and habeas relief and examines why they remain underutilized. * * * [The author summarizes clemency, the resentencing process, compassionate release, and writs of error coram nobis or vobis, none of which has been effective for this population in terms of obtaining their freedom from prison.]

III. PAROLE: A POLITICAL PROCESS

A. California, the Governor, and Parole

Parole has become the most successful route for battered women serving life sentences in California. The particularities of state law, however, render parole a difficult and uncertain option. The greatest obstacle may lie in the fact that parole depends heavily upon the whims of three individuals: the Governor, a Governor-appointed Board of Parole Hearings Commissioner, and a civil servant Deputy Board Commissioner.

The Board has authority over prisoners serving indeterminate sentences. Prisoners sentenced to determinate sentences (sentences for a set number of years, such as for manslaughter convictions) do not need to go before the Board but instead gain release once they have fulfilled the court-imposed sentence. However, because most of the women who are eligible for section 1473.5 relief are serving life sentences with the possibility of parole, the Board and the Governor exercise great control over these women's fates.

The parole process in California is notoriously difficult. One journalist reports that "even one write-up for smoking a cigarette just one time in three decades can keep you from getting parole in California." Obtaining a parole grant from the Board is rare enough: the Board grants parole at a rate of less than 10 percent. However, a prisoner's journey does not end with the Board's finding: California is one of only four states whose governor holds veto power over parole decisions, which allows him to reverse any Board decision for persons serving indeterminate terms on murder convictions. * * *

B. Navigating the Political Current

* * * After overturning a Governor's parole veto, the Second Appellate District concluded its opinion with a plea: "We implore the Governor and his staff to pause and reflect upon these miniature constitutional crises foisted upon the judiciary. We take no pleasure in 'overruling' the Governor in a parole case. But we are obligated to follow the law. . ." Although judicial acknowledgement of the problem provides a promising start, it by no means will prove enough for prisoners without the financial means to challenge their denials through the court system. For these prisoners, parole remains a thorny game of navigating political will, veiled motivations, and arbitrarily applied standards. And for those who can access the courts, the means for doing so are severely limited in the wake of a recent United States Supreme Court decision that effectively withdrew the federal court system as a venue for challenging parole denials. * * *

Public misperceptions about battered women feed into this politicization; no governor wants to be labeled as one who "declared open season on husbands," as the media once labeled Ohio's Governor Celeste after he released twenty-eight abuse survivors through clemency. * * *

C. The Danger of the *Shaputis* Doctrine

* * * In 2008, the Supreme Court of California handed down the companion decisions of *In re Lawrence* and *In re Shaputis. Lawrence* clarified the proper standard for judicial review of a parole denial, and it made clear that the gravity of the commitment offense will "not . . . eternally provide adequate support for a decision that a prisoner is unsuitable for parole." In *Shaputis*, however, the Court demonstrated the limits of *Lawrence* by finding that the petitioner's "lack of insight" supported the Governor's reversal of the Board's suitability finding. This

decision created a curious twist in the legal authority, since "insight" is not listed among the enumerated factors indicating parole suitability or unsuitability, and the term hardly lends itself to concrete interpretation. The court offered no definition of the term but appeared to equate "insight" with an "understanding" of the motivation and circumstances that led the prisoner to commit the crime.

Rather than having the effect of creating fewer parole denials, the two decisions together seem to have prompted the Board and Governor to continue denying parole with regularity while simply tweaking the language of their denials. State officials appear to have taken *Lawrence* and *Shaputis* to mean that it is no longer permissible to deny parole based on the gravity of the commitment offense alone, but that it is now valid to deny parole based on lack of insight. * * *

D. Battered Women's Stereotypes: One Woman's Story

The recent emphasis on insight poses a particular danger for convicted battered women navigating the parole process, for the stereotypes concerning abuse victims create a quick and easy way for the state to deny parole based on "lack of insight." The recent parole denial for one Habeas Project client illustrates these difficulties. This woman had been convicted of second-degree murder for a crime that her abusive husband committed while she sat, some ten yards away, in the car with their infant. She has now served over twenty-five years in prison for her purported role in the crime. * * *

The Board's inability to understand the range of reasons a woman might remain in an abusive relationship translated directly to a denial of parole. The abuse could not have been so bad, the Board reasoned, if she stayed in the relationship. Thus, she must be lying about her motivation, thus she lacks insight into her crime, thus she is still a danger to society, thus she cannot be granted parole. By misapprehending the complexity of a struggle common to many battered women, the Board demonstrated either its disconcerting ignorance of abuse patterns or a conscious disregard for abuse survivors' experiences. Given the large number of women who enter prison with histories of abuse, this calls into question the competency of a Board whose decisions directly determine the outcome of these women's lives. Surmounting the stereotypes on which the Board appears to rely would prove a daunting task for even the most competent attorney.

The difficulty of the task doubles with the additional layer of Governor approval required. In a similar display of misunderstanding, Governor Wilson once developed a test for battered women that involved asking this very question: "Why didn't she just leave?" Though his test applied to clemency, it demonstrates how the biases of one individual can systemically operate to re-victimize an entire class of women. * * *

When the Board and Governor issue denials because the woman's version of insight does not comport with their own, they are potentially violating several state statutes. First, California law specifically prohibits the Board or the Governor from requiring admissions of guilt as a prerequisite to parole. Further, state regulations governing parole suitability list "Battered Woman Syndrome" among the enumerated factors favoring parole, not as a harmful factor weighing against it, as the Board sometimes seems to use it. Finally, in circumstances where the petitioner had no trial or did not receive the benefit of expert testimony on intimate partner battering at her trial, the Board must conduct an investigation into the abuse and consider any information or evidence therein revealed. Finding documents to prove the abuse occurred is challenging. For women convicted prior to the current expert testimony laws, the incidents of abuse would have occurred at least fourteen years, if not decades, earlier. Further, abusers and abused individuals often go to great lengths to hide the abuse from the public. But even in cases where the Board's Investigations Unit substantiates the abuse claims, the Board might still not consider such findings in its decision. In handing down a parole denial to one woman, for example, the Board commissioner stated, "there was an investigation done . . . and [the abuse] was partially substantiated at that time. However, not enough impact to make a difference in today's rendering." With legal, social, and political obstacles preventing women from accessing parole, many double victims will need to turn to the habeas statute to seek relief.

IV. WRITS OF HABEAS CORPUS UNDER CALIFORNIA PENAL CODE § 1473.5

A. Relevant Evidentiary Standards

Under authority granted by the California Penal Code, "[e]very person unlawfully imprisoned or restrained of his liberty, under any pretense whatever, may prosecute a writ of habeas corpus, to inquire into the cause of such imprisonment or restraint." Habeas corpus can be used as a means of obtaining a new trial, which can serve as a route to release if the new trial results in acquittal or in a sentence term shorter than the time the individual has already spent imprisoned. Alternatively, a successful habeas petition can lead to a reduction in sentence, a vacation of the conviction, or a new plea bargain, all of which can result in immediate release depending on the new sentence and the time already served.

* * * [C]onvicted battered women have a specific form of habeas relief available to them under California Penal Code section 1473.5. This statute allows imprisoned women [or men] to file habeas petitions if they did not present expert testimony on the effects of intimate partner battering at their criminal trials. At the heart of this habeas relief lies section 1107 of the Evidence Code, which expressly permits expert witness testimony on intimate partner battering and its effects. In a case involving a woman

charged with a crime committed against or at the coercion of her batterer, such expert testimony can save her from spending her life in prison. This evidentiary rule has been in effect since 1992; the habeas corpus statute that affords relief to women convicted prior to the change in law went into effect in 2001.

To appreciate the significance of Evidence Code section 1107, one must first understand how self-defense operates in California. Under state law, a criminal defendant who has committed homicide can be acquitted upon a showing that she feared imminent danger to her life or great bodily harm. This fear must be both something she actually experienced (the subjective prong) and something that was reasonable or "sufficient to excite the fears of a reasonable person" (the objective prong). A defendant can be acquitted when both prongs of the test are met, constituting what is known as perfect self-defense. Imperfect self-defense, by contrast, exists when the defendant subjectively believed that her life was in danger, but the fact-finder determines that her belief was not objectively reasonable.

While a finding of imperfect self-defense will not result in acquittal, it can make an enormous difference in the amount of time someone will serve in prison. By negating the element of malice necessary for a murder conviction, imperfect self-defense can lead to a voluntary manslaughter conviction, which carries a sentence of three, six, or eleven years in prison, depending on the presence of mitigating or aggravating circumstances. Most significantly, manslaughter carries a determinate sentence, meaning that the prisoner will be released after she serves a set number of years and will not have to wait for a parole suitability finding. First-degree murder, by contrast, carries a minimum indeterminate sentence of twenty-five years in prison, with a maximum sentence of death. Most people convicted of murder receive an indeterminate life sentence, meaning that they must serve a minimum of the base sentence (such as twenty-five years in a first-degree murder case, with possible lengthy enhancements for the use of a knife or gun). Ultimately, release depends on the Board and the Governor finding them suitable for parole, which may never happen.

Expert testimony on battering and its effects, admissible under Evidence Code section 1107, often plays a critical role in helping a woman prove either imperfect or perfect self-defense, which can greatly reduce or eliminate prison time. Expert witnesses can educate the judge and jury; dispel myths; help them understand the woman's mindset; bolster her credibility; and contextualize her actions in the scheme of what are often years of physical, psychological, and sexual abuse. * * *

B. Joyce Walker: An Illustrative Case

Hudie Joyce Walker's case, which produced the first and only published appellate decision to date interpreting the section 1473.5 habeas statute, illustrates what the legislature envisioned when it originally enacted the law. *[This case, found at 147 Cal.App.4th 533 (2007), is the only published appellate decision on point in California as of Jan. 2024.]* Until her imprisonment at the age of forty-nine, Ms. Walker's life consisted of a series of abusive relationships, beginning with sexual abuse as a child and culminating in marriage to a man whose regular beatings sometimes caused Ms. Walker to lose consciousness. On one particular night in May 1990, her intoxicated husband returned home, pointed a gun at Ms. Walker, and told her, "today will be your last goddamned day on this Earth." Ms. Walker fled the house, but on the advice of the local Deputy Sheriff returned home later that night while her husband was away to collect her medications and other personal belongings. Her husband returned home unexpectedly. When he threw a gun down on the table, both parties reached for it simultaneously—Mr. Walker presumably in order to kill his wife, and Ms. Walker to prevent him from doing so. The gun discharged as they were grappling and Mr. Walker died.

At her trial, Ms. Walker's attorney chose not to present expert testimony on battering and its effects. The attorney's case rested on the argument that Ms. Walker shot her husband accidentally; he believed that presenting expert testimony regarding Ms. Walker's history of abuse would undermine this legal theory. He may have worried, as sometimes happens, that evidence of battering would give the jury reason to think Ms. Walker had a motive for the crime. The court heard Ms. Walker's case in 1991, prior to the enactment of Evidence Code section 1107, prior to the decision in *Barton* that would have made a voluntary manslaughter instruction mandatory, and prior to the decision in *Humphrey* that would have made expert testimony on battering clearly relevant and admissible for both subjective and objective self-defense prongs. Having received insufficient instructions and no expert testimony, the jury convicted Ms. Walker of second-degree murder. The court imposed a sentence of nineteen years to life in prison.

Ms. Walker made numerous legal attempts to obtain her freedom before her section 1473.5 writ succeeded. The initial appeal of her conviction failed despite her having included a declaration from her defense counsel that he was wrong not to have presented expert testimony on her experiences of abuse. Ms. Walker's subsequent federal habeas petitions failed for similar reasons: the court did not find her counsel ineffective where he made a tactical decision not to include expert testimony on battering. A state trial court rejected Ms. Walker's first section 1473.5 writ in 2004, based partly on its finding—mirroring the reasoning of the appellate court during Ms. Walker's initial appeal—that any expert testimony would be "irrelevant" given her claim that the shooting was an accident.

Ms. Walker then filed her section 1473.5 petition with the state court of appeals. That court exercised its power to review the petition on the merits and found that exclusion of expert testimony on battering, particularly in light of *Barton* and *Humphrey*, had prejudiced Ms. Walker at her first trial. The court thus vacated her conviction and ordered a new trial. Ms. Walker subsequently pled no contest to voluntary manslaughter, which carried a shorter prison term than the time she had already served. Finally, on May 29, 2007, after sixteen years of incarceration, Ms. Walker became a free woman.

Ms. Walker's case illustrates the overarching purpose of section 1473.5: to grant justice to abused women whose imprisonment or lengthy sentences would not have occurred had today's laws been in effect at the time of their trials. As originally enacted, however, this relief did not benefit the scores of women who fit into the spirit, but not the letter, of the habeas statute. The original version of section 1473.5, passed into law in 2001, applied only to prisoners charged with murder of their abusive partners and who entered into plea agreements or whose trials began prior to 1992, when section 1107 went into effect. However, because of misunderstandings about the admissibility and applicability of expert witness testimony under section 1107, numerous women did not have the opportunity to present expert testimony for years after the section was enacted. Further, by limiting the habeas statute to first- or second-degree murder of the abusive partner, the legislature excluded battered survivors imprisoned for acts committed under duress or at the coercion of their abusers and those convicted of attempted murder or manslaughter of their abusers. Though surely these people should have found equal relief in light of the purpose of section 1473.5, statutory amendments were needed to ensure that this relief could be realized.

C. Expanding the Law, Embracing More Women

In 2004, Senator John Burton introduced Senate Bill 1385 in the California legislature with the purpose of expanding section 1473.5's coverage, correcting its outdated terminology, and eliminating filing deadlines. At legislative hearings, Senator Burton emphasized that the first incarnation of section 1473.5 was "unduly restrictive [and] exclude[d] many in the intended beneficiary class: incarcerated survivors who were not able to use evidence of battering even though their crimes were directly related to their experience of being battered." The bill faced little opposition, and passed with strong bipartisan support. The new version of section 1473.5 went into effect January 1, 2005.

In its final form, S.B. 1385 made three major changes to previous law. First, it expanded the law's beneficiaries to include people convicted of any violent felonies as defined under Penal Code section 667.5(c)—not just those convicted of first- or second-degree murder in the deaths of their abusive partners, as originally prescribed. * * *

The second major extension in S.B. 1385 shifted the eligibility cut-off date from January 1, 1992, to August 29, 1996. Where previously section 1473.5 included only women who had entered into plea agreements or whose trials began before 1992 (when the new Evidence Code section went into effect), it now would include women whose crimes occurred prior to the date the California Supreme Court issued *Humphrey*, August 29, 1996. * * *

Finally, the amended statute changed terminology to eliminate references to "battered woman's syndrome" (BWS) and substitute "battering and its effects." * * *

D. The Limits of Habeas

* * * To date, petitions filed under the amended habeas statute have met with mixed results in the courts. * * * Another petitioner argued for relief based on his experience as the son of an abuser. The district court denied each petition for untimeliness. * * * Even when a petitioner can meet the procedural and merit-based requirements, a successful petition does not necessarily lead to release. A new trial, following a successful petition, may still carry the same risks inherent in the first one. * * *

The numerous pitfalls of section 1473.5 highlight the need for private counsel and for resources more broadly [such as funding for experts and investigators]. * * *

Because they are excluded from the parole and compassionate release processes, section 1473.5 petitions are critical for wrongly imprisoned women serving these extreme sentences [i.e., life without possibility of parole or a death sentence]. * * *

The California habeas statute is unique in this country. The statute addresses the plight of women convicted during a time when the law did not formally recognize the experiences of abuse survivors and, more importantly, the statute has resulted in the release of at least sixteen people as of March 2011. It also serves a critical role in California, where advocates speculate that section 1473.5 may not serve the same function in other states where alternative routes to release have more traction. But its limits—high procedural burdens, eligibility cut-off dates, resource demands, and a perhaps tenuous relationship to release—should prompt advocates to reexamine more traditional routes, which can benefit both women who can and cannot utilize section 1473.5. * * *

[Editor's Note: Ca. Penal Code section 1473.5 was amended effective Jan. 1, 2013 to remove the sunset clause, so there is no deadline to file for relief. The new language also specifies that if domestic violence expert testimony offered at trial was not "competent and substantial," the prisoner is eligible to submit a habeas petition. Similarly, Ca. Penal Code section 4801 was amended to add, "The fact that a prisoner has presented evidence of intimate partner battering cannot be used to support a finding that the prisoner lacks insight into his or her crime and its causes."

Former Ca. Gov. Jerry Brown allowed many more parole recommendations to be implemented than his predecessors had. He stated that he should second-guess the judgment of the parole board only in unusual circumstances. As of 2012, 37 prisoners were released through the efforts of the Ca. Habeas Project: 16 were granted parole after their pro bono attorneys investigated their cases for habeas petitions and then represented the prisoners before the parole board, while 21 were released through habeas petitions to the courts. While the Project disbanded, rates of battered women obtaining parole in Ca. have improved greatly.]

ROSSAKIS V. NEW YORK STATE BOARD OF PAROLE

146 A.D.3d 22 (N.Y. 2016)
(citations and two footnotes omitted)

In this appeal, we take the unusual step of affirming the annulment of a decision of respondent-appellant the New York State Board of Parole (the Board) denying parole to petitioner-respondent Niki Rossakis (petitioner). We agree with the motion court that the Board's decision was so irrational as to border on impropriety and was therefore arbitrarily and capriciously rendered. However, we vacate the portion of the motion court's judgment which directed how the Board was to weigh the statutory factors.

FACTS[1]

On May 17, 1996, petitioner was convicted of murder in the second degree for shooting her husband Gary (decedent) on January 21, 1993. Petitioner has consistently maintained for two decades that decedent abused her physically and sexually throughout their marriage. She claims that he raped her in early 1993, leading to her having an abortion two weeks prior to the shooting. At that time, her physician advised the couple that she should not have sex for six weeks, so that she could heal from the procedure. Nevertheless, on the night before the shooting, decedent forced his fingers inside of her, and threatened to force her to have intercourse. She managed to extricate herself and spent the night downstairs. On the morning of the shooting, decedent reached for her crotch. When she pushed his hand away, he said, "I will get you later bitch." Petitioner then took decedent's gun from a nearby night stand drawer and shot him in the head.

At trial, petitioner testified that she shot decedent because she feared he would rape her. Her expert witness testified that her behavior was not inconsistent with that of an abused woman. The jurors were instructed as to the defenses of justification and extreme emotional disturbance. On May 17, 1996, petitioner was convicted of murder in the second degree and

---

[1] We rely for our statement of facts solely on the record before this Court. That record does not include the minutes of petitioner's underlying criminal trial. In a prior decision of this Court, we denied the Board's motion asking us to take judicial notice of the transcripts of petitioner's criminal trial. Despite our ruling, the Board nonetheless improperly cited to those transcripts in their briefs. Accordingly, we have disregarded these portions of the Board's briefs.

criminal possession of a weapon in the second degree. The Appellate Division Second Department found that her initial sentence of 23 years to life was excessive, and reduced it in the interests of justice to 15 years to life, the minimum for murder in the second degree.

Petitioner has now been in prison for over 20 years. During that time, she has obtained two associate degrees from Marymount Manhattan College and Bard College; successfully completed every rehabilitative program offered to her, including anger management and nonviolent conflict resolution techniques; acted as a teaching assistant and tutor to other inmates; served on the Inmate Grievance Resolution Committee, a committee composed of correctional staff and inmates hearing inmate complaints against the facility; and won praise for her work as a telephone operator for the Department of Motor Vehicles. She has been offered a job at a family violence agency upon her release. If released, she intends to complete her bachelor's and master's degrees, continue in therapy, and become involved with her church. Petitioner, who has no prior history of violent crime, received the best score possible on her Correctional Offender Management Profiling for Alternative Sanction (COMPAS) evaluation, indicating a low likelihood for violence, substance abuse, or criminal behavior.

Petitioner has sought and been denied parole three times: in 2009, 2011, and, most recently, 2013. She challenged the Board's 2011 denial in a proceeding pursuant to article 78 of the CPLR. In a decision dated May 2, 2013 (the May order), Justice Kathryn E. Freed found that the Board had improperly focused on the seriousness of petitioner's offense without considering the other statutory factors, and ordered a new parole hearing. The Board appealed, triggering a stay of the May order. However, before the Board could perfect its appeal, petitioner appeared for a routine parole hearing in 2013.

At the 2013 parole hearing, petitioner testified, "I did the worst thing someone could do, and I killed . . . Gary, and I'm very, very sorry for that. . . . When I first started my bid, I saw myself as the victim. Today I know that Gary is the victim. I no longer harp on the abuse just to justify what I did to my husband. I was wrong. I should have just gotten up and left. I should have made more of an attempt to reach out and talk to people. I didn't do that. I isolated and started to self-destruct. . . . I made a horrible decision, and I'm sorry." The Board denied her most recent request for parole on August 6, 2013, and withdrew its appeal of the May order.

The Board's denial consisted of a brief four-paragraph decision. In its first paragraph, the Board asserted that petitioner's release was incompatible with the welfare of society, largely mirroring the text of the Executive Law itself. The Board's second paragraph described the facts of the underlying offense and made mention of petitioner's substance use around the time of decedent's death. The Board's third paragraph summarily listed petitioner's institutional achievements with no further analysis. In its final paragraph, the Board concluded that petitioner lacked remorse, finding that she continued to blame decedent for his death and continued to identify as an abuse victim despite the jury's guilty verdict. Petitioner then commenced this proceeding, now on appeal before this Court, challenging the 2013 denial.

In an extensive opinion, the motion court found that the Board's 2013 decision was again based almost exclusively on consideration of petitioner's crime, and ignored the other applicable statutory parole factors, including petitioner's institutional achievements and remorse. The motion court ordered that petitioner receive a new parole hearing before a new panel of Commissioners. The order also directed "in the strongest way possible, that the Board consider all of the other factors which emphasize forward-thinking and planning. In other words, this new Board is not authorized to re-sentence or unduly consider the crime. That is but one factor. In other words, . . . the Board is instructed to evaluate the applicant as she is today and how she has prepared herself for her release back into society."

ANALYSIS

In an article 78 petition challenging a parole decision, the petitioner bears the burden to show that the decision is the result of " 'irrationality bordering on impropriety,' " and is thus arbitrary and capricious. The Board must consider eight statutory factors enumerated in the Executive Law in determining whether an inmate should be released on parole, of which the following five are relevant to this appeal:

> "(i) the institutional record including program goals and accomplishments, academic achievements, vocational education, training or work assignments, therapy and interactions with staff and inmates; . . .; (iii) release plans including community resources, employment, education and training and support services available to the inmate . . .; (v) any statement made to the board by the crime victim or the victim's representative, where the crime victim is deceased or is mentally or physically incapacitated . . .; (vii) the seriousness of the offense with due consideration to the type of sentence, length of sentence and recommendations of the sentencing court, the district attorney, the attorney for the inmate, the pre-sentence probation report as well as consideration of any mitigating and aggravating factors, and activities following arrest prior to confinement; and (viii) prior criminal record, including the nature and pattern of offenses, adjustment to any previous probation or parole supervision and institutional confinement."

The Board is not obligated to refer to each factor, or to give every factor equal weight. However, as this Court has previously held, "[i]t is unquestionably the duty of the Board to give fair consideration to each of the applicable statutory factors as to every person who comes before it, and where the record convincingly demonstrates that the Board did in fact fail to consider the proper standards, the courts must intervene." In particular, "[t]he role of the Parole Board is not to resentence petitioner according to the personal opinions of its members as to the appropriate penalty for murder, but to determine whether, as of this moment, given all the relevant statutory factors, he should be released. In that regard, the statute expressly mandates that the prisoner's educational and other achievements affirmatively be taken into consideration in determining whether he meets the general criteria relevant to parole release." The Board may not deny parole based solely on the seriousness of the offense.

Based on the record before us, we conclude that the motion court correctly determined that the Board acted with an irrationality bordering on impropriety in denying petitioner parole. The Board focused exclusively on the seriousness of petitioner's conviction and the decedent's family's victim impact statements (which it incorrectly described as "community opposition to her release") without giving genuine consideration to petitioner's remorse, institutional achievements, release plan, and her lack of any prior violent criminal history.

The Board's statement that, "[d]espite your assertions of abuse being rejected by a jury after hearing you testify for eight days, and having no corroboration on record of the abuse, you continue to blame your victim for his death," disregards petitioner's testimony accepting responsibility and expressing remorse for her actions. It also fails to recognize that petitioner may legitimately view herself as a battered woman, even though the jury did not find that she met New York's exacting requirements for the defenses of justification and extreme emotional disturbance. Indeed, her criminal trial attorneys submitted letters to this effect. As one of those attorneys, now a law professor, highlighted, our collective understanding of domestic violence is far greater today than when petitioner was arrested and tried, and this dearth of knowledge may very well have affected how the jury viewed the instructions as to these defenses. While we cannot and do not attempt to retry petitioner, we agree with the motion court that apologizing for the shooting while steadfastly maintaining that she was an abuse victim does not indicate a lack of remorse for her actions.

The Board summarily listed petitioner's institutional achievements, and then denied parole with no further analysis of them, in violation of the Executive Law's requirement that the reasons for denial not be given in "conclusory terms." Moreover, the Board's decision began by stating that petitioner's release "would be incompatible with the welfare of society and would so deprecate the serious nature of the crime as to undermine respect for the law." These statements came directly from the language of Executive Law § 259–i(2)(c), further violating the Executive Law's ban on the Board making conclusory assertions.

Despite petitioner's impressive COMPAS score, evidencing her low risk for violence or substance abuse upon release, the Board asserted that there is a "reasonable probability" that petitioner would again violate the law, based on the crime of which she was convicted, her addiction to prescription medication around the time of her arrest and trial in the early 1990s, and her use of drugs in the early 1980s, prior to her marriage to decedent. The Board's unsupported finding echoes decedent's family's victim impact statements, which emphasized petitioner's prior drug use and their belief that she is a dangerous person. Decedent's family also emphasized that petitioner would have nowhere to go if released; however, the record makes clear that petitioner had secured a job offer and was taking concrete steps to secure housing. * * * [W]e find that the Board inappropriately relied on claims in decedent's family's victim impact statements that were affirmatively rebutted by the objective evidence supporting petitioner's release.

Among the many factors the Board must consider in granting or denying parole is the "recommendations of the sentencing court." Here, the court that pronounced the sentence petitioner is currently serving * * * reduced petitioner's sentence to 15 years to life, holding that the trial court's sentence of 23 years to life was excessive. However, as the motion court noted, the Board's repeated denials to petitioner of parole have had the effect of undermining this sentence reduction.

For all these reasons, we affirm the motion court's finding that the Board acted with irrationality bordering on impropriety and therefore arbitrarily and capriciously denied petitioner parole. However, we have previously held that "[w]hile the court is empowered to determine whether the administrative body acted arbitrarily, it may not usurp the administrative function by directing the agency to proceed in a specific manner, which is within the jurisdiction and discretion of the administrative body in the first instance." Accordingly, we vacate so much of the motion court's order as may be read to direct the Board to emphasize factors which emphasize forward thinking and planning over the other statutory factors.

We hold that petitioner is entitled to a new parole hearing to take place before new Commissioners who have not sat on any of petitioner's earlier parole hearings. The hearing shall take place within 60 days from the issuance of this decision, and the Board shall render its decision within 30 days after the new hearing. * * *

[Editor's Note: Ms. Rossakis was granted parole at her subsequent parole board interview.]

COURTNEY CROSS, REENTERING SURVIVORS: INVISIBLE AT THE INTERSECTION OF THE CRIMINAL LEGAL SYSTEM AND THE DOMESTIC VIOLENCE MOVEMENT

31 Berkeley J. Gender L. & Just. 60 (2016)
(most footnotes omitted)

INTRODUCTION

When Lauren Walker came home from prison, she discovered that her boyfriend, John Baldwin, had forged his name onto her lease and was living in her apartment.[1] John refused to move out and told Lauren that he would get her sent back to prison if she kicked him out. Lauren tried to end the relationship but she could not get away from John. When she went to work, he called her cell phone constantly. If she turned her cell phone off, he called her office and demanded to speak with her. John frequently went to Lauren's job to check on her. As a result, Lauren was fired. She could not find another job and became extremely depressed. She began self-medicating with crack cocaine, a habit she developed at age fifteen to cope with being sexually abused by several family members and older men.

After Lauren lost her job, John became physically abusive. He blamed his violence on her drug use. He hit her and strangled her several times a week, choking *[i.e., strangling]* her until she passed out multiple times. Lauren frequently had black eyes, split lips, and bruises and burns around her neck. Although he was working, John still repeatedly called Lauren and came to the apartment during the day to make sure she had not left. John did not use drugs himself but he often bought drugs for Lauren, spending his entire income tax return on crack because he did not like her interacting with other men to buy drugs.

John rarely allowed Lauren to leave the house alone: he would drive her to meetings with her parole officer and her addiction support group and wait outside. Although Lauren had confided in her parole officer about the violence, she was too afraid of John and too dependent on his income to call the police or get a protection order like her parole officer recommended.

Because she was embarrassed by her injuries and afraid that her parole officer would have John arrested, Lauren stopped going to her mandatory meetings and drug tests.

Lauren felt trapped. When she had the locks changed to her apartment, John broke in. When she tried to call her family for help, John broke her cell phone. When her parole officer sent her to an in-patient drug treatment program, John entered the same program and forced Lauren to leave when he found out that they could not see each other during the program. On her own, Lauren arranged to attend another treatment

[1] Although names have been changed and personal details have been removed, Ms. Walker's story is true. The author represented her in a parole revocation hearing in front of the United States Parole Commission.

program. When John found out, he became furious and found Lauren outside of her apartment building and dragged her up the stairs to the apartment, breaking her GPS ankle monitor. She refused to go inside so John took her broken GPS monitor and drove off. Lauren immediately left for the program.

When she completed the program, Lauren tried to break off the relationship again. John did move out but continued to come by the apartment to see who she had over and where she went. John's new girlfriend also started coming by Lauren's apartment to harass her. When his girlfriend hit Lauren with her car, John took Lauren to the hospital but made her leave before seeing a doctor because he was afraid the police would be called. Shortly thereafter, Lauren was sent back to prison for a year because she violated the terms of her parole by using drugs, skipping mandatory meetings and drug tests with her parole officer, and tampering with her GPS monitor.

Lauren's story is not unique in its facts or its outcome. Many incarcerated women feel pressure to return to and remain in volatile homes upon their release, only to find the obstacles inherent in the reentry process compounded by domestic violence at home. The reentry requirements imposed upon returning citizens by community supervision make it especially difficult for reentering women who are experiencing domestic violence to leave unsafe and unsupportive homes. These same women often find that they are unable to access domestic violence services due to their criminal backgrounds. Women on community supervision experiencing domestic violence—referred to here as "reentering survivors"—must then choose whether to remain in an unsafe living situation or risk reincarceration if their attempts to escape or ameliorate the violence cause them to violate the terms of their supervision. Reentering survivors' experiences demonstrate how the criminal legal system first ignores how community supervision interacts with and exacerbates violence against women, and then systematically punishes women whose experiences of abuse interfere with their ability to meet supervision requirements. * * *

One cannot fully comprehend the experiences of reentering survivors solely by exploring either the abuse they endure at home or the challenges they face through community supervision. Rather, it is critical to understand the many ways in which the intersection of these two experiences profoundly affect the lives of reentering women. Because many reentering survivors are non-white, low-income women, the violence and coercion inflicted by their abusive partners and the control exerted by the state are further compounded by issues of race, class, and gender. In addition, the convergence of the criminal legal system and the domestic violence movement in supporting "tough on crime" policies has further excluded reentering survivors from social and legal services created for victims of domestic violence and further exposed them to the punitive structure of community supervision. * * *

Experiencing abuse during reentry can aggravate preexisting injuries and trauma. Domestic violence can also cause new physical and psychological afflictions that can impede reentry. Despite the abuse, a reentering survivor's past experiences with law enforcement and incarceration may make her less willing or able to invite state involvement into her life again. For instance, Lauren Walker was incarcerated 200 miles away from home. While in prison, she participated in a drug treatment program, but this program addressed neither her co-occurring mental health diagnosis nor her trauma from having been physically and sexually abused throughout her life. She received minimal vocational training and limited release planning. Although she had been sentenced to be released directly into an in-patient drug treatment facility before living in the community, this transfer was never arranged and she was told to just go home. While incarcerated, Lauren was unable to obtain the skills necessary to navigate her depression, her addiction, and her abuse. Her attempts to get the help she needed once she was released also proved insufficient in the face of barriers in the community and at a home. Yet Lauren also felt she could not turn to the police in her myriad attempts to free herself from domestic violence. Worried about how John Baldwin's arrest might undermine her financial stability, expose her to violence from the police or from John, or result in her own reincarceration, Lauren did not see turning to law enforcement for help as a viable option. Because her previous interactions with the police had resulted in her own arrest and incarceration, Lauren, like many returning citizens and reentering survivors, was unwilling to jeopardize her freedom—even for her safety. * * *

Lauren Walker found herself relying on John Baldwin in order to comply with her community supervision. Lauren became completely financially dependent on John after she was fired from her job. She needed him to take her to all of her required appointments. He also became her primary source of social interaction. Yet his abusive behavior contributed to her relapse, and her lack of sobriety was cited as one reason for her reincarceration. Ironically, Lauren's decision to enter a second drug treatment program to become clean and get away from John was also a violation of her supervision and contributed to her reincarceration. Although Lauren was eventually successful in separating from John, she was unable to reach a point where she could maintain both her safety and her liberty. * * *

Moreover, these studies of [very extensive] pre-incarceration abuse demonstrate how women released from incarceration are particularly vulnerable to abuse in the community. Without access to trauma-informed care during and after incarceration, these women risk returning to past patterns of abuse and harmful coping mechanisms like substance abuse. Women involved in illegal activities or who have had negative experiences with law enforcement are "desirable targets of violence" because their abusive partners know they are unlikely to seek help from the police. That is, reentering survivors are especially vulnerable to forms of domestic violence that target their status as reentering citizens. * * *

In deciding to revoke her parole and reincarcerate her for one year, the parole board saw as irrelevant the ways in which John's behavior undermined and sabotaged Lauren's compliance and chose not to mitigate her violations of community supervision.

II. THE DOMESTIC VIOLENCE MOVEMENT: FROM ACTIVISM TO INSTITUTION

As the criminal legal system moved from rehabilitation toward (increasingly) retributivist policies, so too did the domestic violence movement transition from a woman-centered approach to a greater focus on "tough on crime" advocacy. In doing so, the domestic violence movement left behind many of its founding political principles. Part of this transformation has included a close alliance with the state, premised upon crime control (of batterers) as the primary means of combatting domestic violence. The narrowing of the movement's goals and services has resulted in the systematic exclusion of marginalized women from the domestic violence movement's purview. This exclusion, combined with the adoption of "tough on crime" approaches to domestic violence, has meant that many reentering survivors are not only overlooked by the movement, but also endangered by it. * * *

[W]omen who are seen as "less likely to cause trouble, less likely to have retaliated against her abusive partner, and more likely to want to end her relationship with the abusive partner" are most likely to be found eligible for programming [by domestic violence advocates]. * * * [M]any domestic violence programs insist that the program's address remain confidential, which is problematic because those on community supervision are often required to give their addresses to their supervision officers who may visit unannounced. * * *

Not only do reentering survivors have to face all of these judgments when seeking out services, but they may also be denied assistance because of their criminal records. According to Sue Osthoff, the director of the National Clearinghouse for the Defense of Battered Women, "We all too frequently hear about community-based battered women's programs that will not assist battered women charged with crimes (especially if the alleged crime is an assault against her partner) because, they say, they cannot or will not work with 'perpetrators.' " This exclusion often involves no analysis of the causes behind women's criminal records, including the violence they are currently experiencing. * * *

IV. CONCLUSION

* * * The challenges faced by reentering survivors are largely invisible to both the criminal legal system and the domestic violence movement. Notwithstanding some advocacy around training parole and probation officers on domestic violence among female supervisees, there has yet to be a meaningful discussion regarding how the structure of supervision itself interacts with domestic violence. Nor is there widespread understanding among domestic violence advocates about the obstacles reentering survivors may encounter if they are able to access help. For example, a reentering survivor may be hesitant to file for a protection order if doing so will require an admission that she has violated her community supervision (perhaps by going somewhere she is not allowed to go or seeing someone she was ordered to stay away from). Without a deeper understanding of the intersection between the criminal legal system and the domestic violence advocacy movement, both systems will continue to endanger an already marginalized population.

[The author calls for changes in the criminal legal system, including moving toward decriminalization of low-level drug offenses; expanding not just alternatives to incarceration but also alternatives to conviction programs; improving access to programming and reentry planning in jails and prisons; refocusing community supervision on reintegration as opposed to surveillance; and minimizing collateral consequences of criminal convictions while expanding opportunities for expungement and record sealing. * * * "The domestic violence movement must also build alliances with those advocating for these changes and join the broader movement campaigning for criminal justice reform." She also calls for community-building to prevent crime, and for the domestic violence movement to "return to its explicitly political roots," with a focus on survivors who were once at the movement's periphery and working for widespread economic changes so people have access to adequate jobs and housing.]

Lauren Walker's story illuminates just some of the challenges of women's reentry. Although the barriers she faced proved insurmountable, Lauren was relatively better off than many reentering women: she did not have to look for housing, she was able to quickly obtain employment, she did not have children to support, and she was able to get herself into multiple drug treatment programs. Yet many women must tackle these obstacles, and more, and are similarly reincarcerated for being unable to comply with the terms of their community supervision. The abuse Lauren experienced at home undermined every advantage from which she might have benefited; she did not receive the kind of support that might have facilitated successful reentry and a violence-free life. Had she been released to an individually tailored combination of safe and independent housing with cash assistance, drug and mental health counseling, and trauma-informed community supervision, Lauren may have been better equipped to overcome the many obstacles still inherent in the reentry process. Although there is no quick fix to ensure successful reintegration, reentering survivors would benefit greatly from being able to access appropriate public benefits, social and legal services, and state supervision designed to foster successful outcomes. Without recognizing the many ways in which "tough on crime" policies undermine individuals' and communities' safety and long-term stability, even reforms designed to protect domestic violence survivors risk further marginalizing those survivors already on the periphery. In order to promote truly inclusive reform, domestic violence activists must advocate within both the domestic violence movement and the larger criminal legal system for a returned focus to individuals' needs and strengths.

CHAPTER 14

FEDERAL RESPONSES TO DOMESTIC VIOLENCE: VIOLENCE AGAINST WOMEN ACT, RESTRICTIONS ON FIREARMS, MILITARY RESPONSE

■ ■ ■

This chapter looks at U.S. federal government responses to domestic violence. The first part focuses on the various versions of the Violence Against Women Act, starting with VAWA I, the first time the federal government made a major commitment to address domestic violence. The materials describe the civil rights provision in VAWA I, and the U.S. Supreme court decision holding that section unconstitutional in *U.S. v. Morrison*, but argue that VAWA's impact has been huge in spite of that decision. The 2022 provisions of VAWA's reauthorization are summarized, along with the first U.S. Plan to End Gender Based Violence released in 2023.

The next part of the chapter concerns federal restrictions on possession of firearms by batterers. Given the major developments in jurisprudence, legislation, research, and policies concerning this topic, the section contains entirely new materials. These materials start with a toolkit focused on preventing and reducing domestic violence-related gun injuries and fatalities, followed by an article arguing that these fatalities are preventable if U.S. laws were strengthened and enforced (e.g., requiring universal background checks before selling firearms and enacting strong gun relinquishment protocols). The author also urges family law attorneys and advocates to ask every client about guns in the home and work with clients to create appropriate safety plans.

An article about fatal mass shootings in the U.S. and their connection to domestic violence is summarized, followed by a recent report by the California Dept of Justice Armed & Prohibited Persons System Program regarding confiscation of firearms by the state. Then new statutes from two states requiring courts to play an active role in firearms relinquishment by abusers are described.

Next is an article about the *Rahimi* decision, pending in the U.S. Supreme Court when this book went to press, in which the Fifth Circuit Court of Appeals held unconstitutional the long-standing federal statute prohibiting firearm possession by anyone subject to a domestic violence restraining order, followed by an amicus brief filed with the Court by several groups opposed to the decision. This part of the chapter ends with a post-*Rahimi* decision by a different federal district court, holding that the statute is constitutional under the originalist standard announced in the Court's *Bruen* decision.

The final part of the chapter deals with domestic violence and the U.S. military, with an overview of the issues in general, legal provisions for victims of domestic violence whose abusers are servicemembers, and a new article questioning how well the military deals with such cases. The chapter concludes with a description of specialized "veteran's courts," with a commentator arguing that domestic violence cases should be dealt with in traditional criminal courts rather than in these specialized courts.

A. OVERVIEW, VAWA'S CIVIL RIGHTS REMEDY

CLAIRE M. DEMATTEIS, PROTECTING THE FREEDOM FOR WOMEN TO BE FREE FROM VIOLENCE: THE VIOLENCE AGAINST WOMEN ACT ENDURES

22 Widener L. Rev. 267 (2016)
(most footnotes omitted)

Twenty-five years after it was introduced as novel legislation, and more than fifteen years after its cornerstone civil rights remedy was struck down by a divided U.S. Supreme Court, the Violence Against Women Act endures as the seminal law that has dramatically shifted how we talk about, prosecute and protect women's fundamental freedom to be free from violence—across the country and around the globe.

In 1980, the forcible rape crime rate, primarily against women, was 36.8 per 100,000 women. By 1985, the rate increased to 37.1 per 100,000 women. By 1990, the rate rose again to 41.2 per 100,000. [*Note: The original version of this essay had erroneous statistics, which have been corrected here.*]

These gender-based crime rates were among the violent crime statistics reviewed by then-Chairman of the U.S. Senate Judiciary Committee, Joseph R. Biden, Jr., which led to his introduction in June 1990 of the Violence Against Women Act. This Act became law on September 13, 1994.

Hundreds of scholarly articles, books, reports and studies have been written on the creation, passage and impact of the Violence Against Women Act. This essay is an account by one attorney[8] who witnessed turning the Act into Action. Counter to what some critics, skeptics and objective

[8] The author served as Counsel and Senior Counsel to U.S. Senator Joseph R. Biden, Jr. from 1994–2004.

scholars[10] have argued, this essay seeks to highlight that even without the civil rights remedy, the Violence Against Women Act has endured and has empowered women to report crimes, seek justice and hold their offenders and law enforcement accountable.

Did the Violence Against Women Act end violent crime against women? Of course not. That was never its objective. Nor should the Violence Against Women Act be judged by such a standard. Then-Senator, and now Vice President, Biden said as much himself in a 1990 hearing before the Senate Judiciary Committee, stating he was under "no illusion that this legislation is going to stop violence against women."

In action, the Violence Against Women Act changed attitudes among law enforcement, judges, victims and society as a whole. By changing attitudes and no longer accepting violence against women as a private family matter, the Act has saved lives. Between 1993 and 2012, intimate partner violence [in the U.S.] declined 64 percent. As important a benchmark as this statistic represents, the change in attitude of how we view such violence is immeasurable: 20 years after passage of the Violence Against Women Act, it is no longer a private family matter when an NFL marquee player knocks out his fiancee unconscious in a hotel elevator. The Violence Against Women Act changed the law and changed attitudes so that such violence is no longer tolerated in a civilized country and ensures offenders are held accountable.

I. The "Voluminous Record"

There is no disputing that when it was written and enacted, Title III, the Civil Rights Provision, was considered a cornerstone of the Act. The goal of the civil rights remedy was to create a federal civil rights cause of action for crimes motivated by gender.

Several law review articles have been published regarding Title III, one of the most provocative published recently by Caroline Schmidt entitled What Killed the Violence Against Women Act's Civil Rights Remedy Before the Supreme Court Did? Respectfully, law review articles such as this miss the mark and fail to acknowledge the lasting impact of the Violence Against Women Act—an impact that endures despite the fact that the U.S. Supreme Court reversed a centuries-old interpretation of the Commerce Clause that was the law of the land when the Violence Against Women Act was first introduced in 1990, through the year it was enacted in 1994.

Ms. Schmidt's law review article provides no context of the impact the Violence Against Women Act has had on a woman's right to seek justice

[10] See Caroline S. Schmidt, What Killed the Violence Against Women Act's Civil Rights Remedy Before the Supreme Court Did?, 101 Va. L. Rev. 501 (2015).

against her abuser, despite the court's rejection of the civil rights remedy.[18] With the movement toward specialized Domestic Violence Courts that the Act spurred, as well as the Act's targeted funding, education and prevention programs, women's rights are being protected to a significantly greater extent than had the Violence Against Women Act [] never been enacted.

When the federal civil rights remedy was struck down by the U.S. Supreme Court in 2000, then-Senator Biden rededicated his efforts to protect women's civil rights through criminal justice measures, education, and prevention programs funded by the Violence Against Women Act. This essay will expand upon this point further, but first, it is important to note that from 1990 when the Violence Against Women Act was first introduced until September 13, 1994 when it [was] signed into law, then-Senator Biden, as Chairman of the U.S. Senate Judiciary Committee, held more than a dozen hearings, with candid testimony from victims—which was really the first time victims spoke so openly and graphically about the violence and sexual assaults they experienced. The U.S. House of Representatives held additional hearings to build support for the five sections of the Act:

> Title I, the Safe Streets for Women Act, which seeks to improve safety outside the home by increasing the penalties for federal cases of rape and aggravated rape;
>
> Title II, the Safe Homes for Women Act, which remedies existing defects in state protective orders by requiring that a protective order issued in one state be given "full faith and credit" in all other states;
>
> Title III, the Civil Rights Provision;
>
> Title IV, Violence Against Women Act Improvements, which addressed the increasing problem of sexual assaults on college and university campuses; and
>
> Title V, Equal Justice for Women in the Courts Act, which provided funding to train state court judges and court personnel on issues relating to violent crimes against women.

In June 2000, in a 5–4 ruling written by Chief Justice William Rehnquist in *United States v. Morrison*, the Court agreed with the government that there was a "voluminous congressional record" supporting the "assertion that there is pervasive bias in various state justice systems against victims of gender-motivated violence," and the Court also agreed with the government that "state-sponsored gender discrimination violates equal protection unless it serves important governmental objectives . . . ."

---

[18] In United States v. Morrison, the Supreme Court held that Congress lacked the constitutional authority to enact the civil rights remedy. United States v. Morrison, 529 U.S. 598, 611–612 (2000).

The Court, however, held that the civil rights remedy exceeded Congress' power under the Commerce Clause and under Section 5 of the Fourteenth Amendment to the U.S. Constitution. According to the majority, even if there was unconstitutional state action, that only justified Congress in targeting the state actors, rather than targeting private parties. Further, in the majority opinion, Justice Rehnquist, who had vocally opposed the civil rights remedy as the Violence Against Women Act made its way through Congress, reiterated his previous concern that the civil rights provision would overload the federal courts and would allow Congress to regulate "family law and other areas of state regulation," even "marriage, divorce, and childrearing."

[Editor's Note: Christy Brzonkala was gang-raped in 1994 in her dorm by two school football players shortly after she came to Virginia Polytechnic Institute and State University. She was severely traumatized by the attack and was unable to attend classes. The school held a hearing but allowed both assailants to continue in school, and Morrison, the only one who admitted assaulting Brzonkala, was allowed to retain his full athletic scholarship. Brzonkala then withdrew from school, fearing retaliation and humiliation. She sued under Title IX, state tort and contract law, and Title III of VAWA, the recently enacted civil rights provision allowing private parties to sue their abusers in federal court for gender-motivated violence.

As Professor Sally Goldfarb describes in "No Civilized System of Justice": The Fate of the Violence Against Women Act, 102 W. Va. L. Rev. 499 (2000), "[u]ltimately, a narrow majority of the Supreme Court struck down VAWA's civil rights provision in an opinion that entirely failed to confront the issues of women's equality, sex discrimination, and civil rights, but which served to overturn one of the most important feminist legislative achievements of recent years." She notes that what was a civil rights provision was re-characterized by the courts as a family law provision. Family law has always been the province of states, even though there are some family law cases decided by federal courts. But the Conference of Chief Justices and some groups of state judges had lobbied against Title III when it was in Congress, arguing that it would "plunge the federal government" into "inter-spousal litigation (which) goes to the very core of familial relationships." This history helped overturn Title III, even though gang rape on a college campus obviously has no relationship to family law.]

II. "Killing" the Civil Rights Remedy Did Not Kill the Act

In her detailed examination of the civil rights remedy and "what killed it before the Supreme Court did," Ms. Schmidt's overly-broad conclusions ignore the Violence Against Women Act's effectiveness, which has proven to extend far beyond the civil rights remedy. First, by describing the Violence Against Women Act's civil rights remedy in terms such as "radical" and that "the visionary legislation was used only to send a message rather than make real change," the author completely obscures the fact that the Act has produced "real change" through Domestic Violence Courts, better law enforcement training, enhanced prosecution, and more housing and social services are available to women from the $6 billion in programs and initiatives funded and initiated by the Act.

Moreover, by positing that the civil rights remedy "was a failure" because it failed to achieve its "promises" of "providing victims of gender violence a forum and method to seek redress" and failed to "reduce the amount of violence against women in our society," Ms. Schmidt again, respectfully, leaves her reader with the incorrect conclusion that the Act was a failure. Rather, the progress over the past twenty years demonstrates just how much the Violence Against Women Act has empowered victims of gender-violence crimes and saved lives.

* * *

III. Building Bipartisan Support

Along with pushing for passage of the Violence Against Women Act since 1990, then-Senator Biden also had introduced and fought for passage of a major crime bill since 1986. The two efforts came together in 1994. The Violence Against Women Act passed as part of the Omnibus Crime Law of 1994. The legislation passed a Democratic-controlled Senate and House. * * *

In 2000 and 2005, the Violence Against Women Act was reauthorized by bipartisan majorities in Republican-led sessions of Congress.

Despite bipartisan support throughout its first 18 years, in 2012, the Violence Against Women Act Reauthorization hit roadblocks in the Republican-controlled Congress over protections for battered immigrant women and protections for same-sex couples. *[Editor's Note: In 2012, advocates around the country lobbied Republican members of Congress, urging them to expand protections for immigrant women, to explicitly include measures against same-sex violence, and to restore tribal autonomy over non-Natives who abuse Native American women and children. These efforts were successful.]* * * * . . .[T]he Violence Against Women Act was re-enacted in 2013. * * *

Despite an increasingly divided Congress, the Violence Against Women Act was non-partisan in action in cities, counties and states across America. Sheriffs, police officers, judges, and lawmakers on the city, county and state levels put politics aside to take full advantage of the federal funding available to help prevent and reduce violence against women and children.

IV. The Act in Action

The Violence Against Women Act has been a model of how the federal government can work with state governments, state criminal justice councils, police, sheriffs, prosecutors, public defenders, social agencies, housing authorities, judges and legal advocates. First, after passage of the Violence Against Women Act, then-Senator Biden was instrumental in securing creation of a new Office of Violence Against Women within the U.S. Department of Justice. That Office has been and remains the link with State Domestic Violence Coalitions in all 50 states to establish, implement and monitor the STOP Violence Against Women Formula Grants. From funding for more battered women shelters and transitional housing programs, to funding for training for law enforcement and judges, to establishing specialized prosecution, policing and courts, the Violence Against Women Act has impacted families and women in all 50 states and U.S. territories.

As the White House Report, issued in September 2014 and entitled 1 is 2 Many: Twenty Years Fighting Violence Against Women and Girls, points out: a 1975 national survey recorded that 28 percent of respondents agreed that slapping a spouse was "necessary," "normal" or "good." After implementation of the Violence Against Women Act, a 2006 study showed that 97% of college students surveyed agreed that for a husband to use physical force to make his wife have sex would constitute intimate partner violence. Thus, the Act and national conversation about violence against women have changed attitudes. The Act also has provided more avenues for victims of gender-violence to seek justice.

A. Domestic Violence Courts

One such example is the proliferation of specialized Domestic Violence Courts, the funding for which initially came from Violence Against Women Act grants. * * *

B. Federal Domestic Violence Statutes

The Violence Against Women Act provides for more than twelve federal domestic violence crimes that have proven to be an effective tool for U.S. Attorneys to work with state and local prosecutors to fight for victims and reduce gender-based violence. Many of these statutes criminalized interstate violation of sexual assault and domestic violence laws for the first time. Like Domestic Violence Courts, these statutes have made an impact in the persistent problem of violence against women. These statutes include:

Interstate Travel to Commit Domestic Violence;

Interstate Stalking;

Interstate Travel to Violate an Order of Protection;

Possession of Firearms While Subject to Order of Protection;

Transfer of Firearm to Person Subject to Order of Protection;

Possession of Firearm After Conviction of Misdemeanor Crime of Domestic Violence;

Transfer of Firearm to Person Convicted of a Misdemeanor Crime of Domestic Violence;

Full Faith and Credit to Orders of Protection;

Amendment of the Brady Statement;

Right of Victim to Speak at Bail Hearing;

Other Victim's Rights;

Restitution; and

Self-Petitioning for Battered Immigrant Women and Children.

[Editor's Note: In addition, as discussed in Chapter 5, some states have enacted statutes explicitly allowing survivors of gender-based violence to sue their abusers in civil suits. See e.g., Ca. Civil Code sections 52.4 (suing specifically for gender motivated violence) and 1708.6 (suing for domestic violence generally).]

C. Law Enforcement Efforts, Housing, LBGT Protections

Other notable provisions of the Violence Against Women Act that continue to have a lasting impact include funding to help train more than a half million law enforcement officers, prosecutors, judges and victim advocates every year. The National Domestic Violence Hotline, established by the original Violence Against Women Act, has helped more than 3.5 million people with issues of domestic violence and dating violence. The 2000 reauthorization expanded protection for immigrant victims of abuse. The 2005 and 2013 reauthorizations of the Act included housing protections for battered women and new funding to help health care providers screen for domestic violence. And the 2013 reauthorization extended Violence Against Women Formula Grants administered by the U.S. Department of Justice to LGBT-specific services, recognizing the first time that the Act's protections apply universally regardless of sexual orientation or gender identity. * * *

[Editor's Note: The author describes the impact of the Act on countries around the world. "These international campaigns to protect women and children spurred by the Violence Against Women Act point to a more enduring impact of the Act than could have been contemplated at its introduction and enactment—despite partisan attacks, the Supreme Court's rejection of the civil rights remedy and funding reauthorization challenges. Indeed, the Violence Against Women Act endures in the United States and around the world." See Chapter 17.]

VII. Conclusion

The forcible rape crime rate in 2013 decreased to 25.2 [per 100,000 women in the U.S.], compared with a rate of 41.2 [per 100,000 women] in 1990 when the Violence Against Women Act was first introduced. The FBI estimates 79,770 reported rapes in 2013, which is a reduction of about 16 percent since 2004. *[Editor's Note: Government statistics report that 40 out of 100,000 people were raped in 2022 in the U.S., a similar statistic to the forcible crime rate. The number greatly increased starting in 2014 due in part to a change in the definition of forcible rape.]*

While much progress has been made, as the Obama-Biden Administration's "1 is 2 Many" campaign acknowledges, the violent crime rate against women is still far too high. To put the persistent problem of intimate partner violence in context, the number of American troops killed in Afghanistan and Iraq between 2001 and 2012 was 6,488. The number of American women who were murdered by current or ex-male partners during that same time period was 11,766. Thus, the goal of the "1 is 2 Many" campaign is to renew efforts among parents, teachers and college students to raise awareness about dating violence and sexual assault on college campuses. Moreover, in 2014, [then-]Vice President Biden and the White House Council on Women and Girls issued the first White House report on campus sexual assault, titled "Not Alone," to highlight enhanced efforts to reach victims, prosecute offenders and prevent future sexual assaults. Another public-private sector initiative is to raise money to complete tests on thousands of untested rape kits sitting in evidence lockers in police agencies across this country.

In conclusion, as the Violence Against Women Act's impact continues to endure, it is important to reflect on the progress made on the federal and state levels to change attitudes and laws to better protect women against violence and note the Act's expansion globally. Even without the civil rights remedy, the Violence Against Women Act has made an indelible imprint on protecting the basic civil right and freedom of women to be free from violence—in their home, on college campuses, and on the street against strangers.

THE WHITE HOUSE, FACT SHEET: REAUTHORIZATION OF THE VIOLENCE AGAINST WOMEN ACT (VAWA)

March 16, 2022

This week, President Biden signed into law the Violence Against Women Act Reauthorization Act of 2022, bipartisan legislation passed by Congress as part of the Omnibus appropriations package.

One of the driving forces of President Biden's career has been fighting back against abuses of power. That force led him to write and champion the groundbreaking Violence Against Women Act (VAWA) as a U.S. Senator, landmark legislation that first passed in 1994. In the nearly three decades since, he has worked with Members of Congress from both parties to pass legislation to renew and strengthen VAWA three times: in 2000, 2005, and 2013. Each time, he worked to expand access to safety and support for all survivors and increase prevention efforts. Preventing and responding to gender-based violence wherever it occurs, and in all of its forms, has remained a cornerstone of the President's career in public service—from VAWA reauthorization to a national campaign to combat campus sexual assault to reforms to address sexual assault and harassment in the military.

While incidents of domestic violence and sexual assault have declined significantly since VAWA first took effect—and efforts to increase access to services, healing, and justice for survivors have improved with each iteration of VAWA—much work remains.

The 2022 reauthorization of VAWA strengthens this landmark law, including by:

- Reauthorizing all current VAWA grant programs until 2027 and, in many cases, increasing authorization levels.
- Expanding special criminal jurisdiction of Tribal courts to cover non-Native perpetrators of sexual assault, child abuse, stalking, sex trafficking, and assaults on tribal law enforcement officers on tribal lands; and supporting the development of a pilot project to enhance access to safety for survivors in Alaska Native villages.
- Increasing services and support for survivors from underserved and marginalized communities—including for LGBTQ+ survivors of domestic violence, dating violence, sexual assault and stalking; funding survivor-centered, community-based restorative practice services; and increasing support for culturally specific services and services in rural communities.
- Establishing a federal civil cause of action for individuals whose intimate visual images are disclosed without their consent, allowing a victim to recover damages and legal fees; creating a new National Resource Center on Cybercrimes Against Individuals; and supporting State, Tribal, and local government efforts to prevent and prosecute cybercrimes, including cyberstalking and the nonconsensual distribution of intimate images.
- Improving prevention and response to sexual violence, including through increased support for the Rape Prevention and Education Program and Sexual Assault Services Program; expansion of prevention education for students in institutions of higher education; and enactment of the Fairness for Rape Kit Backlog Survivors Act, which requires state victim compensation programs to allow sexual assault survivors to file for compensation without being unfairly penalized due to rape kit backlogs.

- Strengthening the application of evidence-based practices by law enforcement in responding to gender-based violence, including by promoting the use of trauma-informed, victim-centered training and improving homicide reduction initiatives.
- Improving the healthcare system's response to domestic violence and sexual assault, including through enhanced training for sexual assault forensic examiners.
- Updating the SMART Prevention Program and the CHOOSE Youth Program to reduce dating violence, help children who have been exposed to domestic violence, and engage men in preventing violence.
- Enacting the National Instant Criminal Background Check System (NICS) Denial Notification Act to help state law enforcement investigate and prosecute cases against individuals legally prohibited from purchasing firearms who try to do so.

[In addition to VAWA,] Over the past year, the Biden-Harris Administration has taken significant steps to prevent and respond to gender-based violence at home and abroad: [The following has been edited for length.]

- Directed $1 billion in supplemental funding for domestic violence and sexual assault services through the American Rescue Plan (ARP) in response to the pandemic, including $49.5 million for culturally-specific community-based organizations that help survivors from historically marginalized communities access the services and support they need. The ARP also provided approximately 70,000 housing choice vouchers to local Public Housing Authorities in order to assist individuals and families, including those who are fleeing, or attempting to flee, from domestic violence, dating violence, sexual assault, stalking, or human trafficking.
- Signed into law the National Defense Authorization Act, which included sweeping reforms to the military justice system—the most significant since the Uniform Code of Military Justice was established more than seventy years ago—and implemented the President's campaign promise to address the scourge of sexual assault in our armed forces.
- Signed into law the Ending Forced Arbitration of Sexual Assault and Sexual Harassment Act of 2021—bipartisan legislation that empowers survivors of sexual assault and

harassment by giving them a choice to go to court instead of being forced into arbitration.

- Directed the Department of Education to review Title IX regulations and other agency actions to ensure that all students have an educational environment that is free from discrimination on the basis of sex. The Department is developing a Notice of Proposed Rulemaking currently under review that will address the need for protection for students who experience campus sexual assault while treating all students fairly.
- Signed into law the Amendments to the Victims of Crime Act (VOCA), which passed Congress with strong bipartisan support and expands the allocation of resources for the Crime Victims Fund. This has already resulted in an increase of hundreds of millions of dollars of non-taxpayer funding for essential and lifesaving services to crime victims around the country, including survivors of gender-based violence.
- Launched the Global Partnership for Action on Gender-Based Online Harassment and Abuse during the 2022 meeting of the United Nations Commission on the Status of Women, together with other countries.
- Issued an executive order directing the Departments of Justice, Interior, Homeland Security and Health and Human Services to create a strategy to improve public safety and justice for Native Americans and to address the epidemic of missing or murdered Indigenous peoples, which disproportionately affect Native women, girls, and LGBTQI+ individuals.
- Re-launched the United States' leadership and participation in the Trilateral Working Group on Violence Against Indigenous Women and Girls with the Governments of Mexico and Canada.

On International Women's Day in 2021, President Biden signed an Executive Order creating the White House Gender Policy Council and calling for the development of the first-ever government-wide National Action Plan to End Gender-Based Violence, as well as an update to the 2016 United States Strategy to Prevent and Respond to Gender-Based Violence Globally.

[Editor's Notes: 1. In "Implementation of VAWA 2022 for the Safety of Indian Women," 28(1) Oct/Nov 2022 Domestic Violence Report 3, Leslie A. Hagen of the DOJ summarizes the many significant changes this new statute will bring to Indian Country and Alaskan villages. The main goal is to ensure that tribal courts will be able to exercise jurisdiction over non-

Native perpetrators of sexual assault, domestic violence, and sex trafficking, as well as child abuse.

Hagen notes that American Indian women and Alaskan Native women are 2.5 times more likely than the national average to experience certain violent crimes, such as nonfatal strangulation, as well as the history of forced removal from homelands, boarding school, slavery, and sexual abuse. A lot of these crimes are committed by non-Indian men. When in 1978, in Oliphant, *the U.S. Supreme Court ruled that tribal courts had no power to prosecute defendants who were not Indians, many Indian women and tribes were left with no recourse. Native advocates and allies worked to convince Congress to recognize tribal jurisdiction as part of Indian people's sovereignty.*

Hagen notes that the 2013 VAWA amended the Indian Civil Rights Act, creating a section called "Safety for Indian Women" for the first time. It gave tribes jurisdiction over non-Indian perpetrators but only for domestic or dating violence occurring in the Indian country of the participating tribe or for violations of a qualifying protection order. Tribes had to provide defense counsel and other due process protections to defendants. Notably, the 2013 Act did not grant jurisdiction where a child or tribal police officer was assaulted by the defendant as part of the crime. Again, Native advocates and allies organized and lobbied to address these gaps.

The 2022 VAWA expands the Indian Civil Rights Act again, allowing tribes to prosecute non-Indians for assaulting tribal officers or children or committing dating violence, domestic violence, sexual violence, sex trafficking, stalking, or violating a protection order, including felonies. The defendant or victim/survivor must be an Indian. Trial by an impartial jury must be provided along with licensed defense counsel, a judge who is licensed to practice law, written rules of evidence, recording the proceedings, access to a writ of habeas corpus, etc. The government can reimburse tribes for their expenses. VAWA 2022 also includes a pilot program for Indian tribes in Alaska to exercise such jurisdiction, since they are not included in the Indian Civil Rights Act.

In 2015 the U.S. DOJ launched a program to provide some tribes access to national crime information systems so they can quickly determine the defendant's criminal history and other background information. VAWA 2022 includes $6 million/year for 4 years to support this program. [Some states also allow tribes to access their law enforcement databases, including restraining order registries.]

Hagen concludes, "Upon passage of VAWA 2022, Fawn Sharp, President of the National Congress of American Indians, said the following: 'The historic tribal provisions in this bill attest to years of powerful, collaborative efforts between survivors, tribal leaders, and allies across Indian Country. We commend Congress' momentous action to reauthorize the Violence Against Women Act and now, by exercising our inherent sovereignty and jurisdiction, Tribal Nations will continue to increase safety and justice for victims who had previously seen little of either.' Title VIII of VAWA 2022 equips Tribes with the means to provide justice to victims of crime, hold offenders accountable, strengthen their sovereignty, and make their communities safer."

2. Historically, only a small proportion of Violence Against Women Act funds were allocated to non-criminal options or social services for survivors. See, e.g., Jill Messing, Allison Ward-Lasher, Jonel Thaller, & Meredith Bagwell-Gray, The State of Intimate Partner Violence Intervention: Progress and Continuing Challenges. J Social Work (2015), https://doi.org/10.1093/sw/swv027 ("[I]n 1994, VAWA appropriated approximately 62 percent of funds for criminal justice and 38 percent for social services. Whereas VAWA authorizations nearly doubled to $3.1 billion in 2013, the proportion of funding for social services decreased to approximately 15 percent of the total, resulting in a smaller dollar amount appropriated for social services in 2013 than in 1994.").

This proportion changed in VAWA 2022, in which half the funding is allocated to the criminal justice system (25% to law enforcement, 25% to prosecution). The other half goes to victim services provided by non-profits, tribal entities, or state coalitions. See 24 USC §§ 10446, 12291.

3. In U.S. v. Cline, *986 F.3d 873 (2021), the defendant's convictions for violating two Colorado restraining orders protecting his pregnant girlfriend from his history of harming her physically and verbally were upheld. He was sentenced to over 7 years in prison. When Cline was arrested in Texas by the U.S. border patrol, his girlfriend had a black eye, concussion, and fractured facial bone. She was crying as the defendant was driving her to Mexico or Costa Rica. He argued on appeal that the restraining orders had not been requested by the girlfriend but the court held that that was irrelevant, as Colorado law mandated their issuance when Cline was charged with abusing her. The court held that the federal offense of traveling in interstate or foreign commerce with intent to violate a protective order, a product of VAWA, was properly applied in this case.]*

THE WHITE HOUSE, U.S. NATIONAL PLAN TO END GENDER BASED VIOLENCE

(2023)
Executive Summary
(footnotes omitted)

In this first-ever U.S. National Plan to End Gender-Based Violence (the National Plan or Plan), the Federal Government advances an unprecedented and comprehensive approach to preventing and addressing sexual violence, intimate partner violence, stalking, and other forms of gender-based violence (referred to collectively as GBV). This initiative builds on the lessons learned and progress made as the result of tireless and courageous leadership by GBV survivors, advocates, researchers, and policymakers, as well as other dedicated professionals and community members who lead prevention and response efforts.

Gender-based violence is a public safety and public health crisis, affecting urban, suburban, rural, and Tribal communities in the United States. It is experienced by individuals of all backgrounds and can occur across the life course happens in all spaces and spheres of human interaction, public and private—in homes, schools, and public venues; through social media and other online spaces; and in workplaces. In today's globalized world, it can transcend national boundaries, including through online exploitation and abuse, human trafficking, and individuals fleeing GBV. The risks of GBV are heightened in conditions of disaster, conflict, or crisis, including public health crises such as a pandemic.

We have made significant progress since the days when GBV was widely considered a private matter, with limited services and support for victims, as well as limited protections from legal systems. Today, addressing GBV is an important part of our nation's social consciousness and public policy priorities. Federal, state, local, Tribal, and territorial laws and policies provide important protections to survivors and families. Several landmark pieces of federal legislation—the Violence Against Women Act (VAWA), Family Violence Prevention and Services Act (FVPSA), and Victims of Crime Act (VOCA)—have strengthened protections and provide core funding through grant programs that advance promising practices nationwide. Schools, workplaces, health care facilities, faith-based institutions, community-based organizations, media, and online platforms have adopted GBV prevention and intervention initiatives. Victim service providers and criminal and civil justice system personnel, including public safety officials, are trained to better understand and address different forms of GBV and to hold perpetrators accountable. As a result of these efforts, survivors now have greater access to safety, healing, and justice. We have also developed better tools to measure GBV in its many forms, and to identify populations disproportionately impacted. And we have advanced efforts to prevent GBV through the development of different programs and policies aimed at decreasing risk factors and improving protective factors.

Yet much work remains to be done. Despite this progress, many people experience GBV over the course of their lives. Many survivors and their families face adverse health and economic outcomes, as well as significant challenges in accessing comprehensive support and services. Community resources remain underfunded and often lack culturally specific approaches needed to best serve survivors from historically marginalized and underserved communities. Too often, efforts to address GBV have operated in silos or have failed to address how survivors of GBV may experience multiple forms of victimization. By and large, these approaches tend to concentrate on reacting to victims and perpetrators based on individual incidents. Additionally, victims and survivors of GBV often face numerous obstacles in accessing justice, and many are reluctant to engage with traditional justice systems. These realities underscore the importance of renewed efforts to understand how people experience GBV, what survivors need, and how to better prevent violence, hold abusers accountable, and challenge views that normalize, condone, or rationalize GBV. Strengthening coordination and commitments to advance GBV prevention, intervention, and response will reduce the devastating effects of GBV on health, safety, justice, development, and economic growth, and will support communities where all people can thrive.

On March 8, 2021, International Women's Day, President Biden issued Executive Order 14020, on the Establishment of the White House Gender Policy Council (GPC), creating the first freestanding policy council within the Executive Office of the President focused on advancing gender equity and equality in both domestic and foreign policy. As directed in the Executive Order, GPC released a National Strategy on Gender Equity and Equality (National Gender Strategy) in October 2021 that reflected extensive input from federal agencies and civil society stakeholders. As part of the implementation of the National Gender Strategy, the Executive Order called on the GPC to "create a National Action Plan to End Gender-Based Violence that establishes a government-wide approach to preventing and addressing gender-based violence in the United States," as well as to update the U.S. Strategy to Prevent and Respond to Gender-Based Violence Globally (Global GBV Strategy). These initiatives are aligned with broader efforts of the Biden-Harris Administration to root out systemic barriers and discrimination and pursue equity and equality for all, as set forth in Executive Order 13985, and Executive Order 13988, "Advancing Racial Equity and Support for Underserved Communities Through the Federal Government," and Executive Order 13988, "Preventing and Combating Discrimination on the Basis of Gender Identity or Sexual Orientation."

Building upon existing federal initiatives, this National Plan to End Gender-Based Violence advances a comprehensive, whole-of-government, and intersectional approach to preventing and addressing GBV in the United States. The Plan sets forth a bold vision and gives priority to areas that have been underemphasized in GBV-focused policy and research, such as prevention, racial justice, LGBTQI+ equality, intergenerational healing, community wellness, and social norms change. Moreover, the Plan highlights critical connections between these priorities and areas that have historically received more focus, such as incident-focused interventions and system responses.

This Plan begins with a focus on what we know works to prevent GBV, including efforts to address the root causes of violence and abuse and to change social norms that perpetuate GBV. The Plan also highlights the importance of programs for children, families, and people who perpetrate GBV, recognizing that GBV can be an intergenerational problem. Indeed, childhood exposure to violence, including witnessing or experiencing violence, can increase a person's risk for suffering relationship violence or perpetrating it when they are older.

Complementing the focus on prevention, the Plan recognizes the critically important role of criminal and civil justice systems, victim advocates, law enforcement, health care providers, including mental health and substance use treatment providers, community-based organizations, and other services that protect survivors and families and foster a coordinated community response to GBV that is survivor-centered and trauma-informed. The Plan encourages recognition by justice, health, and other systems of the diverse and complex needs of survivors through a "no wrong door" approach that maximizes survivor agency and choice. To this end, it also supports the development of restorative practices and other community-centered accountability frameworks that are responsive to survivors' needs and preferences and that provide increased options for seeking support, safety, justice, and healing.

Finally, the Plan recognizes the pervasive impacts of GBV across multiple sectors and social issues, and identifies key fields that often lack consideration of GBV issues and where insufficient attention is traditionally paid to survivors' needs, including to ensure survivors' access to housing, economic, and labor protections; address the increasing impact of online harms; and respond to the critical needs of survivors during emergencies and disasters, including in the context of pandemics and climate change.

The priorities in this National Plan to End GBV, as well as those reflected in the 2022 update to the U.S. Global GBV Strategy, reflect our nation's ongoing commitment to continue advancing and integrating efforts to prevent and address gender-based violence both at home and abroad. Ending gender-based violence is, quite simply, a matter of human rights and justice.

The Plan provides an important framework for strengthening ongoing federal action and interagency collaboration in a comprehensive manner through a government-wide approach, while identifying opportunities to expand access to safety, support, healing, and justice for survivors. The Administration will support ongoing efforts to advance further development and implementation of the Plan through collaboration with federal agencies and through ongoing engagement with survivors, advocates, researchers, and representatives of civil society organizations, as well as state, local, and Tribal and territorial government officials, among others. Although the Plan is focused specifically on federal action, it is designed to be accessible and useful to public and private stakeholders across the United States for adaptation and expansion—because all communities are vital to ending GBV.

VISION STATEMENT

The United States will be a place where all people live free from gender-based violence (GBV) in all aspects of their lives.

This vision applies to all people, regardless of gender, sex, gender identity, sex characteristics, sexual orientation, race, ethnicity, religion, age, disability, geographic location, national origin, immigration or citizenship status, socioeconomic circumstance, medical condition or status, or other factors.

B. FIREARMS RESTRICTIONS

CALIFORNIA PARTNERSHIP TO END DOMESTIC VIOLENCE, PREVENTING & REDUCING GUN VIOLENCE INJURIES AND FATALITIES: A CALIFORNIA TOOLKIT FOR COMMUNITIES, SURVIVORS, AND SERVICE PROVIDERS

(2023)

(edited, footnotes omitted)

Domestic gun violence is a devastating problem. From 2001 through 2012, 6410 women were murdered in the United States by an intimate partner using a gun—more than 600 each year. . .

When firearms are present in a situation where domestic violence is being perpetrated, a survivor is more likely to experience more severe physical abuse, and more likely to end up killed than in situations where firearms are not present. When a woman is being abused by a male partner who has access to firearms, she is five times more likely to be killed by her abusive partner. In total, a firearm is used in over half of domestic violence homicides nationwide.

We also see significant racial disparities within these devastating statistics. Black women are twice as likely to be shot and killed by an intimate partner in comparison to white women. . .

This deadly intersection extends to mass shootings too: in more than half of mass shootings, the shooter killed an intimate partner. One study found that nearly one third of mass shooters had a history of domestic violence.

Additionally, nearly 1 million women in the U.S. today reported being shot or shot at by an intimate partner. About 4.5 million women report that an intimate partner threatened them using a gun.

The good news is when laws are implemented that require abusers to turn in their firearms, we see a 16 percent reduction in domestic violence homicides. We can make a difference and save lives by ensuring access to safety planning and key legal remedies where appropriate.

[Editor's Note: Domestic Violence Restraining Orders are much more comprehensive than Gun Violence Restraining Orders. While both types of orders include gun prohibitions, GVROs do not keep the restrained person away from a location or another person. It may be appropriate to request both orders depending on the situation.]

More than 60 percent of people in the U.S. who die from guns die by suicide. Firearms are the most lethal suicide attempt method. Access to a gun in the home increases the risk of suicide more than three-fold. If firearms are not available, the person at risk for suicide is much more likely to survive. Delaying a suicide attempt can also allow suicidal crises to pass and lead to fewer suicides.

Resources: The National Resource Center on Domestic Violence and Firearms of the Battered Women's Justice Project, the National Center on Gun Violence in Relationships and Giffords Law Center to Prevent Gun Violence.

[Editor's Note: The Ca. Little Hoover Commission issued a report in 2021 called "Beyond the Crisis: A Long-Term Approach to Reduce, Prevent, and Recover from Intimate Partner Violence." It found that California's laws preventing firearm possession by abusive people form a solid legal framework, but need to be better enforced. They noted that the DOJ databases of prohibited persons are technologically outdated and cannot automatically cross reference each other properly, and the firearms department is very understaffed due to low pay.]

JANE K. STOEVER, FIREARMS AND DOMESTIC VIOLENCE FATALITIES: PREVENTABLE DEATHS

53 Fam. L. Q. 183 (2020)
(footnotes omitted)

Introduction

. . .Abused individuals experience alarming rates of firearm threats and fatalities in the United States, and part of what makes firearm violence and these tragedies so heartbreaking is that they are preventable. Community members, family law attorneys, judges, mediators, therapists, and others should play key roles in prevention, but they too often fail to broach the subject of gun safety and miss opportunities for intervention.

Recognizing lethality risks, state and federal laws now restrict access to firearms by domestic violence offenders, although implementation and enforcement gaps persist. At the federal level, the Violence Against Women Act of 1994 bans individuals subject to a protection order from possessing a firearm, and the 1968 Gun Control Act and the 1996 enactment of the Lautenberg Amendment impose lifetime firearm possession bans on those convicted of certain domestic violence crimes. Legislators have the power and ability to enact additional reasonable gun laws to prevent many domestic violence fatalities and mass shootings. Universal background checks, for example, are desired by over ninety percent of Americans and have been proven to reduce domestic violence gun murders by forty-seven percent. Importantly, states that restrict domestic abusers' access to firearms have significantly reduced rates of intimate partner homicide. While a majority of Americans desire legislative reform and the enactment of gun-safety measures, firearm legislation is highly politicized, with the National Rifle Association (NRA) funding campaigns and lobbying without regard for research findings on public health and safety.

This Article examines the problem of family violence firearm fatalities in the context of the highly gendered nature of victimization within intimate relationships, intimate partner homicides, and firearm ownership. It surfaces some of the hard realities for practitioners and courts, including the gendered knowledge gap as to whether there are guns in the home, the easy access to firearms in the United States, and the implementation gaps that must be closed for laws to be effective. In proposing reforms, the article posits solutions that should receive broad support from the legal profession and bipartisan political support, especially if politicians resolve to stop playing politics with the deadly combination of firearms and family violence.

I. Firearms and Domestic Violence: A Dangerous Combination

A. Intimate Partner Violence and Fatalities

Rather than a gun in the home increasing the household's safety, which is the most common reason given for gun possession, firearm ownership dramatically increases rates of firearm fatalities and suicide for members of the household, even with safe gun storage practices. Furthermore, a domestically abusive individual is likely to use the firearm to perpetrate abuse against an intimate partner and children. One prominent study found that in nearly three-quarters of battered women's households that contained a gun, the abusive partner had used the gun against the abuse victim by threatening to shoot and kill her or by actually shooting at her. . .

Intimate partner violence and intimate partner homicides are highly gendered. While both women and men experience domestic violence, women account for eighty to eighty-five percent of individuals abused by intimate partners and typically endure more severe injuries than men. . .

Although societal fears focus on stranger violence, "intimate partners with guns present the greatest fatal risk to women." While intimate partners account for four percent of perpetrators of homicides of men, women are more likely to be murdered by an intimate partner or ex-partner than by a stranger. The most consistent risk factor for femicide is prior intimate partner violence, and these homicides are typically committed after a long history of domestic violence. Guns are used in fatal domestic violence more than any other weapon.

Access to a firearm is the primary predictor of intimate homicide, and prior threats with a weapon significantly correlate with femicide. Separation violence and jealousy are also associated with firearm fatalities, with research showing that when the most violent incident of abuse is triggered by the victimized individual leaving the abusive partner for another relationship or the abusive partner otherwise showing extreme jealousy, this produces a nearly fivefold increase in femicide risk. Having a child in the home who is not the abusive partner's biological child more than doubles the femicide risk.

Intimate partner homicides may extend to even broader tragedy, with the murder of children and bystanders. Homicide-suicides are also common in these contexts. Surviving family members and friends are forever affected, as they lose the murdered parent and the perpetrator to prison or suicide and suffer social consequences.

Intervening in firearm-related domestic violence can prevent widespread tragedy. Of the nearly 170,000 domestic violence-related calls to law enforcement in California in 2018, for example, over forty-five percent of calls reported the use of a weapon in the incident. Because the majority of mass shooters have known histories of domestic violence, early intervention enhances individual, household, and community safety. . . .

B. Gender-Based Violence and the Gendered Nature of Firearm Possession

Like the often-gendered nature of intimate partner violence, firearm ownership is highly gendered. Men are considerably more likely to purchase firearms than women and to store these firearms, and the majority of gun owners are white men. . . . In most families, "a gun is viewed by all concerned as the private property of a particular family member," and that person is typically a man. Furthermore, in homes with firearms, approximately eighty-five percent of men and women reported that storing the guns was solely the man's responsibility.

The gun lobby has used social images of masculinity, including "frontier masculinity," to promote gun use and has mythologized rare stories of private citizens defending vulnerable individuals with guns. . .

Research further reveals that firearm ownership is more likely in households in which intimate partner violence occurs. In homes with "chronic" or "severe" violence, firearm ownership is twenty percent higher than in the general population. . .

New research indicates that domestic violence homicides have increased by thirty-three percent in the United States over the past several years, and scholars attribute this to a divided nation and the normalizing of misogyny.

The gun industry has attempted to increase female ownership by targeting women's fears and encouraging their firearm ownership for protective purposes. . . Despite these efforts, ownership of firearms among women has not increased and the market for guns is still mostly male.

C. Teen Dating Violence and Firearm Possession

When seeking to prevent teen firearm fatalities and massacres, it is critical to recognize that teen dating violence is "highly associated with firearm possession." Recent studies show that youth with firearms are more likely to commit dating violence, to have been in recent serious physical fights, and to endorse aggressive attitudes that increase risk for retaliatory violence. Youth firearm possession additionally correlates with male gender, and factors such as young age, possessiveness, impulsivity, lack of dispute resolution skills, and use of force increase the likelihood that young people with guns will die or kill with them. . .

Although many youth have access to guns at home, most firearms possessed by youth are obtained outside of legal channels through illegal, unregistered sales to minors, making minimizing illegal firearm access key to fatality prevention efforts. . .

II. Opportunities for Preventing Intimate Partner Firearm Fatalities

Massacres from recent decades reveal that individuals with histories of domestic violence commit the majority of mass shootings in America. This connection between firearm fatalities and relationship violence demands action, as does the ease of access to firearms, including illegally obtained highly lethal weapons. Many firearm fatalities are preventable, especially if attorneys are asking the right questions, judges are communicating and entering protective court orders, and legislators have the courage to enact the data-driven solutions that abound.

A. Ask About Abuse

. . .Given the high rates of intimate partner violence in the general population, its particular relevance to family court proceedings, and the safety issues at stake, attorneys should ask questions that would prompt safety planning, appropriate court orders, and awareness of lethality factors.

B. Address the Gendered Knowledge Gap

. . . Many men fail to disclose to their partners that there are guns in the home. Multiple national surveys have established that women are often unaware of the existence of guns in the home and, if they are aware that a gun is in the home, studies of married heterosexual couples consistently find that husbands report more guns in the home than wives do. . .

Studies of multiple jurisdictions reveal that "judges either haphazardly mention or completely ignore disarming amendments" that prohibit firearm ownership by domestic violence offenders, even though they are required to order domestic violence respondents to surrender firearms after making findings of domestic violence. . . .[J]udicial officers should directly ask respondents about firearm possession and access, ensure surrender or confiscation of firearms, and instruct all respondents about firearm prohibitions for respondents found to have committed domestic violence; and domestic violence-related court orders must be entered in background check systems.

C. Use Family Court as a Site for Public Health Messaging

Gun violence is a public health issue and should be treated as such. Although gun violence is a leading cause of death in America, the issue receives less funding than nearly every other leading cause of fatality, and research conducted by the Centers for Disease Control and Prevention, National Institute of Health, and National Institute of Justice is legislatively restricted. . .

The American Medical Association, American College of Physicians, and other medical groups encourage their members to ask patients or the parents of patients about firearms in the home as a routine part of childproofing the home and educating patients about the dangers of unsecured firearms; however, a majority of medical professionals still do not ask about firearms due to their discomfort with the conversation. . . . [T]he NRA opposed such communications and lobbied for the Firearms Owners' Privacy Act, which barred medical professionals from asking patients whether they owned guns based on the idea that Second Amendment freedoms prohibit doctors from discussing firearm ownership with their patients. After lengthy legal battles, the Eleventh Circuit Court of Appeals recently struck down key portions of the law, colloquially called "Docs vs. Glocks," on the ground that it violates medical professionals' First Amendment free speech rights.

. . . Many family-court-involved individuals report feeling as if they are "losing everything," and as a Domestic Violence Clinic director, the cases in which the opposing party is denied any visitation with the parties' children cause me pause and concern for my clients' safety. . . This can be an especially important time for someone else to hold their guns.

A public health approach can bring about cultural change around firearms the same way that the campaigns against smoking and against driving drunk did in recent decades. . . . Courts hearing family law and domestic violence matters should make petitioners aware that especially high-risk times for intimate partner homicide are at the time of attempting to separate from an abusive partner, immediately after a civil protection order is issued, and the period after a protective order expires. In Family Court, even if there is not a judicial finding that mandates gun surrender under federal or state laws, courts can message that when going through major relationship and life changes, litigants should voluntarily not be in possession of guns. . .

Attorneys, law enforcement officers, medical professionals, courthouse personnel, judges, mental health professionals, and other "first responders" and "community helpers" have opportunities to intervene in intimate partner violence and prevent future homicide because they often engage with victims prior to their murder. . . Research also shows that abusive partners are less likely to recidivate after police make a report, regardless of whether the police make an arrest. This is significant because some survivors wish to have the police interrupt the violence and put the abusive partner on notice that the partner's behavior is criminal, without desiring arrest and the collateral consequences of arrest and conviction. . .

III. Legislative Remedies

. . .Despite public outcry following school shootings and other massacres, and notwithstanding greater societal attention to suicide, familial firearm homicides, and accidental shootings, gun control at the federal level has remained "essentially unchanged" for the past two decades. In fact, the primary trend in state law over the past thirty years has favored gun owners' access to and ability to carry firearms, including legislation to make guns easier to obtain and to permit the concealed carrying of firearms. Republican-controlled legislatures at the federal and state levels have rolled back gun control and passed laws protecting gun owners' rights, leaving dangerous gaps in the law that proliferate gun ownership, including by those known to be violent.

. . . Following mass shootings, Republican-controlled legislatures pass laws that loosen gun control, and Democrat-controlled legislatures generally fail to pass gun laws of any kind. Thus, mass shootings have paradoxically served as an impetus for Republican legislators to make guns more available and have created dangerous gaps in the law. Firearm and ammunition purchases also spike immediately following mass shootings, and the gun industry uses political moments and the timing of elections to promote sales through provoking fear that gun restrictions will be enacted. . .

As an indication of the politicization of firearms, conservative legislators have occasionally attempted to increase abuse survivors' access to firearms, contrary to research findings that such measures would increase lethality to the abused individual, the survivor's children, and the broader community. . .

Given the homicide risks and tragedies that are all too common in America, politicians across the ideological spectrum should agree that people who assault or endanger family members should be subject to practical and measured restrictions regarding their access to firearms.

Universal background checks would decrease femicides by nearly fifty percent and are now supported by well over ninety percent of Americans, and a majority of Americans want to prohibit high-capacity magazines, prevent gun sales to suspected terrorists, maintain a national registry, and prohibit or limit the sale of automatic weapons, among other gun violence prevention measures. . .

A. Implement Background Checks

. . .Given discrepancies between systems, significant numbers of background checks are delayed for additional review. The Brady Act, however, imposes a three-day limit for a NICS check and allows a firearm purchase or transfer to proceed if a disqualifying record is not found within three days. This loophole allowed approximately 6,700 firearms to be transferred to individuals with "prohibiting domestic violence records" between fiscal years 2006 and 2015. . .

All domestic violence orders should be entered into federal and state background check systems, as mandated by law, and authorities should be given the time needed to complete background checks. Some states have laws and regulations that allow their agencies to deny or delay a firearm transfer if an incomplete record is being researched when the time limit expires; this should become the law across the nation.

B. Close Loopholes Because Gun Safety Laws Work

. . . Researchers concluded that more restrictive state-level legislation correlates with lower rates of female intimate partner homicide. . . Multiple studies of state laws imposing firearm restrictions during restraining orders find that states with purchase restrictions have the most significant reduction in intimate partner homicides, as compared to states that merely restrict possession. Additionally, keeping a registry of all firearm owners is necessary to increase the effectiveness of the current laws prohibiting possession.

. . . States such as California serve as a model for prohibiting firearm possession or purchase by those subject to a domestic violence ex parte order or temporary protection order. . .

State laws concerning firearm possession vary dramatically. For example, laws differ as to whether weapon seizure is mandatory or discretionary, the authorized method for weapon seizure and return, the definition of "intimate relationship," whether weapons must be used in the domestic violence incident to allow seizure, the amount of time for a state to petition for forfeiture of a firearm, and the burden placed on law enforcement and the respondent or defendant regarding firearm return. . .

C. Surrender or Removal of Firearms

Upon making a finding of domestic violence and entering an order for protection, family court judges are supposed to read aloud a statement that the respondent is not legally permitted to possess firearms or ammunition while the domestic violence protection order is in effect. They, however, rarely explicitly address firearm surrender or make orders confiscating weapons, and instead rely on the "honor system."... most domestic violence firearm surrender orders are never enforced....

States should adopt model domestic violence firearm surrender protocols, such as the protocols drafted by the Center for Court Innovation and the National Center on Protection Orders and Full Faith & Credit, to provide direction to law enforcement, judges, mediators, prosecutors, other attorneys, advocates, and courts handling domestic violence matters. Rather than relying on the honor system, judges could order respondents to return to court with proof of compliance...The presiding Domestic Violence Court judge orders return dates and issues arrest warrants for individuals who fail to appear, with the goal being to follow through on weapon confiscation orders...

Additionally, only eighteen states currently have laws that address the seizure of firearms at domestic violence scenes. More states should enact laws that require or, at the very least, allow police to remove firearms at their discretion from domestic violence perpetrators.

... While the United States contains four percent of the world's population, it owns forty-six percent of the global stock of 857 million civilian firearms. Given the ease of accessing firearms in the United States, early intervention and prevention efforts are necessary and lifesaving.

Along with civil domestic violence orders, gun violence restraining orders or extreme risk protection orders allow family members, law enforcement, and others defined by state statute to petition to remove firearm access from persons who pose a danger to themselves or others...

D. Framing Issues to Overcome Political Opposition

Framing domestic violence-related gun safety policies as saving the lives of law enforcement, and therefore building a narrative that these policies are pro-law enforcement, could generate support from law enforcement organizations and voters who otherwise generally oppose gun control policies...

Framing matters. When voters are asked about specific measures, such as universal background checks, federal databases to track all gun sales, and bans on high-capacity ammunition clips and assault weapons, the majority of voters support these policies. However, the question of whether individuals would prioritize "gun ownership" or "gun control" reveals deep political divides. While divided opinion on gun control persists, the framing of solutions reveals real potential for change.

IV. Conclusion

Such high firearm fatality rates are a uniquely American epidemic, but they should not be accepted as inevitable, especially because these deaths are preventable. Lawmakers, justice system actors, and others can make significant change by having courageous conversations, adopting public health approaches in our communities and courts, taking seriously the fatal combination of domestic violence and access to firearms, recognizing the association between teen dating violence and firearm possession, and implementing, enforcing, and working to improve gun violence prevention laws.

[Editor's Notes: 1. Closing the Boyfriend Loophole: See the Bipartisan Safer Communities Act, S. 2938, signed by President Joe Biden 6/25/22.

This Act is the most significant firearm violence reduction-related federal legislation in decades. It expands background checks, addresses gun trafficking, provides funding for community violence interventions, mental health services, suicide prevention, school violence prevention efforts, mental health courts, drug courts, veterans courts, and extreme risk protection order programs.

Most significantly for domestic violence criminal cases, Section 12005 closes the "boyfriend loophole" by changing regulations on firearm purchases by those convicted of domestic assault. Previously, the law regulated only firearms purchases following domestic assault of a spouse, cohabitant or co-parent. The bill expands this restriction to disqualify anyone found guilty of a domestic violence charge in a romantic relationship, regardless of marital status. The restrictions on dating partners apply for five years, after which the right to own a firearm is restored to first time offenders if no additional violent crimes take place or if the conviction is expunged, set aside, or the defendant is pardoned or has their firearm rights restored. Abusers with more than one misdemeanor conviction of domestic violence against a dating partner may not possess a firearm for the rest of their lives. This Section applies only to domestic violence charges after the law takes effect, with no retroactive penalties.

Note that regardless of the federal restrictions, many states provide that domestic violence survivors in dating couples can obtain domestic violence restraining orders which prevent the restrained party from legally possessing guns under state law. Dating partners commit over half of all intimate partner homicides.

In spite of the many legal limitations in past years, e.g., the boyfriend loophole in effect until 2022, a conviction for a misdemeanor crime of DV was the 4th most frequent reason for denial by the FBI of an application to purchase a firearm. (FBI (2022) Federal denials: Reasons why the NICS system denies, Nov. 30, 1998—March 31, 2022. https://www.fbi.gov/file-repository/federal_denials.pdf/view.)

2023 Legislation: On Feb. 10, 2023, three members of the House of Representatives including one Republican and one member of the Senate introduced the Strengthening Protections for Domestic Violence and Stalking Survivors Act of 2023. This was in response to the 5th Circuit Court of Appeals decision in U.S. v Rahimi *(2023), appeal pending in the U.S. Supreme Court when this book went to press.*

The proposed Act has two parts: 1. Expanding the prohibition on gun possession for people subject to domestic violence restraining orders so it includes dating partners (i.e., closing the boyfriend loophole). 2. Expanding the prohibition on gun possession to people convicted of misdemeanor stalking, a clarification of existing law which bans those convicted of misdemeanor domestic violence from possessing a gun. Stalking occurs frequently in domestic violence cases and is often a precursor to murder, but the conviction may not be for domestic violence per se.

The proposed Act builds on the 2022 Bipartisan Safer Communities Act, which banned gun possession by dating partners subject to domestic violence restraining orders, but allowed the restrained person to again possess guns if they had a clean record for five years. Another attempt to fully close the boyfriend loophole as part of reauthorizing VAWA in 2022 was not successful.

In "Domestic Violence and the Home-Centric Second Amendment," 27 Duke J. Gender L. & Pol'y 45 (2020), Joseph Blocher cautions that the emphasis in 2nd Amendment jurisprudence on the importance of firearms for protecting the home has a very different impact on women than on men. The author argues that given that the mere presence of a firearm in the home greatly increases the chances that men in the home will terrorize and murder women in the home, and that women are at much higher danger from the men in their homes than they are from strangers outside the home, the concept that firearms in the home are necessary for self-defense applies only to men. While Blocher wrote before the decisions in Bruen *(2022),* Rahimi *(2023), and* Silvers *(2023), as well as other recent 2nd Amendment cases, his concern that this jurisprudence should take these gender differences into account is well placed. Who indeed is being protected by the 2nd Amendment right to bear arms and from whom?]*

LISA B. GELLER, MARISA BOOTY, AND CASSANDRA K. CRIFASI, THE ROLE OF DOMESTIC VIOLENCE IN MASS SHOOTINGS IN THE UNITED STATES, 2014–2019

8:38 Injury Epidemiology (2021)
(excerpted, citations omitted)

This study explores the role of [domestic violence] DV in mass shootings in the United States.

We found that 59.1% of mass shootings between 2014 and 2019 were DV-related and in 68.2% of mass shootings, the perpetrator either killed at least one partner or family member or had a history of DV. We found significant differences in the average number of injuries and fatalities between DV and history of DV shootings and a higher average case fatality rate [CFR] associated with DV-related mass shootings (83.7%) than non-DV-related (63.1%) or history of DV mass shootings (53.8%). Fifty-five perpetrators died during the shootings; 39 (70.9%) died by firearm suicide, 15 (27.3%) were killed by police, and 1 (1.8%) died from an intentional overdose.

The intent behind a perpetrator who kills a partner or a member of his or her family may differ from someone who kills people seemingly indiscriminately. This may result in a greater intent to make sure all victims in a DV-related mass shooting are killed. The motive behind a DV-related mass shooting may be revenge, jealousy, a desire to assert power and control, divorce, financial problems, or even suicidality. Given the intent of the perpetrator, DV-related mass shootings may be more targeted than non-DV-related mass shootings, which could increase likelihood that the victims involved would be killed.

This paper highlights the importance of including both "public" and "private" mass shootings in discussions around preventing these incidents. By only focusing on "public" mass shootings, many DV-related mass shootings may be left out of the discussion. This oversight may lead to an assumption that most mass shootings occur at random, leading to missed opportunities for intervention, either through policies or programs, that could help reduce the burden of mass shootings. The results of this paper, that most mass shootings are related to domestic violence, highlights the need to focus on mass shootings more broadly.

Prior research has found that restricting access to guns by perpetrators of DV reduces IPH. Civil domestic violence protective orders (DVPOs) that cover dating partners (13%), prohibit firearm possession for temporary orders (13%), or require firearm relinquishment (12%) are all associated with reductions in IPH. However, effective enforcement of these laws is key to ensure that those prohibited because of a DVPO cannot obtain guns. Additionally, some individuals at risk for interpersonal violence (including mass shootings) or self-harm may not be prohibited from purchasing or possessing firearms. To address elevated risk among individuals, 19 states and DC have passed extreme risk protection orders (ERPOs), an evidence-based mechanism to temporarily remove firearms from individuals who are a threat to themselves or others. This study shows that most perpetrators of DV-related mass shootings died by suicide, highlighting that DV-related mass shooting perpetrators may be at an elevated risk for suicide. ERPOs are a promising tool that could be used to prevent suicides, and recent data shows that these laws have also been used in efforts to prevent mass shootings in California. However, ERPOs are a relatively new policy; future research should further explore the association between ERPOs and mass shootings and their potential impact on DV-related mass shootings in particular.

Future research should continue to examine the role that policies that disarm or otherwise restrict access to guns by perpetrators of intimate partner violence (IPV) or DV have in reducing or preventing mass shootings.

Conclusions

DV, whether directly related or through a perpetrator's history, plays an important role in mass shootings in the United States. DV-related mass shootings were associated with fewer casualties but a higher CFR; fewer victims survived the injuries sustained in a mass shooting that was associated with DV, highlighting the lethality of these events. Increased focus should be placed on disarming and restricting access to guns by perpetrators of IPV and DV.

CALIFORNIA DEPARTMENT OF JUSTICE: 2022 ARMED & PROHIBITED PERSONS SYSTEM (APPS) PROGRAM ANNUAL REPORT

(2023)
(edited)

In 2022, the CA Dept of Justice [DOJ] and local law enforcement collected 1,437 firearms through the APPS program, including 521 firearms that were not part of the database and 54 ghost guns. The DOJ contacted more individuals than ever before—approximately 24,000.

In 2006, California became the first and only state in the nation to establish a system for tracking firearm owners who fall into a prohibited status. The APPS database works to identify individuals who procured firearms and later became prohibited from legally owning them. It remains the only system of its kind in the nation. In general, prohibited persons in APPS include individuals who were convicted of a felony or violent misdemeanor, were placed under a domestic violence or other restraining order, or suffer from serious mental illness. Through the APPS program in 2022, DOJ recovered 1,437 firearms—including 712 handguns, 360 rifles, 194 shotguns, 80 assault weapons, 54 ghost guns, 43 receivers or frames, 3 short-barreled shotguns, and 1 machine gun. Agents also seized 308 large-capacity magazines, 2,123 standard capacity magazines, and 281,299 rounds of ammunition through APPS enforcement actions. As of January 1, 2023, there were 3,347,221 known registered firearm owners in California of which 23,869 are prohibited from owning or possessing firearms, making up less than 1%.

Ghost guns are firearms constructed [sometimes using a 3-D printer] by private citizens that do not have a serial number, which means they are not registered. By definition, ghost guns do not appear in the APPS database and cannot be tracked by law enforcement. In 2022, the APPS program collected 38% more ghost guns in California than in 2021. DOJ is actively combating illegal manufacturing and possession of ghost guns by bringing legal action against the Bureau of Alcohol, Tobacco, Firearms and Explosive (ATF) [presumably for not removing blueprint instructions from the internet] and ghost gun manufacturers. [Some states also require anyone manufacturing a ghost gun to first register it with the state, or make it illegal to create a ghost gun.]

Reasons for Prohibitions: The statistics below outline the number of individuals in each prohibiting category of the APPS database, as of January 1, 2023. Persons can be prohibited under more than one category, which is why the total number exceeds 100%.

- 12,745 (51%) were prohibited due to a felony conviction
- 4,985 (20%) were prohibited due to the federal Brady Handgun Violence Prevention Act
- 4,099 (16%) were prohibited due to a restraining order
- 4,837 (19%) were prohibited due to mental health triggering events
- 2,415 (10%) were prohibited due to a qualifying misdemeanor conviction
- 768 (3%) were prohibited per the conditions of their probation.

In 2022, the DOJ received reports of 194 armed and prohibited individuals who attempted to purchase ammunition and were denied through the ammunition eligibility check process. BOF agents used these reports to investigate 194 individuals and seize 56 firearms, four large-capacity magazines, 55 standard magazines, and 6,621 rounds of ammunition.

DOJ collaborates with local law enforcement agencies (LEA) throughout the state in individual APPS operations, as well as sweeps, or operations that occur over multiple days within a specific area. To expand upon collaborative efforts, on January 1, 2022, DOJ awarded the first cycle of grant funding to county sheriff's departments to support seizures of firearms and ammunition from prohibited individuals through the new Gun Violence Reduction Program.

After conducting an examination of the APPS program, DOJ recommends the following steps to improve the removal of firearms from prohibited persons: Automatic Removal Post-Conviction and Automatic

Removal Post-Restraining Order. [Note: See CA SB 320, which addressed these.]

[Editor's Note: Notification of Background Check Denials to Law Enforcement—The Violence Against Women Reauthorization Act of 2022 included the NICS Denial Notification Act of 2022, which requires the U.S. Attorney General to notify local law enforcement—in the state where the person attempted to purchase the firearm and, if different, in the state where the person resides—whenever a person, including someone convicted of a misdemeanor crime of domestic violence or subject to a domestic violence protection order, fails a NICS background check to buy a gun.]

GIFFORDS LAW CENTER TO PREVENT GUN VIOLENCE, CALIFORNIA S.B. 320 SUMMARY, DOMESTIC VIOLENCE AND FIREARMS IN CALIFORNIA FAMILY AND JUVENILE DEPENDENCY COURT MATTERS

(no date)(emphases in original)

Effective 1/1/22, SB 320 codified in statute California Rule of Court 5.495.

The bill added Family Code [FC] section 6322.5 and amended Family Code sections 3044, 6304, 6306, 6323, 6389, Welfare & Institutions Code [WIC] section 213.5, and several Penal Code [PC] sections.

At the scene and at service ([Emergency Protective Orders, Temporary Restraining Orders, and Orders After Hearing] EPO, TRO, OAH), law enforcement MUST remove firearms in plain sight or found through a consensual search (PC 18250). Relinquishment MUST occur immediately upon request by a law enforcement officer serving an order under FC 6389(c)(2).

If not relinquished then, restrained party has 24 hours to relinquish and 48 hours to turn in proof to law enforcement and the court under FC 6389 and per court forms. [Judicial Council Forms] DV-800/JV 252 may be used to provide proof of relinquishment to the court. Therefore, cases involving firearms should have DV-800 or similar information showing compliance in the court file within 48 hours of service.

DV-800-INFO has statewide, general information on how to comply. However, courts MUST provide local info on how to relinquish under FC 6304.

Before a noticed hearing, the court runs a check under FC 6306, including whether respondent/restrained party has firearms. If the check, or other info provided by a party shows firearm possession, the court MUST consider whether there's been a violation (FC 6306 and 6322.5; information might, for example, be available on the request for order in #9 on [Form] DV-100).

Under FC 6322.5(a), when info about firearms is provided to the court, the court MUST consider whether there is a violation, MUST make a written record of the determination, and MUST provide it to the parties (see also FC 6322.5(c)).

To make the determination, courts MAY set review hearings as provided under 6322.5(c).

Under FC 6306(f), the court MUST make a written record of whether a prohibited party has provided proof of relinquishment.

If evidence of compliance is not provided under FC 6389(d), the court MUST notify law enforcement IMMEDIATELY. Law enforcement must then "take all actions necessary" to obtain firearms and ammunition owned, possessed, or controlled by the restrained party.

The court must review the file and report violations to the prosecuting agency within 2 days (FC 6389(c)(2)(B)(4)).

For custody and visitation, the court MUST consider a determination under FC 6322.5 when deciding whether visitation should be suspended, denied, or supervised (FC 6323(e)). A determination that there's been a violation of the firearm prohibition is a factor in considering whether the rebuttable presumption in FC 3044 has been overcome.

NOTE: A respondent at a hearing 1) may have been prohibited under an EPO or a TRO related to the current case; 2) may have been prohibited for another reason; or 3) may become prohibited as a result of the order issued at the hearing. A respondent could be determined to be in violation at the first noticed hearing or subsequently. Firearms prohibitions are in place under state law in all restraining orders and under federal law if the order after hearing is issued. State law allows for certain exemptions only if specific findings are made and procedures followed under FC 6389(h). [e.g., a mental health evaluation is required before a law enforcement officer subject to a domestic violence restraining order is allowed to possess a firearm on duty.]

[Editor's Notes: 1. According to Giffords Law Center to Prevent Gun Violence, 14 states require law enforcement to remove at least some firearms at the scene of a domestic violence incident, and 6 states authorize but do not require this; additionally, 4 states require courts to transmit domestic violence gun prohibitions to the National Instant Criminal Background Check System.

2. NY amended Criminal Procedure Code section 530.14 and Family Code section 842 effective 10/22, to require that courts must suspend firearms licenses automatically if the defendant or restrained party has a violent felony conviction, was issued an order of protection, or violated an order of protection resulting in physical injury, use of or threatened use of a weapon, or stalking. In these situations, the court must order immediate surrender of all firearms by the defendant to law enforcement. In cases of orders of protection, the surrender expires with the order. A hearing may be held regarding the firearm within 14 days (after surrender). The court must notify law enforcement and the state order of protection registry when surrender or revocation of a firearm license is ordered or modified. If the defendant willfully refuses to surrender a firearm, the court must order law enforcement to search for and immediately seize the firearm.]

JULIA WEBER, TEXAS COURT'S RADICAL FIREARMS DECISION JEOPARDIZES DOMESTIC VIOLENCE SURVIVORS

28(4) Domestic Violence Report 57 (April/May 2023)

Introduction

Earlier this year, a federal court in Texas found unconstitutional the prohibition preventing those restrained by qualifying domestic violence orders of protection from having or owning or possessing firearms and ammunition during the time a qualifying civil protective domestic violence order is in place under 18 U.S.C. § 922(g)(8). In striking down the prohibition and vacating the defendant's sentence resulting from a series of violent fi rearms-related incidents, the court came to a dangerous, extreme, and unnecessary conclusion that puts survivors and communities at risk and prevents enforcement of this lifesaving domestic violence prevention policy in the three states directly impacted.

In *United States v. Rahimi*, 61 F.4th 443 (5th Cir. March 2, 2023) the Court of Appeals for the Fifth Circuit referred to last year's U.S. Supreme Court decision in *New York State Rifle & Pistol Association, Inc. v. Bruen (Bruen)*, 142 S. Ct. 2111 (2022). In *Bruen*, the Supreme Court set out a two-part test for firearm regulations: (1) First, determine whether the Second Amendment's plain text covers the conduct and, (2) if so, decide whether the government has demonstrated that the prohibition at issue is consistent with the U.S. historical tradition of firearms regulation. Id. at 2129–30. After determining that § 922(g)(8) addresses Second Amendment conduct, the *Rahimi* court rejected that the extensive examples provided by the government demonstrated a longstanding history of relevantly similar restrictions on fi rearm access. Writing for the panel, the Hon. Cory T. Wilson concluded:

> Doubtless, 18 U.S.C. § 922(g)(8) embodies salutary policy goals meant to protect vulnerable people in our society. Weighing those policy goals' merits through the sort of means-end scrutiny our prior precedent indulged, we previously concluded that the societal benefits of § 922(g)(8) outweighed its burden on Rahimi's Second Amendment rights. But *Bruen* forecloses any such analysis in favor of a historical analogical inquiry into the scope of the allowable burden on the Second Amendment right. Through that lens, we conclude that § 922(g)(8)'s ban on possession of

> firearms is an "outlier[ ] that our ancestors would never have accepted."

United States v. Rahimi, 61 F.4th 443, 461 (5th Cir. March 2, 2023).

The legally problematic ruling in *Rahimi* involved an individual who had committed multiple acts of firearms-related violence after agreeing to a domestic violence restraining order that prohibited him from having firearms and ammunition because of its several dangerous and disconcerting consequences, namely: (1) significantly increasing risks for people being threatened and abused by intimate partners in the states in the court's jurisdiction (Texas, Louisiana, and Mississippi); (2) creating nationwide confusion and enforcement challenges around how this ruling impacts similar state-level firearm prohibitions and other jurisdictions; and (3) highlighting, along with other recent district court rulings, the current precarious nature of firearm and ammunition prohibitions designed to reduce gun violence. *Rahimi* also provides an important opportunity to address issues some federal courts may have understanding the modern way domestic violence is handled in the states nationally.

This is a critical time for those working on domestic violence and gun violence prevention to elevate the history and importance of current regulations in this area to prevent harm and help save lives. Currently, the *Rahimi* case is the only circuit court opinion on § 922(g)(8) since last year's decision in *Bruen*; however, other similar cases have been decided at the trial court level, including a federal district court in the Tenth Circuit that upheld § 922(g)(8) post-*Bruen*. It is anticipated courts will continue to issue a variety of decisions on the prohibitions in § 922(g) as judges across the country wrestle with applying the two-part *Bruen* test. Immediately after the decision, Attorney General Garland issued this statement:

> Nearly 30 years ago, Congress determined that a person who is subject to a court order that restrains him or her from threatening an intimate partner or child cannot lawfully possess a firearm. Whether analyzed through the lens of Supreme Court precedent, or of the text, history, and tradition of the Second Amendment, that statute is constitutional. Accordingly, the Department [of Justice] will seek further review of the Fifth Circuit's contrary decision.

On March 17, the Solicitor General filed a writ of certiorari, requesting the U.S. Supreme Court to hear the appeal. Whatever the outcome, we can assume the issues, analysis, and decision in *Rahimi* will have long-lasting repercussions across the country for efforts to reduce risk around the intersection of guns and intimate partner violence.

Background of the Case, 18 U.S.C. § 922(g)(8), and Related Prohibitions

In 2020, Mr. Zackey Rahimi agreed to a civil domestic violence order of protection in a case involving allegations that he assaulted his ex-girlfriend with whom he shares a child. That order included language prohibiting Mr. Rahimi from having firearms and ammunition pursuant to 18 U.S.C. § 922(g)(8). Within a few months thereafter, Mr. Rahimi had been involved in five separate firearms-violence related incidents in the Arlington, Texas area, including: shooting at someone's home; shooting at a car after he was in a car accident; leaving and coming back to shoot the car again; shooting a constable's car; and firing shots into the air outside a WhataBurger restaurant when his friend's credit card was declined. As part of the investigation into Mr. Rahimi's shooting spree, law enforcement obtained a search warrant and found a handgun and a rifle. He was subsequently indicted by a federal grand jury for possession of a firearm while subject to a qualifying civil domestic violence order of protection (also referred to as a restraining or protective order). *Rahimi,* 61 F.4th at 448–450.

When he agreed to the civil protection order, Mr. Rahimi became what is referred to as a "prohibited purchaser" or "prohibited person." These are individuals who have lost the right to own, buy, or possess firearms and ammunition under either federal or state law (and sometimes both). Many of these prohibitions are permanent, remaining in place for the rest of the person's life unless his or her firearms rights are reinstated at some later date. In the case of § 922(g)(8), the prohibition lasts only as long as the order of protection is in place.

It is important to note that domestic violence cases provide one of several ways people may be deemed "prohibited." People convicted of felonies were first prohibited under federal law pursuant to the Federal Firearms Act of 1934 (FFA). While the FFA was repealed by the Gun Control Act of 1968 (GCA), many of the provisions from the FFA were reenacted as part of the GCA, including the felony prohibition. The first federal domestic-violence-specific prohibition was added to the GCA in 1994 when the Federal Crime Control and Law Enforcement Act (FCCLEA) added certain qualifying protection orders as prohibiting under § 922(g) (8). The GCA was amended again when the Lautenberg Amendment was adopted in 1996 prohibiting those convicted of domestic violence misdemeanors (as defined) from having firearms and ammunition under § 922(g)(9). Today the list of the categories of prohibited persons (i.e., people who cannot have firearms or ammunition under federal law) can be found at 18 U.S.C. § 922(g) and includes any person:

(1) who has been convicted in any court of a crime punishable by imprisonment for a term exceeding one year;

(2) who is a fugitive from justice;

(3) who is an unlawful user of or addicted to any controlled substance. . .

(4) who has been adjudicated as a mental defective or who has been committed to a mental institution;

(5) who, being an alien—

(A) is illegally or unlawfully in the United States; or

(B) except as provided . . ., has been admitted to the United States under a nonimmigrant visa. . .

(6) who has been discharged from the Armed Forces under dishonorable conditions;

(7) who, having been a citizen of the United States, has renounced his citizenship;

(8) who is subject to a court order that—

(A) was issued after a hearing of which such person received actual notice, and at which such person had an opportunity to participate;

(B) restrains such person from harassing, stalking, or threatening an intimate partner of such person or child of such intimate partner or person, or engaging in other conduct that would place an intimate partner in reasonable fear of bodily injury to the partner or child; and

(C)(i) includes a finding that such person represents a credible threat to the physical safety of such intimate partner or child; or (ii) by its terms explicitly prohibits the use, attempted use, or threatened use of physical force against such intimate partner or child that would reasonably be expected to cause bodily injury; or

(9) who has been convicted in any court of a misdemeanor crime of domestic violence.

Given the limiting language and definitions in § 922(g)(8), not all domestic violence civil protection orders result in a prohibition. For the prohibition to apply, the order must meet both: (1) the criteria listed in the statute; and (2) the definition of intimate partner under § 921(a)(32), which requires that the order must be issued against the spouse of the person, a former spouse of the person, an individual who is a parent of a child of the person, or an individual who cohabitates or has cohabited with the person. 18 U.S.C. § 921(a)(32). These orders are issued exclusively by state and municipal courts, not federal court. Therefore, in states that permit dating or former dating partners (who have never lived together) to request orders of protection, the federal firearm and ammunition prohibition does not apply even when those courts find there has been domestic violence and issue the restraining order.

The same is true for criminal domestic violence cases. Like civil orders of protection, these state convictions are handled in state and local courts; however, to be prohibited under § 922(g)(9), the state conviction must meet the federal definition of what constitutes a "misdemeanor crime of domestic violence." Until last year, the lifetime prohibition postconviction applied only in those cases where domestic violence was perpetrated against a current or former spouse, parent, or guardian of the victim, a person with whom the victim shares a child in common, a person who is cohabiting with or has cohabited with the victim as a spouse, parent, or guardian, or a person similarly situated to a spouse, parent, or guardian of the victim. Last year, however, Congress expanded the definition through the Bipartisan Safer Communities Act (BSCA) to include dating partners as defined under 18 U.S.C. § 921(a)(37). The prohibition for dating partners is limited to five years for those with one misdemeanor domestic violence conviction unless during those five years they otherwise become prohibited under § 922(g). Therefore, currently there is significant variation around whether and how long someone identified as engaging in dangerous behavior resulting in a protective order or conviction associated with a domestic violence incident might become prohibited from having firearms and ammunition under federal law:

- Felony conviction (for domestic violence or other crimes) or domestic violence misdemeanor conviction for perpetration against a spouse, former spouse, child in common, or someone similarly situated: lifetime prohibition.
- Domestic violence misdemeanor conviction for perpetration against a serious dating partner: five-year prohibition.
- Domestic violence protective order: spouses, former spouses, child in common: while order is in place.

In addition to the federal framework, states have also adopted various firearm prohibitions. For example, 28 states currently prohibit those subject to a domestic violence protective/ restraining order issued after notice and a hearing from possessing firearms, and another 15 states authorize courts to disarm restrained parties if certain additional conditions are met. Definitions as to what makes an order qualifying or not also vary by state with 29 states and the District of Columbia having closed or partially closed the so-called "dating partner" or "boyfriend loophole" in civil orders of protection. *Rahimi* addressed only the federal civil firearm and ammunition prohibition—not any state prohibition or the federal prohibition for criminal conviction—and the decision applies only in the Court of Appeals for the Fifth Circuit. Of note, Texas and Louisiana have state firearm and ammunition prohibitions not addressed in *Rahimi* associated with civil restraining orders.

Of course, any of these prohibitions can be effective only if implemented. The three ways they are generally enforced are to: (1) have procedures in place at the time the prohibition is issued that separate the prohibited person from any firearms and ammunition they currently possess; (2) ensure information about the prohibition is entered into appropriate databases so that if they attempt to purchase, they will be denied; and (3) enforce the prohibition upon violation, which is what happened with Mr. Rahimi after he engaged in additional violent acts specifically involving firearms while the prohibition was in place.

Significance

[*Editor's Summary*: Removing federal prohibitions for people subject to civil DV orders will increase dangerousness for victims, their children and families, and community members. Batterers in the three affected states who are allowed to possess guns may travel to other states. Over 2/3 of mass shootings involve some connection to DV, and prohibitions on guns for abusers are associated with a 16% reduction in DV homicides.

The Rahimi opinion states that historically, gun prohibitions were designed to "protect the social order" rather than to protect DV victims. But Mr. Rahimi shot at a law enforcement vehicle and various people in the larger community, not just his wife, so his actions, like those of many other batterers, do implicate the social order.

The Rahimi court's distinction between criminal and civil proceedings is incorrect. The court minimizes the due process protections in DV restraining order proceedings: notice, the opportunity to be heard, the right to counsel, and the rules of evidence all apply in DV restraining order cases.

While the Rahimi opinion recognizes that criminal threats of violence are life-threatening and life-altering even if they do not result in violence, the court then states that "civil protective orders are too often misused as a tactical device in divorce proceedings—and issued without any actual threat of danger." The court ignores that fact that there are often parallel criminal proceedings which take a long time to be resolved, and that in the meantime civil protective orders which include firearm prohibitions are essential to protect the victims.

Civil DV orders in the US are the primary form of protection for DV victims, partly because batterers are rarely arrested, charged and convicted. A 2015 ACLU study found that many DV victims do not contact police, having had negative experiences with them in the past—inaction, hostility, not believing survivors, blaming them, and/or not taking the DV or sexual assault seriously. These responses are particularly found when the victim is a woman, poor, a person of color, Muslim, an immigrant, or LGBTQ. This increases chances that the batterer will retaliate against the DV victim for calling the police. Additionally, calling the police can lead to deportation of the DV victim or the batterer, which may be contrary to what the DV victim needs. It can also lead to loss of housing, employment, or welfare benefits for the victim or abuser. Thus, the Rahimi court's assumption that the criminal system will be sufficient to protect DV victims and thus they do not need firearm prohibitions resulting from civil restraining orders is incorrect.

A further complication from the Rahimi decision is that in the three states covered by the Fifth Circuit, there is now a two-tier system, where prohibiting firearms and ammunition in some cases may be federally unconstitutional, but still permissible given the state and/or local laws. This will inevitably create enforcement challenges and increase the potential for gun violence nationally.]

Going forward, advocates and others who work in this field must continue to raise awareness about the importance of maintaining domestic violence remedies informed by the experiences of survivors and grounded in the history of this country's efforts to reduce dangerousness—remedies that include due process safeguards and provide protections necessary to help increase safety for domestic violence victims and the community at large.

BRADY, BATTERED WOMEN'S JUSTICE PROJECT, DC COALITION AGAINST DOMESTIC VIOLENCE, DV LEAP, EVERYTOWN FOR GUN SAFETY ACTION, GIFFORDS LAW CENTER TO PREVENT GUN VIOLENCE, MARCH FOR OUR LIVES, NATIONAL FAMILY VIOLENCE LAW CENTER, NNEDV, THE SAFE SISTERS CIRCLE, AND TEXAS COUNCIL ON FAMILY VIOLENCE, BRIEF OF GUN VIOLENCE AND DOMESTIC VIOLENCE PREVENTION GROUPS AS *AMICI CURIAE* IN SUPPORT OF PETITIONER

(April 20, 2023)

IN THE SUPREME COURT OF THE UNITED STATES

UNITED STATES OF AMERICA v. ZACKEY RAHIMI

On Petition for a Writ of Certiorari to the United States Court of Appeals for the Fifth Circuit

SUMMARY OF THE ARGUMENT

The United States has a deeply rooted tradition of disarming individuals who pose a danger to others or to the community at large. Amici thus agree with petitioner that history and tradition support the constitutionality of laws that disarm dangerous persons. Pet. 7–10. Amici also agree that 18 U.S.C. § 922(g)(8), which prohibits the possession of firearms by persons subject to a domestic-violence restraining order, falls directly within that tradition and thus is valid under *New York State Rifle & Pistol Association v. Bruen,* 142 S. Ct. 2111 (2022). Pet. 11–13. The Fifth

Circuit's invalidation of Section 922(g)(8) warrants review for that reason alone.

Amici submit that certiorari is particularly warranted here for two additional reasons. First, not only is the Fifth Circuit's invalidation of Section 922(g)(8) deeply flawed; it is symptomatic of wider disagreement over *Bruen's* methodology. This Court's intervention is necessary to confirm that *Bruen's* analogical approach is not a "regulatory straightjacket," 142 S. Ct. at 2133, and that it permits disarming dangerous individuals through laws like Section 922(g)(8). Second, this case presents an especially compelling example of why legislatures have historically passed, and why this Court should sustain, laws that disarm dangerous individuals. For thousands of women, children, and other potential victims of domestic violence, as well as potential other victims of mass shootings by domestic abusers, the stakes are literally life or death.

I. This Court's review is necessary to correct the Fifth Circuit's erroneous interpretation of *Bruen* and to dispel confusion in the lower courts over how to apply *Bruen's* historical-analogical test.

In *Bruen,* this Court articulated the Second Amendment framework for reviewing restrictions on the possession and carrying of firearms. Under *Bruen,* the government may justify a modern restriction by showing that it is "relevantly similar" to historical regulations. "[A]nalogical reasoning requires only that the government identify a well-established and representative historical analogue, not a historical twin." *Bruen,* 142 S. Ct. at 2133.

In holding that Section 922(g)(8) violates the Second Amendment on its face, the Fifth Circuit committed two analytical errors in applying *Bruen's* principles.

1. First, the Fifth Circuit applied an excessively restrictive approach to assessing whether Section 922(g)(8) is analogous to historical regulations. The court parsed each historical firearms regulation with an eye to distinguishing it, effectively requiring a "historical twin" to Section 922(g)(8). The court thus missed the broader principle that emerges from multiple lines of historical firearms regulation: jurisdictions have historically—and can today—disarm dangerous people, including persons subject to domestic violence restraining orders.

2. Second, the Fifth Circuit failed to appreciate the significance of modern efforts to grapple with domestic violence. *Bruen* stated that regulations addressing "unprecedented societal concern[s]" require a "nuanced" analysis of historical firearms regulations. 142 S. Ct. at 2132. Only in the past 50 years have governments begun to adopt measures to address the distinctive and heightened risks of intimate partner violence. This emerging

recognition should play a role in evaluating historical analogies, and it makes the Fifth Circuit's narrow approach all the more erroneous.

B. The Fifth Circuit is not alone in struggling to interpret *Bruen*. Other lower courts are similarly grappling with its historical test, with several courts taking unduly narrow approaches. This Court's review is necessary to confirm that the proper approach to reviewing Second Amendment challenges permits governments to rely on historical traditions of the past to disarm dangerous individuals today.

II. This Court's review is also necessary to ensure that federal, state, and local governments can reduce the threat of lethal violence by prohibiting domestic abusers from possessing firearms while subject to protection orders.

A. Domestic violence is pervasive, deadly, and inextricably linked with firearms in the United States. More than one-third of women in the United States report experiencing domestic violence in their lifetime. And domestic-violence offenders regularly use guns to kill or terrorize their intimate partners: every month, on average, 70 women [in this country] are shot and killed by an intimate partner. Domestic abusers also use guns to wound, threaten, intimidate, and terrorize victims. Children are not spared: up to 20% of violent deaths of intimate partners [in the U.S.] also involve deaths of children or other family members. And the risks of violence extend to the public and law enforcement officers. In most recent mass shootings, the perpetrator either had a history of domestic violence or killed at least one partner or family member during the shooting. And for law enforcement officers, responding to domestic violence calls accounts for the highest number of service-related fatalities.

B. In enacting Section 922(g)(8), Congress recognized the gravity of the threat posed by domestic abusers with access to firearms. States have equally recognized the importance of this issue; at least thirty-one states have criminal prohibitions on firearm possession by persons subject to domestic violence restraining orders. These regulations are effective. They are associated with a 13% reduction in intimate-partner firearm homicides statewide, and an even greater 25% reduction in cities within these states.

States have taken a variety of steps to address the dangers of firearms in the domestic-violence context, including enacting regulations that go beyond federal law. Twenty-four states, for example, have extended their laws beyond Section 922(g)(8) to reach dating partners, and twelve states' prohibitions include temporary restraining orders—both of which have proven even more effective than the baseline federal prohibition. Many states also require domestic abusers to relinquish their firearms in connection with protection orders. Others rely on extreme risk protection order ("red flag") laws to disarm persons determined to pose a danger of using firearms to harm others. The Fifth Circuit's decision raises unjustified constitutional questions not only about Section 922(g)(8), but also about the array of measures that states have successfully used to reduce the threat of firearms related domestic violence.

For all of these reasons, this Court should grant certiorari and reverse the Fifth Circuit's erroneous decision.

[Editor's Note: See also Kelly Roskam, Chiara Cooper, Philip Stallworth, and April M. Zeoli, The Case for Domestic Violence Protective Order Firearms Prohibitions under Bruen, 51 Fordham Urb. L. J. 221 (2023), arguing that § 922(g)(8) is constitutional under a Bruen analysis.]

U.S. v. SILVERS

2023 WL 3232605 (U.S. Dist. Ct., W.D. Kentucky)
(footnotes and most citations omitted)

(Note: The facts include descriptions that may be upsetting to some readers.)

OPINION & ORDER

Victor Silvers was federally indicted and convicted for possessing a gun despite a state-court domestic-violence order that told him not to. That order issued after he grabbed his estranged wife by the neck, punched her, and threatened her with his gun. The criminal statute, 18 U.S.C. § 922(g)(8), prohibits gun possession by anyone who, after notice and a hearing, has been found a credible threat to the physical safety of, or ordered not to use or threaten physical force against, an intimate partner or child. This restriction, according to Silvers, violates the U.S. Constitution.

The lawfulness of Silvers's conviction turns on whether the Second Amendment, as publicly understood when ratified, would've barred the government from disarming someone in his position. Silvers offers no real argument or precedent indicating that this constitutional provision (or its state analogues or common-law precursors) ever defeated the criminal prosecution or civil disarmament of someone determined to be a credible threat to the safety of others. Nor has Silvers pointed to any deficiency in the underlying state-court proceeding or order, which cited § 922(g)(8) and expressly commanded him not to possess a gun.

Is Silvers's total (if temporary) disarmament reconcilable with the constitutional right "to keep and bear arms"? The Second Amendment's apparent tension with § 922(g)(8) renders the statutory restriction presumptively unlawful under the Supreme Court's recent decision in *New York State Rifle & Pistol Ass'n v. Bruen*, 142 S. Ct. 2111, 2126 (2022). Viewed in the light of its historical context and the country's tradition of firearm regulation, however, *id.* at 2131, the scope of the constitutional right doesn't shield persons found to be dangerous from laws restricting their possession of firearms.

"The historical evidence," then-Judge Barrett explained in a pre-*Bruen* dissent concerning a different subsection of § 922(g), "support[s]" the "propositio[n] that the legislature may disarm those who have demonstrated a proclivity for violence or whose possession of guns would otherwise threaten the public safety." Kanter v. Barr, 919 F.3d 437, 454 (7th Cir. 2019) (abrogated by *Bruen*, 142 S. Ct. 2111). Other judges—considering similar statutes and a similar historical record—have reached the same conclusion. "Historically, limitations on the right were tied to dangerousness. In England and colonial America, the Government disarmed people who posed a danger to others. Violence was one ground for fearing danger, as were disloyalty and rebellion." "The most cogent principle that can be drawn from traditional limitations on the right to keep and bear arms," another opinion described at length, "is that dangerous persons likely to use firearms for illicit purposes were not understood to be protected by the Second Amendment." This history of laws used to "disarm dangerous and disaffected persons" reaches back to pre-colonial English history.

The Government is wrong to argue that the Second Amendment didn't apply to Silvers at all. He, like other members of our political community protected by the Bill of Rights, enjoyed a right to keep and bear arms. But that right was not unlimited. As historically understood, it did not dislodge traditional governmental authority to restrict his gun possession based on the dangerous threat he posed to his now-deceased wife. Section 922(g)(8), like other laws familiar at or before the Second Amendment's ratification, restricted Silvers for a limited period of time following due process and individual findings of danger to others. This measure looks nothing like the broad and historically anomalous bans addressed in the Supreme Court's Second Amendment trilogy of *Heller*, *McDonald*, and *Bruen*. Consistent with those precedents, the Amendment's text and history indicate that "legislatures have the power to prohibit dangerous people from possessing guns," and did in fact "disqualif[y] categories of people from the right to bear arms"—though "only when they judged that doing so was necessary to protect the public safety." *Kanter*, 919 F.3d at 451 (Barrett, J., dissenting).

I. Victor and Brittney Silvers

Before her death in 2018, Brittney Silvers served as a sergeant in the U.S. Army and lived on post at Fort Campbell, Kentucky. After seven years of marriage, she and her husband, Victor Silvers, had recently separated. That summer, Brittney drove to Clarksville, Tennessee—where Victor had been living since leaving their apartment—to find Victor. Around 1:00 a.m. on July 22, a Clarksville law-enforcement officer responded after Brittney and Victor "got into a verbal argument" and Victor "grabbed her by her neck with one hand and struck her in the face twice with his other hand."

The officer "observed blood on Britt[ney] Silvers' lips and her face appeared to be swollen," as shown in a photo found in the police report.

An officer secured an arrest warrant against Victor Silvers for domestic assault later that morning. And the next day Brittney sent a text message asking Victor to "[t]hink about all the times you put your hands on me." "I'm just fed up," she wrote.

Officers arrested and jailed Victor in Montgomery County, Tennessee for domestic assault on September 22. He was released on bail the same day. As a condition of his release, the state court prohibited Victor from "harassing, annoying, telephoning, contacting or otherwise communicating" with Brittney, and ordered him to "vacate" and "stay away" from her home

Victor and Brittney nevertheless exchanged several text messages that night and the following day. Victor asked her whereabouts and demanded that she answer his calls. "Please don't come near me," Brittney answered. "I don't feel safe." Victor asked if she was at the house of a man Victor suspected she was seeing, and then wrote "Never mind found you!" Once more Brittney responded: "Please don't come near me[.] I don't feel safe."

Three days later Brittney petitioned the Christian County (Ky.) Circuit Court for an order of protection. The petition stated that "my spouse Victor Silvers assaulted me and threatened me with his gun." The state court issued an emergency protective order. Victor received service on October 1 of a protective-order summons, later found at his house in Clarksville, notifying him of an October 9 hearing date at Christian County Circuit Court. Silvers "didn't go" to the hearing "on purpose," as he told Brittney in a subsequent text message.

After the hearing, the state court issued a domestic-violence order [DVO] against Silvers. The judge found "by a preponderance of the evidence that an act or threat of domestic violence occurred and may occur again," that a "weapon" had been "involved," and that Silvers was "Armed and Dangerous." The court ordered that Silvers "be restrained from committing further acts of abuse or threats of abuse, stalking, or sexual assault," and from any "unauthorized contact" with Brittney. "In order to assist in eliminating future acts of domestic violence and abuse," moreover, the judge ordered Silvers "not to possess, purchase or attempt to possess, purchase or obtain a firearm or ammunition during the duration of this order," specifically citing 18 U.S.C. § 922(g)(8). The order didn't expire until October 2021—though Kentucky law allows for reconsideration and permits either party to move to amend an order of protection.

Silvers received notice of this order, too. Officers later discovered pictures of the order on his phone; Brittney had sent the images via text message.

Five days after the state court issued the DVO, Brittney died. She was shot in her head, neck, and chest. Off-duty soldiers who lived nearby heard the gunshots and ran to her apartment. They found Brittney stretched out in the yard, a male friend bleeding nearby, and Victor locked inside his car screaming.

II. This Prosecution

Because these crimes occurred at Fort Campbell, part of the United States' "special maritime and territorial jurisdiction," the federal government investigated and prosecuted them. A federal grand jury sitting in Paducah, Kentucky, charged Victor Silvers with committing seven offenses, including first-degree murder, attempted murder, and—relevant here—carrying a firearm while subject to a DVO in violation of § 922(g)(8). The Government initially sought the death penalty, but later withdrew the request.

On the eve of trial, the Government issued a second superseding indictment, though it added no charges to the counts facing Silvers. In response he moved to dismiss the § 922(g)(8) charge. Relying on the Supreme Court's recent decision in *Bruen*, he argued that the federal statute violates the Second Amendment. Given the complexity and importance of the parties' arguments, and the minimal evidentiary impact that dismissal would have given the overlapping nature of the conduct at issue in the other six counts, the Court deferred ruling on the motion until after the verdict.

Following a six-day trial, the jury found Silvers guilty on all seven counts. The Government offered abundant evidence, apart from the gun and DVO, that led the jury to convict Silvers on the other six counts—one of which carried a mandatory life sentence, another of which required a consecutive ten-year sentence, and three of which authorized sentences of imprisonment up to life.

III. Section 922(g)(8)

The federal Gun Control Act of 1968 prohibits firearm possession by individuals who fall into several categories, including convicted felons, fugitives, drug addicts, and persons who have been committed to a mental institution. *See* § 922(g)(1)–(4). Congress amended that statute in 1994 to introduce a new category, § 922(g)(8), covering individuals subject to some DVOs. Section 922(g)(8), the Sixth Circuit has held, "reflects Congress's determination that persons subject to domestic violence protection orders pose an increased threat to the safety of their intimate partners and children." This provision, the court went on, reflected Congress' "conclu[sion] that keeping firearms away from such individuals represents a reasonable step toward reducing" that threat.

Section 922(g)(8) applies if three conditions exist:

(1) a court issues an order after the individual receives notice and an opportunity to be heard;

(2) the order restrains the individual from "harassing, stalking, or threatening an intimate partner or child of such intimate partner or person, or engaging in other conduct that would place an intimate partner in reasonable fear of bodily injury to the partner or child"; and

(3) the order "includes a finding that such person represents a credible threat to the physical safety of such intimate partner or child" or "explicitly prohibits the use, attempted use, or threatened use of physical force . . . that would reasonably be expected to cause bodily injury."

A person subject to an order that meets these criteria may not possess a firearm.

The jury found Silvers guilty of violating § 922(g)(8). The Government's evidence showed, first, that on the day Brittney died, Victor was subject to a court order issued after notice and a chance to be heard. Second, the order "restrained" him "from committing further acts of abuse or threats of abuse" and "from any unauthorized contact with" Brittney. Third, the order found that "an act or threat of domestic violence occurred and may occur again." Indeed, for purposes of this motion, Silvers doesn't dispute that § 922(g)(8) properly applies to him as a factual and statutory matter. Rather, his motion to dismiss relies solely on the argument that the Second Amendment bars the federal government from prosecuting him for possessing a weapon while subject to the state-court DVO.

IV. The Second Amendment

Did § 922(g)(8) infringe Silvers's right to keep and bear arms by criminalizing his possession of a gun while under the domestic-violence order? The Second Amendment provides that "[a] well regulated Militia, being necessary to the security of a free State, the right of the people to keep and bear Arms, shall not be infringed." The statute at issue undoubtedly affected Silvers's ability to keep arms, as commonly understood at ratification and today. And contrary to the Government's argument, Silvers is a member of "the people" covered by this constitutional provision. That means he is presumptively protected by the Second Amendment. Whether § 922(g)(8) infringes that protection, however, turns on the Second Amendment's public meaning as informed by this country's history and tradition of gun rights and restrictions.

1. **"To keep and bear Arms."** The charged offense rests on Silvers's mere possession (not use or even transport) of a weapon. This restriction plainly implicates his ability to "keep" arms, which simply means his right

"to 'have weapons.'" The Second Amendment presumptively protects the right of individual citizens to possess a handgun in the home for purposes of self-defense. *Heller*, 554 U.S. at 635. The Supreme Court reached that conclusion after evaluating the Amendment's text, historical background, and post-ratification history. These sources, the Court held, rendered the Second Amendment right incompatible with a District of Columbia law that completely banned the possession of handguns in the home.

Other blanket restrictions have met the same fate. The Chicago ordinance at issue in *McDonald v. City of Chicago*, like the law in *Heller*, "effectively bann[ed] handgun possession by almost all private citizens who reside[d] in the City." Although that decision addressed state regulation under the Fourteenth Amendment rather than federal regulation under the Second, the Court held that the right recognized in *Heller* is "deeply rooted in this Nation's history and tradition."

Bruen itself rejected a law that permitted an individual "to carry a handgun for self-defense outside the home" only at the grace of state officials. The New York law in question "condition[ed] issuance of a license to carry on a citizen's showing of some additional special need" and "pro[of] that proper cause exists." This regime conflicted with the "plain text" and historical understanding of the Second Amendment, which protects "'bear[ing]' arms in public for self-defense." "When the Second Amendment's plain text covers an individual's conduct," as is the case here, the *Bruen* Court held that "the Constitution presumptively protects that conduct." . . .

2. **"The people."** Instead, the Government raises a different threshold objection. The Second Amendment offers Silvers no protection, it contends, because persons subject to the sort of domestic-violence order covered by § 922(g)(8) are not among "the people" whose gun rights are guarded by the Second Amendment. "*Heller* and *Bruen*," the argument goes, "defined the right to bear arms as belonging to 'law-abiding, responsible' citizens." Those in Silvers's position are purportedly not "ordinary," "responsible" or "law-abiding," because in "most circumstances . . . the conduct that led to the protective order constitutes an assault, battery, or criminal threat." . . .

This provision, it's worth remembering, codified a preexisting right: "the Amendment acknowledges '*the* right . . . to keep and bear Arms,' a right that pre-existed the Constitution like '*the* freedom of speech.'" By ensuring that the new national government would continue to respect such natural-and common-law rights, the Amendment preserved the status quo for "all members of the political community" subject to the Constitution—rather than bestowing a novel right on "an unspecified subset" of the nation.

Heller explained that "the people" refers to "all Americans." . . . And even in upholding a neighboring provision—§ 922(g)(9)—against constitutional challenge, *Stimmel v. Sessions* recognized that "[b]y acknowledging that 'law-abiding, responsible citizens' are at the core of the Amendment's protections, the *Heller* Court presumed certain individuals *can be* 'disqualified' from exercising Second Amendment rights. In other words, such people did not simply lack any Second Amendment rights in the first place. So Silvers remains with the scope of "the people" addressed by the Amendment.

3. History and Tradition. The relevant question, then, "is whether the government has the power to disable the exercise of a right that [the people] otherwise possess, rather than whether they possess the right at all." That authority turns on whether the legal restriction is consistent with the constitutional text, viewed in its historical context.

a. The premise of *Heller* and *Bruen* is that the Second Amendment right retains an intelligible and justiciable scope, even if its contours are by now somewhat obscured by time and pre-*Heller* practice. . .

Justice Thomas's opinion in *Bruen* accordingly framed the inquiry into the contours of that right as a "presumption" that restrictions are invalid. This focus on historical applications of the text aligns with the Court's previous acknowledgment that, "like most rights, the right secured by the Second Amendment is not unlimited." . . . So the *Bruen* opinion went on to assess whether the Government could overcome that presumption by demonstrating that a "regulation . . . is consistent with the Nation's historical tradition of firearm regulation." "Only then," *Bruen* instructed, "may a court conclude that the individual's conduct falls outside the Second Amendment's 'unqualified command.' "

This "historical tradition" includes the regulations enacted by the states and federal government in the era of the Amendment's ratification. "[W]hether a historical regulation is a proper analogue for a distinctly modern firearm regulation requires a determination of whether the two regulations are 'relevantly similar.' " The Government, however, needn't identify a "historical *twin*"; a "well-established historical *analogue*" will suffice. The *Bruen* Court directed courts toward two ways to ascertain whether a historical regulation is "relevantly similar" to a modern one: "how" and "why" the particular "regulations burden a law-abiding citizen's right to armed self-defense." The question here, as the Fifth Circuit recently framed it, is whether Silvers "forfeited his Second Amendment rights [because] his conduct ran afoul of a 'lawful regulatory measure[ ]' 'prohibiting . . . the possession of firearms,' that is consistent with 'the historical tradition that delimits the outer bounds of the right to keep and bear arms.'. . .

b. The Government maintains that § 922(g)(8) is analogous to laws that disarmed "dangerous" people and "surety" statutes (which also concerned dangerous people). Its historical evidence ranges from 17th-century English statutes to Reconstruction-era laws. . . . Fortunately judges examining § 922(g) today aren't the first to confront this material. . . What becomes apparent is that the Government's position rests on a historical principle that Silvers lacks: These three opinions' "analyses show that the limit on the Second Amendment right was pegged to dangerousness."

. . . Judge Hardiman drew the "dangerous persons" principle from ratifying-convention proposals, English laws, colonial loyalty-oath statutes, and related scholarship. Those materials, he determined, showed that the Second Amendment guaranteed a right to possess weapons for non-violent felons, but *not* for "people who have demonstrated that they are likely to commit violent crimes."

This "[h]istory," Judge Barrett's dissent in *Kanter* explained, "support[s] the proposition that the state can take the right to bear arms away from a category of people that it deems dangerous." . . . She reached this conclusion after reviewing numerous founding-era legal sources (many cited by the Government here) shedding light on the contemporaneous public meaning of the right to keep and bear arms: state ratifying-convention proposals, England's Militia Act of 1662, prohibitions against going "armed to terrify" the public, colonial "loyalty" laws disarming classes of people who refused to swear an oath of allegiance or were otherwise perceived as potential threats to public order (often on a groupwide basis—covering "Catholics," "slaves, [or] Native Americans"—in a manner now rightly perceived as odious), and historical scholarship. The category of "dangerous people" these laws addressed, moreover, includes individuals "who have not been convicted of felonies." The key is a person's "demonstrated . . . proclivity for violence" or conduct showing that "possession of guns would otherwise threaten public safety.". . .

c. . . . Regardless of the rights the Second Amendment preserves for non-dangerous persons, therefore, it does not guarantee gun possession for persons demonstrated to be dangerous, as Victor Silvers had been in 2018. The historical record reveals laws that focus on dangerousness and whose features are analogous to § 922(g)(8). These analogues overcome the presumption recognized in *Bruen,* "inform the meaning of [the] constitutional text," and establish "that dangerous persons likely to use firearms for illicit purposes were not understood to be protected by the Second Amendment." So the federal government may, consistent with the constitutional text as understood at the time of its adoption, prohibit gun possession by those in Silvers's situation.

Three types of laws, described in the decisions and scholarship above, are pertinent to this historical inquiry.

First, "going-armed" laws known to the ratifying generation prohibited persons from "bearing arms in a way that spreads 'fear' or 'terror' among the people." . . . *Second,* other ratification-era laws disarmed people feared to be disloyal. . . Even after the Glorious Revolution, when gun rights expanded thanks in part to the English Bill of Rights, the practice of disarming entire groups on grounds of dangerousness persisted. *Third,* surety statutes required some individuals, including "those threatening to do harm," to post a "surety" (essentially a bond) "before carrying weapons in public." . . . "If he refused he would be liable to imprisonment.". . . *[Editor's Note: These days these peace bonds are still used in Canada, but seldom in the U.S.]*. . .These laws were widespread: . . .

Next, these historical analogues involved civil as well as criminal proceedings. . . The then-existing line between civil and criminal process and punishment, in any case, was not as clear or relevant as implied by Silvers's argument (to the extent he has raised it at all). Surety statutes, for instance, represented a hybrid that involved civilly imposed restrictions that could be enforced by criminal prosecution. English law at times authorized monetary rewards for confiscation of weapons. And nothing in the founding-era precedents or examples cited here appears to have placed significant weight on whether a proceeding was civil or criminal in nature. . . .

And it's unclear why Silvers' civil disarmament following notice, hearing, and a judicial finding of danger would be more objectionable than his disarmament after indictment but before a judicial finding of guilt. . . . Any such procedures, however labeled, must surely comport with separate due-process protections regarding notice, hearing, and decision-making in connection with the deprivation of valuable rights. And the text of § 922(g)(8) itself imposes procedural safeguards on the DVO process before an order is backed by the federal criminal proscription. So Silvers cannot escape the reach of § 922(g)(8) just because the underlying state-court order was civil rather than criminal in origin.

Although these founding-era examples may not represent historical twins of § 922(g)(8), *Bruen* doesn't require an identity of legislation. This makes sense: it's the Second Amendment whose content remains constant, not the statutes regularly enacted and amended by the people's elected representatives. By design, legislatures may alter the form and substance of laws—so long as they remain consistent with the Constitution. The unsurprising fact that the form of gun laws has changed over time shouldn't by itself cast doubt on their constitutionality; as a dissenting Justice Scalia observed in a related context, "[q]uite obviously, not every restriction upon expression that did not exist in 1791 or in 1868 is *ipso facto* unconstitutional." The question is instead "whether the government action under challenge is consonant with the concept of the protected freedom . . . that existed when the constitutional protection was accorded." In this case, that means asking whether the statute's content remains consistent with the scope of the right to keep and bear arms. Legislators, of course, may validly "update" statutes in a manner forbidden to judges interpreting the Constitution.

Whatever the Government's burden for demonstrating the consistency between a statutory restriction and the Second Amendment right, the extensive evidence of the "dangerousness" principle . . . surely suffices to overcome it. These going-armed, loyalty, and surety laws refute Silvers' position that the scope of the common-law right, as codified by the founding generation, privileges gun possession over the dangerous behavior and legal process underlying Silvers' DVO. Rather, our history and tradition show that a "firearms disability can be consistent with the Second Amendment to the extent that . . . its basis credibly indicates a present danger that one will misuse arms against others and . . . redresses that danger."

The limitations Silvers faced are consistent with the relevant aspects of statutes and causes of action that coexisted with the historic right to keep and bear arms: they existed for a similar purpose (prevention of violence and terror) and acted through similar mechanisms (temporary disarmament in response to legal process and a judicial determination of dangerousness). The historical analogues, moreover, all reflect the same background presumption that the people generally have a right to keep and bear arms. . . . Certainly the going-armed, loyalty, and surety laws resemble the targeted restrictions of § 922(g)(8) far more than the blunderbuss disarmament that preceded the English Bill of Rights, or the "severe" and "outlier" restrictions at issue in *Heller*, *McDonald*, and *Bruen*.

4. Silvers' counterarguments are inconsistent with *Bruen* and the original meaning of the Second Amendment. Despite this historical record, Silvers contends that the Government cannot show a historical law "distinctly similar" to § 922(g)(8). Its features, he maintains, differ from those of the analogues discussed above: § 922(g)(8) targets violence against a particular person (instead of the world at large), completely prohibits firearm possession (as opposed to prohibiting only public carry), and may require individuals to wait years to regain their guns (though he doesn't identify what length of time might be tolerably short).

First, he views the loyalty statutes as unanalogous because they were "motivated by a fear of insurrection and rebellion," whereas § 922(g)(8) "seeks to prevent interpersonal violence." But "fear of insurrection and rebellion" surely encompasses fear of the violence that would bring; that's why the laws targeted gun possession as opposed to, say, seditious speech. And disarmament based on fear of threatened violence to a specific person (as opposed to general political heterodoxy) seems more rather than less appropriate; certainly § 922(g)(8) is more particularized than categorical disarmament of large groups of people based on stereotyped and generalized proclivities for dangerousness. If anything, this aspect of the loyalty statutes favors . . . the statute's constitutionality. . .

Second, Silvers cannot overcome § 922(g)(8) on the ground that it proscribes gun possession both inside and outside the home . . .Most important is the principle these going-armed laws reveal and the surety and loyalty statutes reinforce: that Second Amendment rights weren't absolute following a finding of dangerousness or threat. Many of the laws discussed above contemplated disarmament as well as more limited restrictions on use or possession.

Third, although Silvers is right that restrictions imposed under § 922(g)(8) may last more than a year, he is wrong that this presents a distinction of categorical or constitutional magnitude. The disability he faced was time-limited, individualized, and reminiscent of several aspects of the historical provisions discussed above... Here, again, the relevant constitutional principle is a legal determination of dangerousness, not any free-floating temporal restriction (which Silvers hasn't identified in any event).

Finally, Silvers devotes much of his brief to a broader conceptual point: that evidence of "relevantly similar" analogues isn't enough. Instead he maintains that the Government must identify statutes that are "*distinctly* similar" to § 922(g)(8), and may not rely on "analogical reasoning." ... *Bruen* specifically contemplated "reasoning by analogy" when considering unanticipated "modern regulations." ...

5. **Section 922(g)(8) as applied to Silvers.** Even if these historical laws were insufficiently analogous, that alone wouldn't suffice to invalidate Silvers' indictment and conviction under § 922(g)(8) ... Silvers wasn't convicted merely for possessing a gun at home despite the DVO; the jury found him guilty of traveling from Tennessee to a military base in Kentucky to murder his wife with a gun outside *her* home. So this inside/outside distinction isn't enough to render § 922(g)(8) *facially* unconstitutional...

Such an argument—and any other as-applied argument—is undeveloped and therefore forfeited in this case. Regardless, whether Silvers received personal service of the DVO raises a different legal concern than the constitutionality of § 922(g)(8) under the Second Amendment. And on that score, nothing suggests that the state-court judge rubberstamped Brittney's petition or that Brittney sought the DVO for "tactical" reasons. Silvers doesn't challenge the proof or process that led to the DVO. Perhaps for good reason: abundant evidence, as recounted above, supports a finding that he abused his wife while armed and posed a credible threat to her safety. Tragically, as the jury found, Silvers's subsequent actions—fatally shooting his wife—bore out that determination. So even if Silvers had pursued an as-applied challenge on this basis, it would fail...

C. MILITARY RESPONSE TO DOMESTIC VIOLENCE

CHRISTINE ZELLAR CHURCH, THE SERVICEMEMBERS CIVIL RELIEF ACT: PROTECTING VICTIMS OF DOMESTIC VIOLENCE IN PROTECTION ORDER CASES INVOLVING THE MILITARY

12 T.M. Cooley J. Prac. & Clin. L. 335 (2010)
(citations and footnotes omitted)

A. Domestic Violence and the Military

* * * Victims alleging intimate partner violence at the hands of a servicemember may face an uphill battle in the court of public opinion, which can spill over into state courts. Sympathy and public support for those who serve in our military is at an all-time high. When referring to a returning servicemember, our lexicon contains terms like "warriors" and "patriots." There are no similar sympathetic terms that describe the spouse who handles the family household and is a single parent to the children while the servicemember is deployed. Even the language of the United States Supreme Court reflects this patriotic fervor when describing the purpose of the Servicemembers Civil Relief Act (SCRA) as necessary to "protect those who have been obliged to drop their own affairs to take up the burdens of the nation."

Yet domestic violence remains a serious issue among military families. Many family members of returning combat veterans are in need of protection and legal assistance. Domestic violence rates among veterans with post-traumatic stress disorder (PTSD) are higher than those of the general population. A 1995 study found that 63% of veterans seeking help for PTSD had been aggressive to their partners in the last year. A 1996 study of fifty volunteer Vietnam combat veterans and their partners found that 42% of the men had engaged in physical aggression against their partners in the previous year, 92% had been verbally aggressive, and 100% had used psychological aggression. A recent 2006 study suggests that "treatment-seeking veterans with PTSD or depression are more apt to perpetrate violence, especially severe violence, than are numerous other clinical or population-based groups that have been studied." The findings of the study note:

> [A]pproximately 81% of PTSD and 81% of depressed veterans engaged in at least one act of violence toward their partners in the last year. These rates are more than six times higher than rates in the general population and are almost double the rate found when using volunteer Vietnam combat veterans and their partners . . . Further, approximately 45% of PTSD veterans and 42% of depressed veterans perpetrated at least one severe violent

act in the last year (based on a combined report). These rates were 14 times higher than were rates from the general population.

The deep sympathy that Americans have for returning soldiers and sailors who are suffering from depression, post-traumatic stress disorder, or traumatic brain injury must not, consequently, result in underestimating the danger that the servicemember's family may be facing. Deborah Tucker, Executive Director of the National Center on Domestic and Sexual Violence (NCDSV) and Co-chair of the U.S. Department of Defense Task Force on Domestic Violence (DTFDV), warns in her article about domestic violence, PTSD, and traumatic brain injuries: "When we struggle in considering a case of domestic violence assault, it is important that no matter the reason behind the assault that the offender be held accountable; and the victim supported and assisted to ensure her future safety."

The Defense Task Force on Domestic Violence was established in 2000 to study domestic violence within the military system and to make recommendations to the Department of Defense. In 2002, the entire country became aware of a possible link between domestic violence and combat related military service after the highly publicized deaths of the wives of four Ft. Bragg soldiers. Funding for the military's Family Advocacy Program (FAP) increased and additional non-lawyer victim advocates were hired to assist victims of domestic violence who live in or near a military installation. While the increase in support services by FAP victim advocates provided advocacy and support within the military system, there was no additional funding to provide attorneys for these victims of family violence. Also, family members of active duty National Guard or Reservists who do not live in or near a military installation have limited access to any type of advocacy and assistance.

While victims of intimate partner violence have few resources, there are multiple referral services that will provide a pro bono lawyer for the servicemember. The American Bar Association has organized the Military Pro Bono Project, which coordinates with many state bar associations, to refer servicemembers in need of legal assistance to a local attorney. Family members who are seeking protection from a servicemember are not eligible for assistance from this project. * * *

HAILEY GUINN, MILITARY ADJUDICATIONS OF DOMESTIC VIOLENCE

(unpublished, 2021)
(footnotes omitted)

I. Introduction

. . .[D]omestic violence runs rampant in the military. The Department of Defense's Family Advocacy Program (FAP) tracks reports of domestic abuse, both between spouses and between unmarried intimate partners in the military. A 2019 survey of FAP data, conducted by the Department of Defense, showed that roughly 6,800 of the 13,571 reports of spousal abuse collected by the FAP in 2019 met the Department's definitional criteria for domestic abuse. The definition includes emotional or psychological abuse, economic control, and interference with personal liberty. The 6,800 qualifying reports involved 5,505 unique victims. From these statistics, the Department extrapolates that in 2019, for every 1,000 military spouses, there were approximately 10.9 incidents of spousal abuse distributed among 8.8 unique victims. This data suggests that the rate of spousal domestic violence in the military is more than twice that of the national population; 1.1% as compared to 0.42%.

The FAP also collected 1,902 reports of intimate partner violence between unmarried people in the military in 2019, 1,121 of which met the Department of Defense's definition of domestic abuse. Notably, the definitions used cover violence between unmarried couples only if they have cohabitated or if they share a child.

No data is available on the total number of unmarried servicemembers in intimate relationships, so the Department cannot establish a percentage rate of intimate partner abuse incidents and/or victims. To frame this issue on a larger scale, the Department of Defense found more than 40,000 incidents of domestic abuse between 2015 and 2019 (including both married and unmarried individuals), 74% of which were physical.

The lack of public attention regarding the military justice system has allowed many of its shortcomings to go unaddressed, shortcomings that bear particularly heavily on the legions of domestic violence victims who have been battered by servicemembers. . .

II. Background: Military Justice Systems

Military justice proceedings vary from civilian ones in two key ways. First, military servicemembers are governed by an additional set of substantive laws called the Uniform Code of Military Justice (commonly referred to as the UCMJ). Second, servicemembers are subject to different procedures and evidentiary rules than are used in civilian criminal and civil courts. . .Enacted in 1951, the UCMJ is a set of federal laws that applies across all branches of the military to all active duty military members, activated National Guard and Reserve members, military academy students, and select civilians serving the military in wartime. . .

Until 2018, the UCMJ did not enumerate domestic violence as a recognized crime, so commanding officers had complete discretion over whether and how to hold perpetrators accountable for it. Charges for instances of domestic violence could range from assault to rape and maiming. In 2018, the UCMJ was amended to formally classify domestic violence as a type of assault. . .

Public outcry for the reform was spurred, in part, by a mass shooting committed by a former member of the Air Force, former airman Devin Kelley, who stormed a small Texas church with an AR-556 and two handguns, killing 26 people and injuring 20 others, making his attack the worst mass shooting in Texas history. Kelley had previously been ejected from the military pursuant to assault convictions for battering his wife and child. The Lautenburg Amendment restricts firearm ownership for individuals with domestic violence convictions, so Kelley should not have been able to possess the firearms used in the shooting. However, because Kelley was convicted under general assault provisions of the UCMJ instead of under a domestic violence statute, civilian authorities were not properly notified of the crimes that would have disqualified him from purchasing firearms.

This tragedy highlighted the importance of communication between military officials and civilian authorities about martial convictions. By creating a UCMJ offense specifically for domestic violence, legislators such as Rep. Jackie Rosen, D-Nev., intended to "close a dangerous loophole" facing military families by highlighting Lautenburg-disqualifying convictions. The legislation passed relatively quickly with bipartisan support and was signed into law on August 13, 2018.

The new domestic violence provision applies to any servicemember who:

1. commits a *violent* offense against a spouse, an intimate partner, or an immediate family member of such a person; or

2. with intent to threaten or intimidate a victim described above, commits *any* UCMJ offense against any person or property; or

3. violates a protective order with intent to threaten and intimidate or commit a violent offense against one of these victims, or

4. Assaults such a victim by strangling or suffocating.

It is important to note that while "domestic abuse" and "domestic violence" are used interchangeably in common parlance, the military draws an important distinction between the terms. The Department of Defense defines "domestic abuse" broadly as:

> (1) domestic violence or (2) a pattern of behavior resulting in emotional/psychological abuse, economic control, and/or interference with personal liberty that is directed toward a person who is:
>
> > A current or former spouse,
> >
> > A person with whom the abuser shares a child in common, or
> >
> > A current or former intimate partner with whom the abuser shares or has shared a common domicile.

. . .Notably, while "domestic abuse" is defined broadly to include emotional as well as physical abuse, the definition's category of victims is drawn narrowly. Nonmarital relationships fall under this definition only if the parties cohabitate or have a child together. Thus, nearly all casual dating relationships are excluded.

Domestic abuse also includes "spousal neglect," which is "withholding or threatening to withhold access to appropriate, medically indicated [sic] health care, nourishment, shelter, clothing, or hygiene where the spouse is incapable of self-care and the abuser is able to provide care or access to care." Unlike domestic violence, domestic abuse is *not* an enumerated offense in the UCMJ. Rather, it is a big-picture pattern that may, but need not, include discrete offenses of domestic violence.

In practice, this distinction is largely irrelevant to battered victims. Domestic abuse victims are eligible for support from the Department of Defense's Family Advocacy Program . . . even if their batterer's behavior does not satisfy the elements of the domestic violence offense. Furthermore, a lack of domestic violence does not foreclose disciplinary action by the military. Abusive servicemembers can still be charged with other offenses under the UCMJ, just as batterers were charged before the 2018 amendment that made domestic violence a discrete offense.

It is important to note that charging decisions under this framework are completely at the discretion of the perpetrator's commanding officer. . .

a. Military Justice Procedures

Military justice procedures fall into two main categories: Non-judicial punishment under Article 15 and judicial punishment in the courts-martial. . . Either of these proceedings may be conducted in tandem with civilian criminal prosecutions or civil cases. . .redundant prosecutions can occur in civilian criminal courts and courts-martial without violating the Constitution's bar on double jeopardy. . .

i. Article 15 Punishment

Article 15 proceedings allow commanding officers to maintain discipline by unilaterally imposing punishments for relatively minor infractions. . . Article 15 cases are imposed and adjudicated entirely at the commander's discretion, meaning a single person has the power to make charging decisions, decide guilt, and impose a sentence. The only procedural checks on the process are the servicemember's right to present favorable evidence to the commanding officer in a hearing and the servicemember's ability to appeal any punishment to the next highest commanding officer. The servicemember cannot subpoena witnesses nor have the evidence against them reviewed by an independent judge or jury. Article 15 proceedings are common because they are easy for commanders to administer and they are expedient; the entire process can take less than ten minutes if the accused servicemember has no rebuttal argument to make to his [or her] commander.

In the domestic violence context, the informality of Article 15 proceedings is a double-edged sword. The loose evidentiary rules and standards of Article 15 cases facilitate a military equivalent of what civilian prosecutors refer to as "victimless prosecutions:" cases against batterers that do not require victim participation. This option overcomes the biggest obstacle civilian prosecutors face in domestic violence cases: "their inability to rely on their star witnesses." Furthermore, while some victims find that testifying against their abusers "establishes at least a little level of self-respect and self-esteem," others may feel revictimized by forced participation. Victims may also fear that cooperating with the prosecution puts them at risk of retaliation by their abuser. Doing away with live victim testimony also circumvents the safety issues of bringing victims and abusers face-to-face in a courthouse. . .Commanders can use Article 15 proceedings to punish behavior that does not fit the criteria of any particular UCMJ offense, which means they can punish even noncriminal emotional abuse. Finally, the expedience of Article 15 proceedings offers an additional victim safety benefit by allowing earlier specific deterrence.

However, the broad discretion and informality inherent in Article 15 proceedings come with dangers as well as benefits. First, there is the issue of commanders' priorities when issuing Article 15 punishments. In theory, commanders' broad discretion in the Article 15 process gives them room to accommodate individual victims' needs. However, officers are not instructed to account for victims' wishes when filing nonjudicial punishment. For example, Army Regulations instruct commanders to "weigh carefully the interests of the Soldier's career against those of the Army to produce and advance only the most qualified personnel for positions of leadership, trust, and responsibility." Furthermore, commanders are to "use nonpunitive measures to the fullest extent to further the efficiency of the command before resorting to nonjudicial punishment" to, among other reasons, "preserve a Soldier's record of service from unnecessary stigma by record of court-martial conviction."

These instructions reveal that the military's priority in the punitive process is keeping their members' records clean whenever possible and rooting out only conduct that could compromise the integrity of its internal operations. Absent from the directed considerations are securing justice for affected civilians or holding offenders accountable. This conclusion is further supported by the Army's instruction that commanders should consider the "age, previous record, maturity, and experience of the offender" when administering punishment. This is bad news for victims of domestic violence,. . .

Second, the looser procedural requirements mean there are fewer checks to stop litigation abuse [by the batterer, e.g., false allegations toward the servicemember]. . . If the batterer is a fellow servicemember, their commanding officer could levy disciplinary actions against them for their deceit and abusive conduct, but there is no remedy in the military against civilian abusers.

Third, servicemembers are strongly deterred from exercising their right to the procedural protections of a court-martial. Servicemembers do have the option to decline an Article 15 proceeding in favor of a more formal court-martial, but few do because the maximum punishments and consequences under a court-martial are exponentially more severe. A servicemember punished in an Article 15 proceeding faces a maximum of 8 days confinement, while a general court-martial may impose up to 200 days confinement and a discharge from the military. Furthermore, a finding of guilt in a court-martial is a federal criminal conviction, while a finding of guilt in an Article 15 case is noted only on internal military records and may in some cases be removed after two years. The steep increase in possible punishments is a powerful incentive for servicemembers to forego the due process protections of a court-martial even if they feel their Article 15 proceeding was unfair.

Courts-Martial

If a servicemember does opt to exercise their right to a formal judicial proceeding, or if their commanding officer feels their conduct is too serious to adjudicate via Article 15, the servicemember will be tried in a court-martial. . .Now, courts-martial have broad power to try cases under both the UCMJ and state laws. Findings of courts-martial can be appealed to the Courts of Criminal Appeals, the intermediate appellate courts of the military justice system, and subsequently, upon the court's discretion, to the U.S. Court of Appeals for the Armed Forces, the highest civilian court that reviews military tribunal decisions. . .

For domestic violence victims, the implications of court-martial trials are similar to the implications of civilian criminal court proceedings. The victim may be subpoenaed under Article 46 to testify under oath in court and they may be cross-examined by the defense. This is a heavy burden to place upon civilian witnesses who are not even subject to the court-martial's jurisdiction. . .

However, unlike in a civilian criminal trial, a finding of guilt in a court martial requires only three-quarters of the panel to vote to convict. The accused servicemember is presumed innocent and the burden is on the prosecution to establish guilt beyond a reasonable doubt. Charges against batterers are limited to criminal offenses and offenses under the UCMJ, so there is less flexibility to hold batterers accountable for nonphysical abuse than there is via nonjudicial punishment. However, given the breadth of the UCMJ, it is still easier to bring charges in the military than in civilian court. . .

III. Reporting Domestic Violence in the Military

Domestic abuse, domestic violence, and sexual assault can be disclosed to the military in two ways: restricted and unrestricted reports. Unrestricted reports will be disclosed to the alleged perpetrator's command and all personnel who have an "official need to know," while restricted reports remain confidential. Both types of reports enable the victim to access support services, but only unrestricted reports can trigger an investigation. The Department of Defense expressly favors unrestricted reporting. However, it recognizes a "fundamental need to provide a confidential disclosure vehicle" in contexts where unrestricted reporting would create a barrier to care for victimized servicemembers or dependents.

There is a common misconception that victims are free to choose whether their case will be restricted or unrestricted. . . the Department of Defense's preference for unrestricted reporting has led it to severely limit the availability of restricted reporting. Only military beneficiaries (servicemembers and their dependents) can restrict their reports; civilian employees/contractors, their family dependents, and unmarried civilian intimate partners are not eligible. . .Further, reports involving child abuse, child neglect, or sexual assault of a minor can never be restricted. Victims can always opt to unrestrict a restricted report, but they cannot rescind the permission to disclose once a report has been unrestricted.

Whether a report will be restricted or unrestricted is determined primarily by to whom the report is made. Reports first made to law enforcement or a military command will always be unrestricted. Only abuse first reported to Family Advocacy Program (FAP) victim advocates, FAP clinicians, or the victim's healthcare providers can be restricted. If someone other than the victim tells a commander about the abuse, an independent investigation will be initiated and the victim will no longer have the option of restricted reporting. . .If an independent investigation is initiated *after* the victim has already made a restricted report, the victim's report will remain confidential, but the investigation will still move forward using external sources of information.

The Department of Defense's policies on restricted reporting are logical given its priorities and mission, but still carry unfortunate implications for victims of domestic violence. The Department of Defense deems domestic violence "an offense against the institutional values of the Military Services of the United States of America." The military has a vested interest in holding its servicemembers to high character standards, especially members in leadership positions. This agenda logically favors unrestricted reports because they allow commanders to root out servicemembers with violent tendencies and mitigate their ability to cause further harm, especially harm to other servicemembers. While the military has an interest in supporting domestic violence victims, its policies indicate that it is trumped by its interest in upholding servicemember integrity and maintaining internal discipline. Outside of the limited context of restricted reporting, victims have no say in whether or not there will be an investigation and subsequent punitive measures. The availability of independent investigations further undermines victim autonomy in determining how their case will be handled.

This approach parallels prosecutorial "no-drop" policies in the civilian criminal system, under which prosecutors "would not dismiss criminal charges in otherwise winnable cases simply because the victim was not interested in, or was even adamantly opposed to, pursuing the case." The rationales are similar as well: punishment, deterrence, and victim safety. Ironically, some proponents of no-drop policies also include victim empowerment as an additional justification. They presume that victims of abuse will derive strength and validation from testifying. This may be true, but it is also possible that being denied a choice in the matter will make victims feel powerless, and that no-drop approaches uphold the penal interest (or military character and fitness standards in this context) at the expense of victim empowerment.

IV. Military Protective Orders

a. Historical Development

Military Protective Orders (MPOs) go hand-in-hand with the above discussion on reporting because issuing an MPO is generally a commander's first step after receiving an unrestricted report. Historically, commanders protected alleged victims of domestic violence by using their general authority to impose conditions on the liberty of servicemembers suspected of committing offenses. They can order pretrial confinement only in extreme cases, but they can take other safety measures like moving the servicemember into the barracks, issuing no-contact orders, and requiring check-ins. Giving commanders unchecked and unguided discretion over how to handle allegations of domestic assault opened the door to a slew of problems for victims, including inconsistency in what safety measures victims could count on receiving.

To rectify this issue, the Department of Defense formalized the format of protective orders via DD Form 2873, a template for protective orders that includes a checklist of suggested conditions. The accompanying Department of Defense instructions provide further guidance to commanders on what to consider in issuing an MPO. Now, the standard format of an MPO covers the facts of the allegations, the existence of any concurrent civilian orders, and whether the commander is imposing conditions of no-contact, restraining orders, relocation, firearm restrictions, or other case-specific conditions.

b. Notice Requirements

An MPO goes into effect when it is issued to the servicemember. Within seven days of issuing an MPO, the servicemember's commander is supposed to notify the appropriate civilian authorities. If the commander chooses to issue a no-contact order, they are required to provide a written copy within 24 hours to the person the servicemember is ordered not to contact. . .there are no enforcement mechanisms to ensure that commanders actually follow this procedure . . .

c. Function and Duration

One of the most striking differences between MPOs and civilian protection orders is that MPOs are "devoid of due process." MPOs are issued by the restricted servicemember's commanding officer without notice to the servicemember and without giving the servicemember an opportunity to contest the order. The issuance of an MPO is purely discretionary and does not hinge on any evidentiary burden; a simple allegation of abuse is enough to trigger one. Another key difference between military and civilian protective orders is that the duration of MPOs is unlimited by definition, while most states offer only short-term protection orders. An MPO will remain in effect until the commander who issued it either chooses to terminate it or issues a replacement order.

The ease of obtaining MPOs makes them ideal for protecting victims in emergency domestic violence situations. Victims are at a heightened risk of violence when they leave their batterers—a phenomenon known as "separation assault"—and the availability of instantaneous protective orders when a victim reports abuse could mitigate this risk. . .The risks inherent in the loose MPO process parallel the risks of the highly discretionary Article 15 process discussed earlier. In a domestic violence situation where the victim is a servicemember, the abuser could use MPOs as a powerful tool to control them. It would take only one false allegation to trigger an MPO that would keep the victim away from their home and children, and the victim would not have an opportunity to dispute the allegation before the order went into effect. As an MPO is technically just an order from the servicemember's command, there is no formal appellate process for servicemembers to dispute them. However, the servicemember is of course free to speak to their commanding officer and advocate for why the order should be changed.

Given that the primary advantages of MPOs seem to be in emergency contexts, it is difficult to justify their unlimited statutory duration. Unlimited protective orders do benefit victims by circumventing the physical and psychological dangers of repeatedly facing their abusers in court. However, the advantages to the victim come with a weighty burden on the offender, and it seems contrary to the fundamental values of American justice to levy such a burden with no due process at all. The due process concerns could be mitigated without sacrificing the viability of MPOs in emergency contexts by implementing a two-tiered approach: MPOs could initially be issued under the same discretionary standard currently in effect, but their duration could be limited. . .

Enforcement

. . .Because MPOs are issued without even a semblance of due process, they would not warrant full-faith-and-credit enforcement in any civilian court. Thus, they are enforceable only within and by the military. Punishments for violating MPOs are highly variable; commanders are supposed to resolve charges of misconduct at the lowest level possible, but they have complete discretion in deciding what that lowest level is. They can choose to take no action at all, they can impose Article 15 proceedings or other nonjudicial punishment, or they can go as far as to invoke a court-martial trial.

V. Punishments for Domestic Violence

Given the military's unique situation as both an employer and an arbiter of justice for servicemembers, it is able to mete out a broader array of punishments than is the civilian justice system, including job-related penalties. Punishments for a finding of domestic violence under the UCMJ include forfeiture of pay, reduction of rank, and dishonorable discharge, as well as confinement and restraining orders. However, punishments for domestic abuse will vary widely based on the type of punishment administered (nonjudicial versus judicial) and the actual charges levied, which may not include the specific charge of domestic violence. Martial punishment is not limited to the sentence of a court-martial or Article 15 proceeding, either; superior officers can, in select situations, levy additional penalties against guilty servicemembers through administrative processes.

a. Additional Administrative Punishments

One of the most severe service-related punishments the military can administer is dropping a service member from the rolls. For officers, being dropped from the rolls entails separation from military service and termination of all rights and benefits under the Uniformed Services Employment and Reemployment Rights Act (USERRA). In 1996, Congress empowered the President to drop from the rolls of the armed forces any officer who:

1. Goes absent without leave for three or more months,

2. Receives and serves a final sentence of at least six months confinement from a court-martial, or

3. Receives a final sentence of incarceration from a civilian court.

Enlisted personnel can be dropped from the rolls as well if they desert for thirty days or more or they are confined by civilian authorities for at least six months. However, they retain their eligibility to all rights and benefits under USERRA when dropped. . .

b. The Lautenberg Amendment

[Title 18 USC section 922 (g)(8) and (g)(9) make it illegal for anyone in the U.S. who is under a restraining order for domestic violence or convicted of a misdemeanor crime of domestic violence, respectively, to possess a firearm in or affecting interstate commerce. Section (g)(8), the restraining order prohibition, has an exception for on-duty law enforcement and military servicemembers. But Section (g)(9), the Lautenberg Amendment, does not, so a misdemeanor domestic violence conviction will end the servicemember's military career.]

Only criminal convictions or findings of guilt with the weight of criminal convictions fall under the Lautenberg Amendment. Thus, guilty verdicts from special and general courts-martial will qualify along with state and federal court convictions, but Article 15 proceedings and summary courts-martial verdicts will not. . .

VI. Family Advocacy Program

The Family Advocacy Program (FAP) provides domestic-violence-related support, both clinical and nonclinical, to servicemembers and their families. The services offered range from victim advocacy and support to offender rehabilitation. FAP offers support for all types of domestic abuse as defined by the Department of Defense, even when there has been no domestic violence. However, the program does limit eligibility based on offender-victim relationship: the two must be spouses, former spouses, or "intimate partners." As mentioned previously, the Department of Defense defines intimate partners as people who share a child, cohabit, or have cohabitated in the past. This is a narrow definition as it excludes all dating and engagement relationships where the partners have not lived together. This exclusion is arbitrary and should be eliminated. . .

VII. Conclusion

Recommendations for reform in martial adjudications of domestic violence center around a common theme: increased victim consideration and protection. Much of this can be accomplished through greater accountability and transparency in martial justice procedures. Commanding officers should be required to keep records of any choices not to levy discipline in potentially abusive scenarios and to note their reasons for inaction. This would promote accountability and ensure a record could accrue if the abuse became a pattern. Additionally, the charging directions discussed should be amended to include victims' safety and wishes as a consideration. Given that civilian victims are not supposed to be under the jurisdiction of the martial justice system, it is fundamentally unfair that it can compel them to testify against their will in quasi-prosecutions. Finally, the MPO process needs to be fortified with more procedural protections. Adapting the process to resemble California's domestic violence restraining order process would mitigate the unfairness of servicemembers being restrained without an order [based in due process]. It would also benefit victims of domestic violence by ensuring they would have an opportunity to advocate for stronger or extended orders, if needed, before an impartial third party.

PAMELA KRAVETZ, WAY OFF BASE: AN ARGUMENT AGAINST INTIMATE PARTNER VIOLENCE CASES IN VETERANS TREATMENT COURTS

4 Veterans Law Rev. 162 (2012)
(citations and footnotes omitted)

INTRODUCTION

Army Spc. Thomas Delgado served as a combat medic in Iraq and earned a Purple Heart when a bomb struck his vehicle. He returned home in December of 2005. On September 24, 2008, several days after his fifth wedding anniversary, Delgado got into an argument with his wife Shayla while under the influence of alcohol and the anti-anxiety medication, Ativan, grabbed a gun and threatened to kill himself. Shayla attempted to wrestle the gun from him and Delgado pursued her, broke her nose and attempted to choke her. Police records indicate that she reported fear that he was "going to kill her or hurt her very badly." Records also indicate that she got away from him and he pursued her again into the bedroom where he attempted to choke her a second time. Prosecutors charged Delgado with first-degree attempted murder, among other charges. Shayla later stated to reporters that Delgado did not intend to harm or kill her, but that she was injured in the struggle over the weapon because her husband was in a suicidal crisis. Delgado's case was considered as one of the very first cases for the new veterans treatment court near Fort Carson, Colorado.

The concept of problem-solving justice is a criminal justice approach that has developed over the past fifteen years to address the underlying issues and conditions that lead to criminal behavior. Court models employing problem-solving theories vary according to the specific issue, but most include practices such as enhanced information collection, increased community involvement, increased collaboration and tailored access to community-based services and resources for the defendant. Domestic violence has been a prominent issue in the problem-solving justice arena. The U.S. Department of Justice Office on Violence Against Women has used various funding streams, particularly the Grants to Encourage Arrest Policies and Enforcement of Protection Orders Program (GTEAP), and the Court Training and Improvements Program to support the development of Domestic Violence and Integrated Domestic Violence Courts with the overarching goals of increasing victim safety through access to victim advocacy, shelter, safety planning and other resources, and also increasing offender accountability through enhanced monitoring and compliance hearings. Additionally, courts targeting veterans as criminal defendants are among the newer developments in the field of problem-solving justice. As a hybrid of drug treatment and mental health court models, veterans treatment courts seek to address the mental health and addiction issues that often stem from the trauma of active combat and that can lead to criminal activity. Rather than pursuing the normal course of a criminal case, the courts focus on providing access to community-based services and rehabilitation, such as substance abuse treatment, vocational training, education, and mentoring.

The intersection of these two issues, domestic violence and veterans affected by trauma, leads to serious safety and ethical concerns when intimate partner violence cases are heard in a veterans court model. Despite the U.S. Department of Justice's support and guidance on the establishment of veterans courts in conjunction with national technical assistance providers such as the National Association of Drug Court Professionals (NADCP), a clear protocol does not exist as to whether intimate partner violence cases should be eligible for entry into veterans courts. This lack of a coherent policy leads to inconsistent treatment of these cases and potentially dangerous situations for domestic violence victims as well as problematic messages to the community about the nature of domestic violence and the proper criminal justice response.

This note argues that intimate partner violence cases are inappropriate for admission into veterans treatment courts for three reasons. First, the courts do not currently have access to professionals with sufficient expertise in both combat-related trauma and domestic violence dynamics to perform adequate assessments to determine the underlying causes of a veteran's violence against his partner. Second, accepting an intimate partner violence case into a veterans court sends the victim and the community problematic messages about the dynamic of domestic violence and the role of the criminal justice system. Finally, the majority of research has shown that substance abuse, mental health and batterers' intervention treatment has limited, if any, effectiveness on recidivism in intimate partner violence cases.

In many ways, the case involving Thomas and Shayla Delgado is a common domestic violence scenario—a violent incident has occurred where a husband has seriously assaulted his wife, the wife's version of events has either gradually or abruptly changed from what she initially reported to law enforcement on the scene, and she is resistant to participating in her husband's prosecution. The case also raises serious questions regarding admitting perpetrators of domestic violence into veterans treatment court programs. Was Thomas' assault a result of the trauma he experienced while serving in Iraq, or is there a history of abuse in his relationship with Shayla prior to his deployment? How is a court expected to be able to make such a determination in a pre-trial and pre-discovery assessment? What has caused Shayla to revise her perception of what occurred? What communication has taken place between Thomas and Shayla since the incident? Given the severity of the incident and of the charges against Thomas, it is alarming that the veterans treatment court near Colorado Springs, Colorado, a program in its infancy, would attempt to take jurisdiction of the case. Fortunately, prosecutors successfully resisted the transfer and the case was handled in a traditional criminal court. However, given the growing trend to expand the scope of veterans treatment court programs to violent offenses generally, and specifically to domestic violence offenses, it is possible that cases like Delgado's could find their way into an ill-equipped veterans treatment court, with potentially dangerous results. * * *

A. Prevalence of Domestic Violence in the Military

Domestic violence is a serious problem that pervades all branches of the U.S. military. Recent studies have shown that the rates of domestic violence in military families may be two to five times the rate in the general population. Victims of domestic violence at the hands of military servicemembers may be at particular risk of injury or death due to the offender's access to firearms and his specialized training in combat and use of weapons. Numerous high profile cases of intimate partner homicides and violence involving military families have been making headlines over the past several years. This heightened awareness has drawn attention to the military's handling of domestic violence and sexual assault by servicemembers. Exact rates of intimate partner violence among military families, like general domestic violence rates overall, are difficult to determine. Congress has generally granted wide discretion to military base commanders to address domestic violence in their ranks and as a result, the military has been largely unaffected by advocacy efforts to prevent and address the issue. From 1998 to 2007, the Department of Defense Family

Advocacy Program received more than 176,000 reports of spousal abuse, 102,754 of which were determined to be substantiated. The data from 1998 through 2005 includes only reports involving married couples. In 2006, the Department of Defense added the category of "intimate partner" to the data collection, which is defined as "a person of the opposite sex with whom the victim shares a child in common, or a person with whom the victim shares or has shared a common domicile." * * *

IV. ALTERNATIVE SOLUTIONS

A. Recommendation for Blanket Exclusion of Intimate Partner Violence Cases from Veterans Treatment Courts

All intimate partner violence cases should be excluded from veterans treatment courts, at least until research has been completed and replicated and evidence-based screening and assessment tools are developed to ensure that the cases that are accepted are truly reflective of the goals and values of veterans court programs—to rehabilitate veterans whose experience of combat trauma has led them to criminal behavior. Intimate partner cases characterized by a power and control dynamic do not appropriately fit those goals. Currently, there is greater societal and individual harm caused by accepting typical intimate partner violence cases into a veterans treatment court than by excluding cases where PTSD or TBI is a factor. In a traditional court setting, the offender will have defense counsel who is able to protect his rights and raise various defenses on his behalf and a fact-finder can determine whether the offender's experience of combat caused his violence. For serious intimate partner violence offenses, the ideal venue is a specialized felony domestic violence court where all indicted domestic violence felonies within a jurisdiction are concentrated into a single docket to be handled by dedicated judges, court staff and prosecutors who receive ongoing training on domestic violence issues and victims have expanded access to counseling, advocacy and other local resources.

Domestic violence cases are of the most difficult to prosecute in any venue. Victims are frequently reluctant to participate in the prosecution, there can be complicated emotional, family, and cultural dynamics involved, evidence can be difficult to obtain, and there are often few witnesses to intimate partner assaults. Like most criminal prosecutions, the vast majority of cases are resolved through plea negotiations and do not go to trial. The purpose of excluding domestic violence cases from veterans treatment courts is not based on the argument that the cases are prosecuted and convictions are obtained with great success in other venues. Rather, accepting intimate partner violence cases into a veterans treatment court model makes difficult and highly volatile situations even worse due to mixed messages about criminal responsibility, emphasis on treatment, and the risk of victim coercion. * * *

[Editor's Note: In Wounds of War: Symposium Edition: The Aftermath of International Conflicts: Veterans Domestic Violence Cases and Veterans Treatment Courts, 37 Nova. L. Rev. 631 (2013), Linda J. Fresneda describes the devastating effects of international deployments on veterans and their families, which can result in PTSD and veterans battering their partners. She calls for more veterans' courts, noting that it is a form of restorative justice in which defendants can have their criminal charges dropped or reduced after completing the program. As the prior article noted, this approach to domestic violence is controversial, as it may allow the abuser to continue contact with the victim/survivor and may be seen as not taking domestic violence seriously. However, ensuring that people with PTSD receive treatment is a good policy, no matter what court handles the case.]

CHAPTER 15

CONFIDENTIALITY AND SAFETY ISSUES, INCLUDING MANDATORY REPORTING OF DOMESTIC VIOLENCE

■ ■ ■

This chapter deals with issues of privacy and confidentiality, which are key to safety for survivors of domestic violence. The legal system has the potential to increase danger to survivors or to decrease this in a variety of ways.

The chapter starts with materials on working with people who have been abused by their partners to assess what level of danger they are in, including a description of a special tool used by police officers responding to domestic violence calls. These are followed by a case in which a judge appropriately used domestic violence lethality factors she had learned about, applying these in deciding to issue a restraining order. Information about crafting safety plans is next. Then come materials regarding identity confidentiality for survivors fleeing domestic violence, including implications of courts publishing case records online. A criminal case deals with whether conversations between domestic violence survivors and trained domestic violence counselors are admissible in court due to the 6th Amendment Confrontation Clause and due process or are confidential based on a state statute.

The next section focuses on cyberstalking and other misuse of technology by batterers, via an article describing ways the Internet of Things can become tools of abuse in intimate partner battering cases and proposing possible solutions to stop this.

The final section in this chapter deals with the policy question whether intimate partner abuse should be reported over the wishes of the survivor, and if so, to whom. An article describes the advantages and dangers of health practitioners reporting suspected domestic violence to law enforcement agencies, and calls for differing responses depending on the level of severity of the abuse. Then come arguments for and against proposed legislation in one state ending mandatory reporting to police of domestic violence by health care practitioners. The chapter ends with a case in which a hospital that discharged a domestic violence survivor to her batterer was found not liable when the batterer killed her shortly afterward, raising issues about client autonomy and what responsibility medical personnel or others have to protect survivors who choose to stay with their abusers.

A. SAFETY ISSUES FOR VICTIMS GENERALLY

JACQUELYN C. CAMPBELL, DANIEL WEBSTER, JANE KOZIOL MCLAIN, CAROLYN REBECCA BLOCK, DORIS CAMPBELL, MARY ANN CURRY, FAYE GARY, JUDITH MCFARLANE, CAROLYN SACHS, PHYLLIS SHARPS, YVONNE ULRICH AND SUSAN A. WILT, ASSESSING RISK FACTORS FOR INTIMATE PARTNER HOMICIDE

250 National Institute for Justice Journal 14 (2003)
(footnotes omitted)

Why does domestic violence turn to murder? Can we measure the risk of death for a battered woman? Which women in abusive relationships are most likely to be killed? One helpful tool for finding answers to these questions is called the Danger Assessment. The series of 15 questions on the Danger Assessment is designed to measure a woman's risk in an abusive relationship.

THE DANGER ASSESSMENT TOOL

The Danger Assessment Tool was developed in 1985 and revised in 1988 [and 2003] after reliability and validity studies were done. Completing the Danger Assessment can help a woman evaluate the degree of danger she faces and consider what she should do next. Practitioners are reminded that the Danger Assessment is meant to be used with a calendar to enhance the accuracy of the battered woman's recall of events. The Danger Assessment can be printed from https://www.dangerassessment.org, which also gives directions regarding permission for use.

[Editor's Note: The 2004 version of the Danger Assessment Tool has been substituted for the one in the article with the approval of Dr. Jacquelyn Campbell. The following version incorporates corrections to the calendar scale 2/3/2010 and the 2019 update, which added strangulation, cutting off breathing, blacking out, and passing out.]

Several risk factors have been associated with increased risk of homicides (murders) of women and men in violent relationships. We cannot predict what will happen in your case, but we would like you to be aware of the danger of homicide in situations of abuse and for you to see how many of the risk factors apply to your situation.

Using the calendar, please mark the approximate dates during the past year when you were abused by your partner or ex-partner. Write on that date how bad the incident was according to the following scale:

1. Slapping, pushing; no injuries and/or lasting pain

2. Punching, kicking; bruises, cuts, and/or continuing pain

3. "Beating up"; severe contusions, burns, broken bones

4. Threat to use weapon; head injury, internal injury, permanent injury, miscarriage, choking (use a © in the date to indicate choking/strangulation/cutting off your breathing—example 4©

5. Use of weapon; wounds from weapon

(If **any** of the descriptions for the higher number apply, use the higher number.)

Mark Yes or No for each of the following. ("He" refers to your husband, partner, ex-husband, ex-partner, or whoever is currently physically hurting you.)

___ 1. Has the physical violence increased in severity or frequency over the past year?

___ 2. Does he own a gun?

___ 3. Have you left him after living together during the past year?

3a. (If have *never* lived with him, check here: ___)

___ 4. Is he unemployed?

___ 5. Has he ever used a weapon against you or threatened you with a lethal weapon? (If yes, was the weapon a gun? check here:___)

___ 6. Does he threaten to kill you?

___ 7. Has he avoided being arrested for domestic violence?

___ 8. Do you have a child that is not his?

___ 9. Has he ever forced you to have sex when you did not wish to do so?

___ 10. Does he ever try to choke/strangle you or cut off your breathing?

10a. (If yes, has he done it more than once or did it make you pass out or black out or make you dizzy? Check here:___)

___ 11. Does he use illegal drugs? By drugs, I mean "uppers" or amphetamines, "meth," speed, angel dust, cocaine, "crack", street drugs or mixtures.

___ 12. Is he an alcoholic or problem drinker?

___ 13. Does he control most or all of your daily activities? For instance: does he tell you who you can be friends with, when you can see your family, how much money you can use, or when you can take the car? (If he tries, but you do not let him, check here: ___)

___ 14. Is he violently and constantly jealous of you? (For instance, does he say, "If I can't have you, no one can."?)

___ 15. Have you ever been beaten by him while you were pregnant? (If you have never been pregnant by him, check here: ___)

___ 16. Has he ever threatened or tried to commit suicide?

___ 17. Does he threaten to harm your children?

___ 18. Do you believe he is capable of killing you?

___ 19. Does he follow or spy on you, leave threatening notes or messages on answering machine, destroy your property, or call you when you don't want him to?

___ 20. Have you ever threatened or tried to commit suicide?

___ Total "Yes" Answers

Thank you. Please talk to your nurse, advocate or counselor about what the Danger Assessment means in terms of your situation.

A team of researchers studied the Danger Assessment and found that despite certain limitations, the tool can with some reliability identify women who may be at risk of being killed by their intimate partners. *[Editor's Note: Due to weighted scoring, after the yes answers are added, extra points are given, as some answers are more indicative of increased risk (e.g. gun possession). The levels of danger include Variable (less than 8), Increased (8–13), Severe (14–17), and Extreme (18+).]* * * * The findings indicate that the Danger Assessment tool can assist in assessing battered women who may be at risk of being killed as well as those who are not.

The study also found that almost half the murdered women studied did not recognize the high level of their risk. Thus, a tool like the Danger Assessment—or another risk assessment process—may assist women (and the professionals who help them) to better understand the potential for danger and the level of their risk.

LIMITATIONS AND CAVEATS

Eighty-three percent of the women who were killed had scores of 4 or higher, but so did almost 40 percent of the women who were not killed. This finding indicates that practitioners can use the Danger Assessment (like all intimate partner violence risk assessment tools) as a guide in the process rather than as a precise actuarial tool.

It also indicates the need for a more precise cutoff score. Perhaps giving greater weight to certain questions, such as those related to guns and threats, could accomplish greater precision.

Cutoff scores should identify those who are at great risk of being killed, not miscategorize women who are not likely to be killed. Both categories are important because if the cutoff score is too high, women in extreme danger may be missed. If the cutoff score is too low, women with a lower risk of being murdered may be scared unnecessarily, and potential perpetrators' liberty may be restricted unfairly. Although finding a realistic cutoff score is difficult, it is crucial and something the researchers will continue to study.

HIGH CORRELATIONS: GUNS AND THREATS TO KILL

Previous studies have looked at the relationship of gun ownership or possession to intimate partner homicide, particularly when the partners live apart. The Danger Assessment study found that women who were threatened or assaulted with a gun or other weapon were 20 times more likely than other women to be murdered. Women whose partners threatened them with murder were 15 times more likely than other women to be killed. When a gun was in the house, an abused woman was 6 times more likely than other abused women to be killed. [Figure 2 omitted]

Although drug abuse or serious alcohol abuse (where the abuser was drunk every day or almost every day) also translates into increased risk and tends to separate batterers from intimate partners who kill, threats to kill, extreme jealousy, attempts to choke, and forced sex present higher risks.

LOW CORRELATION: THREATENED OR ATTEMPTED SUICIDE

Threatened or attempted suicides by either males or females in the study were not found to be predictors of intimate partner homicide. However, there is an increased risk of homicide when the man is suicidal and there has not been any physical abuse. Approximately one-third of the murders studied were homicide-suicides. Further analysis is needed to learn how a man's potential for suicide increases his partner's risk of becoming a homicide-suicide victim.

This study did not examine the risk faced by men of intimate partner homicide when the woman was suicidal, so this factor's weight was not determined. However, since the question of whether a woman is suicidal is important for prevention efforts, the researchers recommend that it remain on the assessment.

THE SAFETY PLAN

In safety planning, an abuser's threats with a weapon or threats to kill should be rated as particularly serious, as should a possible murderer's access to a gun. Thus, the researchers suggest that the legal prohibition against gun ownership for those convicted of domestic violence is especially important to enforce, and any protection order should include firearms search-and-seizure provisions.

However, criminal justice practitioners making decisions about an alleged batterer's bail or sentencing should keep in mind that more than a third of women who had a score of 4 or higher were not murdered. The research showed that only a score of 8 or 9 reliably identified those women who were killed. Thus, while the current cutoff score of 4 suggests the need for great caution and for protective action, it does not reliably identify a woman's risk of death.

ADDENDUM FROM DANGER ASSESSMENT WEBSITE (VISITED 10/23/05)

We have considered carefully the "choking" language (vs. strangulation) and have decided that women are much more likely to respond to the word "choking" as reflecting their experience, although strangulation is a more accurate medical (and criminal justice) term. We have also carefully thought about the women's perceptions issues and have continued to include it in the "do you believe he is capable of killing you" item along with his threats of killing based on our analysis. We also urge people to consider that women's perceptions of threat of reassault, shown to be important in many studies, may be more accurate than their perception of risk of homicide. Only 47% of our femicide victims (according to proxy informants) and more importantly 53% of our attempted femicide victims accurately predicted their risk before the lethal or near lethal event.

[Editor's Notes: 1. In "Suicide and the Danger Assessment: Links Between Suicide, IPV, and Homicide," 24(6) DVR Aug/Sept 2019, p 85, Jill Messing & Jacquelyn Campbell discuss question 20 in the Danger Assessment survey tool, in which the practitioner asks the DV survivor if they have ever felt suicidal or attempted suicide. They note that this is the only question in the survey that is not linked to a higher risk of being killed by the abuser, and it is not included in the weighted scoring.

It is included so that DV advocates can help the survivor create a safety plan that addresses the issue of suicide if it is still a current possibility (e.g., asking if the survivor has a plan and the means to carry it out). The authors found one in five female victims of IPV had threatened or attempted suicide at some point, so it is important to screen all victims for this. They also state that the risk of suicide, attempted suicide, or threats of suicide is twice as high for female African American IPV survivors, higher for survivors who were sexually assaulted or in the greatest danger of being killed by their abusers and may be higher for young women and those with chronic illness or a disabling disease.

2. In a companion article in the same DVR issue, Casey Gwinn and Gael Strack describe the prosecution of an abuser after his wife of 11 years committed suicide. He was charged with depraved heart murder since his abusive actions showed extreme indifference to human life even though he may not have intended this outcome. He was acquitted of murder but convicted of strangulation and sentenced to prison. The authors cite other cases where similar actions result in convictions and stress the importance of timely prosecution for the crimes that precede the suicide to help prevent victims killing themselves. Note that there are also staged suicides of domestic violence victims which are actually murders and need to be investigated carefully.

3. Admissibility of Danger Assessment in Court: See Amanda Hitt and Lynn McLain, Stop The Killing: Potential Courtroom Use Of A Questionnaire That Predicts The Likelihood That A Victim Of Intimate Partner Violence Will Be Murdered By Her Partner, 24 Wis. J. L. Gender & Soc'y 277 (2009), analyzing whether the Danger Assessment tool is admissible in various court settings, depending on the context. According to www.dangerassessment.org, it has been used by advocates to screen high leathality cases for prosecutors and in perpetrators' pre-sentencing reports.]

EDITOR'S SUMMARY, "INFORMING COLLABORATIVE INTERVENTIONS: INTIMATE PARTNER VIOLENCE RISK ASSESSMENT FOR FRONT LINE POLICE OFFICERS" BY JILL THERESA MESSING & JACQUELYN CAMPBELL

10 Policing 328 (2016)

Approximately 30% of women and girls over 14 internationally and 35% of US women are survivors of intimate partner violence (IPV) during their lifetimes, with a quarter of US women reporting severe lifetime IPV. IPV is the single largest risk factor for femicide by a current or former partner, as it happens in 2/3–4/5 of cases prior to the death. About 20–25% of perpetrators of IPV commit most of the severe, repeated abuse, so identifying and intervening with them in particular could prevent a great deal of IPV and femicide.

The Danger Assessment (DA) survey tool was originally designed for a survivor and a trained practitioner to do together to predict intimate partner femicide and severe reassault. The goal is to empower survivors to make decisions to protect themselves. The score is weighted, and results in a finding of variable danger, increased danger, severe danger, or extreme danger.

Collaborative interventions between social service systems and the criminal justice system raise rates of arrest and conviction of IPV offenders, along with increasing survivors' cooperation, trust, and satisfaction with the criminal justice system. These interventions should not inhibit survivor self-determination. Risk assessments are used to decide conditions of release of offenders before trial, perpetrator treatment, prosecution and sentencing.

In the Lethality Assessment Program (LAP), police officers use a short version of the DA called a Lethality Screen or the DA-LE (Danger Assessment for Law Enforcement) which has 11 risk factors to determine the victim-survivor's level of risk for homicide. If the risk is high, the officer offers the victim-survivor a short call with a domestic violence advocate who helps assess the risk and offers services.

The DA-LE was tested in 7 places in Oklahoma over 4 years, based on two contacts with over 500 IPV survivors, 7 months apart. While it is based on the original DA, it includes 2 new questions: a partner's previous attempts to kill the survivor and multiple strangulation. The study found that neither the DA-LE nor the Lethality Screen was perfect in classifying all attempted homicide cases, partly because the survivors engaged in many protective actions—using DV services, obtaining restraining orders, hiding, developing safety plans, etc.—which affected how much danger they were in. But while they were not perfect at identifying risk of attempted femicide, the use of the DA, the DA-LE, or the Lethality Screen may educate abused women about their risks and encourage them to protect themselves, lowering their risk of subsequent violence. Thus, these risk assessments can be preventative as well as predictive. (The authors note that the study spanned only 7 months so it is possible that some of the perpetrators attempted to kill their former partners after the study ended.)

Because they have direct and immediate contact with victim-survivors, police officers are in a position to gather information about risk factors that others in the criminal justice system (e.g., prosecutors, pre-trial services, judges, probation officers) are often unable to obtain, since those others may not be able to speak with victim-survivors. Or if there is a conversation, the victim-survivor may not be forthcoming with information after some time has passed. [Editor's Note: This may be due to the Cycle of Violence, where after the violent incident, the perpetrator is often apologetic, promises to change, tries to win the victim-survivor back, etc. And some victim-survivors do not want to engage with the criminal justice system except in an emergency.]

In the process of training about how to use a risk assessment tool, officers should be taught to inquire about the history of abuse in the relationship and to be aware of the many femicide risk factors besides physical violence, including coercive control. Partnering with DV practitioners in assessing the risk a victim-survivor is in can also be helpful for officers. Cases that are identified as high risk for femicide can be referred to a DV High Risk Team including DV advocates, law enforcement, prosecution, corrections, parole, and probation working collaboratively to identify, review, and act. Victim-survivors who seek services from DV advocates should be given the full DA including the calendar as a collaborative intervention that helps with safety planning.

[Editor's Note: There is also a 48-item Stalking and Harassment Assessment and Risk Profile (SHARP), available at www.stalkingrisk.com. As mentioned previously in this textbook, stalking and IPV often overlap and stalking is one of the predictors of femicide but sometimes the abuse takes the form of stalking, harassment and threats without any physical abuse.]

PETTINGILL V. PETTINGILL

480 S.W.3d 920 (Ky. 2015)
(citations and footnote omitted)

The Jefferson Circuit Court, Family Division, entered a domestic violence order (DVO) against Jeffrey Pettingill. The Court of Appeals affirmed, and we granted discretionary review. On appeal to this Court, Jeffrey argues that he was deprived of a full appellate review and that the family court erroneously relied on "lethality factors" when entering the DVO. For the reasons stated herein, we affirm the opinion of the Court of Appeals.

I. BACKGROUND.

On July 2, 2013, Sara Pettingill filed a domestic violence petition against her husband, Jeffrey. In her petition, Sara alleged that Jeffrey's violent, controlling, and unstable behavior made her fear for her own safety as well as the wellbeing of their minor daughter. She was particularly afraid because she had recently separated from Jeffrey and was seeking a divorce. Specifically, Sara described an incident when Jeffrey became angry and abused the family pet in front of their daughter. Sara also recounted numerous examples of Jeffrey's controlling behavior, including: setting up surveillance cameras inside their home; locking her out of bank accounts; accessing her private email and social media accounts; and breaking her cell phone. Furthermore, Sara indicated that Jeffrey had become mentally unstable and alleged that he: boasted about keeping a firearm in their home even though he was a convicted felon; threatened the life of his ex-wife who had filed domestic violence charges against him in Tennessee; and claimed to be an ex-CIA agent.

Based on Sara's petition, the Jefferson family court entered an emergency protective order (EPO). The Sheriff was originally unable to serve Jeffrey, noting on the summons, "is avoiding, someone told him about paperwork." Nonetheless, Jeffrey did eventually receive notice of the EPO and summons and appeared, represented by counsel, at the scheduled domestic violence hearing on July 11, 2013.

Following that hearing, the family court entered a DVO against Jeffrey on Administrative Office of the Courts (AOC) Form 275.3. In so doing, the court found by a preponderance of the evidence that acts of domestic violence or abuse had occurred and may occur again. For support, the family court noted further findings of fact on its docket sheet:

> [Jeffrey] avoided service, served 7/10/13
>
> The Court finds: 9 out of 12 top lethality factors in intimate partner
>
> 1) [Jeffrey] has abused the family pet;
>
> 2) Cyber stalking [Sara];

3) Threatened the life of his ex-wife in the presence of [Sara];

4) Shown possessive—jealous behavior by monitoring [Sara]'s cell phone;

5) Damaged property ([Sara]'s cell phone) throwing it against the wall;

6) Engaged in rulemaking behaviors including not allowing [Sara] to drive her own car;

7) Has prior felony conviction;

8) Recently purchased a firearm (3/29/13);

9) Recent separation—of the parties places [Sara] at extreme risk of physical harm.

Jeffrey appealed the DVO to the Court of Appeals. Jeffrey argued, *inter alia,* that the family court erred when it took judicial notice of, and based its decision on, the domestic violence lethality factors rather than the standard set forth in Kentucky Revised Statute (KRS) 403.720 and 403.750.

The Court of Appeals disagreed and affirmed the family court's DVO. However, as an initial matter, the Court noted that its review was "severely hampered" by the lack of a complete record, stating that it had not received the video record of the hearing. The Court concluded, however, that it was Jeffrey's duty, as appellant, to ensure the record on appeal was sufficient and that because it could not review the testimony, it must assume the omitted record supported the decision of the family court.

Notwithstanding the incomplete record, the Court of Appeals found that the family court applied the appropriate standard based on the fact that it properly completed the AOC 275.3 standard form. The Court reasoned that the additional findings noted on the docket sheet could not be seen to indicate the family court's disregard of the correct standard nor did the reference to lethality factors render the decision infirm. Furthermore, the Court found no inference by the family court that it was taking judicial notice of any fact and that comparing its findings to the lethality factors did not change the nature or character of the adjudicated facts adduced during the hearing. * * *

II. ANALYSIS.

On appeal to this Court, Jeffrey makes three assignments of error: (1) that he was denied his constitutional right to an appellate review [based on the lack of the video of the hearing]; (2) that the family court erred when it took judicial notice of the lethality factors; and (3) that the court erred when it used the lethality factors as the standard to enter a DVO. We address each argument in turn. * * *

B. Judicial Notice.

As he did before the Court of Appeals, Jeffrey continues to argue that the family court impermissibly took judicial notice of the lethality factors for intimate partner violence. He alleges the factors are not the kind of facts that are the proper subject of judicial notice and that the court did not follow proper procedure set forth in Kentucky Rule of Evidence (KRE) 201 when adopting them. The Court of Appeals found that this argument was without merit, and we agree.

A trial court may take judicial notice of adjudicative facts that are not subject to reasonable dispute. In other words, KRE 201 allows judicial notice to be taken of facts which can be determined from "unimpeachable sources" such as "encyclopedias, calendars, maps, medical and historical treatises, almanacs, and public records." Classic examples of facts taken by judicial notice include the definition of words, the phases of the moon, and reliability of some scientific tests.

Lethality factors or "lethality predictors" for intimate partner violence are not facts but risk factors used by courts, law enforcement, counselors, and social scientists to evaluate the threat of domestic violence between partners. Louise E. Graham and James E. Keller, 15 Kentucky Practice: Domestic Relations Law § 5:13 (West 2014); Symposium, *Death by Intimacy: Risk Factors for Domestic Violence,* 20 Pace L. Rev. 263 (2000). Common factors include: threats of homicide or suicide, or suicide attempts; history of domestic violence and violent criminal conduct; stalking; depression or other mental illness; obsessive attachment to victim; separation of parties; drug or alcohol involvement; possession or access to weapons; abuse of pets; destruction of victim's property; and access to victim and victim's family and other supporters.

We agree with Jeffrey that these factors are not the type of facts that are normally taken by judicial notice, but we also agree with the Court of Appeals that these factors were not taken by judicial notice. The family court's reorganization of facts elicited during the hearing was not done according to judicial notice; all the adjudicative facts were proven through testimony. The list of lethality factors—presumably contained in the court's mind—was judicial knowledge rather than judicial notice. This Court has previously held that judicial knowledge and notice are inherently different and that "[w]hile a resident judge's background knowledge of an area may 'inform the judge's assessment of the historical facts,' the judge may not actually testify in the proceeding or interject facts (excluding facts for which proper judicial notice is taken)." The family court had permissible judicial knowledge of the lethality factors. In other words, the court employed its background knowledge of domestic violence risk factors to inform its judgment as to whether the facts of this case indicated that domestic violence may occur again.

Because no adjudicative facts were taken according to judicial notice, there was no violation of KRE 201.

C. DVO Standard.

Jeffrey also maintains his argument below that the family court erroneously relied on the lethality factors as the standard for issuing the DVO. Jeffrey asserts that KRS 403.750 and 403.720 make up the proper standard.

A court may issue a DVO if, "[f]ollowing the hearing provided for under KRS 403.740 and 403.745, [it] finds from a preponderance of the evidence that an act or acts of domestic violence and abuse [has] occurred and may again occur. . . ." KRS 403.750. " 'Domestic violence and abuse' means physical injury, serious physical injury, sexual abuse, assault, or the infliction of fear of imminent physical injury, serious physical injury, sexual abuse, or assault between family members or members of an unmarried couple." KRS 403.720. Thus, in this case, the family court was required to determine whether, by a preponderance of the evidence, Jeffrey inflicted fear of imminent physical injury, serious physical injury, sexual abuse, or assault and whether fear, injury, abuse, or assault might occur in the future. The court properly made this finding.

Following the hearing, the family court found that Sara had met the burden above and entered a DVO against Jeffrey. To document this order, the court completely and accurately filled out AOC Form 275.3 and, under the "Additional Findings" header, checked the box corresponding to "for [Sara] against [Jeffrey] in that it was established, by a preponderance of the evidence, that an act(s) of domestic violence or abuse occurred and may again occur." To supplement this finding, the family court made further factual findings on its docket sheet, which are recounted above.

We agree with the Court of Appeals that the family court adhered to the proper standard and that its reference to lethality factors does not indicate otherwise. The finding made on AOC Form 275.3 clearly tracks the language of KRS 403.750 and applies the proper standard. Additionally, the reference to lethality factors on the docket sheet does not negate the court's previous finding. The court merely used its judicial knowledge of common risk factors to evaluate whether domestic abuse may occur in the future, as required by the statutory standard. The predictive nature of the standard requires the family court to consider the totality of the circumstances and weigh the risk of future violence against issuing a protective order. In hindsight, perhaps the family court should not have employed social science terminology in describing its analysis; nonetheless, the substance of the court's reasoning was not erroneous. * * *

Noble, J., concurs but would state that "lethality factors" are merely a series of factors often found to have been present after the fact of domestic violence (and certainly not all of them in every case), and as always, a court must exercise independent judgment as to the weight of the presence of any of the factors in the case before it, as such factors have not been normed nor found to be statistically predictive. *[Editor's Note: Actually, as the Campbell article at the beginning of this chapter explains, the factors in the Danger Assessment have been found to be statistically predictive.]*

CORY HERNANDEZ, RECOMMENDATIONS FOR DRAFTING A SAFETY PLAN FOR DOMESTIC VIOLENCE SURVIVORS

(2017)

Your safety, and the safety of your loved ones (such as your children, pets. and other family members who may be living with you), are paramount. This holds true whether you are, or think you are, in an abusive relationship, and even after you have left one. It is good to craft and frequently update a safety plan to suit your evolving needs. Even after leaving an abusive relationship, the abuse may not end; perpetrators may escalate the violence if they feel rejected or without control over you.

If you are in an abusive relationship and currently do not have plans to leave, it is good to consider some important steps you can take to keep yourself and your loved ones safe. If practicable, teach your loved ones, including children, how to call the police in an emergency, or after receiving a signal from you (like a code word or hand signal). If possible, scout out relatively safe places of retreat, in and around your home, for when you feel the abuse is about to start or become especially violent. Have safe escape routes for emergencies, including potentially lethal situations, even if you are not yet ready to fully leave the relationship. Remove from the home, or hide, weapons and potential weapons—or at least be aware of where they are. You may also want to talk with trusted friends, coworkers, family members, or neighbors, who can keep an eye out and intervene or call the police.

If you are considering permanently or temporarily leaving an abusive relationship, create a basic plan for leaving in an emergency situation. Make sure you and your children know the plan or the plans, and have copies on your persons—including especially copies of important phone numbers, escape routes, and maps to safe locations. In some circumstances, to keep everyone safe, you may need to leave without the children or your pets; practice leaving with and without them, and practice leaving via various avenues: plan for all contingencies. Have more than one place in mind for where you can go and safely stay after leaving—such as with a trusted friend, a family member, or a coworker, or at a domestic violence (DV) shelter or a hotel. Check these places' policies on having children (of certain ages and genders) and pets, and have back-up places in case you and your children or pets have to reside separately for a while. If possible, maintain a credit card and/or bank account in only your name.

Maintain a list of important people (and current contact information), including, for instance: your DV advocate; your attorney; your caseworker or social workers from CPS or another governmental agency you interact with (perhaps your welfare worker); your and your loved ones' doctors, counselors, and therapists; your trusted family members, friends, and coworkers; your employers; your and your children's schools (like teachers, counselors, or administrators); and your children's daycare workers or babysitters.

You and your children should keep packed bags, hidden from the perpetrator, for a quick get-away. Include at least some of the following items:

1. Cash, credit/debit cards, and loose change for calling on a payphone;
2. Extra clothing and shoes for you and your children;
3. Cell phone and charger (unless you're afraid of being tracked through it);
4. Printed map with identified safe locations;
5. Keys to your home, car, and workplace, and to your new safe place;
6. Necessary toiletries, medication, and prescriptions;
7. Important personal papers for you and your loved ones, including birth certificates; social security cards; medical, school, and work records; address books; and legal records, including divorce papers, custody and visitation orders, restraining orders, and welfare benefits documents;
8. Immigration papers, including passports, visas, green cards, and work permits;
9. Car information, including driver's license and car registration;
10. Financial records, including bankbooks and checkbooks, mortgage payment books, unpaid bills, and insurance papers;
11. Mementos, including family photos, heirloom jewelry, and things of importance;
12. Children's personal items, such as favorite toys and books;
13. Your updated safety plan, including a list of important contact information; and
14. Anything else you think would be necessary to take in an emergency.

If after you leave temporarily you decide to leave an abusive relationship permanently, your safety plan will need to be updated. For instance, whether or not you think the abuser knows where you now reside, consider changing your locks (which your state may require a landlord to allow for DV victims), upgrading your home security (such as by installing a security gate, stronger doors, smoke detectors, external perimeter lights, or a code security system, which Victims of Crime funds may cover), and telling your trusted neighbors and/or landlord about the abuser and what you would like them to do if they see the abuser, accompanied with a recent photo of the abuser. You should also look into your state's laws on keeping your personal information, like your address, private and confidential (many states have such programs through the Secretary of State office).

If you obtained a restraining order, keep copies of the order and a photo of the abuser with you, and with your children and any other protected parties, your employer, your children's school and/or daycare, your local police department, your DV advocate, your attorney, any support groups you attend (like group counseling for DV survivors, or AA), any other place you go to a lot (such as your school, your place of worship, or a restaurant or cafe you spend a lot of time at), and any other place where your abuser may come (like a trusted friend's or neighbor's place). *Keep track of the abuser's violations of your order*, and consider telling your DV advocate, your attorney, the police, or the court.

Sometimes, even after obtaining a restraining order, you may still have to interact with the abuser. Often this happens in cases with children: the court may order joint mediation, or you may have to see the abuser during custody exchanges. If possible, try seeking separate mediation sessions and supervised exchanges at a safe and neutral location, like a police department or fire station. Work with trusted support persons in your life—like your DV advocate, counselor, friend, family, clergyperson, attorney, or therapist—to develop coping strategies for these interactions, and *keep a list of people you can contact for when you are feeling down or need emotional support*.

Remember: it is best to go over your personal safety plan often—by yourself and with others, like your DV advocate—and keep printed copies of your current plan with you and your loved ones. In addition to 911 for emergencies, a useful resource to know is the National Domestic Violence Hotline (http://www.thehotline.org/ [chat available online]): 1-800-799-7233 (1-800-787-3224 (TTY)).

*[Editor's Note: If you are working with someone who is being abused, ask them for a safe way to contact them. Block your number (*67) before calling. Be careful when leaving messages. Do not leave anything on an answering machine or voicemail if the abuser might hear it. If the abuser answers the phone, do not hang up but ask for the name of someone who does not live there and say it is a wrong number. If the abused person*

answers, ask them if the abuser is present and if it is safe to talk. If the abuser is present, ask yes and no questions. Keep the abused person's contact information confidential. Do not use letterhead when writing to the abused person, unless you know that you are sending it to a safe location. Let the abused person use your computer and phone. Given them referrals to domestic violence resources. Think about your safety as well as your client's and keep your name and contact information from the abuser.]

KRISTEN M. DRISKELL, IDENTITY CONFIDENTIALITY FOR WOMEN FLEEING DOMESTIC VIOLENCE

20 Hastings Women's L. J. 129 (2009)
(citations and footnotes omitted)

I. INTRODUCTION: MOVING IN

Victims of domestic violence who are fleeing their abusers frequently seek to relocate and change their names, their addresses, and their very identities in order to start a new life, free from violence. Helping these women achieve a fresh start presents a new legal problem: How to resolve the conflict between maintaining publicly accessible records and guaranteeing victims' safety by keeping confidential the names, addresses, and other traditionally public records of victims who fear being tracked by their abusers. Legislative concerns about fraudulent use of confidentiality programs and custodial interference by women fleeing with their children in violation of a custody order further complicate an already complex situation and make it nearly impossible to achieve an easy solution. * * *

Given the inefficacy of these measures [restraining orders, suits against police for failure to enforce these orders, mandatory arrest and no-drop prosecution policies sometimes escalating the abuse], escape and establishment of a new identity may be the only way for some victims of domestic violence to break free from the cycle of abuse. But this solution has its shortcomings. As Mary Lou Leary, Executive Director of the National Center for Victims of Crime, reported to the Senate Committee on the Judiciary in 2006:

> Women fleeing domestic violence or stalking may have to leave their job, their community, and their circle of friends to relocate to a safe place. To keep from being traced by a determined perpetrator, a woman might change her name and her Social Security number. Then she finds she no longer has any work or credit history. With a "clean slate" Social Security number, she's unable to get a job or even a volunteer position. She may have trouble registering her children at school. She often can't even get a library card.

Moreover, advancing internet technologies and the release of personal information by government agencies, courts, and corporations make it easier than ever for an abuser to find and continue to abuse his victim. The problem is further compounded if the woman relocates to a new state, where the laws protecting her confidentiality may differ from those of her home state and where she may have to re-register with—and risk exposure by—the new state's agencies and courts.

Domestic violence shelters, family violence clinics, and lawyers have developed innovative ways to protect the confidential information of women fleeing domestic violence. For example, all federally funded domestic violence shelters are legally required to meet minimum standards of confidentiality, and many family violence clinics keep confidential the location of the clinic, itself, as well as the names and addresses of all its clients to prevent abusers from finding their victims. However, when a domestic violence shelter breaches that confidentiality, a victim may have no legal remedy. Additionally, a court may sometimes order a shelter or clinic to reveal the victim's name and address to the other party (sometimes the abuser) in a court proceeding, and thus frustrate the purpose of such a confidentiality policy for a fleeing victim.

Many documents and forums provide public records that place a heavy burden on efforts to maintain confidentiality, including driver's license information (including name, address, birth date, physical description, and any traffic violations in the last seven years), vehicle registration information, voter registration information, property, court cases, arrests, and change-of-address notifications. Although there are some restrictions on who can obtain such information (except in the case of property records and most court records), a savvy internet user or a charismatic individual can easily obtain such information from either the government agency itself or from corporations willing to sell such information for marketing or other purposes. State and federal courts publish court records on the internet where they are accessible through legal search engines and thereby provide the tools for abusers to track their victims to at least a general community, if not to an exact address. Fear of having identifying information published may deter domestic violence victims from filing necessary court cases or registering restraining orders or custody orders if they relocate to a new state. Even something as simple as buying property and filing the record in a state that publishes such records online poses risks to the woman who fears being tracked by her abuser, or may prove deadly for the woman who underestimates the ease of internet searches and the lengths to which her abuser would go to continue the abuse.

Statutory solutions require a careful balancing of the privacy needs of relocated victims of domestic violence and the desirability of free access to public records for political accountability. Many states have address confidentiality programs ("ACP") for survivors of domestic violence, but other states still leave the problem unaddressed. *[Editor's Note: As of 2017, 34 states plus D.C. have such programs.]* Few states address the more complicated problem of interstate relocation or how to register a protective order in a new state while maintaining one's confidentiality, since many states require notice of the registration to the person against whom the protective order is ordered—the abuser.

This Note will address this conflict in legal interests. Part II will explore current legal remedies for a woman seeking to protect her confidentiality, including name change statutes, Public Records exemptions, and ACPs. Part III will briefly examine the additional obstacles a woman fleeing with her children faces, especially when the abuser has custody rights to the children. Part IV will discuss some proposed remedies from the legal community and also make some recommendations for legal reform. The Note concludes that states need to consider a more uniform application of state law combined with an integrated approach to helping victims of domestic violence, particularly those in poverty, relocate to start a new life free from abuse. * * *

V. CONCLUSION: MOVING OUT

Victims of domestic violence who seek to flee their abusers by relocating and changing their identities can find some support in state statutes that allow them to maintain confidentiality. ACPs enacted in thirty-one states have proved a valuable resource for victims of domestic violence. Confidential name change statutes provide an additional tool for fleeing an abuser, although they are in effect in far fewer states. Public Records exemptions continue to promote respect for the confidential needs of the victim. Nonetheless, this area of the law needs significant legal reform. In balancing the important and legitimate governmental interests in public records and limiting fraudulent uses of confidential programs with the important and legitimate desire of a victim of domestic violence to escape abuse, a state reforming its confidentiality laws and policies should keep in mind the very real effects of domestic violence on an individual—effects that include physical bruising, emotional scarring, and even death.

Uniformity of the laws in this area, as well as actual application of such laws in every state, would greatly increase the opportunity for a victim of domestic violence to start a new life. Utilizing existing structures like domestic violence shelters and clinics to promote and implement existing ACPs and name change statutes would help streamline the relocation process for the victim of domestic violence. Lastly, it is important to promote a respect for victims, now survivors, of domestic violence, and encourage them through education and outreach to take advantage of every opportunity available to start a new life.

SAFETY NET, THE NATIONAL SAFE AND STRATEGIC TECHNOLOGY PROJECT AT THE NATIONAL NETWORK TO END DOMESTIC VIOLENCE, PUBLIC & INTERNET ACCESS TO COURT RECORDS: SAFETY & PRIVACY RISKS FOR VICTIMS OF DOMESTIC VIOLENCE & ALL CITIZENS USING THE JUSTICE SYSTEM

www.nnedv.org (2006)(emphases in original)

Publishing to the Web versus Public Access

- Publishing highly sensitive family law and victim cases to the web is invasive and unnecessary. The most vulnerable members of our communities may choose not to use the court system for protection or common court services to protect their privacy.
- Court Transparency and Accountability can be achieved by creating non-invasive public search engines that can be put on a court website—allowing anyone to search for trends in types of cases, dispositions, etc. . . without publishing party names and sensitive details to the world wide web.
- Expensive technology and personnel are needed to redact social security numbers and other information from family and victim court documents. These security and quality assurance measures outweigh potential cost savings for the court.
- Even password protected "subscription" court websites can be linked to one large national search engine and make locating victims easier than ever. Stalkers & batterers will be adept at obtaining subscriptions.
- Sealing a case or filing under a pseudonym may be possible, but difficult in pro se and criminal cases and not sufficient protection for victims.
- There is no public policy purpose of posting victim and witness identities, addresses, and intimate details of DV, SA, and Family Law cases to the Internet. Posting the details of a domestic violence petition or photos from a sexual assault to the web does not support justice and safety for victims.
- Courts should model their policies on ethical privacy practices: including robust notice, choice, accuracy, security, and enforcement—see Fair Information Principles below [not included here].

I. BACKGROUND

State, Local, and Federal Courts are beginning to publish court records to the Internet, providing terminals and kiosks within courthouses, and scanning documents for electronic access. In late 2000, the National Center for State Courts (NCSC) and Justice Management Institute (JMI) began a grant funded project to develop a model policy governing electronic access to court records. The model policy was intended for state systems and local courts to help develop their own policies and guidelines.

The proposed model policy was reframed as "Guidelines" and presented to the Conference of Chief Justices and Conference of State Court Administrators in July 2002 for endorsement. Some state and local courts are planning to adopt the guidelines as such, though the document explicitly outlines complex issues that must be resolved before implementation. The Guidelines are not intended as a template, but rather a discussion guide to help states resolve issues, some which have life and death implications for victims and other vulnerable citizens in our communities.

The newly termed "Guidelines" have few explicit privacy and safety protections and leave much work to local and state jurisdictions to insure the justice system does not further harm victims & others.

The National Network to End Domestic Violence has created this paper to help advocates and allies minimize the danger to victims and other citizens when courts are contemplating publishing records and indexes to the Internet. When courts move beyond allowing paper access to court records, all citizens face increased risk of privacy invasion, identity theft from social security numbers, as well as possible discrimination from allegations in court documents. Victims of domestic violence face possible fatal consequences from common court proceedings such as minor filings and sensitive victim cases becoming web searchable from anywhere in the world.

II. INCREASED BENEFITS WITHOUT HARMING INDIVIDUALS

Courts can meet their mandate to provide access to public records within the court facility, through paper files or on-site kiosks, without increasing harm and privacy invasions for the most vulnerable citizens in the justice system. The primary purpose of the courts is not to publish stories or sell data. If remote access is desired, it can be done without compromising privacy by developing systems that only allow remote access to the parties in a case.

Court accountability can also be accomplished without harming individual privacy and safety by utilizing internal search engines of summary data, without publishing sensitive identifying case information. For example, a database can provide detailed analysis of numbers, types, and dispositions of cases without compromising the privacy of the individual.

Publishing court records to the Internet is a highly complex endeavor and the quality assurance steps required to insure accurate information can be minimized by not posting family law cases and cases with victims, which usually contain highly sensitive information.

III. RISKS TO VICTIMS & OTHER CITIZENS

There are many members of the public who have heightened privacy needs in every interaction with the court such as police officers, witnesses in dangerous crime cases, all children, and many others. Victims of all crimes including domestic violence, sexual assault, and stalking should not be further victimized by the very system that purports to help them find safety and justice. Any court system contemplating publishing some case information or case records to the Internet must consider the potential harm to the most vulnerable citizens.

Existence of a Record on the World Wide Web

The mere existence of a victim's name on a court website could lead a batterer or stalker to a victim's new community, if not exact address. If a victim moves to a new town to start a new life away from a batterer, she might be found if an online court index lists only her name on the Internet. Failing to expressly exclude victim and witness identities from web or remote access will mark these victims and witnesses for continued violence and harassment by the batterer. This encroachment on privacy and the resulting threat to personal safety will discourage victims of domestic violence from seeking protection from their abusers just as it will discourage witnesses from helping to end the violence through their testimony.

Most public filings can give abusers the information they need to track their victims. Posting such filings on the Web increases their utility and accessibility for some, but also increases the chance that victims will be found. For example, if a victim of domestic violence flees her abuser in Virginia, relocates to Texas, buys property, and files her land record with a court that posts such records on the Web, her abuser can find her with a simple, national HTML search. Many of life's most important events involve the court system. In a jurisdiction where the court posts records on the Internet, a victim of domestic violence must weigh the benefits of the activity against the possibility that her attacker will locate her.

Inaccurate Information or Publishing a Case to the Web in Error

Inaccurate information published to the web is frequently impossible to correct. The nature of this publishing medium allows search engines (Google, Yahoo, etc) to index information as soon as it is posted to the web. Even if a court corrects a web posting, the inaccurate information may be found by the search engines for all of perpetuity. There are even archiving sites (www.archive.org) that document and preserve websites even if inaccurate information on a court website is removed or corrected in the future.

Some Records are not Appropriate for Internet Publication

In the past, the content of some court records: health information, details about children, photos of rape victims, and more, would never be published by the courts, and only published by the media if deemed newsworthy and within the bounds of journalism ethics. For this reason alone courts should not publish sensitive case records to the Internet.

Courts must not publish documents relating to civil protection cases to the Internet. In addition, domestic violence cases often spawn divorce proceedings, child custody disputes, and other matters that fall under the larger umbrella of family law.

A court's failure to adequately notify litigants of its information practices would constitute a serious breach of the public trust. The vulnerability of the people it serves and sensitivity of the information it holds only accentuates the courts' duty in this regard. Without robust and clear notice, it is not possible for anyone with heightened privacy needs to make an informed decision whether the court will adequately protect their sensitive information.

It is likely that even most attempts at adequate notice may not reach some of society's most vulnerable members. For immediate safety, victims of violence may feel forced to compromise their long-term privacy and safety needs by using a court that publishes records to the Internet. When courts publish records, adequate notice includes accessible information to assist battered immigrant women, victims with disabilities, and others.

It is entirely likely that the necessary notice will prevent many who desperately need help from using the justice system. Once victims and witnesses learn that the court will publish their information and documents for literally the entire world to see online . . . they may never use the justice system again.

IV. SAFER SOLUTIONS

A. Exclude documents in civil protection matters, family law, domestic violence, sexual assault, and stalking cases from remote or Internet access

- Public vs Published. A court may consider these cases "public" and provide access at a court facility without "publishing" them to the web.
- People who have a need to look at these cases can come into the courthouse for onsite paper or electronic access.
- We do not want young children learning how to search the Internet in school to find their own custody or parent's divorce petitions and allegations on the Internet.

- These cases do not create high volume access in the courthouse such as a large civil class action case that might have many plaintiffs and attorneys wanting remote or Internet access to reduce time at the courthouse. There is a higher likelihood that remote or Internet access would make it more convenient for people misusing this information.

B. Exclude domestic violence & sexual assault victim and witness identities from any public access and online remote access

- Restrict contact information categorically (home address, phone, email) from any public access if at all possible.
- Restrict remote/Internet access to names in domestic violence, sexual assault, stalking, family law, & protection order cases.
- Allow individuals to restrict access to their names in docket listings (since many docket listings are shared widely and being posted to the web).

C. Apply the access principles to all records maintained by the court including non-court records housed in the courthouse

- The Model Guidelines only apply to judicial case records, not all records maintained by court (marriage licenses, land records, etc) however some courts may automatically move to post all records housed by the courts on the Internet. A victim may relocate and need a common record filed at the court—if the land title is posted to the Internet, it will be easily searchable.
- The executive branch may be responsible for nonjudicial records housed in a courthouse (land records, etc). Communities should work with all branches of government to categorically or case-by-case prevent Internet publication.

D. Prevent the disclosure of protected information in web based summary documents or indexes

- Anyone should be able to petition to restrict access in a variety of ways: file under initials or pseudonym, restrict remote or onsite access to a case—docket number could be listed with no name and a note "case restricted or sealed", etc.
- Many court systems are posting to the Internet their docket lists with summary information including name, address, docket number, case disposition, and other summary data. An online docket listing could put a victim at risk of being located by a batterer or stalker.

E. Allow any petitioner to exclude all court records from remote access

- Any citizen should be able to petition the court to restrict access in a variety of ways: file under initials or pseudonym, restrict remote or onsite access to a case—docket number could be listed with no name and a note "case restricted or sealed", only summary information on the web not the actual documents, etc.

- Many citizens including survivors of domestic violence, sexual assault, and stalking may have legitimate concerns about their information being posted by the courts to the Internet. Since the court can choose to provide access within the courthouse, anyone should be able to petition the court to restrict remote access. Since this is not the same as sealing a case completely, a lower standard may apply. (Consult an attorney in your state for legal advice).

F. Information must be protected from the time of request through decision of the court

- If someone petitions the court to either completely seal a case or restrict remote/Internet access (see D. above) their case and all information about it should be protected from the time of the request until a decision is made.

- If the court posts a case to the web while the request to restrict Internet access is pending review, then a victim's privacy and safety could be violated. If there is no protection of the information while a request is being reviewed, than many victims may need to choose to NOT USE THE COURT—for anything.

G. If a court denies a request to seal or restrict remote/Internet access, a victim must be able to remove her court documents without her papers being posted to the Internet. In some cases, victims might have to choose safety and privacy over using the court system

- If a petition to restrict Internet publication is denied, then a victim must have the ability to withdraw her initial filing without her petition to withdraw being posted to the web.

H. Permit local courts to adopt more restrictive access policies than the National Model "Guidelines"

- The February 2002 proposed Model Policy encouraged states to prohibit local courts from having more restrictive access policies than the state uniformly adopts. This is counterproductive in a state where the uniform policy is harmful to victims and a local court is receptive to protecting victim information.

- Local courts should have the latitude to protect the privacy and safety of their constituents. State courts might want to set a minimum level of privacy so that local courts don't post too much information to the Internet, but should not tell local courts that they must post as much private data as a less conscientious court jurisdiction.

I. Provide robust notification of electronic record management to litigants, victims, witnesses, and the community, including victim advocacy groups

- Any court contemplating increasing access to court records MUST provide robust notice on where the records are posted AND also how to restrict access. Many comparable data privacy doctrines require comprehensive notice.
- Some court staff may be hesitant to include notice on how to restrict access for fear that a) all who use the court will petition for restriction and b) witnesses and victims might not participate in hearings if they understand that information about them will be posted to the Internet. This concern is never a valid reason for limited notice.
- Clear signs posted throughout the courthouse could assist in this notice, as could a brochure to give to witnesses when they are called to the court since frequently court administrators do not know witness identities prior to a hearing. Other officers of the court (prosecutors, etc) can also provide comprehensive notice to victims and witnesses.
- Courts should work with local and state victim advocacy groups if they are contemplating increasing access to sensitive court records and data through the Internet or other electronic means. State coalitions and local programs can assist victims in navigating the petitions to restrict access and planning for safety about potential consequences of using court systems that post victim data.
- Also, notice for pro se litigants is critical. There are many pro se litigants without attorneys to explain the courts publication policy. All victims, witnesses, and pro se litigants need effective notice.

J. Include processes for preventing and remedying failures to properly exclude information from public access

- All good technology initiatives include quality assurance and auditing processes. Courts must include a comprehensive and timely process PRIOR to posting any court records into an electronic system connected to the Web.

- Preferably, an outside neutral office should assist or oversee an audit process to check for errors. Random sampling of all cases and checking cases where restrictions to access were granted would help identify if the court is posting information to the Internet in error. State Courts could oversee an audit process of local courts. Alternatively or in addition, an office in the court that is not responsible for the day-to-day management of the electronic court records could oversee an audit.
- Since it can be assumed that errors will occur, a timely remedy process should be developed prior to implementing an electronic system. Depending on the nature of the error (posted a case to the Internet that was not supposed to be posted at all or an error within a court document) the court might want judicial review—however it should be timely. Victim safety and citizen privacy could be compromised by an error and due to Internet Search engines, selling court data in bulk, and Internet Archives, time is of the essence.
- All court staff including judges should be required to participate in training on any electronic system to reduce errors and assist in granting petitioners appropriate restrictions on Internet publication. All court staff should know the process to request a restriction of access and also the process to remedy an error, even if that process is the correct referral to the appropriate staff person.

[Editor's Notes: 1. In "Address Confidentiality and Real Property Records: Safeguarding Interests in Land While Protecting Battered Women," 100 Minn. L. Rev. 2577 (2016), Jonathan Grant notes that the address confidentiality programs currently in effect in 30 states often do not protect the survivor's name in real property records. He also describes problems such as clouds on title that could develop if this situation is not handled properly. While ". . . no state has offered sufficient protection for victims wishing to permanently relocate and start new lives by purchasing a home," and Minnesota's statute needs amending, the author states that its approach is the most comprehensive.

2. In "Protecting Survivors' Right to Vote: Why Voter Information Should Not be Public," Georgetown Journal of Gender and the Law Online, Volume XXII, Issue (2021) https://www.law.georgetown.edu/gender-journal/online/volume-xii-online/protecting -survivors-right-to-vote-why-voter-registration-information-should-not-be-public/, Ida Adibi notes that not all states offer Address Confidentiality Programs (ACP) for DV survivors, and that many survivors and officials in states with this option are unaware of it or the barriers to access it are too onerous. The author states that voter registration rolls are generally open to the general public unless the voter is enrolled in an ACP, and that the rolls contain a great deal of personal information—e.g., home address, party affiliation, and voter history—which abusers can weaponize against survivors. Adibi calls for state or federal statutes limiting public access to personal information in voter rolls. She cites Massachusetts, where names and addresses of voters are not public information, though there are exceptions for political parties, candidates, and ballot question committees. While she states that the Massachusetts statute needs to be strengthened as it can be circumvented, it is a first step toward ensuring that DV survivors and others can safely participate in voting.]

THE PEOPLE OF THE STATE OF COLORADO V. ROBERT R. TURNER, JR.

109 P.3d 639 (Colo. 2005)
(citations and footnotes omitted)

In this original proceeding pursuant to C.A.R. 21, the Alliance Against Domestic Abuse (the "Alliance") seeks reversal of a Chaffee County Court pretrial order compelling the Alliance to provide certain documents under a subpoena duces tecum relating to M.P. The subpoena was issued by the defendant, Robert Turner Jr., who is charged with domestic violence against his girlfriend, M.P. The Alliance moved to quash the subpoena, and the defendant moved to compel production. The county court held an evidentiary hearing, and ultimately ordered the Alliance to produce a broad outline of any assistance provided to M.P. The court reasoned that the victim-advocate privilege set forth in section 13–90–107, C.R.S. (2004) protects only "communications" from the victim to the victim advocate, and not advice or assistance given by the victim advocate in return.

The Alliance petitioned us for issuance of a Rule to Show Cause, which we granted. We now make that Rule absolute. We hold that the victim-advocate privilege attaches to records of assistance provided by the victim advocate because those records are a part of "any communication" made to such advocate by the victim of domestic violence. Accordingly, the defendant has the burden of demonstrating that the victim waived the privilege either expressly or by implication, which he failed to do. Lastly, we reject the defendant's contention that his right to compulsory process and his right to cross-examine witnesses are violated by our construction of the statute.

I. BACKGROUND

On November 20, 2003, the Chaffee County District Attorney brought two domestic violence charges of assault and harassment against Robert Turner, Jr., stemming from allegations that he battered his girlfriend, M.P.

During pretrial discovery, defense counsel discovered that M.P. had contacted the Alliance, a private, non-profit domestic violence victim advocacy center located in Salida, Colorado, in connection with the charges.

On April 14 and 16, 2004, defense counsel served the Alliance with two separate subpoenas duces tecum demanding production of records of M.P.'s contact with the Alliance. The first subpoena required the Alliance to produce "any and all records, notes and files regarding any and all assistance provided to [M.P.]." The second requested the same information "pursuant to [M.P.'s] reports of domestic violence/abuse on or about November 20, 2003 and thereafter."

On April 20, relying on section 13–90–107, the Alliance noted its refusal to comply with the subpoena in a letter to defense counsel. In response, defense counsel filed a Motion to Compel with the county court, arguing that records of assistance provided by the Alliance to M.P. were properly discoverable because the victim-advocate privilege only applies to communications made by a victim of domestic abuse, and not to "assistance" provided by the organization. On April 29, 2004, contending that the plain language and underlying purpose of the statute attaches the privilege to records of assistance provided, the Alliance moved to quash the subpoena.

The county court conducted an evidentiary hearing on May 5, 2004, taking arguments from the defendant and the Alliance on the question of whether the defendant's request for records or reports of the kinds of assistance the Alliance provided M.P. fell within statutorily privileged "communications" made to victim advocates by a victim of domestic violence.

The court agreed with the defendant that the victim-advocate privilege was not intended to protect records of assistance provided by a domestic abuse agency. The court held that although evidence of housing assistance had "marginal relevance," it was nonetheless not protected by the privilege and was therefore discoverable. Although the court did deny the defendant full access to all records of M.P.'s contact with the agency, it nonetheless ordered the Alliance to "provide a broad outline as to the type of assistance," provided to M.P., including for example, "emergency financial assistance."

The Alliance petitioned from that decision and we accepted original jurisdiction.

II. ORIGINAL JURISDICTION

* * * We choose to exercise our original jurisdiction in this case both because the outcome has a significant impact on these parties, and because the question of discoverability of a victim advocate records is an issue of public importance that this court has not previously addressed.

III. ANALYSIS

We are asked to interpret section 13–90–107(1)(k)(I), which reads as follows:

> A victim's advocate shall not be examined as to any communication made to such victim's advocate by a victim of domestic violence, as defined in section 18–6–800.3(1), C.R.S., or a victim of sexual assault, as described in sections 18–3–401 to 18–3–405.5, 18–6–301, and 18–6–302, C.R.S., in person or through the media of written records or reports without the consent of the victim.

The defendant argues that the privilege does not extend to a victim's identity or the nature of the services provided by a victim's advocate organization. In essence, he asserts that the victim-advocate privilege is a one way protection, governing communications, or more precisely, statements made by the victim to the victim's advocate, but not "advice, information, assistance and/or services provided to the victim by a victim's advocate organization."

The Alliance counters that the victim-advocate privilege must be construed to include all communications between the victim and the agency, including records of assistance provided. Any other construction, in the Alliance's view, would weaken the entire purpose and thrust of the statute—namely, the protection of victims of domestic violence from any further abuse.

We agree with the Alliance. We hold that the plain language of the statute must be construed in a manner designed to serve the underlying objective of the privilege. Accordingly, the defendant may not obtain records of any assistance, advice or other communication provided by a victim's advocate unless he demonstrates that the victim has waived the privilege—which burden he has not here met. We also reject the defendant's contention that his right to compulsory process and confrontational rights are violated by our construction of the statute.

A. Nature of Domestic Violence and Need for Privilege

In order to analyze the statute, we must first put it in context. The General Assembly acted around a time when domestic violence had been recognized as a "disease of epidemic proportions eating at the fabric of our society." Domestic violence is defined in Colorado as "an act or threatened act of violence upon a person with whom the actor is or has been involved in an intimate relationship" and includes harassment, injury, control, terrorism or damage to property. Moreover, domestic violence often does not consist of a single incident; it is recognized instead as a continual state of victimization that involves several crimes.

Significantly, for purpose of this case, and contrary to common understanding, most victims of domestic violence attempt to flee from their abusers but are hampered by enormous economic hurdles, particularly if they have minor children. In 1990, the United States Senate Judiciary Committee reported that 50 percent of all homeless women and children were fleeing abuse. Thus, the availability of services provided by domestic violence organizations, including housing assistance and counseling, is essential to helping victims escape from abusers. Near the time the General Assembly promulgated and implemented the 1994 omnibus domestic violence bill, Colorado battered women shelters housed over 6,000 clients. The same year, Colorado shelters turned away almost 8,000 persons escaping abuse. Non-shelter housing assistance furnished by domestic abuse agencies fills the gap where temporary shelter housing might be unavailable.

Domestic violence organizations also help to reduce the economic gap between abuse victims who can and those who cannot afford to secure the services of paid therapists.

Maintaining and handling client records and collecting information from and about victims of domestic violence are a critical function of any victim advocacy program. The disclosure of the victim's residence or location can make the victim accessible to an abuser from whom he or she is hiding.

It is within this unique societal setting that the General Assembly acted to create the victim-advocate privilege. Much like the psychologist-patient privilege, the assumption of confidentiality is essential to fostering trust between the parties to the relationship. * * *

Indeed, we have likewise validated Colorado's psychologist-patient privilege, concluding that the disclosure of confidential counseling communications can cause the victim embarrassment and shame. We have noted in addition, that, although similar, the privilege is even more critical in the counseling context than in the physician-patient arena because a doctor may sometimes treat a patient's physical symptoms without the need for "trust." If victims fear that their abuser may have access to victim impact statements, pre-sentence reports, and compensation files, they are less likely to seek assistance.

Accordingly, having considered the framework of domestic violence and the privilege, we now proceed to examine the parameters of Colorado's statutory victim-advocate privilege and its application to this case.

B. The Victim-Advocate Privilege

The trial court concluded that the privilege does not protect records of assistance offered by the Alliance. We review the trial court order interpreting the victim-advocate privilege de novo. Generally, privileges are creatures of statute and therefore must be strictly construed. Our task is to ascertain the legislative intent, giving effect to the statute's plain meaning.

* * * The statute provides no exceptions and requires no balancing of competing interests.

Furthermore, the statute recognizes the "victim advocate" as a person "[w]hose primary function is to render advice, counsel, or assist victims of domestic violence." Hence, the language anticipates that any number of services rendered by the advocate may be the subject of the victim's communications. Secure housing, for instance, could become the subject of communications made by a victim seeking to hide from an abuser. Assistance provided by the counselor is necessarily intertwined with information transmitted by the victim to the advocate.

The legislative history supports a conclusion that the General Assembly intended a broad construction of "communications." * * *

More importantly, the clear language of the statute extends the privilege so as to prohibit the disclosure of information contained in records or reports, such that "examined" is not a restrictive term making the privilege effective only at trial.

Accordingly, the plain language of the statute leads us to conclude that the privilege extends to services or assistance provided by the agency to the victim.

The defendant's emphasis on the fact that the subpoena was generic and that the trial court ordered the Alliance to provide a sanitized list of the services rendered to the victim does not negate our conclusion. The mere disclosure that the individual received any services violates confidentiality because it implicitly reveals statements made by the victim to the victim's advocate. Disclosing the victim's identity and the nature and extent of the services compounds the error. The statute's legislative history is consistent with this understanding. * * * Senator Wham explained that it was important for victims to know, even before contacting advocacy centers that their communications would be kept confidential. In total, the victim-advocate privileges "reflect the role of [victim advocates] as the last resort from an abusive relationship and underscore the critical importance of anonymity and secrecy" in protecting the victim from further abuse.

Of course, in the face of any privilege, the defendant may still discover records or reports of assistance by demonstrating waiver. At this point in the proceeding, the defendant has made no such showing.

At the hearing before the trial court, the defendant argued that the prosecution's endorsement of an expert who would testify about the cycle of domestic violence and about reasons why a victim might recant effectively waived the privilege. The defendant now renews that argument, which the trial court did not address because it held the privilege inapplicable. The party seeking to overcome the privilege bears the burden of demonstrating that the privilege has been waived. Waiver is a form of consent to disclosure which must be justified by an evidentiary showing of an expressed or implied waiver. It is undisputed that M.P. did not expressly waive the privilege; thus, we must determine from the circumstances of the case whether she waived the victim-advocate privilege by implication.

The mere endorsement of a domestic violence expert—even if such expert is affiliated with the Alliance—cannot operate to waive the privilege. The defendant cites no law and makes no evidentiary showing to the contrary. We reject any suggestion that such an endorsement constitutes an implied waiver.

C. The Defendant's Due Process Argument

We now consider the defendant's argument that the confrontation clause entitles him to a broad cross-examination of witnesses against him, especially concerning their credibility. In support of that proposition, the defendant asserts that his Sixth Amendment right to examine witnesses is furthered by the exercise of his right of compulsory process, entitling him to compel the Alliance to comply with the subpoena duces tecum.

The United States Supreme Court has identified two types of confrontation clause protections afforded the defendant: the right physically to face those who testify against him, and the right to conduct cross-examination. Here, the defendant argues in essence that the Alliance's argument that the privilege protects records of assistance provided the victim interferes with his ability to prepare his defense adequately because he would be hampered in cross-examining the alleged victim by probing her motive and credibility.

* * * In *District Court*, 719 P.2d at 726, we addressed the issue of whether defining the victim's rights under the psychotherapist-patient privilege as absolute interfered with the defendant's right to confront adverse witnesses. * * * We made clear, however, that the defendant's right to cross-examination is not absolute, explaining that under appropriate circumstances, the trial court may limit the defendant's right of confrontation. As we saw it, the defendant's right to cross-examine adverse witnesses must bow to the strong public policy interest in encouraging victims of sexual assaults to obtain meaningful psychotherapy. We reasoned, "The defendant's constitutional right to confrontation is not so pervasive as to place sexual assault victims in the untenable position of requiring them to choose whether to testify against an assailant or retain the statutory right of confidentiality in post-assault psychotherapy records." We implied, however, that had the defendant made a "particularized factual showing in support of his assertion that access to privileged communications of the victim" was necessary for the effective exercise of his right of confrontation, the result would have been different.

A year after our decision in *District Court*, the Supreme Court decided *Pennsylvania v. Ritchie*, 480 U.S. 39 (1987). The Court dealt with the question of whether and to what extent the State's interest in the confidentiality of its investigative files concerning child abuse must yield to the defendant's confrontational rights. * * * The Supreme Court ultimately * * * held that the right to question adverse witnesses does not include the power to require the pretrial disclosure of any and all information that might be useful in contradicting unfavorable testimony. Rather, the Court concluded that "the right is satisfied if defense counsel receives wide latitude at trial to question witnesses."

* * * [T]he Court held that compulsory process obligates the government (which necessarily includes a state-created protective services agency) to turn over exculpatory evidence to the accused. The Court especially noted that the state confidentiality statute at issue unequivocally qualified the privilege, by contemplating "some use of [the agency's] records in judicial proceedings."

* * * Unlike the state statute in *Ritchie*, moreover, our statute defines the privilege without exceptions. * * *

We hold that neither the defendant's right to cross-examine witnesses, nor his right to compulsory process is violated by withholding records of any assistance the Alliance may have provided M.P. * * *

[Editor's Note: In Necessary Third Parties: Multidisciplinary Collaboration and Inadequate Professional Privileges in Domestic Violence Practice, 21 Colum. J. Gender & L. 283 (2001), Professor Jeffrey R. Baker states that as of 2011, 34 states plus the District of Columbia provided specific testimonial privileges for domestic violence victim advocates or sexual assault victim advocates. While the Federal Rules of Evidence do not contain such a privilege, Rule 501 states that federal courts follow state laws regarding privileges.]

B. CYBERSTALKING

MADISON LO, DOMESTIC VIOLENCE VIA THE INTERNET OF THINGS

26(6) Domestic Violence Report 81 (Aug/Sept 2021)

Our increasingly digital society has unique benefits, but it also brings new dangers. One particular risk deserving of greater attention is the misuse of Internet of Things (IoT) devices as tools of domestic violence. This article explains the unique implications of IoT-facilitated abuse and explores current remedies in civil and criminal law. At the same time, it also questions whether existing legal remedies are sufficient and offers several suggestions for reform.

The IoT and IoT-Facilitated Abuse

The Internet of Things (IoT) is an umbrella term describing the network of stand-alone Internet-connected devices that individuals can monitor or control from a remote location. IoT devices are "smart" because of how they share data, allowing them to communicate with other devices through apps or websites and with each other on shared networks. . . IoT devices are popular and encompass a range of technologies including appliances (speakers, refrigerators, TVs), personal items (toys, watches, health trackers, medical devices, glasses, cars), home systems (thermostats, security cameras, doorbells, lighting), home assistants (Amazon Alexa, Google Nest), and more. A 2017 McKinsey report stated that 29 million homes in the United States had smart technology and that the number was growing by 31% each year. Business Insider estimated that the number of IoT-enabled devices worldwide will increase 12% annually, from 27 billion in 2017 to 125 billion in 2030.

As usage of networked devices grows, consumers and businesses have voiced concerns over privacy and security issues such as massive data generation that leaves sensitive information vulnerable to hackers and unwanted data collection by technology companies. However, they have neglected to consider the privacy, security, and safety risks for survivors of domestic violence specifically. Even if designers of IoT devices added security features to protect against third-party intrusion, the devices still assume that all users within a household trust each other to use the devices properly. But in homes where domestic violence occurs, this assumption is dangerous. Abusers could install IoT devices and misuse the features to monitor, harass, threaten, and isolate survivors. They might know the survivors' passwords or at least have a greater chance at guessing them due to knowledge gained during former partnership or cohabitation. Or, they might have insisted that their partner share the passwords during the relationship.

There are limited statistics on the frequency of IoT-facilitated abuse, but empirical research and anecdotal evidence make clear that it is occurring. . . A 2018 New York Times investigation based on interviews with survivors, lawyers, shelter workers, and emergency responders revealed that survivors were experiencing dystopian activity such as air conditioners being remotely switched off, digital front door passcodes being changed every day, and doorbells ringing incessantly without anyone being outside. Additional tactics include boiling a kettle to remind the survivor that the abuser is watching, using smart sensors on doors to check when the survivor leaves the house, controlling smart locks to restrict the survivor's movement, and monitoring the search history of virtual assistants to make sure the survivor is not seeking help.

. . . While court cases regarding IoT-facilitated abuse remain rare compared to informal reports to shelters and help lines, more incidents will likely reach U.S. courts as IoT devices become more prevalent.

Unique Characteristics and Harms

The legal implications of IoT-facilitated abuse include jurisdictional and evidentiary issues. It can be difficult to determine where a survivor can pursue a suit against an abuser who misuses technology because cyberspace has no territorial borders. This would be particularly acute in cases involving IoT devices, which are intended to be controlled remotely. Some courts have taken expansive views of jurisdiction in tech abuse cases: the California Court of Appeal for the Third District held in 2017 that if a person in another state commits an act of domestic violence against someone in California using social media or electronic communications, California courts have jurisdiction to issue a restraining order. Still, the jurisdictional question has not been resolved in an IoT-related case. [Lack of] Evidence can also be a barrier. The National Network to End Domestic Violence (NNEDV) suggests that survivors document suspicious activity on their accounts, such as password changes, and track strange activity in real time by taking videos or recordings. Another option would be for police and prosecutors to publish lists of what evidence is necessary to investigate IoT-facilitated abuse. This would help advocates to work with survivors to document the necessary information for an incident report. However, because IoT-facilitated abuse is non-physical, the evidence may only exist in data that is difficult for the survivor to obtain.

Beyond legal implications, IoT-facilitated abuse exacerbates the harms of other forms of abuse. Broadly, tech abuse endangers survivors by blurring geographic and spatial boundaries, allowing abusers to harass from a distance and deterring survivors from leaving abusive situations because they feel they cannot escape. IoT-facilitated abuse makes this barrier to safety even harder to overcome because the perpetrator's control extends beyond devices to all corners of the home. IoT-facilitated abuse may also accelerate physical violence and make separation, which is already dangerous for survivors, even riskier. A 2002 study found that 68% of femicide victims or attempted femicide survivors experienced stalking in the 12 months before the actual or attempted femicide. Because abusers can use IoT devices to accomplish the same goals as stalking—locating and surveilling survivors—IoT-facilitated abuse could implicate the same dangers. An Australian study found that 100% of survivors abused by an intimate partner reported that tech abuse began or escalated at separation. Similarly, experts warn that uninstalling IoT devices or trying to regain control of accounts can escalate conflict.

Further, survivors know that society will not always believe them if they share their experiences. In cases of IoT-facilitated abuse, the victim-blaming phenomenon might manifest as blaming survivors for sharing too much personal information that could enable others to compromise their devices or being too eager to purchase new technologies. However, advice to stop using IoT devices fails to address the root cause of abuse and may engender additional dangers by forcing survivors to give up access to devices that can increase safety; for example, if the survivor installs a video doorbell to check whether the abuser is at the door. Law enforcement can also contribute to minimization, consciously or not. Survivors of cyberstalking have been told by police to "[c]all us if he shows up," implying a physicality requirement. This minimizes the survivor's fear and fails to protect against technologically advanced forms of violence. Indeed, in the case of IoT-facilitated abuse, a physicality requirement would nullify almost all complaints. . .

Remedies and Suggestions for Reform

. . .1. Civil Remedies: Tort Law and DVROs.

Some tort law claims, such as a claim for intentional infliction of emotional distress (IIED), offer well-suited remedies for survivors of nonphysical violence including IoT-facilitated abuse. However, one issue is that IIED claims only apply to "extreme and outrageous" conduct but using IoT devices is not generally perceived as outrageous—at least not when they are used as intended. Secondly, IoT devices are located primarily in private households, where courts often prefer not to probe, particularly when it comes to emotional rather than physical injuries.

Some states recognize tort claims for stalking via electronic devices. For example, in 1998, the California legislature expanded its civil stalking statute to include threats made through an "electronic communication device," and, in 2014, broadened it to include "implied" threats made "directly, indirectly, or through third parties, by any action, method, device, or means." No IoT case has tested this law yet. While IoT-facilitated abuse likely satisfies the threat element as contact through a "device," it is clear that legislators did not consider networked devices when making these statutory revisions. The statute covers conduct intended to surveil the plaintiff yet defines surveillance as "remaining present outside of the plaintiff's school, place of employment, vehicle, [or] residence." It thus excludes IoT devices, which would be used to surveil from inside the plaintiff's residence. State civil stalking statutes must be reformed to cover indirect surveillance as well as eliminate any physicality and location requirements.

Another civil remedy is the domestic violence restraining order (DVRO). DVROs are common, but research shows that survivors face barriers in obtaining and enforcing them in the context of tech abuse. . . To ensure that survivors of IoT-facilitated abuse can seek DVROs, legislators should clarify that courts have the authority to issue DVROs based on tech abuse and to include provisions requiring the abuser not to interfere with the survivor's IoT devices. To address confusion around scope, courts should include a definition of "contact" within the order that covers indirect contact through electronic and networked devices. Finally, to deter deliberate violations, courts should enforce compliance through contempt or criminal misdemeanor charges.

2. Criminal Remedies.

Stalking is a crime in all 50 states. However, states vary in their responses to addressing cyberstalking: a few states recognize it as a distinct crime; many incorporate elements within their stalking statutes such that the language could be interpreted to include cyberstalking; and some do not address it at all. Overall, state stalking laws must be reformed (i) to remove any physicality and directness requirements that would disqualify claims of IoT-facilitated abuse, and (ii) to explicitly include networked devices as instruments of stalking. Otherwise, even a statute that covers electronic "communications" would fail to include IoT devices, which are used indirectly. "Jackie's Law" in New York provides a potential model. Seeking to address cyberstalking, Jackie's Law amended a section of New York's stalking statute to include GPS tracking within the meaning of "following." Likewise, a statute inclusive of IoT-facilitated stalking could state: " 'Following' shall include the unauthorized tracking of such person's movements or location through the use of 'smart' or internet-connected devices."

If an abuser's actions do not rise to the level of stalking, a survivor also might be able to use criminal harassment laws. To ensure this remedy is available, states must strive to pass anti-harassment laws that adequately account for remote contact, such as unconsented exposure to IoT-controlled ringing doorbells. Existing surveillance laws can provide additional remedies for survivors of IoT-facilitated abuse, particularly because under federal law and most state laws, it is a crime to intercept conversations without one party's knowing consent. IoT-facilitated abuse could also fall under surveillance laws if the abuser uses IoT devices with cameras—e.g., security cameras, video doorbells, or smart home systems powered by mounted iPads—to capture intimate images, video, or audio of the survivor. Finally, if those recordings are intimate in nature and later disseminated, the conduct could fall under so-called "revenge porn" laws.

3. Non-Legal Remedies.

The legal system alone is not sufficient to address IoT-facilitated abuse. As the prior discussion demonstrates, current laws were not created to address the unique implications of IoT-facilitated abuse. While advocates could (and should) argue to courts that these laws apply to the IoT context, they are bound to face counterarguments by opposing parties and are subject to the uncertainty of judicial discretion as to whether the laws apply. Some people argue that legal remedies are inappropriate as remedies for domestic violence entirely. Contact with the legal system can be expensive, traumatizing, and even dangerous for survivors and their communities. . .

Potential nonlegal remedies include digital safety resources, community accountability strategies, and safer design. Existing digital safety resources from the NNEDV and other organizations cover topics such as keeping data confidential, spotting and engaging with networked devices, and securing passwords. All groups who work with survivors should make such resources available, including at shelters, at Family Justice Centers, and prominently on their websites. Community accountability approaches to harm seek safety and accountability within and by communities. Several organizations have applied community-based models to their work. . .As for safer design, makers of IoT devices must consider the implications of their products on survivors, collaborate with advocates to improve protections, and create user guides that address the risks of shared device ecosystems. Reforms might include supporting multi-user accounts, preventing data-sharing between users without consent or notice, and generating weekly reports informing users about [the history of] their logins. . .

C. MEDICAL RESPONSE TO DOMESTIC VIOLENCE, REPORTING TO POLICE

THOMAS L. HAFEMEISTER, IF ALL YOU HAVE IS A HAMMER: SOCIETY'S INEFFECTIVE RESPONSE TO INTIMATE PARTNER VIOLENCE

60 Cath. U. L. Rev. 919 (2011)
(citations and footnotes omitted)

IV. MANDATORY REPORTING

Unlike mandatory reporting of child abuse, mandatory reporting of Intimate Partner Violence (IPV) has been a relatively recent and sporadic addition to state laws. Support for mandatory reporting of IPV has been much more tepid than the relatively strong support for mandatory reporting of child abuse, possibly due to how the victims are perceived. Children are viewed as vulnerable, innocent, and less able to protect themselves from abuse, whereas adult IPV victims are perceived as able to avoid or escape abuse, more capable of making their own choices, and more autonomous. As a result, many policy-makers believe there is less need or justification for establishing mechanisms, such as mandatory reporting of IPV, that effectively insert the state into associated domestic disputes, even when abuse is involved.

The recent trend toward enacting mandatory reporting of IPV began when California first enacted a specific reporting requirement. The California statute requires health practitioners to file a report with local law enforcement when they know or reasonably suspect that a patient is suffering from wounds or physical injuries caused by assaultive or abusive conduct. When California enacted this change, healthcare providers already had to report certain types of injuries—such as those inflicted by a knife, firearm, or other deadly weapon—under existing statutes. The revision, however, specifically encompassed "[a]buse of [a] spouse or cohabitant," as well as "[e]lder abuse," "[c]hild abuse or endangerment," and a number of other assaultive or abusive actions. Like most child-abuse reporting statutes, this law imposes penalties for failing to report abuse and provides individuals with immunity from liability if they comply with the law by filing such a report.

The enactment of this controversial statute sparked opposition from members of the medical community, but received strong support from many law-enforcement groups. The California Medical Association (CMA) voiced concern that the statute, by requiring documentation and reporting of potential domestic violence, placed a significant burden on physicians. The CMA further expressed its view that the statute's immunity clause for medical providers afforded less protection than is generally conferred by child-abuse reporting laws. * * *

Similar laws soon followed in Kentucky, Rhode Island, and Colorado. Notably though, Rhode Island's law only requires such reports for statistical and training purposes and precludes the reporter from including the victim's name. The New York legislature considered similar bills in 1997 and 1999, which required medical professionals to report suspected domestic violence if they had reasonable cause. Ultimately, the legislature did not enact either bill, possibly because of the American Medical Association's (AMA) opposition to mandated physician reporting. Currently, twenty-one states and the District of Columbia explicitly require some type of mandatory reporting of domestic violence. * * *

C. Penalties for Failure to Report and Immunity from Liability

Like child-abuse reporting laws, IPV reporting laws generally impose penalties for a failure to comply with reporting requirements, which include fines, misdemeanor convictions, or both. However, roughly half of the states with direct or indirect mandatory IPV reporting requirements provide immunity from civil liability to mandated reporters who file a report. Such protection is similar to that provided to child abuse reporters. Fifteen of these states require that the report be filed in "good faith" before affording immunity, but four of the fifteen have adopted a presumption of good faith. Only North Dakota provides good-faith immunity for both filing and not filing a report—the other states provide immunity only for the filing of a report or for compliance with the law. Finally, several states whose laws lack an explicit good-faith safe-harbor provision employ alternate protective language, such as: "any person . . . shall be held harmless from any civil liability for his *reasonable compliance*" with the reporting law.

D. To Whom to Report

Whereas child abuse reporting requirements typically mandate that reports be directed to Child Protective Services (CPS) or a comparable social-service agency charged with responding to child abuse and neglect, almost all IPV-related reports must be filed with a law-enforcement agency. * * *

E. Responses to Filed Reports

Unlike child-abuse reporting laws, IPV-related, mandated reporting statutes rarely include a timetable for initiating and completing an investigation of reported IPV. Instead, law-enforcement agencies receiving these reports typically enjoy broad discretion regarding their response. This latitude may reflect lawmakers' greater confidence that a law-enforcement agency, as opposed to a social-services agency, will respond to such reports in a timely manner. However, a recurrent complaint is that law-enforcement officials fail to either take IPV reports seriously or respond promptly. Some officers have asserted that they do not receive sufficient training to prepare them to respond appropriately when they encounter domestic violence. * * *

F. Critique of Mandatory IPV Reporting

Those opposed to IPV reporting laws argue that they may generate frivolous reports (when filing criteria are too broad or the penalties for failing to file are too great) or spurious reports (when reports are used to obtain revenge or leverage following the dissolution of a relationship). Although such concerns seem to be raised less frequently in the context of IPV than in the context of child abuse, inappropriate reporting of IPV does occur. * * *

A second, more frequent criticism of mandatory IPV reporting is that it disempowers victims by limiting their ability to choose how to respond to the abuse. Critics note that women have endured a long history of paternalistic subjugation by a society that presumes them to be incompetent to make their own decisions, and such critics contend that mandatory IPV-reporting laws similarly categorize women as incompetent to decide how to respond to their IPV experiences. They maintain that victims of IPV are not analogous to abused children, who are highly dependent and vulnerable, lack decision-making capacity as a matter of law, and need proactive intervention to ensure prompt delivery of protective services. These critics maintain that IPV constitutes a complex social dynamic, wherein any number of viable reasons could result in victims not seeking intervention; furthermore, they note that a societal response in some instances may actually be harmful to the victims. Although the critics believe protective and social services should be made readily available to IPV victims, they typically oppose the imposition of automatic societal responses, such as mandatory reporting, and favor allowing the victim to direct what response, if any, occurs. Some states have embraced this critique and attempt to provide IPV victims greater control over these situations by allowing them to block otherwise mandatory IPV reports or by requiring their affirmative consent before reports can be filed.

Although not as widely expressed, another criticism of mandatory IPV-reporting laws is that the generated reports may be a relatively ineffective means of redressing IPV because assessing which party instigated the violence can be a difficult (if not impossible) task. * * *

Another critique of mandatory IPV-reporting laws, particularly those that target physicians, is that mandatory reports may lead abusive partners to prevent their victims from obtaining needed medical assistance. Alternatively, victims themselves may avoid seeking medical treatment out of fear that it will result in an IPV report, which may cause them embarrassment, lead to retaliation by their abusive partner, or have other negative effects.

These laws may also adversely impact doctor-patient confidentiality. The AMA's ethical guidelines advocate for complete doctor-patient confidentiality, although they do provide an exception when the law requires disclosure of confidential information. Not surprisingly, a study in California found that fifty-nine percent of primary care and emergency physicians "might not comply with the mandatory reporting law if a patient objected." Some commentators argue that physicians can provide greater assistance to abuse victims by instead encouraging and empowering them to take affirmative steps on their own. A collaborative approach may also enhance victims' trust in their physicians, encouraging them to confide in their doctors.

Finally, some commentators believe that mandatory reporting of IPV "is potentially the most dangerous" state-mandated intervention. One study found that more than half of domestic-violence perpetrators threaten violent retaliation if they are held criminally responsible for their behavior. Not surprisingly, fifty-two percent of women in another survey said they feared mandatory reporting would increase their risk of abuse. Further, this study determined that sixty-seven percent of women would be less willing to tell their physicians about abuse if they knew of mandatory reporting laws.

In addition to the potential danger they pose, mandatory reporting laws may provide little meaningful relief to women in abusive relationships. As many as thirty percent of individuals charged with IPV continue to batter their victims while being prosecuted. Additionally, in one nationwide study of organizations dedicated to redressing domestic violence, eighty-six percent of the respondents believed that police respond to domestic-violence complaints ineffectively; seventy-one percent stated that domestic-violence cases are rarely prosecuted; and forty-two percent claimed that no perpetrator in their county had ever received a jail sentence for domestic violence. Further, the authors of this study determined that only twenty-five to thirty percent of all domestic-violence calls receiving a police response had been reported as required by law.

Despite the many concerns that critics have voiced about the mandatory reporting of IPV, it still has supporters. Proponents typically note two primary justifications for mandatory reporting laws: to remedy significant under-reporting and to identify otherwise difficult-to-detect and dangerous cases of IPV. Whereas the compulsory school enrollment and related mandatory vaccinations of child-abuse victims typically provide opportunities for third parties—such as teachers, other school officials, and doctors—to observe signs of abuse, adult victims of IPV are more easily isolated by their abusers, to the point where they no longer have daily or even weekly contact with third parties who can spot indications of abuse.

Proponents of mandatory reporting maintain that reporting laws promote early intervention and protection of victims, offer counseling and other rehabilitative services to abusive partners to help them control their abusive conduct, help document a history of abuse in anticipation of future prosecution, and enhance data collection and research regarding the nature and causes of IPV. Others argue that mandatory reporting "force[s] state actors to treat crimes against women in the same manner in which they treat other crimes."

Arguably, assertions of misplaced paternalism may be less compelling to the extent that "battered spouse syndrome," or an equivalent impairment, has debilitated the person experiencing IPV. Indeed, increased manifestation of psychiatric disorders, including depression, is reported among some victims of IPV. These victims may be less capable of protecting themselves or looking out for their own interests. As noted, it has been hypothesized that women who experience chronic abuse can develop a condition of "learned helplessness" over time that prevents them from leaving abusive relationships; this condition is commonly referred to as "battered woman syndrome" or, most recently, "battered spouse" or "battered person" syndrome. This syndrome is now widely viewed as a type of post-traumatic stress disorder, and its presence has been cited to defend battered spouses (particularly women) who injure or kill their batterer. Although somewhat controversial when offered as a criminal defense, *[Editor's Note: There is actually no such thing as a "battered spouse defense." Evidence of domestic violence is introduced to address one of the elements of self-defense, duress, specific intent, etc.—see Chapter 13.]* the presence of an IPV-related disabling psychiatric disorder may provide a stronger rationale for mandatory IPV reporting because it can explain a battered partner's failure to leave an abusive relationship and the necessity for intervention.

Relatedly, some argue that the extreme domination some abusive individuals exercise over their victims justifies intervention. Proponents of this line of reasoning assert that the battered intimate partner is essentially a hostage who is isolated from ordinary means of obtaining help, particularly when the victim has dependent children living in the home. Because the abuser may place the victim in a state of helpless isolation by employing extreme isolation measures such as hiding car keys, forcing the victim to remain in the house, and disconnecting the phone line, some believe that reporting laws for IPV are appropriate.

In attempting to resolve this debate, it is important to recall the two basic and relatively distinguishable forms of IPV—patriarchal terrorism and common couple violence—discussed earlier. Social-science research suggests that patriarchal terrorism (more commonly referred to today as "intimate terrorism" or "intimate partner terrorism") is likely to leave victims debilitated, isolated, unable to take steps to protect themselves, and at considerable risk of future harm. In contrast, common couple violence (more frequently referred to as "situational couple violence" today) generally does not leave victims highly vulnerable, subject to escalating violence, incapable of seeking assistance, or in need of medical treatment.

For incidents of intimate partner terrorism, state intervention may be particularly appropriate as a means to protect the victims' well-being. In these cases, the victims (and any children involved) are at great risk because they are unlikely to be able to escape, avoid violence, or otherwise exercise their autonomy. Intervention is typically less imperative for situational couple violence and is more likely to be counterproductive and contrary to the victims' wishes. For situational couple violence, it will generally be inappropriate to employ highly proactive reporting laws that set a series of required investigations and responses in motion.

Although not perfect, medical injuries can be a relatively reliable indicator of intimate partner terrorism. Healthcare providers, particularly those staffing emergency rooms whose medical assistance may be relatively unavoidable, can thus be appropriately charged with reporting this form of IPV. * * * [The author advocates that mental health professionals also be mandated to report IPV, and other professionals should be encouraged but not mandated to make such reports.] *[Editor's Note: While therapists were originally included in the California mandated reporting law, the legislature removed this at the request of organizations representing therapists.]* * * *

The development of screening instruments that can readily and reliably detect intimate partner terrorism when placed in the hands of these professionals [i.e., therapists] is a critical component of imposing this latter reporting requirement. * * * Only when a sufficiently reliable instrument is available should this reporting requirement of a subjective belief of the occurrence of intimate partner terrorism be imposed. *[Editor's Note: See earlier articles about risk assessment tools.]*

Another key question is who should receive mandated reports of intimate partner terrorism. As discussed, almost all IPV-related mandated reports are currently filed with a law-enforcement agency because such agencies can readily target the abusive individual (often by removing this person from the home). * * *

At the same time, to the extent that local law-enforcement officials have proven incapable of adequately and appropriately handling IPV-related mandated reports, the justification for mandated reporting is considerably diminished. * * *

A more difficult issue to address is whether the victim should be allowed to block mandated reporting of IPV-related intimate partner terrorism. As discussed, at least three states allow victims to prevent IPV reports from being filed. But because victims of intimate partner terrorism may be under considerable pressure from their abusive partner to block these reports and may be otherwise unable to protect themselves, allowing these victims to halt mandated filings may be problematic. However, societal intervention over the objection of the person who is the purported beneficiary carries a considerable risk of harm to the victim, and is generally not permitted, absent procedural checks to respect and protect the person's autonomy and dignity. These procedural checks are particularly appropriate for victims of IPV and for individuals with a psychiatric disorder—two populations that have historically experienced deprivations of liberty and subjugations of their rights, ostensibly to promote and protect their interests.

As a result, it seems appropriate for a mandated reporter to first inform the victim (when possible) that a report of intimate partner terrorism is going to be filed, thereby giving the victim an opportunity to refute what appears to be evidence of this type of IPV. However, because batterers who engage in intimate partner terrorism can effectively deny their victims an opportunity to protect themselves, these victims should not be able to block report filings if a mandated reporter remains convinced that intimate partner terrorism is occurring. Further, the mandated reporter should not be expected to provide this notice to the victim if the reporter does not have a reasonable and timely opportunity to meet with the victim alone, or if circumstances exist that place either the victim or the reporter at risk, such as the abuser being present. It is recognized, however, that this scenario may leave mandated reporters in an uncomfortable and delicate situation that leaves them uncertain whether to file these reports; this scenario is particularly likely if the victim steadfastly denies IPV despite strong evidence to the contrary. As a result, it is imperative to devise appropriate screening mechanisms and to protect mandated reporters with good-faith immunity.

Notwithstanding the justifications for implementing mandated reporting of intimate partner terrorism, exclusive reliance on this mechanism in lieu of social services should be avoided. Society, unfortunately, tends to address a range of social ills by relying heavily on law enforcement—a relatively well-funded and preexisting mechanism—notwithstanding that law-enforcement officers and others caution that these extended duties are outside their expertise, may distract them from their established duties, and may leave them unable to accomplish what society expects of them. Mandated IPV reporting to law-enforcement officials should not be viewed as a panacea for combating IPV. Even when officers receive appropriate training for IPV issues, their efforts should be accompanied by a range of services designed to assist the victim, so that responses do not singularly focus on punishing the offender and fail to provide other forms of assistance that may be more productive. Finally, the risks and adverse consequences associated with situational couple violence should not be overlooked, with needed services made readily available to these victims as well. * * *

[Editor's Note re California AB 1028 (introduced in 2023):

Proponents of CA Assembly Bill 1028 favored amending the Penal Code section that currently mandates reporting to law enforcement by medical personnel when they suspect DV that has caused physical injury; instead, such reporting would take place only with the consent of the survivor or if the injuries were caused by a firearm. The proponents argued that contact with the police may be dangerous for some survivors and may make things worse (e.g., sometimes the survivor is wrongly arrested, or the report may lead to deportation of undocumented survivors or their abusers). They cited studies showing that a majority of doctors say they might not report DV without the consent of the patient. They also argued that survivor autonomy should be paramount and that mandatory reporting erodes trust between patients and doctors. They called for connecting survivors of DV and sexual assault to community-based advocates in lieu of police.

A study based on 2462 callers to the National DV Hotline, "The Impact of Mandatory Reporting Laws on Survivors of Intimate Partner Violence: Intersectionality, Help-Seeking, and the Need for Change," by Carrie Lippy, Selima N. Jumarali, Nkiru A. Nnawulezi, Emma Peyton Williams, and Connie Burk (35 J of Fam Viol 255), was published in 2019. The authors notde that in most states medical personnel are mandated to report DV-related injuries or injuries caused by weapons, in some states DV advocates are mandatory reporters of DV, and in some states everyone is mandated to report DV. Findings of the study indicated that for over a third of DV survivors mandatory reporting reduced help-seeking and reports made things worse for most survivors due to retaliation from the abuser and inadequate response from the criminal justice system (e.g., arresting the abuser and jailing them for one night but not prosecuting, removing children from the home, arresting the survivor). On the other hand, one survivor stated that talking to the police helped her see that the situation was more serious than she had thought.

Opponents of AB 1028 argued that there were many cases where DV survivors were so severely injured that they could not communicate or think rationally, or where they were afraid to tell medical personnel what caused their injuries for fear of retaliation from the abuser but they actually wanted help from the criminal justice system. The opponents noted that many DV survivors were so controlled, coerced and isolated by their abusers that they had few opportunities to obtain such help, and that contact with medical personnel may be their only opportunity to get it. The opponents also stated that many times it is the police who bring DV survivors to the hospital, so in those cases the issue of reporting is moot. They also pointed out that if police are called by medical practitioners, the survivor has the right not to speak to the officer(s). The opponents also stated that best practice is for medical personnel to connect DV survivors to community-based advocates at the bedside of the patient whether or not police are involved—these options are not mutually exclusive.

The bill did not receive the necessary votes in the state Senate to reach the Governor in 2023.]

MCSWANE V. BLOOMINGTON HOSPITAL AND HEALTHCARE

916 N.E.2d 906 (Ind. 2009)
(citations and most footnotes omitted)

The estate of a domestic violence victim whose former husband killed her on the way home after she insisted on leaving the hospital with him sued the hospital and the treating physician for her death. The trial court granted summary judgment on the basis of lack of duty and contributory negligence. We affirm.

Facts and Procedural History

* * * On the morning of November 25, 2002, Malia Vandeneede and Monty Vandeneede, divorced but still living together, arrived at the Bloomington Hospital to request treatment for lacerations on Malia's thigh and hand. She told the hospital staff she had been thrown from a horse into a pile of brush. Triage nurse Jennifer Powell examined Malia in Monty's presence. Malia refused to request an examination of the laceration on her thigh, and the larger circumstances (like the fact that Malia's jeans were not torn) led nurse Powell to suspect that she might have been the victim of domestic assault.

At some point when Monty's attention was diverted, Powell used the opportunity to point Malia's attention toward a domestic violence form taped to the desk. Malia shook her head violently, so Powell dropped the issue. She did report the incident to the surgery nurse on duty.

After some x-rays and other tests, hospital staff referred Malia to Dr. Jean Eelma, an orthopedic surgeon who was on call that day. Dr. Eelma examined Malia, who told her that the injury was the product of falling off a horse into a pile of brush. Monty was present during this examination, but not present when Dr. Eelma and a nurse took Malia to surgery.

Malia was in the custody of nurses during the early period of her recovery. Later in the recovery period, staff permitted Monty to join her. Nurse Brian Guzik found Malia "alert and oriented." Dr. Eelma had written Malia a prescription for Darvocet, but Malia requested that the prescription be rewritten for Oxycontin, saying that Darvocet would not work. Guzik called Dr. Eelma to report Malia's request, as well as Malia's statement that if Eelma would not change the prescription she knew a Dr. Nienevor who would. Eelma did in fact decline, so nurse Guzik called Dr. Nienevor, who likewise refused to prescribe Oxycontin, and Malia then accepted the prescription for Darvocet.

While Malia was still in recovery, her mother Ava McSwane arrived at the hospital and informed a nurse that she believed her daughter had not been in a horse accident at all but rather that Monty had assaulted her with a fireplace poker. After some consultation, Ava McSwane called the State Police, the Monroe County Sheriff's Department, the Owen County Sheriff's Department, and hospital security. None of the law enforcement agencies responded.

In the meantime, Malia was preparing for release from the hospital, telling nurse Guzik that she was ready to go home. As Guzik, Monty, and Malia left the surgery area, two security guards asked Monty to join them in a nearby hallway, where they conducted a search for weapons and a sobriety test. These were both negative.

As Malia was being wheeled out of the hospital, nurse Jennifer Perantoni told her that she need not depart with Monty. Malia's mother pleaded with her not to leave with Monty. Malia responded in no uncertain terms that she wanted to leave with Monty. "Stay out of our business," she said.

Malia and Monty drove away together. They had gone but a few blocks when Monty shot Malia twice, killing her, and then killed himself as well.

McSwane filed a complaint for medical malpractice on behalf of Malia's estate and on behalf of her daughter against Bloomington Hospital and Dr. Eelma. The complaint alleges that the defendants permitted Malia to leave the hospital in the custody of Monty even though they had information suggesting the possibility of further violence. The defendants sought a preliminary determination of law in the Monroe Circuit Court, in the nature of summary judgment. The estate filed a cross-motion for summary judgment.

The trial court granted judgment for the defendants, and they appealed. A divided Indiana Court of Appeals reversed. We granted transfer. * * *

Medical Providers and Domestic Violence

As counsel for McSwane properly observes, the elements of a claim for medical malpractice are the same as for any other claim for negligence. The claimant must show that the defendant owed her a duty of care at the time the injury occurred, that the defendant's behavior did not conform to that standard of care, and that the claimant's injuries were proximately caused by the breach. While the existence of a duty is regarded as a matter of law, summary judgment based on application of law to particular facts is rarely suitable.

The parties have largely argued this appeal based on the trial court's finding that there was no duty and that the claim is barred by contributory negligence. McSwane argues that a duty existed on three grounds: that the hospital had assumed a duty to its patients, that the possibility of injury was foreseeable, and that public policy supports legal imposition of a duty.

The hospital has argued that its duty to McSwane did not extend to protecting her from harm caused by Monty off its premises. It counters McSwane's argument about assumption of duty, which rests on the hospital's implementation of an internal domestic violence policy, by noting that there is no indication McSwane relied upon or knew about its policy. It cites the downside of imposing duties based on an actor's adoption of protocols designed to protect patrons, namely, the risk that doing so will discourage adoption of prophylactic measures.

The parties' debate over assumed duty seems unnecessary. It is straightforward enough to say that a hospital's duty of care to a patient who presents observable signs of domestic abuse includes some reasonable measures to address the patient's risk. The hospital in this instance took several such actions, including direct suggestions that abuse might be the cause, providing a chance to so indicate outside the earshot of the abuser, security examinations of the suspected abuser, facilitating telephone calls to law enforcement, and declarations that Malia need not leave the hospital with him.

While counsel for McSwane argues that the hospital's failure to separate its patient from her ex-husband so that she could safely report his attack, the record reflects that the hospital did keep them apart on multiple occasions. While counsel does not suggest that the hospital should have physically restrained Malia from leaving the building, it appears plain that little short of that would have kept her from leaving with Monty. Holding that the hospital's duty encompassed such measures obviously bumps right up against patient autonomy and informed consent, two touchstones of medical malpractice law.

While the parties and the trial court have analyzed this aspect of the case through debate over extent of duty, it might just as well be analyzed by asking whether the hospital, construing the facts favorably to McSwane, has succeeded in demonstrating that it did not breach its duty, a burden rarely but occasionally met as a matter of law. Considered as whether the hospital's duty extended to off-premises activities or as whether it breached its duty by assenting to Malia's insistence on departing, the trial court was correct to grant judgment for the hospital.[1]

Contributory Negligence

In 1986, the General Assembly altered Indiana's common law by adopting comparative fault as the general rule for negligence actions. The legislature specifically excluded from this alteration actions against qualified healthcare providers for medical negligence, leaving in place contributory negligence for this and certain other claims.

A plaintiff's contributory negligence operates as a complete bar to recovery. While a plaintiff whose own negligence may have contributed as much as 49 percent to her injury may recover under comparative fault from a defendant whose acts provided 51 percent, under contributory negligence a claimant whose own negligence was even slightly causal is barred from recovery. A court should find a plaintiff contributorily negligent if her conduct falls below the standard to which she is required to conform for her own protection. A patient's failure to provide accurate diagnosing information or failure to seek recommended treatment are examples of such contributory negligence. The question of contributory negligence is a question of law for the court when only one reasonable inference or conclusion can be drawn from the evidence.

Counsel for McSwane contends that having received anesthetic and pain medications Malia could not be contributorily negligent as a matter of law. The materials the hospital tendered on summary judgment describe Malia as "alert and oriented" even during her recovery period. Nurse Guzik said Malia was "very aware [of] what was going on. . . . I mean she followed commands very well. Ask her a question, she'd answer appropriately." The surgeon's conclusion about the debate over pain medication was that Malia "was a person in my opinion that probably was very capable of making her own decisions." Counsel for McSwane does not point to any facts that actually contradict this assessment.

---

1 McSwane's central contention about the treating physician was that she failed to report the suspected abuse, relying on Ind.Code § 35–47–7–1. As the Court of Appeals' majority noted, this contention was not made in the trial court and thus is not available on appeal. Counsel does not present any other contentions about Dr. Eelma except those that are congruent with claims about the hospital. Eelma thus prevails.

While negligence is generally a question for the finder of fact, where the evidence permits only a single inference, contributory negligence may be a matter of law for the court. The trial court found that Malia's insistence on leaving with Monty in the face of offers by hospital staff and pleas by her own mother was negligence that contributed to her injury. This was not error.

Conclusion

We affirm the judgment of the trial court.

RUCKER, J., dissenting.

I agree with the majority that "a hospital's duty of care to a patient who presents observable signs of domestic abuse includes some reasonable measures to address the patient's risk." Although the existence of duty is a matter of law for the courts to decide, a breach of duty is usually a matter left to the trier of fact. Only where the facts are undisputed and lead to but a single inference or conclusion may the court as a matter of law determine whether a breach of duty has occurred. Unlike the majority however I do not believe the question of breach in this case can be determined as a matter of law.

The record establishes a lack of communication about suspected domestic abuse between the ER staff and the treating emergency room physician. Although the triage nurse indicated she informed a charge nurse of her suspicions, the record is void of any evidence of an emergency room charge nurse taking any action or informing the treating physician. The fact that the attending physician states that he was not informed of the suspected domestic abuse indicates that the emergency room support staff did not follow the hospital's adopted domestic violence policies, which requires such communication from staff to the treating physician. This concern is amplified because the attending physician was able to spend time alone with Malia before she was heavily medicated and while the "husband" was out of the exam room. Thus the doctor, had he been properly informed, could have asked appropriate questions regarding domestic abuse during that period, which could have given the patient a reasonable opportunity to seek refuge.

In sum, the facts in this case raise genuine issues as to whether the hospital breached its duty of care by, among other things, discharging a patient to the custody of a suspected abuser. This is not a matter that can be resolved by summary disposition.

I also disagree with the majority's determination that Malia was contributorily negligent as a matter of law. It is of course the case that in a contributory negligence regime any negligence on the part of the plaintiff, no matter how slight, will bar any action for damages. But contributory negligence is generally a question of fact that is not appropriate for summary judgment if there are conflicting factual inferences to be drawn from the designated evidence. As the majority correctly declares "the question of contributory negligence is a question of law for the court when only one reasonable inference or conclusion can be drawn from the evidence." In this case the majority apparently is of the view that because there was evidence that Malia was "alert and oriented" during her period of recovery, "very aware [of] what was going on" and was "capable of making her own decisions," op. at 911, she was negligent in some degree and thus the trial court properly granted summary judgment in favor of the Hospital. But summary judgment is rarely appropriate in negligence actions. And this is so because "negligence cases are particularly fact sensitive and are governed by a standard of the objective reasonable person—one best applied by a jury after hearing all of the evidence."

The medical records indicate that, while Malia was present in the emergency room, she received numerous drugs, including Phenergan and the narcotic analgesic Dilaudid to control her pain. It was determined that Malia required general surgery to repair her injuries, which was done in an operating room under general anesthesia, with full intubation. Malia was rendered medically unconscious for over one hour and then given numerous medications, one of which was 10 milligrams of morphine (a narcotic analgesic) for post-operative pain. Although the record indicates that Malia was thereafter alert and oriented, it is unclear what her true decision-making capabilities and mental state were at the time of discharge. Furthermore, from the record before us it appears that Malia was discharged from the hospital approximately 90 minutes after the surgery was completed, which leaves open the likelihood that the she had not fully recovered from the general anesthesia and was thus mentally and/or physically incapable of reasonable decision making, or self-protection, when allowed to leave the hospital.

This Court has held:

> The general rule on the issue of the plaintiff's contributory negligence is that the plaintiff must exercise that degree of care that an ordinary reasonable [person] would exercise in like or similar circumstances. . . . We hold that a departure from the general rule is required where the plaintiff is suffering from physical infirmities which impair [her] ability to function as an "ordinary reasonable [person]." The proper test to be applied in such cases is the test of a reasonable [person] *under the same disabilities and infirmities* in like circumstances. On the issue of contributory negligence, mental condition and/or physical incapacities are factors to be considered.

It is clear to me there are different factual inferences that may be drawn from the evidence concerning Malia's mental, emotional, and physical condition. Thus, a fact-finder should determine whether having received general anesthetic, a relaxant, numerous doses of various opiates for pain, and being advised by Hospital not to make any important decisions, Malia was exercising that degree of care that a reasonable person under the same or similar condition would have been expected to exercise when she decided to leave the hospital with her former husband. This is not in my view a matter that can be disposed of by summary disposition. For the foregoing reasons I respectfully dissent and would reverse the judgment of the trial court.

[Editor's Note: It is not only the medical system that grapples with the issue of reporting intimate partner abuse to law enforcement. In "Mandatory Reporting of Campus Sexual Assault and Domestic Violence: Moving to a Victim-Centric Protocol that Comports with Federal Law," 24 Temp. Pol. & Civ. Rts L. Rev. 401 (2015), Professor Jill Engle discusses the policies and practices that colleges should adopt for faculty reporting when students disclose they are being abused, to comply with federal law while still remaining sensitive to victim needs.]

CHAPTER 16

FINANCIAL, EMPLOYMENT, AND HOUSING ISSUES AFFECTING SURVIVORS OF DOMESTIC VIOLENCE

■ ■ ■

This chapter looks at financial, employment, and housing issues affecting survivors of domestic violence. These economic issues, key to the survival of victims and their children, raise many legal questions.

The chapter starts with a statement that domestic violence policy needs to work for poor women of color, i.e., that this needs to be the yardstick against which any proposed changes are measured. This is followed by an article outlining the history of welfare law, explaining why public benefits are key for those escaping domestic violence, examining how the Family Violence Option is working, and calling for major reforms. A new article describes the role of consumer credit in domestic violence cases, explaining that coerced debt is another tactic used by abusers to control their victims and offering possible solutions to this problem.

The second section of the chapter focuses on survivors of domestic violence as workers. A commentator describes how batterers frequently interfere with their partners' employment, leading to an epidemic of workplace violence and even homicide, and how workplace injunctions can be utilized to help stop this. Next is a short checklist of recommended employment-related protections for survivors of abuse. A case illustrates the right in some jurisdictions to collect unemployment benefits if the survivor is no longer working due to domestic violence. The section ends with a federal case holding an employer not liable when an employee is murdered at work by her former fiance.

The last section looks at tenancy issues faced by victims of domestic violence. A commentator describes how nuisance ordinances, zero tolerance for violence policies, and the right to quiet enjoyment of one's residence often lead to eviction of domestic violence survivors. The author describes various federal, state, and municipal laws designed to protect domestic violence survivors' housing. The next piece outlines the federal guidelines on application of the Fair Housing Act in domestic violence cases, providing that landlords participating in HUD programs have an affirmative obligation to further fair housing policies, as well as refraining from discriminating against survivors of abuse. Then comes a case in which a husband assaulted his wife, then lost his Section 8 voucher; the appellate court held that if the holder of a Section 8 voucher is terminated, the remaining tenant (in this case the wife) must have the opportunity to establish eligibility to receive the voucher. Finally, a case of first impression construes a recently enacted state law creating the affirmative defense in unlawful detainer evictions that "a landlord shall not terminate a tenancy . . . based upon an act or acts against a tenant . . . that constitute domestic violence." The appellate court held that the trial court erred in refusing to allow the jury to consider the tenant's evidence of abuse, and reversed the eviction order.

A. FINANCIAL ISSUES

DONNA COKER, SHIFTING POWER FOR BATTERED WOMEN: LAW, MATERIAL RESOURCES, AND POOR WOMEN OF COLOR

33 U.C. Davis L. Rev. 1009 (2000)
(citations and footnotes omitted)

LatCrit [Latino Critical Race] Theory invites scholarship that centers the experiences of Latinas/os while tying those experiences to the project of social justice for all. This Essay treats as central the experiences of Latinas and other women of color who are battered by intimate partners and suggests a test for evaluating anti-domestic violence measures that builds on those experiences. I argue that every domestic violence intervention strategy should be subjected to a material resources test. This means that in every area of anti-domestic violence law and policy, whether it be determining funding priorities, analyzing appropriate criminal law or arrest policies, developing city ordinances or drafting administrative rules, priority should be given to those laws and policies which improve women's access to material resources. Further, because women's circumstances differ in ways that dramatically affect their access to material resources, the standard for determining the impact on material resources should be the situation of women in the greatest need who are most dramatically affected by inequalities of gender, race, and class. In other words, poor women and, in most circumstances, poor women of color should provide the standard of measurement.

My proposal will not radically reshape structures of racism, sexism, heterosexism, and economic inequality that increase women's vulnerability and limit their responses to violence. Battered women can make few positive claims for material resources because there are few positive claims available for poor people, generally. Rather, in a negative rights world with inadequate and often punitive social services and dramatic inequalities, this proposal is a limited countermeasure designed to increase wherever possible the chances of strengthening women's autonomy. The test is remedial, not revolutionary, but it provides a way to distinguish between different strategies in a manner that accounts for the different material and social conditions that face battered women.

Domestic violence laws and policies may directly provide women with material resources such as housing, food, clothing, or money, or they may increase resources indirectly through the availability of services such as job training, childcare, and transportation. The material resources test requires first that priority be given to those programs, laws, or policies that provide women with direct aid. Second, even when the primary goal of an intervention strategy is not the allocation of material resources, we should prefer methods of implementation that are likely to, directly or indirectly, improve women's access to material resources. Further, we should usually prefer local assessment of the impact of law and policy on women's material resources over universal assessments because the impact of a policy will always be mediated by the particular conditions facing women in a given locale. We should always prefer assessment that is informed by the circumstances of those women who are in the greatest need. In most circumstances this will be poor women of color who are sandwiched by their heightened vulnerability to battering, on the one hand, and their heightened vulnerability to intrusive state control, on the other. Strategies that increase material resources for poor women of color are likely to benefit—or at least not harm—other battered women in the same locale.

* * *

Throughout this Essay, I examine the particular circumstances for Latinas who are battered. I do this to underscore two related points. First, the use of women of color as the standard by which to apply a materials resource test could operate to create an essential "women of color" category that masks important differences that affect the material resources analysis. The literature on battered Latinas illustrates the importance of such differences as immigration status, migration experiences, language, and culture in understanding battered women's experiences. Second, a focus on Latinas also highlights the serious inattention given the study of battered women of color, in general, and Latinas in specific.

I. MATERIAL RESOURCES, DOMESTIC VIOLENCE, AND POOR WOMEN OF COLOR

A. Class, Race, Ethnicity, and Safety in Anti-Domestic Violence Discourse and Law

The material resources test provides a means of operationalizing the feminist goal of empowering battered women through addressing four problems of current domestic violence intervention strategies. The first problem is the tendency to ignore or undervalue the significance of race or ethnicity in shaping the efficacy of universal intervention strategies. A focus on material resources forces an assessment of the impact of intersections of class, immigrant status, race, ethnicity, and gender because these factors will determine the degree to which a policy or law is likely to increase material resources for the women affected.

The second problem with many current domestic violence laws and services is the tendency to ignore the importance of women's economic subordination in their vulnerability to battering. An unstated norm for battered women—those that are white and nonpoor—is created when a policy or law ignores the relationship of poverty to violence and fails to account for racial differences in battered women's experiences. Influenced by the range of services that state and federal funders would pay for, it is this normative client image that is instrumental in constructing battered women's need as primarily psychological, rather than material. Kimberlé Crenshaw's story of the Latina, refused shelter because she was a monolingual Spanish speaker and could not participate in the shelter's English-only support groups, is an extreme example of the devastating effects of this psychological focus.

The third problem a focus on material resources counters is the trend to develop increasingly punitive criminal measures against batterers without evidence that these measures improve the well being of victims. This uncritical resort to increasing criminal sanctions serves to hide the social and political conditions that foster battering. For example, the County Commission in Miami-Dade, Florida enacted an ordinance in 1999 that, among other provisions, requires the clerk of the court to notify the employer of anyone convicted of a domestic violence offense. The sponsors of the legislation argued that "it sends a message," but regardless of the intended message, the result was direct and predictable harm for poor women of color. Professional men are not likely to lose their jobs if their boss is notified of a misdemeanor conviction, but men working in low skill jobs, where men of color are disproportionately represented, are likely to be fired. The ordinance takes money directly from poor women and their children by diminishing their possibility for receiving child support. The ordinance probably increases women's danger, as well, since unemployed men may be more likely to engage in repeat violence.

* * *

The fourth problem with anti-domestic violence discourse and law is the pervasive presumption that women should leave battering partners and that doing so will increase their safety. This presumption that separation equals safety is dangerous for women, and particularly so for poor women of color. First, the safety that presumptively flows from separation is largely fictive for poor women. Women with sufficient money to remove themselves some distance from the batterer may increase their safety from all but the most homicidal batterers. Poor women, however, are often simply unable to hide. Further, separation may create catastrophic results for poor women. Separation threatens women's tenuous hold on economic viability, for without the batterer's income or his assistance with childcare, for example, women may lose jobs, housing, and even their children. It is a cruel trap when the state's legal interventions rest on the presumption that women who are "serious" about ending domestic violence will leave their partner while, at the same time, reducing dramatically the availability of public assistance that makes leaving somewhat possible. Thus, failure to acknowledge the manner in which women's access to material resources frames the separation/safety question is the first problem with the focus on separation.

* * *

The material resources test does not require the state to make judgments about what choices are in battered women's best interest. It operates on only one important presumption: inadequate material resources render women's choices more coerced than would otherwise be the case. Thus resources should be made available to women so that, with assistance, they can make a determination about the best course of action based on their own set of circumstances.

B. Material Resources and Domestic Violence

Inadequate material resources render women more vulnerable to battering. Inadequate resources increase the batterers' access to women who separate, and inadequate resources are a primary reason why women do not attempt to separate. Some battering men appear to seek out women that are economically vulnerable, but even were this not so, the batterer's behavior often has a devastating economic impact on the victim's life. Abusive men cause women to lose jobs, educational opportunities, careers, homes, and savings. Battering renders some women permanently disabled and puts others at greater risk for HIV infection. Women become homeless as a result of battering, their homelessness is made more difficult to remedy because they are battered, and they are more vulnerable to further battering because they are homeless. They frequently become estranged from family and friends who might otherwise provide them with material aid.

Cris Sullivan's research suggests that victims' resources have a relationship to experiencing renewed violence and to increased victim well being. Sullivan compared two sets of women leaving a battered women's shelter. The groups were matched in terms of demographics including race, age, employment status, and severity of violence. Each group contained roughly the same number of women cohabitating with their abuser and women separated from their abuser. The experimental group members were provided with an advocate who met with them twice weekly for ten weeks to assess their needs and set priorities. Advocates assisted women in gaining access to educational resources, legal assistance, employment, services for their children, housing, child care, transportation, financial assistance, health care, and social supports. Participants in the experimental group were compared with the control group on a number of measures at different intervals over the course of two years. The women in the experimental group reported significantly less psychological abuse and depression and significantly higher improvement in quality of life and level of social supports than did those in the control group. Most impressive were the differences in the physical abuse measures: one out of four women in the experimental group experienced no abuse during the twenty four month follow up, while this was true for only one out of ten women in the control group. Sullivan believes that what made the advocacy program succeed was that participants, not advocates, guided the direction of the intervention, and the "activities were designed to make the community more responsive to the woman's needs, not to change the survivor's thinking or belief system." Thus, connection to material resources in areas that the women identified as necessary made significant differences both in terms of their ability to improve their lives and in reducing their victimization.

JoAnn Miller and Amy Krull examined victim interview data gathered in three studies of police response to determine the relationship between the victim's employment status and batterer recidivism. They found that unemployed victims in one study were the victims of significantly more recidivistic violence than were employed victims. While this unemployment effect was not borne out in the other two studies, the length of time the victim was unemployed correlated with recidivism in all three studies: the longer the victim was unemployed, the higher the level of recidivism.

Initial inquiries regarding the importance of battered women's material resources focused on the relative economic position of women vis-à-vis their battering partner and found that economic dependency on the partner was a significant predictor of severe violence and a primary reason women gave for re-uniting with their abusive partner. These studies of relative economic power may inadvertently rest on a middle-class norm in which nuclear family households are understood to be autonomous economic units and the dynamic between the couple is the focus of inquiry. Absolute rates of poverty are likely to be equally critical, if not more so, for many battered women. The ability to relocate or hide, for example, is related as much to absolute rates of poverty as it is to women's relative economic resources compared to that of their abuser. The importance of familial and neighborhood networks for economic survival—networks which are likely to be heavily geographically dependent—are critical in determining a woman's ability to relocate.

Despite the vulnerability of poor women to domestic violence, programs for battered women sometimes fail to address the needs of the very poor, particularly those that are perceived as "deviant." For example, some battered women's shelters refuse admission to "homeless" women because they are believed to be too manipulative, "street-wise," or antisocial. Women with substance addictions may find it particularly difficult to obtain shelter that is safe and that treats addiction. Thus, women's poverty renders them more vulnerable to battering, battering deepens their poverty, and extreme poverty may place a woman outside the scope of services designed to assist battered women.

* * *

CONCLUSION: THE MATERIAL RESOURCES TEST AND SHIFTING POWER FOR BATTERED WOMEN

The most obvious impact of applying the material resources test is to shift significant monies to direct aid for victims and to target more significant aid to poor women and especially poor women of color. There are many possible steps towards this goal. Because of the possible relevance of neighborhood disintegration to domestic violence recidivism, particular services should be focused on increasing the autonomy of women in those neighborhoods through resource enhancement. Current legal remedies that enhance resources for battered women could be made more effective. For example, crime victim compensation requirements that victims cooperate with the prosecution of the batterer, renders the aid useless for many women. In addition, compensation is frequently available for psychological counseling, but not for meeting the material needs of victims. Law reform that increases criminal penalties without evidence of gains for battered women should be disfavored and law that diminishes battered women's material resources should be eliminated.

The material resources test should be incorporated into federal funding criteria for domestic violence intervention projects. Federal dollars should not support universal (state-wide) mandatory arrest policies, as is currently the case. Rather, funding should encourage local assessments of the impact of arrest policies on poor women of color. In addition, funding criteria should support those programs that represent broad based coalitions that are either focused on particular neighborhoods or particular racial/ethnic groups. Such coalitions are more likely to have the local knowledge required to assess the situation for poor women of color.

Application of the material resources test may also suggest changes in the way lawyers engage in their legal representation of battered women. For example, Legal Services in Tampa, Florida formed an organization called ChildNet to respond to the material and social support needs of battered women clients. Jeanie Williamson, Director of ChildNet, explained that staff attorneys were frustrated with the inability of legal remedies to give women freedom from abusive partners. ChildNet provides women with advocates, who assist them in locating community services including education, childcare, and job training. Similarly, Linda Mills has argued for the establishment of domestic violence commissions that would assist women with housing and job needs as well as provide legal remedies such as restraining orders.

Funding for domestic violence research should prioritize research that addresses the needs of poor women, and especially poor women of color. This research must escape the black/white paradigm limitations of current domestic violence research and address the particular needs of Latinas and other women of color who are frequently ignored by research.

The measure of the efficacy of any domestic violence intervention strategy must account for, as much as possible, the various forces that mediate and shape women's experiences of battering. The material resources test attempts to do this by requiring an inquiry into the likelihood that a given intervention strategy will result in increased material resources for women, and particularly for poor women of color. Material resources are critically important in battered women's survival. Without the specific attention that the material resources test provides, this importance will continue to be overlooked.

RACHEL GALLAGHER, WELFARE REFORMS' INADEQUATE IMPLEMENTATION OF THE FAMILY VIOLENCE OPTION: EXPLORING THE DUAL OPPRESSION OF POOR DOMESTIC VIOLENCE VICTIMS

19 Am. U. J. Gender Soc. Policy & L. 987 (2011)
(citations and footnotes omitted)

I. INTRODUCTION

Domestic violence is often a scar of poverty. Welfare reform legislation attempted to address the interplay between domestic violence and socio-economic status by adopting the Family Violence Option in the Temporary Assistance for Needy Families (TANF) program. While the Family Violence Option of TANF might serve as Congressional recognition that domestic violence is an exacerbating issue for low-income women, the exception comes with little teeth for actual victims. The Family Violence Option provides states with the authority to voluntarily waive TANF benefit requirements (such as term limits and child support cooperation mandates) for screened domestic violence victims on their rolls, but despite its good intentions of loosening strict qualifications for victims, it is failing to achieve this result in reality. Across the nation, states are under-utilizing the Family Violence Option. While all states have either formally adopted the Family Violence Option or claim to have adopted a comparable policy, utilization rates of domestic violence waivers are surprisingly low, suggesting that implementing the Family Violence Option has been ineffective. Yet, the welfare system continues to be characterized by strict, punitive requirements, making compliance and benefits impossible for many victims of domestic violence. * * *

II. THE HISTORY OF WELFARE—PUNITIVE, SEXIST, AND RACIST ROOTS

The tradition of inadequate poverty laws in the United States includes a narrative of charity, but it is also pervaded with racist and sexist stereotypes. The state and federal government aid programs we are most familiar with today (i.e., Social Security, unemployment compensation, etc.) were initially developed to support "white, male workers and the white women and children dependent upon their wages while they excluded a huge segment of poor women of color and their children." * * * "[Beneficiaries of welfare] might need aid because their wages were too low to survive on them; or they might need aid due to economic depression or other causes of unemployment that were beyond the individual's control." However, "most able-bodied poor were believed, in the end to be morally responsible for their own poverty," and thus benefits were "stingy" and requirements were "disciplinary" in nature "so as not to encourage dependency." These themes have remained constant throughout the history of welfare initiatives. * * *

C. Contemporary Welfare Policy—[TANF]

Concerns about welfare abuse and debates as to whether or not it was wasteful spending grew in the 1990s. In 1996, Congress enacted the Personal Responsibility and Work Opportunity Reconciliation Act (PRWORA), which dramatically reformed the state of welfare. PRWORA replaced Aid to Families with Dependent Children (AFDC) with TANF and implemented strict maximum time requirements and qualifications for subsidies as well as a block grant system, which does not fluctuate depending on how many people the state is serving. * * * Sexist and racist stereotypes continued to influence welfare reform. * * * John Mica, a Congressman from Florida, "held up a sign during a congressional debate that read, 'Don't feed the alligators.' " On the House floor, he then argued that "providing aid to poor women would do nothing but spur them to reproduce, entice them to return for more free handouts, and threaten the general public safety."

The sexism written into PRWORA is astonishing. The factual findings for Congress explicitly found that marriage was not only an integral piece of the infrastructure for a stable society but an essential support that a society needs for the successful promotion of a child's best interests. * * * The statute explicitly aims to decrease single motherhood by making these women less dependent on the government and more dependent on men. Rather than incorporating programs and educational opportunities statistically proven to lead to economic self-sufficiency, TANF implementation limits these opportunities, encouraging women to turn to marriage instead and diverting precious federal resources to this purpose. "Under the new regulations promulgated under the Deficit Reduction Act of 2006, obtaining a bachelor's or master's degree is specifically excluded from the activities that constitute work for the purposes of TANF." Furthermore, many states then started to abandon programs that included offering post-secondary education for welfare recipients. * * *

Statistics also indicate that poverty laws affect more women in general due to the fact that women constitute the majority of our country's poor. * * * "Women are forty percent more likely to be poor than men." "Women are less likely to be employed than men," and they earn less on each dollar than similarly situated male colleagues. Approximately ninety percent of adult TANF recipients are single mothers who are also more likely to be poor. However, it is noteworthy to distinguish that, while single mothers have an exceptionally high poverty rate of over thirty-five percent, they are not the majority of our underclass, as our societal perceptions tend to assume.

Cultural norms of worthiness and animus toward the poor continue to be evident in contemporary welfare reform. "The federal economic stimulus legislation—the American Recovery and Reinvestment Act [of 2009]—increased benefits for Food Stamp, Social Security, [Supplemental Security Income] and Unemployment Compensation recipients, but did not increase benefits for TANF recipients . . ." This conscious exclusion was made despite the fact that these groups of people were most likely to spend benefit increases quickly, consistent with the Act's underlying economic stimulus intentions. * * * It purposefully omitted cash aid as a federal entitlement for qualified families and instead instituted mandatory work requirements, time limits, child support cooperation, and marriage promotion program participation. TANF's changes greatly constrained serving impoverished American families in general, but also affected domestic violence victims in particular.

III. THE CORRELATION OF WELFARE AND VICTIMS OF DOMESTIC VIOLENCE

* * * There is a critical role of women's agency and autonomy that needs to drive legal remedies for domestic violence. Welfare reform policy, as an economic lifeline for escaping abuse, has to take this into account. If welfare reform serves to punish the "unworthy" poor women who are perceived to comprise its rolls, it also undermines the chances of domestic violence victims to achieve economic autonomy, central to their escape of abuse. It undermines these chances despite the fact that domestic violence victims arguably did not relegate themselves to a position of lazy government dependency, but rather are forced by their dominantly male abusers to seek assistance * * * to escape violence.

Domestic violence is most often associated with physical abuse, but it has psychological and economic repercussions as well. It ultimately makes economic self-sufficiency harder to achieve for its victims. Women are the vast majority of victims of domestic violence and sexual assault. Although domestic violence affects women from all different backgrounds, low-income women are even more likely to be abused. "Studies show that 14% to 32% of welfare recipients are [currently] in abusive relationships, and more than half the women in a study who were welfare recipients had been the victims of violence at some time." Domestic violence exacerbates variables of poverty. It often forces a choice of staying in an abusive relationship or risking homelessness. Women are often coerced to return to their abusers as a result of economic reality, which ironically often follows a period of escalated violence after separation in order to coerce reconciliation. Domestic violence victims also suffer from interference with their employment. "Studies indicate that between 35% and 56% of employed abused women surveyed were harassed at work by their abusive partners, and that between one-fourth and one-half of domestic violence victims reported losing a job at least in part to domestic violence." This interference can often result in destabilizing a victim's economic self-sufficiency capabilities, driving many victims to resort to TANF benefits. * * * For many victims, employment is not a realistic source of income and support because of a lack of childcare, continued abuse, poor health, and poor employment history as a result of abuse. * * *

IV. TANF'S FAMILY VIOLENCE OPTION—AN ATTEMPT TO MITIGATE THE HARSH REQUIREMENTS OF WELFARE REFORM

* * * Including the Family Violence Option in TANF was an explicit legal recognition that domestic violence and poverty are specially linked and that making welfare available to victims is imperative. However[,] what harsh requirements are even eligible to be waived for domestic violence victims varies from state to state. * * *

A. Time Limits

Under TANF, no individual can receive benefits longer than an aggregate period of five years, consecutive or not. This requirement, without some further exception, poses great threat for victims of domestic violence as it often takes decades to break the cycles of violence. Additionally, many states have enacted shorter periods of eligibility, making it even more difficult for victims to benefit from this public assistance.

B. Work Requirements

TANF also imposed strict work requirements, which could be devastating to domestic violence victims. While TANF imposes work requirements generally, the states enact their own specific rules. In Texas, an individual must work at least thirty hours a week or participate for twenty hours a week in an activity established under the job opportunities program. * * * Although education is a proven resource for increasing economic self-sufficiency, post-secondary education is not a legitimate work requirement substitute in many states.

C. Child Support Cooperation

* * * These requirements mandate a victim to disclose the name of her abuser and whether he is the father of her children and to participate in any state claims for child support against him. For domestic violence victims who have experienced the failure of the system when the system did not protect them (whether from violated restraining orders, victim arrests, etc.) time and time again, these requirements ask them to balance whether food on the table or their whereabouts being unknown to their abusers is more important.

D. Marriage Promotion

TANF also makes $150 million a year in federal funding available to states that create projects promoting marriage and responsible fatherhood. States can make participation in these programs mandatory, with the exception of domestic violence victims, but because screening can be so difficult in assessing whether a welfare recipient is a victim, the participation requirements still pose a detriment to victims.

E. Immigrant Restrictions

* * * Legal immigrants cannot receive benefits unless they have resided in the United States for at least five years. This requirement ignores the fact that immigrant women experience poverty at a much higher rate than native-born women and are also more likely to be victims of domestic violence, sexual assault, and human trafficking. Exceptions for battered immigrant victims do exist, and victims of domestic violence who are also immigrants may qualify for TANF once they have a pending or approved VAWA application or approved application for a family sponsored visa. However, qualifying for these exceptions can take lengthy amounts of time and involves navigating confusing bureaucracy. * * *

[Editor's Note: States can opt to provide benefits to immigrants not qualified under federal law, and some do. Also, a former U.S. Attorney General clarified that no immigrant can be denied certain benefits such as emergency Medicaid, school food programs, services for domestic violence victims, and food banks. However, because welfare implementation is inconsistent and arbitrary, and caseworkers are often not well trained, some workers have turned immigrants in to the criminal justice system or INS/ICE. See Leslye Orloff, Lifesaving Welfare Safety Net Access For Battered Immigrant Women And Children: Accomplishments And Next Steps, 7 Wm. & Mary J. of Women & The L. 597 (2001).]

F. Family Caps

As of July 2007, fifteen states had child exclusion policies, capping a family's grant of welfare benefits at the number of children existing at the time of application for benefits. Thus, a child's needs are ignored if a child is born into a family receiving TANF benefits, even though the cost increment averages only an additional $100 per month. These policies are premised on the belief that "women have children to get higher TANF benefits." Seeing as many abusers use sexual violence as abuse, this requirement may further harm domestic violence victims.

G. The Family Violence Option

Recognizing that many of these requirements often exclude domestic violence victims' practical eligibility, Congress included an exception in TANF for domestic violence victims. The Family Violence Option provides states with the opportunity to voluntarily waive some of the harsh program requirements associated with TANF. * * * The legislation also included a Hardship Exception, specifically giving the states the opportunity to opt out domestic violence victims from the TANF's temporal caps. * * * Thus, the Family Violence Option makes it conceivably possible to exempt domestic violence victims from oppressive welfare requirements, such as the harsh time limit, forced child support, and strict work requirements. However, in practice the voluntary waiver on behalf of the states is not yielding results that support the idea that domestic violence victims are being afforded the exceptions they desperately need to survive and escape abuse. The Hardship Exception limits the number of exemptions each state can grant to no more than twenty percent of the average number of families receiving assistance. * * * At a minimum, these limits statutorily exclude up to twelve percent of reporting victims who needed exemptions. Because domestic violence is highly underreported, these limits likely exclude even more victims than these statistics indicate. *[Editor's Note: According to California attorneys specializing in public benefits law, welfare recipients qualifying for exemptions under the Family Violence Option are not counted as part of the 20% of the caseload allowed exemptions due to hardship; thus the welfare system may grant exemptions to domestic violence survivors without the welfare office risking being penalized for exceeding the 20% cap on hardship exemptions.]*

V. THE FAILED IMPLEMENTATION OF THE FAMILY VIOLENCE OPTION

As of 2010, "[a]ll states have either formally certified adoption of the Family Violence Option or reported to the federal government adoption of a comparable policy." However, despite its relatively widespread adoption, the utilization rates of domestic violence waivers are surprising low. Systematic information about Family Violence Option administration is virtually nonexistent. There is, however, substantial evidence that TANF caseworkers often fail to effectively screen for domestic violence and/or to offer waivers and service referrals when appropriate. * * *

A. Case Study: California

In 1998, California adopted the Family Violence Option in what they called the California Work Opportunity and Responsibility to Kids program

(CalWORKS). LIFETIME, a California statewide membership organization of low-income parents in California which provides peer-based support and advocacy services to help hundreds of CalWORKs parents each year, produced a report in 2005 examining the efficacy of the Family Violence Option adopted in California. The report's key findings were clear in illustrating that the program was not effectively serving high percentages of domestic violence victims in the CalWORKs program. * * * [O]ne third of the mothers who participated in the survey reported that "they were victims of domestic violence but never received information about their eligibility for domestic violence counseling and services, and/or have been denied access to domestic violence counseling, and services, or waivers." * * * Of the thirteen counties analyzed from 1999 to 2004, twelve counties provided domestic violence services to less than four percent of their CalWORKs caseload. * * * Although mothers may benefit from domestic violence services, "state data indicated that waivers [from welfare to work requirements] were not being granted at all," demonstrating that the exceptions embodied in the federal Family Violence Option were not actually being extended. * * *

B. National Indications of Failure— The Legal Momentum Report

* * * Legal Momentum and the National Resource Center on Domestic Violence conducted a qualitative national survey in the fall of 2009 * * * [which] indicated that the Family Violence Option is inadequately addressing victims' unique issues across the country. * * * According to the report, victims across the country are not consistently and effectively screened or notified of family violence specific responses, waivers, or protections. Concerns identified by respondents included conducting interviews of applicants in the presence of abusive partners and employing workers who were not trained in family violence or who sought to disqualify applicants from eligibility. Furthermore, those victims who did disclose domestic violence were not consistently receiving the appropriate waivers or necessary protections to be safe. Many respondents rated the Family Violence time limit extension and work requirement exemption policies as ineffective. * * * One respondent reported, " 'Unless a woman was recently beaten by her abuser she is not seen as a victim of domestic violence. . . . There is no consideration of the mental health aspect, ability to get a job, court dates, [or] emotional confusion[. . . .]' " * * *

VI. POLICY IMPLICATIONS OF FAILING TO PROVIDE FOR IMPOVERISHED VICTIMS OF DOMESTIC VIOLENCE

* * * The Legal Momentum Report * * * [suggests] increasing the following: minimum wage to a living wage, access to childcare, training for TANF and welfare caseworkers regarding domestic and sexual violence, transportation service, emergency relocation and other related assistance to victims fleeing domestic violence, screening for family violence,

[increasing] TANF benefit levels, and general access to subsidies and opportunities for victims to pursue higher education. Other advocates of reform echo these concerns. * * *

VII. CONCLUSION AND RECOMMENDATIONS

* * * At a minimum, reauthorization [of welfare reform] must implement federal standards for waivers and give states only the discretion to provide more leniency, not more discipline. * * * If we achieve nothing else, we need to prioritize creating mandatory waivers of time limits, work requirements, and child support cooperation initiatives for screened victims, removing the "option" from the Family Violence Option for these measures, but also leaving the door open and encouraging states to use their discretion for lifting all other restrictions when appropriate. * * * Finally, welfare caseworkers need more sensitivity training to help promote more accurate identification of probable domestic violence victims, including developing a broad definition of "domestic violence victim," [and] recognizing and addressing the realities of the cycle of violence in hopes that the purposes of including the Family Violence Option in TANF will be better served. * * *

MEGAN ADAMS, ASSURING FINANCIAL STABILITY FOR SURVIVORS OF DOMESTIC VIOLENCE: A JUDICIAL REMEDY FOR COERCED DEBT IN NEW YORK'S FAMILY COURTS

84 Brooklyn L. Rev. 1387 (2019)
(footnotes omitted)

INTRODUCTION

When Emma first met Andrew, she was a successful real estate agent who was financially independent and about to buy her first apartment. At first, Andrew supported her success. Shortly into their marriage, the dynamics of their relationship changed drastically. Andrew took complete control over Emma's life. He limited her time with family and friends, restricted access to her computer and phone, and fully managed the couple's finances. He alone had access to her bank accounts, giving her a small, set portion of her own paycheck each week for spending. He depleted the savings she had accrued. Emma tried to leave the relationship no less than five times before she was able to exit for good. Later, she learned that Andrew had spent tens of thousands of dollars on her credit cards and had taken out several loans in her name, saddling her with substantial debt that she alone was responsible for.

Central to a law's effectiveness is the relief it provides. For survivors of domestic violence, like Emma, who have suffered from non-physical abuse, there exists a critical gap between a court's finding of wrongdoing and the available remedies. This is especially true in the context of economic abuse, and specifically in situations involving coerced debt.

Perpetrators of domestic violence exert power and control over their partners using a variety of tactics, including physical or sexual violence, emotional abuse, and economic abuse. In abusive relationships involving coerced debt, an abuser utilizes credit as a means to control, harm, or in other ways, limit their partner. . . Studies suggest economic abuse plays a role in as many as ninety-nine percent of [abusive] relationships. . .

Economic abuse can be experienced in many forms. Abusive partners may withhold funds and other assets, deny or restrict access to bank accounts and statements, prevent a partner from working or receiving an education, or use a partner's name, social security number, or other personal identifying information to open bank accounts or lines of credit without their knowledge. Professor Angela Littwin first coined the term "coerced debt" and defined it as "all non-consensual, credit-related transactions that occur in a violent relationship." The impacts of coerced debt, namely a damaged credit score, can be far-reaching and create a number of devastating challenges for survivors as they attempt to exit abusive relationships and find both physical safety and long-term stability.

Credit scores have become an essential aspect of modern life—not just in terms of an individual's financial identity but also their ability to access utilities, housing, and often employment opportunities. Thus, coerced debt can have wide-ranging and destructive consequences for survivors. Damaged credit makes it even more difficult for a survivor to exit an abusive relationship and access the immediate resources they will need to initially survive, such as housing. Indeed, in a 2018 survey of domestic violence survivors, nearly forty percent of respondents reported damaged credit as a barrier to leaving their abusive relationship. Even if a survivor is able to exit the relationship, their ability to gain lasting independence and stability is complicated because poor credit affects a person's ability to access essential credit lines, banking services, and can subject victims to predatory debt collection practices.

Society's lack of awareness surrounding economic abuse is reflected in the U.S. legal system. There exists no single legal avenue through either the federal or state level in which survivors of economic abuse, let alone survivors of coerced debt, may fully access relief for the harm they have endured. Family courts, the legal bodies that states have entrusted with domestic violence proceedings, have yet to fully recognize economic abuse within their jurisdictions, nor has the criminal legal system allowed certain financial crimes to apply to intimate partner settings. Further, the Violence Against Women Act, the federal statute designed to improve national and community-based responses to domestic violence, has yet to address economic abuse as its own form of domestic violence. Absent a legal remedy, victims of coerced debt are often unable to leave abusive relationships for lack of financial resources or, if they are able to leave, have substantial difficulty repairing their financial standing to access essential resources needed to ensure their safety. . .

An "overarching theme" among studies of economic abuse is the prevalence of coerced debt abuse. Debt coercion tactics can include accessing capital in a partner's name without their knowledge or threatening violence or harm against a partner to establish such credit, among other known methods. In the case of one survivor's account of coerced debt, after her husband had opened several credit cards in her name without her knowledge and charged nearly $19,000 to the accounts, she was saddled with the sole responsibility of paying off the cards as she attempted to leave the relationship. Until she repaired the damaged credit, she was "unable to get a mortgage, buy a new car, or crawl out of the mounting debt incurred from late-payment penalty fees on the cards."

Research into the pervasiveness of coerced debt is far from comprehensive; however, the research that does exist indicates that it is a significant problem that further endangers the most vulnerable of victims at times when they are in urgent need of credit to reach safety. A 2019 national survey of callers to the National Domestic Violence Hotline found that fifty-two percent of participants had endured coerced debt. In another study, more than a quarter of clients that visited victims' services organizations sought assistance repairing their credit due to economic abuse in a relationship. Additionally, sixteen percent of identity theft victims, a crime that manifests similarly to coerced debt, have suffered from domestic violence. Twenty-four percent of identity theft victims identify the thief as a family member, friend, partner, or ex-partner. In a 2018 survey of New York City domestic violence service providers, economic abuse was found to be especially prevalent within the City's population in which "[o]ver one in three survivors receiving legal services relating to domestic violence also [reported] a consumer debt legal issue."

Similar to domestic violence generally, these statistics do not capture the extent of the economic abuse or coerced debt problems. In a study exploring why survivors do not report or seek assistance with economic abuse, respondents most commonly cited "[e]mbarrassment and fear of immigration-related repercussions." Those who do report the abuse attribute the relief they achieved far more to social service organizations than police, government agency services, or credit bureaus. . .

Despite the widespread flaws within the credit reporting system, an individual's credit score not only impacts their immediate daily life but also their long-term financial future. Non-lending entities that the average person ordinarily interacts with are becoming increasingly reliant on credit-screening. From utility and cell phone companies to landlords and even some employers, credit-screening has become an inevitable part of daily life. A damaged credit score thus has far-reaching negative consequences and can adversely impact loan approvals, interest rates on credit, insurance rates, access to utilities, and even employment and housing opportunities.

For survivors of domestic violence, this score is especially important when exiting an abusive relationship. Research suggests that low-income communities, in particular, rely on credit to weather emergencies. If denied access to household funds during the relationship or if a survivor is escaping without first withdrawing their own funds, they will need to rely on credit in the short-term in order to meet their immediate basic needs, not to mention future needs, such as employment and permanent housing. With housing, for example, survivors are typically limited in the length of time they may stay in a domestic violence shelter and thus will need to secure a more permanent housing solution shortly after leaving the abusive relationship. Given these limitations, it is not surprising that "[d]omestic violence is the leading cause of homelessness in [the United States]." Without access to credit, survivors are too often denied access to housing options and left with the difficult choice between returning to their abusive relationship, finding family or friends that can provide shelter, or becoming homeless. . .

[The author argues that current federal and state remedies for coerced debt are insufficient to address the needs of survivors of domestic violence. These include criminal prosecution for identity theft, since law enforcement agencies often will not make reports in such cases and because survivors may not want to involve police. Tort claims might be useful, such as tortious interference with contractual relations, negligent misrepresentation, IIED, and other causes of action, though filing a tort claim may make exiting the relationship and obtaining a divorce more difficult or may subject the survivor to years of being required to interact with the abuser through the court system.

Including coerced debt in domestic violence restraining orders or divorce decrees is another option if the court makes specific orders identifying any debts that were obtained through coercion, assigning those to the abuser, and ending the debt coercion. [Note: See Ca. Fam. Code § 6342.5, allowing family courts to do this, whether or not the parties were/are married.] The author notes that such court orders could be used by domestic violence survivors to show to credit reporting agencies and collection agencies to stop the attempted collection from survivors of debts that were incurred by the abuser and to repair their credit ratings.

The author calls for Congress to include economic abuse in the next reauthorization of VAWA. [Note: VAWA 2022, Title VII, Economic Security for Victims, Sec. 701 (15) adds "economic abuse" for the first time, and defines it to include problems with access to credit and credit card debt, forcing a partner into bankruptcy or to default on household bills, etc. Section 704 of the same Title mandates periodic reports to Congress by

HHS and the Dept of Labor regarding issues affecting survivors of abuse and specifies that this includes economic security and credit history.]

The author also calls on Congress to broaden the definition of identity theft within the Fair and Accurate Credit Transactions Act (FACTA), to capture this unique aspect of coerced debt. Additionally, she notes that Congress should consider methods by which to incentivize or mandate that private actors, including both credit reporting agencies and traditional lending institutions, develop written policies regarding victims of coerced debt that explicitly eliminate the police report requirement. Similarly, she states that the Fair Credit Reporting Act (FCRA) needs to be amended to remove this requirement. [Note: Ca. amended its Civil Code and Penal Code effective 1/22 to allow survivors to submit an identity theft report from the Federal Trade Commission rather than a police report to debt collectors and others.]]

[Editor's Notes: 1. Survivors of domestic violence also may have problems regarding income tax returns. The Internal Revenue Code provides relief for "innocent spouses," who may face tax deficiencies caused by their abusers. Survivors of abuse may not have been aware of such deficiencies, or may have knowingly signed fraudulent returns under duress. However, innocent spouse relief is often hard to attain. In Jacqueline Clarke, (In)equitable Relief: How Judicial Misconceptions about Domestic Violence Prevent Victims from Attaining Innocent Spouse Relief under I.R.C. § 6015(F), 22 Am. U. J. Gender Soc. Pol'y & L. 825 (2013–2014), the author describes a study involving 444 cases. It found that tax court judges dismissed most petitions for innocent spouse relief due to a narrow definition of "abuse," e.g., there was no finding of abuse unless there was an order of protection, or abuse claims were disallowed in cases of joint custody, which is obviously inaccurate. She calls for tax court judges to be educated on the intricacies of domestic violence. In the absence of formal training programs for judges, survivors and their attorneys could educate them through briefing and expert witness testimony.

2. Survivors may also deal with bankruptcy. In A Brief Introduction to the Intersections Between Domestic Violence Law and Bankruptcy Law, 22(2) Domestic Violence Report 21 (Dec/Jan 2017), Danisha Brar and Jared Ellias explain the protections in bankruptcy law for survivors of spousal abuse. These include being able to shield the assets needed to protect themselves from other creditors, which helps them get a fresh start. And abusers who file for bankruptcy are unable to discharge domestic support obligations or tort awards. See Hermosilla v. Hermosilla *in Chapter 5.*

3. Finally, insurance companies may discriminate against survivors of domestic violence. In Stop Re-Victimizing the Victims: A Call for Stronger State Laws Prohibiting Insurance Discrimination Against Victims of Domestic Violence, 23 Am. U. J. Gender Soc. Pol'y & L. 413 (2014–2015), Emily C. Wilson notes that insurance companies often label survivors of abuse as voluntarily engaging in high-risk behavior. She argues that this is untrue, unfair, and against sound public policy. She calls for state laws that keep domestic violence histories confidential, expand the scope of prohibited insurer conduct, and prohibit discrimination in all types of insurance.]

B. EMPLOYMENT ISSUES

1. OVERVIEW

MICHAEL MOBERLY, THE WORKPLACE INJUNCTION: AN EMERGING BUT IMPERFECT WEAPON IN THE FIGHT AGAINST DOMESTIC VIOLENCE

26 Am. U. J. Gender Soc. Pol'y & L. 831 (2018)
(footnotes omitted)

. . . The damaging effects of domestic violence are not limited to its impact on the intended victim and members of her family. As one jurist observed, "the perils of domestic violence are often experienced in the workplace," where the victims may include the employer itself "and too often innocent bystanders, including co-workers, who also may suffer injuries in any violent act." Indeed, like domestic violence generally, workplace domestic violence has become a virtual epidemic, and the problem is—or at least should be—a matter of grave concern to potential victims, their advocates, and employers, all of whom are in need of more effective weapons to combat this growing menace. . .

I. THE WORKPLACE DOMESTIC VIOLENCE PROBLEM

Workplace violence is a matter of significant public concern, and in recent years employers have become increasingly attuned to the issue. Although this violence takes various forms, workplace domestic violence is a particularly vexing problem for employers, not only because of its prevalence, but also because the typical employer may have little or no knowledge of the potential perpetrator's propensity for violence, making it difficult to anticipate a violent workplace incident, let alone prevent one from occurring. . .

This phenomenon [a victim of domestic violence being murdered by her abuser at her workplace] is not altogether surprising. Employment is often confined to a specific and relatively public location, and involves a predictable work schedule, leaving employees who are involved in abusive relationships vulnerable to attack while they are at work. As one commentator explained, domestic violence may spill into the workplace "for no other reason than the perpetrator knows where the victim is going to be at some particular point in time—at work."

. . .[The author states that employers are legally obligated to provide a safe workplace to all employees, but that employers may be immune from tort liability for breaching this duty because workers' compensation is supposed to provide an exclusive remedy for injuries happening at work. However, the fact that domestic violence is usually seen as a personal issue and not work-related may mean that workers' compensation would not apply to an injury or death caused by an abuser of the worker. There are many appellate decisions in which employers were found liable in tort (usually negligence) for such events. Training for all employees about warning signs of domestic violence and instituting routine security precautions can be helpful. But firing domestic violence survivors to prevent these incidents at work is not advised since it could lead to tort liability for wrongful termination. *[Editor's Note: And it is fundamentally unfair to fire survivors of abuse, as well as potentially financially disastrous for them if they cannot quickly find an equivalent job.]*

VI. THE EMERGENCE OF WORKPLACE INJUNCTIONS

Many of the existing strategies for addressing workplace domestic violence "tend to be 'incident-focused' reactive responses," and thus may be of little assistance in preventing a violent workplace incident. However, a more promising option available to employers in a few states is the workplace injunction, sometimes referred to as a workplace restraining order or "TRO." Like a more traditional domestic violence protective order, which a victim can seek without her employer's input or assistance, a workplace injunction may prevent threats or other forms of nonphysical abuse, egregious enough in themselves, from escalating into physical violence.

Traditional domestic violence protective orders typically require the perpetrator to refrain from contacting the victim, which in the case of a victim who is employed means, among other things, staying away from her place of employment. Arizona's "order of protection" statute, for example, authorizes a court to restrain the perpetrator from coming near the victim's "residence, place of employment or school" if there is reasonable cause to believe that physical harm might otherwise occur. However, in most states these protective orders can be obtained only by the victim herself (or, under some circumstances, by another member of her family or household). The victim's employer has no standing to seek relief under the statutes that authorize these types of protective orders.

For any number of reasons, an employee involved in an abusive relationship may be unwilling—or unable—to obtain a protective order on her own behalf, leaving herself and possibly her coworkers vulnerable to a workplace assault. *[Editor's Note: In some cases, employers or attorneys for domestic violence survivors have obtained workplace violence restraining orders in addition to the survivor's domestic violence restraining order.]* Statutes authorizing workplace injunctions are intended to minimize this risk, which they do by enabling employers to obtain "civil injunctive relief against an individual who has harassed, threatened, assaulted, or stalked an employee on the employer's worksite or while conducting the employer's business." As one commentator explained:

> Civil protection orders are generally considered an important tool for domestic violence victims, but they are very distinct from workplace restraining orders. Both orders should accomplish the same goal as it relates to the workplace—to get an unwanted person to stay away and refrain from harassing, threatening, or assaulting the target. . . .The major difference between the civil protection order and the workplace restraining order is the person who initiates the relief.

[The author notes that while most states have not enacted workplace injunctions, these court orders can have significant advantages, including drawing the abuser's attention away from the survivor, thus making her less vulnerable to a retaliatory attack than if she obtained her own order. And many employers have more resources to obtain and enforce court orders than survivors do. Of course, many perpetrators pay no attention to court orders, violating them repeatedly, some perpetrators may be enraged by the court order, and workplace injunctions protect survivors only at the workplace, so it is important for the survivor to obtain their own more comprehensive restraining order. Employers should consult with the employee prior to obtaining a workplace injunction, though due to the duty to protect the entire workplace and members of the public who come there, the employer may decide to seek an injunction even if the survivor objects.]

[Editor's Notes: 1. In 2012, the EEOC posted Questions and Answers: The Application of Title VII and the ADA to Applicants or Employees Who Experience Domestic or Dating Violence, Sexual Assault, or Stalking at http://www.eeoc.gov//eeoc/publications/qa_domestic_violence.cfm, a useful resource.

2. In "Employer Liability and Domestic Violence Victim Advocacy," a chapter in the ABA's The Impact of Domestic Violence on Your Legal Practice *(2005), Robin R. Runge lays out guidelines for attorneys whose clients are employed survivors of domestic violence. She discusses when and how a survivor should tell someone at work about the abuse. This can result in job loss, since most employees in the U.S. are "at-will" and can be fired for no reason unless there is a collective bargaining agreement or a workplace policy that serves as a contract or in cases where discrimination is prohibited under Title VII, the Americans with Disabilities Act (e.g., if the client has PTSD), the Age Discrimination in Employment Act, or state anti-discrimination statutes. The survivor can ask that the employer keep the domestic violence issues confidential though this may not be an enforceable right. She explains that the Family Medical Leave Act provides job guaranteed unpaid leave from work for a "serious health condition" of the employee or a family member, which may be very useful to a survivor of domestic violence.]*

EDITOR'S SUMMARY OF FUTURES WITHOUT VIOLENCE AND LEGAL MOMENTUM, CHECKLIST OF CONSIDERATIONS WHEN DEVELOPING EMPLOYMENT-RELATED PROTECTIONS FOR SURVIVORS OF DOMESTIC VIOLENCE, SEXUAL ASSAULT AND STALKING

(2022)

- Define "domestic violence," "sexual assault" and "stalking" broadly, without requiring that survivors comply with the criminal justice system before receiving other services and including many types of abuse including coercive control.
- Include survivors of domestic violence, sexual assault, and stalking in any anti-discrimination protections.
- Include reasonable accommodations for survivors in workplace settings, e.g., time off, assigning the survivor a new email address and a new phone number, changed locations or shifts, removal from the website, etc.
- Provide paid leave from work for abuse survivors, free from retaliation, and do not limit what exactly the leave can be for or clarify that the list is not exhaustive. Include survivors in unemployment insurance laws.
- Do not require certification of the abuse or allow self-certification, but if certification from third parties is necessary, keep sources broad (e.g., a letter from local domestic violence agency).
- Require training for supervisors regarding employers' obligations in these areas.
- Build in robust confidentiality policies.

2. LEAVE FROM WORK

[Editor's Note: In "This Seattle woman is fighting Amazon to help domestic violence survivors," 10/27/22 Seattle Times, Lauren Rosenblatt reports that Leslie Tullis, a senior product manager and mother of two, was fired in 2017 for requesting leave from work at Amazon as a domestic violence survivor in spite of the law allowing such leave. At the time, no one at the company besides Tullis was aware of the law so there were no protocols for how to comply with it.

Rosenblatt wrote: "To help victims of domestic violence become survivors, Washington lawmakers passed the Domestic Violence Leave Act in 2008. The law requires employers to provide workers experiencing domestic violence, sexual assault or stalking time off—with few parameters and few questions asked. An employee's job is protected by law when using this leave, according to the state Department of Labor & Industries, which can include 'reasonable amounts' of unpaid leave, beyond available paid time off."

Amazon says Tullis was fired for poor performance, not for taking time off, and also said she had taken excessive unpaid leave. Tullis is alleging discrimination and retaliation, and wants her job back. So far the court has ruled in her favor twice and fined Amazon $1000 for violating the law; the company was appealing.

The article notes that abusers may actively try to sabotage and control survivors, forcing them to relocate, go to court multiple times, and/or get to work late when the abuser does not show up for child care or sabotages the survivor's car. This can result in a lot of missed work and financial problems.

Court documents show that at the time she was fired there was already a finding of domestic violence in Tullis' divorce case, where she was granted a restraining order by the trial court and sole custody by the appellate court based on her ex-husband's history of abuse toward her.

The Washington labor director found that Amazon had retaliated against Tullis in violation of Washington state law for taking leave from work. At oral argument on 1/18/24, Amazon urged the Washington Appellate Court to reverse that finding.]

3. UNEMPLOYMENT BENEFITS

E.C. v. RCM OF WASHINGTON, INC.

92 A.3d 305 (D.C. Ct. App. 2014)
(citations and footnotes omitted)

In this appeal, * * * [petitioner] E.C., joined by *amici curiae* and the District of Columbia Office of the Attorney General ("the District"), contends that the ALJ [Administrative Law Judge] erred in his determination that she is disqualified from receiving unemployment compensation benefits on account of engaging in "simple misconduct," by admitting her former boyfriend, who had a history of abusing her, onto the premises of her employer's residential facilities on three occasions, because she is entitled to benefits under D.C. Code § 51–131 (2010 Supp.), enacted to allow victims of domestic violence to receive unemployment compensation benefits in circumstances where they can show they have separated from their employment "due to domestic violence." E.C., *amici,* and the District urge us to interpret the language "due to domestic violence" broadly, to mean that any claimant who shows that domestic violence played a "substantial factor" in the claimant's separation from employment is eligible for unemployment compensation benefits, even if the claimant might otherwise be disqualified from receiving benefits, for reasons including misconduct, as alleged here. [We agree, and reverse the ALJ's ruling partially disqualifying E.C. from benefits.]

* * * [B]ased on the statute's legislative history, remedial purpose to combat domestic violence and its impact on victims in the unemployment compensation context, as well as public policies underlying similar remedial legislation, the statute intends to allow for broad coverage of claimants whose separation from employment is "due to domestic violence." However, we emphasize that in order for a claimant to qualify for benefits under this provision of the statute, the claimant first must establish a causal nexus between the domestic violence and the claimant's separation from employment * * *: (1) the claimant suffered domestic violence that qualifies as an "intrafamily offense" under the Intrafamily Offenses Act ("IFOA"), along with qualifying supporting documentation, and (2) domestic violence played a "substantial factor" in the claimant's separation from employment. * * *

I. FACTUAL BACKGROUND

The uncontroverted evidence demonstrates that E.C. was in an abusive relationship with her ex-boyfriend, M.L., for over eleven months, during which time she tried to end the relationship no less than four separate times. While E.C. was involved with M.L., she began working for RCM, an organization that provides housing for persons with mental and physical disabilities ("residents"). To ensure the safety of the residents under RCM's care, it required all employees to observe a company policy prohibiting those not employed or authorized by RCM from accessing its residential facilities. RCM apprised all new hires, including E.C., of the policy at new hire orientation and company training, as well as in the personnel handbook provided to each employee.

Over the course of E.C.'s relationship with M.L., he exhibited controlling behavior that interfered with her work and became extreme and violent whenever E.C. attempted to end the relationship. For example, in separate instances, M.L. grabbed E.C. around her neck, vandalized her apartment building, kicked in her car window, slashed her tire, and stalked her at work. In another incident, M.L. repeatedly called E.C., came to her workplace, and tapped on the glass patio door of her workplace while he watched her ignore his calls. According to E.C., it was M.L.'s abusive and controlling tactics, specifically his repeated attempts to invade her work space and stalk her at work, which led E.C. to permit him to set foot on RCM property on three separate occasions, in violation of RCM's policy prohibiting access to unauthorized persons, ultimately leading to her termination. * * * According to E.C., M.L. appeared uninvited so often at her workplace that she could not "even give a number" for the times he appeared. In one such instance, E.C. felt compelled to speak with M.L. on a public street by the RCM facility because "it's safer for [her] to allow him to say what he needs to say so that [she] [could] remain safe." E.C.

eventually ended the relationship with M.L. in March 2012, which led to M.L.'s final threat to get E.C. fired. Specifically, M.L. said: "[Y]ou think that you're going to hold your job? You're unfit to work here and I'm going to make sure that I call your employ[er]."

To protect herself against M.L., E.C. filed two temporary protection orders ("TPO's") in August 2011 and March 2012, respectively, in the Domestic Violence Unit of D.C. Superior Court, both of which were granted and ordered M.L. to stay away from E.C.'s work and home, among other places. The court, however, rejected E.C.'s September 2011 request for a [long-term] civil protection order ("CPO"), which resulted in the lapse of her August 2011 TPO, because, according to the court, the parties seemed to agree on their desire to stay away from each other, given that M.L. had similarly filed a TPO against E.C. *[Editor's Note: It is unfortunate that the court penalized E.C. for her abusive boyfriend's misuse of the court system when it allowed E.C.'s TPO to lapse. His filing for a TPO was a not-altogether uncommon tactic of litigation abuse, and a successful tactic.]* E.C. later filed a second CPO against M.L. in March 2012 that the court granted. In that CPO, E.C. described numerous incidents, including how M.L. repeatedly came to RCM's residential facility at 110 Michigan Ave., Northeast, and how during one argument, he grabbed E.C.'s purse and then grabbed her neck.

With regard to her alleged misconduct, E.C. admitted that she voluntarily allowed M.L. onto RCM property on three occasions [to prevent M.L. from " 'mak[ing] a scene at [her] workplace' " and because " 'the last thing [she] needed was to lose her job.' "] * * * RCM eventually terminated E.C. on the basis that she had violated company policy by admitting non-authorized persons onto company property in those three instances. Subsequently, E.C. filed for unemployment insurance benefits under D.C. Code § 51–109 (2001). The District of Columbia Department of Employment Services denied E.C.'s application for benefits on May 29, 2012, because RCM had terminated E.C. for violation of an employer rule, constituting employee misconduct. E.C. appealed that denial of benefits to the Office of Administrative Hearings (OAH).

[At the July 2012 hearing before ALJ James Harmon, RCM produced witnesses from its human resources and similar departments, who testified to E.C.'s alleged misconduct of allowing M.L. onto the premises.] * * * Notably, [one witness] testified that prior to terminating E.C., RCM learned of her domestic violence issues with M.L. E.C. revealed to her employer that she had "a past violent history" with M.L., including "quite a few bad altercations." [This witness] also testified that E.C. described multiple incidents where M.L. either appeared at RCM's residential facilities, or followed E.C. in the community while she served RCM residents. * * * [E.C. also testified about M.L.'s history of abuse, and presented a domestic violence expert witness who] * * * noted that M.L.'s actions made E.C. afraid and willing to comply with some of his requests in order to reduce the possibility of abuse, because M.L. carried out his threats against her, including ultimately depriving E.C. of her employment. Specifically, E.C.'s actions at RCM, including her allowing M.L. onto company property, were consistent with common patterns of abusive relationships involving domestic violence[.] * * *

* * * With regard to her relationship with M.L., the ALJ determined that E.C. engaged in a "turbulent relationship" with him, during which a number of abusive events took place. However, the ALJ also found that E.C. took certain precautionary measures, such as seeking TPOs and CPOs against M.L. From these factual findings, the ALJ drew a series of legal conclusions. Specifically, the ALJ determined that RCM failed to show that E.C. had committed gross or simple misconduct[.] * * * Nonetheless, the ALJ independently determined that E.C.'s behavior constituted simple misconduct because E.C. allowed M.L. onto RCM's residential facilities on three occasions, and that these instances constituted "a willful and deliberate violation of [RCM's] interests." * * * The ALJ also acknowledged that the evidence demonstrated that E.C. was a victim of domestic violence, but found that the evidence in the record "[did] not show that, during those specific times [when E.C. allowed M.L. onto the property] that her actions were so adversely and severely affected by her being a victim of domestic violence, that she lacked the required intent to commit an act or acts that constituted misconduct under the [D.C. Unemployment Compensation] Act." Consequently, the ALJ disagreed with E.C.'s contention that she lost her employment "due to domestic violence," and did not make an explicit ruling under D.C.Code § 51–131. This petition for review followed.

II. DISCUSSION

* * * E.C. claims that the ALJ improperly required her to demonstrate a strict causal nexus between her termination from employment and the alleged domestic violence, effectively placing the burden on E.C. "to show that her exposure to domestic violence negated a finding of misconduct," thus making the "special protection for domestic violence victims superfluous" under the statute. She contends that had the ALJ applied § 51–131, based on its language, purpose, and legislative history, he would have determined that she qualified for benefits under the statute because E.C. proved that domestic violence played a "substantial factor" in her separation from employment, even if it was not the "sole cause." * * *

A. Standard of Review and Statutory Construction

* * * The District of Columbia's unemployment compensation statute creates a presumptive right to unemployment compensation benefits. However, an employee is ineligible to receive benefits if the employee is discharged for "gross" or "other than gross" misconduct—commonly referred to as "simple" misconduct. Although the "gross" and "simple" misconduct provisions operate to disqualify certain claimants from

benefits, D.C. Code § 51–131(a) provides an exception: "Notwithstanding any other provision of this subchapter, no otherwise eligible individual shall be denied [unemployment compensation] benefits for any week because the individual was separated from employment by *discharge* or voluntary or involuntary resignation *due to domestic violence* against the individual. . . ." (emphasis added). * * * To be eligible "to receive [unemployment compensation] benefits for separation from employment due to domestic violence," a claimant must "submit [ ] . . . support [for] the claim of domestic violence[,]" which a claimant can establish through various means, including [reports from police, government agencies, court orders, statements from shelters, social workers, counselors, attorneys, doctors, clergy, etc.]. * * *

B. Interpretation of the Statute's "Notwithstanding" Clause

[T]he "notwithstanding" language of D.C. Code § 51–131 indicates that the legislature intended this provision "to override conflicting provisions of any other section." * * * [T]he plain language of D.C. Code § 51–131 unambiguously overrides any conflicting provision within the same subchapter, which covers eligibility for, and disqualification from, unemployment compensation benefits. Therefore, § 51–131 is intended to supersede § 51–110(b)'s disqualification of a claimant's unemployment compensation benefits for engaging in misconduct when that claimant is a victim of domestic violence, and shows that his or her separation from employment was "due to domestic violence" under §§ 51–131 and 51–132. * * *

C. Domestic Violence As an "Intrafamily Offense"

* * * E.C., *amici,* and the District suggest that this court read "domestic violence" broadly to include all the abusive actions taken by the abuser against a claimant throughout their relationship, that may constitute "intrafamily offenses," not just the specific actions directly leading to the claimant's termination. To support this broad definition of "domestic violence," [we use] our jurisprudence on the IFOA, where we have liberally construed "domestic violence" in order to further the Act's remedial purpose.

First, we must determine whether any of the incidents leading to a claimant's separation from employment constitute "interpersonal" or "intrafamily violence," as well as what proof the claimant must show of this violence. For example, in *Richardson v. Easterling,* we concluded that under the IFOA, an individual does not necessarily have to provide proof of a *criminal* act involving abuse or violence in order to establish an "intrafamily offense," because doing so placed an unintended limitation on the IFOA, which ran contrary to its "paramount consideration" as a remedial piece of legislation. Accordingly, we determined that, contrary to the trial court's ruling, a pattern of harassing behavior by petitioner's boyfriend that was committed "with the intent to cause emotional distress to [petitioner] by willfully, maliciously and repeatedly harassing [him]," was a sufficient, though not necessary, means of proving the "intrafamily offense" of stalking. * * * Thus, like in *Richardson,* any pattern of conduct designed to cause emotional distress is sufficient, though not necessary, to constitute an "intrafamily offense" for purposes of D.C. Code § 51–131, so long as the claimant establishes the pattern of conduct through one of the means of supporting documentation under D.C. Code § 51–132, see *supra* Part II.A.

* * * [W]e must additionally consider what timeframe is relevant in so doing. * * * In *Cruz-Foster,* we assessed whether the trial court erred in denying a request to extend petitioner's CPO for "good cause," and ultimately remanded to the trial court because it had not considered the "entire mosaic" of petitioner's history of abuse, which we recognized "as critical to the determination" of whether petitioner met her burden in showing "good cause." We specifically determined that the trial court improperly limited its consideration of whether petitioner met her evidentiary burden to "an assessment of credibility with respect to the episodes" of abuse by petitioner's perpetrator, Foster, *after* his release from prison, rather than considering the entire history of abuse, spanning the time shortly after petitioner's marriage to Foster, Foster's criminal history of contempt for violation of a CPO, and the final abuse after Foster's imprisonment. * * * [W]e noted the remedial character of the IFOA, which required asking "whether the 'balance of harms' favor[ed] the grant of [petitioner's] application," and the D.C. Council's intended "preference for a generous construction of the remedial provisions of the Act." We find that the same remedial concerns that arose in *Cruz-Foster* similarly arise here, because, if we were to read too narrow a timeframe into the domestic violence statute for purposes of establishing proof of an "intrafamily offense," then claimants who establish proof of an "intrafamily offense" suffered during the entirety of the relationship, but not during the isolated instances leading to their separation from employment would be disqualified from receiving benefits. This result would be anomalous to the underlying considerations of the IFOA—"to protect victims of family abuse from acts and threats of violence" and further its "remedial purpose" by "liberally construing" its provisions. Accordingly, * * * a reviewing court must consider the "entire mosaic" of the claimant's history of abuse, not just the incidents directly leading to her separation from employment.

D. The Causation Standard for Interpreting "Due to Domestic Violence"

* * * [We conclude "a claimant need only show that the 'domestic violence' played a 'substantial factor' in . . . separation from employment," not "that the 'domestic violence' be the 'sole cause.' "] * * * The District of Columbia Council's Committee Report [notes that domestic violence victims are often stalked by their abusers at work and often have to miss

work due to the abuse. Plus, " '[a] lost job and income makes it even more difficult to leave the violent relationship.' "] * * * [The councilmember who introduced the law testified that some " '[s]tudies have shown that 96% of employed domestic violence victims experience problems at work related to the abuse and that 30% lose their jobs due to domestic violence.' " And the councilmember noted that " 'unemployment compensation is vastly greater [than public welfare benefits].' "] * * * [Thus,] the statute's liberal reporting requirements were intended to allow claimants the greatest possible chance to establish the requisite causal nexus needed to show eligibility for unemployment compensation benefits. * * * And, notably, the D.C. Council envisioned extending broad coverage under the statute because in 2010, it amended § 51–131 to extend benefits to individuals whose separation from work was due to domestic violence against "the individual *or any member of the individual's immediate family* [.]" (emphasis added). * * *

E. E.C.'s Eligibility for Benefits under D.C. Code § 51–131

* * * [H]ere, E.C. proved that she suffered "domestic violence" in two ways. First, she showed that at least on one of the three occasions leading to her termination from RCM, M.L. stalked her by following her from Superior Court to RCM's residential facility on Alabama Avenue, which qualifies as "interpersonal" or "intrafamily violence" sufficient to establish an "intrafamily offense," because when M.L. followed E.C. to her work, he did so with the "intent to cause [her] emotional distress." Second, giving due consideration to the "entire mosaic" of abuse committed by M.L. against E.C., E.C. sufficiently showed how M.L.'s actions as a whole constituted "domestic violence" and an "intrafamily offense" under D.C.Code §§ 51–131 and 16–1008 because his actions against E.C. constituted the kind of emotional violence similar to that suffered by petitioner in *Richardson,* against which the IFOA intends to protect. Consequently, we agree with E.C. that, here, the ALJ failed to meaningfully weigh the entire history of abuse perpetrated by M.L. against her in determining that E.C. did not show her separation from employment was "due to domestic violence." [The ALJ failed to consider E.C.'s undisputed testimony, her expert witness, and her documentary evidence, including restraining orders "that satisfy the reporting requirements"—all of which "showed a pattern of abuse."] * * * E.C. specifically testified that M.L. committed physical acts of violence and vandalism against her, as well as harassed and stalked her on multiple occasions, all of which establish "intrafamily offenses." Nonetheless, * * * the ALJ erred by not considering *all* of the evidence proffered by E.C. of the history of domestic violence when he determined that her separation from employment was not "due to domestic violence."

* * * [Additionally], the record shows that domestic violence played a "substantial factor" in each incident of misconduct leading to E.C.'s termination from employment because each incident is linked to the entire

history of E.C.'s relationship with M.L., which shows a continuing pattern of harassment, stalking, and threatening behavior at her place of work that ultimately led M.L. to inform her employer of the three incidents of misconduct, resulting in E.C.'s termination. Moreover, [undisputed testimony showed E.C. allowed M.L. onto the property for her personal safety and job security.] * * * [Thus, w]e hold that E.C.'s evidence at the hearing of "domestic violence" and its effects on her employment shows that "domestic violence" played a "substantial factor" in the incidents of misconduct that led to her termination from employment, such that her separation from employment was "due to domestic violence" pursuant to D.C. Code § 51–131. * * *

E.C.'s case is a prime example of a victim of domestic violence whose experiences with domestic violence impacted her "ability to maintain . . . employment." Rather than stay with the perpetrator, E.C. chose to end the relationship and continue "to [try to] achieve economic security after leaving an abusive relationship." E.C.'s case squarely fits within the purpose of the statute—to provide unemployment compensation to an individual who is "separated from employment by discharge . . . *due to domestic violence* against the individual." (emphasis added). * * * [Reversed and remanded.]

4. EMPLOYER LIABILITY WHEN A DOMESTIC VIOLENCE VICTIM IS INJURED OR KILLED AT WORK

SABRIC V. LOCKHEED

532 Fed.Appx. 286 (3rd Cir. 2013) (unpublished)
(footnotes and citations omitted)

This case arises out of the deadly shooting of Deborah Bachak, a Lockheed Martin Corporation employee, by her former paramour, George Zadolnny. Zadolnny was a security guard with U.S. Security Associates and worked at the Lockheed facility. Bachak's parents and estate brought suit against Lockheed and U.S. Security, alleging defendants' negligence caused Bachak's death. Lockheed asserted a cross-claim against U.S. Security for indemnification.

We will affirm the District Court's order insofar as it granted summary judgment to Lockheed and U.S. Security on plaintiffs' negligence claims. We will reverse as to Lockheed's cross-claim and remand to the District Court with instructions that summary judgment be entered for Lockheed.

I.

Pursuant to a security services contract, U.S. Security provided uniformed security guards to the Lockheed facility. One guard per shift was armed. In May 2004, U.S. Security hired Zadolnny as the first-shift armed security officer for the Lockheed facility. Bachak was a long-time Lockheed employee working in the Document Control Department. Bachak and Zadolnny entered into a romantic relationship in late 2007. They moved in together in early 2008 and became engaged that spring. Bachak terminated the relationship between August and October of 2008.

On December 16, 2008, while on duty, Zadolnny left the guardhouse under the guise of going to the restroom. He walked over to the Document Control Room, encountered Bachak, and asked if she would speak with him in the mailroom. Once Bachak met Zadolnny in the mailroom, he shot her five times. Zadolnny took his own life immediately after killing Bachak.

Bachak's parents (the "Sabrics") brought suit individually and as co-executors of Bachak's estate in the Lackawanna County Court of Common Pleas. Against Lockheed, plaintiffs asserted claims for negligence, vicarious liability, wrongful death, and a survival action. Against U.S. Security, plaintiffs asserted claims for negligence, assault and battery, vicarious liability, wrongful death, and a survival action. Lockheed removed the action to the District Court for the Middle District of Pennsylvania, where both Lockheed and U.S. Security moved to dismiss the action for various reasons. The District Court largely denied their motions. Lockheed then brought a cross-claim against U.S. Security, contending U.S. Security was contractually obligated to indemnify it.

After discovery, defendants moved for summary judgment against plaintiffs. The District Court granted defendants' motion, finding Lockheed and U.S. Security did not owe Bachak any duty and therefore could not be held liable under a negligence theory. Lockheed also moved for summary judgment on its indemnification claim against U.S. Security. The District Court denied this motion and dismissed the cross-claim because U.S. Security was adjudicated non-negligent. The Sabrics appeal, asserting both Lockheed and U.S. Security owed Bachak a duty and breached it. Lockheed cross-appeals the denial of its claim for indemnification.

II.

To establish a claim for negligence, the plaintiff must show: (1) the defendant owed a duty of care to the plaintiff; (2) the defendant breached that duty; (3) there is a causal connection between the defendant's breach and the plaintiff's injury; and (4) the plaintiff incurred actual loss. Whether the defendant owed a duty of care under the first element is a question of law. The inquiry involves "weigh[ing] several discrete factors, including: (1) the relationship between the parties; (2) the social utility of the actor's conduct; (3) the nature of the risk imposed and foreseeability of the harm incurred; (4) the consequences of imposing a duty upon the actor; and (5) the overall public interest in the proposed solution."

Plaintiffs assert defendants owed Bachak a duty under three theories: (A) Section 317 of the Restatement (Second) of Torts; (B) Section 323 of the

Restatement; and (C) non-Restatement Pennsylvania common law. We will address each theory in turn.

A.

Plaintiffs assert that under § 317 of the Restatement (Second) of Torts, defendants had a duty to exercise reasonable care so as to control Zadolnny because defendants knew of his propensity for violent behavior. The District Court found the Pennsylvania Supreme Court's decision in *Dempsey v. Walso Bureau, Inc.,* 431 Pa. 562, 246 A.2d 418 (1968), was on point and precluded a duty under § 317 because Zadolnny's allegedly dangerous disposition was never reported to the management or human resources department of either defendant. On appeal, plaintiffs contend the trial court erred in failing to consider evidence establishing that both Lockheed and U.S. Security knew or should have known of the risk of harm Zadolnny posed to Bachak. * * *

Thus, while a wayward employee need not have committed the *exact same* act in the past (e.g., murder) in order to hold the employer liable under § 317, the wayward employee must have committed prior acts of the same general nature as the one for which the plaintiff brings suit-acts that show the employee is "vicious or dangerous and . . . intended to inflict injury upon others."

Viewing the facts in the light most favorable to plaintiffs, and drawing all inferences in their favor, we find the evidence insufficient to establish a duty under § 317 on the part of either defendant. Supervisors at Lockheed and U.S. Security knew, at best, that Zadolnny had sometimes become agitated and angry, had verbally lashed out, and harbored a vendetta toward his ex-fiancée. This knowledge was insufficient to place defendants on notice that Zadolnny would one day physically harm Bachak.

In their briefs, plaintiffs highlight additional instances of Zadolnny's problematic behavior but fail to establish that reports of these instances were made to defendants' management or human resources personnel. * * * As the District Court explained,

> Decedent and her co-workers did not find Zadolnny's conduct necessary to warrant the lodging of a complaint with Lockheed's Human Resources Department. And, without such a complaint, the Court cannot avoid the inevitable conclusion that the necessity to control Zadolnny's conduct did not exist because he was not known, nor was he believed to be prior to the date of the shooting, to present an unreasonable risk of harm to Decedent.

Given the lack of evidence suggesting Zadolnny was vicious or dangerous or that Lockheed or U.S. Security should have known of the risk he posed, the District Court found that defendants did not owe Bachak a duty under § 317 of the Restatement. We agree.

B.

Plaintiffs assert that by instituting certain policies, defendants undertook to provide a protective service to Bachak, and thereby acquired a duty under § 323 of the Restatement (Second) of Torts to implement these policies with reasonable care. Plaintiffs contend the District Court erred in failing to consider all of the policies that defendants had in place, including Lockheed's Workplace Security policy, Harassment-Free Workplace policy, and Post Orders/Standard Operating Procedures for Contract Guard Force. Plaintiffs also bring our attention to U.S. Security's internal rule prohibiting guards from fraternizing with client-employees. But even assuming that (1) by instituting these policies, defendants undertook to protect Bachak from the harm that occurred here, and (2) at least some of these policies were negligently implemented by Lockheed and U.S. Security personnel, we nonetheless agree with the District Court that these policies did not constitute actionable undertakings under either prong of § 323.

We have said that for § 323(a) to apply, "the defendant's negligent performance must somehow put the plaintiff in a worse situation than if the defendant had never begun the performance."

No policy that plaintiffs assert defendants negligently implemented caused Bachak to be placed in a worse position than she would have been in the absence of the policy. Without Lockheed's anti-harassment policy, Bachak would have been subject to harassment without any internal corporate means to address it. And without Lockheed's Workplace Security policy and Post Orders (both of which directed personnel on how to identify and react to potentially violent situations), there would have been no coordinated effort to prevent or respond to workplace violence. Moreover, it is plaintiffs' position that U.S. Security's no-fraternization policy was effectively ignored with respect to Bachak and Zadolnny. Thus, the existence of the no-fraternization rule did not place Bachak in greater danger than if it had not been implemented at all.

Plaintiffs are no more successful under § 323(b) because Bachak did not rely on any of these policies to her detriment. As mentioned, Bachak and Zadolnny disregarded U.S. Security's no-fraternization rule. Similarly, Bachak never reported any threats or harassment to security, management, or the human resources department as required by Lockheed's policies addressing violence in the workplace. Indeed, when Lockheed employee Richard Lombardo became concerned that Zadolnny was bothering Bachak on the morning of the shooting, Bachak downplayed the situation and asked Lombardo twice to "leave it alone," and not report Zadolnny to the human resources department.

Bachak's failure to invoke the protective policies of Lockheed and U.S. Security precludes a finding of reliance. * * *

Given that there is no genuine issue of material fact that Bachak either (a) was made worse off by defendants' policies, or (b) relied on these policies to her detriment, we agree with the District Court that defendants did not owe Bachak a duty under Restatement § 323.

C.

Plaintiffs contend that even if we decline to find a duty under §§ 317 or 323 of the Restatement, we should nonetheless recognize that defendants had a duty to provide a safe workplace under Pennsylvania non-Restatement common law. But the duty to provide a safe workplace is essentially the duty to prevent foreseeable acts of harm. As we previously stated, Zadolnny's violent act was not reasonably foreseeable to Lockheed and U.S. Security. Thus, any non-Restatement common law claim, if one exists, must fail. * * *

IV.

We will affirm the District Court's grant of summary judgment to defendants Lockheed and U.S. Security on the Sabrics' negligence claims. With respect to Lockheed's indemnity cross-claim [against U.S. Security], we will reverse and remand to the District Court with instructions that summary judgment be entered for Lockheed.

C. HOUSING ISSUES

RYAN SCHAITKIN, DOMESTIC VIOLENCE AND EVICTION: HOUSING PROTECTIONS FOR SURVIVORS, AND WHAT WE CAN LEARN FROM EVICTION DIVERSION PROGRAMS

50 Fordham Urb. L. J. 173 (2022)
(footnotes omitted)

INTRODUCTION

There has been a growing eviction crisis in the United States over the past two decades. The Eviction Lab at Princeton University found that between 2000 and 2016, landlords filed for eviction against 9% of all renters in the United States, with an average 3.6 million eviction cases filed annually. Housing courts entered judgments against 1.5 million renters annually, or about 4% of all renters. These numbers may not fully represent the actual number of tenants forced to relocate. The Brookings Institute, for example, reports that some tenants are more likely to vacate their dwellings before any formal eviction because they expect the court will rule in the landlord's favor.

The eviction crisis impacts survivors of domestic violence in particular because of the ways in which nuisance ordinances, one-strike eviction policies, and the covenant of quiet enjoyment implied in landlord-tenant agreements are enforced against people experiencing domestic violence.

Nuisance ordinances often penalize conduct based on the frequency or amount of police responses to a certain property—the more tenants contact police, the more likely the residence is to be characterized as a nuisance. Once a municipality labels a property a nuisance, the landlord or property owner is often responsible for terminating the nuisance. Notably, approximately one-third of all nuisance claims are brought against women experiencing domestic violence.

Zero-tolerance, one-strike eviction policies can jeopardize a tenant's housing even more quickly than nuisance laws. Under the federal one-strike policy, criminal activity can serve as the basis for eviction even if the tenant is not the person who committed the crime. For tenants experiencing domestic violence, this means that their abusers' criminal acts (i.e., the domestic violence) could lead to an eviction, even without any fault by the tenant.

Meanwhile, through the implied covenant of quiet enjoyment, landlords are liable for breaches of their tenants' quiet enjoyment of the property. Landlords can face steep penalties for violating the covenant, including damages such as rent abatement and other reasonable expenses incurred by injured tenants. These policies incentivize landlords to evict survivors quickly, refuse to renew their leases, or discourage them from seeking police assistance in dangerous situations, to protect the quiet enjoyment of the premises for other tenants.

These policies and laws often do not distinguish between the wrongdoer and the victim, such that a residence may still be labeled as a nuisance even if the tenant is the survivor of domestic violence, rather than the source. This poses significant ramifications for survivors of domestic violence. This is notable because the Centers for Disease Control and Prevention (CDC) estimate that approximately 25% of women and 10% of men have experienced sexual violence, physical violence, or stalking by an intimate partner in their lifetime. They further estimate that approximately 6.6 million women and 5.8 million men experienced this conduct in the year prior to the survey's publishing. With so many annual incidences of domestic violence, nuisance ordinances and implied covenants in leasehold agreements can significantly impact tenants in unsafe living situations, and their ability to maintain a safe and stable housing situation. The result is that more than 50% of homeless women report that domestic violence is the cause of their homelessness.

One of the primary federal tools for protecting the housing of survivors is the Violence Against Women Act (VAWA). After more than a three-year lapse in the law dating back to December 2018, the VAWA was reauthorized by Congress and signed into law by President Joseph R. Biden on March 15, 2022. While the VAWA provides key housing protections for federally-covered housing, the law does not apply to housing beyond the federal framework, leaving many tenants unprotected. Some jurisdictions have attempted to fill these gaps with state- and local-level legislation, typically by providing that domestic violence cannot be grounds for eviction or by allowing for affirmative defenses based on domestic violence. The Uniform Law Commission (ULC), a group of attorneys which provides states with non-partisan draft legislation, also recently attempted to provide states with a statutory framework for combating domestic violence in housing with its Revised Uniform Residential Landlord and Tenant Act (RURLTA). Among other proposals, RURLTA permits tenants to escape unsafe situations by terminating their leases.

While the VAWA, RURLTA, and some state laws provide some protection to survivors of domestic violence, these laws fail to address the financial reality facing many women experiencing domestic violence. One study showed that approximately 94% of women in abusive relationships face some form of economic abuse, where their abuser exercises financial control over them. A significant proportion of women report losing employment because of their abuse. Further, the financial constraints placed on women by their abusers may prevent them from terminating their lease agreements because they are unable to afford new housing.

The VAWA and state and local policies attempt to lighten the burden placed on survivors of domestic violence by reducing the negative ramifications of nuisance ordinances, enforcement of quiet enjoyment covenants, and one-strike policies. Still, they fall short of achieving their goal of protecting housing for victims of domestic violence because they fail to address the financial instability that prevents many survivors from being able to move on from abusive situations. While federal, state, and local policies are crucial to protecting housing for survivors of domestic violence, they do not solve the problem completely. Eviction diversion programs such as rental assistance and right to counsel in housing courts are necessary to fill in statutory gaps in protection. Because statutory protections fall short of solving these problems, municipalities must invest in right to counsel and eviction diversion programs to supplement statutory protections and more thoroughly protect survivors of domestic violence. . . .

Nuisance laws and one strike policies make it more difficult for women to report domestic violence by discouraging survivors from seeking police assistance. For instance, under Norristown, Pennsylvania's nuisance ordinance, Lakisha Briggs was warned by police that one more altercation with her abusive boyfriend would result in an eviction. Ms. Briggs felt that she had no options—if she tried to kick her boyfriend out, somebody would call the police due to the altercation and she would be evicted. If she called the police herself to remove him, she would likewise be evicted. Ultimately, Ms. Briggs suffered another attack by her abuser which sent her to the hospital for emergency treatment. Norristown officials forced her landlord to evict her as a result. 80 Ms. Briggs sued Norristown over the eviction and the parties reached a settlement, one part of which was the repeal of the nuisance ordinance. Even after the Norristown repeal, nuisance ordinances and one-strike laws are still broadly used. More than 2,000 local governments still operate similar laws, which present potentially dangerous consequences for survivors of domestic violence. . .

Whereas nuisance and one-strike laws discourage survivors from engaging with law enforcement, a tenant can be evicted due to the covenant of quiet enjoyment simply based on repeated altercations that disturb their neighbors' peaceful enjoyment of their residences. . . Survivors may bc aware of the disturbances caused by the domestic violence, but may not feel that they can leave because of an inability to financially support themselves, the difficulties of having to raise their children as single parents, or a lack of a safe place to go if they were to leave. . .

III. LEGAL PROTECTIONS FOR SURVIVORS OF DOMESTIC VIOLENCE

. . .A. The Violence Against Women Act

In response to the severe consequences of eviction and the burden that they can place on survivors of domestic violence, legal protections have been instituted at the federal and state level to address these issues. Chief among these protections at the federal level is the VAWA. Initially passed in 1994 and reauthorized by Congress in 2000, 2005, and 2013, the VAWA implements key protections intended to protect survivors of domestic violence in the housing context.

Through the informal rulemaking process, the Department of Housing and Urban Development (HUD) defined the VAWA's housing protections to include: notification of occupancy rights to tenants under the VAWA; a prohibition on landlords from denying an otherwise qualified applicant admission to housing, or evicting a tenant from housing on the basis of domestic violence, dating violence, sexual assault, or stalking; and a prohibition on eviction on the basis of criminal activity directly relating to domestic violence if the tenant is the victim or threatened victim of the crime or if engaged in by someone else in the household.

The rule also provides that an actual or threatened act of domestic violence cannot be construed as good cause for terminating the tenancy; and that all covered housing providers are required to have emergency transfer plans to aid in the relocation of tenants to safe units in the event that a tenant believes they are unsafe in their current unit due to domestic violence. In such cases, the tenant may bifurcate the lease to remove/evict the abuser from the lease, and may be granted reasonable time up to 90 days to establish continued eligibility for covered housing following termination of the lease. . .

President Biden signed the VAWA reauthorization into law on March 15, 2022. . .

Title VI of the new law is dedicated to housing protections for survivors of domestic violence. While there will be some uncertainty about how some of the VAWA 2022 reauthorization provisions will be implemented until the enforcing agencies promulgate regulations through the rulemaking process, the text of the VAWA 2022 illustrates some changes to housing protections for survivors. Title VI, Section 601 expands the list of covered federal housing eligible for the housing protections under the VAWA. Title VI, Section 602 establishes a gender-based violence prevention office and creates a VAWA Director, whose duties include tasks such as coordinating with state and local governments for housing protection for survivors. Title VI, Section 602 also implements several new protections, including regular agency compliance reviews to ensure adherence to the housing protections and prohibitions on retaliation for employment of the protections by tenants.

Title VI, Section 603 attempts to eliminate some of the burden that nuisance ordinances place on survivors by including a right for tenants to report, without penalties, crimes of which they are the victim or for which they are not at fault, and prohibits as a penalty of that criminal activity the designation of the property as a nuisance. By attempting to legislate out the designation of properties as nuisances based on criminal activity, the VAWA 2022 takes an important step toward eliminating a key disincentive for survivors to report abuse to the police in covered federal housing. . .

Title VI, Section 605 of the VAWA 2022 expands funding so that survivors of domestic violence without the resources to obtain safe, permanent housing may be eligible for homeless assistance under the Act. . .Title VII of the VAWA discusses the issues of economic abuse and economic insecurity for survivors, and Section 704 has commissioned a study on economic security for survivors of domestic violence. . .

However, the VAWA's housing protections notably leave key gaps in protection for survivors. While the VAWA sets aside funding for housing grants, the funding is inadequate compared with the need. Congress' findings indicate that domestic violence costs survivors [in the U.S.] eight million hours of work each year, and that the annual cost of domestic violence for survivors is over eight billion dollars. And whereas upwards of 90% of all homeless women have experienced abuse, and more than 50% of homeless women say that domestic violence is the cause of their homelessness, the grant program has been capped annually at just four million dollars total.

Another key weakness is that tenants often do not have the means to find adequate representation to assert their rights in housing court proceedings, so they may not be able to access the protections to which they are entitled. Finally, despite the VAWA 2022's expansion of the list of federal housing entities covered for housing protections, the protections are necessarily limited to covered federal housing, leaving many of the 44.1 million rental households in the United States without the benefit of the VAWA's housing protections.

B. State and Municipal Housing Protections

Considering the VAWA's limitations to covered federal housing entities, it is also important to examine state and local housing protections for private renters. Some local jurisdictions have attempted to protect survivors of domestic violence by providing that domestic violence cannot be grounds for eviction. Other states have implemented statutes that allow tenants to terminate their leases early in response to domestic violence, rape, sexual assault, or stalking.

As with the VAWA, however, these protections may be limited in their efficacy due to various factors. As Langley notes, these laws often assume that the survivor can successfully keep the abuser away from the home, which is not always possible due to the relationship between the survivor and the abuser.

Additionally, when considering the significant financial strain that those with low economic security face with respect to renting, and the financial dependency abusers impose on survivors of domestic violence, it may be unrealistic to expect that survivors have the financial means to take advantage of protections such as opting out of a tenancy because they may not have the financial flexibility to find alternative housing. . .

One potentially effective tool to combat eviction and homelessness among survivors of domestic violence are eviction diversion programs that provide rental assistance [The author states that Congress authorized such assistance during the COVID 19 pandemic], access to legal counsel in housing courts [where only 3% of tenants typically have counsel while 81% of landlords do], and alternatives to court proceedings to mediate housing issues. Such programs may eliminate two key issues confronting survivors who face eviction due to domestic violence—financial instability, and a lack of awareness of their legal options. . .

To solve this problem, three states have recently guaranteed their citizens a right to counsel in housing eviction courts—Washington, Maryland, and Connecticut. Prior to 2021, zero states guaranteed such a right. . .Research has shown that providing tenants with legal assistance throughout the eviction process can save municipalities money as well. For instance, a program in New York City connected 1,300 families with counsel during the eviction process, costing the city approximately $450,000 but saving the city around $700,000 in shelter costs for tenants who may have otherwise been evicted. . .

[Editor's Notes: 1. Landlords who fail to evict a perpetrator of domestic violence upon request may be liable under the duty to provide quiet enjoyment or under the duty to protect tenants from foreseeable criminal

acts of third parties. Landlords may also be liable for a retaliatory eviction of a victim of domestic violence if the basis is that the victim called the police.

2. Maine passed a statute in 2015 allowing the perpetrator of abuse to be removed from the lease and allowing the survivor to stay in the rental unit even if the survivor was not a signatory to the lease. See Maine Statutes, Title 14, section 6001. See also Maine Statutes Title 14, section 6010, allowing survivors to seek civil damages from a perpetrator of abuse for early termination of a lease due to domestic violence, including back rent, current rent, moving costs, damage to the unit, court costs, and attorney fees. Hawaii Statutes, Sec. 521–82, also passed in 2015, has similar provisions.]

U.S. DEPARTMENT OF HOUSING AND URBAN DEVELOPMENT OFFICE OF GENERAL COUNSEL, GUIDANCE ON APPLICATION OF FAIR HOUSING ACT STANDARDS TO THE ENFORCEMENT OF LOCAL NUISANCE AND CRIME-FREE HOUSING ORDINANCES AGAINST VICTIMS OF DOMESTIC VIOLENCE, OTHER CRIME VICTIMS, AND OTHERS WHO REQUIRE POLICE OR EMERGENCY SERVICES

Washington, D.C. (2016)
(footnotes omitted)

I. INTRODUCTION

The Fair Housing Act (or the Act) prohibits discrimination in the sale, rental or financing of dwellings and in other housing-related activities on the basis of race, color, religion, sex, disability, familial status, or national origin. The Department of Housing and Urban Development's (HUD's) Office of General Counsel issues this guidance to explain how the Fair Housing Act applies to ensure that the growing number of local nuisance ordinances and crime-free housing ordinances do not lead to discrimination in violation of the Act. * * * This guidance therefore addresses both the discriminatory effects and disparate treatment methods of proof under the Act, and briefly describes the obligation of HUD fund recipients to consider the impacts of these ordinances in assessing how they will fulfill their affirmative obligation to further fair housing. * * *

II. BACKGROUND

A. Nuisance Ordinances

A growing number of local governments are enacting a variety of nuisance ordinances that can affect housing in potentially discriminatory ways. * * * These ordinances often label various types of conduct associated with a property—whether the conduct is by a resident, guest or other person—a "nuisance" and require the landlord or homeowner to abate the nuisance under the threat of a variety of penalties. The conduct defined as a nuisance varies by ordinance and has ranged from conduct affecting the appearance of the property—such as littering, failing to tend to one's lawn, or abandoning a vehicle, to general prohibitions related to the conduct of a tenant or guest—such as disorderly or disruptive conduct, disrupting the quiet use and enjoyment of neighboring properties, or any criminal conduct occurring on or near the property. Nuisance conduct often includes what is characterized by the ordinance as an "excessive" number of calls for emergency police or ambulance services, typically defined as just a few calls within a specified period of time by a tenant, neighbor, or other third party, whether or not directly associated with the property.

In some jurisdictions, an incident of domestic violence is defined as a nuisance without regard to whether the resident is the victim or the perpetrator[, and in others,] * * * incidents of domestic violence are not specifically defined as nuisances, but may still be categorized as such because the ordinance broadly defines nuisance activity as the violation of any federal, state or local law, or includes conduct such as disturbing the peace, excessive noise, disorderly conduct, or calls for emergency services that exceed a specified number within a given timeframe. Some ordinances specifically define "excessive" calls for police or emergency services as nuisances, even when the person in need of services is a victim of domestic violence or another crime or otherwise in need of police, medical or other emergency assistance. Even where ordinances expressly exclude victims of domestic violence or other crimes, victims are still frequently deemed to have committed nuisance conduct because police and other emergency service providers may not log the call as domestic violence, instead categorizing it incorrectly as property damage, disturbing the peace or another type of nuisance conduct. Some victims also are hesitant or afraid to identify themselves as victims of abuse.

The ordinances generally require housing providers either to abate the alleged nuisance or risk penalties, such as fines, loss of their rental permits, condemnation of their properties and, in some extreme instances, incarceration. Some ordinances may require the housing provider to evict the resident and his or her household after a specified number of alleged nuisance violations—often quite low—within a specific timeframe. For example, in at least one jurisdiction, three calls for emergency police or medical help within a 30-day period is considered to be a nuisance, and in another jurisdiction, two calls for such services within one year qualify as a nuisance. Even when nuisance ordinances do not explicitly require evictions, a number of landlords resort to evicting the household to avoid penalties.

In many jurisdictions, domestic-violence-related calls are the largest category of calls received by police. * * * From 1994 to 2010, approximately 80 percent of the victims of intimate partner violence in the nation were women. Women with disabilities are more likely to be subjected to domestic violence than women without disabilities. * * * Studies have found that victims of domestic violence often do not report their initial incident of domestic violence and instead suffer multiple assaults before contacting the police or seeking a protective order or other assistance. * * * Nuisance ordinances (and crime-free housing ordinances) are becoming an additional factor that operates to discourage victims from reporting domestic violence and obtaining the emergency police and medical assistance they need.

For example, a woman in Norristown, Pennsylvania who had been subjected to domestic violence by her ex-boyfriend was warned by police that if she made one more 911 call, she and her young daughter would be evicted from their home pursuant to the local nuisance ordinance. The ordinance operated under a "three strike" policy, allowing her no more than two calls to 911 for help. As a result, the woman was too afraid to call the police when her ex-boyfriend returned to her home and stabbed her. Rather than call for an ambulance, she ran out of her house in the hope she would not lose her housing. A neighbor called the police and, due to the serious nature of her injuries, the woman was airlifted to the hospital. A few days after she returned home from the hospital, she was served with eviction papers pursuant to the local nuisance ordinance.

B. Crime-Free Lease Ordinances and Crime-Free Housing Programs

A number of local governments enforce crime-free lease ordinances or promote crime-free housing programs that incorporate the use of crime-free lease addenda. Some of these ordinances operate like nuisance ordinances and penalize housing providers who fail to evict tenants when a tenant, resident or other person has allegedly engaged in a violation of a federal, state and/or local law, regardless of whether the tenant or resident was the victim of the crime at issue. Others mandate or strongly encourage housing providers to include lease provisions that require or permit housing providers to evict tenants where a tenant or resident has allegedly engaged in a single incident of criminal activity, regardless of whether the activity occurred on or off the property.

These provisions often allow housing providers to evict tenants when a guest or other person allowed onto the property by the tenant or resident allegedly engages in criminal activity on or near the property, regardless of whether the resident was a victim of the criminal activity or a party to it. The criminal activity that constitutes a lease violation is frequently broadly and ambiguously defined and may include any violation of federal, state or local laws, however minor. Thus, disorderly conduct, excessive noise and similar activity may constitute a crime resulting in eviction. * * *

Furthermore, some crime-free housing ordinances mandate or strongly encourage housing providers to implement lease provisions that require eviction based on an arrest alone, or do not require an arrest or conviction to evict a tenant, but rather allow housing providers to rely on a preponderance of the evidence standard while remaining silent on who is responsible for determining that this standard has been met. The principles discussed in HUD's "Office of General Counsel Guidance on Application of Fair Housing Act Standards to the Use of Criminal Records by Providers of Housing and Real Estate-Related Transactions" are instructive in evaluating the fair housing implications of crime-free lease ordinances and crime-free lease addenda mandated or encouraged by localities and enforced by housing providers.

III. DISCRIMINATORY EFFECTS LIABILITY AND ENFORCEMENT OF NUISANCE ORDINANCES AND CRIME-FREE HOUSING ORDINANCES

A local government's policies and practices to address nuisances, including enactment or enforcement of a nuisance or crime-free housing ordinance, violate the Fair Housing Act when they have an unjustified discriminatory effect, even when the local government had no intent to discriminate. Under this standard, a facially-neutral policy or practice that has a discriminatory effect violates the Act if it is not supported by a legally sufficient justification. Thus, where a policy or practice that restricts the availability of housing on the basis of nuisance conduct has a disparate impact on individuals of a particular protected class, the policy or practice is unlawful under the Fair Housing Act if it is not necessary to serve a substantial, legitimate, nondiscriminatory interest of the local government, or if such interest could be served by another practice that has a less discriminatory effect. * * * Discriminatory effects liability is assessed under a three-step, burden-shifting standard requiring a fact-specific analysis. * * * As explained in Section IV, below, a different analytical framework is used to evaluate claims of intentional discrimination.

A. Evaluating Whether the Challenged Nuisance Ordinance or Crime-Free Housing Ordinance Policy or Practice Has a Discriminatory Effect

In the first step of the analysis, a plaintiff (or HUD in an administrative enforcement action) has the burden to prove that a local government's enforcement of its nuisance or crime-free housing ordinance has a discriminatory effect, that is, that the local government's nuisance or crime-free housing ordinance policy or practice results or predictably will result in a disparate impact on a group of persons because of a protected characteristic. This is also true for a local government's policy or practice encouraging or incentivizing housing providers to adopt crime-free lease addenda (and the discussion throughout the guidance applies equally to such actions). * * *

Different data sources may be available and useful to demonstrate that a government's ordinance actually or predictably results in a disparate impact, which is ultimately a fact-specific and case-specific inquiry. * * * For example, nationally, women comprise approximately 80 percent of all individuals subjected to domestic violence each year, which may provide grounds for HUD to investigate under the Fair Housing Act allegations that the adverse effects of a nuisance ordinance fall more heavily on victims of domestic violence. * * *

B. Evaluating Whether the Challenged Nuisance Ordinance or Crime-Free Housing Ordinance is Necessary to Achieve a Substantial, Legitimate, Nondiscriminatory Interest

In the second step[, * * * t]he interest of the local government may not be hypothetical or speculative, meaning the local government must be able to prove with evidence what the government interest is, that its interest is legitimate, substantial and nondiscriminatory, and that the challenged practice is necessary to achieve that interest. Assertions based on generalizations or stereotypes about persons deemed to engage in nuisance or criminal conduct are not sufficient to prove that an ordinance or its enforcement is necessary to achieve the local government's substantial, legitimate, nondiscriminatory interest.

As explained in the preamble to HUD's 2013 Discriminatory Effects Final Rule, a "substantial" interest is a core interest of the organization that has a direct relationship to the function of that organization. The requirement that an interest be "legitimate" means that the local government's justification must be genuine and not false or fabricated. A number of local governments have [these] ordinances * * * because the residents requested police, medical or other emergency assistance, without regard to whether the calls were reasonable under the circumstances. Where such a practice is challenged and proven to have a disparate impact, the local government would have the difficult burden to prove that cutting off access to emergency services for those in grave need of such services, including victims of domestic violence or other crimes, thereby potentially endangering their lives, safety and security, in fact achieves a core interest of the local government and was not undertaken for discriminatory reasons or in a discriminatory manner. * * *

C. Evaluating Whether There Is a Less Discriminatory Alternative

* * * If the analysis reaches the third step, the burden shifts back to the plaintiff or HUD to prove that such interest could be served by another policy or practice that has a less discriminatory effect[, * * * which] will depend on the particulars of the policy or practice at issue, as well as the specific nature of the underlying problem the ordinance seeks to address.

IV. INTENTIONAL DISCRIMINATION AND ENFORCEMENT OF NUISANCE ORDINANCES OR CRIME-FREE HOUSING ORDINANCES

A local government may also violate the Fair Housing Act if it intentionally discriminates in its adoption or enforcement of a nuisance or crime-free housing ordinance. This occurs when the local government treats a resident differently because of sex, race or another protected characteristic. The analysis is the same as is used to analyze whether any housing ordinance was enacted or enforced for intentionally discriminatory reasons.

Generally, two types of claims of intentional discrimination may arise. One type of intentional discrimination claim arises where a local government enacts a nuisance ordinance or crime-free housing ordinance for discriminatory reasons. Another type is where a government selectively enforces a nuisance or crime-free housing ordinance in a discriminatory manner. For the first type of claim, in determining whether a facially neutral ordinance was enacted for discriminatory reasons, courts generally look to certain factors[, * * *] all of which need not be satisfied, includ[ing], but are not limited to: (1) the *impact* of the ordinance at issue, such as whether the ordinance disproportionately impacts women compared to men, minority residents compared to white residents, or residents with disabilities or a certain type of disability compared to residents without disabilities; (2) the *historical background* of the ordinance, such as whether there is a history of discriminatory conduct by the local government; (3) the *specific sequence of events*, such as whether the locality adopted the ordinance only after significant community opposition motivated by race or another protected characteristic; (4) *departures from the normal procedural sequence*, such as whether the locality deviated from normal procedures for enacting a nuisance ordinance; (5) *substantive departures*, such as whether the factors usually considered important suggest that a local government should have reached a different result; and (6) the *legislative or administrative record*, such as any statements by members of the local decision-making body.

For the second type of intentional discrimination claim, selective enforcement, where there is no "smoking gun" proving that a local government is selectively enforcing a nuisance or crime-free housing ordinance in a discriminatory way, courts look for evidence from which such an inference can be drawn. The evidence might be direct or circumstantial. For example, courts have noted that an inference of intentional sex discrimination could arise directly from evidence that a housing provider seeks to evict female residents shortly after incidents of domestic violence.

A common method of establishing intentional discrimination indirectly, through circumstantial evidence, is through the familiar burden-shifting method of proving intentional discrimination originally established by the Supreme Court in the employment context. In the standard complaint alleging selective enforcement of a nuisance or crime-free ordinance for discriminatory reasons, the plaintiff first must produce evidence to establish a prima facie case of disparate treatment. This may be shown, for example, by evidence that: (1) the plaintiff (or complainant in an administrative enforcement action) is a member of a protected class; (2) a local government official (or housing provider, depending on the circumstances) took action to enforce the nuisance or crime-free ordinance or lease addendum against the plaintiff or complainant because the plaintiff or complainant allegedly engaged in nuisance or criminal conduct; (3) the local government official or housing provider did not take action to enforce the nuisance or crime-free ordinance or lease addendum against a similarly-situated resident not of the plaintiff or complainant's protected class who engaged in comparable conduct; and (4) the local government or housing provider subjected the plaintiff or complainant to an adverse housing action as a result of the enforcement of the nuisance or crime-free ordinance or lease addendum. It is then the burden of the local government and/or housing provider, depending on the circumstances, to offer evidence of a legitimate, nondiscriminatory reason for the adverse housing action. * * * [Then], a plaintiff or HUD may still prevail by showing that the proffered reason was not the true reason for the adverse housing decision, and was instead a mere pretext for unlawful discrimination. * * *

V. ASSESSMENT OF NUISANCE ORDINANCES AND CRIME-FREE HOUSING ORDINANCES AS PART OF THE DUTY TO AFFIRMATIVELY FURTHER FAIR HOUSING

In addition to prohibiting discrimination, the Fair Housing Act requires HUD to administer programs and activities relating to housing and urban development in a manner that affirmatively furthers the policies of the Act * * *: recipients also must take meaningful action to overcome fair housing issues and related barriers to fair housing choice and disparities in access to opportunity based on sex, race, national origin, disability, and other characteristics protected by the Act. Congress has repeatedly reaffirmed th[is] mandate by requiring HUD program participants to certify that they will affirmatively further fair housing as a [funding] condition. * * * In conducting their assessments of fair housing, state and local governments should assess their nuisance ordinances, crime-free housing ordinances and related policies or practices, including the processes by which nuisance ordinance and crime-free housing ordinances are enforced, and consider how these ordinances, policies or practices may affect access to housing and access to police, medical and other governmental services based on sex, race, national origin, disability, and other characteristics protected by the Act. One step a local government may take toward meeting its duty to affirmatively further fair housing is to eliminate disparities by repealing a nuisance or crime-free ordinance that requires or encourages evictions for use of emergency services, including 911 calls, by domestic violence or other crime victims. * * *

[Editor's Note: VAWA 2022 improves tenants' rights in federally subsidized housing (e.g., Section 8) if they are being denied housing or evicted for being survivors of domestic violence, sexual assault, dating violence, or stalking. Complaints can be filed on the Housing and Urban Development (HUD) website.]

A.S. v. BEEN

228 F.Supp.3d 315 (S.D.N.Y. 2017)
(most citations omitted)

Plaintiff A.S. ("Plaintiff") brings this action against Vicki Been, in her capacity as Commissioner of the New York City Department of Housing Preservation and Development ("HPD"), and HPD itself (collectively, "Defendants"), alleging that Defendants deprived Plaintiff of her due process rights, discriminated against her on the basis of her sex, and acted in a manner that was arbitrary, capricious and contrary to federal and local law by denying her the opportunity to be heard at an HPD hearing held to determine the termination of a voucher issued to Plaintiff's husband pursuant to Section of the Housing Act of 1937.

Plaintiff and her husband lived in an apartment together, with the husband receiving a Section 8 voucher pursuant to the HPD Housing Choice Voucher Program. In February 2014, Plaintiff alleged that her husband attempted to rape her. After reporting the incident to the police and obtaining an order of protection against him, Plaintiff submitted a HUD-91066 Form to HPD pursuant to the Violence Against Women Act ("VAWA") to initiate a bifurcation procedure through which the Section 8 voucher held by the husband could be transferred to Plaintiff. In June 2015, after Plaintiff submitted additional paperwork and met with HPD representatives in support of her claim, HPD, without notifying Plaintiff, held a hearing regarding the termination of the husband's Section 8 voucher. After the hearing, HPD notified a representative at Sanctuary for Families that the Section 8 voucher would remain with the husband. In February 2016, HPD sent Plaintiff a letter notifying her that the Section 8 voucher issued to her husband was terminated, with no mention of a process to appeal the decision.

Plaintiff subsequently filed the Complaint alleging six causes of action: (1) violation of due process; (2) disparate treatment under Title VIII of the Civil Rights Act of 1968 ("Title VIII"), 42 U.S.C. Section 3604; (3) disparate impact under Title VIII; (4) disparate treatment under New York City Human Rights Law, N.Y.C. Admin. Code Section 8–107(5); (5) disparate impact under New York City Human Rights Law; and (6) arbitrary and capricious action by Defendants.

At the December 9, 2016 initial conference in this matter counsel for Defendants indicated that they intended to move to dismiss. The Court ordered a briefing schedule for the parties to submit letter briefs regarding Defendants' proposed motion. Defendants filed a letter brief on December 19, 2016, arguing that Plaintiff's Complaint should be dismissed because: (1) Plaintiff had no protected property interest in her husband's Section 8 Voucher because the voucher was not in her name; (2) Plaintiff's Fair Housing Act ("FHA") claim should be dismissed because Plaintiff's claim does not concern a "dwelling" within the scope of the FHA; and (3) the Court should decline to exercise supplemental jurisdiction over Plaintiff's remaining state law claims. Plaintiff's December 30, 2016 opposition letter argues that: (1) VAWA establishes that Plaintiff has a protected property interest in her husband's Section 8 Voucher; and (2) the FHA extends to conduct by actors who affect the availability of housing, such as the HPD.

The Court now construes the correspondence described above as a motion by Defendants to dismiss the Complaint ("Motion"). For the reasons discussed below, Defendants' Motion is DENIED.

I. DISCUSSION

A. Plaintiff's Due Process Claim

When determining whether a plaintiff has an actionable due process claim, courts must determine whether the plaintiff possesses a liberty or property interest and, if so, what process was due before the plaintiff was deprived of such interest.

"A termination of [Section 8 voucher payments] or voucher holders' participation in the program constitutes a deprivation [of property interests] that would entitle them to procedural safeguards." Other courts have held that merely applying for Section 8 housing entitles an individual to certain due process rights where the local housing authority's practices establish procedures applicable to the denial of an application.

The law remains unsettled, however, regarding whether a spouse, who was not the voucher holder herself, has a protected property interest in her spouse's Section 8 voucher. The precedents Defendants cite in their Motion are inapplicable to this case. *Junior v. City of New York, Housing Preservation & Development Corporation* addressed whether due process rights attached when the housing department determined a plaintiff should pay a larger share of rent. *Morales v. Related Management Company* dealt with a plaintiff who was rejected for a specific apartment, but still retained his Section 8 voucher.

In this case, HPD terminated Plaintiff's husband's Section 8 voucher and did not transfer the voucher to Plaintiff. While there is authority that suggests it is common practice in other parts of the country to transfer a voucher from an accused abuser to that person's partner following proper notification under VAWA by the abused partner, no case speaks to this precise question.

A close reading of VAWA suggests that finding Plaintiff has no interest in the husband's Section 8 voucher would run counter to the purpose of the statute to provide certain protections to survivors of domestic violence. VAWA clearly contemplates the circumstances of this case by establishing a bifurcation procedure to allow public housing agencies to terminate assistance to any individual who engages in activity relating to domestic violence without "penalizing a victim of such criminal activity who is also a tenant or lawful occupant of the housing." The statute further states that, if the individual who is removed due to involvement in activity relating to domestic violence is the "sole tenant eligible to receive assistance under a covered housing program," the public housing agency "shall provide any remaining tenant an opportunity to establish eligibility for the covered housing program."

VAWA therefore establishes a system whereby, if the original voucher holder's voucher is terminated, the remaining tenant must have an opportunity to establish eligibility to receive the voucher. In this case, if Plaintiff's husband's Section 8 voucher was terminated, Plaintiff herself would be entitled to an opportunity to establish her eligibility for the Section 8 voucher. The provision of this opportunity to be heard illustrates that other occupants of a residence secured through a Section 8 voucher who are not the voucher holders themselves nonetheless have some interest in the voucher itself. This fact is further underscored by the transfer of vouchers by other housing authorities from the alleged abuser to the survivor pursuant to a VAWA claim.

Furthermore, HPD's own Housing Choice Voucher Program Administrative Plan indicates that a domestic violence survivor has rights when the original Section 8 Voucher was terminated due to activity related to domestic violence. The Administrative Plan states that "HPD may exercise its explicit authority to terminate assistance to any individual who is a tenant or lawful occupant and who engages in criminal activity directly relating to domestic violence, dating violence, sexual assault, or stalking against affiliated individual or other individual . . . without terminating assistance to, or otherwise penalizing the victim of such violence who is also a tenant or lawful occupant." The Administrative Plan further notes that HPD "will consider the role of domestic violence in the family breakup and follow policy when determining who will retain the subsidy."

The Court is persuaded that both VAWA and HPD's own Administrative Plan demonstrates that Plaintiff had a sufficient interest in her husband's voucher, as both establish procedures to allow Plaintiff an opportunity to seek eligibility to receive the voucher if HPD terminated the husband's voucher. VAWA expressly prescribes a bifurcation procedure to provide certain protections with regards to housing, amongst other things, for domestic violence survivors. Were this Court to find that Plaintiff in this case does not have a sufficient property interest in her husband's Section 8 voucher these protections would serve no purpose. Accordingly, the Court finds that Plaintiff has a sufficient property interest in her husband's Section 8 voucher to defeat dismissal of her due process claim.

B. Plaintiff's Fair Housing Act Claim

The FHA makes it unlawful to "refuse to sell or rent after the making of a bone fide offer, or to refuse to negotiate for the sale or rental of, or otherwise make unavailable or deny, a dwelling" on the basis of race, color, religion, sex, familial status, or national origin.

While some courts outside of the Second Circuit have read the FHA to strictly apply to landlords, owners and others who offer dwellings for rent or sale only, within the Second Circuit "[t]he phrase 'otherwise make unavailable' has been interpreted to reach a wide variety of discriminatory housing practices, including discriminatory zoning restrictions[.]"

The Second Circuit has traditionally accorded plaintiffs bringing FHA claims the "broadest possible grounds for standing." Plaintiffs in the Second Circuit have, in the past, brought suit under the FHA because they were denied Section 8 vouchers.

In this case, HPD's decision regarding Plaintiff's Section 8 voucher impacted Plaintiff's ability to secure housing. The Court is persuaded that Defendants, through their administration of the Housing Choice Voucher Program, have the capacity to "otherwise make unavailable" Section 8 vouchers to individuals, such that their actions are subject to the FHA. Therefore, the Court finds that Plaintiff's FHA claim falls within the scope of the statute.

As Plaintiff has a protected property interest in her husband's Section 8 voucher sufficient to support a due process claim at this stage of the proceedings, and Defendants' actions with regards to administering the Housing Choice Voucher Program fall within the purview of the FHA, Defendants Motion to Dismiss is DENIED.

ELMASSIAN V. FLORES

69 Cal.App.5th Supp. 1 (2021)
(footnotes and citations omitted)

In this matter of first impression, we construe the affirmative defense in unlawful detainer evictions that "a landlord shall not terminate a tenancy . . . based upon an act or acts against a tenant . . . that constitute domestic violence." We hold:

(1) A tenant can assert the defense to being evicted based upon domestic violence causing a nuisance on rented property even if non-domestic violence grounds are also asserted in the action. The language of the statute and its legislative history indicate that, although a tenant can be evicted for non-domestic violence grounds even when the tenant is a victim of domestic violence, including due to creating a nuisance for reasons other than domestic violence and/or failing to pay rent, in instances where the action is based on both domestic violence and non-domestic violence grounds, a tenant must be allowed to maintain the [Ca. Code of Civil Procedure] section 1161.3 defense as to the domestic violence grounds.

(2) The requisite documentation needed to support the defense can consist of a report prepared by the police narrating a domestic violence incident

based solely on a tenant's statements which do not name the perpetrator of the violence, do not indicate the relationship between the victim and the perpetrator, and only document one of multiple instances of violence relied on by the landlord to evict the tenant. The statute provides the domestic violence defense must be documented by "[a] copy of a written report, written within the last 180 days, by a peace officer . . . stating that the tenant . . . has filed a report alleging that [the tenant] is a victim of domestic violence. . . ." and the language used and the statute's legislative history do not evince a requirement that further information be provided.

The trial court granted a directed verdict as to the defense by defendant and appellant Noemi Flores that plaintiff and respondent Nora Elmassian terminated the tenancy and brought an unlawful detainer action based upon acts of domestic violence committed in the apartment complex where defendant lived. The jury was thus not allowed to consider whether defendant should prevail on her defense as to domestic violence grounds in the action, and determined plaintiff proved defendant committed a nuisance on the property. The court entered judgment in plaintiff's favor, and defendant appealed.

We conclude the court erred in granting a directed verdict regarding the defense. There was evidence presented of defendant having committed a nuisance based upon domestic violence and non-domestic violence acts, and we cannot tell from the jury's verdict on which grounds the jury rested its decision. Viewing the evidence in the light most favorable to the party opposing the directed verdict and without considering the credibility of the witnesses, as we are required to do on appellate review, we find there was substantial evidence supporting the domestic violence defense. We thus reverse the judgment.

. . .Defendant answered the complaint, generally denying plaintiff's allegations, and asserting several defenses. On the day trial started, during a case management conference, the court determined defendant would be asserting the defenses that the case was brought in retaliation to defendant complaining about her unit's state of disrepair, and because the action was based upon acts of domestic violence.

[The evidence showed that defendant and her partner/co-tenant often argued, resulting in the partner's arrest and a restraining order prohibiting him from coming near defendant and the younger children; he complied. However, another man started coming to defendant's apartment against her wishes and causing trouble, including being violent toward her and breaking her door. Defendant reported these incidents to the police and introduced the reports at trial. The court did not allow the jury to consider the domestic violence evidence, which the court of appeal found was legal error, so it reversed the judgment in favor of the plaintiff.]

[Editor's Notes: 1. In "A Home with Dignity: Domestic Violence and Property Rights," 2014 B.Y.U. L. Rev. 1 (2014), Professor Margaret E.

Johnson discusses protective orders and housing, including "move-out" orders, orders that allow the restrained person to stay but prohibit abuse of the protected person, and orders that require the restrained person to pay for another residence for the protected person. She also discusses laws that prohibit discrimination in renting or selling a home to a survivor of abuse. The author advocates for a comprehensive theory that addresses the rights to a home when there is domestic violence by focusing on each party's dignity, the importance of home, and ending domestic violence, as opposed to merely "safety." This approach includes providing economic support for survivors who want to stay in their homes or find a new one, establishing shelters for abusers, and providing more funding for shelters and transitional housing for survivors.

2. In "Flexible Funding as a Promising Strategy to Prevent Homelessness for Survivors of Intimate Partner Violence," J. of Interpersonal Violence 1 (2016), DOI: 10.1177/0886260516664318, Professor Cris Sullivan, Heather Bomsta, and Margaret Hacskaylo describe a program based on "short-term financial crises [facing survivors of abuse] with spiraling effects that could have been averted by access to a limited amount of cash." The program provides flexible funding to domestic violence programs to help survivors maintain employment, pay moving or storage fees, change locks, and pay security deposits and first month's rent. The authors evaluated a program in Washington, D.C. that gave survivors funding to facilitate either remaining in their homes or obtaining safe and permanent housing. Sometimes advocates also intervened with landlords, agencies, or the legal system at the survivor's request. The average grant was $2000, usually for rent, which enabled recipients to keep their jobs, etc. Almost all the participants were housed 6 months later. Several survivors said this help was "life saving" for them and their children, and many said it greatly lowered their stress and improved their parenting.]

CHAPTER 17

IMMIGRATION AND HUMAN RIGHTS ISSUES

■ ■ ■

This chapter concludes the book by bringing the topic back to the international aspects of domestic violence, which were touched on toward the beginning of the book. It also illustrates two of the ongoing themes in the book: first, whether domestic violence is caused by individual pathology or is a societal epidemic indicative of tolerance or support for of male domination of women, and second, the pattern of social struggle leading to improved policies and laws addressing gender based violence which is followed by backlash.

The first part of the chapter deals with immigration policies involving survivors of domestic violence in the U.S., which have evolved greatly in the past few years. A new article gives an overview of the history of federal laws regarding battered immigrant women, including VAWA. The author states that the motivation behind these policies was "profound compassion and humanity," but that the ways the laws and policies are enforced is frequently "heartlessly rubbing salt into the wounds of immigrant survivors of abuse." Then comes another new article describing a national survey including over 11,000 survivors of domestic violence and concluding that the VAWA self-petition is life-changing. This is followed by a summary of a recent case regarding the federal rule that made immigrants ineligible for entry into the U.S. or becoming a permanent resident if they accepted public benefits, which many survivors of domestic violence must rely on, and how that "public charge" rule came to an end.

The next article discusses the intersections between trafficking, domestic violence, and marriage immigration, also known as the mail-order bride industry.

The second part of the chapter addresses domestic violence as the basis for an asylum claim in U.S. courts. A new article describes the history of this jurisprudence and how significant it was that in 2021 Attorney General Merrick Garland vacated *A-B-*, a case involving a battered Salvadoran woman in which his predecessor, Jeff Sessions, had announced a policy making it very difficult for applicants to qualify for asylum based on domestic violence.

Then comes a recent case, *Rodriguez Tornes v. Garland*, in which a battered Mexican woman was denied asylum by the Board of Immigration

Appeals, but the Ninth Circuit Court of Appeals reversed, holding that she had been persecuted based on her feminist political opinion, and that this met the requirements for asylum. The court quotes expert testimony from the author of this textbook in concluding that domestic violence is not an individual relationship problem, as the BIA claimed, but instead is based in a patriarchal system in which men dominate and control women and the State does not intervene, thus in effect supporting male dominance and violence against women by intimate partners.

The book ends with the big picture: materials describing domestic violence as an international human rights issue. This is still a concept with which many courts have yet to agree, given that human rights law, like most of the legal system, has viewed domestic violence as a private, not a State, issue. The first article explains why the international human rights perspective is so important in the domestic violence context. The next piece argues that rape, including marital rape, should be included in international Conventions covering women's rights and violence against women, since sex without consent is a violation of international human rights.

The third article in this section shows how VAWA has expanded to have international impact. The next article illustrates the human rights dimensions of domestic violence through focusing on a key U.S. Supreme Court decision holding that police are not mandated to enforce restraining orders, *Castle Rock v. Gonzales;* this was followed by a decision in the same matter from the Inter-American Commission on Human Rights, holding that the U.S. had violated the petitioner's human rights and those of her children who were murdered by their father. The commentator calls for a new concept of the State and of the U.S. Constitution, moving from a negative role to a pro-active one in which the State has a duty to protect its citizens from domestic violence.

A new article describes the recent backlash against the Istanbul Convention, the only European international Convention dealing with violence against women, based on accusations that condemning gender-based violence goes against traditional concepts of the family where men are in charge.

The book ends on a positive note, with a resolution passed in many U.S. cities and counties, declaring that "Freedom from Domestic Violence is an International Human Right."

A. IMMIGRATION

1. OVERVIEW, U VISAS, VAWA SELF PETITIONS

MONIKA BATRA KASHYAP, HEARTLESS IMMIGRATION LAW: RUBBING SALT INTO THE WOUNDS OF IMMIGRANT SURVIVORS OF DOMESTIC VIOLENCE

9 Tulane Law Review 51 (2020)
(footnotes and quotations omitted)

. . .II. LEGAL PROTECTIONS CREATED SPECIFICALLY FOR IMMIGRANT SURVIVORS OF DOMESTIC VIOLENCE

Immigrant women survivors of domestic violence experience what Kimberle Crenshaw refers to as "[i]ntersectional subordination"—where systems of oppression such as race, gender, national origin, and class domination "interact[ ] with preexisting vulnerabilities to create yet another dimension of disempowerment." As a result of these intersecting "patterns of subordination," immigrant women survivors of domestic violence—particularly immigrant women of color—are uniquely vulnerable. Several factors exacerbate the experience of domestic violence for immigrant women: (1) language barriers, (2) the fear of deportation and family separation, (3) a lack of familiarity with legal systems and protections, (4) the lack of legal authorization to work and achieve financial independence, (5) a lack of culturally sensitive services and shelters, and (6) the influence of culture-specific notions of traditional gender roles. A recognition of this unique vulnerability led Congress to pass a series of federal immigration provisions over the past thirty years that are designed to protect such survivors. These provisions are the battered spouse waiver, the VAWA self-petition, and the U-Visa. This Part of the Article will set forth the legislative history of the battered spouse waiver, the VAWA self-petition, and the U-Visa in order to reveal their genesis within legislation rooted in profound compassion and humanity.

A. The 1990 Battered Spouse Waiver (Immigration Act of 1990)

The battered spouse waiver was the first immigration provision Congress created that acknowledged the unique barriers faced by immigrant women survivors of domestic violence. The provision was introduced through the Immigration Act of 1990and was designed to correct a specific flaw created by the Immigration Marriage Fraud Amendments of 1986 (IMFA). The IMFA erected additional hurdles in the process of getting a "green card" through marriage to a U.S. citizen or legal permanent resident; namely, the IMFA required completion of a two-year "conditional residency" requirement before an immigrant spouse could be granted full lawful permanent residency. Accordingly, under the IMFA, an immigrant spouse had to file a joint-petition *with her spouse* two years after the marriage—proving that the marriage was bona fide—in order to be granted legal permanent residence. This joint-filing requirement presented an obstacle for an abused immigrant spouse who had to stay with her abuser for the duration of the two-year conditional residency period in order to achieve permanent residency status.

The battered spouse waiver provides an exception for an abused immigrant spouse from the joint-petition requirement if she can show that: (1) the marriage was entered into in good faith, (2) she was battered or subjected to extreme cruelty by the citizen or lawful permanent resident abuser during the marriage, (3) she already has conditional legal permanent residence as a spouse of a citizen or legal permanent resident, and (4) extreme hardship would result if she were to be removed. At the time the waiver was introduced, agency regulations stated that the evidence required to support a waiver "can include, but is not limited to, reports and affidavits from police, medical personnel, psychologists, school officials, and social service agencies." If the application was based on a claim of extreme cruelty, then agency regulations *required* that the waiver application be supported by an evaluation of a "professional recognized by the Service as an expert in the field" such as "[l]icensed clinical social workers, psychologists, and psychiatrists."

While the battered spouse waiver represented Congress's acknowledgement of the unique vulnerabilities faced by immigrant survivors of domestic violence, the evidentiary requirements established were subject to fervent criticism for failing to recognize the difficulties for immigrant survivors in gathering such evidence. As a result, the evidentiary requirements were later amended by the Violence Against Women Act of 1994. The issue of the evidentiary requirements aside, the battered spouse waiver of 1990 reflected a valiant legislative effort by Congress to protect those immigrant survivors of violence who were "entrapped in the abusive relationship by the threat of losing their legal resident status" by sending them a "clear[ ] signal that there is an escape from their dilemma and that the abusing spouse does not have complete control over their lives." In this way, the battered spouse waiver served as the first manifestation of Congress's intent to "ensur[e] the safety and protect[ ] the legal rights of immigrants in situations of domestic violence."

B. The VAWA Self-Petition (Violence Against Women Act of 1994)

The VAWA self-petition was the next provision that reflected Congress's acknowledgement of the unique vulnerabilities faced by immigrant women survivors of domestic violence. The VAWA self-petition was created by the Violence Against Women Act of 1994 (VAWA 1994). While the battered spouse waiver was only available to an immigrant survivor seeking to remove her conditional residency status after she *had already been petitioned for* by her U.S. citizen or legal permanent resident spouse, the VAWA self-petition provided immigrant survivors the ability to "self-petition" for their own immigration status. By creating the VAWA self-petition, Congress acknowledged the unique "double" vulnerability to both abuse and deportation experienced by immigrant women survivors of domestic violence:. . .

In order to address this unique vulnerability, Congress created the VAWA self-petition to provide protection for immigrant women survivors by preventing the petitioning process from being used "as a means to control or abuse." The statutory eligibility requirements for a VAWA self-petition are as follows: the survivor must prove that she (1) entered into the marriage in good faith, (2) suffered battery or extreme cruelty at the hands of her citizen or legal permanent resident spouse (green card holder), (3) is a person of good moral character, and (4) lived with her abuser spouse. If her VAWA self-petition is approved, then the survivor is eligible to apply for legal permanent residence (green card).

Through VAWA 1994, Congress also created a new "any credible evidence" standard for VAWA self-petitions and the battered spouse waiver that did not *require* an evaluation from a licensed mental health professional to demonstrate extreme cruelty. This new standard was in response to Congress's recognition that the previous requirement "may be discriminatory against non-English-speaking individuals who have limited access to bilingual mental health professionals" and that immigrant survivors of domestic violence are not likely to have access to a range of evidentiary documents. Since 1994, Congress has extended the reach of the "any credible evidence" standard to apply to other survivor-based legal protections.

Finally, it is important to highlight the critical limitation of the VAWA petition: like the battered spouse waiver, the VAWA self-petition is only available to survivors of domestic violence whose abusers are U.S. citizens or legal permanent residents. Still, despite its shortcomings, the 1994 VAWA self-petition was the product of a "watershed moment in the domestic violence advocacy movement [that] generally and specifically helped to highlight the plight of immigrant domestic violence victims."

C. The U-Visa (Battered Immigrant Women Protection Act of VAWA 2000)

The U-Visa represents the third immigration provision Congress created in recognition of the unique vulnerabilities and barriers faced by immigrant survivors of domestic violence. The U-Visa was created through the Battered Immigrant Women Protection Act of 2000 (BIPWA) during the 2000 reauthorization of VAWA (VAWA 2000) as part of the Trafficking and Violence Protection Act of 2000 (TVPA). BIPWA was enacted in order to address the "residual immigration law obstacles standing in the path of battered immigrant spouses and children seeking to free themselves from abusive relationships that . . . had not come to the attention of the drafters of VAWA 1994." Congress clarified this intent accordingly:. . .

Both the title of the U-Visa's enacting provision (BIPWA) and the legislative history of the U-Visa make it clear that—like the battered spouse waiver and the VAWA self-petition—the U-Visa was created primarily to protect immigrant survivors of domestic violence. . . .

However, even though the U-Visa was created "most importantly for immigrant victims of domestic violence," and even though the U-Visa provided protection for survivors of domestic violence regardless of the immigration status of their abuser, the U-Visa includes a unique component: the requirement that the immigrant survivor cooperate with law enforcement in the investigation or prosecution of her abuser. Indeed, the U-Visa was also designed as a way to assist law enforcement agencies in prosecuting perpetrators of violent crimes such as domestic violence. . . .

The statutory requirements for the U-Visa further reflect its dual purpose. To be eligible for a U-Visa, a survivor must not only prove that she suffered "substantial physical or mental abuse" as a result of a specific crime of violence, but she must also prove her "helpfulness" to the "investigation or prosecution" of that crime by submitting a "certification" from a "law enforcement official or prosecutor, . . . judge, the Department of Homeland Security (DHS), or other [f]ederal, [s]tate, or local authority investigating or prosecuting criminal activity." This "certification" must attest to the survivor's helpfulness in the detection, investigation, prosecution, conviction or sentencing involving the crime of violence.

As a result of its dual purpose, and because of its helpfulness and certification requirements, the U-Visa statute disregards the particular cultural, economic, political, linguistic, social, and legal barriers that make assisting law enforcement especially difficult for immigrant survivors of domestic violence. For example, limited English skills, distrust or fear of the police due to negative past experiences with law enforcement, fear of arrest or deportation, fear of separation from their families or communities, fear of economic consequences and isolation, and fear of fatal retaliation or "separation violence" make survivors of domestic violence uniquely unable, fearful, or disinclined to engage with law enforcement. Natalie Nanasi makes the point that "requiring battered immigrant women to cooperate with law enforcement in order to receive U visas has ironically made the immigration relief that was specifically created to help them a source of increased risk and danger."

Nonetheless, despite significant limitations and inadequacies, the U-Visa—along with the battered spouse waiver and the VAWA self-petition—represents Congress's attempt to help address the unique vulnerabilities and barriers to legal protection faced by immigrant survivors of domestic violence. As Nanasi acknowledges, the U-Visa reflects Congress' "unmistakable" intention "to connect the visa to the fight against domestic violence."

D. Additional Protections Created in VAWA Reauthorizations (2000, 2005, 2013)

In addition to creating the battered spouse waiver, VAWA self-petition, and U-Visa, Congress continued to express its recognition of the unique obstacles faced by immigrant survivors of domestic violence by enacting numerous survivor-specific legal protections with each of the subsequent reauthorizations of the Violence Against Women Act in 2000, 2005, and 2013. For example, VAWA 2000 eased evidentiary requirements of establishing extreme hardship, expanded the categories of immigrant survivors who may be eligible for VAWA, created a waiver of certain impediments to good moral character determinations in VAWA cases, and created a waiver of the ground of deportation for crimes of domestic violence for immigrant survivors if they are not the primary perpetrator of abuse in the relationship. Notably, VAWA 2000 created survivor-specific waivers of certain grounds of inadmissibility, including a waiver of the unlawful presence inadmissibility ground, waiver of the misrepresentation inadmissibility ground, waivers of certain criminal-related inadmissibility grounds, and a waiver of the health-related inadmissibility grounds for immigrant survivors infected with the HIV virus.

Similarly, the 2005 reauthorization of VAWA provided additional protections that were intended to address the fact that "threat of deportation, cultural and language barriers, lack of a work permit and limited access to legal and social services may make immigrant victims of domestic violence more dependent on their abusive spouses." Some of these protections included: exempting VAWA self-petitioners from penalties imposed for overstaying grants of voluntary departure, exempting VAWA self-petitioners from limits on motions to reopen relief applications for cancellation of removal or suspension of deportation, and incorporating employment authorization benefits for certain immigrant survivors of domestic violence.

The 2013 reauthorization of VAWA (VAWA 2013) provided even more protections for immigrant survivors of domestic violence. These protections included: requiring specific background checks of petitioning spouses to flag potentially abusive relationships, expanding VAWA coverage to derivative children whose self-petitioning parent died during the petition process, protecting children who reach twenty-one years of age before their VAWA petitions were approved, and adding stalking to the list of crimes for U-Visa eligibility. Perhaps the most controversial and far-reaching protection included in VAWA 2013 was the survivor-specific exemption from the public charge ground of inadmissibility.

[Editor's Note: See article below about the public charge rule which was ordered by President Trump and revoked by President Biden in 2021.]

The additional legal protections created by the 2000, 2005, and 2013 reauthorizations of VAWA underscore Congress's enduring awareness of the unique barriers faced by immigrant survivors of gender violence. However, as this Article will show, these very survivors are subjected to the mental health-related inadmissibility ground under IN A section 212(a)(1)(A)(iii) in a way that reflects a profound lack of compassion and humanity—namely, by excluding immigrant survivors of violence who have experienced suicidal behavior as a direct consequence of the abuse and trauma they have suffered.

III. INA'S MENTAL HEALTH INADMISSIBILITY GROUND: § 212(A)(1)(A)(III)

This Part of the Article will provide historical background and an overview of INA's mental health-related ground of inadmissibility, section 212(a)(1)(A)(iii). This Part will also discuss the contours of certain inadmissibility waivers that are provided in the INA, including those that are available specifically for immigrant survivors of violence. This Part will reveal that while Congress has demonstrated great compassion and awareness of the unique barriers faced by immigrant survivors of violence by providing them with waivers and exemptions for numerous grounds of inadmissibility, the same compassion and awareness has not been extended to the mental health-related inadmissibility ground at section 212(a)(1)(A)(iii) of the INA. . .

All immigrants seeking to live in the United States—including those immigrants who are already in the United States without lawful immigration status and those who are applying for a visa or for legal permanent residence—are subject to INA's grounds of inadmissibility. For example, survivor applicants for a battered spouse waiver and VAWA self-petition must be deemed "admissible" in order to obtain legal permanent residency. And a survivor applicant for a U-Visa must prove her admissibility in order to be eligible for the visa itself. If a survivor applicant is deemed inadmissible, she will be subjected to removal or deportation. . . .

C. Survivor-Specific Waivers and Exemptions of Grounds of Inadmissibility

The INA also includes several waivers for certain grounds of inadmissibility specifically for applicants for battered spouse waivers, VAWA self-petitions, and U-Visas. For example, VAWA self-petitioners are eligible for waivers of the following inadmissibility grounds: communicable disease of public health significance, many criminal grounds, fraud or misrepresentation, and reentering or attempting to reenter after removal. The standard for each of these VAWA-specific waivers is different: for a communicable disease of public health significance, she must prove that she has received or is no longer required to receive vaccination for the applicable diseases; for criminal grounds, the VAWA self-petitioner must present positive evidence to warrant favorable discretion; for fraud or misrepresentation, she must prove extreme hardship to a qualifying relative; for reentering or attempting to reenter after removal, she must show a connection between the abuse and her deportation, departure, reentry, or attempted reentry.

Similarly, section 212(d)(14) of the INA provides a special inadmissibility waiver for U-Visa applicants for nearly all grounds of inadmissibility except those related to perpetrators and participants of Nazi persecution, genocide, acts of torture, or extrajudicial killings. The standard for an inadmissibility waiver under section 212(d)(14) of the INA is "if the Secretary of Homeland Security considers it to be in the public or national interest." Agency case law has interpreted "public interest" to mean " 'something in which the public, the community at large, has some pecuniary interest, or some interest by which their legal rights or liabilities are affected" '; and "national interest" has been determined by three factors: (1) the "substantial intrinsic merit" of the immigrant's field of work, (2) whether "the proposed benefit will be national in scope," and (3) whether "the national interest would be adversely affected" by denial of the waiver. In adjudicating the waiver, USCIS balances the adverse factors of inadmissibility against the social and humanitarian considerations presented and may grant the waiver in the exercise of discretion.

It must be noted that while these special waivers are made available to survivor applicants, this only means that they are eligible *to apply* for such a waiver. These waivers are discretionary, very costly, and, more often than not, require the assistance of legal representation. In the U-Visa context, a section 212(d)(14) waiver application requires submission of a $930 application fee. And while a survivor applicant can try to apply for a fee waiver for her inadmissibility waiver application, fee waiver applications have been increasingly denied. Moreover, applications for waivers of health-related inadmissibility grounds often entail submitting medical or mental health evaluations that are retraumatizing and that can themselves be prohibitively costly. Finally, during the adjudication process of inadmissibility waivers, survivor applicants often receive a "Request for Evidence" (RFE) or a "Notice of Intent to Deny" (NOID) requiring survivors to submit additional evidence and testimony, which further prolongs and frustrates the waiver adjudication process.

In addition to special waivers for certain grounds of inadmissibility for survivor applicants, Congress has also created specific *exemptions* from grounds of inadmissibility for immigrant survivor applicants. . . .Moreover, as discussed in Part II, VAWA 2013 created an *exemption* for battered spouse waiver applicants, VAWA self-petitioners, and U-Visa applicants from the public charge ground. Unlike in the inadmissibility waiver context, where it is necessary to file a lengthy and costly waiver application, in the case of an exemption the inadmissibility ground *does not apply*, and therefore, there is no need to file or adjudicate a waiver application.

These survivor-specific inadmissibility waivers and exemptions codify Congress' persisting recognition of the unique barriers faced by immigrant survivors of violence. Notably, the public charge exemption was created in response to advocates who had long argued that the public charge ground contravened legislative intent by penalizing VAWA applicants whom Congress had intended to protect because of their unique vulnerability. By exempting battered-spouse waiver applicants, VAWA self-petitioners, and U-Visa applicants from the public charge ground of inadmissibility, Congress acknowledged the inherent conflict in penalizing survivors of violence whose very vulnerability puts them at a heightened risk of poverty. The next Part of the Article will reveal a similar inherent conflict that has remained unchecked by Congress—the glaring conflict that arises from penalizing survivors of violence for engaging in suicidal behavior when their very experience of abuse and trauma puts them at a heightened risk of suicidality.

IV. THE HEARTLESS ENFORCEMENT OF INA § 212(A)(1)(A)(III) ON IMMIGRANT SURVIVORS

This Part of the Article will show how section 212(a)(1)(A)(iii) of the INA is enforced in ways that heartlessly penalize, stigmatize, and re-traumatize immigrant survivors of violence—whom Congress intended to protect—for engaging in suicidal behavior as a result of the violence and trauma they have suffered. This Part will first describe the procedural steps involved in the enforcement of section 212(a)(1)(A)(iii) and will then turn to exposing how the heartless enforcement of section 212(a)(1)(A)(iii) disregards medical evidence, weaponizes mental health evaluations, reveals inconsistencies within immigration law, and tragically contravenes national suicide prevention efforts led by the U.S. government.

A. How INA Section 212(a)(1)(A)(iii) is Enforced

If a survivor applicant for a battered spouse waiver, VAWA self-petition, or U-Visa offers evidence of past or present suicidal behavior in the course of corroborating the impact of the abuse and violence she suffered, section 212(a)(1)(A)(iii) of the INA will be triggered. As a result, she will be required to undergo a mandatory health screening conducted by a designated physician who is certified by the federal government. All health-related grounds of inadmissibility—including mental health-related grounds—are enforced through a mandatory medical exam conducted by a designated civil surgeon pursuant to instructions issued by the Centers for Disease Control and Prevention (CDC) as part of the U.S. Department of Health and Human Services. The civil surgeon must rely on a specific set of instructions promulgated by the CDC in order to determine the survivor applicant's admissibility.

The CDC instructions require that all medical examiners use the current version of the *Diagnostic and Statistical Manual of Mental Disorders* (DSM-V) published by the American Psychiatric Association when assessing an immigrant's admissibility. Moreover, the CDC instructions list "major depression" as one of the four mental disorders "most frequently associated with harmful behavior," noting that this disorder can be associated with "high rates of suicide." Further, in defining "harmful behavior" the CDC instructions specifically list "suicide attempt[s]" as an example of such behavior.

If, upon examination, or sometimes multiple examinations, the designated civil surgeon finds that the survivor applicant's suicidal behavior renders her inadmissible, the civil surgeon will make a Class A determination. The civil surgeon may also opt to refer her to a psychiatrist or other specialist for yet another evaluation to affirm a Class A determination. If a Class A finding is made and the survivor applicant is deemed inadmissible, she will be subject to deportation. However, as previously discussed, she may still be eligible for a costly and discretionary waiver of inadmissibility. If she cannot afford a waiver, is not eligible for a fee waiver, or her waiver is denied, the survivor applicant will be subject to deportation.

B. Disregarding Medical Evidence Connecting Domestic Violence and Suicidal Behavior

The heartless enforcement of INA section 212(a)(1)(A)(iii) shamelessly disregards authoritative medical evidence establishing the correlation between domestic violence and suicidal behavior. . . .

C. Weaponizing Mental Health Evaluations and Impeding Healing

The heartless enforcement of INA section 212(a)(1)(A)(iii) results in weaponizing mental health evaluations submitted by survivor-applicants to corroborate their abuse. The battered immigrant spouse waiver, VAWA self-petition, and the U-Visa require a showing of either "extreme cruelty" or "substantial physical or mental abuse." Agency regulations define "substantial physical or mental abuse" to mean "injury or harm to the victim's physical person, or harm to or impairment of the emotional or psychological soundness of the victim." This requirement is often met by submitting mental health evaluations that corroborate emotional and psychological harm as a result of the abuse or violence. According to psychologists, the role of evaluations in the immigrant survivor context is "to assess and document psychological constructs" relevant to the determination regarding eligibility:. . .

As a result, out of fear of triggering section 212(a)(1)(A)(iii) of the INA, immigration lawyers who assist immigrant survivors in their applications for immigration protection must explain the risks of disclosing suicidal behavior. Some lawyers will also discourage the inclusion of any reference to suicidal behavior in the record. Moreover, some lawyers will ask mental health evaluators to remove references to suicidal behavior from their evaluations of immigrant survivors to avoid triggering the enforcement of section 212(a)(1)(A)(iii) of the INA. . .

[T]he heartless enforcement of section 212(a)(1)(A)(iii) tragically overlooks the opportunity to benefit the public interest by aiding in an immigrant survivor's post-traumatic growth and path toward resiliency and personal strength. . . .

[Editor's Note: The author argues that the heartless enforcement of INA section 212(a)(1)(A)(iii) also creates inconsistencies in the treatment of suicidal behavior within immigration law, ignores evidence of higher susceptibility of immigrant survivors to suicide, and contravenes suicide destigmatization and prevention efforts led by the U.S. Government. She concludes with a proposal to categorically exempt all immigrant survivors of violence from the requirement to submit a discretionary waiver application, so the applicant could submit a mental health evaluation to corroborate the abuse without fear that it might include a mention of suicidal behavior.]

Finally, such a reform aligns with the legislative intent of immigration provisions created by Congress specifically for immigrant survivors of domestic violence precisely because of the unique vulnerabilities they face. Such a statutory reform is desperately needed to stop immigration laws from heartlessly rubbing salt into the wounds of immigrant survivors of violence.

LESLYE E. ORLOFF, HALEY IESHA MAGWOOD, YASMIN CAMPOS-MENDEZ, AND GISELLE A. HASS, TRANSFORMING LIVES: HOW THE VAWA SELF-PETITION AND U VISA CHANGE THE LIVES OF SURVIVORS AND THEIR CHILDREN AFTER EMPLOYMENT AUTHORIZATION AND LEGAL IMMIGRATION STATUS

National Immigrant Women's Advocacy Project (NIWAP)
American University, Washington College of Law (2021)
(For the full final report see https://niwaplibrary.wcl.american.edu/transforming-lives-study-21.)
(footnotes omitted)

Abstract

Research on immigrant survivors of crime and abuse has focused on learning about their experiences, assessing how social services, healthcare, and justice systems serve immigrant communities, and creating the policy reforms needed to meet immigrant survivors' needs. Research has seldom focused on measuring and learning about how immigrant survivors' lives are transformed as they apply to the U.S. government for immigration relief under the Violence Against Women Act's (VAWA) VAWA and U visa programs. The National Immigrant Women's Advocacy Project (NIWAP), at American University's Washington College of Law, conducted a national survey, collecting data from attorneys, advocates and state government staff at 169 agencies in 42 states serving immigrant survivors of crime and abuse in the U.S. Study participant professionals reported on 11, 171 immigrant clients who applied for VAWA and U visa relief. Of those cases, 6,770 had been granted employment authorization and 2,845 obtained lawful permanent residence through the VAWA or U visa programs. This study sought to learn from professionals how their immigrant survivor clients' lives changed from filing for VAWA and U visa relief through eventually obtaining lawful permanent residence. In the study, participants answered both open and closed-ended questions describing how their VAWA and U visa clients' and their clients' children's lives changed as they moved through the immigration application process and obtained increasing levels of immigration protection. The study found that when immigrant survivors of crime and abuse no longer fear deportation, can legally work, and ultimately become permanent residents in the U.S., they, their families and communities thrive. The transformation from fear to immigration relief leads to better law enforcement, workplace conditions, academic performance, and health outcomes.

The study results show that some of the most significant changes for most survivors occur at the point when the VAWA and U visa applicants are granted employment authorization and deferred action, a form of protection from deportation. The changes consist of significant reductions in immigration- related threats and abuse, threats of child abduction, threats to gain sole custody of children, and workplace-based abuse. After receipt of employment authorization, there is a 114% increase in immigrant survivors' willingness to trust police and 30% of VAWA and U visa applicants who received employment authorization continued to make police reports regarding future crimes. These changes point to reduced fears and greater trust and faith in the law enforcement and justice systems of the U.S. As a result, survivors are more effective participants and witnesses, allowing for greater access to justice, enabling law enforcement agencies to hold perpetrators accountable for their crimes,6 and generating greater safety for victims, law enforcement officers and communities across the country.

When survivors can legally work and no longer fear deportation, they end their isolation by reconnecting with friends, family, and the larger community, including their ethnic/cultural communities. There is a 6-fold increase in immigrant survivors' parental involvement in their children's schools, and a 24% increase in immigrant survivors reaching out to help other victims in their community. Finally, the study results found that with employment authorization, labor force participation, in at least minimum wage employment, increased by 300% among immigrant survivors. Forty three percent of immigrant survivors authorized to work were employed in jobs with healthcare, vacation, and maternity leave benefits. According to study results, after employment authorization, immigrant survivors' participation in English as a Second Language (ESL) classes increased 225%, with 35% obtaining GEDs and 38% pursuing either Associates or Bachelor's degrees, achievements which allow them and their families to make social and economic contributions to society.

Immigrant survivors' and their children's health, well-being and self-esteem also improved and continued to improve as they gained lawful permanent residence through the VAWA and U visa programs. This study demonstrates how and when in the process of gaining legal status, immigrant survivors become more resilient, resourceful, economically stable, socially active, and engaged in helping others in their communities. In particular, data showed that among the gains is an increased adjustment of the immigrant survivors and their children through acculturation and biculturalism, thereby becoming more active and integrated members of the larger U.S. society. The results of this study show that policy reforms that shorten the time from filing to employment authorization and protection from deportation will significantly benefit immigrant survivors and their communities and will promote access to justice. The results also clearly show that the ability of U.S. law enforcement and prosecution agencies to hold perpetrators accountable for their crimes is enhanced by expedited access to employment authorization and deportation protection for immigrant survivors. . .

[Editor's Notes: 1. On June 14, 2021, the Dept of Homeland Security announced changes that will make the process of receiving a U visa with work authorization and protection from deportation up to ten times faster, from 5 years to 6 months. Hopefully these changes will be implemented quickly and will achieve this goal.

2. A U.S. citizen spouse can contract with the federal government and his or her immigrant spouse by signing a federal immigration form called the Form I-864 affidavit of support. (See 8 U.S.C. § 1183a; 8 C.F.R. § 213a.2.) By doing so, the U.S. citizen spouse promises to support the immigrant spouse at an income of at least 125 percent of the federal poverty line for ten years—a promise which the immigrant spouse can enforce in a contractual lawsuit, and for which that spouse has no duty to mitigate damages. See In re Marriage of Kumar, *13 Cal.App.5th 1072 (2017) (holding also that family courts must allow these contractual claims to be raised in divorce actions); see also earlier cases with similar holdings in several jurisdictions. These contracts can enable abused immigrant spouses to leave their marriages and survive economically until they are able to support themselves.*

3. In "Transnational Abandonment Survivors at Maitri," 4/12/23, Zakia Afrin, Director of Survivor Advocacy at Maitri, a South Asian domestic violence agency, reports on another form of domestic violence, husbands abandoning wives who are citizens of South Asian countries. Based on a survey that the agency conducted in four languages, examples of this form of abuse include: Husband canceling the wife's visa petition; hiding her green card or visa papers; filing for divorce in the U.S. after the wife was forced to leave and serving her in South Asia; taking the wife to South Asia under the false pretense that they are visiting and leaving her in the home country without documents or financial support; bringing U.S. citizen children back to the U.S. away from the mother who cannot travel because she has no visa; and taking the child to South Asia while the mother is in the U.S., thereby forcing her to return to the home country from which she will not be able to return due to her lack of a visa in order to be with her child(ren).

Since only two South Asian countries (Pakistan and Sri Lanka) are signatories to the Hague Convention on International Aspects of Child Abduction, the others (including India) are under no legal obligation to return children to their primary caretaker or home country. Similarly, no South Asian countries have signed and ratified the Hague Convention on the Recognition of Divorces and Legal Separations, but this treaty could be helpful in such situations if it were in effect in those countries. In the absence of laws addressing these problems, Maitri advocates with embassies and consulates of South Asian countries and other policy forums in the U.S. regarding these issues.]

NATIONAL NETWORK TO END DOMESTIC VIOLENCE (NNEDV)—PUBLIC CHARGE & IPV—(2022) REGARDING *ARIZONA V. CITY AND COUNTY OF SAN FRANCISCO, CALIFORNIA* (U.S. SUPREME COURT, 2022) 142 S.CT. 1926 (MEM)

In 2019, the Trump Administration expanded the grounds under which an immigrant would be ineligible to enter or become a permanent resident of the United States by defining a "public charge" to include an immigrant who would likely depend on cash benefits and other government assistance (like housing, food, and insurance). Based on the Trump Administration's expanded definition, a greater number of noncitizens could be denied entry or permanent residency based on their likely need for assistance.

The Biden Administration chose to stop enforcing the public charge rule in March 2021, and eventually rescinded it. Several states (including Arizona) attempted to continue enforcing the rule. The states went to the U.S. Court of Appeals for the Ninth Circuit, seeking to intervene there to defend the rule in the hope of having it reinstated. But the Ninth Circuit declined, prompting the states to appeal to the Supreme Court. They asked the Supreme Court to consider whether states with interests should be permitted to intervene to defend a rule when the United States ceases to defend it. The Court in *Arizona v. City and County of San Francisco* dismissed the case, indicating it was wrong to have taken up the dispute in the first place. As a result, the Ninth Circuit's ruling that states could not overrule the federal government and revive the policy stands, and the Trump Administration's expanded definition should not be enforced.

Many immigrant survivors escape to the United States with few resources, and having access to government assistance is often crucial to their journey to leave abusers, heal from trauma, and build safer lives for themselves and their children. For the past several years, when immigrant survivors feared that they would be denied permanent residency based on their need for help, it had a chilling, even life-threatening, effect on their ability to escape abuse. NNEDV is pleased to see that the lower court decision in *Arizona* stands and is grateful that enforcement of the Trump Administration's expanded "public charge" definition has finally come to an end.

2. "MAIL-ORDER BRIDES," OR MARRIAGE IMMIGRATION

OLGA GROSH, FOREIGN WIVES, DOMESTIC VIOLENCE: U.S. LAW STIGMATIZES AND FAILS TO PROTECT "MAIL-ORDER BRIDES"

22 Hastings Women's L.J. 81 (2011)
(citations and footnotes omitted)

I. INTRODUCTION

Susanna Remerata met her husband, Timothy Blackwell, through an online international marriage brokerage firm. They wrote letters to each other for one year before meeting in 1994. They married three days after, and Susanna left her native Philippines to live with her new husband in Washington state. The marriage was violent and short-lived. Physical abuse started when Blackwell [strangled] her the day after their wedding. Susanna reported the abuse and obtained a protective order. While waiting for divorce proceedings outside of a Seattle courtroom, Blackwell shot and killed Susanna and two of her friends. Susanna was eight months pregnant; but the doctors were unable to save the unborn girl.

Susanna's story is unfortunately not unique. ["Informational and power imbalances common in IMB matches increase the incidence of domestic violence above the national average."] * * * Politicians, academics, and non-governmental organizations have successfully lobbied to change immigration law and to provide better resources to prevent immigrant bride abuse. Although monumental, these legislative strides have proven inadequate. * * * This Note argues that the anti-violence laws intended to protect immigrant brides are of limited use as tools of empowerment because U.S. immigration law stigmatizes foreign bride marriages as fraudulent, thus diminishing the brides' rights and protections against abuse. * * *

II. OVERVIEW OF THE MAIL-ORDER BRIDE INDUSTRY

A. Asian Picture Brides

[The author traces the history of the U.S. foreign bride industry, beginning "in the early nineteenth century, during the Industrial Revolution and the California Gold Rush," and through to the early and mid-twentieth century. Ultimately, "[t]he brides were legally bound to their new husbands and could not terminate the marital contracts."]

B. The Modern International Marriage Broker Industry

Today, international marriage brokers (IMBs) play the matchmakers between foreign brides and male U.S. citizens or legal permanent residents. In 1999, over two hundred U.S.-based agencies matched U.S. men with four thousand to six thousand women from Asia and Eastern Europe. In 2005, the number of IMBs operating in the U.S. grew to over five hundred, with an estimated two thousand and seven hundred IMBs operating world-wide. In 2009, the Dept. of Homeland Services (DHS) reported that 27,754 foreign fiancé(e)s and 15,419 foreign spouses entered the United States. Foreign brides comprise one-third to one-half of the foreign fiancé(e)s and spouses admitted to the United States.

IMBs actively recruit women from economically depressed regions to marry foreign men. These businesses then create databases with the women's personal information and, most importantly, their photographs. Male customers may search according to factors such as age, weight, nationality, hair color, and even breast size and underwear preferences. Some sites require women to fill out questionnaires asking, "Do you wear makeup?" or "Have you experienced premarital sex?" Once a male customer decides he is interested in a woman, he pays the broker a fee to obtain her contact information. IMBs also offer package tours for male clients interested in visiting women in their home countries, and help procure entry visas for the selected brides.

C. The Consumer Husbands

Men who use IMBs to shop for wives come primarily from Australia, the European Union, and the United States. These clients are usually white, educated, economically successful, and middle-aged. Consumer husbands from the United States favor foreign women because they think U.S. women are more interested in their careers than family, while foreign women desire nothing more than to be homemakers. "It all started with women's lib. . . . Guys are sick of the North American me, me, me attitude," said Sam Smith, who founded "I Love Latins," an international matchmaking website. John Line, a forty-three-year-old from California explained, "I wanted a wife who isn't career-oriented, who participates very little in the world outside, who doesn't have high aspirations, who is useful, whose life revolves around me. . . . And yes, she had to be a virgin." Line married a twenty-three-year-old Filipina and admitted to strictly controlling her access to money, the telephone, and the car.

Randall Miller, a Washington, D.C. lawyer who represented an abused immigrant bride, explains, "The guy doesn't have to be a predator . . . He wants to be the king of the house and buys into [the] promotional claim that he can get a more traditional woman in Russia—she will cook dinner and have sex and otherwise shut up." The consumer husband is "taken aback when the woman is outspoken and has opinions and wants to get a job." The gap between reality and grooms' expectations of subservient women is an invitation to violence.

D. The Immigrant Brides

Foreign women in the export countries are typically unemployed due to national economic distress, uncontrolled gender subordination, and few work and educational opportunities for women. Some women seek to emigrate in order to escape poverty stemming from legal and social practices, such as preferential treatment of sons regarding inheritance. These women generally come from financially destitute regions, and are often young. Some have no post-secondary education. Unlike the consumer grooms, the women pay no fee to the marriage brokers. Brokers recruit potential brides through newspapers, magazines, and Internet advertisements that promise a foreign husband.

Russia, Eastern Europe, and the Philippines are the major sources of foreign brides. According to a study of IMBs in the former Soviet Union republics, women from this region are recruited for their European appearance. Women are also chosen from urban tourist areas because they have had more contact with U.S. culture. In the Philippines, approximately three hundred thousand to five hundred thousand Filipinas leave each year as foreign brides, hoping to find a U.S. suitor who will help them escape the "plain facts of unemployment, inflation, malnutrition, and militarization [that] permeate their everyday lives." IMBs' recruitment practices take advantage of women who seek emigration as a solution to limited opportunities and desperate lifestyles in their home countries.

E. Impact of the Mail-Order Bride Industry on Foreign Women

Immigrant brides are three to six times more likely to experience domestic violence than other women. In fact, these figures may be much lower than the actual number of incidents of domestic violence against immigrant brides as many go unreported due to language difficulties and the threat of deportation if the marriage is dissolved. The growth of the mail-order bride industry has spurred abuse of immigrant brides because U.S. men who have money to purchase foreign wives are empowered by the industry to exert substantial control over their new wives. An Immigration and Naturalization Services (INS) report documented that the men who use IMB services "seek relationships with women whom they feel they can control."

U.S. Citizenship and Immigration Services (USCIS), the agency responsible for immigration matters today, considers IMBs different from dating services or personal advertisements. Foreign bride marriages create grossly imbalanced relationships where "the consumer husband holds all the cards." Men seeking control choose women who come from economically poor regions, where a woman does not have many alternatives to support herself and her family. The immigrant brides have no family or support networks, and lack the language skills and employment opportunities necessary for financial independence. Furthermore, the brokers provide little or no immigration information to the women because the companies are more concerned with satisfying their paying male customers than with protecting the brides. As a result, many immigrant brides arrive unaware of their immigration rights and remain in abusive relationships because they think their only other option is deportation.

Moreover, the IMB industry perpetuates the idea that men can own and profit from women as sexual objects, reinforcing the discarded notion of coverture. Many of the websites that catalogue brides are venues for pornography and prostitution, and many brides fall victim to sex trafficking. Some brokers openly market the potential brides as "sexual objects, dedicated to subservience and solely oriented toward pleasing the man." Others "sell" women like produce at a supermarket, asking if the customer wants to "add" a particular woman to his shopping cart. Others advertise the process of searching their "voluminous database as easy as ordering a pizza." This process replete with sexual images and the great cost of acquiring an immigrant bride *[Editor's Note: In January 2024, the cost ranges from $10,000 to $30,000.]* reinforce the belief that the consumer husband has purchased and now owns his wife. * * *

III. IMMIGRATION LAW STIGMATIZES FOREIGN BRIDE MARRIAGES AS FRAUDULENT

A. Marriage Fraud for Immigration Benefits

To promote family unity, United States immigration laws bestow certain advantages on family-sponsored immigrants. * * * However, due to quota limitations, spouses and other immediate relatives of permanent residents must wait for about one year to receive a visa, while there is almost no waiting period for spouses of U.S. citizens. * * * In the 1980s, immigration marriage fraud became a significant public policy concern. . . To commit marital fraud outside the immigration context, a spouse must lie about willingness or ability to procreate or engage in sexual intercourse. However, when it comes to investigating immigration fraud, the law focuses on the couple's intention at the time of their marriage. * * * Congress enacted the Immigration Marriage Fraud Amendments of 1986 (IMFA) to balance the competing policies of family reunification and marriage fraud prevention. IMFA granted a two-year "conditional resident" status to immigrant spouses, which immigration officials could revoke if they determined that the marriage was "entered into for the purpose of procuring an alien's admission as an immigrant." * * * Congress insisted on legislating as if foreign bride marriages are fraudulent despite data that suggested otherwise. The rate of fraud Congress attributed to immigration marriages dropped to eight percent in 1996, and one percent in 1999. * * * Despite these findings, an INS-funded study listed as an appendix to the 1999 report claims [otherwise because of the women's " 'self-descriptions they offer and their willingness to marry men of advanced age and dubious character.' "] * * * Congress appears to define marital fraud by regulating the creation and existence of marriages involving foreign spouses. * * *

* * * [B.]3. Policing the Marriage

Immigration officials have great difficulty distinguishing "real marriages" from fraudulent ones, and as a result, some genuine marriages are not recognized. In the case of Agnes Cho, a Chinese citizen, the Board of Immigration Appeals (BIA) held her marriage was a sham despite evidence of a long courtship, cohabitation, a joint health insurance policy, and that the spouses met each other's parents. The BIA found that Cho's marriage was fraudulent from the start because her husband had an affair. The BIA also reasoned that because Cho moved out after her husband's violent abuse, Cho married only to receive permanent residency. Simply because the marriage broke down, the BIA construed the marriage as fraudulent from the start. * * * Although the Court of Appeals for the First Circuit reversed, the BIA's decision shows that immigration officials expect more from marriages involving immigration benefits than from other marriages. * * * "By making spouse a category for gaining immigration status, Congress has necessarily embroiled DHS in the difficult business of passing judgment on individual marriages." * * *

IV. STIGMATIZATION DETERS LEGAL RECOURSE

To ameliorate the harsh effects of immigration law on foreign brides in abusive marriages, Congress passed the Violence Against Women Act (VAWA) in 1994 with subsequent amendments in the years 2000 and 2005 [and 2013 and 2022]. * * *

B. A Negative Presumption of Immigration Fraud Through Marriage Remains

Although VAWA ameliorates the time restrictions IMFA placed on foreign bride marriages, the abused foreign bride still faces several legal hurdles. In addition to proving that the battered spouse entered [the] marriage in good faith, that the marriage was legal, and that she was battered or subjected to extreme cruelty, the battered spouse also carries the burden of proving that the marriage was a bona fide marriage. * * *

The "bona fide marriage" requirement is difficult to prove due to the ambiguity of evidentiary standards and the arbitrary and unpredictable outcomes that result from discretionary power held by immigration officials. * * * Instead of presuming that the marriage is facially valid, the current petitioning requirement places the burden of proof on the immigrant victim. It is particularly difficult for a battered foreign spouse to carry her burden of proof because her abusive marriage, dependent economic status, and language and cultural barriers combine to keep her powerless and uninformed. The negative presumption combined with the language and economic difficulties create an almost insurmountable barrier to a successful petition. The daunting VAWA petition process and the lack of clear standards for applying discretion over petitions present significant obstacles to the battered foreign spouse.

V. INSUFFICIENT IMB INDUSTRY REGULATION

A. The IMB Business and Moral Turpitude

In addition to insufficient protection resulting from heavy immigration burdens, foreign brides are also left unprotected by lack of effective regulation of an industry that sells people. Juries, judges, and the public have been stunned by the IMB industry's disregard for the immigrant brides' safety. In *Fox v. Encounters International*, Nataliya, a Ukrainian bride, sued the IMB agency because the owner, Natasha Spivack, intentionally downplayed the gravity and urgency of the physical and mental abuse that Nataliya suffered from her husband, James Fox. The abuse began as verbal insults, then escalated when Fox attempted to break Nataliya's leg when she was four months pregnant. Nataliya sought Spivack's advice on at least three separate occasions. Despite knowing about VAWA's battered spouse waiver, Spivack falsely told Nataliya that nothing worth complaining about was happening and that Nataliya's only other option would be deportation back to Ukraine. * * * The abuse culminated in Fox severely beating Nataliya and holding a gun to her head for over two hours. After the incident, Nataliya called an ambulance due to chest pain and was diagnosed with a broken collar bone, swelling to her face, numerous contusions, and a human bite to her hand. Not until Nataliya reached a women's shelter with her baby did she discover the existence of the battered spouse waiver.

The jury found that Spivack and her agency, Encounters International (EI), had a fiduciary duty to Nataliya. Furthermore, the court held that Spivack intentionally withheld information about the battered spouse waiver, and that Nataliya reasonably relied on Spivack's advice to her detriment. The jury awarded Nataliya $92,000 in compensatory damages and $341,500 in punitive damages, which the court found not excessive considering Spivack's reprehensible misconduct. The court was especially repulsed by Spivack's immoral conduct to "gain Plaintiff's [Nataliya's] trust, confidence, and loyalty in order that Plaintiff would marry James

Fox, continue to be married to James Fox, and create another EI success story."

In another case, *European Connections v. Gonzales*, a federal district court recognized that for-profit IMBs have incentives to disregard immigrant brides' safety. Matchmaking services are more concerned with the satisfaction of the paying male customers than with safeguarding the female clients. Regulating IMBs' recruiting practices and standards of care toward foreign brides would likely save women's lives.

B. Positive Development of Disclosure Requirements

1. Groom's Background and Criminal History

After more than two decades of investigating husbands' abuse of immigrant brides, Congress passed the International Marriage Broker Regulation Act (IMBRA). IMBRA requires IMBs to collect and distribute to the potential bride information about a particular U.S. male client before that client may initiate contact. The IMBs must search public sex offender registries, obtain the client's criminal history for violent crimes, including domestic violence, sexual abuse, and child abuse, as well as any arrests related to drugs and alcohol. If an IMB gives a client information about a potential bride before conducting the requisite research, that IMB is subject to substantial civil and criminal penalties, including up to a $25,000 penalty for each improper disclosure. * * * The disclosure requirement only applies to organizations that explicitly advertise foreign nationals for marriage with U.S. citizens or legal permanent residents. IMBRA defines IMBs narrowly, so as not to affect domestic matchmaking organizations. * * * This measure explicitly protects the right of adults to court in whatever fashion they choose without passing judgment on Internet dating, but also recognizes the power imbalances involved when the Internet-based industry advertises destitute foreign women.

2. Limits on Fiancée Petitions

In addition to the disclosure requirements, IMBRA limits the number of fiancée petitions a U.S. citizen or legal permanent resident may request within a particular time period. Prior to IMBRA, there was no official limit to the number of fiancée or spouse visas for which an individual citizen could apply. Now, a petitioner must wait two years between petitions. If a citizen or legal permanent resident has petitioned for two K-1 visas in the past ten years, the Department of Homeland Security (DHS) must notify the immigrant fiancée that the petition pertaining to her is the male's third petition.

* * * In 1998, Anastasia, an eighteen-year-old foreign bride, immigrated from Kyrgyzstan to Seattle, Washington, to join her new husband, Indle King [who was 38]. King had abused and divorced his previous wife, and he quickly became violent toward Anastasia as well. By 2000, King decided that he wanted to divorce Anastasia. Because he was

unwilling to pay for divorce proceedings, King recruited an accomplice to help him kill Anastasia. King, who weighed almost three hundred pounds, pinned Anastasia to the ground while his accomplice [strangled] her with a necktie. Anastasia's body was found in a shallow grave. As it turns out, while he plotted to kill Anastasia, King was already seeking another immigrant bride. *[Editor's Note: In 2002, King was sentenced to almost 29 years in prison and his accomplice was later sentenced to 32 years.]* IMBRA-mandated criminal background checks and petition limits potentially protect foreign brides from sorrowful fates such as Anastasia's. * * *

C. IMBRA Falls Short of Protecting Foreign Brides

1. Implementation Roadblocks

A 2008 study conducted by the United States Government Accountability Office (GAO) reported that USCIS, the Department of State (DOS), and the Department of Justice (DOJ) have implemented only some of the key IMBRA provisions. The provisions not implemented were those meant to provide potential immigrant spouses with crucial information about the citizens sponsoring their spouse or fiancée visas. * * * First, the DOS did not comply with the IMBRA mandate that DOS mail a copy of the visa petitioner's background check to the foreign bride. Second, USCIS failed to cross-check fiancée and spouse visa petitions to see if the petitioner had petitioned previously for someone else. In fact, USCIS only investigated petitioners who admitted that they had previously filed petitions. Third, USCIS officials admitted that they no longer tried to notify beneficiaries of petitions approved within the last ten years. USCIS explained that it was too difficult to obtain the correct overseas contact information. As a result, foreign brides have been deprived of required information regarding their potential spouses.

a. Information Pamphlet for Battered Immigrant Spouses

* * * [I]n October 2010, USCIS released a fact sheet relating information about the immigration process and available domestic violence protection. The seven-page fact sheet is divided into two parts, the first dealing with resources available to victims of domestic violence, including calling 911 or requesting protection orders, and the second focusing on victims' immigration rights. * * * However, . . . the pamphlet does not state explicitly that a victim of domestic violence will not be deported if she seeks help from the police or immigration authorities. While USCIS does state that domestic and sexual abuse is illegal in the United States and that "[a]ll people, regardless of immigration or citizenship status, are guaranteed basic protections under both civil and criminal law," frequent recommendations to contact a family or immigration lawyer inspire little confidence in the self-petitioning process. Never lifting the burden from the battered spouse, the fact sheet warns, "Ultimately, you are responsible for deciding whether you feel safe in the relationship." * * * Nor does USCIS define what a "good faith" marriage is and what an immigrant victim must

do to meet the requirements. * * * As a result, USCIS leaves a battered spouse without a guideline by which to decide whether she would qualify as a self-petitioner. The battered spouse faces a gamble that she may not qualify. This consequently diminishes the likelihood that a battered spouse will leave the abusive marriage or report the abuse. Despite USCIS's release of the fact sheet, GAO's concern that foreign brides are more likely to be unaware of their immigration rights and safety resources if the pamphlet is not translated or distributed remains valid. * * * [T]he Tahirih Justice Center, which works to protect female immigrants from gender-based violence, observed that the pamphlet circulation plan proved problematic, as it called for distributing the pamphlet to immigrant brides [when the sponsoring spouse was also present.] * * *

2. Power Imbalance Remains

IMBRA was enacted under the assumption that once informational imbalances are corrected, the foreign bride will be on equal footing with the consumer husband to enter into a marriage contract freely. Such conjecture ignores the pervasive economic imbalances inherent to the IMB industry. Women from countries with meager employment opportunities and social benefits often become foreign brides because the industry has become successful at commodifying women from poor foreign regions as a gender, taking advantage of their hope of improving their lives. Immigrant brides are incentivized to stay in an abusive relationship for at least two years in order to gain permanent residency. * * * In sum, IMBRA protects the immigrant brides as long as they are victims of domestic violence, ignoring that they are also victims of fundamental forces that contribute to the existence and success of the IMB industry. Because IMBRA does not recognize that merely providing foreign brides with information is insufficient protection and that these women are victims of more than domestic violence, IMBRA does not truly correct the power imbalance that endangers immigrant brides. *[Editor's Note: While it is possible for an abused immigrant spouse to file separately to remove the conditional residency, immigrant spouses may not be aware of this option and it may be hard to prove the abuse to the satisfaction of USCIS.]*

VI. RECOMMENDED REMEDIES TO ALLEVIATE STIGMATIZATION

[The author calls for ending the legal stigmatization of foreign bride marriages, including the requirement of marrying within ninety days of arrival. She also calls for shifting the fraudulent marriage presumption away from the victim, so the USCIS has to prove the marriage was fraudulent; and urges more efficient regulation of the IMB industry, allowing a private cause of action by non-governmental organizations against IMB's, and a new government-imposed code of conduct for IMB's. Further, she calls for fostering cooperation between countries to end abuse of foreign brides, informing brides of their rights and the groom's background, and balancing the power between the spouses. She encourages non-governmental organizations to assist foreign brides when they are abused. She then suggests abolishing such marriages, noting that a court in Massachusetts held such contracts are void as against public policy. But she notes that because successful immigrant bride marriages allow some women a chance to escape poverty, foreclosing the opportunity for women in destitute regions to escape poverty in the United States likely will shift the domestic abuse problems and sexual exploitation to other countries. And she states that the foreign bride movement could go underground in the U.S., which may result in even more egregious abuses.]

[Editor's Notes: 1. In 2013, Congress amended VAWA to clarify who is responsible for investigating and prosecuting violations of the IMBRA of 2005 (Title VIII, § 808(a) [S. 47]), prohibiting marketing foreign brides who are under 18 years of age or marketing brides to anyone under 18 years of age (8 U.S.C. § 1375a(d)), strengthening background checks for U.S. citizens using IMB's (id., § 1184), increasing penalties for IMB's who violate the law (id., § 1375a), specifying the penalty if a U.S. citizen fraudulently fails to disclose information required under the Act (Ibid.), and requiring a report to Congress in 2015 by the Comptroller General regarding how the IMBRA is working. (Ibid.) This report, Improvements Needed to Fully Implement the International Marriage Broker Regulation Act, released by the GAO in 2014, found that many of the same problems described in the GAO's 2008 study had not been corrected. These included consular officers apparently not giving the required pamphlet to would-be brides describing the legal rights and resources available to immigrant crime victims, and the USCIS not keeping electronic records of whether would-be husbands had criminal convictions or had filed previous petitions for foreign brides.

2. In Trafficked: Domestic Violence, Exploitation in Marriage, and the Foreign-Bridge Industry, 51 Va. J. Int'l L. 443 (2011), Jane Kim argues, since "trafficking of foreign brides for the purposes of exploitation in marriage . . . violates international law," including the Palermo Protocol, the entire "industry should thus be prohibited and criminalized in order to truly combat modern forms of slavery." Such criminalization process, though, must take place "over a long-term period" and "offer interim and supplementary measures that are equally important and necessary to combat" trafficking, such as implementing "skills-training institutions," awareness-raising campaigns, and programs "to reduce oppression, poverty, gender discrimination, and gender-based violence."]

B. ASYLUM

HARVARD LAW REVIEW MEMBERS, ATTORNEY GENERAL GARLAND VACATES *MATTER OF A-B-*. *MATTER OF A-B-*, 28 I. & N. DEC. 307 (A.G. 2021)

135 Harv. L. Rev. 1174 (2022)
(footnotes omitted)

Under international and domestic law, an asylum seeker must be found to have a "well-founded fear" of persecution—based either upon past persecution or a fear of future persecution—"on account of race, religion, nationality, membership in a particular social group, or political opinion." Even though gender is not explicitly listed as a protected ground, the Board of Immigration Appeals (BIA) and U.S. courts have frequently granted asylum to survivors of gender-based violence on the basis of their "membership in a particular social group." This practice was thrown into flux when former Attorney General Jefferson Sessions held in *Matter of A-B-* (*A-B- I*) that a survivor of domestic violence did not qualify for asylum based on her membership in a gender-based particular social group (PSG). Recently [in 2021], in *Matter of A-B-* (*A-B- III*), Attorney General Merrick Garland vacated this decision. In doing so, the Attorney General provided a welcome return to precedent after *A-B- I* made it exceedingly difficult for survivors of domestic violence to receive asylum.

The respondent in *Matter of A-B-* was Ms. A-B-, a citizen of El Salvador who applied for asylum in the United States after suffering repeated physical, emotional, and sexual abuse from her ex-husband, with whom she had three children. Ms. A-B- married her husband in 1999, after which he began abusing her. In 2008, "tired of [his] violence," she separated from him and moved to a town several hours away. Her husband found her and raped her, beginning a pattern of behavior that continued after they officially obtained a divorce in 2013. After receiving several threats—including from her former brother-in-law, a local police officer, who warned her "to be very careful," as "you don't know where the bullets will land"—Ms. A-B- fled to the United States. She then filed an application for asylum on the ground that she had suffered persecution in El Salvador on the basis of her membership in the PSG of " 'El Salvadoran women who are unable to leave their domestic relationships where they have children in common. with their partners."

The immigration judge denied her asylum request. The judge determined that Ms. A-B- was not credible, that she had failed to establish that membership in her proposed PSG was "a central reason" for the persecution she suffered, and that she had not shown that the El Salvadoran government was unwilling or unable to assist her. The judge also found that her proposed PSG was not valid under 8 U.S.C. § 1101(a)(42)(A) because she had not "show[n] a common immutable characteristic despite her female gender and Salvadoran nationality." Thus, Ms. A-B-'s case did not satisfy the necessary elements for asylum, which required that she (and others applying for asylum on the grounds of membership in a PSG) show:

> (1) membership in a particular group, which is composed of members who share a common immutable characteristic, is defined with particularity, and is socially distinct within the society in question; (2) that her membership in that group is a central reason for her persecution; and (3) that the alleged harm is inflicted by the government of her home country or by persons that the government is unwilling or unable to control.

Ms. A-B- appealed this decision to the BIA.

In 2016, the BIA reversed the immigration judge's decision and remanded, ordering that Ms. A-B- be granted asylum provided that she pass background checks. The BIA held that the immigration judge had clearly erred in finding that Ms. A-B- was not credible. In the BIA's view, her central story remained undisputed, and the smaller discrepancies in the record were sufficiently resolved by her assertion that she had been too focused on escaping her trauma to remember. The BIA also found that her membership in her proposed PSG was a central reason for the persecution she suffered and that the El Salvadoran government was unwilling or unable to protect her. Finally, the BIA held that Ms. A-B-'s proposed PSG *was* valid, chiefly because it was similar to a social group the BIA had recognized in a previous case, *Matter of A-R-C-G-*: "married women in Guatemala who are unable to leave their relationship."

In 2018, then-Attorney General Sessions directed the BIA to refer this case to him for review, inviting briefs on "[w]hether, and under what circumstances, being a victim of private criminal activity constitutes a cognizable 'particular social group' for purposes of. . .asylum." In a decision commonly known as *A-B- I*, then-Attorney General Sessions vacated the BIA's decision and remanded to the immigration judge. He held, inter alia, that asylum claims "pertaining to domestic violence . . . perpetrated by non-governmental actors" would generally not be valid and that Ms. A-B-'s membership in her proposed social group did not qualify her for asylum. The BIA had not cited any evidence that "her husband knew any such social group existed, or that he persecuted [his] wife for reasons unrelated to their relationship"—thus, the BIA had failed to show a nexus between Ms. A-B-'s membership in her PSG and the harm she had suffered. In addition, then-Attorney General Sessions overruled *Matter of A-R-C-G-*, the first precedential BIA decision that unambiguously held PSGs for victims of domestic violence valid. He reasoned that, because the government in *A-R-C-G-* had conceded the key questions regarding Ms. A-R-C-G-'s PSG (including its cognizability), the BIA had "performed only a cursory analysis" of her proposed PSG. As such, the decision lacked precedential value.

Attorney General Garland subsequently vacated *A-B- I* and *A-B-II* in a decision known as *A-B- III*. After reviewing the basic tenets of asylum law and the procedural history of the case, he explained that President Biden had directed the Attorney General and the Secretary of Homeland Security "to promulgate regulations 'addressing the circumstances in which a person should be considered a member of a "particular social group" " ' Because rulemaking necessarily involves public input and a "thorough" analysis of the relevant issues, especially when it implicates immigration law, Attorney General Garland reasoned that vacating *A-B- I* would give the Department of Homeland Security "appropriate flexibility" in the rulemaking process.

Attorney General Garland also challenged former Attorney General Sessions' opinion in *A-B- I*. He explained that, although the opinion was framed as a restatement of existing precedent in asylum cases, it "could be read to create a strong presumption against asylum claims based on private conduct." As such, former Attorney General Sessions' decision had created and would continue to create confusion among lower courts and discourage a thorough case-by-case analysis of asylum claims. Thus, Attorney General Garland concluded that *A-B-I* and *A-B-II* should be vacated and *Matter of A-R-C-G-* reinstated as good precedent.

The Attorney General's decision to vacate is consistent with precedent in the BIA and federal circuits, which has established the validity of PSGs based on sex. Indeed, the BIA has explicitly named sex as an acceptable basis for a PSG since the beginning of the BIA's PSG jurisprudence. In addition, *A-B- III* removes a significant obstacle for survivors of domestic violence seeking asylum and could impact the viability of asylum claims from other survivors of private violence.

The interpretation of the phrase "particular social group" has largely been left to the BIA, since courts often defer to administrative agencies on questions of statutory interpretation. As such, almost exclusively, the BIA's definition rules this area of immigration law. The BIA first defined "particular social group" in *Matter of Acosta*. There, the BIA wrote that all the members of a cognizable PSG must share a "common, immutable characteristic." It then explicitly stated that "sex" was an example of one such shared characteristic.

As PSG jurisprudence progressed, the BIA continued to refine the definition of—and thus the legal test for—a satisfactory PSG. In *Matter of M-E-V-G-* and *Matter of W-G-R-*, the BIA established that a cognizable PSG is a group that not only shares a common, immutable characteristic but is also 1) particular and 2) socially distinct. To be particular, the PSG must be "discrete" rather than "amorphous." To be socially distinct, the PSG's shared characteristic must "meaningfully distinguish[ ]" those in society who have the characteristic from those without it. Moreover, as it did in *Matter of Acosta*, the BIA reiterated that sex was an example of a basis for a PSG that fulfilled these requirements.

Though a few circuits have been hesitant to recognize gender-based PSGs, most have consistently held that these PSGs are cognizable for the purposes of asylum. For example, the First and Eighth Circuits have held that gender-based formulations may establish cognizable PSGs. While there has been some debate over what precise groups of women may constitute PSGs, many other federal circuits have ruled similarly on the issue. Most significantly, the Ninth Circuit has suggested that a combination of sex and nationality (for example, "Somalian females") or even sex generally can constitute a PSG. In its view, both examples are simply "logical application[s]" of circuit and BIA precedent.

Attorneys representing survivors of domestic violence seeking asylum have consistently relied on *Matter of A-R-C-G-'s* allowance of certain PSGs. In friendlier circuits, these proposed PSGs often take the form of "nationality + women." Other circuits have seemingly implied that PSGs formulated as such would be too indistinct to be cognizable, thus giving rise to formulations such as the ones proposed in *De Pena-Paniagua v. Barr*: "Dominican women abused and viewed as property by their romantic partners, who are unable to escape or seek protection, by virtue of their gender"; "Dominican women viewed as property and unable to leave a domestic relationship"; and "Dominican women unable to leave a domestic relationship."

At least equally important as the fact that *A-B- III* returned PSG jurisprudence to established practice are two key normative implications of Attorney General Garland's decision: reduced uncertainty and expanded eligibility for domestic violence survivors seeking asylum. Immigrants—and asylum seekers, specifically—have historically faced considerable unpredictability when seeking lawful presence in the United States. As with all asylum seekers, the success rates of asylum applicants seeking protection on the grounds of gender-based PSGs depend on a number of factors, including the applicants' geographical locations (and thus the circuits in which the applicants would appear should a party petition for review) and the immigration judges before whom the applicants appear. In recent years, the volatility of PSG requirements and changing political tides have created even more unpredictability for domestic violence survivors seeking asylum.

By overruling *Matter of A-R-C-G-*, *A-B- I* added an extra layer of legal uncertainty for these applicants. Over the course of *A-B- I's* reign, some legal advocates had maintained that, although undoubtedly more difficult, obtaining asylum was not impossible for survivors of domestic abuse, especially in federal circuits with favorable precedent. Others, however, argued that *A-B- I* had such wide-ranging implications that it effectively "ordered U.S. immigration courts to stop granting asylum to victims of domestic abuse." Regardless of the varying responses to *A-B- I*, former Attorney General Sessions' decision "put[ ] survivors' lives and safety at grave risk" nationwide, and people who would have otherwise been eligible for asylum were denied relief as a direct result.

By reinstating *Matter of A-R-C-G-* as a precedential BIA decision, *A-B- III* will have a massive impact on the unpredictability faced by asylum seekers who have survived domestic violence. Notably, the Attorney General's decision reinstates formal recognition of domestic violence as a potential basis for asylum. *A-B- III* will have an impact in all circuits, even if the vacatur will naturally be a smaller remedy in circuits that were more willing to minimize the effects of former Attorney General Sessions' decision—thus, the decision provides for some uniformity in a legal realm that has seen circuits apply PSG precedent in various ways.

Indeed, shortly after Attorney General Garland issued his decision, Associate Attorney General Vanita Gupta issued a follow-up memorandum directing government attorneys to "take appropriate steps in light of [*A-B- III*], including seeking remands . . . to allow the Board to reconsider asylum claims." This memorandum illustrates the immediate impact of *A-B- III*: asylum seekers with pending cases were almost instantly more likely to obtain relief. The impact of *A-B- III* may even stretch beyond the domestic violence realm, as this decision also vacates *A-B- I*'s presumption against asylum claims grounded on persecution inflicted by private actors, thus reaffirming support for asylum claims based in other forms of private violence such as gang violence.

By vacating former Attorney General Sessions's decision in *A-B-I*, Attorney General Garland remedied a drastic departure from BIA and federal circuit precedent regarding PSGs based on gender. This decision is significant for immigrants who are seeking asylum on the basis of domestic abuse suffered or feared in their home countries. For asylum seekers like Ms. A-B-, whose seven years of legal turmoil have finally come to an end, *A-B- III* allows for a significantly more hopeful path.

RODRIGUEZ TORNES V. GARLAND

993 F.3d 743 (9th Cir. 2021)
(footnotes and citations omitted)

Petitioner Maria Luisa Rodriguez Tornes, a native and citizen of Mexico, testified to a lifetime of severe abuse from her mother, her estranged husband, and her partner for, in their eyes, being insufficiently subservient to men. An immigration judge ("IJ") granted asylum, and alternatively granted withholding of removal and protection under the Convention Against Torture ("CAT"), in a detailed decision. The Board of Immigration Appeals ("BIA") reversed in part, holding that Petitioner's past persecution and fear of future persecution lacked a nexus to a protected ground. Because the record compels a contrary conclusion, we grant the petition and remand for further proceedings.

FACTUAL AND PROCEDURAL HISTORY

Since the age of five, Petitioner has been told that men will beat her if she does not submit. Her mother demanded that she learn how to do housework, how to accept spousal abuse, and how "to obey everything that [her] husband would say." She beat Petitioner with various objects almost daily, in part to prepare her for future beatings from her husband. Yet Petitioner came to believe that "there should be equality in opinions[ ] and in worth" between men and women. She became a teacher.

Petitioner's husband, Esteban Baron Mata, began a regime of grueling abuse months after they married. When he once wanted food at 1 a.m., for example, he awakened Petitioner by sticking a lit cigarette into her arm and ordered her to cook. She told him to do it himself; he grabbed her hair and dragged her into the kitchen. Petitioner "had to do it because [she] was his woman, [she] was his wife, and it was [her] responsibility to serve him," he said. On another occasion, he burned Petitioner's face with a cigarette because she refused to leave her teaching job. He told her that she had no right to work and that, as a man, it was his duty to provide. "You think that because you studied, you can step on me," he said during one beating. "You're not going to step on me. I'm the man and you're going to do what I say." Petitioner said that she did not report her husband's abuse to the police because doing so would have been futile. When a friend tried to report her own husband, a police officer told her to stop gossiping, return home, and do her "duties."

Baron left Petitioner in 1993 when she was pregnant. Her Catholic family prohibited divorce and required that she live with them until Baron returned. Petitioner fled to the United States. Years later, in phone calls and messages through Facebook, Baron sought Petitioner's location and insisted that they reunite. After Petitioner changed her phone number and deleted her account on Facebook, Baron visited Petitioner's daughter. He appeared aggressive and threatened "revenge." "His family also says that he is still a violent man towards women and beats" his current girlfriend.

Petitioner met Jorge Hernandez Fernandez in Phoenix, Arizona. They moved in together. He, too, beat, raped, burned, and strangled her. Petitioner's assertions of female independence and equality prompted his abuse. When Petitioner declined to give Hernandez money so that she could save for household expenses, he cut her with a broken beer bottle and raped her. "If you're not going to give me money, give me sex," he said. During another instance when Petitioner declined sex, Hernandez responded that she had no choice in the matter because she was his property. When she spoke up in front of his friends in their home, he said that she had to just "come in and not say anything." He then punched her so hard that she suffered a vaginal hemorrhage.

The cycle of abuse occurred almost weekly. Hernandez said that Petitioner, as a woman, was not allowed to have opinions; Petitioner expressed opinions anyway; Hernandez abused Petitioner. When Petitioner took a job in which she would have to speak to men—despite Hernandez's demand that she not take such a job—he left bite marks and visible signs of strangulation on her neck to show other men that she "had an owner." "What's wrong with it? . . . You're my woman, and they need to know it," he said. When she tried to kick him out, he returned and raped her. He also dictated her clothing. "I wasn't allowed to have an opinion about . . . anything," Petitioner wrote in her declaration. "He couldn't stand that I, as the supposedly weaker sex, was the breadwinner. . . ."

Petitioner and Hernandez had three children, all of whom are citizens of the United States. After several foiled attempts, Petitioner escaped the relationship.

In 2017, the government deported Hernandez to Guatemala and Petitioner to Mexico. Hernandez called Petitioner and her children, demanding to know where Petitioner now lived. Because he lacks family in Guatemala, Petitioner believes that Hernandez now lives in Mexico, where he has family and can obtain residency. Fearing for her safety, Petitioner returned to the United States. The government initiated removal proceedings against Petitioner in December 2017.

The IJ found Petitioner credible and granted her asylum. In the alternative, the IJ granted withholding of removal and CAT protection. The IJ found that Petitioner's feminist political opinion was at least one central reason for her past persecution by Baron and for her well-founded fear of future persecution by Baron and Hernandez. The IJ also found that Petitioner's membership in a particular social group of "Mexican females" was at least one central reason for her past persecution by Baron and for her well-founded fear of future persecution by Baron and Hernandez. Citing reams of documentary evidence, the IJ found that if the Mexican government did not condone violence against females, it at least "demonstrated a complete helplessness" to protect Petitioner.

The BIA affirmed the grant of CAT protection but reversed the grants of asylum and withholding of removal. It tersely disposed of the IJ's pages of factual findings. Citing the Attorney General's opinion in *Matter of A-B-*, 27 I. & N. Dec. 316 (A.G. 2018) ("*Matter of A-B- I*"), the BIA held that "the record lacks findings that [Petitioner's] domestic partners abused her for 'reasons unrelated to their relationship[s].' " Nevertheless, the BIA did not disturb the IJ's finding that Petitioner is credible. It also acknowledged that Petitioner "suffered severe mental and physical abuse from her mother, her ex-husband, and her former domestic partner, including, but not limited to, repeated rapes, beatings, burns, and verbal and mental abuse." More broadly, the BIA did "not disturb the [IJ]'s factual findings regarding the 'pandemic' of violence against females in that country or the import of 'culturally constructed' and entrenched identity roles." The government did not challenge the IJ's findings that Petitioner (1) suffered past persecution and torture; (2) has a political opinion; and (3) is a member of a cognizable social group of Mexican females.

In affirming CAT relief, the BIA held that the IJ did not clearly err in finding that authorities acquiesced in Petitioner's torture and that it would be "unreasonable for her to relocate within Mexico." Petitioner timely petitions for review, challenging the denial of asylum and withholding of removal. . . .

DISCUSSION

A. General Principles

To be eligible for asylum, Petitioner must prove that she is "unable or unwilling" to return to her country of origin "because of persecution or a well-founded fear of persecution on account of race, religion, nationality, membership in a particular social group, or political opinion." Thus, Petitioner has the burden of establishing that (1) her treatment rises to the level of persecution or that she has a well-founded fear of future persecution; (2) the persecution was or would be on account of one or more protected grounds; and (3) the persecution was or would be committed by the government, or by forces that the government was unable or unwilling to control. To obtain withholding of removal, Petitioner must show that her "life or freedom would be threatened in [Mexico] because of [her] race, religion, nationality, membership in a particular social group, or political opinion." "Past persecution 'triggers a rebuttable presumption of a well-founded fear of future persecution.'" At issue here is whether Petitioner "establish[ed] a nexus between [the] mistreatment and a protected ground."

For asylum, Petitioner must show that a protected ground "was or will be at least one central reason" for persecution. . . A central reason cannot be "incidental, tangential, superficial, or subordinate to another reason for harm."

That an unprotected ground, such as a personal dispute, *also* constitutes a central reason for persecution does *not* bar asylum. "[I]f a retributory motive exists alongside a protected motive, an applicant need show only that a protected ground is 'one central reason' for his [or her] persecution."

The Acting Attorney General recently agreed that our nexus standard is the correct one. "To establish the necessary nexus, the protected ground: (1) must be a but-for cause of the wrongdoer's act; and (2) must play more than a minor role—in other words, it cannot be incidental or tangential to another reason for the act." *Matter of A-B-*, 28 I. & N. Dec. 199, 208 (A.G. 2021) ("*Matter of A-B- II*"). That test is substantively indistinguishable from our own. Under *Parussimova*, Petitioner must first show that "the persecutor would not have harmed [her] if such motive did not exist," that is, but-for cause. . . As discussed above, *Parussimova* next requires Petitioner to show that her protected ground was not "incidental, tangential, superficial, or subordinate to another reason for harm. In sum, *Matter of A-B- II* did not change the standard for establishing nexus, at least in our circuit. The government's motion to remand so that the BIA can consider *Matter of A-B- II*'s effect on nexus is therefore denied.

B. Political Opinion

Petitioner must establish two facts to show persecution on account of her political opinion. First, she "must show that [s]he held (or that h[er] persecutors believed that [s]he held) a political opinion." Second, she "must show that h[er] persecutors persecuted h[er] because of [that] political opinion."

We have held repeatedly that political opinions "encompass[ ] more than electoral politics or formal political ideology or action." Although "the mere presence of some political element does not require the conclusion that some maltreatment was on account of political opinion," applicants need not "espouse political theory." Like the Third Circuit, we have "little doubt that feminism qualifies as a political opinion within the meaning of the relevant statutes."

Direct and indirect evidence can show that persecution was on account of a political opinion. "Testimony regarding a persecutor's statements serves as direct evidence that the persecution was motivated by a political opinion. . . ." So long as the IJ finds that a petitioner is credible, that testimony can come from the petitioner herself. A short temporal gap between a petitioner's actual or imputed assertion of a political opinion and her mistreatment provides "indirect evidence of a nexus."

Here, substantial evidence does not support the BIA's conclusion that the record lacks evidence of a nexus between Petitioner's persecution and her political opinion. At the outset, it bears repeating that the BIA did not disturb the IJ's factual findings regarding Petitioner's favorable credibility and the severity of her mistreatment. Therefore, the only two pertinent questions are those described above: (1) whether Petitioner had an actual or imputed political opinion, and (2) whether she was persecuted because of that political opinion. We are compelled to answer both questions in the affirmative.

First, Petitioner has a feminist political opinion. The government did not challenge that conclusion before the agency. To the extent that the BIA determined otherwise, Petitioner's testimony, work habits, and insistence on autonomy compel a contrary conclusion. Under our precedents, it is no answer that Petitioner did not engage in feminist "electoral" activities, or "espouse political theory." Petitioner's testimony that "there should be equality in opinions[ ] and in worth" between the sexes suffices.

Second, Petitioner was persecuted because of that political opinion. The record contains episode after episode of men stating, quite plainly, that they were beating, burning, raping, and strangling her *because* she sought an equal perch in the social hierarchy. Hernandez left bite and strangulation marks on Petitioner after she took a job against his wishes, to show other men that she "had an owner." Petitioner's husband, Baron, burned a cigarette into her face because she refused to leave her job and, according to her husband, acknowledge "that [he] and [Petitioner] were not equals." Petitioner was doing something wrong, Baron said, by "providing money" when, "as a man, it was his duty to do [that]." When he said that Petitioner "didn't have th[e] right to have that job," Petitioner countered that she did. Baron responded by hitting her.

Indeed, some of the worst acts of violence came "immediately after" Petitioner asserted her rights as a woman. After Petitioner said that she was not obligated to have sex whenever Hernandez wished, he said that "it was [her] obligation as a woman to serve him when he wanted," and he raped her. Similarly, after Petitioner bought her own trailer with her wages and attempted to prevent Hernandez's entry onto her property, Hernandez raped and strangled her so that she "would understand that he wasn't going to go anywhere."

The government's argument that there is no evidence that Baron and Hernandez were "aware" of Petitioner's political opinion thus lacks any rational basis. Petitioner does not claim that she was persecuted for being a feminist merely because she, a woman, was mistreated by men. Rather, she claims that she was persecuted when those men mistreated her because she expressly asserted to them her political opinion that she was their equal.

That some incidents of abuse may also have reflected a dysfunctional relationship is beside the point. Petitioner need not show that her political opinion—rather than interpersonal dynamics—played the sole or predominant role in her abuse.

Thus, the record compels the conclusion that Petitioner's political opinion is at least one central reason for her past persecution and her presumptively well-founded fear of future persecution. It then follows that Petitioner's political opinion is "a reason" for her persecution for purposes of withholding of removal.

C. Fear of Future Persecution

Because the BIA determined that nexus is lacking, it "f[ound] it [un]necessary to address the [government's] argument that [Petitioner] . . . did not have a well-founded fear of future persecution." Yet it then held that the IJ did not err in granting CAT protection. To receive CAT protection, Petitioner had to prove "that it is more likely than not that . . . she will be tortured in the country of removal."

Thus, this petition presents a recognized exception to the ordinary remand rule that we allow the BIA to decide issues in the first instance. Petitioner "met the high burden of demonstrating that [s]he is likely to be tortured, . . . [s]he necessarily meets the lower burden for eligibility for asylum that [s]he has a well-founded fear of future persecution." In other words, when the agency grants CAT protection, it necessarily has decided that there is a well-founded fear of future persecution. Similarly, Petitioner "has demonstrated the existence of a clear probability of future persecution" for her withholding of removal claim. "Having established a nexus between h[er] persecution and . . . political opinion, and having established a well-founded fear of future persecution, a *Ventura* remand is unnecessary."

D. Inability or Unwillingness to Control Persecution

The BIA did not discuss whether Petitioner fears persecution "by the government, or by forces that the government was unable or unwilling to control." It did, however, affirm the IJ's finding that the Mexican government would acquiesce in Petitioner's torture. As with Petitioner's fear of future persecution, our precedents and the BIA's own opinion show that it necessarily decided that the government was unable or unwilling to control Petitioner's persecutors. "Public officials acquiesce in torture if, 'prior to the activity constituting torture,' the officials: (1) have awareness of the activity (or consciously close their eyes to the fact it is going on); and (2) breach their legal responsibility to intervene to prevent the activity because they are *unable or unwilling* to oppose it."

Thus, on this record, the agency's finding that the government "would acquiesce" in Petitioner's torture necessarily includes the determination that the government would be unable or unwilling to stop Petitioner's future persecution, a less severe form of mistreatment than torture. That is especially so here, because the BIA parroted the Acting Attorney General's own standard for persecution in concluding that the government showed acquiescence by "routinely breach[ing] the duty to intervene in these matters."

E. Ability to Relocate

If the government proves that Petitioner "can reasonably relocate internally to an area of safety," then she is ineligible for asylum. In its analysis of asylum and withholding of removal, the BIA stated that it was unnecessary to address Petitioner's "ability to relocate" because it found nexus to be lacking. Once again, the BIA's holding with respect to Petitioner's CAT claim necessarily resolved that issue.

For purposes of asylum and withholding of removal, assessing Petitioner's ability to relocate "consists of two steps: (1) 'whether [she] could relocate safely,' *and* (2) 'whether it would be *reasonable* to require [her] to do so.' " In resolving Petitioner's CAT claim, the BIA held that country conditions "render it *unreasonable* for [Petitioner] to relocate within Mexico." Accordingly, the BIA necessarily decided that Petitioner also could not relocate for purposes of asylum and withholding of removal.

In sum, we hold that (1) we are compelled to conclude that Petitioner established a nexus between her mistreatment and political opinion and (2) the BIA necessarily concluded that she carried her burden to prove the other elements of her claims for asylum and withholding of removal. Petitioner is thus eligible for asylum and entitled to withholding of removal.

On remand, the Attorney General shall exercise his discretion in determining whether to grant Petitioner asylum. If he does not grant asylum, Petitioner shall receive withholding of removal.

PETITION GRANTED AND REMANDED. The panel shall retain jurisdiction over any future petitions for review.

PAEZ, CIRCUIT JUDGE, concurring:

I join Judge Graber's fine opinion in full. I write separately on a point the court's opinion does not address. In rejecting Ms. Rodriguez Tornes's political opinion claim, the BIA suggests that the presence of a "personal relationship" motivation for intimate partner violence implies that there were no intersectional or additional bases for the violence Ms. Rodriguez Tornes experienced. The court's opinion thoroughly documents the record evidence, which the BIA ignored, demonstrating how Ms. Rodriguez Tornes was targeted for violence by her domestic partners on account of her feminist political opinion. The BIA, however, *also* ignored extensive record evidence from expert witness Prof. Nancy Lemon, a leading authority on domestic violence, that directly rejects the BIA's premise that domestic violence is presumed to be motivated by nothing more than the private dynamics of a "personal relationship."

In contrast to the BIA's "personal relationship" view of domestic violence, Prof. Lemon draws on more than three decades of research, writing, legal representation, and lawmaking to explain that "the socially or culturally constructed and defined identities, roles and responsibilities that are assigned to women, as distinct from those assigned to men, are the root of domestic violence." She analyzes data from the U.S. Department of Justice, Bureau of Justice Statistics and studies from leading medical and social science publications to highlight "compelling evidence that heterosexual domestic violence is, in significant part, motivated by bias against women and the belief that men are entitled to beat and control women." Prof. Lemon summarizes cross-cultural studies within the United States and internationally that demonstrate "a correlation between patriarchal norms that support male dominance and violence against women by intimate partners."

In her report, which the IJ referenced in her decision, Prof. Lemon provides a lengthy examination of social science research exploring how particular behaviors exhibited by male abusers—including emotional abuse, sexual abuse, marital rape, economic abuse, blaming, guilt and using children—are each tied to social belief systems that "men are entitled to dominate and control women because the male sex is considered superior" and operate to "exploit the traditional socially constructed roles, identities, duties and status of women in intimate relationships." In describing the legal, social, cultural, and political structures that lay the foundations for intimate partner violence, Prof. Lemon explains that "*domestic violence is not typically caused by behaviors unique to the victim or by inter-personal dynamics unique to the relationship between the abuser and the abused*. . . .Rather, heterosexual male batterers have certain expectations of intimate relationships with regard to which partner will control the relationship and how control will be exercised. These expectations are premised on a dogmatic adherence to male privilege and rigid, distinct, and unequal roles for women and men." [emphasis added]

The record evidence of Prof. Lemon's rigorous expert analysis undermines the BIA's unsubstantiated premise that, unless otherwise shown, domestic violence is a purely private matter. The BIA makes no mention of the record evidence of Prof. Lemon's expert analysis, let alone the decades of publicly available social science research and public policy that all reject the BIA's outdated view of domestic violence as a quirk within a "personal relationship." Thus, the BIA's assertion that domestic violence is presumptively a private matter is not supported by substantial evidence.

C. DOMESTIC VIOLENCE AS A HUMAN RIGHTS ISSUE

RHONDA COPELON, INTERNATIONAL HUMAN RIGHTS DIMENSIONS OF INTIMATE VIOLENCE: ANOTHER STRAND IN THE DIALECTIC OF FEMINIST LAWMAKING

11(2) Am U J of Gender, Soc. Policy & L 865 (2003)
(citations and footnotes omitted)

* * * The documentation of the history of our movement and [Elizabeth Schneider's] thoughtful reflections on the continuing dialectic and challenges are, indeed, a gift to all of us and to women in many parts of the world who have been struggling to have recognized and to eliminate violence against women. In that process, and unlike most United States activists, many of our sisters abroad have turned to the framework and mechanisms of international human rights to both legitimate and advance their struggles and, in so doing, have contributed to the vision and tools we can be using here. * * *

My comments today will briefly trace the history and theoretical obstacles in this process and elaborate on how the human rights framework and human rights activism can assist us here in the United States, as well as how the dialectic of state dependency, depoliticization and the disaggregation of violence from equality . . . compromise international human rights and present continuing challenges for women's human rights activists and scholars as well.

In 1990, women's human rights issues were barely on the margin of the international human rights agenda. The Convention on the Elimination of All Forms of Discrimination Against Women ("CEDAW") was consigned to little more than window-dressing. Violence against women was almost never addressed in either official or non-governmental human rights documentation and reporting. Even when the state was responsible for rape, for example, it was usually treated as a personal matter, rendered invisible and immunized from accountability. Rape in war was also on shaky ground as it had evolved in international humanitarian law only as implicit in the crime of "humiliating and degrading treatment" or in the "offense against honor and dignity" rather than as an explicit, named crime of violence.

In response, ["visionaries [and] renegades from mainstream thinking or women, in various positions in and out of governments, who themselves were survivors of rape or battering,"] * * * identified violence against women . . . as a priority issue of human rights in. . . preparations for the 1993 World Conference on Human Rights in Vienna ("Vienna Conference").

* * * Leading mainstream human rights non-governmental advocates, however, adhered to a state-centric approach to human rights and were just beginning to recognize the severity of gender-based violence. With narrow exceptions like slavery, the traditional view was that human rights address only the actions of the state, not private individuals. In this view, state action which inflicts violence of sufficient gravity upon women would constitute a human rights violation. But privately inflicted violence, while appropriate for condemnation by municipal criminal laws, did not, they argued, present a human rights concern apart from some form of active state involvement. Thus, when state officials inflicted violence on women—for example, rape in prison—that would be a violation, for example, of the right of personal security. And, if the state treated violence against men and women unequally—e.g., in not enforcing assault laws against domestic violence or in nullifying the killing of women by the defense of honor—that would be discrimination, an appropriate human rights concern. * * * Including private gendered violence, it was said, would "dilute" the human rights framework. Thus feminists had to challenge this incarnation of the public/private distinction, and discovered, in the process, that the international human rights process was not impenetrable to global

organizing and that basic human rights principles include certain positive state responsibilities that should apply to private gender violence.

The Vienna Conference was a watershed. Testimonies as to the gravity and pervasiveness of gender violence, the force of women's broad organizing, and the very concrete fact, brought home by the participation of women from Bosnia and the former Yugoslavia, that women were being raped systematically in Bosnia—just hours from the site of the Conference—prevailed over objections to incorporating gender violence as a human rights problem. They also prevailed over the vigorous chorus of "no's" from defenders of archly patriarchal religions and cultures, who may condemn violence against women but who also contend that it is not an international problem and that sexual subordination in the home should be excluded from the human rights framework. The new consensus is reflected in the official document, the Vienna Declaration and Programme of Action.

The historic achievement of the Vienna Conference was two-fold: the recognition of violence against women as a human rights issue and the setting into motion of a process of integrating or "mainstreaming" issues of women's rights and gender equality into the international system at all levels. * * *

Significant international documents address domestic violence as a human rights problem. These include Recommendation No. 19, "Violence Against Women," of the Committee to End Discrimination Against Women (which monitors implementation of CEDAW); the Inter-American Convention on the Prevention, Punishment and Elimination of Violence Against Women (called the Convention of Belém do Pará), the unanimously approved UN General Assembly Declaration on the Elimination of Violence Against Women, the Beijing Platform for Action, and the reports of Radhika Coomaraswamy as the UN Special Rapporteur on Violence Against Women: Its Causes and Consequences, which reports have been accepted by annual resolutions of the UN Human Rights Commission on the Rights of Women.

While the UN human rights system operates primarily through various shaming techniques, the recent Rome Treaty creating the International Criminal Court ("ICC") is different. Despite vigorous objections from the Vatican and some Islamist countries, the ICC's jurisdiction encompasses rape, sexual slavery, forced pregnancy, enforced sterilization and other sexual violence in time of peace as well as war as crimes against humanity when such violence is widespread or systematic and is the consequence of state or organizational policy. The ICC exists not only as an institution of justice but as an incentive to states to adopt and prosecute these crimes domestically. Thus, for example, acceptance or encouragement of marital rape or battering by law or by organizational leaders is one example of the ICC's potential reach.

At the same time, intimate gender-based violence seems intractable and the obstacles endure. In United Nations arenas, a small band of countries, representing various fundamentalisms, and now joined by representatives of the [George W.] Bush Administration, continues to challenge the Vienna framework. * * *

[Schneider] points out the significance of the international acceptance of the concept that gender violence is per se gender discrimination. International recognition of gender violence as a human rights violation does not depend upon showing that the state inflicted it or that the state treated violence against women differently from violence against men. Rather, gender violence is viewed as inherently discriminatory in that it both reflects inequality and perpetuates it. This approach is rooted in an acknowledgment of the impact of this systemic practice and the necessity to prioritize its elimination. It entrains the positive obligation of the state under the International Covenant on Political and Civil Rights ("ICCPR") to ensure people against attack on their rights by others and the obligation, set forth in CEDAW and the Convention on the Elimination of All Forms of Racial Discrimination ("CERD"), to both eliminate discrimination and take positive steps to achieve full equality.

Recognition by the international human rights system is an important step in transforming private gender violence from a personal to a political issue. Paralleling right-wing anti-federalist opposition to the federal Violence Against Women Act here, opponents of recognizing privately inflicted gender violence as a human rights violation argued that this is a municipal or "domestic" law matter inappropriate for international scrutiny, sanction or redress. * * * State wrongdoing, it was argued, is the appropriate target because the state has a greater capacity to harm and where the state is the wrongdoer, the victim has no recourse. However, feminist advocates around the globe insisted upon and demonstrated—through women's tribunals, testimonies, documentation, statistical compilations, scholarship, and manifestations—that the harm done by the batterer is no less grave than that perpetrated by the state. Further, * * * neither human rights law, nor the state, can claim to be neutral when it does nothing to prevent private abuse, because the impact in fact is to empower the abuser.

Further, . . . to elucidate the gravity and political nature of private gender violence, feminist human rights advocates and scholars analogized battering to enslavement and torture. The issue of torture, for example, was first brought to the table by Latin American women who, while fighting dictatorial repression in their countries, recognized that what they or their sisters were suffering at home had far too much in common with the violence inflicted on political prisoners in the jails. The analogy to torture and slavery challenges the traditional trivialization of private violence as well as shifting the responsibility from the blameful woman to the batterer. These arguments provide an additional lens, illuminating women's dependency, not as a product of their own weakness or pathology, but as a function of the exercise of political power and control. * * * These ends, and not the justification of higher penalties, should be the point of illuminating the discrepancy between the gravity of intimate violence and the impunity traditionally accorded it. * * * [T]he notion that rape and battering can constitute torture or enslavement gained ground in official documents as well as in the jurisprudence of the ad hoc International Criminal Tribunals [, . . . thus situating] intimate violence as a form of political violence and [helping] to illuminate the impossibility of eliminating one without the other. [This notion] also opens the door, for example, to relief for battered women refugees who cannot legally be returned to countries where they are in danger of torture.

The international human rights system also helps us to understand the nature of battering as a "cultural practice." Western media tend to focus on "cultural practices"—honor killings, female genital mutilation, and dowry deaths, for example—as human rights violations. But * * * throughout the world, as well as in the United States, intimate battering of women is a pervasive "cultural practice," * * * [which requires] a cultural response. CEDAW, for example, requires states to "take appropriate measures to . . . modify the social and cultural patterns of conduct of men and women, with a view to achieving the elimination of prejudices and customary and all other practices which are based on the idea of the inferiority or superiority of either of the sexes or on stereotyped roles for men and women."

Contrary to our constitutional system, the international human rights system—including political and civil rights—imposes positive as well as negative state responsibilities. Under our federal constitutional system, claims that the state is responsible for failing to protect, prevent or punish have no force. [Citing to *DeShaney v. Winnebago County* and *Harris v. McRae*, the author concludes that the state has no obligation either to provide a person the means to exercise a fundamental right or even to avoid discriminating against that exercise by favoring one option over another]. Excepting essentially custodial situations, the state has only the duty to refrain from actively harming a person. * * *

The international human rights framework, however, does require murder laws and much more. [The author points to the International Covenant on Political and Civil Rights (ICCPR) to contend states have responsibilities to both "do no harm" (negative rights) and, while exercising "due diligence," "to ensure (positive) the protection of these rights as against private interference as well as the means to exercise basic rights." She also discusses the Convention on the Elimination of all Forms of Discrimination Against Women (CEDAW) to show states' "broader obligation" to positively "eliminate gender-based violence as part and parcel of the obligation to eliminate both intentional and disparate impact discrimination," which is decidedly more than the U.S. Supreme Court has said is required of the federal constitution. Finally, the author notes that "the [Committee on the Elimination of Racial Discrimination] CERD Committee has recently issued Recommendation No. 25, which partially adopts an intersectional analysis of race and gender discrimination with respect to private violence."] * * *

To the extent that our constitutional system embraces international law, the positive obligations of the international framework should eventually bear concrete fruit here despite persistent objections from successive administrations. [The author explains why the ICCPR obligates the United States "to provide appropriate remedies for gender violence, including judicial remedies," which, she argued in an amicus brief to the Court in *Morrison,* should include the VAWA remedy, given "Congress' power to implement treaty obligations and to confer Article III jurisdiction on the federal courts."] * * * The Court, and, most disappointingly, the dissenters in *Morrison*, did not even note this argument as one for the future, which would have been appropriate since the issue had neither been addressed by Congress nor argued below. Nonetheless, unless this increasingly rightist Supreme Court completely reframes the relationship of international and domestic law—which is a very real and immediate risk—these arguments should operate as a counterweight to devolution and enable Congress to legislate enhanced protection of the human right to be free of gender violence as well as other human rights having comparable status in treaty or customary law.

The Vienna Convention's mandate to "mainstream" gender in the human rights system also applies to nations and has been an important tool for local activists. Gender mainstreaming is pro-active. In theory, all governmental and inter-governmental entities are required to take initiative to examine the impact of their policies on women, search out the invisibilized harms and inequalities that result, and develop alternative approaches and remedies. To do this, agencies and institutions are to have a gender focal point—someone who has expertise in the subtleties of gender—with authority to investigate, critique, jump start and implement reforms in a continuing process of consultation with women affected and their representatives. * * * Along with heightening awareness of the human rights system and the seriousness of intimate gender violence, these mainstreaming strategies are among the goals of current efforts in the U.S. to enact CEDAW and CERD on a state or local basis. * * *

While the international system can inspire and legitimate change, international initiatives and impact will wane or rise with the strength of the continued mobilization and monitoring by the women's movement. The long overdue but rapid progress in women's human rights in the 1990s also spawned the proverbial backlash, to slow down or block advances by women both domestically and internationally. Progress is endangered by the rise of various fundamentalisms and their impact on governmental policies. [The author cites to examples of the Vatican, some Islamic governments, and the Clinton Administration as opposing women's human rights from various angles, including "neo-liberal fundamentalism."] * * * Because of the tremendous power of the United States in the United Nations system, it is critical that the women's anti-violence movement, and the women's and progressive movements generally, keep the pressure on the U.S. Administration at home and utilize human rights principles and the human rights system to bring attention to its failures. * * *

All of this is not to deny that the international human rights system still operates more in rhetoric than in reality. * * * While it is undeniably progress that the international system has finally recognized gender violence as a human rights matter, the remedies are primarily state-centric. This raises, in turn, the limitations and dangers of transferring reliance for protection to, and, thereby, enhancing, the policing power of the state. What happens to women's alternative remedies—the protective whistles used in Nicaragua and the shaming tactics, picketing, etc., with which movement in many places, including here, began? Casting women as victims draws attention and support, but victimization approaches can undermine rather than advance the goal of women's empowerment. And dealing only with violence rather than with the broader underlying social, economic, cultural and racial discrimination, as well as poverty, all of which perpetuate the conditions for gender violence, is to focus on the tip of the iceberg.

[Schneider] ends her book with a compelling plea to reinvigorate the struggle against the separation of the problem of gender violence from gender equality. The same problem exists, not as a theoretical but as a practical matter, in the United Nations system when it comes to the fashioning of concrete remedies. For example, the mandate of the Special Rapporteur on Violence against Women, Its Causes and Consequences was the product of women's demand for a rapporteur on violence and discrimination. Closely linked to the separation of gender violence from discrimination is the even greater chasm between the commitment progressively to implement economic and social rights, which is also crucial to addressing the cycle of gender violence and dependency as well as women's inequality.

* * * The human rights system should not be viewed as cabined by the limitations of its official decrees or official mechanisms of enforcement. Human rights is fundamentally a movement and its progress is maintained by the same irrepressible spirit and organized mobilizations that so recently forced recognition of private gender violence as a human rights issue and by those who continue to insist that gender violence, gender inequality and poverty are inextricable.

* * * [Schneider] reminds us of the beginnings of the women's and anti-violence movements in the U.S. Having taken several steps forward, we must recapture these beginnings to propel the dialectic toward the elimination of violence, inequality and poverty here. Integrating human rights and the experience of our sisters abroad will hopefully fuel these efforts and reshape the debate and the remedies in the decades to come.

EDITOR'S SUMMARY OF EXCERPT FROM "TOWARDS A LEGAL REFORM OF RAPE LAWS UNDER INTERNATIONAL HUMAN RIGHTS LAW" BY MARIA ALEJANDRA GOMEZ DUQUE

22 Geo. J. Gender & L. 487 (2021)

II. INTERNATIONAL HUMAN RIGHTS STANDARDS ON LAWS CRIMINALIZING SEXUAL VIOLENCE AND RAPE

A. THE HISTORICAL DEVELOPMENT OF INTERNATIONAL LAW ADDRESSING GENDER-BASED VIOLENCE

The only universal treaty on women's rights is the Convention on the Elimination of All Forms of Discrimination Against Women ("CEDAW") of 1979, ratified by 189 out of 207 countries. While it does not address violence against women explicitly, the CEDAW Committee defined such violence as a form of discrimination. Ratifying countries are thus obligated to eliminate violence against women.

Starting in 1993, the Vienna Declaration and Program of Action prioritized working against violence against women in public and private life. Further achievements occurred in 1994 and 1995: the General Assembly [of the UN] passed the Declaration on the Elimination of Violence Against Women (DEVAW) and created the Special Rapporteur on Violence Against Women, and the Fourth World Conference on Women in Beijing focused on violence against women. Under the DEVAW and the CEDAW, nations should adopt legal and other measures to prevent, criminalize, investigate, prosecute, and punish all acts of violence against women. Additionally, survivors should have an effective judicial remedy without discrimination. The Istanbul Convention, the Belem do Para Convention, and the Maputo Protocol all included these policies.

B. FREE CONSENT AS THE KEY ELEMENT FOR THE LEGAL DEFINITION OF RAPE

Since historically rape was a crime against the victim's husband or father, the concept that women (or men) must consent to sex is still relatively new, but it has been incorporated into international human rights law conventions and protocols. In 1997 the first Special Rapporteur emphasized that the burden of proof should be on the defendant to prove that the victim consented, rather than on the victim to prove lack of consent. Additionally, there should be no requirement of physical violence, threats, or intimidation to prove rape or sexual assault as the crime is often accomplished through coercion and sometimes the victim chooses passivity to avoid further harm. A 2003 landmark case from Bulgaria held that coercive circumstances could be the basis for a rape conviction, and that Bulgaria had violated the duty to prosecute acts of torture, as well as the right to privacy and family life, by its lack of assessment of all the surrounding circumstances and the victim's perspective in the investigation of rape.

Both the Istanbul Convention and the Maputo Protocol incorporate language about the necessity of consent before sexual activity, including considering whether psychological pressure or coercion have overcome the other person's free consent. Decisions from the Inter-American Court of Human Rights also acknowledge this standard and state that nonconsensual sex is a form of gender-based violence. States should adopt these definitions and policies, which emphasize the power relationship inherent in rape, as opposed to the antiquated notion that rape is caused by mere sexual desire.

C. THE PROHIBITION OF DISCRIMINATORY LAWS THAT ALLOW RAPE

Under international human rights law, including CEDAW, the Istanbul Convention and the Belem do Para Convention, there is an obligation to adopt domestic legislation in order to give effect to the rights enshrined in the international treaties that the states have ratified. Thus, any law that allows or has the effect of allowing a human rights violation is a breach of a state's international obligations. International human rights law criminalizes marital rape and inter-partner rape, is gender neutral so male victims are covered, and prohibits forced marriage which includes child marriage and rape-marriage, where victims are required to marry their rapists. Some Conventions also explicitly criminalize rape by a former spouse or partner.

In addition to requiring victim consent, these international laws require States to repeal corroboration requirements and admissibility of the victim's sexual history. However, most of the regional conventions do not include a definition of rape or sexual violence. The international community should create an instrument to help eliminate "rape cultures" by eradicating gender stereotypes and cultural beliefs that interfere with reporting by victims and appropriate response by the criminal justice system.

III. CURRENT CHALLENGES OF RAPE LAWS WORLDWIDE

A. THE LACK OF A CONSENT-BASED DEFINITION OF RAPE LAWS AROUND THE WORLD

The Istanbul Convention obligates States to enact consent-based definitions of rape. While many States have ratified the Convention, only 8 European nations have adopted this definition, 2 of which still require the victim to explicitly state that they do not consent to sex, thus presuming that women consent perpetually unless stating otherwise.

While many States have criminalized marital rape, 112 have not, so judges in those countries are free to decide whether or not such behavior is a crime even though there is no legal justification for not punishing it. And a French divorce court recently ruled that wives have a legal duty to have sex with their husbands, a ruling that is being challenged.

IV. RECOMMENDATIONS FOR LEGAL REFORMS AND ADVANCING HUMAN RIGHTS STANDARDS

All forms of rape should be prohibited by the laws, including marital rape, homosexual rape, rape-marriage, child marriage and dowry. Lack of consent from the victim's point of view should be a key element of the crime, with a legal presumption of veracity of the victim's statements, counteracting universal gender stereotypes about women's propensity to lie. Incorporating a gender perspective into each nation's laws will help end impunity in cases of sexual violence around the world.

CLAIRE M. DEMATTEIS, PROTECTING THE FREEDOM FOR WOMEN TO BE FREE FROM VIOLENCE: THE VIOLENCE AGAINST WOMEN ACT ENDURES

22 Widener L. Rev. 267 (2016)
(footnotes omitted)

V. The Violence Against Women Act Expands Internationally

A community of nations and worldwide organizations have galvanized to spread the impact of the Violence Against Women Act to countries from Australia to Latin America, from Africa to Afghanistan and throughout Europe and the Asia-Pacific region. Through the efforts of organizations, including the United Nations, World Health Organization, Amnesty International USA, the U.S. State Department, Women Thrive Worldwide, the G-8, and the Family [Violence] Prevention Fund (known as Futures without Violence), the sea change in attitudes toward violence against women has spread throughout the world.

This international effort does not rely on a civil rights remedy. Governments, courts, law enforcement, survivors and victims' advocates throughout the world have seen the impact of the Violence Against Women

Act in the United States and are replicating its provisions. Countries throughout Europe, including Britain and Germany, have adopted the Domestic Violence Court model. That is just one example of the increasingly global reach of the Violence Against Women Act. In fact, in Afghanistan—a country formally ruled by the strict anti-women's rights, militant Taliban regime—former President Hamid Karzai decreed into law by executive order in 2009 the Elimination of Violence Against Women (EVAW) law.

Among the first international efforts to recognize the significance of the Violence Against Women Act occurred just one year after its passage. In 1995, the United Nation's Fourth World Conference on Women, held in China, adopted the Beijing Declaration and Platform for Action with the goals of gender equality and the empowerment of women. The UN Commission on the Status of Women has remained relentless in pursuing these goals. Twenty years after it was first adopted, in March 2015, the fifty-ninth session of the UN Commission on the Status of Women held in New York undertook a major review of the progress made implementing the Beijing Declaration and Platform for Action and established further actions and initiatives to continue to confront global challenges to women and children from living free from violence.

Other international efforts include the UNiTE campaign launched in 2008 by UN General Secretary Ban Ki-moon. The goals of UNiTE include adopting and enforcing national laws to address and punish all forms of violence against women and girls in accordance with international human rights standards; establishing data collection and analysis systems on crimes against women and children, similar to crime reports existing in the United States and other industrialized nations; establishing programs to support abused women and girls; and protecting women and girls from rape of war.

At the April 2013 Group of Eight Nations in London, foreign ministers from the G-8 made the "historic" declaration that rape and serious sexual violence in conflicts constitute war crimes and grave breaches of the Geneva Conventions—putting responsibility on nations to search for and prosecute anyone accused of such crimes.

Finally, the International Violence Against Women Act (IVAWA) was first introduced [in Congress] by then-Senator Biden in 2007. It was re-introduced in 2010 in both the U.S. House of Representatives and in the U.S. Senate. The International Violence Against Women Act, despite bipartisan support, has not yet been enacted. While the Act does not require additional funding, its goal is to streamline and better coordinate existing anti-gender-based violence programs across numerous U.S. government agencies. The programs that IVAWA seeks to better coordinate include health programs and women's economic and education opportunities in countries from the Middle East, Africa, Eastern Europe and Central America.

These international campaigns to protect women and children spurred by the Violence Against Women Act point to a more enduring impact of the Act than could have been contemplated at its introduction and enactment—despite partisan attacks, the Supreme Court's rejection of the civil rights remedy and funding reauthorization challenges. Indeed, the Violence Against Women Act endures in the United States and around the world. * * *

MAX D. SIEGEL, SURVIVING *CASTLE ROCK*: THE HUMAN RIGHTS OF DOMESTIC VIOLENCE

18 Cardozo J of L and Gender 727 (2012)
(citations and footnotes omitted)

INTRODUCTION

On June 22, 1999, the police department of Castle Rock, Colorado repeatedly dismissed Jessica Gonzalez' cries for help after her estranged, abusive husband abducted their three young daughters from her front yard. In so doing, law enforcement ignored a permanent restraining order Jessica had taken against her estranged husband explicitly stating on the back of the order that law enforcement "shall" enforce its terms using "every reasonable means" and arrest or seek an arrest warrant following any attempted or actual violation. Within ten hours of learning of her daughters' disappearance, Jessica called and met with law enforcement nine times, but police refused to enforce the order. Again and again, law enforcement instructed Jessica to wait and see and then check back with them hours later, neglecting to take any action when Jessica filed a report at the station; in fact, they never dispatched any officer even after promising that they would take action. While Jessica feared for her daughters' lives, law enforcement took dinner breaks, searched for a lost dog, and sent three officers to investigate a routine traffic stop. Ultimately, despite Jessica's numerous requests for help and personal attempts to find her daughters by phone and by going to her estranged husband's apartment, and without law enforcement making any reasonable effort to enforce the order or locate the children, Jessica's estranged husband opened fire on the Castle Rock Police Station. Law enforcement shot back, killing him, before finding Jessica's three children dead in the back of their father's truck. Law enforcement then detained and interrogated Jessica for twelve hours. Jessica was never allowed to identify the bodies of her children, and she still does not know whether it was the police or her estranged husband that fired the shots that killed her three girls.

Subsequently, Jessica brought suit against Castle Rock, asserting that by failing to enforce the restraining order, the police department had violated her constitutional rights. The United States Court of Appeals for the Tenth Circuit sided with Jessica in her action against the State and found that she had a protected property interest that law enforcement had violated without adequate procedural due process. The Supreme Court of the United States reversed, holding that Jessica did not have a constitutional right to police enforcement of the order because Colorado law did not create a personal entitlement to enforcement and that even if it did create such an entitlement, it would not constitute a property interest warranting due process protections under the Fourteenth Amendment. The Court's opinion invoked earlier decisions in which it had refused to impose affirmative duties on the government, fortifying a deeply ingrained conceptualization of the Constitution of the United States as a "Negative Constitution" that creates a government with restraints on its actions but extremely limited responsibilities to its citizens.

After exhausting her domestic remedies, Jessica petitioned the Inter-American Commission on Human Rights to review her case. The Commission approved Jessica's petition on October 7, 2008. Jessica alleged that law enforcement did not adequately respond to her pleas for assistance and that the State never properly investigated the deaths of her three daughters, whose time, place, and cause of death are still unknown. On August 17, 2011, the Commission ruled that the United States had violated Jessica's human rights as well as the rights of other abuse survivors throughout the country. The Commission's report declared that the United States had continuously failed to fulfill its legal obligation to protect individuals like Jessica from domestic violence, and set forth recommendations to guide the country into compliance with international law. The immediate impact of the report is largely symbolic, as the proceedings before the Commission allowed Jessica to tell her story and realize a sense of justice she did not experience in the American system. The report's most concrete consequence, however, is that the Commission will continue to monitor the United States and release follow up reports about the country's progress. Nevertheless, the Commission's findings draw attention to the stark contrast between the American response to domestic violence and international standards, providing an opportunity for reflection and valuable leverage to advocates for reform.

Accordingly, this Article will view the Commission's report through the lens of the United States' Negative Constitution and examine the source of the country's incapacity to meet international standards for human rights. Part I will explain the global legal framework for the Commission and its findings before placing the United States' mechanisms for protecting survivors in the context of the Negative Constitution, which exacerbates the vulnerability of underprivileged populations and ensures ongoing social inequality. Part II will describe the potential for American courts to incorporate international standards into legal proceedings and assert that respect for outside sources of law accords with both contemporary developments and history. Finally, this Article will argue that a wholesale abdication of negative constitutionalism is necessary to protect the United States against the widely borne economic ramifications of domestic violence, the reputational costs of the nation's failure to participate in the global effort to aid survivors of abuse, and the depreciation of its expressive value as a country with an abysmal legacy of State-sanctioned violence against women.

I. INTERNATIONAL AND AMERICAN STANDARDS FOR DOMESTIC VIOLENCE

Legal reactions to domestic violence vary distinctly between the international and national levels. Global actors like the Organization of American States have recognized a uniform responsibility for government to take affirmative measures in its response to domestic violence, including the exercise of due diligence by the United States. Yet, the Supreme Court has demanded state statutory enactments to achieve government support for survivors while neglecting impediments to implementation and relegating survivors' lives to unlikely protections.

A. The Global Laws of Affirmative Measures and Due Diligence

The Commission's report on Jessica's case emerged from a long tradition of international laws that have strongly favored the intrinsic rights of abuse survivors. The Universal Declaration of Human Rights of 1948, created by a Commission on Human Rights that was newly formed in the wake of the Holocaust, has served as the foundational document for both the United Nations and international human rights. Today, the Universal Declaration of Human Rights remains the most important source of protection for human rights, recognizing that they are inherent to individuals rather than conferred by a sovereign government onto its people. Additional international human rights laws arise from various other treaties, resolutions, and conventions that States have passed. The Inter-American Convention on the Prevention, Punishment and Eradication of Violence against Women is particularly relevant to contemporary international domestic violence law and policy, and it provides that every woman has the right to be free from violence, the State shall exercise due diligence in its response to violence against women, and any person or group may petition the Commission to review a State's noncompliance with its measures.

Global enforcement entities administer justice regionally and based on the extent to which each State has institutionalized these standards. While statutory and constitutional law is a democratic manifestation of majority values, international law is administered by supranational entities of less conventional legitimacy. Particularly relevant to Jessica's case, the Commission supervises human rights in the member states of the Organization of American States (OAS) and, in conjunction with the Inter-American Court of Human Rights, investigates complaints and makes recommendations concerning human rights. The Commission has treated the American Declaration of the Rights and Duties of Man as binding on OAS member states that have not ratified the American Convention on Human Rights, including the United States. According to the Commission, the United States is bound as a matter of law to take affirmative measures to give effect to the rights contained in the Declaration.

After years of correspondence, briefs, and hearings, the Commission ruled in Jessica's favor, holding that the State had deprived her of equal protection, failed to take reasonable measures to protect its citizens, and provided an inadequate response to private violence. First, the Commission found that the United States had violated Article II of the Declaration by failing to protect Jessica and her three daughters from domestic violence. The Commission echoed international and regional systems, announcing that a State's "failure to act with due diligence" to prevent domestic violence constitutes discrimination and denies women equality before the law. Second, the Commission found that the United States had violated Article I and Article VII of the Declaration because it did not take reasonable measures to protect Jessica's children's lives. A person's right to life is the most fundamental human right, and the Commission considered measures to protect the right to life like enforcement of restraining orders critically important for vulnerable populations—especially young girls. Finally, the Commission found that the United States had violated articles V and VI, which pertained to Jessica's right to judicial protection. Specifically, the United States violated Jessica's right to judicial protection when it did not enforce the restraining order and when it failed to adequately investigate and provide access to information about the deaths of Jessica's children.

The report's findings and aspirations extended far beyond Jessica's circumstances. The Commission acknowledged that Jessica's case was one of several instances of the United States having violated citizens' human rights by failing to take reasonable measures to address domestic violence. The Commission specified that the report's conclusions were tailored to the question of whether Jessica had the opportunity to present her claims and be heard and also that "it is not the formal existence of judicial remedies that demonstrates due diligence, but rather that they are available and effective." Thus, while the report focused on Jessica's case, its recommendations encompassed the entire national response to domestic violence.

The Commission's report signaled the systematic failures of the United States to realize widely accepted international standards for human rights, particularly considering that due diligence is a longstanding requirement of State responsibility in the prevention and punishment of violent acts. Moreover, the report pointed to various international instruments to show the existence of a global consensus that states have an obligation to exercise due diligence in response to the problem of violence against women. The report offered four principles highlighted by current law and practice: the State may incur international responsibility if it fails to act with due diligence to address violence against women; international consensus "underscore[s] the link between discrimination, violence against women, and due diligence; due diligence includes adequate judicial remedies for victims; and the State must consider factors like age and minority status that could place individuals at heightened vulnerability for victimization.

The report addressed the United States' response both in terms of law enforcement and the law itself. First, it detailed standards for law enforcement's reaction to abusers' potential violations of restraining orders and made recommendations to better protect the human rights of survivors. Unlike the steps taken by the officers in Jessica's case, minimum standards for officers are that they read an order in its entirety to determine whether it has been violated, verify the existence of an order even when its holder does not have a copy, and attempt to locate the abuser in violation of an order and seize his or her firearms. An adequate response requires defined protocol, and law enforcement should be trained in the complex problem of domestic violence and be able to determine the risks of a particular violation by weighing situational factors, including an aggressor's access to weapons, threats of suicide, and history of violence.

Turning to the judiciary, the report described the pressing need for multifaceted legal reforms across the country. The Commission acknowledged that as a result of the Supreme Court's holdings in *Castle Rock v. Gonzales*, *DeShaney v. Winnebago County Department of Social Services*, and *United States v. Morrison*, the United States might have improperly narrowed the remedies available to domestic violence survivors in legal proceedings against government officials. While legislative developments like the Violence Against Women Act of 1994 are positive, the Supreme Court has left victims of domestic violence with no constitutional or federal statutory remedy when police are grossly negligent in the execution of their duty to protect an individual's physical security. Therefore, the Commission called for new policies and legal approaches that would mandate enforcement of precautionary measures to benefit survivors, better protect children, and help to restructure discriminatory sociocultural patterns that compromise survivors' safety by impeding the American response to domestic violence.

B. American Constitutionalism's Astonishing Disregard for Human Consequences

The Commission called for sweeping legal reforms in a country preoccupied with a conceptualization of law that is antithetical to basic principles of human rights. In stark contrast to international standards, the United States' domestic violence interventions are limited to political processes and subsequent judicial review because citizens do not have a constitutionally guaranteed right to government assistance to meet their most basic needs. Generally, the Constitution limits and empowers government, and it does not create positive rights such as those advocated in the report and widely accepted elsewhere in the world.

The Supreme Court has espoused negative constitutionalism irrespective of the gravity of the human indignity at stake. * * * [The author discusses the example of the child abuse case *DeShaney v. Winnebago County Department of Social Services*, holding that the State did not have a constitutional obligation to protect the child from private violence, and *Webster v. Reproductive Health Services,* upholding prohibitions against the use of public facilities for abortions, public employees' performance of abortion services, and public funding of abortion counseling. Concomitantly, the author notes that the Court sometimes acts to promote a safe, ordered society even when it infringes on the rights of individuals, analyzing *Jacobson v. Massachusetts,* in which the Court upheld a Massachusetts statute that mandated vaccination against smallpox after a citizen who had refused vaccination or to pay the monetary penalty associated with his refusal faced criminal penalties. The author notes that usually it is only when the case involves prisoners that the Court finds the State has a duty to act, citing *Farmer v. Brennan* and *Brown v. Plata*. Justice Scalia, who delivered the opinion of the Court in *Gonzalez v. Castle Rock,* argued in *Plata's* dissent that the majority had decided to uphold "the most radical injunction issued by a court in our Nation's history" and that this was "a case whose proper outcome is so clearly indicated by tradition and common sense . . . [t]he proceedings that led to this result were a judicial travesty." The author also discusses the *Morrison* decision, holding the right to file a civil suit in VAWA I unconstitutional.]

This cycle of unfair governance and individual tragedy is characteristic of an ongoing system of oppression in the United States that stems from the Negative Constitution. Even when laws are applied equally across the country, Americans experience legal outcomes and their social consequences in different ways. Negative constitutionalism disproportionately disadvantages less resourced Americans because in the context of government restraint without affirmative obligations, wealthier individuals are more likely to be able to afford to effectuate their liberties in the absence of government intervention while individuals without enough resources cannot attain the same constitutionally guaranteed entitlements. Thus, negative constitutionalism unfairly hinders communities of color, women, and other lower-resourced populations who might experience reduced employment options, unequal pay, limited access to education and health care, or additional systemic barriers to prosperity.

The Negative Constitution shrouds social injustice and magnifies the subordination of vulnerable populations. At times, the very perception that negative rights exist can be damaging to individuals by mediating the stigmatization of domestic violence survivors and other groups potentially in need of assistance because even when negative rights never realistically enhance the individual's opportunities for constructive change, they create the façade that the individual has choices and is making bad ones. Law does more than regulate society: it creates society. Negative constitutionalism contributes to a nation in which purportedly universal rights are exercised unequally across socioeconomic classes, genders, communities, and survivors of abuse. Under a Negative Constitution, rights are not truly guaranteed, and the entitlements of the collectively disempowered hinge on the moralizing impulses of the social elite.

II. PROTECT THE HUMAN RIGHTS OF ABUSE SURVIVORS

The United States has a long road to travel before it meets the standards in the Commission's report. Recognition for the persuasive value of international law in American courts is a realistic starting point in line with longstanding tradition, but a fundamental shift in the Court's constitutional jurisprudence is necessary to insulate the United States from further damage to its economy, international reputation, and domestic legitimacy.

A. Give International Standards Persuasive Value in Domestic Courts

* * * *Castle Rock* represents a case study in how the Court could have untethered itself from the Negative Constitution and brought the United States into better compliance with international standards. The circumstances in *Castle Rock* more closely resembled *Farmer v. Brennan* and other exceptions to the Negative Constitution than they resembled *DeShaney* because the State limited Jessica's capacity to act on her own behalf. The Court could have distinguished *Castle Rock* from *DeShaney* based on the extent of the State's involvement in each case; while Jessica repeatedly and directly interacted with the State in *Castle Rock* and relied on what she believed was the State's legally mandated duty to arrest her estranged husband, the State had mere knowledge of the private violence taking place in *DeShaney*. In *Castle Rock*, the State possessed an affirmative obligation to respond to Jessica's cries for help, emanating from its promise to act on Jessica's behalf in the restraining order and the legal limits the State places on all citizens' abilities to defend themselves against systematic acts of harassment and private violence.

Once distinguished from *DeShaney* and other cases within the realm of negative constitutionalism, the legal analysis in *Castle Rock* falls apart. As Justice Stevens pointed out in his dissent, the statute giving rise to the restraining order at issue in *Castle Rock* was intended to mandate police enforcement, an order of protection is issued to benefit the specific holder of the order, and the Court had already recognized various nontraditional property rights in other cases, including property without specific monetary value that indirectly benefited its owner. It necessarily followed that the State violated Jessica's constitutional rights because no one on the Court contested that if Jessica had a property interest, then *Castle Rock's* deprivation of Jessica's interest was in violation of the Due Process Clause.

Moreover, the Court should have considered elements of international standards for human rights throughout its process of contemplation. While the Court greatly weighted the importance of police discretion, it should have also valued the vital impact of unchecked police discretion on each domestic violence survivor's right to life. Additionally, the Court should have more thoroughly assessed the human tragedy that led to the proceedings; the deaths of Jessica's children were not irrelevant to Jessica's rights but rather ineradicable consequences of a society that does not take affirmative measures to protect children or other vulnerable populations or to preserve women's equal protection before the law. These considerations need not have been determinative, but should have been at least persuasive. This would have been in line with the *Castle Rock* Court's reliance on legal articles as well as the Court's inspection of international standards for the treatment of sexual minorities in *Lawrence v. Texas* and its recognition that other countries' experiences with emergency power "may not be irrelevant" in *Youngstown Sheet & Tube Co. v. Sawyer.*

* * * [The author discusses *Roper v. Simmons,* in which the Court took into account international human right standards in holding unconstitutional a law under which a juvenile was ordered to be executed.]

Other countries have continuously demonstrated this degree of respect for foreign law—especially American law—and it is becoming necessary for American courts to maintain cognizance of developments outside the United States in order to meaningfully participate in a globalized society. Undoubtedly, countries differ and the world's constitutions are not identical, but the United States has greatly influenced other nations' constitutions and the decisions of foreign courts. Much of international law is not such a significant departure from American standards that it is unwieldy in American courtrooms. Moreover, the application of foreign law in non-American, domestic courtrooms is increasingly common, and a more international perspective is essential for the United States to maintain political, economic, ethical, and social traction in a progressively globalized world. * * *

B. Reject the Negative Constitution

Increasing the persuasive value of international standards in American courtrooms is a realistic mechanism for improving the United States' compliance with global human rights law, but it is the first among many steps toward rectifying the deeper failure of the State to adequately respond to domestic violence. There are no quick fixes that would immediately and everlastingly secure the adequate protection of human rights in the United States. If the Supreme Court ever backs away from the amplified version of the Negative Constitution that it applied in *Castle Rock*, it would have another important decision to make: whether to decisively renounce its violations of international standards by giving fair balance to domestic violence survivors' human rights or to preserve the State's opportunity to avoid its responsibilities for another day by leaving the mantle of *DeShaney* intact. Only through renouncing *DeShaney* and the other cases in which it denied a constitutional right to intervention and by adopting affirmative measures as a nationwide approach to the State's response to domestic violence could the United States curtail the various destructive consequences of its noncompliance with international standards, including the economic and reputational damage that arise from its human rights violations and the depreciative impact of domestic violence on the expressive value of the Constitution. * * *

The Commission's decision in *Castle Rock* highlighted human rights violations in a nation that has been repeatedly put on notice about its inadequate treatment of women. Similar to the Commission's findings that the country's human rights deprivations were multifaceted and ongoing, the Committee on the Elimination of Racial Discrimination has registered concerns in its official capacity under the International Convention on the Elimination of All Forms of Racial Discrimination about the insufficient response among American authorities to violence and abuse against minority women, which deprives them "of their right to access to justice and the right to obtain adequate reparation or satisfaction for damages suffered." Elsewhere, as with the Convention on the Elimination of All Forms of Discrimination Against Women, the United States has averted violations of international treaties by simply refusing to ratify them, although not without disapproval from the global community. * * *

The individual must have a right to government intervention in cases of domestic violence. Strengthening rights-based approaches to government enhances the public's perceived legitimacy of institutions, and the Constitution should accommodate the positive obligation of government protection in light of citizens' persistent expectations that government obligations constitute a normative right and that the government has a duty to protect the public. Constitutional requirements for affirmative measures like mandatory arrest provisions are especially vital in the domestic violence context because they demand affirmative measures from a government that once sanctioned violence against women. Thus, affirmative measures that preserve fundamental human rights are not just the international standard for State conduct; rather, the government's responsibilities to prevent and respond to domestic violence are American values of constitutional import.

CONCLUSION

In its current form, the American response to domestic violence is a troubling violation of international standards for human rights. Now that

Castle Rock has been acknowledged as an injustice on the world's stage, Jessica has given the country the guidance it needs in the Commission's report to improve the State's response and move toward compliance with international laws. Progress requires an entirely new understanding of the realities of surviving abuse, but treating global standards as persuasive in American courts is a feasible starting point. The United States' reputation, financial health, and legitimacy demand reform, warranting a clean break from negative constitutionalism in favor of internationally acceptable affirmative measures to protect human rights.

[Editor's Note: On 10/27/14, the IACHR convened a hearing to follow up on the implementation of its 2011 recommendations in the Gonzales case. Ms. Gonzales' counsel argued that the U.S. had not achieved full implementation of the recommendations, specifically a recommendation that the federal government investigate the deaths of Ms. Gonzales' three daughters, as part of a "pattern and practice" of inappropriate responses by law enforcement in Colorado to domestic violence cases. It is unclear how and when they died—from their father shooting them or from being caught in the cross fire when he started a gun battle with the police. The IACHR also recommended that the U.S. government compensate Ms. Gonzales for this loss, which has not happened.

The U.S. Ambassador to the Organization of American States noted that since the 2011 hearing, Congress passed VAWA 2013, and that the federal government had funded a two-day Violence Against Women Leadership Training for Colorado law enforcement officers. It also convened a 2015 round table for federal staff working on domestic and sexual violence issues to discuss human rights principles. The ambassador stated that the DOJ cannot investigate individual cases, nor can the federal government compensate Ms. Gonzales for the loss of her daughters, absent an act of Congress.

The UN Special Rapporteur on the Status of Women testified in favor of Ms. Gonzales's claims and also called for the U.S. to address both the legislative and structural causes that promulgate violence against women.

The Commissioners unanimously found that the U.S. had failed to fulfill the 2011 recommendations and must do more, including compensation to Ms. Gonzales and an investigation into her daughters' deaths. They concluded by noting, "The key to implementing the Commission's recommendations is not so much about what the Department of Justice can do, but what the United States, as a state, can do to fulfill its obligations under international law."]

MAGGIE WOODS, TRYING TO REMOVE THE *GENDER* FROM "GENDER-BASED VIOLENCE": POLAND'S POLICY FRAMEWORK IS WAR ON WOMEN, NOT DOMESTIC VIOLENCE

(unpublished, 2020)
(footnotes omitted)

Introduction

" 'The most painful thing is that our government is doing nothing to improve the situation. No actions are being taken. As if victims of domestic violence were no more than a difficult topic that's easiest swept under the carpet." So lamented Joanna Gzyra-Iskandar, a coordinator at Poland's Centrum Praw Kobiet (CPK), or Women's Rights Centre, in the early months of the coronavirus pandemic. In 2020, the "shadow pandemic" of domestic violence surged across Europe and the rest of the world where public health restrictions cut domestic violence survivors' freedom and access to support. In March 2020 alone, the number of calls to CPK's helpline in Poland increased by fifty percent.

On July 14, 2020, the United Nations Special Rapporteur on violence against women, its causes, and consequences and the Platform of Independent Expert Mechanisms on Discrimination and Violence Against Women (EDVAW) together called on States to respond immediately to COVID-19's amplifying effects on violence against women globally. The Rapporteur and EDVAW emphasized that due to women's continued underrepresentation in positions of decision-making authority, "different forms of systemic discrimination already faced by women and girls will be exacerbated." They demanded that States implement key measures to recognize the especially vulnerable circumstances of women and girls and "[i]nclude the prevention and redress of violence against women as a key part of national response plans for COVID-19."

On July 25, 2020, in the wake of this international call to intensify efforts against domestic violence, Poland announced that it would withdraw from the Council of Europe Convention on Preventing and Combating Violence Against Women and Domestic Violence. More commonly known as the Istanbul Convention (the Convention), the multilateral treaty is the first and only legally binding instrument in Europe that exclusively focuses on violence against women. The Convention provides a comprehensive framework of prevention, protection, prosecution, and treatment to combat not only idiopathic triggers of domestic violence (such as pathological anger and substance abuse) but also its root cause, the very same that the Special Rapporteur and EDVAW identified in their statement: systemic gender discrimination.

Poland is not alone in its doubt over the Convention. Turkey also announced withdrawal from the treaty in summer 2020, and it has since followed through in March 2021. A slew of other Central and Eastern

European (CEE) States—such as Ukraine, Bulgaria, Croatia, the Czech Republic, Latvia, Lithuania, the Slovak Republic, and Hungary most recently—have experienced heated debates in their national legislatures that ultimately rejected ratification. Prevalent in these debates was concern over the Convention's framing of the problem of domestic violence: governments were uneasy with the idea that gender discrimination is the underlying cause of violence because it implicates predominant, conservative cultural values. Recep Tayyip Erdogan, for example, iterated the common refrain that the Convention attacked traditional Turkish values, and political organizations in Poland have launched domestic and international campaigns that claim the Convention is trying to destroy the Polish family.

This controversy over the Convention is occurring within a convergence of three interrelated political trends that have emerged over the past decade since the Convention opened for signature in 2011: rising right-wing populism, anti-genderism, and political schisms within the European Union (EU). Right-wing populism has swept across Europe and the rest of the world since the 2010s. It has capitalized on general discontent among "the people," usually grounded in economic depression, anti-immigrant sentiment, and resentment toward elite institutions and Western Liberalism. This brand of populism has notably succeeded in Britain's referendum for Brexit, the electoral success of former President Donald Trump, and the election of far-right leadership in various other countries, such as Prawo i Sprawiedliwość (PiS), or the Law and Justice Party, in Poland.

Many of these same populist movements and government parties, like PiS, have similarly espoused anti-genderism, which is a backlash ideology to "gender ideology." "Gender ideology" is the term these groups use to frame and delegitimize activism on behalf of gender and LGBTQ+ equality, and anti-genderism has justified official discrimination against women and LGBTQ+ persons across Europe and in Poland especially. Anti-genderist movements repudiate the use of the term *gender* and the promotion of gender equality in international human rights instruments like the Convention. They consider the term a Western Liberal imposition that threatens not only traditional notions of family and social structure but the very sovereignty of the nation. With the rise of right-wing populism, anti-genderism has gained considerable pull in European national governments. It is the framework under which PiS has justified not only withdrawing from the Istanbul Convention but also curtailing women's reproductive rights in Poland, most notably on October 22, 2020, when a PiS-appointed constitutional tribunal all but banned abortion. Indeed, feminist scholars Agnieszka Graff and Elżbieta Korolczuk have called the combination of PiS's populism and anti-genderism an "opportunistic synergy," and Poland has become the "paradigmatic case" of what human rights abuses can occur when anti-genderism operates in a context that is particularly conducive to it.

As the EU continues to deliberate on ratifying the Convention, this disagreement on national stages threatens both Europe's unity on and international recognition of women's human right to be free from coercion, violence, and death. Poland has managed to reframe the human rights issue of violence against women as not a matter of women's equal humanity but as an issue of protecting Poland's very culture. This emotionally charged appeal is perhaps a familiar refrain even to those outside Europe. Like Prop 8 proponents in California, who in 2008 reframed same-sex marriage from an issue of equal rights to one that would "imperil the exercise of religious and personal belief" and "challeng[e] parental authority over children," opponents of the Convention frame its discourse of structural gender equality as destructive of the wholesomeness of the Polish family and the innocence of its children. Worryingly, this anti-genderist propaganda is not isolated to Poland. In fact, Poland has officially reached out to neighboring countries to sign a homemade convention, rebranding withdrawal from the Istanbul Convention as better protection for both women and Poland.

This Note examines the practical effects of Poland's reframing the issue of gender-based violence and analyzes different possible solutions to address the human rights abuses that Poland is perpetrating under the ideological framework of anti-genderism. The anti-genderist reframe not only shapes Poland's policies on domestic violence, which fall far short of its international obligations, but also threatens its already strained relationship with the EU and women's broader human rights within Europe and without. As Professor Korolczuk has explained, anti-genderism in Poland is not merely an ideology and discourse but an organizational strategy that has paired with the current government's brand of populism. This "opportunistic synergy" of anti-genderist ideology and populist political action makes domestic violence a particularly intransigent problem to solve in Poland.

Professors Korolczuk and Graff have extensively studied the phenomenon of anti-genderism in Poland as it relates to women's rights, feminism, and gender politics, but practicable solutions to combat anti-genderism's effect on domestic violence policies remain elusive. Other scholars have analyzed the frameworks of domestic violence policies in both international and CEE contexts along spectra of women-centered to gender-neutral solutions and strategic to practical gender interests. Although the Istanbul Convention is considered the gold standard among human rights activists, its framework remains on the extremes of both spectra: it is women centered and strategic. It is therefore an easy target to repudiate as an ideological imposition. Nevertheless, the Convention sets an important standard for individual European States, Europe as a whole, and the international community. Locating violence against women within a greater framework of structural gender equality is crucial to addressing the systemic problem of domestic violence in Europe. Poland's failures to protect women speak to that truth.

Part I of this Note first reviews different frameworks to address domestic violence. It then briefly describes the history of the structural equality framework within the United Nations' attempts to address domestic violence as a human rights issue. This is the dominant framework for *international* human rights discourse on domestic violence, but it is not the only—nor even a very popular—framework that States employ to address domestic violence within their borders. This Part concludes with a summary of the Istanbul Convention's framework and provisions.

Part II examines anti-genderism and argues that its ideological framework has caused significant failures in domestic violence policy and implementation strategies in Poland. This Part first reviews Poland's cultural history, which created a socio-political environment conducive to anti-genderism. It then shifts to focus on the anti-genderist movement's effects on domestic discourse and policies concerning gender equality and violence against women. It argues that anti-genderism within PiS has in turn both hindered legislative efforts to address domestic violence and driven official hostility toward victim services organizations for women and gender quality activists. This Part concludes by examining the potential international consequences of Poland's anti-genderist propaganda and its withdrawal from the Convention. Poland's stance is not isolated and has the potential not only to deepen political rifts within the EU but also to diminish human rights protections for women across Europe.

Part III looks at potential solutions to enforce human rights obligations in Poland. This Part first grapples with the difficulty of dismantling anti-genderism's synergy with Polish populist politics. It then reflects on internal solutions—solutions that work within the current ideological environment to improve survivors' lives directly. Then it reflects on external mechanisms—namely, the power of the EU both to sanction and to exert financial pressure on Poland to recommit to its obligations and the jurisdiction of the European Court of Human Rights (ECtHR) to force Poland to adhere to its longstanding obligations under the European Convention on Human Rights (ECHR). What seems necessary is not only an internal solution to push against current public and political attitudes toward gender and domestic violence but also external pressure on the Polish government to change its policies. . . .

IV. Conclusion

In the midst of larger trends of anti-genderism and right-wing populism that have swept across Europe, Poland stands out as an example of how the reactionary framework of anti-genderism cannot provide a satisfactory response to the pandemic of domestic violence because it was never intended to. Domestic violence has, incredibly, become a catalyst for political schism in Europe, and the Istanbul Convention, a symbol of iconoclasm. Poland has taken domestic violence out of the context of structural gender discrimination to protect religious and traditional cultural values. In doing so, it has diminished the gravity of domestic violence and vitiated effective methods to combat it.

This Note has examined the history and effects of anti-genderism in Poland to highlight the real harm that an ideological framework can produce. In the meantime, activists on the ground have developed ways to work within the cultural climate of Poland—"a culture largely hostile to feminism"—to provide women empowerment and protection. These efforts, however, are localized and will not have a broader impact without wider cultural support. This Note presses the urgency of addressing anti-genderism through European political and judicial mechanisms to ensure protection of women's human rights not just in Poland, but throughout Europe.

[Editor's Note: Turkey withdrew from the Istanbul Convention in 2021.

In 2022, Ukraine ratified the Convention. So did the United Kingdom, ten years after signing it, but excluded migrant women whose residency status is dependent on that of an abusive spouse or partner. There was public outcry about this exclusion. The Home Office stated that they are considering including migrant women in the future but it appears that this has not happened as of January 2024.]

The European Union ratified the Convention in 2023.

As of January 2024, Poland had not withdrawn from the Convention but was still considering doing so even as it is considering legislation to better protect survivors of domestic violence. Rates of domestic violence in Poland have been falling since 2014 according to Notes from Poland.com]

CINCINNATI CITY COUNCIL, OHIO, RESOLUTION NO. 47–2011

(2011)

DECLARING that freedom from domestic violence is a fundamental human right and further DECLARING that local governments have a responsibility to continue securing this right on behalf of their citizens.

WHEREAS, according to the Domestic Violence Resource Center, one in four women and one in fourteen men experiences domestic violence in their lifetimes; and

WHEREAS, Hamilton County Pre-Trial Services reports that there were 3,828 domestic violence arrests in 2010, a six percent increase from 2009, and only 28.7 percent (1,098) of those arrested were sentenced; and

WHEREAS, of the 1,098 sentenced, 73 percent received probation, 23 percent were ordered to jail, and 506 protection orders were issued; and

WHEREAS, in Hamilton County between 2008 and 2010, sixteen women and two children were victims of domestic violence homicide and, in each case, the woman had ended her relationship with her abuser and planned to leave or had already done so; and

WHEREAS, the Hamilton County YWCA Battered Women's Shelter responded to 21,778 hotline calls and sheltered 599 women and children in 2010; and

WHEREAS, due to increased demand, the Battered Women's Shelter expanded its shelter capacity from 54 beds to 72 beds in 2010; and

WHEREAS, survivors of domestic violence must deal with the effects of physical injuries, long-term psychological damage, financial instability, and trouble finding safe housing; and

WHEREAS, police and sheriff's departments, courts, cities, social service agencies, and other local government entities constitute the first line of defense against domestic violence; and

WHEREAS, police and sheriff's departments, courts, cities, social service agencies, and other local government entities incur significant monetary costs due to domestic violence; and

WHEREAS, world leaders and leaders within the United States recognize that domestic violence is a human rights concern; and

WHEREAS, the United Nations Declaration on the Elimination of Violence Against Women, adopted in 1993, recognizes the urgent need for the universal application to women of the rights and principles with regard to equality, security, liberty, integrity, and dignity of all human beings, noting that "those rights and principles are enshrined in international instruments, including the Universal Declaration of Human Rights" and;

WHEREAS, the United Nations Commission on Human Rights condemned violence and human rights violations against women in March, 1994; and

WHEREAS, by recognizing that domestic violence is a human rights issue, the City of Cincinnati will raise awareness and enhance domestic violence education in communities, the public and private sectors, and within government agencies; now, therefore,

BE IT RESOLVED by the Council of the City of Cincinnati, State of Ohio:

Section 1. That the City of Cincinnati declares that freedom from domestic violence is a fundamental human right.

Section 2. That the city of Cincinnati declares that state and local governments bear a responsibility to continue securing this human right on behalf of their citizens.

Section 3. That a copy of this resolution be spread upon the minutes of the Council.

Passed: October 5, 2011

(Signed by Mayor, attested by Clerk, submitted by Vice-Mayor Roxanne Qualls)

[Editor's Note: By Feb. 2018, approximately 31 local governments around the U.S. passed similar resolutions, inspired by the Lenahan/Gonzales case, according to Cornell Law School's website, Freedom from Domestic Violence as a Fundamental Human Right: Resolutions, Presidential Proclamations, and Other Statements of Principle. The website has not been updated since 2018. Hopefully more governments throughout the U.S., and perhaps in other countries, have passed similar resolutions since then.

Many of these resolutions have been initiated by students from local law schools. They could be helpful for attorneys and advocates in establishing that there is a government policy protecting victims and survivors of domestic violence and their children when making policy arguments to courts and legislators.]